ENCYCLOPÆDIA
Britannica
2001
YEAR IN REVIEW

ENCYCLOPÆDIA
Britannica

Encyclopædia Britannica, Inc.   Chicago • London • New Delhi • Paris • Seoul • Sydney • Taipei • Tokyo

ENCYCLOPÆDIA
Britannica
2001 YEAR IN REVIEW

Foreword

It is the task of the editors of Britannica's yearbooks to get acquainted intimately with each calendar year, to discern each year's special "personality." We look for themes, or leitmotivs, and try to knit them all together into a coherent whole. The task of sorting out 2001 was both easier and more difficult in that, three-quarters of the way through, it suddenly became a one-story year—and 2001 was turned into one of the most remarkable years ever. The events of September 11 and its aftermath immediately swept other stories to the sidelines.

Our keynote article, written by the *Washington Post*'s Robert G. Kaiser, bears as its title a date, "9-11," and is placed at the head of the section of the book that examines the chronology of the year. Kaiser writes thoughtfully of the changes in the United States and the world after that date, pointing out that the events confirm the concept of the world as a "global village." As the hundreds of contributions to this yearbook began to arrive, the editors were amazed at how many of them referred to the terrorist attacks and the aftermath.

- **Health and Disease** "A few hours after the World Trade Center's twin towers collapsed, five designated city hospitals were prepared for the worst. Triage centres were set up within a few blocks of 'ground zero,' fully staffed and equipped to treat any possible injury and perform lifesaving surgery."

- **Environment** "[A]crid smoke, soot, and ash from tons of pulverized debris complicated the recovery in New York City."

- **Business** "Any hopes that the boom years of the 1990s would extend into the next decade ended for good after the September 11 terrorist attacks."

- **Fashion** "Prominent American buyers . . . refrained from traveling to see the European collections."

- **Museums** "A number of museums sought to upgrade their insurance policies and implement damage-control measures."

- **Architecture** "Architects and others debated the long-term impact of the disaster. Would the world stop building skyscrapers?"

- **International Law** "[B]ecause Osama bin Laden . . . was not the representative of any state, charges against him could not be brought in the [International Court of Justice]." "Were the attacks an act of war? Was a declaration of war required in order to respond with military force?"

- **Media and Publishing** "The September attacks forced first one and later a second postponement of the Emmys, as well as the delay of the TV season's debut by one week. . . . 'The 11th' hastened the decline of an industry already suffering lowered revenues and resulted in the closure of some well-known magazines."

- **Religion** "The [attacks] spurred a worldwide examination of Islamic doctrine. . . . Muslim scholars pointed out . . . that terrorist violence is an interpretation of Islam that most adherents of the faith reject."

Many country articles, such as Afghanistan and Pakistan, were heavily devoted to these events, of course, but other countries were affected as well:

- **Germany** "[Chancellor Gerhard] Schröder jumped ahead even of the U.S. in defining what had happened as a "conflict of cultures" and a "declaration of war on the free world.""

- **U.K.** "[Prime Minister] Tony Blair . . . [won] overwhelming political and public support for his international role in the fight against terrorism."

- **Iraq** "Pres. Saddam publicly opposed the U.S.-led war on terrorism and called on other Islamic countries to help defeat it. He also decried the military action in Afghanistan, calling it a spark that could set 'the world on fire.'"

- **Egypt** "[Pres. Hosni] Mubarak . . . spoke of Egypt's need to coordinate actions with Western countries to combat terrorism."

- **Venezuela** "[Pres. Hugo] Chávez equated civilian casualties from the bombing with the deaths caused by terrorists on September 11."

Of course, there were other important events in 2001. Topping Britannica's list would be the economic downturn, both in the U.S. and around the globe; worldwide protests against globalization; the continuing AIDS epidemic in this the 20th year since it was first identified; foot-and-mouth disease and "mad cow" disease, both of which continued to affect agriculture, diets, and personal freedoms in the U.K. and continental Europe; the improvement in the prospects for peace in Northern Ireland but the deterioration in the Israel/Palestine and Pakistan/ India relationships; and the furor over the death penalty evoked by the execution in June of American terrorist Timothy McVeigh.

Both the Philippines and Indonesia got rid of old, corrupt leaders, and interesting new figures were elected in Israel, Bulgaria, Moldova, Peru, and Japan. Nine members of the Nepali royal family were massacred. Kofi Annan was whisked in for a second term as secretary-general of the United Nations, and the man and the organization shared the Nobel Prize for Peace. Apart from the business turndown, the Microsoft trial and the demise of Enron Corp. were probably the biggest business headlines. Scientific firsts in 2001 included evidence from Australia that Africa may not have been the only location where the human species arose; a spacecraft landed on an asteroid; and an artificial heart was implanted. Disastrous earthquakes shook India, El Salvador, and Chile.

The year's top names in sports included golfer Tiger Woods, baseball slugger Barry Bonds, the formidable Michael Jordan, race-car driver Jeff Gordon, and Jacques Rogge, the Belgian tapped to head the International Olympic Committee. In the realm of culture, Tony Kushner returned to the stage with a play about—do you believe it?—Afghanistan, while *The Producers* made records on Broadway and young Harry Potter performed his wizardry on movie theatre box offices.

All this, plus biographies, obituaries, a day-by-day calendar of events—and much, much more—awaits you in the pages that follow.

Editor

ENCYCLOPÆDIA
Britannica
2001 YEAR IN REVIEW

Contents

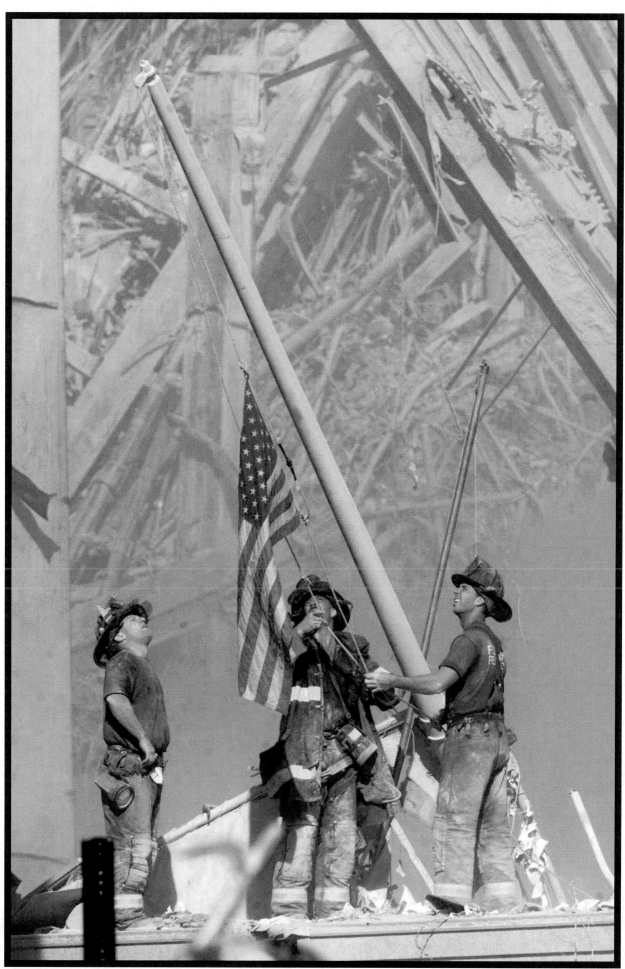

Dates of 2001

The September 11 terrorist attacks in the U.S. changed forever the contours of the world and affected the ways we all interact with one another.

9-11

Robert G. Kaiser

For years we said we lived in a global village. On Sept. 11, 2001, terrorists bent on wreaking havoc in New York City and Washington, D.C., proved that this was so. Never before had the world so intimately shared the same tragic disaster. Because the attacks occurred in the morning on the U.S. East Coast, perhaps 90% of the Earth's population was awake when two airplanes flew into the World Trade Center and another crashed into the Pentagon. Transported to New York by some of the most powerful images ever conveyed by television, billions of people vicariously experienced the horror.

Rare are the events that jolt the entire globe. In truth, there may never have been another that had the impact of September 11. The detonation of the first atomic bomb or the bringing down of the Berlin Wall may have been more important historical events, but neither had an audience as big or as raptly attentive as that on September 11. In part because nearly everyone was jolted, we will need a long time to grasp the true import of that date. It became a cliché almost immediately afterward that "everything has changed." Giving that phrase real content will take years.

Some of the things that changed were quickly obvious. The United States lost its innocence and its isolation, becoming in just a few days a different kind of global power. For 56 years after World War II, Americans had policed the globe as beneficent gendarmes, trying to keep the world safe for democracy and capitalism. Suddenly on September 11 the mission changed. The goal became to keep America itself safe.

For the first time, other nations rushed to America's side, offering condolences and active assistance. The North Atlantic Treaty Organization invoked Article 5 of its founding treaty, declaring that the terrorist actions constituted an attack against all NATO members, which would

The Pentagon from the southwest.

September 9	September 11		
Suicide bombers attack Ahmed Shah Masoud, head of the anti-Taliban opposition	7:59 A.M. American Airlines Flight 11 takes off from Logan International Airport in Boston, bound for Los Angeles.	8:14 A.M. United Airlines Flight 175 takes off from Logan International Airport in Boston, bound for Los Angeles.	8:20 A.M. American Airlines Flight 77 takes off from Washington Dulles International Airport in Washington, D.C., bound for Los Angeles.

Jim LoScalzo for USN&WR

8:42 A.M. United Airlines Flight 93 takes off from Newark International Airport in Newark, N.J., bound for San Francisco.

8:48 A.M. American Airlines Flight 11 crashes into World Trade Center north tower in New York City.

9:03 A.M. United Airlines Flight 175 crashes into World Trade Center south tower in New York City.

9:40 A.M. American Airlines Flight 77 crashes into Pentagon.

9:45 A.M. Federal Aviation Authority orders all flights grounded.

9:59 A.M. South tower of World Trade Center collapses.

10:10 A.M. United Airlines Flight 93 crashes near Shanksville, Pa.

10:28 A.M. North tower of World Trade Center collapses.

5:25 P.M. A third building, 7 World Trade Center, 47 stories tall, collapses.

10:30 P.M. President Bush addresses the nation from the White House.

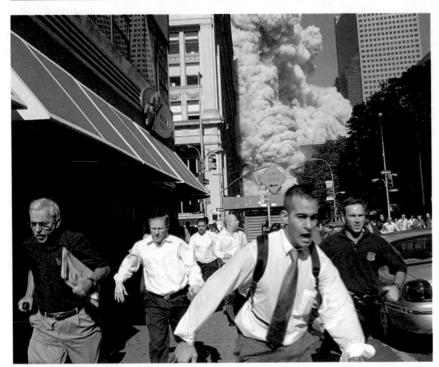

The World Trade Center collapses.

AP/Wide World Photos

respond—as required by the treaty—as if they had been attacked themselves. Article 5 had never before been invoked. In Moscow the young president of Russia phoned the young U.S. president aboard Air Force One and pledged his country's cooperation for a war against terrorism. Vladimir Putin's call was the first the administration of George W. Bush received from a foreign leader. On September 19 the Organization of American States agreed by acclamation to invoke the Rio Treaty, a mutual defense pact. One after another the countries of the world lined up with the United States. Most did so without evident hesitation, a few because Bush made it so clear, in his speech to Congress on September 20, that the U.S. expected their support: "Every nation in every region now has a decision to make: Either you are with us or you are with the terrorists."

Ultimately, only Iraq offered sympathy to the terrorists; no other government would take their side. This was a huge change. The nations of the world had never before been so united on an important global issue. The collapse of international factions into a united front against terrorism signaled power-

fully that, as U.S. Secretary of State Colin Powell put it in a speech in Shanghai on October 18, "not only is the Cold War over, the post-Cold War period is also over." Suddenly the world had a new cause and a new sense of shared challenge. Old alignments seemed to disappear.

But that near unanimity among political leaders was not so evident on the streets of the world's cities, towns, and villages. Within hours of the September 11 attacks, cameras caught Palestinians on the West Bank exulting over the terrorists' successes. Posters carrying the likeness of Osama bin Laden blossomed throughout the Muslim world. Public opinion polls and questioning reporters found that citizens of many lands felt sympathy for the terrorists and antipathy for the United States.

In China government officials had to censor Internet discussions, which included much cheering for a blow struck against American arrogance. A poll taken in Bolivia found that Bin Laden was the most admired man in that Andean nation. In Muslim countries certain myths took hold: that it was not the Arabs on board who hijacked the aircraft and flew them into the Pentagon and the WTC

but, in fact, Israeli intelligence agents who were responsible for the attacks; that the Americans had no proof that Bin Laden was behind what had happened. One of the ugliest myths, written and repeated time and again in the Arab world, was that several thousand Jews who ordinarily worked in the World Trade Center did not show up for work on September 11—an implication that they had been warned of the attacks. In fact, many of the nearly 3,000 victims in the World Trade Center were Jewish.

These expressions of hostility toward the United States and sympathy for those who killed so many innocent people shocked and alarmed many Americans, who wondered how foreigners could wish them ill. Americans hold their country in a high regard, and many did not realize how ambivalent others could be in their attitudes toward the world's only superpower. Anti-Americanism was nothing new, of course, but this latest strain had special characteristics related to America's overwhelming power and the way it had been used and perceived through the 1990s.

Before September 11, Americans had clearly grown comfortable with their cushy position, above the world's frays. Americans liked being richer than the rest and well insulated from their tribulations. In 2001 the new U.S. administration was becoming famous for a go-it-alone approach to international affairs, infuriating allies and rivals by its unilateral policies and decisions and by its reluctance to join other nations in collective action. One example was the international effort to do something about global warming. On September 11 the international community was preparing for a conference that would complete a final agreement on emissions controls, but the U.S., the producer of one-fourth of the world's greenhouse gases, had opted not to participate.

On those occasions when the United States did play an active part in world affairs and did join other countries in some collaborative efforts, it was usually on its own terms. Many Americans considered this reasonable and appropriate. Why should they give others any influence over matters they wanted to, and could, control themselves?

September 11 created a new reality. Beginning with that communication from Russian Pres. Vladimir Putin, President Bush spent most of the first days

FBI investigators scour the crash site of United Airlines Flight 93 in rural Pennsylvania.

after the attacks speaking and meeting with foreign leaders, building what he called a new global coalition against terrorism. "We will rally the world," Bush said, and he did just that. A president regarded warily by many world leaders as a unilateralist and a bit of a cowboy was suddenly courting support from every conceivable precinct. On September 24 the House of Representatives voted to release $582 million of the $819 million in back dues to the United Nations. Concerns that just before September 11 dominated American policy suddenly disappeared. So, for example, Uzbekistan, with its corrupt and authoritarian regime that had been held at arm's length by the United States before September 11, became an important ally and a base for American military operations soon afterward.

"Working well with others" became a category on school report cards in the U.S. in the last generation, but globally, this had not been an American value. George Washington, the founding father, offered his countrymen the vision of a United States totally insulated from foreign entanglements in his famous Farewell Address 205 years before September 11, and that remained a tantalizing goal for many Americans. Washington, of course, could not have imagined the technological changes that would shrink the world in our time. Even Americans who experienced those changes remained reluctant to accept their true implications.

September 11 ended the dream of "fortress America." The 19 Arab terrorists who hijacked four airliners that day obviously were not restrained by any sense that the United States enjoyed special protection from hostile foreign forces. The shock that went through the American population after September 11, all but eliminating air travel and tourism for weeks, also marked a turning point for the American experiment, though it was impossible to explain just how. That might take years to clarify.

The horror planned for September 11 was supposed to be worse, and very nearly was. The fourth hijacked airplane was evidently aimed at the Capitol or the White House in Washington—we may never know its target for certain. A direct hit on either would have been symbolically devastating, adding enormously to the impact of the attacks. But a group of brave and resourceful passengers on United Airlines Flight 93 prevented its hijackers from fulfilling their mission, forcing the plane down in a Pennsylvania farm field, where the lives of everyone on board ended.

The fate of Flight 93 was a demonstration of how the modern global village can function. Passengers on board the flight, who thought they were flying from Newark, N.J., to San Francisco, made calls to relatives on the ground with cellular telephones and learned that a hijacked plane already had been flown into the World Trade Center in New York. One of them was Jeremy Glick, 31, sales manager for a technology firm, who told his wife to "have a good life" and promised to go down fighting against the terrorists. Glick and several other passengers, all apparently held in the galley at the rear of the Boeing 757, were plotting to rush the cockpit of the plane, 110 feet forward of the galley, to disrupt whatever

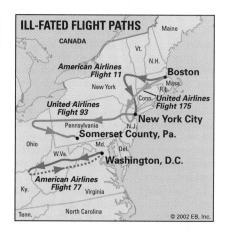

ILL-FATED FLIGHT PATHS

© 2002 EB, Inc.

September 20

President Bush, in a televised speech to the nation, announces the creation of the Office of Homeland Security.

September 24

The U.S. freezes assets of organizations that are connected with the Taliban or Osama bin Laden.

September 26

President Bush authorizes two Air Force generals to order threatening commercial airliners shot down.

September 28

The UN Security Council adopts a resolution requiring all UN members to take steps to eliminate terrorism.

After the World Trade Center collapse.

plan their hijackers had in mind. One of the other plotters, Todd Beamer, told a telephone operator whom he had reached via an onboard "airfone" about this plan. The operator heard him shout to his comrades, "Are you guys ready? Let's roll!" The operator then heard screams and sounds of a scuffle before the line went dead. In the next few moments, the plane took a series of sharp turns and then plunged into the Pennsylvania countryside near the town of Shanksville, just south of Johnstown. Somehow, the passengers had disrupted the hijackers and forced the plane to Earth.

In that case the technological wizardry of the age contributed to heroism and a self-sacrifice that may have saved many lives in Washington. This was one example of how the events of September 11 were made possible by modern technology or modern styles of life. Other examples of the same phenomenon were not so uplifting.

Eerily, the terrorists, avowed enemies of secular modernity, were able to have the enormous impact they had by mastering skills and technologies that were part of what they claimed to detest. Their ability to move freely between their countries of origin, principally Saudi Arabia and Egypt, and the flying schools and Internet cafés of the United States they so ardently hated, and then into the cockpits of those four Boeing jetliners, was perhaps the most powerful symbol of what September 11 really represented—on one hand, angry young Arabs who belonged to a movement dedicated to antimodernism and an anti-American crusade; on the other hand, a hypermodern America open to the world, open even to these fanatics who were determined to inflict great harm on the United States. In an age of irony, this ultimate irony: the terrorists could do the damage they did only by acquiring skills from American flying schools, exploiting America's porous airport-security arrangements, and mastering the arts of hiding in plain sight in a society they abhorred. In the real global village of 2001, we were all startled to discover, such trickery was amazingly simple. On

October 7

The U.S. begins air strikes in Afghanistan and also begins dropping food packets.

October 11

The FBI issues another warning that there may be more terrorist attacks in the next few days.

October 19

U.S. ground troops begin operations in Afghanistan.

October 26

President Bush signs Anti-Terrorism Act into law.

September 10, it soon became clear, we had not understood the world we lived in; a month later we understood it a lot better, though far from thoroughly.

The easy, comforting notion of a global village implies that all the world's peoples are intimate neighbours, sharing more than they do not share. But this is not the global village that September 11 revealed so starkly.

In the real modern world, different peoples have taken what are sometimes radically different paths and reached very different destinations. In Europe and North America, where technology, education, and tradition produced the greatest wealth, the failure of the Muslim world to match this prosperity was just a fact of modern life, little remarked upon before September 11. Most Muslims lived in relative poverty; some were rich from oil; and almost none, rich or poor, occupied the most modern precincts of the global village. The most modern and successful nation in the Middle East, the centre of the Muslim world, was not Muslim at all: Israel. But Israel was a hated symbol to many of its Arab neighbours.

The gulf that divides Muslim, mostly Arab peoples from Europeans and Americans, and also Asians, may be the most significant dividing line in the 21st-century world. Put simply, the secular global economy created by the richer countries gave great benefit to many and was a model to be emulated for many more. South Koreans, Chinese, Cypriots, and Chileans all subscribed to the same broad propositions that animated Americans, Germans, and Japanese: technological progress is good; wealth earned from global trade is desirable; consumerism and the democratization of wealth are goals to be pursued. For most of the adherents of this loose creed, political democracy was also part of the formula—democratic governments, most agreed, were most likely to achieve the prosperity so many were seeking.

Many Muslims and Arabs embraced the rich world's ideals—this is evident from the fact that millions of them have found ways to establish residency in rich countries and pursue new lives in them. The governments and especially the religious establishments of the Arab world, however, were not part of the fledgling consensus joined by so many other nations. No Arab government was a democracy, and no Arab nation was a full par-

ticipant in the technological revolution of the age. Only a few oil-rich autocracies even took a stab at participation.

The Muslim world has never experienced anything comparable to the enlightenment of the 17th and 18th centuries that prepared the Christian nations of Europe for the Industrial Revolution and modernity. For Muslim fundamentalists—for example, the Wahhabi sect that dominates the religious life of Saudi Arabia—nonparticipation in the modern world is seen as a good thing, a way to avoid pollution of Muslim values by infidels. But such fundamentalists are surrounded by the temptations of the wealthy world, and often by neighbours in their own countries who do not share their disdain for modernity. Tens of thousands of well-to-do Saudis, for example, own houses or apartments in Europe or the United States and happily partake of modern pleasures when visiting those places. Yet at home they support a system that denies such pleasures to most of their countrymen and provides few opportunities for citizens to express themselves or influence their government.

The Arab world differs from the modernized West and Asia in another important respect. When countries get rich, their birthrates decline. Birthrates are so low in the developed European nations that they are all facing shrinkage of their native populations. Japan is in a similar position. Conversely, the Arab countries are experiencing rapid population growth. Saudi Arabia is growing more than 3% a year; Egypt, about 2%. Burgeoning populations aggravate tensions in these societies, none of which is creating opportunities for young people sufficient to satisfy the growing number of working-age citizens.

All of these factors are related to the success Bin Laden and his allies have had in building the al-Qaeda terrorist movement that shook the world on September 11. Obviously, only a tiny fraction of the young men of the Arab and Muslim worlds joined al-Qaeda and other like-minded groups. Might there be many more in the future? The possibility could not be dismissed.

Americans took comfort from their own response to September 11. The country found many heroes to thank, from those passengers on Flight 93 to the fire fighters and police officers of New York City, so many of whom gave

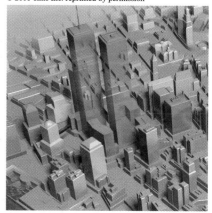

© 2001 Time Inc. reprinted by permission

The World Trade Center area: the shaded buildings were lost or damaged.

their lives that day in service to their country and community. Americans poured hundreds of millions of dollars into charities to support the victims' families and stoically put up with the practical consequences of the attacks, which included a sharp economic downturn, closures and postponements of various meetings and events, and total disruption of domestic airline travel in the United States. Countless Americans remarked on a new mood in the country, a new spirit of cooperation and sharing, and a new recognition, as many put it, of what "really matters" in their lives.

At year's end it was still too early to know the more profound impact of September 11 and its aftermath. Would Americans' lost innocence be translated into a real commitment to confronting the underlying problems confronting the global village? Or would a quick war on terrorism be followed by a relapse into American exceptionalism and another retreat from international engagement? The terrorists of September 11 challenged the United States to confront the fact that it overwhelms all other nations in its wealth, power, and influence and to accept the responsibilities that accompany such preponderance. The terrorists succeeded in making America the target. Americans would have to choose a response to that new status.

Robert G. Kaiser is an associate editor of the Washington Post, *coauthor (with Leonard Downie, Jr.) of* The News About the News: American Journalism in Peril *(forthcoming in 2002), and author of several other books on international affairs.*

November 13

Anti-Taliban forces overrun Kabul, the capital of Afghanistan.

December 7

Kandahar, the Taliban's capital, falls to Northern Alliance troops after allied bombings.

December 22

A new government, backed by the allies, is installed in Afghanistan.

December 31

The Taliban has been routed and the al-Qaeda terrorist network put on the defensive; Bin Laden and Taliban leader Mullah Omar are still at large, however.

January

> *America has never been united by blood or birth or soil. We are bound by ideals that move us beyond our backgrounds, lift us above our interests and teach us what it means to be citizens. Every child must be taught these principles. Every citizen must uphold them. And every immigrant, by embracing these ideals, makes our country more, not less, American.*
>
> George W. Bush, in his inaugural address, January 20

1 In a mass to celebrate the World Day of Peace, Pope John Paul II enjoins people of different cultures to treat one another with respect.

•

Fifteen people parachute from the top of the Petronas Towers in Malaysia to celebrate the arrival of the new millennium. (Photo right.)

•

Tyson Foods, Inc., agrees to acquire IBP, inc., in an agreement that will create the world's largest meat company.

•

El Salvador becomes the third Latin American nation (after Panama and Ecuador) to replace its national currency with the U.S. dollar.

AP/Wide World Photos

2 Two tourist boats, one from Quemoy Island and one from Matsu Island, become the first to travel legally from Taiwanese territory to mainland China.

Cambodia's legislature agrees to create a special tribunal in concert with the United Nations to try Khmer Rouge leaders who carried out a massacre in the 1970s; critics are dubious that this arrangement can be effective.

•

Women enlisting in the German armed forces become the first females eligible for combat duty in Germany; the exclusion of women in units of the military is illegal for all members of the European Union.

3 Hillary Rodham Clinton is sworn in as a senator from New York; it is the first time in U.S. history that a sitting first lady has held a political office.

International Paper Co. agrees to sell for $10.5 million three tracts of land totaling 10,725 ha (26,500 ac) in the Adirondacks in northern New York to the Nature Conservancy, an organization concerned with environmental preservation.

4 The Chief Rabbinate Council in Israel declares that Jewish law forbids allowing any but Jewish sovereignty over the Temple Mount in Jerusalem; earlier the mufti of Jerusalem had said that Islamic law prohibits any but Muslim sovereignty over the same area.

Sawt al-Shaab appears on newsstands in Syria; it is the first newspaper not published by the government or ruling party to be permitted in Syria since 1963.

The publisher of *George* announces that the quasi-political magazine founded in 1995 by John F. Kennedy, Jr., who died in 1999, will close with its March issue.

5 Australia bans the importation of beef and beef products from 30 European countries to prevent "mad cow" disease from entering the country. (*See* January 13.)

U.S. Pres. Bill Clinton signs an order banning logging and the building of roads in more than 23.5 million ha (58 million ac) of national forest land.

6 Elections are held in Thailand; the opposition Thai Rak Thai Party appears to win a majority of the 500 parliamentary seats.

Undeterred by bitterly cold weather, Muslim pilgrims from throughout the world gather in Bangladesh to celebrate the festival of Biswa Ijtema.

South Africa calls for assistance from the World Health Organization in attempting to contain a cholera outbreak that has struck more than 15,000 people in KwaZulu/Natal state.

7 John Kufuor is inaugurated as president of Ghana in that nation's first peaceful transition from one elected government to another.

Groups of soldiers attack the office of broadcast media during an attempted coup in Côte d'Ivoire.

In a referendum in Senegal a new constitution is approved by a margin of more than 92%.

8 The UN's World Food Programme releases a report and map detailing the incidence of undernourishment in the world; one-third of the population of sub-Saharan Africa, including 73% of Somalia's people, is chronically hungry, according to the report.

The French-based construction concern Lafarge Group announces that it will acquire the British company Blue Circle Industries to create the world's biggest cement company.

India's biggest film financier, Bharat Shah, is arrested on suspicion of having colluded with organized crime figures to extort money from the Bollywood film industry, the largest in the world.

9 At a meeting of the American Astronomical Society, Geoffrey W. Marcy announces that his team has found two planetary systems that call into question everything known about such systems; one has anomalous orbits, and the other has planets of seemingly impossible size.

Australian scientists say that analysis of DNA taken from human remains that are about 60,000 years old shows no links with human ancestors from Africa; this suggests that Africa is not the only site of the genesis of the human species.

Sen. Jesse Helms of North Carolina says that he will stop blocking U.S. payment of back dues to the United Nations; the UN estimates that the United States is close to $1.6 billion in arrears. (*See* September 24.)

The president of the Philadelphia Orchestra announces that Christoph Eschenbach will become the orchestra's seventh director in 2003 when Wolfgang Sawallisch retires.

10 American Airlines agrees to buy Trans World Airlines and, in a separate transaction, reveals plans to acquire 20% of US Airways. (*See* April 9.)

Actress Jeanne Moreau is inducted into the French Academy of Fine Arts; she is the first woman to be so honoured.

A controversial statue depicting Franklin Delano Roosevelt, the 32nd president of the U.S., seated in a wheelchair is unveiled in Washington, D.C.

An Asian gaur (an endangered species), cloned and implanted in the womb of a cow in Iowa, dies of dysentery two days after being born.

11 The U.S. Federal Communications Commission approves the megamerger of America Online and Time Warner, which has been in the works for a full year; the new company, AOL Time Warner, begins trading the next morning.

Yoichiro Kaizaki resigns as president and CEO of the Bridgestone Corp., the parent of Bridgestone/Firestone; he denies that he is doing so in order to accept responsibility for the massive tire recall in 2000, although that is how it is interpreted in Japan.

12 Anson Chan, the head of civil service and second-ranked official in Hong Kong, unexpectedly resigns; she had been appointed to her post by the British, and it was felt that her departure did not bode well for Hong Kong's continued autonomy under China.

In a study published in *Science*, scientists report that they inserted a jellyfish gene into the ovum of a rhesus monkey, and the resultant monkey, born in October 2000, carries the gene; it is the first transgenic primate.

13 A magnitude-7.6 earthquake strikes El Salvador; felt in Honduras and Nicaragua and even as far away as Mexico City, the quake shuts down the capital, San Salvador, and sets off landslides that bury the middle-class Las Colinas neighbourhood in Santa Tecla. (*See* February 13.)

A cow that appears to have "mad cow" disease is found in a slaughterhouse in Italy;

it is the first time the disease has been reported in an Italian-born cow. (*See* January 5 and January 30.)

In the worst public transportation accident in Swaziland's history, an overloaded bus crashes, killing 30 people.

14 Jorge Sampaio is reelected president of Portugal in a landslide; the voter turnout, the lowest in the nation's history, is attributed to the perception by many that the popular Sampaio is unbeatable.

15 The East African Community, an economic organization consisting of Kenya, Tanzania, and Uganda, is formally inaugurated; it replaces an organization of the same name and members that had ceased to exist in 1977.

Motorola, Inc., announces that it is closing the Harvard, Ill., plant, its only cellular phone manufacturing facility in the U.S., and laying off 2,500 workers.

In the field of children's literature, the Newbery Medal is awarded to Richard Peck for *A Year Down Yonder,* and David Small wins the Caldecott Medal for his illustration of *So You Want to Be President?* by Judith St. George.

A trilateral partnership for cooperation and research is announced by the Solomon R. Guggenheim Museum in New York City, the State Hermitage Museum in St. Petersburg, and the Kunsthistorisches Museum in Vienna.

Kim Jong Il, leader of North Korea, makes a sudden and secret visit to Shanghai; it is only the second time in 18 years that he has been known to travel outside his country.

16 Swiss food giant Nestlé SA agrees to acquire Ralston Purina Co., the St. Louis, Mo.-based manufacturer of pet foods, for $10.1 billion and create a company called Nestlé Purina Pet Care.

Luther and Johnny Htoo, the twin teenage leaders of the rebel Karen group in Myanmar (Burma) known as God's Army, surrender to Thai authorities at the border, together with 12 followers, mostly children or teenagers.

Dave Winfield, a power hitter who played with several teams and is the only athlete in history to have been drafted in football and basketball as well as baseball, and Kirby Puckett, who led the Minnesota Twins to two World Series championships, are elected to the National Baseball Hall of Fame. (*See* March 6.)

17 Two teams of scientists working in Cambridge, Mass., report that they have brought a beam of light to a full stop and then restarted it; the achievement means that it may be possible to store light.

California's beleaguered electrical power companies institute a series of rolling blackouts, in which blocks of customers are denied power for up to 90 minutes, in order to save power.

The British House of Commons overwhelmingly passes a bill to outlaw fox hunting with hounds; the ban is rejected by the House of Lords on March 26, however.

Alain Rossignol/KTM Sportmotorcycle AG Motorsport

The School of the Americas, run by the U.S. Army and famous for having trained authoritarian Latin American leaders, including Panama's Manuel Noriega and Nicaragua's Anastasio Somoza, reopens (it had closed in December 2000) with the new name Western Hemisphere Institute for Security Cooperation.

18 The government of the Democratic Republic of the Congo acknowledges that Pres. Laurent Kabila has died, two days after reports that he had been assassinated circulated throughout the world. (*See* January 26.)

U.S. civil rights leader Jesse Jackson publicly acknowledges that he fathered and is providing financial support for an out-of-wedlock child born in May 1999.

19 The Ecuadoran oil tanker *Jessica,* which ran aground on a reef in the Galápagos Islands on January 16, suffers a crack in its cargo hold and begins leaking diesel fuel, threatening the fragile and unique ecosystem with disaster.

The man believed to be the head of the Sinaloa drug cartel, Joaquín Guzmán Loera, escapes from a maximum security prison near Guadalajara, Mex.

20 George W. Bush is inaugurated as the 43rd president of the United States; thousands of people who believe that he gained the office through illegitimate or unfair means protest. (*See* January 23.)

Faced with huge demonstrations against him and with the withdrawal of military support, Joseph Estrada resigns the presidency of the

Philippines, and his vice president, Gloria Macapagal Arroyo, is sworn in to replace him. (*See* April 25.)

•

Michelle Kwan wins her fifth U.S. national figure-skating championship.

21 Pope John Paul II names a record 37 men to the Sacred College of Cardinals, 10 of them from Latin America; on January 28 he adds 7 more, bringing the number of voting cardinals to 135, a new high.

•

The annual Paris–Dakar Rally comes to a successful conclusion as threatened interference in Western Sahara fails to materialize; winners are Jutta Kleinschmidt, in a Mitsubishi Pajero; Fabrizio Meoni, on a KTM 660 LC4 motorcycle (photo left); and Karel Loprais, in a Tatra T815 ZER truck.

•

At the Golden Globe Awards in Hollywood, *Gladiator* and *Almost Famous* take home best picture honours; best director is Ang Lee for *Crouching Tiger, Hidden Dragon,* and best screenplay goes to Stephen Gaghan for *Traffic.*

22 Pakistan closes all of Afghanistan's Islamic Taliban's offices in the country and freezes the assets of suspected terrorist Osama bin Laden.

•

Akebono, the first non-Japanese *yokozuna* (grand champion sumo wrestler), announces his retirement at the age of 31, because of chronic knee pain.

23 Matthew Kneale wins the 2000 Whitbread Book of the Year Award for his novel *English Passengers;* the

previous four prizes, awarded for books published in the U.K., had gone to collections of poetry.

•

The Florida State Association of Supervisors of Elections votes on a single standard for conducting recounts and asks the state legislature for uniform statewide voting technology. (*See* January 20.)

•

On the eve of the Chinese New Year, five Falun Gong followers set themselves on fire in Tiananmen Square in Beijing.

24 The year 4699, Year of the Snake, begins and is celebrated by Chinese throughout the world.

•

On the most auspicious day of the Kumbh Mela festival (which began on January 9 and ends on February 21), tens of millions of pilgrims bathe at the confluence of the Ganges, Yamuna, and mythical Saraswati rivers at Allahabad, India.

•

Marine archaeologists announce that they have completed the first archaeological survey of an offshore region in sub-Saharan Africa and have found four sunken ships and submerged Swahili villages off Kenya's coast.

25 The World Economic Forum opens in Davos, Switz.; in response to past criticism, delegates from unions and nongovernmental organizations will be included as well as government officials, and there will be live Internet broadcasts of some sessions.

•

In the ongoing "banana war," Chiquita Brands International sues the European Commission, contending that banana import quotas have nearly bank-

rupted the company. (*See* November 28.)

26 An earthquake of magnitude 7.9 strikes Gujarat state in India; the commercial city of Bhuj, with a population of 150,000, is largely destroyed, and several cities experience damage in the quake, which shakes the entire subcontinent.

•

Joseph Kabila is inaugurated as the president of the Democratic Republic of the Congo. (*See* January 18.)

27 At least 17 people die on the Tanzanian island of Zanzibar when police clash with opposition demonstrators demanding that new elections be held and the results of previous elections annulled.

•

Jennifer Capriati defeats Martina Hingis 6–4, 6–3 to win the Australian Open tennis tournament in the former Olympic champion's first Grand Slam win; on January 28 Andre Agassi beats Arnaud Clement in straight sets in the men's competition to win his seventh Grand Slam title.

28 The Baltimore Ravens, a franchise that has been playing in Baltimore, Md., only since 1996, defeats the New York Giants 34–7 to win Super Bowl XXXV. (*See* January 31.)

•

Kuwait's entire cabinet, including the premier, Crown Prince Sheikh Saad al-Abdullah as-Salim as-Sabah, resigns.

29 The Chrysler division of DaimlerChrysler announces plans to eliminate 26,000 jobs worldwide

over the next three years; on the same day, the Xerox Corp. says it will eliminate 4,000 jobs to cut costs.

•

The New York Philharmonic announces that Lorin Maazel will replace Kurt Masur as music director to start the 2002–03 season.

30 Tiznow, which won the Breeders' Cup Classic race in November 2000, is named Horse of the Year for 2000.

•

Daron Rahlves becomes the first American male skier since 1982 to win a gold medal at the world Alpine championships when he stuns onlookers by winning the supergiant slalom in Sankt Anton, Austria.

•

The U.S. Food and Drug Administration says that it has quarantined 1,222 Texas cattle that have eaten feed containing animal by-products, which creates a risk for "mad cow" disease. (*See* January 13.)

31 A Scottish court convicts Libyan 'Abd al-Baset al-Megrahi of the 1988 bombing of Pan Am Flight 103 and acquits his countryman Lamin Khalifa Fhimah. (*See* February 3.)

•

Reports surface that law-enforcement officials in Tampa, Fla., photographed the face of every spectator at the Super Bowl in order to find out if any of them were wanted on charges by any agency. (*See* January 28.)

•

The new state flag is flown over the Georgia statehouse; approved by the lower house of the legislature on January 24, it features five historical flags and relegates the formerly prominent Confederate battle flag to a small banner near the bottom.

February

1 The major European steelmaker Corus Group announces that it will cut one-fifth of its workforce, more than 6,000 jobs, mostly in depressed regions of Great Britain.

Edward Albee attends the opening of his new play, *The Play About the Baby,* in New York City; the playwright is known for not attending his openings.

2 BellSouth, the telephone company that serves the southeastern United States, announces that it will eliminate all its pay phones by the end of 2002, citing loss of revenue due to competition from cell phones.

A plan to reintroduce elk to the Great Smoky Mountains, from where they disappeared at least 150 years ago, gets under way with the arrival of 25 elk at a 1.2-ha (3-ac) pen in North Carolina.

3 During government-organized protests against the verdict in the case concerning the 1988 terrorist acts against Pan Am Flight 103 over Lockerbie, Scot., four Libyan students stab themselves in Tripoli. (*See* January 31.)

The XFL, a new professional football league founded by Vince McMahon and owned by World Wrestling Federation Entertainment and NBC, opens its season with the Las Vegas (Nev.) Outlaws against the New York/New Jersey Hitmen and the Orlando (Fla.) Rage against the Chicago Enforcers. (*See* May 10.)

4 An official of the Tibetan government in exile says that India has granted refugee status to the teenage Karmapa Lama, number three in the Tibetan Buddhist hierarchy, who had fled to India in January 2000.

At a pole-vault meet named for him in Donetsk, Ukraine, Sergey Bubka, who broke 35 world records in his career and who is widely held to be the best pole-vaulter ever, announces his retirement.

5 The Halifax Group, the largest mortgage bank in the U.K., agrees to buy out the Equitable Life Assurance Society for about $1.5 billion and rename the joint company Halifax Equitable.

The Internet toy retailer eToys announces that it will go out of business on April 6.

The Holy Land Experience, a new theme park that purports to re-create the Jerusalem of biblical times, opens in Orlando; the Jewish Defense League, which believes the park has an evangelical Christian bias, protests. (*See* February 8.)

6 Ariel Sharon defeats Ehud Barak in elections to become prime minister of Israel; his margin of victory is unprecedentedly large, and the voter turnout is unprecedentedly low. (*See* March 7.)

Thousands of people march in Kiev, Ukraine, to demand the resignation of Pres. Leonid Kuchma, who has been implicated in a variety of scandals.

Cipla Ltd., an Indian company that makes generic drugs, announces a plan to sell the drugs used to combat AIDS to Doctors Without Borders at a price substantially lower than that charged by the world's major pharmaceutical manufacturers.

The American household appliances manufacturer Sunbeam Corp. files for bankruptcy protection.

7 Jean-Bertrand Aristide is sworn in as president of Haiti; opposition parties set up what they call a parallel government, arguing that Aristide's election is not legitimate.

Alfred Sirven, a prominent figure in the complex and far-reaching Elf Aquitaine corruption scandal in France, presents himself for trial in Paris after four years in hiding. (*See* May 30.)

The Eagles (Aguilas Cibaeñas), representing the Dominican Republic, win baseball's Caribbean Series with a 4–2 record.

US Coast Guard/AFP Worldwide

8 Former German chancellor Helmut Kohl reaches a plea agreement with prosecutors investigating a fund-raising scandal in which criminal charges against him will be dropped and he will pay a fine; the investigation into Christian Democratic Union practices continues, however.

•

Disney's California Adventure, a new theme park based on the attractions of the Golden State, opens in Anaheim, Calif. (*See* February 5.)

9 *The USS* Greeneville, *a U.S. submarine conducting exercises for a group of VIP tourists, strikes and sinks the* Ehime Maru, *a Japanese fishing boat, after surfacing rapidly near Hawaii; nine people, many of them vocational-high-school students, are killed in spite of the efforts of the U.S. Coast Guard, which arrives on the scene about 30 minutes after the collision. (Photo above.)*

•

Thaksin Shinawatra takes office as prime minister of Thailand.

•

On the eve of the anniversary of Iran's Islamic revolution, a demonstration in Tehran demanding freedom of expression is violently dispersed by police.

10 Members of an Islamic rebel group slaughter 27 people, mostly women and children, in a shantytown near Berrouaghia, Alg.

•

Astronauts Marsha S. Ivins, Robert L. Curbeam, Jr., and Thomas D. Jones install Destiny, the first of five planned scientific research laboratories, on the International Space Station.

11 In accordance with the peace treaty signed in 2000, Ethiopia begins withdrawing its troops from Eritrea.

•

Tens of thousands of nationalists demand early elections in Croatia, opposing the policy of Prime Minister Ivica Racan of cooperating with the UN in investigating possible Croatian war crimes against Serbs.

Ellen MacArthur breaks the women's solo around-the-world sailing record when she completes the Vendee Globe race in 94 days 4 hr 25 min; the previous record, 140 days, was set by Catherine Chabaud in 1997.

12 Omar Hassan al-Bashir is sworn in for a second five-year term as president of The Sudan after elections in December 2000.

•

In Dnipropetrovsk, Ukraine, Russian Pres. Vladimir Putin and Ukrainian Pres. Leonid Kuchma sign an agreement to cooperate in aviation and space research and to reconnect their power grids.

•

The spacecraft NEAR Shoemaker lands on the near-Earth asteroid Eros; the landing, planned at the last minute, is the first time a spacecraft has landed on an asteroid.

•

At a joint news conference, scientists from Celera Genomics and the Human Genome Project say it appears that there are only about 30,000 human genes, far fewer than the 100,000 that had long been assumed.

13 El Salvador is hit with its second earthquake in as many months when a magnitude-6.6 temblor strikes towns to the east of San Salvador, killing 402 (*see* January 13); on February 14 a magnitude-7.3 earthquake with its epicentre in the ocean shakes the island of Sumatra in Indonesia. (*See* February 28.)

•

The Indianapolis (Ind.) Baptist Temple, which denies that the U.S. government has jurisdiction over it, is seized by Internal Revenue Service agents to satisfy a debt of $6 million in unpaid taxes.

14 The European Parliament approves stringent standards governing all aspects of genetically modified foods and seed in hopes of ending an unofficial three-year moratorium on such items.

•

In Trinidad and Tobago, after a 55-day standoff, seven people who had lost elections to the House of Representatives and then had been nominated to the Senate by Prime Minister Basdeo Panday are appointed to the House by Pres. Arthur Robinson; Robinson and Panday had accused each other of undermining the constitution.

•

The Kansas State Board of Education reverses a 1999 decision and restores the teaching of the theory of evolution to the state science curriculum.

•

Violent protests by Hindu nationalist elements against the celebration of Valentine's Day, popular among the younger, more Westernized population, take place in cities throughout India.

•

A bichon frise named Special Times Just Right! wins best in show at the Westminster Kennel Club Dog Show; it is the first time the top prize at the premier American dog show has gone to this breed.

15 Voters in Bahrain approve a measure that changes the form of government to a constitutional monarchy, restores the parliament (which was abolished in 1975), and gives women the right to vote.

•

An official Russian state commission investigating the sinking of the submarine *Kursk* in August 2000 confirms that a torpedo exploded aboard the sub. (*See* October 8.)

•

A court in Frankfurt, Ger., sentences former terrorist Hans-Joachim Klein to nine years in prison for his participation in the 1975 attack on an OPEC conference in Vienna in which three persons were killed.

•

Nature magazine publishes a report that scientists have found two recently active volcanoes on the Gakkel ridge, under the Arctic Ocean off Greenland; the find is surprising because it was thought that such volcanic activity would not occur in slow-spreading seafloor sites.

16 Comoros and the breakaway island of Anjouan sign an agreement that provides for national elections and the adoption of a new constitution.

•

The New China News Agency says that an unusually severe winter has led to the deaths

of 38 newborn babies and several expectant mothers in northern China near the Mongolian border; temperatures in this region have dipped to –51.7 °C (–61 °F).

•

Imelda Marcos opens the Marikina City Footwear Museum near Manila; the exhibits include hundreds of pairs of shoes donated by the former first lady and other local celebrities.

17 An aged, rusting freighter carrying 908 Kurdish men, women, and children runs aground on the French Riviera; the captain and crew have disappeared by the time authorities arrive to rescue the would-be immigrants.

•

The Welsh rock band Manic Street Preachers becomes the first English-language musical group to play in Havana since 1979; their song "Baby Elián" is particularly warmly received.

18 Violence between indigenous Dayak and Madurese migrants from other parts of Indonesia breaks out in Borneo; by the end of the week, well over 200 people are dead and ships are being sent to evacuate thousands of refugees.

•

Riots break out in 18 prisons across the state of São Paulo, Braz., and hundreds of people, most of them visiting family members, are taken hostage.

•

Celebrated stock-car racing star Dale Earnhardt, Sr., is killed in a crash near the end of the Daytona 500 race; Michael Waltrip goes on to win the race.

19 In a $3.1 billion deal, the Luxembourg company Arbed, Usinor of France,

and Aceralia of Spain announce plans to merge to become the world's largest steel company; annual production of the new company is expected to be 46 million metric tons, while the current leader, Nippon Steel of Japan, produced 28 million metric tons in 2000.

•

Lieut. Gen. Tin Oo, a member of Myanmar's (Burma's) ruling junta, is killed in a helicopter crash together with a cabinet minister, seven government officials, and five others.

20 The U.S. Federal Bureau of Investigation acknowledges that one of its top experts on Russian counterintelligence, Robert Philip Hanssen, has been one of Russia's most valuable spies for 15 years.

•

Scientists report that DNA testing of the skeletons of children confirms that there was a major malaria epidemic in the 5th century AD in Rome; the epidemic may have contributed to Rome's decline and may have persuaded Attila to bypass the city.

•

An exhibit of erotic art by Pablo Picasso, featuring work he did from age 13 to age 92, opens at the Musée du Jeu de Paume in Paris.

21 Great Britain suspends all exports of animals and animal products and sets up quarantine areas in an attempt to contain an outbreak of foot-and-mouth disease; another outbreak, in Argentina, causes Brazil to issue a ban on Argentine beef.

•

In a Grammy Awards ceremony at which most of the attention is given to controversial rap artist Eminem, Song of the Year honours go

to U2's "Beautiful Day," and Album of the Year is won by Steely Dan's *Two Against Nature*.

•

Francisco Xabier García Gaztelu, believed to be the top military leader of the Basque separatist group ETA, is arrested in Anglet, France.

•

The foreign ministers of Nigeria and São Tomé and Príncipe sign a treaty allowing the two countries to explore jointly for minerals in the region lying between them in the Gulf of Guinea.

22 For the first time, a non-nationalist government is elected in Bosnia and Herzegovina.

•

Finland wins the men's relay at the world Nordic skiing championships; four days later the result is annulled after several Finnish skiers fail their drug tests.

•

The Society of Stage Directors and Choreographers announces that its nine-year strike against Radio City Music Hall in New York City has been settled.

•

British fashion designer Alexander McQueen closes a deal in which he is selling a majority stake of his design label to the Italian luxury goods maker Gucci Group; the influential couturier served three years as head designer of the Givenchy fashion house.

23 In Moscow a judge rules that the Jehovah's Witnesses have not violated a law prohibiting religious sects that incite violence and thus are permitted to practice their religion freely in Russia.

•

A U.S. Court of Appeals rules that government agencies must give Native Americans a complete tally of how much money should be in their accounts; the accounts have been so badly mismanaged since they were started in 1887 that the Indians bringing suit believe more than $10 billion has been lost.

•

Laurence Olivier Awards are presented in London to,

among others, actors Julie Walters, Samantha Spiro, Conleth Hill, and Daniel Evans; the best new play is *Blue/Orange* by Joe Penhall.

•

Concerto for Cello and Orchestra: In Memoriam F.D.R., a new piece by Peter Schickele commissioned by New Heritage Music, is performed by Paul Tobias and

the Chamber Symphony of the Manhattan School of Music.

24 Violent storms hit the eastern half of the United States, with tornadoes in Mississippi and Arkansas, flooding in Kansas and Missouri, and heavy snowfall in Nebraska and Minnesota.

•

Zapatista leaders begin a 15-day march from Chiapas to Mexico City to demand greater rights and more autonomy for Indians in Mexico.

25 For the first time since independence, the Communist Party is returned to power in legislative elections in Moldova.

In runoff presidential elections held in Cape Verde, PAICV candidate Pedro Pires wins with a margin of 1%.

•

The British Academy of Film and Television Arts presents four awards each to *Gladiator* and *Crouching Tiger, Hidden Dragon*.

26 **The Taliban rulers in Afghanistan order the destruction of all statues, including exquisite ancient statues of Buddha; the world community reacts with horror, but to no avail. (Photo left.)**

A U.S. federal judge orders the income-tax-preparation firm H&R Block to stop advertising its high-interest loans against expected tax refunds as "rapid refunds."

27 Nineteen foreign ministers representing the member states of NATO meet in Brussels to discuss

solutions to, among other problems, growing conflict along the Kosovo border in Yugoslavia.

•

The Polisario Front celebrates the 25th anniversary of its declaration of an independent republic of the Western Sahara; the territory was annexed by Morocco in 1979.

•

The U.S. National Academy of Sciences publishes a report saying scientists at the Johnson Space Center in Houston, Texas, have found a crystal in a meteorite from Mars that resembles Earth crystals formed by bacteria, a finding that points toward the possibility of life on the red planet; many scientists are skeptical, however.

28 France defies the European Union and offers financial aid to farmers suffering from the collapse of beef prices caused by the outbreak of mad-cow disease, throwing into doubt the future ability of the EU to maintain a common agricultural policy among all its members.

•

Rwanda and Uganda begin withdrawing troops from the Democratic Republic of the Congo in accordance with a UN plan to bring peace to the area.

•

The Pacific Northwest is hit by an earthquake of magnitude 6.7 that lasts for 40 seconds, with the most damage occurring in Seattle, Wash.; no deaths are reported and injuries are few, at least in part because the epicentre is some 50 km (30 mi) underground. (*See* February 13.)

•

A panel in Oklahoma City, Okla., recommends the payment of reparations to the survivors and descendants of the victims of the Tulsa race riot of 1921, one of the nation's worst.

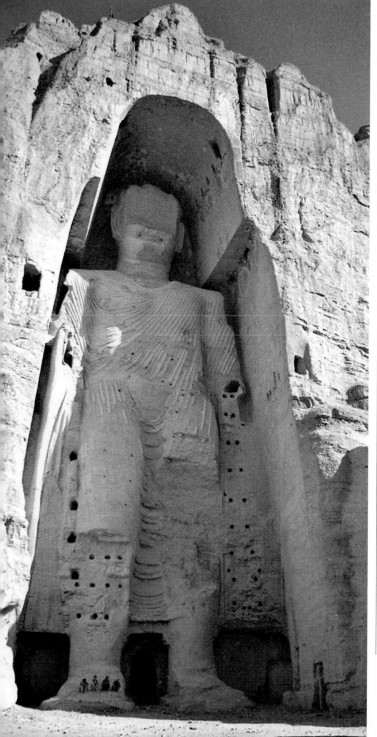

AP/Wide World Photos

March

1 Seven foreign oil workers—four Americans, an Argentine, a Chilean, and a New Zealander—who had been kidnapped in October 2000 in Ecuador are freed after a ransom of some $13 million is paid.

China ceremonially begins construction of what is to be the world's first commercial maglev (magnetic levitation) train, to run from Shanghai's financial district to one of its airports and begin operations in 2003.

A report in the journal *Nature* describes findings that a common compound, magnesium boride, is superconductive at temperatures 16 °C (29 °F) higher than any other simple metallic compound.

2 Jean-Marie Cherestal is sworn in as prime minister of Haiti, as is his cabinet, which includes members of opposition parties.

The U.S. Navy halts bombing exercises on Vieques Island, off Puerto Rico, pending talks with the Puerto Rican government. (*See* April 26.)

U.S. Pres. George W. Bush grants "temporary protected status" to 150,000 illegal immigrants from El Salvador; Salvadoran Pres. Francisco Flores has said that remittances from these immigrants are vital to El Salvador's recovery from the earthquakes that had shaken the country earlier in the year.

3 A supposed bomb placed in the cargo hold under the seat that Thai Prime Minister Thaksin Shinawatra was to occupy explodes, destroying the jet at Bangkok International Airport 35 minutes before its scheduled takeoff.

Senegalese Pres. Abdoulaye Wade replaces Prime Minister Moustapha Niasse; the new prime minister, Madior Boyé, is Senegal's first woman prime minister.

John Ruiz defeats Evander Holyfield in Las Vegas, Nev., to take the World Boxing Association title and become the first Hispanic heavyweight champion.

4 In a referendum, voters in Switzerland resoundingly reject a proposition to begin negotiations toward entering the European Union.

In the village of Castelo de Paiva, Port., a 116-year-old bridge collapses and two cars and a double-decker bus fall into the Douro River, killing about 70 people; it is the worst road accident in the history of Portugal.

5 A fire in a dormitory at a girls' secondary school in Gindiri, Nigeria, kills at least 23 girls; the dormitory had been locked for the night because of the proximity of a boys' school.

A freshman at Santana High School in Santee, Calif., opens fire at school, killing 2 other students and wounding 13.

6 An explosion kills 41 people, mostly children, at an elementary school in Wanzi county in China, and officials blame a lone terrorist; the children were reportedly being made to assemble fireworks by their teachers.

Bill Mazeroski, a second baseman famous for hitting the winning home run in the 1960 World Series, and Negro leagues pitcher Hilton Smith are elected to the National Baseball Hall of Fame. (*See* January 16.)

Russian Pres. Vladimir Putin takes part in a 40-minute live Internet conversation moderated and broadcast over the World Wide Web by the BBC.

7 Ariel Sharon takes office as the prime minister of Israel (*see* February 6); meanwhile, the Knesset (parliament) votes to return to the parliamentary system, whereby the prime minister is elected by legislators.

The government of Fiji is declared illegal by a court and resigns.

8 Bernard Landry, who has expressed aggressively separatist opinions, is sworn in as the pre-

George Serras/National Museum of Australia 2001

Yugoslavia is presented with papers officially reinstating his Yugoslavian citizenship.

13 The first outbreak of foot-and-mouth disease in continental Europe is confirmed by the French Ministry of Agriculture; the disease has been found on a farm at Mayenne.

•

The Japanese stock market falls to its lowest level since 1985 amid political uncertainty and opposition to Prime Minister Yoshiro Mori.

•

The Australian dollar falls to 50.48 U.S. cents, its lowest level in history.

•

The Indian Internet news service Tehelka.com begins showing videotapes of government bribe taking over a defense contract; the exposé throws the government into chaos.

14 The first Albany Medical Center Prize in Medicine and Biomedical Research is awarded to Arnold J. Levine for his discovery of and work on the *p53* gene, which, when mutated, is a major cause of cancer.

•

Bristol-Myers Squibb announces that it no longer opposes other drugmakers' producing low-cost versions of its anti-AIDS drug Zerit for sale in Africa.

•

The Iditarod Trail Sled Dog Race is won for the third year in a row, and the fourth time overall, by Doug Swingley, who completes the 1,770-km (1,100-mi) trip in 9 days 19 hours 55 minutes.

•

A life-size bronze statue of Mother Teresa is unveiled at the Mother House, the headquarters of the Missionaries of Charity order that she founded, in Kolkata (Calcutta).

mier of Quebec, succeeding Lucien Bouchard.

•

Indictments for massive fraud in eBay art auctions on the Internet are brought against three men, none of whom has been arrested and one of whom has not even been located.

9 Flooding caused by snowmelt in Ukraine raises the Tisza River to its highest point in over a century; it is measured at 7.6 m (25 ft) in the Hungarian village of Zahony.

•

In Fort Lauderdale, Fla., Lionel Tate, age 14, who was convicted in January of having killed a six-year-old girl when he was 12, is sentenced to life in prison without parole.

10 German Gunda Niemann-Stirnemann breaks her own world record in speed skating in the 5,000-m race at the world

championships in Salt Lake City, Utah.

•

The Nuu-chah-nulth Tribal Council, representing some 6,500 members of 12 First Nations of Canada, agrees to a treaty with the province of British Columbia and with the federal government that grants it a measure of autonomy and financial benefits in return for cessation of exemption from payment of federal taxes.

11 *Prime Minister John Howard officially opens the National Museum of Australia in Canberra; the innovative museum, devoted to the history of Australia and its peoples, is immediately and immensely popular. (Photo above.)*

•

American astronauts James S. Voss and Susan J. Helms undertake the longest space walk since the shuttle program began, 8 hours 56 minutes; their task is to help move a docking port on the International Space Station.

•

Former secretary of the treasury Lawrence H. Summers is named to replace Neil L. Rudenstine as president of Harvard University.

12 Yoweri Museveni is reelected president of Uganda in a bitterly fought election.

•

In a military training exercise in Kuwait, a U.S. Navy jet mistakenly drops three bombs on an observation post, killing five U.S. military personnel and a New Zealand army major.

•

The largest transatlantic financial services deal to date takes place when Prudential PLC in Great Britain agrees to buy the American insurance company American General Corp. for some $26.5 billion; the merger creates the world's sixth largest insurance group.

•

In the London hotel where he was born, Crown Prince Alexander Karadjordjevic of

15 Uganda, Rwanda, Zimbabwe, and the Democratic Republic of the Congo all begin pulling their troops back from the front lines of the battle in the Congo, as required by an agreement made under the auspices of the United Nations.

•

A boat carrying some 60 would-be refugees who had left the Dominican Republic bound for Puerto Rico 24 days earlier crashes on a coral reef off Haiti; 57 occupants are feared dead.

•

A forensics expert confirms that the skeletons found on a ranch 145 km (90 mi) west of San Antonio, Texas, are those of atheist leader Madalyn Murray O'Hair and her son and granddaughter, who disappeared in 1995.

•

Two antiques dealers are charged with having faked appraisals (by arranging for friends to submit Civil War swords the dealers had given them previously) on the popular television show *Antiques Roadshow*.

16 In a ruling accepted by both disputants, the World Court divides territories long contested between Bahrain and Qatar; Bahrain gets the Hawar Islands and Qit'at Jaradah Island, while Qatar gets the islands of Janan and Hadd Janan and Fasht ad-Dibal reef as well as the coastal area of Zubara.

•

Explosions rip through four different apartment buildings owned by state cotton mills in Shijiazhuang, the capital of Hebei province, China; authorities blame a single former worker and say that only 108 people were killed, though many find both these claims implausible.

•

In Phoenix, Ariz., Swedish golfer Annika Sörenstam sets a new Ladies Professional Golf Association record when she shoots a 59; 59 is also the men's Professional Golfers' Association of America record.

17 In Cornwall, Eng., the Eden Project, the largest botanical garden in the world, opens; it bills itself as "the living theatre of plants and people" and expects to attract 750,000 visitors a day.

•

On the Greek island of Kalymnos, nine marble statues believed to be from the Hellenistic period and more than 2,000 years old are discovered; shepherds unearthed the ancient statues while digging holes for fence posts.

18 Bertrand Delanoë becomes the first elected Socialist mayor of Paris since the 19th century.

•

Aventis CropScience reports that the genetically modified StarLink corn (maize) has accidentally found its way into more than 430 million bushels of corn in the U.S. (*See* June 13.)

19 In a racially charged atmosphere and amid rioting, elections held in Guyana return Pres. Bharrat Jagdeo to power with 53% of the vote for his third consecutive term; he is sworn in on March 24.

•

The Interpublic Group of Companies, based in New York City, announces plans to buy Chicago's True North Communications for some $2.1 billion; the acquisition of True North will make the Interpublic Group of Companies the largest advertising company in the world.

•

The Australian mining concern BHP Co. Ltd. announces plans to merge with Billiton PLC, based in Great Britain, in what is expected to be the largest corporate merger in Australia's history; the value of the new firm, BHP Billiton Ltd., in late June when the merger is completed is U.S. $38 billion.

•

Mary Robinson, possibly the most successful high commissioner for human rights since the UN Commission on Human Rights was established in 1946, unexpectedly says she will leave the office when her term ends in September; she changes her mind on April 2, however.

•

The Rock and Roll Hall of Fame inducts, among others, Solomon Burke, Michael Jackson, Paul Simon, and Ritchie Valens and the bands Aerosmith, Queen, Steely Dan, and the Flamingos.

20 *The largest offshore oil platform in the world, which is owned by the Brazilian company Petrobrás, sinks off the coast of Rio de Janeiro five days after explosions on the platform killed 10 workers. (Photo below.)*

The editor and owner of *Al-Majales* magazine, Hedayet Sultan as-Salem, one of the first women journalists in Kuwait, is shot dead in her car in Kuwait City.

•

The U.S. National Imagery and Mapping Agency says that it believes it has located the Mars Polar Lander in images of Mars; the spacecraft disappeared in December 1999.

21 The Boeing Co. announces that it will move its headquarters from Seattle, Wash., to either Dallas, Texas; Denver, Colo.; or Chicago, setting off shock waves in Seattle and a race to attract the company in the other three cities; on May 10 Boeing announces that it has picked Chicago.

•

The U.S. Department of Agriculture seizes two flocks of sheep, some 370 animals

AP/Wide World Photos

in all, in Vermont because of fears that the sheep, imported from Belgium and The Netherlands in 1996, may carry "mad cow" disease.

•

Ali Ahmeti, the political representative of the National Liberation Army, an Albanian rebel group in Macedonia, announces a unilateral cease-fire, saying his group wants to negotiate with the Macedonian government.

22 South Korean Pres. Kim Dae Jung opens Incheon International Airport, which will replace Seoul's Gimpo Airport as the gateway to South Korea; the facility has the capacity to become a major hub in northeastern Asia.

•

Pres. Mathieu Kérékou easily wins reelection as president of Benin in the second round of voting; there are allegations of election fraud, however.

•

The journal *Nature* publishes a report by paleontologist Maeve G. Leakey on a 3.5-million-year-old hominid skull she found in Kenya in 1999; Leakey believes it is a new genus and species, which she has named *Kenyanthropus platyops*, and it suggests that humans are not necessarily descended from *Australopithicus*.

23 The Russian space station *Mir*, after 5,511 days in space and 86,330 orbits of Earth, splashes down to its final resting place in the South Pacific Ocean.

•

The trust representing the heirs of Margaret Mitchell, author of *Gone with the Wind*, asks a federal judge to issue an injunction stopping the publication of *The Wind Done Gone*, a takeoff on

Mitchell's work by Alice Randall. (*See* May 25.)

24 Michelle Kwan wins the world figure skating championship, her fourth, in Vancouver, B.C.; two days earlier Yevgeny Plushchenko had won the men's championship.

•

A magnitude-6.4 earthquake strikes Hiroshima, Japan, killing at least two people and destroying more than 500 homes.

25 Comedian Steve Martin hosts the annual Academy Awards extravaganza; top winners include *Gladiator*, director Steven Soderbergh, and actors Russell Crowe, Julia Roberts, Benicio Del Toro, and Marcia Gay Harden.

•

In Mariucci Arena in Minneapolis, Minn., the Minnesota-Duluth Bulldogs defeat the St. Lawrence Saints to win the first National Collegiate Athletic Association women's hockey title.

•

Local officials say that they have found more than 200 bodies in mass graves in Kinama, a suburb of Bujumbura, Burundi, that government forces have recently retaken from rebel guerrilla forces.

26 Kazakh Prime Minister Kasymzhomart Tokayev ceremonially opens a 1,580-km (900-mi)-long oil pipeline that will carry hundreds of thousands of barrels of oil daily from the Tengiz oil field in western Kazakhstan to Novorossiysk, a Russian port on the Black Sea.

•

An arson fire in a dormitory of a boys' secondary school in Machakos, Kenya, kills 67

of the students who were sleeping there; one of the exits from the building had been locked.

•

Great Britain calls out its army to bury the carcasses of animals that have been slaughtered to try to contain the spread of foot-and-mouth disease; the animals are being slaughtered too quickly to allow for the burning of the carcasses.

27 The Wellington Arch in London, built in 1828 to commemorate the British victory over Napoleon at Waterloo, is ceremonially reopened after a two-year restoration.

•

California's Public Utilities Commission approves electricity rate hikes of close to 50%, the highest increases in the state's history.

•

The Avery Fisher Career Grants are awarded to violinist Timothy Fain, cellists Daniel Lee and Hai-Ye Ni, and flutist Tara Helen O'Connor.

•

The United States casts its fifth UN Security Council veto since 1990; the issue is the creation of a UN observer force to be deployed in Israeli-occupied Palestinian territories.

28 The White House announces that U.S. Pres. George W. Bush opposes the Kyoto Protocol on greenhouse emissions; while not unexpected, the statement appalls the other signatories of the treaty. (*See* June 12.)

•

The first commercial flight lands at Eleftherios Venizelos Airport, the new facility outside Athens.

•

Henri Loyrette, head of the Orsay Museum in Paris, is

chosen to succeed Pierre Rosenberg as director of the Louvre; Rosenberg will retire in April after 39 years at the Louvre.

29 The San Francisco Bay Bridge is lifted 1.3 cm (0.5 in) so that engineers can insert ball-bearing suspension devices under the bridge supports; the devices are meant to ensure that the bridge would survive an earthquake.

•

NorthPoint Communications becomes the first major digital subscriber line company to go bankrupt as its nationwide network of fast Internet access goes dark.

•

The Czech brewery Budejovicky Budvar announces its introduction to the United States of a lager beer that it is calling Czechvar, in order to avoid trademark problems with Anheuser-Busch, makers of Budweiser.

30 U.S. Pres. George W. Bush announces plans to build a small baseball field for the playing of T-ball on the south lawn of the White House.

31 The United Nations announces that 1996 Nobel Peace laureate José Ramos-Horta will become the head of the interim governing council in East Timor.

•

Ukrainian authorities re-arrest Yuliya Tymoshenko, an opponent of Pres. Leonid Kuchma, who had been accused of corruption but had been released when a court ruled there were no grounds to keep her in custody while she awaited trial; a higher court overruled the decision.

April

1 An international incident is created when a U.S. spy plane collides with a Chinese fighter jet that was tailing it in the South China Sea; the Chinese pilot is killed, but the American plane lands safely on Hainan Island, China, where the crew is held. (*See* April 12.)

After lengthy negotiations during which he threatens to kill himself and his family, former Yugoslav president Slobodan Milosevic is arrested without incident shortly after midnight; Milosevic is charged with corruption and abuse of power, including looting large sums from the government.

The National Collegiate Athletic Association championship in women's basketball is won by the University of Notre Dame, which defeats Purdue University 68–66; on April 2 Duke University defeats the University of Arizona 82–72 in the men's championship.

2 The Swiss architects Jacques Herzog and Pierre de Meuron, designers of London's Tate Modern museum, are announced as the winners of the 2001 Pritzker Architecture Prize; the prize will be awarded in a ceremony on May 7.

NASA scientists announce that a photograph of a supernova explosion 11 billion years ago snapped by the Hubble Space Telescope in 1997 confirms a theory that Einstein formulated, then repudiated, of the existence of dark energy, or negative gravity, as a force permeating the universe. (*See* April 24.)

3 Gao Zhan, a Chinese-born American scholar who has been detained in China for 51 days, is formally charged with espionage; her husband and five-year-old son, who were taken into custody with her, had been allowed to return to the U.S. on March 8. (*See* July 26.)

Japan approves the use of a new middle-school textbook that critics from South Korea and China say distorts Japan's role in World War II, downplaying atrocities and justifying invasions.

4 A Communist, Vladimir Voronin, is elected president of Moldova by an overwhelming margin in Parliament.

The toy manufacturer Mattel Inc. announces that it will close its last American manufacturing plant over the next two years and relocate production to Mexico; the plant, in Murray, Ky., makes Fisher-Price toys.

Astronomers at the Whipple Observatory in Arizona announce that they have observed the third and fourth known "extreme" galaxies; extreme galaxies, the first of which was discovered in 1996, emit very great amounts of gamma radiation.

5 Turkmen Pres. Saparmurad Niyazov orders the closing of the opera and ballet house in Ashgabat, the Turkmenistan capital, saying that these art forms are foreign to Turkmen culture.

The *Far Eastern Economic Review* reports that restoration work is almost complete on a huge reclining Buddha statue made of stone and dating to about the 5th century; the statue, which was unearthed in 1966 near the Afghanistan border in southern Tajikistan and kept out of public view since, will be featured in the Museum of National Antiquities, due to open in Dushanbe, the Tajik capital, in August 2001.

6 Pakistan's Supreme Court vacates the corruption conviction of former prime minister Benazir Bhutto but then orders a new trial; she has been in voluntary exile since 1999.

Pacific Gas and Electric, California's biggest investor-owned utility, files for bankruptcy protection.

7 NASA successfully launches the 2001 Mars Odyssey, which is expected to reach the "red planet" in October, orbit it for two and a half years, and send back data on chemical elements and minerals.

A helicopter carrying among its 16 passengers and crew 7

AP/Wide World Photos

Americans searching for those still listed as missing in action from the Vietnam War (1955–75) crashes into a mountain in central Vietnam; all aboard the aircraft are killed.

8 Victorious in the Masters golf tournament at Augusta, Ga., Tiger Woods becomes the first person in the history of golf to win four consecutive major professional tournaments.

•

In presidential elections held in Peru, Alejandro Toledo bests candidates Alan García and Lourdes Flores; but he wins less than 50% of the vote and therefore must contest a runoff election with second-place finisher García. (*See* June 3.)

•

Sophie, countess of Wessex, wife of Great Britain's Prince Edward, resigns as chairman of her public relations firm after the publication of some indiscreet remarks she made to undercover reporters.

9 American Airlines, having negotiated an agreement with the pilots' union, closes on the acquisition of TWA; American is now the world's largest airline. (*See* January 10 and July 27.)

10 The States-General in The Netherlands passes a bill permitting euthanasia; it is the first such national law in the world.

•

An agreement is reached on how to divide the gold reserves of former Yugoslavia, totaling some $440 million, which have been held in the Bank for International Settlements in Basel, Switz., since 1991: 36.5% to the present Yugoslavia, 28.5% to Croatia, 16.4% to Slovenia, 13.2% to Bosnia and Herzegovina, and 5.4% to Macedonia.

Bulgarian Foreign Minister Nadezhda Mihailova walks across the border to Greece to celebrate the European Union's lifting of visa restrictions on Bulgarians; it is the first time Bulgarians have been allowed to travel freely into Western Europe since World War II.

11 In a stampede at the beginning of an association football (soccer) match at Ellis Park, a stadium in Johannesburg, S.Af., at least 43 people are trampled to death.

•

China executes 89 convicted criminals as part of a crackdown on organized crime.

12 *The crew of the American spy plane that had made an emergency landing in China after colliding with a Chinese fighter jet is released and flown to Guam after days of diplomatic wrangling. (See April 1 and August 11.) (Photo above.)*

•

After three nights of rioting following the fatal shooting of an unarmed African American man by police, Cincinnati, Ohio, Mayor Charlie Luken declares a state of emergency and a citywide curfew.

•

The National Basketball Association approves a series of bold rule changes designed to increase viewer interest: henceforth in professional basketball the zone defense will be allowed; defenders may remain in the lane for only three seconds unless they can reach an opponent; and the 10-second rule will become the 8-second rule.

13 Edward Natapei is elected prime minister of Vanuatu, succeeding Barak Sope, who had lost a no-confidence vote brought in the wake of corruption charges.

•

Workers from five trade unions return to work at Guinness plants after only one day of a strike that had raised fears of a shortage of stout in Ireland over Easter weekend.

14 A conference in the Republic of the Congo chaired by Gabonese Pres. Omar Bongo is brought to a close after adopting a draft constitution.

After a gun battle in Pinheiros jail in São Paulo, Braz., 150 prisoners break out and then hijack cars to make good their escape.

15 Rioting breaks out in the ethnically diverse neighbourhood of Lidget Green in Bradford, Eng.; two pubs are firebombed and a drugstore burned before calm is restored seven hours after the melee began. (*See* June 24.)

16 In New York City the winners of the 2001 Pulitzer Prizes are announced: journalism awards go to *The Oregonian,* the *Miami Herald,* the *Chicago Tribune,* and the *New York Times;* arts and letters winners include Michael Chabon for fiction and Joseph J. Ellis for history.

The 105th Boston Marathon is won by Lee Bong Ju of South Korea, with a time of 2 hr 9 min 43 sec; Catherine Ndereba of Kenya (2 hr 23 min 53 sec) is the women's winner for the second straight year.

The Miho Museum in Japan returns ownership of a rare 6th-century boddhisattva to China after acknowledging that the statue had been stolen from China, which in turn agrees to loan the statue to the Japanese museum until 2007.

17 Mississippi votes overwhelmingly to retain its state flag, which features the Confederate battle flag in its canton; opinions had been

voiced that the inclusion of the Confederate flag is racially offensive.

A Web site that permits users to trace their ancestry through U.S. immigration records from Ellis Island debuts; by the following day the new site is logging 97 million hits per hour.

A frantic international search for the Nigerian-registered ship *MV Etireno* ends when the ship docks in Cotonou, Benin; it was believed to be carrying 180 slave children but proves to have only a few apparently enslaved children.

18 India for the first time successfully launches a rocket capable of placing a satellite into orbit; it is the sixth country to demonstrate that capacity.

In a speech at the Virginia Military Institute, former U.S. senator and Nebraska governor Bob Kerrey for the first time publicly acknowledges and expresses his pain over his role in a U.S. military raid that he led on Feb. 25, 1969, in the Mekong delta in Vietnam in which a number of unarmed women and children were massacred.

The UN announces that a 26-km (16-m)-wide buffer zone has been established between Ethiopia and Eritrea, where fighting over an ill-defined boundary had broken out in 1998.

Spain declines to extradite Vladimir A. Gusinsky to Russia, on the basis that he has done nothing that is illegal in Spain; one of the new breed of Russian oligarchs, Gusinsky is an outspoken critic of the government in Moscow.

The *Journal of the American Medical Association* publishes a study showing that, in

the first large-scale trial of St. John's wort, the herbal remedy did nothing to alleviate major depression.

19 A lawsuit by 39 major pharmaceutical firms that had sought to block a law allowing South Africa to manufacture or import low-priced versions of anti-AIDS drugs is dropped.

Prime Minister Sani Lakatani of Niue complains that, since the grounding of Royal Tonga Airlines, the Pacific island has no access to the outside world and is in economic crisis; he appeals for help from New Zealand.

20 The Peruvian air force shoots down a small plane carrying missionaries, killing American Veronica Bowers and her infant daughter, Charity; the tragedy apparently occurred because of language difficulties between the Peruvians and American CIA personnel working together in a drug-interdiction program.

Thirty-four heads of state and government begin three days of meetings in Quebec for the third Summit of the Americas; thousands of protesters demonstrate energetically in the streets.

The day after it opens in New York City, the musical *The Producers* breaks a Broadway box-office record, selling $3 million worth of tickets in a single day; the previous record, set in 1997, was held by *The Lion King.*

21 China, Vietnam, Malaysia, Brunei, and the Philippines, all of which claim the Spratly Islands in the South China Sea, believed to be rich in oil, agree not to establish new settlements there.

Fernando da Costa, who had escaped from a Brazilian prison where he had been serving a term for trafficking in cocaine in 1996 and who is reputed to be a top drug lord, is arrested in Colombia after a concentrated two-month manhunt.

22 The elevation of Nong Duc Manh as the new leader of the Vietnamese Communist Party, replacing Le Kha Phieu, is announced; Manh is widely rumoured to be the illegitimate son of Ho Chi Minh.

Chris A. Hadfield becomes the first Canadian astronaut to walk in space when he and American astronaut Scott E. Parazynski attach a Canadian-made robot arm to the International Space Station.

In an astonishing upset, virtual unknown Hasim Rahman of the U.S. knocks out favourite Lennox Lewis of the U.K. in the fifth round in Brakpan, S.Af., winning the International Boxing Federation and World Boxing Council heavyweight championships.

The London Marathon is won by Abdelkader El Mouaziz of Morocco, in 2 hr 7 min 11 sec, and Deratu Tulu of Ethiopia, in 2 hr 23 min 57 sec; it is the best time El Mouaziz, winner of the New York Marathon, has ever posted, and it is the first marathon that Olympic 10,000-m champion Tulu has ever won.

23 The Goldman Environmental Prize, the largest prize for grassroots environmentalism, is awarded to American journalists Jane Akre and Steve Wilson, Rwandan conservationist Eugene Rutagarama, Bolivian activist Oscar

Olivera, Yosepha Alomang of Papua New Guinea, Greek biologists Myrsini Malakou and Giorgos Catsadorakis, and reef protector Bruno Van Peteghem of New Caledonia.

About 120 guests and staff of the luxury Swissôtel in Istanbul, Turkey, are released unharmed about 10 hours after being taken hostage by armed men; the terrorists are protesting Russian military presence in Chechnya.

A U.S. Global Hawk spy plane named the *Southern Cross II* becomes the first unmanned aircraft to fly across the Pacific Ocean when it touches down at an air force base near Adelaide, Australia, a day and a half after taking off from Edwards Air Force Base, California.

24 The running of the 94-year-old TT motorcycle road races in the Isle of Man is canceled in an effort to keep the island free of foot-and-mouth disease.

The flooding Mississippi River crests in Davenport, Iowa, as an army of volunteers works to hold the river back.

The 11th anniversary of the launching of the Hubble

Space Telescope is celebrated by pointing it at a target selected by amateur astronomers voting on the Internet—the Horsehead Nebula. (See April 2.) (Photo below.)

25 Former Philippine president Joseph Estrada is arrested on a charge of plunder, the most serious of the charges that have yet been brought against him. (*See* January 20 and May 1.)

On a 3-1 pitch Rickey Henderson takes his 2,063rd career walk, breaking the record set by Babe Ruth; his team, the San Diego Padres, loses the game nonetheless.

26 Two days after the resignation of Yoshiro Mori, Junichiro Koizumi becomes Japan's prime minister.

In San Juan, P.R., 6,000 people turn out to protest the planned resumption of training exercises by the U.S. Navy on the island of Vieques; the exercises begin the following day. (*See* March 2 and June 14.)

American poet Yusuf Komunyakaa is announced as the winner of the Ruth Lilly Poetry Prize; the honour, given for lifetime

achievement, includes a cash award of $100,000.

American singer and actress Jennifer Lopez introduces her own line of casual clothes, J. Lo by Jennifer Lopez; the brand will be carried by top-tier department and specialty stores.

27 A report in *Science* magazine details studies on the archaeological site of Caral in Peru; these studies show that it flourished for five centuries beginning about 2600 BC, which makes it by far the oldest city yet discovered in the Americas and indicates that a civilization began there much earlier than previously believed.

The same issue of *Science* reports that researchers at IBM have created transistors made of carbon nanotubes that are only a few molecules in width; the discovery may enable the creation of vastly smaller and more powerful computers.

John Tobin, an American postgraduate student at Voronezh State University in Russia who had initially been accused of espionage, is sentenced to 37 months in a penal colony for marijuana possession; Tobin contends the drugs were planted.

28 The first antigovernment rally in its 35-year history as an independent state takes place in Singapore as 2,000 people gather in support of Joshua Jeyaretnam, one of only three opposition representatives in the 93-member Parliament.

A Russian Soyuz booster rocket takes off from the Baikonur Cosmodrome in Kazakhstan, carrying two

Russian cosmonauts in addition to the first space tourist, American millionaire Dennis Tito, to visit the International Space Station; NASA had finally dropped its objections to Tito's presence on April 20.

29 John Carlstrom, head of the Degree Angular Scale Interferometer team at the Centre of Astrophysical Research in Antarctica, presents findings that support the theory that tiny distortions in matter from the Big Bang led to the formation of the large structures in the universe; the findings also support the theory of dark matter and the idea that the universe is flat rather than curved.

The inaugural Firehawk 600 race at the Texas Motor Speedway in Fort Worth is canceled when drivers refuse to participate; the speedway's track allows speeds of over 370 km/h (230 mph) and thereby subjects drivers to dangerously high G-forces.

30 Pres. Frederick Chiluba is nominated for a third term as president by his party, although Zambia's constitution forbids presidents to serve more than two terms; on May 4 Chiluba agrees not to run for another term.

Germany proposes a plan to remodel the European Union into a centralized federal system similar to that of Germany's government; while there is general agreement that the present government of the EU is too unwieldy, other members fear loss of autonomy and domination by Germany.

Sweet Basil, a popular jazz club in the Greenwich Village section of New York City, closes.

AFP Worldwide

May

1 In a speech at the National Defense University in Washington, D.C., U.S. Pres. George W. Bush proposes a new defense plan for the country that would include a network of defensive missiles; the initiative is seen by experts to contravene the Anti-Ballistic Missile Treaty signed by the U.S. and the Soviet Union in 1972.

•

Following an attack on Malacañang, the presidential palace, by supporters of ousted former president Joseph Estrada, Philippine Pres. Gloria Macapagal Arroyo declares a "state of rebellion" in Manila; she lifts the order on May 6.

•

Louis J. Freeh, the director of the U.S. Federal Bureau of Investigation, announces that he plans to retire in June; the FBI has been under pressure in recent months following the exposure of one of its agents, Robert P. Hanssen, as a longtime spy for the Russians.

•

Thomas E. Blanton, Jr., formerly a member of the Ku Klux Klan, is convicted of having murdered four African American girls in the bombing of the 16th Street Baptist Church in Birmingham, Ala., in 1963.

2 Novartis Pharmaceuticals, the Swiss drug company, announces that it will make its antimalaria medicine, Riamet, available to the World Health Organization for delivery to Africa for $2 a dose—about one-tenth the price normally charged in the West. (*See* May 7.)

•

The former heads of two leading auction houses, Sotheby's and Christie's, are indicted in New York City on antitrust charges for having fixed commission fees charged to customers over a six-year period.

•

Stanford University is the recipient of the largest gift ever made to an institution of higher learning in the United States (and possibly in the world) when the William and Flora Hewlett Foundation pledges $400 million to the university.

3 In a secret tally among the members of the United Nations Economic and Social Council, the United States is voted off the UN Human Rights Commission for the first time since it was created in 1947; the vote is seen as an expression of growing exasperation with U.S. conduct in international organizations.

•

Leaders of the Florida House of Representatives and Senate agree on a program of election reforms for the state, including the banning of punch-card ballot machinery and the requiring of hand recounts in particularly close elections; the outcome of the 2000 U.S. presidential election was delayed for weeks because of irregularities in balloting procedures in Florida.

4 Pope John Paul II begins a six-day trip to areas of the Mediterranean region associated with Saint Paul, including Syria and Malta, with a highly controversial visit to Greece; he is the first pope to visit Greece in close to 13 centuries. (*See* May 6.)

•

After learning that an American Hindu is suing McDonald's, alleging that the fast-food chain uses beef fat in making its french fries, hundreds of people riot against McDonald's outlets in India; the company maintains that, though it does flavour its fries with beef extract in the U.S., it uses no beef product in India.

5 In the 127th running of the Kentucky Derby, Monarchos, a horse not considered a contender, wins in the second fastest time in the history of the race.

6 After becoming the first pope ever to visit Syria, John Paul II becomes the first ever to set foot in a mosque when he visits the Great Mosque of Damascus. (*See* May 4.)

•

The first space tourist, American businessman Dennis Tito, returns to Earth in Kazakhstan.

7 The Antonov-225, the largest airplane in the world, successfully completes a short test flight in Ukraine; the airplane, reworked from a plane designed to carry the *Buran* space shuttle, has a wingspan of 88.4 m (290 ft).

Novartis Pharmaceuticals announces that it has bought a 20% stake in Roche Holding; market observers are surprised and speculate that it means the two Switzerland-based pharmaceutical corporations plan to merge. (*See* May 2.)

8 The World Trade Organization approves Moldova's application for admission; Moldova becomes the organization's 142nd member on July 26.

9 Police fire tear gas into the crowd at a soccer match in Accra, Ghana, when fans of the losing team begin throwing debris onto the field, triggering a panic in which more than 120 people are trampled to death; it is Africa's worst sports-related disaster ever.

American Susan Sontag receives the biennial Jerusalem Prize for Literature, awarded to writers whose work deals with the freedom of the individual within society; in her fiery acceptance speech, Sontag expresses strong disagreement with Israeli government policy in the Arab settlements.

In a concert at New York City's Carnegie Hall, Peter Wiley ceremonially replaces David Soyer as cellist for the Guarneri String Quartet; Wiley is the first new member to join the quartet since it started 37 years ago.

10 The U.S. Congress approves a budget plan that allows the first major tax cut in 20 years; final approval comes on May 26. (*See* July 22.)

President Bush nominates John P. Walters as director of the Office of National Drug Control Policy; Walters is viewed as being in favour of punishment rather than treatment for drug users.

Nature publishes a report by Carnegie Institute of Washington researchers who applied 25 million psi of pressure and transformed a nitrogen sample into a solid with semiconducting properties; moreover, if low temperatures are maintained, the nitrogen retains its new properties after the release of the pressure.

NBC and World Wrestling Federation Entertainment announce the demise of the XFL football league after one unprofitable and unpopular season. (*See* February 3.)

11 U.S. Attorney General John Ashcroft orders that the execution of Oklahoma City bomber Timothy McVeigh, originally set for May 16, be postponed until June 11 because McVeigh's defense counsel was improperly not given access to large quantities of FBI files before his trial. (*See* June 11.)

Cautious reductions in Germany's pension system are approved by the legislature; the very generous benefits have been strained by demographic changes, and gaining approval for the changes represents a great political victory for Chancellor Gerhard Schröder.

*The **Toronto Globe and Mail** publishes a report saying that a Canadian man owns a portrait said to be of William Shakespeare, painted in 1603 and passed down for 12 generations in his family; it has been authenticated as being from the right time, but scholars are divided on whether the painting does, in fact, portray Shakespeare. (Photo below.)*

12 Kinfe Gebremedhin, the head of the Ethiopian Federal Security and Immigration Authority (the intelligence service), is assassinated as he leaves an officer's club in Addis Ababa.

With their song "Everybody," the Estonian duet of Tanel Padar and Dave Benton (a native of Aruba) are the surprise winners of the 46th Eurovision Song Contest, held in Copenhagen.

The 2001 PEN/Faulkner Award for Fiction is presented to Philip Roth for *The Human Stain*. (*See* May 16.)

At New York City's Madison Square Garden, the undefeated Félix Trinidad wins a championship in his third weight class when he defeats World Boxing Association middleweight champion William Joppy (the fight actually ends shortly after midnight). (*See* September 29.)

More than 50 people riot in Paris to protest the popular reality TV series *LoftStory*.

13 Media tycoon Silvio Berlusconi wins election as prime minister of Italy for the second time.

Elections held in the Basque region of Spain are won by the moderate Basque Nationalist Party.

In Hannover, Ger., the Czech Republic wins its third consecutive International Ice Hockey Federation world championship, defeating Finland 3–2.

14 The sixth International IMPAC Dublin Literary Award is given to Canadian author Alistair MacLeod for his novel *No Great Mischief.*

•

The U.S. Supreme Court rules that under federal law there is no acceptable medical use for marijuana.

15 Japan's Imperial Household Agency confirms that, as long rumoured, Crown Princess Masako is pregnant; Masako, married to Crown Prince Naruhito since 1993, has had no children and suffered a miscarriage in 2000.

•

Acting Gov. Jane Swift of Massachusetts gives birth to twin girls; she had been hospitalized since May 8 but had continued to conduct state business by telephone.

•

Allen Iverson, a guard for the Philadelphia 76ers, is named the National Basketball Association's Most Valuable Player.

16 Richard Serra is awarded the annual Gold Medal for Sculpture by the American Academy of Arts and Letters, while the Gold Medal for Fiction, given every six years, is given to Philip Roth (*see* May 12); 14 new members, including Amiri Baraka and Garrison Keillor, are inducted into the academy.

•

The restored dome of the Choral Synagogue, the most important Jewish temple in Moscow, is officially unveiled amid great celebration; the dome features a large gilded Star of David.

17 Off the coast of Somaliland, a derelict ship is discovered on which more than 86 of 150 persons aboard perished; the ship reportedly developed engine trouble, and the officers forced the Somali passengers, bound for Yemen, to jump into the sea at gunpoint before the crew itself fled the vessel.

The American banking giant Citigroup says it will purchase the second largest bank in Mexico, Grupo Financiero Banamex-Accival.

18 France launches its first new aircraft carrier in nearly 40 years, the *Charles de Gaulle.*

•

Hong Kong orders the slaughter of more than one-third of the territory's poultry—1.2 million birds—and the cessation of imports from mainland China in an effort to stop the spread of a fatal avian influenza.

•

UNESCO inaugurates a new category for its historical preservation role, Masterpieces of Oral and Intangible Heritage, and names 19 cultural spaces and expressions to the list.

19 Point Given, the losing favourite at the Kentucky Derby, returns to form at the 126th running of the Preakness Stakes and is ridden to victory by Gary Stevens. (*See* June 9.)

20 Natsagiyn Bagabandi is reelected president of Mongolia; his party, the former ruling communist party, won control of the Great Hural in 2000.

•

As the Cannes International Film Festival closes, Italian director Nanni Moretti's *The Son's Room* wins the Palme d'Or; the Grand Prix goes to director Michael Haneke for *The Piano Teacher*, and its stars, Isabelle Huppert and Benoit Magimel, take home acting honours.

The media company Vivendi Universal agrees to acquire the on-line music-distribution company MP3.com less than one year after settling a copyright-infringement suit with MP3.

•

In Ireland the three-day St. Patrick's Day celebrations, postponed because of the outbreak of foot-and-mouth disease, conclude with the traditional parade in Dublin. (Photo below.)

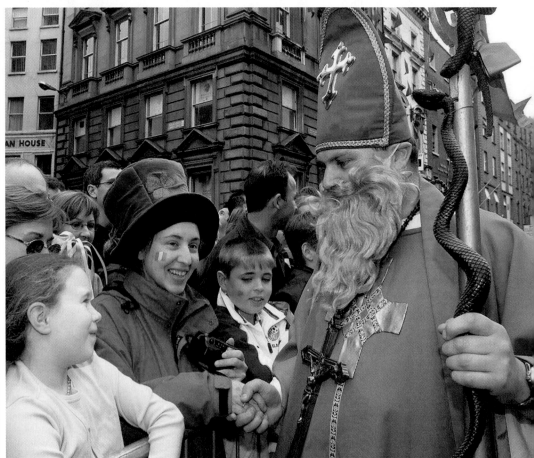

AP/Wide World Photos

21 Procter & Gamble agrees to buy the hair-products company Clairol from Bristol-Myers Squibb in a move that should give it nearly half the U.S. market.

•

Saad ad-Din Ibrahim, a sociology professor and prominent Egyptian human rights activist, is found guilty of antigovernment activities and sentenced to seven years in prison.

22 Reports indicate that the Taliban rulers of Afghanistan have set forth a plan to require non-Muslims in the country (primarily Hindus and Sikhs) to wear an identifying badge.

•

The Ford Motor Co. says that it plans to replace 13 million Firestone Wilderness AT tires, most of them on Ford Explorer sport-utility vehicles, with tires made by other manufacturers.

Embattled Ukrainian Pres. Leonid Kuchma nominates an ally, industrialist Anatoly Kinakh, to replace Viktor Yushchenko as prime minister.

•

The original manuscript of Jack Kerouac's *On the Road* is bought at auction for $2,430,000, a world record price.

23 India ends its six-month-long cease-fire in Kashmir but at the same time says it will invite the head of Pakistan's government, Gen. Pervez Musharraf, to go to New Delhi to discuss the action; the following day Pakistan grudgingly says it will accept the invitation.

•

Canada becomes the first country to ratify the Stockholm Convention, which bans the nonessential use of persistent organic pollutants; this category of chemicals is particularly troublesome in the Arctic, as they tend to accumulate and persist in colder climates.

•

U.S. Secretary of State Colin Powell begins a one-week tour of Africa with a meeting at the presidential palace in Bamako with Alpha Oumar Konaré, the president of Mali.

24 A three-story reception hall in Jerusalem hosting a wedding reception with more than 600 guests collapses, killing at least 25 and injuring hundreds.

•

Vermont Sen. James M. Jeffords announces that he feels the Republican Party is far more conservative than he is and that he is therefore abandoning his party affiliation to become an independent; this throws the balance of power in the evenly split Senate to the Democrats.

•

Horse breeders in central Kentucky are informed that the reason more than 500 thoroughbred foals and fetuses have died in the past few months is that the mares are somehow ingesting naturally occurring cyanide from black cherry trees; scientists suspect fecal matter from Eastern tent caterpillars may be the transmission source.

25 Pres. Chen Shui-bian of Taiwan meets in San Salvador, El Salvador, with leaders of eight Latin American nations that support Taiwan; the Latin American leaders sign a declaration recognizing Taiwan's democracy, a move Chen hopes will bolster Taiwan's efforts to join the UN.

•

The U.S. Court of Appeals for the 11th Circuit over-turns an injunction preventing publication of *The Wind Done Gone*, Alice Randall's parody of *Gone with the Wind*, Margaret Mitchell's 1936 bestseller. (*See* March 23.)

26 Racial strife breaks out in Oldham, Eng., near Manchester, when a group of white youths attacks a home in a South Indian neighbourhood and residents respond by attacking a pub with a largely white clientele; sporadic fighting continues for the next three days.

•

Laurance S. Rockefeller donates his 448-ha (1,106-ac) JY Ranch in Wyoming to Grand Teton National Park; his father, John D. Rockefeller, Jr., had donated most of the land that makes up the park.

27 Brazilian Helio Castroneves, driving for Team Penske in the Indianapolis 500, takes the lead at lap 149 and, in spite of a 16-minute rain delay, holds on to win the auto race.

•

Czech athlete Roman Sebrle sets a new world record for the decathlon of 9,026 points, surpassing the record of 8,944 points set by Tomas Dvorak, also of the Czech Republic, in 1999.

28 In a coup attempt, supporters of André Kolingba fire on the home of Pres. Ange-Félix Patassé in Bangui, Central African Republic; the action sparks 10 days of fighting, but by June 7 the government has regained control.

•

The Women's College World Series of fast-pitch softball is won by the University of Arizona Wildcats when they defeat the UCLA Bruins 1–0; Arizona pitcher Jennie Finch wins the shutout.

29 In a federal courtroom in New York City, the four men on trial for having conspired with accused terrorist leader Osama bin Laden to bomb the American embassies in Kenya and Tanzania in 1998 are found guilty on all 302 charges.

•

Thai Prime Minister Thaksin Shinawatra removes the head of the Bank of Thailand, Chatumongkol Sonakul, for failing to heed his instructions to raise interest rates.

•

The U.S. Supreme Court rules that the Professional Golfers' Association of America tour must permit disabled golfer Casey Martin to use a golf cart when he competes, finding that walking is not fundamental to the game.

30 In the Elf Aquitaine corruption case, which has engulfed the government of France, former foreign minister Roland Dumas is found guilty of having received bribes from Elf and is sentenced to six months in prison. (*See* February 7.)

•

The General Motors Corp. formally offers to take over troubled South Korean car manufacturer Daewoo Motor Co.

31 The Scripps Howard National Spelling Bee, held in Washington, D.C., is won by 13-year-old Sean Conley, an eighth-grader at Minnesota Renaissance School in Anoka, Minn.; he wins the final round by correctly spelling *succedaneum*.

June

> *We have to ask for the opinions of experts on what we should do about the collapse of a safe society.*
>
> Japanese Prime Minister Junichiro Koizumi, responding to the Ikeda school killings, June 8

1 In Kathmandu, Nepal, Crown Prince Dipendra opens fire at a family party, killing King Birendra, Queen Aiswarya, and seven other members of the royal family before turning the gun on himself.

•

A Palestinian suicide bomber sets off his explosives in the midst of a crowd of teenagers outside a discotheque in Tel Aviv, Israel, killing 22 and injuring scores more.

•

Papua New Guinea's secessionist province of Bougainville ends a decade-long war when final terms for peace with Papua New Guinea are negotiated; the island is to have statelike autonomy and the option of total independence by the years 2011–16.

2 A woman taking part in a medical experiment at Johns Hopkins University, Baltimore, Md., becomes the first research subject to die in the university's history; the experiment was intended to help reveal how the human body fights asthma and involved a drug that produced an asthmalike reaction in healthy subjects.

3 Alejandro Toledo wins a runoff presidential election in Peru, defeating Alan García Pérez. (*See* April 8.)

•

The 55th annual Tony Awards are presented at Radio City Music Hall in New York City; winners include the plays *Proof, The Producers* (which wins 12 Tonys, a record number), *One Flew over the Cuckoo's Nest,* and *42nd Street* and the actors Richard Easton, Mary-Louise Parker, Nathan Lane, and Christine Ebersole.

•

Australian Karrie Webb wins the U.S. Women's Open golf tournament in Southern Pines, N.C., for the second year in a row. (*See* June 24.)

4 Utah Gov. Michael Leavitt declares a state of agricultural emergency resulting from what many call the worst infestation of Mormon crickets in 40 years; the insects, which are also bedeviling Nevada, are causing millions of dollars in crop damage, endangering vehicles on the road, and keeping residents indoors.

•

The state legislature of Nevada passes a law that allows regulators to permit casinos to offer Internet gambling.

5 Prosecutors representing the crown in Canada file charges against Inderjit Singh Reyat relating to the bombing of an Air-India flight in 1985; Reyat is serving time for murder in a bombing at Narita International Airport in Japan, and the filing of new charges in such a case is unprecedented.

•

James K. Hahn is elected mayor of Los Angeles over Antonio Villaraigosa in a closely watched runoff election, though in the April election that necessitated the runoff, Villaraigosa had come in ahead of Hahn.

•

A jury in Los Angeles awards over $3 billion to a man who was diagnosed with lung cancer after 40 years of smoking Marlboro cigarettes; Philip Morris Companies Inc. plans to appeal, though it does not deny that its product caused the cancer.

6 The State Duma of Russia votes to allow nuclear waste to be imported and stored in Russia; the bill is opposed by the general public in Russia and by environmentalists elsewhere because of Russia's poor record of nuclear safety.

•

The Democratic Party formally takes control of the U.S. Senate, and Tom Daschle succeeds Trent Lott as majority leader.

7 Prime Minister Tony Blair and the Labour Party coast to an expected victory in elections in the U.K.

•

Former Argentine president Carlos Saúl Menem is arrested in an investigation of his suspected involvement in arms smuggling to Croatia and Ecuador in 1991–95 during his tenure in office.

•

Ireland rejects the Treaty of Nice, which sets forth procedures for admitting new members to the European Union and requires ratification by all members.

8 A man armed with a knife invades an elementary school in Ikeda, Japan, stabs to death

AP/Wide World Photos

the form of a Plateau of Humankind and has exhibitions of visual arts, film, theatre, poetry, and dance.

•

Gilberto Simoni wins the 84th Giro d'Italia bicycle race; one stage of the race had been canceled on June 7 after a dramatic drug raid on the cyclists' hotel rooms during the night.

•

In Switzerland a referendum to allow Swiss members of UN and NATO peacekeeping forces to carry arms passes in a very close vote.

11 In the first federal execution in the U.S. since 1963, Timothy McVeigh is put to death in Terre Haute, Ind., for having carried out what was at the time the worst terrorist attack in U.S. history, the 1995 Oklahoma City bombing. (*See* May 11.)

•

Mud slides caused by heavy rain fall into a road near Quito, Ecuador, killing 38 people.

•

The British pound sterling falls to its lowest point against the U.S. dollar in 16 years, apparently because of fears that the recent Labour electoral victory means that Britain is likely to abandon the pound in favour of the euro.

12 In his first overseas trip as president of the United States, George W. Bush arrives in Spain, where he reiterates his opposition to the Anti-Ballistic Missile Treaty and the Kyoto Protocol. (*See* March 28 and July 23.)

•

The Coalition to Stop the Use of Child Soldiers releases a report saying that at least 300,000 children under the age of 18, some as young as 7 years old, are fighting as soldiers in 41 countries.

seven second-grade girls and one first-grade boy, and also seriously wounds six other students and a teacher, shocking the entire nation.

•

After a week of pounding southeastern Texas, Tropical Storm Allison hits Houston with renewed strength, causing massive flooding that cuts off power and access to most hospitals and forces more than 10,000 residents from their homes. (Photo above.)

•

In elections in Iran reformist Pres. Mohammad Khatami is reelected with 77% of the vote.

•

The 1,700th anniversary of the founding of the Armenian church by St. Gregory the Illuminator is celebrated at the church of St. Gregory in Kayseri, Turkey, by about 300 people, half of whom are Americans of Armenian descent.

9 American Jennifer Capriati defeats Kim Clijsters of Belgium in a hard-fought battle to win the women's French Open tennis title; the following day Brazilian Gustavo Kuerten defeats Alex Corretja of Spain to win the

men's competition for the third time.

•

The Colorado Avalanche defeats the defending National Hockey League champions, the New Jersey Devils, 4 games to 3, to win the Stanley Cup.

•

Preakness winner Point Given runs to a commanding victory in the Belmont Stakes, the last of the U.S. Triple Crown horse races. (*See* May 19.)

10 The 49th Venice Biennale opens to the public; it is in

The International Organization for Migration reports that an increasing number of teenagers from Eastern Europe, Africa, and Asia are being smuggled into Western Europe, most often to work in the sex industry.

13 Israeli Prime Minister Ariel Sharon and Palestinian leader Yasir Arafat reluctantly agree to an American-proposed cease-fire plan.

The U.S. Centers for Disease Control and Prevention announces that it has found no evidence that consumption of corn products tainted with genetically modified StarLink corn produced allergic reactions or illness of any sort. (*See* March 18.)

14 In a startling reversal of position, Pres. George W. Bush announces that the U.S. Navy will end its military exercises on Vieques Island, Puerto Rico, by May 2003. (*See* April 26 and July 29.)

Hundreds of thousands of ethnic Berbers and opposition party supporters march in Algiers, many rioting; Berber unrest has led to many days of rioting and demonstrations since April.

15 The Los Angeles Lakers defeat the Philadelphia 76ers 108–96 to win the National Basketball Association (NBA) championship for the second year in a row; also for the second time, Shaquille O'Neal is named Most Valuable Player of the finals.

In Göteborg, Swed., where a summit meeting of European Union leaders is taking place, thousands of antiglobalization demonstrators engage in 12 hours of sustained rioting.

A new international grouping, the Shanghai Cooperation Organization—made up of China, Kazakhstan, Kyrgyzstan, Russia, Tajikistan, and Uzbekistan—holds its inaugural meeting; delegates criticize the missile defense plan put forth by the U.S. and discuss joint action to counter Muslim separatists.

16 A bomb explodes in Narayanganj, Bangladesh, at a meeting of the Awami League, the country's ruling party, killing 22 people.

© Reuters 2001

The Leaning Tower of Pisa opens for the first time since 1990 as work to keep it from falling over is completed; it now leans only 4.1 m (13.5 ft) off perpendicular, 44 cm (17 in) less than its previous lean. (Photo above.)

17 The party of former king Simeon II wins the parliamentary elections in Bulgaria; the king waits until July 12 to accept the post of prime minister.

Chelsea Clinton, the daughter of former U.S. president Bill Clinton and Sen. Hillary Rodham Clinton, graduates summa cum laude from Stanford University.

18 The Taliban agrees to let the UN World Food Programme employ women to conduct interviews in Afghanistan to determine where and how food should be apportioned; because women are forbidden to speak to men outside their family, the survey cannot be carried out effectively without women as interviewers.

In Tulsa, Okla., Retief Goosen of South Africa defeats American Mark Brooks by two strokes in an 18-hole play-off to win the U.S. Open golf tournament.

19 Authorities in Yemen say they have arrested eight men who they believe were plotting to bomb the U.S. embassy in San'a'; the men are said to have fought with Osama bin Laden against Soviet forces in Afghanistan in the 1980s.

Baltimore Orioles third baseman Cal Ripken, Jr., who played in 2,632 successive games between 1982 and 1998, announces that he will retire at the end of the baseball season.

20 Pervez Musharraf appoints himself president of Pakistan while maintaining that the nation will return to democratic rule after elections in October 2002; Musharraf came to power in a coup in October 1999.

American Lori Berenson is convicted of treason and sentenced to 20 years in prison in open court in Peru; she was convicted and sentenced to life in prison by a closed military court in 1996, but the decision was overturned and a new trial ordered in August 2000.

•

Billy Collins is named the next poet laureate of the U.S.; Collins will replace Stanley Kunitz in the post in October.

21 U.S. federal indictments are brought against 14 men, none of them in custody in the U.S., in the 1996 bombing of the Khobar Towers in Saudi Arabia, in which 19 American airmen were killed; though the men indicted are Saudi Arabian and Lebanese, U.S. officials believe Iran is behind the act.

•

Russia, Azerbaijan, and Kazakhstan agree in Paris to stop fishing sturgeon for the rest of the year to give dwindling stocks a chance to regenerate; 90% of the world's caviar is produced by sturgeon in the Caspian Sea, which these countries border.

22 A 120-year-old bridge over the Kadalundi River in Kerala, India, collapses as a passenger train is crossing it; three cars fall into the river, killing 59 passengers.

•

The Sara Lee Corp. pleads guilty in court to having produced and distributed meat that was infected with listeria in 1998; it is believed that 15 people died as a result of eating the contaminated meat.

•

The Constitutional Court of Turkey votes to ban the Virtue Party, the main opposition party; the pro-Islamic party has 102 deputies in the legislature.

23 A magnitude-7.9 earthquake strikes southern Peru, causing great damage in both Arequipa and Moquegua and killing at least 31 people.

•

Vladimiro Montesinos, the former head of the Peruvian spy agency and right-hand man to Peru's ousted president Alberto Fujimori, is captured in Venezuela; he was wanted on charges of gun running and collaborating with drug traffickers.

•

The Unitarian Universalist Association elects William Sinkford as its president; he is the first African American to lead the largely white church.

24 Three days of small skirmishes escalate into a race riot in the economically depressed town of Burnley in northern England; about 7% of Burnley's population is of South Asian background. (*See* April 15.)

•

Karrie Webb wins the Ladies Professional Golf Association championship and becomes the youngest woman golfer (age 26) ever to complete a career grand slam. (*See* June 3.)

•

Mayon Volcano in the Philippines erupts, forcing over 30,000 people to evacuate their homes.

•

A privately funded peace memorial is dedicated near the site of the Battle of the Little Bighorn, which took place 125 years earlier on June 25; speakers call for peace between whites and Native Americans.

25 The General Assembly of New York passes a law banning the use of a hand-held telephone while driving a motor vehicle; it is the first state in the U.S. to enact such a ban.

•

IBM announces that it has developed the world's fastest silicon-based transistor; the

company expects that the chip will find applications in fibre-optic communications and in cellular telephones.

•

During the pontiff's visit to Kiev, Pope John Paul II and the chief rabbi of Ukraine, Yaakov Dov Bleich, visit the memorial honouring those who were killed by the Nazis in 1941–43 at Baby Yar.

•

A never-before-published novelette by Mark Twain appears in *The Atlantic Monthly;* "A Murder, a Mystery, and a Marriage" was written in 1876 as an entry for a contest Twain proposed to the magazine, but no one else agreed to take part in the contest.

26 In a light heavyweight professional boxing bout taking place aboard the Intrepid Sea-Air-Space Museum in the Hudson River in New York City, Beethavean Scottland suffers severe head injuries in the fight with the undefeated George Khalid Jones; Scottland dies of his injuries on July 2.

27 The United Nations approves the Declaration of Commitment, which treats AIDS as a political and economic threat and sets a goal of a 25% reduction in HIV infections in the worst-affected nations by 2005.

•

The tire manufacturer Bridgestone/Firestone announces plans to close its plant in Decatur, Ill., which produces 10% of the company's output.

•

In the NBA draft, for the first time ever, the first pick (by the Washington Wizards) is a high-school student, Kwame Brown, a 19-year-old senior from Brunswick, Ga.

28 Former Yugoslav president Slobodan Milosevic is extradited to The Hague to face war-crime charges before the UN tribunal; the following day Zoran Zizic, the prime minister of Yugoslavia, resigns in protest. (*See* July 17.)

•

A U.S. Court of Appeals, while upholding the finding of District Court Judge Thomas Penfield Jackson that Microsoft Corp. is a monopoly, voids the order that the computer company be broken up and bars Jackson from further involvement in the case.

29 Kofi Annan is elected with almost no opposition to a second term as secretary-general of the United Nations and swears himself in to the new five-year term. (*See* October 12.)

•

The National Japanese American Memorial is officially opened a few hundred metres north of the Capitol in Washington, D.C.

•

The first of four Russian military bases in Georgia, left over from the Soviet era, is turned over to the government of Georgia; a 1999 treaty gives Russia a deadline of July 1 for completing the transfer of all four bases.

30 The BBC's World Service discontinues its venerable shortwave radio service; its digital satellite radio and Internet service are supplanting it.

•

A rocket carrying the Microwave Anisotropy Probe, which will photograph so-called fossil light in the universe to show what the universe looked like immediately after the big bang, is launched from Cape Canaveral, Florida.

July

1 David Trimble resigns his position as first minister of Northern Ireland, citing as his reason the failure of the Irish Republican Army to disarm; Gerry Adams, head of Sinn Fein, says the failure to disarm is a result of the British inability to produce an acceptable replacement for the Royal Ulster Constabulary. (*See* August 11.)

•

A U.S. law creating a 233-sq-km (90-sq-mi) zone called Tortugas North, for tourists, and a 158-sq-km (61-sq-mi) zone called Tortugas South, for scientists, underwater off the Dry Tortugas National Park, Florida, goes into effect; together called the Tortugas Ecological Reserve, it is the largest area of U.S. coastal waters that is off-limits for fishing.

2 Despite assurances by the Taliban ambassador to Pakistan to the U.S. ambassador to Pakistan that the Taliban would not permit Osama bin Laden to attack U.S. interests, U.S. Pres. George W. Bush signs an executive order to continue economic sanctions against the Taliban for harbouring Bin Laden, whom the U.S. blames for the 1998 bombings of the U.S. embassies in Tanzania and Kenya. (*See* July 30.)

•

The first completely implantable artificial heart, the AbioCor, is placed into a patient on the brink of death; the patient, later revealed to be Robert Tools, age 58, suffers a stroke in November and dies later that month.

•

In a surprise move, Mexican Pres. Vicente Fox Quesada marries his spokesperson, Martha Sahagún, putting an end to gossip about their relationship.

3 In Russia's worst airline disaster since 1996, a Russian passenger airliner flying between Yekaterinburg and Vladivostok crashes on its approach to an intermediate stop, Irkutsk, killing all 143 aboard.

•

Australia and East Timor agree on a plan to share the oil and gas reserves in the Timor Sea between the two countries; the plan will give 90% of the revenues to East Timor.

•

Two weeks after the collapse of the ruling coalition, the head of the Lithuanian Social Democratic Party, Algirdas Brazauskas, becomes prime minister; Brazauskas was Lithuania's president from 1992 to 1998.

4 Scientists from the U.S. and Vietnam meeting in Hanoi agree to work cooperatively on a study examining environmental damage caused by the use of the herbicide Agent Orange by U.S. forces during the Vietnam War.

•

Farmers in Klamath Falls, Ore., open irrigation gates that had been closed in April by order of the federal government to protect the endangered suckerfish; the disappearance of the irrigation water, together with a severe drought, has enraged local farmers.

5 The government of Macedonia signs a cease-fire agreement with leaders of the ethnic Albanian rebels who have been fighting in the northwestern part of the country.

•

In the first of several highly publicized shark attacks in U.S. coastal waters this summer, an eight-year-old boy, Jessie Arbogast, has his right arm bitten off by a 2-m (7-ft) bull shark; the boy's arm is rescued from the shark's mouth and later reattached by surgeons.

•

Susan P. Schoelwer, the curator of the Connecticut Historical Society, tells the press that a flag discovered in the society's storage area in 1998 has been authenticated as one of the five flags that were in the theatre box occupied by U.S. Pres. Abraham Lincoln on the night he was assassinated.

•

Hannelore Kohl, the wife of former German chancellor Helmut Kohl, in despair over the rare, painful, and untreatable allergy to sunlight that she had developed, commits suicide.

6 Scientists at the Stanford (Calif.) Linear Accelerator Center announce that they have found CP violation in the decay of B mesons, confirming results seen only once before, with another particle, the K meson, in 1964; CP violation is an inequality in certain basic processes of particle physics and may explain why vastly more matter than antimatter resulted from the big bang.

7 Maoist insurgents in Nepal kill 39 police officers at various security posts throughout the country, the highest one-day total since the insurgency began five years ago. (*See* July 19.)

Violence breaks out in Kingston, the capital of Jamaica, in the wake of a police raid for illegal weapons; when calm is restored three days later, at least 25 people have died.

Portugal decriminalizes the possession of recreational drugs for personal use, joining Spain and Italy in treating drug use as a medical rather than a criminal matter. (*See* July 30.)

Six people are gored in the first day of an unusually dangerous running of the bulls in Pamplona, Spain.

8 Great Britain's fourth race riot, the worst so far this year, rages for nine hours in the northern town of Bradford.

Officials in Bosnia and Herzegovina say they have found a mass grave containing at least 200 bodies in the village of Liplje.

American tennis star Venus Williams defeats Belgian Justine Henin to win her second consecutive Wimbledon title; a day later Goran Ivanisevic of Croatia becomes the first wild-card entrant to win a major tournament when he defeats Australian Patrick Rafter.

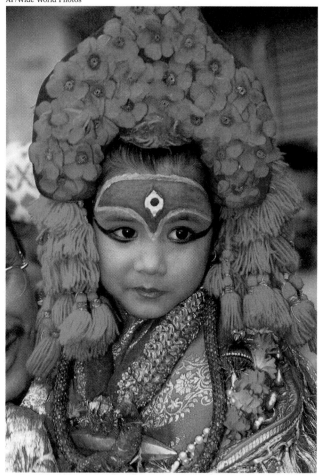
AP/Wide World Photos

The Israeli conductor Daniel Barenboim creates an uproar in Israel when, at the conclusion of a program for the Israel Festival from which a planned piece by Richard Wagner, whom many consider an anti-Semite, had been excised, Barenboim asks the audience whether they would like a Wagner piece as an encore; after a half-hour debate a number of people leave, and the overture to Wagner's *Tristan und Isolde* is performed.

9 An appeals court in Chile rules that Augusto Pinochet Ugarte is too ill to stand trial; this effectively puts an end to efforts to bring him up on charges of human rights abuses during his 17-year tenure as ruler of Chile.

10 Sri Lankan Pres. Chandrika Kumaratunga orders Parliament suspended for two months and calls for a referendum on a proposed new constitution that would give more rights to Tamils.

Preeti Shakya, age four, is enthroned as Kumari, the virgin goddess who brings peace and prosperity to Nepal; she will lead a sequestered life, dressed in red, until her menarche causes her to lose her divinity and a new Kumari must be found. (Photo above.)

Zlatko Lagumdzija, a Bosnian Muslim and foreign minister, is appointed prime minister of Bosnia and Herzegovina, replacing Bozidar Matic, a Bosnian

Croat who had resigned on June 22.

11 On the last day of its summit meeting in Lusaka, Zambia, the Organization of African Unity decides to dissolve the organization after 38 years of existence and transform itself into the African Union, modeled on the European Union.

Police in Washington, D.C., search the apartment of U.S. Rep. Gary Condit of California, looking for clues in the disappearance of Chandra Levy, a Washington intern who was last seen on April 30; Condit's personal life has come under increasingly heavy scrutiny throughout the summer. (*See* August 23.)

Four firefighters die in the deadliest wildfire in the U.S. since 1994; the blaze, in the Okanogan National Forest in Washington, explodes from 40 to 1,012 ha (100 to 2,500 ac).

12 A report issued by Human Rights Watch charges that the human rights record of the opposition to the Taliban in Afghanistan is as bad as that of the Taliban and that the countries supporting the opposition are doing so for their own self-interest.

France orders the extradition of former high-profile antiwar activist Ira Einhorn to the U.S., whence he fled in 1981 to avoid being tried for the 1977 murder of his girlfriend, Holly Maddux; on July 20 Einhorn arrives in the U.S., where he is immediately imprisoned.

13 Beijing is selected to host the 2008 Olympic Games, winning out over Toronto,

Paris, Istanbul, and Osaka; China responds with joy.

14 Pres. Pervez Musharraf of Pakistan arrives in India for a summit meeting with Indian Prime Minister Atal Bihari Vajpayee to discuss the Kashmir dispute; two days later the talks abruptly break off, however. (*See* October 1.)

•

The last original episode of the *Bozo's Circus* television show in the U.S. is broadcast in Chicago; at the height of its popularity in the 1960s, there were about 180 Bozos on the air throughout the nation.

15 Using a Canadian-supplied mechanical arm, the astronauts aboard the International Space Station install a new entryway onto the space station; the new airlock is compatible with NASA spacesuits as well as the Russian spacesuits that the other airlock is able to accommodate.

16 In Moscow Russian Pres. Vladimir Putin and Chinese Pres. Jiang Zemin sign a mutual friendship treaty, the first between the two countries in more than 50 years.

•

Jacques Rogge, a Belgian surgeon and former world champion yachtsman, is elected president of the International Olympic Committee; chosen partly for his personal integrity in the recent IOC scandals, he replaces Juan António Samaranch of Spain.

•

Germany asks the Czech Republic to close down the Temelin nuclear power plant near the border between the countries, contending that the plant is not safe.

•

The 50th anniversary of the publication of *The Catcher in the Rye* by J.D. Salinger is noted; in celebration the online bookseller Amazon.com sells the book at the 1951 price—$3.

•

Fifteen sea lions in Ecuador's Galápagos National Park are discovered butchered on the beach on San Cristóbal Island; the sea lions' sex organs are in demand in Asia, where they are used for folk medicinal purposes.

17 Dragisa Pesic is named by Pres. Vojislav Kostunica to replace Zoran Zizic as prime minister of Yugoslavia. (*See* June 28.)

18 A 60-car train carrying hazardous materials derails in a tunnel under Baltimore, Md., and catches fire, melting fibre-optic cables and slowing Internet and rail traffic throughout the Middle Atlantic region; five days later the tunnel is finally cleared.

•

A special train arrives in Vladivostok, Russia, from Moscow as part of a celebration of the centenary of the 9,267-km (5,758-mi)-long Trans-Siberian Railroad, still the longest railway in the world.

19 Indonesia passes a bill granting increased autonomy to the rebellious province of Aceh.

Faced with an ultimatum from his party, the Nepali Congress Party, as well as a burgeoning Maoist insurgency, Prime Minister Girija Prasad Koirala of Nepal resigns; on July 22 King Gyanendra appoints Sher Bahadur Deuba to replace him. (*See* July 7.)

•

Nearly two-thirds of Argentina's workers participate in a one-day strike, effectively shutting down the country, to protest recently announced austerity measures.

20 Outside the Group of Eight meeting in Genoa, Italy, Carlo Giuliani, one of tens of thousands of protesters, is killed by police; his is the first death among antiglobalization activists.

•

The London Stock Exchange goes public; its shares are traded—on its own exchange—for the first time.

•

A public uproar greets a media report about a study commissioned by the Philip Morris tobacco company in the Czech Republic that spells out the savings to public finances brought about by smokers' dying earlier than nonsmokers.

21 The United Nations Conference on the Illicit Trade in Small Arms and Light Weapons in All Its Aspects approves an agreement, much weakened by the demands of the U.S., to reduce trafficking in small arms.

•

Doctors in Murcia, Spain, report the largest-known outbreak of Legionnaires disease; more than 300 became ill with the disease, which they contracted from cooling towers in six different buildings.

22 David Duval of the U.S. wins his first major golf tournament when he finishes three strokes ahead of Niclas Fasth of Sweden at the 130th British Open.

•

The first of the tax-rebate checks authorized in the new U.S. budget are mailed out to American taxpayers; 91.6 million people are scheduled to receive such a check. (*See* May 10.)

23 A day after the military ignored Indonesian Pres. Abdurrahman Wahid's orders to shut down the People's Consultative Assembly (the legislature), the assembly votes unanimously to oust Wahid in favour of his vice president, Megawati Sukarnoputri.

•

In Bonn, Ger., 178 nations, not including the U.S., reach an agreement on the Kyoto Protocol after three days of marathon bargaining; under the agreement 38 nations must reduce their greenhouse gas emissions to 5.2% below 1990 levels by 2012. (*See* June 12.)

•

Burundi Pres. Pierre Buyoya signs an agreement with Hutu politicians to lead the first transitional government under the Arusha accords, designed to end the civil war in Burundi, as an attempted coup fanned by fears of the power-sharing arrangement is put down.

24 The Liberation Tigers of Tamil Eelam attack Sri Lanka's international airport at Colombo, destroying or disabling 14 commercial and military aircraft and leaving 20 dead.

•

A court in Seoul, S.Kor., finds seven former executives of the Daewoo Corp. guilty of accounting fraud and sentences them to as much as seven years in prison.

•

Phase I of the largest rat eradication program in the world is completed on the 106-sq-km (41-sq-mi) sub-Antarctic Campbell Island, believed to be infested with as many as 200,000 Norway rats.

25 The U.S. rejects an international protocol for compliance with the 1972 treaty banning germ warfare, objecting to provisions that it believes would be detrimental to the business community.

•

Louis G. Spisto, the executive director in New York of the American Ballet Theatre, quits abruptly; his two-year tenure has nearly torn the dance company apart.

26 The Chinese government says that it has released U.S. residents Gao Zhan and Qin Guangguang to the U.S. two days after having sentenced them both to 10 years' imprisonment for spying; U.S. Secretary of State Colin Powell is due to arrive in Beijing on July 28. (*See* April 3.)

•

Congressional Gold Medals are awarded to the 29 Navajo code talkers (only 5 of whom are still living) who were instrumental in the Allied victory over Japan in World War II by relaying military information coded in the Navajo language, which is spoken by only a handful of non-Navajos.

27 Scientists at California's Lawrence Berkeley National Laboratory retract a claim they made in 1999 that they had created a 118th element; with results that could not be reproduced, the researchers reexamined the original data and found they did not support the claim.

•

A judge in Bogotá, Colom., orders a halt to spraying intended to destroy the coca crop; local farmers contend that the herbicide used, glycophosate, is causing health problems and damaging legal crops.

•

United Airlines and US Airways call off their proposed merger as the U.S. Department of Justice threatens to sue to prevent it from taking place. (*See* April 9.)

28 The National Academy of Public Administration finds that the Smithsonian Institution needs about $1.5 billion worth of repairs and renovations and blames management problems for much of the deterioration.

29 American Lance Armstrong wins his third consecutive Tour de France bicycle race.

•

In a nonbinding referendum on the Puerto Rican island of Vieques, 68% of balloters vote for an immediate end to U.S. Navy exercises on the island. (*See* June 14.)

30 New rules go into effect in Canada that permit anyone who is terminally ill or suffers from certain specified chronic illnesses to grow and smoke marijuana for pain relief, provided they have a medical certificate verifying their condition. (*See* July 7.)

•

The UN Security Council approves a plan to appoint experts to monitor and help enforce an arms embargo against the Taliban in Afghanistan; the embargo is intended to press the Taliban into surrendering Osama bin Laden. (*See* July 2.)

31 Prime Minister Atal Bihari Vajpayee, frustrated by work involved in holding his coalition together, shocks the government of India when he offers to resign; he is immediately persuaded to stay on.

•

Lava from Mt. Etna in Sicily, Italy, which has been erupting for two weeks, threatens two villages and forces the closing of tourist and scientific facilities. (Photo below.)

AP/Wide World Photos

August

According to the second paragraph of Article 7,
I have the right to speak the Albanian language.

Arben Xhaferi, ethnic Albanian leader, surprising
participants at the signing of a peace agreement in Macedonia
by addressing them in Albanian, August 13

1 The first book is ceremonially placed in the new Bibliotheca Alexandrina in Egypt, located approximately on the site of the ancient Library at Alexandria; included among the first volumes are a handwritten 7th-century Qur'an, a Bible, and the Microsoft Excel 2000 handbook.

Azerbaijan gives up Cyrillic and adopts the Latin alphabet (in a variant similar to Turkish) for its national language, Azerbaijani; the change, made for nationalist reasons, causes substantial confusion, especially because of a lack of computer fonts and keyboards.

In Germany, for the first time, homosexual couples exchange rings and vows as a new law permitting same-sex partnerships goes into effect; the law permits registered partners to inherit from one another and to share a surname but not to adopt children.

2 Former Bosnian Serb general Radislav Krstic is found guilty of genocide by the UN war crimes tribunal in The Hague

and is sentenced to 46 years in prison; the following day three Bosnian Muslim officers are transferred to The Hague to face the tribunal.

Robert S. Mueller III is confirmed as the new FBI director, replacing Louis J. Freeh; on the same day, Mueller successfully undergoes an operation for prostate cancer.

3 Scientists from the Sloan Digital Sky Survey say they believe they have seen the beginning of the formation of stars; it is believed that, as stars began to form, clouds of hydrogen atoms were floating throughout the universe, and the Sloan scientists think they have seen the shadow of one of these clouds on a quasar.

Thailand's high court for the first time overturns an indictment by the anticorruption commission when it acquits Prime Minister Thaksin Shinawatra of financial irregularities.

4 North Korean leader Kim Jong Il and Russian Pres.

Vladimir Putin issue a joint statement in Moscow in which they pledge to combat international terrorism, among other things; this is Kim's first visit to a noncommunist state.

In a ceremony in Canton, Ohio, players Lynn Swann, Nick Buoniconti, Mike Munchak, Jackie Slater, Ron Yary, and Jack Youngblood, as well as coach Marv Levy, are inducted into the Pro Football Hall of Fame.

Hundreds of First Nations people gather in Montreal in an encampment to reenact the Great Peace of 1701, a treaty signed between the French and the Iroquois, and to celebrate its 300th anniversary. (Photo right.)

5 Officers from the Taliban's Ministry for the Promotion of Virtue and the Prevention of Vice close the Kabul offices of Shelter Now, a Christian relief agency, and arrest 24 of its workers, accusing them of attempting to spread Christianity, which is forbidden in the Taliban-run areas of Afghanistan.

Pak Se Ri of South Korea wins her third major golf tournament when she outplays Australian Karrie Webb to win the Women's British Open in Sunningdale, Eng.

In Edmonton, Alta., American runner Maurice Greene wins the world championship 100-m sprint for the third consecutive time with a time of 9.82 sec; on the following day American sprinter Marion Jones loses her first 100-m race since 1997 to Zhanna Pintusevich-Block of Ukraine, and on August 8 Ethiopian runner Haile Gebrselassie, who had won every 10,000-m event that he had entered since 1993, finishes behind Charles Kamathi of Kenya.

6 The Irish Republican Army agrees to a method for putting its weapons beyond use as a deadline approaches for an agreement to prevent the shutdown of the Northern Ireland Assembly.

The publishing company Alfred A. Knopf, Inc., agrees to pay former U.S. president Bill Clinton an advance of

$10 million to write his memoirs; it is the biggest publishing advance ever paid.

7 Pres. Hugo Bánzer Suárez of Bolivia hands the presidency over to his vice president, Jorge Quiroga Ramírez, because of ill health.

•

In Nairobi, Kenya, on the former site of the U.S. embassy, the August 7 Memorial Park is opened to commemorate the victims (207 Kenyans and 12 Americans) of the terrorist bombing that destroyed the building on Aug. 7, 1998.

8 Bayer AG withdraws its anticholesterol drug, Baycol, from the world market after 31 deaths are linked to it.

•

Kyrgyzstan announces plans to charge Kazakhstan, Tajik-

istan, and Uzbekistan for using water in rivers that originate in Kyrgyzstan, saying that it requires money for the upkeep of reservoirs that provide water for its neighbours.

9 After weeks of well-publicized ruminating, U.S. Pres. George W. Bush announces that the U.S. will support stem-cell research, provided the research is done only on the 60 existing stem-cell lines; it is unclear, however, whether these lines are in fact viable and available to American researchers.

•

The U.S. and Mexico reach an agreement in principle to expand a temporary worker program that will allow many undocumented Mexicans living and working in the U.S. to gain permits and work toward permanent legal residency.

•

Soldiers overthrow the secessionist government of Said Abeid Abderemanein on Anjouan Island; Anjouan had declared independence from Comoros in 1997 but signed a reconciliation agreement in 2000.

10 A passenger train strikes a land mine near Zenza do Itombe, Angola, and more than 250 passengers are killed; UNITA rebels claim responsibility, saying that the train was also carrying military supplies.

•

Cambodia's King Norodom Sihanouk signs a law to create a UN-assisted tribunal to try former Khmer Rouge leaders for war crimes.

11 Home rule is restored in Northern Ireland after a

one-day suspension; the pause allows British authorities to wait another six weeks before calling new elections in the wake of David Trimble's resignation as first minister. (*See* July 1 and November 6.)

China refuses an offer of $34,576 from the U.S. to defray China's costs from the incident wherein a U.S. spy plane and Chinese fighter jet crashed; China had sought $1 million. (*See* April 12.)

12 Two days of heavy rains cause flash flooding and mud slides in northeastern Iran, killing at least 114 people, destroying crops, and leaving thousands homeless; on August 14 New Delhi suffers its heaviest rainfall in 40 years.

The space shuttle *Discovery* delivers a new three-member

crew to the International Space Station for a four-month stay; this crew is the space station's third.

13 Government and ethnic Albanian leaders sign a political deal in Macedonia that gives more representation to ethnic Albanians and recognizes Albanian as an official language. (*See* August 17.)

Japanese Prime Minister Junichiro Koizumi visits the Yasukuni shrine, a Shinto memorial to those who died during World War II; the visit excites a storm of protest in China and South Korea, where 20 young men chop off the tips of their little fingers to demonstrate their distress.

14 Leaders of the 11 African countries with a stake in Air Afrique agree to a restructuring plan whereby the airline will be dissolved and then re-created, with Air France holding a majority stake in return for significant financial support; African heads of state hail the plan, which has saved the airline from going out of business.

In spite of Pres. Daniel arap Moi's support, a bill that would have created the Kenya Anticorruption Authority is defeated in that country's parliament; continued financial aid to Kenya from the International Monetary Fund is contingent upon the creation of the authority.

Emmanuel Milingo, the Roman Catholic archbishop of Zambia—who had risked excommunication to marry Maria Sung of South Korea in a mass wedding in May presided over by the Rev. Sun Myung Moon of the Unification Church—renounces his wife and reconciles with the Roman Catholic Church.

15 A law to give Indian groups in Mexico greater rights goes into effect; in the five years since the law was drafted to satisfy demands of Zapatista rebels in Chiapas state, however, it has lost support among Indians throughout the country.

A new civil code granting women equal legal rights with men is passed in Brazil; the code was first proposed 26 years ago.

16 A six-day auction of the assets of the Amedeo Development Corp., Prince Jefri Bolkiah's defunct construction company, in Brunei comes to a close with total sales of $7.8 million, a fraction of the $15 billion the former finance minister had lost.

The Industry Standard, a respected financial magazine that focused on the dot-com economy, suspends publication.

17 The first of the NATO peace-keeping troops arrive in Macedonia; two days earlier NATO had decided to send only 400 British troops initially and to wait to see if the combatants held to their cease-fire before sending in the full contingent of 3,500 from 12 countries. (*See* August 13.)

Prime Minister Percival Patterson of Jamaica agrees with opposition leader Edward Seaga to create a strategy to reduce violence in the inner city; the following day 7 people are murdered in Kingston, bringing the death total since May to 71.

Because of bad weather, American balloonist Steve Fossett halts his fifth attempt to become the first person to circumnavigate the globe solo in a balloon; he lands in a field in Brazil after making it just past the halfway mark.

18 A hotel in Quezon City, Phil., burns down, killing 73; security bars on windows and inaccessible fire escapes contribute to the death toll.

Danny Almonte, playing for the Bronx, N.Y., Rolando Paulino All-Stars, pitches the first perfect game in the Little League World Series since 1957; it is later proved that Almonte is 14 years old, however, and his team's entire season is struck from the record books because he is two years too old to be eligible to play Little League baseball. (*See* August 26.)

The 10-day consecration of the Great Stupa of Dharmakaya is completed at Red Feather Lakes, Colo.; the stupa, built to honour the teacher Chogyam Trungpa Rinpoche, who died in 1987, attracted 2,000 Buddhists from around the world to the dedication ceremonies.

19 Three days of performances, parades, and fireworks celebrating the 800th anniversary of the city of Riga, the capital of Latvia, come to a close.

American David Toms wins the Professional Golfers' Association of America championship, simultaneously setting a new scoring record for a major tournament championship with a score of 265, breaking the record of 267 set by Greg Norman in 1993.

20 In Gaborone, Botswana, government officials from the Democratic Republic of the Congo, opposition politicians, and rebel leaders begin talks to try to settle the civil war in the country.

An orderly march of 100,000 persons calling for greater recognition of the Berber language and culture takes place in Kabylie, a region in northeastern Algeria considered to be the centre of Berber culture. (*See* October 3.)

21 Two hundred yachts race in the America's Cup Jubilee regatta over the course of the race in which the schooner *America* triumphed 150 years ago, an 80-km (50-mi) course circling the Isle of Wight; the winner is Gianni Agnelli's *Stealth.*

The 14th-century Orthodox monastery at Lesok, Macedonia, is destroyed by an explosion, apparently the work of ethnic Albanian terrorists; the incident is unusual, however, because cultural and religious monuments have not previously been targeted during the current civil strife in Macedonia.

22 Jesse Helms, the ultraconservative Republican senator from North Carolina, announces that he will retire at the end of his term in 2003; Helms turns 80 in October.

The Bush administration releases figures showing that the large projected U.S. budget surplus for the next several years has dwindled to a negligible amount.

New Scientist magazine publishes a report that Hans Beekman of Belgium's Royal Museum for Central Africa found banana fossils in Cameroon dating to 500 BC; experts had believed that bananas did not reach Cameroon until the 10th century AD.

23 Speaking at an elementary school in Crawford, Texas, Pres. George W. Bush says definitively that the U.S. will pull out of the Anti-Ballistic Missile Treaty, though he says the timing of the withdrawal has not been determined.

For the first time, an official of the government of China acknowledges that the country is facing an AIDS epidemic and discloses that HIV infections in China rose 67.4% in the first six months of 2001 compared with the first six months of 2000.

Beleaguered U.S. Rep. Gary Condit of California appears on a prime-time television interview with ABC News investigator Connie Chung; the program is the most-watched show in the summer of 2001, with an estimated audience of 24 million people. (*See* July 11.)

24 An article in *Science* magazine by geneticists for the Mpala Research Centre in Kenya and the U.S. National Cancer Institute reports their findings that forest elephants and savanna elephants in Africa are in fact two different species, which brings to three the number of living elephant species.

Tom Green is sentenced in Provo, Utah, to five years in prison for bigamy and nonsupport, in spite of the pleas of his five wives. (Photo right.)

25 Crown Prince Haakon of Norway marries Mette-Marit Tjessem Høiby, a commoner with a colourful past.

The hero of East Timor's independence struggle, José Alexandre Gusmão, bows to public pressure and announces that he will run for president when elections are held in 2002. (*See* August 30.)

The Women's United Soccer Association holds its first championship game, in Foxboro, Mass.; the Bay Area CyberRays defeat the Atlanta Beat 4–2 to win the Founders Cup.

26 In Williamsport, Pa., Kitasuna of Tokyo, Japan, becomes the 55th world champion Little League team when it beats the nine from Apopka, Fla., 2–1. (*See* August 18.)

Sammy Sosa of the Chicago Cubs becomes the third player in major league baseball history to have four 50-home-run seasons (the other two are Babe Ruth and Mark McGwire); by season's end he has 64.

27 *Physical Review Letters* publishes a study that suggests that the fine structure constant has increased slightly over the life of the universe; if confirmed, the finding would have astonishing inferences for other constants, such as the speed of light.

A parade in Chisinau marks the 10th anniversary of Moldova's independence; Ukraine and Belarus also celebrate the 10th anniversaries of their independence in August.

At the Tonga National Museum in the capital, Nuku'alofa, Prime Minister Prince 'Ulukalala Lavaka Ata officially opens the island country's first major exhibition of prehistoric artifacts, most dating to the Lapita era, about 3,000 years ago.

28 The computer manufacturer and retailer Gateway announces plans to lay off one-quarter of its workforce, eliminate most of its overseas operations, and close one factory and four support centres in the U.S.

Cuba's central bank says that U.S. coins will not be accepted as currency after October 15; the U.S. dollar has been accepted as currency on a temporary basis in Cuba since 1993.

29 Australian troops seize an overcrowded Norwegian container vessel off Christmas Island to prevent it from landing on Australian territory; four days earlier the ship had rescued 434 Afghan, Sri Lankan, and Pakistani asylum seekers from a sinking Indonesian ferry. (*See* September 19.)

Thirty Nigerian families file suit against the pharmaceutical company Pfizer, Inc. in U.S. federal court, contending that the drug company illegally experimented upon their children during a 1996 meningitis outbreak.

The National Black Sports and Entertainment Hall of Fame inducts its first 24 members in New York City; among the honorees are Muhammad Ali, Louis Armstrong, Ella Fitzgerald, and Wilma Rudolph.

30 Voters in East Timor go to the polls for their first free election, to select the assembly that will write the constitution for the new nation; the turnout is estimated at better than 90%. (*See* August 25.)

For the first time, the general public in India may gaze upon the astonishing wealth of jewelry that was accumulated by the Nizams of Hyderabad as the collection goes on exhibit in the National Museum in New Delhi.

31 Papua New Guinea signs a peace agreement with rebels in Bougainville after a decade-long civil war.

The International Labour Organization releases a report showing that Americans worked the longest hours of any country in the world between 1990 and 2000 and increased the hours spent on the job per year by nearly 40 over the course of the decade.

George Frey/AFP Worldwide

September

> *As for those that carried out these attacks, there are no adequate words of condemnation. Their barbarism will stand as their shame for all eternity.*
>
> British Prime Minister Tony Blair,
> in his address to his nation, September 11

1 The Los Angeles Sparks overwhelm the Charlotte Sting to win the Women's National Basketball Association championship, and the team's centre, Lisa Leslie, is named Most Valuable Player.

•

A fire breaks out in a mahjongg parlour in Tokyo's most famous red-light district; the death toll, at 44, makes it Tokyo's deadliest fire since 1982.

2 The Hewlett-Packard Co. announces that it will buy the Compaq Computer Corp.; they are the second and third largest personal computer manufacturers, respectively, in the U.S.

3 Israel and the U.S. abandon the UN World Conference Against Racism in Durban, S.Af., objecting that the proposed declaration unfairly singles out Israel as an offender. (*See* September 8.)

•

Fradique de Menezes is inaugurated as the new president of São Tomé and Príncipe; on September 25 he appoints Evaristo de Carvalho to replace Guilherme Posser da Costa as prime minister.

4 Disney opens its newest theme park, Tokyo DisneySea, which has an aquatic theme, in Japan; in spite of the straitened economy in Japan, theme parks remain popular.

•

An arson fire starting at the Straw Market engulfs the market, the offices of the Ministry of Tourism, an office complex, and a complex of shops and restaurants at the heart of the tourist strip in Nassau, Bahamas.

•

The *Proceedings of the National Academy of Sciences* publishes a report by researchers at the University of Wisconsin at Madison describing how they induced human embryonic stem cells to become blood-making cells.

5 Elections are held in Nagorno-Karabakh, which has declared itself independent; Azerbaijan maintains that the elections are illegal.

•

At a scientific conference in Washington, D.C., scientists describe an observation by the Chandra X-Ray Observatory of energy flares that provide strong evidence of the theorized black hole at the centre of the Milky Way Galaxy.

6 After a summer of media attention devoted to shark attacks on swimmers, the Florida Fish and Wildlife Conservation Commission bans the practice of using bait to attract sharks so tourists can swim with them.

•

The ABC television network announces that it will join CBS in broadcasting most of its offerings in the HDTV (high-definition television) format.

7 Surgeons at Mount Sinai Medical Center in New York City remove a diseased gall bladder from a woman in Strasbourg, France, through the use of robotics and computer imaging; it is the first transoceanic instance of what has come to be called telesurgery.

•

Counting of last week's ballots reveals that Laisenia Qarase has been elected prime minister of Fiji; he had been installed as interim prime minister by the military in July 2000 following the coup in May.

8 Tajikistan's minister of culture, Abdurahim Rahimov, is murdered by a gunman outside his home in Dushanbe.

•

The UN World Conference Against Racism in Durban, S.Af., finally succeeds in hammering out a declaration that the attending nations can agree to, though many are still somewhat dissatisfied; the declaration condemns slavery and discrimination against ethnic minorities, refugees, and women. (*See* September 3.)

•

At the U.S. Open women's tennis finals, telecast in prime time, American Venus Williams defeats her younger sister, Serena, to take her second straight U.S. Open title; the next day Australian Lleyton Hewitt defeats Pete Sampras of the U.S. for the men's title.

Patrick Witty

●

Monsoon Wedding, a film by Indian director Mira Nair, wins the Golden Lion award at the Venice Film Festival.

9 Suicide bombers attack Ahmad Shah Masoud, the leader of the anti-Taliban opposition in Afghanistan; it is initially unclear whether the assassination attempt is successful, but a spokesman finally confirms his death on September 15.

●

In presidential elections held in Belarus, Pres. Alyaksandr Lukashenka declares victory hours before the first returns are in.

●

The Jewish Museum Berlin, designed by Polish-born architect Daniel Libeskind, is opened with a gala attended by 800 dignitaries.

10 Tokyo's benchmark Nikkei Stock Average closes at its lowest point since 1984, while the *Financial Times* Stock Exchange 100 index in London closes below 5,000 for the first time since 1998.

●

A general election in Norway results in the Labour Party's worst showing since 1924. (*See* October 17.)

11 *In a coordinated terrorist attack, two hijacked airliners strike the twin towers of the World Trade Center in New York City, which subsequently collapse (photo above), another strikes the Pentagon near Washington, D.C., and a fourth crashes in rural Pennsylvania, apparently short of its intended goal; the total death toll is in the vicinity of 3,100.*

●

For the first time ever, the U.S. government closes the airspace over the United States, as well as all airports, to commercial traffic in an attempt to prevent any possible further planned terrorist strikes from taking place.

●

An exceptionally violent typhoon kills five people in Tokyo and causes great damage to roads and rail.

12 The North Atlantic Council, the governing council of NATO, agrees to allow the U.S. to invoke Article 5 of the NATO charter, which declares that an attack against any NATO member is to be regarded as an attack against all members; it is the first time in the alliance's 52-year history that Article 5 has been invoked. (*See* October 2.)

●

U.S. authorities say that they have evidence that the hijackers in the September 11 terrorist attacks were followers of Osama bin Laden and also that they have identified accomplices in a number of cities.

●

The Federal Aviation Administration announces that henceforward knives and other cutting implements will not be allowed on U.S. airline flights; evidently the weapons used to hijack airliners on September 11 were of this previously permitted category.

13 U.S. Attorney General John Ashcroft says that federal investigators have identified 18 men who were hijackers in the September 11 terrorist attacks, and the following day the names of the 19 total number of hijackers are released; all were ticketed passengers aboard the airliners that they hijacked.

●

Bond markets in the U.S. resume trading for the first time since September 11; interest rates plummet.

●

The Federal Aviation Administration allows all airports in the U.S. except Logan International Airport in Boston, where two of September 11's hijacked flights originated, and Ronald Reagan Washington National Airport to reopen; few flights take off, however, and most of those are airplanes that had been diverted on September 11 and are returning to hub airports and their original destinations.

●

The government of Nigeria promises to step in to stop

the violence after three days of fighting between Muslims and Christians in the city of Jos leave hundreds dead; violence first broke out in this historically peaceful city on September 7.

•

The New England Journal of Medicine publishes findings that the bacterium that causes stomach ulcers, *Heliobacter pylori*, is also responsible for the vast majority of stomach cancers.

14 Tropical Storm Gabrielle makes landfall in Florida, causing extensive damage and flooding throughout central Florida.

•

Musicians who had gathered (and become stranded) in Los Angeles for the Latin Grammy Awards, scheduled for September 11 and canceled, hold an impromptu benefit concert for the Red Cross and the New York Disaster Relief Fund.

15 Pres. Pervez Musharraf pledges Pakistan's support for U.S. efforts to punish those responsible for the September 11 terrorist attacks; Pakistan borders Afghanistan, and its support is seen as crucial.

•

A barge collides with a piling of the Queen Isabella Causeway in Texas a few hours after midnight, causing two adjacent 24-m (80-ft) segments of the bridge to fall into the Laguna Madre channel and a number of vehicles to drive off the edge in the dark.

16 The Professional Golfers' Association of America announces that the Ryder Cup golf tournament, scheduled for later this month in Sutton Coldfield, Eng., will be postponed until next year

in the wake of the September 11 terrorist attacks.

17 The New York Stock Exchange opens for the first time since it closed the morning of September 11.

•

After a week in abeyance, major league baseball resumes playing games; it is the first major sport to return to the arena.

•

The World Bank and the International Monetary Fund cancel their annual meetings, scheduled for September 29–30 in Washington, D.C.; it is the first time the institutions have ever called off a meeting.

•

The government of Macedonia reluctantly agrees to accept a small NATO security force to help keep the peace after the conclusion of the 30-day weapons-collection effort.

•

The General Motors Corp. agrees to buy about two-thirds of South Korea's bankrupt Daewoo Motor Co. from its creditors.

18 For the second straight day, Typhoon Nari pounds Taiwan with record rainfalls, causing massive flooding and killing 79 people.

•

Two days of talks between cabinet-level negotiators from North and South Korea end with a number of agreements, including plans for a new round of family visits and work to complete a rail link between the countries.

19 The Organization of American States agrees by acclamation to invoke the Rio Treaty, a hemispheric mutual-defense pact.

•

United Airlines announces plans to cut 20% of its workforce; since September 11 several airlines and Boeing have announced job cuts as a result of losses caused by the grounding of all flights and subsequent decreased demand layered onto problems caused by a softening economy.

•

Indonesian Pres. Megawati Sukarnoputri meets with U.S. Pres. George W. Bush in Washington, D.C.; Megawati does not pledge to crack down on Muslim extremists in her fragmented country.

•

The first of the 434 largely Afghan refugees turned away from Australia in late August land in Nauru, where they will be processed by officials from the United Nations High Commissioner for Refugees. (*See* August 29.)

20 In his first formal televised address to the nation since his inauguration, U.S. Pres. George W. Bush announces plans to create a new cabinet-level office to be called the Office of Homeland Security and to be headed by Tom Ridge, currently the governor of Pennsylvania.

•

Fans at an exhibition ice hockey game between the New York Rangers and the Philadelphia Flyers in Philadelphia's First Union Center insist on watching U.S. Pres. George W. Bush's address to the nation rather than the final period of the game.

•

Rwanda adopts a new national anthem, "Rwanda Nziza," replacing "Rwanda Rwacu," which was felt to have ethnically divisive lyrics.

21 *America: A Tribute to Heroes*, a two-hour benefit show to raise money for relief work in New York City and Wash-

ington, D.C., that was put together in less than a week, is broadcast on more than 30 cable and broadcast TV stations in the U.S. and in 200 other countries as well.

•

After the Riigikogu (legislature) fails to decide on a new president, a special assembly chooses Arnold Ruutel to replace Lennart Meri as president of Estonia.

The Lasker Awards for medical research are presented in a ceremony in New York City to Robert Edwards for clinical research; to Mario Capecchi, Martin Evans, and Oliver Smithies for basic medical research; and to William Foege for public service.

22 Deep Space 1, a NASA probe whose primary mission ended in September 1999, surprises scientists by successfully passing within 2,250 km (1,400 mi) of the nucleus of Comet Borrelly and transmitting pictures and other data that will greatly add to scientific understanding of comets.

23 In general elections in Poland, there is a lower-than-usual turnout, and the winning party is the Democratic Left Alliance, the former communist party; Solidarity not only is ousted from power but also receives too few votes to win seats in the National Assembly.

•

The leftist Social Democratic Party, which has governed the German city-state of Hamburg for the past 44 years, is voted out; the gains made by the conservative Christian Democratic Union and the new rightist Law and Order Party are seen as a reaction to the discovery that the terrorist attacks in the U.S. were apparently planned in Hamburg.

The worst U.S. coal mine disaster since 1984 takes place in Brookwood, Ala., when a pair of methane gas explosions kill 3 miners outright as well as 10 other miners who were attempting to rescue them.

24 Pres. George W. Bush announces that all assets of suspected terrorists will be frozen, and he threatens foreign banks that fail to follow suit or cooperate with U.S. efforts with measures that would make it impossible for them to do business in the U.S.

The U.S. House of Representatives votes to release $582 million of the $819 million in back dues that the U.S. owes to the United Nations. (*See* January 9.)

25 Saudi Arabia severs relations with the Taliban rulers of Afghanistan, three days after the United Arab Emirates did so; now only Pakistan recognizes the Taliban as the legitimate government of Afghanistan.

Basketball legend Michael Jordan announces his second comeback from retirement, declaring that he will sign a two-year contract with the Washington Wizards, sell his ownership stake in the team, and donate his salary for the season to the relief efforts in New York City and Washington, D.C.

General Motors announces that the 2002 model year will be the last in which the Chevrolet Camaro and the Pontiac Firebird are produced; four million Camaros have been sold since the model's debut in 1967, but sales of sports cars have fallen 53% since 1990, the company reports.

26 Pres. George W. Bush authorizes two air force generals to order, on their own authority, the shooting down of commercial airplanes that appear to be threatening U.S. cities.

A pro-Taliban mob burns down the long-abandoned U.S. embassy building in Kabul, Afg.

27 In Zug, Switz., an unhinged man armed with a standard Swiss army-issue assault rifle bursts into a cantonal parliament meeting and opens fire, killing 14 legislators; it is the worst mass murder in Switzerland's history.

Ali Ahmeti, political representative of the ethnic Albanian National Liberation Army in Macedonia, gives the rebel force orders to disband as part of the peace process.

28 The UN Security Council unanimously adopts a resolution requiring all UN members to take steps to eliminate terrorism, including cooperating in any international campaign against terrorists.

The Commonwealth cancels its biennial summit, scheduled for October 6–9 in Brisbane, Australia; in the wake of the September 11 terrorist attacks, leaders of the 54 member nations did not want to leave their countries.

In spite of a 10-day-old truce, a flare-up of violence in Palestinian areas in the Middle East marks the first anniversary of the new *intifadah*.

29 Members of the Free Papua Movement, a separatist organization, occupy the city of Ilaga, capital of the Central Highlands district in Irian Jaya, in spite of the fact that Indonesia recently granted Irian Jaya autonomy.

In a stunning upset, American Bernard Hopkins becomes the first unified middleweight champion in 14 years when he knocks out Félix Trinidad of Puerto Rico in the 12th round in front of a capacity crowd of more than 19,000 fans at Madison Square Garden in New York City.

30 Pres. George W. Bush approves the disbursement of funds for the covert support of the opponents of the Taliban in Afghanistan.

Japanese runner Naoko Takahashi sets a new world record for women in the Berlin Marathon, running 42.2 km (26.2 mi) in 2 hr 19 min 46 sec, nearly a full minute faster than the previous record, set in 1999 in Berlin by Kenyan Tegla Loroupe. (*See* October 7.)

A free concert of remembrance in New York City's Carnegie Hall features, among others, conductor James Levine and soprano Leontyne Price, who comes out of retirement for the event. (Photo below.)

AP/Wide World Photos

October

You can not stop us. We have this anthrax. You die now. Are you afraid? Death to America. Death to Israel. Allah is great.

Text of anthrax-laden letter sent to
U.S. Sen. Tom Daschle and opened on October 15

1 The Swissair Group files for bankruptcy protection for most of its operations; the following day the group grounds all its flights, but the Swiss government steps in, and Swissair begins flying an abbreviated schedule on October 4.

A car bomb explodes in the Legislative Assembly building in Srinagar, the summer capital of the Indian state of Jammu and Kashmir, and a gunfight ensues; 38 people are killed in the incident, for which a militant Pakistani group called Jaish-e-Muhammad claims responsibility. (*See* July 14.)

Italy's highest court acquits Prime Minister Silvio Berlusconi of having falsified documents while acquiring a film company in 1987; he had been convicted and sentenced to prison on that charge in 1997.

FOMA, the world's first third-generation (3G) high-speed cellular phone service, is launched in Japan.

Condé Nast announces that the November issue of *Mademoiselle*, a fashion magazine for young women that had been published for 66 years, will be the last.

2 NATO says that the U.S. has proved to its satisfaction that Osama bin Laden and al-Qaeda are responsible for the September 11 terrorist attacks in the U.S. and that it is therefore prepared to support the U.S. in retaliating against them. (*See* September 12.)

Russia and Iran sign a military accord under which Russia will sell missiles and other weapons to Iran; Russia had stopped selling arms to Iran six years earlier under pressure from the U.S.

U.S. Pres. George W. Bush expresses explicit support for the creation of a Palestinian state.

3 A deranged passenger on a Greyhound bus traveling through Tennessee attacks the bus driver; in the ensuing struggle the bus flips over, and six passengers, including the assailant, are killed.

The pharmaceutical giant GlaxoSmithKlein announces a new national discount program for low-income senior citizens whose health insurance coverage does not include a prescription-drug benefit.

A meeting takes place between Algerian Prime Minister Ali Benflis and Berber leaders in which Algeria agrees to give Tamazight, the Berber language, national recognition and promises to punish police brutality against Berbers. (*See* August 20.)

4 A Russian airliner explodes and crashes into the Black Sea, and all 76 aboard die; the cause proves to be an errant Ukrainian surface-to-air missile that went awry during training exercises.

Health officials report that a man in Florida has been hospitalized with the first case of pulmonary anthrax to have occurred in the U.S. since 1976, but they stress that there is no cause for alarm; the man, Robert Stevens, a photo editor for the supermarket tabloid *Sun*, dies the following day.

Parliamentary elections in Bangladesh, believed to be free and fair in spite of a high level of violence throughout the campaign, return a victory to the party of Khaleda Zia, who goes about forming a new government.

San Diego Padres outfielder Rickey Henderson, batting against the Los Angeles Dodgers, hits a home run and scores his 2,246th career run, breaking the record held by Ty Cobb since 1928.

The World Health Organization issues a report urging national governments to devote more resources to mental health; the dearth of such resources is particularly acute in the poorest countries, and the response in this area to the events of September 11 in the U.S. is singled out for praise.

5 The day after Israeli Prime Minister Ariel Sharon shocked the U.S. administration by implicitly comparing its attempts to discourage Israeli reprisals against

Palestinian attacks to former British prime minister Neville Chamberlain's policy of appeasement toward Nazi Germany, Pres. George W. Bush calls Sharon's remarks "unacceptable," an unusually strong rebuke.

•

Philippine authorities announce that Mustapha Ting Emmo, a key leader of the militant Muslim group Abu Sayyaf, has surrendered.

•

Barry Bonds, batting for the San Francisco Giants against the Los Angeles Dodgers, breaks Mark McGwire's single-season home-run record when he hits his 71st and 72nd home runs; he finishes the season with 73.

6 In an outdoor stadium in East Lansing, Mich., a record 72,554 people watch a tie ice hockey game between Michigan State University and the University of Michigan; the previous hockey attendance record, 55,000, was set in 1957 in Moscow.

7 U.S. and British forces launch air strikes against Taliban positions in Afghanistan; at the same time, U.S. forces begin dropping food packets in remote and poverty-stricken areas of Afghanistan.

•

A referendum to turn a number of responsibilities over to regional governments passes in Italy; the decentralizing legislation is the first poll on constitutional change in Italy in close to half a century.

•

Railtrack, the company that owns the railroad tracks in the U.K., undergoes bankruptcy reorganization in order to keep the nation's railway system from financial collapse.

•

Kenyan runner Catherine Ndereba sets a new world record in the women's marathon of 2 hr 18 min 47 sec at the Chicago Marathon (see September 30); the men's winner is Ben Kimondiu of Kenya.

8 It is discovered that a co-worker of Robert Stevens has been exposed to anthrax, and spores are found on Stevens's computer keyboard.

•

Girma Wolde-Giorgis is elected by the parliament as the second federal president of Ethiopia, succeeding Negasso Gidada.

•

The Nobel Prize for Physiology or Medicine is awarded to Leland H. Hartwell, R. Timothy Hunt, and Paul M. Nurse for their work in discovering the mechanisms regulating cell multiplication.

•

In Italy's worst civilian air disaster in nearly 30 years, a Cessna takes a wrong turn on a taxiway in Milan and crashes into an SAS airliner about to take off, which explodes; 118 people, including 4 airport workers, are killed.

9 In accordance with the terms of the peace pact worked out earlier this year, Macedonia grants amnesty to all ethnic Albanian rebels who have disarmed.

•

The Nobel Prize for Physics is awarded to Carl E. Wieman, Eric A. Cornell, and Wolfgang Ketterle for their production of the Bose-Einstein condensate; the Nobel Prize for Chemistry goes to William S. Knowles, Ryoji Noyori, and K. Barry Sharpless; and the Nobel Prize for Economic Sciences is awarded to Americans Joseph E. Stiglitz, George A. Akerlof, and A. Michael Spence.

•

The United Service Organization appoints entertainer Wayne Newton its official celebrity front man, replacing Bob Hope, who had served in that capacity since the early 1950s.

10 In order to avoid a no-confidence vote, Sri Lankan Pres. Chandrika Kumaratunga dissolves the government and calls for new elections. (See December 5.)

•

The five major American television news organizations agree to censor tapes of Osama bin Laden to remove inflammatory propaganda and possibly prevent the airing of clandestine signals to operatives.

11 The Nobel Prize for Literature is awarded to V.S. Naipaul, a Trinidadian-born British writer.

•

The broadcasting system NBC agrees to buy Telemundo Communications Group, the second biggest Spanish-language broadcaster in the U.S.

12 The centennial Nobel Prize for Peace is awarded jointly to the United Nations and its secretary-general, Ghanaian Kofi Annan.

•

The day after a warning from the FBI that more terrorist attacks may occur in the U.S. in the next few days, U.S. government officials say they have received more credible threats of a possible attack in the next two days; citizens are instructed to be calm but wary.

•

Erin M. O'Connor, an assistant to NBC newsman Tom Brokaw, is diagnosed with cutaneous anthrax in New York City; as was the case in Florida, the anthrax spores apparently came in the mail.

•

The Polaroid Corp. files for bankruptcy protection; its core business of instant photographs was decimated by competition from computer imaging.

13 Company officials at American Media, Inc. (owner of the *Sun* tabloid) say that blood tests have shown that five more employees, in addition to the man who died and two others who were infected with anthrax, have been exposed to anthrax.

•

After negotiations between the U.S. Department of Justice and the Microsoft Corp. fail to reach an agreement by a court-imposed deadline, U.S. District Court Judge Colleen Kollar-Kotelly appoints Eric D. Green, a specialist in dispute resolution, to mediate between the parties.

14 Ireland holds a state funeral for 10 Irish Republican Army volunteers who were hanged by British authorities in 1920 and 1921.

•

A large monument to nationalist leader Stepan Bandera is unveiled in Drohobych, Ukraine; Bandera had cooperated with Nazi Germany, believing that German victories would lead to independence for Ukraine.

15 An anthrax-laden letter addressed to Senate Majority Leader Tom Daschle is opened by one of his assistants, and the baby son of an ABC news producer in New York City is diagnosed with cutaneous anthrax; the following day it is revealed that the anthrax is of exceptionally high quality and that the anthrax-laden letters addressed to Daschle and to Tom Brokaw appear to have been sent by the same person.

The venerable Bethlehem Steel Corp. files for bankruptcy protection.

Brill's Content, a magazine about the media, suspends publication; the previous day *Lingua Franca*, a journal chronicling academic life, had stopped publication.

New York City Mayor Rudolph Giuliani is named a Knight Commander of the Most Excellent Order of the British Empire by Queen Elizabeth II for his support to British families affected by the September 11 terrorist attacks. (*See* December 23.)

Comedian Whoopi Goldberg receives the Mark Twain Prize of the John F. Kennedy Center for the Performing Arts in Washington, D.C.; the award is given annually for contributions to American humour.

16 The German pharmaceutical company Bayer AG announces that it will triple its production of Cipro, which is the primary antibiotic used to fight anthrax; on October 24 Bayer agrees to sell Cipro to the U.S. government for half the price it had been charging.

Peace talks to end the war in the Democratic Republic of the Congo begin in Addis Ababa, Eth.

17 Rechavam Ze'evi, the Israeli minister of tourism and a right-wing politician, is assassinated by members of the Popular Front for the Liberation of Palestine. (*See* October 23.)

Norwegian Prime Minister Jens Stoltenberg submits the Labour Party government's

resignation after a poor showing in elections on September 10; a centre-right coalition led by the Christian People's Party under Kjell Magne Bondevik takes over on October 19.

In London the Booker Prize for literature is awarded to Australian author Peter Carey for *True History of the Kelly Gang*.

Daniel S. Goldin announces that he will resign as head of NASA, an agency he has led since 1992.

18 The men who were convicted in May of having conspired with Osama bin Laden to bomb the U.S. embassies in Kenya and Tanzania in 1998 are sentenced to life in prison without parole.

Japan's legislature approves a measure that will allow Japanese troops to go overseas to provide logistic and humanitarian support to U.S. troops fighting in Afghanistan; the Japanese constitution forbids the use of troops in a combat situation, however.

19 U.S. ground forces for the first time enter the war in Afghanistan.

Leszek Miller of the Democratic Left Alliance is inaugurated as prime minister of Poland.

A wooden fishing boat carrying at least 400 refugees from the Middle East sinks in the Java Sea off Indonesia; only 44 survive.

20 *Investigators say that a day after an anthrax-laden letter addressed to "the Editor of the New York Post" was found, anthrax spores have been found in the mail room of the U.S. House of Representatives. (Photo above.)*

In an address at the annual summit meeting of the Asian-Pacific Economic Cooperation forum in Shanghai, Pres. George W. Bush declares that the September 11 terrorist attacks in the U.S. were intended to disrupt the world economy.

21 The San Jose Earthquakes defeat the Los Angeles Galaxy in overtime to win the Major League Soccer championship in Columbus, Ohio; Dwayne DeRosario, who scored the winning goal, is voted Most Valuable Player of the game.

After a long and fractious search, the U.S. Olympic Committee elects Lloyd Ward its new CEO; Ward is the first African American to head the USOC.

22 Two postal workers in Washington, D.C., die of pulmonary anthrax, and two others are hospitalized with the same disease; a fifth postal worker, who works at a different facility from the previous four, is diagnosed with pulmonary anthrax on October 25.

East Timor's new constituent assembly requests that the United Nations, which is administering the territory, grant it independence on May 20, 2002.

23 In an effort to save the peace process in Northern Ireland, the Irish Republican Army begins putting its weapons verifiably beyond use.

•

Israel turns down a U.S. request that Israeli forces be withdrawn from Palestinian-controlled areas of the West Bank, maintaining that the forces will remain until the Palestinian Authority has arrested those responsible for the murder of Rechavam Ze'evi. (*See* October 17.)

•

A UN appeals court overturns the conviction of three Bosnian Croats whom the international war crimes tribunal had found guilty of persecution, saying there was insufficient evidence to convict; it is the first time a ruling by the war crimes tribunal has been reversed.

24 An accident caused by a truck swerving into the path of another truck in a tunnel 17 km (10.6 mi) long in Bellinzona, Switz., results in a conflagration that kills 11 people and closes the heavily used tunnel to all traffic for several weeks.

•

Pope John Paul II apologizes to China for what he calls errors by Roman Catholic missions; relations between China and the Holy See have been particularly tense since the canonization as martyrs on Oct. 1, 2000, of 120 Chinese whom Beijing regards as criminals.

25 The U.S. Congress passes an antiterrorism bill that grants the government expanded right to use electronic surveillance and expands its ability to detain immigrants without charges.

•

The Microsoft Corp. releases the newest version of its personal computer operating system, Windows XP.

26 South Africa and Burundi sign an agreement to allow South African peacekeeping troops to protect the transitional government due to be established in Burundi.

•

Bernadine Healy, the high-profile president of the American Red Cross, suddenly resigns; disagreements between Healy and the board of governors had come to a head over her handling of the September 11 disaster fund.

•

Abdul Haq, an ethnic Pashtun anti-Taliban leader, is executed by the Taliban days after he sneaked into Afghanistan from exile in Pakistan in hopes of putting together a Pashtun-based opposition to the Taliban.

27 A cofounder of the Intel Corp., Gordon Moore, and his wife, Betty Moore, donate $600 million to the California Institute of Technology in the single largest gift ever given to an American university.

•

The Democratic Alliance, a merger of the two majority-white parties, the New National Party and the Democratic Party in South Africa, collapses when former New National Party members pull out.

•

In the Breeders' Cup Classic race at Belmont Park in Elmont, N.Y., Tiznow, ridden by Chris McCarron, becomes the first horse in 18 years to win the event two years in a row.

28 Gunmen enter a Christian church in Bahawalpur, Pak., during services and mow down the worshipers, killing 16; it is assumed that the act is a reaction to the U.S. bombing in Afghanistan.

29 Once again, the U.S. government warns the general public that it has credible information that there may be some sort of terrorist attack against the U.S. in the next few days.

•

The U.S. Supreme Court hears cases outside the Supreme Court building, for the first time since 1935, while the courthouse is searched for evidence of anthrax; no workers are found to have been exposed.

30 Jacques Nasser resigns as chief executive of the Ford Motor Co.; he is replaced by William Clay Ford, Jr.

•

Nelson O. Oduber is sworn in as prime minister of Aruba.

31 A hospital worker in New York City, Kathy T. Nguyen, dies of pulmonary anthrax; investigators are baffled as to where she was exposed to it.

•

Five women who had been hanged as witches in Salem, Mass., more than 300 years earlier are officially exonerated.

•

A bridge designed by Leonardo da Vinci in 1502 to cross the Golden Horn inlet in Istanbul opens near Oslo; while Leonardo's design was for a bridge 352 m (1,155 ft) long, this bridge, over a highway, is 67 m (220 ft) long and proves that the design works. (Photo below.)

Siv Helene Kristensen

November

1 The U.S. recalls its ambassador from Caracas after Venezuelan Pres. Hugo Chávez Frías criticizes the U.S. war in Afghanistan.

•

A transitional power-sharing government, headed by Pierre Buyoya, a Tutsi, is inaugurated in Bujumbura, Burundi; the majority of the population of Burundi is Hutu.

2 The U.S. government and Microsoft Corp. announce that they have reached an agreement to settle the long-running antitrust lawsuit; on November 6, 9 of the 18 states that had joined the lawsuit and the District of Columbia indicate they will not sign the deal.

•

The last issue of the daily newspaper the *Atlanta* (Ga.) *Journal* is published; it is absorbed by the *Atlanta Constitution*, which will henceforward be published as the *Atlanta Journal-Constitution.*

•

King Muhammad VI of Morocco completes a two-day trip to Western Sahara to emphasize his country's claim to the disputed area.

3 The ruling People's Action Party wins its ninth consecutive election in Singapore in elections in which only 29 of the 84 seats were contested.

•

For the first time since it was painted in 1931, the original of the Norman Rockwell painting *The Barefoot Boy,* commissioned by the Coca-Cola Co., is placed on view to the public, in the exhibition "Norman Rockwell: Pictures for the American People" at the Solomon R. Guggenheim Museum in New York City.

4 The Arizona Diamondbacks unexpectedly come from behind in the bottom of the ninth inning of game seven of the World Series to defeat the New York Yankees 3–2 and win the major league baseball championship in Phoenix, Ariz.

•

After being delayed twice, first by the September 11 terrorist attacks and then by the beginning of the war in Afghanistan, the television Emmy Awards are finally presented in Los Angeles; winners include the HBO comedy series *Sex and the City* and the NBC drama *The West Wing.*

•

The much-anticipated film version of J.K. Rowling's best-selling novel *Harry Potter and the Philosopher's Stone* premieres in London; the film, released as *Harry Potter and the Sorcerer's Stone* in the U.S. on November 14, breaks box-office records in both countries.

The New York City Marathon is won by Tesfaye Jifar of Ethiopia with a time of 2 hr 7 min 43 sec; Margaret Okayo of Kenya, with a time of 2 hr 24 min 21 sec, is the first woman across the finish line.

•

Hurricane Michelle makes landfall on Cuba's south coast, killing five people and causing great damage to the sugar-producing area; it is the worst storm to hit Cuba in 50 years.

•

In presidential elections held in Nicaragua, Enrique Bolaños Geyer of the Constitutionalist Liberal Party wins a surprisingly large victory over Daniel Ortega Saavedra of the Sandinista National Liberation Front.

5 IBM announces that it is placing a number of its software tools in the public domain as the first step toward creating a new open-source organization to be called Eclipse.

6 After losing in the first ballot on November 2, David Trimble wins reelection as the head of a renewed power-sharing government in Northern Ireland. (*See* August 11.)

•

The Belgian airline Sabena is declared bankrupt, and its final scheduled flight, from Benin, lands at Brussels International Airport.

•

Republican Michael R. Bloomberg is elected to succeed Rudolph Giuliani as mayor of New York City; it is the first time in New York's history that two consecutive Republicans have become mayor.

7 A federal appeals court in the U.S. vacates the $5.3 billion award Exxon was ordered to pay in 1994 for the *Exxon Valdez* oil spill in 1989, and the case is sent back to the Alaska district court for a reassessment of damages.

•

For the first time since the crash of the Concorde outside Paris in July 2000, the supersonic passenger craft flies again on a commercial flight, from Paris to New York City.

•

Taiwan for the first time in more than 50 years allows direct trade with and investment in China.

•

Registration begins for the new Internet domain designation .biz.

•

John Ashbery is named winner of the Wallace Stevens Award, a lifetime achievement award, by the Academy of American Poets.

8 First Minister Henry McLeish of Scotland resigns in the face of revelations of undeclared income that he realized by subletting his office; Jack McConnell is appointed to replace him on November 22.

•

A U.S. federal judge issues an order to temporarily stop the Department of Justice's plans to revoke the medical license of any Oregon doctor who prescribes lethal medications to terminally ill patients under Oregon's Death with Dignity Act, which has been in effect since 1997.

9 Representatives from some 140 countries gather in Doha, Qatar, for the fourth ministerial conference of the World Trade Organization.

•

With its stock price in free fall, Enron Corp. agrees to be acquired by its rival Dynegy Inc. (*See* November 28.)

10 After 15 years of negotiations, China becomes a member of the World Trade Organization; the following day Taiwan becomes the organization's 144th member.

•

U.S. Pres. George W. Bush makes his first speech to the General Assembly of the United Nations; he emphasizes the responsibility of all UN members to fight terrorism and reminds them that Osama bin Laden has condemned the organization.

•

After several days of battle, anti-Taliban forces capture the northern Afghanistan stronghold of Mazar-e Sharif.

•

Australian Prime Minister John Howard is elected to a third term of office.

11 Canada 3000, Canada's second largest airline company, goes bankrupt and abruptly ceases operations.

•

St. Louis Cardinals slugger Mark McGwire, who broke Roger Maris's single-season home-run record in 1998 only to see his own record broken in 2001 by Barry Bonds, announces his retirement from major league baseball. (*See* November 19.)

12 *American Airlines Flight 587, en route from New York City to Santo Domingo, Dom.Rep., crashes shortly after takeoff into the Rockaway neighbourhood of the New York City borough of Queens, killing 260 people on the airplane and several people on the ground. (Photo right.)*

The immense underground neutrino-detection apparatus known as the Super-Kamiokande at the Kamioka Neutrino Observatory in Japan is nearly destroyed by an accident in which thousands of photomultipliers implode in a chain reaction.

•

A list compiled by the Heritage Foundation and *The Wall Street Journal* finds for the eighth year in a row that Hong Kong has the freest economy in the world.

13 Pres. George W. Bush signs an executive order permitting foreign nationals suspected of terrorism to be tried by military tribunals, with fewer rights than defendants in U.S. civil courts enjoy. (*See* November 23.)

•

Taliban fighters withdraw from Kabul, the capital of Afghanistan, and, though the U.S. government asks that the anti-Taliban forces not occupy the city until a new government has been agreed upon, the forces move in and take control.

•

The U.S. Conference of Catholic Bishops elects Wilton D. Gregory of the diocese of Belleville, Ill., as its new president; he is the first African American to be elected to this position.

14 Unification talks between North and South Korea break off abruptly; at issue is South Korea's maintenance of a military state of alert that began with the start of the war in Afghanistan.

•

The aid workers from Shelter Now who had been arrested on August 5 on charges of proselytizing for Christianity are abandoned by their Taliban captors outside Kabul and are rescued by U.S. military forces.

•

The National Book Awards are presented to Jonathan Franzen for his fiction work *The Corrections*, Andrew Solomon for his nonfiction book *The Noonday Demon: An Atlas of Depression*, Alan Dugan for his poetry collection *Poems Seven: New and Complete Poetry*, and Virginia Euwer Wolff for her young-adult book *True Believer*; playwright Arthur Miller is given a medal for distinguished contribution to American letters.

15 The U.S. Congress agrees on an aviation security bill that will see the federal government take over airport security screening within a year and provide training for the workers; the bill is signed into law on November 20.

•

Philip Morris, which owns Kraft Foods and the Miller Brewing Co. as well as the two major tobacco companies Philip Morris U.S.A. and Philip Morris International, announces that it will change its name next year to the Altria Group; it hopes that the new name will not be associated solely with tobacco products in the public's mind.

•

Roger Clemens, a pitcher for the New York Yankees, wins his sixth Cy Young Award.

16 Investigators sifting through impounded mail sent to Capitol Hill discover an anthrax-laden envelope addressed to Sen. Patrick Leahy that is similar to those sent to Sen. Tom Daschle and newsman Tom Brokaw; evidently, the letter was initially misdirected to the State Department, spreading anthrax spores wherever it went.

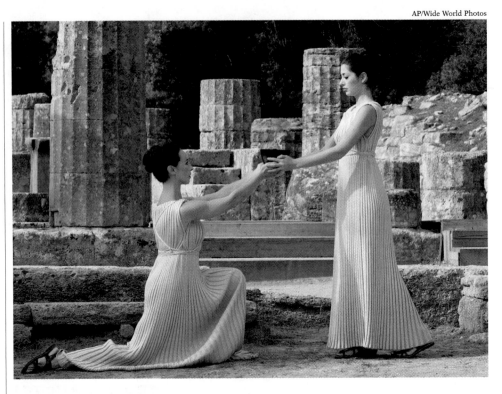

•

German Chancellor Gerhard Schröder narrowly wins a vote to allow German troops to be deployed in the war against terrorism; it would be the first use of German troops outside Europe in a combat role since 1945.

•

Macedonia adopts 15 constitutional amendments to give civil rights to ethnic Albanians.

•

Miss Nigeria, Agbani Darego, is crowned Miss World in Sun City, S.Af.; she is the first black African winner.

17 In Yugoslavia the Serbian province of Kosovo holds its first democratic legislative election; the majority of the seats go to the party of ethnic Albanian nationalist Ibrahim Rugova.

•

After a week of torrential rains causes flooding that kills nine people, the rains in Austin, Texas, ease up.

•

Lennox Lewis defeats Hasim Rahman in Las Vegas, Nev., to retake the World Boxing Council and International Boxing Federation heavyweight titles.

18 The oil companies Conoco Inc. and Phillips Petroleum Co. announce plans to merge into a company to be known as ConocoPhillips.

•

Georgi Parvanov of the Socialist Party is the victor over incumbent Pres. Petar Stoyanov in runoff presidential elections in Bulgaria.

19 *The Olympic torch is lit in a ceremony at Mt. Olympus in Greece; it will be flown to the U.S. and carried throughout the country until it reaches Salt Lake City, Utah, to open the Winter Games in February 2002. (Photo above.)*

•

Barry Bonds is named the National League Most Valuable Player for a record fourth time; the next day Seattle Mariners outfielder Ichiro Suzuki is named the American League's MVP, a week after being voted Rookie of the Year. (*See* November 11.)

20 Danish Prime Minister Poul Nyrup Rasmussen's Social Democratic Party in legislative elections loses to the Liberal Party, which promises to limit immigration to the country; Anders Fogh Rasmussen is appointed prime minister on November 27.

•

The insurgent Moro National Liberation Front announces it is abrogating a 1996 peace agreement with the Philippine government after making a surprise attack on an army base; it is unclear how many former MNLF fighters will heed the renewed call to arms.

21 Ottilie Lundgren, an elderly woman living alone in rural Connecticut, becomes the fifth person in the U.S. to die of pulmonary anthrax; as in the earlier case of Kathy Nguyen, experts have no idea how Lundgren might have been exposed to the disease.

•

The British cruise line P&O Princess Cruises and the Miami, Fla.-based Royal Caribbean Cruises announce that they will merge; the new company, tentatively named RCP Cruise Lines, will surpass Carnival as the world's largest cruise ship company.

•

Four American food companies sign deals with Cuba to sell it food to help make up for the stocks that were destroyed by Hurricane Michelle; they are the first trade deals made by American companies with Cuba since the U.S. trade embargo was established in 1959.

22 Scientists at the American biotechnology company Advanced Cell Technology, Inc., say they have created 24 completely normal cow clones. (*See* November 25.)

•

A landslide kills approximately 80 people illegally working a closed open-pit gold mine in Filadelfia, Colom.

•

The first official papal e-mail is sent by Pope John Paul II from a laptop in his office in the Vatican; the message transmits a document that includes an apology for past injustices to South Pacific islanders committed by Roman Catholic missionaries.

•

Pakistan closes the Taliban embassy in Islamabad.

23 Officials in Spain tell U.S. officials that Spain will not extradite the eight men it has charged with complicity in the September 11 terrorist attacks without a guarantee that they will be tried in a civilian court rather than the military tribunal

that Pres. George. W. Bush has said he would implement for trying suspected terrorists. (*See* November 13.)

•

Marks & Spencer announces that it is selling clothing retailer Brooks Brothers to Retail Brand Alliance Inc., which owns, among other brands, Casual Corner.

24 The Grand National Assembly of Turkey ratifies changes to the country's legal code that make women equal to men before the law and no longer subject to their husbands; the new code will become effective on Jan. 1, 2002.

•

Taliban soldiers surrender their last stronghold in northern Afghanistan, the city of Kunduz.

•

A Crossair jet crashes while coming in to land at the airport in Zürich, Switz., killing 24 of the 32 people aboard; Crossair is the designated successor airline to the defunct Swissair.

25 Taliban prisoners of war being held in a prison outside Mazar-e Sharif, Afg., revolt; by the time the revolt is crushed on November 27, 450 persons are dead, including one CIA operative from the U.S.

•

Advanced Cell Technology, Inc., announces that it has successfully cloned a human embryo; its purpose is to acquire embryonic stem cells for research into cures for various conditions, among them the neurodegenerative diseases. (*See* November 22.)

•

In presidential elections in Honduras, Ricardo Maduro, of the National Party, defeats the ruling Liberal Party's candidate, Rafael Pineda; Maduro had run on an anticrime platform.

26 The National Bureau of Economic Research declares that the U.S. economy officially entered a recession in March, ending a decade of expansion, the longest in history.

•

An AIDS advocacy group goes to court in South Africa to force the government to make a drug widely available that reduces by 50% the chance of transmission of HIV from an infected mother to her newborn baby.

•

A court in Russia orders the closure of TV-6, the last major independent television station in Russia.

27 The Nepalese army launches an air and ground offensive against Maoist insurgents who seek to topple the government; following a weekend of rebel attacks, King Gyanendra declares a state of emergency. (*See* July 19.)

•

The Cayman Islands, known as a haven for tax evaders, signs an agreement with the U.S. to share information that will make it possible for the U.S. to uncover tax violators and money laundering.

28 As the stock prices of the energy giant Enron collapse, Dynegy backs out of the deal it had made to buy the company, saying that Enron failed to disclose the depth of its financial problems. (*See* November 9.)

•

Chiquita Brands International (formerly known as the United Fruit Co.), a major global producer of bananas and other fruit, files a plan for bankruptcy protection. (*See* January 25.)

•

The World Health Organization releases a report saying

that 40 million people in the world have either HIV or AIDS; 28 million live in sub-Saharan Africa, but the highest rates of increase occurred in Eastern Europe and Central Asia.

29 In Gaborone, Botswana, representatives of 30 countries plus the diamond industry agree on a certification process for the diamond trade intended to prevent diamond profits from supporting armed conflict in Africa.

•

Officials in Nigeria disclose that a cholera outbreak has killed at least 700 people in the northern part of the country.

•

Owing to a precipitous decline in advertising revenue, the publisher of *Asiaweek* magazine, based in Hong Kong, announces that it is ceasing publication.

•

Former Beatle George Harrison dies of cancer in Los Angeles.

30 Daniel arap Moi of Kenya, Benjamin Mkapa of Tanzania, and Yoweri Museveni of Uganda ceremoniously reestablish the East African Community in Arusha, Tanz.; the East African Community was originally established in 1967, but it ceased to exist in 1977.

•

The Apartheid Museum, which traces the history of the apartheid system and gives visitors a sense of what it was like to live under South Africa's former policy of racial segregation, opens in Johannesburg.

•

The *Caribbean Journal of Science* publishes a report of the discovery off the coast of the Dominican Republic of a dwarf gecko that is 1.9 cm (0.75 in) long; it is the world's smallest reptile.

December

1 Legislative elections in Taiwan give Pres. Chen Shui-bian's Democratic Progressive Party a majority of the seats in the parliament as it supplants the Kuomintang as the ruling party.

Japanese Crown Prince Naruhito and his wife, Princess Masako, become the parents of a baby girl; on December 7 she is ceremonially named Princess Aiko.

Argentine Pres. Fernando de la Rúa issues an order that no one may withdraw more than $250 a week from a bank account; the previous days had seen bank runs as panicky citizens sought to protect themselves in a collapsing economy.

AP/Wide World Photos

2 In the largest corporate bankruptcy filing in U.S. history, the Enron Corp. asks for bankruptcy protection, at the same time filing a lawsuit against Dynegy Inc. for backing out of a buyout agreement. (*See* December 5.)

The annual John F. Kennedy Center for the Performing Arts Honors Gala celebrates the artistic achievements of actor and singer Julie Andrews, actor Jack Nicholson, pianist Van Cliburn, tenor Luciano Pavarotti, and composer Quincy Jones.

France defeats Australia to win its ninth Davis Cup in tennis competition in Melbourne, Australia.

Voters in Switzerland overwhelmingly reject a proposal to disband its citizen army.

3 It is revealed that one of the last 80 Taliban prisoners who surrendered on December 1 after an uprising in Mazar-e Sharif, Afg., is an American citizen, John Walker.

The long-awaited invention from Dean Kamen that has been variously code-named "It" or "Ginger" and has been touted as being epochal is unveiled; the Segway Human Transporter is a two-wheeled battery-powered gyroscopic scooter with a top speed of about 25 km/h (15 mph). (Photo above.)

A prototype antimissile weapon destroys a dummy warhead in a second consecutive successful test of technology for the proposed U.S. national missile-defense shield.

4 In a breakthrough, Turkish Cypriot leader Rauf Denktash and Greek Cypriot leader Glafcos Clerides agree to hold face-to-face negotiations in an attempt to bring peace to the divided island. (*See* December 29.)

U.S. Pres. George W. Bush freezes the assets of the Holy Land Foundation for Relief and Development, the largest Muslim charity in the U.S., saying it supports the Palestinian organization Hamas, which has claimed responsibility for suicide bombings in Jerusalem over the past few days.

The first bridge over the Mekong River opens to traffic, connecting eastern and western Cambodia by road for the first time.

5 Four Afghan factions, shepherded by a UN envoy and diplomats from the U.S., Great Britain, France, Germany, India, Iran, Pakistan, and Russia, agree to an interim government for Afghanistan. (*See* December 22.)

An Enron spokesman confirms that it paid out $55 million in bonuses to top employees shortly before filing for bankruptcy protection; separately, the U.S. Department of Labor announces that it is investigating the management of Enron employees' 401(k) retirement accounts. (*See* December 2.)

The opposition United National Party wins legislative elections in Sri Lanka; Ranil Wickremesinghe is sworn in to replace Ratnasiri Wickramanayake as prime minister on December 9. (*See* December 24.)

The televangelist Pat Robertson resigns as president of the Christian Coalition, a rightist American political organization.

The principal owner and former CEO of Sotheby's auction house, A. Alfred Taubman, is convicted in a U.S. federal court of having conspired to fix fees charged to sellers.

6 The name of the Canadian province of Newfoundland is officially changed to Newfoundland and Labrador.

Chivas Regal, representing Scotland, defeats the Tigresses, representing the U.S., to win the 20th annual World Elephant Polo Association championship in Chitwan, Nepal.

7 The Taliban abandons its last stronghold in Afghanistan, Kandahar, though U.S. forces are unable to locate either the head of the Taliban government in Afghanistan, Mohammad Omar, or Osama bin Laden.

A dance commissioned for the Olympic Arts Festival in Salt Lake City, Utah, in February 2002, *Here . . . Now,* a tribute to runner Florence Griffith Joyner choreographed by Judith Jamison, has its premiere by the Alvin Ailey Dance Theater in New York City.

The Right Livelihood Awards are presented in Stockholm to Uri and Rachel Avnery, Israeli peace activists; Angie Zelter, Ellen Moxley, and Ulla Roder, campaigners against Britain's Trident nuclear submarines; Leonardo Boff, a Brazilian who was an origi-nator of "liberation theology"; and José Antonio Abreu, a Venezuelan founder of children's and youth orchestras.

8 After a week of rioting over rents charged in a slum on the outskirts of Nairobi, Kenya, that has left 15 people dead, leaders and residents of various ethnic groups hold a peace rally; the tenants are mainly Luo and Luya, and the landlords are mostly Nubians.

9 The World Health Organization confirms that there is an outbreak of Ebola fever in Gabon near the border with the Democratic Republic of the Congo; the Red Cross warns on December 14 that the disease is spreading quickly.

10 Accusations of corruption and political defections force new elections in Trinidad and Tobago less than one year after the last election; the legislative seats are divided equally between the ruling United National Congress and the opposition People's National Movement. (*See* December 24.)

A one-day strike to protest the economic policies of Pres. Hugo Chávez virtually shuts down Venezuela.

The 2001 Nobel Prizes are presented in ceremonies in Stockholm and Oslo.

11 The U.S. government brings its first indictment resulting from the September 11 terrorist attacks against Zacarias Moussaoui, a French citizen whom U.S. officials suspect of originally having been part of the group of airline hijackers; he will be tried in federal court.

The Science and Technology Foundation of Japan announces the winners of the Japan Prize: Timothy Berners-Lee, for inventing the World Wide Web, and Anne McLaren and Andrzej K. Tarkowski, for their work on mammalian embryonic development.

U.S. Attorney General John Ashcroft says that the U.S. has broken up the largest commercial operation to smuggle illegal immigrants in history; the investigation focused on a bus company called Golden State Transportation.

12 Chinese Pres. Jiang Zemin arrives in Myanmar (Burma) for a three-day visit to discuss transportation and trade ties; it is the first visit by a Chinese president since the Myanmar junta came to power in 1988.

The centennial of the first transatlantic telegraph signal is celebrated in a reenactment when, 100 years to the minute after the original, Guglielmo Marconi Giovanelli, the grandson of Guglielmo Marconi, sends a signal from Poldhu in Cornwall, Eng., which is received on Signal Hill in St. John's, Newfoundland and Labrador.

The last jai alai game is played in Connecticut; the first fronton had opened in 1972 as a way to bring gambling revenues to the state.

13 Five armed men attack the Parliament House in New Delhi, and, in a gun battle outside, they are killed before gaining entrance; five police officers, a driver, and a gardener are also killed, and two more people die later. (*See* December 21.)

•

Israel announces that it is breaking off contact with Palestinian leader Yasir Arafat, characterizing him as "irrelevant."

•

Pres. George W. Bush formally announces the U.S. withdrawal from the 1972 Anti-Ballistic Missile Treaty.

•

The U.S. releases an amateur videotape that government officials believe was made on November 9; the tape shows Osama bin Laden gloating about the September 11 terrorist attacks in the U.S.

14 An emergency antiterrorism bill passes both houses of Parliament to become law in Great Britain.

•

A high court judge in South Africa rules that the government must make available to HIV-positive pregnant women a low-cost drug that will reduce the risk of transferring the infection to their babies. (*See* November 26.)

•

Koloa Talake becomes the new prime minister of Tuvalu after Faimalaga Luka loses a no-confidence vote on December 7.

15 European Union leaders agree to set up a constitutional convention to revisit its institutions; the convention, to be headed by former French president Valéry Giscard d'Estaing, is to begin work in March 2002.

Throughout the U.S., 7,500 high-school seniors retake the SAT tests; their original exams were quarantined during the anthrax scare and never reached the Educational Testing Service in New Jersey for scoring.

•

Ethnic clashes break out in the provincial capital of Mendi in Papua New Guinea and continue for the next five days; some 25 people are killed in the fighting.

16 *The beginning of the three-day Eid al-Fitr festival is celebrated in Kabul, Afg., as residents enjoy freedoms and pleasures forbidden to them under Taliban rule. (Photo below.)*

•

The first commercial shipment of food from the U.S. in almost 40 years arrives in Cuba; the consignment consists of frozen chicken thighs sold to the island by Archer Daniels Midland Co. (*See* November 21.)

•

The Philadelphia Orchestra plays its first program in its new home, Verizon Hall in the Kimmel Center for the Performing Arts; the project to build the new hall, first proposed in 1908, got under way in 1986.

•

Champion calf roper Cody Ohl wins the all-around world championship of the Professional Rodeo Cowboys Association in the National Finals Rodeo in Las Vegas, Nev.

17 Armed men storm the National Palace in Port-au-Prince, Haiti, in an apparent coup attempt against Pres. Jean-Bertrand Aristide; they are unsuccessful.

•

Vivendi Universal of France announces that it will buy the television and film units of USA Networks Inc.

•

Portuguese Prime Minister António Guterres announces his resignation after candidates from the opposition Social Democrats are victorious in local elections.

•

The parliament that was elected on December 5 in the first democratic elections in the Solomon Islands since the June 2000 coup selects Sir Allan Kemakeza as the new prime minister.

•

Portuguese association football (soccer) player Luis Figo, of the Real Madrid team, is named FIFA World Player of the Year; American Mia Hamm becomes the first player to win the newly established award for women.

18 A federal judge overturns the death sentence of celebrated black activist Mumia Abu-Jamal, who was convicted in 1982 of having killed a police officer in 1981; the judge lets the conviction stand, however.

•

The Parliament of France approves a bill to give a bit more autonomy to Corsica.

The World Meteorological Organization says that 2001 will have been the second warmest year on record, with an average surface temperature of 14.42 °C (57.96 °F); the warmest year on record is 1998.

19 The U.S. federal government indicts Tyson Foods, Inc., the largest meat producer in the U.S., for smuggling illegal immigrants from Mexico to work in its meat-processing plants.

AT&T agrees to sell its cable television business to Comcast Corp.

Newsmagazine star Katie Couric and the NBC network sign a television news contract for the biggest amount ever—about $60 million over five years.

A botanist in Australia says that he has rediscovered a shrub, *Asterolasia buxifolia*, that for 130 years was believed extinct.

20 After several days of rioting and looting throughout Argentina, Pres. Fernando de la Rúa resigns.

The UN authorizes a security force, to be led by Great Britain, to assist in the transition to a new government in Afghanistan.

A series of wildfires, many of them set by teenagers, begin burning in New South Wales, Australia; at year's end the fires are continuing to destroy houses and land around Sydney.

Fire department officials in New York City declare that the fires from the World Trade Center disaster on September 11 have finally been extinguished.

21 In reaction to the raid on its Parliament House (*see* December 13), India recalls its ambassador to Pakistan and cuts off transportation ties between the countries.

Hamas announces that it is suspending the use of suicide attacks in Israel.

Science magazine documents sightings of a previously unknown squid, unlike known species in many ways, that has been seen on several occasions near the seafloor in many of the world's oceans.

The world's fastest rollercoaster, the Dodonpa, opens at the Fujikyu Highlands amusement park in Japan; it reaches speeds of up to 170 km/h (107 mph).

22 Hamid Karzai is sworn in as head of the interim government in Afghanistan; the ceremonies celebrate the cultural diversity of the country, and two rival leaders, Rashid Dostum and Ismail Khan, attend, which bodes well for the future. (*See* December 5.)

An American Airlines flight from Paris to Miami, Fla., makes an emergency landing in Boston after passengers and crew subdue a British man, Richard Reid, who was attempting to ignite the soles of his shoes, which were filled with powerful explosives.

23 In the biggest debt default in history, after Adolfo Rodríguez Saá is sworn in as interim president he immediately announces the suspension of payments on Argentina's external debt.

24 A truce agreed to by the new government of Sri Lanka and the Liberation Tigers of Tamil Eelam goes into effect. (*See* December 5.)

Patrick Manning takes office as prime minister of Trinidad and Tobago after having been selected by the president. (*See* December 10.)

The Adolph Coors Co. announces that it will acquire the Carling operations of Bass Brewers from Interbrew; Carling is the most popular beer in Britain.

25 In his annual Christmas address, Pope John Paul II enjoins the faithful to save the children of the world, as the hope of humanity rests on the children.

26 The Qatar-based television network Al-Jazeera broadcasts excerpts from a videotaped speech by Osama bin Laden; Bin Laden says that he is speaking three months after the September 11 terrorist attacks and looks rather gaunt and pale.

27 Presidential elections are held in Zambia; the winner, from a field of 11 candidates, is Levy Mwanawasa, but international observers cast doubts on the vote-counting process.

28 The Um-Kalthoum Museum, dedicated to the life and career of the great Egyptian singing star from the 1920s through the 1960s, opens in Cairo.

Bill Cartwright, who played as the centre on the Chicago Bulls championship teams in 1991, 1992, and 1993, is named head coach of the professional basketball team.

29 Nearly 300 people are killed when a firecracker ignites fireworks stands lining narrow streets in Lima, Peru.

For the first time since the Turkish invasion of Cyprus in 1974, Turkish Cypriot leader Rauf Denktash enters the Greek area to have dinner at the home of Pres. Glafcos Clerides in Nicosia; on December 5 Clerides had dined in the home of Denktash. (*See* December 4.)

The city of Buffalo, N.Y., begins digging out after a snowstorm that began on December 24 dumped 206 cm (82.3 in) of snow on the city in five days and thereby made this by far the snowiest December in the city's history.

30 Adolfo Rodríguez Saá resigns as interim president of Argentina; Ramón Puerta declines to resume the position.

In an effort to head off an imminent war with India, Pakistan arrests Hafiz Muhammad Saeed, founder of one of the militant Muslim groups believed to be behind the attack on India's Parliament House.

31 Eduardo Camaño takes the post of interim president of Argentina.

La Scala, Milan's famous opera house, closes for renovation; it is scheduled to reopen in 2004.

Disasters

The following list records the **MAJOR DISASTERS** that occurred in 2001. Events included in this feature involved the loss of **15 OR MORE LIVES** and/or **SIGNIFICANT DAMAGE** to property.

Aviation

January 25, Ciudad Bolívar, Venez. A DC-3 propeller airplane en route to Margarita Island in the Caribbean Sea crashed into a shantytown shortly after takeoff and burst into flames; all 24 persons aboard were killed, and 3 persons on the ground were injured.

March 3, Unadilla, Ga. A military transport plane en route from Florida to Virginia crashed in a field during heavy rain, killing all 21 national guardsmen aboard the craft.

March 24, On the island of Saint-Barthélemy, French overseas *département* of Guadeloupe. An airplane transporting passengers from Saint Martin to Saint-Barthélemy crashed into a house while preparing to land; all 19 persons aboard the plane and 2 persons on the ground were killed. It was the worst aviation disaster in the Caribbean in nearly 20 years.

March 29, Aspen, Colo. A private jet slammed into a hillside while attempting to land in snowy weather; 18 persons died.

April 4, Adaryel, The Sudan. A military plane crashed while attempting to land during a sandstorm; 15 persons were killed, including the Sudanese deputy defense minister, Col. Ibrahim Shams Eddin.

April 7, Quang Binh province, Vietnam. A helicopter carrying a team searching for the remains of U.S. soldiers missing in action from the Vietnam War slammed into a mountainside in hazy weather; all 16 persons aboard were killed.

May 16, Near Akcadag, Turkey. A military plane en route from Diyarbakir to Ankara crashed in a field, apparently after an engine malfunction; all 37 persons aboard the plane were killed.

May 17, Northern Iran. A plane encountered heavy rain and crashed in a mountainous area between the cities of Gorgan and Shahrud; 29 persons died, including Iranian Transport Minister Rahman Dadman and six members of the parliament.

July 3, Near Irkutsk, Russia. An airliner en route from Yekaterinburg in the Ural Mountains to the eastern port city of Vladivostok with 145 persons aboard went down in a Siberian forest; the disaster was blamed on pilot error; there were no survivors.

September 12, Mérida, Mex. A charter plane carrying tourists from a cruise ship to see ancient Mayan ruins crashed shortly after takeoff; 19 persons died, including 16 Americans.

October 4, Over the Black Sea. A Russian airliner en route from Tel Aviv, Israel, to Novosibirsk, Russia, exploded in midair and crashed in the Black Sea, killing all 78 persons aboard the craft. Initial suspicions of terrorism were discounted; the Ukrainian government later acknowledged that a stray surface-to-air missile fired during a Ukrainian air defense exercise had caused the explosion. Ukrainian Defense Minister Oleksandr Kuzmuk resigned over the incident.

October 8, Milan. A Scandinavian Airlines System passenger jet taking off for Copenhagen from Milan's Linate Airport collided with a small private plane in heavy fog and exploded; 118 persons were killed, including all 114 persons aboard the two planes and 4 airport workers. Investigators blamed the absence of ground-level radar at the airport in part. It was Italy's worst aviation disaster.

November 12, New York City. American Airlines Flight 587 crashed on takeoff from John F. Kennedy International Airport; the plane, which was headed to Santo Domingo, Dom.Rep., lost its tail in midair and went down in the borough of Queens, striking several buildings; 260 persons died, including all 255 persons aboard the plane and 5 on the ground. Although no evidence pointed to terrorism, investigators at year's end were still trying to determine why the tail sheared off the plane.

November 24, Near Zürich, Switz. A Swiss airplane en route from Berlin to Zürich crashed in a wooded area after encountering some rain and snow as it made its approach to land; 24 of the 32 persons aboard the plane died.

December 2, Near Okhotsk, Russia. A cargo plane crashed following a fire aboard the aircraft; as many as 18 persons were feared killed.

December 8, Near Taloqan, Afg. Bad weather conditions were blamed in the crash of a helicopter carrying Northern Alliance commandos and captured Taliban fighters; 21 persons aboard the craft died.

December 16, Near Medellín, Colom. A small plane carrying 16 persons crashed in a mountainous area shortly after taking off in rainy weather; there were no survivors.

Fires and Explosions

March 5, Gindiri, Nigeria. A fire, which began when a kerosene lantern overturned, swept through a dormitory of a government high school for girls; at least 23 girls died; rescue efforts were hampered because the dormitory doors had been locked and chained to prevent students from sneaking out or in.

March 6, Jiangxi province, China. An explosion flattened a two-story rural elementary-school building; the blast was believed to have been caused by an illegal fireworks factory located inside the school. According to the Xinhua news agency, 41 persons died, including 37 children and 4 teachers, and 27 persons were injured.

May 20, Northern Chile. An electrical fault in the Iquique penitentiary ignited a blaze that claimed the lives of 26 prisoners.

August 6, Erwady, India. A fire at a mental asylum killed at least 26 persons, many of whom had reportedly been chained to their beds; it was unclear to investigators what had started the blaze.

August 16, Katpadi, India. An accidental explosion at a government-run dynamite factory claimed the lives of at least 25 persons and seriously injured 3.

August 18, Quezon City, Phil. Fire swept through a six-story hotel, killing at least 73 persons, many of whom had been trapped by security bars on the windows of their rooms; 51 persons were injured. The fire was caused by a short circuit in the ceiling of a stockroom; the hotel's owner, who had been cited for safety violations, was later charged with reckless endangerment.

September 1, Tokyo. An explosion and fire in a nightclub in the Kabukicho entertainment district claimed the lives of 44 persons.

September 4–5, Kruger National Park, S.Af. A bush fire of unknown origins swept through the park, killing 15 villagers and 4 game rangers who were trying to rescue them.

September 21, Toulouse, France. A massive explosion at an industrial plant left a 15-m (50-ft) crater at the site and claimed the lives of at least 29 persons and injured some 2,000; officials stated that the blast was likely an accident.

December 17, Southern Italy. A state-run home for the disabled in a remote area of the Apennine Mountains was destroyed in a blaze started by an electrical short circuit; 19 patients were killed; authorities later acknowledged that the home had been constructed of flammable material and should have been torn down.

December 29, Lima, Peru. An explosion at a fireworks shop ignited a blaze that swept through a crowded commercial centre in Lima's historic district; the explosion was thought to have been caused by a fireworks demonstration that went out of control; at least 290 persons were killed.

December 30, Jiangxi province, China. An explosion at a fireworks factory destroyed a warehouse and 10 workshops; more than 40 persons died.

Marine

January 1, Off the coast of Mayaya, Sierra Leone. An overloaded boat en route to Freetown from Rokupr capsized in the Atlantic Ocean, killing some 60 persons.

January 1, Off the coast of Kemer, Turkey. A cargo ship filled with migrants from the Middle East and Asia broke apart in a storm during an attempt to immigrate illegally to Greece; at least 16 persons were confirmed dead, and 30 were missing. Most of the victims had apparently been locked in the cargo area of the ship.

January 23, Off the coast of the Dominican Republic. A motorboat—carrying a group of Dominicans intending to enter Puerto Rico illegally—overturned in rough seas; at least 50 persons were missing and presumed drowned.

January 26, Black Sea. A Ukrainian cargo and passenger ship en route to Yevpatoriya, Ukraine, sank during a storm; 14 persons were confirmed dead, and 5 were missing.

January 29, Off the coast of Karachi, Pak. A fishing boat returning to shore overturned in a storm, killing 35 persons.

March 3, Off the southeastern coast of Haiti. A ship capsized in rough seas; 6 persons were killed, and 17 were missing.

March 15, Off the island of Ile-à-Vache, southwestern Haiti. A boat loaded with Dominicans migrating illegally to Puerto Rico crashed on a coral reef after having drifted off course for 24 days; at least 50 persons died.

April 11, Off the coast of southwestern Japan. A South Korean-registered oil freighter went missing; although no distress signals were received, an oil slick believed to be from the freighter was sighted; 28 persons were feared dead.

April 15, Off the coast of Sulawesi Island, Indonesia. An overloaded boat sank after its engine failed; at least 21 persons drowned.

May 3, Goma, Democratic Republic of the Congo. A ferry sank in Goma harbour on Lake Kivu, apparently after scores of people rushed onto the vessel seeking shelter from a sudden cloudburst; more than 100 persons drowned.

May 12, Off the western coast of Madagascar. A passenger boat sank, claiming the lives of at least 26 persons, most of them members of a local football team.

July 21, Near Katoka, Democratic Republic of the Congo. An overcrowded ferry capsized in a whirlpool on the Kasai River; some 60 persons drowned; the accident occurred at night, and the boat captain who was piloting the craft reportedly was drunk.

July 22, Off the coast of Karachi, Pak. A boat described as old and in poor condition capsized on the Arabian Sea; 19 family members died.

October 19, Java Sea. An overcrowded fishing boat en route from the Indonesian island of Sumatra to Australia with some 400 illegal immigrants aboard broke apart and sank; only 44 persons were rescued.

November 16–17, Florida Straits. A twin-engine speedboat carrying some 30 Cubans intent on illegally entering the U.S. capsized; the U.S. Coast Guard later recovered the boat but no bodies.

November 18, Lake Tanganyika, Democratic Republic of the Congo. A collision between two boats as one was preparing to leave shore and another to dock claimed the lives of at least 19 persons.

November 29, Near Bhola, Bangladesh. A ferryboat sank on the Tetulia River after colliding with a larger vessel; around 90 persons were missing and feared drowned.

Mining and Construction

February 2, Bihar state, India. Water suddenly filled a coal mine, trapping many workers; 38 miners were feared dead.

February 5, Heilongjiang province, China. A gas explosion claimed the lives of 37 miners.

February 22–23, Xinjiang and Hunan provinces, China. Poisonous gas and high temperatures were blamed for the deaths of 11 miners at a coal mine in Xinjiang on February 22. In a separate incident on the following day, a gas explosion was believed to have killed 21 miners in Hunan.

March 4, Entre-os-Rios, Port. A bridge collapsed after one of its support pillars gave way, and a double-decker bus and three cars that were passing over the bridge at the time plunged into the Douro River; 59 persons died.

April 21, Shaanxi province, China. A gas explosion in a coal mine claimed the lives of 47 miners and injured 4.

May 8, Hegang, China. A gas explosion ripped through a coal mine; 54 miners were feared dead.

Mid-May, Urumqi, China. A brick wall surrounding a construction site collapsed onto a bazaar; 19 persons died, and over 30 were injured.

May 18, Sichuan province, China. Water pipes burst in a prison-run coal mine and flooded a shaft; 39 prison labourers were presumed dead.

May 24, West Jerusalem. A three-story banquet hall collapsed while some 700 people were celebrating a wedding; at least 23 persons died; the collapse was attributed to structural failure.

July 17, Shanghai. A massive crane toppled over at a shipbuilding plant; at least 36 persons were killed.

July 22, Xuzhou, China. An explosion occurred at a coal mine that had reopened illegally after having been shut down only a month before; 92 miners died.

August 19, Donetsk, Ukraine. A methane gas explosion ripped through the Zasyadko coal mine, igniting a raging fire and trapping workers; at least 47 miners died, and 44 were injured.

November 22, Filadelfia, Colom. A landslide buried a group of gold miners digging illegally at a condemned mine; about 80 persons were killed, and dozens more were missing and feared dead.

Natural

January, Inner Mongolia, China. A three-day-long blizzard that began on December 31 was followed by freezing temperatures in the region throughout January; of the estimated 1,640,000 persons affected by the storm and cold front, at least 39 lost their lives; more than 200,000 head of livestock also perished during the cold spell.

January 13 and February 13, El Salvador. A magnitude-7.7 earthquake, whose epicentre was off El Salvador's Pacific coast, jolted the country on January 13, leaving some 200,000 persons homeless. On February 13 a second earthquake struck with a magnitude of 6.6 and an onshore epicentre southeast of the capital, San Salvador. At least 1,259 persons died in the two quakes.

January 18, Western Tanzania. A landslide brought on by heavy rains destroyed 30 homes in a fishing village on Lake Tanganyika; at least 15 persons were missing and feared dead.

January 20, North Sulawesi province, Indon. A series of three landslides and the magnitude-5.8 earthquake that followed wreaked havoc on the islands; at least 33 persons died, and numerous houses and two bridges were destroyed.

January 20–late March, Southern Africa. Heavy rains in Zambia, Zimbabwe, and Malawi swelled the Zambezi River watershed, resulting in severe flooding in these countries and along the river in Mozambique. Hundreds of thousands of persons were displaced in Mozambique, where there were more than 80 confirmed deaths by March 28.

January 26, Gujarat state, India. A powerful earthquake of magnitude 7.7 devastated the state. In what was described as the worst earthquake to hit India in a half century, more than 300,000 houses were destroyed, and a further 751,086 homes were damaged, according to official government figures. The quake affected more than 15,000,000 persons and left at least 14,000 dead and more than 166,000 injured. The disaster caused at least $2.3 billion in damage.

January 30, Western Iran. Snow as deep as two metres (six feet) fell in Khuzistan province, burying many villages; 28 persons who had ventured from their homes in search of food and supplies were missing and feared dead in the drifts.

Early February, West Java province, Indon. Heavy rains triggered landslides and extensive flooding; at least 94 persons perished, including 62 in the district of Lebak.

Early February, Western Afghanistan. Frigid temperatures claimed the lives of more than 500 persons in refugee camps in Herat province; since June 2000 thousands of Afghans had been displaced from their homes by severe drought conditions.

May 1, Southwestern China. A landslide that occurred after days of heavy rain caused a nine-story apartment building to collapse, killing at least 65 persons.

May 6–7, Tazeh-Qalel, Iran. Torrential rains triggered floods that killed at least 32 persons and injured 50; 2,500 head of cattle also died in the downpour.

May 9, Bihar state, India. A powerful storm claimed the lives of at least 17 persons, including 9 who died when uprooted trees smashed into their home.

May 11, Bangladesh. A series of storms and landslides caused damage throughout the country; at least 31 persons died, and some 500 were injured.

Mid-May, Haiti. Heavy rains and flooding claimed the lives of at least 21 persons, including 12 killed in a shantytown in Pétionville, a suburb of Port-au-Prince.

A man in Gujarat state, India, combs through the wreckage of a home destroyed by the magnitude-7.7 earthquake that struck on January 26.

AP/Wide World Photos

June 6–17, Southern and eastern U.S. Tropical Storm Allison left a broad swath of destruction in her wake. The hardest-hit area was Houston, Texas, where the storm killed at least 20 persons and damaged up to 27,000 houses, bridges, and other structures. The death toll also included at least 2 persons in Louisiana, 9 in Florida, 9 in North Carolina, 1 in Virginia, and 6 in Pennsylvania.

June 12, Papallacta, Ecuador. Motorists who had been stranded by a landslide and had taken refuge in a mountain hut were buried when a second avalanche swept down on them; at least 36 persons died.

June 23, Southern Peru. An 8.1-magnitude earthquake, whose epicentre was located off the Peruvian coast, jolted the southern Andean region of the country; hardest hit were the cities of Arequipa and Moquegua; at least 102 persons died, 53 were missing, and 1,368 were injured.

June 23–24, Taiwan and Fujian province, China. Typhoon Chebi claimed the lives of 9 persons in Taiwan before sweeping across the Taiwan Strait and striking Fujian, where at least 73 persons died and 87 were missing and feared dead.

June 27, Limbe, Cameroon. Heavy flooding claimed the lives of at least 30 persons.

Early July, Southern Taiwan, northern Philippines, and Guangdong province, China. Typhoon Utor wreaked havoc in lands touching the South China Sea. The storm killed 1 person in Taiwan, at least 121 persons in the Philippines, and 23 persons in Guangdong.

July 15, South Korea. A tropical storm—described as the worst to have hit the country in 37 years—swept across South Korea, setting off landslides and flooding that left at least 40 persons dead and 14 missing. Some 34,000 homes were flooded in Seoul and the surrounding area.

July 23, Mansehra, Swat, and Buner districts, Pak. Monsoonal rains triggered a series of flash

floods that claimed the lives of at least 150 persons and washed away hundreds of houses.

Late July, Southeastern Poland. Heavy flooding and thunderstorms devastated the region. By July 26, when the Vistula River overflowed its banks, at least 26 persons had died.

July 30, Hua-lien and Nan-t'ou counties, Taiwan. Typhoon Toraji ripped through the area, bringing heavy rains that set off landslides and flash floods; by the time the storm receded, 77 persons had been killed, and 133 were missing and presumed dead.

August 1, Nias Island, Indonesia. Massive landslides and floods struck the island following days of torrential rains; more than 70 persons were confirmed dead, and at least 100 were missing.

August 10–12, Northeastern Iran. The worst flooding in the region in 200 years inflicted widespread damage. According to figures announced on state television, 181 persons were known to have died, and at least 168 were missing. Some 10,000 persons were displaced by the disaster, which caused an estimated $25 million in damage.

August 11, Northern Thailand. Flash floods in the mountains of Phetchabun province followed heavy rains and killed about 86 persons.

Late August, Nepal. Heavy rains brought on flash floods and landslides across the country; at least 28 persons lost their lives.

September 16–19, Taiwan. Typhoon Nari pummeled the north of the island; flooding, mud slides, and power outages resulted; at least 94 persons died, including 25 in Taipei.

October 8–9, Southern Belize. Hurricane Iris—described as the worst storm to hit the country in 40 years—devastated much of the southern region; 22 persons died, at least 3,000 houses were destroyed, and some 12,000 persons were left homeless.

October 17, Southern India. A strong storm pummeled towns along the coast, killing at least 31 persons, including 16 in Kurnool.

November 7, Southern and central Philippines. Tropical Storm Lingling battered the regions, triggering flash floods and uprooting trees with winds as strong as 90 km/h (56 mph); particularly hard hit was the island of Camiguin, where hundreds were forced to flee their homes; at least 68 persons were killed, and dozens were missing.

November 9, Kerala state, India. A landslide in the village of Amboori claimed the lives of approximately 50 persons.

November 9–17, Northern Algeria. Torrential rain produced heavy flooding in the region; the official death toll was 750 persons, most of whom died in the Bab el Oued neighbourhood of Algiers; some 24,000 persons were left homeless, and at least 1,500 houses were destroyed in the capital alone.

Late December, Rio de Janeiro state, Braz. Torrential rains and mud slides claimed the lives of at least 52 persons; more than 30 were missing, and some 2,000 were forced to abandon their homes.

Railroad

January 10, Near Mvoungouti, Republic of the Congo. A train en route from Pointe-Noire to Brazzaville reportedly experienced engine problems before colliding with another train that had stopped at the Mvoungouti station; though both were freight trains, they were also carrying passengers; at least 45 persons died, and 98 were injured.

May 23, Near Ovrazhnoye, Russia. A train slammed into a passenger bus that had run a red light and driven onto the tracks at a railroad crossing; at least 14 persons were killed and 18 injured.

May 30, Lucknow, India. A train was struck by an overcrowded bus at a railroad crossing, killing 31 persons and injuring 49.

June 22, Near Kozhikode, India. Several cars of a passenger train en route from Mangalore to Chennai (Madras) derailed as the train was crossing a bridge and plunged more than 30 m (100 ft) into the rain-swollen Kadalundi River; at least 52 persons were killed, and some 230 were injured.

August 16, Ujani, India. An express train bound for Mumbai (Bombay) struck and killed 15 persons between stations at Bodhwad and Achaigaon.

December 25, Brebes, Indon. A head-on collision between two passenger trains crowded with holiday travelers claimed the lives of at least 42 persons; the driver of one of the trains reportedly had fallen asleep and sped past a stop signal.

Traffic

January 15, Mbabane, Swaziland. Two tires on an overloaded bus burst, causing the driver to lose control of the vehicle and crash; at least 28 persons were killed.

January 22, Southern Morocco. A passenger bus overturned on a highway between the cities of Marrakesh and Asni; 29 persons died, and 27 were seriously injured.

January 26, Punjab province, Pak. A collision between two passenger buses near the town of Pattoki claimed the lives of 38 persons and injured 52.

February 12, Zhejiang province, China. A bus fell into Thousand Islands Lake after a landslide struck the area; 10 deaths were confirmed, and 6 persons were missing and feared dead.

March 10, Near Ataye, Eth. A bus plummeted into a ravine after colliding with another vehicle; 22 persons aboard died, and 30 were injured.

April 1, Malindi, Kenya. Two passenger buses collided, and both then fell from a bridge into the rain-swollen Sabaki River; at least 34 persons were killed.

April 4, Tamil Nadu state, India. A head-on collision between a bus and an oil tanker truck claimed the lives of at least 40 persons.

April 7, Songwe, Tanz. A minibus hit a bull that had strayed onto a road; the driver lost control of the vehicle and collided with another bus, and all 32 persons in the minibus died.

April 11, Between Franklin and Kokstad, S.Af. An overloaded bus plummeted 64 m (210 ft) down an embankment after the driver lost control of the vehicle; at least 29 persons died.

April 12, Near N'Djamena, Chad. A trailer truck loaded with passengers, grain, and livestock crashed through the guardrail of a bridge and plunged into the Chari River; at least 40 persons lost their lives.

April 30, Northern India. A bus carrying Hindu pilgrims from the city of Hardwaru to the Badrinath temple plunged into the Alaknanda River; at least 45 persons were feared dead.

June 26, Near St. Louis du Sud, Haiti. A bus crashed in a ditch after its driver swerved to avoid hitting an abandoned truck; at least 41 persons were killed.

July 24, Near Jinju, S.Kor. A tourist bus struck a telephone pole and plunged down a steep hill; 18 persons were killed, and 25 were injured in the crash.

July 24, Punjab state, India. A bus toppled from a road into an irrigation canal after its brakes failed to work; at least 22 persons were feared dead.

August 12, Eastern Zambia. A crowded bus overturned and crashed into a ditch, killing at least 38 persons.

August 15, Near Nairobi, Kenya. An overloaded minibus swerved from a road to avoid hitting another vehicle and plunged into the Mwania River; 23 persons died.

August 18, Southern Iran. A head-on collision between a bus and a truck on a highway between Kerman and Sirjan claimed the lives of 30 persons and injured at least 20.

August 21, Near San Nicolas de los Arroyos, Arg. Some 20 persons lost their lives when a bus slammed into the back of a truck, reportedly after the driver of the bus fell asleep at the wheel.

August 26, Northern Nigeria. A speeding bus blew a tire and careened off a bridge into a river; 49 persons perished.

September 29, Northern Iran. A bus collided head-on with another bus and plummeted into an Alborz mountain valley; 20 persons died.

October 10, Near Calama, Chile. A bus carrying workers to a copper mine collided head-on with a truck, killing 22 persons and injuring 21; a plane carrying investigators to the site also crashed, killing 6.

Late October, Buenavista, Phil. A bus slammed into a house where mourners had gathered for a vigil; at least 21 persons died.

Early November, Karnataka state, India. A head-on collision between two trucks claimed the lives of at least 22 persons and injured 37.

November 14, Near Huelva, Spain. A bus carrying retirees on an excursion to caves in the area crashed after the driver lost control of the vehicle while trying to maneuver a curve in the road; 19 persons died, and 14 were injured.

November 18, Angash, Peru. A bus fell from a mountain road in the central Andes 183 m (600 ft) into a ravine; at least 25 persons died, and 20 were injured.

December 14, Southern Jordan. A bus loaded with Muslim worshipers returning home from a pilgrimage to Mecca crashed through the fence of a truck depot, slammed into other vehicles, and exploded into flames; the driver apparently had lost control of the vehicle after a brake failure; all 52 persons aboard the bus died.

December 31, Mpumalanga, S.Af. A truck carrying more than 100 family members on an annual pilgrimage to their ancestral burial ground overturned on a steep gravel road; at least 48 persons died.

Miscellaneous

March 5, Mina, Saudi Arabia. At least 35 persons died in a stampede on the first day of the hajj, the annual pilgrimage to Mecca; the stampede occurred as thousands of Muslims made their way across a bridge to perform the sacred rite known as "stoning the devil."

March 31, Pakpattan, Pak. A stampede at the gate of a Muslim shrine claimed the lives of at least 35 persons and injured some 125.

April 11, Johannesburg, S.Af. A stampede occurred at an association football (soccer) match between two local teams when thousands of fans who were locked outside Ellis Park stormed into the stadium; 43 persons were killed.

May 9, Accra, Ghana. In what was described as the worst tragedy at a sporting event in Africa's history, at least 130 persons were killed in a stampede toward locked stadium gates at an association football (soccer) match between Accra's Hearts of Oak and Kumasi's Asante Kotoko after Kotoko fans threw debris onto the playing field, and police fired tear gas into the crowd; in addition to the deaths, dozens of people were injured.

August 9, Dhaka, Bangladesh. A faulty fire alarm at a garment factory triggered a stampede; 16 workers, most of them women, were crushed to death in a stairwell as they tried to flee; 50 were injured.

Late August, Near Yamoussoukro, Côte d'Ivoire. At least 27 persons died after drinking corn broth contaminated with rat poison; the woman who sold the broth was detained by authorities and could face manslaughter charges, but officials described the poisoning as accidental.

Mid-September, Southern Estonia. About 60 persons died after drinking illegally brewed vodka—contaminated with methyl alcohol—that had been sold in the resort city of Parnu.

Late November, Sulawesi Utara province, Indon. At least 27 persons died and at least 4 were hospitalized after they drank contaminated homemade liquor.

Late November–early December, Tamil Nadu state, India. At least 50 persons had died by December 1 from drinking contaminated homemade liquor.

Residents of the Bab el Oued neighbourhood of Algiers attempt to move a car in their search for victims following days of torrential rain in November that produced heavy flooding and mudslides.

Hocine/AFP Worldwide

People of 2001

The portraits varied widely—Kumbh Mela pilgrims, refugees, rescue workers, world statesmen, Nobel Prize winners, and terrorists. These were only a few of the indelible images of the people of the year.

Nobel Prizes

The 2001 **NOBEL PRIZES** marked the **100th ANNIVERSARY** of their founding; they were first awarded on **DEC. 10, 1901**, the fifth anniversary of the death of **ALFRED BERNHARD NOBEL**, whose **WILL** had instructed the establishment of **FIVE PRIZES** (the Prize for **ECONOMICS** was added in 1969).

PRIZE FOR PEACE

The 2001 Nobel Prize for Peace was awarded to the United Nations (UN) and to its secretary-general, Kofi Annan. In announcing the prize in its centenary year, the Norwegian Nobel Committee said of the UN, "Today the organization is at the forefront of efforts to achieve peace and security in the world." Annan, who took office on Jan. 1, 1997, and who in 2001 was elected to a second term, was praised both for carrying out administrative reforms and for promoting the goals of the UN.

The UN charter came into effect on Oct. 24, 1945, in San Francisco. With its headquarters in New York City, the UN and its agencies and affiliates made up a worldwide organization of more than 50,000 employees involved not only in the settlement of disputes but also in promoting advances in fields such as health, social welfare, and finance. Through the 1980s the UN often was the victim of Cold War politics, particularly between the U.S. and the U.S.S.R. Nonetheless, it sometimes played an important role in armed conflicts, as in the Korean War (1950–53), and served as an important forum in confrontations, as with the Cuban missile crisis of 1962. During the 1990s the UN expanded its role in helping to settle regional wars, particularly in the Balkans, in East Timor, and in parts of Africa. Although this was the first Nobel Prize for Peace awarded to the UN, several of its agencies had received the honour: the Office of the United Nations High Commissioner for Refugees in 1954 and 1981; the United Nations Children's Fund (UNICEF) in 1965; and United Nations peacekeeping forces in 1988. The International Labour Organization, an affiliated agency, won the prize in 1969.

Annan was praised by the Nobel Committee as being "pre-eminent in bringing new life" to the UN. He was born on April 18, 1938, in Kumasi, Gold Coast (now Ghana), and was educated largely in Kumasi and in the U.S. He earned a degree in economics from Macalester College, St. Paul, Minn., in 1961 and a master's degree in management from the Massachusetts Institute of Technology in 1972. He began working for the UN in 1962 as a budget officer at the World Health Organization in Geneva and, except for the years 1974–76, made his career with the UN. During the 1990s he was an assistant and then an undersecretary-general, performing duties that included overseeing peacekeeping operations in Bosnia and Herzegovina.

Annan was elected secretary-general, the first to come from the ranks of the staff, with a mandate to streamline the UN bureaucracy. He also forcefully promoted human rights and programs to combat AIDS and terrorism. He took an active role in negotiations when necessary but also was forthright in criticizing members when he felt it his duty to do so. Annan was the second UN secretary-general to win the Nobel Prize for Peace. Dag Hammarskjöld was awarded the prize posthumously in 1961, after he had died in a plane crash earlier in the year.

(ROBERT RAUCH)

PRIZE FOR ECONOMICS

The Nobel Memorial Prize in Economic Sciences was awarded in 2001 to Americans George A. Akerlof, A. Michael Spence, and Joseph E. Stiglitz, whose research and analyses had laid the foundations for the theory of markets with asymmetrical information. Their analysis of markets in which one side had better information than the other was fundamental to modern microeconomic theory and changed economists' perceptions of how markets work. It enabled an understanding of the phenomena in real markets that could not be explained by traditional neoclassical theory. The application of the models was wide ranging—from economic development and labour markets to traditional agricultural and modern financial markets. These models were also used to explain the existence of certain economic and social institutions and the introduction of contracts to limit the negative effect of information asymmetries.

Akerlof received the Nobel for his exposition on markets with asymmetrical information, in which sellers of a product have more information than buyers about the product's quality. He demonstrated that this could lead to "adverse selection" of poor-quality products such as—in his well-cited example of a secondhand-car market—a defective car known as a "lemon." In his 1970 seminal work "The Market for Lemons: Quality Uncertainty and the Market Mechanism," Akerlof explained how private or asymmetrical information prevents markets from functioning efficiently and examined the consequences of this. Akerlof suggested that many economic institutions had emerged in the market in order to protect themselves from the consequences of adverse selection, including secondhand-car dealers who offered guarantees to increase consumer confidence. In the context of less-developed countries, Akerlof's analysis explained that interest rates were often excessive because moneylenders lacked adequate information on the borrower's creditworthiness.

Spence developed the theory of "signaling" to demonstrate how the better informed in the market communicate their information to the less-well-informed to avoid the problems associated with adverse selection. In his 1973 seminal paper "Job Market Signaling," Spence demonstrated how education was used as a signal in the labour market. While an employer could not observe the productivity of a potential employee, he could assume that the cost of achieving a freely available educational standard—in terms of effort, expense, or time—was less for a productive than an unproductive person. For signaling to work, its cost had to differ widely between the various job candidates.

Stiglitz concentrated on what could be done by ill-informed individuals and operators to improve their position in a market with asymmetrical information. He found that they could extract information indirectly through screening and self-selection. "Equilibrium in Competitive Insurance Markets: An Essay on the Economics of Imperfect Information," a classic 1976 article on adverse selection written by Stiglitz with Michael Rothschild, examined the insurance market in which the (uninformed) companies lacked information on the individual risk situation of their (informed) customers. The analysis showed that by offering incentives to policyholders to disclose information, insurance companies were able to divide them into different risk classes. The use of a screening process enabled companies to issue a choice of policy contracts in which lower premiums could be exchanged for higher deductibles.

Akerlof was born on June 17, 1940, in New Haven, Conn., and was educated at Yale University (B.A., 1962) and the Massachusetts Institute of Technology (Ph.D., 1966). In 1966 he joined the faculty of the University of California, Berkeley, where he served as Goldman Professor of Economics from 1980. In 2000 the University of Zürich, Switz., awarded him an honorary doctorate.

Spence was born in 1943 in Montclair, N.J., and was educated at Princeton University (B.A., 1966), the University of Oxford (B.A., M.A., 1968), and Harvard University (Ph.D., 1972). He taught economics at Harvard and at Stanford University, where in 1990 he became the Philip H. Knight Professor and dean of the Graduate School of Business.

Stiglitz was born on Feb. 9, 1943, in Gary, Ind., and was educated at Amherst (Mass.) College (B.A., 1964) and the Massachusetts Institute of Technology (Ph.D., 1967), where he began his teaching career in 1966. He later became a professor at Yale, Oxford, Stanford, and Princeton. From 2001 he was professor of economics, business, and international affairs at Columbia University, New York City. Stiglitz was an active member of Pres. Bill Clinton's economic team; a member of the U.S. Council of Economic Advisers (1993–97), of which he became chairman in June 1995; and senior vice president and chief economist of the World Bank (1997–2000).

(JANET H. CLARK)

PRIZE FOR LITERATURE

Trinidadian-born British writer V.S. Naipaul—who merged fiction and reminiscence as well as memoir and reportage to create a compelling oeuvre that reflected his intimate journey through memory and experience toward the realization of self-discovery and truth—was awarded the 2001 Nobel Prize for Literature. The author of more than 25 volumes of fiction, history, travelogue, and journalism, Naipaul was an astute and often condescending observer of a world he perceived to be governed by class consciousness, prejudice, and political injustice. His penetrating, nihilistic vision of contemporary society encompassed both the dark and often brutal realities of colonial imperialism and postcolonial chaos and diaspora. His was an uncompromising voice for the oppressed, disenfranchised, and stateless, who, like himself, migrated from place to place in search of purpose and acceptance in what he deemed "borrowed cultures."

A descendant of Hindu immigrants from northern India whose Brahmin grandfather immigrated to the Caribbean as an indentured labourer, Vidiadhar Surajprasad Naipaul was born Aug. 17, 1932, in Chaguanas, Trinidad. His father, affectionately portrayed in the highly acclaimed *A House for Mr. Biswas* (1961), was a local journalist with literary aspirations of his own and instilled in both Naipaul and his younger brother Shiva, also a celebrated writer, an appreciation for literature and respect for the expressiveness and eloquence of language. Educated in Chaguanas and later in Port of Spain, Naipaul at the age of 18 left Trinidad for Great Britain to continue his studies at University College, Oxford. After graduating with honours in English, he became a freelance journalist with the BBC in London. In 1955 Naipaul married, and in the following year he returned briefly to Trinidad before settling permanently in England, first in London and then in Salisbury, Wiltshire, near Stonehenge.

Early in his career, Naipaul was identified with the emerging generation of politicized West Indian authors—among them Edgar Mittelhölzer, Samuel Selvon, George Lamming, and Derek Walcott—who sought to create a decolonization of English literature. Naipaul's first published novel, *The Mystic Masseur* (1957), was awarded the John Llewellyn Rhys Memorial Prize and combined ethnic humour and layered cynicism to create a satiric composite of Trinidadian society. The condition of the marginalized West Indian also informed both his second novel, *The Suffrage of Elvira* (1958), and *Miguel Street* (1959), a collection of interrelated stories about life in Port of Spain. Naipaul first gained critical recognition with *A House for Mr. Biswas*,

V.S. Naipaul

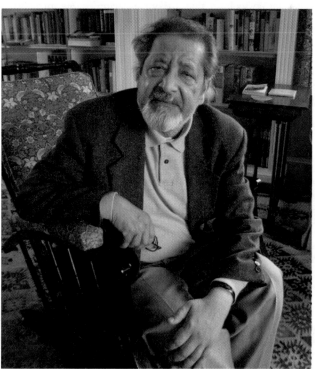

© Reuters/Chris Ison/POOL DC

which reflected the struggle of a modern-day West Indian Everyman forced to endure the humiliation and anguish of servitude and exploitation while desperately searching for both self-preservation and identity.

In 1962 Naipaul released his first work of nonfiction, *The Middle Passage*, which provided an acerbic and often insolent assessment of European colonialism in the West Indies and South America. The following year *Mr. Stone and the Knights Companion*, the first of his novels with an English setting, was published. These were followed by the publication of *An Area of Darkness* (1964), the first volume in his so-called "India" trilogy, which also includes *India: A Wounded Civilization* (1977) and *India: A Million Mutinies Now* (1990). Naipaul broadened his literary perspective of cultural dislocation with *The Mimic Men* (1967), which was followed by one of his best-known fictional works—the Booker Prize-winning *In a Free State* (1971), an experimental novel merging several genres to examine the pervasive decay of postcolonial disorder and disillusionment. The destructive and grim reality of postindependence upheaval was further explored in *Guerrillas* (1975), the first of his works to receive widespread attention in the U.S., and in *A Bend in the River* (1979). Naipaul continued to delve into the boundaries between fiction and autobiography with *The Enigma of Arrival* (1987), a personal reflection on the condition of colonialism and the postcolonial experience.

After being knighted in 1990, Naipaul received the first David Cohen British Literature Prize in 1993 for "lifetime achievement by a living British writer." He remained productive throughout the 1990s, enhancing his reputation with the publication in 1994 of the meditative novel *A Way in the World* and the controversial account of Islamic fundamentalism *Beyond Belief: Islamic Excursions Among the Converted Peoples* (1998). Following the death in 1996 of his first wife, Naipaul remarried that year. In his latest work, *Half a Life* (2001), Naipaul returned to the themes of his earlier fiction—the postcolonial legacy of displacement and exile.

(STEVEN R. SERAFIN)

PRIZE FOR CHEMISTRY

The syntheses of many important chemicals rely on catalysts, substances that speed up reactions without being consumed themselves. The 2001 Nobel Prize for Chemistry went to three scientists who developed the first chiral catalysts, which drive chemical reactions toward just one of two possible outcomes. Their catalysts found almost immediate use, most significantly in the manufacture of new drugs but also in the production of flavouring agents, insecticides, and other industrial products. One-half of the $943,000 prize was shared by William S. Knowles, formerly of the Monsanto Co., St. Louis, Mo., and Ryoji Noyori of Nagoya (Japan) University. The other half of the prize was awarded to K. Barry Sharpless of the Scripps Research Institute, La Jolla, Calif.

Knowles was born on June 1, 1917, in Taunton, Mass. He received a Ph.D. from Columbia University, New York City, in 1942, after which he conducted research at Monsanto until his retirement in 1986. Noyori was born on Sept. 3, 1938, in Kobe, Japan. He took a Ph.D. from Kyoto University (1967) and in 1968 joined the faculty of Nagoya University. In 2000 he assumed directorship of the university's Research Center for Materials Science. Sharpless was born on April 28, 1941, in Philadelphia. He received a Ph.D. from Stanford University (1968) and, after postdoctoral work, joined the Massachusetts Institute of Technology (MIT) in 1970. In 1990 he became W.M. Keck Professor of Chemistry at Scripps.

Many molecules are chiral—they exist in two structural forms (enantiomers) that are nonsuperimposable mirror images, like a pair of human hands. In humans and other living things, one chiral form of a molecule often predominates in the biochemical activities inside cells. For instance, natural sugars, which are the building blocks of carbohydrates, are almost exclusively right-handed. Natural amino acids, the building blocks of proteins, are almost all left-handed. Likewise, the receptors, enzymes, and other cellular components made from these molecules are chiral and tend to interact selectively with only one of two enantiomers of a given substance. For many drugs, however, traditional laboratory synthesis results in a mixture of enantiomers. One form usually has the desired effect, binding with a cellular receptor or interacting in some other way. The other form may be inactive or cause undesirable side effects. The latter happened with the drug thalidomide, prescribed to pregnant women for nausea beginning in the late 1950s. One enantiomer relieved nausea, whereas the other caused birth defects.

Traditional syntheses for thalidomide and other drugs are symmetrical in the sense that they produce equal amounts of both enantiomers. For decades chemists had tried to develop asymmetrical methods that would yield more of one enantiomer or even one enantiomer exclusively. The three Nobel laureates developed asymmetrical catalysts for two important classes of reactions in organic chemistry, hydrogenations and oxidations.

In the early 1960s scientists did not know if catalytic asymmetrical hydrogenation even was possible. In many important syntheses, hydrogenation involves the addition of hydrogen to two atoms that are joined by a double bond in a molecular structure. An asymmetrical hydrogenation reaction would do so in a way that produced more of one enantiomer than the other. The breakthrough came in 1968 when Knowles, working at Monsanto, developed the first chiral catalyst for an asymmetrical hydrogenation reaction. Knowles was seeking an industrial synthesis for the drug L-dopa, which later became a mainstay for treating Parkinson disease. Variations of the new catalyst found almost immediate application in producing very pure preparations of the desired L-dopa enantiomer.

Beginning in the 1980s Noyori, working at Nagoya University, developed more general asymmetrical hydrogen catalysts. They had broader applications, could produce larger proportions of the desired enantiomer, and were suitable for large-scale industrial applications. Noyori's catalysts found wide use in the synthesis of antibiotics and advanced materials.

Sharpless addressed the great need for chiral catalysts for oxidations, another broad family of chemical reactions. Atoms, ions, or molecules that undergo oxidation in reactions lose electrons and, in so doing, increase their functionality, or capacity to form chemical bonds. In 1980, working at MIT, Sharpless carried out key experiments that led to a practical method based on catalytic asymmetrical oxidation for producing epoxide compounds, used in the synthesis of heart medicines such as beta blockers and other products. As was expressed by the Royal Swedish Academy of Sciences, which awarded the chemistry prize to Knowles, Noyori, and Sharpless, "Many scientists have identified Sharpless' epoxidation as the most important discovery in the field of synthesis during the past few decades."

(MICHAEL WOODS)

AP/Wide World Photos

Wolfgang Ketterle (centre), flanked by associates at the Massachusetts Institute of Technology

PRIZE FOR PHYSICS

Three scientists who first created a new ultracold state of matter that Albert Einstein had predicted more than 70 years earlier won the 2001 Nobel Prize for Physics. Eric A. Cornell of the U.S. National Institute of Standards and Technology (NIST), Carl E. Wieman of the University of Colorado at Boulder, and Wolfgang Ketterle of the Massachusetts Institute of Technology (MIT) shared the $943,000 prize for their production in 1995 of the so-called Bose-Einstein condensate (BEC).

Cornell was born on Dec. 19, 1961, in Palo Alto., Calif. He earned a Ph.D. from MIT (1990) and, after postdoctoral work, joined the faculty of the University of Colorado in 1992. That same year he became a staff scientist at NIST. Wieman was born on March 26, 1951, in Corvallis, Ore. After earning a Ph.D. from Stanford University (1977), he taught and conducted research at the University of Michigan at Ann Arbor until 1984, when he moved to the University of Colorado. Both Cornell and Wieman held positions as fellows of the Joint Institute for Laboratory Astrophysics (JILA), a research and teaching centre operated by NIST and

the University of Colorado. Ketterle was born on Oct. 21, 1957, in Heidelberg, Ger. He received a Ph.D. from the University of Munich and the Max Planck Institute for Quantum Optics, Garching (1986). After postdoctoral work he joined the faculty at MIT in 1993. He also served as a principal investigator with the Center for Ultracold Atoms, a joint research institution sponsored by MIT, Harvard University, and the National Science Foundation. Ketterle was a German citizen with permanent residency in the U.S.

Generations of physicists had dreamed of creating a BEC since the concept for this exotic state of matter first emerged in the 1920s. In 1924 the Indian physicist Satyendra Bose made important theoretical calculations about the nature of light particles, or photons. Physicists already had recognized that the propagation of light can be thought to consist of discrete packets of energy traveling through space. Bose presented an alternative derivation of a law about the behaviour of photons that had been developed earlier by the German physicist Max Planck. The kinds of particles that fitted Bose's description eventually were named bosons in his honour. Bosons have a property that allows

them to congregate without number, occupying the same quantum state at the same time.

Einstein translated Bose's work into German, submitted it for publication to a physics journal, and started working on the concept himself. Bose's work focused on particles, such as photons, that have no rest mass. Einstein extended it to particles that have mass, such as the atoms in a dilute gas. He predicted that if a sufficient number of such atoms get close enough together and move slowly enough, they will undergo a phase transition into a new state. That new state of matter became known as a Bose-Einstein condensate.

Physicists recognized the keys to achieving a BEC. The major challenge was to make the gas very cold, about a tenth of a millionth of a degree of absolute zero (-273.15 °C, or -459.67 °F), to slow down the motion of the atoms without causing them to condense to a liquid. Atoms in gases usually move about in an uncoordinated way, ricocheting off each other and nearby objects. Under the specific conditions described by Einstein, however, the atoms "sense" one another and transform from a mass of uncoordinated individuals to a coherent group that acts like a single giant atom.

Cornell and Wieman, working at the University of Colorado in 1995, used a combination of laser and magnetic techniques to slow, trap, and cool about 2,000 rubidium atoms to form a BEC. Ketterle, working independently at MIT, created a BEC from sodium atoms. Ketterle's BEC, which comprised a much larger sample of atoms, was used to carry out additional studies of the condensate, including an interference experiment that provided the first direct evidence of the coherent nature of a BEC. Those first successes led to a flurry of experiments in other laboratories in which physicists expanded the roster of BEC-forming gases and used BECs to produce "atom lasers" that emit coherent beams of matter rather than light.

In 2001 about 20 groups were conducting BEC experiments, which were providing new insights into the laws of physics and pointing to possible practical uses of BECs. (*See* MATHEMATICS AND PHYSICAL SCIENCES: *Physics.*) As the Swedish Academy observed, "Revolutionary applications of BEC in lithography, nanotechnology, and holography appear to be just round the corner." (MICHAEL WOODS)

PRIZE FOR PHYSIOLOGY OR MEDICINE

AP/Wide World Photos

Paul M. Nurse (left) and R. Timothy Hunt; (inset) Leland H. Hartwell

Dan Levine/AFP Worldwide

Three researchers shared the 2001 Nobel Prize for Physiology or Medicine for their pioneering discoveries about one of life's most basic processes. Working independently, Leland H. Hartwell of the Fred Hutchinson Cancer Research Center, Seattle, Wash., and Paul M. Nurse and R. Timothy Hunt of the Imperial Cancer Research Fund (ICRF), London, illuminated the common mechanisms that regulate the cycle of growth and division in cells ranging from yeast to human beings. As was acknowledged by the Nobel Assembly at the Karolinska Institute in Stockholm, which awarded the $943,000 medicine prize, these findings greatly expanded scientific understanding of cancer and other diseases that occur when the machinery of the cell cycle goes awry.

Hartwell was born on Oct. 30, 1939, in Los Angeles. After earning a Ph.D. from the Massachusetts Institute of Technology (1964), he served on the faculty of the University of California, Irvine, from 1965 until 1968, when he moved to the University of Washington. In 1997 he assumed the duties of president and director of the Hutchinson Center. Nurse was born on Jan. 25, 1949, in Great Britain. He received a Ph.D. from the University of East Anglia, Norwich, Eng. (1973), later headed the ICRF Cell Cycle Laboratory (1984–87), and served on the faculty of the University of Oxford (1987–93). In 1996 he became director general of the ICRF and, once again, head of its Cell Cycle Laboratory. Hunt, born on Feb. 19, 1943, in Great Britain, earned a Ph.D. from the University of Cambridge (1968) and later served on its faculty (1981–90). In 1990 he joined the ICRF, rising to principal scientist.

The cell cycle comprises a carefully orchestrated series of events that unfolds countless times each day in the human body. An adult human has about 100 trillion cells, all of which originate from the division of a single fertilized egg cell. Even after a human is fully grown, cells continue to divide to replace those that die. In the first phase of the cell cycle, the cell enlarges. On reaching a certain size, it enters the second phase, in which DNA synthesis occurs—the cell duplicates its genetic material and creates a copy of each chromosome. In the next phase, the cell checks to ensure that DNA replication is accurate and prepares for cell division. In the fourth phase, the chromo-

somes separate into two sets, and the cell divides into two daughter cells, each with one set of chromosomes. The daughter cells then return to the first phase of the cell cycle.

The phases of the cycle must be coordinated with great precision. Each must occur in its proper order and be completed before the next phase begins. Errors in this orchestration may lead to chromosomal abnormalities—for example, chromosomes that have missing or rearranged parts or that are distributed unevenly between the daughter cells. Such abnormalities often occur in cancer cells, which have escaped the normal controls on the cell cycle and multiply in unrestrained fashion. The three Nobel laureates discovered key molecular regulators of the cell cycle, including proteins called cyclins and enzymes called cyclin-dependent kinases.

Hartwell started work in the late 1960s, using baker's yeast as a model organism to study the cell cycle with genetic methods. He identified more than 100 genes, termed cell-division-cycle (CDC) genes, involved in cell-cycle control. For instance, one—named *cdc28*—controls the first phase and so

became known as "start." Hartwell also found that the cycle includes optional pauses, called checkpoints, that allow time for repair of damaged DNA.

Nurse used another type of yeast as his model organism. In the mid-1970s he discovered a gene called *cdc2*, which works as a master switch to regulate the timing of different cell-cycle events. In 1987 Nurse isolated the corresponding gene in humans, which was named cyclin-dependent kinase 1 (*cdk1*). The gene codes for a protein that belongs to a family of key enzymes, the cyclin-dependent kinases (CDKs), that participate in many cell functions. About a half dozen other CDKs were identified in humans.

Hunt isolated the first cyclin in the early 1980s from sea urchins. Cyclins are proteins formed and broken down during each cell cycle. Hunt discovered that cyclin binds to the CDK molecules discovered by Nurse, functioning as a biochemical enabling agent to activate the CDKs. Hunt also showed that the periodic degradation of cyclin is an important general regulatory mechanism in the cell cycle. By 2001 about 10 cyclins had been identified.

(MICHAEL WOODS)

Biographies

The **SUBJECTS** of these biographies are the people who in the editors' opinions captured the **IMAGINATION** of the world in 2001—the most **INTERESTING** and/or **IMPORTANT PERSONALITIES** of the year.

Aerosmith

The year 2001 was one of the highest peaks in the roller-coaster career of hard-rock survivors Aerosmith; the group was inducted into the Rock and Roll Hall of Fame and enjoyed the runaway success of its first self-produced album, *Just Push Play*. Overcoming the legendary excess that had brought its career to a screeching halt in the early 1980s, Aerosmith returned with even greater popularity than it had enjoyed as one of the biggest arena rockers of the '70s. In the process the group passed the 50-million mark in album sales to become the 10th best-selling act in recording history.

Aerosmith was formed in 1970 in New Hampshire by vocalist-drummer-harmonicist Steven Tyler (born Steven Tallarico on March 26, 1948, in New York City), guitar wizard Joe Perry (born Sept. 10, 1950, in Boston), and bassist Tom Hamilton (born Dec. 31, 1951, in Colorado Springs, Colo.). After the addition of guitarist Brad Whitford (born Feb. 23, 1952, in Winchester, Mass.) and drummer Joey Kramer (born June 21, 1950, in New York City), Tyler became a full-time front man. Relocating to Boston, Aerosmith honed its mixture of blues-based heavy metal and Rolling Stones-styled rock before signing with Columbia Records in 1972.

Touring nearly nonstop in support of its first two albums, *Aerosmith* (1973) and *Get Your Wings* (1974), the band won an enthusiastic following before releasing the multimillion-selling *Toys in the Attic* (1975)—featuring "Walk This Way" and "Sweet Emotion"—and *Rocks* (1976). The band's rerelease of "Dream On" in 1976 also became a huge hit, one of rock's first power ballads. In leotards and flowing scarves, Tyler, who resembled the Stones' Mick Jagger, exuded sex both in the band's raucous live shows and in the clever, libidinous lyrics that earned him the nickname the "Shakespeare of the salacious." The group's sex-and-drugs lifestyle took a heavy toll, however; alcohol, cocaine, and barbiturate abuse—and ultimately the heroin addiction of the "toxic twins" (Tyler and Perry)—resulted in rapidly declining creativity and erratic live shows. Perry went solo in 1979, following the release of the uninspired *Night in Ruts*, and Whitford followed. The band pushed on with new guitarists, but by the time *Rock in a Hard Place* (1982) appeared, Tyler was passing out onstage.

In 1984, however, the original members regrouped, and in 1986 Perry and Tyler guested on Run DMC's hip-hop remake of "Walk This Way." Soon after, the band committed to sobriety. As daily workouts replaced all-night parties, Aerosmith found a new generation of fans on MTV with a series of suggestive music videos, charting singles, and hit albums. Hit songs included "Dude (Looks like a Lady)" from *Permanent Vacation* (1987), "Janie's Got a Gun" from *Pump* (1989), and "Cryin'" from *Get a Grip* (1994); the latter album, like the follow-up *Nine Lives* (1997), reached number one. The group garnered Grammy Awards in 1990, 1993, and 1994. (JEFF WALLENFELDT)

Antinori, Severino

On Jan. 25, 2001, Severino Antinori, an Italian physician and research scientist specializing in human fertility, announced that he planned to begin work on a project to clone humans and that he had already found 10 couples who were willing to participate. Joining him as his future partner was American fertility specialist Panayiotis Zavos, who said that he and Antinori expected to produce a viable human embryo within 18 months. On March 9 at a conference in Rome, they stated that the number of volunteers had increased to more than 600 infertile couples.

In order to produce the clones, Antinori and Zavos planned to impregnate women with embryos made with the DNA of the child's intended father. The children would, therefore, be the genetic twins of their fathers, which would thus allow infertile men to pass their genes on to the next generation. Antinori, however, claimed that the babies would have a small amount of the DNA of their mothers and consequently would not be exact clones. Many throughout the world quickly expressed strong opposition to the project. Some objected on moral and religious grounds, while others cited the many miscarriages, stillbirths, and abnormal offspring that had resulted from the efforts to clone large mammals. In regard to the second criticism, Antinori and Zavos claimed that their long experience with in vitro fertilization and other types of assisted pregnancy would greatly increase their chances for success.

Antinori was born about 1945 in Rome. He studied medicine at the University of Rome, graduating in 1972, and then continued to work at the university, specializing in gastroenterology in 1973–74. Later in the 1970s he shifted his specialty to obstetrics and gynecology, working at various hospitals and institutions in Italy and eventually establishing his own clinic in

Hard-rock survivors Steven Tyler (right) and Joe Perry of Aerosmith

Biographies

Rome. Antinori first gained international attention in 1993, when a 59-year-old British woman gave birth to twins as a result of treatment in his fertility clinic; eggs from a young Italian woman had been donated, fertilized with sperm from the British woman's husband, and then implanted in her. A year later, after undergoing the same procedure, a 62-year-old Italian woman gave birth to a son; she was believed to be the oldest woman ever to have given birth. Throughout 2001 Antinori continued to defend himself against those who opposed his cloning project. To his many critics he declared, "I can guarantee at 99% that I will not give birth to any monsters." (DAVID R. CALHOUN)

Arroyo, Gloria Macapagal

On Jan. 20, 2001, after angry protesters had driven Philippines Pres. Joseph Estrada from the presidential residence, Malacañang Palace, in Manila, the country's vice president, Gloria Macapagal Arroyo, assumed power. The demonstrations had been sparked by the Senate's halting of Estrada's impeachment trial on corruption charges. The armed forces withdrew support from Estrada; the Supreme Court unanimously declared the presidency to be vacant; and Arroyo was officially sworn in as his successor. Estrada later claimed that he had not relinquished the presidency, but the Supreme Court ruled her government legitimate.

Born on April 5, 1947, in San Juan, a suburb of Manila, Arroyo lived at Malacañang as a teenager when her father, Diosdado P. Macapagal, was president of the Philippines from 1961 to 1965. She was valedictorian of her high-school class and studied economics at Georgetown University, Washington, D.C., where she began a lasting friendship with classmate and future U.S. president Bill Clinton. After returning to the Philippines and graduating magna cum laude from Assumption College, Manila, in 1968, Arroyo earned a master's degree in economics from Ateneo de Manila University in 1978 and a doctorate of economics from the University of the Philippines, Quezon City, in 1986.

Arroyo was a university professor when Pres. Corazon Aquino appointed her undersecretary of trade and industry in 1986. She won a seat in the Senate in 1992 and was reelected in 1995 by a record 16 million votes. Arroyo, who wrote 55 laws on economic and social reform, was named several times by the media as the country's outstanding senator. The 13 million votes she garnered in her successful bid for the vice presidency in 1998 was the largest mandate ever in a Philippines presidential or vice presidential race, while Estrada, running separately, won the presidency with fewer votes.

Estrada named Arroyo secretary of social welfare and development, an unusual second job for a vice president. As scandal began to envelop Estrada, she resigned the cabinet post on Oct. 12, 2000, to rally opposition against him.

Arroyo brought an unprecedented academic and administrative background to the Philippines presidency. Even so, she enlisted experienced officials to help her tackle national problems, especially poverty. A member of the wealthy elite, she sought to win over the masses who had supported the charismatic Estrada,

Gloria Macapagal Arroyo walks tall as she reviews troops in Manila

Romeo Gacad/AFP Worldwide

adopting a more informal style on visits to poor areas. Unusual for Philippines politics, she had not been known by a nickname, but her publicists encouraged the use of Ate Glo ("Big Sister Gloria"). Although Arroyo tried to be folksy, she showed a steely side by taking a tougher line than Estrada on combating rebellion in the southern Philippines. (HENRY S. BRADSHER)

Bachchan, Amitabh

By far the biggest draw on Indian television in 2001 was *Kaun Banega Crorepati*, the Hindi version of *Who Wants to Be a Millionaire*. The show captured the imagination of millions, and fueling its popularity was *Kaun Banega Crorepati*'s charismatic host, Amitabh Bachchan. The television assignment was a decided departure for Bachchan, a former film star who was once regarded as "the king of Indian cinema."

Born on Oct. 11, 1942, in Allahabad, India, Bachchan was the son of a noted Hindi poet, Harivansh Bachchan. He was educated at Sherwood College, Nainital, and the University of Delhi. After working for a time as a business executive in Calcutta (now Kolkata) and performing in theatre, Bachchan began a long career in film. His screen debut, *Saat Hindustani* (1969; "Seven Indians"), flopped. Initially, Indian audiences found it hard to accept Bachchan's gangly physique and "angry young man" persona. Four years later, however, he tasted his first commercial success with *Zanjeer* (1973; "Chain"). A string of hit action films followed, including *Deewar* (1975; "Wall"), *Sholay* (1975; "Embers"), and *Don* (1978). Bachchan's oeuvre was not confined to action alone, however; his comic flair was showcased in breezier fare such as *Chupke Chupke* (1975) and *Mr. Natwarlal* (1979).

An accident on the set of the film *Coolie* in 1982 left Bachchan comatose, but he eventually made a full recovery. His subsequent films did poorly at the box office, however. Motivated by his friend Indian Prime Minister Rajiv Gandhi, Bachchan entered politics and was elected to Parliament from Allahabad by

an overwhelming majority. His stint in politics proved to be short-lived. In 1989, after being implicated in the bribery scandal that toppled Gandhi's government, Bachchan was forced to resign his post. Returning to film, he won the National Award for his portrayal of a mafia don in *Agneepath* (1990; "Path of Fire").

In 1992 Bachchan took another hiatus from moviemaking, and when he reappeared three years later, it was as head of his own entertainment venture, Amitabh Bachchan Corp. Ltd. (ABCL). The business, which specialized in film production and event management, brought the Miss World beauty pageant to India in 1996 but quickly ran into deep financial trouble. The actor was forced to explore other options. *Kaun Banega Crorepati* first aired in July 2000. Taking a role on the small screen was perceived as a move that Bachchan was forced to make in order to pay off ABCL creditors. The transition was a successful one, however. Bachchan's fluent Hindustani and easygoing charm helped put contestants at ease and *Kaun Banega Crorepati* on top of the ratings chart. His annual salary of $3.2 million made him Indian television's highest-paid star. (SHALAKA PARADKAR)

Barber, Patricia

She rose from Chicago cult performer to international jazz star, but Patricia Barber's rise was slow and far from steady. On one opening night in 1984 at a small club on the city's fashionable Gold Coast, only two people showed up. "A year later there were lines of people around the block waiting to get in," says Barber, and that six-nights-a-week gig stretched into eight years. Her audience grew in the 1990s when she began performing her own subtle, sophisticated songs and her arrangements of modern pop tunes; she also recorded four albums showcasing her originals. For her sixth album, *Nightclub*, Barber returned to interpreting familiar standard songs in her intimate yet dramatic style. The compact disc became a jazz best-seller, spending eight weeks among *Billboard*'s top five jazz albums in

2001. Barber expanded her fame with months of touring clubs, concerts, and jazz festivals in North America, Europe, and Israel.

Barber, the daughter of two musicians, was born on Nov. 8, 1955, in Lisle, Ill. She began taking classical piano lessons when she was six years old. She grew up in Illinois and Iowa, majored in classical music and psychology at the University of Iowa, and initially resisted becoming a jazz musician as "a stupid thing to do for a smart woman."

Jimmy Katz

Patricia Barber's modern cool

But jazz proved an irresistible lure, and in 1979, a year after graduation, she migrated to Chicago, where she scuffled for work for five years, sometimes surviving on a hot-dog diet. Her break came with that 1984 booking at the Gold Star Sardine Bar, where the club owner insisted that Barber sing and play only standards. The intimate quality of her music became evident, as she often chose slow tempos for the familiar songs that she sang quietly, over her lyrical, Bill Evans-influenced piano playing. She continually added new material to her repertoire. She also borrowed money from her sister to record her first album, which she sold from the bandstand.

With her early 1990s move to the Green Mill, a jazz club in a former Chicago speakeasy, she began expanding her horizons, adding unusual selections, from 11th-century Gregorian chants to Santana and Joni Mitchell. Barber began writing songs too, setting poems of E.E. Cummings and Maya Angelou to music and also writing her own lyrics. Songs of hers, including "Touch of Trash" and "Postmodern Blues," revealed veins of ironic humour, melancholy, and whimsy; she began expressing her own worried vision of today's "materialistic" society in song. Dissatisfied with the way a major label handled her second album, Barber began producing her own recordings, using her own loyal musicians, for a small local label. Against all odds, Barber's discs *Café Blue* (1994), *Modern Cool* (1998), and *Companion* (1999) spread her reputation beyond Chicago. When a major label began distributing her albums, sales shot up. Despite the hit status of *Nightclub* and her

increased time on the road, Barber remained based in Chicago and still sang regularly at the Green Mill.   (JOHN LITWEILER)

Beckham, David and Victoria

Even for a country as obsessed with celebrity status as Great Britain, the phenomenon of David and Victoria Beckham grew in 2001 into something remarkable. When David, the captain of England's association football (soccer) team and a key midfielder on Manchester United (England's, and arguably the world's, most famous football club), and Victoria, "Posh Spice" of the Spice Girls pop group, moved into their vast new home in Hertfordshire, north of London, the house quickly acquired the sobriquet "Beckingham Palace," an ironic reference to Buckingham Palace, the London home of Queen Elizabeth II. Yet despite the glitz of stardom, "Posh" and "Becks" gained many admirers beyond the normal ranks of pop music and sports fans, not least for the obvious delight they took in raising their baby son, Brooklyn. Coming from two different popular cultures, both widely associated with rowdy behaviour and personal excess, the couple offered young people gentler and healthier role models.

David Beckham was born on May 2, 1975, in Leytonstone, east London. He joined Manchester United as a trainee in 1991 and first distinguished himself as a special talent in a televised league match in August 1996, when he scored a goal from the halfway line (a feat roughly equivalent to a golfer's hole in one). From 1998 he played regularly for England, and he was made captain of the national team for its 2001 qualifying matches, ahead of the 2002 World Cup. Beckham's autobiography, *David Beckham: My World*, was an immediate best-seller upon publication in 2000. His glamour status was so high that his regular changes of hairstyle caused consternation among hairdressers throughout Britain, who would be flooded with demands from their regular customers to copy Becks's new look.

Posh was born Victoria Caroline Adams on April 17, 1974, in Hertfordshire. In 1994 she was one of the five young women selected to form the Spice Girls. The Spice Girls was the first group to reach number one in the British pop music charts with each of its first four singles, and the five members—both together and individually—became a cultural phenomenon. When Adams met Beckham, their relationship was widely expected to be very short-lived—a view that was not greatly disturbed by the birth of Brooklyn in March 1999. In July of that year, however, the couple married in an ostentatious ceremony at a castle outside Dublin. Conducted by the bishop of Cork, the wedding was reputed to have cost £500,000 (about $750,000). The couple still made a profit, though; they sold photographic rights to the celebrity magazine *OK!* for £1 million (about $1.5 million), including pictures of the bride and groom sitting on red velvet thrones under crown-shaped chandeliers.

Despite criticism for the "vulgarity" of their nuptials, the Beckhams gradually silenced the doubters by presenting themselves as model, if unusual, parents. David would often take Brooklyn to Manchester United matches.

Victoria, who did some fashion modeling and started to make solo records, showed that motherhood could be combined with a successful career. In the fall of 2001, she released her first solo album and her own autobiography, *Learning to Fly*. Few people would hazard a guess as to how long their joint celebrity status would last, but back in 1998 not that many had expected the Posh and Becks show to be still going strong in 2001.   (PETER KELLNER)

Berlusconi, Silvio

On June 11, 2001, Italian media magnate Silvio Berlusconi, a tycoon with an estimated fortune of over $10 billion, was sworn in as the country's new prime minister after his centre-right alliance, the House of Freedoms, scored a resounding victory in the May 13 general elections. His installation followed more than six years of leading the opposition. Though Berlusconi was an articulate and dynamic figure, controversy surrounded him; his numerous entanglements with the judiciary were coupled with the seeming incompatibility of his roles as both a leading politician and Italy's most powerful

AP/Wide World Photos

Silvio Berlusconi and his contract with the Italian people

media magnate. Once in office, he pledged swift action to regulate such "potential conflicts of interest." Following the September 11 attacks, he was quick to offer support to the U.S., but he courted controversy again when in a speech given in Berlin he asserted that Western civilization was superior to the Islamic world. He later said his remarks, which were denounced by European Union and Muslim leaders, were taken out of context.

Berlusconi was born on Sept. 29, 1936, in Milan. As a youth he engaged in moneymaking ventures by putting on puppet shows and then by charging for "ghosting" homework assignments for his classmates. As a law student at the University of Milan, he paid for his tuition by selling vacuum cleaners and by crooning (backed by his own band) on summer cruises. After obtaining a loan from the bank that employed his father, he launched a successful real-estate-development concern in Milan, reportedly with the help of local socialist politicians. The bulk of his fortune, however, was made in television. In 1978 he circumvented a law that guaranteed the national monopoly of RAI, the state TV network, and set up rival TV stations. Then, aided by the socialist government (1983–87) of Bettino Craxi, a friend from university, Berlusconi acquired three national TV channels. They formed the foundation of his media empire.

Berlusconi launched into politics in 1993. Exploiting a gap left by a corruption scandal that wiped out the old political order, he founded the conservative populist Forza Italia ("Go, Italy") movement to fight off a growing challenge from the left wing. After relinquishing his positions in the Fininvest Group, his giant holding company, Berlusconi led the right-wing Freedom Alliance, headed by Forza Italia, to a landslide election triumph in 1994. His government fell after seven months, however, when a vital coalition ally defected amid charges of corruption in Berlusconi's business empire. Since 1994 Berlusconi had been involved in some nine court cases for financial misdeeds ranging from bribing judges to tax evasion. Though proceedings were dropped in four cases, near year's end five cases were still pending, one of them in Spain. Berlusconi, however, rejected all charges, claiming they sprang from a political conspiracy against him by the left wing. (DEREK WILSON)

bin Laden, Osama
Almost as soon as Americans grasped the reality of the Sept. 11, 2001, terrorist attacks, their attention began to focus on the figure of Osama bin Laden. The vehemence of his anti-Americanism, the scope of his resources, and the refinement of planning already exhibited in Bin Laden's previous terrorist attacks had advertised his readiness to resort to such breathtaking brutality. Subsequent investigation confirmed Bin Laden's involvement.

Bin Laden was born on March 10, 1957, in Riyadh, Saudi Arabia, the son of a wealthy contractor with ties to the Saudi royal family. He attended King Abdul Aziz University in Riyadh, where he took a degree in 1981. In 1980 Bin Laden traveled to Peshawar, Pak., and became active in recruiting "Arab Afghans," Muslims from various countries who went to fight with the Afghan mujahideen against the Soviet army. Through associations with these militant Islamists, he began to devote himself to the cause of international jihad. He established al-Qaeda, an organization that was establishing camps inside Afghanistan for the purpose of training Arab Afghans to fight in other countries.

After the Soviet withdrawal from Afghanistan in 1989, Bin Laden returned home to Saudi Arabia, where he opposed the government over the stationing of U.S. troops in the country at the time of Iraq's occupation of Kuwait. In 1991 he was expelled, and three years later his Saudi citizenship was revoked. Meanwhile, the jihad in Afghanistan had lost its focus, and Bin Laden settled in The Sudan, where he invested in several commercial enterprises as support and cover for al-Qaeda. From there he allied himself with other militant Islamist organizations. After 18 U.S. soldiers were killed in Somalia in October 1993—for which Bin Laden later took credit—the U.S. withdrew its forces, which confirmed for Bin Laden the weakness of American resolve.

Forced to leave The Sudan in May 1996, he moved once more to Afghanistan, where the Taliban was now in a position to offer him protection. Early in 1998 al-Qaeda joined militants from other countries in an international jihad against Jews and "Crusaders"—it was announced that every Muslim had the duty to kill or fight Americans and their allies, whether civilian or military. Responsibility for the August 1998 bombing of U.S. embassies in Kenya and Tanzania was laid on Bin Laden, and in response the U.S. launched cruise missiles against targets in The Sudan and Afghanistan. Surviving the attacks and harboured by the Taliban in Afghanistan, Bin Laden became a world figure, as admired in the Muslim world as he was reviled in the U.S.

Despite repeated demands from the West, the Taliban refused to surrender Bin Laden to any form of international justice. After the September 11 attacks, however, the Taliban themselves became the target of U.S. reaction. Bin Laden, meanwhile, demonstrated his mastery of another Western technology—the media—by releasing a series of videotaped interviews to the Qatar-based satellite network Al-Jazeera in which he taunted the U.S. and its allies. At year's end, as allied troops mopped up the remains of Taliban resistance, Bin Laden had still not been apprehended.

(STEPHEN SEGO)

Bloomberg, Michael
In 2001, after 20 successful years of leading the financial information firm he founded, Michael Bloomberg was ready to lead something new. For his next challenge he entered the race for mayor of New York City. The formal announcement of his candidacy in early June sparked two types of speculation: what effect Bloomberg's election as mayor might have on New York City and what effect his absence as CEO might have on his company, Bloomberg LP.

Michael Rubens Bloomberg was born in Medford, Mass., on Feb. 14, 1942. His father was a bookkeeper and his mother a secretary. After earning a bachelor's degree in engineering from Johns Hopkins University, Baltimore, Md., in 1964, he attended Harvard University (M.B.A., 1966) and then took an entry-level job with Salomon Brothers investment bank. Within 15 years he had achieved the level of partner and was leading the firm's block trading operations. A political shake-up at Salomon in 1981 left him without a job, but with his $10 million partnership buyout, he created Innovative Market Systems. By 2001 the renamed Bloomberg LP employed more than 7,000 people around the world. Central to the company's success was the Bloomberg computer terminal, a comprehensive financial news and information source that was leased to users at a price of $1,285 per month. The company's other holdings included the Bloomberg Business News wire service, news radio station WBBR in New York City, Bloomberg Television, and specialty magazines.

While the firm's customers were among the wealthiest people in the world, and Bloomberg—being one of them—operated in a fairly narrow spectrum of privilege and influence, he was generous with his money. Over the years he had donated or pledged roughly $100 million to

Johns Hopkins University. He also served on the boards of leading cultural institutions, including the Metropolitan Museum, Lincoln Center, the Central Park Conservancy, and the Jewish Museum. Reportedly worth about $4.5 billion, Bloomberg funded much of his mayoral campaign himself, spending more than $68 million from his personal fortune. His campaign themes focused on issues of great concern to New Yorkers: improvements in traffic and transit, housing, and education. What helped him most, however, was the endorsement of outgoing New York City Mayor Rudolph Giuliani, whose leadership following the September 11 terrorist attacks was universally praised. After trailing badly in the polls just weeks before the November 6 election, Bloomberg went on to win the mayor's race, defeating Democrat Mark Green by a narrow margin.

Certainly Bloomberg's political and business strategies had been made in tandem. Perhaps to reveal his own concerns about his company's future growth, Bloomberg had chosen the head of Bloomberg's European sales force, Lex Fenwick, to manage the firm's day-to-day business operations during the campaign. As mayor, Bloomberg knew that his old firm would have to fight to retain customers while attracting new ones. (SARAH FORBES ORWIG)

Blunkett, David
Following the U.K.'s 2001 general election, Prime Minister Tony Blair appointed David Blunkett to be home secretary, one of the most senior cabinet positions. Blunkett's sterling reputation amply justified this promotion; it also raised the possibility that Blunkett might eventually succeed Blair as leader of Great Britain's Labour Party. What made this prospect remarkable was the fact that Blunkett had managed to establish himself as one of the U.K.'s leading politicians without ever having been able to see.

Blunkett, who was blind from birth, was born on June 6, 1947, in the northern England city of Sheffield and was brought up in poverty after his father died in an industrial accident at work. He was educated at schools for the blind, but he turned down a course in training to be a piano tuner and insisted on a wider education. He studied part time at a technical college and did well enough on his exams to win a place at the University of Sheffield, where he studied politics. His passion for politics led him at the age of 22 to become the youngest-ever councillor on Sheffield's city council, and he rose to become the council's leader in 1980. Blunkett belonged to Labour's left wing, a position that helped in his election to the party's national executive in 1982.

At that time Labour, having lost power nationally in 1979, was badly divided. In the 1980s these divisions came to a head when party leader Neil Kinnock sought to expel a group of hard-line left-wingers. Blunkett sided with Kinnock on this and on a wider strategy for modernizing the party. In 1987 Blunkett was elected MP for the safe Labour constituency of Sheffield Brightside. In 1994 Labour's new leader, Tony Blair, appointed him the party's shadow minister, or spokesman, on education. It was a key appointment, as Blair announced that on becoming prime minister he would make his three top priorities "education, education, education."

When Labour won the 1997 general election, Blunkett became education secretary, with the task of raising school standards to match those of other prosperous countries. Blunkett introduced a number of reforms, including requiring schools to provide children up to the age of 11 with a daily "literacy hour" and a "numeracy hour" in order to improve basic skills. Blunkett frequently cited his own disability and impoverished background to argue that all children had the potential to succeed and that no school should be allowed to use the fact that its children came from deprived or broken families as an excuse for bad results. Blunkett's tough strategy was widely praised, although he was not always popular with teachers unions. His promotion to home secretary on June 8, 2001—with a brief to be equally tough in tackling crime, disorder, and threats to internal security—was his reward for having been one of the most successful cabinet ministers during Blair's first term in office. After the terrorist attacks in the U.S. on September 11, however, Blunkett's job looked to be an even bigger challenge.

(PETER KELLNER)

Bonds, Barry

On Oct. 5, 2001, Barry Bonds, the left fielder of the San Francisco Giants, set a single-season major league baseball record by hitting his 71st and 72nd home runs, erasing the previous mark of 70 set by Mark McGwire of the St. Louis Cardinals in 1998. Two days later, in the last game of the season, Bonds raised his total to 73. Along with his home runs, he also finished the season with an .863 slugging percentage, breaking the record of .847 set by Babe Ruth in 1920. Bonds surpassed another Ruth mark by walking 177 times, seven more than Ruth had done in 1923. Bonds hit a home run in every 6.52 times at bat, breaking McGwire's 1998 record of 7.27. His efforts were rewarded after the season ended when he was voted the National League's Most Valuable Player (MVP), the fourth time he had earned that honour.

Barry Lamar Bonds was born on July 24, 1964, in Riverside, Calif. He was the son of Bobby Bonds, an All-Star player for the Giants and the Yankees who also played for several other teams. After showing outstanding talent as a centre fielder in high school, Bonds was drafted by the Giants in 1982. Instead, he chose to attend college at Arizona State University, where he won all-conference honours for three straight years. In 1985 the Pittsburgh Pirates drafted Bonds in the first round. In his first major league season in 1986, he led all National League rookies with 16 home runs, 48 runs batted in, and 36 stolen bases in 113 games. In 1990 he hit .301 with 33 home runs and led the Pirates to a division championship. After the season he was voted the league's MVP.

In 1991 Bonds batted .292 and hit 25 home runs and won a second MVP award. In December 1992 he left Pittsburgh as a free agent and signed a six-year, $43,750,000 contract with the Giants, which at that time was the highest pay for any major league player. Bonds enjoyed a remarkable debut season with

San Francisco; he hit a career-high .336 with 46 home runs and collected his third MVP award. During the next four years, Bonds hit 37, 33, 42, and 40 home runs, and he helped his team reach the play-offs in 1997. In 2000 he smacked 49 home runs—his highest single-season total until 2001—but as in several previous years, he struggled in the play-offs, gaining only three hits in 17 at-bats against the New York Mets. Although overshadowed by his hitting, Bonds's fielding prowess also earned him several Gold Glove awards.

As for the future, Bonds expressed a desire to continue playing for the Giants. After nine years with San Francisco, however, he was eligible for free agency, and there was some doubt that the Giants would be able to afford his salary demands.   (DAVID R. CALHOUN)

Bush, George W.

The presidency of George W. Bush, which began on an uncertain note, was transformed by the terrorist attacks in the U.S. on Sept. 11, 2001. He had come into office in January after having lost the popular vote but with a five-vote margin in the electoral college. Although he had campaigned as a "uniter, not a divider," a number of his appointments and policies had a clear right-wing bias. He quickly moved through Congress a huge tax cut favouring those with high incomes, though other proposals—including an education reform bill and a so-called faith-based initiative that would funnel money to religious groups for social services—were significantly altered or simply languished. Nonetheless, the president pushed ahead with his agenda; he rolled back several environmental policies and appointed a study panel that favoured the partial privatization of Social Security. In foreign affairs the administration took a unilateral, even isolationist, approach,

adopting a hard line toward China, vowing to abandon the 1972 Anti-Ballistic Missile Treaty in order to conduct tests for a missile defense system, and withdrawing from work on treaties dealing with matters such as global warming and bioterrorism. The Bush approach did not appear to be playing well, for at midyear barely 50% of Americans approved of the president's performance.

The terrorist attacks dramatically changed the situation. The American people rallied around the president, and a poll taken shortly afterward gave Bush no less than a 90% approval rating. The focus of the administration shifted to what came to be called the "war on terrorism." Abandoning previous policies, the president consulted with governments throughout the world to develop a coalition and support for military action against the Taliban government in Afghanistan, which harboured Osama bin Laden—the apparent mastermind of the attacks—and he won promises of cooperation even from Russia and China. Although the administration had earlier taken a hands-off approach to the Israeli-Palestinian conflict, it now pressured the two sides to settle their dispute. It reversed its stance on the bioterrorism treaty. While bombing Taliban targets, the administration began making plans for a new government in Afghanistan, even though Bush had earlier disdained such "nation building." A critic of big government, Bush now pushed for expanded powers. He created a cabinet-level Office of Homeland Security under Pennsylvania Gov. Thomas Ridge (q.v.) and won a vast expansion of intelligence-gathering powers. Abandoning strict free-market policies, Bush supported the intervention of the government in support of the U.S. economy, including a bailout of airlines. In November he signed legislation authorizing the federal takeover of airport security within one year.

AP/Wide World Photos

George W. Bush at Ground Zero with New York City Mayor Rudolph Guiliani and Fire Commissioner Thomas Van Essen

Bush was born on July 6, 1946, in New Haven, Conn. He graduated from Yale University (B.A., 1968) and Harvard Business School (M.B.A., 1975) and then worked in the oil business in Texas. He was an adviser to his father, George H.W. Bush, in the late 1980s, and after his father was elected to the presidency in 1988, he returned to Texas. He was managing partner of the Texas Rangers baseball team before being elected governor of Texas in 1994 and winning reelection in 1998.

(ROBERT RAUCH)

Calderón, Sila María

On Jan. 2, 2001, Sila María Calderón, who had served as mayor of San Juan from 1997 to 2000, became Puerto Rico's first female governor. Heading the Popular Democratic Party (PPD) ticket, she narrowly defeated the New Progressive Party candidate Carlos Pesquera by a margin of 48.5% to 45.7% in the November 2000 election. Her victory was viewed as a setback for proponents of Puerto Rican statehood; though Calderón pledged to work for greater Puerto Rican autonomy, she supported its status as a commonwealth with the United States.

Calderón was born in San Juan on Sept. 23, 1942, and was influenced by her father, who was a strong supporter of the PPD. Following a conventional upbringing, Calderón was educated at Manhattanville College, Purchase, N.Y., where she earned a bachelor's degree in political science in 1964; she later gained a master's degree in public administration from the University of Puerto Rico. When Luis Silva Recio, a former professor of Calderón's, was chosen as Puerto Rico's secretary of labour in 1973, she became his executive assistant.

Calderón gained valuable experience in both the public and the private sectors in Puerto Rico. In 1984 she served as the special assistant to Gov. Rafael Hernández Colón. The following year Colón appointed her chief of staff, and she then served as secretary of the interior before becoming secretary of state in 1988. During her private-sector career, she served as a vice president of Citibank and as president of the Commonwealth Investment Co., Inc. In 1996 Calderón was elected mayor of San Juan with just over 50% of the vote and was later chosen as head of the PPD. In the 1998 referendum on Puerto Rican statehood organized by pro-statehood governor Pedro Rosselló, she led the pro-commonwealth campaign; her efforts were rewarded when the majority of votes were cast in favour of Puerto Rico's seeking commonwealth status.

In running for governor in 2000, Calderón promised to end corruption and the U.S. Navy's bombing exercises on Vieques, a large island off the east coast of the main island of Puerto Rico that had been used for naval exercises since 1941. Calderón's strong antibombing stance, plus the killing of a security officer by an errant bomb in 1999 and the island's alarmingly high cancer rate (which many attributed to the exercises), catapulted her to victory.

Despite U.S. Pres. Bill Clinton's offer to hold a referendum on the bombings in Vieques in 2001, Calderón vowed immediately after her inauguration that she would step up efforts to end the military use of the island. On April 24

Calderón launched legal action against the U.S. government, basing the lawsuit on the Noise Control Act of 1972. Although U.S. Pres. George W. Bush had initially resisted ending the exercises, in June his administration announced that the bombings would be permanently halted in 2003, and in a nonbinding referendum in July more than two-thirds of the island's residents voted to end the exercises immediately, significant victories for the very visible governor. In September she announced plans to conduct a binding referendum, allowing voters to choose either to halt the exercises in 2003 or to accept a $50 million aid package with continued bombings.

(MICHAEL I. LEVY)

Capriati, Jennifer

In 2001 American tennis player Jennifer Capriati served up one of the greatest comeback stories in sports as she won her first Grand Slam singles titles, the Australian Open and the French Open. Though such success had once been predicted for the former child prodigy, personal problems, including burnout and alleged drug use, had seemingly ended her career.

Jennifer Maria Capriati was born on March 29, 1976, in New York City and lived in Spain until the age of four, when her family moved to Florida so that she could pursue a tennis career. Capriati quickly attracted attention with her innate talent and bubbly personality. By the time she turned professional in 1990, she had earned more than $6 million in endorsements. During her first year on the Women's Tennis Association (WTA) tour, Capriati set a number of records, including becoming the youngest player to reach the semifinals at a Grand Slam event (the French Open) and to win a match at Wimbledon. In late 1990 she won her first professional title, the Puerto Rico Open, and she finished the

AP/Wide World Photos

American tennis ace Jennifer Capriati on a comeback

year ranked in the WTA top 10—the youngest player ever to do so. With powerful strokes and incredible consistency, Capriati continued to impress in 1991, reaching the semifinals at Wimbledon and the U.S. Open. In 1992 she defeated Steffi Graf to capture the gold medal at the Summer Olympics in Barcelona, Spain.

The pressures of professional play and her parents' divorce, however, began to take their toll on Capriati. After an unexpected first-round loss at the U.S. Open in 1993, she took a break from the tour. Her troubles continued, however, as she was arrested for shoplifting and later for possession of marijuana; she was not convicted in either case. Though she returned to the tour in 1994, she lacked commitment and fitness and faced intense media scrutiny. Playing well only sporadically, Capriati managed to win just one match at a Grand Slam tournament between 1994 and 1998.

In 1999 Capriati regained her focus. Dedicating herself to getting into shape, she lost some 14 kg (30 lbs) and that year claimed her first title since 1993. She finished 1999 ranked number 23 in the world, and the following year, with her father as her coach, Capriati climbed in the rankings to number 14. At the 2001 Australian Open, in her first Grand Slam final, she upset top-seeded Martina Hingis 6–4, 6–3. With the victory, Capriati entered the top 10 for the first time in seven years. Her astonishing comeback continued at the French Open. Two points from defeat, she rallied to overcome Kim Clijsters in a three-set thriller (1–6, 6–4, 12–10) to take the title. Her bid for a Grand Slam (winning all four major events in one year), however, ended with a semifinal loss at Wimbledon.

(AMY TIKKANEN)

Carabias Lillo, Julia

In January 2001 the World Wildlife Fund (WWF) awarded its 23rd annual J. Paul Getty Wildlife Conservation Prize to Mexican environmental scientist Julia Carabias Lillo. The WWF commended Carabias for her efforts to promote public participation in the development of environmental policy. During her term as Mexico's secretary of the environment, natural resources, and fisheries, she doubled the size of the nation's protected-area system to more than 6% of the total area of the country and thereby safeguarded such species as the gray whales and pronghorn antelope of Baja California and the manatees and jaguars of Yucatán.

Carabias was born in 1954 in Mexico City. She gained both undergraduate and master's degrees from the science department at the National Autonomous University of Mexico (UNAM) in Mexico City. In 1977 she began teaching at UNAM, and in 1981 she became a full professor of science there, concentrating her research on such subjects as rain forest regeneration, environmental restoration, and the use of natural resources. She served as a member of UNAM's University Council from 1989 to 1993. Among the works she coauthored were *Manejo de recursos naturales y pobreza rural* (1994), *Areas naturales prioritarias para la conservación en la región* (1997), and *Desarrollo sustentable* (1999). She coauthored *For Earth's Sake* for the UN Conference on Environment and Development, held in Brazil in 1992. Carabias entered government service in early 1994 as president of Mexico's National Institute of Ecology. She was a member of the advisory council for the National Conservation Fund and in late 1994 became secretary of the environment, natural resources, and fisheries, a position she held until late 2000.

In June 2000 she arranged a meeting of officials from Mexico and the U.S. to work on the problem of restoring natural water flows to the Rio Grande, and she also helped create an international task force to deal with a water crisis on the middle section of that river. In addition, she played an important role in enforcing the environmental provisions of the North American Free Trade Agreement. After receiving the WWF prize, Carabias donated the $100,000 cash portion of it to the protection of the Chajul region of southern Mexico's Lacandon forests.   (DAVID R. CALHOUN)

Cavallo, Domingo

When Domingo Cavallo was appointed economy minister on March 20, 2001, Argentines hailed him as a reformer who could rescue the economy from its dire straits. It was the second time in a decade that he had been appointed to the position, and he was the third person to hold it within a month. The Argentine economy, the second largest in South America, had been in recession for nearly three years, with an unemployment rate of 15% and large budget deficits. The government had been unable to meet targets set by the International Monetary Fund (IMF), and there was widespread fear that it would default on loans. Thus, the task before Cavallo, both to invigorate the economy and to restore confidence, was enormous.

Cavallo was born on July 21, 1946, in San Francisco, Córdoba province. He was trained as a certified public accountant (1966) and earned master's (1968) and doctoral (1969) degrees in economics from the National University of Córdoba. In 1977 he earned a Ph.D. in economics from Harvard University. He taught at the National University of Córdoba (1969–84), Catholic University of Córdoba (1970–74), and New York University (1996–97). He was the author of a number of books and articles and the publisher of *Forbes Global* in 1998–99. In addition, he received many awards and prizes, as well as a number of honorary degrees.

Cavallo was the head of Argentina's central bank in 1982, minister of foreign affairs from 1989 to 1991, and economy minister from 1991 to 1996. In the early 1990s the Argentine economy was suffering from runaway inflation, which Cavallo controlled by pegging the value of the peso to the U.S. dollar. He also instituted an extensive privatization plan. The economy revived, but in 1996 Cavallo left the government of Pres. Carlos Menem, which was charged with widespread corruption. The following year Cavallo founded the Action for the Republic (AR), a centre-right party, and won his first term to the Chamber of Deputies. He was unsuccessful in a bid for the presidency in 1999 and was defeated in a run for mayor of Buenos Aires in 2000.

Upon his appointment as economy minister by Pres. Fernando de la Rúa in 2001, Cavallo acted quickly. His program called for increased tax revenues coupled with spending cuts, and he took steps to stimulate investment. These measures, however, failed to pull the Argentine economy out of its slump, and public confidence in the government tanked. After a $400 million bank run on November 30, Cavallo limited cash withdrawals to $250 per week—a move that in part triggered the massive street protests that erupted in Buenos Aires in December. Argentina could not avoid defaulting on its $132 billion foreign debt, and both Cavallo and de la Rúa resigned office on December 20.

                          (ROBERT RAUCH)

Corigliano, John

Premieres during the 2000–01 season of new works by the American composer John Corigliano, including his *Symphony No. 2*, continued his reputation as a prolific writer whose compositions were regularly heard in concert halls. Corigliano did not write in a particular style but rather drew from eclectic influences that varied from work to work. Many of his compositions were virtuosic, tailored to the performers who commissioned them. His music was generally tonal and accessible and was often highly expressive. He wrote in many forms, including works for orchestra, solo instruments, and chamber groups, as well as operas, choral works, and film scores.

Corigliano was born on Feb. 16, 1938, in New York City. His father was concertmaster of the New York Philharmonic from 1943 to 1966, and his mother was a well-known piano teacher. He tried many instruments but had only sporadic lessons. In his teens he began analyzing the scores of compositions while listening to recordings, and he demonstrated an ability to transpose and harmonize. He studied at Columbia University, graduating cum laude in 1959, and also studied at the Manhattan School of Music. He then worked for radio stations, assisted Leonard Bernstein in the production of his Young People's Concerts, produced recordings, and did orchestrations for pop albums. In 1964 his *Sonata for Violin and Piano* won first prize in the chamber music competition at the Festival of Two Worlds in Spoleto, Italy. It received its premiere two years later at Carnegie Hall, and his career as a composer was launched.

Among the best known of Corigliano's compositions were *Concerto for Clarinet and Orchestra* (1977), a favourite that remained in the repertoire; *Pied Piper Fantasy* (1982), a work for flute and orchestra commissioned by James Galway; and *A Dylan Thomas Trilogy* (1999), for three male voices with two choruses and orchestras. *Symphony No. 1*, completed when he was composer in residence with the Chicago Symphony Orchestra from 1987 to 1990, was a response to the AIDS epidemic. Its recording by the orchestra received two Grammys, as the best new composition and the best orchestral performance. *String Quartet* (1995), commissioned for the Cleveland Quartet's final tour, also won two Grammys, for best new composition and best performance. It was the first time two recordings of a composer's works had been so honoured. His opera *The Ghosts of Versailles*, commissioned by the Metropolitan Opera and premiered in 1991, was performed throughout the world. *The Red Violin*, his third film score, won an Academy Award in 2000.

Corigliano taught at institutions in New York City, including the Juilliard School. He received numerous prizes and awards. In 1991 the versatile and prolific composer became a member of the American Academy of Arts and Letters.   (ROBERT RAUCH)

Crowe, Russell

All hailed Russell Crowe in 2001 as the New Zealand-born actor captured a best actor Academy Award for his portrayal of Maximus, a general turned gladiator in ancient Rome. His commanding performance, which combined brutal fight scenes with emotional longing, also helped *Gladiator* win an Oscar for best picture and made the epic one of the highest-grossing films of 2000. The role of a warrior was not unfamiliar to Crowe, whose commitment and intensity had led to his reputation for being combative on film sets and during interviews. Such uncompromising behaviour, however, combined with charisma, dry humour, and rugged good looks, made Crowe one of Hollywood's most sought-after and talked-about performers.

Russell Crowe as Maximus the gladiator

Four years after his birth, April 7, 1964, in Wellington, N.Z., Russell Ira Crowe moved with his family to Australia. He was the son of film- and television-set caterers, and he made his acting debut at the age of six on the television series *Spyforce*. After returning to New Zealand in the late 1970s, Crowe cofounded the rock band Roman Antix, serving as songwriter, guitarist, and lead singer; the group later reformed as 30 Odd Foot of Grunts, and in 2001 it released its second full-length compact disc, *Bastard Life or Clarity*. In the mid-1980s Crowe began performing in musicals, and from 1986 to 1988 he toured with *The Rocky Horror Picture Show* as the cross-dressing Dr. Frank N. Furter. In 1990 he moved to the big screen, appearing in *Prisoners of the Sun* and *The Crossing*. Crowe displayed an innate ability to inhabit the characters he portrayed and for his next film, *Proof* (1991), received a best supporting actor award from the Australian Film Institute (AFI). With the controversial *Romper Stomper* (1992), his career reached a turning point. As a menacing neo-Nazi, Crowe earned an AFI best actor award and attracted the attention of Hollywood. In 1995 he appeared in his first American film, *The Quick and the Dead*. The western, however, had little success at the box office, nor did the series of films that followed, including the cyberthriller *Virtuosity* (1995).

Crowe's breakthrough came as the brutish but vulnerable policeman Bud White in the 1950s crime drama *L.A. Confidential* (1997). His complex performance helped make the film a commercial and critical hit and put Crowe on the Hollywood map. After learning to ice-skate for *Mystery, Alaska* (1999), he gained some 18 kg (40 lb) and 20 years to portray a tobacco-industry whistle-blower in *The Insider* (1999). Crowe immersed himself in the role and earned an Academy Award nomination for best actor. After his star-making turn in *Gladiator*, he appeared as a hostage negotiator opposite Meg Ryan in *Proof of Life* (2000). The film, however, attracted more attention for the offscreen relationship that developed between the two costars than for the onscreen action. For his next project, *A Beautiful Mind*, Crowe transformed himself once again, playing John Forbes Nash, a Nobel Prize-winning mathematician suffering from schizophrenia. It was a predictable choice for the unpredictable actor.   (AMY TIKKANEN)

Daschle, Tom

On June 6, 2001, the U.S. Senate passed from Republican to Democratic control, and Tom Daschle of South Dakota became the new majority leader. The shift occurred without a single change in membership when Sen. James Jeffords of Vermont left the Republican Party to become an independent, which gave the Democrats a 50–49 majority. The Democrats under Daschle thus suddenly found themselves with greater power to determine the legislative agenda and to pass judgment on the appointments and judicial nominees of Pres. George W. Bush.

Thomas Andrew Daschle was born on Dec. 9, 1947, in Aberdeen, S.D. The first member of his family to attend college, he graduated from South Dakota State University in 1969 with a B.A. in political science. From 1969 to 1972 he served in intelligence in the Air Force Strategic Air Command. For five years, from 1972 to 1977, he was a congressional aid to U.S. Sen. James Abourezk, and in 1978 he won the first of four terms in the House of Representatives. In 1986 Daschle defeated the incumbent to win election to the Senate, and he was reelected overwhelmingly in 1992 and 1998. He became a member of the powerful Finance Committee while still a freshman senator and in 1988 was appointed cochair of the Democratic Policy Committee. Other legislative interests of Daschle included agriculture and veterans' and Indian affairs. He compiled a record that was generally liberal on economic matters and moderate on social issues. Daschle gained a reputation for looking out for the interests of his constituents, and every year he drove himself throughout South Dakota to visit each of its 66 counties and to talk to voters.

In 1994 Daschle won the position of Democratic leader by one vote, and he became minority leader in the Senate at the beginning of

Tom Daschle on the summit of Capitol Hill

the 1995 session. A soft-spoken man, he had a reputation for being fair and inclusive, but he was a skillful tactician and could be tough when needed. He opposed the tax-cut bill of President Bush on the grounds that it was fiscally irresponsible and that it unduly benefited the wealthy. As he took control of the Senate, he declared that parts of the Bush legislative program, including drilling for oil in the Arctic National Wildlife Refuge and quick deployment of a missile defense system, would not pass the Senate. In the first three weeks under Daschle's leadership, a patients' bill of rights, guaranteeing certain protections to those who were covered under managed-care health insurance, cleared the Senate despite the president's threat to veto it. Later in the year Daschle took the lead in blaming the Bush tax cut for the disappearance of the budget surplus.   (ROBERT RAUCH)

Delanoë, Bertrand

When on March 18, 2001, Bertrand Delanoë became the first Socialist mayor of Paris since 1871 he entered the history books. On a shorter time scale, Delanoë's victory was also noteworthy for having ended nearly a quarter of a century of domination of the City of Light by the former mayor, French Pres. Jacques Chirac, and his neo-Gaullist party, the Rally for the Republic (RPR).

That domination—and the way it finally crumbled into scandals of corruption and internecine warfare among Chirac's political heirs—eventually contributed heavily to Delanoë's victory. Delanoë's avowed homosexuality proved to be a nonissue, and his low-key style and persistence eventually came to be preferred by Parisians to the higher-profile Socialist rivals who at several points looked certain to eclipse him. He was helped mightily by the split in the RPR ranks between Philippe Séguin, the official RPR candidate, who polled 25.7% of the vote in the March 11 first round of balloting, and Jean Tiberi, the incumbent RPR mayor, who had split with his party but still scored 13.9%. Had these two candidates combined, they would have surpassed Delanoë's 31.4%. Delanoë, however, was able to secure backing from the Greens, who made a strong showing, and he won fairly easily in the final round of voting on March 18.

Delanoë was born on May 30, 1950, in Tunis, Tun. After his early years in North Africa, he went to France and finished his education in Toulouse. He plunged into politics, becoming secretary of the Socialist Federation of Aveyron *département* at the age of 23. His potential was spotted by François Mitterrand, the Socialist Party leader, and he rose fast, becoming a Paris city councillor. Delanoë was elected a deputy to the National Assembly in 1981, and in 1983 he became head of the Socialist Party's national federations. At 33 he was effectively number three in the ruling Socialist Party.

In 1986 Delanoë lost his National Assembly seat, though he kept his seat on the Paris city council. He founded a public relations business, mainly on behalf of institutional clients, including teacher and student associations. He returned to prominence when he became leader of the Socialist group on the city council in 1993, and he led it into the 1995 election with modest success, taking 6 of the 20 arrondissements from the right. That same year saw Chirac end his 18 years as mayor of Paris when he became president. The system of government that Chirac had installed in Paris came under growing criticism and judicial investigation for possible "kickbacks." In a campaign manifesto, Delanoë complained that during Chirac's long time as mayor, he had "progressively transformed the capital into an island outside the law."

After becoming mayor in March, Delanoë had his biggest and most controversial impact in 2001 on the city's traffic system. Elected with Green support, he embarked on a series of controversial measures to discriminate against cars in favour of other forms of transport. These included closing the Seine riverbank motorway from mid-July to mid-August, adding new bus lanes on main boulevards, and establishing studies on the reintroduction of trams and more use of the Seine to carry cargo.   (DAVID BUCHAN)

Duncan Smith, Iain
On Sept. 13, 2001, in the wake of its second successive crushing general election defeat, the U.K.'s Conservative Party elected as its leader a right-wing MP whose most distinctive policy was hostility to closer links between the U.K. and the European Union (EU). Iain Duncan Smith's victory was all the more remarkable for the fact that, of the five candidates who sought the Tory leadership, he was alone in never having served before as a government minister.

George Iain Duncan Smith was born on April 9, 1954, in Edinburgh. His father had been a Royal Air Force pilot during World War II and had been credited with shooting down 19 German aircraft. Duncan Smith was educated privately, including a period at HMS Conway, a school in Wales where the sons of officers were brought up in spartan conditions. In 1975 he entered army training at the Royal Military Academy, Sandhurst, and he was subsequently commissioned into the Scots Guards, rising to the rank of captain in 1979. In 1981 he decided that his future lay in civilian life and joined the defense electronics company GEC-Marconi as a sales and marketing executive—a role that took him frequently to the U.S., where he forged links with Pentagon officials and Republican politicians. In 1982 he married the Hon. Elizabeth Wynne Fremantle, daughter of the 5th Baron Cottesloe.

In 1992 Duncan Smith entered the House of Commons as MP for Chingford and Woodford Green, strongly Conservative middle-class suburbs on the outskirts of London. He quickly established himself as a member of the anti-EU "awkward squad" of Conservative backbench MPs who attacked their own party's government for signing the EU's Maastricht Treaty and who frequently voted against the government on European issues. He also established himself as a right-winger on other issues, most notably by arguing that the role of the state should be curbed significantly and that taxes should be sharply reduced.

When the Conservatives lost power in 1997, the party's new leader, William Hague, appointed Duncan Smith to his shadow cabinet, first as the party's official spokesman on social security. He became shadow defense secretary in 1999, but he continued to be best known for his uncompromising views on Europe. When Hague resigned following the party's disastrous performance in the general election held on June 7, 2001, Duncan Smith stood for the party leadership, promising that he would "never" support the entry of Britain into the EU's single currency. In the final runoff against his pro-European (and far more experienced) rival, Kenneth Clarke, Duncan Smith's views proved to be far more in tune with the party membership, and he won 61% of the votes cast. (PETER KELLNER)

Ellroy, James
American author James Ellroy, long regarded as a master of the crime-fiction genre, continued his move into the realm of general fiction with the publication of his novel *The Cold Six Thousand* in May 2001. The book, which

covered the turbulent years between the assassination of U.S. Pres. John F. Kennedy in 1963 and that of his brother Robert in 1968, was the sequel to Ellroy's best-selling 1995 novel *American Tabloid*. As in his earlier crime novels, themes of violence and corruption were still prominently featured, but *The Cold Six Thousand* and *American Tabloid* aimed for a much broader scope; together they represented the author's expressed ambition to "re-create 20th-century American history through fiction."

Lee Earle Ellroy was born on March 4, 1948, in Los Angeles. His parents were divorced in 1954, and Ellroy moved with his mother to El Monte, Calif., a suburb of Los Angeles. In 1958 his mother was murdered there, a crime that was never solved; in his autobiographical *My Dark Places* (1996), Ellroy wrote about the crime and its effect on his life. After his mother's death Ellroy lived with his father. He attended high school in Fairfax, a predominantly Jewish section of Los Angeles, but was expelled before graduation for "ranting about Nazism" in his English class. He then enlisted in the army but soon decided that he did not belong there and convinced an army psychiatrist that he was not mentally fit for combat. After three months he received a dishonourable discharge. Soon afterward his father died, and after a brief stay with a friend of his father, Ellroy landed on the streets of Los Angeles. From the age of 18 he lived in parks and vacant apartments; he spent most of his time drinking, taking drugs, and reading crime novels. After being jailed for breaking into a vacant apartment, Ellroy got a job at a bookstore. Meanwhile, he had become addicted to Benzedrex, a sinus inhaler that he swallowed to gain a euphoric high. With his health deteriorating and fearing for his sanity, Ellroy joined Alcoholics Anonymous and found steady work as a golf caddy. At the age of 30 he wrote and sold his first novel, *Brown's Requiem* (1981).

Most of Ellroy's books dealt with crime and corruption. Among the best known were four novels that constituted the "L.A. Quartet" series: *Black Dahlia* (1987); *The Big Nowhere* (1988); *L.A. Confidential* (1990), made into an acclaimed movie of the same title in 1997; and *White Jazz* (1992).

After publishing *White Jazz*, Ellroy produced *American Tabloid* and *The Cold Six Thousand*. In 2001 Ellroy fans were happy to hear that a cable television miniseries, entitled *James Ellroy's Los Angeles*, was set to air in September 2002 and that a film adaptation of *My Dark Places* was also in the works. (DAVID R. CALHOUN)

Grant, Hugh
Although in real life British film actor Hugh Grant could occasionally be a scoundrel—witness his 1995 arrest with a prostitute and his resultant "I did a bad thing" apology tour of American television talk shows—in "reel" life he was generally known to the public as the boyishly appealing leading man who finally got the girl. That was not the case in 2001, however, when in *Bridget Jones's Diary* he portrayed the womanizing boss and scheming

sometime lover of the film's leading character. According to Grant, his character was closer to his off-screen personality than most of the roles he previously had played. In most people's minds, however, he was not a cad but rather an endearing, stammering, bumbling, and funny love interest—much like the one they had taken to in Grant's first big hit, *Four Weddings and a Funeral* (1994).

Hugh John Mungo Grant was born on Sept. 9, 1960, in London. It was not until his senior year at the University of Oxford, where he was studying English literature, that he became involved in acting. He appeared in a student film, *Privileged* (1982), and joined the Oxford University Dramatic Society. Following graduation (1982), Grant wrote and occasionally performed in radio commercials and attempted to write a novel before turning once again to acting. His stage debut came at the Nottingham (Eng.) Playhouse in 1985. He went from there to London, where he formed the Jockeys of Norfolk comedy troupe, for which he wrote, directed, and performed in revues. He began his professional film career with the James Ivory–Ismail Merchant film *Maurice* (1987), for which he won a best actor award at the Venice Film Festival, and added numerous films and television productions to his credits, including *White Mischief* (1988), *Impromptu* (1991), *The Remains of the Day* (1993), and *Sirens* (1994). It was his charming performance in *Four Weddings and a Funeral*, however, that brought him to the attention of the general public; he also won the Golden Globe best actor award and was named best actor by the British Academy of Film and Television Arts. Grant quickly followed up with *An Awfully Big Adventure, The Englishman Who Went up a Hill but Came down a Mountain, Restoration, Nine Months,* and *Sense and Sensibility,* all of which were released in 1995. He took on a more serious role in *Extreme Measures* (1996) but returned to romantic comedy in *Notting Hill* (1999), *Mickey Blue Eyes* (1999), and *Small Time Crooks* (2000).

Given that one of Grant's most commented-upon physical attributes was his unruly mop of hair, audiences for his forthcoming film, *About a Boy,* were in for another surprise. In addition to playing another irresponsible womanizer—though this time one who wises up—he would be sporting a much shorter and more conventional haircut.

(BARBARA WHITNEY)

Graves, Michael
In a ceremony on Feb. 16, 2001, American architect Michael Graves was honoured with what many in his field considered the ultimate compliment—recognition of excellence by one's own peers—when he was presented with the 2001 Gold Medal of the American Institute of Architects, the AIA's lifetime achievement award. Graves's designs had ranged from large multiuse buildings, office interiors, and hotels to private domestic commissions and a host of consumer products.

Graves was born on July 9, 1934, in Indianapolis, Ind. He earned degrees in architecture from the University of Cincinnati, Ohio, and

Michael Graves reflects on his designs (the Alessi teakettle)

Steve Simon

Harvard University in 1958 and 1959, respectively. In 1960 he attended the American Academy in Rome. The influence of Italian architecture and design was clearly present in his work, as were the colours that reflected the mood of Tuscany and the Mediterranean—warm terra-cotta tones, azures, and reds—and that figured prominently in the overall conception of his projects.

Influential as a theorist as well as a practicing architect and designer, Graves had taught at Princeton University in the school of architecture since 1962; the offices of his firm were also located in the town of Princeton. Though some described Graves as a "Postmodern classicist," he resisted such a categorization. His style was marked by a synthesis of classical elements, strong geometric shapes, and frequent playful touches. In the Renaissance-inspired facade for his design of the Walt Disney Corp. headquarters, figures of the Seven Dwarfs were positioned across the entablature in place of ordinary columns. Some of his other well-known projects included the Swan and Dolphin hotels at Disney World in Orlando, Fla., and the Humana Building in Louisville, Ky.—a 27-story high-rise with a dramatic glass pyramid over its entrance and an open porch area on the 25th floor. Graves's projects were purposefully geared toward capturing public attention. In late 1998 and for the following year and a half, visitors to Washington, D.C., saw his inventive interpretation of scaffolding enshrouding the Washington Memorial during its renovation. Public reactions to Graves's solution were mixed; the nearly 58 km (36 mi) of aluminum scaffolding covered with a layer of blue mesh took four months to erect. The scaffolding was intended to perform on both functional and aesthetic levels, protecting workers while maintaining a certain visual interest during the restoration.

The extra-architectural nature of this project pointed to the breadth of Graves's interests

and the range of his endeavours. In addition to buildings and interior spaces, he designed small accessories and household objects that bore his personal stamp, including lamps, salt and pepper shakers, bookends, watches, picture frames, and, most famously, the Alessi stainless-steel teakettle with instantly recognizable bird spout and blue handle. His design-friendly products were also featured at discount chain Target Corp. stores. Despite the scale or purpose, Graves approached each project with the same humanist philosophy of design that he had worked to refine for nearly 40 years.   (MEGHAN DAILEY)

Gusinsky, Vladimir

Media tycoon Vladimir Gusinsky was the first Russian businessman to recognize the political and financial benefits of the mass media. His holdings included television, radio, newspapers, and magazines known both for their professionalism and for the critical stance they often adopted toward Kremlin policies. In 2001 Gusinsky lost control of his media empire at the end of what some observers depicted as a Kremlin-inspired campaign to destroy him.

Vladimir Aleksandrovich Gusinsky was born into a Jewish family in Moscow on Oct. 6, 1952. He studied at a petrochemical institute and began his career as a theatre actor and director in the provincial city of Tula. In the late 1980s, however, he took advantage of a new mood of economic liberalization to establish himself in private business. Gusinsky differed from the majority of those who made their fortunes at that time by exploiting privileged backgrounds to strip the assets of the Soviet state. In cooperation with an American partner, Gusinsky by contrast set up a consulting company that facilitated joint ventures between Soviet and Western firms. In 1989 he established Most Bank, which soon became one of the most active and innovative com-

mercial banking groups in Russia. In 1993 Most began to handle the accounts of the Moscow city government and the vast amounts of money passing through them. In turn, Mayor Yury Luzhkov's administration reportedly helped Most acquire some of the choicest development plots in Moscow's booming real-estate market. This made Gusinsky many enemies, while the Kremlin suspected him of financing Luzhkov's presidential ambitions. Gusinsky was one of seven "oligarchs" who, alarmed by the prospect of a Communist victory in Russia's presidential election in 1996, bankrolled Pres. Boris Yeltsin's reelection campaign.

In 1992 Gusinsky founded the newspaper *Segodnya* and the independent television channel NTV. Later he acquired the Ekho Moskvy radio station, and in 1996 he launched a weekly political magazine, *Itogi*, a joint venture with *Newsweek*. NTV raised Kremlin hackles both through its critical coverage of Russia's 1994–96 war in Chechnya and through its merciless satirizing of the foibles of Russia's leaders. In 1997 Gusinsky left his post at Most Bank to concentrate on his media interests, run by the private holding company Media-Most.

Following Russia's 1998 financial crash, advertising revenues dried up. To keep his publications afloat, Gusinsky was obliged to borrow large sums of money. He turned for funding to the natural gas monopoly Gazprom. This put him heavily in debt to a company seen by many as an arm of the Russian state. Russia's new president, Vladimir Putin, came to power in 2000 vowing to strip the "oligarchs"—Russia's richest businessmen—of their privileged access to political power. Within weeks of Putin's inauguration, Gusinsky had been jailed on embezzlement charges. Then Gazprom began to demand repayment of its loans. After a bitter court battle, Gusinsky was forced unwillingly to relinquish control of his media holdings and left the country for exile in the Spanish resort of Sotogrande. NTV was placed under new management; *Itogi* and *Segodnya* were closed down. The Russian government demanded Gusinsky's extradition, but the Spanish courts refused.

Gusinsky and his supporters depicted him as a champion of media freedom and victim of Kremlin persecution. The Russian authorities countered that the case was a matter simply of property rights and the repayment of loans. Many felt that the truth contained elements of both interpretations and lay somewhere in between.   (EDITOR)

Haakon, Crown Prince, and Crown Princess Mette-Marit

On Aug. 25, 2001, Crown Prince Haakon of Norway married Mette-Marit Tjessem Høiby, who was not only a commoner but also a single mother when they began dating in 1999. Even in permissive Norway—where in 1998 almost 50% of firstborn children were born to unmarried women—the prince's choice of bride raised eyebrows.

The objection, however, seemed to be less the issue of descent—her four-year-old son,

Mette-Marit, Marius, and Haakon

Marius, could never be king—than the people with whom the new crown princess had associated in her former life. Less than a week before they tied the knot, the crown prince and his bride-to-be held a press conference in which she apologized for her former life and made her statement serve as both a plea and an object lesson. She hoped to curtail future questions about her past and, without admitting she had used drugs, used the occasion to condemn them. For that was the issue Norwegians cared most about; her former boyfriend (and the father of her son) had been sentenced to prison for assault and possession of cocaine. Crown Prince Haakon, who acknowledged in mid-May 2000 that Mette-Merit was his girlfriend, was completely supportive of her, as were his parents, King Harald V and Queen Sonja. The king did not stand in the way of the marriage, perhaps because he had had to wait nine years before his father, King Olav V, and the Norwegian Parliament approved his marrying commoner Sonja Haraldsen.

The crown prince was born on July 20, 1973, in Oslo. Though he had an older sister, Märtha Louise, Haakon Magnus was the only son of then crown prince Harald and crown princess Sonja, and as such he was from birth heir to the throne. (The succession law was changed in the 1990s.) He had a happy childhood, mostly out of the limelight. After four years of service in the navy, including time at the Naval Academy in Bergen, he broke with Norwegian tradition to attend the University of California, Berkeley, where he obtained (1999) a B.A. in political science. Thereafter he enrolled at the University of Oslo to study law and social science. On Dec. 1, 2000, he introduced his fiancée, with whom he was already sharing an apartment, to the public.

Mette-Marit Tjessem Høiby was born on Aug. 19, 1973, in Kristiansand, Nor., and grew up under quite different circumstances, with an ordinary middle-class upbringing. She was an exchange student in Wangaratta, Australia, during six months of her high-school years. Thereafter she experienced what she called a "youth rebellion" that resulted in her "wild life." That life came to an end for her in an almost fairy-tale manner when she met, and ultimately married, a prince.

(KATHLEEN KUIPER)

Handler, Daniel

Capitalizing on the unsentimental tastes of legions of 10–13-year-old readers, American storyteller Daniel Handler (a.k.a. Lemony Snicket) captured the imagination of his youthful audiences with *A Series of Unfortunate Events*. These unhappy morality tales—featuring titillating alliterative titles such as *The Reptile Room* (1999), *The Austere Academy* (2000), and *The Miserable Mill* (2000)—had sold more than one million copies by 2001.

Handler was born on Feb. 28, 1970, in San Francisco. After earning a B.A. in 1992 from Wesleyan University, Middletown, Conn., he received an Olin fellowship to write a novel, which he discarded upon finishing. He returned to his hometown, worked as an administrative assistant and a writer for a radio program, and, in the meantime, wrote another novel before moving to New York City, where he began reviewing movies and reading manuscripts for a literary agent. His novel was rejected so many times that he began hosting a reading series called "Great Writers Who Can't Get Published." Shortly thereafter, he appeared on the literary scene with *The Basic Eight* (1999), a critically acclaimed novel about a high-school student bludgeoned with a croquet mallet wielded by a classmate. *Watch Your Mouth* (2000), written in the form of an opera, was a satiric work centred on the theme of incest.

Remembering his youth, Handler had railed against the number of novels devoted to sports or fantasy themes. When urged to turn his hand to creating the kind of books that he would have enjoyed, Handler resurrected Lemony Snicket—a name he had invented when requesting materials from a right-wing organization for a book project—as the doleful narrator and author of the series. *The Bad Beginning* (1999), which introduced the travails of three orphaned siblings (and also introduced his habit of naming some characters after past literary luminaries, in this case Klaus, Sunny, and Violet Baudelaire), launched the series and established an aura of mystery around Snicket. He was typically featured on the back of the hardcover books as a shadowy figure—his image appearing out of focus or away from the camera.

Handler deftly served as Snicket's representative at book events, regaling his listeners with the travails of Snicket as well as entertaining them with accordion music and dire tales about danger lurking in the most unlikely places. A favourite story recounted how a bug had bitten Snicket in his armpit and prevented him from appearing. Handler also warned readers not to read or purchase the Snicket books, which typically feature unhappy

Daniel Handler a.k.a. Lemony Snicket

beginnings, middles, and endings. Notwithstanding, his fans waited with eager anticipation for each new offering in the projected 13-book series. The latest installments of Snicket's imagination—*The Ersatz Elevator, The Vile Village, The Hostile Hospital*—all appeared in 2001.   (KAREN J. SPARKS)

Harvey, Paul

In 2001 American broadcaster Paul Harvey was off the air for part of the year after damaging a vocal cord. His vastly popular radio programs, however, passed major milestones: *The Rest of the Story*, heard Mondays through Saturdays, turned 25 in May, while *Paul Harvey News and Comment*, on the air twice each weekday, celebrated 50 years of syndication. Harvey's mix of current events news, human-interest anecdotes, and common-sense editorials reached some 24 million listeners via 1,600 radio stations daily. His staccato pacing, bouncing intonation, and signature hooks ("Stand by . . . for news!"; "Paul Harvey . . . good day!") helped make his voice one of the most recognizable in the history of radio.

Paul Harvey Aurandt was born on Sept. 4, 1918, in Tulsa, Okla. He was descended from five generations of Baptist preachers. His mother raised him and his sister alone after their father was shot to death. At 14 he landed a job at KVOO radio in Tulsa, and he was soon doing voice work there. He studied briefly at the University of Tulsa but quit to work full-time in radio; by age 25 he had gained experience at stations across the plains and the Midwest and had covered the activities of the U.S. military for the Office of War Information. In 1940 he married Lynne ("Angel") Cooper, who afterward took control of his business affairs. Following a medical discharge from the Army Air Corps in 1944, he shortened his name to Paul Harvey and began broadcasting for Chicago radio station WENR. *Paul Harvey News and Comment* proved immediately popular in Chicago and was nationally syndicated by the American Broadcasting Company in 1951. In 1976 the program spun off *The Rest of the Story*, whose brief biographical narratives were written by the Harveys' only child, Paul Harvey Aurandt, Jr.

Harvey often opined on rising taxes, bloated government, and the decay of American values. He called his particular conservative cast "political fundamentalism." Though he was associated with prominent figures of the American right—he once hosted Sen. Joseph McCarthy at his home and was short-listed among George C. Wallace's potential vice presidential running mates in 1968—Harvey resisted identification with any ideology but his own. He publicly urged Pres. Richard Nixon to abandon the Vietnam War in 1970, and in the 1980s he decried several of Pres. Ronald Reagan's conservative positions.

Apart from his radio work, Harvey regularly appeared as a television and newspaper commentator and published several books, including *Remember These Things* (1952), *Autumn of Liberty* (1954), and *You Said It, Paul Harvey* (1970). In 2001 his son and actor David Hartman split Harvey's broadcasting duties while he recovered from surgery in May to repair his vocal cord, and he returned to the airwaves in late August.   (COLIN J. MURPHY)

Hau, Lene Vestergaard

In 2001 Danish scientist Lene Vestergaard Hau became one of the all-time most prominent women physicists when the journal *Nature* published a paper in which Hau and a team of physicists at the Rowland Institute for Science in Cambridge, Mass., described how they had sent a pulse of laser light into a tiny cloud of extremely cold gas, halted the light, stored it for a fraction of a second, and then released it. Though Hau's team was not the only one to achieve this feat, the latest research related to altering the speed of light had its roots in an experiment conducted by Hau in 1999. In that experiment Hau and her colleagues at the Rowland Institute shone lasers through a cloud of ultracold sodium atoms—known as a Bose-Einstein condensate—which effectively slowed light from its normal speed of about 299,792 km (186,282 mi) per second to 61 km (38 mi) per hour. It was believed that these advances could translate into practical applications that would substantially improve telecommunications and computers.

Hau was born on Nov. 13, 1959, in Vejle, Den. From an early age she enjoyed mathematics, and she excelled at school, skipping the 10th grade. She entered Aarhus University, where she was drawn to studying physics owing to an interest in mathematics and quantum mechanics. She earned a B.S. degree in mathematics in 1984, an M.S. in physics in 1986, and a Ph.D. in physics in 1991, all from Aarhus University. Her studies included seven months at CERN in Geneva. She accepted a postdoctoral position on the faculty at Harvard University, where she later became the Gordon McKay Professor of Applied Physics. Hau also took a position at the Rowland Institute, serving as principal investigator for the Atom Cooling Group. In 1994, working with Jene A. Golovchenko at the Rowland Institute, Hau developed one of the first elements that led to the slowing of light. Called a "candlestick," the device wicks sodium atoms out of molten sodium metal and projects them into a cooling apparatus that, by using lasers, cools the atoms to a temperature 50 billionths of a degree above absolute zero.

Hau attributed her success in a field dominated by men to her upbringing and her homeland. Her parents, she said, encouraged her in her studies just as much as they did her brother. In addition, in Denmark laypeople and other scientists regarded physicists highly, and research was sometimes funded by private interests. Hau herself had studied for a year on a scholarship subsidized by Carlsberg brewers.   (ANTHONY G. CRAINE)

Herzog, Jacques, and de Meuron, Pierre

The 2001 Pritzker Architecture Prize was awarded to Jacques Herzog and Pierre de Meuron, a pair of Swiss architects whose modernist designs were characterized by a reliance on established architectural principles coupled with imaginative new techniques suited to each individual project. A prime example of this meeting of tradition and innovation was the Dominus Winery in Napa, Calif. Essentially a long, low-slung rectangular box, the building had a facade constructed of local stone held together with wire rather than mortar. Some portions of the stone walls were packed tightly enough to provide insulation from heat and cold, while other sections were stacked loosely enough to allow air and light to penetrate where needed.

Both men were born in Basel, Switz., in 1950, Herzog on April 19 and de Meuron on May 8. Friends and schoolmates during childhood, the two began at an early age to work together on drawings and models. When it came time to attend college, neither chose to study architecture initially. Herzog first studied commercial design before attending the University of Basel to study biology and chemistry. With an interest in drawing and math, de Meuron pursued a degree in civil engineering. Unsatisfied after a year of school, both decided to study architecture, first at the Swiss Federal Institute of Technology and Lausanne, then at the institute's Zürich campus, where they received their degrees in 1975. Among their instructors was Aldo Rossi, who would receive the Pritzker Prize in 1990. After three years as professor's assistants, Herzog and de Meuron established their own architecture firm in Basel. Herzog took the post of visiting professor at Cornell University, Ithaca, N.Y., in 1983, and both men became visiting professors at Harvard University in 1989. Their firm, meanwhile, grew to 120 employees in offices in Basel; London; Munich, Ger.; and San Francisco.

Their most prominent project was the Tate Gallery of Modern Art in London. To create the museum, Herzog and de Meuron converted a former power plant on the South Bank of the River Thames. Incorporating traditional elements with Art Deco and modernism, the architects created what they described as a "building of the 21st century." Upon opening to the public in May 2000, the new Tate Modern received critical acclaim and served as a catalyst for the revitalization of its South Bank neighbourhood. Other high-profile projects included the nearly transparent headquarters of a cough drop manufacturer in Laufen, Switz., in which glass panels made up much of the facade; a railroad utility building in Basel that was sheathed in copper strips; and the Rudin House in Leymen, France—a cartoonish-looking residence that, perched on a platform, appeared to float above the landscape.

Herzog likened the pair's body of work to that of Pop artist Andy Warhol, who used common, recognizable forms and objects and attempted to create something new from them. "We love to destroy the clichés of architecture," Herzog said.   (ANTHONY G. CRAINE)

Hill, Faith

Though American Faith Hill did not release a new album or embark on a concert tour in 2001, the country and pop singer sustained her star status. Besides contributing a song, "There You'll Be," to the sound track for the movie *Pearl Harbor,* she won three Grammy Awards in country categories, including one she shared with her husband, country singer Tim McGraw; she appeared on Barbara Walters's annual Academy Award-night special on ABC; and she performed in the landmark *America: A Tribute to Heroes,* a cross-network TV benefit for victims and rescue workers in the September 11 terrorist attacks in the U.S.

Audrey Faith Perry was born on Sept. 21, 1967, in Jackson, Miss., and was the adopted daughter of Pat and Edna Perry. The family later moved to the nearby town of Star, Miss. Influenced by Elvis Presley, Reba McEntire, and Tammy Wynette, Hill left home at the age of 19 to pursue a career as a professional singer in Nashville, Tenn.

In 1993 she released her first album, *Take Me as I Am,* which included two country chart-topping singles, "Wild One" and "Piece of My Heart." Her second album, *It Matters to Me,* appeared in 1995 and produced a number one single of the same title. It was her third album—*Faith*—issued in 1998, that propelled Hill to major stardom; helped by the crossover success of "This Kiss," a romantic up-tempo song, the album sold five million copies. In the fall of 1998 Hill began appearing as a headliner, and in April 1999 she launched her first major tour as a solo artist. Her four-month This Kiss tour traveled to 50 cities.

Hill's fourth album, *Breathe,* appeared in November 1999 and set the stage for a spectacular run of media exposure, touring, and industry awards. It debuted at the number one spot on the *Billboard* country album chart and on the *Billboard* 200 chart, which measured all music genres. During 2000 Hill sang the national anthem at Super Bowl XXXIV, and she performed at the Academy Awards, during which Pepsi premiered a commercial featuring her. *People* magazine named Hill one of the 50 most beautiful people of 2000, and she served as a celebrity spokesperson for Cover Girl cosmetics and Pepsi.

Hill also starred in the VH1 Divas 2000, together with Diana Ross, Mariah Carey, and Donna Summer. Hill's first network TV special, *Faith!,* aired Thanksgiving Day 2000 on CBS, and her recording of "Where Are You Christmas" was featured in the film *How the Grinch Stole Christmas* (2000). When Hill and McGraw combined talents for their Soul 2 Soul Tour 2000, more than one million fans turned out for more than 60 shows. Both the Los Angeles-based Academy of Country Music and the Nashville-based Country Music Association named Hill top female vocalist for 2000. She had reportedly sold more than 20 million albums worldwide, including more than 7 million copies of *Breathe.*   (JAY ORR)

Iverson, Allen

With his remarkable play during the 2000–01 National Basketball Association (NBA) regular season and a gritty, determined performance during the play-offs, Allen Iverson, a guard for the Philadelphia 76ers, forced the NBA and its fans to accept him as one of the league's elite players. Previously known primarily as a talented but difficult player with a checkered past, Iverson won the league scoring title, earned Most Valuable Player honours, and led his team to the NBA finals, all during a season in which he improved relations with his coach and developed a new reputation as a team player.

Allen Ezail Iverson was born on June 7, 1975, in Hampton, Va. Growing up in poverty with his mother and two sisters, Iverson attended Bethel High School, where he led the school's football and basketball teams to state championships his junior year. At age 17 Iverson was jailed after being accused of starting a racially charged brawl in a bowling alley, but his conviction was later overturned owing to lack of evidence. He was offered a scholarship to Georgetown University, Washington, D.C., where in two years he averaged 23 points per game and won two Big East Conference Defensive Player of the Year awards before making the decision to leave school to play professionally. Iverson was chosen first overall in the 1996 NBA draft by the 76ers.

Despite being one of the smallest players in the league (1.8 m, 75 kg [6 ft, 165 lb]), Iverson made a big splash immediately, scoring 30 points in his first game and, late in the 1996–97 season, stringing together five consecutive games of 40 points or more. He led his team with a 23.5 scoring average and won Rookie of the Year honours. His quickness and his signature crossover dribble often left even the best defenders helpless. His refusal to conform to a conservative off-the-court persona, such as that of Michael Jordan, made Iverson an outcast. His hip-hop-styled clothing, flashy jewelry, and braided hair were not part of the image the league wanted to promote. One NBA publication even went so far as to obscure Iverson's tattoos in a photo. An arrest after his rookie year (all charges were later dropped) tarnished his reputation further.

Iverson led his team in scoring and steals in each of his first five seasons, winning the league scoring title in 1998–99 and being named to the All-NBA first team. During his first several years in the league, however, his clashes with 76ers coach Larry Brown over late arrivals to practice and other issues became as well known as his scoring prowess. He was portrayed by the media as a selfish, disruptive player. At the beginning of the 2000 season, Iverson released a controversial rap song from his upcoming album that contained derogatory lyrics about women and homosexuals, which further cast a negative light. As the season progressed, however, Iverson began to show a new side. He worked harder in practice, praised his teammates in public, and mended his relationship with Brown. The NBA, meanwhile, began to recognize that Iverson had a huge following of young fans who identified with his rebellious image.

During the 2001 play-offs, Iverson staged one brilliant effort after another, averaging 32.9 points despite nagging injuries. During game four of the Eastern Conference finals against the Milwaukee Bucks, Iverson was elbowed in the mouth and knocked to the floor. He went on to score 28 points in a 76ers win, later admitting that he had swallowed the blood from his wound as he ran the court so that the ref-

Hoops marvel Allen Iverson

erees would not force him to leave the game to be treated. The moment typified Iverson's season and helped to define a new image for one of the game's most talked-about players.

(ANTHONY G. CRAINE)

Jo, Sumi

In 2001 South Korean soprano Sumi Jo continued to grace the stages of major opera houses and concert halls throughout the world; she also released a critically acclaimed compact disc (CD), *Prayers,* which featured her renditions of religious songs ranging from Franz Schubert's "Ave Maria" to the hymn "Amazing Grace." *Prayers* followed Jo's release of another highly praised CD, *Only Love* (2000), a collection of songs from Broadway musicals.

Soo Kyong Jo was born in Seoul, S.Kor., on Nov. 22, 1962. She began studying music at an early age. She entered the music school of Seoul National University but left in her second year to attend the Accademia di Santa Cecilia in Rome. There, beginning in 1983, she studied keyboard and vocal music. After graduating in 1985, she came to the attention of Austrian conductor Herbert von Karajan, who praised the beauty of Jo's voice, and on his recommendation she appeared at the Salzburg (Austria) Festival in 1986. In the same year, she made her operatic debut as Gilda in Guiseppe Verdi's *Rigoletto*, and in 1988 she appeared as Oscar in that composer's *Un ballo in maschera*, with Karajan conducting. She recorded the work with Karajan and counted Oscar among her favourite roles. During the late 1980s Jo took first place in a number of international competitions. By the end of the decade her career had been established, and she was on her way to becoming an international star.

Thierry Cohen, Paris, France/Warner Classics International

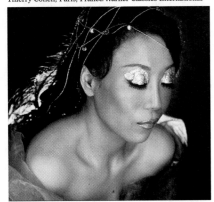

Korean coloratura Sumi Jo

Jo's light, expressive voice made her well suited for the major coloratura roles of the operatic repertoire. She was particularly noted for her portrayal of the Queen of the Night in Mozart's *Die Zauberflöte* and for her title role in Donizetti's *Lucia di Lammermoor*. Among the operas of Richard Strauss, she sang Sophia in *Der Rosenkavalier* and Zerbinetta in *Ariadne auf Naxos*. In the 1992 Grammy Award-winning recording of Strauss's *Die Frau ohne Schatten* by the Vienna Philharmonic, conducted by Georg Solti, Jo was the Voice of the Falcon. She also recorded a number of collections of arias as well as CDs that had crossover appeal to popular music audiences.

In 1993 Jo was named the best soprano of the year at the sixth La Siola Doro in Forli, Italy. She found herself in demand by the leading opera companies of the world. Among European houses, she sang at La Scala (Milan), Covent Garden (London), and the Vienna Staatsoper. In the U.S. she performed at the Metropolitan Opera in New York City and at Lyric Opera of Chicago. Her résumé also included engagements in South America, Australia, and Asia.   (ROBERT RAUCH)

Jung, Andrea

Though Avon Products, Inc., the world's largest direct-selling company, had built its reputation selling women's cosmetics door-to-door, its 115-year-old sales strategy was being revamped to draw on Avon CEO Andrea Jung's background in department store retailing. In 2001 Avon announced plans to sell beauty and lifestyle products through retail stores while maintaining the three million Avon sales representatives in more than 130 countries. The company chose to focus on American department stores with the planned September launch of a new beComing line in 125 Sears and 75 J.C. Penney stores. Before the products were launched, however, Sears canceled its plan to participate, and J.C. Penney was left as the sole retailer opening exclusive Avon boutiques.

Jung was born in 1959 in Toronto but moved to Wellesley, Mass., with her family when she was a young child. Her parents (her father was an architect, and her mother was a chemical engineer) were Chinese immigrants who had high expectations for their daughter. She took piano lessons and was schooled in Mandarin Chinese. After graduating magna cum laude (1979) from Princeton University, Jung followed her interest in fashion and retailing by joining Bloomingdale's executive training program. Her career choice might have shocked her parents—at least until Jung achieved increasingly important positions at I. Magnin (senior vice president and general merchandise manager) and Neiman Marcus (executive vice president).

When she joined Avon in 1993—she began as a consultant but was quickly promoted to president of product marketing for American operations—Jung opposed the company's move into retailing. She saw that the products and the people were not ready to expand beyond the company's traditional direct-selling approach. By the time she was named president in 1998 and CEO in 1999, she and others had already been studying new sales approaches that might take advantage of traditional retailing and Internet marketing while maintaining productive relationships with the company's sales representatives worldwide.

Jung was known for making informed decisions. As an attractive Asian American (Mattel made an Andrea Jung Barbie doll for her), she promoted a glamorous image for the company and served as a role model for customers, company representatives, and rising executives who took cues from her example. She was also a figurehead for the company's commitment to diversity.

Foremost, Avon was a company for and about women, and Jung epitomized the successful woman. Under her leadership Avon continued to prosper—exceeding $5 billion in annual sales—even as it sought new opportunities. In addition, her dedication to women's health was recognized in 2000 when she was named the recipient of the Award for Distinguished Service from the Columbia-Presbyterian Medical Center; the Avon Worldwide Fund for Women's Health had sustained programs in more than 30 countries and provided more than $100 million. Jung pledged to increase that amount to $200 million by the end of 2002.   (SARAH FORBES ORWIG)

Kabila, Joseph

On Jan. 26, 2001, Joseph Kabila was inaugurated as the president of the Democratic Republic of the Congo (DRC). He was the eldest son of the former president, Laurent Kabila, who had been shot by a bodyguard and apparently killed on January 16, although the death was not announced until two days later. (*See* OBITUARIES.) The son—named interim president on January 17 and subsequently chosen to succeed his father—inherited a country that, for the most part, was without a functioning government or basic services and whose economy had largely been ruined during two and a half years of civil war. Almost nothing was known about the new president either inside or outside the country, and the first assessment was that his father's advisers had chosen him as a figurehead. During the following months, however, the son surprised many people by taking the initiative and turning the policies of the government in a different direction.

Kabila was born on June 4, 1971, in Sud-Kivu province and grew up and was educated in Tanzania. He came to speak primarily English and Swahili but was not fluent in French, which along with English was an official language of the DRC. When his father deposed Pres. Mobutu Sese Seko in 1997, the son followed him to Kinshasa. In 1998 he was sent to Rwanda and then to China for military training. Upon his return, he became head of the country's armed forces, with the rank of major general.

Less than a week after being sworn in, Kabila made his first trip abroad as president. He conferred with government leaders in France and Belgium and also traveled to the U.S., where he met with Secretary of State Colin Powell (*q.v.*) and with officials of the World Bank, the International Monetary Fund, and the United Nations. While in the U.S., he also met with Paul Kagame, head of Rwanda, who had been one of his father's principal opponents. In a meeting in Zambia later in February, the new president agreed to begin the implementation of a cease-fire agreement that had been signed in Lusaka in July 1999 but that his father had refused to honour. As part of the agreement, he held talks with rebel groups, and the governments of five neighbouring countries—Rwanda, Uganda, Zimbabwe, Angola, and Namibia—that had troops in the country agreed to begin their withdrawal. UN peacekeepers arrived at the end of March to monitor the cease-fire and the pullback of troops. On April 14 Kabila, having dismissed the cabinet that had been held over from his father's administration, named his own group of ministers.   (ROBERT RAUCH)

Karzai, Hamid

The U.S. bombing of Afghanistan, launched in October 2001, produced dramatic military results before a political framework for reconstructing the country could be established. By mid-November the Taliban regime had collapsed, and there were fears that a destructive power struggle might break out among Afghanistan's conflicting ethnic, religious, and political communities. Talks were hastily arranged in Bonn, Ger., under the auspices of the United Nations; they were to include representatives of the non-Pashtun Northern Alliance as well as factions still loyal to the former Afghan king, Zahir Shah. Agreement was reached on December 5 that Hamid Karzai should chair an interim administration for six months, until a Loya Jirga, a traditional Afghan assembly, could be convened. Karzai was a tribal leader (but not a warlord), educated, fluent in Western and Eastern languages, and, above all, known and trusted in the U.S.

Karzai was born on Dec. 24, 1957, in Kandahar, Afg., son of the chief of the Popalzai Pashtuns. Both his father and his grandfather had served the government of Zahir Shah from the 1930s until he was overthrown in 1973. Under the Soviet-imposed regime in the 1980s, the Karzai family left Afghanistan and settled in Pakistan. Karzai attended university in India, and during the Soviet occupation he worked in Pakistan with the Liberation Front of Sibgatullah Mojaddedi. When the communist government of Mohammad Najibullah fell in April 1992, the mujahideen established a coalition government under Mojaddedi's presidency, and Karzai served as deputy foreign minister. He continued in this position when Burhanuddin Rabbani became president. At this point the mujahideen turned on one another, causing tens of thousands of deaths and countrywide turmoil. In 1994 Karzai again left the country.

Like most Afghans, Karzai was at first optimistic when the Taliban appeared and brought a kind of order to Afghanistan. The Taliban, although they were mostly ethnic Pashtun, had no sympathy for the traditional social and political institutions to which Karzai remained faithful, however. For his part, Karzai opposed the influence that the Pakistanis and other foreigners exerted over the Taliban. Karzai blamed the Taliban when his father was assassinated in July 1999 near the family home in Quetta, Pak. The leadership of the Popalzai now fell to him.

As the U.S. began bombing, Karzai entered southern Afghanistan to rally support against the Taliban. Then he received the call from Germany. He immediately began negotiating the surrender of Kandahar with local Taliban leaders and moved into the compound formerly occupied by Taliban supreme leader Mullah Mohammad Omar.

At ceremonies in late December in Kabul, attended by the Iranian and Pakistani foreign ministers, Karzai and his cabinet were sworn in before a gathering of representatives from most of Afghanistan's ethnic and tribal groups. In his address Karzai spoke in both Pashtu and Dari and wore an Uzbek robe. Behind the platform hung an enormous portrait of the late Tajik leader Ahmad Shah Masoud. The few women present—including two cabinet members—wore head scarfs, not burqas. A smiling Rabbani embraced Karzai and wished him success. (STEPHEN SEGO)

Koizumi, Junichiro

In 2001 the Liberal Democratic Party (LDP), which had dominated Japan's politics since 1955, experienced an intraparty revolt. Unpopular Prime Minister Yoshiro Mori had been selected by backroom party barons, and LDP members and local legislators demanded that the next party president be chosen by the rank and file. Under pressure, Mori resigned on April 6. The candidate favoured to succeed him was 59-year-old Junichiro Koizumi, who was a longtime member of the Diet (parliament) but had only limited cabinet experience and national exposure as a politician. In fact, Koizumi ranked second in most public opinion polls behind a popular woman, Makiko Tanaka (q.v.), who eventually withdrew as a candidate.

Koizumi subsequently opened a whirlwind campaign. With his mop of gray-flecked hair and trendy wardrobe, the new candidate was an interesting and charismatic presence on television and one who proved especially appealing to women. He spoke in a positive fashion. His campaign slogan, "Saa! kaeyo . . ." ("Well! Let's go back . . . [to prosperity]"), was seen on posters all over the country. Among other proposals, Koizumi advocated economic reform as a means of solving Japan's towering debt. He urged that pressure be applied to banks, whose nonperforming loans had risen by 15% during the previous year. He did relatively well in his appeals to voters in urban areas, where the LDP had traditionally managed only slim support.

In the party primaries, Koizumi won significant majorities. On April 24 he was elected president of the LDP by a sizable margin. Two days later he was confirmed by the Diet as the nation's 87th prime minister.

Koizumi was born on Jan. 8, 1942, in Yokosuka, Kanagawa prefecture, Japan. He was a member of an established political family; both his father and grandfather served in the Diet. Koizumi graduated from Keio University, Tokyo, with a degree in economics. While he was a graduate student at the London School of Economics, his father died; Koizumi returned to Japan and ran for the Diet himself but lost. He ran again three years later, however, and was successful, and he thereafter was reelected to the Diet 10 consecutive times.

Since Koizumi's confirmation by the Diet as prime minister was made possible by a strategic alliance between the LDP and a number of smaller parties, the new prime minister's cabinet was quite unusual. It included members of the alliance parties but relatively few representatives of the powerful factions that had long dominated the LDP. For the first time in Japan's history, five women were given portfolios, including Tanaka, who became the first woman to be named foreign minister.

(ARDATH W. BURKS)

Koons, Jeff

In the summer of 2001, the completed paintings from American artist Jeff Koons's much-anticipated and ongoing series of works were exhibited to great acclaim at the Kunsthaus in Bregenz, Austria. They represented his most ambitious project, *Celebration*, an extensive series of large-scale paintings and sculptures that had occupied him since 1993 and that included canvases and sculptural works depicting popular recognizable imagery, notably children's

An exuberant Jeff Koons

Reinhard Kaufhold/Berliner Verlag

toys, snack foods, or a colourful pile of Play-Doh set against a Mylar-silver background.

Koons was born on Jan. 21, 1955, in York, Pa. After studying at the Art Institute of Chicago and the Maryland Institute College of Art, he moved to New York City in 1976. His career as a commodities trader on Wall Street helped fund his artistic endeavours, which in the beginning involved the purchase of consumer goods and the repositioning of them as art objects. Perhaps more than any of his contemporaries in the New York art world of the 1980s, Koons and his art embodied the flashy materialism and technique of appropriation that were associated with that period; for Koons, however, it was a matter of context. One of his first series consisted of brand-new vacuum cleaners placed in glass cases, lit by fluorescent lights, and showcased like precious objects or cultural specimens.

He followed with *Equilibrium Tanks*—ordinary aquariums filled with water in which basketballs were suspended. Many visitors to his exhibits, in addition to critics, dismissed Koons as a fraud, declaring him and his work facile at best and insincere, talentless, and totally corrupt at worst. These opinions were fostered in part because of the atelier of assistants and fabricators who performed much of the labour involved in making a "Jeff Koons." Koons, however, viewed his work in an almost moral dimension; as he explained in a 1997 interview, "I have the need to maintain a spiritual trust in the work, so if somebody is viewing it they will never feel let down."

The provocative nature of his work reached its high point when Koons first showed his controversial *Made in Heaven* series at the Venice Biennale in 1990. This group of works included small glass sculptures and numerous photographic tableaux of Koons and Ilona Staller, the Italian porn star better known as Cicciolina, engaging in sexual acts. A combination of kitsch, theatricality, and explicit sexuality, the works were intended by the artist to celebrate his love for Cicciolina, whom he married in 1991. The couple produced a son, Ludwig, but separated in 1992.

Koons's work was also playful at times, conveying an almost childlike innocence. After *Made in Heaven*, he created a series of three-dimensional brightly painted ceramic figures of dogs and cats and porcelain bouquets of flowers. His monumental sculpture *Puppy* was an example of his desire to create archetypal images that would be understood by everyone. The 12-m (40-ft)-high puppy covered with many thousands of live flowering plants was unveiled in 1992 in Arolsen, Ger., and was later shown in Bilbao, Spain, and it most recently was displayed at Rockefeller Center, New York City, in 2000. *Celebration* signaled that a new, mature phase was under way in Koons's career. (MEGHAN DAILEY)

Kufuor, John

On Jan. 7, 2001, Ghanaian politician John Kufuor of the New Patriotic Party (NPP) began his first term as president of Ghana. His inauguration marked the first peaceful transfer of power between democratically elected governments since Ghanaian independence in 1957.

John Kofi Agyekum Kufuor was born on Dec. 8, 1938, in Kumasi, Ghana's second largest city and the traditional capital of the Asante people. He was the 7th of 10 children and the son of Nana Kwadwo Agyekum, an Asante royal, and Nana Ama Dapaah, a queen mother. Kufuor was educated at Prempeh College, Kumasi, and in Great Britain. He was called to the bar in 1961 at Lincoln's Inn, London, and then studied at the University of Oxford, where he earned (1964) a master's degree in philosophy, politics, and economics.

After completing his education, Kufuor returned to Ghana and launched his political career. In 1967 he became chief legal officer and town clerk for the city of Kumasi. By 1969 he was a member of Parliament and deputy foreign minister in the government of Kofi Busia. After Busia was overthrown in 1972, Kufuor spent several years as a businessman in the private sector. During Ghana's transition back to democracy in 1979, Kufuor returned to public life. He was a member of the assembly that drafted the constitution of the third republic, and he was elected to Parliament in 1979, serving as deputy minority parliamentary leader. After Jerry Rawlings overthrew the government in late 1981, Kufuor stayed on as Rawlings's secretary for local government. He resigned less than a year later, however, expressing his disappointment with the Rawlings regime.

Kufuor spent the rest of the decade as a private citizen until Ghana returned to democratic politics in 1992. He helped found the NPP and in 1996 became the party's candidate for president. Though Kufuor lost to Rawlings in the national elections that year, the NPP nominated him again to stand for the 2000 elections. Running on a platform that emphasized improving the Ghanaian economy and educational system and capitalizing on the mood of voters who were ready for a change in leadership, Kufuor won the election by capturing 57% of the vote in a runoff.

He spent his first year in office concentrating his efforts on the national economy. Though unemployment and inflation remained high, the national currency stabilized, and investment in the country increased. (AMY SETTERGREN)

Landry, Bernard

Bernard Landry was sworn in as Quebec's 28th prime minister (premier) on March 8, 2001. Changes in the leadership of the separatist Parti Québécois (PQ) following the defeat of the province's 1995 referendum on sovereignty had helped bring Landry to the head of the government. The new prime minister's goals for Quebec were clear and uncompromising: independence combined with an economic union with the rest of Canada. Landry asserted that Quebec was more than a "distinct society" within Canada; it was a nation that deserved to be recognized as a state. Only statehood, he believed, would allow Quebec to

fulfill its destiny as a French-language community in North America.

Landry was born on March 9, 1937, near Joliette, Que. He studied law and economics in Montreal and Paris. In the 1970s he joined the PQ, a movement committed to winning independence for Quebec. The PQ came to power in the province in 1976, and Landry was elected to the legislature. He rose rapidly through a number of cabinet posts to become Quebec's minister of finance.

In 1985 the PQ—and Landry—lost office, but nine years later the party was returned to power, and Landry resumed his former position as minister of finance. He was also appointed deputy prime minister, a post that made him second in command of the provincial administration. He threw himself into the important task of reviving the Quebec economy, which had been weakened by years of political uncertainty. He also saw the need to restore a sound basis to Quebec's public finances. Both these tasks were essential, he argued, to give credibility to Quebec's claims of statehood. His efforts were crowned with success when he balanced the books of the provincial government in 1999 for the first time in many years.

Observers expected Landry to face some tough challenges in his mission to secure an independent Quebec. In particular, he had to contend with the province's English-speaking residents and immigrants, who were strongly opposed to separation. Overall popular support for independence had been falling steadily since the 1995 referendum and by 2001 stood at about 40%. Landry had also developed a reputation for being short-tempered and outspoken. Whether he could placate his opponents and revive a flagging Quebec nationalism was open to question. Another referendum would have to be held in order to win the right to negotiate independence, and Landry made it clear that a vote would take place only when conditions were ripe for the referendum's success. By year's end it was still too early to assess whether Landry would become the first head of an independent Quebec. (DAVID M.L. FARR)

Lane, Nathan

American actor Nathan Lane, no stranger to plaudits for his abilities as a performer, reaped new praise in 2001 for his masterfully hilarious turn as con man Max Bialystock in Mel Brooks's blockbuster Broadway musical comedy *The Producers*. For his indefatigable effort he was rewarded with his second Tony Award for best performance by a leading actor in a musical. Brooks said he considered Lane "God's gift to Broadway."

Lane, born Joseph Lane on Feb. 3, 1956, in Jersey City, N.J., discovered his flair for musical comedy when he appeared in a high-school production of *No, No, Nanette*, and following graduation he embarked on a career in theatre. Among his early productions was a dinner-theatre staging of *Guys and Dolls*, in which he played Nathan Detroit, and when he was about to join Actors' Equity and learned that there was already a Joe Lane in the membership, he named himself after that character. He moved to New York City in the late 1970s, appeared in some Off-Broadway productions, and—in addition to taking odd jobs to help support himself—put together a comedy act with another actor, Patrick Stark. Sent to Los Angeles, the team, known as Stark and Lane, spent about two and a half years performing in nightclubs and as the opening act at concerts before Lane returned to New York. He then had a part in a short-lived 1982 television sitcom, *One of the Boys,* and shortly thereafter was cast in a Broadway production of *Present Laughter.* Such plays as *Love* and *She Stoops to Conquer* (both in 1984) followed, and in 1987 Lane made his motion picture debut in *Ironweed.* An Off-Broadway role in *The Lisbon Traviata* (1989) attracted critical praise, as did his performance in *Lips Together, Teeth Apart* (1991) and the film *Frankie and Johnny* (1991). In 1992 he reprised his role in *Guys and Dolls,* this time in a dream-fulfilling run on Broadway. The following year Lane's performance in *Laughter on the 23rd Floor* was singled out as exceptional, and he further charmed audiences with his voicing of the meerkat Timon in the animated film *The Lion King* (1994), his performance in the play *Love! Valour! Compassion!* (1994), and his role as the drag queen Albert in the movie *The Birdcage* (1996). Lane then went on to play the lead character Pseudolus in a Broadway revival of *A Funny Thing Happened on the Way to the Forum* (1996), a performance that garnered him his first Tony Award. In 1999 he starred in the TV series *George and Martha,* and in 2000 he appeared onstage in *The Man Who Came to Dinner* as well as in TV productions of that play and of *Laughter on the 23rd Floor.* (BARBARA WHITNEY)

Lewis, Ray

A year that began with two weeks in jail on a charge of murder ended in triumph for Baltimore Ravens middle linebacker Ray Lewis, who on Jan. 28, 2001, led his team to a convincing 34–7 victory over the New York Giants in Super Bowl XXXV in Tampa, Fla. Lewis was named the game's Most Valuable Player and was also voted the National Football League's (NFL's) Defensive Player of the Year.

One year earlier, on Jan. 31, 2000, Lewis and several friends attended a post-Super Bowl party at a nightclub in Atlanta, Ga., and as the party was breaking up, a fight erupted outside the club. When it was over, two men, Richard Lollar and Jacinth Baker, had been stabbed to death. Lewis was seen driving away from the fight, and he and two companions, Joseph Sweeting and Reginald Oakley, were charged with the murders. During a four-week trial in the spring of 2000, the charge was dropped against Lewis, who pleaded guilty to misdemeanour obstruction of justice and testified against Sweeting and Oakley. The NFL later fined Lewis $250,000; Sweeting and Oakley were subsequently acquitted of the murder charges.

Ray Anthony Lewis was born on May 15, 1975, in Bartow, Fla. After starring in several sports in high school, he enrolled at the University of Miami, Fla., where he became a middle linebacker and was named to the Freshman All-America team. In his junior year, his last at the university, Lewis finished the sea-

son with a team-high 160 tackles and earned first-string All-America honours. After his first season with the Ravens in 1996, he gained recognition as a member of the NFL's all-rookie team. In 1997 he led the league in tackles with 210 and played in the Pro Bowl. Lewis again competed in the Pro Bowl in 1998, and in 1999 he led the NFL with 198 tackles.

In the days leading up to Super Bowl XXXV, Lewis bristled at relentless questions from reporters about the brawl in which Lollar and Baker were killed, and he vowed to take his frustrations out on the field. Spearheading a defense that forced five turnovers and held the Giants to a mere 152 yd on offense, Lewis solidified his reputation as one of the league's best middle linebackers by making three solo tackles and deflecting four passes in the game. He also helped convince many observers that the Baltimore defense was one of the best in NFL history. (DAVID R. CALHOUN)

Lopez, Jennifer

In early 2001 American superstar Jennifer Lopez was burning up multiple entertainment charts with a number one album (*J.Lo*) and a hit movie at the box office (*The Wedding Planner*) in the same week. The multitalented Lopez was known as much for her acting and singing as for her voluptuous curves, revealing evening gowns, highly publicized romance and subsequent breakup during the year with rapper and producer Sean ("Puffy" or "P. Diddy") Combs, and later surprise marriage to dancer Cris Judd. Lopez was the highest-paid Latina actress in the history of Hollywood; she reportedly was negotiating for a fee of over $10 million for her role in the upcoming thriller *Taking Lives.*

Lopez was born on July 24, 1970, in the Bronx, New York City, to a family of Puerto Rican descent. She took dance lessons throughout her childhood and performed internationally with stage musicals, and at age 16 she made her film debut with a small role in *My Little Girl* (1986). Her television break came in 1990 when she was cast as one of the "Fly Girls," dancers who appeared on the comedy show *In Living Color.* After she left the show, she turned her focus to acting, first in a couple of short-lived television series, then in movie roles. Film success came quickly, and by 1995 she was appearing with such big-name stars as Wesley Snipes and Woody Harrelson (*Money Train*), Robin Williams (*Jack;* 1996), and Jack Nicholson (*Blood and Wine;* 1997). Lopez still remained somewhat in the periphery of the public vision, however, until she landed the lead role in *Selena* (1997), a biopic of the murdered Tejana singer. She went on to star in a number of thrillers and action dramas, including *Anaconda* and *U Turn* (both 1997), *Out of Sight* (1998), and *The Cell* (2000), and she gained widespread praise for *The Wedding Planner,* her successful first attempt at romantic comedy. That release was quickly followed by the romantic drama *Angel Eyes* in the middle of the year.

Ambitious, driven, and a self-admitted perfectionist, Lopez was not one to rest on her laurels; in 1999 she added pop artist to her list of titles with the release of her debut album *On the 6.* To the surprise of many critics, the album quickly went platinum and subsequently sold

J.Lo

over eight million copies worldwide. Two years later her second album, *J.Lo,* sold more than 272,000 copies in its first week. By mid-2001 Lopez had a number of films in the works, and there were plans for her to star in and produce specials for television and to develop a sitcom. She also announced that she would launch a clothing line with the help of Andy Hilfiger, which would be available in retail stores by the year's end. (SANDRA LANGENECKERT)

Loyrette, Henri

On March 28, 2001, the French government announced the appointment of Henri Loyrette, head of the Orsay Museum, to be the new director of the Louvre Museum. The 48-year-old arts administrator and historian thus moved across the Seine River on April 14 to take on the responsibility of running the national museum of France, the largest in the country and one of the largest and most important in Europe. He replaced the retiring Pierre Rosenberg, who had been associated with the Louvre for nearly 40 years and who had been its director since 1994. Not only was Loyrette one of the youngest persons ever to head the Louvre, but it was also notable that he had not risen through the ranks at the institution, which was the normal path of advancement to the top.

Loyrette was born on May 31, 1952, in Neuilly-sur-Seine, a suburb of Paris. He received a university degree in history and in 1975–77 studied in Rome at the Academy of France. Upon his return to France in 1978, he was appointed curator at the Orsay, where he remained for 23 years, becoming director in 1994. The Orsay boasted the largest collection of 19th-century art of any French museum, and Loyrette, whose specialties were 19th-century painting and architecture, organized a number of successful exhibitions there. These included exhibitions on Edgar Degas, on whom Loyrette was an expert, on the caricaturist Honoré Daumier, and on the still lifes of Édouard Manet, as well as on lesser-known European artists. Loyrette also organized exhibitions on the origins of Impressionism and on the relation of Impressionism and Art Nouveau, in addition to the 1987–88 exhibition "Chicago, Birth of a Metropolis." Loyrette's writings included three books on Degas, as well as works on a number of other 19th-century artists, on Gustave Eiffel, and on Marcel Proust's views on modern art.

Loyrette held important positions in several French cultural organizations, and he had been widely honoured. He served as secretary-general of the French Committee on Art History and was a member of the board of directors of a number of institutions, including the National Graduate School of Decorative Arts and the Cité de la Musique, an interactive museum in Paris. When he was elected to the Académie des Beaux-Arts in 1997, he was its youngest member.

As the new director of the Louvre, Loyrette faced the kinds of problems museums throughout the world were grappling with, including ensuring sources of adequate funding. This was particularly acute at the Louvre, where the large numbers of visitors put enormous demands on the staff and physical plant. Nonetheless, Loyrette, with his distinguished background and experience, appeared to be a natural fit for the position. (ROBERT RAUCH)

MacLeod, Alistair

For his long-awaited first novel, *No Great Mischief* (2000), Canadian author Alistair MacLeod won the 2001 International IMPAC Dublin Literary Award; a superbly crafted work, the book chronicled the lives of several generations of Scottish immigrants on Cape Breton Island in northeastern Nova Scotia. MacLeod, a meticulous stylist who wrote *No Great Mischief* over the course of 13 years, was the first Canadian writer to receive the $172,000 award, the world's richest literary prize for fiction. Until the award was announced, MacLeod was largely unknown outside his native country, despite his having earlier published two critically acclaimed short-story collections. Fellow Canadian author Michael Ondaatje once called him "one of the great undiscovered writers of our time." Following the publication of *No Great Mischief*, the *Toronto Globe and Mail* went farther, describing MacLeod as "the greatest living Canadian writer."

MacLeod was born in North Battleford, Sask., on July 20, 1936. His parents were natives of Cape Breton, and when MacLeod was 10 years old, he returned with his family to the island. He worked as a miner and logger before earning a teacher's certificate from Nova Scotia Teachers College. He went on to obtain his B.A. and B.Ed. from St. Francis Xavier University, Antigonish, N.S., in 1960, his M.A. from the University of New Brunswick at Saint John, in 1961, and his Ph.D. from the University of Notre Dame in 1968. He taught at Indiana University at Fort Wayne from 1966 to 1969, then returned to Canada

as a professor of English and creative writing at the University of Windsor, Ont. For many years MacLeod also taught writing at the Banff (Alta.) Centre for Continuing Education. He was named professor emeritus at the University of Windsor in 2000.

MacLeod's writing career began in 1968 with the publication of his short story "The Boat," which was included in the 1969 anthology *The Best American Short Stories*. Many critics acknowledged him as a master of the short-story form after the appearance of his first collection, *The Lost Salt Gift of Blood*, in 1976, and a second volume of stories, *As Birds Bring Forth the Sun* (1986), further solidified his reputation. MacLeod's fiction dwelled mostly on the working people of Cape Breton—miners, loggers, fishermen, and small farmers—and sensitively explored family relationships as well as examining the relationship of the islanders to their Celtic past.

MacLeod's literary oeuvre was notable for its smallness. Together, *The Lost Salt Gift of Blood* and *As Birds Bring Forth the Sun* included only 16 stories, and each book took some 10 years to write. His lean output might be explained by his admitted perfectionism; MacLeod revised constantly and read each of his sentences aloud in his belief that "the ear is a good editor." In part to satisfy the growing numbers of admirers of his work, he followed up *No Great Mischief* with *Island* (2000), which collected all of his previously published stories and included one new one. (SHERMAN HOLLAR)

Mami, Cheb

In 2001 internationally renowned Algerian *rai* singer Cheb Mami continued his efforts to cultivate an American fan base. Before his 1999 collaboration with British pop singer Sting on the smash-hit single "Desert Rose," Mami, a popular figure in Europe and North Africa, had been virtually unknown in the U.S. The success of "Desert Rose," however, propelled Mami into the spotlight; he was a guest on *The Tonight Show* and *The Late Show with David Letterman*, performed with Sting at the 2000 Grammy Awards, and saw his celebrated song used in a Jaguar television commercial. In 2001 Mami performed with Sting at the Super Bowl and embarked on a seven-city U.S. tour following the July release of *Dellali*, his seventh album.

The performer known as the "prince of *rai*" was born Khelifati Muhammad on July 11, 1966, in Saida, Alg. He initially followed in the occupational footsteps of his father and took a job as a welder. At the age of 12, Mami began singing in the streets and at weddings. In 1982 he placed second in a radio talent contest and was approached by record producers. Under a local record label, the newly discovered Cheb Mami (Arabic for "the young mourner") released cassettes that sold well but made little money. In 1985 he performed in the nearby port city of Oran (the birthplace of *rai* music) at a festival that had been organized by Khaled, the "king of *rai*." The frank, often racy lyrics of *rai* music coupled with what some believed were undertones of political protest made *rai* a controversial art form amid the growing volatility of the Algerian political scene during the 1980s. As a result,

many of the genre's artists began to leave the country in fear for their lives. Like many others, Mami moved to France, where he found an enthusiastic audience among the second-generation North Africans living there.

In the years following the move, Mami became a French club favourite before emerging as an international star. Though his style was an eclectic fusion of reggae, funk, salsa, hip-hop, and North African rhythms, *rai*'s distinct flavour was apparent. Mami's first album, *Prince of Raï*, was released in 1989 and was followed by *Let Me Raï* (1990), *Saida* (1995), *Let Me Cry* (1998), *Douni el Bladi* (1998), *Meli Meli* (1999), and *Dellali*. (SHANDA SILER)

McCartney, Stella

When Stella McCartney was asked by a London fashion critic why the clothes she designed for French fashion label Chloé held so much appeal for young women, she quipped, "I know what makes chicks tick." McCartney's words were validated in April 2001 when, after protracted negotiations with the Gucci Group, Gucci chairman Domenico de Sole announced that the Italian luxury goods conglomerate would provide at least 51% of the funds to back a new design label produced under McCartney's name.

McCartney, born in 1972 in London, was the daughter of Sir Paul McCartney (a former Beatle) and Linda McCartney, a noted photographer and animal rights activist. She graduated (1995) from Central Saint Martin's College of Art and Design, London, and rose quickly to the forefront of the international fashion world. She was hired in 1997 by the Vendome Group to revitalize its 47-year-old design label, Chloé. McCartney replaced legendary designer Karl Lagerfeld, who expressed skepticism about her design skill. "I think they should have taken a big name," he said. "They did, but in music, not fashion." Indeed, McCartney's design experience had been limited. Prior to her formal schooling, she worked for a time at the French couture house Christian Lacroix and as an intern at

Mary McCartney Donald

Stella McCartney—knows what makes chicks tick

British *Vogue*. Though she produced a blockbuster graduation show that featured supermodel Naomi Campbell, one of McCartney's tutors admitted that she was "a very hardworking girl, but she did not really stand out in her year."

McCartney did, however, succeed in establishing Chloé as a desirable brand; its sales reportedly increased fivefold. Her first collection, featuring lacy petticoat skirts and dainty camisoles, silenced critics, and her 2001 Paris romantic offerings—sexy silk pants set off by midriff-baring tops, signature body-hugging jeans paired with showier tunic tops or jackets, and fake-fur coats and vests splashed with jeweled appliqués—cemented her reputation. McCartney also built the brand a celebrity cult following. This in part was due to her high-profile customers and friends, notably Madonna (for whom she designed a wedding dress), Kate Hudson (whom McCartney outfitted for the 2001 Academy Award ceremonies), actresses Liv Tyler and Gwyneth Paltrow, and model Kate Moss.

Rumours that McCartney had met with Tom Ford, the Gucci Group's design director, began circulating early in 2000. Some suspected that she would take over design at Gucci, because Ford had been named design director of Yves Saint Laurent. McCartney's position as a staunch animal rights activist (shortly after her mother's death, she made a video supporting animal rights for People for the Ethical Treatment of Animals) prevented her from signing a deal, however. She refused to work with leather or fur—both central design elements for Gucci. In hiring McCartney, Gucci both acquired the design talent that it had long sought and, it seemed, concluded that an animal-friendly label could potentially turn a profit.   (BRONWYN COSGRAVE)

Middelhoff, Thomas

Could signal success in publishing be translated into the music business as well? In 2001 Thomas Middelhoff, the dynamic chairman and CEO of Bertelsmann AG, the German global media giant, was betting that it would.

Middelhoff was born in Düsseldorf, Ger., on May 11, 1953. He earned an MBA (Westphalian Wilhelm University of Münster) and studied marketing before joining his family's textile business in 1984. He took his first position with a Bertelsmann subsidiary in 1986 and moved up the corporate ranks quickly.

Renowned for his high-tech savvy, Middelhoff met America Online (AOL) founder Steve Case in 1994 and was so impressed with the Internet service provider that he urged his company to invest millions in AOL and its European counterpart. The value of that investment soared, as did Middelhoff's standing with Bertelsmann. These and other successes propelled Middelhoff, then aged 45, into Bertelsmann's CEO position in 1998. Shortly thereafter, Bertelsmann sold its interests in AOL and AOL Europe for nearly $9 billion and turned to investing in other on-line technologies, specifically the Internet file-sharing company Napster, Inc.

At the same time Middelhoff was making a name for himself, Bertelsmann was accelerating its global strategy to acquire publishing houses and other media assets throughout the world. Key subsidiaries included newspaper and magazine publisher Gruner+Jahr, American book publishers Bantam Doubleday Dell and Random House, science and business publisher BertelsmannSpringer, and BMG Entertainment (which owned more than 200 record labels in more than 50 countries, including Arista and RCA in the United States). In February 2001 the firm gained a controlling interest in the Luxembourg-based RTL Group, Europe's largest producer of radio, television, and movie content and operator of 18 radio and 24 TV stations across the continent. Still, American markets accounted for much of the company's international growth, and Bertelsmann chose New York City—where Middelhoff spent roughly half his time—as the seat of its book-publishing operations in 1999. In mid-2001 Bertelsmann enjoyed annual revenues of €16.5 billion (about $15 billion).

As CEO, Middelhoff set out to shed unprofitable businesses (such as AOL and pay television), reinvigorate traditional ones (European book clubs), and, principally, make Bertelsmann a leading provider of content. Middelhoff's Napster gamble surprised many observers. Napster provided software that allowed individuals to swap electronic music files without paying for them, and the service spent much of 2000 mired in legal battles brought on by music companies. To the chagrin of Bertelsmann executives, however, Middelhoff came down in support of Napster, assuming that users would be willing to pay for the legal acquisition of music files over the Internet. In July Konrad Hilbers, a Bertelsmann executive, was named CEO of Napster. Middelhoff showed his commitment to the agreement by anteing up $50 million intended to help Napster comply with copyright laws. Early signs, however, suggested that Napster's customers might not be willing to pay the price of copyrights, and they turned to competing companies such as FastTrack, Gnutella, and Audiogalaxy. At year's end the chips were still out on Middelhoff's bet.

(SARAH FORBES ORWIG)

Morris, Mark

American dancer-choreographer Mark Morris had special reason to celebrate the 20th anniversary season of his company, the Mark Morris Dance Group, in 2001—the opening of the troupe's first permanent American home, the Mark Morris Dance Center in Brooklyn, N.Y. The $6 million building, conveniently across the street from the company's usual home performing venue, the Brooklyn Academy of Music (BAM), included such amenities as offices, kitchens, dressing rooms and showers, and rehearsal studios that could double as performance spaces for smaller, more experimental works. Having such a sumptuous home was a unique accomplishment in the world of American modern dance.

Morris was born on Aug. 29, 1956, in Seattle, Wash., and at age eight, after attending a performance by the José Greco flamenco company, decided to become a Spanish dancer. He took classes, began performing professionally at age 11, joined the Koleda Folk Ensemble at 13, and began choreographing professionally at 14. He spent part of 1974 studying in Spain and in 1976 moved to New York City, where he danced in the companies of such choreographers as Eliot Feld, Lar Lubovitch, Laura Dean, and Hannah Kahn. In 1980 Morris launched his company when he and 10 fellow dancers presented a concert of five of his works, and its reputation was solidified at BAM's 1984 Next Wave Festival. Only two years later Morris won a Guggenheim fellowship, was choreographing for major ballet companies, began taking his company on tour, and was the subject of an hour-long public television special. In 1988 Morris accepted an invitation to become the resident choreographer of the Théâtre Royal de la Monnaie in Brussels, expanded the membership of the company, and renamed it the Monnaie Dance Group/Mark Morris. Even at home many considered him the "bad boy of modern dance" and especially did not appreciate or understand his outrageous humour or his more innovative works, and the Belgians, not accustomed to his style of dance, were even less receptive. Nonetheless, during his three years in Belgium, Morris choreographed some of his most acclaimed and enduring creations, including *L'Allegro, il penseroso ed il moderato* (1988), his first full-evening work and the subject of a photo and essay book by that name in 2001; *Dido and Aeneas* (1989), a dance version of the opera, in which Morris danced the parts of both Dido and the Sorceress; and *The Hard Nut* (1991), his version of *The Nutcracker*. He was awarded a MacArthur fellowship in 1991. While Morris was out of the U.S., Mikhail Baryshnikov and the White Oak Dance Project kept Morris's works before the American public.

Following the company's return to the U.S. in 1991, Morris created an average of five or six new works each year for his company—including *Beautiful Day* (1992), *The Office* (1994), *Somebody's Coming to See Me Tonight* (1995), and *Four Saints in Three Acts* (2000), his version of the Gertrude Stein–Virgil Thomson opera—and by 2001 had choreographed more than 100 numbers. Noted for his musicality, he also created classical ballets for numerous companies, including the American Ballet Theatre, the San Francisco Ballet, and Les Grands Ballets Canadiens. The onetime enfant terrible of modern dance had become a setter of standards and a solid member of the dance establishment.   (BARBARA WHITNEY)

Mueller, Robert

Just days after taking the oath of office (Sept. 4, 2001) as director of the Federal Bureau of Investigation, Robert Mueller was confronted with the daunting task of assigning some 4,000 FBI agents to pursue thousands of leads and gather intelligence relating to the activities and identities of the perpetrators behind the September 11 terrorist attacks in the U.S. In the wake of the national crisis, Mueller sent agents to at least 30 countries, but it soon became clear that more investigators fluent in

Arabic, Farsi, and Pashtu were needed by the FBI; he appealed to the general population to contact the agency via a hotline if anyone was fluent in any of these languages. Mueller had little time to recover from the major surgery he had undergone in early August.

In his years investigating everything from street-corner crimes to terrorist bombings and bank fraud, Mueller had established himself as a top-notch law enforcer who emphasized the government's responsibility "to protect its citizens from criminal harm within the framework of the Constitution." Pres. George W. Bush characterized him as a man of "fidelity, bravery, and integrity." The nation's top crime-fighting organization was sorely in need of such a leader; after years of critical missteps, the FBI had come to be identified by its failures rather than its successes. These included the disappearance of computer laptops and firearms, the tardiness in identifying FBI agent Robert Hanssen as a Russian spy, and the mishandling of evidence in the Oklahoma City bombing case that came to light only days before convicted bomber Timothy McVeigh was to be put to death.

Robert Swan Mueller III was born Aug. 7, 1944, in New York City and was raised in Philadelphia. He earned some ribbing among fellow law enforcers, who—because of the "III" after his name—called him "Bobby Three Sticks." After attending St. Paul's, a private school in Concord, N.H., Mueller studied at Princeton University (B.A., 1966). He served as a Marine Corps officer for three years, including one year in Vietnam, and was awarded the Bronze Star, the Purple Heart, and the Vietnamese Cross of Gallantry. He next pursued a master's degree in international studies from New York University and earned his law degree from the University of Virginia School of Law.

Though Mueller had worked in private law practices in San Francisco, Boston, and Washington, D.C., he left each position for work in public law enforcement. As the assistant attorney general for the criminal division of the Department of Justice (1990–93), he supervised the investigation of the Pan Am Flight 103 bombing. Among his various other appointments, he served as U.S. attorney in two regions: the District of Massachusetts (Boston, 1986–87) and the Northern District of California (San Francisco, 1998–2001). In San Francisco Mueller improved performance by reassigning supervisors, implementing tough new rules, and emphasizing productivity. Despite the fact that he sometimes stepped on toes, California's leading politicians were impressed. Though his no-nonsense style was unlike the star-quality public persona the White House sought for its new FBI director, Mueller was catapulted to the centre of international affairs following the September terrorist attacks.   (SARAH FORBES ORWIG)

Newton, Helmut
A larger-than-life nude photograph of a statuesque female model overshadowed the entrance to the spring show at the Barbican Gallery in London in 2001. It was one of 200 images by German-born fashion photographer Helmut Newton, shown on the occasion of his 80th birthday, and it loomed large over visitors to the exhibit, which had previously been mounted at the New National Gallery in Berlin. Similarly, the retrospective proved that Newton himself loomed large; he had cast a shadow over the field of fashion photography since the 1960s and had influenced scores of camera buffs and advertising campaigns with his provocative photos, which explored the eroticism of glamour. Sex and power were constant themes in his work, with hints of violence and fetish that earned his cold, sophisticated photos the label "porno-chic."

Newton was born on Oct. 31, 1920, in Berlin to well-to-do Jewish parents. He came of age during the bourgeois decadence of Berlin society in the 1930s. As a teenager, Newton took up photography and set up homemade fashion shoots. Dropping out of school at age 16, he became apprenticed to the fashion photographer Yva (Else Simon). In 1938, when his family fled the Nazi regime and moved to South America, Newton went his separate way, eventually settling in Australia, where in 1947 he became a citizen. The following year he married June Browne, who later would also find success as a photographer under the name Alice Springs. Initially, Newton struggled as a freelance in Melbourne, but by the late 1950s he was working primarily for high-fashion magazines in Paris, where he lived from 1961 to 1981.

Newton made his name on the pages of *Vogue, Elle, Marie-Claire, Jardin des modes, Stern,* and *Nova,* with carefully composed voyeuristic images known for their staged fin de siècle settings and sexually charged content. The shock of a heart attack in 1971 caused him to reassess his career, and from that point forward he began exercising greater creative control over his shoots, helping to establish French *Vogue* as the height of fashion photography in the 1970s. Sometimes controversial, his sensationalistic images prompted attacks from feminists as well as from disparaging art critics when his work began appearing in museums. In 1981 he moved to Monte-Carlo and began photographing nudes; his oversized images appeared in the book *Big Nudes* (1982). Newton was also sought after for his celebrity poses, which were collected in *Portraits* (1987). Other published works included *White Women* (1976), *Sleepless Nights* (1978), *World Without Men* (1984), and *SUMO* (2000), a massive 480-page tome, which at 50 × 70 cm (20 × 27.5 in) and 30 kg (66 lb) was less a coffee-table book than a coffee table itself.   (TOM MICHAEL)

Obaid, Thoraya

On Jan. 1, 2001, Thoraya Ahmed Obaid became the executive director of the United Nations Population Fund (UNFPA) and the first Saudi national to head a UN agency. The UNFPA, the largest internationally funded source of population assistance, actively promoted equality between the sexes and universal education and health care, especially better reproductive health care for women. Its campaigns to battle AIDS, expand the availability of reproductive information and services for adolescents, and end violence against women, including female genital mutilation, met with resistance in many conservative areas of the world, especially those that were reluctant to address such concomitant issues as homosexuality, teen sexuality, and women's rights. It was believed that Obaid, a Muslim woman (like her predecessor, Nafis Sadik of Pakistan), would be sensitive to Muslim concerns and serve as a role model in Muslim countries where the status of women was still low. In Saudi Arabia, for example, where women could not appear in public unless covered from head to toe, were not permitted to drive, and could not travel without written permission from male relatives, Obaid's success and visibility contributed to changes in government policy, including an agreement by the government to sign the Convention on the Elimination of All Forms of Discrimination Against Women. Indeed, the Saudi government fully supported Obaid's candidacy for the UNFPA position. Obaid herself had expressed the hope that she could, from her own personal experience, tell less-developed countries, especially in Muslim societies, that educating women, allowing them to work, and enabling them to make choices about their lives were Islamic rather than un-Islamic in nature.

Obaid was born on March 2, 1945, in Baghdad, Iraq. Her parents were devout Muslims, and they took as a literal command the instruction in the Qur'an's very first *surah*—"Read." They believed in educating their daughter as well as their sons and enrolled her in an Islamic school in Mecca, Saudi Arabia, when she was three. Because education for girls was limited in Saudi Arabia at the time, Obaid was sent in 1951 to the American College for Girls in Cairo. She later became the first Saudi woman to receive a government scholarship to study in the United States. She earned a B.A. (1966) in English literature from Mills College, Oakland, Calif., and M.A. (1968) and Ph.D. (1974) degrees from Wayne State University, Detroit. In 1975 Obaid began working for the UN Economic and Social Commission for Western Asia, and she became that agency's deputy executive secretary in 1993. In 1998 she was appointed director of the UNFPA's Division for Arab States and Europe. Her 25 years of experience at the UN and her demonstrated commitment to empowering women moved UN Secretary-General Kofi Annan to describe her as "the ideal candidate" to head the UNFPA.   (AMY R. TAO)

Parker, Sarah Jessica
Although Sarah Jessica Parker struggled to define the rules of dating as Carrie Bradshaw on *Sex and the City,* the American actress knew the secrets to a successful relationship with television viewers: sex, friends, and fashion. In 2001 Parker returned for the highly anticipated fourth season of *Sex and the City,* and millions tuned in for the candid look at four friends—Bradshaw, Miranda (played by Cynthia Nixon), Samantha (Kim Cattrall), and

Trendsetter Sarah Jessica Parker
Craig Blankenhorn/Getty Images

Charlotte (Kristin Davis)—searching for Mr. Right in New York City. Broadcast on the cable channel HBO, the series offered an uncensored, humorous, and, at times, risqué look at the lives of thirtysomethings. Swearing, nudity, and graphic discussions about sex were common features, as were the cosmopolitan cocktail, Manolo Blahnik high heels, and designer fashions. At the centre was Parker, who combined comedy, sensuality, and compassion to create a character to whom single women could relate. Critics also applauded her performance, and in 2001 she won her second Golden Globe Award for best actress in a television comedy or musical series.

Parker was born on March 25, 1965, in Nelsonville, Ohio. Although her family was far from wealthy, young Sarah was encouraged to participate in the arts and took ballet and acting classes as a child. At the age of 11, Parker moved with her family to New York City so that she and her siblings could pursue careers in entertainment.

In 1978 she landed the lead role in Broadway's *Annie*, and she stayed with the musical for some three years. Other stage work followed, and in 1979 she made her film debut in *Rich Kids*. In 1982 Parker portrayed a high-school nerd in the television series *Square Pegs*. Although the show lasted only one season, it developed a cultlike following and led to several film offers for Parker, including *Footloose* (1984) and *Girls Just Want to Have Fun* (1985). Parker continued her work in the theatre, appearing in *The Heidi Chronicles* (1989), *The Substance of Fire* (1991), *Sylvia* (1995), for which she earned critical praise for her portrayal of a dog, and *How to Succeed in Business Without Really Trying* (1996), in which she appeared with her longtime boyfriend, Matthew Broderick; the couple married the following year.

In 1991 Parker's film career received a boost with her performance opposite Steve Martin as the bouncy SanDeE* in *L.A. Story*. Other movies quickly followed, notably *Honeymoon in Vegas* (1992), *Ed Wood* (1994), and *The First Wives Club* (1996), but the roles failed to establish Parker as a leading lady. That changed, however, with *Sex and the City*. Premiering in 1998, the series, inspired by the best-selling book by Candace Bushnell, brought Parker unprecedented attention. The show, however, was not without its detractors. In addition to complaints concerning the ribald nature of the show, some charged that it objectified men—Carrie's former boyfriend, for example, is known only as Mr. Big. Quite a few others, however, believed that such a role reversal in American television was long overdue.   (AMY TIKKANEN)

Parsons, Timothy

Capping a career of more than 40 years in which he had established himself among the world's leading marine biologists, Canadian Timothy Parsons was named a winner of the Japan Prize in 2001. The award recognized Parsons's pioneering exploration of the complex relationships between fish and the physical, chemical, and biological aspects of their environment and the application of that new understanding to reversing the decline in fishery resources. In contrast to the traditional population-dynamics approach to fishery management, Parsons's work concentrated on the entire marine ecosystem and led to methods for nurturing the environment to help increase fish populations that had become depleted owing to overfishing and pollution. His advances helped create an alternative, holistic approach to marine conservation and management and influenced a new school of oceanographers and fishery managers. Parsons also conducted important research on the effects of pollution on the marine environment through the innovative use of mesocosms—large floating tubes of water that simulated natural ecosystems—and computer modeling.

Timothy Richard Parsons was born on Nov. 1, 1932, in Colombo, Ceylon (now Sri Lanka). He attended McGill University, Montreal, where he earned a bachelor's degree (1953), a master's degree (1955), and a doctorate (1958). He took a position as a research scientist at the Fisheries Research Board of Canada but left in 1962 for a post in the Office of Oceanography at UNESCO in Paris; he returned to the Fisheries Research Board in 1964. In 1971 Parsons joined the faculty at the University of British Columbia, where he remained until he retired to the post of professor emeritus in 1992. He also served as honorary scientist emeritus at the Institute of Ocean Sciences in Sidney, B.C.

During his career Parsons served as president of the International Association of Biological Oceanography (1976–82), won numerous awards and honours, including a fellowship of the Royal Society of Canada (1979), the Oceanographic Society of Japan Prize (1988), and the Killam Research Prize (1990). He published more than 150 works, including three textbooks.

Parsons was the first Canadian recipient of the Japan Prize, given by the Science and Technology Foundation of Japan; the award was considered comparable in stature to a Nobel Prize.   (ANTHONY G. CRAINE)

Paterno, Joe

On a cool autumn day, in a small American town called State College, Pa., in an area called Happy Valley, a group of young men in plain uniforms gathered to play amateur football. This game was no small affair, especially for a bespectacled old man on the sidelines in cuffed khaki pants. That man was coach Joe Paterno of Pennsylvania State University. On that day, Oct. 27, 2001, he became the winningest football coach in major college history, and he did it in front of a jubilant home crowd in the nation's second largest college stadium. Both the size of the stadium and the success of the football program were testimony to Paterno's brilliant reign as head coach of the Penn State Nittany Lions. In the final quarter of the game, the Nittany Lions roared back from an 18-point deficit to hand Ohio State University a 29–27 loss and to give their coach his 324th career win, surpassing the record held by Paul ("Bear") Bryant of the University of Alabama.

Paterno finished the year with 327 total wins over 36 seasons. His long career sparkled with highlights, including two national championships (1982, 1986), five undefeated seasons, and five seasons with only one loss. There were also 20 victories in bowl games, 20 top-10 finishes, and 34 shutouts. The Nittany Lions were especially dominant in the 1990s, during which the team joined the Big Ten Conference and posted 97 wins with only 26 losses. Paterno saw 250 of his players advance to playing in the professional National Football League. Known for his conservative, brass-tacks approach to the game, Paterno excelled at developing first-rate linebackers, some of whom were among his 31 players named to the All-America first team.

In January 2002 Paterno became the first active coach in 20 years to receive the Amos Alonzo Stagg Award, the highest honour given by the American Football Coaches Association. A four-time winner of the association's Coach of the Year award, he was also the first coach to be named Sportsman of the Year by *Sports Illustrated* magazine (1986). Not content only to build the football program, Paterno was an advocate for academic integrity and donated millions to build up the nonsporting programs of the university.

Joseph Vincent Paterno was born on Dec. 21, 1926, in Brooklyn, N.Y., where he attended Catholic schools and played football. He served in the U.S. Army in the final year of World War II before accepting an athletic scholarship to Brown University, Providence, R.I., where he studied English literature and led the team as quarterback. Upon graduation in 1950 he intended to enroll in law school at Boston University but was lured away when his former coach at Brown, Charles ("Rip") Engle, became head coach at Penn State. After 16 years as Engle's assistant, Paterno succeeded him in 1966.   (TOM MICHAEL)

Peacocke, the Rev. Canon Arthur Robert

The winner of the 2001 Templeton Prize for Progress in Religion was the Rev. Arthur Peacocke, a biochemist, theologian, and Anglican priest who had spent most of his career encouraging cooperation between science and religion. Peacocke was the sixth scientist, and the third in a row, to receive the lucrative ($1 million in 2001) award created to serve as the equivalent of a Nobel Prize for religion. Peacocke, who took part in some of the earliest work on the DNA molecule, compared the relationship between science and religion to that of the two helical strands that make up DNA. The search for intelligibility and the search for meaning, he said, are necessary, complementary approaches to answering the same questions about how things came to be. Most scientists dismissed attempts to integrate faith and science because of a lack of proof of a supreme being, but Peacocke countered that theologians had successfully used supporting evidence for their claims in the same fashion that scientists did for theirs.

Peacocke was born Nov. 29, 1924 in Watford, Eng. He received a doctorate in physical biochemistry from the University of Oxford in 1948 and during the 1950s, while working at the virus laboratory at the University of California, was part of a team that identified properties of the recently discovered DNA molecule. A self-described mild agnostic during his college years, Peacocke found himself searching for answers to questions he considered too broad for science alone to answer. He began theology studies and received a bachelor of divinity degree from the University of Birmingham, Eng., in 1971, when he was also ordained a priest in the Church of England. He took a post teaching biochemistry and theology at the University of Cambridge before returning to Oxford, where he served two terms (1985–88 and 1995–99) as director of the Ian Ramsey Centre, which promoted teaching and research in science and religion. He also founded the Science and Religion Forum (1972) and the Society of Ordained Scientists (1985). In 1993 Peacocke was made an MBE. He was the author of a number of books that examined the ties between science and religion, including *Theology for a Scientific Age* (1990) and *Paths from Science Towards God: The End of All Our Exploring* (2001).

An early adherent to the anthropic principle—the notion that the universe contains conditions ideal for the development of living beings—Peacocke concluded that a likely explanation for the existence of life was the existence of a supreme being. Advances in astronomy were shedding new light on what scientists knew about the creation of the universe; advances in genetics were forcing scientists to grapple with new ethical considerations. Peacocke maintained that it was time for science and theology to work together to draw meaning and guidance from what was being learned.   (ANTHONY G. CRAINE)

Powell, Colin

On Jan. 20, 2001, the engaging former chairman of the U.S. Joint Chiefs of Staff Colin Powell—whose leadership role in the 1991 Persian Gulf War had brought him to the attention of the American public—was sworn in as U.S. secretary of state.

Born on April 5, 1937, in New York City, Colin Luther Powell was the son of Jamaican immigrants. While attending the City College of New York, Powell joined the Reserve Officers' Training Corps program and rose to become commander of the college's Army ROTC unit. After graduation in 1958, Powell was commissioned a second lieutenant in the U.S. Army, and he served two separate tours (1962–63; 1968–69) in Vietnam. He earned an M.B.A. from George Washington University in Washington, D.C., in 1971, after which he became an assistant to Frank Carlucci, the deputy director of the Office of Management and Budget. Powell later served as a battalion commander in South Korea (1973–74) and in positions at the Pentagon (1974–75). In 1975 he was promoted to the rank of colonel, and in the early 1980s he became a major general and the senior military assistant to the secretary of defense.

In 1986 Powell was appointed deputy director of the National Security Council under Carlucci, who was then Pres. Ronald Reagan's national security affairs assistant. The following year Powell succeeded Carlucci, and in early 1989 he assumed command of the Army Forces Command. In April of that year he was elevated to the rank of four-star general, and in August he was appointed chairman of the Joint Chiefs of Staff, the first African American and at age 52 the youngest person to occupy the highest post in the military.

After retiring from the army in 1993, Powell remained active in politics, helping to broker a compromise in which Haiti's military regime ceded power to elected Pres. Jean-Bertrand Aristide. Popular with broad segments of the electorate, Powell was lobbied by both the Democratic and Republican parties to run for national office. Although polls in 1995 showed Powell a formidable contender for president, he declined to run. Nonetheless, he publicly declared himself a Republican, despite his support for abortion rights and affirmative action—two issues that put him outside the Republican Party's mainstream.

As secretary of state Powell spent the early months of 2001 attempting to broker an end to hostilities between Israel and the Palestinians and to gain support for loosening the UN-imposed trade sanctions against Iraq. In June he attended a UN AIDS conference and pledged U.S. financial support for an international fund to combat the disease. Though he was scheduled to attend the UN World Conference Against Racism, which began on August 31, Powell led a U.S. boycott in response to Arab efforts to single out Israel as racist. In the wake of the September 11 terrorist attacks in the U.S., Powell focused on building international support for U.S. actions against the Taliban to force it to cease harbouring Osama bin Laden (*q.v.*), whom the U.S. blamed for the attacks.

(MICHAEL I. LEVY)

Redstone, Sumner

"The words *step down*, the word *retire* . . . is not in my dictionary. I love what I'm doing. I know I'm at the top of my game." These sentiments were expressed in June 2001 by Sumner Redstone, the 78-year-old chief executive officer and chairman of the board of Viacom Inc., a media conglomerate whose holdings included, among others, Paramount Pictures, CBS, Blockbuster, Simon & Schuster, and MTV. Also in 2001, along with his executive duties, Redstone published his autobiography, *A Passion to Win*, written with Peter Knobler.

Redstone was born Sumner Rothstein on May 27, 1923, in Boston. He graduated with a B.A. degree from Harvard University in 1944. Because he had become fluent in Japanese, he was chosen to join a U.S. Army team charged

Statesman Colin Powell, in Mali

AP/Wide World Photos

with cracking secret Japanese military and diplomatic communication codes during the remainder of World War II. After the war he entered Harvard Law School, from which he graduated in 1947. During the next few years, he worked for the U.S. Court of Appeals and served as an instructor at the University of San Francisco and as special assistant to U.S. Attorney General Tom Clark. In 1951 he became a partner in the Washington, D.C., law firm of Ford, Bergson, Adams, Borkland, & Redstone.

Stating that "litigation is generally offensive to me," Redstone in 1954 returned to Boston and began working for Northeast Theater Corp., a motion picture-exhibition business that his father had established. By 1964 he had expanded Northeast Theater to 59 screens in the Boston area, and three years later he became president and chief executive officer of the firm, which was renamed National Amusements. During the next few years, he continued to increase the company's number of movie theatres. Although prosperous and successful, he concluded that the real money and power in the movie business was in Hollywood. After seeing the film *Star Wars* in 1977, he began buying shares in Twentieth Century Fox, the movie's producer, and he later sold them at a large profit.

In 1979 Redstone suffered severe burns in a hotel fire in Boston. At the time, he had increased the number of National Amusements theatres to 180. With time to reflect during his recovery, he began to think, however, that his ambitions had been too limited. In 1987 he purchased Viacom, which was then a somewhat obscure television company. With that acquisition he became the largest producer of programs for cable television subscribers, owning Showtime, the Movie Channel, MTV, five network-affiliated TV stations, and syndication rights to *The Cosby Show,* one of the most popular programs on television; at the same time, his movie-theatre chain had expanded to 1,300 screens.

In 1994 Redstone added to his empire by winning hard-fought battles to acquire Paramount Communications and Blockbuster, and in 2000 he merged Viacom with CBS to create the second largest media company in the world, behind only AOL Time Warner.

(DAVID R. CALHOUN)

Reza, Yasmina

During the 2000–01 theatre season, French playwright and actress Yasmina Reza seemed to be everywhere. Her hit plays were being staged throughout the world, and she herself took a role in a Paris production. Though best known for *Art,* she was enjoying renewed attention for her latest stage work, *Trois versions de la vie.* It had its premiere in Vienna in October 2000 and opened the following month in Paris, with the author in the cast, and in December in London under the title *Life × 3.* The work showed a ticklish situation—a couple arriving a day early for a dinner party—working itself out in three ways.

Reza, born on May 1, 1959, in Paris, was the daughter of Jewish parents who had immigrated to France. Her father was an Iranian born in Moscow, and her mother was from Budapest. The father was an engineer and businessman who was also a pianist, and her

mother was a violinist. The daughter studied at the University of Paris X, Nanterre, and at the drama school of Jacques Lecoq before working as an actress. Her first plays, both winners of a Molière Award, were *Conversations After a Burial* (1987), involving death and sex, and *Winter Crossing* (1990). It was *Art,* however, which premiered in 1994, that brought her wide notice. In the play three friends quarrel over a work of modern art and thereby show just how fragile friendship can be. The play was in production on major stages worldwide virtually continuously after its opening. It won Molière Awards for best author, play, and production, Olivier and *Evening Standard* awards in London, and a Tony Award in New York as best play. Another hit, *The Unexpected Man* (1995), was a two-hander set on a train. Following long monologues by a male author and his female seatmate and fan, the play ends with a brief dialogue between the two that centres on people's need for one another.

Included in Reza's other writings was *Hammerklavier,* novelized vignettes of memories of her father, published in 1997. She did a French translation of an adaptation of Franz Kafka's *Metamorphosis* for the filmmaker Roman Polanski and wrote two screenplays, including *Le Pique-nique de Lulu Kreutz* for a film directed by her companion, Didier Martigny. Returning to her first profession, she took part in the filming of *Loin* (also known as *Terminus des anges*), directed by André Téchiné, in 2000.

Critics said that not since Jean Anouilh in the 1950s had a French playwright been so exportable. Reza's brief dramas with small casts, written in a spare, witty language, offered satire in the tradition of Molière. At the same time, the playwright spoke to contemporary anxieties, and critics compared her to Harold Pinter and Edward Albee.

(ROBERT RAUCH)

Ridge, Tom

In response to the Sept. 11, 2001, terrorist attacks in the U.S., Pres. George W. Bush created by executive order a new department to counter future domestic threats—the Office of Homeland Security—and on September 20 selected his friend Tom Ridge to head it. Taking the post required Ridge to step down as governor of Pennsylvania. No sooner had he been sworn in on October 8 than he found himself reacting to widespread public fear and outrage over bioterrorism in the form of anonymous letters mailed to public figures carrying lethal amounts of anthrax, an infectious disease, that resulted in several deaths. Ridge hit the ground running, developing a program of antiterrorist training, preventive technologies, and emergency responses. One outcome was the mobilization of the National Guard to augment security at the nation's airports. His new cabinet-level position put him squarely in the national spotlight as he issued general alerts of suspected future threats, however vague, with a public wary of any new acts of terror. Despite his high profile, there was concern in Washington that, even with high-level council members, a 100-member staff, a $25 million start-up budget, and the executive backing of the president, Ridge would be unable to coordinate the myriad activities of some 46 dif-

ferent state and federal agencies related to his chain of command.

A popular two-term governor who had been due to leave office in 2003, Ridge was a leading figure in the Republican Party. He had been considered as a running mate for presidential candidates in 1996 and 2000, despite being pro-choice on the volatile issue of abortion. In office he was a moderate Republican, fiscally conservative with a streak of independence, known for his hard-working, pleasant demeanour.

Thomas Joseph Ridge was born on Aug. 26, 1945, to Slovak-Irish-Cherokee parents in a blue-collar family in Erie, Pa. Educated at private schools, he earned a scholarship to Harvard University (B.S., 1967). In 1969, after his first year at Dickinson School of Law, Carlisle, Pa., he was drafted to serve in the Vietnam War, becoming a staff sergeant in the army and winning the Bronze Star for Valor, among other decorations. After returning to complete his J.D. (1972) at Dickinson, he practiced law in Erie and in 1982 narrowly won election to the U.S. Congress. Ridge steadily improved his margins of victory in succeeding elections and served a total of six terms in Congress.

A long shot in the 1994 gubernatorial elections, Ridge defeated the incumbent lieu-

Tom Ridge: on his shoulders, America's security

tenant governor but stumbled in his first years in office, with failed attempts to institute school vouchers and privatize liquor stores. Soon afterward, though, buoyed by a strong economy and budget surplus, Ridge found his footing and launched his programs with success. When on September 11 one of the four hijacked planes crashed in the countryside of his home state, Ridge was at the site within hours.

(TOM MICHAEL)

Rogge, Jacques

As a former Olympic yachtsman, Belgian Jacques Rogge was no stranger to rough waters, but he faced a flood of problems when he took

Biographies

over the helm of the International Olympic Committee (IOC) in July 2001, succeeding outgoing president Juan António Samaranch of Spain, a figure who became nearly synonymous with the triumphs and excesses of the modern Olympic movement. Rogge was elected in the hope that he would clear away the aura of scandal that had imperiled the IOC in recent years, particularly the high-profile resignations and felony charges of bribery that grew out of the successful Salt Lake City, Utah, bid for the 2002 Winter Games. Rogge, a medical doctor who served on the board of the World Anti-Doping Agency, was chosen to cleanse the public image of the IOC and bring some down-to-earth governance to what had become the most opulent sports organization in the world.

Rogge won election to the eight-year post (with a possible four-year extension) over rivals Kim Un Yong of South Korea, Dick Pound of Canada, and Pal Schmitt of Hungary. His first challenge prior to the Olympic Games at Salt Lake City was to maintain calm and tighten security in the wake of the terrorist attacks in the United States on September 11. Though Rogge was granted emergency powers to cancel the Games without the vote of the full committee, he had no intention of backing out. Voicing his confidence in the safety of the event, he declared that he would take lodging in the Olympic Village dormitories along with the athletes, rather than in a hotel.

Rogge was born on May 2, 1942, in Ghent, Belg. In Great Britain he studied sports medicine and earned his medical degree before returning to Belgium to work as an orthopedic surgeon in Deinze, where he performed as many as 800 operations a year. He also lectured at Free University in Brussels and the University of Ghent. A successful athlete, he was a 16-time national champion in rugby and one-time yachting world champion. He competed in the Finn class of sailing at the Summer Games in 1968, 1972, and 1976 before he left competition but not the Olympic movement. As the head official of Belgium's Olympic team in 1980, he refused to join the U.S.-led boycott of the Moscow Summer Games protesting the Soviet invasion of Afghanistan. Despite intense pressure on Rogge, Belgian athletes competed in Moscow. "This was a milestone in my life," Rogge declared later. "We thought it was our duty to participate in the Olympic Games."

In 1989 he became president of the European Olympic Committee, and in 1991 he joined the IOC; he became a member of various IOC commissions, including the medical committee, and in 1998 he joined the IOC executive board. Rogge was instrumental in coordinating the successful 2000 Summer Games in Sydney, Australia, and in helping to formulate the 2004 Games in Athens. The new IOC president—the eighth in the 107-year history of the organization—planned to leave his medical practice and take up residence in Lausanne, Switz., home to the IOC headquarters. (TOM MICHAEL)

Sa'd ad-Din Ibrahim

On May 21, 2001, less than two hours after the defense lawyers had completed their summation, Egypt's High Security Court found Sa'd ad-Din Ibrahim, a respected university professor, guilty of having accepted money from overseas without government approval, embezzled grant funds, and defamed Egypt abroad. Sentenced together with 27 co-defendants, Ibrahim received seven years' imprisonment at hard labour, despite the fact that he was 62 years old and in poor health.

Ibrahim was born on Dec. 3, 1938, in Mansurah, a city in Egypt's Nile Delta. He graduated from Cairo University (B.A., 1960) and was awarded a government scholarship to study sociology at the University of Washington (Ph.D., 1968). He took U.S. citizenship and, while teaching at DePauw University, Greencastle, Ind., met his future wife, Barbara Lethem. In 1975, however, Ibrahim returned to Cairo, where he won a tenured position at the American University. He performed pioneering research on militant Islamic movements in Egypt. In 1988 he founded the Ibn Khaldun Center for Development Studies, which soon became a leading institution in the Muslim world for the study of human rights, civil society, and minority rights.

On June 30, 2000, Ibrahim was arrested and imprisoned by the authorities. Two of the charges against him were related to a $250,000 European Commission grant Ibrahim had won to make a documentary about voting rights in Egypt. The charge that he had received funds from foreign organizations without government approval was considered suspect by many because the Ibn Khaldun Center was a registered organization that paid Egyptian taxes and therefore was entitled to make such transactions. Similarly, the embezzlement charge was shaky because Ibrahim's handling of the grant money had been properly audited. The third accusation—that Ibrahim had defamed Egypt's reputation abroad—stemmed from his participation in seminars on the plight of Christian Copts, who had suffered widespread discrimination at the hands of the Egyptian authorities, and from his studies on parliamentary elections that proved unflattering to the Mubarak regime. On Aug. 10, 2000, Ibrahim was released on bail, and his trial opened in Cairo some three months later, on November 18.

At the end of 2001, many Egyptian people felt themselves squeezed between the authoritarian Mubarak regime and the radical Islamists. The possibility of a third alternative—a country in which the citizens enjoyed democracy and the rule of law as well as their Islamic faith—seemed quite distant as long as men like Ibrahim languished in prison.

(MARIUS K. DEEB)

Sade

The year 2001 witnessed the reunion of a beloved pop icon and an adoring fan base as Nigerian-born British singer Sade emerged from an almost decade-long hiatus to embark on a world tour with new material from her latest album, *Lovers Rock* (2000). The singer renowned for her sensual voice and exotic looks had lapsed into silence after the release in 1992 of the wildly successful *Love Deluxe* and a subsequent tour.

Helen Folasade Adu was born to a Nigerian economics professor and an English nurse on

AP/Wide World Photos

Sade returns to the stage

Jan. 16, 1959, in Ibadan. Because people in the community refused to address her by her English first name, her parents began calling her Sade, a shortened form of her Yoruba middle name. When she was four years old, her parents separated, and she moved with her mother and younger brother to Essex, Eng. At 17 Sade began a three-year program in fashion and design at Central St. Martin's College of Art and Design in London. After graduating, she worked as a menswear designer and did some modeling. Her foray into music was the result of her agreement to fill in temporarily as lead singer for Arriva, a funk band that had been put together by her friends. Sade later sang with another funk band, Pride, before breaking away with fellow Pride members Stuart Matthewman, Andrew Hale, and Paul Spencer Denman to form the band that would eventually bear her own name.

Sade's music was a sophisticated blend of soul, funk, jazz, and Afro-Cuban rhythms that defied easy categorization. The sound was exemplified by the songs "Your Love Is King" and "Smooth Operator," both tracks from Sade's Grammy Award-winning debut album *Diamond Life* (1984). A second album, *Promise* (1985), enjoyed similar popularity and was followed by a world tour. The album featured the hit song "The Sweetest Taboo," which stayed on the American pop charts for six months. In 1988 Sade embarked on a second world tour to coincide with the release of a third album, *Stronger than Pride*.

After *Love Deluxe*, Sade enjoyed life away from the limelight. She became a mother, while other members of her band recorded separately as Sweetback. They reunited to produce the long-awaited *Lovers Rock*, and Sade completed her comeback with a triumphant return to the concert stage. Fans were so overjoyed that tickets to many of her performances sold out within an hour. (SHANDA SILER)

Saxecoburggotski, Simeon

On July 24, 2001, Simeon Saxecoburggotski became prime minister of Bulgaria. The new head of government had ruled the country as King Simeon II from 1943 to 1945. In early April 2001 he formed a party that, in the elections held in June, won exactly half of the seats in the National Assembly. He then formed a coalition government dedicated to economic reform and to ending corruption.

The future tsar was born on June 16, 1937, in Sofia. His father, Tsar Boris III, died suddenly on Aug. 28, 1943, and at the age of six the boy ascended the throne as Simeon II. By late 1944 the Red Army had occupied Bulgaria, and regents ruling in the boy's name were executed in 1945. A referendum in September 1946 ended the monarchy, and Simeon II and his mother were forced into exile. They lived first in Egypt, where the boy studied in Alexandria at Victoria College (1946–51), and then went to Spain. He graduated from the Lycée Français in Madrid in 1957, attended the Valley Forge Military Academy in Wayne, Pa., in 1958–59, and became a successful businessman in Madrid. In 1962 he married the daughter of a Spanish banking family. He first returned to Bulgaria as a visitor in 1996, and most of the royal property was later returned to him.

In April 2001 he announced the formation of the National Movement for Simeon II to field candidates in the national legislative elections scheduled for June 17. When the courts ruled that the party had not met all of the requirements for registration, two minor parties allowed the movement to join them in a coalition, which allowed it to participate in the election. Although the former tsar was not himself a candidate, he campaigned for those running under the party banner. The party won 120 of the 240 seats and formed a coalition with the Movement for Rights and Freedoms, which represented the country's Turkish minority.

Upon taking office, the new prime minister took as his surname Saxecoburggotski, the Bulgarian form of the name of his royal house, Saxe-Coburg-Gotha. His cabinet was notable for including a large number of professionals, particularly people trained in finance and economics, and for its youth. Few members had previous political experience, and none had ever been a member of a cabinet; two of the positions went to Turks. The new prime minister announced an 800-day reform plan that called for lower taxes, a balanced budget, increased investment, and improved living standards, and he stressed the importance of preparing Bulgaria for membership in the European Union and NATO. He brushed aside charges from opponents that his ultimate aim was to restore the monarchy.   (ROBERT RAUCH)

Schumacher, Michael

On Oct. 14, 2001, German racing car driver Michael Schumacher completed a record-breaking year by winning the Japan Grand Prix, the final event of the Formula One automobile racing season. The victory was Schumacher's ninth in the season's 17 Grand Prix races, a tally he had achieved twice before, in 1995 and 2000. Briton Nigel Mansell (in 1992) was the only other driver to win nine races in one season.

Even more noteworthy for Schumacher, however, was his season-ending career total of 53 Grand Prix triumphs, the most ever by a Formula One driver and two more than the previous record of 51 held by retired French driver Alain Prost. His achievements also won for Schumacher his fourth drivers' world title. Only Juan Manuel Fangio of Argentina, with five championships in the 1950s, had won more.

Schumacher was born Jan. 3, 1969, in Hürth-Hermülhein, W.Ger. As a young boy he became interested in go-kart racing, an enthusiasm that was supported by his father's management of a go-kart track in the town of Kerpen. In 1984 and 1985 Schumacher won the German junior karting championship, and in 1987 he gained the German and European karting titles. The next year, at the age of 19, he left karting and became a driver of Formula Three cars, vehicles that were less powerful than the Formula One racers. Two years later, in 1990, he won the German Formula Three championship.

In 1991 Schumacher moved up to Formula One competition as a driver for the Jordan team. He switched to Benetton the following year and won the drivers' world championship for that team in 1994 and 1995. Before the 1996 season he moved to the Ferrari team, though many thought that he might have won a third consecutive world title if he had remained with Benetton. When questioned about that possibility, Schumacher commented, "I've always been more interested in the way I achieve victories rather than just to achieve them. I had won two championships, so I needed something different." His younger brother, Ralf, joined him on the Grand Prix circuit in 1997.

In the 1999 British Grand Prix at Silverstone, Michael Schumacher veered off the track at Stowe corner, plowed through a wall of tires at 160 km/h (100 mph), and crashed into a concrete wall. With ambulances and medical teams rushing to the ruined Ferrari, many in the crowd feared that Schumacher would not survive the accident. He emerged from the car, however, with nothing worse than a broken leg. He recovered from this setback to win the drivers' championship in 2000, Ferrari's first drivers' title since 1979. The triumphs of 2001 followed. In May it was announced that Schumacher had signed a contract to drive for Ferrari until 2004. In October, two weeks after completing his triumphant Grand Prix season, he returned to Kerpen and finished second in the karting world championship.

(DAVID R. CALHOUN)

Sharon, Ariel

In elections in Israel on Feb. 6, 2001, Ariel ("Arik") Sharon, leader of the right-wing Likud, defeated Ehud Barak of the Labor Party by a margin of 62.4% to 37.6%. After assembling a broad-based coalition government, Sharon took office as the country's 11th prime minister on March 7. Ironically, it was Sharon's visit to Jerusalem's Temple Mount in September 2000 that sparked the Palestinian uprising that in turn discredited Barak's peace policies and paved the way for Sharon's landslide victory.

As prime minister, Sharon set up a national unity government with Labor and announced two major policy changes—there would be no negotiations with the Palestinians as long as violence continued, and interim, rather than final, arrangements would be made when the shooting stopped.

Ariel Sheinerman was born on Feb. 26, 1928, in Kfar Malal, a small farming village north of Tel Aviv, Palestine. The village often came under Arab attack, and from the age of 13, Sharon, armed with a club and dagger, helped patrol the fields at night. In Israel's 1948 War of Independence, he made a name for himself as a fearless young officer, and in 1953 he was handpicked to set up a commando unit to retaliate against relentless Arab incursions. The unit, known as 101, did more than carry out reprisal raids; it transformed the Israel Defense

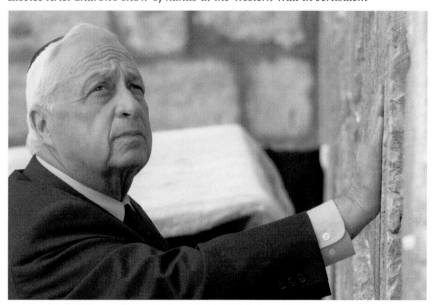

Electee Ariel Sharon's show of hands at the Western Wall in Jerusalem

Forces' ethos, with a strategy that emphasized taking the attack to the enemy.

His command of Unit 101 highlighted failings that would dog Sharon in later life: his headstrong belief in his own better judgment and his penchant for exceeding orders. The most blatant case was a 1953 raid on the West Bank village of Qibya, where Sharon's men blew up more than 40 houses and left 69 civilians dead.

Sharon's brilliance as a field commander was never in question. He led one of three lightning armour thrusts into Sinai in the 1967 Six-Day War and in 1971, as head of Southern Command, crushed Palestinian terror in Gaza. When he was denied the post of chief of staff, however, he left the army in 1973, and within months unified political forces on the right to form the present-day Likud. Recalled to service in the 1973 Yom Kippur War, he made a daring crossing of the Suez Canal that turned the tide and made him a national hero.

His star waned when, as defense minister in 1982, he masterminded Israel's ill-fated invasion of Lebanon and was forced to resign after a commission of inquiry found him indirectly responsible for a massacre by Israel's Christian allies in the Sabra and Shatila Palestinian refugee camps.

Sharon, however, continued to serve in Likud-led governments, incurring U.S. wrath for persistent promotion of Jewish settlement activity in occupied territory. In 1998 he became foreign minister, a platform from which he took over as party leader when Benjamin Netanyahu lost the premiership to Barak in 1999. With elections looming, Netanyahu launched a comeback in November 2000 and seemed set to recapture the leadership. He withdrew, however, at the 11th hour, paving the way for what months before had seemed a highly improbable victory for Sharon at the polls. (LESLIE D. SUSSER)

Soderbergh, Steven

Onetime independent film prodigy Steven Soderbergh had two films competing against one another in two categories at the 2001 Academy Awards. Both his David-versus-Goliath tale *Erin Brockovich* (2000) and his drug-trade pseudodocumentary *Traffic* (2000) vied for best picture and best director awards. Critics feared that the double nominations would cause a split vote in the Academy and ultimately result in both films' defeat. In the end both movies won laurels—Julia Roberts won the best actress award for *Brockovich*, and Soderbergh won the best director award for *Traffic*, which took three other awards but lost out to *Gladiator* for best picture.

Steven Andrew Soderbergh was born on Jan. 14, 1963, in Atlanta, Ga. When he was 13, his family relocated to Baton Rouge, La., where his father assumed the post of professor and administrator at Louisiana State University. Soderbergh enrolled in a film animation course at the university while still a high-school student, and it was then that he began making short films. After graduating from high school, he moved to Hollywood to pursue a career as a screenwriter, but his efforts were met with rejection. A year later he returned to Baton Rouge, where he worked at a video arcade while continuing to write and shoot low-budget short

pieces. His change of fortune came in 1986 when he was asked to develop one such project into a full-length promotional film for the rock band Yes. This relatively small beginning emboldened Soderbergh to set out for Hollywood once more. He then completed the celebrated *sex, lies, and videotape* (1989), which explored the complexities of modern relationships. The film was a surprise hit at the Cannes International Film Festival that year, picking up three awards, including the Palme d'Or, and catapulting the 26-year-old Soderbergh to fame. *Kafka* (1991), *King of the Hill* (1993), *Underneath* (1995), *Gray's Anatomy* (1996), and *Schizopolis* (1996) followed, but they were not as well received. At the height of his return to obscurity, a shunned Soderbergh was forced to make a living as a freelance, but he persisted in making films. He again found commercial and critical success with *Out of Sight* (1998), the story of a bank heist and unlikely romance between the lead characters, played by George Clooney and Jennifer Lopez (*q.v.*). *The Limey* (1999), a gritty gangster's tale, enjoyed similar kudos. That year he published the memoir *Getting Away with It: or, The Further Adventures of the Luckiest Bastard You Ever Saw*. Soderbergh continued to explore crime and its implications in *Brockovich* and *Traffic*. After the excitement of the 2001 Oscars, Soderbergh began work on *Ocean's Eleven*—a star-studded remake of the 1960 classic—which was released in December.

(SHANDA SILER)

Sontag, Susan

American essayist, cultural and literary critic, and novelist Susan Sontag had been honoured with numerous awards for her work, but when she was named the recipient of the Jerusalem Prize for the Freedom of the Individual in Society, there was an outcry among those who felt that she should not accept the prize. Sontag was reluctant to refuse, however, an action she deemed would be "boorish, unconvivial, pretentious."

At the award ceremony, she was disinclined to voice opinions on the situation in Israel, but she spoke against "the doctrine of collective responsibility as a rationale for collective punishment." She decried "the use of disproportionate firepower" and other military actions against civilian Palestinians. She called for the dismantling of Jewish settlements. In the end, however, she gratefully accepted the prize "in the name of peace and the reconciliation of injured and fearful communities" and because it "honours, above all, the international republic of letters."

Sontag seemed destined for life as a public intellectual. She was born on Jan. 16, 1933, in New York City and reared there, until age five, by her grandparents. When her father, who was a fur trader working mostly in China, died, her mother returned home. The family ultimately settled in Los Angeles. Sontag

started school at age six and was quickly advanced to the third grade. At 15 she entered the University of California, Berkeley, and a year later she transferred to the University of Chicago. She married intellectual Philip Rieff in her sophomore year (they divorced in the late 1950s) and graduated with a B.A. (philosophy) in 1951. She took master's degrees in English literature (1954) and philosophy (1955) at Harvard University and taught before publishing her first novel in 1963.

Sontag first came to national attention in 1964 with an essay entitled "Notes on 'Camp,'" in which she discussed the attributes of taste in gay culture. This and other essays were some of the earliest to treat modern culture in a serious philosophical manner. She wrote on theatre and film, as well as on 20th-century cultural figures such as writer Nathalie Sarraute, director Robert Bresson, and painter Francis Bacon, among others. Many of the essays and reviews collected in early volumes were first published in *The New York Review of Books*, *Commentary*, and *Partisan Review*. Her later critical works included the award-winning *On Photography* (1977), *Illness as Metaphor* (1977), and *AIDS and Its Metaphors* (1988). Her most popular novel was *The Volcano Lover* (1992), a postmodern romance about the life of Sir William Hamilton. *In America* (2000), a work of fiction based on the life of actress Helena Modjeska, won a National Book Award in 2000.

(KATHLEEN KUIPER)

Sörenstam, Annika

Swedish golfer Annika Sörenstam reestablished herself in 2001 as the top player on the Ladies Professional Golf Association (LPGA) tour. Although she had led all LPGA golfers by winning 18 tournaments during the 1990s, Sörenstam had watched Australian Karrie Webb grab all the headlines and dominate the tour in 1999 and 2000. Sörenstam played well in 2000, winning five tournaments. Though her victory at the Welch's/Circle K Championship in Tucson, Ariz., qualified her for the Hall of Fame, her season went largely unnoticed, owing to the attention Webb received. This did not sit well with the notoriously competitive Sörenstam. Determined to recapture the number one spot on the tour, she spent the off-season working on a new physical fitness regimen and concentrating on her short game and her putting. The result was a resurgence that at times caught even Sörenstam herself by surprise. A prime example was her record-setting 10-stroke comeback victory in the last round of the Office Depot tournament in Los Angeles, which broke the previous last-round comeback record of eight strokes. She characterized the amazing performance as "more than a miracle"; it gave Sörenstam her fourth win in a row and made her one of only four women golfers ever to string together that many victories. During that stretch she also became the first woman golfer to break 60 when she shot a 59 in the second round of the Standard Register Ping tournament in Phoenix, Ariz. At the same tournament, she set a new 72-hole mark with her 27-under-par performance.

Sörenstam was born Oct. 9, 1970, in Stockholm. She began playing golf at the age of 12, and she was a member of the Swedish national team from 1987 to 1992. She attended the University of Arizona, where she won a National Collegiate Athletic Association title in 1991 and earned All-America honours in 1991 and 1992. In 1992 she won the world amateur championship, finished second at the U.S. women's amateur championship, and posted the second lowest score among amateurs at the U.S. Women's Open. She was the European tour's Rookie of the Year in 1993 and with three top-10 finishes on the LPGA tour the following year, including one tie for second, was named that tour's Rookie of the Year. In 1995 she posted her first LPGA tour victory at the U.S. Women's Open and went on to win Player of the Year honours while capturing the Vare Trophy for lowest scoring average (71.0). She also became the first player to lead the LPGA tour and the European tour in winnings in the same season. In 1996 she successfully defended her title at the U.S. Women's Open and won the Vare Trophy (70.47) again. Six titles in 1997 earned her Player of the Year laurels for a second time, then she repeated as Player of the Year in 1998, when she became the first player on the LPGA tour to finish the season with a scoring average below 70 (69.99).

Other highlights of 2001 included a victory with Tiger Woods in a made-for-TV match-play event against Webb and David Duval. By the end of her remarkable season, Sörenstam had won her first major title (the Nabisco Championship) since 1996, led the tour in earnings for the year, and become the first woman golfer to break the $7 million mark for career earnings. (ANTHONY G. CRAINE)

Stella, Frank

After keeping a low profile throughout the 1990s, American artist Frank Stella returned to the limelight in a big way, with large public sculptures. In 2001 the 65-year-old completed work on *The Prince of Homburg*, a massive

mostly metal sculpture for the plaza outside the National Gallery of Art in Washington, D.C. The 9,100-kg (20,000-lb) piece followed on the heels of public art murals for the Princess of Wales Theatre in Toronto (1992–93), designs for a museum addition in Dresden, Ger., and a bandshell in Miami, Fla. A pioneer of Minimalism in the 1960s, Stella traced a gradual arc from the stark flatness of his first paintings, through three-dimensional constructions, and finally to architecture. All the while, though, he continued to sharpen the cutting edge of modern art with innovative work upheld by sound theories.

Stella was born on May 12, 1936, in Malden, Mass. He was educated at Phillips Academy, Andover, Mass., and at Princeton University (B.A., 1958), where he was taught appreciation for the New York school of Abstract Expressionism by Stephen Greene and William Seitz. After graduation Stella moved to New York City and became an instant sensation when his paintings appeared in a group show at the Museum of Modern Art in 1959–60. His "black paintings" were shockingly two dimensional: cruciform stripes of common black house paint bordered by narrow strips of raw canvas. Inspired by the object-oriented work of Jasper Johns and troubled by what he saw as growing ambiguity in Abstract Expressionism, Stella promoted a Gestalt theory of "What you see is what you see" that became the credo for Minimalism, which rejected illusionism, narrative, and symbolism, and he concentrated on fundamental shapes of primary colours. In exhibits at the influential Leo Castelli Gallery, Stella helped minimalism eclipse Action painting to become (along with Pop art) the driving force of the New York school by the mid-1960s.

Stella furthered his nonobjective aesthetic by achieving greater flatness through the use of aluminum paints and by notching his rectangular canvases so that no negative space appeared. He was one of the first artists to use

shaped canvases. He explored colour and shape with the *Benjamin Moore* series (1961), *Concentric Square* series (1963), and *Irregular Polygon* series (1966), culminating with the *Protractor* series (1967–69). Never bound by the movement he helped launch, Stella shifted to a larger colour field with *Irregular Polygons* (1966–67) and *Polish Village* (1971–73). He edged toward sculpture with the "maximalist" protrusive relief series of the 1970s: *Brazilian* (1974–75), *Exotic Bird* (1976–80), and *Indian Bird* (1977–79). This period also introduced the French curve into Stella's art, a dominant feature in his later work.

While visiting Rome in 1982–83, Stella was taken with the historical Baroque response to the decline of Renaissance art, particularly through artists such as Caravaggio, and he sought to revive abstract art in the same manner. He gave a series of lectures at Harvard University, later published as *Working Space* (1986), and created a group of Baroque-influenced abstract paintings called *Circuit and Shards* (1983), which was followed by the *Cones and Pillars* series (1987); the latter showed Stella toying with illusionism and spatial dynamics. He was the subject of two retrospectives by the Museum of Modern Art (1970, 1987) and was the only American to mount a solo show in 2000 at the Royal Academy of Arts in London.

(TOM MICHAEL)

Stroman, Susan

Of the record-breaking 12 Tony Awards won by the musical comedy *The Producers* in 2001, two went to Susan Stroman, the show's innovative director and choreographer. No stranger to honours, she had previously amassed three other Tonys, as well as multiple Outer Critics Circle, Drama Desk, and Laurence Olivier awards.

"Stro," as she was known, was born on Oct. 17, 1954, in Wilmington, Del., and grew up in a home in which music was prized. She loved watching Fred Astaire movies and later admitted that, even when she was very young, she visualized dance when she heard music. She began dance classes at age five and learned to play musical instruments. Stroman got some choreographing experience in local theatres during her student years in high school and at the University of Delaware, and in 1977, a year after graduation, she headed for New York City. Knowing that she would need to have some performing credentials before she could break into choreographing professionally, Stroman secured work in several shows and in 1980 became assistant director, assistant choreographer, and dance captain of a little-known show, *Musical Chairs*. In 1987, after spending several years at small choreographing jobs, she and a member of that show's cast, Scott Ellis, collaborated on an Off-Broadway revival of *Flora, the Red Menace*. It became a cult success and helped them make some important connections, which led to further work on such shows as the New York City Opera's *Don Giovanni* (1989) and the John Kander and Fred Ebb revue *And the World Goes 'Round* (1991). For the latter, Stroman won her first Outer Critics Circle Award for choreography. In 1992, her inventiveness was showcased to great success when

Jim McHugh, February 1993

Frank Stella in the limelight

she choreographed *Crazy for You* and took Broadway by storm, winning Tony, Drama Desk, Outer Critics Circle, and later—for the London production—Olivier awards. Among shows that followed were *Show Boat* (1994), for which she was honoured with another Outer Critics Circle Award, *Big* (1996), *Steel Pier* (1997), and the London revival of *Oklahoma!* (1998), which won her another Olivier Award. Stroman's imagination took a different direction for *Contact* (1999), telling three separate stories almost entirely through dance; among that show's awards were Tonys for both choreography and best new musical. Another award-winning musical was the revival of *The Music Man* in 2000. Stroman also choreographed for film and television and counted such ballets as *But Not for Me* for the Martha Graham Company in 1998 and *Blossom Got Kissed* for the New York City Ballet in 1999 among her credits.

Originally, Stroman's husband since 1995, *Crazy for You* director Mike Ockrent, was to have been director of *The Producers*, with Stroman as choreographer, but after he died in 1999, Stroman took over the directorship as well. In October 2001 yet another of her efforts as director-choreographer opened in New York City—*Thou Shalt Not*, a musical version of Émile Zola's *Thérèse Raquin*. *Oklahoma!*, with Stroman's London choreography, was scheduled to open in New York in March 2002, Broadway's first production of that play without the original Agnes de Mille choreography. (BARBARA WHITNEY)

Tanaka, Makiko

Dubbed "the Lady with the Big Mouth" by *Time* magazine, Japanese Foreign Minister Makiko Tanaka made headlines in 2001 for her outspoken comments and her skirmishes with Japan's senior political bureaucrats. She was criticized by members of the Diet, Japan's parliament, which did not permit her to represent Japan at the United Nations General Assembly in November, and officials of her own Liberal Democratic Party (LDP) for, among other comments, suggesting that the best way former prime minister Yoshiro Mori could help Japan was by putting a big adhesive bandage over his mouth; characterizing most party elections as "like a garage sale full of senior politicians who've been in office too long," some of whom she said should be strapped to satellites; and making decisions and expressing opinions that veered from the official government policy. Her supporters, however, praised her as a reformer who spoke only the truth and provided a much-needed shake-up of the old scandal-ridden system.

Many observers found it ironic that Tanaka was challenging the LDP old guard, since her father, former prime minister Kakuei Tanaka, had been instrumental in establishing the powerful political machine. Some analysts attributed her motives to the belief that her

father had been betrayed when Noboru Takeshita (who later became prime minister) took over the ruling LDP faction that Kakuei Tanaka had helped found.

Maki, as she was affectionately known, was born on Jan. 14, 1944. She attended high school in the United States before graduating from the School of Commerce at Waseda University in 1968. She frequently served as an unofficial first lady during her father's prime ministership (1972–74). In 1983 she campaigned for her husband, Naoki Tanaka, who was elected to the Diet, but she retreated from the public eye to care for her father when he suffered a stroke in 1985. In 1993 Tanaka was elected to the Diet, and she served as head of the Science and Technology Agency from 1994 to 1995. She was reelected in 1996 and 2000, and by 2001 her relaxed, informal personal style and sharp wit had made her one of the most popular political figures in Japan. Her active support of reformist candidate Junichiro Koizumi (*q.v.*) contributed to his election as prime minister in April 2001, and he promptly appointed her Japan's first female foreign minister. She just as promptly began making waves, describing traditional Japanese diplomacy as "an exercise in telling nothing with as many words as possible." In contrast, she remarked, "I usually like to say what's on my mind. I think that's what diplomacy is about." She proved her point in the following months, even criticizing several of Koizumi's decisions, but the controversies served only to boost Tanaka's popularity with the public. (AMY R. TAO)

Thaksin Shinawatra

Though he came late to politics after spectacular successes in the telecommunications industry, Thaksin Shinawatra, one of Thailand's richest men, captured the imagination of voters with his promises of a fresh approach to politics and led his newly created Thai Rak Thai Party to a convincing win in national elections on Jan. 6, 2001. He was appointed prime minister by King Bhumibol Adulyadej on February 9. Thaksin's tenure in office, however, came perilously close to an abrupt end when the independent National Counationrcorruption Commission prosecuted him on April 3 before the Constitutional Court on charges of having concealed assets in a mandatory declaration of wealth. Acquitted by a vote of 8–7 on August 3, Thaksin was left free to pursue his populist political platform.

Thaksin was born on July 26, 1949, in the northern Thailand city of Chiang Mai. He was a descendant of Chinese merchants who had settled in the area before World War I. Although his father was a politician, Thaksin originally planned for a career in the police force. He graduated from the Police Cadet Academy in 1973, winning a scholarship to study criminal justice at Eastern Kentucky University. On his return to Thailand, Thaksin first taught at the Police Academy before being tapped for special duties in the office of Prime Minister Seni Pramoj. In 1978 Thaksin completed a doctorate at Sam Houston (Texas) State University. Back in Thailand, he worked in police planning and public relations positions and became adept in computer technol-

Thaksin Shinawatra: saluting or giving thanks?

ogy. After having attained the rank of lieutenant colonel in the police force, he left the force in 1987 to run his business in the computer field alongside his wife, Potjaman.

It was an era when business fortunes were inextricably linked with political influence. After a brush with bankruptcy, Thaksin eventually obtained a monopoly on satellite communications and a cell phone concession, and he rapidly translated these into a vast fortune. In 1994 he was asked to be foreign minister; he served three months until the fall of the government. The following year he assumed leadership of the Palang Dharma Party, and on the party's entrance into Prime Minister Banharn Silpa-archa's government coalition in 1995, he served as deputy prime minister. Thaksin served as deputy prime minister a second time under Chavalit Yongchaiyudh in 1997.

In his new position as prime minister, Thaksin injected a corporate CEO-style of leadership, brushing aside the objections of bureaucrats and implementing a "workshop" approach to problem solving. His platform had great popular appeal. Thaksin promised the creation of a new bank for small businesses, a three-year debt moratorium for delinquent farmers, and a development fund for each of Thailand's 70,000 villages. (ROBERT WOODROW)

Thomson, James

On Aug. 9, 2001, U.S. Pres. George W. Bush (*q.v.*) announced that the federal government would support research on the approximately 60 existing lines (self-sustaining colonies) of human embryonic stem cells, microscopically tiny undifferentiated cells that have the potential capability of growing into any one of the approximately 200 cell types that compose a human. Because of this capability, scientists believed that stem cells could be used as replacement cells in transplantation therapies in humans to treat such ailments as Parkinson disease, diabetes, spinal-cord injuries, and Alzheimer disease.

President Bush's decision was the culmination of a series of developments that began in 1998 when James Thomson, a biologist at the University of Wisconsin at Madison, became the first person to isolate stem cells from human embryos. For Thomson this achievement was the result of a long process of research and experimentation that began when he was an undergraduate at the University of Illinois at Urbana-Champaign.

Thomson was born in Chicago on Dec. 20, 1958, and grew up in the Chicago suburb of Oak Park. At the University of Illinois, he was encouraged to work in the biology laboratories, where he became interested in the process of early development—the explosive surge of biological activity that occurs when a fertilized egg implants itself in a womb and then begins to divide and form the specialized cells that eventually become the great variety of tissues in the body. Continuing his education and research at the University of Pennsylvania, where he gained a Ph.D. in molecular biology, Thomson learned that biologists in 1980 had succeeded in extracting embryonic stem cells from mice. Because embryonic development in mice differs considerably from that in humans, Thomson then decided to conduct stem cell research on a species much more similar to humans; he chose the rhesus monkey.

In 1991 Thomson moved to the University of Wisconsin, where he continued his research at the primate centre. After many months of painstaking work, he succeeded in isolating the rhesus monkey embryonic stem cells in 1995. The obvious next step, to Thomson, was to try to extract stem cells from human embryos. This, however, confronted him with a moral dilemma, because such an extraction kills the embryo. After consulting with bioethicists at the university, Thomson decided that continued research was "the better ethical choice" as long as the embryos, created by couples who no longer wanted them in order to have children, would otherwise be destroyed.

After he succeeded in isolating the human embryonic stem cells, Thomson assigned the patent for his discovery to the Wisconsin Alumni Research Foundation; the patent covered both the method of isolating the cells and the cells themselves. Consequently, the National Institutes of Health, the agency responsible for implementing President Bush's decision, planned to negotiate with the foundation in order to gain access to the stem cells. As for Thomson, he commented that he was somewhat disappointed that the Bush edict would restrict the creation of new cell lines, but he was generally pleased that the research would go forward. (DAVID R. CALHOUN)

Thorpe, Ian

In July 2001 at the world swimming championships in Fukuoka, Japan, Australian freestyler Ian Thorpe added to his already formidable reputation by winning six gold medals, setting four world records, and leading his nation to a team victory. Living up to his nickname of "the Thorpedo," he set individual world marks of 1 min 44.06 sec in the 200-m freestyle, 3 min 40.17 sec in the 400-m freestyle, and 7 min 39.16 sec in the 800-m freestyle. He was also a member of the 4 × 200-m freestyle relay team, which set a world record of 7 min 4.66 sec. Thorpe's additional gold medals were won in the 4 × 100-m freestyle relay and the 4 × 100-m medley relay. Named both best male and best performer of the meet, he credited his coach, Doug Frost, with playing a major role in his success.

Thorpe first attracted widespread international attention at the Olympic Games in September 2000 before a hometown crowd in Sydney. In that competition he won gold medals and achieved world records in the 400-m freestyle, the 4 × 100-m freestyle relay, and the 4 × 200-m freestyle relay. His only defeat was a second-place finish in the 200-m freestyle.

Thorpe was born on Oct. 13, 1982, in the Paddington district of Sydney. Inspired by the success in the pool of his older sister, Christina, he began swimming competitively at the age of eight under coach Jenny McAdam. He later commented that as a young boy he had felt like a "fish out of water" at other sports, including cricket, at which his father had gained recognition. A high-school classmate described him as having "no coordination at all on land." At the age of 13, Thorpe broke 10 national age-group records in one meet, and one year later he became the youngest swimmer to make Australia's national team. At the 1998 world championships, he became at the age of 15 the youngest world swimming champion with his world-record victory in the 400-m freestyle. At the Pan Pacific championships in August 1999, Thorpe, (now 2 m [6 ft 4 in] tall and taking full advantage of his extraordinarily large feet, which some compared to flippers), set world long-course records in the 200-m and 400-m freestyle events. Remarking on his subsequent celebrity status, he said, "Nothing can really prepare you for this." According to 1984 Olympic swimming champion Rowdy Gaines, Thorpe has "revolutionized freestyle. He is doing the 400 free with a six beat [per arm cycle] kick the whole way. The only other people doing that are sprinters." In addition, his stroke length of 2.7 m (8 ft 8.5 in) is longer than that of his competitors.

Thorpe also became notable for his generosity. After setting his first world record at the Pan Pacific championships, he donated his $25,000 prize money to two charities, and for several years he spent much time helping a childhood friend through a difficult bout with cancer. (DAVID R. CALHOUN)

Toledo, Alejandro

On July 28, 2001, nearly five centuries after Europeans conquered the Incas—and after two years of campaigning—Alejandro Toledo was sworn in as Peru's first democratically elected president of Quechua ethnicity. Although easily half of Peruvians were Amerindians, the white and mestizo minorities had held the key to economic, scholastic, and political power since colonial times. Excepting the dictatorship of "El Indio" ("the Indian"), Juan Velasco Alvarado (1968–75), Peru's first president to break the colour barrier was Alberto Fujimori (1990–2000), who quickly became known as "El Chino" ("the Chinaman"), although he was of Japanese ancestry. Toledo accepted the moniker "El Cholo" (also "the Indian") with pride. He spent his last campaign day in Cuzco, the former Inca capital, and, a day after taking office, the shoeshine-boy-turned-economist paid homage to his ancestors and the Andean mountain *apus* (gods, or spirits) at the ruins of Machu Picchu.

Alejandro Toledo Manrique, the son of peasant farmers, was born on March 28, 1946, in Cabana, Ancash department, and grew up on the northern coast at Chimbote. An academic scholarship took him to the United States and the University of San Francisco (B.S., 1970). After earning a Ph.D. (1976) in economics of human resources from Stanford University, he worked in international economics at the United Nations (1976–78, 1989), the World Bank (1979–81), and Harvard's Institute for International Development (1991–94). In 1998 he became director of international affairs at the Graduate School of Business Administration (ESAN) in Lima.

The smear tactics used by the Fujimori camp against the other candidates unwittingly paved the way for Toledo, who led the centrist Perú Posible party in the 2000 presidential race. Toledo withdrew from the runoff in protest and launched a series of popular demonstrations against Fujimori's victory. After a bribery scandal toppled Fujimori's government, Toledo led the pack of new candidates for the April 2001 elections and won 36.5% of the vote in the first round.

AP/Wide World Photos

Alejandro Toledo takes the measure of his land at Machu Picchu

Toledo's image was marred somewhat by allegations of infidelity, immoral behaviour, and cocaine use. He also had a falling out with campaign chief Álvaro Vargas Llosa (son of the novelist Mario Vargas Llosa, who lost the 1990 presidential race to Fujimori), who began to advocate blank ballots to protest the candidacies of both Toledo and former president Alan García Pérez. On the positive side, Toledo was aided by his daughter and his wife, the anthropologist Eliane Karp, who gave campaign speeches in Quechua. In the second round of voting, on June 3, Toledo took 53.1% of the ballots. Fewer than 3% of votes were blank. In his inaugural speech, Toledo promised to create new jobs, partly by increasing tourism, and to fight corruption, narcotraffic, and human rights abuses—in short, "to be the president of all Peruvians and of all races."

(STEPHEN P. DAVIS)

Whitman, Meg

During a year when many Internet ventures had either failed or were struggling to survive, the on-line auction firm eBay Inc. continued to flourish in 2001. At the head of this thriving enterprise was president and CEO Meg Whitman. Under her leadership, revenues in 2000 totaled more than $430 million, an increase of 92% over 1999, and the percentage of sales that came from international business doubled between 2000 and 2001. Visitors to the firm's Internet site could find an array of offerings in more than 4,500 categories, ranging from automobiles to clothing, jewelry, books, and dolls.

When a corporate headhunter first approached her for the position in 1998, Whitman, then an executive with toy and game manufacturer Hasbro, Inc., was not interested. A visit to eBay's headquarters and the testimonies of many enthusiastic users impressed her, however, and she accepted the offer to lead the company. Whitman later commented that she quickly realized that eBay's strength lay in the fact that its services could not be duplicated by old-economy brick-and-mortar concerns because its job was to connect people rather than to sell them things.

Margaret Whitman was born in 1957 and grew up in Cold Spring Harbor, N.Y., on Long Island. She earned her undergraduate degree from Princeton University in 1977 and a master's degree in business administration from Harvard University in 1979. From 1979 to 1981 she worked in brand management for Procter & Gamble in Cincinnati, Ohio. After moving with her husband to California in 1981, she joined the consulting firm Bain & Co. as a vice president and remained there until 1989. From 1989 to 1992 Whitman served as senior vice president of marketing at the Consumer Products Division of Walt Disney Co., where she played a major role in Disney's acquisition of *Discover* magazine. Again moving with her husband, this time to Boston in 1992, she became president of the children's shoe manufacturer Stride Rite, a division of Stride Rite Corp. Leaving Stride Rite in 1995, she accepted an offer to become CEO of Florists Transworld Delivery (FTD), a federation of commercial florists. There Whitman encountered opposition from staff members and member florists, who strongly objected to FTD's transformation into a privately held firm. She resigned from FTD in 1997 and became general manager of the Playskool division of Hasbro.

One of Whitman's first responsibilities at eBay was to prepare the company for its initial public offering (IPO) in September 1998. She brightened the design of eBay's Web pages and walled off all firearm and pornography auctions into separate age-restricted sites; eBay later banned auctions of firearms and prohibited sales of tobacco, drugs, alcohol, animals, and body parts. At the IPO 3.5 million shares of eBay were offered at $18 per share; at the end of the first day, each share was valued at $47.1875. Whitman was described as "relentlessly optimistic," and those who worked with her said that her ability to stay focused and positive set her apart from most executives.

(DAVID R. CALHOUN)

Wirtz, Jacques

Even after a 50-year career in which he had designed more than 100 gardens, Belgian landscape architect Jacques Wirtz was far from considering retirement; in fact, he seemed to be hitting his stride in 2001. A decade earlier Wirtz's work was not well known outside Belgium, but during the 1990s he took on more high-profile projects, including gardens at the Louvre in Paris, the headquarters of the Bank of Luxembourg, and gardens for celebrities, notably one for actress Catherine Deneuve. His work became internationally known, and he was hailed as one of the most talented and influential landscape designers in Europe. During the year Wirtz continued to work in England on one of his larger projects, a $20-million commission by the duchess of Northumberland to redesign the 5-ha (12-ac) walled garden at Alnwick Castle, a spectacular undertaking that would feature waterfalls and Wirtz's famous (and often duplicated) mass plantings of geometric-shaped hedges of beech, box, hornbeam, and yew. Some of his hedges were carefully sculpted and pruned for years in order to achieve the desired effect.

Wirtz was born in 1924 in Antwerp; his family moved to the environs outside the city when he was 12, and he was influenced by the natural beauty of the countryside. He studied landscape architecture at a horticultural college in Vilvoorde before starting his own business growing and selling flowers and maintaining local gardens. In 1950 Wirtz designed his first complete garden; the majority of his creations were for private residences. His style was inspired by gardens of his childhood as well as those seen on visits to other European countries and Japan. He came to be known for designs that served to complement rather than conceal the natural surroundings, and he favoured flowering plants, grasses, clipped trees and hedges, and water, rather than the harsh man-made materials that adorned many other modern gardens.

His career received a boost in the 1970s when he won a competition to design the garden for Belgium's pavilion at the International Exhibition in Osaka, Japan. During this time he also designed the campus of the University of Antwerp, a plan that featured an ivy ground cover and an abundance of flowering trees. Wirtz gained wider recognition in the early '90s when he won a contest to redesign the Carrousel Garden, which connected the Louvre with the 25-ha (63-ac) Tuileries Gardens, redesigned in 1664 by celebrated French landscape architect André Le Nôtre. At the end of the year, Wirtz and his two sons, who shared in his business, had a number of projects in the works, including a garden at Canary Wharf in London, a small Jewish cemetery in Switzerland, and gardens around a law court in Italy, all scheduled for completion by 2003 or 2004. He was also poised to begin his first work in the U.S., designing private gardens in Los Angeles, Chicago, and Florida.

(SANDRA LANGENECKERT)

Yang Yang

Chinese short-track speed skater Yang Yang—known as Yang Yang (A)—confirmed her dominance on the ice in 2001 by winning her fifth consecutive world championship overall title. During three days of competition in Chonju, S.Kor., Yang reached the finals of all five women's events, taking gold in the 1,000-, 1,500-, and 3,000-m individual races and the 3,000-m relay and silver in the 500-m race. Her decisive win came as little surprise. After a season in which she had reached the finals in 14 of the 17 events she competed in and had tallied eight individual wins, she entered the world championships as the top-ranked woman on the World Cup circuit. The letter A often appended to Yang's name stood for her birth month of August and distinguished her from teammate Yang Yang (S), who was born in September and with whom Yang often shared the medalists' podium. The written distinction between Yang Yangs (A) and (S) was for the benefit of non-Chinese speakers, because their names were pronounced differently in Chinese.

Yang was born on Aug. 24, 1976, in the northeastern Chinese province of Heilongjiang, near the Russian border. She began skating in 1984, and by age 13 she had reached the finals of an International Skating Union test competition. Yang qualified for the Chinese short-track team in 1995, but she overtrained for the 1996 world championships and achieved only mediocre results. By the next season she had perfected her training, and at the 1997 world championships she split an overall win with two-time world champion Chun Lee Kyung of South Korea. In doing so she became China's first world short-track champion.

Yang had a mixed showing at the 1998 Winter Olympics in Nagano, Japan, where she failed to win any individual medals. She was strong in early heats and, in fact, set a world record (1 min 31.991 sec) in the 1,000-m quarterfinal. In the 1,000-m final, she again met Chun, the defending Olympic champion, whom she led for most of the race. The two tangled arms at the finish, however, and Chun kicked forward to win by centimetres before falling to the ice. Compounding the loss, judges then disqualified Yang for interference.

Kim Jae-Hwan/AFP Worldwide

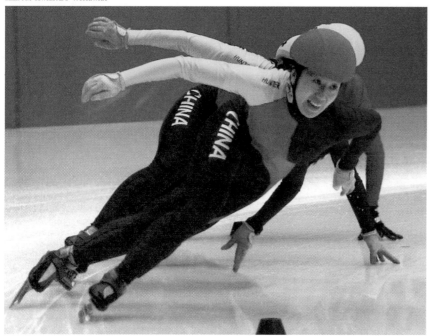

Yang Yang roars ahead

The only medal Yang took home from Nagano was a silver for the 3,000-m relay. She blamed poor mental preparation for the results. Later in 1998, however, Yang won her second world championship—this one hers alone—and she thereafter dominated the World Cup circuit and the world championships. After the 2001 win, her hopes settled on the 2002 Winter Olympics in Salt Lake City, Utah, where she promised to be a strong contender to capture China's first-ever winter gold.

(COLIN J. MURPHY)

Yoshimoto, Banana

"Banana mania" was not an enthusiasm triggered by potassium deprivation but rather the way journalists around the world referred in 2001 to the wild popularity of Japanese writer Banana Yoshimoto. Her stories were light, their action slight, and their characters unusual. They were not entirely evanescent; they briefly budded, flowered, and faded, leaving behind a lingering scent of great beauty and loss.

Born in Tokyo on July 24, 1964, Mahoko Yoshimoto appeared to have a genetic predilection for both writing and nonconformity; her father, Takaaki ("Ryumei") Yoshimoto, was an intellectual, critic, and leader in the radical student movement in the late 1960s. Reared in a much freer environment than that of most Japanese children, Yoshimoto entered the College of Art at Nihon University, Tokyo. There her graduation story, *Moonlight Shadow* (1986), was an immediate

hit and earned her the Izumi Kyoka Prize from the faculty. About this time, by her own account, she chose the pen name Banana Yoshimoto because it was both cute and androgynous. While working as a waitress, she wrote the novella *Kitchin* (Kitchen), published in 1988. Two more books—*Kanashii yokan* ("Sad Foreboding") and *Utakata/Sankuchuari* ("Bubble/Sanctuary")—were published in Japan that year. Yoshimoto never looked back.

The Chinese were the first to catch Banana mania, translating and publishing *Kitchin* in 1989. A translation of *Tsugumi* (1989) appeared the following year in South Korea. Her first English-language book, which contained both *Moonlight Shadow* and *Kitchen,* was published as *Kitchen* in 1993, and her reputation spread to readers throughout the United States and England. Soon her work had also been translated into German, Hebrew, Spanish, Italian, and Albanian. Two Japanese directors, Jun Ishikawa (*Tsugumi,* 1990) and Yoshimitsu Morita (*Kitchin,* 1990), adapted her novels to the large screen, and in 1997 Hong Kong director Ho Yim made a Cantonese-language version of *Kitchin.* While her name spread, Yoshimoto continued to write, producing the novels *NP* (1990; *N.P.*) and *Amrita* (1994; *Amrita*) and several volumes of essays (*Painatsupurin* [1989; "Pinenuts Pudding"], *Songs from Banana Note* [1991], *Yume ni tsuite* [1994; "About a Dream"], and *Painappuru heddo* [1995; "Pineapple Head"]) and short stories (*Shirakawa yofune* [1989; *Asleep*] and *Tokage* [1993; *Lizard*]). In 2000–01 a one-volume author's selection came out, and four volumes of collected works were published. Yoshimoto was just 36.

Her Japanese fans continued to respond to elements in her writing that were both old and new. Though her characters, settings, and ti-

tles were modern and influenced by American culture, they were unmistakably Japanese at the core. Some cited the Japanese sensibility known as *mono no aware,* usually translated as "the pathos of things," as the essence of her style. The phenomenal appeal of her work was not always evident to English-language critics, some of whom called her writing superficial and simplistic and her characters unbelievable. Her appeal appeared to lie deep in her identity and her personal response to life, in a biography that was as quirky as her writing.

(KATHLEEN KUIPER)

Zöggeler, Armin

After having closed out the 2000 international luge racing season with victories in three of the final four events and clinching the year's World Cup overall luge championship, Armin Zöggeler of Italy barely skipped a beat to kick off the 2001 season. Zöggeler defeated defending Olympic champion Georg Hackl of Germany in the two-track European championships in January. He finished third in a subsequent race in Austria but returned to the top of the medalists' podium in Altenberg, Ger., by posting a time of 1 min 49.685 sec. In early February the luge circuit moved on to Nagano, Japan, where Zöggeler finished second behind Germany's Wilfried Huber. Two weeks later, in Park City, Utah, Zöggeler was victorious once again as he recorded the year's fastest time, 1 min 29.391 sec.

Zöggeler capped off a tremendous 2001 season in Calgary, Alta., by capturing his third world championship with a time of 1 min 30.139 sec. In the process, he again defeated Hackl as well as nine-time overall World Cup champion Markus Prock, who placed second and third, respectively. Zöggeler also led his Italian squad to a fourth-place finish in the team event in Calgary.

Zöggeler was born on Jan. 4, 1974, in Merano, in Italy's South Tirol region. He broke onto the luge racing scene as a 15-year-old in 1989; his 14th-place finish in an international competition was a sure sign of things to come. He joined the Italian national team that year. In 1994, competing as a 20-year-old in the Lillehammer (Nor.) Olympic Games, he finished third behind Hackl and Prock. In 1995 he returned to Lillehammer and captured his first world championship and took second place in the overall World Cup standings. In 1997 he moved his performances up a notch and was able to claim the World Cup title. One year later, in the 1998 Winter Olympics in Nagano, he lost to Hackl and took the silver medal. Later that year Zöggeler's Italian team won the silver in the European championships in Oberhof, Ger. From that point on, Zöggeler dominated the world luging scene. In 1999 he captured five of the seven races he entered on his way to taking his second World Cup championship.

By the close of the 2001 season, Zöggeler, who lived and trained in Völlan, Italy, where he supported himself and his family by working as a police officer, was looking to the future. With silver and bronze medals already in his Olympic collection, he vowed to go for the gold in the 2002 Winter Games in Salt Lake City, Utah.

(BILL BRADLEY)

Obituaries

In 2001 THE WORLD LOST many leaders, PATHFINDERS, news-makers, HEROES, cultural icons, and ROGUES. The pages below RECAPTURE the LIVES and accomplishments of those we REMEMBER best.

Aaliyah (Aaliyah Dana Haughton), American rhythm and blues singer and actress (b. Jan. 16, 1979, Brooklyn, N.Y.—d. Aug. 25, 2001, Abaco Islands, The Bahamas), was considered on the verge of superstardom after the success of her first two albums—*Age Ain't Nothing but a Number* (1994), with its hit singles "Back and Forth" and "At Your Best (You Are Love)," and *One in a Million* (1996)—and her Grammy nominations for her singles "Are You That Somebody?" (1998) and "Try Again" (2000), as well as her starring role in the movie *Romeo Must Die* (2000); she recently had released a third album, *Aaliyah*, had finished work on the film *Queen of the Damned*, and was beginning two sequels to the movie *The Matrix* (1999) when she was killed in a plane crash as she was leaving The Bahamas after filming a music video.

Abu Ali Mustafa (Mustafa az-Zibri), Palestinian nationalist (b. 1938, Arabeh, Palestine—d. Aug. 27, 2001, Ram Allah, West Bank), was a cofounder and, from July 2000, secretary-general of the Popular Front for the Liberation of Palestine (PFLP), a radical faction of the Palestine Liberation Organization (PLO). He was born Mustafa az-Zibri and later took the nom de guerre Abu Ali Mustafa. As a young man he joined George Habash's Arab National Movement, and in 1967 he and Habash formed the Marxist-oriented PFLP, based in Damascus, Syria. The PFLP, which staunchly rejected PLO peace talks with Israel, was believed to have been responsible for several terrorist attacks and hijackings. Mustafa eventually acknowledged the Palestinian Authority, however, and in September 1999 he unexpectedly returned to the West Bank. He was killed in an Israeli rocket attack on his offices.

Adams, Douglas Noël, British novelist (b. March 11, 1952, Cambridge, Eng.—d. May 11, 2001, Santa Barbara, Calif.), was the creator of the satiric science-fiction whimsy *The Hitchhiker's Guide to the Galaxy,* which first saw life as a radio series and then became a book, a television series, a play, record albums, comic books, and a computer game, gaining cult status along the way. The book and its sequels feature British suburbanite Arthur Dent, who—after being rescued by Ford Prefect, a visitor from the planet Betelgeuse, just before Earth is destroyed to clear the way for a hyperspace freeway—encounters such characters as the two-headed alien Zaphod Beeblebrox and learns that the secret of the universe is the number 42. More than 14 million copies of the books were sold worldwide. Adams was edu-

Rising star Aaliyah

AP/ Wide World Photos

cated at St. John's College, Cambridge, earning an M.A. in English literature in 1974. At Cambridge he wrote comedy sketches for the Footlights revue, and following graduation he occasionally worked on writing projects while making his living at a series of odd jobs, including serving as a bodyguard for the Qatari royal family. From 1978 to 1980 Adams wrote scripts for the BBC and worked as a script editor for the *Dr. Who* TV series. In 1978 *The Hitchhiker's Guide,* the culmination of an idea he had had while hitchhiking in Europe in 1971, began on BBC radio. It quickly gained a huge following, and a stage version was produced in 1979. Adams turned it into a novel that same year, and it became a TV series in 1981. The first book was joined by four sequels—*The Restaurant at the End of the Universe* (1980), *Life, the Universe and Everything* (1982), *So Long, and Thanks for All the Fish* (1985), and *Mostly Harmless* (1992)—to become what Adams called his five-part trilogy. Adams also wrote such books as *The Meaning of Liff* (with John Lloyd; 1983) and two detective-story satires—*Dirk Gently's Holistic Detective Agency* (1987) and *The Long*

Dark Tea-Time of the Soul (1988)—as well as the nonfiction *Last Chance to See* (with Mark Carwardine; 1990), which reflected his interest in ecology and his concerns about endangered species. He also formed (1996) a multimedia company, the Digital Village, and shortly before his death finished writing the script for a Hollywood film version of *The Hitchhiker's Guide to the Galaxy.* The day before Adams died, his main character achieved immortality when asteroid 18610 was named Arthurdent.

Adler, Lawrence Cecil ("Larry"), American musician, composer, writer, and entertainer (b. Feb. 10, 1914, Baltimore, Md.—d. Aug. 6, 2001, London, Eng.), played classical music on the harmonica, which he insisted on calling a "mouth organ"; he then enjoyed a long career as a humorist, telling stories of his encounters with celebrity friends and British royalty. Though the harmonica had previously been associated only with folk music, in his hands it became a highly versatile and expressive instrument. At age 10 Adler became the youngest cantor in Baltimore, and the following year he ordered an expensive piano, which he then persuaded his parents to accept; he also began playing the harmonica. In 1927 he won the Maryland Harmonica Championship by playing a Beethoven minuet. The next year, at 14, Adler left home for New York City and played harmonica on the streets, then in nightclubs; by age 17 he was performing with Fred Astaire on Broadway in *Smiles.* He also appeared in

AP/Wide World Photos

Harmonica virtuoso Larry Adler

small film roles and became a favourite of New York City and Hollywood stars before playing his first of many concerts with symphony orchestras in Sydney, Australia, in 1939. Adler learned music by listening and memorizing; he did not learn to read music until 1940, when French composer Jean Berger wrote a concerto for him. Among others who composed music for him were Ralph Vaughan Williams and Darius Milhaud; William Walton called him a "genius," and George Gershwin praised his performance of *Rhapsody in Blue*. A liberal who entertained American troops during World War II and the Korean War and in Israel during its 1967 and 1973 wars, Adler opposed the House Committee on Un-American Activities; as a result, he was blacklisted in the U.S., and in 1949 he moved to England, where he had long been popular. There he composed for the stage, films, and television, and he performed as a stand-up comedian-storyteller as well as a musician in nightclubs, in theatres, and on the air. At age 80 Adler issued the disc *The Glory of Gershwin* with guest stars that included Elvis Costello and Elton John; it made him the oldest performer to have placed an album on the British hit record charts. In later life Adler also became a successful book, film, and restaurant critic, as well as the author of *Jokes and How to Tell Them* (1963) and the autobiography *It Ain't Necessarily So* (1984).

Adler, Mortimer Jerome, American educator, philosopher, editor, and writer (b. Dec. 28, 1902, New York, N.Y.—d. June 28, 2001, San Mateo, Calif.), influenced by the ideas espoused by his heroes, Aristotle and St. Thomas Aquinas, championed the notion that a liberal education—

the study of the great literature of the Western world—could provide the foundation of education for all people and lead to an understanding of the human condition. To that end he, along with Robert Maynard Hutchins, created (1947) the Great Books Foundation, which led members of the public in reading and meeting to discuss classic works. He was a cofounder and regular lecturer at the Aspen (Colo.) Institute. He also had a long association with Encyclopædia Britannica, during which he counted the compilation of the 54-volume *Great Books of the Western World* (1952) and its *Syntopicon*, a two-volume index based on 102 great ideas, and the restructuring of the *Encyclopædia Britannica* for its 15th edition (1974) among the numerous projects he guided; he served on the board of editors from its inception in 1948 and was its chairman from 1974 until 1995, when he retired. Adler dropped out of high school at age 15 and was working for the *New York Sun* when he determined that he would become a philosopher and enrolled in Columbia University, New York City. Although he completed the course work in three years, his refusal to take a required swimming test kept him from graduating (his bachelor's degree

was, however, finally awarded in 1983). Nevertheless, he became (1923) a psychology instructor there, and in 1928 he was awarded a Ph.D. In 1930 Hutchins created the position of associate professor of the philosophy of law for Adler at the University of Chicago, and in 1942 Adler became a full professor. He left the university in 1952 and founded the Institute for Philosophical Research in San Francisco. Among the works created there was the two-volume *The Idea of Freedom* (1958 and 1961). The institute was moved to Chicago in 1963, and Adler then edited the 10-volume *Gateway to the Great Books* (1963) and the 20-volume *Annals of America* (1968) for Encyclopædia Britannica. In the early 1980s he conceived the Paideia Project, a plan for a humanist education in the elementary and secondary grades, which he put forth in the books *The Paideia Proposal: An Educational Manifesto* (1982), *Paideia Problems and Possibilities* (1983), and *The Paideia Program: An Educational Syllabus* (1984). Among the dozens of Adler's other books were *How to Read a Book* (1940; rev. ed., 1972), *The Difference of Man and the Difference It Makes* (1967), *How to Think About God* (1980), and *Six Great Ideas* (1981). Adler served (1988–91) as a professor at the University of North Carolina at Chapel Hill and was a cofounder (1990) of the Center for the Study of Great Ideas in Chicago. His memoirs were published in *Philosopher at Large: An Intellectual Autobiography* (1977) and *A Second Look in the Rearview Mirror* (1992).

Akesson, Birgit, Swedish dancer and choreographer (b. March 24, 1908, Malmö, Swed.—d. March 24, 2001, Stockholm, Swed.), sought to replace conventional expressionistic modern dance techniques with a new idiom of dance as pure nonrepresentational form. As a dancer she created stark solos that relied on slow movement and almost sculptural abstract shapes, often performed without music. In 1963 she founded the Choreographic Institute in Stockholm (later the State Dance School), where she headed the choreography department after her retirement as a dancer in 1965. Akesson, who later studied dance forms in Africa and East Asia, was awarded the title of professor by the Swedish government in 1992.

Alboreto, Michele, Italian race-car driver (b. Dec. 23, 1956, Milan, Italy—d. April 25, 2001, Klettwitz, Ger.), was one of Italy's most popular and successful Formula One (F1) drivers in the early 1980s. After being the European Formula Three champion in 1980, Alboreto won five F1 Grand Prix races, including three during his years driving for Ferrari (1984–88). He finished second to Alain Prost in the 1985 F1 drivers' championship, but thereafter he was plagued with mechanical failures. After leaving F1 racing in 1994 and switching to sports-car racing, Alboreto, with co-drivers Stefan Johansson and Tom Kristensen, won the 1997 24-hour Le Mans Grand Prix d'Endurance. He died in a crash at the Lausitzring circuit while test-driving a new Audi in preparation for the 2001 Le Mans race.

Alekan, Henri, French cinematographer (b. Feb. 10, 1909, Paris, France—d. June 15, 2001, Auxerre, France), was one of the most accom-

plished filmmakers of the 20th century. After working for a time as a puppeteer, Alekan broke into the film industry as an assistant camera operator in 1927. His career was interrupted by the German occupation of France during World War II. After the war Alekan became a director of photography. He worked with film director René Clément to create *La Bataille du rail* (1946) and *Les Maudits* (1947) and with poet Jean Cocteau to create the film *La Belle et la bête* (1946). In 1953, under director William Wyler, Alekan shot his first American film, *Roman Holiday*, for which he received an Academy Award nomination. He remained in demand throughout the rest of the 1950s and early '60s; however, interest in his work waned thereafter until German film director Wim Wenders drafted Alekan to handle the photography for *The State of Things* (1982) and *Wings of Desire* (1987).

Amado, Jorge, Brazilian novelist (b. Aug. 10, 1912, Ferradas, near Ilhéus, Braz.—d. Aug. 6, 2001, Salvador, Braz.), was the literary patriarch of his country. The first half of his career was characterized by ideological works and the second by humorous, often ribald, novels of Brazilian life. The publication of Amado's second novel, in 1933, led to his being briefly detained, the first of many harassments by the government. This book was followed by others dealing with the exploitation of plantation workers and with the brutality of life in Brazil. He was forced into exile from 1938 to 1942. The masterpiece of his first period was *Terras do sem fim* (1942; *The Violent Land*, 1965), an epic novel about the struggles of workers. In 1946 he was elected to Congress as a member of the Communist Party, but two years later the party was banned, and he was again forced into exile. After returning to Brazil in 1952, Amado began to write the novels that made him famous. He became known particularly for his celebration of the Afro-Brazilian culture, including the candomblé religion, of his native Bahia state. He was called the author of "whores and tramps," a title he embraced. The best known of his later works were *Gabriela, cravo e canela* (1958; *Gabriela, Clove and Cinnamon*, 1962) and *Dona Flor e seus dois maridos* (1966; *Dona Flor and Her Two Husbands*, 1969). Both were made into films and adapted as soap operas for Brazilian television. To charges that he had abandoned his earlier views, he replied that it was important to portray the dreams of the poor. In all, he published 32 books, which were translated into some 50 languages and sold 20 million copies. Among his many honours were France's Legion of Honor and the Graça Aranha Prize of the Brazilian Academy of Letters.

Ammons, A(rchie) R(andolph), American poet and scholar (b. Feb. 18, 1926, near Whiteville, N.C.—d. Feb. 25, 2001, Ithaca, N.Y.), won almost every major American poetry award during a career that spanned nearly half a century. Regarded as a 20th-century Transcendentalist poet, Ammons explored the relationship between man, nature, and the self through free verse. In his work, which also often dealt with the quotidian, he skillfully maintained a philosophical yet conversational tone. Ammons, who grew up on a farm during the Depression, joined the U.S. Naval Reserve at the age of 18, at the height of World War II. It was during his service aboard a navy destroyer in the Pacific that he began writing poetry. After the war Ammons earned a degree in biology (1949) from Wake Forest College (now Wake Forest University), Winston-Salem, N.C., and attended graduate school at the University of California, Berkeley. He worked as an elementary school principal, a real-estate agent, and a sales executive at a New Jersey glass company before publishing his first volume of poetry, *Ommateum: With Doxology* (1955). It was followed by *Expressions of Sea Level* (1963) and *Tape for the Turn of the Year* (1965; written on adding-machine tape), which was published the year after he became a teacher of creative writing at Cornell University, Ithaca, where he spent the rest of his career. Ammons published nearly 30 books, including *Uplands* (1970), *A Coast of Trees* (1981; winner of the National Book Critics Circle Award), and National Book Award winner *Garbage* (1993), a book-length poem about a huge pile of decomposing trash he spotted near Interstate 95 in Florida. *Glare*, his last volume, appeared in 1997.

Anderson, Maceo, American tap dancer (b. Sept. 3, 1910, Charleston, S.C.—d. July 4, 2001, Los Angeles, Calif.), was a founding member of the Four Step Brothers, a widely popular tap-dance act. Anderson danced from the age of three. In his early teens he formed a trio of dancers that eventually began performing at the famed Cotton Club in New York City in the mid-1920s. The group became a quartet in the mid-1930s. By the 1940s the Four Step Brothers were the best-known tap-dance act in the nation. Anderson and his fellow dancers regularly appeared at Radio City Music Hall and the Roxy and Paramount theatres in New York City and on *The Ed Sullivan Show* until they disbanded in the late 1960s. Anderson later taught at his own dance school in Las Vegas, Nev.

Anderson, Poul William, American science-fiction writer (b. Nov. 25, 1926, Bristol, Pa.—d. July 31, 2001, Orinda, Calif.), was the prolific author of more than 100 books of science fiction and fantasy. Over a period of about half a century, he tapped his knowledge of both science and Scandinavian folklore and mythology to create powerfully imaginative depictions of the future, writing in such varied styles as farce, adventure tales, romantic and heroic fantasy, mystery, sociopolitical drama, and serious science fiction. Anderson lived in Denmark for a short time when he was a child and there developed the interest in and acquaintance with Scandinavian mythology that would inform his later fiction, as would his bachelor's degree in physics from the University of Minnesota. In 1947, a year before graduation—during the time known as the golden age of science fiction—he had his first story, "Tomorrow's Children," published in *Astounding Science Fiction* magazine. Following graduation, Anderson began his career as a freelance and had his stories published in a number of pulp magazines. His first novel, *Vault of the Ages*, was published in 1952, and in 1954 his first successful novel, *Brain Wave*, ap-

peared. The latter reflected one of Anderson's primary interests—how people draw on their resources of courage in the face of challenges. Considered his best novel was *Tau Zero* (1970); its theme was the life and death of the universe. Other notable novels included *A Midsummer Tempest* (1974), in which William Shakespeare's works come true; *The Boat of a Million Years* (1989), which addresses immortality; and *Genesis* (2000), which deals with the intelligence of machines and which won the John W. Campbell Memorial Award. Anderson also counted numerous Hugo and Nebula awards among his many honours; served as president of the Science Fiction Writers of America (1972–73), which presented him its Grand Master Award in 1997; and was inducted into the Science Fiction and Fantasy Hall of Fame in 2000.

Anscombe, G(ertrude) E(lizabeth) M(argaret), British philosopher (b. March 18, 1919, Limerick, Ire.—d. Jan. 5, 2001, Cambridge, Eng.), was a close associate of Ludwig Wittgenstein and served as one of the executors of his literary estate; in addition, she was an important philosopher in her own right. Anscombe attended Sydenham School, London, and St. Hugh's College, Oxford. While working in the early 1940s as a research fellow at Newnham College, Cambridge, she met Wittgenstein, to whom she became philosophically and personally close. She translated his late masterwork *Bemerkungen über die Grundlagen der Mathematik* (1956; *Remarks on the Foundations of Mathematics*) and his *Philosophische Untersuchungen* (1953; *Philosophical Investigations*). Anscombe explicated the development of his philosophy in *An Introduction to Wittgenstein's Tractatus* (1959). Her own work centred on questions of the philosophy of action and ethics. *Intention* (1957) stressed reasons rather than causes in the analysis of action. In the "Modern Moral Philosophy" (1958), she argued for a return to an Aristotelian notion of virtue over modern consequentialism. Anscombe converted to Roman Catholicism in 1940 and was an advocate of many of the church's philosophical and moral teachings. She condemned contraception in *Contraception and Chastity* (1975) and defended the ontological argument for the existence of God. Her acceptance of the Catholic notion of just war led her to criticize British entry into World War II and to oppose an honorary Oxford degree for former U.S. president Harry Truman in 1956. Anscombe was a research fellow of Somerville College, Oxford (1946–64), and she taught at the University of Chicago. In 1970 she was called to the chair of philosophy at Cambridge, where Wittgenstein had taught. Anscombe, who wore a tunic and trousers at a time when trousers were not completely acceptable for women, also sported a monocle and smoked cigars. She married (1941) philosopher Peter Geach, with whom she had seven children.

Anthony, Earl, American bowler (b. April 27, 1938, Kent, Wash.—found dead Aug. 14, 2001, New Berlin, Wis.), was the winningest player in the history of the Professional Bowlers Association (PBA); he also became the first bowler to earn $1 million in his career. Anthony, whose

childhood dream of becoming a major league baseball player was derailed by an ankle injury, joined the PBA Tour in 1963. After a slow start he went on to dominate professional bowling during the 1970s and early '80s. He won a record 41 PBA tournaments from 1970 to 1983, including 10 major titles. During this time professional bowling was regularly broadcast on television, and Anthony achieved widespread fame. He was named PBA Player of the Year six times and was the tour scoring leader five times. He retired from the sport in 1984 but made a brief comeback in 1987 and a year later joined the PBA Senior Tour, on which he won seven senior titles. He garnered a career total of $1,441,061 in prize money. Anthony was inducted into the PBA Hall of Fame in 1981. In later years he worked in television as a commentator on bowling broadcasts. He died from head trauma after falling down a flight of stairs.

Asahina, Takashi, Japanese conductor (b. July 9, 1908, Tokyo, Japan—d. Dec. 29, 2001, Kobe, Japan), was credited with popularizing the Austro-German repertoire—especially Bruckner, Beethoven, and Mahler—in Japan and had one of the longest careers of any conductor, remaining professionally active virtually right up until his death at the age of 93. A self-taught violinist, Asahina abandoned a legal career and worked as a department-store clerk and a railroad engineer before apprenticing himself to Russian conductor Emmanuel Metter in the early 1930s. Asahina made his conducting debut in 1939 and founded the Kansai Symphony Orchestra (now the Osaka Philharmonic Orchestra) in 1947. He became widely known internationally after conducting the Berlin Philharmonic in 1956. Asahina conducted more than 60 orchestras in 15 countries and in 1994 was awarded the Japanese Order of Culture in recognition of his achievements in the arts.

Ash, Mary Kay (Mary Kathlyn Wagner), American entrepreneur (b. May 12, 1918, Hot

Ed Lallo/Getty Images

Cosmetics queen Mary Kay Ash in her pink cadillac

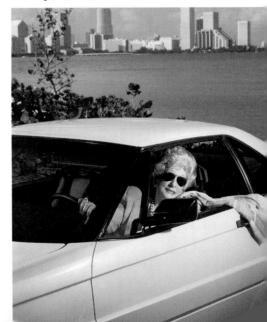

Wells, Texas—d. Nov. 22, 2001, Dallas, Texas), was the founder of cosmetics giant Mary Kay Inc. and one of the most famous business-women in the world. Ash had held relatively modest jobs in direct sales before establishing her own business in 1963. Mary Kay Cosmetics (as the company was originally known) was an almost instant success, recording nearly $1 million in sales by 1965. By 2000 the company's wholesale revenue was estimated at $1.2 billion. Ash cultivated a flashy image as an executive and was known for lavishly rewarding productive employees with such gifts as diamonds, minks, and pink Cadillacs. She wrote a number of best-selling books, including *Mary Kay: You Can Have It All* (1995).

Astafyev, Viktor Petrovich, Soviet-Russian novelist (b. May 1, 1924, Ovsyanka, Krasnoyarsk *kray*, Russia—d. Nov. 29, 2001, Krasnoyarsk, Krasnoyarsk *kray*), drew on his experiences living in a rural village as well as his stint as a volunteer in the front lines during World War II to pen novels that chronicled the bleakness and despair of life in Siberia and the madness and horror of war. As one of the *derevenshchiki* ("village writers"), Astafyev was renowned for the stark realism of his narratives, which centred on rural people who were removed from Communist Party discipline. Among his most acclaimed works were *Tsarryba* (1980; *Queen Fish* [1982]), an epic tale about the threat of ecological destruction in Siberia; *Pechalny detektiv* (1986; "The Sad Detective Story"), a gruesome look at the alcoholism, violence, and animosity among Soviet people; and *Proklyaty i ubity* (1993; "The Damned and the Dead"), considered one of the most authentic yet disturbing depictions of the effect of World War II on Russian villages. Astafyev's collected works were published by Molodaya Gvardiya in four volumes in 1979–81. He was the recipient of the Hero of Socialist Labour (1989).

Aston, Kenneth George, British association football (soccer) referee (b. Sept. 1, 1915, Colchester, Essex, Eng.—d. Oct. 23, 2001, Ilford, Essex), invented the yellow (caution) and red (ejection) disciplinary cards, which were first employed during play at the 1970 World Cup finals and were quickly introduced around the world. Aston qualified as a referee in 1936. In 1962, having worked successfully for the Football Association in England, he was invited to officiate at the World Cup finals in Chile. He replaced the designated referee for the contentious first-round game between Chile and Italy, but the players resisted all attempts to control violent play, and the match deteriorated into a brawl that came to be known as "the Battle of Santiago." Although he never officiated another World Cup match, Aston supervised all officials at the 1966 and 1970 World Cups. In 1970 he introduced the red and yellow cards (inspired, he said, by the colours used in traffic lights) to help referees clarify disciplinary actions on the field. He was made MBE in 1997.

Astor, Francis David Langhorne, British newspaper editor (b. March 5, 1912, London,

Eng.—d. Dec. 7, 2001, London), as editor of *The Observer* from 1948 to 1975, was largely responsible for turning the paper's viewpoint from a conservative, establishment-supporting one to espousal of a number of liberal causes, including anticolonialism, human rights, and prison reform. He came to be considered one of the most outstanding and influential 20th-century editors.

Atef, Muhammad (Sobhi Abu Sitta), Egyptian-born Islamist militant (b. 1944?, Egypt—d. Nov. 14/15, 2001, near Kabul, Afg.), was believed to have been a close associate of Osama bin Laden (in early 2001 his daughter married Bin Laden's son) and chief military strategist for the Islamic terrorist organization al-Qaeda. He reportedly trained as a police officer before joining the radical Egyptian Islamic Jihad, members of which assassinated Pres. Anwar as-Sadat in 1981. Atef, whose other suspected noms de guerre included Abu Hafs al-Misri and Abu Khadijah, fled to Afghanistan in the 1980s. In 1999 he was one of more than 100 defendants convicted of subversion in Egypt and sentenced to prison in absentia. Intelligence sources indicated that Atef was involved in terrorist attacks on Americans in Somalia as well as the 1998 bombings of the U.S. embassies in Kenya and Tanzania and the terrorist attacks in the U.S. on Sept. 11, 2001. The U.S. government placed him on the FBI's list of "most wanted terrorists" and offered a $5 million reward for his capture. He was reported to have been killed in a bombing raid on an al-Qaeda stronghold outside Kabul.

Atkins, Chet (Chester Burton Atkins), American guitarist and record producer (b. June 20, 1924, Luttrell, Tenn.—d. June 30, 2001, Nashville, Tenn.), was a major figure in country music. Atkins shone as a guitarist, talent scout, and record producer who created the "Nashville sound" of the 1960s; Don Gibson,

Dolly Parton, Charley Pride, Waylon Jennings, Willie Nelson, Elvis Presley, and Perry Como (*q.v.*) were among the stars he produced or discovered for RCA Records. Atkins played fiddle and guitar with country bands on several Southern and Midwestern radio stations before making his first records as a singer-guitarist in 1946 (he later tried to destroy the master recordings on which he sang). After appearances on the Grand Ole Opry and hit guitar solos, including "Galloping on the Guitar" (1949), he played at many recording sessions with Hank Williams and others. Atkins became an assistant producer in 1952 and urged RCA to sign Presley, which led to the latter's rise to stardom; in 1957 Atkins became manager of RCA's Nashville recording operations. He then championed a modern country music sound that abandoned banjos, fiddles, and steel guitars in favour of string sections and vocal choruses. Atkins became an RCA vice president in 1967 but soon began to perform more actively. He made over 100 albums under his own name, playing the guitar in his signature fingerpicking style that he had adapted from that of Merle Travis. Atkins won a total of 14 Grammy Awards during his career and costarred on albums with guitar legends Travis, Les Paul, Doc Watson, Jerry Reed, and Mark Knopfler as well as his Nashville cronies Boots Randolph, Floyd Cramer, Danny Davis, and the Nashville String Band, among others. He toured the world playing country music, pop, and jazz and was sometimes featured with symphony orchestras. In the 1980s Atkins left RCA to record for Columbia. The guitarmaker Gretsch introduced its Chet Atkins Country Gentleman model in the 1960s. Atkins was inducted into the Country Music Hall of Fame in 1973.

Aumont, Jean-Pierre (Jean-Pierre Philippe Salomons), French actor (b. Jan. 5, 1911, Paris, France—d. Jan. 30, 2001, St. Tropez,

Fingerpicker extraordinaire Chet Atkins

France), employed his suave good looks and Gallic charm in more than 60 French and American motion pictures during a 70-year stage and screen career. Although Aumont was often cast in B-grade movies, his films included Marcel Carné's *Hôtel du Nord* (1938), François Truffaut's *La Nuit américaine* (1972; *Day for Night*), and Claude Lelouch's *Le Chat et la souris* (1975; *Cat and Mouse*). He also starred in the original stage production of Jean Cocteau's *La Machine infernale* (1934; *The Infernal Machine*) and the 1963 Broadway musical *Tovarich* opposite British actress Vivien Leigh; on television Aumont appeared in such miniseries as *A Tale of Two Cities* (1989) and *Le Comte de Monte Cristo* (1998; *The Count of Monte Cristo*). In 1991 he received an honorary César (French Oscar) for lifetime achievement.

Babu Chhiri Sherpa, Nepalese mountaineer (b. June 22, 1965, Taksindu, Nepal—d. April 29, 2001, Mt. Everest), was a legendary guide who reached the summit of Mt. Everest 10 times and set two records on the world's tallest peak; in May 1999 he survived for more than 21 hours without bottled oxygen while "camping" overnight on the 8,850-m (29,035-ft) summit, and in May 2000 he ascended from Base Camp (about 5,350 m [17,600 ft]) to the summit in an astounding 16 hours 56 minutes. Babu Chhiri reportedly fell into a crevasse while taking photographs near Camp II at about 6,500 m (21,300 ft).

Balthus (Balthazar Klossowski), French artist (b. Feb. 29, 1908, Paris, France—d. Feb. 18, 2001, Rossinière, Switz.), was one of the greatest figurative painters of the 20th century. His works included street scenes, portraits of fellow artists, and provocative depictions of young girls, who were often shown with cats. Balthus was largely self-taught and had a strong sense of tradition, with Piero della Francesca and Nicolas Poussin among his important influences. He was the son of Polish artists and grew up in Paris, Berlin, and Switzerland. In 1921, when he was 16, he published *Mitsou*, a series of drawings depicting his cat, with a preface by Rainer Maria Rilke. In 1924 Balthus went to Paris to study, and early in his career he supported himself by painting portraits and working as a stage designer and illustrator. Balthus had his first one-man show in Paris in 1934, and he subsequently became well known in the U.S., with eight exhibitions at the Pierre Matisse Gallery in New York City from 1938 to 1977. From 1961 to 1977 he was director of the French Academy in Rome, and it was during this period that he began to paint the Japanese model Setsuko Ideta, who in 1967 became his second wife. Balthus had a number of retrospectives, including exhibitions at museums in Paris, New York City, London, and Venice. Although he was reclusive and shunned publicity about

Figurative painting master Balthus

his personal life, he collaborated with Nicholas Fox Weber on a biography, *Balthus* (1999). Among his paintings were *Guitar Lesson* (1934), depicting a young girl spread over the knees of an older woman and described variously as an erotic portrait of lesbianism or as a pietà; *The Mountain* (1937), one of his best-known landscapes, combining realistic detail with a sense of fantasy; and *Therese* (1938), one of his many suggestive portraits featuring a young girl.

Barnard, Christiaan Neethling, South African surgeon (b. Nov. 8, 1922, Beaufort West, S.Af.—d. Sept. 2, 2001, Paphos, Cyprus), performed the first transplant of a heart from one human to another (1967), the first "piggyback" heart transplant, in which a second heart was inserted in order to aid the patient's own weak one (1974), the first transplantation of an animal's heart into a human, again to assist the patient's heart and give it time to heal (1977), and the first heart-lung transplant (1981). His early transplants were daring and controversial, in part because they set a precedent for the consideration of brain death as acceptable for the harvesting of organs for transplant and in part because he flouted the racial barriers of apartheid. They also gained the handsome and charismatic doctor instant fame both professionally and socially, and he became an international celebrity and member of the jet set. Barnard graduated from the University of Cape Town in 1946, spent some time in private practice, and then returned to the university to conduct research. He earned his M.D. degree in 1953, became a surgeon at Groote Schuur

Hospital in Cape Town, and in 1956–58 studied at the University of Minnesota, earning a Ph.D. There Barnard developed his interest and expertise in open-heart surgery, and when he returned (1958) to South Africa, he took a U.S. government-donated heart-lung machine with him. At Groote Schuur he formed one of the world's finest heart-surgery units, where he had especially good results with valve surgery and with correcting children's congenital cardiac problems and where he also began experimenting with heart transplantation, generally in dogs. Although Barnard's first heart-transplant patient died of double pneumonia 18 days after surgery because his dosage of immunosuppressant drugs was too high, his second patient lived more than 19 months. More experience and the development of better antirejection drugs eventually made heart transplant surgery standard, and some 100,000 such operations had been performed by late 2001. Barnard suffered from rheumatoid arthritis and in 1983 was forced to retire from the practice of surgery. He thereafter included conducting research in Oklahoma, running his farm in South Africa, and writing a weekly newspaper column among his activities. In addition to the autobiography *One Life* (1969; with Curtis Bill Pepper)—whose royalties were donated to the Chris Barnard Foundation, which supported research and made it possible for children from all over the world to travel to South Africa for heart surgery—Barnard also wrote papers for scholarly journals and a number of other books, including another autobiography, *The Second Life* (1993), such works on health topics as *Heart*

South African transplant surgeon Christiaan Barnard

Attack: You Don't Have to Die (1971), *The Arthritis Handbook* (1984), and *50 Ways to a Healthy Heart* (2001), and several novels.

Basov, Nikolay Gennadiyevich, Soviet physicist (b. Dec. 14, 1922, Usman, near Voronezh, Russia—d. July 1, 2001, Moscow, Russia), was corecipient of the Nobel Prize for Physics in 1964 with Aleksandr M. Prokhorov, his colleague at the P.N. Lebedev Physical Institute in Moscow, and Charles H. Townes of the United States. The award was given for fundamental research in quantum electronics that led to the development of the maser and the laser, which produce parallel monochromatic coherent beams of microwaves and light, respectively. Basov studied theoretical and experimental physics at the Moscow Engineering Physics Institute, graduating in 1950. From 1952 he did postgraduate work in quantum radiophysics under Prokhorov at the Lebedev Institute. By 1954 Basov and Prokhorov had developed the concept for a device that would emit microwave radiation of a single wavelength. The next year they learned that Townes's team at Columbia University, New York City, had already built such a device, which they called a maser (microwave amplification by stimulated emission of radiation). Basov and Prokhorov soon constructed a maser, and by 1958 other teams had applied the maser principle to the optical spectrum to lay the groundwork for the laser (light amplification by stimulated emission of radiation), the first of which was built in 1960. Basov served as deputy director (1958–73) and director (1973–89) of the Lebedev Institute and as director (1989–2001) of its Institute of Quantum Radiophysics. He was a deputy in the Supreme Soviet (1974–89) and a member of the Presidium (1982–89). In 1982 Basov was among 97 Nobel laureates to call for an international freeze on nuclear weapons.

Beame, Abraham David (Abraham David Birnbaum), British-born American politician (b. March 20, 1906, London, Eng.—d. Feb. 10, 2001, New York, N.Y.), served as mayor of New York City from 1974 to 1977; he was the city's first Jewish mayor. An accountant by profession, Beame worked in the city's budget office from 1946 to 1961, when he was elected city comptroller. He failed in his first mayoral bid in 1965, and he later served another term as comptroller. Beame was successful in his second campaign for mayor, though the outgoing administration left him to contend with severe financial problems. The ensuing fiscal crisis dominated Beame's one term in office and drove the city to the brink of bankruptcy in 1975. Beame's solutions, which included raising taxes, cutting services, and reducing the municipal workforce by 65,000, proved unpopular, and he was defeated in his reelection bid.

Bebey, Francis, Cameroonian-born writer, composer, and musician (b. July 15, 1929, Douala, Cameroon—d. May 28, 2001, Paris, France), achieved international kudos both as a novelist and poet and as an influential "Afropop" musical performer. Bebey was educated in literature and musicology at the Sorbonne and at New York University. He ex-

perimented with jazz and classical guitar before expanding his eclectic musical repertoire with traditional African rhythms and instruments, notably the *sanza* (thumb piano) and *ndewhoo* (a one-note pygmy flute). He recorded and performed worldwide, singing in English, French, and Douala. Bebey's first novel, *Le Fils d'Agatha Moudio* (1967; *Agatha Moudio's Son*, 1971), won the Grand Literary Prize of Black Africa in 1968. His wide-ranging literary output also included musicology studies, such as *Musique de l'Afrique* (1969; *African Music*, 1975); poetry, such as *Nouvelle saison des fruits* (1980); and fiction, notably *Le Roi Albert d'Effidi* (1973; *King Albert*, 1981).

Bécaud, Gilbert (François Gilbert Silly), French singer-songwriter (b. Oct. 24, 1927, Toulon, France—d. Dec. 18, 2001, Paris, France), composed "chansons françaises," romantic melodies that became pop hits for him as well as for many other French- and English-language performers. Bécaud, who earned the nickname "Monsieur 100,000 volts" for his dynamic stage presence, wrote more than 400 songs, most notably "Et Maintenant" ("What Now, My Love"), "Je t'appartiens" ("Let It Be Me"), "L'Important c'est la rose" ("What's Important Is the Rose"), and "Seul sur son étoile" ("It Must Be Him").

Beti, Mongo (Alexandre Biyidi), Cameroonian novelist and political writer (b. June 30, 1932, Mbalmayo, Cameroon—d. Oct. 8, 2001, Douala, Cameroon), was a critic of colonialism, which he believed destroyed traditional African society, and of the authoritarian regime that ruled Cameroon after independence in 1960. He was widely translated and gained an international reputation. He was the son of the owner of a cocoa plantation and was educated in Cameroon before going to France in 1951 to study at the Sorbonne. In the late 1950s he took a position teaching literature at the Lycée Corneille in Rouen, France, where he remained for 30 years. He published his first novel, *Ville cruelle* (1954), on the exploitation of peasants, under the pseudonym Eza Boto. His second novel, *Le Pauvre Christ de Bomba* (1956), appeared under the name Mongo Beti, which he used thereafter. Considered his most important work, the book was a satire on the influence of Roman Catholic missionaries in Africa. *Mission terminée* (1957), published in the U.K. as *Mission to Kala* and in the U.S. as *Mission Accomplished*, was an attack on French colonial policy. *Maine basse sur le Cameroun* (1972) was banned in both France and Cameroon. Other novels included *Remember Ruben* (1974) and its sequel, *La Ruine presque cocasse d'un polichinelle* (1979), which told of revolutionaries who defeated a French-backed regime in their native country. Later novels, such as *Les Deux Mères de Guillaume Ismaël Dzewatama, futur camionneur* (1982), dealt with mixed marriages. In 1978, with his French-born wife, he founded *Peuples Noirs/Peuples Africains*, a journal opposing neocolonialism in Africa. He returned to Cameroon in the 1990s.

Bibby, (Thomas) Geoffrey, British archaeologist (b. Oct. 14, 1917, Heversham, Cumbria,

Eng.—d. Feb. 6, 2001, Odder, near Århus, Den.), unearthed, with his Danish colleague Peter Vilhelm Glob, the 4,000-year-old remnants of the ancient kingdom of Dilmun beneath the modern city of Manama, Bahrain. The excavations, which began in 1953 and eventually extended over several countries, verified that the legendary Dilmun was a real trading centre and confirmed the Persian Gulf region's historic significance. Bibby's books included *Testimony of the Spade* (1956), *Four Thousand Years Ago* (1961), and *Looking for Dilmun* (1969).

Birendra Bir Bikram Shah Dev, Nepalese royal (b. Dec. 28, 1945, Kathmandu, Nepal—d. June 1, 2001, Kathmandu), was king of Nepal for 29 years. Educated at St. Joseph's School, Darjeeling, India, Eton (Eng.) College, the University of Tokyo, and Harvard University, he was the first Nepalese royal to study abroad. Upon the death of his father, King Mahendra, on Jan. 31, 1972, Birendra acceded to the throne. He was a popular, though autocratic, ruler. During his reign he opened up Nepal to extensive tourism and managed to maintain the country's independence despite political pressure from India, China, and the Soviet Union. In November 1990 he approved a new constitution that, while preserving his status as monarch, restored the multiparty democracy that his father had abolished. Along with his wife, Queen Aishwarya, and six other royal family members, Birendra was shot and killed at the Royal Palace; the massacre was carried out by Birendra's eldest son, Crown Prince Dipendra, who afterward turned the gun on himself and died three days later. Dipendra reportedly had been enraged by his mother's opposition to his choice of bride.

Black, Charles Lund, Jr., American legal scholar and educator (b. Sept. 22, 1915, Austin, Texas—d. May 5, 2001, New York, N.Y.), was a renowned authority on constitutional law; his 1974 book *Impeachment: A Handbook* was widely studied during the Watergate Scandal and was reissued during the impeachment proceedings against Pres. Bill Clinton in 1999. Black, who held a law degree from Yale University, taught at Columbia University, New York City, from 1947 to 1956, at Yale from 1956 to 1986, and again at Columbia from 1986 to 1999. A noted champion of civil rights, he helped write the legal brief for the plaintiff in the landmark *Brown* v. *Board of Education of Topeka* (Kan.), the 1954 case in which the U.S. Supreme Court ruled that racial segregation in public schools violated the 14th Amendment to the Constitution.

Blake, Sir Peter James, New Zealand yachtsman and explorer (b. Oct. 1, 1948, Auckland, N.Z.—d. Dec. 6, 2001, off Macapá, Braz.), was the winner of the two most important yachting competitions—the Whitbread Round the World Race (1989–90) and the America's Cup (1995 and 2000)—and in 1994 in the *ENZA New Zealand* won the Jules Verne Trophy when he set a nonstop circumnavigation world record of 74 days 22 hours 17 minutes 22 seconds, which went unbroken for three years. He later combined his enthusiasm for sailing with

America's Cup winner Sir Peter Blake

his environmental interests and investigated pollution and global warming in Antarctica and South America. Blake began sailing when he was a young boy and at age 16 participated in his first long ocean race. In 1973–74 he served as a crew member in the first Whitbread race—and the first of the five in which he sailed—and when he finally won, in *Steinlager 2*, he did it by being the first competitor ever to win all six of the race's legs. Blake made an unsuccessful effort to win the America's Cup for New Zealand in 1992 but saw victory on board the *Black Magic* in the next challenge three years later. For his success in winning the cup, Blake, who had been created MBE in 1983 and OBE in 1991, was rewarded with a knighthood in 1995. He went on to manage *Black Magic*'s victorious defense in 2000, but he also had already begun his environmental activities. He served as head of the Jacques Cousteau Society, formed his own company, blakexpeditions, to promote interest in the oceans' ecology, and was appointed special envoy of the UN Environment Program. Blake, on a pollution-monitoring exploration of the Amazon River and the Rio Negro in Brazil, was murdered when robbers boarded his boat and he rushed on deck to try to protect the vessel and its crew.

Boetticher, Budd (Oscar Boetticher, Jr.), American film director and screenwriter (b. July 29, 1916, Chicago, Ill.—d. Nov. 29, 2001, Ramona, Calif.), was a professional matador in Mexico before becoming a leading director of classic western movies. Much of his reputation was based on seven films he directed from 1956 to 1960, including *Seven Men from Now*, *The Tall T*, and *Decision at Sundown*; they starred Randolph Scott as a lonely but resolute cowpoke hero confronted by villains, and Boetticher called them "morality plays." He was also acclaimed for directing *Bullfighter and the Lady* (1951), a story based on his own experiences; he directed his last feature film, *A Time for Dying*, in 1971.

Bonfá, Luiz Floriano, Brazilian guitarist and songwriter (b. Oct. 17, 1922, Rio de Janeiro,

Braz.—d. Jan. 12, 2001, Rio de Janeiro), was one of the originators of bossa nova, a musical style that blended samba and jazz. In the late 1940s and early '50s, Bonfá played with a popular Brazilian band called the Quitandinha Serenaders, but he left the group to concentrate on songwriting. He achieved international fame after performing on the sound track of the 1958 film *Orfeu negro* (*Black Orpheus*). In 1962 he was a featured performer at a widely publicized bossa nova concert held at Carnegie Hall in New York City. Several Bonfá recordings became hits and pop/jazz standards, including "Manhã de Carnaval" and "Samba de Orfeu."

Bosch Gaviño, Juan, Dominican writer and politician (b. June 30, 1909, La Vega, Dom. Rep.—d. Nov. 1, 2001, Santo Domingo, Dom. Rep.), was the country's first democratically elected president. Serving only seven months in 1963 before being deposed, he nonetheless remained a power in Dominican politics. He left secondary school at the end of his third year. A foe of dictator Rafael Trujillo, he went into exile in the late 1930s. In 1939 he founded the Dominican Revolutionary Party (PRD), the country first political party. After Trujillo's assassination in 1961, Bosch returned and ran for president in the election of Dec. 20, 1962. With the support of the poor, the middle class, and intellectuals, he won almost two-thirds of

Dominican political and literary lion Juan Bosch

AP/Wide World Photos

the votes. Bosch took office on Feb. 27, 1963, with a program of land reform, nationalization of certain businesses, and curbs on the power of the military; a new constitution was adopted in April. Although he was a cautious reformer, he earned the enmity of landowners, businessmen, and the military, as well as of the Roman Catholic Church and of the U.S., which saw him as a leftist. On Sept. 25, 1963, he was overthrown in a military coup, which was followed by civil war and, in April 1965, an invasion by U.S. troops. He returned from exile to run in the election of 1966 but lost. In 1973 he split with the PRD to form the Dominican Liberation Party. Although he ran for president another five times, he never regained power. A charismatic orator, he also was a prolific writer and published essays, novels and short stories, biographies of Pablo Duarte and Simón Bolívar, and historical works that included a history of the Caribbean.

Boudreau, Louis ("Lou"), American baseball player and manager (b. July 17, 1917, Harvey, Ill.—d. Aug. 10, 2001, Olympia Fields, Ill.), began his professional career as a dazzling defensive shortstop, became the second youngest manager in major league history, and went on to lead the American League in batting and manage the Cleveland Indians to their last world championship; he then managed three more teams and broadcast major league games for nearly three decades. Boudreau signed a baseball contract with the Cleveland Indians in 1938. By 1940 he was playing in the All-Star Game, and the following year he nominated himself to become the next player-manager of the Indians. Team president Alva Bradley surprised everyone by naming the 24-year-old Boudreau to the post; his fellow players responded by winning 728 games for him, the most victories for any Cleveland manager, during the next nine seasons. He was noted for inspiring self-confidence in his players. His most famous innovation was the "Williams shift," in which he moved all defensive players except the left fielder to the right side of the field, to stymie the Boston Red Sox's power-hitting Ted Williams. On offense as well as defense, he was his own best player, hitting over .300 four times; his .327 was best in the league in 1944, and his lifetime batting average was .295. He was a favourite among fans as well as fellow players, and when new team owner Bill Veeck threatened to replace him in 1947, Cleveland fans held pro-Boudreau rallies to protest. The next year, after his team had added the league's first African American players—slugging outfielder Larry Doby and pitcher Satchel Paige—Boudreau hit .355, with 18 homers and 106 runs batted in, and led the Indians to their first World Series victory in 28 years. After Boudreau's playing career ended, he managed the Red Sox (1952–54) and the Kansas City Athletics (1955–57) and then became the Chicago Cubs radio announcer in 1958. Apart from a season off, during which he managed the Cubs to a seventh-place finish in 1960, he remained the team's radio voice until 1987. He was elected to the National Baseball Hall of Fame in 1970.

Boulting, Roy, British filmmaker (b. Nov. 21, 1913, Bray, Berkshire, Eng.—d. Nov. 5, 2001, Eynsham, Oxfordshire, Eng.), created, in partnership with his twin brother, John, some of Great Britain's most popular motion pictures of the 1940s and '50s. In 1937 the Boultings founded Charter Film Productions Ltd. and began making movies, usually with one brother serving as producer of the films that the other directed. During World War II Roy directed documentaries for the Army Film and Photographic Unit, notably the Academy Award-winning *Desert Victory* (1943). After the war the Boultings reteamed and made films ranging from the thriller *Brighton Rock* (1947) to social dramas such as *Fame Is the Spur* (1946), *The Guinea Pig* (1948), and *Seven Days to Noon* (1950). They were best known for their satiric comedies, including *Private's Progress* (1956), *Lucky Jim* (1957), and *I'm All Right, Jack* (1959), many of which served as star vehicles for Ian Carmichael and Peter Sellers. Roy Boulting's final films included *The Family Way* (1966), *Twisted Nerve* (1968), and *There's a Girl in My Soup* (1970). John Boulting died in 1985.

Bradman, Sir Donald George ("the Don"), Australian cricketer (b. Aug. 27, 1908, Cootamundra, N.S.W., Australia—d. Feb. 25, 2001, Adelaide, Australia), was the most effective batsman in the history of the game and one of the most celebrated Australians of the 20th century. Bradman's achievements far surpassed those of any other cricket batsman. His career averages of 99.94 in Tests and 95.14 in first-class matches were well ahead of those in second place: R.G. Pollock (60.97) in Tests and V.M. Merchant (71.22) in first-class matches. He made a world-record 37 scores of 200 or greater in a total of 338 first-class innings, compared with runner-up W. Hammond (36 in 634 innings), and scored his hundredth first-class hundred in his 295th innings, while the next-fastest, D.C.S. Compton, needed 552 innings. Bradman's 452 not out, against Queensland in 1930, remained the highest first-class score for almost 30 years, and his 334 against England in 1930 (309 in one day) was the highest Test score at the time. In 234 first-class matches for New South Wales, South Australia, and Australia, he made 28,067 runs, including 117 hundreds and six scores of 300 or more runs (another world record), with one score of more than 400. In 52 Tests he scored 6,996 runs, with 29 hundreds, including 2 triple and 10 double centuries. After playing for Bowral Cricket Club, Bradman was invited (1927) to play for New South Wales, scoring 118 not out in his first match. His Test debut came the next year against England at Brisbane. He batted poorly and was dropped, but he soon was recalled and batted 79 and 112. The Australian tour of England in 1930, in which he scored 974 runs in the Test series (average 139.14), established him as the game's dominant batsman. He continued his high scoring against the West Indies (1930–31) and South Africa (1931–32). To counter Bradman's devastating batting, England captain D.R. Jardine devised the infamous "bodyline" bowling for the 1932–33 tour of Australia. In a bitterly contentious atmosphere, England won the series and "contained" Bradman to an average of

Legendary batsman Sir Donald Bradman

Allsport Hulton/Archive/ Allsport

56.57 for the Test series, with only one century. After bodyline was condemned and outlawed, Bradman resumed his assault on the bowlers and never averaged less than 84.16 for any season until World War II interrupted his career in 1940. Bradman, who had been named captain in 1936, was well into his 30s and plagued with health problems when cricket resumed after the war. Nevertheless, he led Australia to victory in four Test series (15 wins, 3 losses, and 6 draws). Although only 1.7 m (5 ft 7 in) tall, Bradman had deft footwork and strong wrists and forearms, combined with intense powers of concentration and an insatiable appetite for runs. After retiring in 1948, he served as a selector, and he was twice chairman of the Australian Board of Control. He was knighted in 1949 and appointed Companion of the Order of Australia in 1979. The Bradman Museum was opened in Bowral in 1989. The 2000 *Wisden Cricketers' Almanack* named Bradman the top cricketer of the 20th century.

Braun, Victor, Canadian opera singer (b. Aug. 4, 1935, Windsor, Ont.—d. Jan. 6, 2001, Ulm, Ger.), was an internationally renowned baritone. After studying opera at the Royal Conservatory of Music, Toronto, he made his professional debut in a 1957 Canadian Opera Company production of Puccini's *Tosca.* He was the grand prize winner of the International Mozart Competition in 1963. Braun joined the Bavarian State Opera in Munich, Ger., in 1968, and a year later he debuted at Covent Garden in London in the title role of Humphrey Searle's *Hamlet.* His repertory included more than 100 roles, most notably the title roles of Verdi's *Falstaff* and Tchaikovsky's *Eugene Onegin.*

Brown, Lester Raymond ("Les"), American bandleader (b. March 14, 1912, Reinerton, Penn.—d. Jan. 4, 2001, Pacific Palisades, Calif.),

led a top swing-era dance band that went on to long-term Hollywood and television success and spent 40 years accompanying comedian Bob Hope's stage and broadcast shows. Excellent arrangers and musicians contributed to the Brown band, notably singer Doris Day, who joined when she was 17 years old. While the dance-band business was collapsing in the late 1940s, Brown's band thrived by appearing on Hope's weekly radio programs, and it was featured on television with Hope, Steve Allen, and Dean Martin. Brown began playing soprano saxophone in boyhood; he later attended Duke University, Durham, N.C., where he led the student dance band. The big band he formed in 1938 won popular success, especially after Day joined in 1940, and made a musical breakthrough with its 1941 hit "Joltin' Joe Dimaggio." Brown's arrangers, influenced by the Jimmie Lunceford, Count Basie, Woody Herman, and other top jazz bands, crafted a modern swing style; Brown's musicians, including his brother, trombonist Clyde ("Stumpy") Brown, played with singular precision and technical skill. The band scored a number of hit records, including "Mexican Hat Dance," "I've Got My Love to Keep Me Warm," and, most famously, "Sentimental Journey," a number one song in 1945 featuring Day's vocals. Two years later the Brown band first appeared with Hope; it made 18 overseas Christmas tours with him to entertain troops, including 7 trips to wartime Vietnam, and appeared in over 800 shows with Hope. Brown led his band at inauguration balls for Presidents Richard Nixon and Ronald Reagan, as well as for the U.K.'s Queen Elizabeth. The band—often introduced as "Les Brown and His Band of Renown"—continued to perform at concerts and dances and record throughout the rock era, although in 1990, a decade before his retirement, he maintained, "There won't be much demand for big bands soon."

Callaway, Ely Reeves, American golf-equipment manufacturer (b. June 3, 1919, La Grange, Ga.—d. July 5, 2001, Rancho Santa Fe, Calif.), founded the Callaway Golf Co. in 1982; under his leadership the company became the world's leading manufacturer of golf equipment. His most popular golf club, the oversized "Big Bertha" driver, introduced in 1991, was credited with revolutionizing the sport by making the driver one of the easiest golf clubs to use. Another Callaway driver, the ERC, was banned by the U.S. Golf Association for allegedly propelling the golf ball too far. Callaway had been president of a textile company and a vineyard owner before launching his golf company.

Campanelli, Pauline Eblé, American artist (b. Jan. 25, 1943, Bronx, N.Y.—d. Nov. 29, 2001, Pohatcong township, N.J.), painted superrealist still lifes that, while never of much interest to prestigious, expensive galleries and art museums, sold by the thousands through catalogs, furniture stores, and print and poster shops, rivaling only Andrew Wyeth in sales by a living artist. Purchases of prints of her most popular picture, *Wild Rose Berries,* topped 600,000.

Carver, Richard Michael Power Carver, Baron, British field marshal (b. April 24, 1915, Bletchingley, Surrey, Eng.—d. Dec. 9, 2001, Fareham, Hampshire, Eng.), rose steadily through the military ranks from 1935, when he graduated from Sandhurst and was commissioned into the Royal Tank Corps, until he was promoted to field marshal and made chief of the defense staff in 1973. During the intervening years he saw action in the World War II campaigns in North Africa and Europe and held a series of prominent military posts, notably chief of staff (1955) in Kenya during the Mau Mau uprising, head (1964) of the UN peacekeeping forces on Cyprus, and commander (1967–69) of all British troops in the Far East. After retiring in 1976, Carver spent a year (1977–78) in Rhodesia (later Zimbabwe) as the British resident commissioner. Having been knighted in 1966, he was made a life peer in 1977 and served in the House of Lords, where he was openly critical of NATO and the concept of nuclear deterrence. Carver also wrote a dozen books, including several volumes on military strategy and an autobiography, *Out of Step* (1989).

Cavagnoud, Régine, French skier (b. June 27, 1970, La Clusaz, France—d. Oct. 31, 2001, Vienna, Austria), was one of France's finest young Alpine skiers and a top prospect for the 2002 Winter Olympic Games. Cavagnoud first qualified for the World Cup circuit in December 1994. Despite recurrent injuries, she steadily improved, eventually winning eight World Cup races and representing France at three Winter Olympics. In January 2001 she won the gold medal in the supergiant slalom (super G) at the world championships in St. Anton, Austria; a month later she clinched her first super G title in the 2000–01 World Cup and finished third for the overall title. Cavagnoud died from severe brain injuries she sustained when she collided with a German ski coach during a high-speed training run on October 28.

Chang Hsüeh-liang, Chinese warlord (b. June 3, 1901, Haicheng, China—d. Oct. 14, 2001, Honolulu, Hawaii), kidnapped Nationalist leader Chiang Kai-shek in 1936 in an attempt to force him to fight the Japanese rather than the Communists. His action had a decisive effect on subsequent Chinese history. Chang was the son of the warlord Chang Tso-lin, who dominated Manchuria. The son took military training, joined his father's army at age 19, and soon became a general commanding his own troops. When the Japanese murdered his father in 1928, Chang assumed power, proving to be an able ruler and forming an alliance with Chiang. In 1931, however, the Japanese invaded Manchuria, forcing Chang and his troops to the south. He was cured of an opium addiction and then traveled throughout Europe. Chang returned to China in 1934, and in 1935–36 Chiang used his troops against Communist forces. Chang was intent on persuading Chiang to form an alliance with the Communists to fight the Japanese invaders, and in 1936 the Nationalist leader went to Sian to meet with him. Chang took Chiang hostage and held him for two weeks, until he agreed to Chang's demand. This so-called Sian Incident temporarily took pressure off the Communists, who had been pushed to northwestern China at the end of their Long March, and allowed them to rebuild. The Nationalists later court-martialed Chang, and he was put under house arrest. When the Nationalists fled to Taiwan in 1949, they took Chang with them, and he remained under arrest until 1990, gaining the distinction of becoming the world's longest-serving political prisoner. In 1991 he was allowed to visit his children in the U.S., and three years later he settled there. At his death he was honoured by the presidents of both China and Taiwan.

Chavis, Wilson Anthony ("Boozoo"), American singer and accordion player (b. Oct. 23, 1930, Dog Hill, Lake Charles, La.—d. May 5, 2001, Austin, Texas), helped popularize zydeco music with such hits as "Paper in My Shoe" (1954). Chavis made numerous recordings in the 1950s but, after a dispute with his record company, gave up performing for more than two decades. He launched a successful comeback in the 1980s, touring widely and releasing a string of new albums, including *Louisiana Zydeco Music* (1986) and *Zydeco Homebrew* (1988). Chavis, who by the 1990s had earned the nickname "king of Zydeco," was especially noted for his mastery of the diatonic button accordion.

Chelimo, Richard, Kenyan athlete (b. Feb. 24, 1972?, Marakwet region, Kenya—d. Aug. 15, 2001, Eldoret, Kenya), was one of his country's top long-distance runners in the early 1990s, but his many achievements were marred by controversy and disappointment. Chelimo captured the world junior 10,000-m title in 1990. The next year he won a silver medal at that distance at the world championships in Tokyo after having yielded the lead on the last lap to his teammate Moses Tanui. At the 1992 Olympic Games in Barcelona, Spain, Chelimo was awarded the gold medal in the 10,000 m when the winner, Khalid Skah, was disqualified because a fellow Moroccan had cheated on his behalf, but the decision was reversed controversially on appeal. In 1993 Chelimo set a world record of 27 min 7.91 sec for the 10,000-m event only to watch it fall to his Kenyan compatriot Yobes Ondieki less than a week later.

Christensen, Willam (William Farr Christensen), American ballet company director (b. Aug. 27, 1902, Brigham City, Utah—d. Oct. 14, 2001, Salt Lake City, Utah), began dancing at a time when men could not expect to have a career in ballet in the U.S. and, with his brothers Harold and Lew, was instrumental in establishing important companies in the country. He also staged the first full-length American productions of the ballet classics *Coppélia* (1939), *Swan Lake* (1940), and *The Nutcracker* (1944). Christensen and his brothers received a thorough education in music and classical dance, primarily from their relatives, and toured in vaudeville in the late 1920s and early '30s. In 1932 Christensen moved to Portland, Ore., where he taught ballet and started a company. He became a soloist with the San Francisco Opera Ballet in 1937, and the following year he was named director of the company. Although programs composed of several short works were customary in the U.S. at that time, Christensen introduced evening-length ballets in addition to choreographing a number of shorter works, including *In Vienna* (1938), *Winter Carnival* (1942), and *Nothin' Doin' Bar* (1950). In 1951 Christensen left the company, which by then had become the San Francisco Ballet, and moved to Salt Lake City to serve as professor of theatre ballet at the University of Utah. There he developed a department of ballet and choreography and in 1952 founded a company, the Utah Ballet. That company became professional in 1963 and in 1968 took the name Ballet West. Christensen remained with Ballet West until 1978, and from that time until he was in his late 90s, he ran his Christensen Ballet Academy.

Chukhrai, Grigory Naumovich, Soviet motion picture director (b. May 23, 1921, Melitopol, Ukraine, Soviet Russia—d. Oct. 28, 2001, Moscow, Russia), broke away from the restrictions of hagiographic Socialist Realism during the relatively censorship-free late 1950s to create poignant films about simple people in wartime. His finest work included *The Forty-First* (1956), which won the special jury prize at the Cannes Film Festival; *Ballad of a Soldier* (1959), which won major awards at film festivals in San Francisco, Cannes, London, and other cities and earned its director the Lenin Prize; and *Clear Skies* (1961), which won first prize at the Moscow Film Festival. In 1963 Chukhrai was barred from traveling abroad when he spurned orders to withhold the Moscow Film Festival's top prize from Frederico Fellini's *8 1/2;* his later films suffered after official censorship was reintroduced.

Chung Ju Yung, South Korean businessman (b. Nov. 25, 1915, Tongchon, Korea—d. March 21, 2001, Seoul, S.Kor.), was the founder of the Hyundai Group, one of the world's largest business conglomerates. He was credited with having played a leading role in the revival of the South Korean economy in the aftermath of the Korean War. Born into a poor farming family, Chung got his start in business as the owner of an auto repair shop. He poured his earnings into other ventures and established Hyundai Engineering and Construction in 1947. Chung was awarded lucrative contracts by South Korean leader Park Chung Hee and was eventually able to acquire the Hyundai Motor Co. and the Hyundai Electronics Industries Co., among other firms, as part of his business empire. He ran unsuccessfully for president in 1992. Although Hyundai's overall sales approached $80 billion per year in the 1990s, the conglomerate fell heavily into debt and was forced to accept government mandates to downsize its global operations. In later years Chung helped South Korean Pres. Kim Dae Jung in his efforts to engage North Korea in dialogue; Chung donated cattle and corn (maize) to the North in 1998 and sponsored a tourism project in the North's Mt. Kumgang region. He officially retired from Hyundai in 2000.

Coca, Imogene Fernandez de, American actress and comedian (b. Nov. 18, 1908, Philadelphia, Pa.—d. June 2, 2001, Westport, Conn.), employed her expressive, elastic face—enhanced by saucer eyes and a huge smile—as well as her energetic physicality and improvisational abilities to great effect, most notably in skits with comedian Sid Caesar on live television during American TV's Golden Age. For the five years from 1949 to 1954, their acts—lampooning everything from opera, ballet, and movies to everyday life and marriage (via their husband-and-wife team "The Hickenloopers")—brought 90 minutes of hilarity weekly to the Saturday-night viewing public and set the standard for TV comedy. The daughter of professional performers, Coca began piano lessons at age 5, singing lessons at 6, and dance lessons at 7, and by the time she was 11, she was work-

Durable comedian Imogene Coca

ing in vaudeville. Her Broadway debut came in 1925 in the chorus of the short-run *When You Smile,* and after appearances in a variety of shows, she got her lucky break. While rehearsing in a cold theatre, Coca donned a massively oversized coat and began to clown around with some other cast members. The producer added her bit to the show, *New Faces of 1934,* and Coca caught the attention of both the critics and the public. Performances at summer vacation resorts and in such Broadway shows as *New Faces of 1936* and *The Straw Hat Revue* (1939) followed, but it was 10 years later, when she was paired with Caesar on the TV show *Admiral Broadway Revue,* that she finally achieved stardom. The pairing lasted through 160 editions of the show that succeeded it, *Your Show of Shows.* Coca won the Emmy Award in 1951 for her work on that program. She later starred in her own half-hour TV show, *The Imogene Coca Show,* for a season and appeared in nightclubs, TV specials, films, including *Under the Yum Yum Tree* (1963), and Broadway plays, including *On the Twentieth Century* (1979).

Como, Perry (Pierino Roland Como), American singer and entertainer (b. May 18, 1912, Canonsburg, Pa.—d. May 12, 2001, Jupiter, Fla.), had a mellow baritone voice and a relaxed, easygoing manner—typified by his trademark cardigan sweaters—that made him an audience favourite dur-

ing a career that lasted over six decades and in which he sold more than 100 million records. For 15 years (1948–63) he hosted weekly television variety shows, winning Emmy Awards in 1954, 1955, 1956, and 1959, and his annual Christmas TV shows became a staple of the holiday season. Como began sweeping up in a barber shop when he was about 10 years old, and by the time he was in his mid-teens, he was the owner of his own shop, where he sang while he worked. Encouraged by his customers and his family, he became a singer with Freddy Carlone's band in 1933, and in 1936 he was signed by Ted Weems to sing with his orchestra. Como recorded and broadcast with Weems until 1942 and was about to give up singing for a return to barbering when in 1943 he accepted a contract to record and appear on radio. His first single, "Goodbye Sue," was released later that year. In 1944 Como had his first hit record, "Long Ago and Far Away," and the first of his over a dozen million-selling hits, "Till the End of Time," followed in 1945. Among his other popular recordings of the 1940s and '50s were "If I Loved You," "I'm Always Chasing Rainbows," "Hot," "Temptation," "Don't Let the Stars Get in Your Eyes," which was the first of his 14 number one records, and "Catch a Falling Star," for which he won a Grammy Award in 1958. Between 1944 and 1950 Como starred in his own NBC radio show, *The Chesterfield Supper Club,* which from 1948 was also televised. *The Perry Como Show* began broadcasting on CBS

in 1950 and from 1955 to 1959 appeared on NBC, where the show opened with the theme "Dream Along with Me" and included the popular "Letters, we get letters" segment. Beginning in 1959 Como served as host of the *Kraft Music Hall;* he ended his weekly TV appearances in 1963 and thereafter, until 1992, headlined occasional specials. During the later years of his career, he kept his name on the charts with such hits as "It's Impossible," "And I Love You So," and "For the Good Times." Como was awarded a Kennedy Center Honor in 1987.

Cooper, Malcolm, British marksman (b. Dec. 20, 1947, Camberley, Surrey, Eng.—d. June 9, 2001, Eastergate, West Sussex, Eng.), won consecutive Olympic gold medals in rifle shooting; he claimed his first gold in the small-bore rifle event at the 1984 Summer Olympic Games in Los Angeles and successfully defended the title at the 1988 Olympics in Seoul, S.Kor. Cooper was the first shooter ever to win consecutive gold medals in the event and the first British athlete since 1908 to win a rifle-shooting gold. Throughout the 1980s he dominated the sport; his achievements included winning individual gold medals in all five shooting events at the 1985 European championships in Zürich, Switz. A naval architect by profession, Cooper retired from competition in 1991 to concentrate on designing weapons for the British army.

Corso, Gregory Nunzio, American poet, playwright, and novelist (b. March 26, 1930, New York, N.Y.—d. Jan. 17, 2001, Robbinsdale, Minn.), was—along with Allen Ginsberg and Jack Kerouac—at the centre of the bohemian Beat literary and social movement from its beginning in the mid-1950s and was the last of that movement's original leading members. His poetry, with its unconventional spontaneity, could be candid and inelegant while at the same time inspiring and influential, and his public poetry readings were equally unconventional. Corso had a troubled childhood, living in a succession of orphanages and foster homes and having run-ins with the law, and at age 16 he began a three-year prison term for theft. During his imprisonment he began to read classic poetry and literature voraciously and then to write his own poetry. In 1950 Corso met Ginsberg in a bar in New York City's Greenwich Village, and Ginsberg—seeing promise in Corso's writing—took him into his circle and guided him in writing in a more experimental style. Corso later spent some time in the Boston area. His works were first published in the *Harvard Advocate* in 1954, and in 1955 his play *In This Hung-Up Age* was performed by Harvard University students. Students at Harvard and nearby Radcliffe College also financed his first book, *The Vestal Lady on Brattle, and Other Poems* (1955). The following year, soon after the famous public reading in San Francisco that included Ginsberg's "Howl" and that marked the rise of the Beats, Corso moved there and became recognized as one of the major figures of the movement. *Gasoline,* his first major book of poems, was published in 1958. Corso also wrote one of his most famous poems, "Bomb," in 1958; when printed, it was typed in the shape of a mushroom cloud. It was included in the volume of poetry *The Happy Birthday of Death* (1960). Other notable works included the novel *The American Express* (1961) and the poetry volumes *Long Live Man* (1962), *The Mutation of the Spirit* (1964), *Elegiac Feelings American* (1970), *Earth Egg* (1974), *Herald of the Autochthonic Spirit* (1981), and *Mindfield* (1989).

Costa Gomes, Francisco da, Portuguese military leader (b. June 30, 1914, Chaves, Port.—d. July 31, 2001, Lisbon, Port.), was the president of Portugal's ruling military junta from 1974 to 1976. Costa Gomes was chief of staff of Portugal's armed forces from 1972 until March 1974, when he reportedly was dismissed because of his support for decolonization. In April of that year, army officers overthrew Prime Minister Marcelo Caetano in a bloodless coup that came to be known as the Revolution of the Carnations. Costa Gomes took power when the junta's interim president, Gen. António de Spínola, went into self-exile in September. As head of state, Costa Gomes presided over the granting of independence to Portuguese colonies in Africa and Asia. After guiding Portugal through two attempted countercoups and parliamentary elections, he relinquished power in June 1976 to Gen. António dos Santos Ramalho Eanes, the newly elected president. In 1981 Costa Gomes was promoted to marshall, Portugal's highest military rank.

Counts, Ira Wilmer, Jr. ("Will"), American photographer (b. Aug. 24, 1931, Little Rock, Ark.—d. Oct. 6, 2001, Bloomington, Ind.), was on the staff of the *Arkansas Democrat* when he took his most famous photos, which captured the turmoil that attended the integration of Little Rock Central High School in 1957. In his best-known image, an African American student is being jeered as she makes her way past a white mob. Another, of a black journalist being kicked by a white man wielding a brick, was said to have led Pres. Dwight D. Eisenhower to send federal troops to Little Rock. Counts went on to work for the Associated Press in Chicago and Indianapolis, Ind., and later spent 32 years (1963–95) on the faculty of Indiana University.

Covas, Mário, Brazilian politician (b. April 21, 1930, Santos, Braz.—d. March 6, 2001, São Paulo, Braz.), was one of Brazil's most influential and respected politicians and a founder of the Brazilian Social Democratic Party. Covas served two terms in Congress before being appointed mayor of São Paulo in 1983. He later served as senator for São Paulo from 1986 to 1994 and as governor of São Paulo state from 1995 to 2001. A close ally of Pres. Fernando Henrique Cardoso, Covas had been planning a presidential campaign for 2002 when he succumbed to cancer.

Craighead, Frank Cooper, Jr., American naturalist (b. Aug. 14, 1916, Washington, D.C.—d. Oct. 21, 2001, Jackson, Wyo.), with his identical twin, John, spent 12 years studying grizzly bears in the Yellowstone National Park area, elucidating details about their lives and habits and demonstrating their importance to the ecosystem. The Craigheads' work helped prevent the extinction of grizzlies.

Cram, Donald James, American chemist (b. April 22, 1919, Chester, Vt.—d. June 17, 2001, Palm Desert, Calif.), was awarded the 1987 Nobel Prize for Chemistry for his development of ways to build molecules that could mimic the functioning of molecules in living organisms; he shared the prize with Charles J. Pedersen and Jean-Marie Lehn. After earning his bachelor's degree from Rollins College, Winter Park, Fla., and his master's degree from the University of Nebraska, Cram received a Ph.D. in organic chemistry from Harvard University in 1947. That same year he joined the faculty of the University of California, Los Angeles. He was appointed a full professor at UCLA in 1956 and became professor emeritus in 1997. Working independently from Pedersen and Lehn, Cram helped pioneer the field of host-guest chemistry. He synthesized an array of large organic molecules that—because of their differently shaped three-dimensional structures—could interact selectively with other, smaller molecules in a process analogous to the interactions between enzymes and other biological molecules. Molecules of the type developed by Cram were later widely used in sensors and electrodes. Cram was a renowned teacher and author of more than 400 research papers and seven books, including *Organic Chemistry* (1959, with George Hammond), a standard college textbook.

Curnow, (Thomas) Allen Monro, New Zealand poet and writer (b. June 17, 1911, Timaru, N.Z.—d. Sept. 23, 2001, Auckland, N.Z.), gained an international reputation for his verse. He was also known as the editor of two anthologies of New Zealand poetry. Curnow's father

Nigel Gardiner
Poetic powerhouse Allen Curnow

was an Anglican clergyman and an amateur poet. Curnow also studied for the ministry from 1931 to 1933 but then turned to journalism, working for the *Christchurch Press* from 1935 to 1948. The first of 20 volumes of poems appeared in 1933, and in 1938 he received a B.A. degree from the University of Canterbury, Christchurch. In 1948 he worked as a journalist in London. In 1951 Curnow joined the faculty of the English department at the University of Auckland, where he remained until his retirement in 1976. Much of his early poetry consisted of social and political satire; this was followed by a period in which he focused on the history of New Zealand and on national identity. Later he wrote of the Auckland landscape as well as on universal and metaphysical themes. Among major collections were *Trees, Effigies, Moving Objects: A Sequence of Poems* (1972), *You Will Know When You Get There: Poems 1979–81* (1982), and *Early Days Yet: New and Collected Poems 1941–1997* (1997). He was the editor of *A Book of New Zealand Verse 1923–45* (1945), considered to be the first serious study of poetry in New Zealand. He also edited *The Penguin Book of New Zealand Verse* (1960), an anthology that generated intense controversy, partly because of his selection of those to be included. Curnow received six New Zealand Book Awards, the Commonwealth Poetry Prize (1988), and the Queen's Gold Medal for Poetry (1989). He was made a Companion of the Order of the British Empire (1986) and was a member of the Order of New Zealand (1990).

Dagmar (Virginia Ruth Egnor), American comic actress (b. Nov. 29, 1921, Logan, W.Va.—d. Oct. 9, 2001, Ceredo, W.Va.), portrayed a stereotypical sexy dumb blonde in early 1950s television, most notably on the late-night talk show *Broadway Open House*, the prototype for *The Tonight Show* and similar programs. With a repertoire of silly poetry and mangled-language lectures—which she dubbed treasises—Dagmar became an overnight sensation.

Davidsen, Arthur, American astrophysicist (b. May 26, 1944, Freeport, N.Y.—d. July 19, 2001, Baltimore, Md.), was a leading researcher in the fields of high-energy astrophysics and ultraviolet space astronomy. After service in the U.S. Navy during the Vietnam War, Davidsen earned a Ph.D. in astronomy from the University of California, Berkeley, in 1975. That year he joined the faculty of Johns Hopkins University, Baltimore, where he spent the rest of his career. Davidsen oversaw the construction of the Hopkins Ultraviolet Telescope (HUT), a project he began in 1979 to study intergalactic space. HUT was carried aboard the space shuttle *Columbia* in 1990 and the space shuttle *Endeavour* in 1995. Davidsen served (1985–88) as the founding director of the Center for Astrophysical Sciences at Johns Hopkins.

Dawson, John Myrick, American physicist (b. Sept. 30, 1930, Champaign, Ill.—d. Nov. 17, 2001, Los Angeles, Calif.), was one of the world's foremost authorities on plasma physics. Dawson was known for his development of the so-called particle-in-cell computer model, a technique for simulating plasmas on computers; he was also the first to suggest using plasma in particle accelerators in order to make them more powerful without increasing their size. Dawson was a research physicist at Princeton University from 1956 to 1962 and a professor of physics at the University of California, Los Angeles, from 1973 until his death. Dawson, who published more than 300 papers on plasma physics, was elected to the National Academy of Sciences in 1977.

Dertouzos, Michael Leonidas, Greek-born computer scientist (b. Nov. 5, 1936, Athens, Greece—d. Aug. 27, 2001, Boston, Mass.), as director of the Massachusetts Institute of Technology's computer science laboratory from 1974, provided valuable support that helped enable the World Wide Web Consortium to develop the standards that made the Internet accessible to individual users throughout the world.

Desio, Ardito, Italian geologist and explorer (b. April. 18, 1897, Palmanova, Italy—d. Dec. 12, 2001, Rome, Italy), led the first successful expedition to scale K2, the world's second tallest mountain; he did not make the final assault to the peak, however, owing to his age. The 1954 feat was largely attributed to his meticulous planning and disciplined military strategy. During World War I Desio served as lieutenant of the Alpine Troops. He later attended the University of Florence, where he studied natural sciences; he then began what became a lifetime post as a professor at the University of Milan. Desio was the author of more than 400 geologic publications. He served as president (1966–73) of the Italian Geological Committee and was the recipient of numerous honours related to the 1954 climb. Desio traveled extensively; he led scientific expeditions in Africa, the Middle and Near East, and Antarctica. He was credited with the discovery of the first deposits of natural oil and gas in Libya (1939) and with having been the first Italian to reach the South Pole (1962). His book *Ascent of K2* (1955) was translated into 11 languages.

de Valois, Dame Ninette (Edris Stannus), Irish-born British dancer and choreographer (b. June 6, 1898, Baltiboys, Blessington, County Wicklow, Ire.—d. March 8, 2001, London, Eng.), was the founder and first director of what became England's Royal Ballet and its renowned school. One of the most influential and highly revered individuals in the arts world in the 20th century—she was generally referred to simply as Madam—she guided the development of a British ballet style and tradition and led the company to international repute. Her family had moved to England when she was a child, and when she was a young teenager, she began her performing career, as one of Lila Field's Wonder Children, and studied dance with such noted teachers as Enrico Cecchetti. In 1923 de Valois began dancing with Sergey Diaghilev's Ballets Russes, but in 1926, having discovered that she was suffering the aftereffects of a childhood case of polio that had gone undiagnosed, she gave up performing and

founded a school in London, the Academy of Choreographic Art. She also worked with Dublin's Abbey Theatre and Cambridge's Festival Theatre and began an association with Lilian Baylis at the Old Vic theatre. Baylis had another theatre, the Sadler's Wells, where in 1931 de Valois's dancers presented their first full-length program. This marked the launch of the Vic-Wells Ballet Company. With Frederick Ashton as chief choreographer and Constant Lambert as musical director, the company, later called the Sadler's Wells Ballet, grew in size and stature, and in 1946 it moved to the Royal Opera House at Covent Garden. It was granted a royal charter in 1956 and became the Royal Ballet. De Valois in the meantime had formed a second company, the Sadler's Wells Theatre Ballet, which later became one of England's top regional dance companies, the Birmingham Royal Ballet. She retired as the Royal Ballet's director in 1963 but continued leading the school until 1972. De Valois choreographed

Hulton/Archive/Getty Images

Dame Ninette de Valois, doyenne of British ballet

such works as *La Création du monde* (1931), *Job* (1931), *The Haunted Ballroom* (1934), *The Rake's Progress* (1935), and *Checkmate* (1937; with Arthur Bliss) and wrote three books. She was made a Chevalier of the Legion of Honour

in 1950, Dame of the British Empire in 1951, and a Companion of Honour in 1982, and in 1992 she was awarded the Order of Merit.

Devi, Phoolan, Indian bandit and politician

(b. Aug. 10, 1963, Uttar Pradesh state, India—d. July 25, 2001, New Delhi, India), was the notorious "Bandit Queen" who became legendary for both her acts of revenge on those who had abused her and her Robin Hood-like activities to aid the lower castes. After being imprisoned, however, she became a member of the Lok Sabha, the lower house of Parliament, where she continued as a champion of the poor and oppressed. Devi's life story was a mixture of fact and legend, beginning with her arranged marriage at age 11 to a man three times her age. A year later, having been brutalized by him, she returned home, an act her family considered disgraceful. By the time she was in her early 20s, she had joined (or been kidnapped into) a gang of *dacoits* (bandits), been sexually assaulted numerous times—once by upper-caste landowners, Thakurs, in the village of Behmai—and left barren, and become the mistress of a *dacoit* leader. On Feb. 14, 1981, Devi led a notorious act of revenge known as the Saint Valentine's Day massacre; some 20 of Behmai's Thakurs were rounded up and shot in retribution for her gang rape. This act intensified both her status in modern folklore and the police search for her. In 1983, in poor health and exhausted by the struggle to stay hidden, Devi negotiated her surrender to avoid a death sentence. Although she agreed to 8 years' imprisonment, she ended up being jailed for 11 years, without trial, and gained release only through the efforts of the lower-caste chief minister of Uttar Pradesh. In 1994, shortly before her release, she was the subject of the Bollywood film *Bandit Queen*. In 1996, Devi took advantage of her cult status and, as a member of the Samajwadi Party, won election to Parliament. She lost her seat two years later but regained it in 1999. Devi was killed when masked assassins opened fire on her outside her home.

Diamond, John, British journalist (b. May 10, 1953, London, Eng.—d. March 2, 2001, London), chronicled his four years with cancer with unflinching honesty, humour, and unsentimental insight through his weekly column in *The Sunday Times* magazine and the best-selling book *C: Because Cowards Get Cancer Too* (1998). Diamond was already a successful consumer writer, newspaper columnist, television presenter, and frequent talk-show guest when he was diagnosed with throat cancer in 1997. Diamond continued to write about the daily minutiae of life with cancer until his death.

Dickson, Gordon Rupert, Canadian-born American science-fiction writer (b. Nov. 1, 1923, Edmonton, Alta.—d. Jan. 31, 2001,

Minneapolis, Minn.), was one of the world's most prominent science-fiction writers; he published more than 80 novels and some 200 short stories. Among Dickson's best-known science-fiction works were *Dorsai!* (1960), *Soldier, Ask Not* (1967), and *Tactics of Mistake* (1971). He also excelled in the fantasy genre; his 1976 novel *The Dragon and the George* won the British Fantasy Society's August Derleth Award.

Didi (Waldir Pereira), Brazilian association football (soccer) player (b. Oct. 8, 1928/29, Campos, Braz.—d. May 12, 2001, Rio de Janeiro, Braz.), was a key inside-right midfielder on the Brazilian national team from 1952 until 1962, scoring 31 goals in 85 international matches. On the field Didi was a masterful playmaking strategist and ball handler, but he was most admired for his devastating *folha seca* ("dry leaf") free kicks. He played for Brazil in the 1954 World Cup and was captain of the teams that won the World Cup in 1958 (when he was named Most Valuable Player) and 1962. Except for a brief, unsatisfactory stint in Spain (1959–60) with Real Madrid and Valencia, Didi played professionally in Brazil. In 1950 he signed with Fluminense, which won the Rio League title the next year; in 1956 he transferred to Botafogo, which won the title in 1961 and 1962. After retiring in 1965 he coached club teams in Brazil and other countries and in 1970 led Peru to the World Cup quarterfinals. Didi was inducted into the International Football Hall of Champions in 2000.

Dionne, Yvonne, Canadian personality (b. May 28, 1934, Callander, Ont.—d. June 23, 2001, Montreal, Que.), was one of the celebrated Dionne quintuplets, whose birth was hailed as a medical miracle; the five identical sisters were the first documented set of quintuplets to have survived more than a few days. In 1935, after the Ontario government deemed the parents of the quintuplets unfit to care for them, the five were placed in a compound called Quintland, where tourists were allowed to view them through one-way glass; during the 1930s up to 6,000 tourists per day visited Quintland. The sisters also appeared in films and advertisements. The Dionne parents regained custody of the girls in 1941. Years later the quintuplets successfully sued the Ontario government for having separated them from their family and put them on display. Yvonne eventually became a librarian and an activist on behalf of Canadian orphans. With her two surviving sisters, Annette and Cécile, she published a book, *Family Secrets: The Dionne Quintuplets' Autobiography,* in 1994.

Donahue, Troy (Merle Johnson, Jr.), American actor (b. Jan. 27, 1936, New York, N.Y.—d. Sept. 2, 2001, Santa Monica, Calif.), was a teen heartthrob in the late 1950s and early '60s, with starring roles in movies, including *A Summer Place* (1959), *Parrish* (1961), *Rome Adventure* (1962), and *Palm Springs Weekend* (1963), and the television series *Surfside Six* (1960–62) and *Hawaiian Eye* (1962); after overcoming substance-abuse problems in the early 1980s, he appeared in some two dozen more movies, including *Cry-Baby* (1990).

Downey, (Sean) Morton, Jr., American television talk-show host (b. Dec. 9, 1933, New York, N.Y.—d. March 12, 2001, Los Angeles, Calif.), pioneered tabloid-style television as the abrasive host of *The Morton Downey Jr. Show,* which aired from 1987 to 1989. Downey worked as an actor, singer-songwriter, and record producer before breaking into radio as a talk-show host in the 1980s. His show became an instant, albeit controversial, hit after moving to television. Known as "Mort the Mouth," Downey frequently insulted his guests, and his outbursts sometimes provoked raucous arguments and fistfights.

Drobny, Jaroslav, Czechoslovak-born sportsman (b. Oct. 12, 1921, Prague, Czechoslovakia—d. Sept. 13, 2001, London, Eng.), during the 1940s was one of his country's finest tennis players and a key member of the national ice hockey team, but he achieved his greatest success on the tennis court after his defection to the West in 1950. Drobny played at Wimbledon in 1938 (representing Czechoslovakia) and in 1939 (representing "Bohemia-Moravia," that part of Czechoslovakia not then under German occupation). After working in a munitions factory during World War II, he led Czechoslovakia to victory in the European zone of the 1947 and 1948 Davis Cup tennis tournaments. At the same time, he guided the Czechoslovak national ice hockey team to a gold medal at the 1947 world championships and a silver at the 1948 Winter Olympic Games. After his defection Drobny played tennis on an Egyptian passport and won the French (1951 and 1952) and Italian (1950, 1951, and 1953) championships. He lost in the final at Wimbledon in 1949 and 1952, but in 1954 he finally captured the All-England title in a thrilling four-set final against Ken Rosewall. In 1960 Drobny took British citizenship and retired from elite-level tennis, although he continued to compete for Britain in veterans' events. In 1983 he was inducted into the International Tennis Hall of Fame.

Dudek, Louis, Canadian poet (b. Feb. 6, 1918, Montreal, Que.—d. March 22, 2001, Montreal), was one of Canada's most influential poets; he was particularly noted for his book-length poems, including *Europe* (1955), *En México* (1958), and *Atlantis* (1967). Dudek was a professor at McGill University, Montreal, from 1951 until the time of his death. In 1952 he helped launch Contact Press, which published leading Canadian poets of the 1950s and '60s. Dudek also published his own literary journal, *Delta,* from 1957 to 1966. He was named a member of the Order of Canada in 1984. His last book, *Surface of Time,* appeared in 2000.

Dudley, Jane, American dancer, choreographer, and teacher (b. April 3, 1912, New York, N.Y.—d. Sept. 19, 2001, London, Eng.), was influential in the development of modern dance in three countries. In the U.S. she danced with Martha Graham's company from 1937 to 1944 and frequently thereafter as a guest artist, as well as teaching for Graham and at colleges and universities and dancing with and choreographing for the New Dance Group and the Dudley-Maslow-Bales Trio. In

1968 she went to Tel Aviv, Israel, as artistic director of the Batsheva Dance Company, and in 1970 she moved to England to join the staff of the London Contemporary Dance School. Dudley left the post of director of contemporary dance studies in 1990 but remained affiliated with the school until 1998.

Duong Van Minh ("Big Minh"), South Vietnamese general (b. Feb. 16, 1916, Long An province, French Indochina—d. Aug. 6, 2001, Pasadena, Calif.), was a key member of the military coup that overthrew South Vietnamese Pres. Ngo Dinh Diem in November 1963; in April 1975 he succeeded Nguyen Van Thieu (*q.v.*) as president just days before North Vietnamese forces captured Saigon. Minh was a French-educated officer in the colonial army before the bifurcation of newly independent Vietnam in 1954. Although he was credited with having authorized the execution of Diem and Diem's brother Ngo Dinh Nhu in 1963, Minh proved to be a cautious and ineffectual leader. After officially surrendering Saigon, Minh was placed in detention, but he was allowed to emigrate in 1983.

Earnhardt, (Ralph) Dale, Sr., American race-car driver (b. April 29, 1951, Kannapolis, N.C.—d. Feb. 18, 2001, Daytona Beach, Fla.), was one of the most successful stock-car racing drivers in history. He won a total of 76 races in his career, and he captured the National Association for Stock Car Auto Racing's (NASCAR's) Winston Cup season points championship seven times—a feat equaled by only one other driver, racing legend Richard Petty. Earnhardt also won NASCAR's American Driver of the Year award twice, in 1987 and 1994. Earnhardt, who began racing at the age of 19 on dirt tracks, claimed his first NASCAR victory in 1979. His aggressive driving style earned him the nickname "the Intimidator" and also helped to make him one of the most

Brian Cleary/AFP Worldwide

"The Intimidator" Dale Earnhardt

popular drivers of his era. He won NASCAR's 1979 Rookie of the Year award. In 1980 he took his first Winston Cup title and, with $588,926 in earnings that year, established a new single-season earnings record. He won back-to-back Winston Cup championships in 1986–87, 1990–91, and 1993–94. His earnings of $3,083,056 in 1990 made him the first NASCAR driver to top the $3 million mark. In 1996 Earnhardt became only the third driver in NASCAR history to start 500 consecutive Winston Cup races, and the following year he became the first driver to earn more than $30 million. His victory in the Daytona 500 in 1998, after 19 unsuccessful bids to win the event, was another major milestone for Earnhardt. His last victory came in October 2000 when he triumphed in the Winston 500 in Talladega, Ala. He was killed on the last turn of the last lap of the Daytona 500 in a crash that involved cars driven by Sterling Marlin and Ken Schrader. At the time of his death, Earnhardt had amassed $41,742,384 in career earnings—an all-time record.

Egan, Msgr. John Joseph, American clergyman (b. Oct. 9, 1916, New York, N.Y.—d. May 19, 2001, Chicago, Ill.), was a Roman Catholic priest who became a noted social activist. Egan was ordained in 1943. As director of the Chicago Archdiocese Office of Urban Affairs from 1958 to 1969, he attracted attention by championing racial integration and criticizing the effects of urban-renewal projects on the poor. Egan was among the clergymen who joined the Rev. Martin Luther King, Jr., on his historic 1965 protest march from Selma to Montgomery, Ala. Egan served as director of the Institute for Pastoral and Social Ministry at the University of Notre Dame from 1970 to 1983. From 1987 until his death, he was head of the Office of Community Affairs at DePaul University, Chicago. In 2001 he again attracted headlines by calling for the Roman Catholic Church to ordain women and married men. An acclaimed biography of Egan, *An Alley in Chicago: The Ministry of a City Priest,* by Margery Frisbie, appeared in 1991.

Enebish, Lhamsurengiyn, Mongolian politician (b. 1947, Mogod Sum, Mong.—d. Sept. 29, 2001, Ulaanbaatar, Mong.), was secretary-general (from 1996) of the Mongolian People's Revolutionary Party (MPRP) and speaker (from July 19, 2000) of the country's Great Hural (parliament). Enebish studied engineering at Mongolian National University and after graduation worked as an engineer (1970–75) and as director of the engineering and architecture bureau in Ulaanbaatar (1975–77). After serving (1980–83) as an economic adviser at the Mongolian embassy in Moscow, he returned to Ulaanbaatar, where he was deputy mayor (1983–90) and mayor (1990–92). Enebish became Mongolia's first deputy prime minister in 1993. He was elected speaker after the MPRP won an overwhelming majority in the July 2000 parliamentary elections.

Evans, Dale (Frances Octavia Smith), American actress, singer, songwriter, and writer (b. Oct. 31, 1912, Uvalde, Texas—d. Feb. 7, 2001, Apple Valley, Calif.), reigned as "queen of the West" alongside her "king of the cowboys" husband, Roy Rogers, in films in the 1940s and early '50s and on television in the 1950s and '60s. These shows featured lavish costumes for the stars, straightforward story lines, and wholesome family values. The couple also recorded some 400 songs together, among them their theme song, "Happy Trails," one of the about 25 that she wrote. Evans was working as a stenographer when, at the suggestion of her boss, she sang on a local radio program. This led to further radio appearances, including a stint as a regular vocalist on a CBS network show, *News and Rhythm,* in addition to employment as a nightclub vocalist. Evans's first notable motion picture appearance was in 1943 in the John Wayne film *In Old Oklahoma* (later titled *The War of the Wildcats*), and the following year found her cast opposite Rogers for the first time, in *The Cowboy and the Señorita.* Besides leading to their marriage (1947), the pairing also was a hit with the public, and they made more than two dozen westerns together. From 1951 to 1957 Evans and Rogers starred in a television series, *The Roy Rogers Show,* and they returned in 1962 for *The Roy Rogers and Dale Evans Show. Happy Trails Theatre* (1986–89) brought their films to the TV audience on cable television's Nashville Network. The deeply religious Evans also wrote more than 20 inspirational books. In the best known of her works, *Angel Unaware* (1953), she told the story of Robin, the only child born to the couple, who had Down syndrome and heart problems and died shortly before her second birthday. Evans and Rogers opened the Roy Rogers–Dale Evans Museum in Victorville, Calif., in 1964 and featured in it much of their career memorabilia, including the preserved bodies of their horses, Buttermilk and Trigger. They were inducted into the National Cowboy Hall of Fame, Oklahoma City, Okla., in 1976. Rogers died in 1998 after nearly 51 years of marriage to Evans.

Evans, Rowland, American journalist (b. April 28, 1921, Whitemarsh, Pa.—d. March 23, 2001, Washington, D.C.), advocated conservative causes as a prominent newspaper columnist and television host. With journalist Robert Novak, Evans published a syndicated column, called "Inside Report," from 1963 to 1993. From 1980 the pair served as cohosts of Cable News Network's political talk show *Evans & Novak,* which was renamed *Evans, Novak, Hunt & Shields* in 1998 after fellow pundits Al Hunt and Mark Shields joined the program. In his columns Evans correctly predicted that Barry Goldwater would win the Republican presidential nomination in 1964 and celebrated the demise of the Soviet Union. With Novak he wrote several books, including *Nixon in the White House: The Frustration of Power* (1971) and *The Reagan Revolution* (1981).

Fahey, John Aloysius, American guitarist (b. Feb. 28, 1939, Takoma Park, Md.—d. Feb. 22, 2001, Salem, Ore.), created extended, serene guitar compositions that fused American folk, country music, and rural blues traditions on noted underground albums of the 1960s; his style, which he called "American primitive guitar," made him a major influence on 1980s New Age music, an idiom that he disliked.

Fano, Ugo, Italian-born American physicist (b. July 28, 1912, Turin, Italy—d. Feb. 13, 2001, Chicago, Ill.), was a pioneering nuclear physicist who helped identify the hazards of radioactivity for humans and whose research provided the groundwork for the development of the gas laser, among other inventions. In 1939, after studying under Enrico Fermi, Fano left Italy for the U.S. in order to escape fascism. Working for the National Bureau of Standards in the 1940s and '50s, he led research into the effects of radiation on biological systems. Fano joined the University of Chicago as a professor in 1966, became chairman of the university's physics department in 1972, and was named professor emeritus in 1982. Among the numerous honours he received was the U.S. Department of Energy's Enrico Fermi Award for lifetime achievement (1995).

Fariña, Mimi (Mimi Margharita Baez), American folk singer and social activist (b. April 30, 1945, Stanford, Calif.—d. July 18, 2001, Mill Valley, Calif.), was the younger sister of folk singer Joan Baez and was also a well-known performer in her own right. With her first husband, Richard Fariña, she made two popular albums in the mid-1960s, *Reflections in a Crystal Wind* and *Celebrations for a Grey Day.* After her husband's death in a motorcycle accident in 1966, she continued to make recordings, including *Take Heart* (1971), a duo album with Tom Jans. Fariña was also known as the founder of Bread & Roses, a charity that organized musical shows for audiences in nursing homes, hospitals, homeless and drug rehabilitation centres, and correctional facilities.

Finster, the Rev. Howard, American artist and preacher (b. Dec. 2, 1916, Valley Head, Ala.—d. Oct. 22, 2001, Rome, Ga.), with his simple colourful works that combined his evangelistic messages with pop culture icons, became one of the most noted folk artists of the 20th century. He was best known for Paradise Garden in Pennville, Ga., which he concocted from items he retrieved from a dump, and his designs also appeared on album covers for such rock groups as R.E.M. and the Talking Heads.

Flanagan, Tommy Lee, American jazz pianist (b. March 16, 1930, Detroit, Mich.—d. Nov. 16, 2001, New York, N.Y.), improvised fluent melodies with swing, harmonic ingenuity, and a light touch. A sensitive accompanist, he made his first recording with Miles Davis; played on classic modern albums, notably Sonny Rollins's *Saxophone Colossus* (1956) and John Coltrane's *Giant Steps* (1959); and toured with tenor saxophonist Coleman Hawkins, singer Tony Bennett, and especially Ella Fitzgerald (1963–65, 1968–78) before becoming leader of his own trio.

Fock, Jeno, Hungarian politician (b. May 17, 1916, Budapest, Austria-Hungary—d. May 23, 2001, Budapest, Hung.), was a moderate communist who tried to institute economic reforms during his service as Hungarian deputy prime minister (1961–67) and prime minister (1967–75). His efforts were blocked by the Soviet Union, however, and he was pushed out of office in 1975. Fock continued to criticize General Secretary Janos Kadar's hard-line regime from within the Politburo for another five years, and he was considered a moderating influence on the Central Committee until he was retired in 1989.

Francis, Arlene (Arlene Francis Kazanjian), American actress and television personality (b. Oct. 20, 1907, Boston, Mass.—d. May 31, 2001, San Francisco, Calif.), enjoyed widespread popularity as a regular panelist on the long-running television quiz show *What's My Line?* and as host of the variety show *Talent Patrol.* She was also a cohost of the television morning show *Home.* Francis appeared on Broadway from 1936 and starred in the hit play *The Doughgirls* in 1942. Work in film and television followed. She appeared on *What's My Line?* from 1950 to 1975.

Freeman, Kathleen, American character actress (b. Feb. 17, 1919, Chicago, Ill.—d. Aug. 23, 2001, New York, N.Y.), appeared in some 100 films, including nearly a dozen Jerry Lewis movies and, most memorably, in the role of vocal coach Phoebe Dinsmore in *Singin' in the Rain* (1952); in her last movie role, she was the voice of an old woman in the animated *Shrek* (2001). In addition to showing up in most of the popular television sitcoms from the late 1950s on, she also had a notable stage career that included tours as Miss Hannigan in *Annie* and Helga Ten Dorp in *Deathtrap* and the role of sassy piano player Jeanette Burmeister in the Broadway production *The Full Monty,* for which she received a Tony nomination and which she played until five days before her death.

Furnas, J(oseph) C(hamberlain), American author and social historian (b. Nov. 24, 1905, Indianapolis, Ind.—d. June 3, 2001, Stanton, N.J.), published a noted social history of the U.S. The three-volume work included *The Americans: A Social History of the United States, 1587–1914* (1969), *Great Times: An Informal Social History of the United States, 1914–1929* (1974), and *Stormy Weather* (1977), covering the years 1929–45. Furnas, a prolific contributor to newspapers and magazines, wrote one of the most widely circulated articles in history, ". . . And Sudden Death," about driving fatalities and the need for automobile safety; some eight million reprints were issued after the article was originally published in *Reader's Digest* in August 1935. Furnas's autobiography, *My Life in Writing: Memoirs of a Maverick,* appeared in 1989.

Futch, Edward ("Eddie"), American boxing trainer (b. Aug. 9, 1911, Hillsboro, Miss.—d. Oct. 10, 2001, Las Vegas, Nev.), was dubbed "the professor of pugilism" for the sharp observation, compassion, and determination that he used to coach more than 20 world champions, including heavyweights Joe Frazier, Ken Norton, Trevor Berbick, Larry Holmes, Michael Spinks, and Riddick Bowe; light heavyweights Bob Foster and Montell Griffin; and welterweights Don Jordan and Marion Starling.

Futch's observation that heavyweight champion Muhammad Ali was vulnerable to left-handed punches helped Frazier become the first boxer to defeat Ali, in 1971; two years later Futch trained Norton, only the second to defeat Ali. Futch became controversial in 1975 while handling Frazier in the boxer's historic 15-round Manila bout with Ali ("the Thrilla in Manila"). Blinded and wounded after 14 three-minute rounds of Ali's brutal blows, Frazier wanted to continue, but Futch withdrew his man from the match. He grew up in Detroit, where he won a local Golden Gloves lightweight title in 1933; altogether he won 37 fights and lost 3 before a heart murmur finished him as an amateur boxer. For a time he was Joe Louis's sparring partner; Futch went on to work for four decades in factories, in a post office, in a restaurant, and as a labourer while training boxers in Detroit and Los Angeles. The first boxer whom he transformed into a world champion was welterweight Jordan in 1958, but Futch did not become a major figure in boxing until he began training Frazier in 1971. Sometimes he had to train under difficult conditions, notably when he was hired in 1981 to train Michael Spinks just two hours before the boxer won an important light heavyweight bout. Often he had to train difficult-to-handle fighters such as Bowe, his last heavyweight champion (1992–93). Futch entered boxing's International Hall of Fame in 1994.

Ganesan, Sivaji (Villupuram Chiniah Pillai Ganesan), Indian actor (b. Oct. 1, 1927, Tamil Nadu, India—d. July 21, 2001, Chennai [Madras], India), was a legendary star in southern India's Tamil film industry, employing his expressive face and eloquent voice in some 300 motion pictures over nearly 50 years. Ganesan began his stage career as a child and achieved almost instant fame with his screen debut in *Parasakthi* (1952). He took his professional name from the 17th-century Maratha warrior king Sivaji, whom he portrayed onstage and later in a 1956 film. Ganesan brought an intense screen presence to scores of historical and dramatic films, notably *Navarathri,* in which he portrayed nine roles. In the 1980s he had a brief unsuccessful political career in Tamil Nadu. In 1995 Ganesan was presented with the French government's highest civilian award, the Chevalier of the Order of Arts and Letters; in 1997 he received the Dada Saheb Phalke from the Indian government for his lifetime contribution to Indian cinema.

Gascoyne, David Emery, British poet (b. Oct. 10, 1916, Harrow, Middlesex, Eng.—d. Nov. 25, 2001, Newport, Isle of Wight, Eng.), introduced French Surrealism to Great Britain. He was acquainted with many of the leading intellectual and artistic figures in England and France and became a noted translator and critic. Unusual among British poets of the time, he was not university educated. He published his first book of poems, *Roman Balcony,* in 1932 at the age of 16 and his only full-length novel, *Opening Day,* the following year. Influenced by writers such as André Breton and Paul Éluard, he published *A Short Survey of Surrealism,* the first such work in English, in 1935. This was followed by *Man's*

Surrealist poet David Gascoyne

Life Is This Meat (1935), a volume of Surrealist verse, as well as by a translation of Breton's *What Is Surrealism?* His years in Paris during the 1930s were recorded in two works published much later: *Paris Journal 1937–1939* (1978) and *Journal 1936–1937* (1980). Although he had at first been interested primarily in the visionary and mystical elements of Surrealism, he later became more interested in its religious aspects. *Poems 1937–42,* which was published in 1943, was his first book of religious verse. *Night Thoughts,* written for the radio, was performed in 1955 and published in 1956. *Collected Poems* appeared in 1965. Addicted to amphetamines and afflicted with depression, he suffered a breakdown in the early 1960s and in 1964 went to live in his father's house on the Isle of Wight, where he remained to the end of his life. He published little poetry after the 1950s, although a number of collections continued to appear.

Gebel-Williams, Gunther, German-born American circus animal trainer (b. Sept. 12, 1934, Schweidnitz, Ger. [now Swidnica, Pol.]—d. July 19, 2001, Venice, Fla.), was one of the most celebrated circus entertainers in history. As animal trainer for the Ringling Brothers and Barnum & Bailey Circus, he was particularly known for his work with big cats; among other feats, he trained lions to ride on the backs of elephants, taught leopards and tigers to jump through flaming hoops, and wrapped panthers around his neck and shoulders. His act also included horses, zebras, camels, and llamas. After beginning his career in a Munich-based circus, Gebel-Williams made his American debut in 1969. The star performer of the Ringling Brothers and Barnum & Bailey Circus for the following 22 years, he appeared in some 12,000 shows. An autobiography, *Untamed,* was published in 1991.

Gierek, Edward, Polish politician (b. Jan. 6, 1913, Porabka, Pol., Austria-Hungary—d. July

29, 2001, Cieszyn, Pol.), as the first secretary of the Polish Communist Party for almost a decade (1970–80), sought to modernize Poland's economy and introduce social reforms, but his attempts ultimately led to financial insolvency and political unrest. After Gierek's father died (1923) in a coal-mining accident, his mother moved the family to France, where Gierek worked as a coal miner and joined the Communist Party (1931). He fought with the Belgian Resistance during World War II. In 1948 he returned to Upper Silesia, Poland's most industrialized region, and within three years he had risen to local party leader. He succeeded Wladyslaw Gomulka as first secretary in December 1970 after price increases had led to major strikes and civil unrest. Gierek eased foreign travel restrictions and allowed greater intellectual freedom. He tried to raise living standards through expanded industrialization and Western-style consumerism, financed by massive foreign investment and loans. Instead, mismanagement, corruption, and a deepening international recession left Poland with crushing national debts. Strikes in 1976 and again in 1980 led to the formation of the powerful new trade union Solidarity. Gierek was replaced as first secretary in September 1980 and was expelled from the party the next year.

Gilbreth, Frank Bunker, Jr., American novelist and journalist (b. March 17, 1911, Plainfield, N.J.—d. Feb. 18, 2001, Charleston, S.C.), drew on his madcap experiences as one of 12 children in a household run by parents who were engineers and efficiency experts to co-write (with his sister Ernestine Gilbreth Carey) the best-selling memoir *Cheaper by the Dozen* (1948; filmed 1950) and its popular sequel, *Belles on Their Toes* (1950; filmed 1952). He was also the longtime writer (1947–93), under the name Ashley Cooper, of the "Doing the Charleston" column for the *News and Courier* (now the *Post and Courier*) newspaper in Charleston.

Gombrich, Sir Ernst Hans Josef, Austrian-born art historian (b. March 30, 1909, Vienna, Austria-Hungary—d. Nov. 3, 2001, London, Eng.), as one of the field's greatest popularizers, introduced millions of people to art through his best-known book, *The Story of Art* (1950; 16th rev. ed. 1995), a clearly written, accessible work that was originally intended for young people but eventually sold millions of copies in more than 20 languages. Gombrich eschewed aesthetics and art criticism, which he considered too deeply rooted in personal emotions, preferring to focus on iconography and innovations in technique, taste, and form as demonstrated in specific works by individual artists. He had little use for modernism, which he derided as overly commercial and too often bent on novelty for its own sake. Gombrich studied art history under Julius von Schlosser at Vienna University and in 1936 moved to London, where he joined the staff at the Warburg Institute. During World War II he translated German-language radio broadcasts for the BBC, which greatly improved his English. Gombrich's first book, *Weltgeschichte für Kinder* (1936), led to the idea of an art book for children, and the eventual result was *The Story of Art*. His later books

included *Art and Illusion* (1960), *Meditations on a Hobby Horse, and Other Essays on the Theory of Art* (1963), *The Sense of Order* (1979), and *The Image and the Eye* (1981). Gombrich served as director of the Warburg Institute from 1959 until his retirement in 1976; he also held appointments at the Universities of Oxford, London, and Cambridge, as well as at Harvard and Cornell universities in the U.S. He was elected a fellow of the British Academy in 1960, made CBE in 1966, knighted in 1972, and appointed a member of the Order of Merit in 1988.

Graham, Katharine Meyer, American newspaper executive (b. June 16, 1917, New York, N.Y.—d. July 17, 2001, Boise, Idaho), took over the leadership position at the *Washington Post* following the death of her pub-

lisher husband and guided it to a position of new success, influence, and respect. Among her most important actions were the decisions to publish the Pentagon Papers—secret government documents concerning decisions about the conduct of the Vietnam War—and to allow two of the paper's reporters, Bob Woodward and Carl Bernstein, to investigate what became known as the Watergate scandal and led to the resignation of Pres. Richard M. Nixon. She was the first woman to serve as the head of a *Fortune* 500 company and was considered the most powerful woman in the U.S. Graham attended Vassar College, Poughkeepsie, N.Y., from 1934 to 1936 and then transferred to the University of Chicago, from which she graduated in 1938. After working as a reporter for the *San Francisco News*, she went (1939) to the *Washington Post*, where her father was editor and publisher. In 1940 she married Philip L. Graham and moved with him to Florida. In 1946 they returned to Washington when, at his father-in-law's behest, he became associate publisher and then publisher of the *Post*. Her husband became increasingly troubled by mental illness, however, and in 1963 committed suicide; Graham became sole owner of the paper and took over its presidency. Though she initially was uneasy about running the company, which by then included *Newsweek* magazine, other publications, and a number of television stations, she persevered and, with the addition of Benjamin Bradlee, whom she hired as executive editor in 1965, the paper thrived. Graham became publisher in 1969. In 1971 the *Post* gained new prominence when it published the Pentagon Papers after the *New York Times*, which had begun publishing them, was stopped by a federal restraining order. When the Supreme Court sided with the newspapers, freedom of the press prevailed. The next year, following a break-in at Democratic National Committee headquarters in the Watergate complex in Washington, D.C., the *Post* relentlessly investigated the action and its connection to the Nixon reelection campaign. The paper was awarded the 1973 Pulitzer Prize for public serv-

ice. Graham became CEO and chairman of the board in 1973 and served in those capacities until 1991 and 1993, respectively. In 1979 she turned over the post of publisher to her son, Donald E. Graham, and he also succeeded her when she left her other positions. Graham won her own Pulitzer in 1998—for her autobiography, *Personal History* (1997).

Granz, Norman, American concert and record producer (b. Aug. 6, 1918, Los Angeles, Calif.—d. Nov. 22, 2001, Geneva, Switz.), presented top musicians in Jazz at the Philharmonic (JATP) concerts around the world and documented them on records for over four decades. At JATP shows, soloists won wild applause for frantic honking-horn "battles," but they also created music of lasting merit. Virtually every major black swing-era musician played and recorded for him—among them the Duke Ellington and Count Basie bands, pianist Art Tatum, saxophonists Lester Young, Coleman Hawkins, and Benny Carter, and singers Billie Holiday and Louis Armstrong—as did modernists such as Dizzy Gillespie (trumpet), Charlie Parker, Stan Getz, John Coltrane (saxophones), and Bud Powell (piano). Pianist Oscar Peterson was his favourite JATP accompanist and by far his most prolific recording artist; Granz also produced Ella Fitzgerald's concerts and her popular series of *Songbook* albums. Though Granz lost revenue when he refused to present concerts before racially segregated audiences, his enterprises were valued at $5 million by the mid-1950s. After service in the U.S. Army Air Force, Granz became an MGM film editor and produced the Academy Award-nominated short film *Jammin' the Blues* (1944). That year he produced the concert that began his globe-trotting career of staged jam sessions. He founded Clef Records in 1946 and Norgran Records in 1953 and combined them into Verve Records in 1956; in 1973 he formed Pablo Records, but he sold it in 1987.

Graves, Morris Cole, American artist (b. Aug. 28, 1910, Fox Valley, Ore.—d. May 5, 2001, Loleta, Calif.), was a self-taught painter whose works expressed a deeply felt connection with nature. After dropping out of high school, Graves became a seaman and, between 1928 and 1930, made three trips to China and Japan, where he developed an interest in East Asian art and religion, especially Zen Buddhism. He worked for the Federal Art Project in the early 1930s, and in 1936 at the Seattle (Wash.) Art Museum, he held his first one-man show. Living as a recluse on an island in Puget Sound, Graves completed some of his best-known paintings, including *Blind Bird* (1940) and *Little Known Bird of the Inner Eye* (1941). In his early works he frequently painted birds, insects, and other woodland animals. A number of his paintings were included in "Americans 1942: 18 Artists from 9 States," a show at the Museum of Modern Art in New York City that attracted widespread attention. A pacifist, Graves was confined to a military jail for 11 months during World War II and settled in Dublin after his release. In 1954–56 he painted the birds and animals of Ireland. Graves eventually returned to the U.S., where he turned his attention to creating floral paintings rather than depictions of animals.

Greenberg, Joseph Harold, American anthropologist and linguist (b. May 28, 1915, New York, N.Y.—d. May 7, 2001, Stanford, Calif.), proposed influential theories regarding relationships between the world's languages. After receiving a Ph.D. in anthropology from Northwestern University, Evanston, Ill., in 1940 and serving in the Army Signal Intelligence Service during World War II, Greenberg embarked on an academic career. He was a professor of anthropology and linguistics at Columbia University, New York City, from 1948 to 1962 and at Stanford University from 1962 until 1985. He was primarily interested in language universals. In *The Languages of Africa* (1955; rev. 1963), Greenberg grouped African languages into four families: Niger-Kordofanian, Afroasiatic, Nilo-Saharan, and Khoisan. He later argued that most of the world's languages could be categorized into 12 "superfamilies." Among his other notable works were *Language in the Americas* (1987) and *Indo-European and Its Closest Relatives: The Eurasiatic Language Family* (2000). He also edited *Universals of Language* (1963) and *Universals of Human Language*, 4 vol. (1978).

Greer, Jane (Bettejane Greer), American actress (b. Sept. 9, 1924, Washington, D.C.—d. Aug. 24, 2001, Los Angeles, Calif.), made only a few notable motion pictures but secured her image as a femme fatale with her portrayal of Kathie Moffat, the quintessential film noir temptress, in the classic *Out of the Past* (1947); when the movie was remade in 1984—as *Against All Odds*—she appeared as that character's mother.

Hailsham of St. Marylebone, Quintin McGarel Hogg, Baron, British politician (b. Oct. 9, 1907, London, Eng.—d. Oct. 12, 2001, London), between 1938 and 1987 served six Conservative governments in a variety of posts, most notably 12 years (1970–74, 1979–87) as lord high chancellor (head of the British judiciary), a position his father, Viscount Hailsham, had held in the 1920s. Hogg was educated at Eton and Christ Church, Oxford, called to the bar in 1932, and took silk in 1953. He was elected to the House of Commons in 1938 but was forced to move to the House of Lords on his father's death (1950). A passionate and often eccentric politician, he was finally allowed in 1963 to relinquish the title 2nd Viscount Hailsham, which he had never wanted. He lost in his bid for Conservative Party leader that year but was reelected to the Commons. In 1970 he was granted his own peerage and returned to the Lords. When he retired in 1987, he was the longest-serving lord chancellor of the 20th century.

Hamburger, Viktor, German-born American embryologist (b. July 9, 1900, Landeshut, Ger. [now Kamienna Gora, Pol.]—d. June 12, 2001, St. Louis, Mo.), was a pioneer in the field of neuroembryology; he was noted for having defined and classified the different stages of embryonic development and for having helped identify a chemical substance called nerve growth factor, which stimulates the growth of nerve cells and promotes the development of the nervous system. While earning his Ph.D. from the University of Freiburg, Ger., he performed research under experimental embryologist Hans Spemann. Hamburger received a fellowship to study at the University of Chicago in 1932. Because of his Jewish ancestry, he was not allowed to return to Germany after the Nazis took power in 1933. In 1935 Hamburger joined the faculty of Washington University, St. Louis. Within six years he had advanced to full professor. He served as chairman of the university's biology department from 1941 to 1966 and assumed emeritus status in 1969. Among numerous honours for his contributions to the field of neuroembryology, Hamburger was elected to the U.S. National Academy of Sciences in 1953 and to the American Academy of Arts and Sciences in 1959. He was awarded a National Medal of Science in 1989.

Hank González, Carlos, Mexican politician (b. Aug. 28, 1927, Santiago Tianguistenco, Mex.—d. Aug. 11, 2001, Santiago Tianguistenco), was a highly influential member of Mexico's long-ruling Institutional Revolutionary Party and held public office almost continuously from 1955 to 1994. During his career he served as the mayor of Mexico City, the governor of Mexico state, and agriculture secretary, among other posts. He was also a successful businessman, with a fortune estimated at $1.3 billion in 1993.

Hanna, William Denby, American animator (b. July 14, 1910, Melrose, N.M.—d. March 22, 2001, Los Angeles, Calif.), in his more than 50-year collaboration with Joseph Barbera, created such popular cartoon characters as Tom and

Animator William Hanna (right) with Joseph Barbera and friends

Jerry, Yogi and Boo Boo Bear, Huckleberry Hound, and the Flintstones; Fred Flintstone's frequent exclamation "yabba dabba doo" became part of the contemporary vocabulary. The Hanna-Barbera team produced 113 Tom and Jerry cartoons and over 3,000 half-hour shows for 150 television cartoon series, and they won seven Academy Awards and eight Emmy Awards, including the Governors Award of the Academy of Television Arts and Sciences (1988). Hanna dropped out of college and was working as a construction engineer, but when he lost his job during the Depression, he took a job at Pacific Art and Title, which produced cartoons. In 1930 he moved to another cartoon-production company, Harman-Ising Studios, the home of the Looney Tunes and Merrie Melodies series. Metro-Goldwyn-Mayer hired the company to produce some cartoons, for which Hanna, besides inking and painting, created songs and lyrics. When MGM added its own cartoon section in 1937, Hanna became a director there. He soon discovered that the gag-writing and sketching talents of another new employee, Barbera, were a perfect complement to his sense of timing and knack for story construction. They teamed up, and when their first cartoon, "Puss Gets the Boot" (1940), was nominated for an Academy Award, MGM allowed them to develop its cat-and-mouse theme. Fifteen years' worth of Tom and Jerry cartoons were the result, including the innovative teaming of cartoon and live action when Jerry danced with Gene Kelly in *Anchors Aweigh* (1944) and both characters swam with Esther Williams in *Dangerous When Wet* (1953). MGM, however, closed its animation department in 1957, whereupon the two men formed their own company, Hanna-Barbera Productions, and began creating cartoons for television. Because of TV's budget limitations, Hanna and Barbera developed a "limited animation" technique that allowed them to produce cartoons much more cheaply by stressing character and witty dialogue instead of the action that had highlighted the Tom and Jerry cartoons. Their first TV show, *The Ruff and Ready Show* (1957), was followed by *Huckleberry Hound* (1958), the first animated series to be awarded an Emmy. In 1960 *The Flintstones*, a Stone Age parody of the hit television series *The Honeymooners*, made its appearance. Equally appealing to children and adults, it was the first half-hour animated situation comedy and came to be considered Hanna-Barbera's greatest hit. A Space Age version, *The Jetsons*, debuted in 1962, and series featuring numerous other characters, including Magilla Gorilla and Scooby Doo, followed. In 1996 Warner Brothers bought Hanna-Barbera, but Hanna continued working.

Haq, Abdul (Humayoun Arsala), Afghan resistance leader (b. 1957/58, Nangarhar province, Afg.—d. Oct. 26, 2001, Kabul, Afg.), was an audacious guerrilla commander in Afghanistan's war against the Soviet Union and later became an internationally known English-language spokesman for the anti-Taliban resistance. In 1977 he joined the fight against the Soviets, eventually taking the nom de guerre Abdul Haq. He was a strong supporter of Afghanistan's exiled king, Mohammad Zahir Shah, and served in Prime Minister Gulbuddin Hekmatyar's interim government in the mid-1990s. When war again broke out among the Afghan warlords, Haq left the country and became a successful businessman in Pakistan and the United Arab Emirates. In September 2001, after the assassination of Northern Alliance leader Ahmad Shah Masood (*q.v.*), a political and military rival, and the terrorist attacks in the U.S., Haq tried to dissuade the Western allies from bombing Afghanistan. He reportedly was attempting to negotiate with anti-Taliban supporters when he was captured by Taliban forces and, within hours, executed as a spy.

Harris, Marvin, American anthropologist and theoretician (b. Aug. 18, 1927, New York, N.Y.—d. Oct. 25, 2001, Gainesville, Fla.), was a prominent anthropologist known for his research on cultural materialism, which led him to pose a number of controversial theories, including that warfare was a means of reducing population numbers when protein became scarce and that cannibalism among the Aztecs arose from a need for protein sufficiency. From 1952 to 1980 Harris taught at Columbia University, New York City, where he earned a Ph.D. in 1953. From 1980 to 2000 he was a research professor at the University of Florida. Harris conducted extensive fieldwork in Brazil and Mozambique. Drawing parallels between functionalism in the social sciences with adaptation in biology, he came to see the social life of humans as shaped by practical problems of existence. He expressed his views in such works as *The Rise of Anthropological Theory* (1968), *Cannibals and Kings: The Origins of Cultures* (1977), *Cultural Materialism: The Struggle for a Science of Culture* (1979), and *Cultural Anthropology* (1983).

Harrison, George, British musician, singer, and songwriter (b. Feb. 25, 1943, Liverpool, Eng.—d. Nov. 29, 2001, Los Angeles, Calif.), was the lead guitarist of the Beatles, who infused rock and roll with new depth and sophistication and became one of the most important and influential bands in the history of rock music; he later also achieved singular success as a songwriter and performer. Harrison was the youngest of the "Fab Four" and was known as the "quiet Beatle," and though he had wanted to be successful, he never became comfortable with fame. He met fellow Beatle Paul McCartney when the two were grammar-school students at the Liverpool Institute. McCartney and John Lennon had formed a rock band, the Quarrymen—which changed its name to Johnny and the Moondogs and then the Silver Beatles before it became the Beatles—and eventually invited Harrison and later Ringo Starr to join. Although Lennon and McCartney wrote most of the songs the Beatles performed, Harrison contributed some of their finest ones, including "While My Guitar Gently Weeps," "Here Comes the Sun," and "Something"—the latter eventually recorded by some 150 other artists, second only to "Yesterday" among Beatles tunes covered. In 1965 Harrison, having become intrigued with the sound of the sitar, studied with Ravi Shankar so that sitar music could be used in Beatles songs. After it was

AP/Wide World Photos

Rock and roll icon George Harrison

heard in "Norwegian Wood" (1965), musicians in other groups also began featuring it. Harrison was also becoming increasingly interested in Eastern religions and culture, and in 1968 he and the Beatles, as well as a number of other celebrities, explored transcendental meditation with the Maharishi Mahesh Yogi in India. This trip helped bring Eastern religion to the attention of the West and influenced dozens of subsequent Beatles songs, but Harrison was the only Beatle to actually make these religious principles part of his life. Following the breakup of the Beatles in 1970, Harrison released the first of his many post-Beatles recordings, the highly successful triple album *All Things Must Pass* (1970); in 1971 he staged two concerts to raise money to fight starvation in Bangladesh—the prototype for later star-studded fund-raising events; and in 1979 he ventured into a new field, film production, as a founder of Handmade Films. Among the company's efforts were the Monty Python film *Life of Brian* (1979), *Time Bandits* (1981), and *Mona Lisa* (1986). In 1987 Harrison scored one of his biggest solo successes with the album *Cloud Nine*. Some of his most memorable songs as a solo artist included "My Sweet Lord," "Give Me Love (Give Me Peace on Earth)," and "I Got My Mind Set on You." Although Harrison spent much of his time in near seclusion with his family following the murder of Lennon in 1980, in the late 1980s he recorded and performed with the Traveling Wilburys, which also included Bob Dylan, Roy Orbison, Tom Petty, and Jeff Lynne, and in the mid-1990s he took part in the Beatles anthology project. The last years of Harrison's life were difficult. In 1997 he was treated for throat cancer, and in late 1999 he was attacked in his home by a deranged intruder and suffered multiple stab wounds. The cancer recurred in mid-2001, and treatments were unsuccessful.

Hartford, John, American musician and singer-songwriter (b. Dec. 30, 1937, New York, N.Y.—d. June 4, 2001, Madison, Tenn.), was a virtuoso banjoist, fiddler, and guitarist whose best-known song, "Gentle on My Mind" (1967), earned two Grammy Awards; the song was later recorded by Glen Campbell, Elvis Presley, Dean Martin, and others. A passionate performer, Hartford became a popular attraction on the bluegrass circuit after his debut album, *John Hartford Looks at Life,* appeared in 1966. He went on to record some 40 albums, including *The Love Album* (1968), *Aereo-Plain* (1971), and *Morning Bugle* (1972). He recorded his final album, *Good Old Boys,* in 1999, and two of his songs, "Man of Constant Sorrow" and "Indian War Whoop," were included on the sound track for the 2000 film *O Brother, Where Art Thou?*

Hartwell of Peterborough Court in the City of London, William Michael Berry, Baron, British newspaper magnate (b. May 18, 1911, Merthyr Tydfil, Wales—d. April 2, 2001, London, Eng.), was chairman and editor in chief of the *Daily Telegraph* for more than 30 years, from when he inherited the newspaper from his father, Viscount Camrose, in 1954 until his retirement in 1987. He built the *Daily Telegraph* into one of Britain's most admired quality newspapers and launched the equally successful *Sunday Telegraph* in 1960. Lord Hartwell was slow to modernize, however, and lost financial control to Canadian entrepreneur Conrad Black in 1985. He was granted a life peerage in 1968 and inherited the viscountcy, which he disclaimed for life, on the death of his older brother in 1995.

Hawthorne, Sir Nigel Barnard, British actor (b. April 5, 1929, Coventry, Eng.—d. Dec. 26, 2001, Baldock, Hertfordshire, Eng.), displayed his versatility in roles both comic and classic during a half-century-long career that saw him gain his first real fame only after some 30 years in the profession, when he was in his 50s and costarred as the quintessential civil servant Sir Humphrey Appleby in the satiric BBC series *Yes, Minister* (1980–83, 1985–86) and its sequel, *Yes, Prime Minister* (1986–87), a role that won him four British Academy of Film and Television Arts Awards. His reputation grew even more with his Oscar-nominated role as the title character in *The Madness of King George* (1994). Hawthorne made his professional stage debut in 1950 in *The Shop at Sly Corner*. The following year he moved to England and, although he appeared on the London stage in *You Can't Take It with You* in 1951, he had little other success and moved back to South Africa. There Hawthorne performed a number of leading roles, and in 1961 he toured in *Beyond the Fringe*. Upon returning to London in 1962, he made his West End debut in *Talking to You*, and besides touring as Field Marshal Haig in *Oh! What a Lovely War*, played Major Flack in *Privates on Parade* (1977). That role led to his being cast in *Yes, Minister*. Hawthorne went on to stage triumphs in *Shadowlands* in London (1989) and on Broadway (1990), where he won a Tony Award, and then *The Madness of George III* (1991) in London, for which he won an Olivier Award. The lead role in the film adaptation of the latter followed. Hawthorne was created CBE in 1987 and was knighted in 1999. Also in 1999 came his final stage role, the title character in the Royal Shakespeare Company's *King Lear*. Although Hawthorne had been undergoing treatment for cancer for some 18 months, he died of a heart attack in the home he shared with his longtime partner, screenwriter Trevor Bentham.

Heckart, (Anna) Eileen, American actress (b. March 29, 1919, Columbus, Ohio—d. Dec. 31, 2001, Norwalk, Conn.), took advantage of her lanky stature, smoky voice, and winning smile to enjoy a long career on the stage, in film, and on television, often playing eccentric characters. Besides her Oscar-winning role as an overbearing mother in *Butterflies Are Free* (1972)—a role she also had filled on Broadway (1969)—and her Emmy Award-winning roles in *Save Me a Place at Forest Lawn* (1966) and an episode of *Love & War* (1994), she was especially remembered for performances on Broadway in *Picnic* (1953), *Barefoot in the Park* (1965), and *The Waverly Gallery* (2000) and on television as Mary Richards's Aunt Flo on *The Mary Tyler Moore Show* (1975 and 1976). Heckart was presented with a special Tony Award for Excellence in Theatre in 2000, which honoured her body of theatre work.

Hélou, Charles Alexandre, Lebanese politician (b. Dec. 25, 1912, Beirut, Lebanon—d. Jan. 7, 2001, Beirut), served as president of Lebanon from 1964 to 1970. After receiving a law degree, Hélou edited two French-language newspapers, *L'Eclair du Nord* in 1932 and *Le Jour* in 1935–46. He was ambassador to the Vatican in 1947 and later held several cabinet posts, including minister of justice and health (1954–55) and minister of education (1964). Hélou earned the sup-

port of Pres. Fuad Chehab and became his successor when Chehab retired in 1964. Not long after his inauguration as president, Hélou agreed at an Arab summit meeting to Arab sponsorship of the Palestine Liberation Organization (PLO), but he refused to allow the stationing of PLO bases in Lebanon, an issue that grew increasingly explosive during the course of his term. In 1968–69 a pattern emerged in which Hélou—a Christian—and the army command opposed the stationing of Palestinian guerrillas in Lebanon, while the Muslim prime minister, Rashid Karami, favoured it. Under great pressure from Arab nations and from Lebanese Muslims, Hélou in 1969 moved to avert a crisis by accepting Karami's proposed policy of coordination between the PLO and the Lebanese army, whereby the PLO secured the right to establish armed units in Lebanese refugee camps. After leaving office in 1970, Hélou had little involvement in public affairs, though he served briefly as minister of state in 1979.

Henderson, Joseph A. ("Joe"), American jazz tenor saxophonist (b. April 24, 1937, Lima, Ohio—d. June 30, 2001, San Francisco, Calif.), was among the handful of important saxophonists from the heyday of hard bop who remained active at the end of the 20th century. Henderson first won acclaim for solos on 1960s hard-bop hits (Lee Morgan's "The Sidewinder" and Horace Silver's "Song for My Father") and he played in avant-garde and jazz-rock settings before achieving his greatest success in the 1990s by playing the standard repertoire. The phrasing of modern tenor sax giants Sonny Rollins and John Coltrane influenced his less-vivid style; Henderson was notable for high harmonic sophistication, complex lines, abstract forms, and, especially in later years, lyricism. He attended Kentucky State College (now University) briefly, then while studying at Wayne State University, he soon became active in Detroit's lively modern jazz scene. Following two years in the army, he settled in New York City in 1962 and worked in Kenny Dorham's and Horace Silver's combos. Henderson also recorded often for Blue Note, adapting to Andrew Hill's experiments in harmony and form as readily as he adapted to Morgan's and Silver's blues-oriented pieces. Later he played for a time in the popular rock-jazz band Blood, Sweat and Tears and with the Herbie Hancock sextet and pianist Chick Corea. From 1963 he also recorded his own albums, which eventually totaled 34, and he included his own tunes such as "Recordame" and "Isotope." Henderson's greatest success began in 1985 with his live trio album, *The State of the Tenor;* it was followed by compact disc tributes to Billy Strayhorn, Miles Davis, and Antônio Carlos Jobim; a big-band collection; and the album *Porgy and Bess*, with an all-star band and singers Chaka Khan and Sting. With these he became a best-selling recording artist; Henderson went on to win four Grammy Awards.

Herblock (Herbert Lawrence Block), American political cartoonist (b. Oct. 13, 1909, Chicago, Ill.—d. Oct. 7, 2001, Washington, D.C.), had a 72-year-long career, through the terms of

13 presidents, during which his drawings, syndicated in hundreds of newspapers throughout the U.S. and in several other countries, simply and clearly spotlighted his support of civil liberties and civil rights and his view of the political issues of the day. He was awarded three Pulitzer Prizes (1942, 1954, and 1979—the last for his entire body of cartoon work) and shared a fourth (1973) with the *Washington Post*. Herblock's talent was apparent early, and at age 11 he began classes at the Art Institute of Chicago, which the following year awarded him a scholarship. He attended Lake Forest (Ill.) College for two years but dropped out (1929) to work for the *Chicago Daily News*. Before long, his cartoons were being syndicated. Herblock was employed by the Newspaper Enterprise Association in Cleveland, Ohio, from 1933 to 1943, during which his work focused attention on the dangers of the rise of fascism in Europe. Following World War II army service (1943–46), Herblock joined the *Washington Post* and began producing six cartoons a week; only late in life did he cut back to five a week. An early target was Sen. Joseph McCarthy and his communist witch-hunts, and it was Herblock who coined the term *McCarthyism*. Another favourite target was Richard M. Nixon, whom Herblock's cartoons always showed sporting a five o'clock shadow until he became president, at which time Herblock desisted out of respect for the office. Besides his cartoon work, Herblock wrote 12 books, including *Herblock: A Cartoonist's Life* (1993). He was awarded the Presidential Medal of Freedom in 1994, and his final cartoon appeared on Aug. 26, 2001.

Hewlett, William Redington, American engineer and businessman (b. May 20, 1913, Ann Arbor, Mich.—d. Jan. 12, 2001, Palo Alto, Calif.), was the cofounder of the Hewlett-Packard Co. (HP), the electronics and computer giant credited with pioneering California's Silicon Valley and thus the computer age. He and his partner, David Packard, promoted an innovative management style that stressed creativity, flexibility, openness, and teamwork, and they both became noted philanthropists. Hewlett's interest in science and electronics began when he was a child,

Computer pioneer William Hewlett (standing) with David Packard

and in 1930 he began studying engineering at Stanford University. It was there that he met Packard, and the two became lifelong friends. After graduation (1934) Hewlett earned (1936) a master's degree at the Massachusetts Institute of Technology and then returned to Stanford for further study. On Jan. 1, 1939, at the suggestion of engineering professor Frederick Terman and with start-up funds of $538, Hewlett and Packard set up a small electronics business in a rented garage in Palo Alto. That garage was later (1989) designated a California historical landmark. One of HP's products, an audio oscillator, brought the company its first success when Walt Disney Productions purchased eight of the devices to test sound equipment for the animated film *Fantasia* (1940). Following service in the U.S. Army Signal Corps during World War II, Hewlett returned to HP (1947) and was made a vice president, and in 1964 he became president, a position he retained until 1977. The company expanded rapidly and in 1968 produced the first desktop scientific calculator. The pocket scientific calculator followed in 1972, rendering slide rules largely obsolete. HP became even better known in 1984 with its laserjet printer. The company eventually became the second largest computer maker and Hewlett became one of the 50 wealthiest Americans. Hewlett served as HP's CEO (1969–78), chairman of the executive committee (1977–83), vice chairman of the board (1983– 87), and director emeritus (from 1987). In 1966 he and his first wife, Flora, established the William and Flora Hewlett Foundation. In 1985 Hewlett was honoured with the National Medal of Science, the highest scientific award in the U.S.

Heym, Stefan (Helmut Flieg), German writer and political activist (b. April 10, 1913, Chemnitz, Ger.—d. Dec. 16, 2001, Jerusalem, Israel), as the author of over a dozen novels, including *The Crusaders (*1948), provoked controversy with his dissident writings. Although he was an avowed Marxist-Leninist, he was a steady critic of East Germany's government throughout that regime's existence, and when German reunification came, he held out hope for socialism to prevail. To that end, he ran for election to the Bundestag (second house of parliament) in 1994, served for a year, and thereafter continued in his activist dissent.

Hibbler, Albert ("Al"), American singer (b. Aug. 16, 1915, Tyro, Miss.—d. April 24, 2001, Chicago, Ill.), rose to fame with the Duke Ellington band (1943–51), singing some of composer Ellington's most enduring songs—"I'm Just a Lucky So and So," "Don't Get Around Much Anymore," and "Do Nothin' Till You Hear from Me"—in a low baritone voice and with eccentric vocal effects. On his own the blind performer recorded his biggest hit, the ballad "Unchained Melody" (1955), followed by "After the Lights Go Down Low." During the civil rights movement, Hibbler was arrested twice during protest marches; he continued to perform regularly into the 1970s.

Higgins, Billy, American drummer (b. Oct. 11, 1936, Los Angeles, Calif.—d. May 3, 2001, Inglewood, Calif.), helped create the free jazz

© Jimmy Katz

Effervescent drummer Billy Higgins

idiom while a member of Ornette Coleman's classic 1950s groups and later became the busiest drummer in jazz; he played on dozens of Blue Note albums and accompanied top jazz artists from Thelonious Monk, Cecil Taylor, and John Coltrane in the early 1960s to latter-day young lions Joshua Redman and Roy Hargrove. Higgins's drumming was characterized by his enthusiastic swing, very precise beat, and crisp-sounding, stimulating, often complex interplay with soloists. In his teens Higgins began playing drums with trumpeter Don Cherry and other Los Angeles bop musicians; by 1957 Coleman was teaching Higgins and Cherry to play his new kind of jazz, with improvisations based on melodies rather than on traditional harmonic patterns. The Coleman quartet created a sensation when it debuted in New York City in November 1959, but Higgins left the group in 1960. He played with Sonny Rollins's quartet, then became a top hard bop drummer and recorded prolifically with masters such as Lee Morgan, Hank Mobley, Dexter Gordon, Jackie McLean, Herbie Hancock, and Cedar Walton. Higgins seldom led groups but was constantly in demand, even after he moved back to Los Angeles in 1978. Besides participating in international tours with the Timeless All Stars and reunions with Coleman and Cherry, he played and acted in Bertrand Tavernier's 1986 jazz film *Round Midnight.* He then cofounded the World Stage, a Los Angeles storefront arts centre where he enticed noted jazz musicians to perform and teach; he also taught at the University of California, Los Angeles. Though liver disease curtailed his career in the 1990s, he resumed performing after a liver transplant in 1995. Two years later Higgins received a Jazz Master Award from the National Endowment for the Humanities. In 2000 liver failure again halted his playing.

Hlavsa, Milan (Mejla Hlavsa), Czech musician (b. March 6, 1951, Prague, Czech. [now Czech Rep.]—d. Jan. 5, 2001, Prague), founded (1968) and served as songwriter and bass guitarist for the underground rock and roll band Plastic People of the Universe, which became a symbol of political unrest in communist Czechoslovakia. Plastic People, which sang in English until the early 1970s, was banned by the Czech government in 1970. The band continued to perform, however, and to make recordings, which were surreptitiously distributed and smuggled out of the country to the West. The arrest of Hlavsa and other rock musicians in 1976 helped to galvanize the formation of the Czech human rights movement Charter 77.

Hohenemser, Kurt, German-born American aerospace engineer (b. Jan. 3, 1906, Berlin, Ger.—d. April 7, 2001, St. Louis, Mo.), was a pioneer in the field of helicopter design. During World War II, Hohenemser worked in Germany for inventor Anton Flettner, helping Flettner build the F1 282 Kolibri, one of the first helicopters used in combat. Hohenemser relocated to the U.S. in 1947. Working as an engineer for the McDonnell Aircraft Corp., he designed, among other helicopters, the XV-1, a precursor of the Osprey military aircraft. From 1966 until his retirement in 1975, he was a professor of aerospace engineering at Washington University, St. Louis.

Hooker, John Lee, American blues artist (b. Aug. 22, 1917, Clarksdale, Miss.—d. June 21, 2001, Los Altos, Calif.), sang and played guitar with a passionately intense feeling that made him one of the most emotionally compelling of all bluesmen. His voice was a big strong baritone; he shouted fast blues over simple, repeated, driving boogie guitar, and he sang bleak slow blues, often muffling the lyrics, over stark guitar chords; he wore dark glasses when singing because, he said, the blues often moved him to tears. Hooker was one of 11 children in a Mississippi sharecropping family; he learned to play guitar from his stepfather and became interested in gospel music and blues in boyhood. In 1943 he moved to Detroit, where he made his first recordings, including "Boogie Chillen," "Crawling King Snake," and "Weeping Willow" (1948–49), hit singles notable for the

© Neal Preston/Corbis

Emotive bluesman John Lee Hooker

raw power of his singing, accompanied only by his riveting guitar. Though his unrhyming lines, pentatonic melodies, and one-chord modal harmonic structures sounded primitive, his swinging energy and his electric guitar, which was just becoming popular among blues audiences, marked him as an urban blues performer with a unique sound. In later hits such as "Dimples" (1956) and "Boom Boom" (1962), he was accompanied by bands. One of the most prolific blues recording artists, he recorded for many labels, often using pseudonyms such as John Lee Booker, John Lee Cooker, Texas Slim, and Birmingham Sam and his Magic Guitar. As the black blues audience dwindled, Hooker gradually became popular with white listeners, first playing unamplified guitar and singing traditional blues in folk music venues and recordings; he eventually sang with rock stars Bonnie Raitt, Van Morrison, and Canned Heat. Hooker toured widely for most of his career and appeared in the films *The Blues Brothers* (1980) and *The Color Purple* (1985). He was inducted into the Rock and Roll Hall of Fame in 1991.

Horwich, Frances Rappaport, American educator and television host (b. July 16, 1908, Ottawa, Ohio—d. July 25, 2001, Scottsdale, Ariz.), was host of the popular children's educational television show *Ding Dong School* from 1952 to 1967. Horwich earned a Ph.D. in education from Northwestern University, Evanston, Ill., in 1942. Before her career in television, she worked as a primary-school teacher, kindergarten director, and college professor. *Ding Dong School* was an immediate hit and helped pave the way for later educational shows aimed at children, including *Sesame Street* and *Mister Rogers' Neighborhood*. Horwich received a George Foster Peabody Award in 1953. After leaving television she worked as an educational consultant.

Hoyle, Sir Fred, British astrophysicist (b. June 24, 1915, Bingley, Yorkshire, Eng.—d. Aug. 20, 2001, Bournemouth, Dorset, Eng.), was the foremost promoter of the "steady-state theory," which holds that the universe is always expanding and that new matter is being continuously created to maintain a constant mean density in space. To his great consternation, however, Hoyle was forever associated with the term *big bang*, which he coined in the early 1950s as a term of derision to denigrate the opposing cosmological theory that the universe began in a sudden explosive expansion of matter and energy from a highly compressed primordial state. Hoyle never accepted the growing evidence in favour of the big-bang model, but in *A Different Approach to Cosmology* (2000), he submitted a modified "quasi-steady state" model in which an infinite universe expands and contracts over time. Hoyle studied mathematics at Emmanuel College, Cambridge, and, after working on military radar development during World War II, returned to Cambridge, where he was a mathematics lecturer (1945–58), Plumian Professor of Astronomy (1958–72), and founding director (1967–73) of the Institute of Theoretical Astronomy. In 1948 Hoyle formulated the steady-state model in collaboration with mathematician Hermann Bondi and as-

tronomer Thomas Gold. During the 1950s he turned to research on the chemical composition of stars. In 1957 Hoyle, William Fowler, and Geoffrey and Margaret Burbridge jointly published the breakthrough paper "Synthesis of the Elements in Stars," in which they explained how all but the lightest chemical elements were created through nuclear reactions within the interiors of stars or during stellar explosions known as supernovas. In 1983 Fowler won the Nobel Prize for Physics for this work, while a disappointed Hoyle eventually was awarded the Royal Swedish Academy of Science's Crafoord Prize (1997). Hoyle was equally well known for his other theories, including his belief that life on Earth evolved from biological material formed in outer space and that some diseases are caused by viruses that originated in space. A prolific science writer and successful popularizer of difficult scientific concepts, Hoyle also wrote several science-fiction novels, notably *The Black Cloud* (1957), *A for Andromeda* (1962), and *October the First Is Too Late* (1966). Hoyle was elected a fellow of the Royal Society in 1957 and served (1971–73) as president of the Royal Astronomical Society. He was knighted in 1972.

Hubley, Faith Elliott, American film animator (b. Sept. 16, 1924, New York, N.Y.—d. Dec. 7, 2001, New Haven, Conn.), made films that combined music, magic, and myth in their celebration of life and humanity. Of the many animated works on which she collaborated with her husband, John Hubley, three won Academy Awards—in 1959, 1962, and 1966.

Hughes, Glenn, American singer (b. July 18, 1950, New York, N.Y.—d. March 4, 2001, New York), performed as a leather-clad biker in the flamboyant disco band the Village People. Hughes had been working as a toll collector before successfully auditioning for the openly gay band in 1977. The Village People went on to record a string of international hits, including "Macho Man" (1978), "Y.M.C.A." (1978), and "In the Navy" (1979). Hughes sang with the group until 1996. At his own request, he was buried in his leather biker's outfit.

Hume, Paul Chandler, American music critic (b. Dec. 13, 1915, Chicago, Ill.—d. Nov. 26, 2001, Baltimore, Md.), wrote highly esteemed reviews for the *Washington Post* for 35 years (from 1947), taught music history at Georgetown University, Washington, D.C. (1950–77), and served as a visiting professor at Yale University (1975–83). In 1950, in a review that brought him to the attention of the general public, he infuriated Pres. Harry Truman when he expressed a less-than-complimentary opinion of a voice recital given by the president's daughter, Margaret Truman.

Hunter, Maxwell White, American aeronautical engineer (b. March 11, 1922, Hollidaysburg, Pa.—d. Nov. 10, 2001, Los Angeles, Calif.), was a leading rocket scientist who was influential in the development of the U.S. space program. After earning a Ph.D. from the Massachusetts Institute of Technology in 1944, Hunter went to work for Douglas Aircraft. While at Douglas

he designed early versions of the B-42 and B-43 bombers, rockets for the Apollo Moon-landing program, Nike antiaircraft missiles, and an intermediate-range ballistic missile known as Thor. In the 1960s he served as space policy adviser to Presidents John F. Kennedy and Lyndon B. Johnson. From 1965 to 1987 Hunter worked for the Lockheed Missiles and Space Co. He reportedly helped sell the administration of Pres. Ronald Reagan on the idea for the U.S. Strategic Defense Initiative, known as "Star Wars." In later years Hunter established a consulting firm, SpaceGuild Inc., and worked on designs for a reusable launch vehicle to replace the space shuttle.

Hunzvi, Chenjerai ("Hitler"), Zimbabwean political activist (b. Oct. 23, 1949, Chikomba district, Southern Rhodesia—d. June 4, 2001, Harare, Zimb.), as chairman (from 1996) of the War Veterans' Association of Zimbabwe, built that formerly small organization into a huge political force; during the last months of his life, he engineered increasingly violent attacks on government opponents as well as the forcible occupation of hundreds of white-owned farms by malcontent Zimbabwean black "veterans." Hunzvi, who took the nom de guerre Hitler during the guerrilla war against white-minority rule in Rhodesia, pursued medical studies in Poland before returning to his homeland in 1990 to practice medicine. Despite reports that he had never fought in the war, Hunzvi proclaimed himself a lifelong freedom fighter, and his successful demands to Pres. Robert Mugabe on behalf of government-funded veterans' pensions earned him a considerable power base. He was elected to the Zimbabwean parliament in 2000.

Husseini, Faisal ibn 'Abd al-Qadir al-, Palestinian political leader (b. July 17, 1940, Baghdad, Iraq—d. May 31, 2001, Kuwait City, Kuwait), was the most senior Palestine Liberation Organization (PLO) official in Jerusalem and a pragmatic but persistent spokesman for Palestinian claims to East Jerusalem. Much of Husseini's influence within the Palestinian community was due to respect for his illustrious family. His father was a Palestinian military hero who died in battle against Zionist forces outside Jerusalem in 1948; a more distant relative, Amin al-Husayni, had been the grand mufti of Jerusalem (1921–48). Husseini studied science in Egypt and military tactics in Syria and joined Yasir Arafat's Fatah movement in 1961 and the PLO in 1965. When most other PLO leaders left Israel, Husseini remained in Jerusalem. He was repeatedly arrested by Israeli authorities and learned Hebrew while in prison. In later years he joined other moderates on both sides in support of U.S.-mediated peace negotiations, and he was often invited to represent the Palestinian point of view on Israeli radio and television. Husseini's home, Orient House, served as the unofficial PLO headquarters in East Jerusalem. He died of a heart attack while on a PLO peace mission to Kuwait.

Ingstad, Helge Marcus, Norwegian writer and adventurer (b. Dec. 30, 1899, Meraaker, Nor.—d. March 29, 2001, Oslo, Nor.), proved the long-debated theory that Vikings established a settlement in North America in about AD 1000. From the early 1950s Ingstad and his wife, archaeologist Anne Stine, explored the sites of known Viking settlements in Greenland and, using information garnered from Norse histories and sagas, began searching for the legendary "Vinland." In 1960 the pair unearthed ruins of an ancient village near L'Anse aux Meadows on the north coast of Newfoundland. By 1964 excavations on the site had revealed Norse artifacts and had provided conclusive evidence of a 1,000-year-old Viking settlement. In 1978 L'Anse aux Meadows was made a UN-ESCO World Heritage site. Ingstad, who trained as a lawyer in Norway before becoming a fur trapper and explorer in Canada, published several books on his adventures, notably *Landet under Leidarstjernen* (1959; *Land Under the Pole Star*, 1965) and *Vestervej til Vinland* (1965; *Westward to Vinland*, 1969).

Ireland, George, American basketball coach (b. June 15, 1913, Madison, Wis.—d. Sept. 14, 2001, Addison, Ill.), served at Loyola University (Chicago) for 24 seasons beginning in 1951 and retired with a 321–255 record. His most famous victory came in 1963, when the Loyola Ramblers won the National Collegiate Athletic Association championship, defeating the defending champion University of Cincinnati (Ohio) team 60–58 in overtime after having been 15 points behind in the second half of the game.

Jansson, Tove Marika, Finnish author and artist (b. Aug. 9, 1914, Helsinki, Fin., Russian Empire—d. June 27, 2001, Helsinki, Fin.), was the author-illustrator of the popular series of children's books that recounted the adventures of the Moomins, a family of hippopotamus-like trolls that spent much of its time sleeping when

Moomin creator Tove Jansson

not coping with floodwaters, comets, and other, less-perilous situations. Following the publication of her first book, *Småtrollen och den stora översvämningen* (1945; "The Small Trolls and the Large Flood"), Jansson released *Kometjakten* (1946; *Comet in Moominland*, 1951). She produced several more Moomintroll books, more than 2,000 other Moomin products—plush toys, wallpaper, pens, jewelry, candles—and a comic strip, *Moomins,* which appeared (1953–60) in the *Evening News* (London). Jansson's books were written in Swedish, the language that she spoke with her parents; her juvenile works, however, were translated into more than 30 languages. Among her other works were plays for children, short stories, adult fiction, and an autobiography, *Bildhuggarens dotter* (1968; *Sculptors' Daughter,* 1969).

Jennings, Elizabeth Joan, British poet (b. July 18, 1926, Boston, Lincolnshire, Eng.—d. Oct. 26, 2001, Bampton, Oxfordshire, Eng.), wrote traditional verse that was both intensely personal and universal. Her poetry was direct and understated, and it reflected her devout Roman Catholicism. She read English at St. Anne's College, Oxford, where her friends included Kingsley Amis and Philip Larkin. From 1950 to 1958 she worked at the Oxford City Library and then briefly for a publisher. Beginning in 1960 she supported herself by writing and reviewing. *Poems,* which appeared in 1953, won the first of her three Arts Council Awards, and *A Way of Looking* (1955) won the Somerset Maugham Award. Robert Conquest selected her work for his 1956 anthology *New Lines,* which also included poems by Amis and Larkin, among others, and which led to her being grouped with the Movement poets. Unlike the other members of this group, however, she was not an ironist. After a trip to Italy she published *A Sense of the World* (1958), expressing her passion for that country. *Song for a Birth or a Death* (1961), which suggested a somewhat fierce view of love, led critics to call her a confessional poet, a label she firmly rejected. She suffered a breakdown in the early 1960s, and a number of subsequent poems, as in *Recoveries* (1964), reflected on her illness. Later volumes such as *Growing-Points* (1975) and *Extending the Territory* (1985) showed an expansion of technique. Major collections included *Collected Poems 1967* (1967), *Selected Poems* (1979), and *Collected Poems 1953–1985* (1986), which won the W.H. Smith Award. *The Sonnets of Michelangelo,* published in 1961 and revised in 1969, came to be considered the standard translation. She also published criticism, a biography of Robert Frost, and poetry for children. She was made CBE in 1992.

Jia Lanpo, Chinese archaeologist (b. Nov. 25, 1908, Hebei province, China—d. July 8, 2001, Beijing, China), was internationally known for his work as director of the Peking man excavation at the Zhoukoudian cave complex near Beijing. In 1929, while still a graduate student, Jia was named interim overseer of the excavation; he became director in 1935. At the site, Jia helped unearth the first Chinese hominid fossils ever discovered; the Peking man fossils, which were about 900,000 to 130,000 years

old and belonged to the Middle Pleistocene Era, included 14 skullcaps, several mandibles, facial and limb bones, and the teeth of about 40 individuals. Though many of the fossils were lost during World War II, Jia had made casts of all of them and had taken some 2,000 photographs of the excavation site. He later directed excavations at other Pleistocene sites in China. A prolific writer, Jia published more than 180 scientific articles as well as two highly regarded books, *Chinese Homo Erectus* (1950) and *Early Man in China* (1980).

Johnson, J.J. (James Louis Johnson), American jazz musician and composer (b. Jan. 22, 1924, Indianapolis, Ind.—d. Feb. 4, 2001, Indianapolis, Ind.), was the first trombonist to improvise in the fast, complex phrases of bebop, and he was considered by many the most important modern jazz artist on his instrument. The Johnson style was dominant during the 1950s and '60s; virtually all other bop-era and modal trombonists based their styles on his lyric art. He played

Improvisational trombonist J.J. Johnson

in the Benny Carter and Count Basie big bands before becoming active in 1945 in New York-centred bebop circles and working and recording with Charlie Parker, Miles Davis, Illinois Jacquet, Sonny Stitt, and others. In addition, Johnson led his own groups. By then his sound was smooth in all ranges of his horn, and he played fast melodic phrases, full of short, staccato notes, with great ease. Remarkably, he developed his virtuoso technique on the slide trombone, a singularly unwieldy horn; hearing his early recordings, many listeners assumed he was playing the valve trombone, a far easier instrument to manipulate. For a time Johnson also worked as a blueprint inspector, but the popularity of the unusual Jay and Kai Quintet (1954–56), which included fellow trombonist Kai Winding, enabled him to concentrate on music full-time. The middle and late 1950s were the height of Johnson's career as a soloist; he led his own groups, toured and recorded often, and appeared on noted albums, including *Stan Getz and J.J. Johnson at the Opera House* (1957) and ones for Miles Davis and Sonny Rollins. He also began composing large-scale works, including *Poem for Brass* (1956), *El Camino Real* (1959), *Sketch for Trombone and Orchestra*

(1959), and the suite *Perceptions* (1961). During 1967–87 he concentrated on composing and arranging for commercials, films (*Cleopatra Jones*, *Barefoot in the Park*, and *Shaft*), and television (*That Girl*, *The Mod Squad*, and *Starsky and Hutch*). When Johnson returned to the limelight (1987–97), his jazz improvisations recaptured the vigour and mastery of his early work.

Johnson, Nkosi (Xolani Nkosi), South African activist (b. Feb. 4, 1989, Daveytown, S.Af.—d. June 1, 2001, Johannesburg, S.Af.), became the human face of AIDS in South Africa and an iconic figure in the campaign to raise money and public awareness about the disease. Johnson, who was born HIV-positive, was abandoned by his birth mother (who later died of AIDS) and was reared by a white foster mother. At the age of seven he was identified as his country's longest-surviving AIDS baby. Later his foster mother went to court to force the local primary school to enroll him as a pupil. Johnson attracted international attention in July 2000 when he made an impassioned speech at the opening ceremony of the XIII International AIDS Conference in Durban, S.Af., in which he called for compassion and improved medical treatment for AIDS sufferers, especially children and pregnant women, and implicitly criticized official South African government policy.

Jovanovich, William (Vladimir Jovanovich), American publisher (b. Feb. 6, 1920, Louisville, Colo.—d. Dec. 4, 2001, San Diego, Calif.), joined the Harcourt Brace and Co. publishing company as a college textbook salesman in 1947 and by 1954 was president. Under his leadership the company—renamed Harcourt Brace Jovanovich in 1970—incorporated such innovations as the use of colourful illustrations and detailed teachers' guides and grew to be one of the largest textbook publishers. He also published his own works, including *The World's Last Night* (1990).

Kabila, Laurent-Désiré, Congolese political leader (b. Nov. 27, 1939, Jadotville, Katanga province, Belgian Congo—confirmed dead on Jan. 18, 2001, Kinshasa, Democratic Republic of the Congo [DRC; formerly Zaire]), was president of the DRC from 1997 until his death. In 1960, after studying in France and Tanzania, Kabila became a youth leader in a political party allied to Congo's first postindependence prime minister, Marxist-Maoist Patrice Lumumba. Lumumba was deposed in 1961 by Mobutu Sese Seko and later killed. Assisted for a time in 1964 by guerrilla leader Che Guevara, Kabila helped Lumumba supporters lead a revolt, but it was eventually suppressed in 1965 by the Congolese army led by Mobutu. Kabila then founded (1967) the People's Revolutionary Party, which established a Marxist territory in the Kivu region of eastern Zaire and managed to sustain itself through gold mining and ivory trading. When that enterprise came to an end during the 1980s, he ran a business selling gold in Dar es Salaam, Tanz., until he resurfaced in Zaire in 1996 as leader of the newly formed Alliance of Democratic Forces for the Liberation of Congo-Zaire. Supported by a nation outraged by the dictatorial leadership of Mobutu,

AP/Wide World Photos

Assassin's target Laurent Kabila

Kabila rallied forces consisting mostly of Tutsi from eastern Zaire. Marching west toward the capital city of Kinshasa, Kabila's troops forced Mobutu to flee the country before their arrival. On May 17, 1997, Kabila installed himself as head of state. He also rejected the name Zaire, which Mobutu had given the country in 1971, and reverted its name to the DRC. Kabila was able to secure regional support, and his plan to revive the economy was welcomed both internationally and at home. Humanitarian organizations, however, soon voiced reservations. Reportedly, Kabila's troops had been responsible for the murder of thousands of Hutu refugees who had fled Rwanda into Zaire in 1994; Kabila ignored UN demands for an inquiry into the massacre. Resorting to many of the same dictatorial methods as his predecessor, Kabila refused to hold new elections, banned political parties, imprisoned journalists and human rights workers, and invited members of his family into the government. His years in office were largely consumed by a fierce conflict in the eastern part of the country between government forces and rebels backed by Uganda and Rwanda. Kabila was shot dead in the presidential mansion, allegedly by one of his bodyguards.

Kael, Pauline, American film critic (b. June 19, 1919, Petaluma, Calif.—d. Sept. 3, 2001, Great Barrington, Mass.), was an outspoken reviewer for *The New Yorker* magazine from 1968 to 1979 and 1980 to 1991, wielding untold influence among film fans and perhaps even moviemakers themselves. Celebrated as much for the provocative style of her writing as for the content, she honed a swordlike sharpness that would eviscerate a faulty work as deftly as it would crown a new piece of art. Thoughtful and high-minded, she nonetheless was wary of over-

intellectualizing the cinematic experience and encouraged her readers and imitators, known as "Paulettes," to trust their emotions. As such, she became a keen observer of popular culture and championed her favourite actors with fervour. She supported many filmmakers who came to prominence in the 1970s, including Francis Ford Coppola, Martin Scorsese, and Robert Altman. Fans and detractors alike found her pans as quotable and opinionated as her praises. "In love" with movies, as she defined it, from childhood, Kael attended the University of California, Berkeley, and began working as a critic in her mid-30s for *City Lights* magazine in San Francisco. She had begun to appear frequently in film journals and on the radio by the time she first published her reviews in the best-selling collection *I Lost It at the Movies* (1965). Thereafter she was a regular contributor to such mainstream titles as *Life, McCall's,* and *The New Republic,* and her work at these publications eventually earned her a spot at *The New Yorker.* During her hiatus from *The New Yorker* in 1979–80, she worked for the motion picture industry. Her other collections included *Kiss Kiss Bang Bang* (1968), *Deeper into Movies* (1973), *When the Lights Go Down* (1980), *Taking It All In* (1984), *Hooked* (1989), and *For Keeps* (1994).

Kato, Shizue Hirota, Japanese feminist and political leader (b. March 2, 1897, Tokyo, Japan—d. Dec. 22, 2001, Tokyo), began in the 1920s to campaign for women's rights and was the first woman to promote family planning in Japan. When women received the vote in 1946, she became one of the first to be elected to the Diet (parliament), serving first in the lower house (1946–50) and then in the upper (1950–74). In 1988, in recognition of her work in less-developed countries, she was given the UN Population Award, the first Japanese person to be so honoured.

Kazantzidis, Stelios, Greek folk singer (b. Aug. 29, 1931, Athens, Greece—d. Sept. 14, 2001, Athens), used his expressive vocal interpretations to capture the joys as well as the melancholy longings of Greeks everywhere, especially those in the working class and emigrants in the Greek diaspora. Kazantzidis had little formal education and began singing professionally in 1950. Although he made scores of recordings in his career, he did not fare well during the military junta (1967–74) and made no recordings between 1975 and 1987. Kazantzidis made a comeback to a new generation of fans in the 1990s.

Keïta, Seydou, Malian photographer (b. 1921/23?, French Sudan—d. Nov. 21, 2001, Paris, France), fashioned insightful studio portraits of ordinary Malian people, usually posed with intriguing combinations of African and Western clothing and props that he provided. Keïta, who was entirely self-trained, founded a small photography studio in the city of Bamako in 1948 and quickly gained a reputation for formal portraiture. He was designated the Republic of Mali's official photographer in 1962 and closed his studio to concentrate on his new duties, but he carefully preserved and stored thousands of black-and-white images. He retired

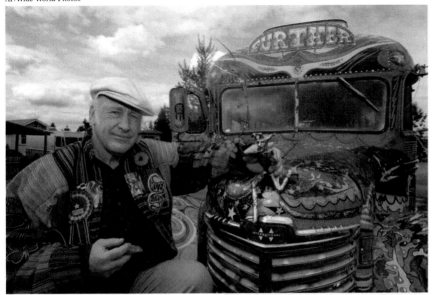

Ken Kesey, a Merry Prankster

from government service in 1977. In the late 1990s Keïta's early work was discovered by André Magnin of the Contemporary African Art Collection in Paris. Thereafter, Keïta's portraits were exhibited in Paris and across the U.S. A book dedicated to his photography was published in 1997, and in early 2001 the Seydou Keïta Foundation was established in Bamako to preserve his work and to support young African artists.

Kepes, Gyorgy, Hungarian-born American artist and theorist (b. Oct. 4, 1906, Selyp, Hung.—d. Dec. 29, 2001, Cambridge, Mass.), experimented with new technologies for art through design, photography, and painting. He headed the Light and Color Department at the New Bauhaus in Chicago (later renamed the Chicago Institute of Design) from 1937 until 1945, when he began teaching at the School of Architecture and Planning of the Massachusetts Institute of Technology. There he founded (1967) the Center for Advanced Visual Studies, a collective that fostered the marriage between art and science and art and modernity. His books included *The Language of Vision* (1944) and *The New Landscape in Art and Science* (1956).

Kesey, Ken Elton, American writer (b. Sept. 17, 1935, La Junta, Colo.—d. Nov. 10, 2001, Eugene, Ore.), became an icon of the counterculture with both his first book, *One Flew over the Cuckoo's Nest* (1962), and his hippie lifestyle as he and a group of friends— the Merry Pranksters—made a cross-country school-bus trip, along the way staging LSD-inspired "happenings." That trip, which helped bring the antiestablishment's antics into the public eye, was chronicled in Tom Wolfe's *The Electric Kool-Aid Acid Test* (1968). While a student at the University of Oregon, Kesey performed in some student productions, and following graduation (1957) he did some acting in Hollywood. His chief interest was in writ-

ing, however, so he spent a year in the graduate program at Stanford University. In 1959 Kesey became a subject of mind-altering-drug experiments at a veterans hospital, and when the tests ended, he remained at the hospital as an orderly in the mental ward. These experiences gave him the basis for *One Flew over the Cuckoo's Nest*, which achieved both critical and popular acclaim. A stage version was produced on Broadway in 1963–64, and a film version was released in 1975; the movie won five Academy Awards, including best picture. To prepare for his next book, *Sometimes a Great Notion* (1964)—a saga about a logging family—Kesey returned to Oregon and worked as a logger. That book also was filmed (1971). Following his school-bus trip with the Merry Pranksters and some trouble with the law, Kesey returned once again to Oregon and settled on his farm. Over the next several years, he wrote short fiction, children's books, and magazine articles; published two collections of his writings, *Kesey's Garage Sale* (1973) and *Demon Box* (1986); founded (1973) and published an underground magazine, *Spit in the Ocean;* and taught writing at the University of Oregon. In 1992 Kesey published another major novel, *Sailor Song,* and in 1994, in collaboration with fellow Prankster Ken Babbs, he published his final novel, *Last Go Round.*

Ketcham, Henry King ("Hank"), American cartoonist (b. March 14, 1920, Seattle, Wash.—d. June 1, 2001, Pebble Beach, Calif.), was the creator of the *Dennis the Menace* comic strip, which daily chronicled the antics and misadventures of a blond, freckle-faced scamp perpetually "five-ana-half" years old. The 50-year-old strip appeared in some 1,000 newspapers in 48 countries and 19 languages. Ketcham discovered his desire to become a cartoonist when he was six years old; after watching a family friend draw some comic-strip characters, he asked to borrow the man's "magic pencil." He attended the University of

Washington but dropped out in order to pursue his career. Ketcham worked as an animator first for Woody Woodpecker creator Walter Lantz and then for Walt Disney. At Disney he worked on animated films, including *Fantasia* (1940), *Pinocchio* (1940), and *Bambi* (1942). During World War II Ketcham served in the navy, where he drew cartoons to be used on posters and in material for training and war-bond-sales purposes, and following the war he became a freelance cartoonist. Ketcham's inspiration for the character of Dennis came (1950) from his rambunctious son of the same name; the child's mother—complaining that when Dennis was supposed to be taking a nap, he instead wrecked his room—exclaimed to Ketcham, "Your son is a menace!" Within five months the strip was running in 16 newspapers, and by 1953 it was being enjoyed by 30 million readers of 193 newspapers in the U.S. and 52 abroad. Cartoon books, a television series (1959–63), a musical, films, games, and toys followed. Ketcham ceased drawing the Sunday strips himself in the mid-1980s and in 1994 turned the daily strips over to a team of artists and writers. He thereupon devoted his artistic skills to oil and watercolour painting.

Kharibian, Leo, American-born dancer, choreographer, and director (b. April 27, 1927, Boston, Mass.—d. Aug. 23, 2001, Leicestershire, Eng.?), helped change the face of musical theatre choreography in Great Britain by incorporating American jazz dance movement in works for the stage, film, and television. He was best known for the "We're Knights of the Round Table" number in the movie *Monty Python and the Holy Grail* (1975).

Kiam, Victor Kermit, II, American businessman (b. Dec. 7, 1926, New Orleans, La.—d. May 27, 2001, Stamford, Conn.), was the innovative owner of Remington Products, a company that specialized in selling electric shavers; he became widely known after appearing in a series of television advertisements in which he proclaimed, "I liked the shaver so much, I bought the company." After receiving a master's of business administration degree from Harvard University, Kiam worked from 1951 to 1955 in the sales and marketing divisions of Lever Bros., maker of Pepsodent toothpaste, among other products. He was an executive at Playtex for the following 13 years before buying his first company, watchmaker Wells-Benrus, in 1968. He acquired a failing Remington from the Sperry Rand Corp. in 1979 and made the company profitable within a year, in part through his unique approach to advertising. Kiam was the majority owner (1988–92) of the New England Patriots of the National Football League.

Kilburn, Tom, British computer engineer (b. Aug. 11, 1921, Dewsbury, Yorkshire, Eng.—d. Jan. 17, 2001, Manchester, Eng.), was a key member of Frederic (later Sir Frederic) Williams's team that designed the first cathode-ray-tube memory system (known as the Williams tube) and built the first working stored-program electronic digital computer. Kilburn, who trained as a mathematician, wrote the original software program, which was successfully tested at the University of Manchester in June 1948. Kilburn was named the university's first professor of computer science in 1964, was made a fellow of the Royal Society in 1965, and was appointed CBE in 1973.

Klaus, Josef, Austrian politician (b. Aug. 15, 1910, Mauthen, Austria, Austria-Hungary—d. July 26, 2001, Vienna, Austria), as chairman of the centre-right People's Party (ÖVP), was Austria's chancellor in an uneasy coalition with the Socialist Party for two years (1964–66); after the ÖVP won a narrow parliamentary majority in 1966, he served at the head of the country's first post-World War II noncoalition, single-party government (1966–70). Klaus, who had been finance minister (1961–64), was admired for his financial reforms and for forging improved ties with Western European nations, but his unwillingness to pursue former Nazis was widely criticized.

Knapp, (Geoffrey Goodman) James ("Jimmy"), British labour leader (b. Sept. 29, 1940, Hurlford, Ayrshire, Scot.—d. Aug. 13, 2001), was, from 1983, general secretary of the U.K.'s largest railway workers' federation, the National Union of Railwaymen (NUR), and its successor, the Rail, Maritime and Transport Union (RMT). A lifelong socialist, Knapp supported the contentious miners' strike of 1984 and successfully managed a series of one-day railway stoppages in 1989 as well as a 15-week signalmen's strike in 1994. He was unable to sustain the union's power amid privatization and increasing globalization, however, and membership declined, even after the NUR merged with the seamen's union in 1990 to form the RMT.

Knowles, John, American writer (b. Sept. 16, 1926, Fairmont, W.Va.—d. Nov. 29, 2001, near Fort Lauderdale, Fla.), won instant acclaim for his first novel, *A Separate Peace* (1959), which sold more than eight million copies. The enduring classic became a part of the syllabus of high-school English classes throughout the U.S. In 1942, at the age of 15, Knowles entered Phillips Exeter (N.H.) Academy. Following graduation in 1945, he received training as a pilot in the U.S. Army Air Corps. In 1946 he entered Yale University, from which he graduated in 1949 with a B.A., and from 1950 to 1952 he worked as a reporter and drama critic for the *Hartford* (Conn.) *Courant*. He then went to Europe, where he was befriended by Thornton Wilder, who encouraged Knowles to write about his experiences. Returning to New York City in 1955, he worked as associate editor of *Holiday* magazine from 1957 to 1960. *A Separate Peace*, a story of the inner conflicts of adolescents, dealt with questions of loyalty and betrayal among boys at a New England boarding school. The novel won the Rosenthal Award of the National Institute of Arts and Letters and the William Faulkner Foundation Award. It was made into a film in 1972. In a 1998 poll of students at Radcliffe College, Cambridge, Mass., it was named the 67th best novel ever written in English. Neither a sequel, *Peace Breaks Out* (1981), nor his other books,

including seven additional novels and a book of short stories, enjoyed much success, however. During the 1960s he was writer in residence at the University of North Carolina at Chapel Hill and at Princeton University, and in the 1990s he taught creative writing at Florida Atlantic University.

Kohl, Hannelore Renner, German political wife (b. March 7, 1933, Berlin, Ger.—d. July 5, 2001, Ludwigshafen, Ger.), as the wife of Helmut Kohl (from 1960), was the de facto first lady during his 16 years as chancellor of West Germany (1982–90) and reunified Germany (1990–98). Trained as an interpreter in French and English, she used superb language skills as well as her personal warmth and charm to enhance the traditional role of political wife. Kohl elicited sympathetic public support as she stood by her husband during the difficult period be-

Germany's "first lady" Hannelore Kohl

fore and after West German reunification with East Germany, the hard-fought national election he lost in 1998, and the financial scandal that engulfed him after he left office. In 1993 she was stricken with photodermatitis, a rare allergy to sunlight, and the escalating isolation and physical pain she experienced eventually led her to take her own life.

Koner, Pauline, American dancer and choreographer (b. 1912, New York, N.Y.—d. Feb. 8, 2001, New York), created works for stage shows at New York City's Roxy Theater, for ice shows, and for television programs and from 1946 to 1960 performed with the José Limón Dance Company. She worked closely with modern dance pioneer Doris Humphrey and choreographed her best-known piece, *The Farewell* (1962), to honour Humphrey's memory. Koner also led the Pauline Koner Dance Consort (1976–82) and at a number of schools taught a course, Elements of Performing, that gained her additional fame.

Korda, Alberto (Alberto Díaz Gutiérrez), Cuban photographer (b. Sept. 14, 1928, Havana, Cuba—d. May 25, 2001, Paris, France), took one of the most famous photographs of the 20th century—a 1960 image of guerrilla leader Che Guevara that was widely reproduced on posters, cards, and T-shirts. Korda had been a prominent fashion photographer in the 1950s before deciding to chronicle the lives of Cuba's revolutionary leaders, including Guevara and Fidel Castro. Exhibits of his photographs were later staged in France and the U.S., among other countries. In the 1990s Korda waged a legal battle against the commercial reproduction of his iconic portrait of Guevara.

Kramer, Stanley Earl, American film producer and director (b. Sept. 29, 1913, New York, N.Y.—d. Feb. 19, 2001, Woodland Hills, Calif.), created unconventional, socially conscious works on a variety of issues not usually addressed in mainstream Hollywood fare, including racial prejudice (e.g., *The Defiant Ones* [1958]), nuclear annihilation (*On the Beach* [1959]), and war crimes (*Judgment at Nuremberg* [1961]), and in tackling such themes acquired a reputation as a maker of "message" pictures, a label he disliked. He also showed support for blacklisted writers by hiring those who could not secure work under their own names following the communist witch-hunts. His nearly three dozen films were nominated for some 80 Academy Awards and won 16, and three—*High Noon* (1952), *Guess Who's Coming to Dinner* (1967), and *It's a Mad Mad Mad Mad World* (1963)—were placed on the American Film Institute's list of the 100 all-time best movies. Kramer graduated from high school at age 15 and earned a bachelor's degree in business administration from New York University in 1933. Soon thereafter, he moved to Hollywood and entered the film industry, working first in such capacities as researcher, editor, and writer, and during World War II service with the Army Signal Corps, he made training and orientation films. Following the war Kramer established an independent production company, and in 1948 its first motion picture, *So This Is New York*, was released. Kramer's first success, *Champion*, followed in 1949 and, in dealing with the ruthlessness of an ambitious prizefighter and the corruption in the fight profession, established the moral tone his best-known future films would reflect. It also sparked the career of Kirk Douglas. The next year he launched Marlon Brando's film career with *The Men*, which explored the challenges faced by disabled war veterans. Later notable films either produced or produced and directed by Kramer included *Cyrano de Bergerac* (1950), *Death of a Salesman* (1951), *The Member of the Wedding* (1952), *The Wild One* (1954), *The Caine Mutiny* (1954), *Inherit the Wind* (1960), and *Ship of Fools* (1965). Kramer was honoured with the Academy of Motion Picture Arts and Sciences' Irving G. Thalberg Memorial Award in 1962. Such later films as *R.P.M.* (1970), *The Domino Principle* (1977), and *The Runner Stumbles* (1979) were not successful. He retired from filmmaking in 1980.

Kumar, Ashok (Kumadlal Kunjilal Ganguly), Indian actor (b. Oct. 13, 1911, Bhagalpur, Bihar, India—d. Dec. 10, 2001, Mumbai [Bombay], India), became one of the most popular, best-loved, and longest-lasting stars of India's "Bollywood" motion picture industry in a career that spanned more than 60 years and some 300 films. He had a natural style of acting that allowed him to be effective and believable in a variety of characters that included both romantic leading men and roguish antiheroes, and he set a style—especially for cigarette smoking—that was copied by young men all across the country. Kumar studied law but was more interested in the direction and technical aspects of film. He was hired (1934) as a laboratory technician trainee and camera assistant at Bombay Talkies, but in 1936, when a replacement was needed for the star of *Jeevan naya* ("New Life"), Kumar was tapped for the role. That same year his next film, *Achhut kanya* ("Untouchable Girl"), made him a star. Among his most notable and most successful films—and one that brought him even greater fame—was *Kismet* ("Fate"; 1943), in which he portrayed a lovable pickpocket and made criminal behaviour appear glamorous. It set box-office longevity records that held for some three decades. Among later films were *Jewel Thief* (1967) and two for which his performances won him the Filmfare Award, India's equivalent of the Academy Award, for best actor: *Raakhi* ("Filial Bond"; 1962) and *Ashirwad* ("Blessings"; 1968). Kumar was also honoured with India's highest cinema prize, the Dada Saheb Phalke Award (1989), and the Filmfare Lifetime Achievement Award (1996).

Kushida, Fuki, Japanese peace and women's rights activist (b. Feb. 17, 1899, Yamaguchi prefecture, Japan—d. Feb. 5, 2001, Tokyo, Japan), was a noted campaigner for world peace and the advancement of women. She became the first secretary-general of the Women's Democratic Club, a feminist and peace organization, in 1946 and worked with feminist writer Yuriko Miyamoto. Kushida was elected president of the Federation of Japanese Women's Organizations in 1958. In 2000 the centenarian attracted attention as the leader of demonstrations against U.S. military bases on Okinawa.

Kuwa Mekki, Yousif, Sudanese resistance leader (b. August 1945, Al-Akhwal, The Sudan—d. March 31, 2001, Norwich, Eng.), as the charismatic commander of the Sudan People's Liberation Army (SPLA), led a guerrilla rebellion on behalf of non-Muslim blacks in southern Sudan against the Islamic fundamentalist rulers based in the Arab north of the country. Kuwa was a member of the Miri tribe, an ethnic subgroup of the Nuba people, and was reared as a Muslim with little knowledge of his ethnic heritage. He studied political science and Nuba history at the University of Khartoum, qualified as a teacher, and was elected (1981) to the regional assembly. As The Sudan slipped into civil war between the north and the south, Kuwa abandoned his teaching career to join the SPLA in 1984.

Lachmon, Jaggernath, Surinamese politician (b. Sept. 21, 1916, Nieuw Nickerie, Dutch Guiana [now Suriname]—d. Oct. 19, 2001, Amsterdam, Neth.), was a prominent figure in Surinamese politics for over half a century. He helped found two political parties, was an MP from 1949 (except during the 1980–87 military dictatorship), and served for many years (1964–67, 1969–73, and 1988–2001) as speaker of the National Assembly.

Lal, (Chaudhuri) Devi, Indian politician (b. Sept. 25, 1914, Chautala, Punjab [now in Haryana state], India—d. April 6, 2001, New Delhi, India), served (1989–91) as India's deputy prime minister under two prime ministers. Lal was appointed deputy prime minister in Prime Minister V.P. Singh's National Front government in 1989; after being dismissed in August 1990, Lal helped engineer Singh's ouster by Chandra Shekhar, who reappointed him to the post. Lal, a vigorous champion of the interests of peasant farmers, was also a longtime member of the Haryana legislature and was Haryana's chief minister (1977–80 and 1987–89); his son Om Prakash Chautala later became chief minister.

Lapidus, Morris, Russian-born American architect (b. Nov. 25, 1902, Odessa, Russia [now Ukraine]—d. Jan. 18, 2001, Miami Beach, Fla.), designed some 1,200 buildings, including 250 hotels; his flamboyant style was long scorned by critics but gained a measure of respect late in his career. Lapidus, who graduated from Columbia University, New York City, with a degree in architecture in 1927, designed retail spaces for 20 years before turning his attention to buildings. He was best known for his glitzy Miami Beach hotels, such as the Fontainebleau (1954), the Eden Roc (1955), and the Americana (1956; now the Sheraton Bal Harbour). His designs were always popular with the general public, but it was not until the 1980s and '90s that critics began to appreciate his work. In 2000 Lapidus received a National Design Award from the Smithsonian Institution's Cooper-Hewitt, National Design Museum. His autobiography, *Too Much Is Never Enough,* appeared in 1996.

Lechín Oquendo, Juan, Bolivian trade union leader and revolutionary politician (b. May 19, 1914, Corocoro, Bol.—d. Aug. 27, 2001, La Paz, Bol.), was the key founder (1946) and longtime leader of the Trade Union Confederation and as such was commander of a workers' uprising that, with its triumph in 1952 and the reforms it brought, began what became known as a "golden decade"; during that decade he served as minister of mines and petroleum (1952–56), senator (1956–60), and vice president (1960–62). Though the government was soon thereafter ousted in a military coup, Lechín remained prominent in Bolivian politics—as the radical opposition—until the mid-1980s.

Lemmon, Jack (John Uhler Lemmon III), American actor (b. Feb. 8, 1925, Boston, Mass.—d. June 27, 2001, Los Angeles, Calif.), excelled in both comic and dramatic character roles, especially in portrayals of a beleaguered everyman beset by the quirks and trials of everyday life; his career was especially defined by two partnerships—with Billy Wilder, who directed him in 7 films, and with his good friend and fellow actor Walter Matthau, with whom he costarred in 10 films and who preceded him in death by almost exactly a year. Lemmon first discovered his passion for acting when he was a young boy, participated in amateur theatre during his years as a student at Harvard University, and, following navy service toward the end of World War II and graduation from Harvard (1947), moved to New York City to pursue a performing career. Having earlier taught himself to play the piano by ear, he supported himself by supplying the music for silent films in a beer hall as he began getting roles on radio and in the live television series *Robert Montgomery Presents, Danger, Studio One,* and *Suspense.* Lemmon's Off-Broadway debut came in *Power of Darkness* in 1947, and in 1953 he made his Broadway debut in a revival of *Room Service.* That performance caught the attention of a film talent scout, and the following year Lemmon was cast opposite Judy Holliday in *It Should Happen to You.* A year later he played Ensign Pulver in *Mr. Roberts,* for which he won the best supporting actor Oscar. *Some Like It Hot* (1959), Lemmon's first movie with Wilder, and *The Apartment* (1960), his second, provided two of his definitive performances, and another Wilder film, *The Fortune Cookie* (1966), introduced his partnership with Matthau. That collaboration was highlighted by the two friends' performances as a neat freak (Lemmon, as Felix Unger) and a slob (Matthau, as Oscar Madison) attempting to survive each other as roommates in Neil Simon's *The Odd Couple* (1968). Late in their careers their teaming found them in *Grumpy Old Men* (1993) and its sequel (1995), *Out to Sea* (1997), and *The Odd Couple II* (1998). In addition, Lemmon excelled in dramatic films—including *Days of Wine and Roses* (1962), *Save the Tiger* (1973), for which he won a best actor Oscar, *The China Syndrome* (1979), *Missing* (1982), and *Glengarry Glen Ross* (1992)—and throughout his career he also returned to the stage, notably in *Tribute* (1978) and *Long Day's*

Getty Images

Versatile actor Jack Lemmon

Journey into Night (1986). He was last seen in the TV production *Tuesdays with Morrie* (1999), for which he won an Emmy. Among Lemmon's many other honours were the American Film Institute's Life Achievement Award in 1988, the Screen Actors Guild's Life Achievement Award in 1990, and a Kennedy Center Honor in 1996.

Leone, Giovanni, Italian politician (b. Nov. 3, 1908, Pomigliano d'Arco, Italy—d. Nov. 9, 2001, Rome, Italy), was a respected member of the Christian Democratic Party, a practicing attorney and professor of criminal law (from 1933), a longtime member of the Italian parliament (1948–67), a life senator (from 1967), and twice interim prime minister (1963 and 1968). In 1971 he was a compromise choice for president, but his term as Italy's head of state came during a tumultuous period of terrorist attacks and political scandal. Despite his reputation for honesty, Leone was forced to resign in 1978 amid allegations that he had taken bribes from the American firm Lockheed Aircraft Corp. Years later Leone's accusers admitted that they had had no proof against him and apologized.

Léotard, (Ange-)Philippe, French actor, poet, and chansonnier (b. Aug. 28, 1940, Nice, France—d. Aug. 25, 2001, Paris, France), appeared in more than 70 French- and English-language films, including *French Connection II* (1975), *Les Misérables* (1995), and *La Balance* (1982; *The Nark*), for which he won a César, France's highest cinema award, as best actor. He also cofounded the avant-garde Théâtre de Soleil, recorded several albums of "chansons française," and published poetry, notably the collection *Pas un jour sans une ligne* (1992; *Not a Day Without a Line*). In his 1997 autobiography Léotard detailed his long struggle with alcoholism and drug abuse.

Lewis, David Kellogg, American philosopher (b. Sept. 28, 1941, Oberlin, Ohio—d. Oct. 14, 2001, Princeton, N.J.), created the theory of "modal realism," which considered possible worlds—that is, all conceivable states of affairs that do not involve logical contradictions—as actually existing rather than as mere heuristic devices. Lewis's actuality of other possible worlds was comparable to that of previous times in this world. For an analytic philosopher, Lewis was systematic in his approach to philosophical problems. He employed a principle he called "Humean supervenience," according to which the world is composed of a "vast mosaic" of local physical facts, upon which all other states of affairs depend. Lewis was educated at Swarthmore (Pa.) College, the University of Oxford, and Harvard University. He taught at the University of California, Los Angeles, from 1966 to 1970 and at Princeton University from 1970 until his death. His paper "Convention: A Philosophical Study" (1969) was awarded the Matchette Prize in philosophy for scholars under 40. Among his other publications were *Counterfactuals* (1973) and *On the Plurality of Worlds* (1986).

Lewis, John Aaron, American composer and pianist (b. May 3, 1920, La Grange, Ill.—d.

March 29, 2001, New York, N.Y.), brought elegance and charm to jazz while leading the Modern Jazz Quartet (MJQ) to musical and popular success for over four decades. He played piano in a spare, graceful style, and his compositions included sophisticated modern melodies as well as breaks, ostinatos, riffs, and

© Francis Wolff/Mosaic Images/Corbis

Modern Jazz Quartet pianist John Lewis

other devices from the early jazz and swing eras. Lewis, inspired by bebop and Bach, was especially noted for creating forms derived from classical music; he joined Baroque canons and fugues to modern improvisation. Lewis grew up in Albuquerque, N.M., and studied music and anthropology at the University of New Mexico; later he attended New York City's Manhattan School of Music (M.A., 1953). After army service during World War II, he became a vital figure in the bebop avant-garde, playing in and composing ("Two Bass Hit" and "Emanon") for Dizzy Gillespie's big band and accompanying Charlie Parker in classic recordings; Lewis also helped create the cool jazz idiom by composing for Miles Davis's 1948 *Birth of the Cool* nonet. In 1952 Lewis began leading the MJQ, one of the longest-lived of all jazz groups. It featured Lewis's piano interplay with the great vibraphone soloist Milt Jackson, accompanied sensitively by Percy Heath, bass, and Connie Kay, drums, and it was active until the late 1990s, apart from a 1975–80 hiatus. Lewis's compositions for the MJQ included songs (his most famed was "Django"), fugues ("Concorde" and "Vendome"), extended works (*The Comedy* and *A Day in Dubrovnik*), and film scores (*Sait-on jamais?* [*No Sun in Venice*] and *Odds Against Tomorrow*). Apart from the MJQ, the versatile Lewis encouraged Third Stream music, which united jazz and classical elements, by composing for orchestras and small ensembles and by coleading Orchestra U.S.A. (1962–65). He was musical director of the Monterey (Calif.) Jazz Festival (1958–82) and of the American Jazz Orchestra (1985–92), a repertory big band. Meanwhile, he also played his intimate style of piano in a variety of jazz combos; in his last major concert (New York City, January 2001), he played

unaccompanied solos and directed the Lincoln Center Jazz Orchestra.

Li Kwoh-ting, Chinese-born Taiwanese economist and government official (b. Jan. 28, 1910, Nanjing, China—d. May 31, 2001, Taipei, Taiwan), helped spearhead the effort to transform Taiwan's economy from a relatively poor, agrarian-based system into one of the world's leading producers of information and telecommunications technology. Li, a Nationalist Party member who fled from China to Taiwan in 1949, served as the country's economics minister from 1965 to 1969 and as finance minister from 1969 to 1976. As a minister without portfolio from 1976 to 1988, he remained an influential policy maker in those fields. In 1979 Li created a large industrial park in the port city of Hsinchu that came to be known as Taiwan's "Silicon Valley." In later years he served as an adviser to Pres. Lee Teng-hui and to Lee's successor, Chen Shui-bian.

Lilburn, Douglas Gordon, New Zealand composer (b. Nov. 2, 1915, Wanganui, N.Z.—d. June 6, 2001, Wellington, N.Z.), was one of New Zealand's most distinctive composers, fusing European musical traditions with inspirations from the literature, landscape, and culture of his native land. Lilburn studied journalism, history, and music at Canterbury University College. After winning (1936) the Grainger Prize for his symphonic tone poem *In the Forest,* he was sent to study under Ralph Vaughan Williams at the Royal College of Music in London. He returned to New Zealand in 1940. Lilburn's powerful earlier compositions, most notably his three symphonies, demonstrated strong influence from such contemporary composers as Vaughan Williams, Jean Sibelius, Igor Stravinsky, Bela Bartok, Arnold Schoenberg, and Aaron Copland. Later, however, he experimented with electronic music. Lilburn was on the music faculty (1947–79) of Victoria University in Wellington and was the founding director (1966–79) of the university's Electronic Music Studio. In addition to his many chamber orchestra and symphonic works, he also composed film, television, theatre, and ballet music. He was awarded the Order of New Zealand in 1983.

Lindbergh, Anne Spencer Morrow, American writer and aviator (b. June 22, 1906, Englewood, N.J.—d. Feb. 7, 2001, Passumpsic, Vt.), was perhaps best known as the wife of Charles ("Lucky Lindy") Lindbergh—the pilot who had made (1927) the first solo transatlantic flight—and the mother of the 20-month-old baby whose kidnapping and subsequent murder in 1932 was sensationalized in the press and labeled the "crime of the century." In her own right, however, she was a renowned pilot and the author of a number of popular books of fiction, diaries, and poetry. Her best-known work, *Gift from the Sea* (1955)—a series of meditative essays on the struggle, especially by women, to achieve balance and serenity in life—sold more than five million copies in its first 20 years in print. Lindbergh met her husband when he was her family's guest during the Christmas 1927 season. She graduated from Smith College, Northampton, Mass., in 1928, and the couple was married the following year. Lindbergh took up flying herself and in 1930 became the first woman in the U.S. to be granted a glider pilot's license. She became her husband's co-pilot, navigator, and radio operator and in 1930 helped him set a new transcontinental speed record of 14 hours 45 minutes from Los Angeles to New York City. In 1931 they made a three-month-long journey to survey air routes over Canada and Alaska to East Asia, and that trip later became the subject of Lindbergh's first book, *North to the Orient* (1935), which was an instant success. Lindbergh solidified her reputation with her second book, *Listen! The Wind* (1938), which recounted a 1933–34 survey of transatlantic air routes. The excessive attention surrounding their first son's kidnap-murder and the trial and death sentence of accused killer Bruno Hauptmann, as well as threats made on the life of their second son, had prompted the family to move to England in 1935, and they remained in Europe until the eve of World War II. Lindbergh's controversial next book, *The Wave of the Future, a Confession of Faith* (1940), supported the isolationist stance her husband was taking and diminished her popularity for a time, but her first novel, *The Steep Ascent* (1944), was well received, and *Gift from the Sea* spent many weeks on the best-seller list. Later works included *The Unicorn, and Other Poems, 1935–1955* (1956) and her five volumes of diaries covering the years 1922–44: *Bring Me a Unicorn* (1972), *Hour of Gold, Hour*

Bettmann/Corbis

Aviatrix Anne Morrow Lindbergh, with son Charles Jr.

of *Lead* (1973), *Locked Rooms and Open Doors* (1974), *The Flower and the Nettle* (1976), and *War Within and Without* (1980).

Lindon, Jérôme, French publisher (b. June 9, 1925, Paris, France—d. April 9, 2001, Paris), took control of the small independent publishing house Les Éditions de Minuit in 1948, at age 23, and thereafter was a central figure in the *nouveau roman* ("new novel," or antinovel) literary movement of the 1950s and '60s. Lindon personally oversaw the publication of significant works by Nathalie Sarraute, Alain Robbe-Grillet, Marguerite Duras, Michel Butor, Claude Simon, and, especially, Samuel Beckett. Other prizewinning novelists followed, notably Jean Rouaud and Jean Échenoz in the 1990s. Lindon also published the literary review *Critique*, several nonfiction books critical of French involvement in Algeria, and works by such prominent philosophers as Pierre Bourdieu, Michel Serres, and Jacques Derrida.

Lions, Jacques-Louis, French mathematician (b. May 2, 1928, Grasse, France—d. May 17, 2001, Paris, France), as a leading figure in the field of applied mathematics, was remarkably proficient at developing and systematizing methods for analyzing nonlinear partial differential equations and thereby increasing the potential scientific and industrial applications. A mathematics professor from 1954 until his retirement in 1986, Lions was an early proponent of the use of computer simulations to assist in nonlinear analysis. He was elected to the French Academy of Sciences in 1973 (president 1996–98) and was president of the National Centre for Space Study (1984–92) and the International Mathematical Union (1991–94). Lions also won numerous international prizes in mathematics, held scientific and industrial advisory posts, and published some 500 scientific papers and more than 20 books. His son, Pierre-Louis, won the Fields Medal in 1994 for his own work in nonlinear partial differential equations.

Livingston, Jay Harold, American songwriter (b. March 28, 1915, McDonald, Pa.—d. Oct. 17, 2001, Los Angeles, Calif.), in collaboration with Ray Evans, created songs for some 80 motion pictures, including three songs that won Academy Awards—"Buttons and Bows" from the Bob Hope western comedy *The Paleface* (1948); "Mona Lisa" from *Captain Carey, U.S.A.* (1950) and later made famous by Nat ("King") Cole; and "Que Sera, Sera," sung by Doris Day in *The Man Who Knew Too Much* (1956). Among their numerous other popular movie songs was "Silver Bells" from another Hope feature, *The Lemon Drop Kid* (1951); it became a Christmas standard and sold over 140 million records. The team also wrote television theme music for such shows as *Bonanza* and *Mr. Ed*, and it was Livingston's voice that was heard singing the latter.

Longford, Francis Aungier Pakenham, 7th earl of, British politician and social reformer (b. Dec. 5, 1905, London, Eng.—d. Aug. 3, 2001, London), was admired as an active, though sometimes eccentric, social reformer in a long political career as a government minister in the

1940s and '50s and later as an outspoken member of the House of Lords, of which he was leader 1964–68. The son of the 5th earl of Longford, he was educated at Eton College and New College, Oxford, where he specialized in banking. During the 1930s he converted from Anglo-Irish Protestantism to Roman Catholicism and from the Conservative Party to the socialist Labour Party. He held a variety of ministerial posts under Prime Minister Clement Attlee, notably undersecretary of state for war (1946–47), chancellor of the duchy of Lancaster overseeing the British zone in occupied Germany (1947–48), minister of civil aviation (1948–51), and first lord of the admiralty (1951). He was created Baron Pakenham in 1945, succeeded to the earldom on the death of his older brother in 1961, and was made a knight of the garter in 1971. As a member of the House of Lords for 40 years, Longford was most often associated with his vigorous campaigns against pornography and for prison reform. Longford was also chairman (1955–63) of the National Bank in London, chairman (1970–80) and director (1980–85) of the publishing house Sidgwick and Jackson, and the author of a score of books.

Lowe, Jacques, German-born American photographer (b. Jan. 24, 1930, Cologne, Ger.—d. May 12, 2001, New York, N.Y.), served as Pres. John F. Kennedy's campaign and personal photographer. Lowe took more than 40,000 photographs of Kennedy and his family, many of them touching candid shots that helped create the image of the Kennedy White House as "Camelot." Lowe collected his photographs in several books, including *JFK Remembered: An Intimate Portrait by His Personal Photographer* (1993), and in a 1996 traveling exhibition.

Ludlum, Robert, American writer (b. May 25, 1927, New York, N.Y.—d. March 12, 2001, Naples, Fla.), was a best-selling author of suspense novels; his books sold more than 220 million copies in some 40 countries. After working as an actor and theatrical producer for 20 years, Ludlum wrote his first novel, *The Scarlatti Inheritance* (1971), which was an instant commercial hit. The book was followed by several more equally successful thrillers, including *The Osterman Weekend* (1972), *The Bourne Identity* (1980), *The Icarus Agenda* (1988), and *The Prometheus Deception* (2000). Three novels by Ludlum were scheduled to be published posthumously.

Maas, Peter, American writer (b. June 27, 1929, New York, N.Y.—d. Aug. 23, 2001, New York), had a half-century-long career during which he published over a dozen books as well as numerous magazine articles. He counted among his works such fact-based investigative best-sellers as *The Valachi Papers* (1969) and *Underboss* (1997), both of which detailed Mafia life and secrets, and *Serpico* (1972; filmed 1973), a whistleblower's revelation of New York City police corruption.

MacNeish, Richard Stockton ("Scotty"), American agricultural archaeologist (b. April 29, 1918, New York, N.Y.—d. Jan. 16, Belize City, Belize), conducted fieldwork investigating the origins of corn (maize) and rice under the auspices of the Andover (Mass.) Foundation for Archaeologic Research and stirred controversy with some of his interpretations derived from his work. His most notable discovery came during the 1960s when he found tiny ears of corn in a cave in the Tehuacán Valley in Mexico; these forebears of modern corn at first were believed to be as much as 7,000 years old but later were dated at 5,500 years old. During the 1990s MacNeish found remnants of cultivated rice paddies that were 9,000 years old along the Chang Jiang (Yangtze River) basin. MacNeish's 1992 discovery in New Mexico of human fingerprints on human-made hearths that were believed as old as 38,000 years led him to discredit a widely held theory that humans first set foot in the Americas about 12,000 years ago by crossing the Bering land bridge from Asia, a hypothesis that raised the hackles of proponents of that theory. MacNeish was killed when he crashed after losing control of his car while driving between two archaeological sites.

MacStiofain, Sean (John Edward Drayton Stephenson), British-born Irish militant (b. Feb. 17, 1928, London, Eng.—d. May 17, 2001, Navan, County Meath, Ire.), was the first chief of staff of the Provisional Irish Republican Army after the hard-line militarist wing's split from the Official IRA in 1969. Originally drawn to the Irish republican cause by his Belfast, N.Ire.-born mother, he joined the IRA in his 20s and later changed his name. As the leader of the Provos, he advocated implacable violent resistance to British rule in Northern Ireland and was credited with waging a terrorist campaign, including at least one fatal bombing. In 1973, however, after an unsuccessful hunger strike while in prison, he was ousted from his post. MacStiofain, who published *Memoirs of a Revolutionary* in 1975, never fully recovered from a stroke he suffered in the mid-1980s.

Magloire, Paul, Haitian military ruler (b. July 19, 1907, Cap-Haitien, Haiti—d. July 12, 2001, Port-au-Prince, Haiti), ruled Haiti from 1950 to 1956. The son of a general, Magloire rose through the ranks of the Haitian army to become a general himself by the late 1940s. He orchestrated the overthrow of Pres. Dumarsais Estimé in 1950 and installed himself as ruler. During his reign Magloire developed tourism, started an ambitious program of modernization, and cultivated good relations with the Dominican Republic and the U.S. Corruption scandals and the severe economic problems that followed Hurricane Hazel in 1954, however, eventually turned the public against Magloire. He was ousted by the military in 1956 and went into exile in New York. After the reign of Jean-Claude Duvalier ended in 1986, Magloire returned to Haiti.

Majali, Habes al-, Jordanian field marshall (b. 1913?—d. April 22, 2001, Amman, Jordan), was one of Jordan's most successful military leaders. Majali joined the army in 1932 and in 1948 led an Arab force that defeated Israeli troops near Latrun. He was placed in charge of the personal guard for Jordan's King Abdullah in 1949, though he failed to prevent the king's as-sassination two years later. This failure did not destroy his career, however, and in 1957 King Hussein named him armed forces chief of staff. Majali served Hussein as defense minister from June 1967 until 1970, when he was reappointed commander of the army in order to crush a Palestinian uprising. He also commanded troops in the 1973 Yom Kippur War. After retiring from the army, Majali was appointed to the upper house of the parliament.

Mansfield, Michael Joseph ("Mike"), American politician and diplomat (b. March 16, 1903, New York, N.Y.—d. Oct. 5, 2001, Washington, D.C.), served as majority leader of the U.S. Senate from 1961 to 1977 under four presidents—the longest anyone had held that post. During that time he was instrumental in guiding a number of vital acts of legislation to passage, among them the Civil Rights Act of 1964, the Voting Rights Act of 1965, legislation that paved the way to ratification of the 26th Amendment, which lowered the voting age to 18 (1971), and the War Powers Act (1973). Mansfield was reared by an aunt and uncle in Montana, and when he was not yet 15, he joined the navy just before the U.S. entered World War I. Because he had lied about his age, he was discharged after 19 months, whereupon he joined the army, served for a year, and then joined the marines. Service in East Asia ignited a lifelong interest in that area. After returning to Montana, Mansfield worked in the copper mines and then, at the urging of his future wife, resumed his education, studying at the Montana State School of Mines, earning a high-school diploma through a correspondence course, and in 1930 entering the University of Montana. He received a bachelor's degree in 1933, joined the university's faculty, and the following year was awarded a master's. A growing interest in politics led Mansfield to seek the Democratic nomination for Montana's seat in the House of Representatives in the 1940 primary election, and though unsuccessful, he ran again in 1942 and won. He served in Congress for 10 years and in 1952 won election to the Senate, despite the anticommunist, red-baiting tactics of Sen. Joseph McCarthy, who campaigned for his opponent. Mansfield served on the Foreign Relations Committee, was named assistant majority leader in 1957, and in 1961, when Lyndon B. Johnson became vice president, moved up to majority leader. He remained in that position—guiding the increasing opposition to U.S. involvement in the Vietnam War and being a leading voice against the Richard M. Nixon administration during the Watergate scandal—until he retired from the Senate in 1977. Mansfield then was appointed ambassador to Japan, a post he held for 10 years, and upon his return to the U.S. in 1988, he became a senior adviser at the investment banking firm Goldman Sachs.

Maria José of Savoy, Queen (Maria José Charlotte Henrietta Gabriella of Saxe-Coburg), Belgian-born Italian royal (b. Aug. 4, 1906, Ostend, Belg.—d. Jan. 27, 2001, Geneva, Switz.), was the last queen of Italy for 27 days, from May 9, 1946, when her husband succeeded his father as King Umberto II, until the Italian electorate voted to abolish the monarchy on June 2. While living in forced exile in Switzerland, Maria José, the daughter of King Albert I of Belgium, wrote books on Italian and Belgian royals. Although the Italian constitution banished all members of the royal House of Savoy, after her husband's death (1983) she was allowed (1988) to visit Italy as a private citizen.

Masoud, Ahmad Shah, Afghan resistance leader and politician (b. 1953, Bazarak, Afg.—death reported on Sept. 15, 2001, Takhar, Afg.), was a military leader in the Afghan mujahideen, first against the Soviets and the Soviet-backed Afghan government (1978–89) and then against the Taliban (from 1992). Masoud, an ethnic Tajik, studied engineering before the Soviet intervention in Afghanistan and then moved to Pakistan for military training. A clever and persistent guerrilla leader, he earned the sobriquet "the lion of Panjshir." Masoud briefly served as defense minister during the mujahideen interim government set up in 1989. After the Taliban took control of most of Afghanistan, including the capital, in 1996, he was the chief commander of the anti-Taliban forces that came to be known as the Northern Alliance. Masoud died of wounds suffered during an attack by two suicide bombers on September 9, two days before the September 11 terrorist attacks in the U.S.

Masters, William Howell, American gynecologist (b. Dec. 27, 1915, Cleveland, Ohio—d. Feb. 16, 2001, Tucson, Ariz.), was a pioneer in the field of human sexuality research and therapy. With partner Virginia Johnson, who later (1971) became his wife, he founded what was known as the Masters & Johnson Institute and conducted hundreds of interviews and observations in extensive—and controversial—investigations of the physiological aspects of sexual activity; they published their findings in a series of best-selling books. Masters graduated from Hamilton College, Clinton, N.Y., in 1938 and received his medical degree from the University of Rochester (N.Y.) School of Medicine and Dentistry in 1943. After further study, including an internship in obstetrics and gynecology at the St. Louis (Mo.) Maternity Hospital and Barnes Hospital in St. Louis, he took (1947) a faculty position at the Washington University School of Medicine, also in St. Louis. His first work there was on hormone-replacement therapy. In 1954 Masters began the research that would bring him renown, and two years later he hired Johnson. During their studies they observed volunteers performing a vast range of sexual acts, and they often employed electronic monitors to note physiological changes their subjects experienced. Masters and Johnson's first book, *Human Sexual Response* (1966), reported the results of these studies. Although it was written in a clinical manner and was intended mainly for medical professionals, it

Researcher William Masters, with his colleague Virginia Johnson
© Bettmann/Corbis

became a best-seller. With the information they garnered from their research, Masters and Johnson devised new methods of treating sexual dysfunction. Especially controversial was their use of prostitutes as sexual surrogates to work with people suffering from sexual performance and enjoyment difficulties; this practice was later dropped, and "ordinary people" volunteers were used. The book *Human Sexual Inadequacy* (1970) described results of their therapeutic methods. As they continued their work, Masters and Johnson published such further books as *The Pleasure Bond* (1975; with Robert J. Levin); *Homosexuality in Perspective* (1979), in which they claimed the ability to change homosexuals' sexual orientation; *Human Sexuality* (1982; with Robert C. Kolodny); and *Crisis: Heterosexual Behavior in the Age of AIDS* (1988; with Kolodny). Masters and Johnson divorced in 1992 but continued working together until Masters closed the institute in 1994.

Mathews, Edwin Lee ("Eddie"), American professional baseball player (b. Oct. 13, 1931, Texarkana, Texas—d. Feb. 18, 2001, San Diego, Calif.), was one of major league baseball's most prolific hitters, with 512 home runs and 2,315 hits in his 17-year career, and was widely regarded as the best third baseman of the 1950s and early '60s. Mathews made his major league debut with the Boston Braves in 1952 and remained with the franchise when it moved to Milwaukee, Wis., in 1953 and to Atlanta, Ga., in 1966; he was the only person to play with the Braves in all three cities. He helped Milwaukee win the World Series in 1957. In Atlanta, Mathews and Hank Aaron established the all-time home-run record for teammates, with 863 between 1954 and 1966. Mathews played in 10 All-Star Games, and he was inducted into the Baseball Hall of Fame in 1978.

Maxim, Joey (Giuseppe Antonio Berardinelli), American boxer (b. March 28, 1922, Cleveland, Ohio—d. June 2, 2001, West Palm Beach, Fla.), was the world light heavyweight champion from 1950 to 1952. On Jan. 24, 1950, Maxim knocked out heavily favoured Englishman Freddie Mills in London to win the world light

heavyweight title. In one of the most memorable boxing matches in history, Maxim defended his title against Sugar Ray Robinson on June 25, 1952, at Yankee Stadium in New York City. The fight took place before a crowd of 48,000 spectators and with the temperature above 38 °C (100 °F). Late in the bout Robinson, who was ahead on the scorecards, began to suffer from fatigue and dehydration and failed to answer the bell for the 14th round. Maxim was awarded the victory by technical knockout. He lost the light heavyweight crown to Archie Moore later that year. Maxim was inducted into the International Boxing Hall of Fame in 1994.

Maximos V (Georges Hakim), Egyptian cleric (b. May 18, 1908, Tanta, Egypt—d. June 29, 2001, Beirut, Lebanon), was spiritual leader of the Greek Catholic Church from 1967 to 2000; his formal title was patriarch of Antioch and all the East and Alexandria and Jerusalem. He was ordained in 1930 and served as archbishop of Acre, Haifa, Nazareth and all Galilee from 1943 until his elevation to patriarch. Maximos V was regarded as a popular and politically shrewd leader to more than one million Greek Catholics. He was known for advocating closer ties with the Eastern Orthodox Church, and he was successful in cultivating good relations with leaders in the predominantly Muslim countries of Syria, Egypt, and Lebanon, where most of his followers lived.

Mayer, Hans Heinrich, German literary scholar (b. March 19, 1907, Cologne, Ger.—d. May 18, 2001, Tübingen, Ger.), was a distinguished academic and critic who sought to achieve a greater understanding of German literature and culture through the application of Marxist-socialist analysis. Mayer, a member of the German Jewish bourgeoisie, trained as a lawyer. He left Germany for France shortly after Hitler's rise to power in 1933 and spent most of World War II in Switzerland, returning to Frankfurt in the U.S.-occupied zone after the war. In 1948 he joined the faculty of the University of Leipzig (in the Soviet-controlled zone), where he was professor of cultural his-

tory (1948–50) and of German literature (1950–64). Increasingly dismayed by the restrictions of East Germany's officially sanctioned socialist realism, he defected to West Germany, where he was professor of German language and literature at the Polytechnical University in Hannover (1965–73). Mayer's authoritative works included studies on Georg Büchner, Bertolt Brecht, Thomas Mann, Johann Wolfgang von Goethe, Martin Luther, Friedrich Dürrenmatt, Richard Wagner, and Friedrich von Schiller.

Mbeki, Govan Archibald Mvuyelwa, South African nationalist (b. July 9, 1910, Nqamakwe, S.Af.—d. Aug. 30, 2001, Port Elizabeth, S.Af.), as a teacher, writer, labour organizer, and editor of the leftist newspaper *New Age*, was in the vanguard of the antiapartheid struggle against the South African government. Mbeki joined the African National Congress (ANC) in 1935 and rose to become national chairman in 1956. Arrested in 1963 for plotting to overthrow the government, he was one of the eight ANC leaders tried in the celebrated Rivonia Trial and sentenced to life imprisonment on Robben Island. His best-known book, *South Africa: The Peasants' Revolt*, reportedly was written on toilet paper in jail and smuggled to London, where it was published in 1964. Mbeki was released from prison in 1987. He won a seat in the country's first all-race Parliament in 1994 and five years later watched as his son, Thabo Mbeki, was sworn in as president.

McCorkle, Susannah, American jazz singer (b. Jan. 4, 1946, Berkeley, Calif.—d. May 19, 2001, New York, N.Y.), brought fresh meaning to popular songs through subtle inflections, rhythmic wit, and a sense of dramatic nuance; she sang in an unforced, smoky voice, and her swing made her a success in jazz clubs as well as cabarets. McCorkle's extensive repertoire ranged widely from Broadway to bop to contemporary jazz and pop material. She also wrote magazine articles about classic jazz singers; authored short stories, notably "Ramona by the Sea," which won a 1973 O. Henry Award; and conducted interactive music workshops for children. McCorkle, who reportedly suffered from depression, took her own life.

McGuire, Alfred James ("Al"), American

basketball coach and broadcaster (b. Sept. 7, 1928, New York, N.Y.—d. Jan. 26, 2001, Milwaukee, Wis.), was one of college basketball's most talented and innovative coaches, and he enjoyed a second career as a popular television broadcaster for collegiate games. McGuire played guard on the basketball teams at St. John's Preparatory School and St. John's University, both in Brooklyn, N.Y. He went on to play in the professional National Basketball Association, with the New York Knickerbockers (1951–54) and the Baltimore Bullets (1954–55), before coaching at Dartmouth College, Hanover,

N.H., from 1955 to 1957 and at Belmont (N.C.) Abbey College from 1957 to 1964. In 1965 he became basketball coach at Marquette University, Milwaukee, where he also served as athletic director from 1971 until his retirement in 1977. His career record was 404 games won and 114 lost. At Marquette his teams won 295 games and lost 80 and appeared in 11 postseason tournaments; McGuire led Marquette to the National Collegiate Athletic Association championship in 1977. He was a master of tactics in the final minutes of games. His penchant for drawing technical fouls from officials was viewed as a weakness by his critics and as a psychological ploy by his admirers. After 1977 he worked briefly as a sports equipment manufacturing executive before embarking on a highly successful 23-year broadcasting career. He was inducted into the Basketball Hall of Fame in 1992.

McGuire, Dorothy Hackett, American actress (b. June 14, 1918, Omaha, Neb.—d. Sept. 14, 2001, Santa Monica, Calif.), had a long stage and screen career in which she specialized in portraying gentle, warm, and intelligent women.

Kobal Collection/Powolny, Frank

Dorothy McGuire: integrity and strength

The qualities she projected—kindness, integrity, and inner strength—did not rely on glamour, and she was thus able to make a smooth transition into motherly roles in her later years. By age 13 McGuire had made her stage debut, opposite Henry Fonda in an Omaha Community Playhouse production of *A Kiss for Cinderella*. After moving to New York City, she acted on radio in a soap opera and in 1938 became an understudy in *Our Town*, taking over the character of Emily—and thus making her Broadway debut—when Martha Scott left the show. Three years later McGuire landed the lead in *Claudia;* she made her film debut in that role in 1943. She portrayed leading roles in numerous films, including *A Tree Grows in Brooklyn* and *The Enchanted Cottage* (both 1945); *The Spiral Staircase* (1946); *Gentlemen's Agreement* (1947), for which she was nominated for an Academy Award; and *Three Coins in the Fountain* (1954).

McGuire also continued performing onstage, with a tour in *Summer and Smoke* (1950) and a Broadway appearance in *Legend of Lovers* (1951) among her credits. Her transition to motherly roles began with *Friendly Persuasion* (1956) and continued in *Old Yeller* (1957), *The Remarkable Mr. Pennypacker* (1959), *Swiss Family Robinson* (1960), *The Dark at the Top of the Stairs* (1960), and, most notably, *The Greatest Story Ever Told* (1965), in which she portrayed the Virgin Mary.

McKay, (George Cadogan) Gardner, American actor, playwright, and novelist (b. June 10, 1932, New York, N.Y.—d. Nov. 21, 2001, Honolulu, Hawaii), achieved fame as the star of the popular television series *Adventures in Paradise*, which aired from 1959 to 1962. McKay abruptly abandoned his acting career when the series ended. After a number of years spent traveling around the world, he returned to the U.S. and became a playwright. One of his many plays, *Sea Marks* (1983), won the Los Angeles Drama Critics Circle Award. From 1977 to 1982 McKay was the drama critic for the *Los Angeles Herald-Examiner*. A novel, *Toyer*, appeared in 1999.

McKay, John Harvey, American football coach (b. July 5, 1923, Everettsville, W.Va.—d. June 10, 2001, Tampa, Fla.), guided the University of Southern California football team to four national titles—in 1962, 1967, 1972, and 1974. McKay also led the team to five Rose Bowl victories and was voted the national collegiate Coach of the Year in 1962 and 1972. From 1976 to 1984 he coached the Tampa Bay Buccaneers of the National Football League, but he achieved only a lacklustre record—44 victories, 88 losses, and 1 draw. McKay was elected to the College Football Hall of Fame in 1988.

McTaggart, David Fraser, Canadian environmental activist (b. June 24, 1932, Vancouver, B.C.—d. March 23, 2001, Perugia, Italy), as chairman of Greenpeace International from 1979 to 1991, was responsible for leading the environmental organization to worldwide prominence. McTaggart's involvement with Greenpeace began in 1972, when he sailed a yacht to Mururoa—an isolated atoll in the South Pacific—as part of a protest against the French government's nuclear testing in the area. He later organized other demonstrations against nuclear testing as well as campaigns to save whales, to protect Antarctica from mineral exploitation, and to end the practice of dumping nuclear waste at sea.

McVeigh, Timothy James, American terrorist (b. April 23, 1968, Pendleton, N.Y.—d. June 11, 2001, Terre Haute, Ind.), was put to death after having been convicted of bombing the Alfred P. Murrah Federal Building in Oklahoma City, Okla., on April 19, 1995; 168 persons died in the blast. McVeigh was the first federal prisoner to be executed since 1963.

Mérieux, Charles, French virologist (b. Jan. 9, 1907, Lyon, France—d. Jan. 18, 2001, Lyon), devised an efficient industrial technique for mass producing vaccines to fight such human

and veterinary viruses as those for polio, rabies, meningitis, diphtheria, tetanus, and foot-and-mouth disease. During World War II he expanded operations at the microbiological laboratory set up by his father, a protégé of Louis Pasteur, distributing blood plasma to members of the Resistance and a serum to help malnourished children. In 1947 Mérieux founded the French Institute of Foot-and-Mouth Disease (later renamed the Mérieux Institute), which fought an outbreak of that virus in the 1960s and stopped a 1974 outbreak of meningitis in Brazil by producing enough vaccine to inoculate some 90 million people. The Mériuex Institute later formed joint ventures with the Pasteur Institute and the pharmaceutical company Rhône-Poulenc. Mérieux also established foundations to train public health technicians, an epidemiological teaching centre, and a laboratory in Lyon to study hemorrhagic fever.

Metlitzki, Dorothee, American literary scholar, educator, and Jewish activist (b. July 27, 1914, Königsberg, East Prussia [now Kaliningrad, Russia]—d. April 14, 2001, Hamden, Conn.), was a noted scholar of medieval English and Arabic literature and of the works of Herman Melville. After completing her education at the University of London, Metlitzki moved to Jerusalem, where she helped found the English department at Hebrew University and, after the establishment of Israel in 1948, mustered support for the country while traveling around the world. She settled in the U.S. in 1954. Metlitzki taught at Yale University from 1964 until her retirement in 1984. In 1977 she published a major work in comparative literature, *The Matter of Araby in Medieval England*.

Meyer, Harry Martin, Jr., American pediatric virologist (b. Nov. 25, 1928, Palestine, Texas—d. Aug. 19, 2001, Kenmore, Wash.), was co-developer of the first vaccine against rubella (German measles), refinement of which resulted in the MMR (measles, mumps, and rubella) vaccine; he contributed to textbooks, published over 100 scientific papers, and achieved worldwide acclaim for his research on infectious diseases and vaccines to protect against them.

Mishin, Vasily Pavlovich, Soviet rocket scientist (b. Jan. 18, 1917, Orekhovo-Zuyevo, Russia—d. Oct. 10, 2001, Moscow, Russia), was named the chief designer of the Soviet lunar program when Sergey P. Korolyov died in 1966. Despite his accomplishments as an engineer on the Sputnik satellite program, Mishin lacked his charismatic predecessor's knack of maneuvering within the political bureaucracy. Faced with insufficient funding and a stifling level of secrecy imposed upon the Soviet space agency, Mishin's team failed to beat the U.S. in the race to the Moon. Mishin was removed from his post in 1974, but he reemerged in the 1980s.

Modjadji V, South African tribal ruler (b. 1936/37, Ga-Modjadji, Northern province, S.Af.—d. June 28, 2001, Pietersburg, S.Af.), was the revered Rain Queen of the Bantu-speaking Lovedu tribe, the latest representative of a 400-year-old matriarchal dynasty believed to have magical rainmaking powers, and South Africa's only reigning queen. As Rain Queen, Modjadji V served as the secular and religious leader of her people, although her brother handled most administrative details because of the seclusion her position traditionally required. Modjadji V was initiated into the dynasty's rainmaking secrets after her mother, Queen Modjadji IV, succeeded to the crown in 1960, and she gained the throne upon the latter's death in 1982. In recent years she was seldom called on to make rain, but Modjadji V, like her predecessors, was respected and consulted by tribes throughout the region as well as by national leaders, including former president Nelson Mandela. Her great-grandmother, Queen Modjadji II, was the inspiration for H. Rider Haggard's 1887 novel *She*.

Moore, Francis Daniels, American surgeon (b. April 17, 1913, Evanston, Ill.—d. Nov. 24, 2001, Westwood, Mass.), was the chief surgeon at Peter Bent Brigham Hospital in Boston when in 1954 a team under his direction performed the first successful human organ transplant—a kidney transplant between identical twins. Moore graduated from Harvard University in 1935 and from Harvard Medical School in 1939. After an internship and residency at Massachusetts General Hospital, he worked at Brigham Hospital from 1948 to 1976. He also served as professor of surgery at Harvard Medical School until his retirement in 1981. In addition, Moore helped develop procedures for the care of postoperative patients. His memoirs, *A Miracle & a Privilege: Recounting a Half Century of Surgical Advance,* appeared in 1995.

Muhlstock, Louis, Polish-born Canadian painter (b. April 23, 1904, Narajow, Pol.—d. Aug. 26, 2001, Montreal, Que.), was celebrated for his artistic depictions of the Great Depression. Muhlstock emigrated with his family to Montreal in 1911. He studied art in Paris from 1928 to 1931, then returned to Montreal to become a full-time painter. Many of his works, rendered in a modernist style, portrayed street scenes and unemployed workers in Montreal. Muhlstock was a founding member of the Contemporary Art Society of Montreal and of the Federation of Canadian Artists. He was made an Officer of the Order of Canada in 1990.

Muñoz, Juan, Spanish sculptor (b. June 17, 1953, Madrid, Spain—d. Aug. 28, 2001, Ibiza, Spain), created moody and challenging installation artworks, most of which featured monochromatic human figures placed amid unnerving architectural spaces and often incorporating animatronics and sound. In 2000 Muñoz received Spain's highest cultural award, the Premio Nacional de Belles Artes. His last completed significant work, which was installed in London's Tate Modern in June 2001, was "Double Bind," a vast structure that filled half the museum's grand turbine hall with a false suspended floor, a working elevator, and sculpted figures seemingly frozen in time. A retrospective of Muñoz's work opened at the Smithsonian Institution's Hirshhorn Museum in Washington, D.C., on October 18.

Narayan, R.K. (Rasipuram Krishnaswami Narayanswami), Indian novelist, short-story writer, and essayist (b. Oct. 10, 1906, Madras [now Chennai], India—d. May 13, 2001, Chennai), was a spellbinding storyteller whose fictional creation, the small town of Malgudi, enchanted readers around the world with its dusty milieu and endearingly eccentric inhabitants; his gentle prose and wry humour brought small-town India alive. Narayan, the third of eight children born into a liberal Tamil family, spent an idyllic childhood in his grandmother's Madras house. He was schooled at Maharaja's College, Mysore, and after graduation (1930) briefly worked as a schoolteacher and a newspaper reporter before turning to writing full time. In September 1935 Malgudi, a town bearing the palimpsests of both Mysore and Madras but smaller than either, debuted in *Swami and Friends*. Narayan's first novel suffered several rejections before Graham Greene recommended it to Hamish Hamilton, who published the work. Greene also shortened Narayanswami's last name to Narayan. (Their correspondence lasted until Greene's death in 1991, and they met once, in 1956.) Narayan's next books, *The Bachelor of Arts* (1937) and *The Dark Room* (1938), also won critical praise. Disregarding the tradition of arranged matches, Narayan fell in love with and married Rajam in 1933. Her death in 1939 plunged him into desolate literary sterility, broken by the autobiographical *The English Teacher* (1945). Narayan never remarried, and he raised his daughter, Hema, alone. *Mr. Sampath* (1949), *The Financial Expert* (1952), and *Waiting for the Mahatma* (1955) were followed by his finest work, *The Guide* (1958). The latter—about a conman turned swami who discovers sanctity through self-sacrifice—was filmed in Hindi. *The Vendor of Sweets* (1967), *The Painter of Signs* (1976), and *A Tiger for Malgudi* (1983) also visited Malgudi and its characters. Besides 15 novels, Narayan published the short-story collections *Lawley Road* (1956) and *Under the Banyan Tree and Other Stories* (1985), as well as a 1974 memoir, *My Days*. He was awarded the Padma Bhushan and membership to the upper house of Parliament, and he was also short-listed twice for the Nobel Prize. Later novels included *Talkative Man* (1986), *The World of Nagaraj* (1990), and *Grandmother's Tale* (1992), his last and the only one not set in Malgudi. His works were widely translated.

Nguyen Van Thieu, Vietnamese military leader and politician (b. April 5, 1923, Tri Thuy, French Indochina [now in Vietnam]—d. Sept. 29, 2001, Boston, Mass.), was president of the Republic of Vietnam (South Vietnam) from 1967 to 1975. Although he had U.S. support, he eventually blamed American policies for the collapse of South Vietnam. In 1945 Thieu, the son of a small landowner, joined the Viet Minh against the French. He soon left the Viet Minh, however,

because of its communist orientation. In 1947 he entered the National Military Academy in Da Lat, and in 1949 he was commissioned as an officer in the army organized by the French. Thieu later undertook military studies in France, in the U.S., and elsewhere, and for four years beginning in 1954, he was head of the National Military Academy. In 1963 he helped organize a coup, undertaken with U.S. approval, against South Vietnamese Pres. Ngo Dinh Diem. Thieu emerged as chief of state in 1965. In 1967 he won election as president, and he was reelected without opposition in 1971. He headed the government during the period of the major U.S. intervention in the war against the Viet Cong and North Vietnam. An authoritarian president, he was at the same time generally considered to be a weak and indecisive political and military leader. He opposed the Paris peace agreements of 1973 but was forced to accept a cease-fire and the withdrawal of U.S. troops, with the promise that other military assistance would continue. By early 1975 North Vietnamese troops had overrun the northern and central provinces of South Vietnam. On April 21, 1975, only days before the fall of the capital, Saigon, he fled the country, leaving his successor, Duong Van Minh (*q.v.*), to surrender. Thieu lived at first in London and then in the U.S., where he remained almost entirely out of public view.

Noble, Maurice, American animator (b. May 1, 1910, Spooner, Minn.—d. May 18, 2001, La Crescenta, Calif.), helped create some of the most famous animated features in entertainment history. Noble's career began at Walt Disney Productions, where he worked on such classic films as *Snow White and the Seven Dwarfs* (1937), *Fantasia* (1940), *Dumbo* (1941), and *Bambi* (1942). He later worked for Warner Bros. and Metro-Goldwyn-Mayer. With Chuck Jones, Noble designed highly popular animated versions of several Dr. Seuss books, including *How the Grinch Stole Christmas!* (1966) and *The Cat in the Hat* (1971).

Nygaard, Jens, American pianist and conductor (b. Oct. 26, 1931, Stephens, Ark.—d. Sept. 24, 2001, New York, N.Y.), was the maverick founder and director of the Jupiter Symphony, which for more than two decades offered concerts of rare and unusual classical music in New York City. Nygaard was noted for conducting obscure works by early 19th-century composers—among them, Louis Spohr, Carl Reinecke, and Carl Czerny—and for finding forgotten works by Wolfgang and Leopold Mozart, among others. As his Jupiter Symphony staggered from one financial crisis to the next, Nygaard was criticized for overworking and underpaying his young musicians—after one concert he could afford to pay each of them only subway tokens and a book of Shakespeare's sonnets. Nonetheless, he ensured that the orchestra played a third of its concerts for charities. Nygaard's mother gave him his first piano lessons, and his father had played clarinet in John Philip Sousa's band; Nygaard himself could play most orchestra instruments by the time he entered Louisiana State University on a clarinet scholarship. He received his bachelor's (1957) and master's (1958) degrees from the

Juilliard School of Music in New York City. After suffering a mental breakdown in 1959, he endured a period of homelessness. During the 1960s and '70s, he made his reputation for wide-ranging musical tastes by leading orchestras, sometimes featuring himself as piano soloist, in and around New York. In 1979 he formed the Jupiter Symphony, named for Wolfgang Mozart's last symphony, and the Rockefeller Foundation contributed a $35,000 grant, but the iconoclastic Nygaard refused further Rockefeller aid rather than establish a conventional orchestra board.

Oakes, John Bertram, American newspaper editor (b. April 23, 1913, Elkins Park, Pa.—d. April 5, 2001, New York, N.Y.), was the editorial-page editor for the *New York Times* from 1961 to 1976; he was credited with devising the modern op-ed page format by including opinion articles written by both the newspaper's own columnists and outside writers. Oakes worked as a reporter for the *Washington Post* and served in the U.S. Army during World War II before joining the *Times* in 1946. Until 1961 the paper's editorial page was largely viewed as impartial, but under Oakes's guidance, it began to champion liberal causes. Oakes was a contributing columnist at the *Times* from 1978 into the early 1990s. He received a George Polk Award for lifetime achievement in the field of journalism in 2001.

O'Connor, Carroll, American character actor (b. Aug. 2, 1924, New York, N.Y.—d. June 21, 2001, Culver City, Calif.), was classically trained and appeared in scores of movies and television programs, but to the majority of the viewing public, he was the irascible but lovable bigot Archie Bunker, the lead character in the groundbreaking sitcom *All in the Family* (1971–79) and its sequel *Archie Bunker's Place* (1979–83). Although Bunker was outspoken in his beliefs in ethnic and gender stereotypes, O'Connor brought out the character's humanity and made sympathetic his bewilderment at the rapidly changing society he was attempting to cope with. O'Connor served in the merchant marine during World War II and afterward attended the University of Montana and then the National University of Ireland in Dublin (B.A., 1952). He appeared in productions presented by the Gate Theatre in Dublin and also toured other European cities, but after returning to the U.S. (1954), he found it difficult to find acting jobs and instead earned a master's degree (University of Montana, 1956) and became a teacher. In 1958, however, O'Connor was cast in an Off-Broadway production of *Ulysses in Nighttown*, and his success in that show led to another Off-Broadway role, in *The Big Knife* (1959). He also amassed numerous TV and movie credits, including roles in the films *Lonely Are the Brave* (1962), *Cleopatra* (1963), and *What Did You Do in the War, Daddy?* (1966), but he was still relatively unknown when he was cast as Bunker in *All in the Family*, an adaptation of the edgier BBC series *Till Death Us Do Part*. Although the character initially stirred up enormous controversy with the outrageous closed-mindedness that Archie Bunker spouted at every op-

Carroll O'Connor (centre) as curmudgeon Archie Bunker

portunity—views that were the exact opposite of those held by O'Connor himself—the show grew in popularity as most of the audience came to recognize that it was the evident absurdity of Bunker's beliefs that was the target of the humour. The show spent five years in the number one spot, at its peak counting some 50 million weekly viewers, and O'Connor's performance as Bunker won him four best actor Emmy Awards. In 1989 he won a fifth Emmy for another successful series, *In the Heat of the Night* (1987–94). Following the 1995 suicide of his son, who had been struggling with alcohol and drug addiction, O'Connor dedicated much of his time to a crusade against drug abuse. His last film role was in *Return to Me* (2000).

Okawa, Isao, Japanese businessman (b. 1926, Osaka, Japan—d. March 16, 2001, Tokyo, Japan), was chairman of the Sega Corp. from 1984 until his death. Okawa was involved with a number of Japanese technology companies. He founded CSK Corp., a computer services company that was Sega's largest shareholder, and served on the boards of several other companies, including the ASCII Corp. and Bellsystem 24, Inc. As chairman of Sega he became responsible for shifting the company's emphasis away from the production of video games and toward software development.

Parker, Eddie ("Fast Eddie"), American billiards player (b. June 2, 1931, Springfield, Mo.—d. Feb. 2, 2001, Brownsville, Texas), was

a legendary pool player whose exploits reportedly inspired the critically acclaimed 1961 film *The Hustler*. Parker played the game from the age of nine and, after a stint in the U.S. Navy in the early 1950s, toured extensively as a money player. In 1959 Walter Tevis, a young pool hall worker whom Parker had befriended, published a novel entitled *The Hustler*, on which the hit film was based. Actor Paul Newman portrayed the Parker-like character "Fast Eddie" Felson in the movie and reprised the role in the film's 1986 sequel, *The Color of Money*. In later years Parker made appearances at billiards tournaments, gave exhibitions, and created instructional videotapes and books.

Paz Estenssoro, Víctor, Bolivian statesman (b. Oct. 2, 1907, Tarija, Bol.—d. June 7, 2001, Tarija), was elected president of Bolivia a record four times and was a founder of the Nationalist Revolutionary Movement (MNR) in 1941. During the course of his political career, Paz Estenssoro moved from leftist to free-market policies. He earned a law degree (1927) from the University of San Andrés in La Paz, where he later (1939–41) taught economics. Beginning in the late 1920s, he held a number of government positions, and in 1932–35 he fought in the Chaco War against Paraguay. In 1938 and 1940 Paz Estenssoro was elected to the Chamber of Deputies, and in 1951 he was elected president. A military junta prevented his taking office until, after three days of fighting, the MNR seized power in 1952. As president Paz Estenssoro instituted radical changes, expropriating and nationalizing foreign-owned tin mines, extending suffrage to the 80% of Bolivians who had never voted before, and beginning a land-reform program. In 1956 he became ambassador to Britain, and in 1960 he was elected to a second term as president. Paz Estenssoro then began to turn rightward, but he was reelected in 1964 with 70% of the vote. Three months later, however, he was ousted in a military coup. He went into exile in Peru, where he taught economics at the University of Lima until, in 1971, he returned to Bolivia to become an adviser in the military government of Gen. Hugo Banzer Suárez. In 1979 he ran unsuccessfully for president, and in the election of 1985 he ran again. He finished second to Banzer in the popular vote in 1985, but neither had a majority. Congress chose Paz Estenssoro as president, and during his last term he reversed a number of earlier policies. He shut unprofitable tin mines and privatized others, instituted austerity measures to reduce the country's hyperinflation, and introduced a number of financial reforms. In 1989 he resigned as leader of the MNR.

Popular Bolivian Pres. Víctor Paz Estenssoro

Pérez Jiménez, Marcos, Venezuelan military dictator (b. April 25, 1914, Michelena, Venez.—d. Sept. 20, 2001, Madrid, Spain), headed a regime (1952–58) that was defined by its brutal suppression of dissent, ambitious public-works schemes, and widespread corruption. Pérez Jiménez attended the Venezuelan Military Academy from 1931 to 1934, graduating as a second lieutenant. In 1939–40 he studied at the Superior War School in Peru. He held a number of powerful positions in the military, including chief of the army staff (1945), chairman of the joint chiefs of staff (1946), and minister of defense (1946–52). Pérez Jiménez took part in a military coup in 1945 that ousted the dictator Gen. Isaias Medina Angarita and installed the democratic government of Rómulo Gallegos. In 1948 he was part of a three-man junta that overthrew Gallegos and then ruled until 1952. In 1952 Pérez Jiménez was declared president, and his appointment was confirmed by the parliament in 1953. Using his dreaded National Security police, he repressed all opposition—jailing and torturing critics—and censored the press, abolished labour unions, closed the national university, and earned the enmity of the Roman Catholic Church. His public-works projects included tunneling a highway from Caracas through the mountains to the Caribbean Sea. His regime was corrupt, and the country suffered high inflation. Nonetheless, as an anticommunist who controlled major oil supplies, he was supported by the U.S. In a plebiscite in 1957, Pérez Jiménez was confirmed for a second five-year term, but increasing unrest, which culminated in a general strike, forced him to flee the country on Jan. 23, 1958. He went to the Dominican Republic and then to the U.S. He was extradited in 1963 to stand trial for embezzlement but was freed in 1968 and went to live in Madrid.

Phillips, James Frederick ("the Fox"), American environmentalist (b. Nov. 20, 1930, Aurora, Ill.—d. Oct. 3, 2001, Aurora), employed a number of creative means of demonstrating his displeasure with pollution, especially that caused by corporations, and he acknowledged his efforts by leaving a note signed "the Fox," with a fox's face drawn in the o. Among his methods were the dumping of sewage in the reception room of the company that had released it into Lake Michigan and the placement of skunks on the doorsteps of executives of companies that polluted. In 1986 he started the Fox River Conservation Foundation.

Phillips, John Edmund Andrew, American singer and songwriter (b. Aug. 30, 1935, Parris Island, S.C.—d. March 18, 2001, Los Angeles, Calif.), was the guiding force behind the Mamas and the Papas, the folk-pop-rock group that in only about two years in the mid-1960s had six numbers in the top 10 and worldwide sales in the millions. They came to epitomize the hippy "flower power" era in the U.S. In the mid-1960s Phillips and his second wife, Michelle (Holly Michelle Gilliam), teamed up with Dennis Doherty and later Cass Elliot, moved to Los Angeles, and named themselves the Mamas and the Papas. Their first single, "California Dreamin'" (1965), reached the number four spot on the charts, and their next, "Monday, Monday" (1966), reached number one and won a Grammy Award. Eleven other hit singles followed. The group disbanded in 1968, reuniting only briefly in 1971. Phillips released a solo album, *John Phillips: The Wolfking of L.A.,* in 1970, and although he struggled with alcohol- and drug-abuse problems in the 1970s, he wrote music for films. In 1982 he toured with a new lineup of the Mamas and the Papas that included one of his daughters as well as Doherty. Phillips's autobiography, *Papa John,* was published in 1986, and in 1998 the Mamas and the Papas were inducted into the Rock and Roll Hall of Fame. Phillips had recently completed a new solo album.

Plumb, Sir John Harold, British historian and academic (b. Aug. 20, 1911, Leicester, Eng.—d. Oct. 21, 2001, Cambridge, Eng.), was a prolific author and a noted expert on the social and political history of 18th-century England, but he was almost as well-known for his sumptuous epicurean lifestyle, acerbic tongue, and reputation as a cantankerous eccentric. Plumb came from a working-class background and was educated at the University of Leicester before studying under historian G.M. Trevelyan at the University of Cambridge. In 1946 Plumb became a fellow at Christ's College, Cambridge, where he held numerous positions during his long academic career, including chairman of the history faculty (1966–68) and master of Christ's (1978–82). His learned and elegantly written books included *England in the Eighteenth Century* (1950), two biographical volumes on Sir Robert Walpole (1956 and 1960), and the text for the *Royal Heritage* television series (1977). Plumb was knighted in 1982.

Porter, Nyree Dawn (Ngaire Dawn Porter), New Zealand-born British actress (b. Jan. 22, 1940, Napier, N.Z.—d. April 10, 2001, London, Eng.), became one of British television's first romantic sex symbols for her portrayal of the mistreated beauty Irene Forsyte in *The Forsyte Saga,* the BBC's 26-part adaptation of John Galsworthy's novel sequence. The series, which was first broadcast in 1967, achieved equal success in the U.S. and numerous other countries and brought Porter international fame. Although she starred in the TV series *The Protectors* in the 1970s and had a successful stage and screen career, she never fully escaped the image of Irene. Porter was appointed OBE in 1970.

Pusey, Nathan Marsh, American educator (b. April 4, 1907, Council Bluffs, Iowa—d. Nov. 14, 2001, New York, N.Y.), was president of Harvard University from 1953 to 1971. Despite his success in revitalizing the university, he left the post embittered by confrontations with antiwar protesters in the late 1960s. He was educated at Harvard and earned a B.A. (1928), an M.A. (1932), and a Ph.D. (1937); his field was ancient history. In 1935 Pusey undertook the development of a great books program at Lawrence College, Appleton, Wis., and he later taught briefly at Scripps College, Claremont, Calif. Beginning in 1940 he taught at Wesleyan University, Middletown, Conn., and in 1944 he returned to Lawrence College as its president.

Verner Reed/TimePix

Harvard humanities booster Nathan Pusey

After becoming president of Harvard in 1953, Pusey led the university in a program of expansion, increasing the endowment, building new facilities, and hiring additional faculty, including many women. The university once again came to emphasize the humanities. Under his leadership the university adopted a "need blind" policy, admitting qualified students irrespective of their ability to pay. As a result of his policies, Harvard became a much more diverse university. In the 1950s Pusey defended the university against attacks by Sen. Joseph McCarthy that the faculty harboured members of the Communist Party. In the late 1960s he opposed equally strongly the tactics of antiwar protesters. When they took over the administration building in 1969, the president called in state and local police, and violence ensued. After leaving Harvard, he was president of the Andrew W. Mellon Foundation (1971–75) and of the United Board for Christian Higher Education in Asia (1979–80). Among his writings was the book *American Higher Education, 1945–70* (1978).

Quinn, Anthony Rudolph Oaxaca, Mexican-born American actor (b. April 21, 1915, Chihuahua, Mex.—d. June 3, 2001, Boston, Mass.), appeared in more than 150 films but was universally identified with one role especially—the earthy full-of-life title character in *Zorba the Greek* (1964), whom he inhabited so completely and comfortably that many of his later parts seemed also to be infused with that character's spirit. He embraced his offscreen life with the same gusto, a fact that was evidenced in part by the fact that his 13th child was born when he was in his 80s. Quinn had a variety of jobs—prizefighter, painter, and musician and preacher for an evangelist among them—and, besides studying for the priesthood, considered becoming an architect. To aid him in the latter, he began taking acting lessons after Frank Lloyd Wright suggested that he improve his speech, and before long he had been cast in the play *Clean Beds.* In 1936 Quinn appeared in a small part in the movie *Parole,* and he thereafter garnered a number of roles of various ethnic and/or outlaw characters in the films *They Died with Their Boots On* (1941), *The Ox-Bow Incident* (1943), *Guadalcanal Diary* (1943), and *Back to Bataan* (1945). His first lead role came in 1947 in *Black Gold*. That same year Quinn went to New York City and made his Broadway debut in *The Gentleman from Athens*. He followed that with touring as Stanley Kowalski in *A Streetcar Named Desire*, returning to New York in 1950 to replace Marlon Brando in that role, and then touring in *Born Yesterday* and *Let Me Hear the Melody*. He also appeared in a number of live television programs. Returning to Hollywood, Quinn had roles in *The Brave Bulls* (1951) and *Viva Zapata!* (1952), for which he won the first of his two Academy Awards for best supporting actor. He then made a few films in Italy, the most notable of which was Federico Fellini's *La Strada* (1954), in which he gave one of his finest performances. Quinn won his second Oscar for *Lust for Life* (1956) and went on to roles in the memorable motion pictures *Wild Is the Wind* (1957), *The Savage Innocents* (1959), *The Guns of Navarone* (1961), *Requiem for a Heavyweight* (1962), and *Lawrence of Arabia* (1962). Quinn returned to the stage in 1982 to tour with and appear on Broadway in a revival of the musical version of *Zorba*, and he also became a successful artist and sculptor. His final movie role was in the not-yet-released *Avenging Angelo*.

Rabal Valera, Francisco ("Paco"), Spanish actor (b. March 8, 1925, Aguilas, Spain—d. Aug. 29, 2001, Bordeaux, France), during his nearly 60-year stage and screen career, evolved from a handsome leading man into an impressive character actor, notably in films directed by Luis Buñuel—including *Nazarín* (1958), *Viridiana* (1961), and *Belle de jour* (1967)—and in Pedro Almodóvar's *¡Átame!* (1990; *Tie Me Up! Tie Me Down!*). Rabal was named best actor at the 1984 Cannes Film Festival for *Los santos inocentes* (*The Holy Innocents*) and at the 1991 Montreal Film Festival for *L'Homme qui a perdu son ombre* (*The Man Who Lost His Shadow*). In 2000 he won the Goya, Spain's highest acting award, for his leading role in *Goya* (1999; *Goya in Bordeaux*). Rabal had just been given a lifetime prize at the Montreal Festival and was flying back to Spain, where he was to receive the Donostia Lifetime Achievement Award at the San Sebastián Film Festival, when he suddenly was taken ill.

Rabbani, Mullah Mohammad, Afghan Muslim cleric (b. 1956?, Kandahar province, Afg.—d. April 16, 2001, Rawalpindi, Pak.), was the second most powerful man in Afghanistan's Taliban regime and the de facto chairman of the Taliban Council of Ministers (the equivalent of a prime minister). Rabbani attended an Islamic seminary before joining the jihad against the communist government installed after the Soviet Union's military intervention in Afghanistan in 1979. During the ensuing civil war, he was a founding member of the fundamentalist Muslim Taliban, originally a religious students' militia. It was widely reported that Rabbani had ordered the execution of former president Mohammad Najibullah after Taliban forces captured the capital, Kabul, in 1996.

Ramone, Joey (Jeffrey Hyman), American rock singer (b. May 19, 1951, New York, N.Y.—d. April 15, 2001, New York), was the lead singer for the influential punk rock band the Ramones. Founded in 1974, the Ramones created a new style of vigorous, thrashing music that became the foundation of punk rock; the first of the band's 21 albums, *Ramones*, appeared in 1976. A tall, gangly man with limited singing ability, Ramone was an unlikely rock star. Nevertheless, his feverish live performances helped the band develop a loyal following, and he was credited with sparking a fashion trend by always wearing torn jeans, black leather, and tinted sunglasses. The band's tour of England in 1976 proved a major inspiration for the punk movement in Great Britain, where the Ramones enjoyed greater commercial success than at home. With a shifting lineup, the group continued to record and perform into the 1990s before disbanding in 1996.

Rascher, Sigurd, German-born Scandinavian saxophonist (b. May 15, 1907, Elberfeld [now Wuppertal], Ger.—d. Feb. 25, 2001, Shushan, N.Y.), was a virtuoso performer who established the saxophone as a classical instrument and expanded its range to four octaves. A number of composers created works for him, and during his career he appeared with virtually all major orchestras in Europe and the U.S. From 1933 to 1938 he taught at the Royal Danish Conservatory in Copenhagen and at the Conservatory of Music in Malmö, Swed.

Raven, Simon Arthur Noël, British writer (b. Dec. 28, 1927, Leicester, Leicestershire, Eng.—d. May 12, 2001, London, Eng.), was a prolific author whose sardonic wit was showcased in the 10-novel sequence *Alms for Oblivion*. Raven's education in the classics influenced his moral outlook, and as a satirist he was often compared to Evelyn Waugh. He attended Charterhouse in Godalming, Surrey, but was expelled in 1945 for homosexual activity. Raven then joined the National Service and was stationed in India. In 1948 he won a scholarship to King's College, Cambridge, but he left in 1952 without finishing his work. He joined the army and served in Africa before resigning in 1956 to avoid a court-martial for gambling debts. Raven wrote essays and reviews for periodicals, including *The Spectator*, and his first published novel, *The Feathers of Death*, on homosexuality in the army, appeared in 1959. In 1961 Raven's publisher subsidized his move to Deal, Kent, to help him avoid the temptations of London, and he lived there for more than 30 years. *Alms for Oblivion*, a portrait of the upper classes from the end of World War II to the mid-1970s, began appearing in 1964. The novels were romans à clef, with the central character, Fielding Gray, loosely modeled on the author and other characters on classmates and friends, some of whom became prominent in British public life. A seven-volume sequel, *The First-Born of Egypt* (1984–92), was less successful. Raven had both artistic and financial success with his adaptations for television, including Aldous Huxley's *Point Counter Point* (1968), Anthony Trollope's *The Way We Live Now* (1969) and *The Pallisers* (1974), and *Edward and Mrs. Simpson* (1978).

Among his nonfiction was the collection of essays *The English Gentleman* (1961) and the memoir *Shadows on the Grass* (1982). Raven was a cricketer and an accomplished writer on the sport.

Reagan, Maureen, American political activist (b. Jan. 4, 1941, Los Angeles, Calif.—d. Aug. 8, 2001, Granite Bay, Calif.), was the daughter of former president Ronald Reagan and his first wife, Jane Wyman; a lifelong Republican, she was nevertheless an outspoken advocate of feminism and abortion rights—positions that clashed with her father's conservative views. After a brief career in film, television, and radio, Reagan devoted herself to political causes. Between 1985 and 1992 she directed a

Activist "first daughter" Maureen Reagan

political action committee that supported more than 100 women candidates across the country. She twice ran unsuccessfully for office herself, losing bids for the U.S. Senate in 1982 and for the U.S. House of Representatives in 1992. She served (1987–89) as cochair of the Republican National Committee. After her father was diagnosed with Alzheimer disease in 1994, Reagan became a spokeswoman for the Alzheimer's Association. She published a best-selling memoir, *First Father, First Daughter*, in 1989.

Reynolds, Peter John, British archaeologist (b. June 11, 1939, Shifnal, Shropshire, Eng.—d. Sept. 26, 2001, Kemer, Turkey), was one of the world's experts on the Iron Age and a pioneer in the field of experimental archaeology. Reynolds refused to accept theories about pre-Roman Iron Age life without practical testing, and he reconstructed Iron Age technologies, agricultural techniques, and building construction as authentically as possible. His work was most fully expressed at Butser

Ancient Farm, an open-air laboratory in Hampshire, which was established in 1972 as a replica of a working British farming settlement from about 300 BC.

Rhodes, James Allen, American politician (b. Sept. 13, 1909, Coalton, Ohio—d. March 4, 2001, Columbus, Ohio), was Ohio's longest-serving governor; although he was credited with improving his state's economy, infrastructure, and educational system, his career was overshadowed by his decision to quell an antiwar protest by sending National Guard troops to Kent (Ohio) State University—an action that led to the shooting deaths of four students on May 4, 1970. Rhodes worked his way up through the local ranks of the Republican Party to become mayor of Columbus at the age of 33. He lost his first bid for the governorship in 1954 but was elected eight years later; he held the post from 1962 to 1970. The day after the Kent State shootings, Rhodes lost the Republican primary for the U.S. Senate, but four years later he was reelected governor. He stepped down in 1982 and lost a bid for a fifth term as governor in 1986.

Richler, Mordecai, Canadian writer (b. Jan. 27, 1931, Montreal, Que.—d. July 3, 2001, Montreal), was celebrated for his vivid, boldly satiric portraits of the haves and have-nots of his native Quebec. His wickedly acerbic novels and essays often garnered outrage from offended parties (of which there were many) while consistently earning him critical acclaim. Born the son of a Jewish scrap-metal merchant in the largely Francophone province of Quebec, Richler considered himself "a minority within a minority" and continually returned to the examination of his experiences as such in his writings. After two years of study at Sir George Williams University in Montreal, Richler abandoned school to cultivate his dream of becoming a novelist and moved to Paris. His first novel, *The Acrobats* (1954), told the story of disillusioned expatriates in Spain à la Ernest Hemingway; Richler subsequently disowned this book owing to its lack of maturity. He spent the next several years in London, where he continued to produce novels. His first major recognition came with the publication of *The Apprenticeship of Duddy Kravitz* (1959), a coming-of-age story of a shrewd, street-smart young Jewish man making a way for himself in postwar Montreal; a literary success before it became a commercial one, the novel was made into a major motion picture in 1974. The film's screenplay (written by Richler) was nominated for an Academy Award. His next book to win critical acclaim was *Cocksure* (1968), a racy portrait of life in 1960s London; though banned in some places, it won the Canadian Governor General's Award. Richler won that award a second time for *St. Urbain's Horseman* (1971). That book was also short-listed for the Booker Prize,

as was a later book, *Solomon Gursky Was Here* (1989). In 1972 Richler moved back to Montreal with a wife and children in tow; his popular children's books chronicling the adventures of Jacob Two-Two developed out of the stories Richler made up to entertain his own children. Richler remained primarily in Montreal for the rest of his life, continuing simultaneously to delight and dismay in fiction and in fact. He contributed essays on various political concerns to leading publications and was most notably a stringent opponent of Quebec's anti-English language laws. His last book of fiction, *Barney's Version*, appeared in 1997, and *Mordecai Richler on Snooker* was published posthumously.

Ridler, Anne Barbara Bradby, British poet (b. July 30, 1912, Rugby, Warwickshire, Eng.—d. Oct. 15, 2001, Oxford, Eng.), wrote verse that was devotional and meditative, reflecting her Christian faith, and that dealt with domestic concerns such as marriage and motherhood. Her Elizabethan sense of form and her use of complex metaphors led critics to compare her to the 17th-century Metaphysical poets, particularly George Herbert and Thomas Traherne. She also wrote verse dramas, wrote and translated opera librettos, and served as the editor of a number of anthologies and collections. Ridler's father, a poet, was headmaster of Rugby School, and her mother was a children's writer. Members on both sides of the family were distinguished in literary, artistic, and clerical circles. She earned a degree from King's College, London, in 1932. From 1935 to 1940 she worked for Faber and Faber, part of this time as secretary to T.S. Eliot and as an assistant in publishing *The Criterion*. In 1938 she married Vivian Ridler, who later (1958–78) was printer to the University of Oxford. He published *Poems*, her first volume, in 1939. Other volumes included *Some Time After and Other Poems* (1972), *New and Selected Poems* (1988), and *Collected Poems* (1994; rev. ed. 1997). Verse dramas included *Cain* (1943) and *The Trial of Thomas Cranmer* (1956). She collaborated with composers as a librettist and did highly regarded performing translations of the librettos of operas by Cavalli, Monteverdi, and Mozart. *The Little Book of Modern Verse* (1941) and the *Faber Book of Modern Verse* (1951; rev. ed. 1960) were among the anthologies she edited. She also edited the poems of Traherne and the writings of Charles Williams, an early influence. In 1998 she received the Cholmondeley Prize for Poetry, and in 2001 she was appointed OBE.

Ridley, Sir (Nicholas) Harold Lloyd, British ophthalmologist (b. July 10, 1906, Kibworth Harcourt, Leicestershire, Eng.—d. May 25, 2001, Salisbury, Wiltshire, Eng.), devised the first successful artificial intraocular lens (IOL) transplant surgery for cataract patients. During World War II, Ridley observed that, when splinters of Perspex from cockpit canopies became lodged in the eyes of wounded pilots, they did not trigger immune reactions. Traditionally, following surgical removal of cataracts, patients were fitted with thick-lensed eyeglasses, but Ridley, on the basis of his wartime observations, developed IOL implants. The British medical community rejected the procedure as too risky,

so in 1949 Ridley conducted his first implant operation in secret. Despite some initial problems with complications, by the 1970s improved instrumentation and microsurgical techniques had made the procedure the most common treatment for cataracts in the U.S. British doctors eventually followed suit, and in 1986, some 15 years after his retirement from medical practice, Ridley was elected to the Fellowship of the Royal Society. He was knighted in 2000.

Riegner, Gerhart Moritz, German-born lawyer and human rights activist (b. Sept. 12, 1911, Berlin, Ger.—d. Dec. 3, 2001, Geneva, Switz.), was the first to warn government officials in London and Washington, D.C. (in August 1942, in what came to be known as the "Riegner telegram"), that the Nazis had made the decision to exterminate the Jews in Europe and had begun putting their plans in motion. To Riegner's horror, however, only in December did the Allies condemn the plan, and not until January 1944 did U.S. Pres. Franklin D. Roosevelt create the War Refugee Board to aid the Jews.

Ripley, S(idney) Dillon, II, American museum director, educator, and author (b. Sept. 20, 1913, New York, N.Y.—d. March 12, 2001, Washington, D.C.), was secretary of the Smithsonian Institution in Washington, D.C., from 1964 to 1984 and was responsible for greatly expanding the museum complex's activities and popularity. Ripley earned a Ph.D. from Harvard University in 1943 and served in the Office of Strategic Services during World War II. He joined the Yale University faculty as a professor of zoology and biology in 1946, and from 1959 to 1964 he was director of the university's Peabody Museum. During Ripley's tenure at the Smithsonian, the number of annual visitors to the complex rose from 10.8 million to more than 30 million. He added eight new museums to the institution, began television programs, and launched *Smithsonian* magazine.

Rogers, William Pierce, American lawyer and politician (b. June 23, 1913, Norfolk, N.Y.—d. Jan. 2, 2001, Bethesda, Md.), served as U.S. deputy attorney general (1953–57) and then attorney general (1957–61) during the administration of Pres. Dwight D. Eisenhower and was secretary of state (1969–73) under Pres. Richard M. Nixon. Though he had long been a close and loyal friend to Nixon, he was greatly overshadowed and rendered largely ineffectual by Nixon's national security adviser, Henry Kissinger, and was replaced by him early in Nixon's second term. Rogers was educated at Colgate University, Hamilton, N.Y., and Cornell University Law School, Ithaca, N.Y., and then became an assistant district attorney in New York City. Following World War II navy service, he returned to that office, and in 1947 he moved to Washington, D.C., and went to work on Capitol Hill. Rogers became friends with Nixon when he assisted Nixon in the House Committee on Un-American Activities investigation of the Alger Hiss case—the case that made Nixon's reputation. Rogers again came to Nixon's aid by first supporting him when, as Eisenhower's vice presidential candidate, Nixon was accused of having benefited from a political slush fund and then by helping him prepare his famous "Checkers" speech. While serving as attorney general, Rogers was central to the drafting of the Civil Rights Act of 1957 and to the establishment of the Justice Department's Civil Rights Division. Rogers returned to private law practice in 1961, and in 1964 he played a prominent role in a landmark Supreme Court case that further defined libel law and increased protection for journalists. While serving as Nixon's secretary of state, Rogers was generally kept in the dark about most foreign policy concerns, though he did get involved in seeking peace in the Middle East. After leaving office, untainted by the Watergate scandal, he once again went into private practice. In 1986 he served as chair of the commission that investigated the explosion of the space shuttle *Challenger*.

Ross, Herbert David, American dancer, choreographer, and film director (b. May 13, 1927, Brooklyn, N.Y.—d. Oct. 9, 2001, New York, N.Y.), had a career as a dancer on Broadway and choreographed for ballet companies, the stage, and motion pictures before turning to film directing. Among his numerous popular movies were five Neil Simon comedies—*The Sunshine Boys* (1975), *The Goodbye Girl* (1977), *California Suite* (1978), *I Ought to Be in Pictures* (1982), and *Max Dugan Returns* (1983)—and a drama that tapped his knowledge of the dance world, *The Turning Point* (1977); one of the main characters in the latter was modeled on his first wife, ballerina Nora Kaye. Ross dropped out of high school to pursue a performing career in New York City, where he danced in the choruses of several shows. While attending an exhibition of artworks by Francisco de Goya, he was especially impressed by the series "Los caprichos" and decided to choreograph a ballet inspired by them. *Caprichos* (1950) was so successful in a workshop that American Ballet Theatre included it in its 10th anniversary season. Ross created more ballets for the company during the following several years, most notably *The Maids* (1957), as well as choreographing for television and supper-club acts; he also did the choreography for a number of Broadway hits, including *A Tree Grows in Brooklyn* (1951), *I Can Get It for You Wholesale* (1962), which launched Barbra Streisand's career, *Anyone Can Whistle* (1964), and *On a Clear Day You Can See Forever* (1965), as well as such films as *Carmen Jones* (1954) and *Funny Girl* (1968). Ross made his film-directing debut with the musical version of *Goodbye Mr. Chips* (1969), and his hit movies included *The Owl and the Pussycat* (1970), *Play It Again, Sam* (1972), *The Last of Sheila* (1973), *Footloose* (1984), and *Steel Magnolias* (1989).

Roy, Pankaj Khirod, Indian cricketer (b. May 31, 1928, Calcutta [Kolkata], India—d. Feb. 4, 2001, Kolkata), was a solid opening batsman for Bengal (1946–68) and India (1951–60), scoring 11,868 first-class runs (average 42.38), including 2,442 runs in 43 Tests (average 32.56). Although Roy's highest individual first-class score was 202 not out, in 1955 he made 173 runs in a world-record 413 opening stand with Vinoo Mankad against New Zealand.

Their record for a first-wicket Test partnership still stood at the time of Roy's death.

Saddler, Joseph ("Sandy"), American boxer (b. June 23, 1926, Boston, Mass.—d. Sept. 18, 2001, Bronx, N.Y.), won 144 of his 162 professional fights, was world junior lightweight champion in 1949–51, and was world featherweight champion in 1948–49 and 1950–57. He was known as one of the hardest-punching small men in boxing, a reputation he most notably lived up to in his four extremely brutal title bouts with Willie Pep, three of which he won. Saddler was voted into the International Boxing Hall of Fame in 1990.

Salahuddin Abdul Aziz Shah (Tuanku Salahuddin Abdul Aziz Shah ibni al-Marhum Sultan Hisamuddin Alam Shah), Malaysian monarch (b. March 8, 1926, Klang, Malaya—d. Nov. 21, 2001, Kuala Lumpur, Malaysia), was the ceremonial head of state, or *yang dipertuan agong* (paramount ruler), of Malaysia from April 26, 1999. Salahuddin was educated in Malaya and at the University of London. In 1960 he succeeded his father as sultan of Selangor, and in 1999 he assumed the throne as independent Malaysia's 11th king (*agong*), in a constitutional monarchy that rotated among the sultans of the country's nine constituent states. Although he occasionally clashed with the prime minister, Salahuddin was particularly popular among the common people. In 1974 he declared that a great mosque should be built in the capital, Kuala Lumpur, which was located under his jurisdiction in Selangor; some 14 years later Southeast Asia's largest mosque was completed and named after Salahuddin.

Salem, Hidaya Sultan as-, Kuwaiti journalist and social activist (b. 1936, Ash-Shuwaykh, Kuwait—d. March 20, 2001, Kuwait City, Kuwait), campaigned against official corruption and for women's suffrage in Kuwait. Salem, one of her country's first female teachers and journalists, was a founding member (1964) of the Kuwaiti Literary League, a board member of the Kuwait Journalists Association, owner and editor in chief of *Al-Majalis* magazine, and the author of several books, notably *Women in the Koran*. She was assassinated on her way to a conference.

Sampson, Nikos (Nikos Georghiades), Greek Cypriot journalist and militant nationalist (b. Dec. 16, 1934, Famagusta, Cyprus—d. May 9, 2001, Nicosia, Cyprus), was president of Cyprus for eight days in 1974, but the coup of which he was a part led directly to the Turkish invasion that resulted in the island nation's division into two antagonistic parts. Sampson, a member of the EOKA guerrilla movement, was sentenced to death in 1957 for having assassinated British servicemen stationed in Cyprus, but he was released from prison when the island gained its independence in 1960. On July 15, 1974, when military forces under the direction of Greek officers overthrew the Cypriot government under Archbishop Makarios III, Sampson was named president. Turkish forces landed on Cyprus on July 20,

and three days later Sampson resigned in favour of Glafkos Clerides. In 1977 Sampson was the only participant in the coup to face trial. He was sentenced to 20 years' imprisonment, but in 1979 he was permitted to go to France for medical treatment. He returned to prison in 1990, but he was freed again because of his continuing poor health.

Sawaki, Kin'ichi, Japanese haiku poet (b.

Oct. 6, 1919, Toyama, Japan—d. Nov. 5, 2001, Tokyo, Japan), was one of the preeminent Japanese *haijin* during the second half of the 20th century; he served as president of the Haiku Poets Association from 1987 to 1993. Sawaki founded *Kaze* ("Wind"), an influential journal for new-style haiku, in 1946. His last haiku collection was *Ayako no te* (2000; "Ayako's Hand"). *Hakucho* (1995; "White Swan") won the 1996 Iida Dakotsu Prize, and his book of essays, *Showa haiku no seishun* (1996; "Springtime of Showa Era Haiku"), received the Haiku Poets Association Criticism Prize in the same year.

Schaap, Richard Jay ("Dick"), American journalist, biographer, and talk-show host (b. Sept. 27, 1934, Brooklyn, N.Y.—d. Dec. 21, 2001, New York, N.Y.), zestfully documented the inner workings of public figures, notably sports heroes. He came to notice in the 1960s alongside New York City newspapermen such as Jimmy Breslin, Pete Hamill, and Tom Wolfe—creators of a forceful, emotive style known as New Journalism. Genial and prolific, Schaap traveled easily among celebrities, penning best-selling autobiographies for sporting legends. He was an editor at *Newsweek*, the *New York Herald Tribune*, and *Sport Magazine*, and he won six Emmy Awards for his radio and television work, which included stints on NBC, ABC, and ESPN. His autobiography, *Flashing Before My Eyes*, appeared in 2001.

Schach, Rabbi Eliezer Menachem, Lithuanian-born Israeli Orthodox Jewish scholar and political leader (b. 1896?, Wabolnick [now Vabalninkas], Lithuania, Russian Empire—d. Nov. 2, 2001, Tel Aviv, Israel), as the spiritual leader of Israel's non-Zionist ultra-Orthodox political parties—Agudat Yisrael, Shas, and Degel Hatorah—wielded great influence on Israeli government policies. In 1940 Schach emigrated from Lithuania to British Palestine, where he was a revered scholar at the Ponevezh Yeshiva in Bnei Brak, near Tel Aviv. In 1984 he sided with Sephardic Jews who broke away from the predominantly Ashkenazic Agudat Yisrael to form Shas. Four years later he founded Degel Hatorah, which in 1992 joined with Agudat Yisrael in a new political bloc, United Torah Judaism. Schach preached moderation in Arab-Israeli relations, opposed Jewish settlements in the occupied territories, and supported trading land for peace, but his fierce contempt for the liberal secularism of the Labor Party led him to support right-wing governments.

Schindler, Emilie Pelzl, German-born industrialist (b. Oct. 22, 1907, Alt Moletein, Sudetenland, Austria-Hungary [now Czech Republic]—d. Oct. 5, 2001, Strausberg, Ger.), was the wife of Oskar Schindler, whom she helped in saving some 1,300 Jews during World War II. She married Schindler in 1928 and worked closely with her industrialist husband throughout the war, scrounging on the black market for food and other supplies for the Jews in their employ, as well as personally protecting them and caring for those too ill to work. In 1949 the bankrupt Schindlers moved to Argentina, where Emilie lived in poverty after her husband returned to Germany in 1957. She eventually was granted a small pension. She received Israel's Righteous Among the Nations award in 1993, and two years later Argentina bestowed its highest honour for foreigners, the Order of May. She delineated her wartime efforts in her 1997 memoir, *Where Light and Shadow Meet.*

Schultes, Richard Evans, American scientist (b. Jan. 12, 1915, Boston, Mass.—d. April 10, 2001, Boston), pioneered the field of ethnobotany, the study of indigenous peoples and their uses of hallucinogenic and medicinal plants. Schultes spent extensive time among native tribes in South America and collected more than 24,000 plant specimens from the Amazon region. Although his books on hallucinogenic plants were widely read by drug experimenters during the 1960s, he dismissed the notion of "mind expansion" espoused by counterculture figures such as Timothy Leary and maintained that such plants should be studied for their medicinal value. Schultes had a long association with Harvard University, where he earned a Ph.D. in biology in 1941 and worked as a curator, lecturer, and professor from 1954 to 1985. Among Schultes's numerous awards were the Tyler Prize for Environmental Achievement in 1987 and the Linnean Society Gold Medal in 1992.

Scindia, Madhavrao, Indian Hindu prince and politician (b. March 10, 1945, Bombay [now Mumbai], India—d. Sept. 30, 2001, Mainpur, India), succeeded (1961) his father as maharaja of the ancient princely state of Gwalior (which was absorbed by independent India in 1948 and incorporated into the modern state of Madhya Pradesh in 1956); after the government abolished Indian royalty, he went into national politics. Scindia was educated in England at Winchester College and New College, Oxford. He was first elected to Parliament in 1971 as a member of the Hindu nationalist party Jan Sangh (later the Bharatiya Janata Party), co-founded by his mother, Vijayraje Scindia. Later in the decade he switched to the Congress (I) Party. The charismatic and popular "commoner-king" was reelected eight times, regardless of his party affiliation. The switch, however, generated a permanent rift with his mother (who had been imprisoned briefly by the government in 1975) and led to years of legal battles between the two over the family estates. Before Vijayraje died in January 2001, she disinherited her son; her will

indicated that he should not have the honour of lighting her funeral pyre—a public ritual he undertook all the same. Scindia held several cabinet ministries in the 1980s and '90s and was deputy leader of Congress (I) at the time of his death. A sports enthusiast, he served as president (1990–93) of the Indian Cricket Control Board and had a cricket trophy named after him. Scindia was killed when the small plane in which he was a passenger crashed.

Sebald, Winifred Georg, German-born novelist and scholar (b. May 18, 1944, Wertach im Allgäu, Ger.—d. Dec. 14, 2001, Norwich, Eng.), entranced casual readers and critics alike with his haunting, richly imaginative, nonchronologically constructed stories. His work often explored themes of memory as they related to the Holocaust. Sebald's novels included *Schwindel, Gefühle* (1990; *Vertigo,* 1999), *Die Ausgewanderten* (1992; *The Emigrants,* 1996), *Die Ringe des Saturn* (1995; *The Rings of Saturn,* 1998), and *Austerlitz* (2001, in German and English).

Secombe, Sir Harry Donald, British comedian, actor, and writer (b. Sept. 8, 1921, Swansea, Wales—d. April 11, 2001, Guildford, Surrey, Eng.), starred as the gullible Neddie Seagoon in the revolutionary 1950s radio program *The Goon Show,* a zany, satiric, anarchic series that became a cult favourite and paved the way for such shows as the TV cult hit *Monty Python's Flying Circus.* Secombe left school at age 15 and worked as a clerk before joining the army during World War II. After the war he appeared as a comic at the Windmill Theatre in London's Soho district, in provincial variety theatres, and on such radio programs as *Variety Bandbox* and *Welsh Rarebit.* He also began gathering with Peter Sellers, Spike Milligan, and Michael Bentine in the Grafton Arms pub, where they shaped their jokes and banter into radio scripts. The quartet's work was accepted by BBC radio, and they began presenting *Crazy People* in 1951. It was renamed *The Goon Show* in 1952 and continued until early 1960 (without Bentine after the second season); a reunion, "The Last Goon Show of All," was broadcast in April 1972 to honour the BBC's 50th anniver-

sary. Secombe's most notable stage appearances were in the musical *Pickwick* (1963)—which featured "If I Ruled the World," a song he made famous—and *The Four Musketeers* (1967); his best-known film was *Oliver!* (1968), in which he played Mr. Bumble. He also contributed to *Punch* magazine and published the novels *Twice Brightly* (1974) and *Welsh Fargo* (1981), as well as two autobiographical works, short stories, and children's books. From 1983 to 1993 he was host of the Sunday evening religious TV program *Highway,* and from 1995 he presented another religious program, *Songs of Praise.* Secombe was made CBE in 1963 and was knighted in 1981.

Senghor, Léopold Sédar, Senegalese poet, philosopher, politician, and statesman (b. Oct. 9, 1906, Joal, Senegal, French West Africa—d. Dec. 20, 2001, Verson, Normandy, France), straddled the literary and political spheres in his dual roles—as Senegal's first president from 1960 until he voluntarily stepped down 20 years later and as one of Africa's most distinguished French-language poets and the leading figure of the "Négritude" movement, which reassessed African culture in the 1930s and '40s and affirmed the literary and artistic expression of the black African experience. Senghor studied at the Sorbonne in Paris and taught school in France until he was drafted into the military in 1939. Captured by German forces in 1940, he composed what later were acknowledged as some of his finest poems while being held in a prison camp. He was released in 1942 and joined the French Resistance. After the war he entered politics and represented his native land in the French National Assembly as the head of the Senegalese Democratic Bloc. Back home Senghor founded the socialist Senegalese Progressive Union (later the Socialist Party) and advocated a confederacy of former French colonies in West Africa. When the so-called Mali Federation broke apart and Senegal was granted separate independence, Senghor was unanimously elected president. Throughout his five terms in office, he worked to modernize his country, fight official corruption, and enhance international cooperation. In 1975 he

Harry Secombe as Mr. Bumble in Oliver!

authorized the formation of two opposition parties; five years later he was the first black African leader to hand over the reins of office in a peaceful transfer of power. As an acclaimed poet, Senghor's literary contributions included *Chants d'ombre* (1945), *Hosties noires* (1948), *Ethiopiques* (1956), *Nocturnes* (1961; Eng. trans. 1969), and *Oeuvre poétique* (1990), and he also edited a 1948 French-language verse anthology. In addition, he wrote numerous philosophical treatises on Négritude and published critical essays under the pseudonyms Silmang Diamano and Patrice Maguilene Kaymor. Senghor received scores of international awards, and in 1984 he became the first black member of the French Academy.

Shaffer, Anthony Joshua, British playwright and screenwriter (b. May 15, 1926, Liverpool, Eng.—d. Nov. 6, 2001, London, Eng.), delighted audiences with his ingenious comic thriller *Sleuth,* which played 2,359 performances in London's West End and more than 2,000 performances on Broadway, where it won the Tony Award for best play of 1970. He went on to write the screenplay for the 1972 Oscar-nominated film version. Shaffer devised several additional plays, notably *Murderer* (1975). He had far greater success, however, with his many other screenplays, including Alfred Hitchcock's *Frenzy* (1972), *The Wicker Man* (1973), *Sommersby* (1993), and three Agatha Christie adaptations, *Death on the Nile* (1978), *Evil Under the Sun* (1983), and *Appointment with Death* (1988). Shaffer also wrote novels in collaboration with his twin brother, Sir Peter Shaffer, playwright of *Equus* and *Amadeus.*

Shakhnazarov, Georgy Khosroevich, Armenian-born Soviet political analyst (b. Oct. 4, 1924, Baku, Transcaucasia, U.S.S.R. [now Baku, Azerbaijan]—d. May 15, 2001, Tula, Russia), as an advocate of glasnost and other political and social reforms, was one of Soviet Pres. Mikhail S. Gorbachev's most loyal and trusted political advisers. Shakhnazarov studied law at Azerbaijan State University and earned a doctorate in political science and philosophy from the Moscow Institute of Law. He worked as a writer and editor for the political publisher Politizdat and later for an international communist magazine based in Prague, where he quietly endorsed the unsuccessful reform movement. A senior official in the Central Committee, Shakhnazarov was responsible (1972–88) for guiding Moscow's relations with its Eastern European allies. In 1988, however, he was invited to join Gorbachev's personal staff. After the president's departure from office in 1991, Shakhnazarov devoted himself to analyzing globalization issues for the Gorbachev Foundation.

Shanahan, Eileen, American journalist (b. Feb. 29, 1924, Washington, D.C.—d. Nov. 2, 2001, Washington), was a pioneering journalist at the *New York Times* and, from 1977 to 1979, a spokeswoman for the administration of U.S. Pres. Jimmy Carter. Shanahan was hired to work in the Washington bureau of the *Times* in 1962. She covered national economic policy and was the first female reporter at the bureau to handle an assignment other than coverage of

presidential wives. Shanahan attracted widespread attention in 1974 when she and six other female employees at the *Times* successfully sued the newspaper for sex discrimination; the case was the subject of a 1992 book, *The Girls in the Balcony,* by one of Shanahan's fellow plaintiffs, Nan Robertson. After her service in the Carter administration, Shanahan worked as an assistant managing editor at the *Washington Star* and the *Pittsburgh* (Pa.) *Post-Gazette.* In 1987 she also helped found a magazine, *Governing,* devoted to covering developments in state and local governments.

Shannon, Claude Elwood, American mathematician and computer scientist (b. April 30, 1916, Petoskey, Mich.—d. Feb. 24, 2001, Medford, Mass.), laid the theoretical foundations for modern mass communications and came to be regarded as the "father of the information age." After graduating from the University of Michigan at Ann Arbor in 1936, he earned (1940) both a master's degree in

Hulton/Archive/Getty Images

Mathematician Claude Shannon with his electronic mouse

electrical engineering and a Ph.D. in mathematics from the Massachusetts Institute of Technology (MIT). He joined the mathematics department at Bell Labs in 1941, where he contributed to work on antiaircraft missile control systems. He remained affiliated with Bell Labs until 1972. Shannon became a visiting professor at MIT in 1956, a permanent member of the faculty in 1958, and professor emeritus in 1978. Shannon's master's thesis, "A Symbolic Analysis of Relay and Switching Circuits" (1940), used Boolean algebra to establish the theoretical underpinnings of digital circuits, which became fundamental to the operation of modern computers and telecommunications equipment. In 1948 Shannon published a paper entitled "A Mathematical Theory of Communication," which established basic tenets of information theory and contained the first published use of the term *bit* to designate a single binary digit. His formulation of information theory was an immediate success with communications engineers and continued to prove useful to later researchers. It also inspired many attempts to apply information theory in other areas, such as cognition, biology, linguistics, psychology,

economics, and physics. Aside from producing many provocative and influential articles on information theory, cryptography, and chess-playing computers, Shannon also designed various mechanical devices, including an electromechanical mouse—one of the first experiments in artificial intelligence.

Sherlock, Dame Sheila Patricia Violet, British hepatologist (b. March 18, 1918, Dublin, Ire.—d. Dec. 30, 2001, London, Eng.), was one of the world's leading authorities on diseases of the liver and served as professor of medicine (1959–83) at London's Royal Free Hospital School of Medicine, where the distinguished liver clinic and research centre was named in her honour. Sherlock received (1941) her medical degree from the University of Edinburgh. During her long career she did breakthrough research on different forms of hepatitis, cirrhosis, and liver cancer. She published hundreds of papers; edited several periodicals, notably the *European Journal of Hepatology* and the journal of the British Society of Gastroenterology, of which she was president; and wrote the classic textbook *Diseases of the Liver and Biliary System* (1955; 11th ed., 2001). Sherlock was appointed DBE in 1978 and was made a fellow of the Royal Society in 2001.

Shull, Clifford Glenwood, American physicist (b. Sept. 23, 1915, Pittsburgh, Pa.—d. March 31, 2001, Medford, Mass.), shared the 1994 Nobel Prize for Physics for his development of neutron-scattering techniques—in particular, neutron diffraction, a process that enabled scientists to better explore the atomic structure of matter. He shared the prize with Canadian physicist Bertram N. Brockhouse, who conducted separate but concurrent work in the field. After graduating from New York University with a Ph.D. in 1941, Shull began a career as a research physicist. His award-winning work was completed at Oak Ridge (Tenn.) National Laboratory from 1946 to 1955. In Shull's technique of neutron diffraction, a beam of single-wavelength neutrons was passed through the solid or liquid material under study. Neutrons interacting with atoms of the target material were scattered into a pattern that, when recorded on photographic film, yielded information about the relative positions of atoms in the material. Shull was also one of the first to demonstrate a way to use neutron scattering to study the structure of magnetic materials. From 1955 until his retirement in 1986, he was a professor at the Massachusetts Institute of Technology.

Sieff of Brimpton, Marcus Joseph Sieff, Baron, British businessman (b. July 2, 1913, Manchester, Eng.—d. Feb. 23, 2001, London, Eng.), succeeded his father, Baron Sieff, and uncle, Simon Marks, in the family business—retailer Marks and Spencer, which was founded by his maternal grandfather, Michael Marks, in 1884. Under Sieff's stewardship—as assistant managing director (1963–65), vice chairman (1965–67), joint managing director (1967–83), deputy chairman (1971), chairman (1972–84), president (1984–85), and honorary president (1985–2001)—the company, popularly known as M&S or "Marks & Sparks," grew into Britain's most profitable retailer and an international concern with outlets in several countries. Sieff was also a prominent fund-raiser for Zionist causes and the nonexecutive chairman (1986–93) of *The Independent* newspaper. In 1980 he became the first son of a life peer to be awarded his own life peerage.

Silva, Adhemar Ferreira da, Brazilian track star (b. Sept. 29, 1927, São Paulo, Braz.—d. Jan. 12, 2001, São Paulo), broke the triple-jump world record seven times and won two Olympic gold medals in the event. Between 1950 and 1956 Silva won 60 consecutive triple jumps. At the 1952 Olympics in Helsinki, Fin., he captured his first gold with a world-record jump of 16.22 m (53 ft 2³/₄ in). He broke the world record for a final time in 1955 with a jump of 16.56 m (54 ft 4 in) at the Pan American Games in Mexico City. A year later, at the Olympics in Melbourne, Australia, he won his second gold with a jump of 16.35 m (53 ft 8 in), an Olympic record. Silva was Brazil's cultural attaché to Nigeria from 1964 to 1966 and later worked as a film actor.

Silverstein, Abe, American aerospace engineer and researcher (b. Sept. 15, 1908, Terre Haute, Ind.—d. June 1, 2001, Fairview Park, Ohio), was an early space researcher who coined the name Apollo for the missions that resulted in placing the first human on the Moon's surface in 1969. Silverstein began his career with the National Advisory Committee for Aeronautics (NACA), the forerunner of the National Aeronautics and Space Administration (NASA). At NACA he helped create and direct the efforts leading to the Mercury series of manned spaceflights. From 1961 until his retirement in 1969, Silverstein was director of the NASA Lewis Research Center, Cleveland, Ohio.

Simon, Herbert Alexander, American social scientist (b. June 15, 1916, Milwaukee, Wis.—d. Feb. 9, 2001, Pittsburgh, Pa.), was awarded the 1978 Nobel Prize for Economics for his theory regarding decision-making processes in economic organizations. Simon studied political science at the University of Chicago, where he received a B.A. in 1936 and a Ph.D. in 1943. After holding various administrative posts, he was appointed (1949) a professor at Carnegie Mellon University, Pittsburgh, where he helped form several departments and schools, including the Graduate School of Industrial Administration and the School of Computer Science. He was best known for a theory of corporate decision making known as behaviourism. In his book *Administrative Behavior* (1947), he sought to replace the highly simplified classical approach to economic modeling and its concept of the single decision-making, profit-maximizing entrepreneur with an approach to decision making that recognized a multiplicity of factors. According to Simon, this framework provided a more sat-

isfactory theoretical approach for a world in which decision-making units were large enough for each one to have significant effects on prices and outputs. Crucial to this theory was the concept of satisfying behaviour—the achievement of acceptable levels of economic variables while keeping complications and risks at a minimum—as contrasted with the traditional emphasis on the achievement of maximum profits as the primary motivating factor. Simon's theory thus attempted to consider the psychological factors involved in decision making that classical economists tended not to take into account. Later in his career, Simon increasingly became involved in an attempt to create artificial intelligence by computer technology. He was the author of 27 books, including *Models of My Life* (1991), an autobiography.

Sinopoli, Giuseppe, Italian conductor and composer (b. Nov. 2, 1946, Venice, Italy—d. April 20, 2001, Berlin, Ger.), performed with an intensity and daring that made him one of Europe's most controversial orchestra leaders. Sinopoli simultaneously studied medicine, psychiatry, and anthropology at the University of Padua, Italy (M.D., 1971), and composition at the Venice Conservatory, whose faculty he joined in 1972. He founded the Bruno Maderna Ensemble for contemporary music in 1975. Sinopoli was principal conductor and music director of London's Philharmonia Orchestra (1984–94) and principal conductor of the Dresden (Ger.) State Opera (from 1991), as well as a frequent guest conductor throughout Europe. Known for his use of extreme tempos and psychological interpretations of the Romantic opera repertory, Sinopoli also conducted his own avant-garde compositions, notably his two-act opera *Lou Salomé* (1981). He recorded extensively for the Deutsche Grammophon label. Sinopoli died of a heart attack he suffered while conducting a performance of Verdi's *Aida* at the Berlin Opera House.

Slaughter, Frank Gill, American author and physician (b. Feb. 25, 1908, Washington, D.C.—d. May 17, 2001, Jacksonville, Fla.), was a surgeon-turned-writer who wrote some 56 best-selling novels, many of which dealt with medical issues. After earning a medical degree from Johns Hopkins University, Baltimore, Md., Slaughter worked as a surgeon in Florida from 1934 to 1942. He published his first novel, *That None Should Die,* a book about socialized medicine, in 1941, and after service in the U.S. Army during World War II, he devoted himself to writing full-time. Other novels with medical themes included *Doctors' Wives* (1967) and *No Greater Love* (1985). He was also noted for his historical novels, including *Constantine: The Miracle of the Flaming Cross* (1965), about the Roman emperor. Slaughter's books sold more than 60 million copies worldwide.

Söderbaum, Kristina, Swedish-born German film actress (b. Sept. 5, 1912, Stockholm, Swed.—d. Feb. 12, 2001, Hitzacker, Ger.), portrayed the Aryan ideal heroine in a series of films in the 1930s and '40s, particularly those directed by her husband, Veit Harlan, under the aegis of Nazi propaganda minister Joseph

Goebbels. The blonde, blue-eyed star's credits included *Jugend* (1938), *Die Reise nach Tilsit* (1939), and *Der Grosse König* (1942). Most controversial were her lead roles in the blatantly anti-Semitic propaganda film *Jud Süss* (1940; *Jew Süss*) and *Kolberg* (1943), said to be Goebbels's imitation of the American epic *Gone with the Wind.* After World War II Harlan was indicted for war crimes several times, but he was never convicted; he died in 1964. Söderbaum too was unapologetic for her role in Nazi filmmaking. She spent the postwar years photographing other film stars and occasionally acting in films and television programs.

Sørensen, Villy, Danish writer and philosopher (b. Jan. 13, 1929, Copenhagen, Den.—d. Dec. 16, 2001, Copenhagen), became one of the most influential Danish intellectuals of his generation. A prominent literary critic after World War II, he began his career writing modernist short stories whose subjects often drew upon the rich allegorical traditions of myth and religion and whose themes earned the writer comparisons to Hans Christian Andersen and Franz Kafka. These themes, which later were expanded in Sørensen's philosophical writings, dealt with notions of the extraordinary in the everyday and with the isolation of the self in society. His first short-story collection, *Sære historier* (1953; *Tiger in the Kitchen and Other Strange Stories,* 1957) was followed by *Ufarlige historier* (1955; *Harmless Tales,* 1991). His philosophical texts included *Digtere og dæmoner* (1959) and *Hverken-eller* (1961), which were both published during the period in which he was coeditor of *Vindrosen,* the leading Danish modernist journal of its time. During the 1960s he edited Karl Marx's *Økonomi of filosofi* (1962) and translated Kafka's short stories and works on Friedrich Nietzsche and Arthur Schopenhauer. Along with Niels I. Meyer and K. Helveg Petersen, Sørensen wrote *Oprør fra midten* (1978), a widely discussed treatise that put forth a nonpartisan, utopian vision of the future. Other notable works by Sørensen included *Formynderfortællinger* (1964; *Tutelary Tales,* 1988), *Ragnarok* (1982), and *Apollons oprør* (1989).

Sothern, Ann (Harriette Lake), American actress (b. Jan. 22, 1909, Valley City, N.D.—d. March 15, 2001, Ketchum, Idaho), achieved fame with her roles in films that included *Maisie* (1939) and *Lady Be Good* (1941) and as the star of the 1950s television series *Private Secretary.* Sothern began her film career after performing in Broadway musicals. Her success in the title role of *Maisie* led to a series of films that included *Maisie Was a Lady* (1941) and *Undercover Maisie* (1947). *Private Secretary* aired from 1953 to 1957, and another television series, *The Ann Sothern Show,* ran from 1958 to 1961. Sothern was nominated for an Academy Award for best supporting actress for her performance in the 1987 film *The Whales of August.*

Southern, Sir Richard William, British historian (b. Feb. 8, 1912, Newcastle upon Tyne, Eng.—d. Feb. 6, 2001, Oxford, Eng.), brought his love of medieval European history to an international audience with the publication of his first book, *The Making of the Middle Ages* (1953), which was later translated into more than two dozen languages. Southern, who spent his entire professional career (1933–81) at the University of Oxford, was knighted in 1974. His other books included *Western Views of Islam in the Middle Ages* (1962), *Saint Anselm and His Biographer* (1963), and *Scholastic Humanism and the Unification of Europe* (vol. 1, 1995; vol. 2, 2000).

Spedding, Sir David Rolland, British intelligence agent and administrator (b. March 7, 1943—d. June 13, 2001, London, Eng.), was from 1994 to 1999 chief of the Secret Intelligence Service (MI-6), the branch of the British government responsible for foreign intelligence and espionage activities. Under the traditional code name "C," Spedding, an Arabist who studied at Hertford College, Oxford, and the Middle East Centre for Arabic Studies, reorganized the post-Cold War MI-6 into a modern operation dealing with such international crimes as drug trafficking, money laundering, and terrorism. Although Spedding's appointment was officially announced in 1994, he never appeared in public, and no photographs of him were published until after his death. He was knighted in 1996.

Stanley, Kim (Patricia Beth Reid), American actress (b. Feb. 11, 1925, Tularosa, N.M.—d. Aug. 20, 2001, Santa Fe, N.M.), achieved renown on the Broadway stage in roles that ranged from the tomboyish Millie in *Picnic* (1953) to the nightclub singer Cherie in *Bus Stop* (1955) and to Masha in *The Three Sisters* (1964), attracting both critical and popular acclaim. She won Emmy Awards for two of her numerous television performances, in an episode of *Ben Casey* (1963) and as Big Mama in *Cat on a Hot Tin Roof* (1984), and although she acted in only five films, she garnered Academy Award nominations for two of her roles, a scheming medium in *Séance on a Wet Afternoon* (1964) and actress Frances Farmer's overpowering mother in *Frances* (1982).

Stargell, Wilver Dornel ("Willie"; "Pops"), American professional baseball player (b. March 6, 1940, Earlsboro, Okla.—d. April 9, 2001, Wilmington, N.C.), was one of the greatest hit-

© Bettmann/Corbis
Powerful Pirate Willie Stargell

ters in the history of baseball; he led the Pittsburgh Pirates to two World Series championships, in 1971 and 1979. He spent his entire major-league career with the Pirates, playing with the team from 1962 until his retirement in 1982. Stargell was a powerful and prolific hitter known for his ability to knock long home runs; he once held longest-home-run records in nearly half of the National League ballparks. Stargell swatted a total of 475 home runs, 2,232 hits, and 1,540 runs batted in. His career batting average was .282. After retiring as a player, Stargell coached briefly for the Pirates and, later, for the Atlanta Braves. He was inducted into the Baseball Hall of Fame in 1988. Stargell died of a stroke only two days after the Pirates unveiled a 3.65-m (12-ft) bronze statue of him in front of the team's new home in Pittsburgh, PNC Park.

Stassen, Harold Edward, American politician (b. April 13, 1907, West St. Paul, Minn.—d. March 4, 2001, Bloomington, Minn.), was the youngest governor of Minnesota, though his early political triumphs were overshadowed by his nine unsuccessful presidential campaigns. Stassen was elected Dakota county attorney at the age of 23 and governor at the age of 31; he served in the latter office from 1938 to 1943. He made his first bid to capture the Republican presidential nomination in 1948 and his last in 1992. Stassen was a delegate to the 1945 San Francisco Conference, which created the United Nations charter. He served as president of the University of Pennsylvania from 1948 to 1953 and later as a disarmament adviser in the Dwight D. Eisenhower administration.

Stern, Isaac, American violinist (b. July 21, 1920, Kremenets, Ukraine—d. Sept. 22, 2001, New York, N.Y.), was one of the 20th century's best-known musicians and an influential teacher and advocate for the arts. His parents immigrated to the U.S. in 1921, and he grew up in San Francisco, where he began violin studies at the age of eight. Stern made his Carnegie Hall, New York City, debut in 1943 and performed there more than 200 times during his life. His repertoire ranged from Bach to 20th-century composers and included contemporary music. With pianist Eugene Istomin and cellist Leonard Rose, he formed one of the greatest of modern piano trios, which performed from the 1960s until Rose's death in 1984. He made more than 100 recordings, and in 1995 Sony Classical issued the 44-compact disc set *Isaac Stern: A Life in Music*. He performed on a number of Hollywood sound tracks, and the documentary *From Mao to Mozart: Isaac Stern in China*, based on a 1979 tour, won an Academy Award in 1981. He promoted the careers of a number of younger musicians, including the violinists Itzhak Perlman and Pinchas Zukerman and the cellist Yo-Yo Ma. In 1960 Stern organized a campaign to save Carnegie Hall from demolition, and he served as chairman of the Carnegie Hall Corp. until his death. He oversaw the hall's restoration in 1986 and the celebration of its centenary in 1991. Stern, active in political causes, took a role in the creation of the U.S. National

AP/Wide World Photos

Carnegie Hall hero Isaac Stern

Endowment for the Arts in the 1960s and became chairman of the America-Israel Cultural Foundation in 1964. A supporter of Israel, he refused to perform in Germany. His autobiography, *My First 79 Years*, written with novelist Chaim Potok, was published in 1999. Among his many honours was the first Albert Schweitzer Music Award (1975).

Stix, Thomas Howard, American physicist (b. July 12, 1924, St. Louis, Mo.—d. April 16, 2001, Princeton, N.J.), was a pioneer in the field of plasma physics. After serving (1943–46) as a radio technician in the U.S. Army, Stix earned a B.A. from the California Institute of Technology and a Ph.D. from Princeton University. In 1953 he was recruited to join Project Matterhorn, an effort by scientists at Princeton to induce a controlled thermonuclear fusion reaction in a confined plasma, or electrified gas, in order to generate energy. Stix developed an antenna—later known as a Stix coil—that generated microwaves to heat plasma to the high temperatures necessary for fusion. Much of his later research involved refining the process of heating plasma with waves. Stix published an influential book, *The Theory of Plasma Waves*, in 1962. He was also responsible for establishing a graduate program in plasma physics at Princeton—the first of its kind. He received the Maxwell Prize, the highest award in plasma physics, in 1980.

Straight, Beatrice Whitney, American actress (b. Aug. 2, 1914, Old Westbury, N.Y.—d. April 7, 2001, Los Angeles, Calif.), won an Academy Award for best supporting actress in 1976 for her portrayal of a spurned wife in the motion picture *Network*. In 1953 she also earned a Tony Award for best supporting actress for her performance in Arthur Miller's play *The Crucible*, in which she portrayed a Puritan woman accused of witchcraft. Straight was a versatile actress whose career onstage, in films, and on television spanned more than half a century. She made her Broadway debut in *Bitter Oleander* in 1935 and appeared in her last film, *Deceived*, in 1991.

Sucksdorff, Arne, Swedish motion-picture director and cinematographer (b. Feb. 3, 1917, Stockholm, Swed.—d. May 4, 2001, Stockholm), was a noted documentary filmmaker and nature photographer. Sucksdorff studied painting and natural history before becoming a still photographer. He made his first documentary in 1939, and in 1949 his impressionistic study of Stockholm, *Människor i stad* (1946; "The Rhythm of the City"), won an Academy Award for best short subject. His feature-length films included *Det stora äventyret* (1953; *The Great Adventure*), a lyrical story of two boys and a wild otter, which captured the same beauty and love of nature as his nonfiction works. In the early 1950s he directed two films in India. Sucksdorff lived in Brazil for some 30 years, working with children and teaching documentary filmmaking for UNESCO. He made only one film while in Brazil, *Mitt hem är Copacabana* (1965; *My Home Is Copacabana*). In the 1990s Sucksdorff returned to Sweden, where he received a lifetime achievement award from the Göteborg Film Festival in 1997.

Sullivan, Leon Howard, American clergyman and civil rights leader (b. Oct. 16, 1922, Charleston, W.Va.—d. April 24, 2001, Scottsdale, Ariz.), was instrumental in helping to end apartheid in South Africa, in part by developing the "Sullivan Principles," a code of conduct for companies operating in that country. After graduating from West Virginia State College, Sullivan studied theology at Union Theological Seminary, New York City, and sociology at Columbia University, New York City. In 1950 he became pastor of the Mt. Zion Baptist Church in Philadelphia, a post he held until 1988. In 1964 Sullivan founded the Opportunities Industrialization Center, a job-training program for minorities. In 1977, six years after being named the first African American board member of General Motors Corp., he drew up the Sullivan Principles, which called for, among other things, equal pay and training opportunities for South African workers, regardless of race. In the mid-1980s Sullivan called for a multinational boycott of South Africa and persuaded many companies to pull out of the country. After Nelson Mandela was freed from prison in 1990, Sullivan worked with him to encourage companies to return to South Africa. Sullivan was awarded the U.S. Presidential Medal of Freedom in 1992.

Sylvester, (Anthony) David Bernard, British art critic and exhibition curator (b. Sept. 21, 1924, London, Eng.—d. June 19, 2001, London), was a towering figure in the British art world and a champion of Modernism, most notably the works of Francis Bacon, Henry Moore, Alberto Giacometti, and René Magritte. Although he had no formal training, Sylvester discovered an interest in art at age 17, unsuccessfully tried his hand at painting, and began writing art reviews in 1942 for the socialist weekly *Tribune*, of which George Orwell was literary editor. In 1945 Sylvester's last article for the magazine, a review of a book on Moore, attracted the notice of the artist, who hired him as a part-time assistant. Sylvester curated his first exhibition, a Moore retrospective, at the Tate Gallery in 1951. By the 1960s Sylvester had gained tremendous influence through his lectures and exhibitions, as well as his pithy reviews, articles, and catalog essays. He also had broadened his zeal to include nonfigurative artists, such as Jackson Pollock (whose work he had initially disparaged) and Willem de Kooning (he organized a de Kooning exhibition at the Serpentine Gallery in 1977), and Pop art. Sylvester appeared on the 1964 BBC television series *Ten Modern Artists* and at various times served on the Arts Council, the British Film Institute production board, the board of trustees for the Tate and Serpentine galleries, and the acquisitions board of the National Museum of Modern Art in Paris. His books included *Henry Moore* (1968), *Magritte: The Silence of the World* (1992), *About Modern Art: Critical Essays, 1948–1996* (1996), and the five-volume Magritte catalogue raisonné, which took him 25 years to complete. Sylvester was made CBE in 1983.

Szulc, Tadeusz Witold ("Tad"), Polish-born American journalist and author (b. July 25, 1926, Warsaw, Pol.—d. May 21, 2001, Washington, D.C.), was working as a foreign correspondent for the *New York Times* when he broke the story of the abortive 1961 invasion of Cuba by U.S.-financed Cuban exiles at the Bay of Pigs (Bahía de los Cochinos). Szulc later wrote at greater length about the incident in *The Cuban Invasion: The Chronicle of a Disaster* (1962) and published a biography of Fidel Castro, entitled *Fidel: A Critical Portrait*, in 1986. Szulc worked at the *Times* from 1953 to 1972, when he left to become a freelance writer. Among his other books were *Pope John Paul II: The Biography* (1995) and *Chopin in Paris* (1998).

Taglioni, Fabio, Italian engineer and motorcycle designer (b. Sept. 10, 1920, Lugo di Romagna, Italy—d. July 18, 2001, Bologna, Italy), during his 35-year career as the chief engineer for the state-owned Ducati (1954–89), transformed that company's motorcycles from cheap, low-powered scooters that were little more than motorized bicycles into high-priced, high-performance road-racing cycles. Taglioni was responsible for both the elegant appearance and the state-of-the-art engines for a series of Ducati motorcycles that won plaudits for their quality, styling, and speed and quickly came to dominate the world Superbike championships.

Tate, Buddy (George Holmes Tate), American tenor saxophonist (b. Feb. 22, 1915, Sherman, Texas—d. Feb. 10, 2001, Chandler, Ariz.), played with a big, rich tone and fluent melodic imagination, first with traveling swing bands in the Midwest. As a featured soloist with Count Basie (1939–48), he incorporated some of Lester Young's innovative melodic and harmonic concepts; he then led a popular band at the Celebrity Club in New York City (1953–74), toured internationally with all-star swing revival groups, and occasionally played lyric clarinet.

Teshigahara, Hiroshi, Japanese film director and flower arranger (b. Jan. 28, 1927, Tokyo, Japan—d. April 14, 2001, Tokyo), was a leading avant-garde film director who achieved worldwide fame with the release of *Suna no onna* (1964; *Woman in the Dunes*). Teshigahara made his directorial debut with *Otoshiana* in 1962. He was nominated for an Academy Award for best director for *Suna no onna*, which also won a Special Jury Prize at the Cannes International Film Festival and was nominated for an Academy Award for best film. After directing *Natsu no heitai* (1972; *Summer Soldiers*), Teshigahara turned his attention to flower arrangement and in 1980 he became grand master of the prominent Sogetsu School of Ikebana. He returned to directing films with *Rikyu* (1989). Teshigahara's last film was *Gohime* (1992; *Basara: The Princess Goh*).

Thérond, Roger Jean, French photojournalist and editor (b. Oct. 24, 1924, Sète, France—d. June 23, 2001, Paris, France), transformed *Paris-Match* from a conventional news weekly into one of Europe's most controversial and popular tabloids. Thérond joined *Paris-Match* in 1949; he was named senior editor the next year and editor in chief in 1962. After having left the magazine to work for a rival weekly, *L'Express*, in 1968, he returned in 1976. Thereafter he boosted flagging sales by switching to a steady diet of sensational news scoops, candid photographs (most of which he personally selected), and juicy gossip about public figures. *Paris-Match* often triggered international outrage and lawsuits, most notably when it published embarrassing snapshots of Monaco's royal family; Britain's Diana, princess of Wales; and former president François Mitterrand on his deathbed. Thérond, however, claimed that the peoples' right to know made all news coverage equally valid. Shortly before his death Thérond was honoured with an award from the International Center of Photography in New York City for his role in shaping European photojournalism.

Tjio, Joe Hin, Indonesian-born American geneticist (b. Nov. 2, 1919, Java, Indon.—d. Nov. 27, 2001, Gaithersburg, Md.), dispelled a 50-year-held belief that the number of chromosomes in the human cell was 48 when he established that the majority of human cells contain 46 chromosomes, arranged in 23 pairs. While working in 1955 at the Institute of Genetics in Lund, Swed., Tjio used a newly discovered technique to separate chromosomes from the nucleus of a cell; he helped establish modern cytogenetics—the study of the relationship between the structure and activities of chromosomes and the mechanisms of heredity—as a major branch of genetics. His work led to the discovery in 1959 that those people afflicted with Down syndrome have an additional chromosome in their cells. Tjio's early education was in strict Dutch schools in Indonesia, and he also became a student of photography (his father was a professional portrait photographer). After earning a degree in agriculture from the School of Agronomy in Bogor, he conducted research to develop hybrid plants that would be resistant to disease. His photographic skills were instrumental in preparing slide samples. Following a three-year imprisonment in a Japanese prison camp during World War II, he traveled to The Netherlands, where he secured a fellowship to study in Europe. He relaunched his studies on plant and insect cytogenetics and became a noted expert in the field. The government of Spain invited him to conduct studies on a plant-improvement program, and he spent 11 years in Zaragoza. During holidays, however, he carried out research at the Institute of Genetics, where he turned his attention to mammalian tissue. When Tjio published his findings about the correct number of chromosomes in the Scandinavian journal *Hereditas* in 1956, he created a stir because he failed to cite Albert Levan, the head of the Institute of Genetics, as first author of the paper, a longstanding European convention. Tjio threatened to throw the work away unless he was named first author. In the interests of scientific advancement, Levan relented. During the last 37 years of his career, Tjio worked in the U.S. at the National Institutes of Health, Washington, D.C., where he compiled a remarkable collection of scientific photographs that documented his work.

Tjupurrula, Johnny Warrangkula, Australian Aboriginal artist (b. 1925?, Minjilpiri, N.Terr., Australia—d. Feb. 12, 2001, Papunya, N.Terr.), was a pioneer of modern Aboriginal abstract art; his innovative works, which combined intricate calligraphic lines and tiny dots, drew international praise and defined the Aboriginal style known as "dot painting." In the 1960s Tjupurrula was transported with other nomadic Aboriginals from their tribal lands to Papunya, a bleak government settlement west of Alice Springs. There, encouraged by a local white schoolteacher, many residents began painting acrylic artwork and decorated trinkets. In 1997 one of Tjupurrula's early paintings, *Water Dreaming at Kalipinya* (1972), sold for a record price for Aboriginal art, A$206,000 (U.S. $263,145); the painting set another record three years later when it sold for more than double that price. Tjupurrula, however, who originally sold the painting for A$150 (about U.S. $75), struggled for years with alcoholism and poor health and died in poverty.

Trenet, Charles (Louis Charles Augustin Claude Trenet), French singer and songwriter (b. May 18, 1913, Narbonne, France—d. Feb. 19, 2001, Créteil, France), was for more than 60 years one of the most celebrated practitioners of the French chanson, a form of cabaret ballad distinguished by catchy tunes and sophisticated, witty lyrics. Trenet's exuberant stage presence and signature rumpled fedora helped earn him the nickname "la Fou chantant" ("the Singing Fool"). He composed more than 1,000 songs, most notably "Douce France" ("Sweet France"), "Que reste-t-il de nos amour?" ("I Wish You Love"), and "La Mer." The latter reportedly had some 4,000 recordings, the best known of which was Bobby Darin's "Beyond the Sea." Trenet, who also painted and wrote several novels, was made a member of the Legion of Honour in 1998.

Trigano, Gilbert, French businessman (b. July 28, 1920, St.-Maurice, Val-de-Marne, France—d. Feb. 4, 2001, Paris, France), was cofounder (1950), with his Belgian partner, Gérard Blitz, of Club Méditeranée, which introduced a revolutionary style of all-inclusive, cash-free holiday "villages." By the early 1980s there were more than 100 Club Med resorts, offering club "members" sun-drenched locations, group activities that included sports under the direction of attractive young "organizers," and a relaxed social environment that was conducive to sexual freedom. Trigano, a member of the Legion of Honour, retired as CEO in 1993 in favour of his son; in 1997 Club Méditerranée was reorganized under new ownership. In the 1980s Trigano also supervised an ambitious government program to install computers in French schools.

Trinh Cong Son, Vietnamese singer and songwriter (b. 1939, Dac Lac province, Vietnam, French Indochina—d. April 1, 2001, Ho Chi Minh City, Vietnam), composed more than 600 songs, but he was dubbed the "Bob Dylan of Vietnam" in the West for his poignant antiwar songs during the 1960s and '70s. After his first hit, "Uot Mi" ("Crying Eyes"), in 1957, Son became one of South Vietnam's best-known singer-songwriters. He was often under pressure from the government, which was disturbed by the pacifist lyrics of such songs as "Ngu Di Con" ("Lullaby," about a mother grieving for her soldier son). After the reunification of Vietnam in 1975, the new communist government sentenced Son to "reeducation" in a labour camp. In later years, however, his often melancholy songs about love and postwar reconciliation gained new acceptance and popularity.

Tupolev, Aleksey Andreyevich, Russian aircraft designer (b. May 20, 1925, Moscow, U.S.S.R.—d. May 12, 2001, Moscow, Russia), designed many of the Soviet Union's most successful jet airplanes, including the Tu-104 (the country's first commercial jetliner), the Tu-134, and the Tu-154, as well as the Tu-26 medium-range bomber and the Tu-160 swing-wing long-range strategic bomber; however, his most ambitious enterprise, the world's first supersonic passenger jet, the Tu-144, ended in failure. Tupolev became chief designer at Tupolev Design Bureau in 1963 and succeeded his father, the celebrated aircraft designer Andrey N. Tupolev, as chief of the design bureau in 1972. The Tu-144 had its first test flight in 1968, two months before the Concorde, and flew more than 100 scheduled flights within the Soviet Union, but fatal crashes in 1973 and 1977 spelled the project's end.

Tutin, Dame Dorothy, British actress (b. April 8, 1931, London, Eng.—d. Aug. 6, 2001, London), was one of the British theatre's most accomplished leading ladies during a 50-year stage career. Tutin's varied repertoire included most of the leading female characters in Shakespeare, Chekhov, and Ibsen, as well as Sally Bowles in the original 1954 London production of *I Am a Camera* and modern plays by John Osborne, Tom Stoppard, and Harold Pinter. Although Tutin concentrated on the theatre, she occasionally appeared on television and in motion pictures, notably as Cecily Cardew in her first film, *The Importance of Being Earnest* (1952), and as Polly Peachum in *The Beggar's Opera* (1953). Tutin was made CBE in 1967 and was elevated to DBE in 2000.

Uhse, Beate (Beate Köstlin Rotermund-Uhse), German entrepreneur (b. Oct. 25, 1919, Wargenau, German East Prussia [now in Poland]—d. July 16, 2001, Switzerland), revolutionized sexual attitudes in post-World War II Germany as the founder of Beate Uhse AG, Europe's largest chain of shops selling erotic products and the first sex-related company to be listed (1999) on the Frankfurt stock exchange. She obtained her pilot's license at age 18 and, after qualifying as a Luftwaffe fighter pilot, ferried planes to the front during the war. After her pilot husband was killed in action, Uhse settled in Flensburg, W.Ger., where she began printing and distributing advice on sex and contraceptive information, which was at that time illegal. Although often faced with official writs and public condemnation, Uhse was admired by many for her honest, even humorous, approach to sex. By the time her company went public, she controlled a mail-order catalog, a Web site, a chain of adult cinemas, an erotica museum, and boutiques throughout Germany that sold everything from contraceptive devices to lingerie to adult videos and sex toys.

Uslar Pietri, Arturo, Venezuelan novelist, journalist, and politician (b. May 16, 1906, Caracas, Venez.—d. Feb. 26, 2001, Caracas), was one of the world's leading Spanish-language writers and a fierce critic of political corruption in Venezuela. His novels included, most notably, *Las lanzas coloradas* (1931), *El camino de El Dorado* (1947), and *La isla de Robinson* (1981). In his fiction Uslar Pietri often used magic realism, and he was one of the first Latin American writers to employ that technique. He edited the Venezuelan daily newspaper *El Nacional* from 1969 to 1974. He also served as a senator from 1958 to 1973 and ran unsuccessfully for president in 1963. Uslar Pietri was outspoken in his belief that Venezuela's lucrative oil business had a corrupting influence on the country in general and on the government of Hugo Chávez Frías in particular.

Utaemon VI, Nakamura (Fujio Kawamura), Japanese actor (b. Jan. 20, 1917, Tokyo, Japan—d. March 31, 2001, Tokyo), was regarded as the preeminent performer of Japan's traditional kabuki theatre during his lifetime. Born into a family of kabuki actors, Utaemon VI made his theatrical debut in 1921. He specialized in *onnagata* (female) roles, considered the most demanding in the highly stylized art form. During his career he played more than 500 different roles. In the 1960s Utaemon VI toured the U.S., Europe, and the Soviet Union. He attempted to preserve the classical style, and to this end he encouraged novelist Mishima Yukio and others to write new kabuki plays in a style that conformed to traditional practices. He also helped revive old plays that were seldom performed. In 1968 the Japanese government designated Utaemon VI a Living National Treasure.

Uzaemon XVII, Ichimura (Bandô Mamoru), Japanese actor (b. 1916, Tokyo, Japan—d. July 8, 2001, Tokyo), was one of the greatest *tachiyaku* (male-role) actors in the traditional kabuki theatre of Japan. Ichimura was the nephew of Kikugoro Onoe VI, one of the foremost interpreters of kabuki plays. After debuting at the Imperial Theatre in Tokyo at the age of five, Ichimura went on to star in numerous dramas, one of the most memorable of which was an elaborately staged performance of the play *Shibaraku* ("Wait!") during the Tokyo Olympics in 1964. In 1990 the Japanese government designated him a Living National Treasure.

Vanden Boeynants, Paul, Belgian politician (b. May 22, 1919, Brussels, Belg.—d. Jan. 9, 2001, Aalst, Belg.), was a longtime member of Parliament (1952–85), the French-speaking leader of the centrist Social Christian Party (from 1961), defense minister (1972–79), and twice prime minister of Belgium (1966–68 and 1978–79). Although he was criticized for his handling of Belgium's 1968 language crisis and for his drastic policy of urban renewal in Brussels, it was a conviction for fraud and corruption in 1986 (and a subsequent three-year suspended sentence) that ended his career. In 1989 Vanden Boeynants returned to the headlines when he was kidnapped by a left-wing group; he was released a month later after payment of the 60 million Belgian franc (over $2 million) ransom.

Verdet, Ilie, Romanian politician (b. May 10, 1925, Comanesti, Rom.—d. March 20, 2001, Bucharest, Rom.), as the brother-in-law of Romanian dictator Nicolae Ceausescu, held a variety of government posts, including first deputy prime minster (1966–74) and prime minister (1979–82). After Ceausescu's overthrow and execution (1989), Verdet declared himself head of a provisional government that lasted about 20 minutes. In 1990 Verdet cofounded the opposition Socialist Labour Party.

Verey, Rosemary Isabel Baird Sandilands, British garden designer and writer (b. Dec. 21, 1918, Chatham, Kent, Eng.—d. May 31, 2001, London, Eng.), inspired horticulturists and amateur gardeners alike through her books and the award-winning 1.6-ha (4-ac) English garden at her home, Barnsley House. Verey was particularly known for her attention to detail and historical perspective and for her inspired use of textures, ornamental vegetables, and a year-round colour scheme. She studied mathematics and economics at University College, London, and married architectural historian David Verey in 1939. In 1951 her husband's parents ceded control of the family home, a 17th-century former rectory near Cirencester, Gloucestershire. In 1970 she opened the house's redesigned gardens to the public, and by the 1990s Barnsley House was welcoming up to 30,000 visitors a year. Verey lectured widely and appeared on the BBC television series *The English Country Garden* in the 1990s. She also designed plans for clients and friends, notably for the gardens at Highgrove for Charles, prince of Wales. Her books included *Classic Garden Design* (1984), *The Garden in Winter* (1988), and *Rosemary Verey's Making of a Garden* (1995). Verey was made OBE in 1996 and in 1999 received both the Victoria Medal of Honour from the Royal Horticultural Society

and a special award from the Massachusetts Horticultural Society.

Vicente, Esteban, Spanish-born American painter (b. Jan. 20, 1903, Turégano, Spain—d. Jan. 10, 2001, Bridgehampton, N.Y.), was a first-generation member of the avant-garde New York school of painting, which flourished from the 1940s to the '80s and established New York City as the epicentre of the international art world. In 1929, after training at the Royal Academy of Fine Arts of San Fernando in Madrid, Vicente moved to Paris, where he met Pablo Picasso. Vicente divided his time between Paris, Madrid, and Barcelona until 1936, when he relocated to New York City. During the 1940s Vicente began to create abstract paintings. He contributed to the highly publicized "Talent 1950" exhibition at the Kootz Gallery, which showcased paintings by New York school artists, and for awhile he shared a studio with Willem de Kooning. From 1964 until the mid-1980s, Vicente taught art at a number of universities, including Black Mountain (N.C.) College, New York University, and Yale University. In 1998 the Spanish government opened the Esteban Vicente Contemporary Art Museum in Segovia.

Wade, Henry Menasco, American attorney and prosecutor (b. Nov. 11, 1914, Rockwall, Texas—d. March 1, 2001, Dallas, Texas), served as district attorney of Dallas county from 1951 to 1987; he attracted national attention for his prosecution of Jack Ruby and for his role in the landmark abortion case *Roe v. Wade*. After Ruby shot and killed Lee Harvey Oswald, John F. Kennedy's assassin, in 1963, Wade successfully led the prosecution of Ruby the following year. In 1970 Wade was sued by Jane Roe (a fictional name used to protect the identity of Norma McCorvey), who sought to keep him from enforcing a state law that prohibited abortion; Wade's office defended the law, which the U.S. Supreme Court ultimately, in 1973, declared unconstitutional. Wade served as counsel to a Dallas law firm after stepping down as district attorney in 1987.

Walker, Arthur Bertram Cuthbert, II, American physicist and educator (b. Aug. 24, 1936, Cleveland, Ohio—d. April 29, 2001, Stanford, Calif.), helped develop solar telescopes used in 1987 to capture the first detailed images of the Sun's outermost atmosphere. Walker, a professor of physics at Stanford University from 1974 until his death, encouraged minorities and women to pursue careers in science, and among his students was Sally Ride, the first American woman to fly into outer space. Walker was appointed by Pres. Ronald Reagan to serve on the commission that investigated the causes of the 1986 space shuttle *Challenger* disaster.

Walker, David Mathieson, American astronaut (b. May 20, 1944, Columbus, Ga.—d. April 23, 2001, Houston, Texas), was the pilot of the space shuttle *Discovery* in 1984 and the commander of three later space shuttle missions. After graduating from the U.S. Naval Academy, Annapolis, Md., in 1966, Walker be-

AP/Wide World Photos

Space shuttle pilot David Walker

came one of the navy's "top gun" fighter pilots; he earned six Navy Air Medals for combat duty during the Vietnam War. NASA selected him to become an astronaut in 1978. As pilot of the *Discovery* shuttle, he played an integral part in the first space salvage mission in history; the crew successfully retrieved two communications satellites that had been stranded in the wrong orbits. Walker later served as mission commander of the *Atlantis* shuttle in 1989, *Discovery* in 1992, and *Endeavour* in 1995.

Walston, Ray, American actor (b. Nov. 22, 1914?, New Orleans, La.—d. Jan. 1, 2001, Beverly Hills, Calif.), had a long career filled with quirky, endearingly cranky characters on the stage, in movies, and on television but was especially popular as the extraterrestrial masquerading as Bill Bixby's earthling Uncle Martin in the TV series *My Favorite Martian* in the mid-1960s. Indeed, his portrayal of the antennaed alien was so successful that he thereafter had trouble shaking that image. Walston began his professional acting career in the late 1930s in Houston, Texas, and in 1943 went to the Cleveland (Ohio) Play House. He made his Broadway debut in 1945 in a small part in Maurice Evans's production of *Hamlet*. Appearances followed in such shows as *Summer and Smoke* (1948), for which he won the Clarence Derwent Award, and *The Rat Race* (1949), and in 1950 he began touring in *South Pacific* in the role of Luther Billis, a part he also played in the film version (1958). In 1955 Walston opened in his breakthrough role, Mr. Applegate—the devil—in *Damn Yankees*, for which he won a Tony Award and which he also repeated in the film version (1958). Walston went on to roles in such films as *The Apartment* (1960), *Paint Your Wagon* (1969), *The Sting* (1973), *Silver Streak* (1976), *Popeye* (1980), and *Fast Times at Ridgemont High* (1982). He appeared in TV series, most notably *Picket Fences* (1992–96). Walston's portrayal of the irascible Judge Henry Bone won him Emmy Awards in 1995 and 1996.

Warmerdam, Cornelius Anthony ("Dutch"), American pole-vaulter (b. June 22, 1915, Long Beach, Calif.—d. Nov. 13, 2001, Fresno, Calif.), was the first in his sport to clear 4.57 m (15 ft), which he attained on April 13, 1940, with a bamboo pole, and he went on to break the outdoor record another six times. His outdoor record of 4.77 m (15 ft 7³/4 in), set in 1942, and indoor record of 4.79 m (15 ft 8¹/2 in), set in 1943, were not broken until 1957 and 1959, respectively, and the men who broke them used more flexible aluminum poles.

Waugh, Auberon Alexander, British writer and satirist (b. Nov. 17, 1939, Dulverton, Somerset, Eng.—d. Jan. 16, 2001, Combe Florey, near Taunton, Somerset), simultaneously delighted and outraged readers with acerbic wit and conservative snobbery in his pointed, pithy, and cruelly funny commentaries on British politics and society. The eldest son of novelist Evelyn Waugh, "Bron" published five novels, beginning in 1960, but in 1972 he renounced fiction for journalism. Thereafter, his often vitriolic columns appeared in such publications as *The Independent, Daily Telegraph, Daily Mirror, New Statesman, Spectator, Evening Standard,* and *Private Eye,* for which he wrote a regular column from 1970 to 1986. As editor (1986–2000) and editor in chief (2000–01) of *Literary Review,* Waugh annually bestowed the good-humoured Bad Sex Award, granted to the novel containing the year's worst prose describing sex. Waugh published several collections of his writings and an autobiography, *Will This Do?* (1991).

Waxman, Albert Samuel ("Al"), Canadian actor (b. March 2, 1935, Toronto, Ont.—d. Jan. 17, 2001, Toronto), achieved fame with his roles on the television series *The King of Kensington* and *Cagney & Lacey.* Waxman studied acting at the Playhouse Theatre in New York City and appeared in a number of films, including *The War Lover* (1962) and *Vengeance Is Mine* (1974), before turning to television. In his most memorable role, he played shopkeeper Larry King on the Canadian Broadcasting Corp. sitcom *The King of Kensington* from 1975 to 1980. From 1981 to 1988 he portrayed Lieut. Bert Samuels on the popular police drama *Cagney & Lacey.* Among later roles, Waxman played a prison warden in the critically acclaimed motion picture *The Hurricane* (1999).

Welty, Eudora Alice, American short-story writer and novelist (b. April 13, 1909, Jackson, Miss.—d. July 23, 2001, Jackson), was known for the lyricism, perception, wit, and humanity that infused her works. Although she wrote primarily about the inhabitants of her native Deep South and their everyday lives, her characters and stories had an appealing universality in their depictions of human emotions and relationships, and her stories were included in numerous anthologies. Welty was educated at Mississippi State College (now University) for Women (1926–27), the University of Wisconsin (B.A., 1929), and the Columbia University Graduate School of Business (1930–31), New York City, but returned home when her father

died in 1931. In 1933 she began traveling throughout Mississippi as a publicity agent for the Works Progress Administration (WPA), interviewing and photographing people of all classes and writing stories. Welty had her first story, "Death of a Traveling Salesman," published in 1936 in *Manuscript,* a small literary magazine, and more stories appeared in such publications as the *Southern Review, The Atlantic Monthly,* and *The New Yorker.* One of these, "Why I Live at the P.O.," became a classic, and Welty was especially pleased that it inspired Steven Dorner to name the Eudora e-mail program after her. For another story, "A Worn Path," she won the first of her six O.

© Philip Gould/Corbis

Southern novelist Eudora Welty

Henry Awards. A collection of short stories, *A Curtain of Green* (1941), was Welty's first book. Among those that followed were the novella *The Robber Bridegroom* (1942), which was later adapted for the musical stage; *Delta Wedding* (1946), her first full-length novel; *The Ponder Heart* (1954), an adaptation of which became a Broadway hit; and the autobiographical *The Optimist's Daughter* (1972), for which she received a Pulitzer Prize. Welty was also noted for her photographs, which reflected the dignity and humanity of their subjects. A collection of pictures she took while with the WPA was exhibited in New York City in 1936 and years later achieved greater acclaim; 100 of the photos were published in *One Time, One Place: Mississippi in the Depression* in 1971, and many were included in a book of more than 200 pictures, *Eudora Welty Photographs* (1989). Another book of images, *Country Churchyards* (2000), was her last published work. Welty counted among her many awards the Presidential Medal of Freedom (1980) and the French Legion of Honour (1996), and she became (1998) the first living writer to be included in the Library of America series.

Whitehouse, Mary Hutcheson, British schoolteacher and campaigner (b. June 13, 1910, Nuneaton, Warwickshire, Eng.—d. Nov. 23, 2001, Colchester, Eng.), was a founder (1964) and president of the Clean Up TV Campaign (later [1965] the National Viewers' and Listeners' Association and then [1994] Mediawatch) and for some three decades pursued her goal of removing sexual and violent content from television, stage, and film. Although she did not achieve most of her goals, she came to be considered a national institution and had a few victories, such as the Indecent Displays Act (1981). She was made CBE in 1980.

Wildenstein, Daniel Leopold, French-born art historian, art dealer, and thoroughbred race horse owner (b. Sept. 11, 1917, Verrières-le-Buisson, France—d. Oct. 23, 2001, Paris, France), was the head of Wildenstein & Co., a secretive and tightly controlled billion-dollar art dynasty that was founded in the 1870s by his grandfather and later moved to New York City by his father. The family company, which Daniel Wildenstein joined in New York in 1940, owned a vast collection of valuable art (including many works by the French Impressionists), as well as art galleries in Japan and New York. Wildenstein, a respected art historian, compiled the catalogues raisonnés for Monet, Manet, and Gauguin. As the owner of a major horse-racing stable in France, Wildenstein was named Owner of the Year six times; his horses won the Prix l'Arc de Triomphe, France's most prestigious race, on four occasions.

Williams, Harrison Arlington, Jr., American politician (b. Dec. 10, 1919, Plainfield, N.J.—d. Nov. 17, 2001, Denville, N.J.), was a prominent Democrat who later served time in federal prison after being convicted of bribery and conspiracy in the Abscam scandal. An advocate of liberal policies, Williams served in the U.S. House of Representatives from 1953 to 1957 and in the U.S. Senate from 1959 to 1982. Williams was one of a number of politicians implicated in Abscam, a sting operation carried out by federal agents who posed as wealthy Middle Eastern businessmen and offered bribes in exchange for political favours. After his conviction on May 1, 1981, Williams resigned from office and eventually served three years in prison. Pres. Bill Clinton refused his request for a pardon in 2000.

Winning, Thomas Joseph Cardinal, Scottish cleric (b. June 3, 1925, Wishaw, Scot.—d. June 17, 2001, Glasgow, Scot.), was the spiritual leader of Roman Catholics in Scotland; his service as archbishop of Glasgow from 1974 until his death—cardinal from 1994—was marked by his unflinching defense of Catholic views on abortion and homosexuality. He supported the Pro-Life Initiative, a program that gave money and other aid to women who agreed not to have abortions, and forcefully argued against equating homosexual relationships with traditional marriage. He was also a notable advocate of public efforts to combat poverty and homelessness. Winning studied at the Pontifical Scots College in Rome. He was ordained in 1948, and became a bishop in 1971, three years before his elevation to archbishop.

Withers, (Elizabeth) Audrey, British journalist (b. March 28, 1905, Hale, Cheshire, Eng.—d. Oct. 26, 2001), was appointed editor of *Vogue* in 1940 and over the following two decades increased both the magazine's size and its subscription base through her transformation and modernization of its content. She was made OBE in 1953, and she published two books: *The Palaces of Leningrad* (1973), in collaboration with her second husband, Victor Kennett, and her autobiography, *Lifespan* (1994).

Woodcock, Leonard Freel, American labour leader and diplomat (b. Feb. 15, 1911, Providence, R.I.—d. Jan. 16, 2001, Ann Arbor, Mich.), served as president of the United Automobile Workers (UAW) from 1970 to 1977. Woodcock dropped out of Detroit City College for financial reasons in 1933 and went to work as a machine assembler; he later joined a small union that eventually became affiliated with the UAW. Woodcock served as an international representative for the UAW from 1940 to 1946 and held a number of posts within the union before being elected its vice president in 1955. He was elevated to president in 1970 and in that year led the union through a highly publicized strike against General Motors Corp., which ended after General Motors agreed to significant wage increases and cost-of-living protection for employees. Woodcock was chosen by Pres. Jimmy Carter to serve as an envoy to China in 1977 and succeeded in negotiating the reestablishment of U.S.-Chinese diplomatic relations. Woodcock served as ambassador to China in 1979–80, after which he worked as an adjunct professor of political science at the University of Michigan at Ann Arbor.

Woods, Donald, South African journalist and antiapartheid campaigner (b. Dec. 15, 1933, Elliotdale, S.Af.—d. Aug. 19, 2001, Sutton, Surrey, Eng.), captured the attention of the world in 1977 with an exposé on the death while in police custody of his friend Steve Biko, a prominent young black activist and founder of the Black Consciousness Movement. Woods, who trained as a lawyer, was a veteran editor (from 1965) of the liberal white *Daily Dispatch* newspaper in East London, S.Af., and was arrested repeatedly by the government for his antiapartheid activities. When he published details regarding Biko's death at the hands of the South African police, Woods was banned and the newspaper was shut down. He escaped to Lesotho and then to the U.K., where he wrote and campaigned for international sanctions against the racist South African government. Woods's book *Biko* (1978) and his personal experiences as described in his autobiography, *Asking for Trouble* (1981), inspired the 1987 film *Cry Freedom*. In 1978 he was the first private citizen invited to address the UN Security Council. Woods was made CBE in 2000, shortly before *Rainbow Nation Revisited* was published.

Wright, L(aurali) R(ose) ("Bunny"), Canadian novelist (b. 1939, Saskatoon, Sask.—d. Feb. 25, 2001, Vancouver, B.C.), was internationally known for her crime novels, many of which featured detective Karl Alberg of the Royal Canadian Mounted Police, Wright's most popular character. Her first novel, *Neighbours* (1979), won the Alberta Best First Novel Award. The first title in her Karl Alberg series, *The Suspect* (1985), was awarded the Mystery Writers of America's Edgar Allen Poe Award for best crime novel. Two later Alberg mysteries, *A Chill Rain in January* (1990) and *Mother Love* (1995), received the Crime Writers of Canada's Arthur Ellis Award. Wright's final novel, *Menace*, was published posthumously.

Xenakis, Iannis, Romanian-born Greek-French composer and architect (b. May 29, 1922, Braila, Rom.—d. Feb. 4, 2001, Paris, France), based his music on mathematical principles, particularly theories of probability. Although his music was generated by the rigorous application of nonmusical ideas, the results were often powerful and moving. He created orchestral, ensemble, and solo works for traditional instruments and also used electronically generated sounds. He studied music as a child, but he was trained principally as an engineer and architect, entering the Polytechnic School in Athens in 1940. A member of the Greek resistance during World War II, he was wounded in 1945 and lost sight in one eye. He received a degree in 1947 but, under a sentence of death for his political activities, fled to Paris. From 1947 to 1959 he worked at the studio of Swiss architect Le Corbusier; there Xenakis was involved in the design of projects that included the Philips Pavilion at the 1958 Brussels World's Fair. During this time he also studied with a number of prominent French musicians, including Olivier Messiaen, and in 1953–54 he completed *Metastasis*, a work for orchestra and his first to gain widespread attention. Other early works included *Pithoprakta*, for trombones, percussion, and strings, which

Musical innovator Iannis Xenakis

Hulton-Deutsch Collection/Corbis

George Balanchine later combined with *Metastasis* to form a ballet. *Concerto PH*, using the amplified sound of burning charcoal, was created for the Philips Pavilion. Xenakis also produced electronic music to accompany laser projections, as at the site of ancient Persepolis, now in Iran, in 1971. He created a number of works for solo percussion, as well as *Pleiades* for percussion sextet, along with works using literary texts. In 1966 he formed a centre for the study of mathematical music. He taught at Indiana University at Bloomington (1967–72) and at the Sorbonne (1973–89).

Yardley, John Finley, American aeronautical engineer (b. Feb. 1, 1925, St. Louis, Mo.—d. June 26, 2001, Chesterfield, Mo.), was responsible for helping to coordinate the first manned spaceflights conducted by the U.S. Yardley began his career as a structural and aeronautical engineer at McDonnell Aircraft Corp. in 1946. He was recruited as a project engineer in the U.S. space program in 1958. After managing the launching operations for the Mercury series of manned spaceflights from 1961 to 1963, he served as technical director of the Gemini program from 1964 to 1967. As an associate administrator for spaceflights for NASA from 1974 to 1981, he helped develop the space shuttle program and oversaw the launch in 1981 of *Columbia*, the first reusable rocket-launched space vehicle. That same year he returned to work at McDonnell Douglas; he retired from the company as senior vice president in 1989.

Ze'evi, Rechavam, Israeli soldier and politician (b. Aug. 20, 1926, Jerusalem, Palestine—d. Oct. 17, 2001, Jerusalem, Israel), pursued hard-line ultranationalist policies, most notably in support of his outspoken belief that all Palestinians should be removed from the Israel-occupied territories in Gaza and the West Bank and transferred to Arab countries and his claim that the kingdom of Jordan should belong to Israel. Ze'evi joined the fight for an independent Israel at age 18 and rose through the army ranks to become military commander in the West Bank. After retiring as a major general in 1974, he served (1974–77) as an antiterrorism adviser to Prime Minister Yitzhak Rabin. In 1988 Ze'evi, who often drew criticism for his inflammatory remarks, entered politics at the head of the tiny ultranationalist Moledet (Homeland) party. Two days after he resigned as minister for tourism, Ze'evi was shot dead, reportedly by the militant Popular Front for the Liberation of Palestine in retaliation for the Israeli assassination of PFLP leader Abu Ali Mustafa (*q.v.*).

Zubkovskaya, Inna (Inna Borisovna Izraelyeva), Russian ballerina and teacher (b. Nov. 29, 1923, Moscow, U.S.S.R.—d. Feb. 5, 2001, St. Petersburg, Russia), as a member of the Kirov (now Mariinsky) Ballet from 1941 to 1970, distinguished herself in most of the leading roles in the classic ballets, including Phrygia in *Spartacus*, one of the roles created on her. She continued to teach and coach until her death.

Events of 2001

Worldwide protests against government policy, globalization, war, and other concerns took centre stage in 2001.

Agriculture and Food Supplies

Food SUPPLIES in 2001 were plentiful, and PRICES remained low. The WTO adjudicated trade DISPUTES between the U.S. and Europe, while many Europeans stopped eating BEEF because of livestock DISEASES. Agriculture felt the tugs of a DECLINING world ECONOMY.

NATIONAL AND INTERNATIONAL ISSUES

Food Production. Total agricultural and food production increased slightly in 2001, while global per capita food production was 1.1% lower. (*See* TABLE I.) Taken together, less-developed countries increased output, while production in developed countries was slightly lower; per capita food production in both regions fell.

Two regions had persistently weak production compared with the 1989–91 period. Transitional countries in the former Soviet Union and Eastern Europe continued to have agricultural and food production at levels 70% of those for 1989–91, and little recovery was evident in 2001. These countries faced agricultural bottlenecks due to poor infrastructure, weak credit markets, underdeveloped input and land markets, weak macroeconomic performance, and incomplete privatization. Moreover, reduced agricultural production in some of these economies may have been affected by market forces. Production difficulties experienced by sub-Saharan Africa during the 1990s also continued into the new millennium. Some African countries expanded total output but saw declining per capita output, primarily because of quickly rising populations. Other countries experienced total and per capita output declines owing to environmental degradation and war. In the Democratic Republic of the Congo, per capita food output was 37% lower than in 1989–91. Ethiopia experienced a substantial fall in per capita output beginning in 1997 as a result of drought and its war with Eritrea.

Food Aid. International food aid continued to be critical for several countries. (*See* TABLE II.) Shipments of cereal grains for aid in 2000–01 declined sharply from the previous year, largely owing to reduced contributions from the United States. The U.S. remained the largest international donor, but American shipments fell by 35%. Meanwhile, Japan moved past the European Union (EU) to become the second largest donor.

The main aid recipients were largely the same as in previous years. Somalia

Table I. Selected Indexes of World Agricultural and Food Production (1989–91 = 100)

Region and country	Total agricultural production					Total food production					Per capita food production				
	1997	1998	1999	2000	2001	1997	1998	1999	2000	2001	1997	1998	1999	2000	2001
Developed countries	**98.9**	**98.1**	**99.8**	**100.7**	**99.9**	**99.6**	**99.0**	**100.7**	**101.7**	**100.6**	**96.1**	**95.2**	**96.5**	**97.1**	**95.9**
Australia	118.3	123.5	131.5	131.2	132.6	129.6	136.8	147.4	146.1	146.8	118.2	123.4	131.4	128.9	128.2
Canada	116.2	124.0	131.7	132.6	120.2	116.1	123.7	131.7	133.2	120.5	107.4	113.4	119.7	120.0	107.6
European Union	102.2	102.5	104.9	105.0	103.4	102.2	102.4	104.7	104.9	103.3	99.6	99.6	101.7	101.7	100.0
Japan	95.2	91.0	92.3	91.7	91.0	95.6	91.5	92.8	92.2	91.6	93.6	89.4	90.4	89.6	88.8
South Africa	100.8	95.8	101.8	105.6	99.3	103.6	98.2	104.2	108.9	102.2	90.9	84.7	88.6	91.4	84.8
Transition countries	72.5	67.6	68.0	67.9	70.8	73.7	68.6	69.0	69.0	71.6	73.3	68.3	68.8	68.8	71.6
United States	118.7	119.5	120.9	123.6	120.6	118.6	120.7	121.6	124.6	121.4	110.0	110.8	110.4	112.0	108.2
Less-developed countries	**131.0**	**134.8**	**138.9**	**141.2**	**142.7**	**132.8**	**137.2**	**141.8**	**144.0**	**145.5**	**117.5**	**119.5**	**121.4**	**121.5**	**120.8**
Argentina	122.4	131.7	134.8	134.1	139.1	125.0	135.0	139.1	139.1	144.4	114.1	121.6	123.8	122.3	125.4
Bangladesh	111.6	114.4	127.0	130.4	129.1	111.3	115.2	129.0	132.4	130.9	94.9	96.1	105.4	106.0	102.6
Brazil	126.5	128.8	139.2	145.0	148.7	130.1	131.4	142.1	147.3	151.6	117.4	117.1	124.9	127.9	129.9
China	153.9	159.8	164.1	169.5	173.5	157.2	165.4	170.6	175.7	179.5	146.1	152.4	155.8	159.1	161.3
Congo, Dem. Rep. of the	93.7	93.4	90.4	87.8	87.8	94.5	94.6	91.8	89.6	89.6	74.1	72.4	68.6	65.1	63.2
Egypt	141.8	140.5	149.0	152.2	152.2	143.5	144.2	153.2	156.7	156.7	125.5	123.8	129.2	129.8	127.6
Ethiopia	124.8	115.7	122.5	118.6	118.6	121.7	116.2	123.4	119.4	119.4	102.6	92.2	95.6	90.2	88.1
India	121.1	122.0	127.3	126.8	125.3	121.7	122.2	127.8	127.8	126.0	107.1	105.8	108.7	107.0	103.8
Indonesia	119.4	117.2	119.5	121.4	122.4	119.8	117.2	120.1	122.2	123.4	107.4	103.6	104.7	105.1	104.8
Malaysia	121.2	119.2	124.6	127.4	131.8	131.2	130.1	138.7	142.8	148.4	112.0	108.8	113.6	114.7	117.1
Mexico	121.8	122.9	128.2	131.8	134.8	122.7	123.8	130.1	134.4	137.4	108.4	107.5	111.3	113.2	114.0
Nigeria	142.8	149.2	153.3	157.2	157.2	143.2	149.7	153.8	157.8	157.8	117.4	119.4	119.4	119.2	116.1
Philippines	122.3	112.5	123.7	126.6	126.5	123.9	113.8	125.8	129.0	128.6	106.1	95.5	103.5	104.1	101.8
Turkey	108.5	116.4	110.4	109.6	108.4	107.7	116.0	110.1	109.2	107.9	95.0	100.7	94.0	91.9	89.5
Venezuela	117.7	113.2	117.5	115.2	115.4	119.3	114.9	119.7	117.8	117.5	102.1	96.4	98.4	95.0	93.0
Vietnam	143.5	150.7	162.0	170.2	167.3	138.8	146.2	155.9	160.3	155.8	121.1	126.9	133.5	135.5	130.0
World	**116.5**	**118.2**	**121.2**	**122.9**	**123.3**	**117.5**	**119.6**	**122.8**	**124.5**	**124.8**	**106.1**	**106.5**	**107.9**	**108.0**	**106.9**

Source: World Wide Web site for UN Food and Agriculture Organization: <http://apps.fao.org> (Dec. 14, 2001).

faced drought and war and was a major target of aid programs. Although North Korea's harvest improved in 2001, that country continued to be short of food and sought assistance through the UN's World Food Programme. When Hurricane Michelle damaged Cuban agriculture, U.S. producers sold food to Cuba despite the trade embargo that had been in effect since the early 1960s. Fighting in Afghanistan and a huge refugee population created a food emergency, for which the U.S. and other donor countries provided supplies. At the time the U.S. bombing began, food-aid packets were also delivered by air drop, but ground fighting disrupted the delivery of food and other aid to civilians.

World Trade Organization. The members of the World Trade Organization (WTO) met in Qatar in November and launched a new round of global trade liberalization negotiations. China and Taiwan were both accepted for WTO membership. Problem areas in agricultural trade negotiations were discussed, including further limits on export subsidies.

During 2001 the WTO heard a number of international trade disputes. The U.S. complained about Mexico's adoption of tariff measures against the U.S., Canadian dairy policy, and South Korean beef-import rules. Argentina and the EU quarreled over import barriers on bovine hides, while the EU and the U.S. confronted each other over wheat gluten and continued their long-running dispute over the EU ban on hormone-treated beef. The U.S. had filed a case in the WTO against the EU banana-import policy that relied on import quotas for various countries. The WTO had ruled in favour of the U.S., but the EU had not complied. In April the parties agreed that the EU would adopt a tar-iff-only import regime effective Jan. 1, 2006, and until then would institute a system of licensing based on historical trade levels, with increased quotas for Latin American bananas.

In July 1999 the U.S. had introduced import barriers against lamb meat to protect its domestic industry. Australia and New Zealand filed complaints that were upheld by the WTO, and in November the U.S. restrictions were removed.

Agricultural Policy. U.S. farm-support regulations, which were to expire in 2002, had been adopted in 1996 when global agricultural markets were tight and farm prices were strong. Since 1998, however, Congress had been obligated to provide special annual supplemental assistance and spend far more than anticipated to maintain adequate levels of farm income. New legislation passed by the House of Representatives in October 2001 formalized this supplemental spending and made a 10-year commitment to continue substantial government subsidies to farming. Another concern in the U.S. was the granting of trade-promotion authority. The U.S. was finding itself at a disadvantage when it participated in WTO talks to liberalize agricultural trade. Other countries were reluctant to negotiate with the executive branch when it was Congress that enjoyed the authority of final approval of trade agreements. Pres. George W. Bush sought the renewal of presidential authority for "fast-track" trade negotiation, which had lapsed in the mid-1990s, but the measure was controversial and opposed by groups that opposed liberalizing trade. On December 6 the House approved trade-promotion authority by a one-vote margin, but by year's end the Senate had yet to consider the matter.

Agricultural policy was proving a significant obstacle to the ongoing negotiations to enlarge the EU to embrace Central and Eastern European countries. EU farm-support policies were quite generous to farmers but were costly, consuming about half of the EU's annual budget. A number of the countries that were seeking admission had large agricultural sectors, and some, such as Poland, had numerous small farms. If the existing EU farm policy was expanded to take in those countries, cost would rise steeply. Farm policy reform was unpopular with EU farmers, but farmers in countries applying for membership wanted equal treatment, even while fearing competition with highly efficient, highly subsidized Western European agriculture.

Livestock Diseases. Foot-and-mouth disease (FMD) outbreaks occurred in many countries, including Great Britain and Argentina, beginning in late February. (*See* Special Report.) Measures were quickly undertaken to restrict the spread of the disease. Infected animals in Britain were placed in quarantine and slaughtered. Britain destroyed over four million animals, or about 8% of its animal inventory. Movements of products in rural areas were restricted or banned, and tourists were prohibited from visiting certain areas; large economic losses resulted. Fresh-meat exports from countries with the infection were banned, and travelers faced increased security. Although FMD is rarely transmissible to humans, the outbreaks following the experience with bovine spongiform encephalopathy (BSE) caused a reduction in European meat consumption. By late summer the disease appeared to have been contained, and few new cases were being reported.

In late September BSE, which does seem to be transmissible to humans, appeared in Japan. Demand for beef in Japan plummeted; wholesale beef prices fell by 50%; and other countries prohibited beef imports from Japan. Although Japan was a large net importer of beef, it exported some specialty beef products.

Hong Kong experienced an outbreak of influenza in poultry, and about one million birds were eradicated. Trade in poultry meat through Hong Kong was disrupted as China tightened inspections on poultry originating in Hong Kong and on frozen poultry from other countries transported through Hong Kong. South Korea, the Philippines, and Japan banned poultry imports from Hong Kong, and Taiwan introduced tighter screening of travelers.

Table II. Shipment of Food Aid in Cereals[1] (in 000,000 metric tons)				
	1997–98	1998–99	1999–2000	2000–01
Shipments from				
United States	2,787	6,403	7,247	4,697
Canada	384	332	421	192
European Union	890	1,557	1,387	707
Norway	45	65	63	58
Switzerland	42	37	47	25
Australia	296	267	264	240
Japan	356	1,149	331	720
Others	1,441	1,440	1,408	1,825
Total	**6,241**	**11,250**	**11,168**	**8,464**
Shipments to				
To LIFDC[2]	5,480	8,404	7,561	7,399
Sub-Saharan Africa	*2,172*	*2,530*	*2,853*	*2,733*
To other countries	761	2,876	3,607	1,065

[1]July–June years.   [2]Low-income food-deficit countries.
Source: World Wide Web site for UN Food and Agriculture Organization: <http://apps.fao.org> (Dec. 14, 2001).

(continued on page 156)

Trouble on the Hoof:
Disease Outbreaks in Europe

by Brian J. Ford

Farmers rarely celebrate good fortune in the modern world, but British agriculture seemed to be emerging from a period of darkness as 2001 began. The scourge of "mad cow" disease was in retreat.

After mad cow disease (bovine spongiform encephalopathy [BSE]) had first been causally related to a human brain illness in March 1996, British beef farming had plunged into crisis. It was evident that eating infected beef in Great Britain had led to a newly recognized fatal illness in humans, initially dubbed new variant Creutzfeldt-Jakob disease ($_{nv}$CJD) and later shortened to variant CJD (vCJD).

Sufferers of vCJD have an average age of around 30. When stricken, they become depressed and apprehensive, and they suffer delusions of being attacked and persecuted by others. They lose the ability to walk and howl like animals as they wither. No cure has been found and little treatment is available.

The causative agent of vCJD is a prion, a form of infectious protein devoid of any genetic material, that causes malformation of brain cells. There are other theories, including one that posits that organophosphate pesticides have given rise to vCJD, but these pesticides are in use elsewhere around the world, and yet vCJD is confined to Britain. Only in the U.K. has the processing of animal feed dramatically changed. Since the early 1980s lower processing temperatures have been authorized, and it is claimed that this allows infectious prions to spread. The incidence of vCJD in Britons rose to a total of about 90 cases at the start of 2001, but it was still showing no signs of the widely forecast dramatic increase. The prions seemed, to humans, to be mercifully uninfectious.

The annual cases of BSE in British cattle rose from 447 by the end of 1987 to 37,280 in 1992. From that date the incidence fell until by the start of 2001 the annual figure was down to 1,537

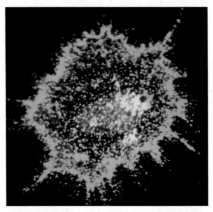

Prions (shown in gold) are thought to be the pathogenic agents of diseases such as variant Creutzfeldt-Jakob disease.

James King-Holmes/Institute of Animal Health/Science Photo Library, Photo Researchers

cases. The figure continued to fall. In the final week of March—five years since the link between BSE and disease in humans had been announced—there were only five new cases of BSE reported. By June, however, the unthinkable had happened: there were 214 new cases of BSE in Britain, while mainland Europe, which had remained largely free of BSE and had placed severe restrictions on the U.K. meat producers ever since the epidemic emerged, now had more confirmed cases—313—than the U.K.

In the meantime, the hopes prevailing early in the year had already been dashed by a devastating outbreak of foot-and-mouth disease (also known as hoof-and-mouth disease in the U.S.). According to the Northumberland (Eng.) County Council, a farmer had been illegally feeding unprocessed kitchen waste to his pigs. Among the scraps was meat from a restaurant that had illicitly imported supplies of produce from East Asia, and some of this was infected with the virus.

Council officials who were prosecuting the farmer stated that he had noticed

symptoms among his pigs but did not report them. As his animals were moved from farm to marketplace, the virus spread, and within weeks Britain was in the throes of the outbreak. British agriculture was crippled once again.

A government ban on the movement of livestock meant that newborn lambs were left to die in the wet mud of open ground instead of being returned to the warmth and safety of the lambing shed. Slaughtermen at infected farms killed all the animals they found. Thousands of decomposing carcasses were left piled high in farmyards. In July the government canceled the sterilization of infected farms because of the high cost involved. A ban on exports meant that British farmers once more had no access to the open market.

Foot-and-mouth disease had last caused a major outbreak in the U.S. in 1929. It was one of the illnesses most feared by farmers. Infected animals dribble saliva and develop sores on hooves and around the mouth. Curiously, the disease is rarely fatal. Tropical animals carry the virus as a matter of course, and in water buffaloes it produces few effects. The worldwide extent of the virus means that there will be no end to it in the foreseeable future.

For months the story was featured in the media, but eventually the press coverage diminished. Many people imagined that the disease outbreak had been controlled, yet figures from the U.K.'s new Department for Environment, Food and Rural Affairs—which replaced the Ministry of Agriculture,

Hundreds of slaughtered cows are burned near Elonby, Eng., in April to help prevent the spread of foot-and-mouth disease.

AP/Wide World Photos

Fisheries and Food following the British general election in June 2001—showed that there were between three and five new outbreaks in some parts of the U.K. every day. Among those were 12 new cases in Cumbria and 17 in Yorkshire.

In July sheep grazing free on the Brecon Beacons in Wales were corralled together and tested for the virus; 10% of them showed positive results. The rural affairs minister for Wales, Carwyn Jones, announced that the unfenced sheep would be slaughtered. The survival of the British landscape depends on grazing animals. From the sweeping grandeur of the Lake District to the rugged headlands of Cornwall and the wild Welsh hills, grazing sheep and cattle are the principal agents of land management.

By midyear almost five million animals had been slaughtered. Stories circulated of farmers' buying infected sheep in order to claim compensation. Fears of a

resurgence in the fall, when animals were brought down from the hills, proved to be unfounded, and by mid-January 2002 the British farm herds were declared officially free of infection.

Nations around the world adopted antivirus measures, with disinfecting hand washes and shoe mats imposed upon tourists. Most governments in areas normally free from the virus relied on a policy of slaughtering infected herds whenever there was an outbreak. This method worked when outbreaks were rare, but many observers expected that the practice of vaccination might become necessary in the future. Meanwhile, the global reach of the Internet has given people the chance to import exotic meats from around the world—free of import restrictions and usually falsely labeled. This fact leads to speculation that local diseases could become global epidemics in the new millennium.

The effect of foot-and-mouth disease on tourism is severe, despite the fact

that there are very few cases of the disease infecting people, and the human illness is fleeting and mild. The tourism industry has lost millions, and for all the promises of financial assistance offered by the British government, little benefit was reported by rural communities themselves. Some apparently unrelated businesses also face extinction. Hot-air balloon companies, for example, have been unable to operate, and thousands of employees have been laid off. The Institute of Directors claimed that the total cost of the epidemic would be £20 billion (about $30 billion).

Nearing year's end, the number of victims of vCJD rose beyond 100. They were not the only people to die. After watching in utter despair as their livestock were shot, more than 100 British farmers turned their shotguns on themselves.

Brian J. Ford is a biologist and the author of many books, including BSE: The Facts *(1996) and* The Future of Food *(2000).*

(continued from page 153)

Global Economic Developments. Agricultural trade was adversely affected by global economic developments in 2001, notably the spread of recession. Consumption of agricultural products is linked to income. As incomes fall, demand for agricultural goods declines and trade shrinks. In 2001 every major economy experienced weaker economic activity, and a recession began in the United States in March. The terrorist attacks in September further weakened both the U.S. and the world economies. Japan continued to have a poor economic performance, and European economies saw lower growth rates. Reduced U.S. imports of technology lowered growth in Pacific Rim countries. Argentina was mired in a multiyear recession and by the end of the year was facing a default on $132 billion in international debt obligations.

Currency values affect international trade for agricultural products. Most trade occurs in U.S. dollars, and a strong U.S. dollar weakens the purchasing power of countries importing U.S. agricultural goods. While the U.S. dollar weakened during much of the year, it remained high by historical standards and strengthened against the currencies of rival exporting countries, which thus reduced the competitiveness abroad of U.S. agricultural products.

GLOBAL MARKETS IN 2001

Grains, Oilseeds, and Livestock. Global production of grains and oilseed was higher in 2001, and prices for farm commodities remained weak. World grain production in the 2001 crop year rose from 1,836,000,000 tons to 1,843,000,000 tons (tons here and throughout are metric tons). Coarse grains output was 2% higher. Coarse grain production in the U.S. fell 11 million tons, or 1%, from the large 2000 crop. Major exporters had smaller coarse grains crops, but several key importing countries harvested larger crops. Russia, Ukraine, and other Eastern European countries had significantly larger harvests. China recovered from a drought, and 2001 production was up by two million tons. World rice production dropped 1.1%. This was the second year of smaller global rice production and marked a break with the steadily rising harvests experienced in the 1990s. World wheat production fell nearly 1% to 577 million tons, dragged down by the decline in the U.S. The U.S. had been experiencing a long-run decline in area planted in wheat because farmers found

Mormon crickets like this one— which was found in a barley field in Idaho—caused millions of dollars of crop damage in Utah and Nevada during 2001.

Agricultural Research Service, USDA

other crops more attractive. Improved wheat crops were recorded by Eastern Europe, North Africa, Russia, and Kazakhstan. Chinese wheat production decreased from 100 million tons to 94 million tons. India and Pakistan saw output declines of 10%. World coarse grains trade fell 4%. Rice trade remained 24 million tons. With reduced global production, world wheat trade was 4% higher. With global wheat consumption greater than production, global stocks fell to the lowest level since 1995–96. Even with a larger global coarse grains crop, expanded consumption in 2001–02 reduced stocks. For rice, growing use combined with lower output caused a stock reduction. The tightening global supply and use balance caused higher wheat and coarse grains prices; however, price levels remained low.

World oilseed production had continuously increased since 1991, and production expanded by 3.6% in 2001, a new record. The U.S. harvested a huge soybean crop, 4.8% above even the large 2000 crop. Soybean outputs in Argentina and Brazil were also large. Oilseed trade rose 5.6%, and ending stocks were 1.9% lower. Oilseed meal and vegetable oil outputs rose with trade increasing owing to expansion of meal and oil use. Prices remained low.

Global meat production expanded in 2001. Beef and pork output rose by nearly 1% to 133.1 million tons. That rise was not matched by increased demand, however, and trade in meat dropped from 9.1 million tons to 8.8 million tons. Both global production and trade of poultry meat expanded. Output increased 2.8%, and trade was 3% higher, which resulted in a 3% increase in consumption. Worldwide output of dairy products grew; cow's milk output was greater in 2001 at 378.5 million tons, compared with 377.1 million tons in 2000. Production declines in the

U.S. and the EU were offset by increased production in Oceania. The U.S. and the EU saw butter production decline because of low prices relative to other dairy products, but trade in butter remained unchanged. Cheese production grew 2%, but total world exports were unchanged because increases from Oceania were offset by reduced EU trade. Nonfat dry milk production was 5% below the 2000 level owing to lower milk and stable cheese output in the U.S. and the EU and to expectations that prospects for nonfat dry milk were not as favourable as those for cheese.

Tropical Products. World sugar production for 2001–02 was down 2% from the previous year. Brazilian output, down sharply in 2000–01, recovered by 8.1% in 2001–02, while EU sugar production during the year fell 12.5% below the 2000–01 level. At 34.2 million tons, global sugar trade was down by 2 million tons. Brazilian exports rose 23%, but exports from the EU dropped 44%. World sugar consumption in 2001–02 rose by 1.5%. Owing to the tighter global supply, prices that had been low for two years strengthened somewhat.

Coffee production in 2001–02 rose slightly above the level of the previous year. This, added to the large beginning stock, meant that total supply was 4% greater. Brazilian coffee output was 1% lower, but large stocks permitted a 16% increase in exports. These large supplies put downward pressure on coffee prices worldwide. In September 2000 the Association of Coffee Producing Countries agreed to reduce export supplies by 20% in order to boost prices, but one year later, with prices at new lows, the attempt was abandoned. Some members could not bear the costs of withholding coffee exports as nonmembers expanded their exports to take up the slack.

(PHILIP L. PAARLBERG)

FISHERIES

Total world fish-catch figures for 1999, the latest year for which figures were available in 2001, were finalized by the UN Food and Agriculture Organization and showed a recovery from the disastrous effects of the El Niño weather patterns the previous year to reach 92,866,600 metric tons. The total catch of fish, crustaceans, and mollusks from marine and inland waters rose 7% over the 1998 figure of 86,933,100 metric tons. (*See* GRAPH.)

The leading fishing nation in 1999 again was China, with a figure of 17,240,000 metric tons. (*See* GRAPH.) This total was similar to the 1998 figure and was expected to remain relatively constant while the country's main focus remained the continued growth in farmed production. There was also an increase in China's farmed production to a massive 22,790,000 metric tons.

Peru recovered second position in the world catch league in 1999 with a haul of 8,430,000 metric tons, a staggering 94% increase over the previous year, when El Niño decimated the anchoveta stocks off the Pacific coast of South America. (*See* GRAPH.) While the recovery was welcome for the Peruvian fishing fleet and fishmeal industry, it would go only a short way to offset the debts incurred by the industry when El Niño's warm waters devastated the fish catch.

Chile, which was also affected by the decline in anchoveta resources, recorded a large recovery with a 55% rise to 5,050,528 from 3,265,383 metric tons in 1998. Despite this, there was continued serious concern over the country's jack mackerel stocks, which registered a 30% decrease in catch from 2,060,000 metric tons in 1998 to 1,420,000 metric tons in 1999. Tight fishing controls on the jack mackerel fishery were in place.

The U.S. managed only a 2% increase in its catch of 4,749,645 metric tons. Russia, which was dependent on its Alaska pollock catch, reported a 7% decrease to 4,141,157 metric tons. The Russian fishing industry was finding the going tough, and unless it could reverse the trend, it was likely to find itself below 4,000,000 metric tons. A change in economic policy by the Russian Central Fisheries Committee had left the industry having to cope with high fuel prices and bid for its fishing quotas against foreign fishing interests in government-organized auctions.

Morocco, in 25th place with a relatively modest catch of 750,000 metric tons, was growing in importance. In

2001 the European Union failed to agree on the renewal of a third-party access agreement with Morocco that would allow significant access to Spanish and Portuguese vessels. Morocco was therefore preparing to see its own landings rise significantly in the coming years.

(MARTIN GILL)

Production trends for the top ten catching nations, 1990–99 (in metric tons)

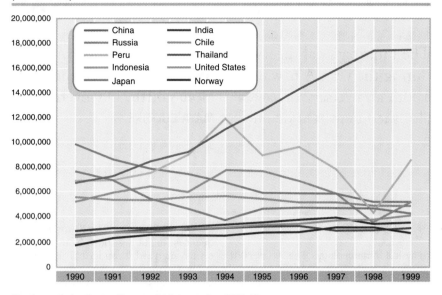

Catch trends for the top five caught fish species, 1990–99 (in metric tons)

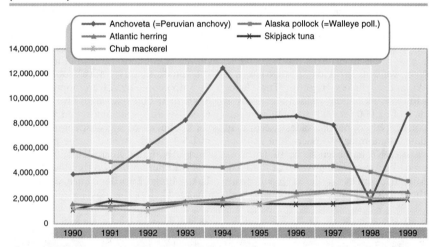

Total world production (aquaculture and capture fisheries) (in metric tons)

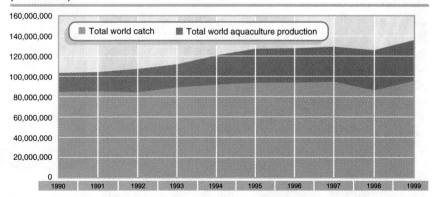

Anthropology and Archaeology

The multiregional theory of human ORIGINS gained support during the year. A new exhibition commemorated the 100th anniversary of MARGARET MEAD's birth. Discoveries also shed new light on ancient MAYA CULTURE.

ANTHROPOLOGY

Physical Anthropology. The year 2001 turned out to be an extraordinary period for the study of human origins. An Australian research team published a molecular analysis of mitochondrial DNA (mtDNA) extracted from 10 southeastern Australian skeletal remains dating from approximately 2,000 to 60,000 years before the present (BP). Six specimens came from Kow Swamp, while four were from Lake Mungo in the Willandra Lakes region. The Lake Mungo 3 individual yielded a consensus date of 62,000 (±6,000) years BP and was considered to be the oldest accurately dated anatomically modern human from which DNA had been successfully recovered. The key finding was that the Lake Mungo 3 mtDNA differed greatly from the mtDNA of all living humans as well

as from all other fossil mtDNA sequences, including those from three recently analyzed Neanderthal individuals from Germany, Russia, and Croatia. Unexpectedly, the Lake Mungo 3 mtDNA fragment did survive as a geographically widespread remnant inserted on chromosome 11 in the modern human nuclear genome. Although the four Lake Mungo individuals spanned the entire aforementioned time range, they all displayed a modern (gracile) form, while the anatomically more robust Kow Swamp people lived from approximately 8,000 to 15,000 years ago. Five of the six Kow Swamp specimens and the other three Lake Mungo specimens had mtDNA closely related to the mtDNA of living Aboriginal Australians.

The authors proposed that the aberrant Lake Mungo 3 mtDNA lineage probably diverged before the most recent common

ancestor of all contemporary mtDNA. Thus, the earliest known human mtDNA lineage occurred in Australia, rather than in Africa, as had been inferred from studies of mtDNA from living populations. Even though this finding did not prove that modern humans originated in Australia, according to one of the authors it provided support for the multiregional theory of human origins rather than for the more widely held out-of-Africa replacement theory.

Also during the year, two new genera of African hominins (a taxonomic grouping that includes modern humans and fossil species more closely related to *Homo sapiens* than to any other living species) were proposed, and additional, older specimens of a previously named genus (*Ardipithecus*) were described. First, a joint French and Kenyan research team published a report based on 13 fossils representing at least five individuals from the Lukeino formation in the Tugen Hills region of Kenya. An isolated molar was described in 1975. Newly discovered fossils found in October and November 2000 included two mandibular fragments (containing a total of three molars), five isolated teeth, three partial femora, the shaft of a humerus, and a finger bone. Volcanic tuffs in the Lukeino formation were radiometrically dated at 5.9 (±0.3) million years, which made these remains the

(Left) The age of this skull and mandible specimen from Kow Swamp in southeastern Australia was estimated to be 13,000 years. (Above) The calvarium of the Lake Mungo 3 skeleton.

left and above: © Peter Brown

oldest-known reputed hominins in the fossil record. They were named *Orrorin tugenensis* ("original man" from Tugen). The femora indicated that *Orrorin* was about the size of a female chimpanzee and walked bipedally when on the ground; however, the humerus and finger bone suggested arboreal adaptations and good climbing ability as well. The teeth exhibited a complex mixture of humanlike, apelike, and intermediate characteristics. The small, thickly enameled molars confirmed that this condition was an archaic feature for the lineage that eventually led to *H. sapiens* and implied that the vast majority of the large-molared australopithecines did not have a direct ancestral-descendant relationship with the genus *Homo*.

The second new African hominin taxon was named *Kenyanthropus platyops* ("flat-faced man" from Kenya). An almost complete, though distorted, cranium (WT 40000) was found at Lomekwi on the western side of Lake Turkana. Although more than 30 skull and dental fragments were discovered in 1998 and 1999 at various Lomekwi localities by an international team of researchers, only this 3.5-million-year-old cranium and a 3.3-million-year-old mandibular fragment (WT 38350) were placed in the new taxon. The cranium exhibited derived facial and primitive craniodental features unlike those of its only hominin contemporary, *Australopithecus afarensis*, or of any earlier hominin. The transverse facial contour was flat below the nasal bones, which resulted in a comparatively flat face with only moderate subnasal prognathism. The malar (cheek) region was particularly tall, and there were no large depressions behind the brow ridges. On the other hand, WT 40000 possessed a small chimpanzee-sized brain and had a small, thickly enameled molar, reminiscent of the primitive condition found in *Orrorin*. Of all the subsequent hominin specimens, WT 40000 most closely approximated the overall facial morphology of ER 1470, the 1,870,000-year-old East Turkana specimen currently placed in the taxon *H. rudolfensis*. The authors suggested that in light of the new *Kenyanthropus* material, *Homo rudolfensis* should now be named *Kenyapithecus rudolfensis*.

Eleven new specimens (representing at least five individuals) of *Ardipithecus* from 5.2 million to 5.8 million years BP were discovered between 1997 and 2001 in the Middle Awash area of Ethiopia. This material was associated with a wet woodland paleoenvironment and was

American anthropologist Margaret Mead is pictured on a field trip to Bali in 1957; the year 2001 marked the 100th anniversary of Mead's birth.

thought to represent a new bipedal hominin subspecies, *Ardipithecus ramidus kadabba*. The chief evolutionary lesson provided by the new *Ardipithecus* specimens combined with the discovery of *Orrorin* and *Kenyanthropus* was that the substantial hominin taxonomic diversity characteristic of the time period from 1.5 million to 3 million years ago might also extend back to just after the time that human and chimpanzee lineages diverged, which thereby made the drawing of clear-cut evolutionary connections within the 6-million-year-old hominin lineage an even more difficult endeavour. (*See also* LIFE SCIENCES: *Zoology*.)

(STEPHEN L. ZEGURA)

Cultural Anthropology. The year 2001 was significant for U.S. anthropology, as it marked both the 100th anniversary of the birth of Margaret Mead and the 100th annual meeting of the American Anthropological Association (AAA), November 28–December 2 in Washington, D.C. To commemorate both, an exhibition entitled "Margaret Mead: Human Nature and the Power of Culture" was organized at the Library of Congress to document Mead's life and works and the events that shaped them. Exhibit curators selected some of the letters, photographs, artworks, films by and about Mead, and field notes to convey to the wider public the scope of Mead's accomplishments and insights. The exhibit was scheduled to run until May 2002. Numerous other exhibits and programs

were organized around the world to remember Mead, the best-known and most-engaged and public American anthropologist of the 20th century.

The AAA recognized Laura Nader, a social and cultural anthropologist from the University of California, Berkeley, with its highest honour by inviting her to deliver the Distinguished Lecture at its November 2000 meeting. Nader gave an overview of anthropology by discussing issues concerning ethics, ethnography, and fieldwork. This emphasis continued the effort to redirect American anthropology to its empirical foundations as well as to public and world issues.

In June 2001 a conference was held in Agrigento, Italy, on "Children and Young People in a Changing World: A Holistic Approach." The meeting was cosponsored by the International Union of Anthropological and Ethnographical Studies and the University of Florence's International Institute for the Study of Man, which produces the *International Journal of Anthropology*. The Agrigento conference discussed the effects on children and young people of such developments as the rise of new nationalisms and cultural diversity. Some stressed the environments in which children are raised, focusing on such subjects as high stress levels among single mothers in Australia, adolescent children of divorced parents in Mexico, and women in the U.S. caught between raising children and caring for aging parents. One study compared children's stages of physical development in New Guinea and in the U.S. and challenged claims that child development is the same everywhere. For example, despite claims by some physicians and researchers, this study argued, an infant's crawling stage is not universal.

Overall, presentations warned against hegemony of models from a few countries or international organizations and the imposition of social programs without prior careful studies that take into account local practices and knowledge. It was strongly recommended that youths be involved in social programs intended for them. From Egypt a visual ethnographic study of a birth ceremony showed how the family functions as the locus of identity and as the basis of the cultural construction of childhood through which the transmission of values and ideals takes place.

A different situation was presented regarding postcommunist southeastern Europe as well as postapartheid South Africa. Remedies for the social crisis in southeastern Europe are not readily available, since key cultural institutions lay dormant for many years under communism. In what could be described as a transitional situation there, children had to work because of low family incomes, so the social structure changed from children-oriented to non-children-oriented. Consequently, children spent more time in the streets and exhibited new patterns of aggression, including sexual abuse and other dysfunctional behaviours, such as involvement in the male sex industry and the trafficking of young women and drugs. A shift in the Balkan countries from coexistence of ethnicities to nationalism and a new focus on homogeneity of ethnic groups had implications for inclusion and exclusion in societies, presenting conflict for people with local identities and displaced children.

In New York City in September, the 54th Annual DPI/NGO Conference for nongovernmental organizations associated with the United Nations Department of Public Information heard an anthropological paper on "Roots of Volunteerism in Arabo-Islamic Society & Culture: Insights from the Bottom Up," read by Fadwa El Guindi. She made the point that the notion of "civil society," which had been adopted by international institutions, was merely a new name for age-old practices in traditional societies and that the notion of "diversity" must be accompanied by the established fact of "a common humanity." In their work

UN organizations and committees could and should benefit from voluntary participation of local citizens already part of their traditional practices—i.e., establish volunteerism from the bottom up.

Renewed scholarly energy—and a resurgence of old concerns—in visual anthropology was manifest in the increase in book-length publications and in a recent international conference. "Beyond Picturing Culture: A Critique of a Critique," published in the *American Anthropologist* in June, included all prominent founders and theorists in the field of visual anthropology and practitioners of ethnographic film and photography worldwide. Discussions ranged from personal narratives, to the role of ethnographic film, to photography as a research tool. Plans were made to publish the proceedings of this seminal meeting.　　　(FADWA EL GUINDI)

ARCHAEOLOGY

Eastern Hemisphere. The dawn of the new millennium proved bountiful for Old World archaeology. Nauticos, a deep-ocean exploration firm hired to recover an Israeli submarine that had sunk in the eastern Mediterranean, found instead the remains of a 2,300-year-old shipwreck that had foundered in 3,000 m (1 m=3.28 ft) of water. Located between Alexandria, Egypt, and the Greek island of Rhodes, the ship, an estimated 26 m long and 16 m wide, challenged a long-held assumption that ancient mariners lacked the navigational skills necessary to sail great distances over open water and were thus restricted to coastal sailing.

Neolithic rock paintings and carvings found on the Greek island of Andros showed a level of Stone Age art previously unknown in the Aegean. The petroglyphs, believed to date to between 4500 and 3300 BC, included images of six ships, measuring between 20 and 30 cm (7.8 and 11.8 in), geometric shapes that may represent the Aegean, and 17 animals, including deer. Archaeologists believed they collectively constituted a larger composition, the earliest complex rendering ever found in the Cyclades. A 5th-century BC gold wreath was discovered by a farmer plowing his fields in Apollonia, near Thessaloniki, Greece. Composed of 30 hammered gold ivy leaves and two bunches of molded berries, the well-preserved wreath was similar to two gold wreaths previously discovered in the region.

A memo signed by the Egyptian queen Cleopatra VII was discovered among

hundreds of documents recycled for use in the construction of a mummy case found by a German expedition at Abusir in 1904. Now in the collection of Berlin's Ägyptisches Museum und Papyrussammlung, the two-column text was dated to Feb. 23, 33 BC.

The excavation of some 3,000 mid-2nd-century BC bullae, or clay document seals, within an administrative building that was destroyed by fire in c. 145 BC at Tel Kadesh in Israel's northern Galilee suggested that the Phoenicians had continued to exercise their cultural and religious authority in the region much longer than previously thought.

In Great Britain a number of Roman finds came to light, including two waterwheels dating to between AD 63 and 108, which were unearthed within ancient wells in London and were the first of their kind to be discovered in the U.K. The waterwheels apparently had been powered by slaves walking on treadmills. More recently, a contractor outside the village of Lopen happened upon a Roman mosaic; it measured 6 × 10 m and featured a dolphin, wine urns, and twining vines. The floor had apparently been made by craftsmen based at Cirencester in the late 4th century AD. This area previously had borne no hint of Roman occupation. Exploration of a medieval manor complex at Wetwang, east Yorkshire, revealed a chariot burial dating from the 3rd or 4th century BC, the earliest Iron Age burial of its kind ever discovered in England. This was the seventh chariot burial found in the area, thought to have been a tribal centre of a Celtic people—known by the Romans as the Parisi.

Among the most ancient relics discovered recently were stone tools, animal bones, and an incised mammoth tusk unearthed at a 40,000-year-old campsite at Mamontovaya Kurya, Russia, near the Arctic Ocean. The finds predated the oldest documented evidence for human activity in the far north by more than 20,000 years. Researchers believed that the date of the site implied either that Neanderthals had expanded much farther north than previously thought or that modern humans were present in the Arctic only a few thousand years after their appearance in Europe. If the toolmakers were modern humans, the timing was significant; the period corresponded to the transition from the Middle to the Upper Paleolithic, a turning point in the history of human evolution in Europe heralded by the arrival of the rich culture associated specifically with modern humans.

Mammoths, rhinoceroses, deer, horses, bison, birds, and unknown animals with elongated muzzles and open mouths were among the more than 200 newly discovered Upper Paleolithic engravings found in Cussac Cave in southern France. Also depicted were line drawings of women and schematic vulvas. Most of the figures appeared to have been engraved with stone tools; there were no paintings. The archaic nature of the figures, some of which were more than four metres in height, suggested that they were done during the Gravettian period (c. 26,000–20,000 BC). Hundreds of fine ceramic vessels used for drinking, feasting, and fertility rites—possibly of an orgiastic nature—were discovered along with a phallic-shaped stalagmite in a cave near the abandoned village of Nakovana, Croatia, on the Adriatic Sea. According to site excavators Tim Kaiser of the Royal Ontario Museum and Staso Forenbaher of the Institute for Anthropological Research in Zagreb, Croatia, the cult site should clarify previously hazy theories about the religious beliefs

of the Illyrians, warriors and neighbours of the Greeks, who lived in the area during the 1st and 2nd centuries BC.

A number of important finds were unearthed in China, including 20 carts and the remains of dozens of horses found during rescue excavations at a Zhou dynasty (770 BC–AD 221) site in the central Chinese city of Xicheng. Within a tomb belonging to the Yangshao culture (c. 5000–3000 BC) in northwestern Shaanxi province, archaeologists found the remains of numerous adults and children, who had been buried separately. A large site thought to have been used by the royal family for sacrificial rituals 3,000 years ago was discovered in Yanshi, one-time capital of the Shang dynasty (1600–1046 BC) in western Henan province. The sacred site lay within one of the largest Shang sites discovered to date.

After toiling for more than a year, Chinese archaeologists discovered a large pit adjacent to that containing the well-known terra-cotta warriors and horses buried with Qin Shihuangdi,

China's first emperor (reigned 221–210 BC). Rather than warriors, however, the newfound pit contained terra-cotta statues representing civilians.

A nine-year excavation at the site of Dholavira in the western Indian state of Gujarat yielded a walled Indus Valley city dated to the middle of the 3rd millennium BC and covering nearly 50.6 ha (125 ac). The Archaeological Survey of India team uncovered a sophisticated water-management system with a series of giant reservoirs—the largest 80 × 12 m wide and 7 m deep—used to conserve rainwater.

For all of the richness of these new discoveries, the field of archaeology had suffered setbacks in terms of site destruction, mainly through flooding. Emerging nations—e.g., Turkey, India, and China—needed to balance their requirement for hydroelectric power with heritage management. Conflict was running a close second in destroying the collective heritage, particularly in Afghanistan, as witnessed by the deliberate destruction of the Bamiyan Buddhas in

Archaeological Survey of India

During the year an ancient walled city was uncovered at the Dholavira site in Gujarat state, India.

the spring of 2001. In addition, much of that country's heritage was in peril from the pillaging of sites; many ancient objects had already appeared on the art market. (ANGELA M.H. SCHUSTER)

Western Hemisphere. Recent discoveries shed new light on ancient Maya civilization. Arthur Demarest and Tomás Barrientos excavated and surveyed an important Maya centre named Cancuén, the "Place of Serpents," in a remote area of Guatemala. Cancuén was first located in 1905 by Harvard University archaeologist Teobert Maler, but it was largely forgotten until Demarest deciphered Maya glyphs at the nearby Dos Pilas site that told of a great lord's conquest of Cancuén. Demarest and his colleagues mapped approximately 13 sq km (5 sq mi) of the site, identifying a three-story limestone palace with 170 rooms grouped around 11 courtyards. The ruling dynasty of Cancuén dates back to the 2nd or 3rd century BC. Its lords flourished by forming alliances with other states such as Teotihuacán on the Mexican highlands and the Maya cities of Calakmul, Dos Pilas, and Tikal. Cancuén boasted a palace close in size to that in Tikal, surrounded by workshops where artisans laboured on jade plaques, pyrite mirrors, and obsidian artifacts. A nearby and still unexplored cave complex may have been the ritual centre for Cancuén. This important site would fill major gaps in the understanding of Maya history.

Archaeologist Norman Hammond of Boston University uncovered a 2,900-year-old sweat house at Cuello in northern Belize. Cuello was the oldest Maya settlement in the lowlands, with occupation beginning perhaps as early as 2000 BC and continuing for 16 centuries. Elite residences or public buildings surrounded a courtyard enclosed on three sides. When the excavators investigated the fourth side, they unearthed a structure, about 2.4 × 2.5 m (8 × 9 ft), that had a domed roof and an outside firebox chamber. Hot embers and stones were pushed down a channel into the house through an opening in the wall. As many as six bathers could sit on benches with their feet stretched above the channel. Hammond compared the Cuello sweat house to the elaborate royal bathhouses at Tikal and other later Maya cities.

Archaeology continued to make important discoveries concerning more recent American history. Tainter Cave near La Crosse, Wis., yielded the most comprehensive set of Native American rock paintings in the Upper Midwest. Found by an amateur archaeologist in 1998 but announced only in 2001, the paintings included images of birds, humans, deer, and numerous geometric shapes. There

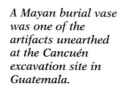

A Mayan burial vase was one of the artifacts unearthed at the Cancuén excavation site in Guatemala.

© Christopher Talbot/AFP Worldwide

were also scenes of an infant bound to a cradle board and nine hunters with bows taking six or seven deer in late winter. This panel lay below a group of birds, bird feet, and feathers, representing the classic Native American separation of earth and sky. Rolled birchbark torches and a 500-year-old moccasin fragment lay on the cave floor. One of the drawings was radiocarbon-dated to AD 900, but some could be earlier. The style of the paintings linked them to the Late Woodland Effigy Mound Culture.

In 1863 an African American named William A.G. Brown went to Virginia City, Nev., hoping to profit from the gold and silver boom at the nearby Comstock Lode. He opened the Boston Saloon, which catered to the small black population in the region, and operated it until 1875. The saloon burned to the ground soon after he closed shop. In mid-2000 a team of archaeologists excavated portions of the Boston Saloon. They recovered thousands of artifacts, including bottle fragments, crystal and glassware, and clay pipes. This was the fourth bar to be excavated in Virginia City, among them Piper's Old Corner Bar, which catered to an upscale clientele. Virginia City was reasonably well integrated for the day, but its black population nonetheless lived under severe social constraints. A preliminary examination of the Boston Saloon artifacts suggested, however, that the African Americans were drinking the same drinks and using similar glassware to what passed over the counters at the upscale Piper's bar.

In 1864 a group of Confederate volunteers under Lieut. George Dixon manned the submarine *H.L. Hunley* and torpedoed the Union sloop USS *Housatonic* off Charleston (S.C.) harbour. The missile hit the sloop's torpedo magazine, and the ship exploded with a massive roar. The *H.L. Hunley* never returned to port and sank 6.4 km (4 mi) offshore. In 1995 a dive team located the sunken vessel with sonar and global positioning technology. The submarine was finally raised on Aug. 8, 2000. An intricate structure of suction piles and nylon slings combined with a polyurethane foam cushion protected the fragile hull during its eight-hour journey to the surface. The archaeologists then attempted to X-ray the steel plates, but sediment blocked the radiation. Eventually they excavated the hull by removing individual steel plates. By late 2001 the partial skeletal remains of eight crew members had been found.

Dos Cabezas ("Two Heads"), a 32-m (105-ft)-high Moche pyramid, lies in Peru's lower Jequetepeque Valley, close to the Pacific Ocean. Three richly decorated tombs of nobles dating to AD 450–550 were excavated from the south side of the pyramid. The three men were remarkable for their exceptional stature. Average Moche males stood between about 1.5 m (4 ft 10 in) and 1.7 m (5 ft 6 in) in height. The Dos Cabezas men, however, towered between 1.75 m (5 ft 9 in) and 1.8 m (6 ft) and died between the ages of 18 and 22 years. Biological anthropologists suspected that they may have suffered from a chronic genetic disorder such as Marfan syndrome, which causes thin, elongated bones. The three appeared to have died within a few weeks of one another. The most important of them lay in Tomb 2, cocooned in clay and wrapped in textiles with his ceremonial possessions. The man had a copper funerary mask with shell eyes, golden eyebrows and nose ornament, and beardlike bangles. He wore a tunic adorned with a cloth human figure with gilded head, hands, and feet. He was buried with an exquisite ceramic bat (an animal sacred to the Moche), a headdress adorned with gilded copper bats, and a nose ornament of solid gold—also a bat. The lord held metalworking chisels and lay with a funerary bundle crammed with war clubs, spear throwers, and gold-plated shields. Sacrificial offerings, a llama and a young woman, lay at a slightly higher level. The excavators believed that the three men were related to one another, but their exact role in early Moche society remained a mystery. (BRIAN FAGAN)

Architecture and Civil Engineering

STAR architects designed a number of EYE-POPPING buildings that were stars in themselves, but their CREATIVITY was overshadowed by the collapse of the TWIN TOWERS of the World Trade Center in September.

ARCHITECTURE

The top architectural story in 2001 was the collapse of the World Trade Center towers in New York City following the September 11 terrorist attacks. Architects and others debated the long-term impact of the disaster. Would the world stop building skyscrapers? Would the threat of terrorism lead people to abandon cities? A number of groups in New York City, including the American Institute of Architects (AIA), the Regional Plan Association, and the Municipal Art Society, joined with city planners and business leaders in informal task-force groups to formulate a redevelopment plan for the site. Proposals ranged from reconstructing the towers exactly as they were to leaving the entire 6.5-ha (16-ac) site as an open-space memorial. Some businesses left the area in fear of further attacks. As a result, a preservation group, the World Monuments Fund, added "Historic Lower Manhattan" to its list of Most Endangered Sites in the world. The twin collapse was scrutinized by engineers, who noted that the intense fire and heat—(upwards of 1,093 °C [2,000 °F]) generated by the explosion of jet fuel aboard the two jetliners that slammed into the towers—had weakened the towers' steel supports and thus caused them to buckle and the floors to cascade nearly straight down. The towers, capable of withstanding hurricane-force winds and ordinary fires, had not been built to withstand an assault of this magnitude. Though they had never been widely admired as works of architecture, the towers' departure was viewed as a human tragedy, an economic disaster, and a blow to Manhattan's great architectural skyline.

Awards. The world's most coveted architectural honour, the $100,000 Pritzker Architecture Prize, was awarded to the Swiss partnership of Jacques Herzog and Pierre de Meuron. (*See* BIOGRAPHIES.) They were also the architects of a proposed addition to the de Young Museum in San Francisco's Golden Gate Park, a design some thought a bit too imposing for the site; it had not been approved by year's end.

Jean Nouvel of France received the Praemium Imperiale of the Japan Art Association for lifetime achievement. He also was the recipient of the Gold Medal of the Royal Institute of British Architects. Nouvel was best known for his transparent all-glass buildings, such as the Arab Institute and Cartier Foundation, both in Paris. Japanese architect Tadao Ando was the winner of the Gold Medal of the American Institute of Architects. Ando's Pulitzer Foundation for the Arts, housing a collection of modern art, opened in St. Louis, Mo., in October. Like such Ando works as the Naoshima Contemporary Art Museum and the Church on the Water in Japan, it was an elegant, minimal building of pale concrete.

The AIA 25-Year Award, for a building that had proved its merit over time, went to the Weyerhaeuser Headquarters (1971) near Tacoma, Wash.; it was designed by Skidmore, Owings & Merrill and landscape architect Peter Walker. The AIA also announced 14 recipients of its annual architecture Honor Awards. Among the more notable were Antunovich Associates and McClier's restoration and recycling of the Burnham Hotel (named after its original architect, Daniel Burnham) in Chicago; Fox & Fowle Architects' exterior design of the Condé Nast Building office tower in Times Square, New York City; and Tod Williams Billie Tsien & Associates' design of the Williams Natatorium, a skylighted pool at Cranbrook Academy of Art in Bloomfield Hills, Mich. Among the 12 recipients for interior spaces were Skidmore, Owings & Merrill's Jin Mao Tower in Shanghai and Hardy Holzman Pfeiffer Associates' restoration of Radio City Music Hall in New York City. "A Civic Vision for Turnpike Air Rights in Boston," an urban-design plan by Goody, Clancy & Associates in collaboration with neighbourhood groups, claimed one of the four awards for urban design.

The Aga Khan Award for Architecture, given every three years for architecture in the Islamic world, was presented as scheduled in Aleppo, Syria, on November 6. Among the world's most respected prizes, the Aga Khan Awards dealt with social as well as purely architectural issues. Among the nine project winners were "New Life for Old Structures," a program to restore buildings in Iran; Barefoot Architects, a rural self-help group in Tilonia, India; and the Nubia Museum, Aswan, Egypt, which housed the culture of Nubia ("Land of Gold"), an ancient area that was partly submerged by the Aswan High Dam in 1971.

Civic and Cultural Buildings. Perhaps the most notable new building of 2001 was the Bibliotheca Alexandrina, the new library located on the harbour in Alexandria, Egypt, designed by the firm Snøhetta of Oslo. Snøhetta's members were unknown in 1989 when their design was selected in a competition that received 524 entries from 77 countries. The library's outstanding feature was a circular reading room with floors that terraced down under a dramatic sloped roof; as one critic described, "A huge inclined silver disk appears to be rising over the sea." The round reading room was undoubtedly influenced by the famous 1857 reading room in the British Museum in London. (*See* LIBRARIES AND MUSEUMS: *Sidebar.*) A notable renovation was that of a courtyard around the reading room of the British Museum. In British architect Sir Norman Foster's design, the courtyard was roofed in a delicate glass structure that curved like a hanging fabric, creating a memorable space that was renamed the Queen Elizabeth II Great Court.

The vast new chancellery building designed by architects Axel Schultes and Charlotte Frank opened near Foster's glass-domed Reichstag in Berlin. The new structure was criticized by some as being bombastic and inefficient. In Sendai, Japan, architect Toyo Ito created a new arts centre called the Sendai Mediatheque. Though the transparent glass structure looked like a watery aquarium from the outside—its seven floors were held up by clusters of slanting columns meant to look like seaweed swaying underwater—inside it housed a great variety of art and media centres for public use.

In Wisconsin Spanish architect and engineer Santiago Calatrava created a new entrance wing for the Milwaukee Art Museum. Its outstanding feature was a 66-m (217-ft)-wide sunshade, which was intended to open and close like a bird's wings over the glass roof of the entry pavilion. The museum hoped that the spectacular building would put the city on the world tourist map and thus do for Milwaukee what architect Frank Gehry's

The interior of Skidmore, Owings & Merrill's 88-story Jin Mao Tower in Shanghai, the tallest building in China, won an AIA Honor Award in 2001.

Guggenheim Museum in Bilbao, Spain, did for that city. In that regard, Milwaukee typified the recent rush by cities and institutions to hire one of the 20 or 30 world "star" architects who, like Gehry, were capable of producing memorably sculptural buildings.

Two small chapels in Japan were also notable. Ando's Komyo-ji, a temple for a Buddhist sect in Saijo, was a symphony of elaborately interlocking wood columns and beams, a type of architectural forest.

Takashi Yamaguchi's White Temple near Kyoto, by contrast, was a tiny one-room box, pure white both inside and out, bathed in mysterious light that made it feel as if it were floating.

Commercial Buildings. One of the most amazing efforts to date of American architect Frank Gehry was the DG Bank in Berlin, located on the Pariser Platz near the Brandenburg Gate. The building's exterior was straitjacketed by rigid rules that were established by the city of Berlin in an effort to make new buildings on the famous square look compatible with one another. Gehry responded by designing a simple, elegant limestone building on the outside, but he broke loose in the interior with a dramatic atrium. The atrium had a delicate glass floor and roof, both warped into improbable shapes, and in its middle, seeming to float in the space, was a conference room sheathed in stainless steel and shaped like a horse's head.

Though the Austrian firm Coop Himmelblau, led by Wolf Dieter Prix and Helmut Swiczinsky, had long been known for its radically modern, or "deconstructivist," buildings that were so pitched that they seemed to be frozen at the moment before they collapsed—its SEG Apartment Tower in Vienna was less unconventional than some of its other designs. The publicly funded "social housing" development tilted in a way that reminded some of the Leaning Tower of Pisa in Italy, but it also contained a 14-story "climate lobby" that helped the building ventilate itself naturally. In Sydney, Australia, Italian Renzo Piano designed Aurora Place, a 41-story office tower with an 18-story apartment building next to it. Sail-like glass shapes rose from the top of the tower, recalling the shapes of the Sydney Opera House nearby. In New York City high-fashion French architect Philippe Starck converted a 1920s brick women's residence into a super elegant hotel called Hudson, which featured inventively theatrical indoor and outdoor lobby spaces.

Exhibitions. The year's most remarkable exhibitions were all in New York City. "Frank Gehry, Architect" filled the great spiral of Frank Lloyd Wright's Guggenheim Museum. On display were 40 projects by the master Los Angeles architect rendered in photos, drawings, and hundreds of models. Among the projects shown was a design for a new branch of the Guggenheim, to be built over the water in New York's East River, which would be 10 times the size of Wright's Guggenheim. By year's end, however, a downturn in the American economy had

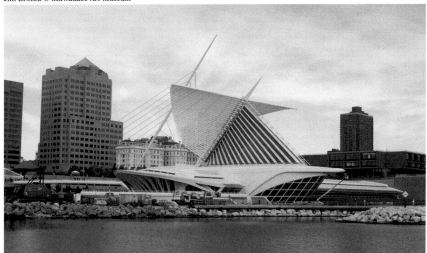

The Milwaukee (Wis.) Art Museum, with a new entrance wing by Santiago Calatrava, features an immense, movable sunshade.

dampened enthusiasm for the proposal. A double exhibit on the modernist Ludwig Mies van der Rohe opened simultaneously at the Whitney Museum of American Art and the Museum of Modern Art (MoMA). "Mies in Berlin" at MoMA showcased his early work in Europe, including such masterpieces as the Barcelona Pavilion and Tugendhat House. The exhibit also explored Mies's early development and the sources from which he learned. "Mies in America" at the Whitney focused on his later work after he immigrated to the United States, including such icons as the Seagram Building in Manhattan and the Farnsworth House in Plano, Ill. The latter had been a concern to preservationists, but during the year it was purchased from a private owner by the state of Illinois, which would maintain it and open it to the public. "Exploring the City: The Norman Foster Studio" filled a large space in the British Museum, next door to the architect's new Queen Elizabeth II Great Court. The exhibit included detailed models of projects from all over the world as well as some of the 900 sketchbooks the architect had filled over the years. "The Architecture of R.M. Schindler," at the Los Angeles Museum of Contemporary Art, showcased the work of the visionary early California modernist. "Albert Kahn: Inspiration for the Modern," at the University of Michigan at Ann Arbor, displayed the work of the designer of such industrial giants as the Ford River Rouge Plant. "Out of the Ordinary: The Architecture and Design of Robert Venturi, Denise Scott Brown & Associates," at the Philadelphia Museum of Art, was a summary of the life work

of the influential firm, whose members espoused the virtues of ordinary vernacular and commercial architecture. "Frank Lloyd Wright and the Art of Japan: The Architect's Other Passion," at the Japan Society in New York City, explored the architect's secondary career as a collector and dealer in Japanese prints.

Preservation. The Leaning Tower of Pisa was at last stabilized by the simple method of removing earth from its high side so that side would settle. The tower was slowly straightened by one degree to restore it to its tilting angle of 163 years earlier, considered safe. The Kaufmann Conference Center, a Manhattan interior that was one of only four American works by the great Finnish architect Alvar Aalto, was withdrawn from a proposed sale and was to be preserved. Preservationists in New York were also concerned about the fate of the TWA Terminal at John F. Kennedy International Airport (1962) by Eero Saarinen. The owner wished to remove part of the building and convert the remainder into a restaurant or another use. The National Trust for Historic Preservation released its annual "Eleven Most Endangered Places" in the U.S. Among them was another modern building—the CIGNA Campus in Bloomfield, Conn., a classic example of "corporate modernism" designed in 1957 (as the Connecticut General Life Insurance headquarters) by Gordon Bunshaft—which was slated to become a golf course. Others on the list were Ford Island at Pearl Harbor, Hawaii, threatened by redevelopment, and Los Caminos del Rio, a 322-km (200-mi) stretch of land along the lower Rio Grande in

Texas, home to Hispanic and Anglo historic sites. At Yale University it was announced that the landmark Art and Architecture Building (1963) by Paul Rudolph would be restored by New York architect David Childs of Skidmore, Owings & Merrill.

Controversies and Future Buildings. The World War II Memorial, on the Mall in Washington, D.C., was under construction at year's end after having survived a court challenge by its critics, who hoped to overturn a law passed by Congress in May that cleared the way for the project. The designer, whose proposal won a national competition, was Friedrich St. Florian of Providence, R.I. Meanwhile, a federal task force published a Memorials and Museums Master Plan, which suggested that future memorials in Washington be sited elsewhere than on the Mall. In San Francisco the city's planning board approved—over the objection of its staff—a design by Pritzker Prize winner Rem Koolhaas of The Netherlands for a new headquarters for Italian clothier Prada, but the company later delayed the project. In New York City hotelier Ian Schrager nixed plans for a new hotel by Koolhaas and Herzog & de Meuron that would have featured a differently shaped window for each room. A design for a presidential library in Arkansas for former president Bill Clinton was unveiled by architect James Stewart Polshek of New York, but the project was delayed by cost problems and by an owner who sued to prevent the city from taking the land. Polshek's design, in a park by the Arkansas River, included a wing that cantilevered out over the water. In Chicago a new lakefront Millennium Park, including a band shell by Frank Gehry, was also troubled by cost overruns. Diller + Scofidio of New York City, a partnership long known for its art installations, was chosen for its first major architectural job, a new Institute of Contemporary Art in Boston. A slowing economy also put this project in jeopardy.

Deaths. Among the notable architects who died during the year were Morris Lapidus, famed for the gaudy hotels he built in Miami, Fla., notably the Fontainebleau and Eden Roc (*see* OBITUARIES); Ian McHarg, considered by many the founder of modern landscape architecture and planning in the U.S. and the author of the seminal book *Design with Nature* (1969); and Steven Izenour, a longtime partner in Venturi, Scott Brown and Associates and coauthor of *Learning from Las Vegas* (1972).

(ROBERT CAMPBELL)

Notable Civil Engineering Projects (in work or completed, 2001)

Name	Location		Year of completion	Notes
Airports		Terminal area (sq m)		
Incheon International (new airport)	Incheon (Inchon), South Korea (near Seoul)	369,000	2001	Landfill between islands; opened March 22
Guangzhou Int'l (new replacement airport)	Guangzhou (Canton), China	300,000	2002	
Pearson International	Toronto, Ont., Canada	332,000	2003	New horseshoe-shaped terminal at Canada's busiest airport
Athens International (new airport)	Spata, Greece	209,000	2001	Europe's biggest airport project; opened March 28
JFK Int'l (new Terminal 4)	Queens, New York City, N.Y.	139,000	2001	Connected by 13-km light rail to Manhattan by 2003; opened May 24
Nong Ngu Hao (new int'l airport)	Bangkok, Thailand	?	2004	Construction began December 2001
Aqueduct		Length (m)		
Great Man-Made River (phase 2)	Libyan interior to Tripoli area	1,650,000	2001	Phase 1 to Benghazi area (1983–93); phase 2 begun 1990
Bridges		Length (main span; m)		
Carquinez (#3)	Crockett, Calif.–Vallejo, Calif.	728	2003	Begun 2000; first major U.S. suspension bridge since 1965
Rion Antirion	Patrai, Greece (across Gulf of Corinth)	560	2004	Multicable-stayed; complex deepwater foundations
San Francisco–Oakland Bay (East Span)	Yerba Buena Is., Calif.–Oakland, Calif.	385	2006	2-km causeway + world's largest suspension bridge hung from single tower
William Natcher	Owensboro, Ky.–near Rockport, Ind.	366	2002	To be longest cable-stayed bridge over U.S. inland waterway
Rosario–Victoria	Rosario to Victoria, Argentina	350	2002	Bridges/viaducts across 59-km wide Paraná wetlands
Millau Viaduct	Tarn Gorge, west of Millau, France	342	2004	8 cable-stayed spans; world's highest (285 m) road viaduct
Leonard P. Zakim Bunker Hill	Boston, Mass.	227	2002	Widest (56 m) cable-stayed bridge in world (see **Urban Developments**)
Maria Valeria (cross-Danube link)	Esztergom, Hungary–Sturovo, Slovakia	119	2001	Replication of 106-year-old bridge destroyed in 1944; opened Oct. 11
Kizuna	Mekong River, near Kampong Cham, Cambodia	?	2001	First bridge across Mekong in Cambodia; opened December 4
Buildings		Height (m)		
Lotte World Tower	Busan (Pusan), South Korea	464.5	2005	Begun December 2000; will be world's tallest
Taipei Financial Center	Taipei, Taiwan	448	2003	Begun 1999; will be world's second tallest to rooftop (with spire, 508 m)
Two International Finance Centre	Hong Kong, China	412	2003	Begun 2000; to be world's fourth tallest building
Plaza Rakyat	Kuala Lumpur, Malaysia	382	2002	Will be tallest reinforced-concrete complex; seventh tallest overall
Migdal (Tower) Egged	Tel Aviv, Israel	326	2006	Begun 2001
Trump World Tower	New York City, N.Y.	262	2001	Tallest residential development in the world
Torre Generali	Panama City, Panama	250	2003	Begun mid-2000; will be Latin America's tallest building
City Tower	Birmingham, England	245	2004	Will be tallest building in the U.K.
Torre Mayor	Mexico City, Mexico	225	2003	Will be tallest building in Mexico
Canal		Length (m)		
Sheikh Zayed	into bedrock of Lake Nasser, Egypt	72,000	2002	Feeds irrigation system for central Egypt oases
Dams		Crest length (m)		
Birecik Dam	Euphrates River, Turkey	2,507	2001	First major hydroelectric plant in Turkey
Three Gorges	west of Yichang, China	1,983	2009	World's largest hydroelectric project; begun 1993
San Roque Multipurpose	Agno River, Luzon, Philippines	1,100	2003	Irrigation and flood control; tallest earth-and-rock fill dam in Asia
Mohale (Lesotho Highlands Water Project, phase 1B)	Senqunyane River, 100 km east of Maseru	700	2002	First transfer of water to South Africa in 1998, second transfer in 2003
Sardar Sarovar Project	Narmada River, Madhya Pradesh, India	?	?	Construction halted 1995, resumed 2000
Alqueva Dam	Guadiana River, 180 km SE of Lisbon, Portugal	?	2002	Will create Europe's largest (250 sq km) reservoir; extends into Spain
Bakun Dam	Balui River, Sarawak, Borneo, Malaysia	?	2006	Hydroelectricity to peninsular Malaysia via world's longest submarine cable
Highways		Length (km)		
Indus Highway	Karachi–Peshawar, Pakistan	1,265	?	59% complete as of September 2001
Beijing–Shanghai Expressway or "Jinghu"	Beijing–Shanghai, China	1,262	2000	Opened late December; construction began in 1987
Egnatia Motorway	Ignoumenitsa–Thessaloniki, Greece	687	2006	First Greek highway at modern int'l standards; 70 tunnels
Railways (Heavy)		Length (km)		
Qinghai–Tibet	Golmud, Qinghai, China–Lhasa, Tibet, China	1,118	2007	Highest world rail (5,072 m at summit); half across permafrost
Guangdong–Hainan	Zhanjiang, China–northern tip of Hainan at Haikou	568	2001	Rail with container ship to Hainan
Panama Canal	Cristóbal–Balboa, Panama	89	2001	Rebuilt railroad for transcontinental container traffic
Kyongui (51-year-old reconnection)	Munsan, S.Kor.–Kaesong, N.Kor.	24	2002?	6.8 km South Korean part complete as of September 2001
Railways (High Speed)		Length (km)		
Spanish High Speed (second line)	Madrid–Barcelona, Spain	760	2004	Madrid–Lleida to be completed by 2002
Kyongbu	Seoul–Busan (Pusan), South Korea	323	2004	Connects largest and third largest cities
TGV Méditerranée	Valence–Marseille, France (branch to Montpellier)	249	2001	Completes high-speed rail across France ("Calais to Marseille")
German High Speed (third line)	Frankfurt–Cologne, Germany	226	2002	Connects Ruhr to Frankfurt International Airport
Italian High Speed (second line)	Rome–Naples, Italy	222	2004	Begun 1994; part of planned 1,300-km high-speed network
Shanghai maglev ("magnetic levitation")	Pudong Int'l airport–metro line 2, Shanghai, China	29.9	2003	World's first maglev train for public use; 430 km/h
Subways/Metros/Light Rails		Length (km)		
Oporto Light Rail	Oporto, Portugal	70.0	2003	Europe's largest total rail system project; first line opened in 2001
Hong Kong Railway (West Rail, phase 1)	Western New Territories to Kowloon, Hong Kong	30.3	2003	5,500-m tunnel and viaduct
Los Angeles Metro (Blue Line ext.)	L.A. Union Station to Pasadena, Calif.	22.0	2003	
Copenhagen Metro	Copenhagen, Denmark	21.0	2002–05	Line 1: 2002; most extensive driverless system in world
Tren Urbano (phase 1)	San Juan, P.R.	17.2	2003	Bayamón (western suburbs) to north San Juan; 60% elevated
Istanbul Metro (phase 2)	Istanbul, Turkey	5.4	2001	Bridge link across Golden Horn; extends under historic city centre
Tunnels		Length (m)		
Apennine Range tunnels (9)	Bologna–Florence, Italy (high-speed railway)	66,000	2006	Begun 1996; longest tunnel, 18.6 km; tunnels to cover 90% of railway
Qinling	between Xi'an and Ankang, China	18,457	2001	World's ninth largest railway tunnel
A86 Ring Road	around Paris, France	17,700	2008	Two tunnels (to east [10,100 m], to west [7,600 m])
Södra Länken	part of Stockholm, Sweden, ring road	16,600	2004	Complex underground interchanges
Pinglin Highway	near Taipei, Taiwan	12,900	2003	Twin tunnels under Sheuhshan Range; Taipei-I-lan expressway link
Westerschelde	Terneuzen to Ellewoutsdijk, Neth.	6,600	2003	Longest world tunnel in "bored weak soil"
Vestmannasund Subsea Tunnel	Streym (Streymoy) and Vágar islands, Faroe Is.	4,700	2002	First subsea tunnel in the Faroe Islands
Urban Developments		Area (ha)		
Putrajaya	25 km south of Kuala Lumpur, Malaysia	4,581	2012	Planned national capital begun 1996; first staff moved in June 1999
Central Artery/Tunnel	Boston, Mass.	–	2004	Complex highway/tunnel/bridge project begun in 1991

1 m=3.28 ft; 1 km=0.62 mi; 1 ha=2.47 ac

Art, Antiques, and Collections

In 2001 the **VENICE BIENALE** and other exhibitions featured **NONTRADITIONAL** mediums—notably video, film, and sculpture-as-architecture—as well as **SNAPSHOTS** of New York City after September 11. A **LEONARDO** drawing and a **JACK KEROUAC** manuscript fetched record auction prices.

PAINTING AND SCULPTURE

At the 49th Venice Biennale, directed for the second time (his first was in 1999) by Harald Szeemann, the international art world gathered to experience what was considered the most significant show of the new and important. Painting and sculpture were not as well represented as other mediums, particularly video and film, which were high in quantity but not always quality. Painting and sculpture were not entirely absent, however. One of the iconic works in Venice was the Australian-born British artist Ron Mueck's 4.8-m (16-ft)-high fibreglass sculpture of a crouching boy, which greeted visitors as they entered one of the Biennale's main exhibition spaces. The piece was a gesture toward a kind of monumental figuration, and it was as immediately imposing as one of Richard Serra's steel-torqued ellipses shown nearby. Subtler were the works by Robert Gober, who used bronze to interpret the light and porous quality of Styrofoam. Gober also presented one of his vaguely anatomic forms cast in wax and set into a wicker basket.

One alternative to the massive scale and unmet goals of the Biennale was Site Santa Fe. "Beau Monde: Toward a Redeemed Cosmopolitanism," curated by Las Vegas, Nev.-based critic Dave Hickey, was the fourth installment of this biannual exhibition. "Beau Monde" featured many established names—notably Ed Ruscha, Jo Baer, Ellsworth Kelly, and Bridget Riley—among emerging and trendier artists. One of these was Japan's Takashi Murakami, who received attention for his two solo exhibitions and his installation in New York City's Grand Central Station. Murakami's signature "superflat" mode of painting featured smiley-faced flowers set against silver backgrounds; he also made sculptures inspired by Japanese comics and animation. An important venue featuring emerging talent was New York City's Studio Museum in Harlem, which mounted "Freestyle," a show of young black artists curated by Thelma Golden. Some standouts included Eric Wesley's full-scale sculpture of a donkey kicking through a gallery wall and Kori Newkirk's paintings made from plastic beads, artificial hair, and hair pomade, which was applied directly to the museum wall to create one work.

Several artists explored the familiar dialectic of sculpture-as-architecture, and vice versa. Gregor Schneider's *Dead House ur* (created for the German pavilion at the Venice Biennale) was an extension of a project that had occupied him for several years. This reconstruction of his family home, a standard tenement construction in Rheydt, Ger., was an elaborately conceived interior within an interior. The pathos of the domestic also fascinated British artist Rachel Whiteread, who made monumental casts of two architectural spaces: a basement staircase and the entire interior space of a small apartment, both of which were created from spaces in her new home, a former London synagogue. Whiteread, whose Holocaust Memorial in Vienna was completed at the end of 2000 to great critical success, followed up with a smaller public commission. Known for making casts of ordinary objects using plaster or synthetic resin, Whiteread most recently cast a replica of a plinth in clear resin. The piece, entitled *Monument*, was installed in June atop an actual stone plinth in Trafalgar Square, London; it was scheduled to remain there until sometime in 2002. An interest in architecture also informed the work of Brooklyn,

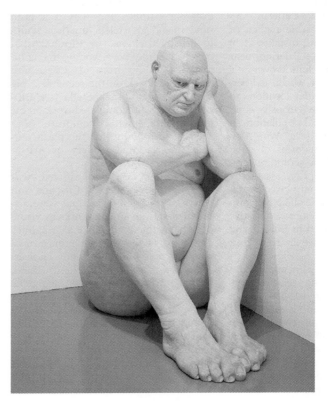

Ron Mueck's **Untitled (Big Man)** *(2000) was emblematic of his oversized sculptures of human figures; the work was acquired by the Smithsonian Institution's Hirshhorn Museum and Sculpture Garden in 2001.*

N.Y.-based Ricci Albenda, who used building materials such as drywall and metal sheeting to construct "spaces within spaces," including a large cube suspended nearly a metre from the floor that almost entirely filled the space of a gallery, giving onlookers only a narrow area of space in which to move between the piece and the wall.

Tate Britain's Turner Prize, worth £20,000 (about $29,000) in 2001, triggered even more controversy than usual when it was awarded to Martin Creed in December for "The Lights Going On and Off," which consisted of an empty gallery with a pair of ceiling lights that flashed on and off.

Combining performance with sculptural and installation elements in a collaborative practice that defied easy definition, the Austrian collective known as Gelatin sparked critical interest. For a large-scale installation called *Total Osmosis*, they transformed an outdoor area into a swampy, toxic backyard. Abandoned toys and other refuse filled a pungent muddy area that was traversable only via narrow wooden planks. Another project involved stuffed animals, semipornographic photo collages, and a series of "lectures," during which, in a disorienting mix of fact and fiction, the artists described their previous projects while executing a wall drawing to illustrate the given topic, ranging from "Hawaii" to "Autopsy."

Italian artist Maurizio Cattelan constructed a larger-than-scale replica of the Hollywood sign and installed it in Sicily in the hills above Palermo, near a garbage dump. Cattelan, known as a provocateur in the art world, deliberately chose this particular location, an action that raised the curiosity—and the hackles—of the local population. In another provocative move, Wim Delvoye pushed the boundaries of good taste with his machine-sculpture entitled *Cloaca*. His contraption, essentially a defecation machine, employed mechanisms that were controlled by computer to duplicate the human digestive process. *Cloaca* traveled in Europe and was scheduled to arrive in New York City in 2002.

There was plenty of painting by both established figures and relative newcomers. James Rosenquist, best known for his mural-sized Pop art works that depicted the motifs of consumerism and mass production, exhibited a new group of works that were studies in dynamism—large canvases filled with shiny geometric shapes that appeared to change and morph when viewed.

Courtesy: Marian Goodman Gallery, New York

The works also reflected Rosenquist's movement forward as an artist; he had succeeded in creating a formidable body of work late in his career. New paintings by Cy Twombly, another artist who had emerged in the 1960s, continued his very recognizable style of calligraphic drips executed in springlike colours. Like a small-scale warm-up for his upcoming 2002 major retrospective at the Museum of Modern Art in New York City, Gerhard Richter showed a group of new, mostly abstract paintings, many of which were executed by means of his "squeegee" method; the squeegee was dragged across a freshly painted canvas, and the layers of wet pigment were smeared into an entirely different composition that was both random and controlled. American sculptor-artist Jeff Koons (*see* BIOGRAPHIES) unveiled some new works, the completed paintings from his *Celebration* series. Also back on the scene in a big way was artist Frank Stella (*see* BIOGRAPHIES), who completed work on his monumental metal sculpture, *The Prince of Homburg*, for the plaza outside the National Gallery of Art in Washington, D.C.

Abstraction, newly interpreted, was seen in many galleries. Charline von Heyl's large-scale abstractions were distinguished from similar works by virtue of her tangible confidence as a painter as well as of the works' compositional strength and unusual colour choices. Another artist who made sophisticated, formally oriented work was Jacqueline Humphries, who exhibited a group of new paintings that worked within the boundaries of the medium—paint and canvas—while incorporating extra-painterly considerations, including the kind of light emitted from computer screens. The intersection of art and technology (or the limits of such an ex-

Gerhard Richter's Moritz *(2000) was among the paintings featured in a show of the German artist's works at the Marian Goodman Gallery in New York City.*

change) was on the minds of many artists, and the traditional methods of art making—painting, photography, and sculpture—continued to be expanded or even replaced by new methods. Though Jeremy Blake's "moving paintings," as he called them, were actually animated digital video discs that mobilized the language of painting and made many historical art references, his colour-saturated works emphatically pointed toward the future.

(MEGHAN DAILEY)

ART EXHIBITIONS

Several important architecture shows were among the critical and popular successes of 2001. Preeminent modernist Ludwig Mies van der Rohe had two distinct phases in his long career: his early years in his native Berlin and those after his 1938 arrival in the U.S. Together, "Mies in Berlin" (at the Museum of Modern Art [MoMA] in New York City and Altes Museum, Berlin) and "Mies in America" (at the Whitney Museum of American Art, New York City, and then the Canadian Centre for Architecture, Montreal) explored the rationality of Mies's International Style of architecture as well as his more expressionistic bent in the years before he coined the dictum "Less is more." In the 1920s Vienna-born architect R.M. Schindler made his home in Los Angeles and captured its casual elegance in domestic dwellings that were perfectly integrated into the landscape. The Museum of Contemporary Art, Los Angeles, mounted the largest show to date covering Schindler's career. Another architect synonymous with Los Angeles was Frank Gehry, whose projects were marked by his signature use of unusual materials and strong, undulating forms. A major exhibition spanning his 40-year career was held at the Solomon R. Guggenheim Museum, New York City, and also traveled to the museum's outpost in Bilbao, Spain, which Gehry himself designed.

Three cultural institutions in Chicago (where the ethnic Polish population numbered second only to Warsaw) hosted the ambitious "In Between: Art from Poland, 1945–2000." The Museum of Contemporary Art, the Renaissance

Society, and the Chicago Cultural Center presented surveys of the work of nearly 40 avant-garde and contemporary artists in addition to projects commissioned especially for the occasion.

The 500th anniversary of the European discovery of Brazil sparked several important exhibitions in the U.S. that celebrated the dynamic range of Brazil's art and culture. With about 350 objects, "Brazil: Body & Soul," which opened at the Guggenheim Museum, New York City, on October 19, was the largest of these. The centrepiece of the show was a large gilded 18th-century altar that filled the museum's rotunda. At El Museo del Barrio in New York City, "O Fio da Trama/The Thread Unraveled" focused on recent Brazilian art that used fabric and weaving as metaphors for social and personal narratives. Several Brazilian-born contemporary artists had solo exhibitions, including Beatriz Milhazes at the Birmingham (Ala.) Museum of Art, and the influential work of Hélio Oiticica was featured at the Wexner Center, Columbus, Ohio. Organized by the Museum of Contemporary Art in San Diego, Calif. (and also shown at the Museum of Modern Art, San Francisco), "Ultrabaroque: Aspects of Post-Latin American Art" featured 16 artists whose work reconsidered the use of the

"baroque" as a metaphor for contemporary experience. Twenty-five contemporary artists considered the contentious dynamics between colonizer and colonized in Brazil in "Virgin Territory" at the National Museum of Women in the Arts, Washington, D.C.

At other Washington museums the focus was on American artists. Jacob Lawrence was the subject of a retrospective at the Phillips Collection that was also scheduled to travel extensively. More than 200 works from Lawrence's long career were shown, among them works from his seminal "Migration" series, which tells the story of the northern exodus of African Americans and what was experienced during and after that epic journey. At the Hirshhorn Museum 39 of Clyfford Still's large colour field paintings were presented, with many related works shown together for the first time. From high abstraction to 19th-century American Realism, Thomas Eakins's masterful figurative works (portraits, photographs, sculpture, and drawing) were presented in several venues in his native Philadelphia, including the Pennsylvania Academy of Fine Arts, where Eakins taught in the 1870s and '80s.

Interestingly, an exhibition of one of the most influential American artists of the past 30 years did not have a venue in

the U.S. Conceptual art maverick Dan Graham's important retrospective opened at the Museu de Arte Contemporânea de Serralves, Pôrto, Port., and continued on to museums in Paris; Helsinki, Fin.; and Otterlo, Neth. The influence of Graham's practice, particularly his use of seriality in photography, was clearly visible in the work of German photographer Andreas Gursky—the subject of an exhibition at the MoMA. Gursky had garnered international attention for his images of contemporary scenes: global exchange markets, hotel interiors, airports, drab apartment-block facades, crowded sports or music events, often on a monumental scale—with some as large as 4.8 m (16 ft) wide.

The styles that constituted what was known as early Modernism were as diverse and varied as the artists who created them, as several important international exhibitions revealed. Henri Rousseau was a self-taught painter whose "naive" style drew the admiration of artists Pablo Picasso and Paul Gauguin, poet Guillaume Appolinaire, and others. The Kunsthalle in Tübingen, Ger., showed a number of important and lesser-known paintings by Rousseau as well as a selection of works that demonstrated his influence over others, among them Fernand Léger, Franz Marc, and Wassily Kandinsky. Though often overshadowed by his contemporary Georges Seurat, Paul Signac was nonetheless an important figure for early Modernism. The Grand Palais, Paris, was the first venue for a large-scale retrospective (the first of the artist's work in 40 years) that included Signac's well-known Pointillist paintings as well as works dating to the end of his life in 1935. Decorative, sumptuous, and often fraught with psychological tension, Gustav Klimt's Art Nouveau embodies the spirit of fin de siècle Vienna. The National Gallery of Canada, Ottawa, presented the first major retrospective of Klimt's work at a North American venue, including 35 paintings and nearly 90 drawings. The Jewish Museum, New York City, showed an unprecedented selection of early works by Marc Chagall culled from Russian collections, including some never before exhibited in the West. Chagall's influence on early 20th-century art was often considered minor, an assumption that this show meant to call into question.

In Paris the Centre Georges Pompidou organized a retrospective of Raymond Hains, a founding member of the Nouveaux Réalistes. The group emerged in France in the late 1950s

The altar of the Monastery of São Bento in Olinda, Braz., was the centrepiece of "Brazil: Body & Soul" at the Guggenheim Museum in New York City.

Juan J. Real/Notimex

and reacted against the refinement of Abstract Expressionism by using found objects to make their work. The Nouveaux Réalistes were included in another exhibition at the Pompidou, the blockbuster "Les Années Pop"—which presented a distinctively European perspective on Pop art, so often labeled a quintessential American style—a showcase of the broad and varied range and meaning of Pop and the breadth of work created beyond American shores. A movement that emerged in Italy in the years after the triumph of Pop, Arte Povera emphasized the tactile, physical qualities of the work of art and the use of "poor" or common materials—concrete, twigs, discarded newspapers, or rags. London's Tate Gallery presented 140 works in "Zero to Infinity: Arte Povera 1962–1972." Elsewhere in London, at the National Gallery, "Vermeer and the Delft School," co-organized by the Metropolitan Museum of Art in New York City, featured paintings by Vermeer and Pieter de Hooch, both of whom helped establish Delft as one of the most significant 17th-century artistic centres, as well as some 50 works by other artists of the period. An enormous selection of Romantic poet and artist William Blake's many paintings, watercolours, and illustrated books was presented at the Tate Britain, and a smaller version of the exhibition traveled to New York's Metropolitan Museum, where visitors could partake of Blake's imaginative world, in which poetry, dream life, and the imaginary become reality.   (MEGHAN DAILEY)

Hiroshi Sugimoto's photograph of a wax likeness of Napoleon Bonaparte was included in the exhibition "Sugimoto: Portraits" in the Guggenheim Museum SoHo.

PHOTOGRAPHY

As scenes of carnage and destruction were repeatedly aired and published following the September 11 terrorist acts in the U.S., people around the world compulsively gaped in horror and disbelief at the images that had been captured on film and magnetic media. From snapshots grabbed with cheap single-use cameras to images made with the most expensive professional video equipment, photography once again demonstrated its shattering power as eyewitness. Hundreds of these photographs gained a life-affirming purpose in late September with the opening of "Here Is New York." At this busy SoHo storefront show, professional and amateur pictures of the World Trade Center attacks and their aftermath could be bought for $25 each, with the proceeds going to aid the children of the victims.

During 2001 Walker Evans received superstar treatment with two major exhibitions. "Walker Evans & Company," a loan exhibition put together by the Museum of Modern Art (MoMA) in New York City, displayed some 60 photographs by Evans himself plus nearly 200 images from other photographers, painters, sculptors, and graphic artists strongly influenced by his penetrating vision and powerful personality. Complementing the MoMA exhibition was "The American Tradition & Walker Evans," which featured more than 100 images from the collection of the J. Paul Getty Museum in Los Angeles. The show explored how American photographers such as Carlton Watkins, Lewis Hine, Paul Strand, and Dorothea Lange were shaped by Evans's seminal insights into the American character

and the power of a straight documentary esthetic to illuminate it.

The busy Getty Museum dipped into its collection of work by the German documentary portraitist August Sander to mount an important retrospective, "August Sander: German Portraits, 1918–1933." During those hectic years of the Weimar Republic and Adolf Hitler's rise to power, Sander worked on an ambitious visual document, "Man in the Twentieth Century." His goal was to make "simple, natural portraits that portray the subject in an environment corresponding to their own individuality" while "simultaneously revealing the social and cultural dimensions of a highly stratified society." To accomplish this, he photographed an "arc" of subjects ranging from artists, intellectuals, business executives, teachers, skilled workmen, and common labourers to the unemployed and the handicapped. When the Nazis came to power, their opposition to his broad, humanistic view of German life forced him to discontinue the project, but, fortunately, both Sander and a representative fraction of his thousands of pre-World War II photographs survived the war.

During the year ink-jet printing technology achieved stunning new levels of photographic reality and exhibition-quality reproduction. Ink-jet printing involved the spraying of minuscule dots of ink onto paper or other absorbent material to form graphic images, which could be derived from digitally recorded photographs or conventional photographs that had been digitized. In particular, recently developed ink products from Iris Graphics and printing equipment from Epson were used to create giant photographic prints with hyper-realistic detail and flamboyant colour. Among highly praised examples were 40 prints exhibited by Stephen Wilkes. This collection, of which the largest print measured about $2\frac{1}{2} \times 1$ m (8×3 ft), included a splendid "Horse in Meadow, Belle Fourche, S.D."

The questions "What is a photograph?" and "What are its dimensions as visual reality when the subject is itself a representation?" were explored by conceptual artist Hiroshi Sugimoto with eerie twice-life-size black-and-white "portraits" of waxwork figures. His photographs of the wax effigies of 20th-century celebrities including Yasir Arafat, Salvador Dalí, and Diana, princess of Wales, were briefly displayed at New York City's Sonnabend Gallery. Scheduled for a longer engagement at New York's Guggenheim Museum SoHo was a collection that also included historical figures such as Napoleon, Voltaire, and Henry VIII and his six wives. Sugimoto used only conventional photographic and printing techniques to achieve effects that some found confusing or unsettling. As he commented, "People think these are photos of a painting, or an actor posed in a historical costume."

Spring sales at major photographic auction houses such as Sotheby's, Swann, and Phillips were affected by the continuing economic slowdown in the U.S. Significant numbers of lots up for auction went unsold, and some individual images that had been expected to command top prices failed to do so. Prints of "Chairs, The Medici Fountain, Paris," by André Kertész, which had been expected to fetch $100,000–

$150,000, and of Diane Arbus's classic "Identical Twins, Roselle, N.J.," which had been estimated to bring $120,000–$180,000, were both withdrawn after they failed to meet their reserve prices. A signed photogravure of Alfred Stieglitz's "Gossip, Katwyck," about the size of a credit card, exceeded its high estimate, however, and sold for $29,900 at Swann in February.

A definite chill settled in as the year wore on toward the critical autumn photo auctions, and it was not for lack of attractive, valuable photographs. Well before the terrorist attacks, there was concern in the art world because of conditions closely linked to what seemed to be a failing economy and loss of consumer confidence. After the traumatic events of September 11, many art dealers and collectors became pessimistic. Nevertheless, as the year ended, other collectors such as Donald Rubell remained enthusiastic. "I'm like one of those overeaters who can't stop," he commented. "There's not a time when I don't feel like buying art."

The 2001 Pulitzer Prize for breaking news photography went to Alan Diaz of the Associated Press for his photograph of U.S. federal agents removing six-year-old Elián González from his relatives' Miami, Fla., home. Matt Rainey of the *Newark* (N.J.) *Star-Ledger* took the Pulitzer for feature photography for his sensitive photographs documenting the care and recovery of two students critically burned in a dormitory fire at Seton Hall University, South Orange, N.J. At the 58th Annual Pictures of the Year competition, sponsored by the National Press Photographers Association and the University of Missouri School of Journalism, Scott Strazzante of the *Herald News*/Copley Chicago Newspapers and CITY 2000 (Chicago in the Year 2000) photo project won the award for Newspaper Photographer of the Year, while Jon Lowenstein of CITY 2000 was named Magazine Photographer of the Year.

Notable people in the photographic field who died during the year included American photojournalist Will Counts, Cuban photographer Alberto Korda, German-born American photographer Jacques Lowe, French photojournalist and editor Roger-Jean Thérond, and Malian photographer Seydou Keïta. (*See* OBITUARIES.) Another loss was Jack Manning, veteran freelance photographer for the *New York Times* who was particularly well-known for his candid portraits of Cuban leader Fidel Castro.   (ARTHUR GOLDSMITH)

ART AUCTIONS AND SALES

The art market continued to thrive in 2001 despite consumer reticence in some markets, and Christie's and Sotheby's continued to sustain challenges for domination from competitors. The two auction houses once again battled for the privilege of offering some of the most coveted art collections in the world, and both managed to secure strong art- and antique-related sales. In December Sotheby's co-owner and former CEO A. Alfred Taubman was convicted in a New York court of conspiring with London-based Christie's chairman Sir Anthony Tennant to fix sellers' fees and other illegal business practices between 1993 and 1999. The auction houses already had settled a related civil suit, but the scandal had little or no effect on sale prices.

Sotheby's Old Master paintings sale held in New York City once again attained impressive results—$32,320,475—and included *Hare in the Forest*, a work by Hans Hoffman that was purchased by the J. Paul Getty Museum for $2,645,750. Sotheby's then offered a selection of Old Master and Modern drawings and prints from the Franz Koenigs collection, which brought $4,895,900; the highlight of that sale was Hans Bol's *Cycle of the Twelve Months*, which hammered at $1,800,000.

Leonardo da Vinci's **Horse and Rider** *was auctioned at Christie's London in July.*

In January Christie's New York offered an extraordinary collection that totaled $26,276,500. At Christie's London in July, a rare drawing—a masterpiece by Leonardo da Vinci, *Horse and Rider*—sold for a resounding £8,143,750 (about $11,533,000), a record for a Leonardo.

The most notable sales in the art world, the spring series of Impressionist and Modern Art and Contemporary Art, registered record sales at both auction houses. In May at Sotheby's New York, the totals for these sales outdid all of the competition and reached a staggering $222.3 million, led by the works in the collection of Stanley J. Seeger. Top lots from the Seeger collection were Francis Bacon's triptych *Study of the Human Body*, which sold for the world-record price of $8,585,750, and Joan Miró's *Nocturne*, which brought $5,615,750, a record for works on paper by the artist. Also offered in the Impressionist series was Claude Monet's *Le Parlement*, a piece that fetched $14,580,750, and *Self Portrait with Horn*, a haunting painting by Max Beckmann, which made a record $22,555,750. An innovative porcelain sculptural work by American artist Jeff Koons (*see* BIOGRAPHIES), *Michael Jackson and Bubbles*, reached a record $5,615,750.

Christie's New York May sale of Impressionist and Modern Art also achieved exciting results, especially when *Nymphéas*, a work by Monet, sold for $9,906,000. In the same evening, Christie's New York also offered three important Picassos from the estate of Patricia A. Withofs; they brought $16,628,000. The unquestionable standout of the trio, *Figure*, a surrealistic depiction of Marie Thérèse Walter, fetched $7,156,000.

In its Masters of the Post-War sale, Christie's sold more than 10 works for more than $1 million each. The focal point of the sale was Andy Warhol's *Large Flowers*, which set a record as the second highest price for the artist at auction—$8,476,000.

Sales remained robust across the Atlantic as well. At Sotheby's London in June, the Impressionist and Modern Art sales totaled some $47 million, with Monet's *Haystacks, Last Rays of the Sun* contributing to the total $14,286,620, an auction record for a work from his iconic series. Another Monet, *Au parc*, which had been forcibly sold in Nazi Germany in 1935, sold for $5,282,950. The painting was offered under an agreement between the current owners and the original heirs.

Christie's Impressionist and Modern June sales in London were equally strong and totaled a decade-high total of $47,241,190. Maurice de Vlaminck's *Peniche sur la Seine* went for $6,698,256. That evening Juan Gris's *Le Gueridon* achieved $6,231,306, a world auction record for the artist.

Also in fine form were the sales of Contemporary and 20th-century art in London. Sotheby's London sale brought the highest total in 10 years—$16,728,841. Attention centred on a colour chart painted by Gerard Richter, which made $2,582,360, a world record for colour charts.

Christie's American Paintings sale in New York in May reached $31,607,175, the second highest total for this category in the auction house's history. Accenting the sale was Georgia O'Keeffe's *Calla Lillies with Red Anemone*, which sold for $6,166,000. Maurice Brazil Prendergast's painting *The Stony Beach* brought $3,526,000. In May Sotheby's American paintings, drawings, and sculpture sale in New York commanded $20,511,125. The apex of the sale was John Singer Sargent's *Rosina-Capri*, which fetched $5,395,750.

Latin American art enjoyed another successful year. In May at Sotheby's New York the sale totaled $7,189,075 and was once again led by an exceptional Frida Kahlo, *Portrait of Christina, My Sister*, which topped the auction at $1,655,750. The May sale at Christie's New York of Latin American paintings achieved $5,753,057, including a $556,000 tag for Rufino Tamayo's *Madre Feliz*.

Both Christie's and Sotheby's celebrated continued success in the jewelry market. In April, Property of a Lady, Christie's New York sale of magnificent jewels, totaled $6,956,477; the real dazzler in the sale was a diamond ring by Bulgari, which realized $3,636,000. Shortly thereafter, Christie's New York offered important jewels from the house of Harry Winston, which brought $1,145,566. Christie's Geneva boasted the highest sales of the spring series, approximately $22 million. The April sale of jewelry at Sotheby's New York brought $11,154,665; an emerald-cut diamond ring fetched $709,750. At Sotheby's spring jewelry sale in Geneva, which totaled $17,018,001, a heart-shaped diamond pendant went for $1,588,230.

In April the front-runner of Sotheby's New York sale of photographs was the single-owner collection from the archives of the Museum of Modern Art, New York City, which totaled a record $4 million. The top lot of this landmark sale was Walker Evans's *Penny Picture Display, Savannah*, which brought $181,750 and established a world auction record for the artist. Christie's New York also offered some rare Brassaï photographs in a sale totaling $2,539,175.

A new world auction record for a literary manuscript was set when the original 36.6-m (120-ft) scroll of *On the Road* (1957), Jack Kerouac's Beat classic that was written in three weeks, fetched a staggering $2,430,000 at Christie's New York in May. In January in New York, Sotheby's offered the scientific library of Joseph A. Freilich, which realized $10,675,080; an intense battle for a first edition of Aristotle's *Opera* ended with a winning bid of $583,250. In a private Christie's sale in June, a fragment of an unfinished work by Mozart sold for a record £355,750 (about $510,600).

At Sotheby's in June the three-day sale of fine art, fashion drawings, and furnishings from the collection of Gianni Versace achieved $10,177,340.

(AMY TODD MIDDLETON)

ANTIQUES AND COLLECTIBLES

Like the economy, the collectibles market in 2001 showed signs of softening. Collectibles that were offered on the Internet sold for about 30% less than they had a year earlier, and fewer items sold at major auctions. Both serious and novice collectors learned more about the value or popularity of items as a result of various reports on trends as well as the plethora of television shows devoted to antiques and collectibles. (*See* Sidebar.)

Among the standout items that sold at auction were a Philadelphia Chippendale card table, which commanded $1,320,000 at a regional auction house in Northfield, Mass., and brought the second highest auction price ever for a card table; a plain beaker-shaped 17th-century silver wine cup (c. 1660) by Hull and Sanderson of Boston, which sold for $775,750 at an international auction house in New York City; and a Southern California American Indian olla (basket), which brought $145,875 in San Francisco.

Costume jewelry, Danish silver jewelry, and theme pieces, including Christmas tree pins or flag pendants, sold as well as in 2000. Bakelite jewelry, perhaps because of the many reproductions, dropped almost 20% in price for all but the greatest rarities. Average California and Czech pottery pieces went for under $200, but prices began rising, especially in the West.

This ski poster fetched a record price for poster art when it was auctioned in New York City in February.

The most newsworthy sale of the year was the auction in Waterville, Maine, of the Buddy "L" Corp.'s toy archives. The Buddy "L" Express truck brought $33,000; the Insurance Patrol truck with box fetched $40,700; and the 1930s International truck-mounted steam shovel with box went for $35,200. Though all toys continued to sell well, robots, cars, and mechanical banks were especially popular.

Rare 19th-century bottles also commanded record-setting prices, including $46,200 for a Corn for the World purple quart flask, $11,200 for a Double Eagle half-pint amethyst flask, and $55,000 for a Masonic-Eagle flask; an aquamarine and milk glass Mason fruit jar sold for $21,280.

Though Arts and Crafts decorative objects sold well, the only record was $195,500 for a Gustav Stickley music cabinet designed by Harvey Ellis. Other furniture records included $36,400 for a carved walnut hat rack (c. 1868) by Mitchell & Rammelsberg of Cincinnati,

Ohio, and $138,000 for an 18th-century American sack-back Windsor armchair. Collectors favouring expensive formal 18th-century furniture began substituting moderately priced good reproductions made in the 1930s. Large old dining-room sets were in demand, and prices for them had doubled in the past few years. Tramp art and unrestored rustic and country furniture continued to sell well.

Late 19th- and 20th-century art pottery remained a best-seller at shows, at auctions, and on the Internet. A 23-cm (1 cm = 0.39 in) Grueby tile decorated with geese sold for a record $11,500, and a Marblehead Pottery vase decorated with Ipswich marsh scenes brought $108,640. As prices rose for Roseville—the most popular of American potteries—Grueby, Rookwood, and Weller, collectors turned to Hull, Shawnee, and other less-famous wares. Late 19th-century majolica remained popular and expensive. Mochaware, an early 1800s ware, set records when a 23-cm jug with twig designs and blue and rust bands sold for $14,950; that record was surpassed a few weeks later when a 14.6-cm mug decorated with lime green and rust-coloured bands brought $19,250.

Swann Auction Galleries in New York City sold a ski poster titled "Yosemite Winter Sports," for a record $6,325. A major poster auction in Ohio set a number of records—$4,312 for Eric Von Stroheim's poster for the 1925 film *Greed;* $3,910 for a lobby card advertising the 1920 movie *Terror Island,* starring Harry Houdini; and $2,185 for a 1920 Tom Mix six-sheet *Days of Daring* movie poster. The Academy Award statuette won by Bette Davis for *Jezebel* (1938) went for $578,000.

Some sports memorabilia also set records. An astounding $577,610 was paid via an Internet auction for "Shoeless" Joe Jackson's baseball bat, Black Betsy, and $275,000 was paid in a private sale for a Mickey Mantle mint 1952 Topps card. The press book for the 1920 sports movie *Play Ball with Babe Ruth* sold for $2,415.

Other interesting record sales for the year included an 1880 Edison Spectacle phonograph, $49,500; a 1946 Phantom camera, $220,000; a Remington claw & ball gun cane (c. 1859), $16,240; an 1880 occupational shaving mug decorated with a lunch wagon, $42,550; a 1950 George Lawrence fishing creel of split willow with leather trim, $9,020; and a cobalt blue glass whale-oil lamp, $26,795.   (RALPH AND TERRY KOVEL)

173

Antiquing for the Ages: The Search for Hidden Treasures

The promise of huge payoffs sent droves of treasure seekers to attics, basements, yard sales, and trash piles in 2001. Fueling the antique mania was the popularity and high visibility of television shows, including *Antiques Road Show, Treasures in Your Attic,* and *Appraisal Fair,* featuring experts who revealed in a number of instances that items thought to be worthless relics were priceless antiques.

Author and appraiser Helaine Fendelman stated that as the new millennium dawned, Americans became more aware that objects they owned might have monetary value. At the same time, the Internet drew more and more individuals on-line, and Internet auctioneers eBay and Antique Networking brought additional attention to the antiques market.

Americans began to wonder about the real value of their own possessions. Unless one was careful, someone more knowledgeable might scoop up castoffs and sell them in turn for a profit. As a result, would-be fortune seekers were sent scrambling to learn everything they could about their family heirlooms and attic treasures. They read trade papers, notably *Collectors News* and *Maine Antique Digest,* listened to radio shows (*Whatcha Got,* hosted by Harry L. Rinker), and watched special TV spots shown on *Martha Stewart Living* and ABC's *PrimeTime.*

It was the television programs devoted to appraisals, however, that spurred the antiquing phenomenon of the 21st century. Antiques experts were virtually transported into the average American living room, where they discussed common misconceptions about antiques, told the difference between an antique and a reproduction, assessed the values of antiques, and exposed unscrupulous practices in the industry. Appraisers shared the history and lore of items and their status as collectibles, whereas owners shared their own personal stories.

Noncollectors were finding that they owned valuable treasures and that the value of the objects increased if they remained in their original condition. An old Depression glass pitcher, found in a box at a flea market, was revealed to be a sought-after piece in the Cameo pattern valued at $1,500–$2,000. Great-grandfather's old railroad conductor's lantern, dating from the 1860s, was assessed at $700–$900. A table lamp, handed down in the family, turned out to be signed by Tiffany Studios and worth $10,000–$12,000.

During these "at-home" courses on collecting, hopefuls also learned the hard reality that not everything "old" was collectible and worth substantial amounts of money. Though a number of items were preserved, owners found in many cases that their keepsakes' only value was sentimental.

Nonetheless, the dream of being one of the lucky owners of a precious possession could not be dampened. It was that dream that brought hundreds of collectibles to the surface and that would continue to send Americans on a search for hidden treasures.

(LINDA M. KRUGER)

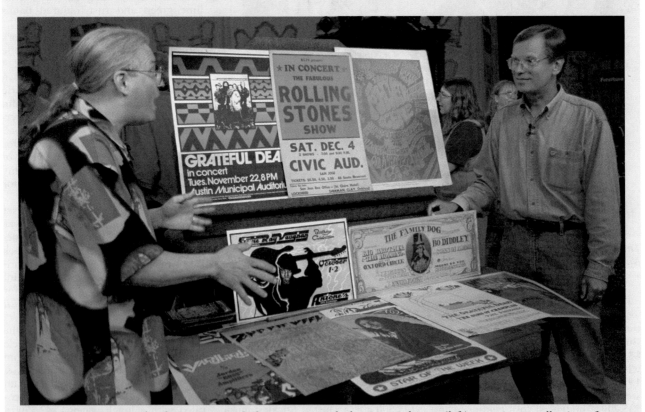

On a February 19 episode of Antiques Road Show, *antiques dealer Gary Sohmers (left) appraises a collection of concert posters and other rock-and-roll memorabilia from the 1960s and '70s at $15,000.*

Jeff Dunn for WGBH

Computers and
Information Systems

Corporate **CUTBACKS, LAYOFFS, AND MERGERS** dominated information systems sectors in 2001 as the U.S. recession pushed high-tech stocks even lower; **MICROSOFT** released Windows XP and reached a tentative settlement in its widely followed court case; the first **THIRD-GENERATION (3G) CELLULAR PHONE** service was introduced in Japan.

The recession year 2001 hit the computers and information systems sector hard. Already reeling from the collapse of dot-com companies a year earlier, the industry had to deal with reduced demand for its products and services. That in turn produced a steady stream of corporate cutbacks and layoffs. The terrorist attacks in the U.S. on September 11, which stunned the world and sent the U.S. stock market tumbling, dealt the troubled technology sector yet another blow.

The computer industry laid off tens of thousands of workers in 2001 as a slowing U.S. economy combined with fallout from the previous year's meltdown of high-tech dot-com companies to reduce demand for information technology products. Cisco Systems, reporting its first quarterly loss in its 11-year history in May, took more than $3 billion in charges against earnings. The charges were mainly related to inventory Cisco believed it might never sell because of the downturn in demand. Layoffs were announced at dozens of computer-related companies, including AOL Time Warner, Inc., Dell Computer Corp., IBM Corp., Sun Microsystems, Inc., Oracle Corp., Texas Instruments, Inc., Siemens AG of Germany, and the Japanese companies Fujitsu, Ltd., Hitachi, Ltd., and Toshiba Corp.

Yet out of the decline a new industry was taking shape. The Hewlett-Packard Co. said it would purchase competitor Compaq Computer Corp., combining two major competitors in the personal computer (PC) market. In the long-running Microsoft Corp. antitrust trial, an appeals court freed Microsoft from the threat of a breakup, and the Department of Justice (DOJ), under the new Republican administration of Pres. George W. Bush, indicated that it

would not pursue the software-bundling issues that had been the heart of the original lawsuit.

The Internet became less competitive. The contracting economy left even strong electronic-commerce (e-commerce) companies struggling with losses, and brick-and-mortar companies began to see their e-commerce operations less as profit centres and more as strategic efforts. The huge declines in the value of technology stocks and the dearth of new capital for technology companies resulted in the collapse of alternative high-speed digital subscriber line (DSL) Internet access providers.

The music industry won its battle against Napster but not the war against free Internet music. Napster, the renegade World Wide Web site that stood accused of aiding copyright infringement by allowing consumers to trade music files for free, was shut down by court order, but other file-sharing Web sites rose up to take its place.

Attitudes toward computer security changed in the wake of the September 11 terrorist attacks. Personal privacy on the Internet seemed likely to decline as the government gained additional freedom to track e-mail, instant messaging, and Web surfing. Several devastating attacks by malicious Internet software resulted in coordinated government and business efforts to prevent future threats.

Microsoft. The Microsoft antitrust case ended the year without a resolution, but the year was a busy one in the ongoing battle over Microsoft's behaviour. The company appeared to have avoided being broken up, but it still faced court penalties for violating antitrust laws.

A federal court previously had found that Microsoft violated federal antitrust laws through actions intended to maintain Microsoft's monopoly on PC operating system (OS) software. That find-

ing was confirmed in June by a seven-judge panel from the U.S. Court of Appeals for the District of Columbia Circuit, which held that Microsoft had violated antitrust laws repeatedly.

The appeals court judges vacated, or nullified, the breakup of Microsoft imposed the previous year by U.S. District Judge Thomas Penfield Jackson, who had put his ruling on hold pending appeals. At the same time, the appeals court removed Jackson from the case, an unusual action, and criticized him for comments about the case he had made outside the courtroom. A newly appointed federal judge, Colleen Kollar-Kotelly, ordered settlement talks. In October the U.S. Supreme Court declined to hear Microsoft's appeal, which requested that the high court dismiss the lower court's findings against the company on the basis of the appeal courts reprimand of Judge Jackson. It was a setback for Microsoft, but one that many who followed the case had expected.

The Bush administration signaled late in the year that it did not have as much enthusiasm for pursuing the Microsoft case as former president Bill Clinton's administration had. The DOJ said in September that it had decided not to seek a breakup of Microsoft or to insist that Microsoft's bundling, or inclusion, of its Internet Explorer browser with the Windows OS was illegal. Instead, the DOJ said it would pursue limitations on Microsoft's business conduct similar to those Jackson previously ordered. Those restrictions included requiring Microsoft to share Windows technical information with other software companies, to offer PC manufacturers "unbundled" versions of Windows that did not include extra Microsoft software, and to sell Windows to all PC makers at the same price. Microsoft previously had resisted efforts to place any restrictions on what it could bundle into its operating system. Some legal experts said that at least part of the government's announcement was a practical move—a breakup of Microsoft was unlikely to occur because the federal appeals court had already vacated Jackson's initial breakup order.

In early November Microsoft and the DOJ reached a tentative settlement, but half of the 18 states that had joined the federal government in the case appeared unwilling to compromise. Some of the states threatened to carry on their antitrust cases independently if the DOJ settled with Microsoft on terms the states considered too easy. Nine states—California, Connecticut, Florida, Iowa, Kansas, Massachusetts, Minnesota, Utah, and West Virginia, plus the District of Columbia—rejected the federal government's settlement with Microsoft because they said it let the company off too easily, and planned to continue the antitrust suit. California, one of the largest states in the group, was expected to pay much of the cost involved. It appeared that a hearing on what action the federal court should take against Microsoft would occur in March 2002.

The states wanted rules to prevent Microsoft from combining or "bundling" with Windows any additional free software features—a move that worked to the disadvantage of Microsoft's competitors. In addition, states wanted the court to prevent Microsoft from offering incentives to PC manufacturers to put Microsoft applications software on new PCs instead of applications from competitors. (The states said the federal settlement would only prevent Microsoft from penalizing PC makers for not using its software.) The states also wanted competitors to have better access to underlying Windows software code than required under the proposed federal settlement.

The states also continued to be concerned about recent Microsoft behaviour not directly related to the antitrust case: Microsoft's new Windows XP operating system, which bundled new technologies—such as streaming video and instant messaging—that could adversely affect Microsoft's competitors. Windows XP went on sale on October 25, but details of what it contained had been disclosed by Microsoft months earlier. In a separate class-action suit, Microsoft offered a settlement that would include donating computer equipment and software to schools. Opponents, led by Apple Computer Corp., objected that this action would effectively expand Microsoft's inroads into education, where it did not yet have a monopoly.

Personal Computers. The PC industry was in decline in 2001 as demand dropped, and a price war broke out between PC manufacturers. It was a sharp reversal for a traditional growth industry. When worldwide PC shipments dropped 1.9% in the second quarter, it was the first decline since 1986.

A revised outlook issued in early September by market research firm IDC predicted that PC shipments worldwide would decline 1.6% in 2001, to about 130 million units. That was in sharp contrast to IDC's June prediction that shipments would grow 5.8% and far less than IDC's earlier prediction that shipments would grow 10.3% for the year. The consumer portion of the PC market declined even more than the overall market; unit shipments were expected to drop 9.6% worldwide.

The slack demand resulted in a price war between manufacturers that was expected to lower revenues for the PC industry. IDC predicted a 10.8% drop in worldwide PC revenue for the year. Some PC companies decided they had had enough. Micron Electronics dropped out of the PC business and laid off 400 people who worked in that business unit.

It was unclear how the IDC projections would be affected by the September 11 terrorist attacks, which shook consumer confidence and rattled the U.S. economy. Merrill Lynch & Co. said in late September that the struggling PC market had been hurt further by the attacks as well as by a likely global recession and that a recovery from the decline in PC unit shipments, revenues, and average sale prices was not expected for at least a year.

In the first quarter of 2001, Dell replaced Compaq as the world's largest PC maker. It was the first change in the top position in several years. Later in the year Dell aggressively courted additional customers by continuing the price war it had begun in 2000. The company said its goal was to increase its mid-2001 global market share of 13% to 40% over several years.

Windows XP was considered by many to be the PC industry's best hope to boost demand. Because many older PCs lacked the processing power and memory required for running XP, industry observers expected the product launch to increase sales of new PCs. Windows XP featured higher reliability than earlier versions of Windows, plus new features dealing with instant messaging, digital photography, and security (in the form of a "personal firewall" to block Internet intruders). While some feared that the ongoing Microsoft antitrust case might lead government regulators to try to block the introduction of XP or force it to be altered, that did not happen, and the product was launched as expected.

By the time Windows XP was introduced in October, many industry watchers were predicting that it would not make a significant difference in 2001 PC sales, both because of concerns about the economy and because XP did not offer enough incremental benefits to boost sales of PCs that came equipped with the new operating system.

Another potential roadblock to the XP introduction did not have much impact. Some privacy advocates asked the Federal Trade Commission to take action against Microsoft based on their contention that Windows XP facilitated the collection of too much personal information about consumers through the sign-up for Microsoft's on-line e-commerce services.

Microsoft made some changes to Windows XP on its own in response to industry complaints. In June the company removed XP's "smart tags," which could link any word on any Web page to another Web site selected by Microsoft. The implication was that Microsoft would be able to use XP to divert e-commerce customers to its own Web sites. Another controversial XP technology, called product activation, remained. To prevent customers from installing one copy of XP on multiple computers, the software took the "electronic fingerprint" of the PC on which it was installed. Substantial changes in that computer would cause XP to deactivate, on the theory that the operating system had been installed on a different machine. Some industry watchers said merely upgrading a computer could cause the deactivation; Microsoft said the changes to the machine would have to be more elaborate than that but did not provide details.

Apple's rival operating system, Mac OS X, which was released for public beta testing in 2000, began shipping in early 2001. A much-anticipated upgrade, OS X version 10.1, followed in the autumn. During the year Apple opened the first of a series of company-owned retail stores in high-traffic shopping malls, veering away from its strategy of selling strictly through independent resellers, large electronics retailers, and its own Web site. The firm hoped to attract some current users of Windows-based PCs at a time when Apple's share of the PC market was about 4.5%. The company's independent dealers believed the new stores were a necessary evil that would take some sales away from dealers but would ultimately help Apple compete against the market domination of Windows-based PCs. Apple also discontinued its Power Mac G4 Cube, a small cube-shaped computer introduced a year earlier, blaming lower-than-expected sales. The company, in a move to remain competitive with Windows-based PC prices, brought back a $799 iMac desktop computer that had been replaced by higher-priced models.

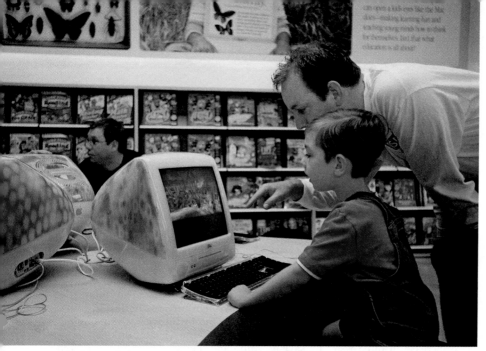

A father and son try out a Flower Power iMac during the grand opening of an Apple retail store in McLean, Va., on May 19.

AP/Wide World Photos

In October Apple introduced iPod, a pocket-sized portable music player that could download and play up to 10 hours of music in the popular MP3 format. A Windows version was expected to follow.

PCs got faster, but as the price of chips came down, they debuted at lower prices than previous top-of-the-line models. In August PCs installed with Intel Corp.'s 2-GHz (gigahertz) Pentium 4 chips (operating at two billion computing cycles per second) arrived. Their beginning prices were as low as $1,500, a switch from the previous generation of new computers; less than a year and a half earlier, a low-end 1-GHz PC had cost $3,000. In large part the price declines were related to lower selling prices for microprocessor chips.

Another kind of PC, the handheld personal digital assistant (PDA), continued to make inroads with consumers and business customers, although sales growth slowed and manufacturers cut prices in response. The best-known PDA brands from Palm, Inc., and Handspring were more than handheld organizers but less than laptop computers. They had date and address books, to-do lists, and memo pads and used handwriting-recognition software. Handspring licensed the Palm OS, but more capable and expensive devices running the Microsoft Pocket PC operating system were being positioned to compete in the business market.

Acquisitions and Mergers. The biggest industry deal of the year was announced in September. Hewlett-Packard, the third largest PC maker, said it would buy Compaq, the second largest, for $25 billion in stock. The merged firm would control about 70% of the retail PC market and would rank second in sales to IBM, with $87.4 billion. To realize cost savings, the two firms would need to cut some 15,000 jobs, leaving the combined company with about 135,000 workers. Carly Fiorina, chairman and chief executive of Hewlett-Packard, was to retain those positions in the combined company, and Michael Capellas, chairman and CEO of Compaq, would be president. The acquisition was not viewed positively by Wall Street. Between the September announcement and mid-October, when a shareholder group voiced opposition to the combination, Hewlett-Packard shares fell 22% and Compaq shares fell 20%. Analysts said one concern was that there was too much overlap between the operations of the two firms. Shareholder opposition to the deal grew as members of the Hewlett and Packard families, who held 18% of the company's shares, publicly opposed the merger. Should shareholders vote against the merger, it was widely believed that Fiorina would lose her top post at Hewlett-Packard. A shareholder vote on the deal was expected in early 2002.

In January Ariba, Inc., a business transaction software company, announced plans to acquire Agile Software Corp., which helped manufacturing companies collaborate on the Internet, for $2,550,000,000 in stock. LSI Logic Corp., which manufactured communications and storage chips, bought C-Cube Microsystems, Inc., for $878 million in stock. TMP Worldwide Inc., the parent company of Internet jobs Web site Monster.com, tried to acquire HotJobs.com, its biggest competitor, but was outbid by Yahoo! Inc., which agreed to pay $436 million.

Jupiter Media Metrix, Inc., which measured the popularity of top Web sites and advised companies on Internet use, was acquired by NetRatings, another Web audience-measurement firm, for $71.2 million. Computer Associates International, Inc., successfully resisted an effort to take over its board of directors, turning back a bid by investor Sam Wyly to replace four directors, including the company's founder and chairman.

On-Line Music. On-line music downloading continued to blossom, despite the music industry's efforts to stop unauthorized free distribution of copyrighted music and the industry's own slowly unfolding plan to sell music over the Internet.

There was a major development in the Recording Industry Association of America's lawsuit against Napster, the high-profile Web service that popularized free music downloads. A federal judge in July ordered Napster to halt its music-file-sharing service until it could show that it had taken all possible steps to prevent the free exchange of copyrighted music. Napster was later allowed to resume Internet operations but chose not to in order to prepare for the 2002 launch of its new membership service. In addition, Napster settled separate copyright-infringement suits filed against it by the heavy-metal band Metallica and the rap artist Dr. Dre, although settlement terms were not disclosed.

Other free file-sharing services took Napster's place, and one, Fast Track, even exceeded the volume that Napster had had at its peak. In October some 30 music and film studios filed suit in federal court against three Internet music Web sites—MusicCity.com, Grokster Ltd., and Consumer Empowerment BV—alleging that they improperly allowed the exchange of music, images, and movies that were copyrighted.

The new free music services on the Internet presented the music industry with vexing legal problems. Court injunctions might be unable to shut down the new services, which allowed music sharing directly between PCs instead of relying on a centralized corporate Web site, as Napster did. Shutting down the Web sites might not end the file sharing among users.

The music industry announced plans to offer, by year's end, two for-pay subscription services for on-line music. Sony Music Entertainment Inc. and Universal Music Group cooperated on a service to be called Pressplay, while EMI Group PLC, AOL Time Warner, Bertelsmann AG's BMG, and RealNetworks, Inc., were behind a competing service to be called MusicNet. Other, similar services were likely to emerge. The exact nature of the music offerings was not disclosed, but the industry's licensing arrangements with music publishers and songwriters covered streaming music—a technique that would let customers listen to music but not record it—and music file downloads that would be limited by how much or how long they could be used. The music industry's efforts to move into for-pay on-line music distribution prompted the DOJ to launch an antitrust investigation aimed at determining whether the music industry was attempting to dominate Internet music illegally. It also was uncertain how successful the initially limited for-pay offerings would be against the free file-sharing services.

The Internet. Despite growing demand for high-speed Internet service, the declining economy effectively reduced the number of competitors, and the DSL service was left largely in the hands of the former regional Bell telephone companies. Several independent companies that provided DSL either failed or were in serious trouble. NorthPoint Communications Group, Inc., and Rhythms NetConnections Inc. shut down. DSL firm Covad Communications Co., which sought protection from creditors in bankruptcy court, said it hoped to attract $200 million in cash investments that would make it profitable again by the end of 2003.

The cable modem service offered by cable TV system operators, which was DSL's chief competitor for high-speed Internet access, had fewer spectacular declines, but even there business failure occurred. At Home Corp. (which did business as Excite@Home), a provider of high-speed Internet access to about four million subscribers through various cable TV systems, filed for bankruptcy protection in September but continued to serve its customers. A month earlier Excite@Home's auditing firm, which had already been slated to be fired, had raised doubts about the company's ability to continue in business. These doubts were confirmed in early December as hundreds of thousands of AT&T Broadband subscribers were left temporarily without Internet access when Excite@Home canceled its contract with AT&T and cut off their

service. Excite@Home said it would cease operations in February 2002.

Wireless high-speed networking companies also ran into trouble. Metricom, Inc., which offered wireless Internet access for notebook computer users in several cities, filed for bankruptcy in July and began selling its assets. MobileStar Network Corp., which provided high-speed wireless Internet access to Starbucks Corp.'s coffee outlets and to several hotels, laid off its workforce and planned to sell its assets.

The world's largest Internet access provider raised prices for its dial-up modem service. America Online, a part of AOL Time Warner, boosted its popular unlimited-use plan by about 9%, to $23.90 a month. AOL justified its first price increase in three years by saying usage of its service by customers had increased more than 50% in that time. AOL remained the market leader in U.S. Internet access. At the time of the price increase, AOL had about 30 million subscribers, MSN (Microsoft Network) was second with about 5 million, and Earth-Link, Inc., was third with about 4.8 million. Freeserve remained the most widely used provider in the U.K., with AOL second.

Late in the year President Bush signed legislation that extended a moratorium on Internet-related taxes for two years, at least temporarily preventing states from levying their own Internet taxes on billions of dollars in e-commerce sales as well as on the sale of Internet access services. There had been fears that Internet taxation by states might contribute to the nation's economic problems.

The virtual world of the Internet proved to be vulnerable to natural disasters in the real world. In July a fire in a Baltimore, Md., train tunnel burned fibre-optic telecommunications cables. Rerouting Internet traffic to other cables resulted in slowdowns in Internet traffic. Damage to undersea cables near China, probably caused by cargo ships dragging their anchors, disrupted Internet traffic between Asia and the U.S. in September.

The U.S. Census Bureau reported in 2001 that 51% of the households in the nation had one or more personal computers in 2000 and that more than 40% of households were connected to the Internet. The results were based on a survey of about 50,000 U.S. households in August 2000.

An Internet-oriented product, the Web appliance, began to disappear from the market owing to lack of demand. Web appliances were intended to offer consumers an easier way to browse the

Web and often were less complex than a PC. They were not much less expensive than a PC, however, and never sold in significant numbers. Sony, 3Com Corp., and Gateway, Inc., dropped Web appliance products in 2001.

E-Commerce. E-commerce continued the downward slide that had begun in early 2000. In the first half of 2001, U.S. Internet advertising revenues declined 7.8% from the same period a year earlier. The on-line ad sales decline compared with revenue growth of 78% in 2000 and marked the end of several years of substantial growth in on-line ad revenues. The Interactive Advertising Bureau, a trade group, said the decline in Internet advertising had come at a time when traditional TV, radio, and newspaper advertising revenues also had dropped.

Many smaller e-commerce players dropped out of the market, and even top players such as Yahoo! were troubled. A 44% decline in revenue caused a third-quarter net loss at Yahoo! and led the company to warn that difficult times and layoffs lay just ahead. Amazon.com, another big player, eliminated 1,300 jobs on January 30, 450 of them by shutting down a distribution centre in McDonough, Ga. One of the few Internet ventures to buck the downward trend was the on-line auction firm eBay Inc., which was flourishing under its president and CEO, Meg Whitman. (*See* BIOGRAPHIES.)

For big corporations e-commerce took on a different tone. On-line business units of brick-and-mortar retailers were valued less as profit centres and more as on-line testing grounds for measuring the appeal of new products and identifying customer buying patterns. In addition, the automobile industry, which knew that consumers were inclined to do their car-buying research on the Web, concentrated on using the Internet as a means to draw people into traditional showrooms rather than as a way to sell cars directly.

E-commerce companies, which relied heavily on credit card purchases, became concerned about increasing credit card fraud. Some claimed that Web fraud expanded after credit card companies ruled that sellers would be liable for disputed card purchases unless the seller had a copy of the buyer's credit card or of the buyer's signature. E-commerce marketers who did business over the Web usually did not have those copies and as a result found themselves stuck for purchases that buyers said they did not make.

In tough times new, unorthodox methods of competition arose. When customers visited some e-commerce sites, free software that ran in the background of a customer's computer would flash ads for competing services on the PC's screen. This software, typically downloaded for free from sites such as Gator.com, offered to make Web browsing easier. In another unusual move, many search engine Web sites, unable to make enough money with advertising, sold listings. This essentially guaranteed that a paid customer would show up near the top of search query results on a particular topic. Web sites that did not sell listings in their

TRIOT Act, which gave law-enforcement officials greater ability to tap telephones and track Internet users.

The new law expanded the use of a federal government Internet spying technology formerly called Carnivore. Carnivore allowed the government to collect, through an Internet service provider (ISP) network, a person's e-mail, instant messaging, and Web surfing activities. The law also expanded the way information was shared between government agencies and made it easier for government investigators to obtain wiretapping permission for Internet activity. In addition, ISPs would be required to make it easier for

locations by using the Internet were considered potentially vulnerable. The Internet Corporation for Assigned Names and Numbers planned to review the security of the Internet's domain name system.

Computerized disaster-recovery services, originally envisioned to help corporations recover data lost in natural disasters such as fires or storms, got more attention as corporations and Wall Street firms recovered from the terrorist attacks. Disaster-recovery firms provided crucial computer network repairs, temporary data-processing centres, and replacement computers.

Following the terrorist attacks, there was much discussion of increased security. Microsoft said it would increase internal security after six employees in its Reno, Nev., office were exposed to life-threatening anthrax spores sent by mail from Malaysia. Elaborate computer security schemes for airports were discussed, including facial-recognition systems that would pick out people whose features matched those of suspected terrorists. Fear of flying also produced a surge of interest in video-conferencing, which enabled business-people to meet face-to-face even though they were hundreds or thousands of kilometres apart.

Meg Whitman, president and CEO of eBay Inc., shakes hands with Microsoft CEO Steve Ballmer after the announcement on March 12 of a new strategic alliance between the two companies.

AP/Wide World Photos

The CERT (originally the computer emergency response team) Coordination Center, a government-funded group that monitored computer security threats, estimated that the number of Internet attacks could double in 2001 compared with 2000, when there were nearly 22,000 recorded attacks, each representing a report filed by a company or an organization. The projected increase was attributed to growth in the Internet as well as to an increase in the number of attackers.

The Code Red worm attracted national attention when it struck in July and reappeared in August. (A "worm" is a malicious Internet program that reproduces itself. Unlike a virus, which tricks a computer user into starting it, a worm acts without human intervention and thus spreads rapidly.) Code Red attempted to attack the White House Web page in mid-July by first infecting an estimated 225,000 Internet Web server computers worldwide. It did so by taking advantage of a well-known Microsoft server software flaw, for which Microsoft had issued a software "patch." Many companies operating these Web servers had not put the patch in place. Code Red then used those servers to launch a "denial of service attack," in which the

searches were able to differentiate themselves from the competition.

Microsoft was undeterred by the e-commerce downturn and introduced its new .NET strategy for selling more services on-line to consumers and businesses. Microsoft said its .NET My Services would sell subscription-based Internet services revolving around on-line content, banking, shopping, and entertainment.

Crime, Security, and Law. After a year in which malicious attacks by creators of Internet viruses and worms made headlines for weeks, it was the U.S. government's actions following the September 11 terrorist attacks that had the greatest potential impact. In October President Bush signed into law the USA PA-

the government to install wiretaps on their systems. Unlike some other parts of the new law that would not expire, the Internet surveillance portion would expire at the end of 2005.

Privacy advocates criticized the new law as a hasty action that unnecessarily expanded the governments surveillance powers, particularly when there was not much evidence that greater surveillance would have warned of the September 11 terrorist attacks.

Some observers worried that another wave of terrorist attacks could be made against "infrastructure" computer systems, including those that ran the electric power grid. Utilities, telecommunications plants, and factories that ran process-control equipment at remote infected computers tried to overload the White House Web page by sending thousands of simultaneous requests for information. Some 350,000 computers were ultimately infected.

Code Red provoked major concern about the Internet's ability to withstand the attack. The FBI's National Infrastructure Protection Center called Code Red a significant threat that could "degrade services running on the Internet." Those fears were heightened when a second version of Code Red appeared in early August; that version of the worm left open a "back door" on a server that would allow a hacker to gain access to the server. The Internet as a whole never was seriously affected by Code Red. Other high-profile attacks included the "SirCam" virus, which arrived as an e-mail attachment and could delete or e-mail files from infected PCs, and the Nimda worm, which infected both Web server computers and PCs and caused damage by overwriting computer files.

There were some high-profile computer-related crimes and court cases during 2001. Dmitry Sklyarov, a Russian cryptographer, was one of the first people to be prosecuted for allegedly violating the Digital Millennium Copyright Act, a 1998 law that limited unauthorized copying of digital material. Sklyarov was arrested after he gave a presentation at a hacker convention on how to decode software used to protect electronic books. About 100 people were arrested in August for what federal officials said was participation in a global Internet child pornography ring. The investigation revolved around Landslide Productions Inc. of Fort Worth, Texas, which offered subscribers access to foreign-based Web sites containing child pornography.

The FBI and the DOJ said 90 individuals and companies were charged as part of an Internet fraud investigation called "Operation Cyber Loss." Based on losses by thousands of people totaling $117 million, the unnamed defendants faced federal and state charges that included wire fraud, mail fraud, bank fraud, money laundering, and violation of intellectual property rights. The charges revolved around on-line auction fraud, nondelivery of products

bought on-line, bank fraud, and pyramid schemes.

The Securities and Exchange Commission (SEC) accused two former top executives at software company AremisSoft Corp. of having defrauded investors of at least $200 million. In a civil suit the SEC said the two had used untrue financial statements in order to sell millions of shares of company stock at inflated prices.

The U.S. Supreme Court ruled in favour of a group of freelance writers who had sued newspaper and magazine publishers for infringing on the writers' copyrights. The suit claimed the publications had infringed by not obtaining permission to make articles available in computer databases following publication. (*See* MEDIA AND PUBLISHING: *Newspapers.*) Another case scheduled to go before the court was a challenge to the 1996 Child Pornography Prevention Act, which had widened the definition of child pornography. The law extended a ban on images of real children engaging in sexual acts to cover computer-generated images that did not involve real children. Civil libertarians argued that the law set a dangerous precedent by

At Lawrence Livermore National Laboratory near San Francisco, a Unix system administrator opens the back door of a node of ASCI White, the world's most powerful computer.

punishing creators of computer-generated pictures; proponents of the law said the wider definition was needed to protect children from pedophiles who wanted such images.

Other Developments. Lernout & Hauspie Speech Products NV, the Belgian firm that was Europes largest developer of speech-recognition and translation software, was declared insolvent, and a court ordered its assets liquidated. The firm had sought protection under the bankruptcy laws of Belgium and the U.S. in late 2000 after a $100 million cash shortfall was discovered in its South Korean unit and an investigation showed that the company's questionable accounting practices had overstated overall company sales by $373 million from 1998 to 2000.

IBM designed the world's most powerful supercomputer for the U.S. government's Lawrence Livermore National Laboratory, Livermore, Calif. The supercomputer was to be used to simulate nuclear weapons explosions. It was funded by the Accelerated Strategic Computing Initiative, which paid computer manufacturers to build supercomputers from ordinary computer components.

IBM also said it had found a way to speed up computer chips by using conventional chip-manufacturing technologies to reduce electrical resistance in chips, which resulted in processing speeds up to 35% faster. Meanwhile, scientists believed that nanotubes, cylinder-shaped molecules 1.4 nanometres (billionths of a metre) in diameter, held out the promise of improving future computer chip designs. Researchers from Michigan State University and IBM said the molecules could help chips run cooler by conducting heat away and might be used as structurally stronger replacements for the tiny metal wires connecting transistors on a chip.

Computer chip manufacturers also were seeking higher chip performance by switching from aluminum to copper (which conducts electricity better than aluminum) for the tiny wires on a chip. In addition, Intel said it was considering using strands of fibre-optic material in place of aluminum and copper wires inside computers. Initially that would mean connecting separate computer components with fibre optics, but eventually the technology could be used on computer chips too. The fibre-optic technology could help boost chip performance because it required less power than wires.

Bell Labs, the research unit of Lucent Technologies Inc., said it had created a tiny organic transistor by assembling carbon molecules. Scientists said the technology might one day be used to make computer chips that were faster, smaller, and easier to manufacture.

Video game enthusiasts had a good year in 2001. Nintendo Co., Ltd., introduced its new Game Boy Advance handheld game machine, and in November two next-generation game console machines, the Microsoft Xbox and the Nintendo GameCube, were introduced. Xbox and GameCube competed with the Sony PlayStation 2. Another competitor, Sega Enterprises Ltd., ended production of its game console, the Dreamcast.

The game industry was attacked in a study from Japan's Tohoku University that said video games might adversely affect brain development in children. A game industry group, the European Leisure Software Publishers Association, claimed that the Japanese research had only a "very limited focus" and that game playing developed several skills.

Gordon Moore, cofounder and retired chairman of Intel, and his wife, Betty, donated $600 million to the California Institute of Technology, from which Moore had graduated with a Ph.D. in chemistry in 1954. It was believed to be the biggest gift ever received by an individual American school. Moore, age 72, was CEO of Intel from 1975 to 1987 and was chairman until 1997.

(STEVE ALEXANDER)

MICROELECTRONICS

In 2001 the global semiconductor industry suffered its worst-ever decline, with projected worldwide sales of semiconductors down 31% to $141 billion, according to the U.S.-based Semiconductor Industry Association (SIA). The association predicted, however, that sales of personal computers (PCs), wireless communications solutions, and consumer products would enable the global semiconductor industry to recover from the inventory buildup that occurred in 2000 and the weak demand for end-market equipment in 2001. After the beginnings of recovery in the fourth quarter of 2001, the industry was expected to continue with slow growth of 6% to $150 billion in 2002 and then return to a traditional growth pattern

with 21% increases in sales to $181 billion in 2003 and $218 billion in 2004.

Sales of flash memory decreased 27% to $7.8 billion in 2001 after having grown 133% in 2000. The SIA predicted that demand for flash-memory devices, led by cellular deployment, digital photography, and automotive applications, would bring growth of 5% to $8.1 billion in 2002. Advances of 23% in 2003 and 25% in 2004 to $12 billion would make flash memory one of the fastest-growing semiconductor sectors. Digital signal processors (DSPs) were another fast-growing sector, for which the SIA expected the key drivers to be wireless and wired communications, emerging digital consumer applications, and portable information devices. Despite having declined 34% to $4 billion in 2001, sales of DSPs were predicted to grow 16% in 2002, 33% in 2003, and 29% in 2004 to $8 billion. The dynamic random access memory sector decreased 60% to $12 billion in 2001, but the SIA expected it to increase 16% in 2002, 44% in 2003, and 54% in 2004 to $29 billion. The microcontroller market declined 17% in 2001 to $10 billion, but it was predicted to rise to $16 billion by 2004. The market for programmable logic devices, which included display drivers for flat-panel displays, declined 28% in 2001 to $25 billion but was expected to grow 6% in 2002, 21% in 2003, and 19% in 2004 to $38 billion. The microprocessors found in PCs, servers, and embedded applications decreased 28% in 2001 to $23 billion. Growth of 7% in 2002, 16% in 2003, and 10% in 2004 to $31 billion was predicted by the SIA, however. The optical storage market was expected to be driven by a rapid shift to compact disc-read/read and write (CD-R/RW) and digital versatile (or video) disc-read only memory (DVD-ROM), especially as more CD-R/RW and DVD-ROM drives were being preinstalled in PCs. In 2001 the optoelectronics market declined 22% to $7.6 billion, but it was predicted to grow 0.1% in 2002, 15% in 2003, and 20% in 2004 to $11 billion.

Although all four major world markets decreased in 2001, the Asia-Pacific market declined least (23% to $39 billion) and therefore took over from the Americas as the world's biggest semiconductor market. The SIA predicted that Asia-Pacific would be the fastest-growing region over the next three years and was likely to reach $67 billion in 2004. The Americas market declined 43% in 2001 to $36 billion, but it was expected to grow to $56 billion in 2004. The market in Japan, which declined 26% in 2001 to

$35 billion, was projected to reach $52 billion in sales by 2004. The European market (down 29% in 2001 to $30 billion) was predicted to rise to $44 billion.

In July 2001 U.S. integrated circuit analyst IC Insights listed the worldwide top 10 semiconductor suppliers (on the basis of sales in the first half of the year). U.S.-based Intel Corp. remained at the top, followed by Toshiba Corp. (Japan), NEC Corp. (Japan), STMicroelectronics (France), Texas Instruments Inc. (U.S.), Samsung Electronics Co., Ltd. (South Korea), Hitachi, Ltd. (Japan), Motorola, Inc. (U.S.), Infineon Technologies AG (spun off from Siemens AG of Germany), and Mitsubishi Electric Corp. (Japan). The top three positions were unchanged from 2000.

On August 27 Intel introduced the world's first 2 GHz (gigahertz) microprocessor in the form of the latest version of its Pentium 4 chip. The company also demonstrated a Pentium 4 running at 3.5 GHz, noting that the chip's microarchitecture was expected to scale to 10 GHz eventually. In September Intel introduced its 845 chipset for Pentium 4-based PCs. Microsoft Corp.'s Windows XP operating system, released on October 25, was optimized for the Pentium 4 for processor-intensive applications. In August Intel demonstrated a new technology called hyper-threading, which enabled microprocessors to handle more information concurrently by sharing resources more efficiently. This was achieved through multiprocessing on a single chip, which the company intended to bring to market in its Xeon processor family in 2002. The company also disclosed details of its forthcoming Banias mobile processor architecture, which would deploy new low-power circuitry and design techniques.

In August Advanced Micro Devices, Inc., the world's second largest microprocessor supplier (with around 22% of the market; Intel was first with 77%), marked the second anniversary of its Athlon processor by announcing that its new 1.2 GHz mobile Athlon 4 processor would be used by Compaq Computer Corp. in its Presario notebook computers and introducing its Windows XP-compatible 1.6 GHz Athlon 1900+.

(ALAN STEWART)

TELECOMMUNICATIONS

In 2001 telecommunications companies around the world experienced a year of tumbling stock prices and huge job losses. By September the stock market valuation of the world's telecom carriers and suppliers had declined by $3.8 trillion from a peak of $6.3 trillion in March 2000. More than a quarter of a million jobs were lost throughout the world in the second quarter of 2001 alone. The major equipment manufacturers—Motorola, Inc., Lucent Technologies, Inc., and Cisco Systems (U.S.), Marconi Corp. PLC (U.K.), Siemens AG (Germany), Ericsson (Sweden), and Nokia Corp. (Finland)—all announced job cuts both in their home countries and in subsidiaries around the world. Some of the biggest losses were announced by the Canadian supplier Nortel Networks Ltd., which shed 50% of its workforce (almost 50,000 jobs). In France equipment manufacturer Alcatel cut 33,000 jobs—almost a third of its employees.

On October 1 FOMA, the world's first third-generation (3G) cellular phone service, was launched in Japan on a fully commercialized basis by NTT DoCoMo, Inc., the wireless operator in which Nippon Telegraph & Telephone (NTT) had a 64% holding. A pilot version of the service had been running since May 30. FOMA (which stood for Freedom Of Mobile multimedia Access) was initially available in the Tokyo area only, but it was to be extended to other major cities in late 2001 and early 2002. As well as a voice service, the 3G handset also provided 64-Kbps (kilobits-per-second) digital communication for a videophone service and a maximum 384-Kbps data downlink for DoCoMo's i-mode mobile Internet service. On November 19 DoCoMo introduced i-motion, a video-clip distribution service using FOMA at speeds of up to 384 Kbps. Movie trailers, news highlights, and music tracks were provided by 28 content providers from 37 i-motion sites accessed via DoCoMo's official i-mode portal. Full video- and music-distribution services were planned to begin in the spring of 2002.

In October Motorola forecast that mobile phone sales would fall for the first time ever in 2001, predicting global sales of 380 million–400 million, compared with around 400 million in 2000. To counter this trend, rival Nokia unveiled an "entertainment phone," featuring a full keyboard, digital music player, FM radio, five games, and advanced messaging capabilities. In April Ericsson and Sony Corp. of Japan announced that they were setting up a joint venture, based in London, to combine the two companies' cellular handset manufacturing businesses. Bell Labs, the research and development arm of Lucent Technologies, introduced the first high-capacity all-optical router.

An NTT DoCoMo, Inc., employee poses while a colleague videotapes her with a FOMA handset, which featured videophone and mobile Internet service.

Bermuda-based international carrier Global Crossing Ltd. was the first customer for the technology, deploying the router on its global fibre-optic network.

During 2001 much of the telecom industry was dominated by spin-offs, mergers, and acquisitions. AT&T Corp. and British Telecommunications PLC (BT) implemented restructuring plans announced in late 2000, which included demerging their wireless businesses. AT&T Wireless became an independent company on July 9. In October AT&T Wireless Services, Inc., which held a 23% stake in American wireless provider TeleCorp PCS, Inc., acquired the rest of that company for $4.7 billion. AT&T had paid $135 million in March for the assets of the bankrupt American digital subscriber line provider NorthPoint Communications Group, Inc. In October AT&T and BT decided to unwind their loss-making international joint venture Concert, set up in 1998, and return its assets to the parent companies in the first half of 2002. In December Comcast Corp. agreed to pay $72 billion to acquire AT&T's cable television business, AT&T Broadband, to form a new company to be called AT&T Comcast Corp. The transaction was subject to regulatory and shareholder approval.

In January BT confirmed that it would buy 45% of VIAG Interkom from German energy conglomerate E.ON AG for €7,250,000,000 (about $6.5 billion), giving it complete ownership of the German fixed and mobile operator. BT took full ownership of Irish mobile operator Esat Digifone in February, acquiring the 49.5% stake held by Norwegian carrier Telenor ASA for $1,240,000,000. As of March 31, BT's debt stood at £27.9 billion (£1=about $1.42). Calls from shareholders for changes at the top led to the departure of Sir Iain Vallance as chairman in April, to be replaced by Sir Christopher Bland, chairman of the BBC. During the summer the new management seemed to reverse course. BT sold to Vodafone Group PLC, the U.K.'s largest wireless operator, its 17% stake in the Spanish mobile operator Airtel Móvil, SA, for £1.1 billion, as well as its interests in Japan Telecom and J-Phone Co., Ltd., for £3.7 billion, and announced that it had agreed to sell its interest in Rogers Wireless Communications Inc. in Canada to AT&T Wireless for £269 million. In October it was announced that Sir Peter Bonfield would stand down at the end of January 2002 after six years as BT's chief executive. BT Wireless (which had been renamed mmO2 in September) became independent on November 19.

The main French carrier, France Telecom, in June relaunched its Itineris wireless network (which had a 48% market share) under the Orange brand. In 2000 Vodafone had acquired U.K. rival Orange plc as part of its purchase of German wireless network Mannesmann AG and had then sold Orange to France Telecom, the majority of whose wireless interests were merged with Orange's to become the Orange SA group. On June 12 BT Wireless and T-Mobile International, the wireless business of Germany's main carrier, Deutsche Telekom AG, announced that they would cooperate on the rollout of 3G networks by their subsidiaries in the U.K. and in Germany.

A similar agreement was announced in October by two of the largest American wireless communications companies. VoiceStream Wireless Corp. (which was acquired by Deutsche Telekom in May) and Cingular Wireless (a joint venture between SBC Communications Inc. and BellSouth Corp.) agreed to share their networks in New York City, California, and Nevada. In November the U.S. Federal Communications Commission voted to relax rules imposing a cap of 45 MHz on ownership of wireless spectrum capacity in cities. The spectrum cap was raised to the rural level of 55 MHz immediately and was to be abolished completely as of Jan. 1, 2003.

(ALAN STEWART)

Earth Sciences

Scientists in 2001 reported finding an ASTONISHING field of white CARBONATE TOWERS on the Atlantic SEAFLOOR; data from a space probe orbiting MARS showed images of SEDIMENTARY FORMATIONS. Climatologists projected 2001 to be the SECOND WARMEST year on record.

GEOLOGY AND GEOCHEMISTRY

In June 2001 geology and geochemistry were successfully merged in Edinburgh at the novel Earth System Processes: A Global Meeting (June 24–28, 2001), coconvened by the Geological Society of America and the Geological Society of London (cosponsored by the Edinburgh Geological Society, University of Edinburgh, and Geological Surveys of the U.S. and the U.K.). The concept was that the plate tectonics revolution of the 1960s was only a first step in understanding the whole Earth system. In order to understand the dynamic whole, interdisciplinary studies of interactions between its component parts are required. The sessions were designed to emphasize the linkages between geologic, chemical, physical, and biological processes, along with their social and economic implications.

The linkages between geology, geochemistry, and the biosphere are clearly displayed by the submarine hydrothermal vents that spew hot water and deposit minerals that form chimneys. A report from a project of the University of Washington and the American Museum of Natural History, New York City, to characterize a suite of large sulfide chimneys from the Juan de Fuca Ridge was published during the year by John Delaney and Deborah Kelley of the University of Washington and seven coauthors. Using a centimetre-scale navigation-control system, optical- and sonar-imaging sensors, and real-time navigation techniques, the researchers produced the highest-quality fine-scale map of a complex with more than 13 chimneys ranging in height from 8.5 to 23 m (1 m=3.28 ft). Water venting from the chimneys reached 300 °C (570 °F). Dense clusters of tubeworms,

snails, crabs, and microbial communities covered the structures. In a remarkable feat of remote engineering in water 2,250 m deep, the team sawed off and recovered four samples of chimneys about two metres in length. These were digitally imaged, cored, split, and immediately subjected to geochemical and microbiological examination. The research team discovered complex vertical zones of minerals, networks of flow channels lined with sulfides, and microorganisms distributed within well-defined mineral zones. The proportions of specific bacteria varied from the hot interior to the cooler exterior of the chimneys and were clearly related to, and perhaps even modifiers of, the geochemistry of their local environment.

The largest submarine hydrothermal towers yet discovered were described and explained in 2001 by Kelley, Donna Blackman (Scripps Institution of Oceanography), and many coauthors from the U.S. and Europe. The submersible research vessel *Alvin* revealed to its three astonished crew members a large field of white towers at a water depth of 700–800 m. This "Lost City Hydrothermal Field" extends across a terrace on the steep southern wall of the Atlantis Massif, about 15 km (1 km=0.62 mi) west of the Mid-Atlantic Ridge near 30° N. It consists of about 30 pinnacle-like chimney structures, the largest reaching 60 m in height and more than 10 m in diameter. In contrast to the black, high-temperature, sulfide-rich chimneys associated with the volcanically active oceanic ridge axes, these white towers vent relatively cool water of less than 70 °C (160 °F); the water precipitates carbonates and hydrated minerals, and there is no evidence for recent volcanism. The mineralogy of the carbonate chimneys and the fluid composition are consistent with re-

actions occurring between percolating seawater and the mantle rock that underlies the Atlantis Massif. The water is heated by the chemical reactions that convert the peridotite rock to serpentinite. Although few mobile creatures were found around these structures, there were abundant, dense microbial communities. These low-temperature carbonate chimneys may be widespread on older oceanic crust, supporting chemosynthetic microbial populations in environments similar to those in early Earth systems when life first evolved.

There was a new claim for the oldest rock on Earth, arising from the geochemistry of tiny minerals, zircons, in Western Australia. Igneous gneisses there are about 3,750,000,000 years old. The zircons, collected from a series of sedimentary rocks formed in a large delta, had previously been dated at 4,276,000,000 years. Detailed investigations by two teams from Australia, the U.S., and Scotland (Simon Wilde and three coauthors, and Stephen Mojzsis and two coauthors), however, yielded an age of 4,404,000,000 years, closer by 128,000,000 years to the formation of the Earth. Measurements of isotope concentrations were made on the sliced zircons by means of a precise ion microprobe that bombards the mineral in tiny spots, releasing atoms that are then weighed in a mass spectrometer. Both groups also measured the oxygen isotope ratios in the zircons and concluded that the minerals were derived from preexisting igneous rocks that had been involved with water at near-surface conditions. The existence of liquid water within 150,000,000 years of the Earth's formation 4,550,000,000 years ago was unexpected, given the intense bombardment of the Earth by asteroids at the time. Perhaps there was early formation of oceans and primitive life-forms, which were periodically destroyed on a global scale and then reformed through an interval of about 400,000,000 years earlier than life on Earth is currently thought to have begun.

Insight into the periodic disruptions caused more recently by asteroid impacts was provided by the study of helium in a sequence of limestones deposited in deep seas between 75 million and 40 million years ago. Graduate student Sujoy Mukhopadhyay, working with Kenneth Farley at the California Institute of Technology, and Alessandro

Montanari of the Geological Observatory, Apiro, Italy, studied the limestones near Gubbio in Italy. This series of limestones, composed predominantly of the calcite skeletons of plankton, includes a finger-thick clay layer at the boundary between the Cretaceous and Tertiary periods corresponding in time to the extinction 65 million years ago of 75% of all living species, including the dinosaurs. The sharp boundary at the top of the Cretaceous limestones indicates an abrupt reduction in productivity of plankton, which then rather suddenly increased above the clay layer with different plankton species forming more limestones. Analyses of the rare element iridium in the clay layer, reported in the early 1980s, had provided the first evidence that the mass extinction was caused by the impact of an extraterrestrial body, accompanied by a huge explosion and the global distribution of dust through the stratosphere. The new analyses of isotopes of helium confirmed that no comet shower had passed near the Earth at that time, and a single large extraterrestrial body was thus left as the destructive agent. The analyses also permitted calculations of rates of sedimentation, which led to the conclusion that, following the impact and destruction of global life, the food chain became reestablished in only 10,000 years. Repopulation of the ocean was then achieved within a short time interval. This rapid turnover contrasts with the longer time interval recognized by many paleontologists for the progressive extinction of larger land animals, such as the dinosaurs.

Some significant steps for the parallel development of experiment and theory were achieved during 2001 in defining the framework of phase relationships that control the geology and geochemistry of rock-melt reactions. Two publications by Tim Holland (University of Cambridge), Roger Powell, and R.W. White (both of the University of Melbourne, Australia) presented a comprehensive thermodynamic model for granitic melts in a synthetic system with eight oxide components, including water. The internally consistent dataset with software Thermo-Calc makes possible calculation of the melting relationships for many rocks through the entire thickness of the continental crust. Manipulations of the complex phase diagrams permit the evaluation of processes, including the extent of melt loss during high-temperature metamorphism.

The continuing dependence of thermodynamic databases on new experiments at higher pressures and with additional components was demonstrated by Robert Luth (University of Alberta). The nature of the melting reaction in the Earth's upper mantle under conditions in which carbon dioxide is present is significantly affected by the position of a particular reaction among calcium-magnesium carbonates. Earlier experimental measurements for this reaction at pressures up to 55 kilobars (1 kilobar=1,000 atmospheres) and a temperature of 600 °C (1,100 °F) had been extrapolated by calculations using Thermo-Calc, yielding the result that dolomite (calcium magnesium carbonate) would not be involved in mantle melting at pressures greater than 60 kilobars, corresponding to a depth of 180 km. When Luth measured the reaction experimentally, however, he determined that dolomite does persist as the carbonate relevant for melting reactions in the upper mantle. The presence of dolomitic carbonate-rich melts in mantle rocks beneath an island off the coast of Brazil was demonstrated in 2001 by Lia Kogarko (Vernadsky Institute, Moscow), Gero Kurat (Natural History Museum, Vienna), and Theodoros Ntaflos (University of Vienna). Textures indicated the formation of immiscible (incapable of being mixed) carbonate, sulfide, and silicate liquids.

The "Lost City Hydrothermal Field" discovered below the North Atlantic Ocean includes this white carbonate chimney more than 9 m (30 ft) tall. In contrast to the high-temperature, sulfide-rich chimneys associated with volcanism at seafloor spreading centres, the spires of the Lost City field expel comparatively cool water that precipitates carbonates and hydrated minerals.

University of Washington/ Woods Hole Oceanographic Institution

Experiments by Roland Stalder, Peter Ulmer, A.B. Thompson, and Detlef Günther of the Swiss Federal Institute of Technology, Zürich, on the effect of water on the conditions for melting in the Earth's mantle provided convincing evidence for the occurrence of a critical endpoint on the melting reaction, at a temperature of 1,150 °C (2,100 °F) and a pressure (130 kilobars) corresponding to a depth of about 400 km. At that point the melt and the coexisting aqueous fluid phase become identical in composition and properties. Despite the advances in thermodynamic calculations, experimental data were still insufficient to calculate the high-pressure behaviour of aqueous fluids under those conditions. (PETER J. WYLLIE)

GEOPHYSICS

An intraplate earthquake of magnitude 7.7 (moment magnitude) shook the Indian state of Gujarat on the morning of Jan. 26, 2001, India's Republic Day. Called the Bhuj earthquake, it was one of the deadliest ever recorded in the country. At least 20,000 people were killed, 166,000 injured, and 600,000 displaced. More than 350,000 houses were destroyed; property damage and economic losses were estimated in the billions of dollars.

The Bhuj earthquake occurred on a fault system adjacent to one on which a major shock (moment magnitude 7.8) took place in the Great Rann of Kachchh in 1819. Its focus was determined to be as deep as 23 km (1 km=about 0.62 mi). In a review of geophysical data from seismology, geology, and tectonics, Roger Bilham and Peter Molnar of the University of Colorado at Boulder and Vinod K. Gaur of the Indian Institute of Astrophysics, Bangalore, demonstrated how this earthquake was triggered by the release of elastic strain energy generated and replenished by the stress resulting from the ongoing collision of the Indian plate with the Asian plate, which began between 40 million and 50 million years ago. In this scenario the top surface (basement rock) of the Indian plate south of the Himalayas flexes and slides under the Himalayas in an uneven, lurching manner, similar to the behaviour observed in rapidly converging lithospheric plates beneath the ocean.

The researchers also showed, on the basis of Global Positioning System (GPS) satellite measurements, that India and southern Tibet were converging at a rate of 20 mm (about 0.8 in) per year, consistent with the rate deduced from concurrent field observations. Moreover, they pointed out that the convergence region along the Himalayas held an increased hazard for earthquakes and that 60% of the Himalayas were overdue for a great earthquake. The Bhuj earthquake did not occur along the Himalayan arc and so did nothing to relieve the accumulating strain on the arc. An earthquake of magnitude 8 would be catastrophic for the densely populated region in the Ganges Plain to the south.

In addition to the Bhuj earthquake, major earthquakes (magnitude 7 and greater) with high casualties occurred on January 13 in El Salvador (magnitude 7.7, with more than 800 people killed and 100,000 homes destroyed) and June 23 off coastal Peru (magnitude 8.4, with at least 100 people killed—many by tsunami—and 150,000 homes destroyed).

Sicily's Mt. Etna, Europe's largest and most active volcano, erupted on July 17 in a dramatic display that continued into August. The flow of molten magma, which emerged from fissures along Etna's southeastern slopes, caused tremendous damage to the tourist complex of Rifugio Sapienza and set fire to a cable-car base station. The July–August event, which was the first flank eruption of the volcano since 1993, aroused wide interest from both the scientific community and emergency managers. It occurred from five short vent segments over a linear distance of six kilometres at an elevation of 2,950–2,100 m (9,680–6,890 ft) and discharged 30 million cu m (1.1 billion cu ft) of new magma. Significant losses were avoided when the lava stopped a few kilometres short of the first major mountain community, Nicolosi. Interest for scientists lay in the simultaneous eruption of two magma types, of contrasting chemistry and residence time in the volcano, and in the wide diversity of eruption intensities observed over short distance and time scales.

The economically crippling eruption of Soufrière Hills volcano on the Caribbean island of Montserrat continued through the growth and collapse of the lava dome in 2001. This long-lived (since 1995) and complex event prompted the publication of a major analytic memoir by the Geological Society of London. The even more protracted eruption of Kilauea volcano in Hawaii, which began in 1983, also carried on unabated throughout the year.

Christopher G. Fox of Oregon State University and colleagues reported on the first detailed observation of the eruption of a submarine volcano—Axial volcano on the Juan de Fuca Ridge off the Oregon coast—by a seafloor instrument serendipitously positioned very close to the event. The instrument, a Volcanic System Monitor, carried several sensors, including one for measuring bottom pressure, which served as an indicator for vertical deformation of the seafloor associated with magma movements. Although the instrument was overrun by a lava flow, the scientific data were retrieved.

The mantle, that part of Earth that lies beneath the crust and above the central core, constitutes 82% of Earth's volume and 65% of its weight. Progress was being made in the use of seismic tomography to infer temperature anomalies associated with thermal convection in the mantle. Analogous to the use of X-rays in medical tomography, seismic tomography yielded accurate maps of variations in the velocities of seismic waves produced by earthquakes. By combining this information with a knowledge of the elastic properties (wave-propagation velocities) of various mantle mineral phases as a function of pressure and temperature, scientists could make accurate estimates of the temperature distribution in Earth's mantle. Such velocity data for a number of mantle mineral phases, for example, $(Mg, Fe)SiO_3$ (perovskite) and $(Mg, Fe)_2SiO_4$ (ringwoodite), were being obtained in various laboratories.

Surface geophysical data (e.g., geodetic measurements and observed tectonic plate motions) and global seismic tomographic models were together providing useful information on the flow and thermochemical structure in the deep mantle. In this respect, A.M. Forte of the University of Western Ontario and J.X. Mitrovica of the University of Toronto suggested the existence of a very high effective viscosity near 2,000 km depth, which would suppress flow-induced deformation and convective mixing in the deep mantle.

Leonid Dubrovinsky of Uppsala (Swed.) University and associates suggested that the observed heterogeneity in composition, density, and thermal state (revealed by seismological data) at Earth's core-mantle boundary and in the inner core could plausibly be explained by chemical interaction. They based their reasoning on experimental data on the chemical interaction of iron and aluminum oxide (Al_2O_3) with $MgSiO_3$ (perovskite phase) under simulated conditions of pressure and temperature at the core.

High-resolution images gathered by the Mars Global Surveyor (MGS), which began orbiting the planet in 1997, yielded exciting views of massive layered outcrops of sedimentary rock, as thick as four kilometres, as reported by Michael C. Malin and Kenneth S. Edgett of Malin Space Science Systems, San Diego, Calif. Although the age relationships of these erosional landforms and the processes of deposition and transport that created them, including the possible role of liquid water, remained to be ascertained, their discovery provided some initial clues to the previously unknown geologic and atmospheric history of Mars.

Mars currently lacks a global dipole magnetic field like that of Earth, but the detection of strongly magnetized ancient crust on Mars by the MGS spacecraft was indicative of the presence of a liquid core and an active magnetic dynamo early in the planet's history. Building on this information, David J. Stevenson of the California Institute of Technology reported important new interpretations

and insights about the Martian interior—the nature and history of the iron-rich Martian core and the influence of the core on the early climate and possible life on Mars. According to Stevenson, heat flow from the Martian core also appeared to have contributed to volcanic activity and feeding of mantle plumes, as in the case of Earth's core.

(MURLI H. MANGHNANI)

METEOROLOGY AND CLIMATE

A revived La Niña—the condition of below-normal sea-surface temperatures dominating the central and eastern equatorial Pacific—influenced the weather over parts of the Earth early in 2001. By April equatorial temperatures had returned to normal, which suggested that La Niña, which had begun in 1998, had finally ended.

The upward trend in global surface temperatures continued, while NASA estimates from land and ocean data for the first ten months of 2001 had the year on track to be the second warmest

on record. In contrast, lower tropospheric temperatures as measured by satellite averaged close to the 1979–98 mean, suggesting no significant recent warming trend above the surface. La Niña played a role in aggravating long-term drought over the southeastern United States, particularly Florida, where the 12-month period that ended in April was the third driest in 107 years. Drought also developed over the northwestern U.S. during the 2000–01 winter as blocking high pressure aloft steered storms to the north and south. November–April precipitation in the region was the second lowest since records began in 1895.

For other parts of the U.S., winter brought abundant snowfall, especially in the Northeast and the Great Plains. Major winter storms struck the Northeast in February and March, with a particularly severe storm burying New England and the northern mid-Atlantic region on March 4–5. A wet and stormy April in the upper Midwest led to serious flooding and considerable property damage along the upper reaches of the Mississippi and other rivers.

The first tropical storm in the Atlantic basin, Allison, made landfall June 5 on Galveston Island, Texas. Although the storm was relatively weak, its historic two-week odyssey across the South and up the mid-Atlantic coast cost about $5 billion and left 50 dead. The storm, which turned Houston's streets into raging rivers after depositing up to 890 mm (1 mm=0.04 in) of rain, ended up as the costliest tropical storm in U.S. history.

In central and western Texas a persistent high-pressure system aloft brought drought to the region for the second consecutive summer. Rainfall totaled well under 50% of normal in both June and July, and temperatures above 37.8 °C (100 °F) worsened the dryness. Rains exceeding 300 mm in late August and early September ended dryness in eastern Texas but triggered flooding.

Over the central U.S., the high-pressure ridge responsible for the heat and dryness in the southern plains expanded northward in late July and early August, bringing dangerous heat to the upper Midwest. The ridge further broadened, which resulted in a nearly coast-to-coast heat wave August 6–9. Nationwide, widespread heat during June–August resulted in the fifth warmest summer on record for the U.S., while above-normal temperatures during September–November across all but the Southeast caused autumn to rank as the fourth warmest on record. Drought intensified along the

The layered floor of Mars's western Candor Chasma is revealed in a high-resolution image taken by the Mars Global Surveyor spacecraft. On Earth such a pattern is evidence of sediment deposited at the bottom of a lake or stream.

NASA/JPL/Malin Space Science Systems

Shimmering colours of the aurora borealis paint the sky over Rockford, Mich., in early November. Beginning in late September, a series of coronal mass ejections from the Sun triggered unusually vivid and far-reaching auroral displays, to the delight of sky watchers worldwide.

Eastern Seaboard in autumn as rainfall totaled under 50% of normal from North Carolina to Massachusetts. In contrast, a series of Pacific storms in November and December eased drought in the West.

The Atlantic tropical storm season was active, with 15 named storms of which 9 became hurricanes. The bulk of activity occurred in the last three months of the season—September to November—during which 11 of the named storms formed. For the second consecutive year, no hurricanes made U.S. landfall. Two storms, Barry and Gabrielle, brought some flooding to Florida but also relieved its long-term drought.

In Central America drought in June and July damaged crops from Nicaragua to Guatemala. Hurricane Iris, a category 4 storm packing winds of 233 km (145 mi) per hour, caused severe damage to southern Belize on October 8. The tropical depression that later became Hurricane Michelle brought extremely heavy rains to portions of Nicaragua and Honduras at the end of October. On November 4, Michelle slammed into the coastal islands of Cuba as a category 4 hurricane and into the main island as a category 3 hurricane. Michelle was the strongest hurricane to hit Cuba since 1952.

Across the Middle East and south-central Asia, another dry winter and spring resulted in countries from Syria to Pakistan enduring a third consecutive year of drought. Much of the region experienced four straight months (January–April) with precipitation below half of normal. The drought slashed crop production and depleted rivers and reservoirs. In Algeria, an intense storm struck the north coast on November 9–11. Up to 260 mm of rain led to catastrophic floods and mud slides in Algiers, leaving more than 700 people dead.

Crops dependent on rain failed almost totally in Afghanistan again in 2001. Major drought during the first half of the year also affected northern China and North and South Korea. March–May rainfall in Beijing totaled about one-third of normal. The opposite extreme prevailed in southern China, where torrential June rains exceeding 800 mm killed hundreds of people. An active storm season also affected the region, with Taiwan enduring damage from Typhoons Chebi in June, Toraji in July, and Nari and Lekima in September. Other storms hit the Philippines, China, and Japan, with two typhoons, Pabuk and Danas, striking the Tokyo area within one month of each other (August 21 and September 10). In the Philippines, Typhoon Utor left more than 150 dead in July, and Tropical Storm Lingling caused at least 180 deaths in early November. Monsoon flooding hit South and Southeast Asia, although on a smaller scale than in 2000. India suffered severely again as floodwaters affected millions during July and August.   (DOUGLAS LE COMTE)

Economic Affairs

Even before the **TERRORIST ATTACKS** in the U.S. on Sept. 11, 2001, the world economy was **SLOWING DOWN** faster than expected. By the end of the year, most world **STOCK MARKETS** were down, numerous companies were implementing **LAYOFFS** or filing for **BANKRUPTCY,** and there were fears of a global **RECESSION.**

Expectations of an economic slowdown at the start of 2001 proved to be well founded, and as the year drew to a close, fears of a global recession were being expressed. In the year 2000 the global economy had grown by 4.7%, its fastest rate in a decade and a half. In November the International Monetary Fund (IMF) revised down its projection for 2001 to 2.4%, but by year's end this looked too optimistic. Growth in the 30 industrialized countries of the Organisation for Economic Co-operation and Development (OECD), which accounted for most world output, was not expected to exceed 1%, which in turn constrained growth of the less-developed countries (LDCs).

The slowdown in the first half of 2001 was more severe than had been expected. The world's stock markets were already falling, and interest rates were being steadily lowered in the U.S. and the European Union (EU) to stimulate economic activity. While several factors had contributed to the global slowdown, the various regions and countries were differently affected. A key factor was a stronger-than-predicted fall in demand for information technology (IT) products. This particularly affected the producer countries in Asia, which were heavily dependent on technology exports.

In Western Europe and other industrialized areas, growth slowed more than expected—partly because of the effects of tighter monetary policies and the need to adapt to higher oil prices—and corporate profits were falling. The Japanese economy was still bordering on recession, but its imports continued to rise strongly. China's economy remained buoyant, with strong domestic demand and a stable currency in terms

of the U.S. dollar. In the first half of the year, China's trade was slowing, but it was still recording double-digit growth in imports and a 9% increase in exports.

While the slowdown had been more severe than expected, it was the unprecedented terrorist attacks in the U.S. that really shook world confidence. While the initial impact was felt in the U.S., where there was a huge loss of life and the physical destruction of much of

the business infrastructure of lower Manhattan, the attacks created fear and uncertainty across the world. The economic might of the U.S., which had been a driving force behind much of the world's economic growth, was seriously undermined. The insurance cost of the damage was likely to reach $50 billion, according to early estimates by the U.S. Bureau of Economic Analysis. This was well in excess of the $19 billion in damage caused when Hurricane Andrew hit Louisiana and Florida in 1992, previously the largest claim to date.

The loss of confidence was quickly reflected in the world's leading financial markets, and acceleration in corporate failures and job losses; major European firms laid off 97,000 workers in October alone, almost twice as many as in September. At the end of November, one of the world's largest conglomerates, the energy trader Enron Corp., filed for Chapter 11 protection in what would be

Table I. Real Gross Domestic Products of Selected OECD Countries
% annual change

Country	1997	1998	1999	2000	2001[1]
United States	4.4	4.3	4.1	4.1	1.3
Japan	1.9	–1.1	0.8	1.5	–0.5
Germany	1.4	2.0	1.8	3.0	0.8
France	1.9	3.5	3.0	3.4	2.0
Italy	2.0	1.8	1.6	2.9	1.8
United Kingdom	3.5	2.6	2.3	3.1	2.0
Canada	4.3	3.9	5.1	4.4	2.0
All developed countries	3.5	2.7	3.4	3.8	1.3
Seven major countries above	3.2	2.8	3.0	3.4	1.1
European Union	2.6	2.9	2.7	3.4	1.8

[1]Estimated.
Note: Seasonally adjusted at annual rates.
Source: International Monetary Fund, *World Economic Outlook,* October 2001.

Table II. Standardized Unemployment Rates in Selected Developed Countries
% of total labour force

Country	1997	1998	1999	2000	2001[1]
United States	4.9	4.5	4.2	4.0	4.8
Japan	3.4	4.1	4.7	4.7	5.0
Germany	9.5	9.3	8.6	7.9	8.1
France	12.2	11.8	11.2	9.5	8.9
Italy	11.8	11.8	11.4	10.5	10.0
United Kingdom	6.5	6.3	6.1	5.5	5.1
Canada	9.1	8.3	7.6	6.8	7.3
All developed countries	6.8	7.1	6.8	6.4	6.5
Seven major countries above	6.4	6.4	6.1	5.7	—
European Union	11.4	9.9	9.1	8.2	8.5

[1]Projected.
Source: OECD, *Economic Outlook,* November 2001.

the world's biggest-ever bankruptcy. Possibly the most lasting impact was on transport and world travel and tourism. Within weeks once-strong national airlines Swissair and Belgium's Sabena were being declared bankrupt as a result of the slump in demand for air travel. The number of international tourist arrivals in 2000 reached 699 million and generated $476 billion. Before the terrorist attacks international tourism in 2001 was on track for a 3–4% increase; in November the World Tourism Organization lowered its forecast to 1%.

On a more positive note, despite the critics of trade liberalization, the World Trade Organization (WTO) meeting in Doha, Qatar, on November 11–14 went ahead as planned, and a new agreement was reached. Most countries were continuing to make efforts to participate in globalization by attracting foreign investment. Of the 150 regulatory chan-ges in investment conditions made by 69 countries in 2000, 147 were more favourable. As a result, foreign direct investment (FDI) continued to be a major influence on economic development, increasing at a much faster rate than world trade or production. In 2000 world FDI reached a record $4,270,000,000,000, 18% up on the previous year and well in excess of forecasts. Sales of the over 800,000 affiliates of transnational corporations also rose by 18% to reach $15,680,000,000,000, while the number of employees, which had doubled over the previous decade, reached 45,600,000. In 2001, however, the slackening in merger and acquisition (M&A) activity was expected to result in a decline in overall FDI.

Against the overall trend, FDI into the LDCs of Asia rose 44% to a record $143 billion in 2000. This was due to an investment boom in Hong Kong associated with China's forthcoming membership in the WTO. At $643 billion in 2000, Hong Kong's share of the total inflow into Asia rose to 45% and overtook that of China. Nevertheless, China was making policy changes in advance of joining the WTO, and it received 12% more FDI in the first four months of 2001 than in the same 2000 period. Southeast Asia's share fell to 10% in 2000, mainly because of divestments in Indonesia. In South Asia, India continued to be the largest recipient, with $2.3 billion.

Outward investment from Asia doubled to a record $85 billion, led by Hong Kong but with increasing flows from China and India. Investment in Latin America and the Caribbean declined from the particularly high level of 1999.

NATIONAL ECONOMIC POLICIES

The revised IMF growth forecast for output in the advanced countries was 1% (in November), compared with the 3.8% achieved in 2000. By the middle of the year, economic activity in many of the advanced countries was, at best, stagnating. The effects of the terrorist attacks in the U.S. in September led to output falls in the final months of the year, for the first time in 20 years.

United States. The longest period of continuous expansion since the National Bureau of Economic Research (NBER) began keeping records in 1854 came to an abrupt halt in 2001, just 10 years after it began. Following expansion of 4.1% in both 1999 and 2000, it was doubtful whether the U.S. economy would grow by the revised IMF economic forecast of 1%. From being the dynamo of world growth, the U.S. suddenly became the generator of a serious global slowdown. After lengthy deliberations the NBER concluded on November 28 that the U.S. had slid into recession in March.

The slowdown in the economy had begun in the second half of 2000 when demand for information and communications equipment began to slump, bringing an 80% drop in high-tech company share prices. It gathered momentum in 2001 as the loss of confidence in high-tech companies, which then had to meet the higher costs of investment, and in the "new economy"

was followed by a general deterioration in business and consumer confidence. An easing of monetary policy from the start of 2001 contributed, however, to continuing strong investment in housing as the cost of mortgages fell. Household spending remained buoyant, with retail sales in April and May up 3.9% on year-earlier levels.

The downturn in demand led companies to reduce output to lower stock levels. As a consequence, manufacturing activity in May reached a 10-year low. Job losses pushed unemployment to 4.9% by August, and reductions in overtime led to shorter workweeks. Nevertheless, by historic standards the unemployment level remained compatible with "full employment" conditions. An easing of the tight labour market was desirable insofar as it brought some stability to employee compensation, which had been spiraling out of control. While rises in average earnings slowed down, however, there was an acceleration in unit labour costs. Company profits fell 13% in the year to the second quarter, with a bigger decline in the year to the third quarter.

By midyear there were mixed signals and some speculation that economic growth would resume by the end of the year. Consumer spending, which accounted for more than two-thirds of U.S. gross domestic product (GDP), was expected to accelerate in the second half of the year as a result of tax cuts and repeated reductions in interest rates.

Inflation Rate
(percentage change from December to December)

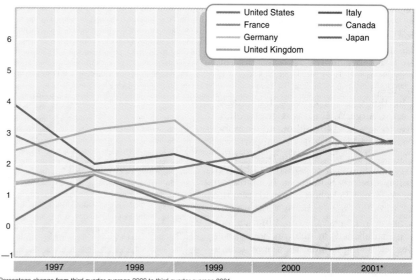

*Percentage change from third quarter average 2000 to third quarter average 2001.
Source: International Monetary Fund, *International Financial Statistics*.

Industrial Production
semiannual averages: 1995 = 100

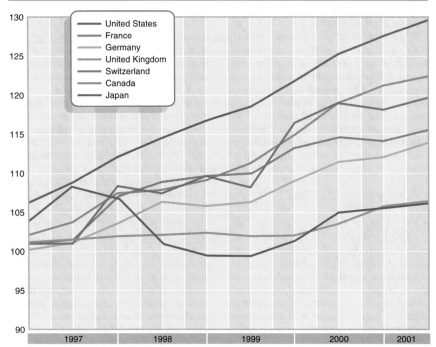

Source: International Monetary Fund, *International Financial Statistics*.

United Kingdom. During the year the U.K. had one of the most resilient economies among the major advanced countries. The growth in output was forecast at 2–2.25%, compared with 3.1% in 2000, which made it the fastest of the industrialized Group of Seven (G-7) countries.

While economic growth had been strong since the summer of 2000, this was largely because of global factors. The collapse of the information and communications technology sector, the U.S. recession, and a general slowdown in overseas demand constrained exports of goods and services, which were expected to rise only 3–4%, compared with 10.6% in 2000.

On the domestic front, however, the combination of a foot-and-mouth epidemic and poor weather conditions proved disastrous for much of the agricultural sector and the tourism industry. In theory, the relative strength of sterling against the euro was eroding the competitiveness of U.K. goods and services, especially in continental European markets. At the same time, however, it was prompting industry to take measures to increase efficiency, particularly in manufacturing.

The main stimulus to the British economy once again came from domestic demand, which increased by 3.7% in 2000 and was expected to rise in 2001. Household spending rose 1.2% in the first quarter and gathered momentum in the

After the September 11 terrorist attacks, however, the downside risks to the economy were intensified. The U.S. was making the hard landing that had been the subject of speculation and fear just a year earlier, when there had been no suggestion that the country could be the target of such terrorism. In October industrial output fell (–1.1%) for the 13th consecutive month, which made it the longest unbroken decline since 1932. There were glimmers of hope, with consumer confidence rising in November for the second straight month. At the same time, new claims for unemployment benefits, at 427,000, fell for the fourth consecutive month. In December it was reported that unemployment had risen to 5.8%, the highest in more than six years.

In the weeks following the attacks, Pres. George W. Bush was given authority to spend $40 billion to respond. Another $15 billion of support was granted to help the American airline companies, many of which had been in trouble before September 11. A further package of $75 billion was being planned to stimulate the economy. This was beginning to reverse the trend in fiscal policy established in the previous seven years, during which the large federal budget deficit had been eliminated and replaced with a healthy surplus. A return to a federal deficit was likely in 2002. On

November 6 the Federal Reserve (Fed) cut the federal funds rate for the 10th time in 2001, by half a percentage point to 2%, which brought it to a 40-year low and nearly 70% below the end-of-2000 level. Another cut in December brought the rate down to 1.75%.

Interest Rates: Short-term
three-month money market rates

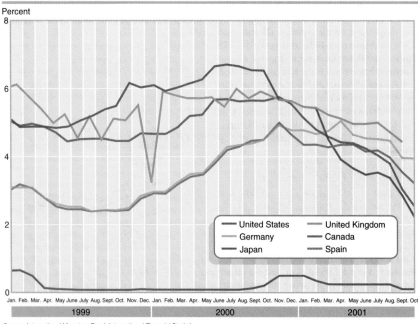

Source: International Monetary Fund, *International Financial Statistics*.

second, when it rose 3.7% above the year-earlier level—the biggest increase in more than a year—and underpinned increased retail sales. Buoyant conditions continued through the third quarter. In September retail sales rose 5.9% over the same year-earlier period, which made the third-quarter year-on-year growth the fastest in 13 years. Prospects for the retail sector remained positive, with a Confederation of British Industry survey showing the strongest outlook for the sector since October 1966. By contrast, survey results for the services sector indicated a weaker outlook, with signs that contracts had been deferred because of the September 11 attacks.

A strong influence on consumer confidence was the high level of employment. In September unemployment was 5.1% (5.4% a year before), compared with an average 8.3% in the euro zone. The number of jobless increased in October and again in November, however, the first time since 1992 unemployment had increased for two straight months. On a claimant-count basis, it was the lowest in 26 years. As a result, wage pressure remained strong and was reflected in higher average earnings, which nevertheless eased back to 4.4% in September, year on year. Unusually, public-sector earnings were rising faster than those in the private sector, a reflection of the priority the government was giving to the public services.

Japan. During the year the Japanese economy deteriorated sharply, and output was estimated to have fallen by 0.9%. The modest recovery in 2000, when the economy grew 1.5%, was due mainly to the strong growth in capital investment and was not sustainable. The 2001 recession was the fourth in 10 years and was predictable, given the decline in technology-related demand in Asia. The harsher-than-expected slowdown in the global IT industry was particularly damaging to Japan, and this had implications for the region. Although Japan's economic role in the Asia-Pacific region had diminished over recent years, it remained important. Reciprocal trade with East Asia in particular was badly affected by the downturn.

First-quarter economic indicators reflected the economic stagnation, which was to continue unabated. Capital-goods shipments were falling, industrial production was down, household incomes were deteriorating, and unemployment was continuing to rise. Real GDP shrank by 0.2% and was followed by a 2% drop in the second quarter. The

AP/Wide World Photos

Unemployed workers in Tokyo check job advertisements at Hello Work, a government-run placement centre, on November 30.

outlook deteriorated further in the wake of the September 11 terrorist attacks in the U.S., and in that month industrial output fell 12.7% (from a year earlier). Retail sales continued to decline, not helped by declines in average earnings because of reductions in overtime. Consumer prices continued to fall and in September were 0.8% lower than one year earlier.

Unemployment was becoming a growing problem. Although the rate had dipped temporarily in 2000, reflecting the improvement in the economy, the trend had been generally upward. From just over 3% in early 1997, the rate had climbed to a record high of 5.3% by September 2001, and it continued to rise in October (5.4%) and November (5.5%). Of particular concern was the mismatch in the labour market.

The emergency economic package unveiled by the Japanese government in April 2001 aimed to stimulate employment through measures that included deregulation, provision of child care, and vocational training. This was in marked contrast to previous policies, which were directed toward preventing layoffs through subsidies, but it was unlikely to produce an early solution to the mismatch problem.

Euro Zone. The belief among many eurozone policy makers that somehow the region would be, at worst, only marginally affected by a global downturn (which in

Interest Rates: Long-term

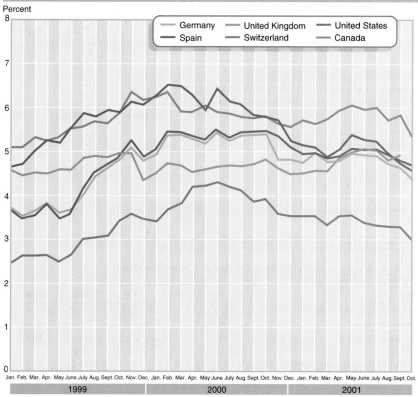

Source: International Monetary Fund, *International Financial Statistics.*

turn depended on what happened in the U.S.) gradually became discredited. GDP growth in the euro zone increasingly weakened as the year progressed. Sluggish trade and a stagnation in business investment were exacerbated by the September 11 attacks. Nevertheless, the European Commission at the end of November optimistically estimated that euro-zone growth would outpace that of the U.S. at 1.6% in 2001 and 1.3% in 2002. This was in sharp contrast to the record growth of 3.5% in 2000, when many of the smaller countries, such as Ireland (11.5% growth) and Luxembourg (8.5%), outperformed, making a contribution to output that was disproportionate to their size.

The final outcome was heavily dependent on Germany, the zone's largest economy and the country leading the downturn. Economic indicators suggested that there would be no early upturn. In the third quarter, GDP contracted by 0.6% (annual rate), industrial output was down 2.6%, and retail sales fell 2.1%. Unemployment, at 9.5% in October, was marginally higher than a year earlier. France, Germany's largest European neighbour, proved more resilient to the downturn in the first half of the year, being supported by tax cuts and employment growth.

Across the euro zone the improvement in the labour market had come to a halt, and unemployment was a cause of growing concern. It remained intractably high in several countries, led by Spain (13% according to national statistics), Belgium (11.7%), Germany (9.5%), Italy (9.4%), and France (8.9%), but it was not an issue in Luxembourg or The Netherlands.

The rate of inflation was rising for much of the year. The initial problem was the euro's weakness against the dollar and then the rapid rise of commodity prices, particularly of oil. In the second half of the year, however, the effect of lower energy prices brought the consumer price rise to 2.7% in the September quarter over the year before. Food prices, which accounted for about 20% of the index, escalated for much of the year as a result of the foot-and-mouth and "mad cow" diseases. Unprocessed-food prices were running at 7.8% up on the year earlier in August and September, having peaked at 9.1% in June.

The Former Centrally Planned Economies. The former centrally planned economies (also called the countries in transition) saw an increase in output for the third year in succession. Nevertheless, at around 2% the rate represented a con-

siderable decline from the record 6.3% growth in 2000 and a bigger fall in output growth than that sustained by any other region. Several factors contributed to the decline, including the slowdown in the world economy and the uncertainty created by the attacks on September 11. More specifically, export growth fell sharply from 12% in 2000 to around 5% in 2001, largely as a result of the reduction in import demand from Western Europe, which accounted for half the region's exports.

The fall in economic activity was most marked in the Commonwealth of Independent States (CIS), where output was expected to rise at around half the rate of increase of 7.8% achieved in 2000. Growth was constrained in 2001 by a slowdown in Russia, where output growth was unlikely to exceed 4% following on from an exceptional 8.3% rise in 2000 that was largely the result of increased oil revenues. Output in Central and Eastern Europe also moderated from a 3.8% increase in 2000, but steep declines were averted by a strengthening of domestic demand in many member countries.

Rates of inflation were contained in most countries, and over the region the rate was expected to fall for the third consecutive year to around 15% (20% in 2000), with rates much lower in Central and Eastern Europe (around 9%). Inflation in Russia continued to be a problem, with the annual rate running at around 20%, as in the previous year.

Less-Developed Countries. The weaker-than-expected global economy led to adjustments in output forecasts. The IMF projection for LDCs of 4% for 2001 was, if achieved, the same as the 1999 outcome but well below the 5.8% growth in 2000. The wide regional disparities, which had long been a characteristic of the less-developed world, narrowed considerably in 2000 but were expected to reemerge in 2001, with conditions in Latin America and the Middle East deteriorating more sharply than expected at the start of the year. Within regions, too, wide disparities persisted.

Asia, excluding the newly industrializing countries (NICs) such as South Korea, Taiwan, and Singapore, continued to drive growth in the LDCs, although the 5.6% IMF projection appeared overly optimistic, given the dramatic falloff in trade, on which many Asian countries depended. While some countries, including China and Malaysia, increased fiscal spending to mitigate the effects, for most this could be only a short-term solution because of concerns about raising the level of public debt. In Indonesia and the Philippines, for example, this was already too high. The increase in China's GDP was expected to fall to 7–7.5% from 8% in 2000.

South Asia, which remained one of the world's poorest regions, relied less on trade. Output in this area was expected to fall from 4.9% in 2000 to 4.5%. Because of the military response in Afghanistan to the September 11 at-

Table III. Changes in Output in Less-Developed Countries
% annual change in real gross domestic product

Area	1997	1998	1999	2000	2001[1]
All less-developed countries	5.8	3.5	3.9	5.8	4.3
Regional groups					
Africa	3.1	3.3	2.5	2.8	3.8
Asia	6.5	4.0	6.1	6.8	5.8
Middle East, Europe, Malta, & Turkey	5.1	4.1	1.0	6.0	2.3
Western Hemisphere	5.3	2.3	0.2	4.2	1.7
Countries in transition	1.6	−0.8	3.6	6.3	4.0

[1]Projected.
Source: International Monetary Fund, *World Economic Outlook*, October 2001.

Table IV. Changes in Consumer Prices in Less-Developed Countries
% change from preceding year

Area	1997	1998	1999	2000	2001[1]
All less-developed countries	9.7	10.5	6.8	6.0	5.9
Regional groups					
Africa	14.2	10.8	11.5	13.6	12.6
Asia	4.8	7.7	2.5	1.9	2.8
Middle East, Europe, Malta, & Turkey	27.7	27.6	23.2	19.2	18.9
Western Hemisphere	12.9	9.9	8.8	8.1	6.2

[1]Projected.
Source: International Monetary Fund, *World Economic Outlook*, October 2001.

tacks, the region faced special risks. Pakistan was most affected, with its trade being severely disrupted. That country reduced its fiscal deficit to 5.2% of GDP, but its external debt was a large $38 billion and its reserves were low. India was more insulated from the global slowdown because of its relatively closed economy. By contrast, in neighbouring Bangladesh agricultural output was well up after the flood-induced 2000 slowdown, and tax revenue increased strongly.

In Africa output accelerated from 2.8% in 2000 to 3.5%. Improvements in the Mahgreb countries (Algeria, Morocco, and Tunisia), where output was projected to more than double over the year before, made a major contribution to overall growth.

In sub-Saharan Africa output growth declined (from 3% to 2.7%) because of the global slowdown. Nevertheless, in many countries, including Kenya, Ethiopia, and Mozambique, agriculture and, hence, household incomes were helped by better weather. Political instability continued to hamper growth in several countries, including Angola and The Sudan, while the politico-economic crisis in Zimbabwe intensified as elections due in early 2002 approached. In South Africa, the region's largest economy, sound macroeconomic policies reduced the country's vulnerability to external shocks.

Output in Latin America rose by 1% at most, following on from the strong 4.2% export-driven growth of 2000. The largest three countries, Argentina, Brazil, and Mexico, were worst affected by the global and U.S. slowdown, and lower interest rates did little to help. Political and financial problems in Argentina led to a dramatic decrease in confidence, and output was declining.

Middle East output was not likely to exceed half the 5.5% advance in 2000. The reduction in oil quotas and lower oil prices, combined with lowered global demand for goods and services, constrained economic activity.

INTERNATIONAL TRADE, EXCHANGE, AND PAYMENTS

International Trade and Payments. The increase in the volume of world trade in 2001 was expected to be just 1% in 2001, following a record 13.3% in 2000. The contraction created a new and unfamiliar situation in which the growth in world output exceeded the volume of world trade. For at least two decades, annual rises in world output had exceeded

export growth. During the 1990s the annual rise in the volume of merchandise exports had outpaced the growth of GDP by three to one, and in each major region exports increased faster than domestic demand. Trade in services, too, had expanded rapidly over the previous decade and accounted for a quarter of all cross-border trade.

In 2001, in contrast to the year before, when all regions had participated in the upsurge in trade, there were many individual country and regional losers in the downturn. The volume of exports from the advanced countries had risen 11.5% in 2000 and by 16.1% (25% in U.S. dollar value) from LDCs. In 2001 the simultaneous slowdown in the U.S., Europe, and Japan meant that any increase in exports of either group would be close to negligible. Even before September 11 it was evident that the world slowdown, which centred on the recession in the high-tech sector, was deeper than expected.

The most affected was the East Asia–Pacific region, which relied on the U.S. and Japanese markets for around 40% of its exports. Exports in the first half of the year were already running at levels well below the year earlier, by up to 25% in Taiwan, South Korea, Malaysia, Singapore, and the Philippines. South Asia was expecting to see a modest increase, as some countries had depreciated their currencies to increase their competitiveness. In Latin America little growth could be expected. In the first half of the year, Mexico's export growth rate fell from 23% in 2000 to zero. Like many other countries in the region, its exports were mainly destined for the U.S. market. The severe slowdown in the EU was affecting many of the former centrally planned economies, and few would see any increases.

The overall current account of the balance of payments in the advanced economies remained in deficit for the third straight year after six years of surplus. It was expected to fall to $223 billion, from a higher-than-expected $248 billion in 2000. The U.S. deficit once again exceeded the total surplus but at $407 billion had fallen from the year before ($445 billion). Among the major G-7 countries, the U.S. and the U.K., as usual, had substantial deficits. The euro zone moved from a deficit in 2000 to a $16 billion surplus, with member countries Germany and Spain each sustaining $14 billion surpluses. The U.K. deficit, at $23 billion, was little changed from the year before. By contrast, Japan's traditional surplus fell quite heav-

ily, from $117 billion to $89 billion. Of the other advanced countries, only Portugal and Australia had significant deficits—$10 billion and $11 billion, respectively. All four of the Asian NICs remained in surplus, with a total of $48 billion, just slightly down on the year before.

After many years of deficits, the LDCs had a surplus for the second year running. It fell sharply, however, from $60 billion to $20 billion owing to a halving of the Asian LDCs' surplus to $22 billion and an increase in Latin America's deficit to $58 billion. Indebtedness of the LDCs eased up slightly to $2,155,400,000,000.

Globalization. Events during the year demonstrated the extent to which world trade and financial markets had become interlinked and global. The synchronized downturn by the Triad (the U.S., Europe, and Japan) could not have occurred even a decade before. Nevertheless, the debate on whether the continued liberalization of world trade was desirable continued. There was no evidence to show that imports led to a widening of the gap between rich and poor. On the contrary, research published in 2001 showed that a representative sample of LDCs that had globalized since 1980 had benefited strongly from rising incomes and a reduction of poverty.

The annual meeting of WTO international trade ministers in Seattle, Wash., in 2000 had been disrupted by violent protests against the perceived capitalist ambitions behind any attempts to increase globalization. The 2001 meeting to expand and extend the multilateral trading system was held in Qatar at a time of increased uncertainty fueled by the sharp downturn in world trade and the terrorist attacks in the U.S. It took place amid the highest security, which limited access of antiglobalization protesters, and most nongovernmental organizations were too busy to protest.

The meeting was successfully concluded. Of great international significance (because of its massive market and trading potential) was the November 11 ratification of membership for China, which became the 143rd member of the WTO a month later. China's membership followed drawn-out preliminary negotiations on various issues dating back to 1986, when it first applied to join the General Agreement on Tariffs and Trade, the WTO's predecessor. In 2001 these issues included a China-U.S. agreement reached on June 8. This limited the amount of support and export subsidies the Chinese government could give to its agricultural sector, as well as easing and clarifying the conditions on various aspects of foreign investment. On the day after China's ratification, membership for Taiwan was approved. To satisfy Beijing (which considered Taiwan part of its sovereign territory), the newest member was designated "a separate customs territory" of Taiwan and its offshore islands of P'eng-hu, Quemoy, and Matsu. The two countries were committed to opening their markets and gradually liberalizing sectors in which the government was involved. China would also have more export opportunities, which many other countries feared would erode their competitiveness.

Exchange and Interest Rates. The global slowdown in 2001 and the September 11 attacks were the major influences on interest and exchange rates during the year. The U.S. started cutting interest rates in January, and Canada quickly followed suit. As the year got under way, most central banks in the industrialized countries outside the euro zone were cutting interest rates, and fiscal policy was being directed toward boosting confidence at household, corporate, and market levels to prevent outright recession. In March these included Australia, Canada, New Zealand, and Switzerland.

The U.S. wasted no time in cutting rates to prevent the "hard landing" that much of the world had been fearing since the middle of 2000. Weak data over the Christmas 2000 period, as well as low business and consumer-confidence indicators, prompted Fed Chairman Alan Greenspan to take early action. On January 3 the Fed cut its Fed funds interest-rate target from 6.5% to 6%. The move came before formal meetings and was on a scale that surprised many observers. It was intended to boost confidence but was not enough, and it was quickly followed by a second cut on January 31 and then a third on March 20, bringing the target down to 5%. Markets reacted positively, and the dollar remained firm against sterling, the euro, and the yen. Further cuts brought the Fed rate to 3.75% in June, down 275 basis points since the start of the year. In the wake of the terrorist attacks on September 11, more reductions were made. By early November the Fed rate was down to 2%, its lowest since 1961. At the start of December, there were positive signs that some sectors of the economy were growing again; equity prices were rallying, and long-term bond yields were up.

Euros are coined on this assembly line in Sérifontaine, France, in October.

Despite this, interest rates were cut again, for the 11th time, to 1.75%.

In the U.K. interest rates moved almost in tandem with the U.S. through most of the year. To reduce vulnerability to the effects of the global slowdown, the Bank of England steadily cut the interest rates from February 8. By August 2 the rate had been reduced four times, by 100 basis points, to 5%. After September 11 raised more recession concerns, three more reductions were made. The last, on November 8, was the most aggressive at half a percentage point and brought the rate to 4%, the lowest in nearly 40 years. The Bank of England, which took the view that inflationary pressures were continuing to ease and the global slowdown might last longer than previously thought, did not cut rates again in December.

The euro zone was widened on January 2 to include Greece, which was relinquishing its drachma in favour of the euro and became the 12th EU member to join the euro system. The European Central Bank (ECB) was slow to experience and recognize the extent of the global slowdown. Its economic output accelerated slightly in the fourth quarter of 2000 over the previous three months, and going into 2001 consumer confidence was higher because of falling oil prices, tax cuts, and lower unemployment. Over the three months to the end of January 2001, the euro appreciated by 15% against the dollar and 8% against sterling. By mid-March, however, there were clear signs

of a serious economic downturn, and sentiment turned against the euro. The ECB was widely criticized for not cutting interest rates. The ECB justified its inaction on the grounds that inflation was too high and that growth over the year would exceed 2.25%, a view not shared by the market.

In the following weeks all sectors of the economy were affected by falling demand, and the euro continued to weaken against the dollar and even the yen, despite the ailing Japan. Finally, on May 10 the ECB cut its interest rates by 25 basis points to 4.5%, which was seen as too little too late. It was not until August 30, after the euro had softened against most major currencies, that the ECB cut the rate again, by a meagre 25 basis points to 4.25%. The events of September 11 prompted a final and more decisive cut of 50 basis points to 3.75%. By the end of November, compared with a year earlier, the euro was trading slightly less than a percentage point lower.

A major preoccupation of consumers, businesses, and banks as the year drew to a close was the likely effect of the arrival and circulation of some 10 billion euro notes and several hundred thousand metric tons of coins on Jan. 1, 2002. These were to replace the 12 national currencies in the euro zone. The Deutsche Mark was to cease to be legal tender in Germany on January 1, while most other currencies had until the end of February.

In Japan nominal interest rates had been below 1% since the mid-1990s, underlying inflation was negative, and land

and stock prices were declining, which left little room for maneuver on interest rates. The year 2001 started on a gloomy note as fears rose that the economic recovery in the second half of 2000 was not as strong as expected, despite large injections of capital. There was speculation that the Bank of Japan (BOJ) would reverse the interest-rate increase implemented in August 2000. This had followed an 18-month zero-interest-rate policy. Growing doubts about the recovery led to a weakening of the yen against the dollar, and by March 8 the exchange rate had reached ¥120 to the dollar for the first time in 20 months.

On March 21 the BOJ announced a further easing of its monetary policy, increasing liquidity and effectively reinstating zero rates. The yen had reached a new two-and-a-half-year low at ¥126 to the dollar on April 6 when the government announced an emergency package that included a proposal to force the banking sector to deal with its bad-debt problems.

In mid-May it briefly rose to ¥118 to the dollar before returning to the ¥121–¥124 range, in which it remained until September 11. The BOJ intervened in the market with large-scale yen selling. This steadied the yen, which remained around ¥120 to the dollar for a while—just half its value of a year earlier—before sliding again to end the year at around ¥131.　　　(IEIS)

STOCK EXCHANGES

Globalization works both ways: just as the internationalization of financial markets can power worldwide growth, it can equally throw the development into reverse. By the end of 2001, all the signs of impending global contraction were in place. The United States, usually the driver of international growth, had entered recession, dragging most of Asia with it and forcing Europe almost to a standstill.

The third-quarter 0.4% drop in gross domestic product (GDP) signaled that the recession had started in the U.S. in March, following the longest period of expansion in U.S. history—121 months, compared with the earlier record of 106 months between 1961 and 1970. Long before the terrorist attacks in the U.S. on September 11 and their aftermath, the year had produced a succession of bleak facts for the record books.

As early as midyear, operating earnings per share in the U.S. were recorded to be down nearly 40% overall, the worst performance since the Great Depression

of the 1930s. Consumers, the backbone of the stock markets' long bull run, had been nervous months before the terrorist attacks, and after September 11 they all but stopped spending. Business investment fell 11.9% that month, and by

year's end the Federal Reserve (Fed) had cut the base interest rate for the 11th time in the year to just 1.75%.

For more than a year, investors had been grappling with a seemingly endless succession of bad news about company

Table V. Selected Major World Stock Market Indexes[1]

Country and Index	2001 range[2] High	Low	Year-end close	Percent change from 12/31/00
Australia, Sydney All Ordinaries	3425	2867	3360	6
Belgium, Brussels BEL20	3030	2323	2782	–8
Brazil, Bovespa	17,889	10,006	13,578	–11
Canada, Toronto Composite	9348	6513	7688	–14
Denmark, KFX	348	236	272	–13
Finland, HEX General	12,872	5584	8805	–32
France, Paris CAC 40	5998	3653	4625	–22
Germany, Frankfurt Xextra DAX	6795	3787	5160	–20
Hong Kong, Hang Seng	16,164	8934	11,397	–25
Ireland, ISEQ Overall	6458	4650	5673	–1
Italy, Milan Banca Commerciale Italiana	1948	1083	1433	–25
Japan, Nikkei Average	14,529	9504	10,543	–24
Mexico, IPC	6869	5082	6372	13
Netherlands, The, CBS All Share	906	557	708	–21
Philippines, Manila Composite	1712	979	1168	–22
Singapore, SES All-Singapore	515	335	426	–15
South Africa, Johannesburg Industrials	8720	6155	7764	–4
South Korea, Composite Index	705	469	694	37
Spain, Madrid Stock Exchange	964	649	824	–6
Switzerland, SBC General	5604	3547	4383	–22
Taiwan, Weighted Price	6104	3446	5551	17
Thailand, Bangkok SET	343	265	304	13
United Kingdom, FT-SE 100	6335	4434	5217	–16
United States, Dow Jones Industrials	11,338	8236	10,022	–7
World, MS Capital International	1249	854	1009	–17

[1]Index numbers are rounded. [2]Based on daily closing price.
Source: *Financial Times*.

Financial Times **Industrial Ordinary Share Index annual averages, 1978–2001**

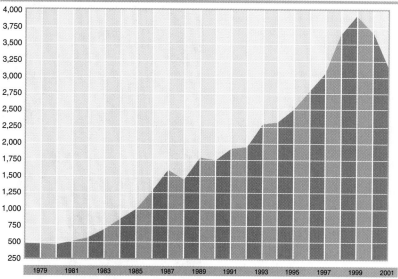

Source: *Financial Times*.

earnings, not only in the high-technology sectors devastated by the bursting of the dot-com bubble but also increasingly across all sectors. In summer the corporate news had looked far worse than the economic fundamentals: by October the whole picture had darkened, even though stock markets soon recovered to pre-September 11 levels. The rout when markets reopened after the attacks was only partly the result of the deep uncertainty the events induced.

According to the Organisation for Economic Co-operation and Development (OECD), the industrial world had contracted for the first time in 20 years. It was, said the organization, the cumulative effect of the collapse of the high-tech sector and a slump in equity values generally, reduction in inventories, rises in the price of oil, which tripled in 1999–2000, and the rise in interest rates over the same period.

The extent of the slowdown elsewhere varied in severity according to countries' trading links with the U.S. Although Europe was undergoing a less-severe contraction, forecasts for the region were revised down. Much of Asia was hard hit, and Japan, suffering a fourth recession in 10 years, was expected to contract more in the coming year.

It was perhaps not surprising that the year ended with nearly all the major developed country stock exchange indexes well down on the year before, in both local currency and U.S. dollar terms. Austria was an exception (up 11.7% in dollar terms), while Japan's Nikkei index declined 23.5%. Germany, France, The Netherlands, and Italy all suffered market falls in excess of 20% over the year. In the U.K. the *Financial Times* Stock Exchange 100 (FTSE 100) index was down 16.2% and was closer to the Morgan Stanley Capital International (MSCI) World Index drop of 16.9%. In the less-developed countries, stock market performances were more mixed, but by December 31 most were sharply down on year-end 2000, with the Hong Kong Hang Seng index slumping 24.5%. The major exceptions were South Korea, Taiwan, Mexico, and Russia, all of which were up for the year. (IEIS)

United States. Falling corporate profits, recession, and the continuing decline of the Internet sector combined to make 2001 a down year for stocks. The technology-driven plunge in stock prices from the heights of the previous year persisted and broadened to create a bear market affecting nearly all sectors. It was the second year in a row that stock prices had declined after a nearly

decade-long bull market. The Fed cut the federal funds rate a record 11 times throughout the year, motivated by a manufacturing-led downturn that had evolved into a recession by March. The terrorist attacks on September 11 shocked the markets and the nation, forcing the longest closure of the U.S. stock exchanges since the Great Depression. Stocks rallied at year's end but did not make up for earlier losses.

All three of the major indexes were down for the second year in a row. The Dow Jones Industrial Average (DJIA) of 30 blue-chip stocks fell 7.10% on the year; the broader Standard & Poor's index of 500 large-company stocks (S&P 500) slid 13.04%; and the National Association of Securities Dealers automated quotation (Nasdaq) composite index, made up largely of technology stocks, suffered the worst, dropping 21.05%. The Russell 2000 index of small market-capitalization (small-cap) stocks fared better, eking out a 1% increase, while the broadest market measure, the Wilshire 5000 index, fell 12.06%.

The DJIA began the year at 10,786.85 and showed no major movement through January and February. The index fell more than a thousand points in March but largely recovered in April, rallying to its yearlong peak of 11,337.92 on May 21. This was followed by a steady decline that progressed largely uninterrupted through the summer months.

The Nasdaq began the year at 2470.52 and showed respectable gains through January, briefly reaching a yearlong peak of 2859.15 on January 24. A decline through February and March cost the index more than a thousand points; some of that loss was recovered in an April rally that gave way to a long, slow decline lasting through the summer.

The S&P 500 index began at 1320.28 and roughly mirrored the Nasdaq's path, pointing to the relatively new prominence of technology stocks in the overall stock market. The S&P 500 hit its yearlong peak of 1373.73 on January 30. On November 30 the S&P 500 had an estimated price-to-earnings (P/E) ratio of 30.97, up from 24.59 at the year's beginning, which reflected a sharp decrease in earnings.

The terrorist attacks on the World Trade Center towers crippled the financial district of New York City. The New York Stock Exchange (NYSE), the Nasdaq stock market, and the American Stock Exchange (Amex) remained closed until September 17, the longest the NYSE had been closed since 1933 and the longest closure ever for the other exchanges. In the first week of trading following the attack, the DJIA fell 14.26%, the Nasdaq was down 16.05%, and the S&P 500 slid 11.6%. Each of these three indexes hit its yearlong low on September 21, with the DJIA falling to 8235.81, the Nasdaq at

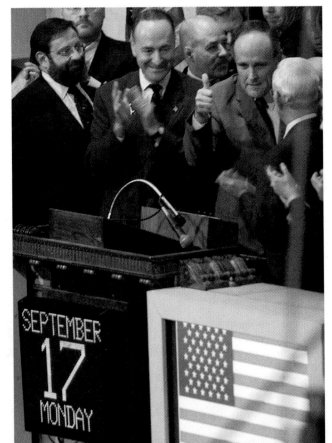

New York City Mayor Rudolph Giuliani gives a thumbs up to traders at the reopening of the New York Stock Exchange on September 17.

AP/Wide World Photos

1423.19, and the S&P 500 at 965.80. The energy-heavy Amex reached its yearlong low, 780.46, on September 25.

Markets then embarked on a rally lasting through year's end, fueled by expectations of economic recovery. The major stock indexes' decline reflected the influential role of technology stocks. JDS Uniphase went from single-digit value in 1999 to over $100 per share in early 2000, gained entrance to the S&P 500 in 2000, and fell back down to single-digits in 2001. Cisco Systems, the leading Internet networking company, fell by more than 50% over the course of 2001. Dramatic price declines were also seen in the stocks of other Internet-related companies such as Amazon.com and Yahoo! and in a wide range of technology firms, including Oracle, Compaq, Advanced Micro Devices, and Vitesse Semiconductor, all of which had risen dramatically in recent years.

Stock prices largely followed expectations about the state of the economy. The year began with an economic downturn centred in the manufacturing sector and marked by excess inventories. By February this slump had broadened, affecting many sectors, including media, telecommunications, and pharmaceuticals. Stock prices plunged in February and March, and the economy entered recession.

Corporate profits, already declining, fell sharply in the first three quarters, as did businesses' capital spending. Third-quarter profits were 22.1% lower than a year before, marking the largest 12-month drop in the 47 years that the government had tracked these statistics. The National Association of Purchasing Management's PMI index showed reduced manufacturing activity in every month through November. In mid-November 4,420,000 people were collecting or had filed for unemployment insurance, the largest such number since 1982. By the end of the month, firms had announced 1,795,000 layoffs, according to outplacement firm Challenger, Gray & Christmas. At the same time, the unemployment rate had climbed to 5.7%, already its highest level in six years; it rose again in December to 5.8%.

Investors' enthusiasm for stocks waned in 2001. According to the Investment Company Institute, through October a net of only $14.9 billion had entered stock funds in 2001, down from $292.8 billion for the same period in 2000. The two largest stock mutual funds, Fidelity's Magellan Fund and Vanguard's 500 Index Fund, both large-cap blend funds, were down 11.7% and 12%, respectively,

for the year, while the average large-cap blend fund declined 12.9%. By the end of November, four out of five U.S. stock mutual funds were down on the year.

Caution and pessimism dominated the investment landscape. Venture capital investment, which had topped $20 billion in every quarter of 2000, was at $12 billion in the first quarter of 2001 and declined to $7.7 billion in the third quarter, matching the level of the first quarter of 1999. Through September there were

Table VI. Selected U.S. Stock Market Indexes[1]

	2001 range[2] High	2001 range[2] Low	Year-end close	Percent change from 12/31/00
Dow Jones Averages				
30 Industrials	11,338	8236	10,022	−7
20 Transportation	3146	2034	2640	−10
15 Utilities	399	275	294	−29
65 Composite	3392	2489	2892	−13
Standard & Poor's				
500 Index	1374	966	1148	−13
Industrials	1613	1113	1334	−13
Utilities	342	219	237	−32
Others				
NYSE Composite	667	504	590	−10
Nasdaq Composite	2859	1423	1950	−21
Amex Composite	959	780	848	−6
Russell 2000	517	379	489	1

[1]Index numbers are rounded. [2]Based on daily closing price.
Sources: *Financial Times; The Wall Street Journal.*

New York Stock Exchange Composite Index, 2001 stock prices (Dec. 31, 1965 = 100)

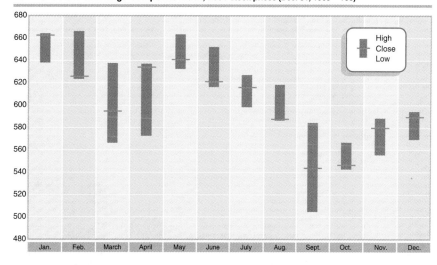

Average daily share volume
in thousands of shares

Sources: *Barron's National Business and Financial Weekly; The Wall Street Journal.*

New York Stock Exchange Common Stock Index Closing Prices
stock prices (Dec. 31, 1965 = 50)

Number of shares sold
In billions of shares

Sources: *Barron's National Business and Financial Weekly; The Wall Street Journal.*

NYSE average daily trading through October was 1,240,000,000 shares, up slightly from the previous year. Dollar volume was $42.6 billion, down slightly. Of the 3,973 equities traded on the NYSE, 2,370 advanced on the year, 1,569 declined, and 34 ended the year unchanged. The most actively traded stocks on the exchange were Lucent Technologies (6.4 billion shares traded), General Electric, EMC Corp., Enron Corp., AOL Time Warner, and Nortel Networks. Enron, which traded 4.4 billion shares, peaked above $84 before collapsing to end the year at 60 cents.

On January 29 the NYSE completed its conversion mandated by the Securities and Exchange Commission (SEC) to a system of decimalized trading, wherein stocks were traded in dollars and cents rather than in the traditional sixteenths of a dollar. Preliminary evidence suggested that decimalization had reduced bid-ask spreads by 37%, according to SEC staff analysis, which resulted in lower transaction costs. This particularly benefited small investors and active traders and improved trading capacity and transparency. A seat on the NYSE sold for $2,200,000 on October 29, down from its peak of $2,650,000 on Aug. 23, 1999.

Average daily trading on the Nasdaq stock market was 1.9 billion shares, up slightly from 2000; dollar volume, however, was $46.6 billion, down sharply from $88.3 billion in 2000, reflecting the lower average price per share. Some Nasdaq stocks began a slow recovery, and at year's end advancers led decliners 2,690 to 2,450, with 32 unchanged. The most active shares traded on the Nasdaq were all high-tech companies—Cisco, Intel, Sun Microsystems, Microsoft, JDS Uniphase, and Dell Computer.

The Nasdaq completed its decimalization on April 9. The SEC reported that bid-ask spreads had been reduced by 50%. The Nasdaq temporarily loosened its continued listing requirements to accommodate stocks hit by the market drop in the week following the September 11 attacks. The $1 minimum bid and public float requirements were suspended until Jan. 2, 2002.

The Amex composite reached a year-long high of 958.75 in mid-May and slid thereafter to close at 849.92, down 5.59% for the year. Advancers narrowly led decliners 550 to 539, and only 9 issues were unchanged. Surprisingly, the most actively traded issue was the Nasdaq 100.

In 2001 the Chicago Mercantile Exchange for the first time became the largest futures exchange in the U.S.,

only 65 initial public offerings (IPOs) in U.S. markets, with another 32 IPOs between October and December, down from a total of 451 in 2000. Mergers and acquisitions activity was at about $99.9 million a month on average, a 30% decline from the 2000 average monthly activity, according to Thomson Financial. The risky practice of margin borrowing fell sharply; in June margin debt stood at $157.9 billion, down from its peak of $299.9 billion in March 2000. Short sell-

ing—wherein investors bet that a stock would decline—was up.

Through November 12 short interest on the New York Stock Exchange had increased to a record 6.3 billion shares, up from 4.9 billion shares in December 2000. Through October investors filed 5,690 arbitration claims with NASD Dispute Resolution Inc. (a unit of the National Association of Securities Dealers), up from 4,646 for the same period in 2000.

surpassing its annual trading record in August. This record volume was attributed to continuous interest-rate adjustments by the Fed and stock market uncertainty. In November the Chicago Board of Trade recorded the highest monthly trading volume in its history, at 30,009,125 contracts, reflecting a positive shift in market sentiment. Volume was up 10.3% on the year. On September 14 the New York Mercantile Exchange introduced its Internet-based version of NYMEX ACCESS, which led to heavier-than-normal volume.

The Commodity Futures Trading Commission, which regulated the U.S. futures and options markets, issued a warning to the public to be wary of companies promising profits from commodity futures and options trading based on information relating to the September terrorist attacks.

Electronic communications networks (ECNs)—computerized systems used to match buyers and sellers of securities without using the traditional trading venues—continued to grow in importance. During October the nine registered ECNs accounted for 34.5% of the reported share volume in Nasdaq trading, up from 26.8% a year earlier. In January the SEC approved Nasdaq's SuperMontage, a redesign of the market's stock-trading platform intended to provide a range of improvements, including better access to price information and simpler order executions in the Nasdaq market.

It was a good year for bonds as investors avoided stocks. Bond prices rose for most of the year, falling only during the stock rallies in January, April, and May, before dropping sharply in November and December as stocks recovered. High bond returns coincided with the slowing of the economy. The Lehman Brothers U.S. Aggregate Bond Index showed a return of 3.03% in the first quarter, 0.56% in the second, and 4.61% in the third, well down from 2000 figures.

The Fed's repeated rate cuts resulted in a steep yield curve for Treasuries. In December the spread, or difference, between 2-year Treasury notes and 30-year Treasury bonds was 2.3%. In October the U.S. Treasury announced that it would no longer issue its 30-year bond; this prompted an immediate 30-basis-point drop in yields. Many bond experts saw this discontinuation as an attempt to drive down long-term interest rates. The spread between the yields of high-yield corporate, or junk, bonds and 7-year Treasuries rose sharply, nearing

10%, a level last seen in 1990. This spread reflected concern over the risk of default among troubled firms, driven by several high-profile bankruptcies, notably Pacific Gas & Electric, which was caught up in California's energy crisis, and Enron.

In 2001 the SEC cracked down on accounting fraud, investigating between 240 and 260 cases. The first antifraud injunction against a Big Five accounting firm in more than 20 years was entered against Arthur Andersen, which agreed to a settlement of $7 million, the largest civil penalty ever imposed on a major accounting firm. In June the SEC issued an alert to investors, urging them not to rely solely on analyst recommendations. The SEC reported widespread conflicts of interest among analysts who covered stocks underwritten by their firms or those they personally owned.

The fortunes of traditional blue-chip stocks were mixed. Philip Morris gained 4.2% and Procter and Gamble 0.9%, while General Motors lost 4.6% and Minnesota Mining & Manufacturing lost 1.9%. Media giant Disney lost 28.4%, and pharmaceutical company Merck & Co. lost 37.2%.

In November, after more than three years of litigation, the Microsoft Corp. reached a settlement with the Department of Justice and 9 of the 18 states that had joined the suit. This settlement was widely seen as a victory for Microsoft, despite the fact that the nine other states had refused to sign on. The software giant's stock ended the year up by about 53%. Personal computer manufacturer Dell was up some 55%, and technology blue chip IBM rose by roughly 42% on the year.

At year's end 8 of the 10 stock sectors tracked by Dow Jones were down on the year, with only consumer cyclicals (+0.18) and noncyclicals (+1.12) in positive territory. The best-performing individual industries were consumer services (+57.12%), office equipment (+50.38%), toys (+38.89%), and water utilities (+37.07%), while the worst were gas utilities (−71.60%), communications technology (−56.58%), advanced industrial equipment (−46.85%), nonferrous metals (−39.85%), and airlines (−34.13%).

Profits and payrolls at many brokerage firms tumbled. Discount broker Charles Schwab reduced its staff by 17% through the third quarter of 2001 as its new assets fell from $31 billion in the first quarter to $11 billion in the second and $18 billion in the third. Merrill Lynch, the largest full-service broker, saw new assets drop from $35

billion in the first quarter of 2001 to only $5 billion in the second and $13 billion in the third.

Canada. The Canadian stock market declined considerably in 2001. The primary measure of the Canadian market, the Toronto Stock Exchange (TSE) 300, fell by 13.94% over the year. The Dow Jones Global Index for Canada fell by about 20% in U.S. dollar terms.

Through October the TSE reported average daily trading of 147.3 million shares, 11.4% lower than the same period in the previous year, and dollar volume of $2.9 billion, 23.7% lower than the same period of 2000. A total of 1,322 companies were listed on the exchange, down from 1,430. IPOs were roughly steady at 42, compared with 43 for the same period of 2000.

Nortel Networks, the largest TSE stock by market capitalization, lost more than 75% of its value on the year and closed at Can$11.90 (Can$1 = about U.S. $0.63) from its yearly high of Can$61.10. The next largest, Thomson Corp., lost 16% of its value and ended the year at Can$48.35, down from a high of Can$57.85. Canada 3000, the country's second biggest airline, received bankruptcy protection in November.

The two-year-old Canadian Venture Stock Exchange (CDNX) was up 8.7% through December 7, though it was down 11.1% from its peak of June 8. On December 10, the main CDNX index was replaced by the new S&P/CDNX Composite index, introduced as a broad indicator of the venture capital market in Canada. Through September, 113 IPOs were completed on the CDNX, up from 101 in the same period of 2000. Average market capitalization was down to $3,820,000 on September 30, from $5,740,000 at the end of the previous year. The TSE and CDNX merged on August 1, but the exchanges continued to operate separately under joint ownership.

The terrorist attacks in the U.S. on September 11 caused a 294-point drop in the TSE 300, and trading was halted. The exchange reopened on September 13, but interlisted American companies were not traded until September 17, the day the major U.S. markets reopened.

On November 14 the Securities Industry Committee on Analyst Standards issued a report recommending that securities firms require their analysts to disclose conflicts of interest and prohibit certain activities.

Foreign investment in Canadian shares plummeted. Through July foreign investors made net investments of only $3.8 billion in Canadian stocks, compared with $36 billion in the same period of the previous year. Canadians made net withdrawals of $26.8 billion from foreign stock markets, continuing the trend from the previous year. The Canadian brokerage industry reported an operating profit of $1.4 billion through July, 31% below the same period of the previous year. Mergers and acquisitions totaled $71 billion in the first six months, less than half the $149 billion of the same period of 2000.

The Canadian central bank, the Bank of Canada, followed the Fed for much of the year and reduced its overnight interest rate nine times, from 5.75% to 2.25%. The Canadian unemployment rate was 7.5% in November, the highest since mid-1999.   (BETH KOBLINER)

Western Europe. Early in the year most investors judged the European Union to be the only relatively safe place for their money as problems mounted in Japan and in the United States. Yet as early as March—and despite the confidence of many in the region that the euro zone would continue to grow—European equity funds suffered their first overall outflows in six years. Investors sold two billion in fund holdings. By year's end many more were disappointed.

Europe's main stock markets approached the winter holiday season firmly in negative territory. Most had lost around a quarter of their value, with the German Xetra DAX down 25%, France's CAC 40 down 27.4%, and Italy down 28.6% (all in U.S. dollar terms). The U.K.'s FTSE 100 fared a little better, recording a sterling loss of 17.7% (20.4% in dollars). Dollar investors who lost least were those invested in the constituents of Spain's Madrid Stock Exchange, down 8.9% late in the year. The newest entrant to the euro zone, Greece, continued to perform poorly. Early in the year a 3.7% drop in the level of the Athens index dashed hopes that investors would pile in when interest rates fell to euro-zone levels. Within a month of the country's May 31 upgrading by the MSCI index series from an emerging to a developed market, investors fled, sending the market down by 12%. Emerging market investment funds reportedly had pulled out an estimated $1 billion.

Markets had reacted positively to the surge in U.S. markets that followed the surprise New Year's cut in the federal funds interest rate by the Fed. The European Central Bank (ECB) left interest rates unchanged in January, concerned that inflation was above the bank's target ceiling of 2%, and through the year the continued reluctance of the ECB to cut rates made investors increasingly nervous.

By midyear short-term prospects had deteriorated further with a spike in oil prices. Manufacturing activity declined as big exporting companies in Germany, France, Italy, and Spain faced slowing demand from the U.S. and Japan. Industrial production fell sharply in the second quarter, down 1.4% in July alone. Europe's slowdown was exacerbated by the effects of the sharp tightening of monetary policy by the ECB between the end of 1999 and October 2000, weakening retail sales. Inflation, however, rose well above the central bank's 2% target to 2.9%, again choking off any likelihood of rate cuts.

In June additional signs of global weakness disappointed investors awaiting a second-quarter revival. Little progress could be made in markets dominated by concerns over corporate weakness and the ECB's failure to deliver rate cuts as expected. It was August before the bank made a quarter-point base-rate cut to 4.25%. By contrast the Fed had, between January and June, cut its rate by 2.5 percentage points. In November the U.S. rate was 2%, compared with the euro-zone rate of 3.25%. Profit warnings, especially from Finnish mobile phone company Nokia, sent the Helsinki exchange down 16.7% in June and undermined the position of other technology stocks, especially when U.S. high-tech companies also reduced their profit forecasts. Pessimism was deepened by falling demand for factory goods, inducing greater declines in activity in Europe and the U.S. Amid anxiety over the slowdown in the U.S. and Japan and another spike in oil prices, euro-zone GDP growth dropped to 2.5%, against 2.9% achieved in the last quarter of 2000.

As the summer wore on, European investors' sentiment increasingly matched that of U.S. investors as prospects for euro-zone growth deteriorated. They were concerned about the continued weakness of the euro and the ECB's resistance to calls for rate cuts. Manufacturing activity declined more than expected, and unemployment rose sharply. Germany's influential Ifo Business Climate Index fell to a five-year low, and the U.K. manufacturing sector entered recession, output having fallen for a second successive quarter.

Other Countries. While all eyes were on the United States, most of Asia became engulfed by a deeper and possibly more dangerous downturn. In Japan, which set the pattern for the region, the recession continued unabated, and the market was volatile. The fall in the yen and tumbling share prices raised fears of a credit crisis. The level of prices had fallen in five of the past six years and was forecast to fall further. As the year began, Japan's retail sales slumped 0.9% year-on-year as household spending fell and retail sales were down for a fourth successive year. Unemployment hit 5% at the end of November, outstripping a post-World War II record high of 4.9%, and ended the year at an estimated 5.4%. Consumer prices had registered their steepest drop in 30 years during 2000, and by January 2001 foreign investors were deserting the market in droves, forcing share prices down.

Nevertheless, the Japanese market enjoyed a brief respite in January 2001 when the unexpected rate cut by the U.S. Fed lifted sentiment. Soon after, equity markets sank, weighed down by reports of weak corporate earnings. The election of a new Japanese prime minister on April 24 triggered a 6% rise in the Topix index, but again this was short lived. In July the market fell when the Tankan survey showed a further weakening of the economy, only to rise again in August on news that the Bank of Japan would boost the money supply. It reverted to a downward trend when it became clear that the earnings of Japan's healthiest companies were set to decline.

The contraction of Singapore's and Taiwan's economies—5.6% and 4.2% of GDP, respectively—was unprecedented. By the end of November, output was stagnating in Malaysia, Hong Kong, and Thailand, and export growth was slowing sharply in China, although domestic demand was helping to sustain output. Despite this, a lack of confidence in the global economy pushed the China market down by more than 20%.

Argentina was the focus of attention in South American markets. Early in the year the U.S. interest-rate cuts briefly lifted investor confidence, but on July 10 the failure of an Argentine government bond auction precipitated another financial crisis. In September the International Monetary Fund agreed to increase its loan to $22 billion. In November, however, the Argentine government announced that it would restructure its debts through exchanging loans, which involved both local and international investors. The proposal was seen by many as debt default, and the country quickly moved into a deeper crisis, with the markets ending down 29% in dollar terms. The problem in Argentina had a contagious effect on Brazil, which was already suffering an energy crisis. The Brazilian currency depreciated 28% in the first 10 months of the year, and although it recovered slightly, the Brazilian stock market ended the year down almost 24% in dollar terms.

According to the investment bank Morgan Stanley Dean Witter, the risk of global deflation was higher at the end of 2001 than at any time in the previous 70 years. Yet in the final quarter of 2001, there was consensus among professional investors in global equities that the "bear" market had hit bottom on September 21. The attacks on September 11, they judged, might have helped to resolve more quickly the problem of past overinvesting by prompting faster rate cuts and reducing capacity in the travel and leisure sectors.

Commodity Prices. Commodity prices were expected to weaken generally as global growth slowed. Amid the general gloom, however, there were a few winners. Cocoa prices rose during October and November by around 30% to reach a three-year high. The market expected production to fall by around 200,000 metric tons over the year to September 2002, mainly because of disease and poor farm maintenance in Côte d'Ivoire, the chief producer. Another more marginal winner was gold. Even before September 11, sentiment for the yellow metal was positive. As the year drew to a close, it had regained some of its attraction as a store of value to reach a price of more than $278 an ounce, a three-year high. Demand had eroded over the previous few years to make a high level of precautionary investment necessary to offset that erosion.

The prices of other metals had fallen steadily despite lower levels of stock, which indicated low expectation of demand. Aluminum fell 11% between April and August and was expected to slide further in the short term. Copper, however, which followed a similar pattern, was always the metal to watch. Traditionally, copper was the first metal to recover from a stock market correction, as the liquidity that results when investors cash in their stock market holdings usually lifts construction activity. (Historically, the price of copper shows a statistical feature known as an "absorbing state." When the price reaches a certain level, it tends to remain there until an unexpected event jars it and sends it back to its long-term average price of around 91 cents a pound. Absorbing

states arise from the tendency of each phase of the economic cycle to linger.) Copper entered an absorbing state in July 2001 at below 70 cents a pound and ended the year at 67 cents; analysts were not expecting an early "breakout."

The price of oil had been highly volatile, and the outlook remained deeply uncertain by the end of the year. In 2000 production cuts, low stocks, and high demand driven by global growth had pushed prices well above the target price range of $22–$28 dollars a barrel set by OPEC. By the third quarter of 2001, demand from the U.S., the world's biggest oil consumer, was 300,000 bbl a day lower than in the third quarter of 2000. The slowdown and the need to sell oil caused producers outside OPEC to be less inclined to cooperate in cutting production, and it was thought that their need to keep up production and sales could keep prices, which ended 2001 below $20 a barrel, depressed. Any extension of the war in Afghanistan, though, could cause interruptions to supply that would force prices up in 2002.   (IEIS)

BANKING

The September 11 attacks in the United States and the resulting international efforts to cut off the source of terrorist funding gave rise to sweeping new legislative and other measures that brought the global banking and financial services industry to the front lines of the war on terrorism in 2001.

On October 26, U.S. Pres. George W. Bush signed into law the U.S.A. Patriot Act, which granted the government broad new investigative and surveillance powers and provided for a significant expansion of anti-money-laundering requirements applicable to banks and other financial institutions. The U.S. measures were part of an intensive global campaign against terrorist-funding sources. International groups such as the Financial Action Task Force (FATF), the anti-money-laundering arm of the Organisation for Economic Co-operation and Development, were deeply involved in the global war against terrorism.

Even before the September 11 attacks, actions had been taken or were under consideration in a number of countries to combat money laundering. Particularly notable were the actions taken by countries identified in the June 2000 report by the FATF as jurisdictions where existing measures to combat money laundering were deemed to be inadequate. The Cayman Islands and Panama instituted a number of remedial actions

in response to the FATF report, and in June 2001 they were removed from the FATF list. Israel for the first time enacted an anti-money-laundering law, an action recognized by the FATF as "welcome" progress.

In other places, including Bermuda and Luxembourg, legislation was enacted expanding the coverage of anti-money-laundering laws. The European Union (EU) had under consideration revisions to its 1991 directive in order to expand its scope. Actions to enhance the effectiveness of reporting on suspicious activity were instituted in Argentina and Canada. Italy adopted guidelines (commonly known as the "Ten Commandments") that provided for significant enhancements to anti-money-laundering practices.

There were also widespread efforts in 2001 to adapt existing laws and regulatory structures to the requirements of an increasingly globalized and integrated financial system. A number of countries continued to grapple with the problem of how to modernize their financial services laws to permit their domestic institutions to meet the challenges presented by advances in information and

World's 25 Largest Banks[1]	
Bank	**Assets** (in U.S. $000,000)
1 Mizuho Holdings (Japan)	1,428,928
2 Sumitomo Mitsui Banking (Japan)	991,791
3 Citigroup (U.S.)	902,210
4 Deutsche Bank (Germany)	885,135
5 Allianz (Germany)	869,561
6 United Financial of Japan	844,692
7 Mitsubishi Tokyo Financial Group	817,280
8 J.P. Morgan Chase (U.S.)	715,348
9 HypoVereinsbank (Germany)	674,670
10 UBS (Switzerland)	673,876
11 HSBC Holdings (U.K.)	673,312
12 BNP Paribas (France)	653,505
13 Bank of America	642,191
14 Credit Suisse (Switzerland)	613,084
15 ING Group (Netherlands)	612,202
16 ABN Amro (Netherlands)	511,448
17 Royal Bank of Scotland (U.K.)	477,903
18 Barclays (U.K.)	472,207
19 AXA (France)	446,899
20 Commerzbank (Germany)	432,818
21 Société Générale de France	429,258
22 Morgan Stanley (U.S.)	426,794
23 Fortis Group (Belgium/Netherlands)	412,499
24 HBOS (U.K.)	401,175
25 Grupo Santander Central Hispano (Spain)	328,551

[1]Ranked by asset size as of Dec. 31, 2000.
Source: *The Wall Street Journal*, Oct. 1, 2001.

communications technology that make possible the delivery of a broad array of financial services and intensify the competitive pressures on those institutions to provide their customers with banking, investment, insurance, and other financial services on an integrated basis. Canada passed Bill C-8, which revised the policy framework for its financial services sector and for the first time provided bank financial groups the option of organizing their business activities in Canada under a holding company structure. Equally significant changes were under way in Denmark, which passed the Act on Financial Undertakings unifying in a single legislative act provisions relating to banking, investment, insurance, and mortgage activities.

Similarly, reform of domestic regulatory systems to enable them to meet the challenges presented by the formation of complex financial groups engaged in a diverse array of activities both at home and abroad was high on the legislative agenda in many countries. In Austria a Financial Market Supervisory Authority Bill was introduced. It would provide for the devolution of banking supervision from the Ministry of Finance while also creating a central supervisory authority for financial services. Germany had under consideration legislation that would significantly revise the financial supervisory system by combining the three supervisory offices for banking, insurance, and securities activities into a single organization. This Federal Agency for Financial Service and Financial Market Supervision would be affiliated with the German Ministry of Finance.

Ireland contemplated legislation that would provide for a new structure for the regulation of financial services. It proposed that the Central Bank of Ireland be restructured and called the Central Bank of Ireland and Financial Services Authority, which would consist of two functional divisions, one responsible for prudential regulation of all financial services (the Irish Financial Services Regulatory Authority) and the other charged with the management of external reserves and the country's participation in the European System of Central Banks (the Irish Monetary Authority). Portugal adopted legislation creating a National Council of Financial Supervisors to promote coordination between the three existing financial supervisors responsible for oversight of the banking, securities, and insurance industries.

Reviews of existing regulatory and supervisory relationships were under way in other countries. In Finland the government assigned a special advisory body the task of preparing a proposal on how to integrate insurance companies into the financial markets' supervisory structure. South Africa continued to debate whether to follow the route taken by Australia and the U.K. and establish a single financial regulator outside the central bank, while in Switzerland debate centred on a recommendation that the Swiss Federal Banking Commission and the Federal Office of Private Insurance be melded into a single integrated financial-market supervisory authority.

The global trend clearly continued to be in the direction of some form of consolidated oversight, but there was as yet no international consensus in 2001 on what kind of governmental authority should exercise this responsibility.

Another important development in 2001 was the pending transition to the euro in the 12 euro-zone countries and the ultimate disappearance of their local currencies in favour of euro banknotes and coins as legal tender for cash transactions. This was scheduled to occur on Jan. 1, 2002, and extensive efforts were under way to ensure that the changeover occurred with minimal disruption. The possible shortage of euro cash in the first weeks of 2002 and the logistic and security challenges of moving euro and legacy currencies at the end of the transition phase were the two major concerns of this gigantic project. In some countries special security arrangements were instituted to protect the new euro banknotes and coins as they were shipped to banks for distribution.

There was also extensive debate surrounding the changes to the Basel Capital Accord proposed in January 2001 by the Basel Committee on Banking Supervision. Key issues in these debates included the use of an "internal ratings-based approach" to setting risk-based capital standards and whether (and how) to incorporate measurements of operational risk into the standards. Another important issue was the role of home and host country authorities in the supervisory review process contemplated under Pillar 2 of the proposal as well as in connection with the application of disclosure standards contemplated under the market discipline principles set forth in Pillar 3.

Deposit insurance schemes were introduced or strengthened in several countries, including Luxembourg, South Africa, and Turkey, while in South Korea deposit insurance coverage was reduced. In the U.S., reform of deposit insurance coverage was the subject of heightened scrutiny by Congress, which considered several proposals to raise coverage limits as well as premium payments. This issue drew public attention in late July when the U.S. Federal Deposit Insurance Corp. seized Illinois-based Superior Bank FSB in a bailout that analysts suggested could cost as much as $500 million. Important revisions to bank-liquidation procedures, including enhancements to depositor protection, also were under consideration in Switzerland.

A number of countries, including India, Pakistan, and Panama, implemented changes to enhance their banks'

Daniel Janin/AFP Worldwide

A special police unit in Paris guards the arrival of new euro bank notes at the Bank of France on November 20.

practices regarding classification of assets and loan loss provisions. In this connection an initiative was undertaken in Spain, where an "insolvency statistical coverage fund" was created. The idea behind the fund was to accumulate additional resources during healthy economic periods to be used in the worst periods of the cycle.

Corporate governance issues also received increasing attention in several jurisdictions, notably Singapore, where a Corporate Governance Code was introduced, and Germany, where consideration was given to a Corporate Governance "Best Practices" Code.

In addition, there were extensive efforts to adapt legal and regulatory systems to the changing world of electronic banking and commerce. Luxembourg adopted a law on electronic commerce, and several countries, including Belgium, Italy, and Sweden, adopted measures to establish the legal framework for electronic signatures. Germany and Singapore undertook efforts to promote Internet payment systems and virtual banking. Legislation on electronic funds transfers (EFT) was adopted in Belgium, while Australia adopted an EFT Code of Conduct.

Privatization of banks continued in a number of countries, including the Czech Republic and Romania. Pressures for cross-industry consolidation resulted in several large mergers. In Germany Allianz AG took control of Dresdner Bank in a $21 billion deal that created the world's sixth largest financial services institution. (*See* TABLE.) Kookmin Bank and Housing & Commercial Bank combined under the Kookmin name to create South Korea's largest commercial bank, with some $121 billion in assets. In the U.S. two North Carolina-based institutions, First Union and Wachovia, joined forces to create the nation's fourth largest bank holding company, with assets estimated at $322 billion.

Cross-border merger activity also continued, as witnessed by the ongoing integration occurring within the Nordic region. BNP Paribas of France increased its presence in the U.S. market by purchasing 55% of BancWest in early 2001 and then acquiring United California Bank from UFJ Holding of Japan in a $2.4 billion buyout. Several countries, notably Israel and Poland, took measures to promote an expanded foreign bank presence in their domestic markets, while in Japan such actions focused on the rescue of failed institutions. Japan was also notable in that it

permitted nonfinancial enterprises to establish commercial banking operations. At year's end the regional Ishikawa Bank became the first middle-level Japanese bank to file for bankruptcy since 1999.

(LAWRENCE R. UHLICK)

BUSINESS OVERVIEW

It was a new, unstable era in 2001. Any hopes that the boom years of the 1990s would extend into the next decade ended for good after the September 11 terrorist attacks that destroyed the World Trade Center, launched the United States into war, and sent the business world into chaos.

The U.S. economy was skirting the edge of recession before the attacks; afterward it tumbled. Already-suffering industry sectors begged for government bailouts, and what had been known as the "new economy" of technology companies and Internet-based start-ups—the stars of the 1990s boom—fell further into disrepair. (*See* COMPUTERS AND INFORMATION SYSTEMS.)

The stock market had been deflating in value throughout the year, equally reducing valuations of traditional companies such as the ExxonMobil Corp. and new economy titans such as Yahoo! Inc. By year's end all signs of a recession were in place. Real gross domestic product (GDP) growth in the U.S. fell at a 0.4% annual rate in third-quarter 2001, the biggest drop since the 1991 first quarter, and real GDP was expected to fall by 1% in the fourth quarter, compared with an annual growth rate of 5% for full-year 2000. In October the Consumer Confidence Index hit 85.5, its lowest standing in seven years, while manufacturing activity fell to its lowest level since February 1991.

For many industries the havoc caused by the terrorist attacks was more toxic than a typical recession. The worst affected were those sectors connected to travel, in particular the airlines, which were rattled to the point of near collapse. Analysts expected the U.S. airline industry to have an after-tax loss of $5.6 billion in 2001.

The airlines already had been in fragile financial health for most of 2001—the result of years of price wars and rising fuel costs. The U.S. government's freeze on air travel for two days in September, combined with the public's overall fear of flying in the weeks after the hijackings, pushed many airlines to the brink of bankruptcy. U.S. airlines lobbied for a government bailout to help compensate for the loss of revenues and ultimately

came away with a $15 billion package that, while enormous, still was not enough to prevent most leading airlines from posting severe losses. Almost all the major U.S. and foreign airlines cut staff by the thousands and slowed production drastically in the last few months of 2001. In mid-October, UAL Chairman James Goodwin warned that the airline could "perish" in the next year; soon afterward he was forced to resign and was replaced by UAL board member John W. Creighton.

European airlines, faced with the economic downturn and a drop in passenger traffic to North America, also registered massive losses. In early October Swissair briefly grounded all flights as it sought an infusion of cash. Sabena, jointly owned by Swissair and the Belgian government, was formally declared bankrupt in November. Out of the ashes of Sabena, Belgian investors created a successor of sorts, former Sabena unit Delta Air Transport, which seemed likely to merge with Virgin Express in early 2002. Air France announced staff cuts and reorganization plans for troubled Air Afrique, which it had acquired in August after the 11 African countries that shared ownership relinquished control of the airline.

Aircraft manufacturers were in equally rough shape. The Boeing Co., which moved its headquarters to Chicago in 2001, planned to cut up to 30,000 employees by the end of 2002 and slashed its airplane deliveries for 2001 to roughly 500, down from an expected 538. That

Air travelers stranded in Brussels on November 6 wait at a Sabena baggage claim that was closed due to demonstrations by employees of the debt-ridden Belgian airline.

Jacques Collet/AFP Worldwide

total was anticipated to fall to about 350 deliveries in 2002. Boeing's chief rival, European manufacturer Airbus, announced plans to deliver 320 aircraft in 2001 but acknowledged that cutbacks by airlines would reduce future orders. On a positive note, the Anglo-French Concorde aircraft, grounded since a fatal accident in July 2000, officially returned to the air in November.

Other industries linked to travel suffered as well. The lodging industry's profits for the year were expected to decline to between $18 billion and $20 billion, compared with 2000's record profit of $23.5 billion; revenue per available room was expected to fall by as much as 5% in 2001, the worst performance in 33 years. Industry occupancy rates were anticipated to fall to 60% of capacity, the lowest since the Persian Gulf War. The damage was such that some analysts predicted 6–10 hotel-chain bankruptcies by early 2002.

In the American automotive sector, sales were weakened by a reduction in rental car usage as well as consumer wariness about making large purchases. After September 11 all of the Big Three auto manufacturers initiated layoffs and began reducing production. The Ford Motor Co. planned to reduce its output by 13%, or up to 120,000 units, and stop production at five North American assembly plants. Ford posted a $692 million loss in the third quarter, and its worldwide automotive revenues fell by 12.4% in the quarter. Ford's woes were compounded by the expenses incurred because of the Firestone tire recall in 2000 and what critics termed a costly acquisition spree. By year's end Ford Chairman Jacques Nasser had been ousted in favour of William Clay Ford, Jr., the great-grandson of company founder Henry Ford. The General Motors Corp., although it posted a loss for the third quarter of $368 million, seemed to be in better shape. Sales of GM pickup trucks and sports utility vehicles shot up by 10% in the otherwise grim month of September. On September 21 GM revealed an agreement to buy the bankrupt South Korean Daewoo Motor and its international subsidiaries. DaimlerChrysler AG, which saw net income fall by 69% in the third quarter, was shaking out its operations to improve productivity. The company planned to slash more than 2,700 jobs and close three plants to get its troubled Freightliner LLC truck subsidiary to profitability by 2003.

As of September, 1,560,000 import cars had been sold year-to-date in the U.S., compared with 1,550,000 in the 2000 pe-

riod. Imported light-vehicle sales rose to an estimated 2.2 million cars, compared with 2.1 million in 2000. It was good news for Japan's Nissan Motor Co., which said it would post $2.7 billion in profits for its fiscal year ending in March 2002. In November German carmaker BMW AG reported strong international sales and higher-than-expected revenue, with net profits (before taxes) up 63.3% for the first nine months of 2001.

The overall market volatility also had an impact on the energy sector, which was coming off one of its best years in recent history. As many analysts had predicted, the spike in oil prices that had helped deliver record revenues to oil and gas companies in 2000 began to abate in mid-2001. Where oil had been in the $30-per-barrel range for much of 2000, prices cooled down to roughly $24 per barrel by August. With jet-fuel usage dramatically down in the third quarter owing to reduced flight loads, many oil players lost revenues.

The oil market continued to tier into the ranks of global superpowers—The ExxonMobil Corp., The ChevronTexaco Corp., BP PLC (formerly BP Amoco), and the Royal Dutch/Shell Group—and lesser, regional players. Many of the latter went on acquisition binges to increase their meagre market shares. The Canadian oil and gas market was ripe for American companies looking for acquisitions, and some observers predicted that the Canadian energy market would no longer be independent by mid-2002. American energy players that bought Canadian energy companies included the Anadarko Petroleum Corp., the Duke Energy Corp., and Conoco Inc. There were signs that some companies had grown overextended during the energy boom of 1999–2000. The most prominent case was the fall of Enron Corp. After a string of accounting irregularities came to light in late 2001, Enron's stock value collapsed to pennies per share, as the company faced charges of massively defrauding its shareholders and formally declared bankruptcy in December. Controversy over ties between Pres. George W. Bush's administration and the ruined company was expected to be a major political issue in 2002.

Heightened demand for electricity also fueled a rebirth in the coal industry, which grew at a rate of about 4.5%, more than double the average growth rate. Spot prices for western coal soared from $5 a ton to as much as $14 a ton. The Peabody Energy Corp., the largest coal company in the U.S., beat analyst expectations when it posted

$4.1 million in net income for third-quarter 2001.

The chemicals industry was hammered by continued high oil and gas prices and declines in business and consumer demand for plastics and other products. Earnings eroded across the board. Market leader E.I. DuPont de Nemours and Co. continued to struggle; total revenues fell by 11% in the first half of 2001. DuPont, which already had sold its oil subsidiary, Conoco, in 1999, pulled out of the pharmaceuticals sector by selling its pharmaceuticals subsidiary to the Bristol-Myers Squibb Co. for $7.8 billion. The Dow Chemical Co. started the year by completing a $10 billion acquisition of the Union Carbide Corp. but wound up posting severe declines in revenues and net income by year's end. A host of smaller chemical manufacturers had declining earnings, including the Cambrex Corp., the Crompton Corp., Cytec Industries Inc., the PolyOne Corp., and Praxair Technology, Inc.

Few sectors were as hard-pressed as the U.S. steel industry, which appeared to be on the verge of collapse throughout the year. When Bethlehem Steel Corp. filed for Chapter 11 bankruptcy protection in October, it was the 25th domestic steel company to have done so since 1998. Other steel companies filing for bankruptcy in 2001 included the Riverview Steel Corp., Edgewater Steel Ltd., GS Industries, Inc., the LTV Corp., and CSC Ltd. The industry was reeling with losses in 2001, recording a $1.4 billion loss in the third quarter alone. Steel manufacturers pointed to high energy costs and, most emphatically, extremely low import prices as the causes of their industry's troubles. The steel manufacturers that managed to avoid bankruptcy often took drastic measures to keep afloat. Top steelmaker USX Corp., which owned the U.S. Steel Group and the energy company Marathon Group, decided to separate the two companies to give them more flexibility to expand through acquisitions. U.S. Steel, which posted an $18 million net loss in third-quarter 2001, was spun off in October into a publicly traded company called United States Steel Corp. The merger of three European companies—Usinor of France, Aceralia of Spain, and Luxembourg's Arbed—was announced in February. The deal would create the world's largest steel group.

Other metals industries were also on the decline. In aluminum, year-to-date shipments as of August were down 14.4%, in part because of the slowdown

Exchange rates of major currencies to U.S.$, 2001

Source: International Monetary Fund, *International Financial Statistics.*

in automobile production. American exports of aluminum ingot and mill products were 725.8 million kg (1.6 billion lb) year-to-date as of August, down from 861.8 million kg (1.9 billion lb) in the same period in 2000, while imports were down 11.7% for the year. The leading worldwide aluminum producer, Alcoa Inc., remained strong, however, with revenues of $17.7 billion for the first three quarters, up from $16.4 billion in the comparable 2000 period. The company's health was in part due to an intensive cost-cutting initiative designed to offset falling demand. In November Alcoa reported that it was buying an 8% stake in China's largest aluminum producer.

Gold demand held up fairly well against signs of a growing worldwide economic slowdown. After a 17-month low of about $260 per ounce in February, gold prices rebounded to the $270–$290-per-ounce range for much of the year, and prices shot up after September 11, as investors poured into the market for security. Top worldwide gold producer AngloGold Ltd., based in Johannesburg, S.Af., bought Normandy Mining Ltd. of Australia for $2.3 billion in September. This followed an earlier $2.3 billion merger of Canada's Barrick Gold Corp. and its American rival, the Homestake Mining Co., which had created the world's second largest gold producer. Analysts approved of the mergers, hoping that less competition and production would improve the market's overall health.

The forest-products industry foundered owing to overall industry volatility, declining prices, and collapsing markets. The U.S. imposed higher duties on Canadian softwood lumber, which it claimed had been dumped on the American market at artificially low prices. (See WORLD AFFAIRS: *Canada.*) In 2000 there had been a divide between

rising pulp prices and falling lumber prices, which provided many manufacturers with steady earnings, but in 2001 all paper markets suffered.

Top paper manufacturers such as the Weyerhaeuser Co. and Bowater Inc. reported serious declines in business for the year. Weyerhaeuser reported a 54% drop in quarterly profits in third-quarter 2001, and its net earnings were $369 million for the first nine months of 2001, compared with $646 million in the same period in 2000. The International Paper Co. posted a $632 million net loss for the first nine months of 2001, and the Georgia-Pacific Corp. had a $289 million loss from continuing operations in the same period.

Home building had enough ballast from yearlong low mortgage rates to withstand a declining economy. Total new houses sold were 8.1 million through September, up slightly from the 8 million in the same period in 2000. Total construction starts for 2001 were estimated to be worth $481.4 billion. Commercial space construction, however, was expected to fall by 16% in 2001 and by 9% in 2002, with the steepest declines hailing from the industries most afflicted by the September 11 attacks, including hotels and office spaces. The weaker economy also caused banks, which had seen their earnings erode in 2001, to be more stringent with funds for commercial development, and this caused some projects to be delayed or canceled. Other sectors were expected to improve, including public-works projects, health care facilities, and multifamily housing.

The tobacco industry was healthy overall, in good part owing to rising product prices.

The pharmaceutical industry was resilient for much of the year, and top players were thriving. Market leader

Pfizer Inc. had a 153% increase in net income for the first nine months of 2001, driven by worldwide sales increases for its key products, including a 13% increase for Viagra and a 37% increase for Lipitor, its cholesterol-reducing drug that in 2001 became the largest-selling pharmaceutical in the world. Heightened competition between generic and patent drug manufacturers threatened to erode revenues for top pharmaceuticals. About $50 billion in drug patents were scheduled to expire in the next five years, and already generic players were profiting at the expense of patent manufacturers. Eli Lilly and Co. lost about 80% of its market share in Prozac once Barr Laboratories, Inc.'s generic reached the shelves.

Drug companies, faced with criticism of high drug prices and the threat of competition from cheaper generics, reached agreements to provide drugs to combat AIDS in several less-developed countries at a fraction of the Western prices, but demands for cheaper drugs continued. When mailborne anthrax hit newsrooms and government offices in September and October, the German pharmaceutical company Bayer AG faced intense pressure from the U.S. government to either reduce the price of its antibiotic Cipro or face the loss of its patent. Waiting in the wings with their generic versions of Cipro were manufacturers, including Barr, that offered their products free or at a steep discount to the government for its stockpiles. While Bayer managed to hold onto its patent by agreeing to reduce Cipro prices, the continuing threat of chemical and biological war ensured that the rivalry between generics and patent drug manufacturers had taken on new, unknowable connotations.

(CHRISTOPHER O'LEARY)

Education

Significant educational developments during 2001 included the expansion of ACHIEVEMENT-TESTING programs, educational alternatives to public schools, controversies over RELIGION in schools, limitations on freedom of inquiry, and ETHNIC QUOTAS in college admission policies.

PRIMARY AND SECONDARY EDUCATION

Newly inaugurated U.S. Pres. George W. Bush made the improvement of education a central goal of his administration. He began the year by appointing Houston (Texas) superintendent of schools Roderick R. Paige the nation's secretary of education. The president adopted the motto "No child left behind" and sent Congress proposed legislation featuring his four pillars of comprehensive educational reform: accountability, local control and flexibility, expanded parental choice, and a focus on what works. Whereas Congress endorsed such key provisions of the bill as nationwide achievement testing and money for poor schools, the legislators eliminated Bush's voucher plan that would have provided public funds for parents to send their children to any school of their choice, including private schools administered by religious groups.

Around the world the rapidly growing popularity of nationwide achievement testing was accompanied by several vexing problems. In the U.S. the nation's largest teachers union, the National Education Association (NEA), passed resolutions denouncing high-stakes testing. Parents' and students' rejection of "test-driven education" led to student boycotts of state achievement testing in several school districts. (*See* Special Report.) When school systems in Florida paid bonuses to schools whose students scored above average on the state achievement test, critics charged that such rewards placed undue emphasis on test passing in contrast to gaining a well-rounded education. Officials in states, notably New York, that already had ambitious testing requirements questioned why more exams, imposed by the federal government, were necessary. An expanded national testing program in Great Britain for students 14 years old and above drew complaints from teachers and parents and motivated the minister of education and skills, Estelle Morris, to order a review of the recently revised curriculum, which had produced what was described as an examination logjam. At the same time, the Labour government's proposal that private companies take over the operation of underperforming public schools met strong opposition from teachers unions.

Tax-supported alternatives to regular public schools continued to increase in the U.S. The Bush legislation included additional money for charter schools, which were established by private groups financed by tax funds and were permitted to offer a curriculum different from that of public schools. About 518,000 (1%) of the country's 50 million schoolchildren attended charter schools. The NEA announced its endorsement of charter schools that hired certified teachers, were subject to the same student-assessment measures as other public schools, honoured teachers' collective-bargaining rights, and had initial construction funds that did not rely heavily on tax revenue. As a further educational option, 850,000 (1.7%) American schoolchildren studied at home under parental guidance. About 18% of homeschoolers were also enrolled in regular schools part-time; 11% used books or materials from a public school; and 8% followed a public-school curriculum. A newly established Patrick Henry College opened in Virginia specifically for youths who had been homeschooled and who chose to pursue higher education in a Christian-based institution.

Private-school enrollments increased in Canada, rising over a 10-year period from 4.6% to 5.6% of all school-age children. Contrary to the impression that only wealthy families sent their children to private institutions, a survey reported that 29% of children enrolled in private schools across Canada came from families with incomes below Can$50,000 (about U.S. $32,000); that percentage rose to 46.1% in the western provinces of Manitoba, Saskatchewan, Alberta, and British Columbia.

Delegates from nine countries' ministries of education met in Beijing to outline steps they would take to upgrade schooling, especially to slash the rate of school dropouts and to turn around low school enrollment and poor classroom performance. The plan was signed by Bangladesh, Brazil, China, Egypt, India, Indonesia, Mexico, Nigeria, and Pakistan.

The South Korean government intended to improve the standard of education in the nation by limiting the number of students per class to 35 by 2004; the head count was currently 35.7 in elementary schools, 38 in middle schools, and 42.7 in high schools. To facilitate the program the government expected to hire 23,600 additional teachers and open 1,208 new schools with a total of 14,494 classrooms.

The Anglican Church of Canada faced the threat of bankruptcy as the result of lawsuits filed by native peoples (American Indians and Inuits) for mistreatment they allegedly had suffered in residential schools that were operated for more than a century by Anglicans, Roman Catholics, Presbyterians, and the United Church of Canada and were financed by the Canadian government. Between 1998 and 2001 more than 7,000 suits were registered, charging sexual-physical abuse and cultural damage to native inhabitants, with by far the largest number of claims focusing on cultural damage. The only cases accepted in the courts by the end of 2001 concerned sexual-physical abuse.

Efforts to curb violence and improve discipline in schools appeared in Israel, Japan, and the U.S. In an effort to reduce the number of incidents of youth violence, which had quadrupled over the past decade, Israel's Education Ministry permitted teachers to search pupils' bags for weapons and toughened legislation that barred the sale of alcohol to minors. Violence-prevention teams composed of teachers, parents, and students were authorized at every school to monitor incidents of hostility.

Japan's central legislative body, the Diet, sought to protect students' "right to learn" by means of a bill empowering school personnel to suspend students who disrupted classes, damaged school property, or attacked fellow students or teachers or caused them psychological distress. In early June a knife-wielding man on a stabbing rampage killed 8 children and injured 13 others at Ikeda Elementary School in Osaka prefecture. The school's children were so traumatized by the setting in which the stabbings took place that the Ministry of Education ordered the construction of a prefabricated building on a nearby site to serve the 680 pupils until the original building could be razed and replaced by a new permanent structure. In response to the incident, other schools introduced such safety measures as the distribution of personal alarms to teachers and the establishment of telephone hot lines between schools and police.

In the U.S. steps to make schools safer included assigning more police to schools as resource officers, instituting "red-code drills" in which students practiced protecting themselves against armed attacks, training teachers to identify potentially dangerous students, and having the courts assign stricter prison sentences to weapon-carrying teenagers. In addition, more schools were installing video surveillance systems, providing hot lines for reporting incidents of violence, encouraging students to take greater responsibility for maintaining a secure school environment, and engaging parents in safe-schooling campaigns. California's Supreme Court strengthened the authority of school personnel by ruling that schools could detain students without first having to prove "reasonable suspicion" of wrongdoing.

Countries differed in the adequacy of their present and future supplies of teachers. In England and Wales a survey revealed 10,000 unfilled permanent jobs in secondary schools; this represented the most serious teacher shortage in 36 years. The British government attempted to lure college graduates into teaching with attractive salaries during their training period, accelerated promotion schemes, and cheaper mortgages, but the incentives had limited success. The booming economy and tight labour market were blamed for the teacher shortage, since graduates, especially women, could easily find better-paid careers. To fill the shortages teacher-placement agencies continued to search abroad, particularly in New Zealand, Australia, South Africa, and Canada, which had furnished the United Kingdom with more than 25,000 teachers over the previous decade.

An investigative team was appointed in Australia to determine the reasons why 1,700 men had dropped out of the nation's corps of teachers since 1990. By 2001 males made up only 17.1% of all teachers in state primary schools and 48.7% in high schools.

Scotland's declining population of school-age children was expected to result in an overabundance of teachers in the coming decade. According to government predictions, the number of pupils in state primary schools would fall from the 2001 level of 425,200 to 368,600 in 2011, a 13% decrease. Students in state secondary schools would decrease from 319,000 to 286,500 by 2011, 10% fewer than in 2001. As a result, the number of full-time secondary teachers would drop to 22,900 in 2011, 7% fewer than in 2001.

Russian Pres. Vladimir Putin announced that in 2002, for the first time, the country planned to spend more on education than on defense. Putin also pledged to double teachers' salaries, which in 2001 averaged about $35 a month.

In India's Punjab province education officials in mid-August sought to fill 7,230 public-school teaching vacancies and 1,200 lecturerships in colleges. The AIDS epidemic in Africa seriously damaged many of the continent's education systems. Delegates at an Education International conference learned that HIV/AIDS had a greater effect on teaching than on any other profession and might nearly wipe out the supply of teachers in Africa within 10 years. An estimated 35–40% of secondary-school teachers in Botswana were reported to carry HIV, and the incidence of HIV infection also was high among teachers in Zimbabwe, South Africa, Swaziland, Malawi, and Zambia. Hadino Hishongwa, deputy minister of higher education for Namibia, reported that 25% of Namibians had tested positive for HIV/AIDS, a level he attributed partly to a lack of sufficient AIDS education for youths, who made up 72% of the country's population.

For the first time in the history of schooling in the U.S., an entire state's public schools were shut down by teachers striking for higher pay. Throughout the state of Hawaii, 13,000 teachers and 3,100 university faculty members abandoned their classrooms in early April in an effort to force legislators to authorize a salary increase, which the teachers union claimed was necessary to keep up with the rising cost of living. The walkout affected 180,000 students.

Controversies continued in India and the U.S. over allowing religious doctrine and practices in public schools. Opponents of India's ruling Bharatiya Janata Party accused the government of attempting to "saffronize" the nation's public-education system by fostering Hindu religious beliefs in schools, a

(continued on page 210)

AP/Wide World Photos

During a rally in Seoul on July 16, South Korean students wear traditional masks to protest Japanese textbooks that play down the aggressive role of the Japanese in their invasions of Asian countries during World War II.

Does Testing Deserve a Passing Grade?

by Charles D. Claiborn

High-Stakes Testing. As the term suggests, high-stakes testing is the use of educational and psychological tests to make decisions of often considerable consequence to individuals and institutions. Some tests assess the achievement or competencies of students at specific grade levels to determine whether they should be advanced to the next grade or, upon completing the secondary-school curriculum, be awarded a high-school diploma. Results of these tests additionally may be taken as an indicator of how well particular schools are educating their students and may in turn be used in allocating resources to schools or determining whether changes in their governance are warranted. Other tests assess the aptitude of applicants to be successful in college or graduate school and are used to make admissions decisions that dramatically affect the educational and professional futures of individuals. The differential impact these tests have on various racial, ethnic, and socioeconomic groups makes high-stakes-testing practices highly controversial.

Characteristics of High-Stakes Tests. According to some, high-stakes tests are "cognitively loaded" in that they measure the primarily cognitive constructs of knowledge and skill and, in some cases, potential or aptitude for gaining further knowledge and skill. The tests are also standardized—developed according to accepted practices of test development, such as those put forth jointly in 1999 by the American Educational Research Association, the American Psychological Association, and the National Council on Measurement in Education—and have thus been validated for their intended purpose and normed for populations with which they will be used. The psychometric adequacy of a test depends on the extent to which these practices have been followed.

The validity of a test is the adequacy of the test to perform a specific function. The types of validity that should be established for high-stakes tests thus vary according to the function of the test. For competency tests, such as minimum-competency tests used for grade advancement or graduation decisions, content validity is of particular concern, since it is important for the test to represent a designated domain of knowledge and skill adequately. A content-valid test of 10th-grade mathematics knowledge and skills, for example, is one that fairly and representatively reflects the range of mathematics topics and problems learned in the 10th grade, as determined by professionals in the area and, in some cases, the public at large. Different interest groups—a teachers union and a state legislature, for example—may naturally have different ideas about what a particular test should contain and who should determine that content. Content validity of competency tests can clearly be a source of controversy.

A second type of validity, criterion-related validity, is important for tests used in the selection of students. The value of a college entrance examination, notably the ACT (American College Testing Program) or SAT (Scholastic Assessment Test), depends on its ability to predict academic performance, which is the criterion of interest. The usefulness of any test for screening or selecting applicants for a position is based on the test's ability to predict job performance, the criterion in this case. It would be highly problematic, scientifically and legally, if a test used for selection or screening of applicants measured something that was not clearly related to criteria of school performance. The test-criterion relationship is the very heart of validity for this sort of test. It would also be problematic if the relationship between test scores and performance differed for different groups within the population, such as ethnic minority groups. The use of a test in such circumstances would constitute bias, though some experts have indicated that standardized tests used in selection do not generally suffer from this sort of distortion.

High-Stakes Testing in Selection—the Diversity Dilemma. Even when high-stakes tests have established validity, they are still open to controversy, especially with respect to issues involving ethnic diversity. In a recent review it was argued that the weight of the scientific evidence supports the validity of high-stakes tests used in selection. Standardized tests of knowledge and skill are indeed effective in predicting performance, at least within the cognitive domain. However, the authors of the review and others have also noted the well-established findings that African Americans and Latinos consistently score lower than whites on such tests and that Asian Americans score higher than whites on measures of quantitative ability and lower than whites on measures of verbal ability. Such ethnic-group differences are typically confounded with socioeconomic status, with members of lower socioeconomic groups typically scoring lower on such tests than members of higher socioeconomic groups. Nevertheless, such findings present a dilemma, that of choosing between the goal of using the most valid tests—those making the best predictions of performance—and the goal of having a more diverse student body or workforce. Several ways of resolving this dilemma have been proposed, though none has been researched thoroughly enough to merit recommendation.

Competency Assessment in Education. The widespread and growing use of competency assessment in schools brings high-stakes testing into the public and political spotlight. Minimum-competency tests are now used in some 23 states to determine grade advancement and graduation. In December the U.S. Senate passed a landmark education bill that would require mandatory annual state math and reading tests for all students in grades three through eight. In addition, the results of such tests are used to assess the perform-

ance of teachers, schools, and school districts and for this reason are made available to the public and are subject to scrutiny by state legislatures and agencies. The rationale for state-mandated minimum competency testing is generally to hold teachers and schools accountable for the education they are providing and to improve education by holding education professionals to a higher standard, namely, that imposed by the state. The practical effect of such practice is to reward those teachers and schools who do well, through financial incentives and public recognition, and punish those who do not.

Criticism of minimum-competency testing as a means to improve education has been considerable. First, there is little evidence to suggest that such testing really improves education. A 1990 report found that the use of minimum-competency tests is associated with higher dropout rates, though the reason for this is unclear. A number of researchers have documented the negative effects of minimum-competency testing on the curriculum and instruction. These include narrowing the curriculum to what is covered on the test ("teaching to the test"), taking time away from instruction in order to prepare students for the test, and limiting instruction to the types of knowledge and problem solving required by the test format (for example, emphasizing the recognition of information as emphasized on multiple-choice tests). Second, minimum-compe-

tency-testing policies often take important educational decisions away from professional educators and place them in the hands of those with little or no expertise—legislators or school-board members. These include decisions about test content and format as well as about standards for passing and the consequences of failure. Inexpert decisions about test development and use can undermine test validity and make unfair testing practices more likely. Third, minimum-competency tests, like all high-stakes tests, have a disproportionately negative impact on ethnic-minority students, students from lower socioeconomic groups, and students with learning disabilities. Finally, though the rationale for minimum-competency testing is to improve education, the focus of testing is often not in line with the instructional goals of particular teachers and schools. Consequently, the results of such tests are not particularly useful as feedback regarding how well teachers and schools are meeting the goals they set for themselves and their students. Though the use of minimum-competency testing has considerable public relations value by appearing to provide hard data on how well or how poorly schools are doing—with an accompanying set of high standards to which students, teachers, and schools are held—the reality of such testing falls short, in regard to both the flawed tests themselves and the often unhelpful, even hurtful, use to which the test results are put.

Charles D. Claiborn is professor of psychology in education at Arizona State University. He is the author of more than 60 articles and book chapters on psychotherapy process, including "Feedback" in Psychotherapy Relationships That Work: Therapists' Relational Contributions to Effective Psychotherapy.

(continued from page 207)
violation of the secular status of public schools prescribed in the nation's constitution. Saffron was the colour of the flag flown by the Rashtriya Swayamsevak Sangh, a Hindu-supremacist organization that administered 14,000 schools. Practices that drew the critics' complaints included government subsidies to universities that offered astrology or ancient Vedic mathematics in the curriculum and practiced Vedic rituals, including the chanting of the Saraswati Vandana hymn to the Hindu goddess of education at the beginning of all educational events.

In the U.S., although the Oregon Senate voted to prohibit posting the biblical Ten Commandments in public schools, the North Carolina Senate voted to permit it. The Hawaii state board of education struck down a proposal that would have permitted the Judeo-Christian biblical version of the world's creation to be taught in science classes as a proper theory of human beginnings along with Darwin's theory of evolution. The U.S. Supreme Court, in a 6–3 decision, ruled that church-sponsored groups, including Christian youth clubs, could use public-school buildings for after-school meetings along with other nonschool clubs. Observers speculated that the court's action could give impetus to the Bush administration's effort to furnish government funds to finance religious groups' programs for assisting people in poverty.

All but a handful of Japanese junior high schools rejected a controversial new history textbook, *Atarashii rekishi kyokasho*, which critics said glossed over Japan's wartime atrocities. The book, compiled by the nationalistic Japanese Society for History Textbook Reform, was scheduled for use beginning in April 2002.

HIGHER EDUCATION

Eight nations that bordered the Arctic Circle launched a University of the Arctic that was designed to offer circumpolar studies and prepare students to help maintain the quality of life in the polar region against destructive intrusions by global-development forces. The cooperating nations included Canada, Denmark (with its territories of Greenland and the Faroe Islands), Finland, Iceland, Norway, Russia, Sweden, and the U.S. Courses were offered via the Internet and on existing campuses of the eight nations. Students were required to spend at least one se-

Newly appointed U.S. Secretary of Education Roderick R. Paige speaks to students, teachers, and parents at an elementary school in Portland, Maine, on April 12.

AP/Wide World Photos

mester of study in a circumpolar neighbour institution before graduating.

The Chinese government, as a means of promoting the progress of universities in the nation's less-developed western regions, paired 13 western universities with advanced institutions in the east, including Beijing University, Xinjiang Shihezi University, and Tsinghua University. The partnerships, funded by loans from commercial banks and world financial organizations, were designed to develop key universities in the west, particularly by training over 1,000 teachers and administrators for the western institutions over a three-year period.

New restrictions on freedom of inquiry appeared in Russia, Egypt, and Cuba. The Russian Academy of Sciences instructed its hundreds of affiliated institutions to curtail the nation's 53,000 researchers by requiring them to report any attempt by scholars to apply for foreign grants. The academy also required institutions to report all visits by foreigners and to submit articles for inspection before they were published abroad. Egypt's premier Islamic higher-learning institution—Al-Azhar University, Cairo—instituted a policy of outlawing any publication that, according to university president Ahmad Omar Hashem, lacked "respect for God, His Prophet [Muhammad], and all religious values." After Cuban Pres. Fidel Castro had announced in 1998 that "in Cuba there are no prohibited books," economist Berta Mexidor started a system of independent libraries that stocked publications formerly banned in the country. By 2001 the network had grown to 65 small private libraries. Some claimed that the arrest of four leaders of the movement on various charges was politically motivated, while government officials asserted that the "libraries"

were created to promote the views of antigovernment parties (with aid from abroad) and denied that the detentions represented an attempt to curb intellectual freedom.

Problems arising from basing college admissions on ethnic quotas continued in Malaysia and the U.S. Malaysia's education minister, Musa Mohamed, announced that the nation's existing laws favouring Malay applicants over citizens of Chinese and Indian heritage in public universities would likely be extended to private institutions as well. At the same time, statistics released by the Ministry of Education showed that 7,168 university places were unfilled because not enough Malay students had applied and that 560 Chinese Malaysians who had scored at the highest levels on university entrance tests had been denied a place at a public institution. The government, however, approved the long-stalled plans by the Malaysian Chinese Association to establish a university to be governed by the association and, according to association spokespersons, to be open to all ethnic groups. In the U.S. advocates of affirmative-action programs that gave preferential admissions treatment to blacks and Hispanics argued that such programs increased the racial diversity on campuses and thereby had the educational benefit of helping all students develop enlightened attitudes and learn to work with people of different cultural backgrounds. Opponents of such programs contended that the research needed to adequately support the diversity argument had not been forthcoming and that special admissions opportunities for selected minorities not only violated the principle of basing admissions on academic merit but also placed other minorities at an unfair disadvantage.

Students' use of illegal drugs drew attention in Great Britain and the U.S. A survey of colleges in the U.K. reported a recent fivefold increase in the number of students using cocaine, which made the drug the second favourite narcotic, after cannabis. Investigators attributed much of the growing popularity of cocaine to its dramatic drop in price. As a result of a law in the United States that denied government financial aid to students with drug convictions, an estimated 34,000 students were denied loans and grants in 2001, more than triple the number in 2000.

The autonomy of higher-education institutions was challenged in Taiwan when a college student, after having been dismissed from Shih Hsin University, Taipei, for failing half his courses during a single semester, filed a lawsuit against the university, contending that the institution's dismissal policy violated his right to continue his education. A national debate was sparked when the Administrative High Court supported the student's claim by ruling that individual universities lacked the authority to oust students for weak academic performance. Although such authority had been awarded to institutions by a Ministry of Education directive, representatives of the Taiwan Association for Human Rights argued that decisions about dismissals would need to be based on regulations passed by the Taiwan legislature, which would thereby ensure uniform practice nationwide.

The Korean Council for University Education initiated an international internship plan to further student-exchange programs and to address problems arising from the fast rise in the number of South Korean students studying abroad. Under the program, about 2,000 students from 63 South Korean universities would travel overseas in 2002. The council currently had exchange agreements with 30 U.S. universities and intended to forge bonds with institutions in Australia, New Zealand, Japan, China, and Europe. Recent reforms of the education system in Greece failed to stem the flow of youths seeking higher education in other nations. Over 55,000 Greek students entered foreign universities in 2001, 65% more than in 1998.

As an effort to revitalize the traditional influence of French culture in Egypt, leaders of the Egypt-based French University Friends' Association announced the establishment of a new French University in Cairo, scheduled to accept students in 2002.

(R. MURRAY THOMAS)

The Environment

The adoption of ALTERNATIVE ENERGY methods, talks leading to agreement on the KYOTO PROTOCOL, and demonstrations over the transportation of spent NUCLEAR FUEL were among 2001's environmental issues. ARTIFICIAL INSEMINATION of zoo animals topped CONSERVATION EFFORTS, and measures to save the ANIMALS at the KABUL ZOO were implemented.

INTERNATIONAL ACTIVITIES

On June 5, 2001, World Environment Day, UN Secretary-General Kofi Annan announced a $21-million, four-year study of the condition of the global environment. With the participation of 1,500 scientists and many organizations, the Millennium Ecosystem Assessment would be the first comprehensive assessment of this kind ever attempted.

At a meeting held in Johannesburg, S.Af., Dec. 4–9, 2000, representatives from 122 governments had finalized an international treaty to reduce or eliminate the production and use of the persistent organic pollutants aldrin, chlordane, dieldrin, endrin, heptachlor, mirex, toxaphene, and hexachlorobenzene. Tropical countries were allowed to continue using DDT for malaria control until a suitable substitute became available. The phasing out of polychlorinated biphenyls would be gradual so that equipment containing them could remain in use until 2025. The treaty was opened for signature in Stockholm in May 2001 and would come into force once 50 countries had ratified it.

Eight people shared the $750,000 Goldman Environmental Prize at a presentation in San Francisco on April 23. The winners were Eugène Rutagarama of Rwanda, who worked to save his country's last mountain gorillas; Yosepha Alomang of Indonesia for helping to reverse some of the damage caused by mining in Irian Jaya; Oscar Olivera of Brazil, who helped reverse the privatization of the Brazilian water industry that had led to sharp increases in water prices; Bruno Van Peteghem of New Caledonia for his opposition to nickel mining in the New Caledonia coral reef; Myrsini Malakou and Giorgos Catsadorakis of Greece, who helped establish the Prespa Park conservation zone in wetlands with the friendly collaboration of Albania, Macedonia, and Greece; and American journalists Jane Akre and Steve Wilson for their investigation into health risks from the agricultural use of recombinant bovine growth hormone.

On September 7 the European Union (EU) formally approved a directive on renewable energy. This required member states to ensure that 12% of gross internal energy consumption and 22.1% of electricity consumption would come from renewable sources by 2010.

NATIONAL DEVELOPMENTS

Germany. On June 11 the federal government and leading energy companies signed a formal agreement to phase out nuclear power. The core of the agreement was a limit on the amount of power each of Germany's nuclear power plants would be permitted to produce. On the basis of an average life of 32 years for each reactor, this would mean the newest reactor would have to close in about 2021. The government published a draft of the necessary legislation on July 9, and after a period for consultation, the cabinet approved it on September 5. As well as setting a limit to the life span of existing nuclear plants, the law required power generators to provide intermediate storage

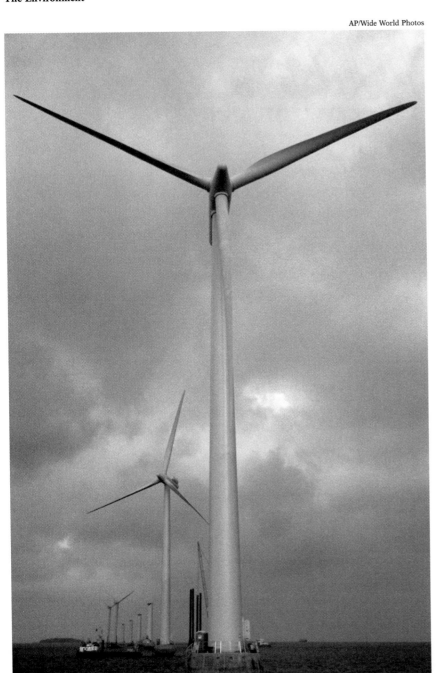

Middelgrunden, a wind park off the coast of Copenhagen that included the world's largest windmill, began producing energy on May 6.

Spain. On September 5 Boliden Ltd., the Swedish-Canadian company operating the Los Frailes iron pyrite mine at Aznalcóllar in Andalusia, said production at the mine would cease immediately. The mine was the source of the 1998 leakage of waste upstream of the Coto Doñana National Park. The cost of cleaning up the leakage was estimated at €180 million (about $165 million), and compensation also would have to be paid. The company, which filed for bankruptcy in 2000, said these costs were a significant factor in the closure.

United Kingdom. On July 18 the British government announced that there would be no further reprocessing of nuclear fuel at the Dounreay plant in Caithness, Scot. Reprocessing at Dounreay had been suspended in 1996 owing to an equipment failure, and almost 25 metric tons of spent fuel remained on-site. This would either be stored at Dounreay or be transported to Sellafield, Eng., for reprocessing.

Ukraine. On Dec. 15, 2000, the last of the four Chernobyl reactors was closed down permanently. In fact, reactor 3 had closed some weeks earlier for technical reasons and had to be restarted in order to be shut down formally. Pres. Leonid Kuchma had issued the command through a television link from the Ukraina Palace in Kiev. On April 26, 2001, the 15th anniversary of the accident at Chernobyl, Kuchma led a memorial service in Kiev. Meanwhile, scientists continued to study the long-term effects of low-level radiation released in the accident.

United States. In its annual *Toxic Release Inventory*, published in April, the Environmental Protection Agency (EPA) reported that two-thirds of the over 3.5 billion kg (1 kg=2.2 lb) of toxic chemicals released into the U.S. environment in 1999 came from hard-rock mining companies and operators of electric power plants. The highest releases were from Nevada and Utah, with nearly 530 million kg and 527 million kg, respectively; Arizona, 437 million kg; and Alaska, 196 million kg. Hard-rock mining companies released some 1.8 billion kg of chemicals into the air, land, and water, and electricity utilities released more than 527 million kg, mostly from stack emissions from coal-burning plants.

On April 25 the Senate unanimously passed legislation authorizing an annual expenditure of $200 million for cleaning up more than 500,000 abandoned industrial sites. On June 7 a

facilities close to their plants for spent fuel and banned all shipments of waste for reprocessing from 2005.

On June 6 Environment Minister Jürgen Trittin announced that the government planned a major expansion of offshore wind-power generation. By 2030 offshore wind parks, using 4,000 generators, would be generating between 75 and 80 terawatts of power annually. Two North Sea areas had been identified as suitable because they were clear of all marine- and bird-conservation areas. The required investment would be made possible by the German renewable energy support law, which guaranteed a price of €0.09 (about $0.08) per kilowatt-hour for wind power.

Republican-led subcommittee of the House of Representatives rejected Pres. George W. Bush's request for $2 million for preparatory studies on oil drilling in the Alaskan Arctic National Wildlife Refuge (AANW). Though on August 2 the House passed the energy bill by 240 votes to 189, complete with its provision allowing oil exploration and drilling in the refuge, on December 3 the Senate roundly rejected a bill (94–1) that would allow drilling in the AANW.

In the wake of the September 11 terrorist attacks in the U.S., acrid smoke, soot, and ash from tons of pulverized debris complicated the recovery in New York City. The EPA reported that asbestos levels did not appear to be dangerous, but doctors recommended that people use special air filters and masks to avoid inhaling particulate matter even during the smallest clean-up operations.

ENVIRONMENTAL ISSUES

Climate Change. The sixth conference of parties to the 1992 UN Convention on Climate Change was held at The Hague in November 2000. There was disagreement over the issues of carbon sinks and nuclear power. The umbrella group of countries, led by the U.S. and including Australia, Austria, Canada, Japan, New Zealand, Norway, Russia, Switzerland, and Ukraine, opposed any restriction on the means used to meet the cost of implementing the Kyoto Protocol. In particular, the group wanted forests (including forests planted long ago), as well as agricultural land, to be counted as sinks that absorb carbon dioxide. Although the EU agreed in the course of negotiations to limit the amount of carbon dioxide counted in this way, EU members rejected the offer on the ground that it would allow countries to claim reductions in greenhouse gas emissions without taking actual steps to reduce them. Negotiations continued during the winter.

On March 13, 2001, however, in a letter to four senior politicians, newly inaugurated President Bush said he would not accept mandatory controls on emissions of carbon dioxide because this would force utilities to switch from coal to gas, which was more expensive and would raise electricity prices. EPA administrator Christine Whitman confirmed the U.S. position on the protocol on March 27, though on March 29 Bush said he would remain open-minded on ways to address the problem of global warming. The EU sent a delegation to Washington to try to per-

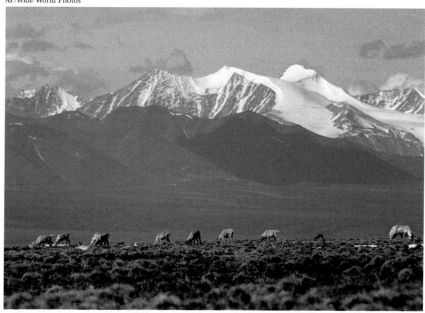

AP/Wide World Photos

Caribou graze in the Alaskan Arctic National Wildlife Refuge. Whether or not to allow oil exploration and drilling in the refuge was the subject of debate in the U.S. House of Representatives during the year.

suade Bush to change his mind. They met Whitman and other EPA officials on April 3, but the effort failed.

The conference of parties resumed in Bonn, Ger., on July 16 and concluded on July 27. Detailed rules for attaining Kyoto targets were finally accepted on July 23 by 178 countries (including Japan but not the U.S.) after the EU had made major concessions over carbon sinks. In another round of talks that was held in Marrakesh, Mor., and ended in November after two weeks of bargaining, negotiators reached agreement on the details of the treaty and hammered out a compliance scheme to insure that pollution levels were met. Some 40 industrialized countries would be required to reduce emissions of carbon dioxide and other greenhouse gases by an average of 5% below 1990 levels by 2012. Before the Kyoto Protocol could come into force, however, the pact needed to be ratified by 55 countries.

The 2,600-page latest report from the Intergovernmental Panel on Climate Change was published on July 12. It estimated that temperatures might rise 1.4–5.8 °C (2.5–10.4 °F) by 2100 and assumed that carbon dioxide levels would reach 540–970 parts per million by that year. The report also concluded that the burning of fossil fuels and the emission of man-made chemicals "have contributed substantially to the observed warming over the last 50 years."

Air Pollution. Figures published on June 5 by the German electricity-supply industry showed that sulfur dioxide emissions from power plants fell 92% between 1991 and 2000. Most of the improvement resulted from retrofitting desulfurization equipment in former East Germany and closing plants that could not be retrofitted economically.

The Norwegian Pollution Control Authority reported in August that acid-rain precipitation increased in 2000 over the southern and eastern parts of the country. In some areas heavy rain and snowfall increased sulfur deposition to levels comparable to those of the late 1980s, causing damage rated from "marked" to "severe."

In September the Mexican Metropolitan Environmental Commission unveiled a 10-year plan to improve air quality. This replaced a five-year program that had ended in 2000. Claudia Sheinbaum, Mexico City's environment secretary, said the aim was to reduce levels of ozone and fine particulate matter.

Freshwater Pollution. In January thousands of fish were killed by cyanide that had spilled into the Siret River near the town of Lespezi, Rom., 340 km (210 mi) northeast of Bucharest, and nearly 60 people required hospital treatment after eating the contaminated fish. The cyanide level in the Siret and one of its tributaries peaked at 128 times acceptable levels. The spill was thought to have originated at a chemical factory owned by Metadet, and the company was immediately fined. The authorities released additional water into the rivers, and the cyanide concentration was quickly reduced.

On July 27 the U.S. House of Representatives voted to maintain the limits for arsenic in drinking water set by former president Bill Clinton's administration. These reduced permitted levels from 50 to 10 parts per billion (ppb). The Bush administration asked a National Academy of Sciences panel to review the risks. Their report, *Arsenic in Drinking Water: 2001 Update*, was released in September. The panel found that the dangers were higher than had been supposed and concluded the proposed 10-ppb limit, based on a study done in southwestern Taiwan, had underestimated risks. The previous study had estimated 0.8 extra cancer cases per 1,000 people, whereas the new panel estimated 1.3–3.7 extra cases, depending on whether it used the background cancer rate in Taiwan or the rate in the U.S. In October the EPA adopted the Clinton arsenic standard.

The Austrian Environment Ministry announced in August that testing for 100 pollutants at 2,000 sites showed that streams and rivers were becoming cleaner. Nitrates in groundwater continued to cause concern, with levels having risen at 13% of measuring stations.

Marine Pollution. On January 16 the Ecuadorian-registered cargo ship *Jessica* ran aground in a bay close to the harbour on San Cristóbal in the Galápagos Islands, spilling about 700,000 litres (1 litre=about 0.26 gal) of diesel and bunker fuel oil from its cargo of about 920,000 litres. About 200,000 litres were removed from the ship safely, and U.S. Coast Guard vessels arrived quickly to help in the effort to contain and recover the oil. The spilled oil formed a slick that reached the islands of Santa Cruz and Santa Fe but caused little harm. Attempts to remove the ship, lying at an angle of about 45° some 800 m (2,600 ft) from the shore, were defeated by heavy seas, and it was decided to make the wreck into an artificial reef.

The Helsinki Commission (Helcom) announced on August 24 that the amount of 47 hazardous substances entering the Baltic Sea had been halved since the late 1980s and that it would aim for discharges to be phased out completely by 2020. At a Helcom meeting in Copenhagen on September 10, transport and environment ministers from countries bordering the Baltic

agreed on tighter rules to prevent oil spills. The need for new rules arose following a collision on March 28 between a cargo ship and a tanker that released about 2,700 metric tons of heavy fuel oil into the southwestern Baltic, causing the worst oil spill in the region in at least six years.

A meeting of parties to the Ospar Convention, held in Valencia, Spain, in late June, finalized an agreement on the discharge of oil into the northeast Atlantic. The oil content of produced water (a by-product of oil pumping) would be reduced by about 15%, calculated from a 2000 deadline. The meeting also added neodecanoic acid, ethenyl ester, and triphenyl phosphine to the list of substances to be phased out as a priority, bringing the total of such substances to 29.

Radioactive Waste. On March 29 the first shipment since 1997 of nuclear waste from the Cogema reprocessing facility at Cap de la Hague, France, arrived at a temporary storage site at Gorleben, Ger. The three-day journey was marked by antinuclear protests, and over 15,000 police were employed to guard the six armoured containers. On May 17 the second shipment, of about 54 spent fuel rods from Germany to Cap de la Hague, was halted for more than an hour by about 20 protesters who blocked the train at Amiens, France. About 15 protesters also blocked the rail track near Caen, France, and on May 16 some 40 protesters threw red smoke generators at the train near Strasbourg, France. Another such incident occurred in November when about 100 protesters attempted to block the motion of a train carrying nuclear waste from Cap de la Hague to Gorleben; they chained themselves to signal boxes and trees along the 600-km (375-mi) route.

Twelve Greenpeace protesters chained themselves to the track beneath an empty wagon at a railhead in Mannheim, Ger., on April 23 to demonstrate against the first shipment in three years of nuclear waste to Sellafield.

Genetically Modified Food. The first meeting of the intergovernmental committee for the Cartagena Protocol took place in Montpellier, France, in December 2000. Representatives from more than 80 countries began developing detailed rules to govern the international movement of live genetically modified organisms (GMOs). The discussions covered information sharing, traceability of GMOs, packaging, handling and transport, national capacity building, and the formation of an expert advisory

group. It was agreed to establish a pilot biosafety clearinghouse to give countries access to up-to-date lists of GMOs and information about national policies and regulations.

The UN Codex Alimentarius Commission agreed in July to require exporters of GM foods to undertake risk assessments, primarily of the foods' allergenicity, before placing them on the market. Findings by the Royal Commission on Genetic Modification in New Zealand were published on July 30. The commission recommended that GM agriculture be introduced "selectively with appropriate care" and rejected outright the idea of a GM-free New Zealand as incompatible with the modern world and the nation's future.

A report published on September 10 found that windborne pollen from corn (maize) plants genetically modified to express *Bacillus turingiensis* toxins posed a negligible risk to monarch butterflies. The study was prepared for the National Academy of Sciences by researchers at the University of Illinois at Urbana-Champaign, Iowa State University, the University of Minnesota, and private biotech companies.

Pesticides. An integrated crop production (ICP) plan announced on July 6 by Dutch Agriculture Minister Laurens Jan Brinkhorst aimed to reduce pesticide use in The Netherlands dramatically. Farmers would be required to adopt such measures as choosing pest-resistant crop varieties and growing "companion" plants. Farmers would be allowed to use pesticides only as a last resort, and in 2003 a tax would be imposed on pesticides. It was hoped that farmers would adopt the ICP plan voluntarily, but unless 90% of farmers had gained ICP certification by 2004, noncertified farms would be forbidden to use any pesticides.

On May 9 a report from the UN Food and Agriculture Organization (FAO) called on leading pesticide manufacturers to help pay for the safe destruction of an estimated 500,000 metric tons of obsolete pesticides that had been dumped in various parts of the world. The FAO reminded the Global Crop Protection Federation (GCPF) of its past commitment to pay up to $1 per litre or kilogram for safe destruction. Chris Waller, coordinator of the GCPF obsolete stocks team, said the industry was waiting for the FAO to devise a scheme that would ensure that money was used to deal only with products made or distributed by the companies contributing to the fund.

Electromagnetic Fields. It was reported in March that a study had found that 0.5% of children exposed to electromagnetic fields of 0.4 microteslas or more could double their risk of contracting leukemia before age 15, from 1 in 1,400 to 1 in 700. The study, commissioned by the U.K. National Radiological Protection Board, analyzed 3,247 childhood leukemia cases in Europe, North America, and New Zealand. Epidemiologist Sir Richard Doll of the Cancer Studies Unit at the University of Oxford said that taken by themselves these results might be due to chance, but there was a possibility that intense and prolonged exposure to magnetic fields could increase the risk of leukemia in children.

On September 11 the results of a study by researchers led by Tom Sorahan at the University of Birmingham, Eng., was published in *Occupational and Environmental Medicine*. The study found that workers in the electricity industry were no more likely to develop brain tumours than the general population. The study looked at the causes of death of some 84,000 electricity workers in England and Wales and found the death rate from brain cancer similar to that for the general population. (MICHAEL ALLABY)

WILDLIFE CONSERVATION

In January 2001 Mexico's former environment secretary Julia Carabias Lillo received the J. Paul Getty Wildlife Conservation Prize from the World Wildlife Fund (WWF). Carabias Lillo (*see* BIOGRAPHIES) was credited with doubling the protected-habitat system in Mexico. Thirty years of conservation effort were rewarded in March when the birth of a male golden tamarin (*Leontopithecus rosalia*) took the number living in the wild to 1,000. The native habitat of the species was in the lowland coastal forest in the Brazilian state of Rio de Janeiro, where habitat destruction had reduced numbers to 200 by the early 1970s.

A celebrated discovery of a new mammal in 1993 was reported as a fake in February. The wild ox *Pseudonovibos spiralis* was described from unusual-shaped horns collected from markets in Vietnam and Cambodia. Local hunters claimed it came from a mysterious beast in the forest, but genetic and morphological tests revealed that the horns were of the domestic cow. The horns had been twisted and carved by local people in a long-standing folk industry.

A report in *Science* in January indicated that Arctic species were suffering as Arctic ice continued to decline, covering 15% less area than it had in 1978. A long-term study indicated that emperor penguins (*Aptenodytes forsteri*) in the Antarctic were highly susceptible to climate change and that their numbers were declining markedly in warm periods with reduced sea ice.

While concern continued over the effects of global climate change on wild species and habitats, some scientists thought that demand for food by a wealthier and larger human population would be the major driver of environmental change in the next 50 years, causing unprecedented ecosystem simplification, loss of ecosystem services, and species extinctions. In May the UN Environment Programme launched the Great Apes Survival Project because poaching and habitat loss could drive the apes of Africa and Southeast Asia to extinction in 5–10 years. The project would help police forests, link patches of habitat, encourage ecotourism, and educate local people. Harvard University biologist Edward O. Wilson argued that large-scale private investment was needed to augment government protection for lands of high value for biodiversity. He said that an investment of $28 billion would protect up to 70% of the species on Earth.

The ornithological literature reported several new birds, including two new flycatchers: the Mishana tyrannulet (*Zimmerius villarejoi*) from the white-sand forest near Iquitos, Peru, where an ongoing study had revealed the presence of at least four bird species new to science, and the Chapada flycatcher (*Suiriri islerorum*) from the Cerrado region of Brazil and adjacent eastern Bolivia. A new species of petrel, the Vanuatu petrel (*Pterodroma occulta*), was described from specimens collected at sea. It was presumed to breed in the Banks Islands or elsewhere in northern Vanuatu. The chestnut-eared laughing thrush (*Garrulax konkakinhensis*) was identified from a narrow altitudinal range on Mount Kon Ka Kinh in central Vietnam. There were plans to extend an existing reserve to include the sites where it had been found.

Populations of some seabirds hit by the *Exxon Valdez* oil spill in Alaska in 1989 had still to show signs of recovery, according to scientists in Anchorage, who believed that food species in the intertidal zone were still contaminated with oil. The wreck of the oil tanker *Jessica* in the Galápagos Islands (*see* Marine Pollution, above) highlighted the fragility of the islands and the inadequacy of conservation legislation. On July 16, 15 sea lions in the Galápagos National Park were butchered on the beach on San Cristóbal for their sex organs, which were in demand in Asia for use as aphrodisiacs. Suspicion rested on foreign fishermen harvesting sea cucumbers in the area.

Many wild species used traditionally as human food were in decline because of increased commercial use, including sharks captured for shark fin soup and sturgeon killed for caviar. The U.S. and Australia had banned the capture of sharks for their fins, and there were calls for other nations to follow. Three caviar-producing states (Russia, Kazakhstan, and Azerbaijan) bordering the Caspian Sea (source of 90% of the world's caviar) halted sturgeon fishing on June 21 in response to plummeting stocks. India gave legal protection to whale sharks (*Rhinocodon typus*) on May 28 because trade threatened them with extinction. A workshop convened by the World Conservation Union (IUCN), the UN Food and Agriculture Organization, and TRAFFIC (the joint wildlife trade monitoring program of the IUCN and the WWF) was held in Cameroon in September. More than 40 representatives from 18 organizations met to find solutions to the problems of declining populations of wild animals used traditionally for human food.

Only six Bali starlings (*Leucopsar rothschildi*) remained in the wild, all in Indonesia's Bali Barat National Park, where relentless trapping for the pet trade threatened them. Saving species created problems for some people. Wolves brought back from the brink of extinction in northern Italy were reported to be hunting farmers' livestock, and legally protected wild boars in Germany caused problems for Berliners by digging up gardens, raiding trash cans, and attacking dogs. In Norway wolves were culled despite court action brought by conservationists.

The 834 species of the mainly insectivorous bats in the order Microchiroptera faced numerous threats from human activities; some species had experienced precipitous declines. The publication of *Microchiropteran Bats: Global Status Survey and Conservation Action Plan* in May aimed to stimulate conservation action for these mammals, which occurred in every continent except in the polar regions and constituted a quarter of all known mammal species.

In September participants in the British Association Festival of Science

African elephants wander in Great Limpopo Transfrontier Park in Mozambique on October 4 after having been moved from Kruger National Park in South Africa.

were warned that coral reefs would disappear in 30–50 years because global warming would cause widespread coral bleaching (a condition in which high water temperatures kill the algal partners of coral). Experiments also showed, however, that corals can evict their algae as an adaptation to warmer seas and may be recolonized by partners better suited to higher temperatures.

New molecular evidence showed that forest and savanna elephants, heretofore classified as a single species, *Loxodonta africana*, merited separate taxonomic status. This had implications for conservation, since one-third of the 500,000 elephants in Africa were forest dwellers. On October 4 South Africa announced that the first 40 of a total of 1,000 African elephants were to be moved from Kruger National Park to Mozambique as part of a plan to establish the world's biggest reserve and to reopen natural migratory routes. (JACQUI M. MORRIS)

ZOOS

Zoos and aquariums continued to be immensely popular in 2001, attracting some 130 million visitors in the U.S.

alone. On May 3 officials at the National Zoo in Washington, D.C., welcomed the one millionth person to see the giant pandas Tian Tian and Mei Xiang since the pair went on display on January 10. The pandas, which arrived in the U.S. in December 2000, were on loan from the China Research and Conservation Center for the Giant Panda in Wolong, Sichuan province. In return for the loan of the pandas for research and exhibit purposes, the Smithsonian Institution, which operated the National Zoo, agreed to donate $10 million to support China's panda preservation and research projects.

Throughout the year Chinese officials relayed exciting news from Wolong; by the end of October five giant pandas at the centre had given birth to healthy twins, and it was reported that there were several more giant pandas waiting to give birth. The practice of artificially inseminating zoo animals, especially those belonging to threatened or endangered species, was followed elsewhere. At the Colchester (Eng.) Zoo in March, an African elephant named Tanya became the first elephant in the country to become pregnant through

artificial insemination. German scientists from the Berlin Institute of Wildlife Medicine and Research performed the procedure.

Animals at the Kabul Zoo were found to be in poor condition after the Taliban was routed from Afghanistan in December. Overseas zoos and well-wishers raised thousands of dollars in pledges to care for the starving animals.

Public interest in aquatic environments helped drive a rapid expansion of aquariums. In the past decade new aquariums were opened in Charleston, S.C.; Denver, Colo.; Newport, Ky.; Myrtle Beach, S.C.; Gatlinburg, Tenn.; Pittsburgh, Pa.; Columbus, Ohio; and Long Beach, Calif. Several smaller aquatic facilities within American zoos also opened. In addition, by 2001 major expansions and renovations were under way in almost every major public aquarium in the country.

The John G. Shedd Aquarium in Chicago undertook a five-year, $85 million renovation and expansion program. Its "Amazon Rising" exhibit, which opened in 2000, was recognized by both the American Zoo and Aquarium Association and the American Association of

Museums as the best new exhibit of the year. The Shedd was constructing a 1,860-sq-m (20,000-sq-ft) addition to house a new exhibit portraying the coral reefs of the Philippines. This exhibit promised to give visitors the sensation of walking on the ocean floor as they moved through a series of marine habitats featuring living corals and the many species that depended on reefs for food and shelter. One of the exhibit's highlights was to be a 1,890,000-litre (500,000-gal) shark habitat, which would give the Shedd an opportunity to exhibit larger sharks for the first time.

North Carolina's three state aquariums—all located along the coast—also were undergoing major expansion and rebuilding projects. The aquarium-building boom even prompted a name change by one of the country's major zoological institutions. The venerable Columbus (Ohio) Zoo, which opened in 1927, was renamed the Columbus Zoo and Aquarium as a result of the new aquatic facility built on its grounds. One of its most popular features was a new manatee exhibit. The Cincinnati (Ohio) Zoo and Botanical Garden also opened a "Manatee Springs" exhibit. Both of these facilities supported manatee-conservation programs in collaboration with the state of Florida.

New aquariums were planned for or under construction in Cleveland, Ohio; Atlanta, Ga.; West Palm Beach, Fla.; Portland, Maine; New Bedford, Mass.; and several other areas. In addition, new aquariums were set to open in several European locations, including Rotterdam, Neth.; Lisbon, Port.; Hirtshals, Den.; and Plymouth, Eng., and in Japan.

Aquariums offered research scientists opportunities to observe marine species, especially cetaceans, in ways that would be impossible from research vessels. Sea World in Orlando, Fla.; the Mystic and Shedd aquariums; and facilities in Vancouver, B.C., and New York state were all participating in and contributing to the research and husbandry of beluga whales as well as cetaceans and other marine mammals.

Also increasing in popularity were butterfly gardens, which offered visitors something new and pleasing to the eyes while raising awareness of the importance of invertebrates, especially pollinators, and the need for habitat-conservation measures to protect these often-overlooked animals. Zoological institutions that had expanded their collections with butterflies included the Bronx (N.Y.) Zoo, the Cincinnati Zoo, and the St. Louis (Mo.) Zoo.

(TED A. BEATTIE)

The "Amazon Rising" exhibit at the John G. Shedd Aquarium in Chicago was recognized as a top new exhibit during the year.

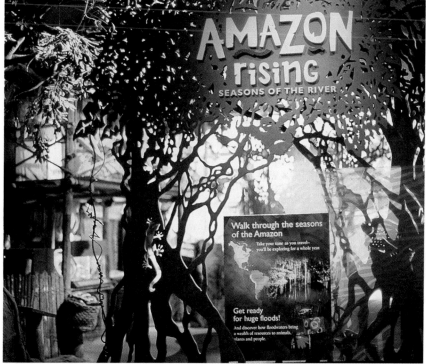

GARDENING

Recent trends in gardening continued unabated in 2001. In the horticultural industry, buying patterns moved farther away from seed toward plants and from mail order to garden centres and mass-market retailers. Consumer interest in heirloom and "organic" seed increased, but commercial growers of flowers and vegetables chose cultivars bred for high yield, disease resistance, and long shelf life, characteristics that were important to their production and distribution methods.

Foster and Gallagher, which in 2000 claimed that it was the largest horticultural retailer in the United States, filed for bankruptcy protection and ceased operations at its subsidiaries, some of which, including Stark Brothers, Breck's, and Spring Hill Nurseries, were among the most well-established horticultural enterprises in the U.S. The 125-year-old W. Atlee Burpee & Co. also filed for bankruptcy protection; it had acquired some of the assets of the defunct on-line marketer GARDEN.COM, purchased the renowned West Coast Heronswood Nursery, and failed in an attempt to enter the retail sector with a chain of garden stores. Operations were expected to continue under new ownership.

The European association Fleuroselect chose 34 cultivars for recognition in the upcoming 2002 season, including three that won a Gold Medal. *Dianthus barbatus* Noverna Purple won for its ability to bloom without vernalization—exposure to a cold period—a first for the species known to generations of gardeners as Sweet William. The 40-cm (1 cm=0.4 in) diploid hybrid bloomed only 80–100 days from sowing and bore light purple 1.5-cm single flowers arranged in 7–10-cm clusters.

A new colour in the Wave series of cascading or spreading petunias also received a Gold Medal. *Petunia hybrida* Lavender Wave produced large numbers of 5.5-cm light lavender single blooms on plants that, though they reached 10 cm in height, spread to 120 cm, which made them ideal for baskets and containers. Good weather tolerance also made Lavender Wave useful for ground-cover applications in sunny locations.

The final Gold Medal was given to *Viola X wittrockiana* Ultima Morpho for its uniquely coloured flowers. The small (5-cm) blossoms had a gradient of blue to white above a lemon-yellow ray petal at the bottom, with radial black markings. Plants of this tetraploid hybrid were a compact 15 cm high and across and bloomed for three to four months in the spring and fall.

All-America Rose Selections presented two awards. The hybrid tea rose Love & Peace—bred by Jerry Twomey and Ping Lim and introduced by Bailey Nurseries in St. Paul, Minn.—was created by crossing the famous Peace rose with an unnamed seedling. Disease-resistant and upright, with glossy dark green foliage, Love & Peace grew in height to 120–150 cm and had a diameter of 90 cm; it produced 12.5-cm-diameter spiraform golden-yellow blooms that had a pink edge and a fruity scent.

Shrub rose Starry Night was recognized for its wide adaptability and pure white dogwoodlike blossoms. Bred by Pierre Orard of Feyzin, France, by combining the cultivar Anisley Dickson with the species *Rosa wichurianna* and introduced by Edmunds' Roses of Wilsonville, Ore., Starry Night had a height and width of 90 cm in cool climates but a height and width of 180 cm in mild-to-warm climates. The pure white five-petaled single blossoms, 6–8 cm in diameter, contrasted well with the glossy medium green foliage.

All-America Selections (AAS) did not award a Gold Medal in either the vegetable or the flower category for the 2002 season. Fleuroselect Gold Medal winners *Petunia* Lavender Wave and *Viola* Ultima Morpho received the lesser designation of flower award, along with *Petunia hybrida* Tidal Wave Silver, chosen for its tall plant habit and unique colouring; *Cleome spinosa* Sparkler Blush, chosen for its dwarf habit and because it was the first commercial hybrid cleome; *Pelargonium zonale* Black Magic Rose, selected for its strongly contrasting foliage and flowers; *Rudbeckia hirta* Cherokee Sunset, recognized for its unique colour range of dou-

Belgian landscape architect Jacques Wirtz's redesign for the walled garden at Alnwick Castle, Northumberland, Eng., featured waterfalls and geometric-shaped hedges of beech, box, hornbeam, and yew.

© Wirtz International

ble and semidouble flowers; and *Catharanthus roseus* (Vinca) Jaio Scarlet Eye, acknowledged for its single bicolour rose and scarlet blooms. In addition, ornamental pepper (*Capsicum annum*) Chilly Chili won a flower award for its decorative fruits, which, unlike others of its class, were nonpungent and thus made it suitable as a potted plant in homes with small children.

AAS vegetable awards were given to basil Magical Michael for its attractive flowers with purple calices and white corollas and to Diva—a cucumber bred by Janika Eckert of Johnny's Selected Seeds—for its superior yields of high-quality seedless fruits. Two pumpkins were honoured: Sorcerer for its uniformity in the 6.8–9.9-kg (15–22-lb) jack-o'-lantern class and Orange Smoothie for its compact plant habit, high resistance to disease, small 1.8–3.2-kg (4–7-lb) size,

and exceptionally smooth skin, which made it ideal for painting rather than carving. Finally, AAS granted a vegetable award to winter squash Cornell's Bush Delicata for its compact plant habit, improved flavour, and exceptional disease resistance.

The Perennial Plant Association in the U.S. chose as its Perennial Plant of the Year *Calamagrostis xacutiflora* Karl Foerster, a natural hybrid of *Calamagrostis epigejos* and *Calamagrostis arundinacea;* the long-blooming grass was first found in the Hamburg (Ger.) Botanical Garden collection and was introduced to the nursery trade by Karl Foerster in his 1957 book *Einzug der Gräser und Farne in die Gärten.*

In England Belgian landscape architect Jacques Wirtz (*see* BIOGRAPHIES) continued work on the 5-ha (12-ac) walled garden at Alnwick Castle; he was commissioned by the duchess of Northumberland to redesign the enclosure. Wirtz's garden designs, featuring mass plantings of geometric-shaped hedges, were much in demand in Europe.

On the lighter side, the ubiquitous garden gnome—a fixture in British lawns and gardens for more than 100 years—fell out of favour during the year. Gnome ownership declined from about 5 million in 1990 to 3.8 million in 2001. In France matters were taken a step or two further; the self-styled Liberation Front for Garden Gnomes took hundreds of the figures from suburban residences and "returned" them to woodland settings.

(SHEPHERD OGDEN)

Fashions

Black-and-white **CONFECTIONS** and looks that featured nautical, opulent, and **TRAILER-TRASH** themes edged out the **MILITARY-INSPIRED** creations that were featured prominently prior to the September 11 terrorist attacks in the U.S.

The international fashion industry, already suffering from early signs of recession, found its gloomy outlook compounded following the Sept. 11, 2001, terrorist attacks in the U.S. Prior to the attacks, the Gap, an American retail giant, had laid off 800 employees and reported that company earnings had decreased by 22%. Luxury goods companies LVMH Moët Hennessy Louis Vuitton and the Gucci Group revised their strategies in the wake of the attacks and admitted that earnings would slow and that they were preparing for a "prolonged slowdown." Wolfgang Ley, chief executive of the German fashion empire Escada, confirmed that his company's American sales had dropped by half following September 11.

The attacks in New York City coincided with 7th on Sixth, the Council of Fashion Designers of America's (CFDA) spring-summer 2002 shows. Though the international fashion community had gathered in the city to celebrate, critique, and acquire merchandise for the upcoming season, business ground to a halt as the disaster unfolded. The CFDA canceled the runway shows. A week or two later several New York designers presented their collections in their showrooms. Prominent American buyers, frightened

A dramatic catwalk setting dramatized the staging in Milan of Antonio Marras's fall-winter collection, which featured styles ranging from military overcoats adorned with medals to frothy ensembles.

AP/Wide World Photos

by the prospect of more terrorist hijackings and aware of the lean financial times ahead, refrained from traveling to see the European collections.

That fashion reflected the change in society was a point that became apparent when the U.S. and Great Britain declared war on terrorism in October. The trappings of battle—military-inspired clothing and camouflage print as well as a range of urban-guerrilla graffiti art—had dominated the international spring-summer catwalks. To the sound of a coronet and battle drums, Miguel Adrover offered suits modeled on 1940s army uniforms and trousers based on army fatigues. Miuccia Prada wore a belted military jacket and platform shoes to the unveiling of her collection—plain gray, navy, and black cotton skirts and sweaters that were reminiscent of the drab Mao uniform. In Paris camouflage was seen at Comme des Garçons, Jean-Charles de Castelbajac, and Christian Dior; at Celine, Michael Kors accessorized bikini bottoms, hot pants, and mesh tank-top dresses with bullet-studded belts. Marc Jacobs at Louis Vuitton featured jackets with epaulets. The onset of war, however, forced the fashion industry to reconsider its direction. Violent imagery and terrorist-chic styling were reappraised.

At the autumn-winter 2001 collections—shown in the summer—designers explored the Middle East. Heads were wrapped and faces were hidden behind scarves at Raf Simons's menswear show. Adrover looked to Egypt for inspiration; his collection made its debut in a nomad's tent, where a female model wore a white headdress and a djellaba, a male model donned harem pants, and pantsuits were layered over tunics and kaftans. Though Gucci showed harem pants for spring-summer 2002, the look failed to take off on the street.

Luella Bartley and Jacobs's punkish sensibility was shared by designers Donatella Versace, Balenciaga, Anna Sui, and Junya Watanabe, who for inspiration also looked to the New Wave scene that dominated popular music in the early 1980s. Prom dresses, cocktail sheaths, full 1950s-style skirts (which

were favoured in the '80s), minis, pedal pushers, leather jackets worn over slips, fur stoles, and rhinestones showed up on their catwalks. For spring-summer, playful trends were plentiful. Modern floral prints—roses, hydrangeas, and wildflowers that had been digitally enhanced by computer technology—looked more abstract than realistic after the images were transferred onto skirts and dresses designed by Cacharel (which presented its first collection in Paris designed by the London duo Clements Ribeiro), Louis Vuitton, Dries Van Noten, Dolce & Gabbana, Eley Kishimoto, Marni, and Jean-Paul Gaultier. A nautical look—interpreted as striped shirts—appeared at Prada and Marni, and a trailer-trash look—handbags inspired by 1950s Cadillacs and chiffon dresses featuring silver YKK zippers and strips of denim—was the theme behind John Galliano's collection for his own line as well as Christian Dior. Nicolas Ghesquiere's collection for Callaghan, which included draped jersey dresses, revealed a Grecian influence. At their spring-summer

Emblematic of the colours favoured by top designers during the year was this frilly black and white gown for Frank Sorbier's spring-summer collection.

Pierre Verdy/
AFP Worldwide

shows, John Bartlett, Kors, Gucci, and Chanel introduced the white shirt as a new staple. Both seasons also signified a return to black dressing. Karan's and Ralph Lauren's spring-summer shows were composed of black and white (Lauren also included chocolate-brown pieces). Tom Ford's much-anticipated debut collection for Yves Saint Laurent ready-to-wear, almost entirely composed of black and white clothes, disappointed critics who were waiting for something more spectacular. The focal point of the collection was Saint Laurent's iconic 1960s tuxedo suit, Le Smoking.

Opulence was a theme at autumn-winter shows. Designer Ford presented satin clothes in deep purple at Yves Saint Laurent and hot pink at Gucci. The Versace and Valentino shows were laden with fur, and Milanese designer Roberto Cavalli incorporated ostrich feathers into his collection; he also lined distressed denim dresses with fur and encrusted silk blousons with semiprecious jewels. Amid the fun and frivolity, sensible styles prevailed.

Basic black and white did not disappoint critics at the autumn-winter 2001 collections. Particular standouts were Nicolas Ghesquiere's work for Balenciaga, which included items ranging from reworked Victorian corset tops to biker jackets and combat trousers made from oiled cotton; "little black dresses" featured by Jacobs and Diane von Furstenberg; Gucci baby dolls; Viktor & Rolf's entirely black collection; Fendi's white Courrèges-style Mod look—composed of white boots, handbags, and patent coats—and Jacobs's Doctor Zhivago-themed collection for Louis Vuitton; it featured black-and-white fur hats, black lace-up boots, and structured, Cossack-inspired black coats that were trimmed with white mink.

Women also responded to the black-and-white theme. Socialites and celebrities at high-profile parties wore ensembles composed of a solid shade of either colour or a combination of both. Black dresses proved to be the chic choices on Oscar night—Julia Roberts looked refined in a silver-trimmed black 1982 Valentino couture gown; Catherine Zeta-Jones chose a black strapless Versace dress; and Sarah Jessica Parker (*see* BIOGRAPHIES) appeared in a chic black mini dress.

Parker's eclectic wardrobe for her role as Carrie Bradshaw in the hit show *Sex & the City* was talked about as much as the show's plotline. Discussion about shoes designed by Manolo Blahnik figured prominently in the script, and designs by Marni, Fendi, Prada, Chanel, Dolce & Gabbana, Givenchy, and Dior were just some of the labels that Carrie and her fellow characters—Samantha, Charlotte, and Miranda—could be seen in each week. The show also launched trends—including a craze for the fabric corsages Carrie frequently wore as accessories—and designers who supplied clothes for the show saw incredible returns; Timmy Woods, a Beverly Hills, Calif.–based designer, reported taking 1,000 orders for a horse-head purse that appeared on the show for only two seconds.

On the street, however, young women embraced "reality dressing," a casual chic uniform that was composed of three essential pieces: designer jeans, a deconstructed T-shirt, and high heels or athletic shoes. This style emerged in response to the popularity of reality TV programs. (*See* MEDIA AND PUBLISHING: *Sidebar.*)

American designer Sean "P. Diddy" Combs's Sean Jean line for fall featured a suede shearling wrap coat that partially concealed a white thermal crewneck pullover and wool pinstriped five-pocket pants.

Throngs of celebrities appeared at the spring-summer and autumn-winter shows. Tickets for the presentation of rap star Sean ("P. Diddy") Combs's label, Sean John, were in great demand; the event occurred in the midst of his trial on weapons and bribery charges. The CFDA's decision in February to sell 7th on Sixth to the International Management Group, an agency that represented athletes and entertainers, heightened the sense that fashion was increasingly becoming part of the entertainment industry. Further proof was evidenced in the launch of more fashion brands by celebrity and personality designers, including the jeans line J. Lo by Jennifer Lopez (*see* BIOGRAPHIES); Intimates, a line of lingerie by model Elle MacPherson; and Marie-Chantal, upscale baby clothes labels designed by Princess Marie-Chantal Miller of Greece. Reinvigorated brands appeared on the retail frontier. Under the direction of its new designer in chief Scott Fellows, Bally of Switzerland debuted on Milan catwalks clothing lines for men and women as well as its more fashion-forward line of bags and shoes. At Burberry, CEO Rose Marie Bravo appointed Christopher Bailey, who had worked with Tom Ford at Gucci, to the position of designer. In March, Narciso Rodríguez announced his departure from Spanish leather-goods house LVMH. Loewe and LVMH appointed Julien MacDonald design director of Givenchy, where he replaced Alexander McQueen, who in December 2000 had sold 51% of his company to the Gucci Group. In April, Gucci announced that, in a similar joint venture, it would back Stella McCartney (*see* BIOGRAPHIES), Chloé's former designer, in establishing her own design label. Phoebe Philo became Chloé's new creative director. Gucci also acquired Balenciaga and Bottega Veneta. Asprey & Garrard announced that it would split into two labels with two distinct retail operations. Jade Jagger and Hussein Chalayan were asked to form an in-house design team that would create a new luxury label.

In the realm of modeling, Karolina Kurkova, a 17-year-old Czech model, became the new face of glamour; Brazilian supermodel Gisele Bündchen announced her retirement from runway shows; Elizabeth Jagger—the daughter of Mick Jagger and Jerry Hall—launched her modeling career; and Carolyn Murphy replaced actress Elizabeth Hurley as the new face of Estée Lauder.

(BRONWYN COSGRAVE)

Health and Disease

The deliberate mailing of **ANTHRAX**-tainted letters in the U.S. in October resulted in deadly **OUTBREAKS** of the disease on the East Coast and heightened fears of **BIOTERRORISM**. During the year researchers took the first steps toward **CLONING** human embryos, and several critically ill patients received a new type of implantable **ARTIFICIAL HEART**.

The medical response to the havoc wreaked by four jetliner crashes on September 11 due to terrorist activity was massive and rapid at all three impact sites: Lower Manhattan, the Pentagon in Virginia, and rural Shanksville, Pa. It was in New York City, however, that the need for an unprecedented level of trauma care seemed likely, at least at first. A few hours after the World Trade Center's twin towers collapsed, five designated city hospitals were prepared for the worst. Triage centres were set up within a few blocks of "ground zero," fully staffed and equipped to treat any possible injury and perform lifesaving surgery. To be sure, about 600 people were treated on September 11, about 150 of whom were critically injured, but as the day wore on, the numbers of new patients dwindled, and the anticipated deluge never materialized.

It soon became obvious that far more people had perished than had survived with injuries. It was the rescue crews, not medical personnel, who had their work cut out for them—digging through the rubble day and night in a mostly vain search for the still living, at significant risk to themselves. In fact, the need was greater for specially trained rescue dogs than for doctors to aid in the on-site search and recovery.

Fears of bioterrorism in the wake of the September 11 terrorist attacks led the U.S. government to evaluate its supply of vaccines against anthrax and smallpox. The available anthrax vaccine was of questionable potency and had safety risks. Whereas new vaccines were in development, they were not available when in early October a smattering of anonymous letters carrying spores of *Bacillus anthracis* began arriving in the mailboxes of broadcast and print media on the East Coast and federal offices in Washington, D.C. Dissemination of the spores as the letters were processed through postal machinery and handled at their destinations was believed responsible for nearly 20 confirmed cases of cutaneous and inhalation (pulmonary) anthrax and several deaths from the rapidly fatal inhalation form.

Because anthrax was preventable and treatable with antibiotics, the U.S. government's strategy was not to vaccinate but to treat everyone who may have been exposed to the bacterium with the antibiotic ciprofloxacin (Cipro). The Food and Drug Administration (FDA) took action to approve two other widely available generic antibiotics, doxycycline and penicillin, for treatment of inhalation anthrax in the event of a large-scale terrorist attack. Anthrax could not be spread by infected individuals, which rendered many of the usual communicable-disease-prevention measures unnecessary. Various actions, including widespread testing of suspected locations for the presence of spores and decontamination of spore-tainted buildings, offices, and mail-sorting equipment, were taken in an attempt to limit further dispersal. Mail from contaminated postal facilities was impounded for several weeks until it could be sanitized by irradiation and returned to the mail stream for delivery. Government authorities also moved to install equipment in post offices that would kill anthrax spores during regular mail processing.

Smallpox, unlike anthrax, was highly contagious, and an estimated 80% of the U.S. population was thought to be susceptible. The devastating viral disease was effectively eradicated from the world in 1977, but samples of the virus still existed and could get into the hands of terrorists. Consequently, the federal government sought to increase its relatively meagre supply of vaccine, 15.4 million doses. Medical scientists at several universities were exploring the possibility of diluting the existing supply to increase the number of doses. At the same time, the government arranged to acquire new smallpox vaccine from several pharmaceutical companies—up to the 300 million doses needed to protect everyone in the U.S.

Stem Cell Research and Human Cloning. Although the tragedy of September 11 and the threat of bioterrorism overshadowed so many events of the year, there were myriad noteworthy developments in health and disease. The field that probably generated the most excitement, and the most heated political debate, was research on human stem cells. These unspecialized cells have the potential to become specific cells—i.e., cells of almost any organ or tissue—and their ideal source was considered to be a five-day-old human embryo, comprising about 200–250 cells. (Stem cells from adults appeared to have less therapeutic promise.)

A long-awaited pronouncement on embryonic stem cell research in the U.S. came on August 9. In a television address Pres. George W. Bush said that he would allow federal support of such research, but only on cell lines that already had been derived from "leftover" embryos grown in infertility clinics. Many research scientists considered the decision severely limiting, and in September the Institute of Medicine (IOM) issued a report concluding that new cell lines would still be needed down the road, in part because existing lines were likely to accumulate genetic mutations.

In November a private Massachusetts biotechnology firm, Advanced Cell Technology, provoked much sound and fury when it announced that it had taken the first steps toward cloning human embryos. According to the company, the goal was not to clone a human being but to produce stem cells for treating disease. In fact, most of the embryos died before reaching even an eight-cell stage, without producing the desired stem cells. President Bush, religious and political leaders, and many scientists condemned the work as immoral and a dangerous move in the wrong direction.

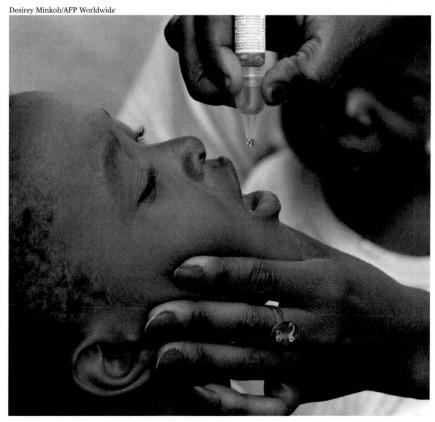

A medical worker in Gabon vaccinates a child against polio on August 12.

Infectious Disease. The World Health Organization's (WHO) Communicable Disease Surveillance and Response service, which tracked major infectious diseases worldwide, reported a number of major outbreaks. They included cholera in West Africa, Chad, Tanzania, South Africa, Pakistan, and India; Ebola hemorrhagic fever in Uganda; measles in South Korea; yellow fever in Brazil, Peru, Côte d'Ivoire, Liberia, and Guinea; plague in Zambia; dengue fever in Venezuela; meningococcal disease in Angola, Ethiopia, the Democratic Republic of the Congo, and the "African meningitis belt," an area that extended across the middle of the continent and included all or part of at least 15 countries between Senegal and Ethiopia; Crimean-Congo hemorrhagic fever in Pakistan and the Kosovo province of Yugoslavia; legionellosis in Spain and Norway; and an illness described as a "highly lethal variant of measles" in India.

One of the greatest scourges of all time, poliomyelitis, came closer to being a thing of the past, thanks to a massive global eradication effort coordinated by WHO, UNICEF, Rotary International, and the U.S. Centers for Disease Control and Prevention (CDC). From 1999 to 2000 the number of polio cases in the world was cut in half to 3,500, and the number of endemic countries (those with naturally occurring poliovirus) dropped from 50 to 20. As of mid-2001, India, which once bore the world's greatest polio burden, had only 10 confirmed cases. The target date for global eradication was 2005, but completion of the task would require an all-out vaccination effort in Southeast Asia, the eastern Mediterranean, and Africa, at a cost of $400 million.

Although childhood vaccines had saved millions of youngsters the world over from infectious disease, deformity, and death, their safety continued to be a source of controversy. Studies published during the year demonstrated that some alleged risks of vaccine use were not real. Combination vaccines against diphtheria, pertussis, and tetanus (DPT) and measles, mumps, and rubella (MMR) were shown not to be associated with long-term risks of seizures or other neurological problems in children. Furthermore, no evidence was found that hepatitis B vaccine caused or aggravated multiple sclerosis. Public health professionals hoped these and other "negative results" would alleviate some of the public's fears.

HIV and AIDS. The year 2001 was the 20th anniversary of the initial reports of a mysterious deadly immune-system disorder that came to be known as AIDS. The medical community, international AIDS organizations, and especially the media saw the occasion as a time to reflect upon the relentless epidemic that had killed more than 21 million people on every continent and from every walk of life. In 2001 an estimated 36 million people were living with HIV infection.

The long-held hope for an AIDS vaccine continued to be pursued. Although as many as 80 potential vaccines had been tried in humans, only one had reached large-scale human trials. About 8,000 volunteers at high risk for HIV in North America, The Netherlands, and Thailand had received either an experimental preventive vaccine developed by the California-based firm VaxGen or a placebo. Periodically they were being tested for HIV. The trials would continue until 2002–03.

At the 8th Conference on Retroviruses and Opportunistic Infections, held in Chicago in February, HIV/AIDS treatment specialists voiced a loud cry for newer and safer drugs and pointed out that the highly lauded combination-drug therapies, also known as AIDS "drug cocktails," were not working for thousands of patients. Clinicians reported a range of adverse effects associated with the life-prolonging drugs, including high cholesterol, diabetes, fat accumulations in the neck and abdomen, weakened bones, and nerve damage in the extremities. Among the many experimental drugs that were described at the conference, perhaps most promising was a new class called entry inhibitors, which blocked the binding of HIV to key receptors on the cell surface.

Excitement about new treatments, however, had little relevance for the millions of people in less-developed countries living with HIV, many of whom had no access to treatment. The high cost of existing drugs and their unavailability to the vast majority of HIV/AIDS sufferers had aroused considerable ire among government officials and others trying to combat AIDS in less-developed countries. To make treatment more accessible, a handful of pharmaceutical companies in India, Thailand, and other countries began producing cheaper generic versions of the patented agents used in drug cocktails, a move vigorously opposed by the multinational companies holding the patents. As sentiments against the drug giants mounted, however, several conceded to pressure and slashed their prices on AIDS drugs for less-developed countries, and a few waived their patent rights. Some 39 major companies that manufactured AIDS drugs had sued South Africa in 1998 in an effort to bar the country from importing cheaper drugs. In April 2001 the companies dropped their case.

UN Secretary-General Kofi Annan called the battle against AIDS one of his personal priorities when he initiated a global fund to allot between $7 billion and $10 billion annually to combat a trio of diseases that continued to ravage the Third World—AIDS, tuberculosis, and malaria. Addressing the delegates to the first UN summit on AIDS, held in New York City in June, Annan said, "This year we have seen a turning point. AIDS can no longer do its deadly work in the dark. The world has started to wake up."

China was one country that "woke up" to its AIDS crisis. In August its deputy health minister, Yin Dakui, admitted that the country was "facing a very serious epidemic of HIV/AIDS" and that the government had "not effectively stemmed the epidemic." An estimated 70% of China's cases were among intravenous drug users. The Chinese government claimed that about 600,000 citizens were infected with HIV, whereas the UN estimated the number at more than one million.

In the U.S. the incidence of new HIV infections among homosexual African American men aged 23 to 29 was called "explosive." CDC surveys found that 30% of men in this group were HIV-positive.

Cancer. Rarely do research scientists become unmitigatedly exuberant over a new treatment. Nevertheless, this was the overwhelming sentiment among cancer specialists about a new drug, imatinib (marketed as Gleevec in the U.S. and Glivec in Europe). Imatinib was one of a new class of anticancer agents known as growth-factor inhibitors, which targeted cancer cells by recognizing their unique molecular defects. The FDA approved imatinib in record time after tests showed that it had induced remissions in 53 of 54 patients with chronic myelogenous leukemia (CML). Less than a month after publication of the CML results, scientists reported that 60% of nearly 200 patients with gastrointestinal stromal cancer (GIST) treated with imatinib had became symptom-free. GIST is a rare intestinal malignancy for which there had been no known treatment.

An IOM report issued in June put some of the fanfare about new cancer treatments in perspective. "The reality is that half of all patients diagnosed with cancer will die of their disease within a few years," the report stated. The expert panel that prepared the report was highly critical of the "almost single-minded focus on attempts to cure every patient at every stage of disease." It found that at least half of dying cancer patients suffered symptoms for which they received little or no treatment; these included pain, difficulty breathing, emotional distress, nausea, and confusion. The report called for a vastly stepped-up program to ensure that suffering cancer patients received palliative (symptom-abating) treatments.

Diabetes. Diabetes was fast becoming one of the most worrisome epidemics of the 21st century. In 2001 more than 135 million people worldwide were affected, and the number was expected to reach 300 million by 2025. The vast majority had type 2, or non-insulin-dependent, diabetes. With globalization, less-developed countries were experiencing some of the steepest increases. A survey published in September indicated that during the decade of the 1990s the proportion of Americans with diabetes increased 49%. Duly alarmed, CDC Director Jeffrey Koplan said, "If we continue on this course for the next decade, the public health implications in terms of both disease and health care costs will be staggering."

As a counterpoint to these dire predictions, a study carried out in Finland found that overweight middle-aged women and men who increased their activity level and ate a low-fat, high-fibre diet were unlikely to develop diabetes, even if their weight loss was minimal. In August a similar study in the U.S. was cut short when it became clear that lifestyle changes were overwhelmingly effective at staving off diabetes in those at high risk.

Three studies reported during the year showed that a common class of drugs for high blood pressure, angiotensin II receptor blockers, could significantly delay inexorable deterioration of the kidneys in people with diabetes. Commenting on these results, one of the investigators said, "For pennies . . . we can prevent a lot of disease and ultimately save billions of dollars in treatment."

A novel antidiabetes drug, nateglinide (Starlix), which became available in a number of countries, offered a new option for people with poorly controlled blood sugar. Studies found that when taken just before a meal, nateglinide triggered an immediate release of insulin by the pancreas. The insulin prevented spikes in postmeal glucose levels; such spikes were associated with blood vessel damage.

Cardiovascular Disease. Balloon angioplasty was among the most frequently performed procedures for restoring blood flow to partially obstructed coro-

On July 2 surgeons in Louisville, Ky., prepare to implant a self-contained artificial heart in the chest of Robert Tools.

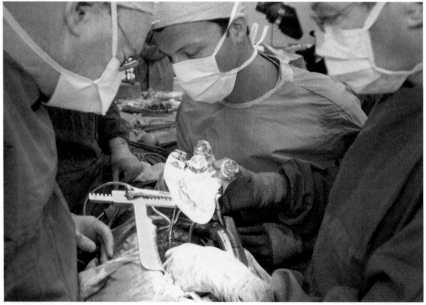

Alzheimer Disease: Clues from Convents

An ongoing study of a highly cooperative group of long-lived nuns has been shedding considerable light on aging and Alzheimer disease. The Nun Study, led by neurologist David Snowdon of the University of Kentucky, began in 1986 and has focused on 678 American members of the School Sisters of Notre Dame, a Roman Catholic religious congregation. When the study began, the sisters ranged in age from 75 to 102 years. All agreed to undergo yearly physical and cognitive-function exams and to donate their brains for study at death.

As a piece of scientific research, the Nun Study has obvious limitations—the outcomes cannot always be generalized to the population at large. On the other hand, because the nuns share so many key lifestyle factors—e.g., ethnicity (Caucasian), reproductive history, occupation, and access to health care—the conclusions drawn about their aging processes are less likely to be confounded by differences in individual experiences.

Another singular aspect of the Nun Study is the researchers' access to the convent archives, ranging from birth certificates to socioeconomic, educational, residential, social, and occupational data. The data that have excited Snowdon the most, however, are those acquired in face-to-face interviews. Recalling his first meeting with residents of a Minnesota convent, Snowdon said, "It shattered all my stereotypes of how 80- and 90-year-old people are supposed to behave."

The insights that scientists have gleaned from this distinctive group are varied. For example, results of studies published in 2001 noted a connection between the nuns' outlook early in life and their longevity. Investigators analyzed autobiographies composed by 180 sisters at the time they took their vows (between ages 18 and 32). Although the majority of this group lived to a ripe old age, those who revealed positive emotions in young adulthood lived about seven years longer—to a median age of 93$\frac{1}{2}$—than their more negative-thinking counterparts.

Snowdon's team also found links in the nuns' autobiographies to changes in their cognitive abilities with age. Sisters who showed "low linguistic ability" as young adults were found more likely to experience declines in language facility as they aged and to develop dementia in later life. In postmortem studies the brains of nuns whose linguistic ability had been rated low had clear pathological evidence of Alzheimer disease. The researchers surmised that less-than-optimal brain development might have predisposed those nuns to the disease.

Although these and other results from the Nun Study are highly intriguing and suggestive, they are not yet conclusive. As Snowdon and his team gather more data on their subjects, they will undoubtedly establish clearer cause-and-effect relationships.

(ELLEN BERNSTEIN)

---

nary arteries. In 90% of angioplasties, after a catheter-delivered balloon had been inflated to widen the artery, a tiny mesh coil (stent) was inserted to help keep the artery open. In as many as 20% of cases, however, the artery renarrowed at the site of treatment within six months as a result of scar formation, a process called restenosis. During the year an experimental technique for preventing restenosis after angioplasty was hailed as a "major breakthrough" by the American Heart Association. The approach used stents that were coated with an antibiotic and designed to release the medication slowly over a one-month period to prevent local scar-tissue formation. In a European trial more than 100 patients who received antibiotic-coated stents had no incidence of restenosis seven months after angioplasty.

In July the first of a new type of artificial heart, developed by the Massachusetts-based firm Abiomed, Inc., was implanted in Robert Tools, aged 58, at Jewish Hospital in Louisville, Ky. Tools had diabetes and end-stage heart disease and was far too sick to be considered for a heart transplant. After removing most of his diseased heart, the surgical team attached the grapefruit-sized device, made mostly of titanium and plastic, to the remains of the two

upper heart chambers and aorta. A battery pack worn outside the body transmitted power to the implanted device with no skin penetration. By contrast, the first artificial heart, the Jarvik-7, which had been given to a few deathly ill patients in the early 1980s, had tubes leading from an internal pump to external compressors and consoles. Tools's recovery exceeded his surgeons' expectations over the first four months, but in November his condition worsened, and he died from severe abdominal bleeding associated with his pre-implant illness. Four subsequent patients successfully received artificial hearts during the year. The goal of these first implants was to enable the severely ill recipients to live an extra six months with a satisfactory quality of life. Abiomed expressed the hope that later generations of its device would be suitable for a broader group of patients, who would gain five or more years of life.

Alzheimer Disease. The Alzheimer's Association estimated that about 4 million people in the U.S. had Alzheimer disease (AD) at the start of the 21st century and predicted that by 2050 the number would jump to 14 million. WHO estimated that there were 37 million people worldwide with dementia, the large majority of whom had AD. As of 2001, there was still no cure or treat-

ment that could significantly halt the progression of the disease.

During the year about three dozen clinical trials were either under way or in the recruitment stage to test potential AD treatments. At the University of California, San Diego, medical researchers began testing the first gene therapy procedure for AD. Their first volunteer was a 60-year-old woman with early-stage disease. Initially, skin cells were taken from the woman and genetically modified to produce large amounts of nerve growth factor. Then, in an 11-hour operation, neurosurgeons implanted the cells into diseased tissue in her brain. The primary goal was to see if the treatment was safe. The researchers hoped that ultimately the therapy would prevent the death of specific nerve cells that are affected by AD and enhance the function of others, which would thereby delay the onset of major symptoms.

An optimistic report published in the March 13 *Proceedings of the National Academy of Sciences* found that people who were physically and mentally active in early adulthood and middle age had an excellent chance of avoiding AD. Similar findings were emerging from a unique ongoing investigation known as the Nun Study. (*See* Sidebar.)

(ELLEN BERNSTEIN)

Law, Crime, and Law Enforcement

The prosecution of **TERRORISTS** and those charged with war crimes, the federal **EXECUTION** of American terrorist Timothy **McVEIGH**, and the move toward the abolition of the **DEATH PENALTY** in a number of countries were among the **LEGAL MATTERS** that captured the headlines during 2001.

INTERNATIONAL LAW

Throughout 2001 countries continued to work toward a common understanding of international law, particularly on the issue of "universal jurisdiction," the concept that war criminals may be punished anywhere regardless of where or against whom they committed their crimes. The September terrorist attacks in the United States raised critical questions for international law, including how terrorists should be punished and what the rules were for taking action against countries alleged to have harboured those responsible.

Peru continued to seek the extradition of former president Alberto Fujimori, who was living in exile in Japan. Fujimori was accused of abandonment of his office, dereliction of duty in the wake of corruption scandals, and failure to appear for court hearings. Japan refused to extradite Fujimori and said the case would be handled according to Japanese domestic law. Chile's former dictator Gen. Augusto Pinochet Ugarte, who faced allegations of war crimes committed during his tenure, was found medically unfit to stand trial.

The collision of a Chinese fighter jet with an American surveillance jet caused the American plane to land on Chinese soil in distress, while the Chinese aircraft was lost at sea. The U.S. questioned whether the Chinese had the right to board the downed American plane, hold its crew, and remove equipment from the plane, all of which the Chinese did. Although there was no international law directly applicable to such a situation, the U.S. raised two legal points: first, the U.S. plane had not overflown China's 19-km (12-mi) recognized territorial seas and therefore did not violate China's sovereignty or break

international law, and, second, customary international law recognizes that a ship in distress can enter a harbour unannounced; furthermore, a foreign military ship in port is not subject to the jurisdiction of the port state. These laws could be interpreted to cover aircraft as well as ships. Chinese authorities claimed that since the aircraft had no right to be on Chinese territory, it was not immune to being searched.

The International Court of Justice. In July the International Court of Justice (ICJ) found that the U.S. had breached its obligations to Germany under Article 36 of the Vienna Convention on Consular Relations. Walter LaGrand, a German national, was sentenced to death for his involvement in a 1982 murder in Arizona. The night before the execution, Germany brought suit in the ICJ. Germany argued that LaGrand had not been informed of his rights under the Vienna Convention, under which he could have notified the German consulate of his arrest and incarceration. Despite the ICJ's issuance of a "provisional measure of protection," LaGrand was executed as scheduled. The court held that the U.S. violated the convention's requirements. It determined that individual rights in one's nation of origin might be invoked in the World Court when the individual was being detained in another country.

The principality of Liechtenstein brought suit in the ICJ against Germany, claiming that Germany had improperly disposed of property belonging to Liechtenstein. After World War II, Czechoslovakia, one of the Allies, seized property without compensation in defeated Germany, including some objects owned by Liechtensteiners. Subsequently, in 1952 Germany and Liechtenstein agreed that although Germany had given up the right to pursue the recovery of its own goods, those objects be-

longing to Liechtenstein had been illegally taken by Czechoslovakia. When in 1991 a Czechoslovak museum sent to Germany on loan a painting that was among those claimed by Liechtenstein, that principality's leader, Prince Hans Adam II, sued the Germans, claiming that the painting had been illegally seized in 1945 and that Germany should relinquish it. The German courts disagreed, finding that the painting was properly seized German property; it was later returned to the Czech Republic. The ICJ had not reached a decision as of year's end.

Universal Jurisdiction. In June a Belgian jury sentenced two nuns and two men to jail terms from 12 to 20 years for crimes committed during the 1994 genocide in Rwanda. A 1993 Belgian law gave its courts jurisdiction over violations of the Geneva Conventions regardless of where the crimes were committed, by whom, or against whom. The Geneva Conventions call for the humane treatment of noncombatants, and they prohibit murder, mutilation, and cruel or degrading treatment. This was the first jury trial to address violations of international humanitarian law that occurred in another country. A Belgian court delayed until November a preliminary hearing to determine whether that country had jurisdiction to bring charges against Israeli Prime Minister Ariel Sharon (*see* BIOGRAPHIES) for his role in a 1982 Palestinian massacre. The court's decision to hear arguments on the case prompted outrage from some countries and caused the Belgian government to consider exempting sitting prime ministers and presidents from the reach of the 1993 law. In a similar case, Senegal's high court ruled that it did not have jurisdiction over Chad's exiled president Hissène Habré for crimes he committed while in Chad. Habré's victims spoke of seeking his extradition to Belgium instead. Similarly, a Cuban American group threatened to file suit in Belgian court against Cuban leader Fidel Castro, alleging crimes against humanity.

International Criminal Tribunal for the Former Yugoslavia. There were several landmark decisions from the International Criminal Tribunal for the Former Yugoslavia (ICTY). Three eth-

AP/Wide World Photos

Former Yugoslav president Slobodan Milosevic is escorted by a security guard into the courtroom of the International Criminal Tribunal for the Former Yugoslavia on July 3 in The Hague.

ism. The September 11 terrorist attacks in the U.S. could cause that to change, however. On September 28 the UN Security Council adopted Resolution 1373, which was legally binding on all members and called for states to take measures to combat terrorism, including bringing terrorists to justice.

Most international law concerned interstate disputes and had little to do with individuals. Thus, because Osama bin Laden, the prime suspect in the terrorist attacks, was not the representative of any state, charges against him could not be brought in the ICJ. The proper forum would have been the International Criminal Court, but the act enabling the ICC had not been ratified by the requisite number of countries—the U.S. being among the nonratifiers. What constituted a legal response to the September attacks was also moot. Were the attacks an act of war? Was a declaration of war required in order to respond with military force?

On October 18 a New York judge handed down life sentences to three foreigners and a naturalized American found guilty of involvement in the 1998 attacks on the U.S. embassies in Kenya and Tanzania. Bin Laden was linked to these attacks as well, but he and 12 others indicted for the bombings remained at large.   (VICTORIA C. WILLIAMS)

COURT DECISIONS

Between Oct. 2, 2000, and June 28, 2001, the United States Supreme Court decided 79 cases. While the term would be forever remembered for *Bush* v. *Gore*, a number of other significant cases also attracted attention. Statistically, if not rhetorically, the term ranked as the most divisive since the current composition of the court was established in 1994. In one-third of the cases, the court ruled 5–4; in the area of civil rights, the "faction-fraction" rose to two-thirds. Not surprisingly, many of the most divisive cases raised salient constitutional questions, and the court's answers to them clarified not only the tenuous status of individual rights but patterns of judicial decision making as well. This was especially true in the fields of civil rights, civil liberties, and criminal law.

The cases of *Alexander* v. *Sandoval, Board of Trustees of the University of Alabama* v. *Garrett,* and *Easley* (formerly *Hunt*) v. *Cromartie* exemplified the dividing line in civil rights jurisprudence. In the first pair of cases, the philosophical split was identical: Justices

nic Serbs were convicted on charges of rape and torture for their abuse in 1992 of women in a "rape camp" in Bosnia and Herzegovina. This was the first case to issue convictions for rape as a crime against humanity. In June Serbia surrendered former Yugoslav president Slobodan Milosevic to the ICTY. He would be the first former head of state to stand trial at an international tribunal. Article 7 of the ICTY specifically denies immunity to heads of state. Milosevic was indicted in 1999 on charges of crimes against humanity and war crimes for the killings of ethnic Albanians in Kosovo. He was indicted in October for crimes in Croatia in 1991–92 and in November for crimes in Bosnia in 1992–96. Gen. Radislav Krstic was sentenced to 46 years in prison for his role in the execution of 7,000 unarmed Muslim men and boys near the Bosnian town of Srebrenica in 1995. According to the verdict issued in the case, "ethnic cleansing became genocide." Former Bosnian Serb leader Radovan Karadzic and his top general, Ratko Mladic, indicted by the tribunal

on charges of genocide and crimes against humanity, were still fugitives, as were many others. In October, after six years of refusing to cooperate, the Bosnian Serb parliament passed a law supporting the ICTY and calling for the arrest of war-crimes suspects living in Republika Srpska (Serb Republic).

Terrorism. A Scottish court found a Libyan, 'Abd al-Baset al-Megrahi, guilty of the bombing of Pan Am Flight 103 over Lockerbie, Scot., in 1988. A second Libyan was acquitted, and al-Megrahi planned to appeal. The court placed responsibility for the bombing on Libya but did not specify who might have been involved. An American federal grand jury indicted 14 men (13 Saudi nationals) in connection with the 1996 bombing of the U.S. military barracks in Saudi Arabia. Saudi Arabia protested, claiming that the U.S. did not have the jurisdiction to prosecute a crime that occurred on Saudi territory, nor did it have the right to prosecute Saudi nationals. Although universal jurisdiction had been recognized for war crimes and genocide, it was less accepted for acts of terror-

William Rehnquist, Antonin Scalia, Anthony Kennedy, Sandra Day O'Connor, and Clarence Thomas formed the conservative majority, with the more liberal Stephen Breyer, Ruth Bader Ginsburg, John Paul Stevens, and David Souter constituting the minority.

Alexander v. *Sandoval* involved a challenge to Alabama's English-only driver's license examinations. Arguing that Title VI of the Civil Rights Act of 1964 and related federal regulations prohibiting discrimination in federally funded programs were never intended to permit or award lawsuits filed by private individuals, Scalia held that there is no private cause of action to enforce such regulations. In the second Alabama-based case, the court ruled that the states are immune from lawsuits claiming discrimination under the Americans with Disabilities Act. Just as the former case limited the application of federal law owing to a narrow interpretation of congressional intent, the latter restricted congressional authority in the area of equal protection, reaffirming a stellar commitment to a state-centred theory of federalism. The notable exception to this trend was established in the case of *PGA Tour, Inc.* v. *Martin*. By a vote of 7–2, the court ruled that Casey Martin, a profes-

sional golfer with diminished ambulatory ability, had a legal right under the Disabilities Act to use a golf cart during the Professional Golfers' Association of America (PGA) tour. Despite the PGA's insistence that such a decision would give Martin an unfair advantage, the court ruled that the use of a cart constituted a reasonable accommodation of the petitioner's disability.

In the area where civil rights, civil liberties, and electoral politics converged, the Supreme Court addressed two important cases. In *Easley* v. *Cromartie*, the minority in *Alexander* and *University of Alabama* gained the support of Justice O'Connor, producing the one-vote margin necessary to uphold the configuration of North Carolina's 12th Congressional District. In ruling that the district, which was 47% black, was crafted through a bipartisan effort and not according to racial identity, the level of suspicion historically associated with apparently race-based districts was relaxed enough to facilitate a judicial inclusion of intent and method, rather than simply racial composition. The inclusion of O'Connor in this case indicated a unique flexibility in terms of both the law and the justice's own position. Since her appointment O'Connor

had been an opponent of presumably race-based districting, and the cases were decided along those relatively rigid lines. By taking into consideration other variables—the source, method, and motives of redistricting—a new jurisprudential flexibility emerged.

In the related field of campaign finance, the same majority upheld limitations on coordinated campaign expenditures. The court held in *Federal Election Commission* v. *Colorado Republican Federal Campaign Committee* that party expenditures were substantively different from individual expenditures and therefore ineligible for the full First Amendment protection offered to citizens. Also, by rejecting party exemptions, the court avoided setting a standard that could conceivably have facilitated the circumvention of other campaign finance rules and regulations.

Although political parties were limited in the expression of support they may give, the speech and actions of attorneys employed by a government corporation may not be subjected to congressional restrictions. Compatible with its philosophy of limited congressional authority, the court ruled in the consolidated cases of *Legal Services Corporation* v. *Velazquez* and *United States* v. *Velazquez* that a 1996 provision limiting various modes of conduct including, but not limited to, lobbying, class-action litigation, immigrant representation, and welfare reform violated the First Amendment rights of the attorneys and their clients.

In *Good News Club* v. *Milford Central School*, the court revisited the controversial issue of speech rights and religious liberty in public schools. Arguing that the school's attempt to deny Christian groups access to facilities for religious instruction amounted to viewpoint discrimination, the court held that public schools must provide the same after-hours privileges for religious organizations as they do for nonreligious organizations. Because the school itself was not sponsoring or requiring religious instruction, the establishment clause was not violated.

In the area of criminal law, the court decided at least four major Fourth Amendment cases: *Illinois* v. *McArthur*, *Atwater* v. *City of Lago Vista*, *Kyllo* v. *United States*, and *Ferguson* v. *City of Charleston*. The *Illinois* and *Atwater* cases were similar in that they involved police conduct relating to the execution of warrants and arrests. In *Illinois* v. *McArthur*, the court ruled that the Fourth Amendment was not violated when police, while awaiting a warrant

Disabled golfer Casey Martin rides down a fairway at Quail Hollow Country Club in Concord, Ohio, on June 14 following the U.S. Supreme Court's decision that he had a legal right to use a golf cart during PGA competition.

to search property for evidence of a controlled dangerous substance, prohibited a man from entering his home. Because police had probable cause to believe the home contained evidence of a crime, because of the reasonable suspicion that such evidence would be destroyed by the suspect if he was allowed to enter the home, and because there was a minimal intrusion into the man's personal privacy, the warrantless seizure was considered constitutionally permissible.

Atwater v. *City of Lago Vista* involved the related question of warrantless arrests. Writing for the court, Justice Souter argued that the Fourth Amendment does not forbid warrantless arrests for minor criminal offenses. The offense in this case was the failure of an adult driver to secure herself and her children with safety belts while in an automobile. Despite competing claims regarding the applicability of common-law traditions and the presumed severity of the penalty, there simply is no constitutional prohibition of the legal action in question.

Kyllo v. *United States* and *Ferguson* v. *City of Charleston* both involved questions of illegal searches—the former involving a home, the latter involving a person. In *Kyllo* v. *United States*, the court ruled that police use of thermal imaging devices aimed at a private residence constituted an unconstitutional search of private property. According to Justice Scalia, using the device to detect heat and light necessary for growing marijuana amounted to a search under the Fourth Amendment, which would have required a warrant. In the *Ferguson* case, the court was asked to determine whether a hospital's policy of testing for drug use and providing such results to police in order to deter pregnant women from using cocaine violated the generally recognized prohibition of warrantless nonconsensual searches. Striking down the law, Stevens wrote that the policy, which emanated from a program designed at the height of the "crack babies" epidemic and ultimately resulted in the use of medical procedures to alert police to criminal conduct, was unconstitutional.

In *Whitman* v. *American Trucking Associations, Inc.*, which was proclaimed by the *New York Times* to be "the most important regulatory ruling" of the term, the court unanimously defended the Clean Air Act against a legal challenge by the ATA. The legal challenge was two-pronged: to argue that the Environmental Protection Agency's power was derived from an unconstitutional delegation of legislative authority to an administrative agency and that cost-benefit analysis should be part of the calculus for developing environmental standards. The court rejected both claims, finding that public-health matters should constitute the sole determinant of new clean-air standards.

The court's 2001–02 term could well be remembered for the manner in which the institution began its session in October: with the unprecedented necessity of acknowledging the impact of terrorism on American soil in the wake of the September 11 attacks and, for the first time since the completion of the Supreme Court building, holding its session outside the historic structure. The dramatic events relating to war and conflict had an immediate impact on the operation, if not the judgment, of the court—so much so, in fact, that one of the court's first orders of business, upholding the prohibition of former president Bill Clinton's privilege of practicing law before the bench, went largely unnoticed. (BRIAN SMENTKOWSKI)

CRIME

Terrorism. On Sept. 11, 2001, terrorist attacks of unprecedented savagery and destruction were launched against the United States. In a coordinated assault terrorists simultaneously hijacked four commercial airliners flying from Newark, N.J.; Boston, Mass.; and Washington, D.C. Two of the planes were then flown into the twin towers of the World Trade Center (WTC) in New York City, while a third plowed into the country's military nerve centre, the Pentagon, outside Washington, D.C. The fourth aircraft crashed into a field in Pennsylvania, apparently after passengers struggled to overpower the hijackers following news received over their cell phones of what had just occurred in New York. This aircraft was believed to have been targeted to fly into either the White House or the U.S. Capitol building in Washington. (*See* Special Report, pp. 8–13.)

More than 3,000 persons were thought to have perished during the course of these attacks, most having been buried amid the rubble of the WTC towers, which collapsed about one hour after being struck. The death toll made this the deadliest single day of violent action against the U.S. since the American Civil War, exceeding the 2,403 deaths in Japan's attack on Pearl Harbor in 1941. In the wake of the September 11 attacks, Pres. George W. Bush declared the U.S. to be "at war" with international terrorism and readied the nation for military retaliation against the perpetrators of the assault. While no terrorist group made immediate claim to have assisted the 19 hijackers identified by the FBI as having been aboard the doomed flights, a massive criminal investigation garnered compelling evidence that the attacks were the work of al-Qaeda ("the Base"), a network of Islamic terrorist organizations led by Saudi-born Osama bin Laden. (*See* BIOGRAPHIES.) Al-Qaeda, according to extensive testimony given at a number of highly publicized terrorist trials in the U.S. during recent years, was a well-organized and sophisticated body that acted as a facilitator and coordinator of terrorist activities in many countries. Al-Qaeda was known to support at least four elite training camps in Afghanistan for its adherents, where instruction was given in bomb making, sabotage, intelligence gathering, abduction, hijacking, and related terrorist activities. When conducting an operation like the attacks upon two U.S. embassies in East Africa in August 1998, al-Qaeda used teams composed of long-term "sleepers," who had been resident in a country for years, as well as "cleanskins," who had never been involved in an operation before. It was believed that Bin Laden and his aides adopted a similar strategy when planning and executing the September 11 assault from their shadowy base within Afghanistan, where they continued to be given sanctuary by that nation's extremist Islamic regime, the Taliban. Despite the imposition upon Afghanistan of severe international sanctions and armed intervention by the U.S. and its allies, the Taliban refused to meet demands that they cease their support for al-Qaeda and hand over Bin Laden and his associates to face justice.

The level of international support and assistance offered to the U.S. in responding to the events of September 11 was demonstrated by NATO, which declared that the attacks were against the alliance as a whole. On October 7 U.S.-led military strikes commenced against a range of targets within Afghanistan, including suspected terrorist bases. Shortly after the attacks began, a prerecorded message from Bin Laden, speaking from an undisclosed location, was broadcast by the Qatar-based satellite TV network al-Jazeera to millions of television screens around the world. During the broadcast Bin Laden implicitly admitted his involvement in the September 11 assault, called upon Muslims to engage in a holy war against the U.S., and suggested that his actions were in part a response to Israeli reprisals against Palestinians.

Drug Trafficking. As required under U.S. law, President Bush delivered to Congress in March a report certifying which governments of the major drug-producing countries and drug-transit countries had cooperated fully with the U.S., or taken adequate steps on their own, to curb drug use and trafficking. Failure to gain certification made a government ineligible for most forms of U.S. assistance. U.S. drug-enforcement officials claimed that the certification process resulted in certain countries eradicating drug crops, capturing seemingly elusive drug barons, and taking other actions to ensure that they met the deadline set each year to receive a favourable presidential ruling. Two countries, Afghanistan and Myanmar (Burma), were denied certification in 2001. U.S. officials observed that during 2000 the cultivation of the opium poppy in Afghanistan increased by 25% and that the country accounted for about 72% of the global supply. Earlier in the year, however, there had been credible reports of decreased poppy cultivation in Taliban-controlled areas. Large opiate stockpiles remained in the country, and drug trafficking continued unabated from Afghanistan to Europe and other regions of the world.

On April 20 an American missionary, Veronica Bowers, and her seven-month-old daughter were killed when the light aircraft in which they were flying was shot down by a Peruvian air force fighter plane in the mistaken belief that it was engaged in a drug-trafficking operation. The incident prompted an extensive examination by the U.S. Senate Select Committee on Intelligence of a six-year-old agreement between the U.S. and Peru under which U.S. assistance was provided in tracking drug smugglers. At the time of the shooting down of the missionaries' aircraft, it was under the surveillance of a U.S. tracking plane flown under CIA contract. As a result of the mistaken attack, the U.S. suspended all of its drug-surveillance flights in Central and South America while officials reassessed the rules and procedures they followed.

Murder and Other Violence. Preliminary figures released in May from the FBI's nationwide Uniform Crime Reporting Program indicated that in 2000 the Crime Index, comprising murder, forcible rape, robbery, aggravated assault, burglary, larceny, theft, and motor-vehicle theft, remained relatively unchanged from 1999. This was the first time in eight years that a decline had not been reported in the number of serious crimes in the U.S. Experts and law-enforcement officials had long cautioned that the crime rate could not drop indefinitely, and this FBI report tended to confirm that the trend had run its course. In the past a large increase or decrease in homicide, or in crime in the biggest cities, had tended to predict significant fluctuations in general rates of serious crime. No indicators of this type were contained in the 2000 figures.

On March 5, in a tragic repeat of school shootings in the past several years that had traumatized rural and suburban communities in the U.S., a 15-year-old high-school freshman, Charles Andrew Williams, killed two fellow students and wounded 13 others at Santana High School in Santee, a suburb of San Diego, Calif. The shooting was the worst episode of school violence since the mass slayings in April 1999 at Columbine High School in Littleton, Colo.

On June 8, in an incident that shocked the entire nation of Japan, a knife-wielding man burst into an elementary school in Ikeda and stabbed to death eight children—seven second-grade girls and one first-grade boy—and also seriously wounded six more students and a teacher. Police arrested Mamoru Takuma, a 37-year-old who had a history of mental illness.

War Crimes. Slobodan Milosevic, the past president of Yugoslavia, became the first former head of state to sit in a defendant's dock facing charges of war crimes and crimes against humanity. On July 3 Milosevic made his initial appearance before the International Criminal Tribunal for the Former Yugoslavia in The Hague following his dramatic nighttime transfer from a Belgrade prison on June 28. Milosevic, who had been placed under arrest by the Yugoslav government on April 1 on unrelated corruption charges, remained defiant before the international tribunal and challenged its legitimacy to place him on trial. Experts predicted that the proceedings against Milosevic could last for years and that his testimony could embarrass a number of Western leaders who had negotiated and dealt with him for much of his period in office. By surrendering Milosevic to the international tribunal, the Yugoslav government received immediate pledges of substantial aid from the U.S. and other nations to assist in rebuilding its shattered economy.

White-Collar Crime, Corruption, and Fraud. "A worldwide corruption crisis" was identified by Transparency International (TI), a Berlin-based nongovernmental organization established to expose and prevent corruption. Releasing its annual Corruption Perceptions Index in June, TI ranked 91 countries on a 10-point scale. A high score, indicating very low levels of perceived corruption, was obtained by some of the world's richest nations—Finland, Denmark, New Zealand, Iceland, Singapore, and Sweden. In contrast, low scores were recorded by some of the world's poorest countries, with Azerbaijan, Bolivia, Cameroon, Kenya, Indonesia, Uganda, Nigeria, and Bangladesh ranked at the bottom of the list. TI's chairman said that the index illustrated once more "the vicious circle of poverty and corruption" as vast amounts of public funds were squandered and stolen by corrupt governments and their officials.

In the Philippines in January, a wave of public anger against corruption forced Pres. Joseph Estrada from office in a bloodless coup. In April Estrada became the first Philippine president to be jailed on suspicion of corruption. Prosecutors alleged that he had pocketed more than $76 million in tax money and illegal gambling receipts during his two and a half years in office. If convicted of plunder, the most serious charge against him, Estrada faced the possibility of a death sentence or life imprisonment.

Law Enforcement. The FBI came under sustained scrutiny during the year as a result of a number of well-publicized incidents that suggested that failures had occurred in its management and information network. The most damaging and embarrassing revelation came in February when it was announced that a veteran FBI counterintelligence agent, Robert Philip Hanssen, had been arrested and charged with committing espionage by providing highly classified national security information to Russia and the former Soviet Union. At the time of his arrest at a park in Vienna, Va., Hanssen was clandestinely placing a garbage bag containing secret information at a prearranged "dead drop" for pickup by his Russian handlers. Hanssen had previously received large sums of money from the Russians for the information he disclosed to them. In July Hanssen pleaded guilty to 15 counts of having spied for Moscow since 1979. As part of a plea deal, Hanssen was given a sentence of life imprisonment rather than death after he agreed to participate in extensive debriefing with government agents and cooperated truthfully and fully with them. Prosecutors said that Hanssen betrayed nine double agents, including two who were later executed. He also provided Moscow with details of several top-secret communication programs, U.S. nuclear war preparations, and a listening tunnel underneath the Soviet embassy in Washington, D.C. A few weeks before this plea bargain, U.S. Attorney General John Ashcroft stated that a review would be conducted of the FBI's security program to try to ensure that the lapses that allowed Hanssen to operate as a spy would not happen again.

(DUNCAN CHAPPELL)

PRISONS AND PENOLOGY

In 2001 the prison population throughout the world continued to exceed the eight-million mark. Accounting for a quarter of this total, the U.S. held more of its inhabitants in prison (702 per 100,000 inhabitants) than any other country. Elsewhere, prison population rates declined in Russia and South Africa to 465 and 385, respectively, while the rate for China remained stable at 112. In Europe the prison population rate for England and Wales rose to 128, which made it the highest of any country in the European Union; Portugal's rate remained at 127, while Finland (52), Northern Ireland (60), and Denmark (61) had the lowest rates.

Various countries announced measures intended to reduce prison numbers. The ruler of Bahrain announced an amnesty for some 400 political prisoners jailed for crimes during the 1990s. Malawi Pres. Bakili Muluzi released 880 prisoners to celebrate nationhood, and 40,000 prisoners were released in Kazakhstan to honour the 10th anniversary of the nation's independence. In Kyrgyzstan an amnesty involving at least 5,000 prisoners was agreed upon. The Russian State Duma approved legislation intended to reduce the prison population by 300,000 through the wider use of bail and settlement colonies.

Violence, death, and disease continued to surface in prisons around the globe. The most serious disturbances in Brazil's penal history occurred in the state of São Paulo's prison system, with prisoners at 29 institutions across the state taking some 8,000 prisoners, prison guards, and visitors hostage as part of a protest

against the removal of gang leaders from one of the prisons. Twenty prisoners were reported killed as paramilitary police secured the release of the hostages and regained control of the prisons. In Chile 26 inmates serving sentences in the Iquique penitentiary were killed in a fire caused by an electrical fault. (*See* DISASTERS.) In Mexico a prison governor was shot dead, apparently as a reprisal for a security clampdown recently ordered at his prison. Serious overcrowding and health problems continued to blight many prisons across Africa. In Morocco it was reported that prison regimes were immersed in corruption, violence, and the sexual abuse of children. In Malawi overcrowding and lack of proper sanitation facilities reportedly led to a dramatic rise in the spread of infectious diseases, including scabies and tuberculosis. Eighty-three prisoners died of suffocation, hunger, and thirst in November 2000 in a

Timothy McVeigh, convicted of the bombing of the federal building in Oklahoma City in 1995, was executed by lethal injection on June 11 at the U.S. Penitentiary in Terre Haute, Ind.

Mozambique prison where 120 prisoners were held in a cell measuring 21 sq m (226 sq ft). In South Africa poor hygiene and water facilities were cited as the cause of a cholera outbreak that infected 600 prisoners. Problems caused by overcrowding and poor conditions were also experienced in various European countries. In Russia, where some 100,000 prisoners were suffering from tuberculosis, the World Bank announced a $50

million credit to combat the disease and to assist HIV-positive prisoners. In Turkey some 250 prisoners joined a hunger strike (resulting in more than 30 deaths of prisoners and their supporters) to protest the transfer of inmates to new prisons where, it was claimed, conditions breached international standards.

DEATH PENALTY

A gradual movement toward abolition of capital punishment continued in 2001. Chile, where the last execution took place in 1985, enacted legislation to abolish the death penalty for peacetime offenses. The Lebanese parliament repealed legislation that had sought to expand the scope of the death penalty by abolishing judicial discretion to consider mitigating factors. In Russia, despite renewed calls for the death penalty from many quarters, Pres. Vladimir Putin stated that he favoured abolition and urged upholding a five-year-old moratorium on the practice. Elsewhere, judicial decisions sought to reduce the scope of the death penalty. In a number of eastern Caribbean countries, including Antigua and Barbuda, Dominica, and Grenada, mandatory death sentences were declared unconstitutional.

Against this global trend, executions took place for the first time in 17 years in Guinea, 6 years in Indonesia, and 3 years in Bangladesh. The Council of Europe found the treatment of prisoners awaiting execution in Japan to be "inhumane" and drew particular attention to the practice of the condemned persons' being given only one hour's notice of their impending deaths. Japan had, however, refused to abandon executions on the grounds that 80% of its population found the practice to be useful. In April the Chinese government embarked upon a "Strike Hard" anticrime campaign during which hundreds of prisoners were paraded at public rallies prior to their executions. A Western diplomat recorded 801 deaths in China in the final three weeks of April, while Amnesty International reported that 89 people had been executed during a single day. In the U.S. 66 prisoners were put to death during the year—a sharp reduction from the 85 executions that took place in 2000. Those put to death included Timothy McVeigh (*see* OBITUARIES), who had been convicted of having placed a bomb in the federal building in Oklahoma City, Okla., that killed 168 people; he was the first federal prisoner executed in the U.S. in 38 years.

(ANDREW RUTHERFORD)

Libraries and Museums

Egypt's Bibliotheca ALEXANDRINA and the JEWISH Museum Berlin were among the new libraries and museums completed in 2001; many other facilities faced LEGAL challenges, natural DISASTERS, and abrupt changes in DIRECTORSHIP.

LIBRARIES

Though in recent years the most newsworthy events pertaining to libraries worldwide had involved war damage, fires, floods, earthquakes, and other tragedies, there were fewer such disasters in 2001 and proportionally more instances that demonstrated the synergies between networked computing and the traditional library functions of organizing knowledge and making it accessible.

Images and information on 20,000 magnificent pre-Columbian textiles created by the Incas and other indigenous cultures were mounted on the Internet —<http://textiles.perucultural.org.pe>— by the National Museum of Archaeology, Anthropology and History, Lima, Peru, with financial support from Fundación Telefónica. In Cambridge, Mass., Genomics Collaborative, Inc. (GCI), began building the world's largest library of genetic material—human tissue and blood. Samples were being collected from around the country, classified, and stored. GCI believed that the collection would be invaluable in developing new drugs to treat cancer, diabetes, and many other diseases. The government of South Australia established the Digital Library of Indigenous Australia to collect and disseminate information about Aboriginal Australians: <http://www.dosaa.sa.gov.au>.

A host of new and unique libraries opened. In France a government-financed automotive research centre began building a compact-disc library of automobile noises that would be available to engineers in pursuit of sweet sounds, including the desirable resonance made by the solid sound of a door closing on a BMW 7-Series sedan. In October the Bibliotheca Alexandrina was completed. (*See* Sidebar.)

New public libraries offered hope to residents of war-torn or impoverished areas. The first large-scale public library opened in Beirut, Lebanon. In Rwanda the design for the country's first-ever public library, in Kigali, was finalized. It was hoped that the library, scheduled to open in 2002, would help raise the country's literacy rate, which at 47% was one of the lowest in the world. The Jaffna Public Library in Sri Lanka, which had been the repository of the history and culture of the island's minority Tamil people, was in the process of rebuilding, 20 years after it had been incinerated by Sinhalese police officers.

In the U.S., technology brought not only new services and capabilities but also conflict and legislation that threatened to alter basic tenets of the library ethos. In 2001 a federal law took effect that mandated the installation of Internet-filtering software in all libraries that received federal funding. Suits filed by the American Library Association (ALA) and the American Civil Liberties Union challenged the law's constitutionality. ALA president Nancy Kranich maintained that "blocking technologies come between librarians and their mission—to connect people with a broad range of information." The ALA position of resisting any action that might keep information from anyone drew fierce censure from socially conservative critics, including radio host Laura Schlessinger and *The Wall Street Journal*. On the other hand, a librarian at the Chicago Public Library sued her employer on the grounds that the pornography viewed by library users created a hostile workplace for library workers.

American libraries also found their missions endangered by other legislative initiatives and legal challenges that surrounded information technology. Provisions of the federal Digital Millennium Copyright Act (DMCA), passed in 1998, markedly restricted the "fair use" policies of former copyright laws, on which libraries and educators had long relied to permit the copying of documents for educational purposes. In 2001, however, some relief was in the offing, as an amendment to the DMCA was under consideration.

Not all library travails, however, arose from technology. Novelist Nicholson Baker's *Double Fold* offered a scathing indictment of library preservation policies, particularly in regard to the practice of discarding newspapers after they were microfilmed. Baker was well remembered by librarians for his similarly vituperative attack in the April 1994 issue of *The New Yorker*, in which he scorned libraries' abandonment of the venerable card catalog in favour of automated versions. Though libraries traditionally landed "below the radar" of august publications, critically acclaimed authors, and outspoken radio talk-show hosts, their importance in contemporary society might be gauged by the quality of their critics. Conversely, it might also be measured by the behaviour of ordinary citizens. In 2001 the Australian Bureau of Statistics reported that more Australians visited libraries than went to the movies.

Shelving was torqued in academic, public, and special libraries, and hundreds of thousands of volumes were launched onto the floor when an earthquake hit western Washington. One public library in the region suffered structural damage from the magnitude-6.8 temblor that struck in February. A month earlier a 7.6–7.9 quake shattered libraries in El Salvador. The Biblioteca Gallardo, a private 80,000-volume library that housed rare manuscripts, art works, and other materials dating back to the 16th century, was virtually destroyed. The country's national library, which never fully recovered from a 1986 quake, was also further damaged. Plans for a June renovation financed by Spain were postponed while the new damage was assessed.

Floods ravaged libraries in West Virginia, where some eight libraries sustained varying degrees of damage in one of the worst disasters to hit the state in decades. In Houston, Texas, Tropical Storm Allison dumped nearly 0.9 m (3 ft) of rain in July, causing billions of dollars of damage. Numerous

Bibliotheca Alexandrina

In a sense, all libraries serve a totemic function. They symbolize man's efforts to preserve knowledge, culture, and wisdom and transmit it to future generations. Large national libraries and university libraries are especially powerful symbols.

No other library, however, has the totemic power of the lost ancient Library of Alexandria, Egypt. Though little is known with certainty about this wonder of the classical world, it has come to be viewed as a kind of scholarly Camelot. Sometime in the 3rd century BC, the library's founder, probably Ptolemy I Soter, began to collect all the written information from throughout the known world. In time, the library held 500,000—or as many as 700,000—papyrus documents, mainly in Greek, including the works of Plato, Socrates, Thucydides, Euclid, Hippocrates, and Sophocles. The library at Alexandria was the world's first think tank, providing a home for many of the greatest minds of the time. Euclid completed his seminal *Elements* there; Eratosthenes accurately calculated the circumference of the Earth.

The circumstances of the library's destruction are still a mystery. Scholarly guesses on the date of its loss range from 48 BC to AD 600. Despite—or because of—the many unknowns, fascination with the institution has persisted for nearly two millennia.

In Alexandria, Egypt, construction was completed during the year on the Bibliotheca Alexandrina, which opened its doors to the public in October.

Snohetta/Hamza Consortium courtesy of the Bibliotheca Alexandrina

In 2001 construction was completed on a new Library of Alexandria, officially known as the Bibliotheca Alexandrina. Scholars around the world are transfixed by the dramatic architecture and the hope that the $200 million structure will recapture the glory of the original. The design has drawn worldwide praise. Essentially, it is a massive cylinder, emerging from the ground at a shallow angle only about 40 m (130 ft) from the sea. The disk-shaped roof suggests the sun rising over the Mediterranean, and the roof pattern of aluminum and glass panels resembles a microchip. One outer wall of the structure is made up of some 6,400 granite panels bearing characters from all the known alphabets. The symbolism of these elements seems ideal.

The Bibliotheca will ultimately house four million volumes on seven cascading levels. The collection will be shelved with the oldest materials on the lowest level, forming a metaphoric foundation for later works. In addition, the library will house a planetarium, a school of library and information science, facilities for the digital preservation of rare books and manuscripts, and a conference centre. The new library will be the most modern facility in the region and will surely become a key node in the expanding Internet.

Despite the allure of the library's revival, critics point to difficulties that may compromise the institution's success. The greatest concern is inadequate funding for maintenance and collections. An architect from the Norwegian firm that designed the library has questioned the lack of funding for upkeep of the spectacular structure. The library will open with a collection of some 400,000 books, many donated but some inappropriate to the library's interests. Moreover, during 2001 the Egyptian government banned some publications that Islamic fundamentalists found objectionable. It remains to be seen if potential difficulties such as these will undermine either the reality or the symbolism of the library. The official inauguration of the Bibliotheca Alexandrina is set for April 23, 2002.

(THOMAS M. GAUGHAN)

---

branch libraries of the Houston Public Library and the libraries of Houston Academy of Medicine–Texas Medical Center and the Houston Symphony all suffered extensive damage to collections, furnishings, and equipment.

(THOMAS M. GAUGHAN)

MUSEUMS

Following the Sept. 11, 2001, terrorist attacks in the United States, the role of museums as custodians and guardians of cultural heritage was underscored worldwide. In an effort to safeguard the value of their collections, a number of museums sought to upgrade their insurance policies and implement damage-control measures.

Earlier in the year the International Council of Museums, along with the Canadian Museum Association and the

United Nations Security Council, publicly condemned the Taliban's destruction in Bamian, Afg., of two several-centuries-old giant Buddha statues that had been carved into a cliff. The Taliban claimed that these priceless treasures were idolatrous symbols.

A number of new museums as well as additions to existing structures appeared during the year. In Germany the Jewish Museum Berlin, designed by Polish-born American architect Daniel Libeskind, opened its doors on September 9. The $60 million zinc-clad structure, meant to symbolize a deconstructed Star of David, was the first Jewish museum in the city in 60 years; the Nazis had destroyed the previous museum in 1938. The centrepiece of the new museum—which chronicled Jewish history from Roman times—was the Holocaust Tower, where visitors found themselves enclosed in a

dimly lit concrete chamber after a door slammed closed behind them.

When the new National Museum of Australia (NMA) debuted in March in Canberra following 20 years of planning, it opened to mixed reviews. Though some praised architect Howard Raggatt's design as a "masterpiece," others deemed the design plagiarized from the Jewish Museum Berlin, which, though it opened in September, had been completed two years earlier. Aerial photographs comparing the two museums had disclosed a disturbingly similar zigzag shape. The director of the NMA, Dawn Casey, maintained that the design was "brilliant," and she downplayed the similarity of the roof designs. The NMA was the first museum devoted exclusively to the country's social history and would house five permanent exhibitions—Nation, Horizons, Eternity,

Tangled Destinies, and the First Australians Gallery. For its opening the NMA featured the temporary blockbuster exhibit "Gold and Civilisation."

On February 15, Singapore opened a new war museum, which chronicled the experiences of the people held at the Changi prison camp in that city during the Japanese World War II occupation. The museum courtyard featured a replica of a chapel built by prisoners of war. After 10 years of planning, Ronald S. Lauder, chairman of Estée Lauder International, opened the Neue Galerie in New York City in November. The museum was devoted exclusively to German and Austrian fine and decorative arts.

In Johannesburg, S.Af., the Apartheid Museum opened in November. The privately financed museum was the first of several planned exhibits to examine the history of apartheid. Upon entering the new museum all visitors were arbitrarily assigned a racial classification ("white" or "nonwhite") and then directed down separate hallways with appropriate "white" and "nonwhite" displays before being allowed to mingle in the final rooms.

Beginning on January 1 the M.H. de Young Memorial Museum in San Francisco's Golden Gate Park, which featured collections of American, African, and Oceanic art, among other objets d'art, shuttered its doors. A new museum—expected to open on the site in the spring of 2005—would showcase the design of Swiss architects Jacques Herzog and Pierre de Meuron. (*See* BIOGRAPHIES.)

A few institutions made significant additions to their structures, notably the British Museum in London, where architect Sir Norman Foster redesigned the central courtyard, which opened in December 2000. In May 2001 the museum unveiled a priceless 17th-century Indian jewel collection that had been looted by Iraq from Kuwait during the Persian Gulf War but later returned. The collection—many of the pieces had never before been seen in the West—was on loan from the Kuwaiti government. Kuwait was rebuilding its museum, which Iraq had burned to the ground during the war. In Wisconsin the Milwaukee Art Museum on October 11 unveiled its gigantic $75 million movable sunshade, designed by Spanish architect Santiago Calatrava. (*See* ARCHITECTURE.)

A number of museums saw changes in directorship. The Victoria and Albert (V&A) Museum, London, announced in February that Mark Jones would succeed Alan Borg. Jones had spent 15 years at the British Museum before becoming founding director of the new National Museum in Edinburgh. On May 2, the day after starting his new job, Jones announced that the V&A would take the lead in abolishing all entrance fees, beginning in November. The Natural History Museum and the Imperial War Museum would be the only top London museums to continue to charge admission.

Following the announcement of Smithsonian Institution secretary Lawrence M. Small's "new strategic direction for science," Robert Fri, director of the National Museum of Natural History, Washington, D.C., tendered his resignation. Fri cited his lack of enthusiasm for the new personnel structure, which would have left control of the scientists to J. Dennis O'Connor, the undersecretary for science. Small had also raised the ire of Smithsonian officials, curators there and at other museums, and Washington lawmakers when he announced the closure of the Smithsonian's wildlife conservation centre in Virginia; he later retracted that decision. Spencer Crew, the director of the Smithsonian Institution's National Museum of American History, Washington, D.C., also departed.

In Venezuela, Pres. Hugo Chávez Frías purged the leadership at 36 government cultural institutions in his effort to rid the country of a "rancid oligarchy." Art critic Sofía Imber, the founding director in 1971 of the Caracas Museum of Contemporary Art (which was later given her name), was one of the most prominent figures to have been removed.

In a surprise move David A. Ross, director of the San Francisco Museum of Modern Art, announced his resignation after three years. During his tenure he had boosted membership from 24,000 to 44,000 and had spent $140 million to enhance the museum's collection. Henri Loyrette, head of the Orsay Museum in Paris, was named the new director of the Louvre. (*See* BIOGRAPHIES.)

The Internet continued to play a major role in museums. The Solomon R. Guggenheim Foundation launched Guggenheim.com, a premium arts centre site, and the U.S. federal government awarded $1.4 million to 6 of 32 applicants—the Exploratorium in San Francisco; the Illinois State Museum Society; the Lowell Observatory, Flagstaff, Ariz.; the North Carolina Zoological Society, Asheboro; the Skyscraper Museum, New York City; and the Wildlife Conservation Society/Bronx Zoo, New York City—in the second year of its Museums Online grant program. (KAREN J. SPARKS)

Visitors at the National Museum of Emerging Science and Innovation in Tokyo walk past a new exhibit called GEO-COSMOS, a huge sphere equipped with 951,040 light-emitting diodes that can display, for instance, real-time weather conditions and carbon monoxide density around the world.

Toru Yamanaka/AFP Worldwide

Life Sciences

Scientists in 2001 announced the COMPLETE SEQUENCING of the RICE GENOME and reported INSIGHTS into the genetics of congenital HEARING AND VISION impairments. The value of a primary CONSERVATION strategy was challenged by results of a study of a PANDA reserve in China. A new look at filamentous structures in DINOSAUR fossils fueled debate over the origin of bird FEATHERS.

ZOOLOGY

Zoological researchers in 2001 continued to assess the effectiveness of the protection mechanisms that animals use against predators. Such knowledge was fundamental to the understanding of certain aspects of population dynamics—the ways in which the size and composition of a population change over time and the factors that influence those changes. A basic principle of Batesian mimicry is that an edible prey species, the mimic, is afforded some level of protection from predators when it closely resembles a venomous or distasteful species, the model. By definition such protection should be less effective or absent in regions where the mimic, but not the model, is present. David W. Pfennig and William R. Harcombe of the University of North Carolina at Chapel Hill and Karin S. Pfennig of the University of Texas at Austin conducted field experiments to test whether the close likeness between nonvenomous king snakes and venomous coral snakes should be regarded as a case of Batesian mimicry.

The investigators used three-coloured snake-shaped replicas made of plasticine (a nontoxic modeling substance) that duplicated the conspicuous red, black, and yellow-to-white ringed pattern of either scarlet king snakes (*Lampropeltis triangulum elapsoides*) or Sonoran mountain king snakes (*L. pyromelana*). The patterns of these nonvenomous snakes are similar to the ringed patterns of the eastern coral snake (*Micrurus fulvius*) and western, or Arizona, coral snake (*Micruroides euryxanthus*), respectively. Regional predators avoid the venomous coral snakes, which are presumed to be the models that the king snakes mimic. The investigators placed their king snake replicas at a series of eastern sites in North Carolina and South Carolina and at western sites in Arizona in tests to determine whether predators would avoid them. Two other kinds of snake replicas, one plain brown and one with conspicuous longitudinal stripes, were placed within 2 m (6.6 ft) of the ringed replicas as controls. Tests were conducted using 480 replicas at 16 eastern sites where scarlet king snakes occurred—at 8 sites where they occupied the same range as coral snakes and at 8 sites where they were outside the coral snake's range. In Arizona 720 replicas were used at 14 sites where king snakes and coral snakes occurred together and at 10 sites where only king snakes occurred. The replicas were removed from the eastern sites after four weeks and from the western sites after two weeks.

Studies of bite and gouge marks left in the replicas revealed that predators had attacked the king snake replicas significantly more often at sites outside the coral snakes' ranges than at sites where king snakes and coral snakes co-existed. Furthermore, outside the coral snakes' ranges, the three types of replicas were attacked indiscriminately, whereas in the coral snakes' ranges, king snake replicas were attacked significantly less often than the others. The results supported the premise of Batesian mimicry that the benefit of being a mimic depends on the model's being present in the same area.

A universal challenge in investigations of the demography and population dynamics of animals has been to deter-

Field experiments reported during the year used replicas of venomous coral snakes and nonvenomous king snakes to study Batesian mimicry. A coral snake (left) and a king snake (right) are shown below.

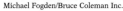
Michael Fogden/Bruce Coleman Inc.

mine how different factors influence the sometimes large fluctuations in population size that are observed in some species over time. Distinctive regulators of population size include those that depend on population density (the population size in a given area) and those, resulting from environmental effects, that are independent of density. To determine the relative influence of various factors on population dynamics, Tim Coulson of the Zoological Society of London and colleagues studied the effects of age, sex, density, and winter weather over more than a decade on fluctuations in the population of Soay sheep (*Ovis aries*) on the island of Hirta, northwest of Scotland. One objective was to quantify how interactions between different variables affected the population fluctuations. Since the 1950s the Soay sheep population has varied in size from fewer than 600 individuals to more than 2,000, with the proportion of various sex and age categories (e.g., numbers of male and female lambs, prime adults, and old adults) varying independently of population density.

The severity of winter weather can differentially affect survivorship in the various age and sex categories; through such interaction with the population demography, it can increase or decrease the total size of the population. For example, during periods of high population density, lambs and old females were observed to fare worse at survival than female yearlings and prime adults. On the other hand, in response to winter weather, survival rates for lambs and males were negatively affected by bad weather throughout the winter, whereas those for yearlings and prime adult females were negatively affected primarily by heavier rainfall at the end of winter. Thus, the dynamics of a population of large mammals can take dramatically different courses depending on differences in the age structure and sex-ratio pattern of the population and in the weather conditions that it experiences. The investigators concluded that management and conservation models that rely on predictions of population size must incorporate the effects of demographic variations and their interaction with climate.

Although all species respond to natural threats to individuals through either evolution or extinction, the current decline in biodiversity observed in terrestrial, freshwater, and marine habitats as a consequence of human activities

was causing alarm on a global scale. Understanding the natural processes that regulate species diversity and abundance was seen as an important step toward developing conservation and management approaches that address the human-based causes of species loss. David R. Bellwood and Terry P. Hughes of James Cook University, Townsville, Australia, studied the distribution patterns of species of fish and corals in Indo-Pacific waters to determine what factors influence the variation in species composition in coral reefs, which are highly diverse habitats. Of four major variables that were examined because of their potential to explain such variation, the available area of shallow-water habitat was found to be the most influential. Two other variables, latitude and longitude, were of minor significance in explaining the species diversity of fish and corals. The fourth variable, reef type, was found to be of little importance. The investigators concluded that suitable habitat had to be protected on a regional scale if the diversity of coral reef assemblages was to remain intact in the Indo-Australian archipelago—a principle that presumably would be applicable globally.

Setting aside protected areas for wildlife is traditionally accepted as a primary conservation strategy to guard against the detrimental effects of human activity. Jianguo Liu of Michigan State University and colleagues, however, challenged the effectiveness of the approach at the Wolong Nature Reserve for giant pandas (*Ailuropoda melanoleuca*) in Sichuan province, China. The investigators used Landsat and declassified spy-satellite data collected before and after establishment (1975) of the 200,000-ha (500,000-ac) reserve to assess the rates of change in giant panda habitat. In addition to forest cover, the slope of the terrain and elevation are also important habitat variables that affect pandas. Two key observations were made in the analysis of habitat changes from 1965 to 1997. First, panda habitat within the reserve continued to decrease in quality and quantity and became even more fragmented after 1975. Second, the habitat areas most severely affected were those deemed to be of high quality for pandas. The direct cause of the ecological degradation was attributed to the presence and rapid increase in numbers of humans living within the reserve, most of whom were minority ethnic groups that were exempt from China's one-

child-per-family policy. A variety of socioeconomic activities, including tourism, collection of wood for fuel, and road construction all contributed to habitat loss. One conclusion of the study was that the development of effective conservation policies for protected lands required the integration of ecological principles with human demography, behaviour, and socioeconomics.

Further insights into the ancestry of humans were provided during the year through the use of molecular techniques. Li Jin of Fudan University, Shanghai, and the University of Texas at Houston and colleagues sampled genetic material from 163 populations of living humans in 13 geographic regions in Asia, ranging from India to Siberia, to test competing hypotheses of the origin of modern humans. The so-called out-of-Africa hypothesis maintained that the ancestors of present-day humans originated in Africa approximately 100,000 years ago and totally replaced all other hominids, such as Neanderthals (an early form of *Homo sapiens*), during their dispersal to other regions. The alternative view was that some genetic mixing occurred between dispersing Africans and other hominids, such as Peking man and Java man (*H. erectus*), in Asia. The investigators tested for genetic markers on the Y chromosome of more than 12,000 human males to determine if all carried one of three chromosome polymorphisms (distinct genetic variations) characteristic of an African origin. Without exception, all of the individuals sampled had genetic markers of African derivation; this supported the hypothesis that hominids dispersing onto the Asian continent from Africa displaced all other hominids already present. (*See also* ANTHROPOLOGY AND ARCHAEOLOGY: *Physical Anthropology*.)

(J. WHITFIELD GIBBONS)

BOTANY

Among milestones in plant science that became widely acknowledged in 2001 was the mapping of the genomes of two plants. The entire DNA blueprint of thale cress (*Arabidopsis thaliana*), a weed related to cabbage and mustard and long a favourite laboratory organism in plant research, was published at the end of 2000. The sequencing of its more than 115 million pairs of chemical bases, the molecular building blocks of DNA and the basis of the genetic code, was the culmination of a six-year, $70 million project involving 300 scientists worldwide. The achievement, the first for a plant genome, promised new types of genetically modified crop plants and a better understanding of the process of evolution.

Early in 2001 scientists announced completion of the sequence of the larger genome of the rice plant (*Oryza sativa*), which comprises 430 million base pairs representing some 50,000 genes. It was anticipated that, as the functions of many of these genes were worked out, the information could lead to significant improvements in the major cereal crops, which are all closely related to rice. Unraveling of the rice genome by the Swiss agribusiness firm Syngenta International AG and the American firm Myriad Genetics, Inc., beat the efforts of a publicly funded international team to map the same genome. The two companies indicated that they would make the rice genome data publicly available through collaboration agreements.

Research into the evolution of plants also made great progress during the year. The Deep Green project, which had been established to investigate the ancestry of green land plants, was completed after five years' work involving more than 200 scientists worldwide. Data were integrated from morphology, biochemistry, and fossil sources to construct the most complete "tree of life" for any group of living things on Earth. Results indicated that green algae and land plants form the plant kingdom, clearly separated from other algae such as red algae, brown algae, diatoms, and dinoflagellates. It was also revealed that the first plants to grow on land were members of a class of freshwater green algae called Charophyceae; this overturned the idea that seawater algae spearheaded the land-plant invasion. Another surprise from the project was that the Charophyceae are the ancestors of all green land plants now alive. Although some other plant groups established themselves on land, they later died out for reasons not yet understood. In the animal kingdom, by contrast, many different groups made the jump from water to land successfully.

Another mystery of plant evolution came one step closer to being understood—the sudden appearance of flowering plants around 130 million years ago. Biologists at the University of California, San Diego, led by Martin Yanofsky, converted leaves of *Arabidopsis* plants into petals by activating five different genes involved in the formation of flower organs lying dormant in

© James Manhart

An intriguing study of the flower movements of the Arctic gentian (Gentiana algida) *appeared in 2001.*

leaves. This achievement indicated that flowers evolved from modified leaves. It also could lead to the development of interesting genetically modified plants, such as ornamental flowering varieties that have colourful petals growing along their stems.

One of the most significant genetic-engineering breakthroughs of the year was the creation of a tomato plant that thrives in salty water, even seawater. A gene for salt tolerance, discovered in *Arabidopsis* in the late 1990s by plant biologists at the University of California, Davis, and the University of Toronto, was introduced into tomato plants. The gene protects the plants from salt damage by coding for a protein that pumps salt into sealed compartments inside leaf cells; the tomato fruit produced was claimed to have no salty taste. Salty water blights 40% of the world's irrigated land, and engineering salt tolerance into crops could exploit huge tracts of this

poisoned land. In addition, the modified tomato plants soaked up so much salt that they could be used to help clean up salty water supplies. Field trials were needed to make sure that the gene would not cross to other plants to create salt-tolerant weeds.

The possibility of unintentional transfer of genes from genetically modified crops was spotlighted in November when researchers from the University of California, Berkeley, reported detection of transgenic DNA in native maize (corn) from remote regions of Mexico, despite a ban in that country on planting genetically modified maize since 1998. Native maize and other ancestors of crop plants were considered a vital genetic resource for crop-breeding programs, and their contamination with foreign genes could threaten global food security.

Many plant roots form partnerships with fungi that live in the soil. Typically the fungi supply phosphorus from the soil to the plant in exchange for carbohydrates and other nutrients. John Klironomos and Miranda Hart of the University of Guelph, Ont., revealed that the roots of the eastern white pine (*Pinus strobus*) support a carnivorous fungus that kills and devours small insects in the soil. Radioactively labeled nitrogen was used to track nutrients as they were absorbed from the animal bodies into the fungus, which then passed them into the tree. Klironomos speculated that, because similar root fungi are nearly ubiquitous among trees, the relationship could be very common and that scientists might have to rethink their ideas about how woodland ecosystems work.

In a rare example of research on flower movements, Michael Bynum of the University of Wyoming and William Smith of Wake Forest University, Winston-Salem, N.C., made a fascinating study of the flowers of the Arctic gentian (*Gentiana algida*) at several field sites in Wyoming. The plant blooms in August, the peak month for thunderstorms in the region. As rain approaches, the flower pinches its petal tube shut and reopens after the rain has passed. The investigators determined that these movements protect the pollen and nectar from being ruined by rain, which in turn helps both pollination and seed set. The movements are a response to the drop in air temperature that often precedes a storm.

The importance of biodiversity was highlighted by scientists at the Imperial College of Science, Technology and Medicine, London, and the École Normale Supérieure, Paris. They found that communities of plants are more productive when they consist of "teams" of different species that specialize in roles that are complementary to one another. It may mean that some plants, and therefore their entire ecosystems, grow more poorly when team members become extinct. This finding gave support to conservationists campaigning to preserve natural environments in their totality.

Scientists were heartened when a tree species, *Trochetia parviflora*, thought to have gone extinct in 1863 on the island of Mauritius, was rediscovered. Vincent Florens and Jean-Claude Svathian of the Mauritius Herbarium recognized the tree from old herbarium specimens. The scientists collected cuttings and seeds to try to propagate the species in hopes of boosting the remaining wild population. (PAUL SIMONS)

MOLECULAR BIOLOGY

A Bucket Brigade for Copper. Soluble copper—copper in its +2 oxidation state [written Cu(II)]—is an effective and nonspecific catalyst of oxidation. As such, it can facilitate the oxidation of many biologically essential molecules such as ascorbic acid, glutathione, and polyunsaturated lipids and thereby prevent them from participating in vital reactions. For this reason, free Cu(II) cannot be tolerated by living cells and is considered a poison. Nevertheless, Cu(II) is found at the active sites of several enzymes and is essential for their catalytic functions. One such enzyme present in cells is superoxide dismutase, a protein that contains both Cu(II) and zinc at its active site. The enzyme catalyzes the elimination of the dangerously reactive superoxide radical produced as a by-product of respiration and thus serves as a defense against oxygen toxicity. Without such defense, aerobic life would not be sustainable.

One intriguing question that life scientists had posed about superoxide dismutase was how Cu(II) is delivered to the enzyme during its synthesis in the cell without harming the cell. In 1997 a team of researchers from three U.S. universities reported that they had discovered part of the answer. Working with the yeast *Saccharomyces cerevisiae*, they found a protein that serves to deliver Cu(II) specifically to the active site of newly synthesized superoxide dismutase. They named it copper chaperone for superoxide dismutase (CCS). In 2001 the structure of CCS bound to superoxide dismutase was determined by X-ray crystallography, and that structure illuminated how CCS works. CCS contains two distinct structural parts, or domains. One domain has the same structure as a protein called Atx1, which was known to pick up Cu(II) ions from a transmembrane Cu(II) transporter, a protein embedded in the cell membrane that brings Cu(II) into the cell. The second domain of CCS is strikingly similar in structure to one-half of the mature form of superoxide dismutase, which is a homodimer, a molecule made of two identical subunits (monomers).

The scenario that emerged from the most recent findings resembles a bucket brigade for passing Cu(II) ions from the outside of the cell to the superoxide dismutase without "spilling" them—i.e., without ever allowing the Cu(II) the freedom to catalyze unwanted oxidations. First, a Cu(II) ion outside the cell is bound by the transmembrane transporter, which moves it to the inside of the cell. Next, using its Atx1-like domain, CCS picks up the Cu(II) from the transporter and diffuses with it to a newly synthesized superoxide dismutase monomer, to which, using its superoxide dismutase domain, CCS then transiently binds and delivers the Cu(II). After receiving the Cu(II), the superoxide dismutase monomer binds with a second monomer (dimerizes) to form the stable and active mature enzyme.

An analog of the yeast CCS was found in human cells, an indication that this type of Cu(II) delivery system is likely widespread in living species. If CCS is needed to deliver Cu(II) to superoxide dismutase in the cell, then a mutant organism that lacks functional CCS should also lack superoxide dismutase activity. This was demonstrated to be the case in mice. Importantly, the mutant mice were normal with respect to the activities of other Cu(II)-containing enzymes. This was evidence for the existence of additional chaperones for delivering Cu(II) to other copper-containing enzymes. In 2001 these other chaperones were under investigation.

Progress in DNA Vaccines. Immunization of humans and other animals is traditionally accomplished by injecting a heat-killed bacterium or virus, or a component protein of it. The administered proteins are recognized as foreign by cells of the immune system, which respond by producing antibodies that circulate in the blood plasma and bind to the foreign proteins with great specificity and affinity. If the protein is from the surface of a bacterium or virus, the elicited antibody binds to and inactivates the bacterium or virus. To partially circumvent this defense, pathogens frequently mutate their surface proteins so that antibodies elicited against one variety cannot recognize and bind to a future variety.

Another aspect of immunity involves the generation of specialized white blood cells, called T cells, that can recognize foreign proteins, or parts of them, displayed on the surface of cells and then kill those cells. Many virus-infected cells, within which virus proteins are being made for the assembly of new virus particles, will display fragments of those proteins on their surface. The killing of these infected cells by T cells sensitized to the foreign proteins serves to abort the infection. A problem with conventional heat-killed or protein-based vaccines, however, is that they do not cause foreign proteins to display on cell surfaces and thus do not elicit sensitized T cells.

A relatively new approach to vaccines has focused on preparations of foreign DNA rather than foreign protein. The DNA is in the form of small circular molecules, called plasmids, that can be taken into cells and cause the cells to produce those proteins encoded by the plasmid. One might anticipate that a plasmid encoding a foreign protein or protein fragment would elicit both specific soluble antibodies and sensitized T cells and thus give rise to effective and long-lasting immunity.

This approach was first tested in chickens, mice, and other animals, where it was found to work spectacularly well even against pathogens hard to target by traditional means. Unfortunately, when tested in humans, DNA vaccines proved disappointing in that much higher doses of the plasmid DNA were found to be required than had been anticipated from the prior studies with animals. These high doses would make the DNA vaccines prohibitively expensive.

Because an essential step in the immune response occurs in lymphoid tissue, it seemed possible that the response to DNA vaccines could be increased if they were administered directly into lymph nodes, rather than into the skin or muscle tissue. During the year Thomas M. Kündig of Zürich (Switz.) University Hospital and his associates tried this approach and reported a 100–1,000-fold gain in response after injecting the vaccine into the peripheral lymph nodes of mice. If tests in humans proved successful, medical science could see the development of DNA vaccines vastly superior to the classic vaccines.

An Antimicrobial Peptide. All multicellular organisms have evolved a constellation of natural defenses to ward off infection from myriad disease-causing agents. One such defense is the production of peptides (molecules structurally like proteins but smaller) with antimicrobial properties. Families of cationic, cystine-rich antimicrobial peptides are found in plants (thionins and plant defensins), insects (heliomycin, thanatin, and insect defensins), mollusks (mytilin and myticin), and mammals (protegrins and alpha and beta defensins).

During the year Tomas Ganz and co-workers at the Harbor-UCLA Medical Center, Torrance, Calif., reported the isolation of a defensin-type antimicro-

bial peptide from human urine and named it hepcidin because it is made in the liver. It is apparently common to vertebrates because the DNA sequence coding for hepcidin was identified in pigs, rats, and flounder. Hepcidin is antifungal as well as antibacterial, and it also inhibits the germination of fungal spores. In keeping with a defensive function, the synthesis of hepcidin in the liver is stimulated by specific molecules, called lipopolysaccharides, present on the surface of bacteria. The peptide could someday prove useful as an antibiotic or antifungal agent.

(IRWIN FRIDOVICH)

Genetics of the Senses. Humans, like all other species on Earth, have myriad systems for acquiring information about their surroundings. For humans and other mammals, these systems include the senses of sight, hearing, touch, smell, and taste. Humans and many other animals also have a sense of balance, which enables them to move and orient their bodies with reference to Earth's gravitational field. Some species, although not necessarily humans, even have a sense of direction based on the presence of tiny magnetic deposits in their bodies, which allows them to sense Earth's magnetic field.

Although many species share a given sense, the exact range of that sense can vary between species according to need. For example, whereas the typical frequency range of human hearing is 20–20,000 Hz, dogs can hear sounds at much higher frequencies, and whales and elephants can hear sounds at much lower frequencies. Similarly, human vision responds to colours of light that range from 400 nm (nanometres; violet) to 700 nm (red), the so-called visible wavelengths. Bees and other pollinating insects, by contrast, can see into the ultraviolet range.

Research by a number of teams has begun to reveal the genetics underlying the human senses, helping to explain how these complex systems work and enabling better diagnosis and intervention for those with genetic impairments of these systems. Results and implications of this effort were summarized in several papers published during the year. Some highlights regarding hearing and vision are discussed below, as well as legal and ethical dilemmas that have surfaced as a consequence.

Congenital Hearing Loss. Optimal human hearing requires not only proper structure and function of the outer, middle, and inner ears but also proper reception and interpretation of the

electrical signals sent along the auditory nerve to the brain. Compromise at any level, due to gene defects or other causes, can result in impaired hearing. At least one in 10 adults aged 65 years or older experiences significant hearing loss, and about one in every 1,000 infants demonstrates profound congenital hearing loss.

Most hearing loss, especially among older adults, is not considered genetic in origin but is typically the result of accumulated damage from trauma or infection. On the other hand, a majority of the cases of isolated hearing loss—hearing loss unaccompanied by other symptoms (such as blindness)—seen in young infants are genetic. Recent studies show that hearing loss in these infants is the result of mutations in one or more of an extraordinary number of different genes. Identification of the relevant genes and mutations has given powerful insight into the broad range of gene products that must function together to achieve normal hearing. They include intracellular motor proteins, ion channels and pumps, transcription factors that regulate the expression of other genes, and extracellular matrix proteins that help to form the tectorial membrane of the inner ear. More will likely be identified in the years to come. Perhaps the mutated genes seen most often in these patients, however, are those that code for the connexins. Connexins are gap junction proteins—proteins spanning the cell membrane that control the passage of small molecules directly from the interior of one cell to that of another. These gap junction proteins contribute to the communication between supporting, nonsensory cells of the inner ear. Mutations in the gene CX26, which codes for the protein connexin 26, account for almost half of all cases of isolated congenital deafness in Caucasian populations.

In 2001 knowledge of the identities and functions of these genes and their products was leading to improved early diagnosis, which in turn was offering improved options for intervention, including cochlear implants. Early diagnosis followed by prompt intervention is important because the auditory regions of the brains of infants born with profound hearing loss will not develop properly unless hearing is restored quickly. Partly in recognition of this urgency, congenital hearing loss joined the list of other, mostly metabolic, impairments for which newborn screening procedures were mandated in some U.S. states and other parts of the world.

Colour Blindness. Like hearing, human vision involves the function and interaction of a multitude of gene products that together make up the sensing organ—the eye—as well as the proper transmission, reception, and interpretation of the electrical signals sent by the eye to the appropriate regions of the brain. Also like hearing, visual impairment is extremely common and complex, involving the interplay of genetic and environmental influences, including normal processes of aging. The underlying cause of late adult-onset farsightedness, for example, is generally considered to be a natural loss of flexibility of the lens with age. Late adult-onset cataracts are believed to result from progressive processes that alter the chemical properties of the lens.

In contrast, hereditary loss of vision generally appears much earlier in life (childhood to early adulthood) and can be either accompanied by other symptoms (syndromic) or isolated. Examples range from albinism, a syndrome that includes severe visual impairment, to such isolated conditions as congenital glaucoma, progressive retinitis pigmentosa, and myopia (nearsightedness). Perhaps one of the best understood of the isolated hereditary causes of vision loss is colour blindness, a fairly common congenital inability to see or distinguish specific colours.

Black-and-white vision is mediated by rhodopsin, a protein located in specialized cells, called rods, in the retina at the back of each eye. Three independent but related proteins, expressed individually in the cone cells of the retina, are responsible for normal human trichromatic colour vision. The gene coding for the protein most sensitive to blue light is located on chromosome 7, whereas the genes coding for the red-sensitive and green-sensitive proteins are both located on the X chromosome. This physical proximity, coupled with a close resemblance in the sequences of the red and green genes, results in a high frequency of unequal recombination events (regrouping of maternal and paternal genes during the formation of sex cells) involving these genes. This, in turn, can lead to either deletion or duplication of one or both genes on the resulting chromosomes. Because the chromosome involved is the X, females who inherit a deleted gene on one X chromosome will most likely carry a compensating normal copy on their other X chromosome, and so they will not experience visual impairment. In contrast, males, who carry only one X (and one Y) chromosome, will have no compensating copy, and so they will experience a form of colour blindness corresponding to the specific gene deletion inherited—either red or green. Indeed, in some studies close to 8% of all males demonstrated some form of colour blindness, generally characterized as red-green colour confusion.

Although treatments for colour blindness were still lacking, studies to elucidate its genetic basis were leading to improved diagnosis and prognosis. In addition, the results of those studies were helping scientists and physicians gain a better understanding of the normal functioning of the human eye and thus of other, in some cases more debilitating, forms of visual impairment.

Legal and Ethical Issues. The recent gains in understanding the genetic basis of sensory impairments in humans have raised moral and legal questions, in large part because of the possibilities presented for prenatal diagnosis of these impairments and for their early diagnosis and intervention after birth. Issues that must be considered include, for example, whether the option of terminating a pregnancy should be offered to "hearing" parents of a child who will be born deaf or to deaf parents of a child who will be born "hearing." Similarly, mandated newborn screening for profound hearing impairment, with the clear intent to encourage early intervention, has been taken by some members of the deaf community as a threat to the continued existence of the well-established deaf language and culture. Clearly, these issues emerge from differing opinions of what is a disease and what is simply a trait. In 2001 such dilemmas over sensory impairment remained but the tip of the iceberg with regard to human genetics. How individuals and societies handled these specific questions would set a precedent for the many similar problems that lay ahead.

(JUDITH L. FRIDOVICH-KEIL)

PALEONTOLOGY

The most primitive plants in the fossil record lack both seeds and leaves. In 2001 a study of the main lineages of living land plants, which considered both genetic and morphological features, concluded that horsetails and ferns belong to a monophyletic group (group with a single common ancestor) that includes the closest living relatives to modern seed-bearing plants. This finding refuted the prevailing view that horsetails and ferns, both of which are spore-bearing plants, represent transitional evolutionary steps from which seed plants eventually were derived. A second plant study suggested that the origin of leaves was caused by falling levels of carbon dioxide in the atmosphere during the Devonian Period (417 million to 354 million years ago), which drove plants to evolve structures for gas exchange and photosynthesis that were more efficient than simple green stems.

For many years paleontologists had assumed that the complex tribosphenic molars typical of marsupial and placental mammals had a single origin in some fossil mammal group from one of the northern continents. A U.S.-Polish study published during the year suggested that fossil tribosphenic mammals recently discovered from Gondwana, the ancient landmass that included all of the present southern continents and India, might have had a separate origin from their northern counterparts more than 100 million years ago. The investigators in the study speculated that this southern lineage gave rise to the monotremes, represented today by the egg-laying platypus and echidna, while the northern lineage produced all other modern mammals, both marsupials and placentals.

Madagascar continued to yield fossils of unusual new Cretaceous dinosaurs. One report described a large sauropod belonging to the Titanosauria, the only group of sauropods that survived until the end of the Cretaceous Period, 65 million years ago. While most titanosaur material was very fragmentary, the new Madagascar genus, *Rapetosaurus*, was the most complete titanosaur skeleton found to date. A phylogenetic study that included this specimen confirmed that titanosaurs were closely related to brachiosaurs. Another new titanosaur, *Paralititan*, was discovered in Egypt's Bahariya Formation of the Late Cretaceous (99 million to 65 million years ago). With a length of nearly 1.7 m (5.6 ft), its humerus (upper forelimb bone) was the largest of any known Cretaceous sauropod. *Paralititan* was the first tetrapod reported from the Bahariya Formation since 1935.

A second new dinosaur from Madagascar, *Masiakasaurus*, was shown to belong to the unusual group of Gondwana theropods called abelisauroids. Measuring 1.8 m (5.9 ft) long, it was unique in being the only theropod known with heterodont dentition (different teeth specialized for different functions). Whereas other theropods (and most other dinosaurs) were homodont (all teeth similar in shape), *Masiakasaurus* had distinctly differently shaped teeth in the lower jaw.

A report by Chinese and American paleontologists revisited the controversial topic of the origin of feathers. Previous studies had suggested that some filamentous covering structures observed in the fossils of several theropod dinosaurs represent primitive feathers. Other analyses, however, had disputed the relationship between these structures and feathers. Moreover, two genera that had been described as having true feathers (*Caudipteryx* and *Protarchaeopteryx*) may have been flightless birds rather than theropods. The new study examined the filamentous covering structures in fossils of *Sinornithosaurus*, a basal dromaeosaurid dinosaur first described in 1999. The investigators concluded that the structures are composed of multiple filaments and show types of branching structure that are unique to bird feathers. If confirmed, this finding would substantiate the theropod origin of bird feathers.

A recent reexamination of skulls of the ornithomimids *Gallimimus* and *Ornithomimus* showed that these toothless dinosaurs may have had keratinized beaks—i.e., beaks made of the fibrous protein keratin, the chemical basis of horny tissue. These animals appear to have had a comblike keratinized plate in the mouth, somewhat similar to the jaw comb of a duck. The researchers involved in the study speculated that the animals may have used their beaks to filter small invertebrates from the water and sediment—certainly a new idea about the diets of toothless theropods.

A study combining medical scanning techniques and engineering analytic methodology analyzed the bite of the well-known theropod dinosaur *Allosaurus* of the Late Jurassic (159 million to 144 million years ago). While conventional wisdom assigned *Allosaurus* a very powerful bite, this research concluded that its bite force was quite low, similar to that of smaller living carnivorous mammals such as wolves and leopards and a sixth of the bite force calculated for *Tyrannosaurus*.

The investigators suggested that, because of its comparatively weak bite, *Allosaurus* had to be discriminating in how and where it attacked its prey.

Late Cretaceous sediments in Mongolia yielded *Apsaravis*, a new fossil bird. According to a description published during the year, the specimen was one of the best ever found of a group of

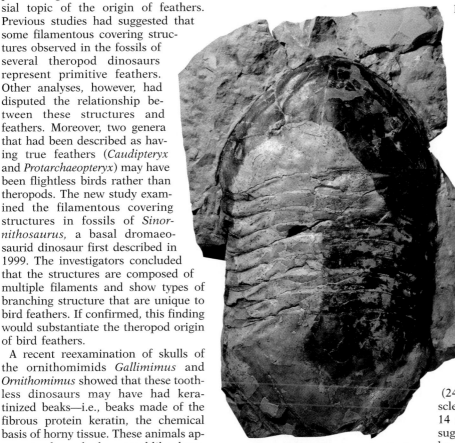

Canadian paleontologists unearthed the world's largest recorded trilobite fossil in late 2000.

Manitoba Museum of Man and Nature

birds known as ornithurines. The new genus appeared to fill an important gap in avian evolution. *Apsaravis* also indicated that the Mesozoic relatives of modern birds were not restricted to nearshore and marine environments, as previously speculated, and it provided new insight into the evolution of flight following its appearance.

A mass of juvenile bird bones reported from the Early Cretaceous of Spain (144 million to 99 million years ago) appeared to represent a regurgitated pellet. The mass contained bones from four individuals and provided the first positive evidence that Mesozoic birds

were prey for other animals. Whereas the predator may have been an early mammal, lizard, crocodile, pterosaur, theropod dinosaur, or another bird, mammals and crocodiles typically do not regurgitate bones in pellets, and the lizards and birds found at the same site appeared too small to have been the predators. That means that either a nonavian theropod dinosaur or a pterosaur most likely produced the pellet.

In October 2000 a group of Canadian invertebrate paleontologists reported finding the world's largest recorded trilobite in rocks of Late Ordovician age (458 million to 443 million years ago) near Manitoba. At more than 70 cm (28 in) long, the specimen was 70% larger than the previous record-sized trilobite. Another invertebrate study addressed the origin of modern corals. The primary reef-forming corals belong to the order Scleractinia, the stony corals. It had been postulated that the scleractinians may have evolved from a group of Paleozoic corals called rugosids (rugose corals). One problem with the theory was that the rugosids disappear from the fossil record at the end of the Permian Period (248 million years ago), whereas the scleractinians do not appear until some 14 million years later. The new study suggested that skeletons in corals may be ephemeral—that is, they are produced only when ocean chemistry is favourable for the precipitation of calcium carbonate. This idea would account for the gap in fossil evidence for the origin of modern corals from Paleozoic forms if conditions in the Early Triassic were unfavourable for skeleton formation.

The Herefordshire Lagerstätte is a Silurian deposit in England of about 425 million years in age that has yielded marine invertebrate fossils in exceptional three-dimensional detail. A wormlike mollusk from this collection was described during the year as a plated aplacophoran. The Aplacophora, along with the chitons, are considered to be the most primitive living mollusks, but up until this discovery they had been unknown from the fossil record.   (WILLIAM R. HAMMER)

Literature

V.S. NAIPAUL netted the Nobel, while Peter Carey took his second BOOKER. PHILIP ROTH and J.G. BALLARD mused on the end of literature. Novelists in many countries wrote about the PAST, while SOCIAL and POLITICAL themes attracted the talents of others. OBSCENITIES, eroticism, and PROMISCUITY also crept into literary works.

ENGLISH

United Kingdom. The Booker Prize chairman of judges, Lord Kenneth Baker, reported that the many entries he had read during 2001 proved that the novel was thriving and keeping abreast of developments within British life. Displacement, often depicted through the uprooted feelings of émigrés or refugees, was a strong presence in many novels considered by the panel. Though historical themes remained popular, World War I was less in evidence as a subject. Instead, writers moved on to World War II and the years leading up to and spanning the 1970s, decades that, though conjuring up a sense of difference, were within living memory. Lord Baker also praised many of the year's novelists for their vivid and unsentimental treatment of childhood. Stories were told from the point of view of children with unusual and forceful personalities, and romanticization was successfully avoided, as evidenced in Philip Pullman's *The Amber Spyglass* (2000), which narrowly missed the Booker shortlist but marked the first time that a children's book read widely by adults had made the long list.

The six titles short-listed included Rachel Seiffert's assured literary debut, *The Dark Room*, a Holocaust story from the German perspective that *The Observer* newspaper praised as a "simply phrased and understated" book that "shatters prejudices"; Andrew Miller's *Oxygen*, an intricate story about a Hungarian writer and his play of the same name, which was tipped as third favourite to win; David Mitchell's fast-paced Postmodern *number9dream*, an ambitious and complex tour de force about a young man's search for his father in a brash futuristic Tokyo; Ali Smith's *Hotel World*, which was also nominated for the Orange Prize and featured a cinematic blend of five different female narratives; and Ian McEwan's best-selling *Atonement*, which opens in 1935 and follows its protagonists to the century's end. McEwan's handling of time, memory, and revisionism was hailed as "impressive, engrossing, deep, and surprising" by *The Observer*. McEwan had won the Booker in 1998 for his last novel, *Amsterdam*.

The 6–4 favourite, *True History of the Kelly Gang* (2000) by Australian Peter Carey, was named the prizewinner. Carey, who had also won the Booker for his *Oscar & Lucinda* (1988), declared that he was "wildly excited and exhilarated" and that, as a result of a private bet between him and McEwan, he owed the latter a sumptuous dinner. Lord Baker observed that both Carey's and McEwan's offerings were their best books ever. In Carey's "magnificent story of the early settler days in Australia," he re-created the character of the outlaw Ned Kelly, sometimes described as an Australian Robin Hood. Carey admitted that were Kelly alive today he might not recognize himself in the book's narrator. A piece of literary ventriloquism, the work was inspired by a 56-page letter Kelly once wrote in justification of a bank robbery.

The Orange Prize for Fiction, awarded annually to a woman writer, was also won by an Australian. Kate Grenville's *The Idea of Perfection* (1999) was acclaimed for its touching and humorous depiction of love between two unlikely rustics in a farming community in the outback. It beat, among other strong contenders, Smith's *Hotel World* and Margaret Atwood's odds-on favourite *The Blind Assassin* (2000). A male panel of judges, set up as a research project in tandem with the actual female panel, sharply criticized the shortlist. Novelist Paul Bailey, who admitted that he did not approve of the prize because "sexes should not be separated like this in art," said the women judges had gone "soft when it came to the crunch" and had chosen big names and dull, soppy stories instead of seeking out grittier stories by lesser-known writers. Despite his objections, his male "shadow panel" admitted that Grenville's book, which had hitherto been little known in Great Britain, was the one worthy contender on the shortlist.

The other major literary award, the 2000 Whitbread Book of the Year—in which novels, volumes of poetry, and nonfiction vied for the prize—was won by novelist Matthew Kneale. This was the first time in five years that the award had not been given to a volume of poetry. Kneale's *English Passengers* (2000), a story of an 1857 expedition to Tasmania, was praised by jury chairman Sir Tim Rice for the way several of its characters, both English and Aboriginal, came together "to tell a story which is at times hilarious and at times tragic." A close contender was Lorna Sage's *Bad Blood* (2000), a forthright memoir of teenage pregnancy and family tensions in postwar Britain. The panel of 10 judges had been evenly divided, and Rice had been obliged to cast the deciding vote. Unexpectedly, Sage died 13 days before the award was announced in January. Her agent, Faith Evans, divulged that the book had been the result of 15 years' work.

The David Cohen British Literature Prize for lifetime achievement went to 81-year-old veteran Doris Lessing. The award, administered by the Arts Council, was given every two years to a writer who had significantly contributed to literature. Arts Council Chairman Gerry Robinson characterized Lessing's novels as "an accumulation of excellence—a body of work that has in its unique and determined way shaped the literary landscape." Meanwhile, a previous recipient of the David Cohen Prize, Trinidadian-born V.S. Naipaul, was awarded the Nobel Prize for Literature. (*See* NOBEL PRIZES.) Both he and Lessing published novels (*Half a Life* and *The Sweetest Dream*, respectively) in a year in which reviewers found strong elements of nonfiction.

WORLD LITERARY PRIZES 2001

All prizes are annual and were awarded in 2001 unless otherwise stated

Nobel Prize for Literature

Awarded since 1901; included in the behest of Alfred Nobel, who specified a prize for those who "shall have produced in the field of literature the most outstanding work in an ideal direction." The prizewinners are selected in October by the Swedish Academy and receive the award on December 10 in Stockholm. Prize: a gold medal and an award that varies from year to year; in 2001 the award was SKr 10,000,000 (about $943,000).

V.S. Naipaul (British, born in Trinidad)

International IMPAC Dublin Literary Award

Awarded since 1996; the largest and most international prize of its kind and is open to books written in any language, the Award is a joint initiative of Dublin Corporation, the Municipal Government of Dublin City, and the productivity improvement company IMPAC. It is administered by Dublin Corporation Public Libraries. Prize: £Ir 100,000 (about $110,000) of which 25% goes to the translator. The awards are given at Dublin Castle by the president of Ireland in June.

No Great Mischief by Alistair MacLeod (Canada)

Neustadt International Prize for Literature

Established in 1969 and awarded biennially by the University of Oklahoma and World Literature Today. Novelists, poets, and dramatists are equally eligible. Prize: $50,000, a replica of an eagle feather cast in silver, and a certificate. Last awarded in 2000.

David Malouf (Australia)

Commonwealth Writers Prize

Established in 1987 by the Commonwealth Foundation. In 2001 there was one award of £10,000 (about $14,500) for the best book submitted and an award of £3,000 (about $4,360) for the best first book. In each of the four regions of the Commonwealth two prizes of £1,000 (about $1,450) are awarded: one for the best book and one for the best first book.

Best Book	True History of the Kelly Gang by Peter Carey (Australia)
Best First Book	White Teeth by Zadie Smith (U.K.)
Regional winners—Best Book	
Africa	The Heart of Redness by Zakes Mda (South Africa)
Caribbean & Canada	The Hero's Walk by Anita Rau Badami (Canada)
Eurasia	Super-Cannes by J.G. Ballard (U.K.)
South East Asia & South Pacific	True History of the Kelly Gang by Peter Carey (Australia)

Booker Prize

Established in 1969, sponsored by Booker McConnell Ltd., and administered by the National Book League in the U.K. Awarded to the best full-length novel written by a citizen of the U.K., Ireland, Pakistan, South Africa, or the Commonwealth and published in the U.K. during the 12 months ending September 30. Prize: £20,000 (about $28,500).

True History of the Kelly Gang by Peter Carey (Australia)

Whitbread Book of the Year

Established in 1971. The winners of the Whitbread Book Awards for Poetry, Biography, Novel, and First Novel as well as the Whitbread Children's Book of the Year are eligible for the £25,000 Whitbread Book of the Year prize.

English Passengers by Matthew Kneale (2000 award)

Orange Prize for Fiction

Established in 1996. Awarded to a work of published fiction written by a woman in English and published in the U.K. during the 12 months ending March 31. Prize: £30,000 (about $42,800).

The Idea of Perfection by Kate Grenville

PEN/Faulkner Award

The PEN/Faulkner Foundation each year recognizes the best published works of fiction by contemporary American writers. Named for William Faulkner, the PEN/Faulkner Award was founded by writers in 1980 to honour their peers and is now the largest juried award for fiction in the United States. Prize: $15,000.

The Human Stain by Philip Roth

Pulitzer Prizes in Letters and Drama

Begun in 1917 and awarded by Columbia University, New York City, on the recommendation of the Pulitzer Prize Board for books published in the previous year. Five categories in Letters are honored with prizes: Fiction, Biography, and General Non-Fiction (authors of works in these categories must be American citizens); History (the subject must be American history); and Poetry (for original verse by an American author). The Drama prize is for "a distinguished play by an American author, preferably original in its source and dealing with American life." Prize: $7,500 in each category.

Fiction	The Amazing Adventures of Kavalier & Clay by Michael Chabon
Biography	W.E.B. Du Bois: The Fight for Equality and the American Century, 1919–1963 by David Levering Lewis
Poetry	Different Hours by Stephen Dunn
History	Founding Brothers: The Revolutionary Generation by Joseph J. Ellis
General Non-Fiction	Hirohito and the Making of Modern Japan by Herbert P. Bix
Drama	Proof by David Auburn

National Book Awards

Awarded since 1950 by the National Book Foundation, a consortium of American publishing groups. Categories have varied, beginning with three—Fiction, Nonfiction, and Poetry—swelling to 22 awards in 1983, and returning to four (the initial three plus Young People's Literature) in 2001. Prize: $10,000 and a crystal sculpture.

Fiction The Corrections by Jonathan Franzen
Nonfiction The Noonday Demon: An Atlas of Depression by Andrew Solomon
Poetry Poems Seven: New and Complete Poetry by Alan Dugan

Frost Medal

Awarded annually since 1930 by the Poetry Society of America for distinguished lifetime service to American poetry.

Sonia Sanchez

Governor-General's Literary Awards

Canada's premier literary awards. Prizes are given in 14 categories altogether: Fiction, Poetry, Drama, Translation, Nonfiction, and Children's Literature (Text and Illustration), each in English and French. Established in 1937. Prize: Can$15,000 (about U.S. $9,540).

Fiction (English)	Clara Callan by Richard B. Wright
Fiction (French)	Le Ravissement by Andrée A. Michaud
Poetry (English)	Execution Poems by George Elliott Clarke
Poetry (French)	Des ombres portées by Paul Chanel Malenfant

Griffin Poetry Award

Established in 2001 and administered by the Griffin Trust for Excellence in Poetry. Prize: Can$40,000 (about U.S. $25,300) each for the two awards.

Canadian Award	Men in the Off Hours by Anne Carson
International Award	Glottal Stop: 101 Poems by Paul Celan translated by Heather McHugh and Nikolai Popov (United States)

Büchner Prize

Georg-Büchner Preis. Awarded for a body of literary work in the German language. First awarded in 1923; now administered by the German Academy for Language and Literature. Prize: DM 60,000 (about $27,700).

Friederike Mayröcker (Austria)

Hooft Prize

P.C. Hooftprijs. The Dutch national prize for literature, established in 1947. Prize: f. 75,000 (about $31,000).

Gerrit Krol, for his prose works

Nordic Council Literary Prize

Established in 1961. Selections are made by a 10-member jury from among original works first published in Danish, Norwegian, or Swedish during the past two years or other Nordic languages (Finnish, Faroese, Sami, etc.) during the past four years. Prize: DKr 350,000 (about $42,000).

Oppdageren (1999) by Jan Kjærstad (Norway)

Prix Goncourt

Prix de l'Académie Goncourt. First awarded in 1903 from the estate of French literary figure Edmond Huot de Goncourt to memorialize him and his brother, Jules. Prize: F 50 (about $6.75).

Rouge Brésil by Jean-Christophe Rufin

Prix Femina

Established in 1904. The awards for works "of imagination" are announced by an all-woman jury in the categories of French fiction, fiction in translation, and nonfiction. Announced in October together with the Prix Médicis. Prize: F 5,000 (about $690).

French Fiction   Rosie Carpe by Marie Ndiaye

Cervantes Prize for Hispanic Literature

Premio Cervantes. Established in 1976 and awarded for a body of work in the Spanish language. Announced in December and awarded the following April. Prize: €90,000 (about $80,000).

Álvaro Mutis (Colombia)

Planeta Prize

Premio Planeta de Novela. Established in 1951 by the Planeta Publishing House for the best unpublished, original novel in Spanish. Awarded in Barcelona in October. Prize: Ptas 100 million (about $550,000) and publication by Planeta.

La canción de Dorotea by Rosa Regás

Camões Prize

Premio Luis de Camões da Literatura. Established in 1988 by the governments of Portugal and Brazil to honor a "representative" author writing in the Portuguese language. Prize: $100,000.

Eugénio de Andrade (Portugal)

Smirnoff Russian Booker Prize

Awarded since 1992; sponsored principally since 1997 by Guinness UDV's Smirnoff brand. Prize: $12,500 for the winner; $1,000 for each finalist.

Kazus Kukotskogo ("Kukotsky's Case") by Lyudmila Ulitskaya

Naguib Mahfouz Medal for Literature

Established in 1996 and awarded for the best contemporary novel published in Arabic. The winning work is translated into English and published in Cairo, London, and New York. Prize: a silver medal and $1,000.

Awrāq an-narjis ("Narcissus Leaves") by Sumayya Ramadān

Jun'ichirō Tanizaki Prize

Tanizaki Jun'ichirō Shō. Established in 1965 to honor the memory of novelist Jun'ichirō Tanizaki. Awarded annually to a Japanese author for an exemplary literary work. Prize: ¥1,000,000 (about $8,170) and a trophy.

Hiromi Kawakami, for her novel Sensei no kaban ("The Teacher's Briefcase")

Ryūnosuke Akutagawa Prize

Akutagawa Ryūnosuke Shō. Established in 1935 and awarded semiannually for the best serious work of fiction by a promising new Japanese writer. Short stories or novellas win the prize more frequently than do full-length novels.

"Kuma no shikiishi" ("The Bear's Pavement") by Toshiyuki Horie
"Seisui" ("Holy Water") by Yūichi Seirai
"Chūin no hana" ("The Mourning Flower") by Sōkyū Gen'yū

Mao Dun Literary Award

Established in 1981 to honour contemporary Chinese novels and named after novelist Shen Yanbing (1896–1981), whose nom de plume was Mao Dun; awarded every four years. Latest awards were announced on October 19, 2000.

Jueze ("Hard Choice") by Zhang Ping

Chang hen ge (1996; "Song of Everlasting Sorrow") by Wang Anyi

Chen'ai luo ding (1999; "When the Dust Settles") by Ah Lai

Nanfang you jiamu ("Fine Tree Possessed in Southland") and Buye zhi hou ("Delightful Marquis to Break Drowsiness"), from Charen sanbuqu ("Trilogy of Tea Men") by Wang Xufeng

Visibly missing from the Booker short-list was Beryl Bainbridge. Her *According to Queeney*, described by *The Literary Review* as "the grimmest but also the funniest book Bainbridge has written," was an unflinching treatment of the subject of death. Other prominent novelists whose offerings similarly failed to attract enthusiasm from the judges included Salman Rushdie, whose *Fury* was coolly received by critics, and Pat Barker, whose *Border Crossing* was much praised. Hanif Kureishi's *Gabriel's Gift*—a quirky, stalwart tale about a 15-year-old boy whose parents split up—was another lacuna, as was Jonathan Coe's *The Rotters' Club,* an artful comedy, with moving interludes set in 1970s Britain. Elaine Feinstein's *Dark Inheritance* (2000) was an elegant evocation of an academic woman's unhealthy fascination with Rome.

The children's book market remained buoyant. South African-born writer Beverley Naidoo was a surprise winner of the Carnegie Medal. Her story for children aged 10 and up, *The Other Side of Truth* (2000), addressed the sensitive issue of asylum seekers and beat tough competition from David Almond, Melvyn Burgess, and Philip Pullman. Naidoo hoped that her book would "encourage readers to make leaps of imagination, heart and mind as they explore our common humanity."

Claims that the novel was dead had been made since the 1950s, and the author J.G. Ballard, on publication of what he termed his "complete" short stories, claimed that these too were "heading for extinction" because people had "lost the knack of reading them" and there was almost "nowhere to publish them."

The memoir, however, enjoyed continued popularity. Paul Arnott's *A Good Likeness: A Personal Story of Adoption* (2000) described the author's sometimes hilarious quest for his natural parents and was greeted by *The Literary Review* as a "wonderful, multifaceted voyage of discovery." Also praised was Penelope Lively's *A House Unlocked,* an ingenious depiction of nine decades of family history woven around her grandmother's Edwardian home in Somerset.

There were a number of notable biographies, including Adrian Tinniswood's *His Invention So Fertile: A Life of Christopher Wren,* a vivid portrait of an era that had been dubbed the "Wrenaissance" and a versatile accolade to Wren's scientific and architectural achievement. Antonia Fraser's *Marie Antoinette: The Journey* was an intelligent consideration of a much-misunderstood life. Susan Watkins tackled another legend in *Mary, Queen of Scots* and achieved a succinct story of an intelligent woman whose Achilles heel was a lack of discrimination in her love life. At 674 pages, Alison Weir's *Henry VIII: King and Court* was a well-paced, ambitious retelling of this larger-than-life monarch; his queens and counselors were vividly drawn alongside an analysis of his political legacy. The witty, urbane, and sometimes pompous Roman writer was the deftly handled subject of Anthony Everitt's biography *Cicero: A Turbulent Life.* One of the last Republicans in a time of civil discord, Cicero enjoyed telling jokes—a predilection that Everitt demonstrated proved part of his undoing.

History painted across large canvases appeared in three notable books. Barry W. Cunliffe's 600-page *Facing the Ocean: The Atlantic and Its Peoples, 8000 BC–AD 1500* was a confident and erudite charting of developments across nearly 10 millennia in the Atlantic world, based largely on archaeological evidence. John E. Wills attempted a lateral approach with his *1688: A Global History.* He mined historical sources from a time of global change in such diverse parts of the world as Bolivia, Japan, China, Africa, and Europe. Niall Ferguson presented a 300-year consideration of whether economics alone drove world events with his *The Cash Nexus: Money and Power in the Modern World 1700–2000;* he concluded that the explanation of global change could be attributed only partly to the traffic of money and that people, with their often irrational actions, also affected the course of history.

An immense and impressive historical offering was Hew Strachan's 1,190-page *The First World War, Volume 1: To Arms.* The first of three planned volumes, the book examined the war's origins and its launch, demonstrating that the conflict was doomed to be global in its extent from the start. This work was complemented by Margaret MacMillan's probe of the ensuing peace agreement, *Peacemakers: The Paris Conference of 1919 and Its Attempt to End War,* which argued that the decisions made that year, and subsequently, made World War II inevitable. Meanwhile, the British mandate in Palestine came under the unbiased eye of Israeli journalist Tom Segev. His *One Palestine, Complete: Jews and Arabs Under the Mandate* (2000) explored new research resources and reached a verdict—that the British were chiefly pro-Zionist, not pro-Arab. Moving on through the postwar era, the culture of spies as it waxed and waned was the arena of Richard Aldrich's fascinating *The Hidden Hand: Britain, America and Cold War Secret Intelligence.*

Two notable edited collections were a volume of Bertrand Russell's letters—presented with helpful commentary by Nicholas Griffin to portray a long life of intensity and brilliance—and *The Oxford Dictionary of Phrase and Fable* (2000), a 1,223-page treasury assembled by Elizabeth Knowles containing apocrypha, outré stories, and unusual turns of phrase.

Among the literary deaths during the year were those of novelist, book reviewer, and editor of *The Literary Review* Auberon Waugh, who admitted in later life that he was overshadowed by his father, Evelyn Waugh; Douglas Adams, the creator of the quirky and original tale of Arthur Dent's trip around the universe, *The Hitchhiker's Guide to the Galaxy,* which was first broadcast on radio in 1978 and spawned an industry of TV shows, stage adaptations, books, and a huge following of fans; poet and dramatist Anne Ridler, whose devotional verse evoked that of T.S. Eliot; writer Simon Raven, whose 10-novel sequence *Alms for Oblivion* highlighted his sardonic wit; and poet Elizabeth Jennings, whose verse reflected her devout Roman Catholicism and her love of Italy. (*See* OBITUARIES.)

(SIOBHAN DOWD)

United States. In a talk in August 2001, novelist Philip Roth put forward the proposition that in 25 years literature as it had been known to the present time would be relegated to the dust. Roth argued that the popularity of the screen and the image, currently riding high, would ride even higher in the future.

One might wonder, however, if David Kepesh, the main character in a number of other Roth novels and now an aging professor-journalist with a sex drive still rampant, would agree. Kepesh stands as the main figure in Roth's brilliant short novel *The Dying Animal,* an erotically charged story that reads as a kind of satyr play following the novelist's prizewinning *The Human Stain.* The metaphor-making power of *The Dying Animal* rivaled anything that Henry Miller had written on the sexual encounter and made pornographic images look pallid by comparison. ("You feel it and you get a sense of this other-world fauna, something from the sea. As though it were related to the oyster or the octopus or the squid, a creature from miles down and eons back. . . . The secret ecstatically exposed.")

Literature dying? *Après moi, pas de deluge,* Roth seemed to be arguing.

Writers would say almost anything, however, to gain public attention. Speaking rather immodestly as someone who probably still would be around and writing in 25 years, novelist Jonathan Franzen, author of the much-touted best-selling (and National-Book-Award-winning) novel *The Corrections,* gave an interview to *The New York Times Magazine* in which he suggested that his own work was going to turn contemporary fiction on its head. He also won the distinction of having his book chosen for Oprah Winfrey's book club—then un-chosen.

The rest of the American writers who came out with new publications let the works speak for themselves. Unsurprisingly, the results were mixed. Veteran fiction writer James Salter revised his 1961 novel *The Arm of Flesh* and in late 2000 published it as *Cassada,* a moody and brilliant homage to fighter pilots between wars, in which his evocative lyric prose worked heroically to evoke landscape or, in this case, skyscape. ("[The sun] was in the last quarter of its elevation, the light flat. The white of the clouds had faded like an old wall. Everything seemed silent and still. . . . There was a strange, lost feeling, as though they were in an empty house, in rooms without furniture, looking through windows that had no glass.") Paul Theroux signed in with *Hotel Honolulu,* in which the prose was flat but the linked stories about the inhabitants of a downtown Honolulu tourist spot led the reader on and on. Amy Tan's *The Bonesetter's Daughter* was a successful reworking of the pattern that Tan used in her biggest hit, *The Joy Luck Club*—the reader was taken from contemporary San Francisco to historical China and back again.

Santa Cruz novelist James Houston, the uncrowned laureate of contemporary California fiction, turned to the 19th century and the material of the Donner party and a few of its members for *Snow Mountain Passage,* a solid hit. In *Carry Me Across the Water,* Ethan Canin, a Californian living half the year in self-imposed exile in Iowa, went from the Pacific theatre in World War II to the present for his quiet, lyrical study of a Jewish-American man assessing his life. Reginald McKnight sent his anthropologist hero to Africa for an engaging study of a black man abroad in *He Sleeps.* Percival Everett stayed home to parody black middle-class culture and the American publishing industry in *Erasure.*

With mixed success octogenarian novelist Mary Lee Settle turned to America's colonial past for her novel *I, Roger Williams,* and William T. Vollmann, her junior by more than 40 years, added *Argall,* another huge—flawed—volume, to his already gargantuan "Seven Dreams" series, this one taking up the matter of the colonization of Virginia. At least Vollmann had a sense of humour; he reviewed his own book in the *Los Angeles Times Book Review* and basically dismissed it. Puerto Rican novelist Rosario Ferré worked on the story of Russian ballerina Anna Pavlova and her sojourn in the Caribbean in the slow-moving *Flight of the Swan.* The accomplished Louise Erdrich created an engaging epic out of the material of the lonely North Dakota landscape and its inhabitants, European and Native American, in *The Last Report on the Miracles at Little No Horse.* The talented young African American writer Colson Whitehead made variations out of myth and history in *John Henry Days.* Gifted Brooklyn, N.Y., writer Jonathan Lethem amused his fans with a 55-page novella he called *This Shape We're In.*

After years of writing for television, fiction writer Michael Malone returned to the novel with a wonderfully entertaining murder mystery set in North Carolina called *First Lady.* Novelist Chaim Potok came out with a collection of three linked novellas in *Old Men at Midnight,* and novelist and short-story writer Ward Just turned to the one-act play and published *Lowell Limpett,* along with two previously unpublished stories with a Washington, D.C., setting. Published posthumously was a nearly 600-page novel by Tennessee writer Richard Marius, *An Affair of Honor,* a bulky old-fashioned and splendid story about a double murder in rural Tennessee. ("Saturday night, August 8, 1953. It had been miserably hot. The temperature broke slightly when the sun sank in the west, turning off the fire that baked the world. The round thermometer with the needle and the dial over the door of Kelly Parmalee's clothing store on the square showed ninety-four degrees.")

Chuck Kinder and Peggy Rambach turned their associations with writers Raymond Carver and Andre Dubus into gossipy romans à clef, titled *Honeymooners* and *Fighting Gravity,* respectively. The two best first novels of the year also took historical material as their subjects, often in highly charged prose, as in David Anthony Durham's *Gabriel's Story,* about a young black cowboy on a quest from Kansas across the Southwest ("The mountains before them rose like sand blankets draped around skeletons of rock . . . ancient carcasses of some giant creatures—backbones, ribs, limbs and digits stretched out and decaying beneath a godawful sun."), and the Armenian genocide in Micheline Aharonian Marcom's intensely lyrical *Three Apples Fell from Heaven* ("In the desert, the Mesopotamian beetles drink blood and soup. There is a lake that overflows its bounds, transshapen by flesh.").

A couple of volumes of collected stories, both by influential stylists, deserved serious notice: a more than 440-page volume from Saul Bellow and the posthumously published *The Collected Stories of Richard Yates.* Also published posthumously was *Meteor in the Madhouse,* several novellas by Leon Forrest, an African American writer from Chicago. From established story writers came *Faithless* by Joyce Carol Oates, *Perfect Recall* by Ann Beattie, *Drinking with the Cook* by Laura Furman, *Zigzagging down a Wild Trail* by Bobbie Ann Mason, and *Bargains in the Real World* by Elizabeth Cox. Chitra Banerjee Divakaruni focused on Asian American transplants in *The Unknown Errors of Our Lives,* and Rick Moody jazzed the usually more placid melodies of Anglo-Americans in *Demonology.* Extremely promising, if somewhat uneven, first books of stories came from Baltimore, Md., writer Christine Lincoln—*Sap Rising*—and Vermont-based writer Arthur Bradford —*Dogwalker.*

Poetry became more prosaic as Billy Collins, the new U.S. poet laureate, pub-

U.S. Poet Laureate Billy Collins

lished his low-key, sometimes even trivial verses in *Sailing Alone Around the Room.* J.D. McClatchy and Stephen Yenser edited the *Collected Poems* of the late James Merrill. Louise Glück presented *The Seven Ages.* ("In my first dream the world appeared/ the salt, the bitter, the forbidden, the sweet/ In my second I descended// I was human, I couldn't just see a thing/ beast that I am/ I had to touch.") The subtle nuances of familiar emotions packed the pages of Jane Hirschfield's lyrical collection *Given Sugar, Given Salt.* ("It is foolish/ to let a young redwood/ grow next to a house.// Even in this/ one lifetime,/ you will have to choose.// That great calm being,/ this clutter of soup pots and books—// Already the first branch-tips brush at the window./ Softly, calmly, immensity taps at your life.")

Al Young, in *The Sound of Dreams Remembered,* rhymed "sixties" and "striptease." *The Darkness and the Light* came from Washington, D.C., poet Anthony Hecht, and *Poems Seven: New and Complete Poetry* was released by Alan Dugan. Old hand Robert Bly issued *The Night Abraham Called to the Stars,* and younger poets Forrest Gander and Mark Doty signed in with *Torn Awake* and *Source,* respectively. Novelist John Updike produced a collection of occasional verse titled *Americana.*

Some fine translations by American poets were released, among them Brooks Haxton's *Fragments: The Collected Wisdom of Heraclitus* ("The river/ where you set/ your foot just now/ is gone—those waters/ giving way to this,/ now this.") and Arthur Sze's translations from a number of classical Chinese poets in *The Silk Dragon* (including this gem from the 8th-century poet Wang Wei—"Sir, you come from my native home/ and should know the affairs there./ The day you left, beside the silk-paned window—/ did the cold plum sprout flowers or not?").

A number of fiction writers and poets turned to autobiography and memoir. John Edgar Wideman explained the importance of basketball in his life in *Hoop Roots;* Horton Foote told of his early life in the theatre in *Beginnings;* Jimmy Santiago Baca chronicled his emergence as a poet in *A Place to Stand;* Deborah Digges described her relationship with her difficult son in *The Stardust Lounge;* Tess Gallagher detailed her relationship with Raymond Carver in *Soul Barnacles;* and novelist and essayist Edward Hoagland recounted his descent into blindness in *Compass Points: How I Lived.*

A number of fiction writers published essay collections, criticism, and journalism. The first essay in Tom Wolfe's *Hooking Up* (2000) was his attempt to sum up "What Life Was Like at the Turn of the Century." In *Political Fictions,* Joan Didion collected her columns from the *New York Review of Books.* Native American writer Louis Owens weighed in with *I Hear the Train: Reflections, Inventions, Refractions;* Alan Cheuse produced *Listening to the Page: Adventures in Reading and Writing;* and Clarence Major collected a number of essays and reviews in *Necessary Distance.* Adrienne Rich offered *Arts of the Possible: Essays and Conversations.* Farther afield, if not entirely trivial was Jay McInerny's wine book *Bacchus & Me* (2000). A much more interesting example of a novelist writing on a subject other than literature was Nicholas Delbanco's short history of a Niccolò Paganini cello in *The Countess of Stanlein Restored.* An example of a non-fiction writer working with the imagination of a novelist was *Red,* Terry Tempest Williams's evocative book about the Utah desert. In *Halls of Fame,* essayist John D'Agata explodes the form of the nonfiction collection as he explores the various Americana exhibitions around the nation, ranging from ones devoted to bowling to those honouring modern dance. ("Woman in black [Clytemnestra] enters empty stage from right flanked by two attendants who carry red cloth. Clytemnestra moves stage left & sits on throne. Man dressed in gold [Agamemnon] enters from stage right on litter.")

Various artists served as the subject for some interesting biographies. Nancy Milford's *Savage Beauty: The Life of Edna St. Vincent Millay* won a lot of praise among reviewers. Less well noticed were *Isadora: A Sensational Life* by Peter Kurth and *Norman Rockwell* by Laura Claridge. Biographer Alfred Habegger released *My Wars Are Laid Away in Books: The Life of Emily Dickinson,* and crime-fiction writer James Sallis worked on *Chester Himes.* African American scholar Emily Bernard edited *Remember Me to Harlem: The Letters of Langston Hughes and Carl Van Vechten, 1925– 1964.* In the political realm, Tom Wells recounted the life and times of Daniel Ellsberg in *Wild Man.* In the world of therapy, Charles B. Strozier concentrated on *Heinz Kohut: The Making of a Psychoanalyst.* The most widely read biography of the year was David McCullough's *John Adams.*

Roth captured the PEN/Faulkner Award for Fiction for *The Human Stain,* and the PEN/Malamud Award for Excellence in the Short Story went to Richard Ford and Sherman Alexie. Chabon won the Pulitzer Prize for fiction for *The Amazing Adventures of Kavalier & Clay,* and Stephen Dunn took the Pulitzer in poetry for *Different Hours.* The latest volume in David Levering Lewis's biography of W.E.B. Du Bois—*W.E.B. Du Bois: The Fight for Equality and the American Century, 1919–1963*—won the Pulitzer for biography. The Pulitzer for history was captured by Joseph Ellis for *Founding Brothers: The Revolutionary Generation.*

Among the literary luminaries who died during the year were poet A.R. Ammons, poet, playwright, and novelist Gregory Corso, novelists Frank Gilbreth, Jr., Ken Kesey, and John Knowles, suspense writer Robert Ludlum, crime novelist Peter Maas, and short-story writer and novelist Eudora Welty. (See OBITUARIES.)   (ALAN CHEUSE)

Canada. The past—personal, historical, and imaginary—was the chosen ground for many Canadian novels in 2001, ranging from Nega Mezlekia's exploration of precolonial Africa from a postcolonial perspective in *The God Who Begat a Jackal* to Robert Hough's 20th-century circus saga about a tiger-taming woman, *The Final Confession of Mabel Stark,* and including along the way the globe-encompassing 18th-century quest for the infinite book in Thomas Wharton's *Salamander.* In addition, early 19th-century Newfoundland was powerfully evoked in Michael Crummey's *River Thieves;* prerevolutionary Russia and beyond, where the focus was on the trials of Mennonite families, were explored in both Sandra Birdsell's *The Russlander* and Rudy Wiebe's *Sweeter than All the World;* and World War I Ontario and France were the disparate locales of Jane Urquhart's *The Stone Carvers,* which revealed the complex relations between workers, immigrants, and other nomads. Richard B. Wright's *Clara Callan* and her sister survive the Depression in their separate ways, and the postwar Hiroshima of *The Ash Garden* was thoroughly cultivated by Dennis Bock.

More contemporary times were reflected in myriad facets in Nancy Huston's *Dolce Agonia,* a town-and-gown tale set in New England; Timothy Taylor's *Stanley Park,* in which a young chef and his father meet on the cutting edge of experience and self-knowledge; Kelli Deeth's *The Girl Without Anyone,* exploring the search for self through self-imposed exile; poet Michael Redhill's first novel, *Martin Sloane,* an excursion through minutia to obsession; Kelly Watt's *Mad Dog*, depicting a chaos of characters crazy as foxes; and Diane Schoemperlen's *Our Lady of the Lost and Found*, in which some of the many apparitions of Mary are chronicled during the Lady's weeklong retreat in the author's home. Yann Martel's *Life of Pi* seemed to occur in no time at all.

The fact that single acts could have far-reaching consequences was apparent in a number of works. In Kenneth Radu's *Flesh and Blood*, falling in love with someone of a different race liberates and confounds both lovers in unexpected ways; in *Critical Injuries*, Joan Barfoot dissected the long-term consequences—good, bad, and ambivalent—of a happenstance encounter between a middle-aged woman and a teenager ripe for trouble; and in *Spadework*, Timothy Findley played with the interlocking fates of people whose lives are disrupted by a single stroke of a gardener's spade.

Short fiction as usual ranged widely in theme and content. In *Hateship, Friendship, Courtship, Loveship, Marriage*, Alice Munro framed her latest collection of stories in the vagaries of a childhood game; in *The Path of Totality*, Audrey Thomas observed the darkness, metaphoric and personal, of those blinded by the light of a sun studied too closely. P.K.

Page's *A Kind of Fiction* was an odd assortment of tales drawn from a poet's point of view by a prosaic pen, while the *Simple Recipes* of Madeleine Thien combined the shifting alliances of family relationships in bold new flavours of character and intrigue. Joseph Boyden's *Born with a Tooth* traced the paths of those caught between two worlds, native and white, while Adam Lewis Schroeder's *Kingdom of Monkeys* took the reader into the jungles of Southeast Asia and the human heart.

Poetry is founded in the ever-present tension between senses and meaning, exemplified in George Elliott Clarke's *Execution Poems* or the communion of romance and reality that distinguished *This Tremor Love Is* by Daphne Marlatt. Robert Kroetsch elucidated the mysteries of passion in *The Hornbooks of Rita K.;* Zoë Landale ventured with brave foolishness into the conundrums of parenthood in *Blue in This Country;* David Zieroth examined the conflicting claims and alliances of the spirit and the flesh in *Crows Do Not Have Retirement;* Rhea Tregebov tested the connections between grief and joy in *The Strength of Materials;* and David Helwig presented four epic poems in *Telling Stories*.

New voices included those of Billie Livingston in *The Chick at the Back of*

the Church, singing the sad, triumphant songs of a survivor, and Shani Mootoo in a mouthwatering concoction of native-English vocabulary and syntax, *The Predicament of Or*. Voices that became silent included those of poet Louis Dudek, essayist and novelist Mordecai Richler, and crime novelist L.R. Wright. (*See* OBITUARIES.)

(ELIZABETH WOODS)

Other Literature in English. Australia, New Zealand, and South Africa continued to provide critically acclaimed and commercially successful literary works in English in 2001. Australian Peter Carey became only the second two-time winner of Great Britain's Booker Prize. His fictional treatment of 19th-century Australian folk hero and outlaw Ned Kelly in *True History of the Kelly Gang* (2000) also garnered the author his second top Commonwealth Writers Prize and eclipsed much notice of Carey's other published work of the year, *30 Days in Sydney: A Wildly Distorted Account*. Another Australian, Arabella Edge, won the South East Asia and South Pacific regional Commonwealth Writers Prize for Best First Book with her historical novel *The Company: The Story of a Murderer* (2000), which was set in 17th-century Amsterdam. Frank Moorhouse won the 2001 Miles Franklin Award for *Dark Palace* (2000), and Hannie Rayson's *Life After George* (2000) represented the first time in the award's history that a play had been short-listed. Tim Winton drew praise

Peter Carey's True History

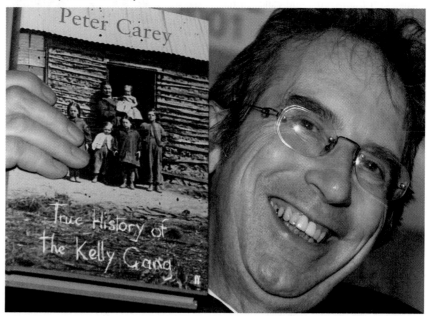

for his *Dirt Music*, a novel that explored the complexities of existence and of marginal relationships. Anna Rutherford—Australian editor, publisher, and scholar of Commonwealth literature—died in February.

Literary highlights in nearby New Zealand were dominated by poets and included the publication of the inaugural poet laureate Bill Manhire's *Collected Poems;* Ian Wedde's long-awaited collection inspired by Horace, *The Commonplace Odes;* the final and posthumously published verse collection *Late Song* (2000) by much-loved poet Lauris Edmond; and the latest collection by veteran Allen Curnow, *The Bells of Saint Babel's: Poems 1997–2001*, his first book in four years. Before his death in September, Curnow had been revered by many as the country's greatest living poet. (*See* OBITUARIES.)

South Africa offered its usual fare of outstanding works and award-winning authors. The much-heralded novelist J.M. Coetzee brought out *Stranger Shores: Literary Essays 1986–1999*, a selection of 26 pieces on literature and writing, and Nobel laureate Nadine Gordimer released her 13th novel, *The Pickup*, the story of a provocative and complex relationship between a wealthy white woman and an Arab mechanic. Countrymen Zakes Mda (*The Heart of Redness* [2000]) and K. Sello Duiker (*Thirteen Cents* [2000]) were honoured as the African regional winners of the Commonwealth Writers Prize for Best Book and Best First Book, respectively.

Also of note was Tanzanian Abdulrazak Gurnah's latest novel, *By the Sea*, which focused on immigrants and exiles in its depiction of two very different refugees who both left the same seaside town in Zanzibar to be reunited many years later in Great Britain. Elsewhere, internationally acclaimed Somalian-born novelist and essayist Nuruddin Farah received the 2001 Fonlon-Nichols Award, conferred by the African Literature Association. (DAVID DRAPER CLARK)

GERMANIC

German. In his 2001 novel *Rot*, Uwe Timm sought to come to terms with the experiences of the generation of so-called 68ers, people who went through the cultural and political turmoil of the 1960s and '70s in West Germany. The protagonist of *Rot* is Thomas Linde, a 68er who makes his living as a eulogist at burials, a profession that becomes a metaphor for the death of the utopian dreams for social and political renewal

of an entire generation—one that now holds the reins of political power in both Germany and the United States. In the end the protagonist dies, and the novel was, in a sense, a eulogy for him and his generation.

Bodo Kirchhoff's novel *Parlando* dealt with the experiences of the children born to the 68ers. The novel's main character, Karl Faller, is in his mid-30s and is a screenwriter for television; he attempts to free himself from the influence of an oppressive father who was once, like so many other 68ers, a social revolutionary and is now a cynic. Like many of Kirchhoff's other works, *Parlando* was also an erotic journey.

In his novel *Die Vertreibung aus der Hölle*, Austrian writer Robert Menasse wove together two stories, one from contemporary Europe and the other from the Europe of the 17th century. The contemporary story deals with a semiautobiographical 68er who experiences the political turmoil of the late

© Jerry Bauer

Erotic journeyman Bodo Kirchhoff

1960s and early '70s, and the other story chronicles the life of a distant ancestor of the contemporary Central European, a Jewish philosopher who must contend with Christian anti-Semitism. Although the novel suggested parallels between the two life stories, the fundamental differences between the kinds of persecution that the two protagonists endure suggested that there is such a thing as progress in human history. In his novel *Fräulein Stark*, Swiss author Thomas Hürlimann told an autobiographical story about a teenager coming of age in

provincial Switzerland in a devout Roman Catholic milieu.

Friedrich Christian Delius also combined contemporary narrative and historical fiction in his novel *Der Königsmacher*, which told the story of Minna—the illegitimate daughter of William of Orange and Marie Hoffmann—a working-class girl in Berlin, and on another level followed the life of the fictional novelist Albert Rusch, Minna's descendent and biographer. *Der Königsmacher* was also a satire of contemporary literary life in Germany, notably the tendency to turn certain authors into pop stars. Martin Walser's *Der Lebenslauf der Liebe* told the pathetic story of Susi Gern, a woman who rises from humble beginnings to riches following her marriage but then falls into degradation and despair.

Juli Zeh's first novel, *Adler und Engel*, was a serious political and crime thriller that offered a devastating critique of contemporary European society. Its protagonist, Max, finds himself mixed up in criminality through his relationship with Jessie, the daughter of a wealthy businessman who happens to be a major drug dealer. In the end the novel told the story of Max's disillusionment and, like Bertolt Brecht's *Die Dreigroschenoper* (1928), suggested an identity between capitalism on the one hand and criminality on the other. In his novel *1979*, Christian Kracht explored the tensions between the European world and Islamic fundamentalism at the time of the 1978–79 Iranian revolution. Both of these novels by young authors produced strong evidence that the much-discussed younger generation of German writers was by no means ready to banish politics completely from their thinking.

Ursula Krechel's novel *Der Übergriff* told a far less overtly political story of loneliness and aging. Its protagonist is a middle-aged woman who must gradually learn to assert herself and to overcome her tendency toward self-deprecation. Norman Ohler's novel *Mitte*, set in the lively Berlin neighbourhood of the novel's title, showed a colourful counterculture coexisting uneasily with Germany's government. The protagonist moves into one of the many old apartment buildings in the centre of Berlin, where he makes a number of mysterious discoveries that lead him to an understanding of the haunted nature of the German capital. Georg Klein's *Barbar Rosa* was set in early 1990s Berlin at the time of German reunification.

Ralf Rothmann's short-story collection *Ein Winter unter Hirschen* explored the miracles of everyday life and the possibility that a book with a Christian theme could find an audience in contemporary Germany. Thomas Hettche's novel *Der Fall Arbogast* was a postmodern thriller exploring the relationship between sex and death in the story of a coroner on the trail of an erroneous verdict handed down many years earlier.

On May 18 Germany lost its most distinguished literary critic, Hans Mayer, who during his 94 years had experienced six states and political systems as well as their writers. Stefan Heym, one of the former German Democratic Republic's most respected dissident writers, died on December 16. (*See* OBITUARIES.)   (STEPHEN BROCKMANN)

Netherlandic. In 2001 well-known novelist and essayist Louis Ferron was awarded the Dutch national Constantijn Huygens Prijs for his uncompromisingly singular and "completely unfashionable and contrary" body of work. The Libris Literatuur Prijs went to Tomas Lieske for his novel *Franklin* (2000), which showcased his brilliant style and bold wit.

Jeroen Brouwers's novel *Geheime Kamers* (2000) was awarded three literary prizes—the Gouden Uil, the Multuli Prijs, and the AKO Literatuur Prijs, the most lucrative award for Dutch literature. The work was lauded as a great novel that "sounds like a symphony and is constructed like a cathedral"; it featured a complex plot in which all the narrative lines connected in the end, grounded in the dark underworld of myth, forgotten fears, and suppressed needs and desires. In his acceptance speech for the Gouden Uil, Brouwers criticized the practice of making the presentation of the AKO Literatuur Prijs in a televised ceremony (as Arnon Grunberg had also done the previous year), and he declined to attend the ceremony. Brouwers maintained that the "circus" surrounding literary prizes debased the literature itself and fostered an inappropriate sense of competition between authors.

In his novel *De mensheid zij geprezen*, Grunberg radically questioned Erasmus's humanist legacy—the lawyer who defends humankind's offenses (hatred, opportunism, lies, and war) sports great rhetorical skill. Harry Mulisch published *Siegfried*, a novel that takes on the relationships between fiction, imagination, and reality in a story about a writer who decides to undo Adolf Hitler by way of fiction. In *Als op de eerste dag* Stefan Hertmans explored the sublime and the sinister potential of fantasy. A younger writer, Floor Haakman, also considered thoughts of fantasy in *Oneetbaar brood*, a suspenseful philosophical novel.

More Dutch works were also being published in English, notably Oscar van den Boogaard's novel *Love's Death*, translated by Ina Rilke, and Grunberg's *Silent Extras* (2000), translated by Sam Garrett. *Love's Death*, written in a fluid and virtuoso style, told a compelling story in a narrative that revealed surprises and complicated motives.

(JOLANDA VANDERWAL TAYLOR)

Danish. Danish writers cast reality to the wind and explored "surreality" in 2001. Per Højholt's novel *Auricula* described a universal silence that is followed by the marvelous conception of actual ears that witness pivotal events of the 20th century; gossip with artists, philosophers, and politicians; and serve as "ear witnesses to history." Søren Jessen's novel *Zambesi* focused on odd characters whose Kafkaesque lives conclude at Café Zambesi, the place where everyone meets and reality unravels. Grete Roulund's *Kvinden fra Sáez* was a tale of intrigue and crime close to home. Hans-Otto Jørgensen's novel *Molly—historien om en engel* (2000) focused on a Juttish farmer, Jens Thorstensen, and the missing moments in his life. The novellas in Jens-Martin Eriksen's *Jonatan Svidts forbyrdelse. Nye beretninger* (2000) depicted ominous outsiders who wreak havoc on serene villages.

In *Fiske i livets flod* (2000), Merete Pryds Helle created a wonderful palimpsest of stories dealing with the written word. Nina Belling and Nina Bolt recaptured other times and places in their works. Belling's *Til en fremmed* (2000) concerned a young Florentine illuminator whose inheritance proves very dangerous. *Spejlmageren* (2000), Bolt's novel of early Renaissance Venice, focused on Bartolomeo, a Murano glassmaker searching for perfection, and on a company of players whose dramas both reflect and transform life. Maria Helleberg's historical novel *Rigets frue* concerned Danish Queen Margrethe I.

In *Til sidst* Asger Baunsbak-Jensen offered a poignant look at the final days of a sadly forgotten and very ill office executive. Jens Christian Grøndahl's *Virginia* (2000) traced wartime love between a 16-year-old girl and an English pilot, as witnessed by a 14-year-old boy. A problematic love lasting through time was the subject of *Bonsai* (2000), Kirsten Thorup's first novel in six years. Anne Strandvad's *Hvor er svalerne om vinteren?* (2000) focused on young Karina's meeting with love and death—and with dire consequences. Kirsten Hammann's *Bruger De ord i kaffen?* conjoined a novel about a novelist with "poetics," discussions on writing. In *Sjælen marineret* Benny Andersen combined a suite from younger days, surrealistic lyrics, and cityscape poems. Christian Yde Frostholm's poems in *Mellem stationerne* (2000) dealt with urban rhythms, personal journeys, and loves. The Children's Book of the Year Prize went to Henrik Einspor for *Med døden i hælene*, and Joakim Garff garnered both the Georg Brandes Prize and *Weekendavisen's* Literary Prize for *SAK*, his biography of Søren Kierkegaard. Kirsten Thorup claimed the Annual Award of the Danish Academy. Essayist and short-story writer Villy Sørensen died in December. (*See* OBITUARIES.)

(LANAE HJORTSVANG ISAACSON)

Norwegian. The year 2001 was a successful one for established authors in Norway. The 2001 Nordic Council Literature Prize was awarded to Jan Kjærstad for *Oppdageren* (1999). Lars Saabye Christensen won acclaim for his gigantic novel *Halvbroren*, which chronicled three generations in Oslo; it was awarded the Brage Prize and Bokhandlerprisen and was nominated for the 2002 Nordic Council Literature Prize. Ingvar Ambjørnsen released *Dukken i taket*, which portrayed the psychological perversity of revenge, and he was awarded a Tabuprisen for his openness about angst. In *Om bare* Vigdis Hjorth returned to the tangles of love, a theme she excelled in exploring.

Hans Herbjørnsrud's short-story collection *Vi vet så mye* investigated the tension between the unexpected and the familiar; it was also nominated for the 2002 Nordic Council Literature Prize. Frode Grytten received rave reviews for *Popsongar*, which spun each story around a pop song. *Svømmetak*, by acclaimed short-story writer Laila Stien, followed the everyday life of women.

In addition, several young authors made their debuts during the year. Many of their works were inspired by the dirty realism launched by cult figure Ari Behn in 1999 and rebelled against the authority of well-established social realism. *The Cocka Hola Company—Skandinavisk misantropi* by Abo Rasul (Matias Faldbakken's pseudonym) instigated controversy with its obscenities. Grethe Nestor's *Kryp* turned the popular genre of the urban single woman à la Bridget Jones into a disturbing tale of venereal disease and crawling insects. Espen Dennis Kristoffersen's *Hvit* was a Lolita-like story, told from the girl's perspective, that was loaded with swearing.

Mystery novels concerned with contemporary issues flourished, notably Jon Michelet's *Den frosne kvinnen* and Fredrik Skagen's *Blitz*. Tom Kristensen's and Jon Lyng's debuts *En Kule* and *Valgets kval*, respectively, described Oslo's financial and political circles.

Annie Riis was awarded the Brage Prize for poetry for *Himmel av stål*, which was praised for its thematic scope and imagery. Veteran poet Cecilie Løveid's *Split* delighted with its cheerfulness and confident language. Endre Ruset's promising debut, *Ribbeinas Vingespenn*, plumbed the possibilities of transgressing physical limits in language and content.

Numerous biographies were welcomed. Sven Kærup Bjørneboe used humour and melancholy in the revealing portrayal of his uncle Jens Bjørneboe. With *Jæger* Ketil Bjørnstad completed his work on the Christiania Bohemians.

(ANNE G. SABO)

Swedish. A feeling of lost control and an urge to use language to beseech a present and a past that had gone out of hand served as a rough summary of preferred themes in Swedish literature in 2001. Per Olov Enquist's *Lewis resa* portrayed revivalist Lewi Pethrus, the founding father of the Swedish branch of the Pentecostal Movement. The 600-page factual novel told the story not only of the man but of the time, and it was also discussed as a biography and 20th-century document.

One observed an inclination for the subjective and a biographical turn, explicit in Lisbeth Larsson's *Sanning och konsekvens*, a study of the art of biographical narration. Using personal experience, many writers found ways to formulate a growing feeling of social estrangement, notably Stig Claesson in *Det lyckliga Europa*, Theodor Kallifatides in *Ett nytt land utanför mitt fönster*, and Bodil Malmsten in *Priset på vatten i Finistère*.

The inspired preacher, a patriarch lost or abandoned, turned out to be somewhat of an icon in Kerstin Norborg's well-written first novel, *Min faders hus*, in senior poet Ragnar Thoursie's first prose book, *Ditt ord är ljus*, and in lyrical form in Jesper Svenbro's *Pastorn,*

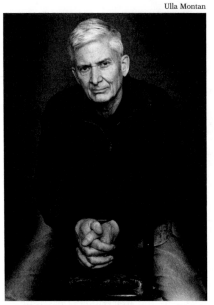

Per Olov Enquist—purveyor of documentary-style fiction

min far. The murdered prime minister Olof Palme turned up as a lost secular father figure in Lars Åke Augustsson's *Sveavägen.* In Ellen Mattson's impressive short novel *Snö*, the ambivalence surfaced in a bravely unheroic historical version of the theme staged at the death of King Charles XII in 1718. History—convincingly studied and deliberately animated—acted as a possible mirror for the present in Maja Lundgren's novel *Pompeji*.

As for genre, short—often hybridic—forms were frequent. Along with the explicit subjective focus, there was an opposing trend that brought out a marked impersonal attitude. Interesting examples, including Magnus Florin's *Cirkulation* and Lotta Lotass's *Aerodynamiska tal*, left realism behind, whereas Mare Kandre's *Hetta och vitt*, Mats Kempe's *Saknar dig sällan så mycket som nu*, Mats Kolmisoppi's *Jag menar nu*, and Alejandro Leiva Wenger's *Till vår ära* used other techniques to estrange everyday life, often by focusing on the effects of migration on identity and language. (IMMI LUNDIN)

FRENCH

France. In 2001 French literature's marked inclination toward gloom continued unabated as it had for over a decade, leaving no permutation of familial misery. Death in the family was a favourite topic, and Laure Adler's *À ce soir* described the death of her son and the subsequent guilt that has consumed her for the past 20 years. François

Bon's autobiographical *Mécanique* traced childhood memories of an existence surrounded by cars, recollections that were stirred by the death of his father, a Citroën car dealer. In *Des phrases courtes, ma chérie*, Pierrette Fleutiaux chronicled a voyage of self-discovery that a daughter took as she accompanied her mother during her final months, while conversely, Isabelle Hausser's *La Table des enfants* depicted the death of a daughter and a distraught mother's attempt to dispel the shroud of mystery concealing the person she was. Marie Darrieussecq covered mourning from several angles at once in *Bref séjour chez les vivants*, in which she examined the devastation wreaked upon a family member one at a time by the drowning of Pierre, their youngest son and brother. Though Anne Sibran's *Ma vie en l'air* did not revolve around death, it did relate the young heroine's insane delusions of flying, which stemmed from incestuous sexual abuse.

Amid the horrors of family life, cracks appeared in the monolithic depressiveness with novels noteworthy for the strategies they used to overcome bleakness. In the undisputed literary event of the year, Michel Houellebecq's *Plateforme* fully recognized and even wallowed in the ills of directionless Western life but reversed conventional values by seemingly singing the praises of Europeans' sexual tourism to poor countries such as Thailand, a twist that aroused a storm of controversy even before the novel was released. In *La Vie sexuelle de Catherine M.*, Catherine Millet also overturned sexual taboos to make promiscuity a banner of individual freedom by describing in explicit, even scandalous, detail her encounters with men of every stripe and perversion. Eric-Emmanuel Schmitt's strategy was even more original; in his *La Part de l'autre*—in contrast to a utopia, or place that never existed—he created a *uchronia*, or time that never existed, to invent the happy 20th century that would have been if only young Adolf Hilter had been accepted into the Viennese art school to which he applied in 1908.

Though dealing with death, Jean d'Ormesson's *Voyez comme on danse*, which began at a funeral, used the normally mournful occasion to resurrect the joy of a man whose love of life and women blazed through the nightmares of Nazism and Stalinism from the Greek Mediterranean to the war zone of Algeria. In *Paulette et Roger*, the ever-sunny Daniel Picouly avoided the blandness of the present by tenderly and lovingly reconstructing what his parents' life as a couple must have been before children came along. Eric Chevillard sidestepped the real world altogether with perhaps the most original work of the year, *Les Absences du Capitaine Cook*, a feast of the absurd in which the usual unities of character and plot were abandoned in favour of a series of insane episodes strung together by far-fetched analogies, word games, and proverbs taken literally that served to reaffirm the author's reputa-

tion as one of the most dazzling writers on the literary scene.

Two perennial favourites also published new works; Nobel laureate Claude Simon's *Le Tramway* reconstructed the world of the author's childhood by the freewheeling analogies of memory as one thought resurrected another with the connecting thread of the trolley rides Simon had taken as a youth. Alain Robbe-Grillet returned to fiction after a long foray into autobiography and a nine-year silence with *La Reprise*, which, in a style familiar to readers of his earlier experimental works, used the trap-

pings of a conventional spy novel to present the story of a secret agent sent in 1949 to bombed-out Berlin to carry out a mission about which he himself knows nothing, a mystery only deepened by the strange memories the city seems to awaken in him.

The Prix Femina went to Marie Ndiaye's *Rosie Carpe*, in which the protagonist and her brother, adrift in the world and on the run from themselves, progressively decline into misery as they reproduce upon their own children the same loveless environment their parents had inflicted on them. The Prix Médicis was awarded to Benoît Duteurtre's *Le Voyage en France*, which presented modern-day France as seen through the disillusioned and shocked eyes of a young man, the illegitimate son of an American woman and a French father he never knew. After years of idealizing the country from afar, the protagonist at last decides to take the trip from New York to see Paris for himself. Martine Le Coz won the Prix Renaudot for *Céleste*, the story of the love between a white woman and a black doctor in cholera-stricken 1830s Paris, a love threatened by the incestuous passion of her uncle, who rages with the jealousy of one forbidden love for another. The Prix Goncourt went to Jean-Christophe Rufin's *Rouge Brésil*, a tale of bitingly ironic wit set against the backdrop of the 16th-century French conquest of Brazil, in which the Europeans' religious fury contrasts with the native Indians' pristine simplicity. (VINCENT AURORA)

Canada. Though the French literary community in Canada viewed itself as a society distinct from the rest of the country, its tastes remained entirely global in 2001. The third installation of Pierre Godin's ongoing biography about the late René Lévesque, the popular provincial politician, attracted attention among parliamentarians and ordinary citizens alike, but readers also were captivated by the adventures of Harry Potter and anything that would shed light on Afghanistan following the September 11 terrorist attacks in the U.S. Nothing, however, could match the outpouring of love for Marie Laberge, the author of several best-selling works of romantic fiction. Her popularity—always strong—was unstoppable, especially with the completion of her trilogy *Le Goût du bonheur* (2000). Another female voice that had fallen by the wayside reemerged with new strength—that of Acadian novelist Antonine Maillet, who in 1979 had be-

© Jerry Bauer

Michel Houellebecq—directionless in France

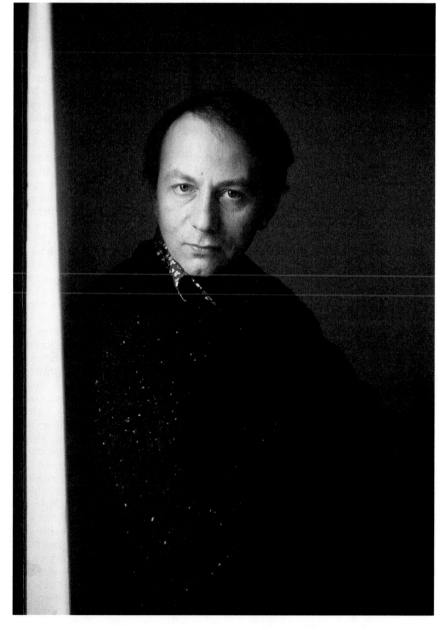

come the first non-French person to win France's Prix Goncourt. Her new novel was *Madame Perfecta*.

Another worldwide trend, pornography written by women, was evidenced in Quebec-born writer Nelly Arcan's *Putain*, the story of a girl who engages in the world's oldest profession and who makes her confession to a nameless psychiatrist. The question of whether the author actually experienced the scenarios described in the book occupied many readers' minds. Madness among women continued to be a favourite topic in French Canada, and writer Andrée A. Michaud produced *Le Ravissement;* her efforts were recognized with the Governor-General's Award, Canada's premier French-language fiction prize. Though plays were rarely published for their literary merit, Normand Chaurette's *Le Petit Köchel* was an exception; it picked up the Governor-General's Award for French-language drama.

One positive trend in publishing was the solidifying of the so-called outlaw small presses, including Les Intouchables, Planète Rebelle, and Trait d'Union, which relied on daring and worked at poverty wages to give younger writers a forum for their works. Though writers in English-speaking markets faced a crisis with the downfall of Chapters, the coun-

Pierre Longtin

Pushing the envelope in French Canadian literature—Nelly Arcan

try's largest retail bookstore chain, French-Canadian authors were largely unaffected by the closure, owing to the strength of independent bookstores in French-speaking Canada.

(DAVID HOMEL)

ITALIAN

The most distinctive feature of Italian literature in 2001 was the publication of several novels whose settings in the recent past served as a framework for a reflection on history. Davide Longo's *Un mattino a Irgalem* takes place during the Italian colonization of Ethiopia, a topic traditionally neglected by historians and creative writers. In the action a short and failed investigation into the crimes of a bloodthirsty sergeant unveils the brutality of colonialism, as well as the dilemmas facing those who are not willing to justify it on ideological grounds. Antonio Franchini's *L'abusivo* focused on more recent history and on the parallel lives of Giancarlo Siani—a young journalist killed by the camorra in 1985 for his reportage on organized crime—and the author-narrator, a former colleague of Siani's, who left journalism and Naples for literature and Northern Italy and tried to reconstruct the dramatic events that led to Siani's death.

Bruno Arpaia, Laura Pariani, and Massimiliano Melilli also looked to the past and anchored their fiction in the biographies of three philosophers: Walter Benjamin, Friedrich Nietzsche, and Antonio Gramsci, respectively. In *L'angelo della storia*, Arpaia alternated scenes from Benjamin's life with those of Laureano Mahojo, a republican fighter in the Spanish Civil War (1936–39). Reflection and action and different perspectives and narrative rhythms run parallel until the two protagonists meet at Port Bou, where Benjamin tragically ends his life. More introspective and lyrical was Pariani's *La foto di Orta*, centred on an 1882 photo of Nietzsche with Lou Salomé and the glimpse at love and happiness it symbolized in the eyes of the philosopher, bound to loneliness and insanity. Largely based on Gramsci's letters and notebooks, Melilli's *Punta Galera* reconstructed the 43 days the antifascist intellectual spent in confinement on the island of Ustica before being sent to prison on the Italian mainland. Melilli re-created Gramsci's relationship with the other exiles and paid special attention to a school of science and humanities they established for the is-

land community. What emerged was the portrayal of a curious, active, and generous man, determined to defy the infamous sentence pronounced at the 1928 trial by the Fascist tribunal that sought "to prevent Gramsci's mind from functioning for twenty years."

Andrea Camilleri confirmed his success with a new adventure for his hero, police inspector Montalbano. More than for its plot, *L'odore della notte* was remarkable for the protagonist's evolution: the inspector, just over 50, longs for human warmth and love and views globalization and the new economy with bitter irony. Antonio Tabucchi ingeniously played with the conventions of the epistolary genre in his *Si sta facendo sempre più tardi*, where the perturbing letters sent by 17 men to their beloved ones (be they real or imaginary, dead or alive) are answered by a single, pointed female response.

Writing outside current trends, Paola Mastrocola and Niccolò Ammaniti received widespread public acclaim. Mastrocola's *Palline di pane* treated with lightness and humour the uneasiness of family life, whereas Ammaniti's *Io non ho paura* chronicled the adventures of Michele, a boy struggling to save a newly found friend, in the incomprehensible world of grown-ups.

Strong theatrical features marked Claudio Magris's *La mostra*, centred on the life of Vito Timmel, a painter from Trieste who died in 1949 in a psychiatric hospital. The title alludes to an exhibit organized after Timmel's death, but it could also be interpreted as a reference to the structural characteristics of the text, in which a life is reconstructed through the fragmented discussions of friends, fellow inmates, and hospital personnel as well as through the visionary monologue of the artist himself. Alternating between different chronological periods and voices, Magris developed an analysis of the relationship between sanity and insanity and explored madness as a refuge from the persecution of life.

Some of the most relevant poetic production of the year was written not in Italian but in dialect, notably in *Rimis te sachete*, Flavio Santi's latest collection. The 28-year-old Santi chose the dialect of the Friuli region for poems that allude to international music and cinema (from rock star Jimi Hendrix to film director David Cronenberg) without losing sight of the dramatic recent history of the area (from the 1976 earthquake to Pier Paolo Pasolini's death). Andrea Zanzotto also employed some dialect in *Sovrimpressioni,* in which the poet revisited the natural landscape he had celebrated in *Dietro il paesaggio* (1951); 40 years later that environment was almost unrecognizable, altered by pollution and cement and devastated by consumerism.

Following the disappearance and death of Geno Pampaloni (1918–2001) —a scholar as well as a militant critic and the author of hundreds of articles for newspapers and magazines— Giuseppe Leonelli edited a collection of Pampaloni's selected essays, *Il critico giornaliero,* which paid tribute to the activity of this intellectual of subtle irony and masterful synthetic precision.

(LAURA BENEDETTI)

SPANISH

Spain. Readers looking for novels with a historical base, for novels presenting stories about real people, for history books, or for poetry about the passage of time, would find many possibilities in the literature published in 2001 in Spain. Juan Marsé won the National Prize for Narrative with *Rabos de lagartija* (2000), another of his works set in the postwar years of the Spanish Civil War (1936–39). The novel centred on David, an adolescent who had a love-hate relationship with his parents; his father was an anarchist sought by the police, and his mother had an ambiguous relationship with the officer looking for her husband. Antonio Muñoz Molina's *Sefarad* was an account of the history of the 20th century through the voices of the persecuted and forgotten. The novel contained thousands of stories, some true and some fictionalized, that recalled cruel episodes in history, including the Holocaust and the communist repression. In Juan Manuel de Prada's most recent work, *Desgarrados y excéntricos,* he rescued from oblivion 15 frustrated 20th-century Spanish writers. Each portrait was the result of a meticulous investigation about the writers, all of whom were ignored in the literary canon. The Planeta Prize, which awarded approximately $550,000 on its 50th anniversary, was given to Rosa Regás's *La canción de Dorotea,* a story of mystery and intrigue involving a woman hired to take care of an ailing man in a country house.

In *El oro del rey,* the fourth and final volume of Arturo Pérez-Reverte's series of adventure novels about the mysterious Capitán Alatriste, the captain and his partner become involved in a mis-

sion concerning the smuggling of gold aboard Spanish galleons arriving from the Indies. One of the most applauded novels of the year was Eduardo Mendoza's *El tocador de señoras,* a funny, clever, and satiric X-ray of certain guilds (politicians and journalists) as well as several members of the Catalonian bourgeoisie. Lucía Etxebarria published her fourth novel, *De todo lo visible y lo invisible,* which began with the second suicide attempt of Ruth, a film director; Ruth meets Juan, a poet who has just arrived in Madrid to write a novel, and these two narcissistic and insecure characters develop a passionate dependence that degenerates into a terribly destructive relationship. Enrique Vila-Matas was the winner of the Rómulo Gallegos Prize of Venezuela for *El viaje vertical* (1999), his traveling book framed in the Spanish Civil War. Promising young author Javier Lucini weighed in with *La canción del mal amado, y otras desmitologías,* a collection of short stories based on Greek mythologies.

© Jerry Bauer

Antonio Muñoz Molina, spokesman for the persecuted and forgotten

A year after his death, José Ángel Valente was awarded the National Prize for Poetry for *Fragmentos de un libro futuro* (2000), which appeared posthumously and encompassed more than 90

poems and some brief prose pieces. The coveted Cervantes Prize, the highest distinction in Spanish letters, went to Colombian Álvaro Mutis. After nine years of silence, Ángel González published *Otoños y otras luces,* which explored the endless autumn, the extinguishing life, and the silence discovered by the poetic creation.

(VERÓNICA ESTEBAN)

Latin America. In 2001 many works explored Latin America's past and present social and political realities as well as offering variations on the theme of love. From Mexico, writer Carlos Fuentes returned to fantastic literature and to the theme of love's difficulties in *Instinto de Inez.* In *La piel del cielo,* Elena Poniatowska, winner of the 2001 Alfaguara Prize, offered an overview of science in Mexico as well as a political social history of that country's past 70 years as seen through the eyes of an astronomer. Laura Esquivel brought indigenous and Spanish-speaking cultures together in *Tan veloz como el deseo,* a tale in which love is the redeeming force in the difficult years following the Mexican Revolution. In *El espía del aire,* Ignacio Solares returned to the charged atmosphere of Mexico in the late 1960s. Other fiction from Mexico included Federico Campbell's novella *La clave Morse,* the story of an alcoholic telegraph operator and amateur writer told through the eyes of his daughters; Ana García Bergua's *Púrpura* (1999), which presented another vision of 20th-century Mexico and the political transformations of that country; and Álvaro Uribe's *Por su nombre,* a tale of obsessive love. In the realm of awards, novelist Juan García Ponce won the Juan Rulfo Prize, and the poet José Emilio Pacheco was awarded the first José Donoso Prize for his extensive body of work, which spanned over four decades. The literary world was saddened by the death of Juan José Arreola, author of a small but brilliant narrative corpus.

Sergio Ramírez of Nicaragua released *Catalina y Catalina,* a collection of stories that presented his country's harsh social and political realities. Rey Rosa of Guatemala published the short novel *Piedras encantadas,* which told the story of children in the streets of Guatemala City and the mysterious death of an adopted boy. *Milagro en Miami* by Zoé Valdés of Cuba explored the theme of exile involving a girl kidnapped from the island to become a supermodel in Milan. More than 10 years after the death of Reinaldo Arenas of Cuba, Alfaguara published his *El palacio de las blanquísimas mofetas,* the story of a boy growing up in rural poverty during the last years of the Fulgencio Batista regime. In *La fábula de José,* Eliseo Alberto of Cuba chronicled the life of a 33-year-old Cuban who arrives during the 1960s in Florida on a raft; he is given a choice of staying in jail or being exhibited in a zoo.

From Colombia, Álvaro Mutis's seven novels dealing with the popular protagonist Gaviero were republished in a volume entitled *Empresas y tribulaciones de Maqroll el Gaviero.* In December Mutis was named the recipient of the Cervantes Prize. Héctor Abad Faciolince published *Basura,* which explored the relationship between reading and writing. Medardo Arias Satizábal wrote *Que es un soplo la vida* about Carlos Gardel's death and the transporting of his body across Colombia. Making significant international literary news was the widely anticipated auction of the galleys of Gabriel García Márquez's *Cien años de soledad,* but the minimum opening bid of $530,000 was not met.

Chilean novelist Antonio Skármeta released *La chica del trombón,* a story of a young girl looking for her identity in the days prior to the election of Salvador Allende. Marcela Serrano's novel *Antigua vida mía,* a finalist for the Planeta Prize, was a narrative about a depressed woman who travels with a friend to Chiapas after the death of her son. Chilean poet Raúl Zurita won the national literature prize, awarded in August 2001.

From Argentina came Federico Andahazi's political novel *El príncipe,* which chronicled the rise to power of the son of a diabolical and fantastic father. Juan Forn published *Puras mentiras,* the tale of a man who finds his life unraveling and ends up traveling anonymously to a small coastal village. Marcelo Birmajer published *Tres mosqueteros,* a novel in which a Jewish man returns to Argentina on an unknown mission after having lived 20 years in Israel and is kidnapped in the airport. Tulio Stella's novel *La familia Fortuna,* in the tradition of Julio Cortázar's *Rayuela,* allows the reader to freely combine the seven "novels" in the text. Juan Gelman, one of Argentina's leading poets, published *Valer la pena,* a collection of 149 poems he wrote between 1966 and 2000.

Uruguayan authors had a banner year. Hugo Burel won the Lengua de Trapo Prize for Narrative for *El guerrero del crepúsculo,* about an encyclopaedia salesman who leaves the hospital after a brain operation only to enter a comic Kafkaesque world and end up in a

house of prostitution, and Rafael Courtoisie showcased his narrative talent with the stories in *Tajos* (1999). In Hugo Fontana's *Veneno,* a friend from childhood narrates the story of a man who is condemned to death in the U.S. for alleged arson of a hotel frequented by gays. Mario Benedetti received the José Martí Iberoamerican Prize for his vast contributions to literature over almost 50 years. (JOHN BARRY)

PORTUGUESE

Portugal. The Association of Portuguese Writers awarded its 2001 Great Prize for Fiction to Maria Velho da Costa for her novel *Irene ou o contrato social* (2000). Velho da Costa, who first gained international acclaim with the publication in 1972 of *Novas cartas portuguesas,* turned to the subject of euthanasia in her latest prizewinning novel, in which a contract is made between a female patient and a male friend who helps her to die. The story was told in a complex and tangled way, challenging the reader to decipher literary allusions and echoes and associations with characters from her previous novels.

Short-listed for the same prize was Helder Macedo's novel *Vícios e virtudes,* a story about a fiction writer whose reputation is on the rise. Macedo used the literary technique of a narrative within a narrative to tell the story of an intriguing woman who is having an affair with a friend, who in turn is writing his own novel based on her. The interplay of situations and affections, the suspicions that assail the narrator, the ambiguities of language that prevail, changing everything into its opposite, confuse the narrator in the pursuit of the obscure object of his own desire. This most entertaining novel, written in an elegant and witty style, possessed a depth of thought that was never sacrificed to literary effect. Vices could become virtues, and virtues could masquerade as vices, depending on the way in which the cards were played.

Concern with language was pursued with great rigour and discipline by Gastão Cruz in his book of poems *Crateras* (2000), which was awarded the D. Dinis Prize for Literature. The sound of the word and the music of the verse served as the essence of his poetry, and meaning was subordinate to them. A simple description of a place had to convey its presence in the tone and colour of the word.

The Camões Prize was awarded to Eugénio de Andrade for his exceptional

body of work. His poems breathed the air of nature and reflected an intense contemplation of nature-related objects, including leaves, seeds, roots, water, and birds. They all combined in a symphony of the four elements. In his *O sal da língua* (1995), the complexity of thought was matched by simplicity of expression. (L.S. REBELO)

Brazil. Brazilians mourned the death in August 2001 of Jorge Amado (*see* OBITUARIES), who for some 70 years was the country's most distinguished writer. In the 1930s and '40s he produced a body of Social Realist fiction that was totally committed to an ideal of communism, a factor that led to periods of his enforced exile from Brazil. From the mid-1950s he developed a unique style of "utopian realism," in which social dilemmas were dealt with from a more comical perspective. Amado claimed that his favourite among his works was *The Violent Land* (1942), which presented the cacao land struggles in his native state of Bahia. It was with his later group of works—including *Gabriela, Clove and Cinnamon* (1958) and *Dona Flor and Her Two Husbands* (1966)—and their adaptation to film, stage, and television that he earned international fame. These and other later novels were notable for highlighting the lives of blacks in Brazilian society and for their sympathetic portrayal of female characters in a traditionally macho society, approaches that caused these works to be praised and detested at the same time.

Fabrício Carpi Nejar published a new poetry collection, *Um terno de pássaros do Sul,* and the *Complete Poetical Works* of the symbolist poet Alphonsus de Guimaraens was published by his son and his grandson, both poets, Alphonsus Filho and Afonso Henriques da Costa Guimarães, respectively. The Guimaraens family continued its long tradition in Brazilian letters—dating back to 19th-century poet and novelist Bernardo Guimaraens—with the publication of Alphonsus Filho's own volume of poems, *O tecelão do assombro.*

Notable works of fiction included Joyce Cavalcante's novel *O cão chupando manga* and new short fiction by Luci Collin, *Precioso Impreciso.*

Two quite insightful volumes of cultural criticism appeared in late 2000. The essays in *Brasil, país do passado?,* edited by Lígia Chiappini, Antônio Dimas, and Berthold Zilly, took Stefan Zweig's classic *Brasil, país do futuro* (1941) as the starting point for a reevaluation of the concept of past, present, and future within the Brazilian

© Jerry Bauer

Brazilian literary giant Jorge Amado died during the year.

context. Fiction and essays by many of Brazil's leading militant intellectuals of the past 50 years, including Antônio Callado, Darcy Ribeiro, Paulo Freire, Paulo Francis, and Herbert José de Souza ("Betinho"), were analyzed to decipher the significance of the national past and what might occur in the future. An interdisciplinary study of the social role of Brazilian soap operas appeared in English: *Living with the Rubbish Queen: Telenovelas, Culture and Modernity in Brazil* by Thomas Tufte. In addition to analyzing the relevance of their themes and contents, the author sought to determine the impact of soap operas on the typical Brazilian viewer—the low-income urban woman.   (IRWIN STERN)

RUSSIAN

The year 2001 was one of losses and gains for Russian literature. Several leading figures died, among them Viktor Krivulin, a major poet, critic, and organizational force in Russia's 1970s "underground"; Vadim Kozhonov—critic, literary scholar, and an intellectual leader of the "populist" wing of Russian literature; and Viktor Golyavkin, a prose writer in the absurdist vein who was a prominent figure in the 1960s. The suicide of 27-year-old Yekaterinburg poet Boris Rizhy received considerable attention in literary circles, especially after the news that he had been posthumously awarded the Northern Palmyra Prize.

Skirmishes continued between the two major literary "parties." The first, led by critics Pavel Basinsky and Andrey Nemzer, stood for values associated with the best traditions of Soviet literature—"humanness," "emotionality," and the "accurate depiction of the realities of daily life." Much of the success of poets Rizhy and Vera Pavlova, winner in 2001 of the Apollon Grigoryev Prize, was attributed to their appeal to this segment of the Russian reading public. Pavlova's poetry was especially interesting in this regard, combining traditional Soviet poetic devices with explicit eroticism.

The opposing literary party, whose primary bastions were the journal of literary criticism *Novaya russkaya kniga* ("The New Russian Book") and the Andrey Bely literary prizes, looked upon the literary Conceptualists (Dmitry Prigov, Lev Rubinshteyn, Vladimir Sorokin, and other postmodernists) as the driving force of contemporary literature. Yaroslav Mogutin was awarded the Andrey Bely Prize for poetry for his militantly homosexual verse, and the prize for prose went to Aleksandr Pyatigorsky for his postmodern combination of scholarship and play in *Vspomnish strannogo cheloveka* (1999; "You Remember That Strange Man"). At the same time, postmodern and avant-garde writing sought a wider audience through publishing ventures (the Amfora Publishing House in St. Petersburg was a typical example) and new literary prizes, including the National Best-Seller. This prize, which attempted to merge serious and escapist literature, was awarded to Leonid Yuzefovich for *Knyaz vetr* ("The Wind King"), an intellectual mystery that took place at the end of the 19th century in Russia and Mongolia. None of the nominated books, however, could be called true best-sellers; the only real crossover author continued to be Boris Akunin, whose novels—like those of Yuzefovich—combined history, fantasy, and the mystery genre.

The nominees for the Russian Booker Prize in 2001 included Tatyana Tolstaya's anti-utopian novel *Kys;* Lyudmila Ulitskaya's *Kazus Kukotskogo* ("Kukotsky's Case"); Alan Cherchesov's *Venok na mogilu vetra* (2000; "A Wreath on the Wind's Grave"), written in the magic realism style; Sergey Nosov's postmodern *Khozyayku istorii* (2000; "To the Master of History"); and two fictionalized memoirs, Anatoly Nayman's *Ser* ("Sir"), about Isaiah Berlin, and Aleksandr Chudakov's *Lozhitsya mgla na staryye stupeni* ("Darkness Falls on the Old Stairs"). The winner was Ulitskaya's *Kazus Kukotskogo.*

© Jerry Bauer

Anti-utopian Tatyana Tolstaya, short-listed for the Russian Booker

Some more aesthetically daring works were published, including a volume of short stories from Nikolay Kononov, nonfiction from essayist Kirill Kobrin, and a novel from Oleg Yuryev, *Poluostrov zhidyatin* ("Jews' Peninsula"), which described the encounter of a group of descendants of 15th-century Jewish heretics with contemporary assimilated Jews.

The most important poetry publications were Yelena Shvarts's *Dikopis poslednego vremeni* ("A Nonsense of Recent Times") and the four volumes released by *Novoye literaturnoye obozreniye* ("New Literary Review") of the 2000 Andrey Bely Prize for poetry finalists: Yelena Fanaylova (who won the

award), Sergey Stratanovsky, Mikhail Ayzenberg, and Aleksandra Petrova. Soon after Krivulin's death, a powerful last book appeared, *Stikhi posle stikhov* ("Verse After Verse"). Viktor Sosnora also published a new book, as did his less-well-known contemporary Sergey Volf. Other notable volumes were released by Prigov, Dmitry Vodennikov, Aleksandr Levin, and Kirill Reshetnikov (who also wrote under the pseudonym Shish Bryansky). The work of the 24-year-old Reshetnikov, very much characteristic of his generation, was marked by a combination of exalted lyricism, weary sarcasm, and provocative vulgarity.

In criticism Olga Slavnikova and Nikita Yeliseyev were singled out for the quality and variety of their publications. Two works of the typically Russian genre of *publitsistika* (social and political commentary) were also superior: Aleksandr Solzhenitsyn's examination of the "Jewish question" in Russia, *Dvesti let vmeste, 1795–1995* ("Two Centuries Together"), and Mikhail Epshteyn's rather different but no less lively futurological study *Debut de siècle.*

The role of the "thick journals" continued to diminish, and all attempted to compensate for lower print runs (each now below 10,000 copies) with an Internet version, sometimes in tandem with their journals, but sometimes—like *Text Only*—as stand-alone Web sites. Finally, the Little Booker Prize was awarded to the Yuratin Foundation from the city of Perm for its publishing and literary activities. Following that award the Little Booker ceased to exist; part of the rationale for eliminating the prize was the optimistic view that contemporary Russian literature was ready to stand on its own feet and no longer needed external support.

(VALERY SHUBINSKY)

JEWISH

Hebrew. The quantitative prosperity of Hebrew fiction in 2001 produced mixed results. The few impressive achievements included Gabriela Avigur-Rotem's *Hamsin vetziporim meshuga'ot* ("Heatwave and Crazy Birds"), Yoel Hoffmann's *The Shunra and the Schmetterling* ("The Cat and the Butterfly"), Daniella Carmi's *Lesha'hrer pil* ("To Free an Elephant"), and Reuven Miran's *Shalosh sigariot bema'afera* ("Three Cigarettes in an Ashtray"). A noticeable improvement was marked by the new collection of short stories

of Gafi Amir (*Dash mine'ura'yich* ["Regards from Your Youth"]) and the new novel of Yael Ichilov (*Zman ptsiot* ["Overtime"]).

A.B. Yehoshua published his most pretentious work by far, *Hakala ha-mesh'hreret* ("The Liberating Bride"), which sums up his canon by implicit allusions to his stories and novels and on the other hand copes with the difficulties of understanding the Palestinians and their culture from a Jewish-Israeli point of view. The novel, however, did not match Yehoshua's previous literary achievements. Several other works by veteran writers failed to match previous accomplishments. Among them were Joshua Kenaz's *Nof im shlosha etzim* (2000; "Landscape with Three Trees"), Avram Heffner's *Kemo Abelar, Kemo Elu'yiz* ("Like Abelard, Like Héloïse"), Yoram Kaniuk's *Hamalka ve'ani* ("The Queen and I"), and Sammi Michael's *Ma'yim noshkim lema'yim* ("Water Kissing Water"). First novels were penned by Rachel Talshir (*Ha'ahava mesha'hreret* ["Liebe Macht Frei"]) and Marina Groslerner (*Lalya*). Ronit Matalon published a spellbinding collection of autobiographical essays along with articles about art and literature (*Kro ukhtov* ["Read and Write"]).

Louis Monier

A.B. Yehoshua looks at Palestinian culture

Perhaps the best collection of poetry was *Isha shemitamenet belih'yot* ("A Woman Who Practices How to Live") by Shin Shifra. Other notable books of poetry included Aryeh Sivan's *Eravon*

("Pledge"), Dory Manor's *Mi'ut* (2000; "Minority"), Ronny Someck's *Hametofef shel hamahapekha* ("The Revolution Drummer"), Maya Bejerano's *Ha'yofi hu ka'as* ("Beauty Is Rage"), Yohai Openhaimer's *Beshesh a'hrei hatzohora'yim* (2000; "At Six in the Afternoon"), Dalia Kaveh's *Geshem* ("Rain"), and Ariel Rathaus's *Sefer hazikhronot* ("The Memories' Book").

The most intriguing work of literary scholarship was Dan Miron's *Parpar min hatola'at* ("From the Worm a Butterfly Emerges"), which studied the life and work of young Nathan Alterman. Hannan Hever examined nationality and violence in Hebrew poetry of the 1940s (*Pitom mar'e hamilhama* ["Suddenly, the Sight of War"]); Hillel Barzel published the fifth volume of the *History of Hebrew Poetry*, which deals with the poetry of Abraham Shlonsky, Nathan Alterman, and Lea Goldberg; and Aharon Komem discussed David Vogel's poetry and fiction in *Ha'ofel vehapele* ("Darkness and Wonder").

(AVRAHAM BALABAN)

Yiddish. The year 2001 was a stellar one for Yiddish poetry, but only a few other Yiddish works were noteworthy.

Baym rand fun kholem ("At the Edge of a Dream"), by master of the short novella Tsvi Ayznman, was a family chronicle of tales and sketches that traced a life journey from Poland to the Soviet Union, with sojourns in the Czech lands, Italy, and Cyprus. After finally settling in Israel, an Auschwitz survivor finds a terrorist on his doorstep whose appearance, in the wake of a bloody outrage, presents the protagonist with a series of moral dilemmas.

Another notable work was Ite Taub's authoritative reminiscence in rich Ukrainian Yiddish, *Ikh gedenk* ("I Remember"). Her narrative began with a retelling of childhood memories in the shtetl of Stidenitse, Ukraine, and provided incisive commentary about the pre- and post-October Revolution years and the political currents that had an impact on the Jewish communities of that republic.

Azarya Dobrushkes's ambitious three-volume miscellany, *Shpeter shnit* ("Late Harvest"), included vignettes about pre-World War II Vilna together with essays on a variety of literary themes.

Dvoyre Kosman's *Yidish: heymish, geshmak* ("The Yiddish Language: Native and Tasty") was a capacious anthology of prose and poetry. Eli Beyder's *Fun bolshevistishn "gan-eydn" in emesn heymland* ("From the Bolshevik 'Paradise' to My Real Homeland") portrayed a hegira

in verse and provided a stinging indictment and eyewitness account of Soviet attitudes toward the national minorities.

In the thought-provoking volume *Velfisher nign* ("Lupine Melody"), author Velvl Chernin, a recent arrival from Russia, explored the life, people, and history of Jerusalem; the book's title was a pun on the author's name. Chernin employed Hebrew chapter titles and found biblical resonances in the perennial political tensions of his adopted country. Gele Shveyd Fishman's *In shtile shoen* ("In Quiet Hours") was an inspirational collection of lyric poetry. Beyle Schaechter-Gottesman's *Mume Blume di makhsheyfe* ("Aunt Blume the Witch") was a charming fairy tale in verse that featured animal protagonists and richly embellished colour illustrations by Adam Whiteman.

(THOMAS E. BIRD)

TURKISH

The Turkish literary field proved fertile in 2001. Many impressive works of fiction with wide-ranging themes and topics appeared, including Ahmet Altan's *İsyan günlerinde aşk* ("Love in Days of Rebellion"), about an early 20th-century fundamentalist uprising; Buket Uzuner's *Uzun beyaz bulut—Gelibolu* ("Tall White Cloud—Gallipoli"); Ayla Kutlu's *Zehir zıkkım hikâyeler* ("Bitter Stories"); Ömer Zülfü Livaneli's *Bir kedi, bir adam, bir ölüm* ("A Cat, a Man, a Death"), winner of the Yunus Nadi Award; Yashar Kemal's *Tanyeri horozları* ("Roosters of the East"); Erhan Bener's *Sonbahar yaprakları* ("Leaves of Autumn"); Hasan Ali Toptaş's chilling neosurrealistic *Ölü zaman gezginleri* ("Planets of Dead Times"); Oya Baydar's *Sıcak külleri kaldı* (2000; "Hot Ashes Remain"), which won the Orhan Kemal Prize; and Hıfzı Topuz's *Gazi ve fikriye*, a semifictionalized account of Kemal Atatürk's love affair and its tragic end.

A new genre appeared—book-length interviews dubbed *"nehir söyleşileri"* ("interview *fleuves*"). The first two books in the series featured two major novelists, Adalet Ağaoğlu and Tahsin Yücel. A welcome event was the publication, in 13 volumes, of the complete short stories of the late satirist Aziz Nesin. A succès d'estime was Emre Kongar's *Kızlarıma mektuplar*, his collection of letters written to his twin daughters. In other literary news, eminent poet Fazıl Hüsnü Dağlarca was awarded an honorary doctorate by Mersin University, UNESCO designated 2002 as "the Year of Nazim

Hikmet" in honour of the centennial of Hikmet's birth, and Orhan Pamuk's *My Name Is Red* (translation from Turkish by Erdağ Göknar) was featured on the September 2 cover of the *New York Times Book Review*. In addition, a number of important collections of poetry appeared, including those by Hilmi Yavuz, Küçük İskender, and Lale Müldür, among others. The publication of critic Mehmet H. Doğan's anthology of modern poetry generated controversy after numerous omissions were noted.

It was a banner year for essays and criticism, with impressive collections published by Melih Cevdet Anday, Enis Batur, Memet Fuad, Erendiz Atasü, Doğan Hızlan, and Ahmet Oktay. Memoirs and autobiographies attracting wide attention included those by Ayfer Tunç, Abidin Dino, Vedat Türkali, Hilmi Yavuz, and Uğur Kökden.

(TALAT S. HALMAN)

PERSIAN

By all accounts, 2001 was an eventful year for Persian literature, both in revisiting the achievements of the previous century from fresh perspectives and in providing glimpses into new literary experiments. Two important international conferences examined the literature of the 20th century, one by focusing on M.T. Bahār (1880–1951) and the other by surveying the entire literary canon of the Persian-speaking world. In the United States, Harvard Film Archive published the bilingual edition of *Hamrāh bā bād*. Titled *Walking with the Wind*, the collection featured haikulike poems by renowned Iranian filmmaker Abbas Kiarostami, who was prevented from participating in scheduled appearances and readings in several American cities following the terrorist attacks in September.

In Iran the granting of several literary awards by private cultural organizations signaled further loosening of state-imposed restrictions on creative writing and greater attention to literary works produced by secular writers. The foundation named for novelist Hūshang Gulshīrī awarded prizes to two newly published novels, Abū Turāb Khusravī's *Asfār-i kātibān* ("Books of the Scribes") and Khusraw Hamzavi's *Shahrī kih zīr-i dirākhtān-i sidr murd* ("The Kingdom That Died Beneath the Cedar Trees"). The foundation's lifetime achievement award went to Aḥmad Maḥmūd. The Kārnāmah Cultural Association awarded its poetry prize to Ali Āmūkhtah-nijād's *Yak panjshanbah*, *yak piādahrow* ("One Thursday, One Sidewalk").

The most notable literary event of the Iranian diaspora was the publication in Sweden of the original Persian version of Gulshīrī's *Shāh-i siyāh Pūshān*, a haunting narrative of a prison encounter between a secular poet and a turncoat political activist. Though Abbas Milani's 1990 *King of the Benighted*, the English translation of Gulshīrī's novella, had already been recognized as a notable work, Gulshīrī's original work was not released for publication until after his death in 2000. 'Izzat Gūshahgīr's collection of short stories . . . *Va nāgahān palang guft: zan* (". . . And Suddenly the Panther Cried: Woman!") contributed to an emerging and significant trend in writing by Iranian women, audacious articulations of gender relations in narratives of deep psychological insight. The most significant work by a Tajik author was Askar Hakim's long poem *Sang-i man almās ast* ("My Stone Is Diamond").

(AHMAD KARIMI-HAKKAK)

ARABIC

The predominant theme of 2001 was literature that chronicled the ordeals of political prisoners in a number of Arab countries. Works defined as "prison literature" were authored by freed political prisoners motivated to speak out by the relative freedom in the past two years in their countries. Writing in French, Moroccan Ahmad Marzouki published *Tazmamart, cellule 10* (2000), and Jaouad Mdidech followed with *La Chambre noire; ou, Derb Moulay Chérif* (2000), with a preface by another freed prisoner, Abraham Serfaty. Moroccan Tahar Ben Jelloun fictionalized the experience of a prisoner in Tazmamart in his novel *Cette aveuglante absence de lumière*. Before his death in April, Egyptian 'Ali ash-Shūbāshī published *Madrasat al-thūwār* ("The School of Revolutionaries"), in which he recounted his prison experience between 1950 and 1964.

Though modern Arabic literature was increasingly targeted by conservative religious groups, a number of Arab writers addressed the issue of fanaticism critically in an effort to protect the freedom of expression in their societies. Egyptian critic Jābir 'Aṣfūr published *Ḍidd al-ta'assub* ("Against Fanaticism"), and Moroccan Zuhūr Guerrām wrote *Fī ḍiyāfat al-Riqābah* ("A Guest of the Censor") in support of Kuwaiti writer Laylā al-'Uthmān, who was fined and condemned with 'Āliyā

Shu'ayb to a two-month suspended prison sentence; they were accused of producing texts damaging to religion and morality.

The Arab intellectuals' preoccupation with the threatening spectre of globalization continued. Writers again analyzed the damaging effects of globalization on the economy and culture of the region. Two Moroccan critics sounded the alarm, Sa'īd Yaqṭīn in *Al-adab waalmu'assasuah* (2000; "Literature and the Institution") and Mahdī al-Manjara in *Intifāḍāt fī zamān al-dhuluqrāṭiyyah* ("Upheavals in the Era of Disgrace"). They deplored increased government control and interference in everyday life, the stifling of creativity, and the deterioration of intellectual thinking. Al-Manjara viewed globalization as a cultural war on Arab-Islamic values.

Ironically, the author who had recently attracted the critics' attention and praise was Leila Aboulela, a veiled Sudanese woman who wrote in English and was inspired by her Islamic faith. Her novel, *The Translator* (1999), was hailed by critics, and her collection of short stories, *Coloured Lights*, showcased her creativity and the harmonious coexistence of Islamic and Western values.

The short story made a noticeable comeback. Two important collections were published in Egypt. Ibrāhīm 'Abd al-Majīd's *Sufun qadīmah* ("Old Boats") portrayed aspects of social and psychological disorientation in Alexandria, and Idwār al-Kharrāt's *Raqṣat al-ashwāq* ("The Dance of Longing") was a collection of previously published short stories. Prolific Moroccan novelist Muḥammad 'Izz ad-Dīn at-Tāzī published *Shams sawdā'* (2000; "A Black Sun"), which reflected the melancholic mood of his society. The regular publication of a number of reputable literary journals, including *Al-Ādāb* in Lebanon, *Manārāt* in Morocco, *Aqwās* in the West Bank city of Rām Allāh, and *Al-Hilāl* in Egypt, provided a platform for a new generation of young writers who, in the absence of government-subsidized presses, would find it difficult to publish their work independently.

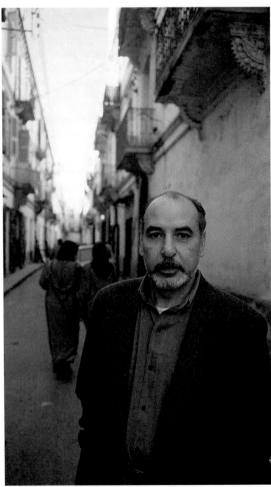

Moroccan novelist, poet, and dramatist Tahar Ben Jelloun

© Andersen/SIPA

Poetry, on the other hand, found the Internet a suitable outlet. A Web site dedicated to *intifāḍah* poetry featured verse by established writers, notably Maḥmūd Darwīsh's *Muḥammad*, following the tragic killing of Muḥammad ad-Durrah in 2000; Ḥanān 'Ashrāwī's *Hadīl's Song;* Fadwā Tūqān's *Martyrs of the Intifada;* and Naomi Shihab Nye's *For the 500th Dead Palestinian Ibtisām Bozieh.* Noteworthy printed collections included those of two Moroccan female poets, Malīkah al-'Āṣimī's *Dimā' al-shams* ("The Blood of the Sun"), a daring thematic and artistic work; and Thurayyā Mājdūlīn's second collection, *Al-mut'abūn* (2000; "The Weary"). Another woman, Egyptian Sumayya Ramaḍān, received the 2001 Naguib Mahfouz Medal for her novel *Awrāq an-narjis* ("Narcissus Leaves").

Departing from his usual interest in social issues, Egyptian Bahā' Ṭāhir portrayed characters striving to fill a spiritual void in their lives in his novel *Nuqṭat al-nūr* ("The Point of Light"). Al-Kharrāt, on the other hand, focused on his Coptic roots and his Upper Egyptian traditions in his novel *Ṣukhūr al-samā'* ("The Rocks of the Sky"). Morocco lost a great writer when Muḥammad Zifzāf died in July; Egyptian short-story writer Jāḍibiyya Sidqī died in December.

(AIDA A. BAMIA)

CHINESE

Three novels were particularly eye-catching to the Chinese literati in 2001. The first was You Fengwei's *Zhongguo 1957* ("China 1957"). Written in the first person, the novel told a series of tragic stories about the victims—mostly university students and teachers—of the antirightist campaign of 1957 in which more than 550,000 Chinese were subjected to severe criticism and, in some cases, retribution by the Communist government. The book detailed the hardships that followed for some of the victims, including imprisonment, forced labour, and public humiliation. The novel was considered one of the most important literary works to address this dark chapter in Chinese history.

The second novel was Wang Anyi's *Fuping.* It told the story of a young girl, Fuping, from a rural area who settles in 1950s Shanghai in hopes of making a better life for herself. The book offered a vivid description of the city, with a wonderful presentation of the

Mo Yan: the headsman and the rebel

various styles and customs of everyday life in Shanghai at the time.

The third novel was Mo Yan's *Tanxiang xing* ("Penalty of Sandalwood"). On display were the author's active imagination and his characteristic use of inflated language and satire, but this story was darker than his previous works. It was a portrait of a royal executioner at the beginning of the 20th century and gave a very detailed description of how he did his job; the executioner's story is intertwined with that of a peasant rebel who becomes the target of the headsman after his revolt against German merchants and soldiers fails. The novel contained so many cultural and political hints about contemporary conditions in China that it drew great attention when it was published.

In the field of Chinese poetry only one important work appeared, *Mengchao shuibi* ("Writing in Dream-Nest") by dissident poet Huang Xiang, who was living in the U.S. and whose works had been banned by the Chinese government. *Mengchao shuibi*, which included both poetry and prose, was published in Taipei, Taiwan. Huang's unrestrained imagination and unyielding spirit made the book attractive.

So-called Internet literature continued to appear in 2001, with more literary Web sites emerging in China, Taiwan, and Hong Kong. The largest Web site featuring Chinese literature was Rongshu.com, which boasted some 1,600,000 registered users and more than 600,000 manuscripts in its data-

base. The site reportedly received more than 6,000 literary submissions per day. Although the boundary between electronic and print literature was becoming indistinct, with an increasing number of writers publishing their works on the Internet, many highly touted e-books failed to find a good market during the year. It seemed that Chinese readers still paid most attention to traditional writers such as Wang Anyi and Mo Yan.

(WANG XIAOMING)

JAPANESE

In the first half of 2001, the Akutagawa Prize, awarded semiannually to the most promising new Japanese writers of fiction, went to Toshiyuki Horie for his story "Kuma no shikiishi" ("The Bear's Pavement," published in the December 2000 issue of *Gunzō*), and to Yūichi Seirai for his story "Seisui" ("Holy Water," from the December 2000 *Bungakukai*). In Horie's work a Japanese narrator visits an old friend, a Frenchman of Jewish descent, in the Normandy countryside. During the visit the friend tells the narrator the harrowing story of his family's experiences during the Holocaust. On one level the work explored the relationship between two friends from vastly different cultures; on a broader level it critiqued the Japanese reaction to events in modern European history.

Seirai's "Seisui" told the story of a son and his dying father. Although alienated by conflicting beliefs and desires (the father is a fervent Christian who wants his son to take over the family business; the son is a religious skeptic who has his own plans for the future), the two attempt to resolve their differences before the father's death. Such themes as family loyalty and the nature of faith were sensitively addressed in "Seisui."

In the second half of the year, the Akutagawa Prize went to Sōkyū Gen'yū for his story "Chūin no hana" ("The Mourning Flower," from *Bungakukai*, May 2001). Gen'yū, a Buddhist priest, used the story as a means to expound a profound vision of life and death.

One of Japan's most prominent—and prolific—writers, Banana Yoshimoto, continued to attract attention. (See BIOGRAPHIES.) Her best-selling collection of novellas, *Asleep*, first published in Japanese in 1989, appeared in English during the year, earning her an even wider international audience. A new English translation of *Genji monogatari* (*The Tale of Genji*) was wel-

In Celebration of the World's First Novel

One thousand years ago in Heian Japan, a woman of whom little is known was widowed. But for her personal loss, that woman, known as Murasaki Shikibu, might never have written *Genji monogatari* (c. 1010; *The Tale of Genji*), which is considered the greatest work of Japanese literature and the world's first novel.

The details of the author's life are sketchy. Even her actual name is unknown; Murasaki Shikibu was assigned by scholars—who used the name of the book's dominant female character (Murasaki) and the author's father's position (Shikibu) at the Bureau of Rites to identify her. Born into a lesser branch of the noble and highly influential Fujiwara family, she had been well educated, learning Chinese (generally the exclusive sphere of males). She had married a much older distant cousin and borne a daughter by him, and after two years of marriage, he had died. It is not known how, four years later, she came to be summoned to the court. In any case, her new position within what was then a leading literary centre enabled her to produce a diary, a collection of poetry, and, most famously, the classic romance *Genji monogatari*.

Because Chinese was the scholarly language of the Japanese court, works written in Japanese (the literary language used by women) were not taken very seriously. Nor was prose considered the equal of poetry. What made Lady Murasaki's work different is this: although it is prose, it is clearly informed by a comprehensive knowledge of Chinese and Japanese poetry; it is a graceful work of imaginative fiction, not a personal account of life at court; it incorporates some 800 *waka*, courtly poems purported to be the writing of the main character; and its supple narrative sustains the story through 54 chapters of one character and his legacy.

At its most basic, *Genji* is an absorbing introduction to the culture of the aristocracy in early Heian Japan, its forms of entertainment, its manner of dress, its daily life, and its moral code. The era is exquisitely re-created by the author through the story of Genji, the handsome, sensitive, gifted courtier, an excellent lover, and a worthy friend.

Eminent British sinologist Arthur Waley was the first to translate *Genji monogatari* into English, completing the last of six volumes in 1933. Waley's was a beautiful and inspiring translation, but it was also very free and proved disappointing to serious students. Edward

Seidensticker's 1976 translation was true to the original in both content and tone, but its notes and reader aids were very sparse, an assessment not lost on *Genji*'s third translator, American scholar Royall Tyler of Australian National University. The publication of Tyler's version in 2001—nearly a millennium after *Genji monogatari* was written—attests to a continuing fascination with early Japanese culture and the durability of one remarkable woman's literary achievement.

(KATHLEEN KUIPER)

Murasaki Shikibu as depicted in a screen painting by 17th-century Japanese artist Ogata Korin

comed as the world's first novel approached its 1,000th anniversary. (*See* Sidebar.)

A more recent classic, *Kuroi ame* (1966; "Black Rain") by Masuji Ibuse, who died in 1993, was again the subject of literary discussion. Ibuse's book chronicled, in diary and documentary form, the effects of the atomic bomb on the people of Hiroshima and especially on a young girl, Yasuko, who could not marry because of her exposure to radiation. Readers had assumed that the diary in the novel was the product of Ibuse's imagination, but critic Naoki Inose pointed out in his

work *Pikaresuku* (2000; "Picaresque") that there actually existed a real diary on which the novel was based, and he claimed that in some instances Ibuse had copied directly from this text. The controversy intensified after the diary, entitled *Shigematsu nikki* ("Shigematsu's Diary"), was published in 2001. Comparing the two works, however, most critics were reluctant to suggest plagiarism and agreed that the device of the diary simply shed light on Ibuse's fictional technique.

The Tanizaki Prize went to Hiromi Kawakami for her novel *Sensei no kaban* ("The Teacher's Briefcase"), a love

story about a teacher and a student. The Yomiuri Prize for Literature was awarded to Naoyuki Ii's short-story collection *Nigotta gekiryū ni kakaru hashi* (2000; "A Bridge over a Muddy Torrent"), which portrayed the lives of rural Japanese, and Eimi Yamada's *A2Z* (2000; "A to Z"). Best-selling literary works that appeared during the year included Haruki Murakami's essay on the Sydney Olympic Games, *Shidoni!* ("Sydney!"), Randy Taguchi's novel *Mozaiku* ("Mosaic"), and Yasutaka Tsutsui's *Daimajin* ("Daimajin, the Stone Samurai").

(YOSHIHIKO KAZAMARU)

Mathematics and Physical Sciences

The LANDING of a spacecraft on an ASTEROID, an incisive CRITIQUE of various ELECTORAL SYSTEMS, and the report of an EXPERIMENT that STOPPED A LIGHT PULSE and STARTED IT AGAIN were among the scientific and mathematical headliners of 2001.

MATHEMATICS

The closeness of the 2000 U.S. presidential election highlighted the unusual characteristics of the American electoral system, such as the electoral college, in which all but a few states assign electoral votes on a winner-take-all basis, and simple plurality elections, in which the leading candidate wins without having a runoff election to establish a majority winner. Mathematicians and others had investigated voting systems in the past, and this contentious election inspired further research and discoveries in 2001. (*See* WORLD AFFAIRS: *United States:* Sidebar.)

When there are only two candidates, the situation is very simple. In 1952 the American mathematician Kenneth May proved that there is only one voting system that treats all voters equally, that treats both candidates equally, and where the winning candidate would still win if he or she received more votes. That system is majority rule.

When there are more than two candidates, as was the case in the 2000 presidential election, the situation is most unsatisfactory. Two notable voting systems have been proposed as better for multicandidate races. The first is commonly attributed to the 18th-century French mathematician Jean-Charles, chevalier de Borda. Borda's method requires each voter to rank the candidates, with the lowest candidate getting 1 point, the next lowest candidate 2 points, and so forth, up to the highest candidate, who gets as many points as there are candidates. The points from all voters are added, and the candidate with the most points wins. This system was actually first described in 1433 by Nicholas of Cusa, a German cardinal who was concerned with how to elect German kings. Today it is used in the United States to rank collegiate football and basketball teams.

Borda believed that his system was better than the one devised by his French contemporary Marie-Jean-Antoine-Nicolas de Caritat, marquis de Condorcet. Condorcet felt that the winner should be able to defeat every other candidate in a one-on-one contest. Unfortunately, not every election has a Condorcet winner. In the 2000 presidential election, however, polls indicated that Al Gore would have been a Condorcet winner, since—with the help of supporters of Ralph Nader—he would have beaten George W. Bush in a one-on-one contest (or in a runoff election).

Like the Borda system, the Condorcet system had already been proposed for ecclesiastical elections; it was first described in the 13th century by the Catalan philosopher and missionary Ramon Llull, who was interested in how to elect the abbess of a convent. Nicholas of Cusa made a copy of one of Llull's manuscripts before deciding he could do better, by devising the Borda system. Another of Llull's manuscripts, with a more complete description of his voting system, was discovered and published in 2001, by Friedrich Pukelsheim and others at the University of Augsberg, Germany.

Part of the reason for the great controversy between Borda and Condorcet was that neither of their systems was ideal. In fact, the American Nobel Prize-winning economist Kenneth Arrow showed in 1951 that no voting system for multicandidate elections can be both decisive (produce a Condorcet winner) and completely fair (candidates change position only with a change in their rankings). Nevertheless, after the 2000 presidential election, Americans Donald Saari and Steven Brams argued persuasively for modifying the U.S. system.

Saari used geometry in order to reveal hidden assumptions in voting methods. He favoured the Borda system, which he believed more accurately reflects the true sentiment of voters, as well as having a tendency to produce more centrist winners than the plurality method. In practice, ranking all the candidates can be onerous, and the "broadly supported" winner may just be everybody's third or fourth choice.

Another criticism of the Borda system is that the electorate may vote strategically, rather than sincerely, in order to manipulate the election. Such strategic voting takes place under the current system; in the 2000 presidential election, many voters who preferred Nader voted for Gore out of fear of giving the election to Bush.

Brams favoured approval voting, which is used by some professional societies; Venetians first used it in the 13th century to help elect their magistrates. Under approval voting, voters cast one vote for every candidate they regard as acceptable; the winner is the candidate with the most votes. Approval voting has several attractive features, such as the winner always having the broadest approval and voters never having to choose between two favoured candidates.

Saari and Brams both agreed that the plurality method, together with the winner-take-all feature of the electoral college, has fundamentally flawed the American electoral process, preventing the election of candidates with broad support and frustrating the will of the electorate. (PAUL J. CAMPBELL)

CHEMISTRY

Carbon Chemistry. In 2001 Hendrik Schön and associates of Lucent Technologies' Bell Laboratories, Murray Hill, N.J., announced the production of buckminsterfullerene crystals that become superconducting at substantially warmer temperatures than previously possible. Superconductors conduct electric current without losses due to resistance when they are cooled below a certain critical temperature. In 1991 a Bell Labs team first showed that buckminsterfullerene molecules (C_{60}), which are spherical hollow-cage structures made of 60 carbon atoms each, can act as superconductors at very low temperatures when doped with potassium atoms.

Schön's group mixed C_{60} with chloroform ($CHCl_3$) or its bromine analogue, bromoform, to create "stretched" C_{60} crystals. In the modified crystal structure, chloroform or bromoform molecules were wedged between C_{60} spheres, moving them farther apart. The altered spacing between neighbouring C_{60} molecules, coupled with the experimenters' use of a setup that took advantage of transistor-like effects, raised the critical temperature of the material. Tests showed that C_{60} mixed with bromoform became superconducting below 117 K (–249 °F), which is more than double the previous temperature record of 52 K (–366 °F) for a C_{60}-based material set the previous year.

Although still very cold, the record-breaking temperature was warm enough for the C_{60} superconductor to function while cooled by liquid nitrogen (boiling point 77 K [–321 °F]), instead of the lower-boiling and much more expensive liquid helium. The only other superconductors that operate at higher temperatures are copper oxide ceramic superconductors. These materials were used in powerful magnets, superconductive wires for power-transmission systems, and other applications, but they were expensive and had other drawbacks. Schön speculated that C_{60} superconductors could turn out to be cheaper. He also believed that increasing the spacing between C_{60} spheres in the crystal by just a small percentage could boost the critical temperature even more.

Physical Chemistry. Water can flow uphill, as chemical engineer Manoj K. Chaudhury demonstrated in a notable 1992 experiment that delighted and perplexed the public. Chaudhury, then at Dow Corning Corp., and George M. Whitesides of Harvard University coaxed microlitre-sized droplets of water to run uphill on the surface of a polished silicon wafer at a rate of about one millimetre per second. The secret involved the creation of a surface tension gradient—a swath of continually decreasing hydrophobicity, or tendency to repel water—across the silicon wafer. The wafer was then tilted from the horizontal so that the most hydrophobic end was lower than the least hydrophobic end. Water droplets deposited at the low end were propelled across the surface against gravity by the imbalance of surface tension forces between the uphill and downhill ends of the drop.

In a report published during the year, Chaudhury and co-workers at Lehigh

Susan Daniel and Manoj K. Chaudhury

Water drops condense on a level silicon surface given a radial surface tension gradient and then merge and travel rapidly from centre to edge in this image sequence (A–D) taken from a video covering a half-second period. The labels 1, 2, and 3 identify individual drops and their trails after movement.

University, Bethlehem, Pa., described a technique for making water droplets move across a silicon surface hundreds of times faster than in the previous experiment, at rates of centimetres to a metre or more per second. The speeds were achieved by passing saturated steam over a relatively cool silicon surface possessing a surface tension gradient. In this case the gradient was applied radially, with the wafer's surface being most hydrophobic at the centre and least so at the circumference. As water droplets condensed on the surface from the steam, they first moved slowly outward but then rapidly accelerated as they merged with neighbouring drops. The energy that was released during drop coalescence and directionally channeled by the surface tension gradient accounted for the increased speed of the drops. Chaudhury suggested that the phenomenon could be put to practical use in heat exchangers and other heat-transfer applications and in microfabricated devices where tiny amounts of fluid need to be pumped from one component to another.

Analytic Chemistry. Nuclear magnetic resonance (NMR) spectroscopy was among the chemist's most important tools for studying the physical and chemical properties of plastics, glasses and ceramics, catalysts, DNA and proteins, and myriad other materials. Spectroscopy is the study of interactions between electromagnetic radiation and matter. NMR spectroscopy is based on a phenomenon that occurs when atoms of certain elements are immersed in a strong static magnetic field and exposed to radio-frequency waves. In response, the atomic nuclei emit their own radio signals that can be detected and used to understand a material's properties.

Researchers from the U.S., France, and Denmark reported a technique for ob-

taining more precise NMR information about a material's atomic structure. The group, headed by Philip Grandinetti of Ohio State University at Columbus, found that spinning samples at speeds as high as 30,000 cycles per second can often boost the NMR signal strength by 10-fold or more. They termed the new technique FASTER (for "fast spinning gives transfer enhancement at rotary resonance"). Spinning materials during NMR was not new. A technique known as magic-angle spinning rotated materials at a certain angle in relation to the NMR's static magnetic field. Unfortunately, magic-angle spinning did not work well for about 70% of the chemical elements, including the common elements oxygen, aluminum, and sodium. Analysis required the averaging of weeks of test results and the use of expensive high-power amplifiers. FASTER could produce results in hours with a much less costly low-power amplifier, according to Grandinetti.

Organic Chemistry. French chemist Louis Pasteur, who established the basics of stereochemistry in the 1840s, tried unsuccessfully to influence biological and chemical processes toward a preference for molecules with a right-handed or a left-handed structure. For example, Pasteur rotated growing plants in an effort to change the handedness of their naturally produced chemical compounds, and he performed chemical reactions while spinning the reactants in centrifuges. Over the next century and a half, chemists tried other ways of producing an excess of either left- or right-handed chiral molecules from achiral precursors, a process termed absolute asymmetric synthesis. (Molecules that exist in right- and left-handed versions, like a pair of gloves, are said to be chiral. Molecules lacking such handedness are said to be achiral.) To date, the only acknowledged successes had come with sophisticated approaches such as the induction of reactions with circularly polarized light and chiral selection based on the electroweak force, a fundamental interaction of nature that has asymmetric characteristics. Scientists had uniformly dismissed reports of asymmetric synthesis by simple stirring—clockwise or counterclockwise rotation during the chemical conversion of an achiral compound.

During the year Josep M. Ribó and associates of the University of Barcelona, Spain, reported convincing evidence that chiral assemblies of molecules can be produced by stirring. They used achiral porphyrins, large disk-shaped molecules made of connected organic rings. The porphyrins had a zwitterionic structure—each molecule contained both positively and negatively charged regions—which allowed them to aggregate through electrostatic interactions and hydrogen bonding. Individual porphyrin disks can assemble linearly into left-handed or right-handed helices, and when left undisturbed they formed equal amounts of each kind. Ribó showed that stirring caused the formation of chiral assemblies, with the chirality controlled by the direction of the stirring.

The findings could shed light on the mystery of homochirality in biological systems on Earth—why the essential molecules in living things are single-handed. Natural sugars, for example, are almost exclusively right-handed; natural amino acids, left-handed. Ribó's work suggested that vortex action during early stages of chemical evolution could be the explanation.

Nuclear Chemistry. During the year scientists at Lawrence Berkeley National Laboratory (LBNL), Berkeley, Calif., retracted their two-year-old claim for the synthesis of the superheavy element 118. The original announcement in 1999 had gained worldwide attention because element 118 was considered to be the heaviest chemical element ever produced and was regarded as evidence for existence of the so-called island of stability, a region of the periodic table consisting of superheavy elements with half-lives significantly longer than their slightly lighter superheavy neighbours on the table.

The retraction came after confirmation experiments at LBNL and in Japan, Germany, and France had failed to reproduce the earlier results. In addition, after reviewing the original data using different analytic software, an LBNL committee of experts found no evidence for the decay chains that pointed to

the existence of element 118. The LBNL researchers in 1999 had not directly observed the element. Rather, after bombarding a target of lead-208 with high-energy krypton-86 ions at LBNL's 224-cm (88-in) cyclotron, they inferred the production of three atoms of element 118 from data that they interpreted as characteristic of the way that the atoms decayed into a series of lighter elements.

(MICHAEL WOODS)

PHYSICS

Particle Physics. In the field of neutrino physics, years of work by large teams of researchers worldwide finally bore fruit in 2001. Of the fundamental particles that make up the standard model of the universe, neutrinos are the most enigmatic. Their existence was postulated in 1930 to explain a mysterious loss of energy seen in the nuclear beta-decay process. Because neutrinos interact so weakly with matter, however, they are extraordinarily difficult to observe, and experimental confirmation of their existence came only a quarter century later. Three types of neutrinos were known—electron, muon, and tau neutrinos. They were generally assumed to be massless, but the question remained open until 1998 when a team at Super-Kamiokande, a mammoth neutrino detector located in a Japanese zinc mine, found the strongest evidence to that time that neutrinos indeed possess a tiny mass.

During the year, this work was extended to solve a major puzzle concerning solar physics. The accepted physical model for the nuclear reactions taking place in the Sun required the emission of a large number of electron neutrinos, but decades of experimental measurement had shown only a third of the expected number arriving at Earth. Physicists working at the Sudbury Neutrino Observatory, a neutrino detector built in a Canadian nickel mine, combined their data with complementary data from Super-Kamiokande to produce direct evidence for the remaining two-thirds. Their results confirmed the theory that electron neutrinos oscillate, or transform, among the three types as they travel through space from the Sun, which explained why earlier work had found a shortfall of two-thirds from that predicted. For neutrinos to oscillate, they must have a finite mass, which was consistent with the 1998 finding from Super-Kamiokande.

The new results enabled the theoretical model of the Sun's nuclear reactions to be confirmed with great accuracy. The

number of emitted neutrinos depends very sensitively on the Sun's central temperature, giving this as 15.7 million K, precise to 1%. At the same time, the oscillation between neutrino types would enable a better estimate for the neutrino mass, which had implications for cosmology. (See *Astronomy,* below.)

Another result from particle physics that affected an understanding of the universe as a whole came from work on a phenomenon known as CP violation. In the standard model every matter particle has an antiparticle with the same mass but with properties such as electric charge and spin reversed—for example, electrons and their positron counterparts. When a particle meets its antiparticle, mutual annihilation takes place with the release of energy. Conversely, a particle and its antiparticle can be created from energy. When the formation of particles and antiparticles in the hot early universe is modeled, a difficulty arises. If particles and antiparticles are identical, an equal number of both sorts should now exist. Because particles vastly outnumber antiparticles in the observable universe, however, there must be some kind of asymmetry in properties between the two types of matter. In present theories a very small asymmetry would do the job, and CP violation appeared to be a possible explanation.

Until the 1950s it was assumed that nature is symmetrical in a number of ways. One example is parity—any reaction involving particles must be identical to the equivalent antiparticle reaction viewed in a mirror. In 1957 it was discovered that nuclear beta decay violated this symmetry. It was assumed, however, that symmetry in particle reactions involving both a change of parity (P) and a change of charge sign (C)—for example, the exchange of a negatively charged electron for a positively charged positron—was not violated. This conservation of charge and parity considered together is called CP symmetry. In 1964 decays of K mesons were found to violate CP symmetry. During 2001 independent teams of physicists at the Stanford Linear Accelerator Center and the High Energy Accelerator Research Organization, Tsukuba, Japan, reported evidence for CP violation in the decay of another particle, the B meson. The experimental results also yielded a numerical value representing the amount of CP violation, which turned out to be about half of the required value predicted by the standard model to produce the known universe. The work was preliminary, however, and further refinement was needed to determine whether the standard model as currently formulated was an accurate picture of nature.

Lasers and Light. Two achievements reported during the year could be said to span the speed range of research in optical physics. Harm Geert Muller of the FOM Institute for Atomic and Molecular Physics, Amsterdam, and collaborators produced the shortest light pulses ever measured—just 220 attoseconds (billionths of a billionth of a second, or 10^{-18} second) in duration. The investigators focused an intense pulse of infrared laser light on a jet of dilute argon gas, which converted some of the light into a collection of higher harmonics (multiples of the original frequency) in the ultraviolet range. The relative phases of the harmonics were such that the frequencies interfered in a special way, canceling each other except for very brief time intervals when they all added constructively. The result was a train of extremely short light spikes. Pulses this short could enable the study of a range of very fast phenomena and perhaps even follow electron motion around atomic nuclei.

In 1999, working at the other end of the speed range, a group led by Lene Vestergaard Hau (*see* BIOGRAPHIES) of Harvard University and the Rowland Institute for Science had demonstrated techniques for slowing a light pulse in a cloud of extremely cold gas from its normal speed of about 300,000 km (186,000 mi) per second to roughly the speed of urban automobile traffic. In 2001 Hau and her colleagues reported on a technique to halt a light pulse in a cold gas and release it at a later time. They first prepared a gas of ultracold sodium atoms and treated it with light from a so-called coupling laser, which altered the optical characteristics of the gas. They then fired a probe pulse from a second laser into the gas. Switching off the coupling beam while the probe pulse was traversing the gas brought the light to a stop and allowed all the information about it to be imprinted on the sodium atoms as a "quantum coherence pattern." Switching on the coupling laser again regenerated a perfect copy of the original pulse. This technique could have applications for controlling and storing information in optical computers.

Condensed-Matter Physics. In 1995 researchers first produced a new state of matter in the laboratory—an achievement that was recognized with the 2001 Nobel Prize for Physics. (*See* NOBEL PRIZES.) Called a Bose-Einstein condensate, it comprises a collection of gaseous atoms at a temperature just above ab-

solute zero (–273.15 °C, or –459.67 °F) locked together in a single quantum state—as uniform and coherent as a single atom. Until 2001 condensates of elements such as rubidium, lithium, and sodium had been prepared by cooling a dilute gas of atoms in their ground states. During the year separate research groups at the University of Paris XI, Orsay, and the École Normale Supérieure, Paris, succeeded in making a condensate from a gas of excited helium atoms. Because no existing lasers operated in the far-ultraviolet wavelength needed to excite helium from the ground state, the researchers used an electrical discharge to supply the excitation energy.

Although each helium atom possessed an excitation energy of 20 eV (which was more than 100 billion times its thermal energy in the condensate), the atoms within the condensate were stabilized against release of this energy by polarization (alignment) of their spins, which greatly reduced the probability that excited atoms would collide. When the condensate came into contact with some other atom, however, all the excitation energy in its atoms was released together. This suggested the possibility of a new kind of laser that emits in the far ultraviolet.

Practical devices based on such advanced techniques of atomic and optical physics were coming closer to realization. During the year a team led by Scott Diddams of the U.S. National Institute of Standards and Technology, Boulder, Colo., used the interaction between a single cooled mercury atom and a laser beam to produce the world's most stable clock, with a precision of about one second in 100 million years. Such precision could well be needed in future high-speed data transmission.

(DAVID G.C. JONES)

ASTRONOMY

Solar System. On Feb. 12, 2001, the unmanned spacecraft NEAR (Near Earth Asteroid Rendezvous) Shoemaker gently touched down on asteroid 433 Eros. NEAR had spent the previous 12 months in orbit about the potato-shaped object, photographing its surface features. After it landed, its onboard gamma-ray spectrometer showed that Eros has a low abundance of iron and aluminum relative to magnesium. Such proportions are found in the Sun and in meteorites called chondrites, thought to be among the oldest objects in the solar system. The observations suggested that Eros was formed some 4.5 billion years

ago and did not undergo significant chemical changes after that time. In another postlanding study, a magnetometer aboard NEAR confirmed the lack of a detectable magnetic field on Eros. This finding suggested that magnetized meteorites (which constitute the majority of meteorites found on Earth) may be fragments knocked from other types of asteroids or that they acquired their magnetization on their journey to Earth.

On September 22 another spacecraft, Deep Space 1, successfully navigated its way past Comet Borrelly, providing the best view ever of the ice particles, dust, and gas leaving comets. The spacecraft came within 2,200 km (1,360 mi) of the roughly 8 × 4-km (5 × 2.5-mi) cometary nucleus. It sent back images that showed a rough surface terrain, with rolling plains and deep fractures—a hint that the comet may have formed as a collection of icy and stony rubble rather than as a coherent solid object. From the amount of reflected light—only about 4%—the surface appeared to be composed of very dark matter. Cosmochemists proposed that the surface was most likely covered with carbon and substances rich in organic compounds.

In mid-2001 an international group of astronomers using 11 different telescopes around the world reported the discovery of 12 new moons of Saturn. This brought the total to 30, the largest number so far detected for any planet in the solar system. The moons range in diameter from 6 to 32 km (4 to 20 mi). Saturn previously had been known to have six large moons, Titan being the largest, and 12 small ones, all but one of which were classified as regular moons because they move in circular orbits in the planet's orbital plane. All of the new moons move in highly eccentric orbits, which suggested that they are remnants of larger objects that were captured into orbit around Saturn early in its history and subsequently broken up by collisions.

Stars. One of the most perplexing problems in modern astrophysics, an observed shortage in the predicted number of neutrinos emanating from the Sun, appeared to be finally resolved during the year. Detailed theoretical studies of nuclear reactions in the Sun's core had predicted that energy is released in the form of gamma rays, thermal energy, and neutrinos. The gamma rays and thermal energy slowly diffuse to the solar surface and are eventually observed as visible light and other electromagnetic radiation. Neutrinos are electrically neutral particles that travel almost

NASA, J. Bell (Cornell University), M. Wolff (SSI), and the Hubble Heritage Team (STScI/AURA)

Two strikingly different visages of Mars appear in Hubble Space Telescope images made in late June and less than three months later, when a global dust storm— the biggest in decades—obscured all surface features.

unaffected through the Sun and interplanetary space on their way to Earth. Beginning in the late 1960s, scientists sought to detect these elusive particles directly. Because neutrinos interact so weakly with matter, detectors containing enormous quantities of mass were built to detect them. These were placed deep underground to allow neutrinos originating in the Sun to be distinguished from background galactic cosmic rays. Despite many experiments employing a variety of detectors, scientists consistently had observed only about a third of the predicted neutrino flux.

Neutrinos come in three varieties, or flavours—electron, muon, and tau. Because nuclear fusion in the Sun's core should produce only electron neutrinos, most of the earlier experiments had been designed to detect only that flavour. The Sudbury Neutrino Observatory (SNO), sited deep inside a Canadian nickel mine, was built to have enhanced sensitivity to muon and tau neutrinos. It used as its detector a 1,000-ton sphere of extremely pure heavy water (water molecules in which the two hydrogen atoms are replaced with deuterium, one of hydrogen's heavier isotopes). A second facility, called Super-Kamiokande and located in a zinc mine in Japan, employed a tank of 50,000 tons of ultrapure ordinary water to detect electron and muon neutrinos. In 2001 the international collaboration running SNO, headed by Art McDonald of Queen's University at Kingston, Ont., reported evidence derived from SNO and Super-Kamiokande data for the detection of the missing two-thirds of the neutrino flux. The results confirmed the theory that electron neu-

trinos transform, or oscillate, among the three possible flavours on their journey to Earth. Oscillation also implied that neutrinos have a tiny but finite mass and thus make a contribution to the nonluminous, unobserved "dark matter" in the universe. (See *Physics,* above.)

The detection of planets orbiting other stars was first announced in 1995. By the beginning of 2001 about 50 extrasolar planets had been reported, and by year's end the number had risen to more than 70. Most of the planets found to date are quite different from those in Earth's solar system. Many are large (as much as 20 times the mass of Jupiter) and often move in elliptical orbits quite close to their parent stars.

During the year, for the first time, a planetary system remarkably similar to Earth's solar system was detected. Geoffrey Marcy of the University of California, Berkeley, Paul Butler of the Carnegie Institution of Washington, D.C., and their collaborators reported that a star visible to the naked eye, 47 Ursae Majoris, is orbited by at least two planets. The presence of one planet had been known since 1996, but the discovery of the second companion changed astronomers' picture of the system in important ways. One planet has a mass at least three-fourths that of Jupiter, and the other has at least two and a half times Jupiter's mass. Interestingly, the ratio of their masses is close to the ratio of the masses of Saturn and Jupiter. Both extrasolar planets move in nearly circular orbits, a property that was thought to increase the odds that the system contains Earth-like planets as well.

Galaxies and Cosmology. Over the past 75 years, observations and theory have combined to produce a consistent model of the origin and evolution of the universe, beginning with a big-bang explosion some 10 billion to 20 billion years ago. Left behind and detectable today as a relic of this hot event is a highly uniform flux of cosmic microwave background radiation. Because the matter that is observed filling the universe attracts other matter gravitationally, the expansion rate of the universe should be slowing down. Nevertheless, observations in 1998 of the brightness of fairly distant exploding stars called Type Ia supernovas suggested that the expansion is currently accelerating. The findings were interpreted as evidence for the existence throughout space of a kind of cosmic repulsion force first hypothesized by Albert Einstein in 1917 and represented by a term, the cosmological constant, in his equations of general relativity. The supernovas observed in the studies were found to be dimmer than expected, which implied that they were farther away than a decelerating universe could account for.

During the year Adam G. Riess of the Space Telescope Science Institute, Baltimore, Md., and collaborators reported new studies of the most distant supernova yet found, designated SN 1997ff. Their analysis of observations of the supernova, which were made with the Hubble Space Telescope, indicated that the expansion rate of the universe was slower at the time of the supernova explosion billions of years ago than it is now. Their results also refuted the possibility that intervening dust or other astrophysical effects could be an explanation for the unexpectedly dim supernovas seen in the earlier studies. SN 1997ff provided the best evidence to date that the expansion of the universe is indeed accelerating.

The existence of galaxies and their current distribution in space to form clusters, filaments, and voids indicated that large-scale fluctuations in the density of matter were present in the very early universe, and theoretical studies indicated that the cosmic background radiation should also carry an imprint of those fluctuations in the form of slight variations in brightness across the sky. In 2001 the combined findings of three recent experiments designed to study the cosmic background radiation provided dramatic evidence for this prediction. First reported on in 2000, two of the experiments—Maxima (Millimeter Anisotropy Experiment Imaging Array) and

Boomerang (Balloon Observations of Millimetric Extragalactic Radiation and Geophysics)—used balloons to carry detectors high above most of Earth's atmosphere. The third experiment—DASI (Degree Angular Scale Interferometer)—was a ground-based interferometer located at the South Pole. All three measured fluctuations in the intensity of the cosmic background radiation on various angular scales across the sky and with an accuracy of one part in 100,000. Taken

Earth Perihelion and Aphelion, 2002

| Jan. 2 | Perihelion, 147,098,130 km (91,402,370 mi) from the Sun |
| July 6 | Aphelion, 152,094,370 km (94,506,880 mi) from the Sun |

Equinoxes and Solstices, 2002

March 20	Vernal equinox, 19:16[1]
June 21	Summer solstice, 13:24[1]
Sept. 23	Autumnal equinox, 04:55[1]
Dec. 22	Winter solstice, 01:14[1]

Eclipses, 2002

May 26	Moon, penumbral (begins 10:12[1]), the beginning visible in North America (except the northeast), Central America, western South America, eastern Asia, the Pacific Ocean, the southeastern Indian Ocean; the end visible in southwestern Alaska, Asia (except the far north), Australia, the eastern Indian Ocean, the Pacific Ocean.
June 10–11	Sun, annular (begins 23:48[1]), the beginning visible in western Indonesia, southwestern Asia, northern Australia, the western Pacific Ocean; the end visible in North America (except northeastern Canada), the eastern Pacific Ocean, the Caribbean Sea.
June 24	Moon, penumbral (begins 20:18[1]), the beginning visible in Australia, southern and western Asia, Europe, Africa, eastern South America, the eastern and southern Atlantic Ocean, the southwestern Pacific Ocean; the end visible in Africa, Europe, South America (except the northwest), western Australia, the southeastern Pacific Ocean.
Nov. 19–20	Moon, penumbral (begins 23:32[1]), the beginning visible in Africa, Europe, North America (except the west), Central and South America, extreme western Asia, the Atlantic Ocean, the western Indian Ocean; the end visible in North, Central, and South America, Greenland, Europe, northwestern Russia, western Africa, the Atlantic Ocean, the eastern Pacific Ocean.
Dec. 4	Sun, total (begins 07:38[1]), the beginning visible in central and southern Africa, the eastern South Atlantic Ocean, the extreme southern Indian Ocean; the end visible in Australia, southern New Zealand, southern Indonesia, the southern Indian Ocean.

[1] Universal time.
Source: The Astronomical Almanac for the Year 2002 (2001).

together, their results implied that more than 95% of the material content of the universe is made up of at least two kinds of dark exotic matter that has gravitational effects on the observed matter. Furthermore, the studies reinforced the idea that about two-thirds of the energy content of the universe exists in the form of the repulsive gravitational force represented by the cosmological constant or some equivalent. (KENNETH BRECHER)

SPACE EXPLORATION

Manned Spaceflight. Human activity in space faced an uncertain future as the International Space Station (ISS) encountered massive cost overruns and as cuts in general space spending were anticipated in response to the Sept. 11, 2001, terrorist attacks.

Following the start of full-time manned operations in late 2000, the ISS underwent rapid expansion with the addition of several key elements. First to arrive was the U.S.-built Destiny laboratory module, taken into orbit February 7 by the space shuttle Atlantis. Destiny, about the size of a bus, was designed to hold 24 standard payload racks, about half of them housing equipment for research into human adaptation to space travel, materials fabrication, and the behaviour of fluids and fires in microgravity. Because of weight limitations on shuttle cargos, the module was only partially outfitted inside and out at launch. The next mission, conducted in March by the shuttle Discovery, took up the Leonardo Multi-Purpose Logistics Module. Contributed by the Italian Space Agency as a reusable cargo carrier, Leonardo carried supplies and equipment for the station and transported trash back to Earth. Astronauts also conducted space walks to prepare the ISS for attachment of the Canadian-built robot arm. Three of Discovery's crew stayed aboard the station as the Expedition Two crew, while the original Expedition One crew, which had occupied the ISS since Nov. 2, 2000, returned to Earth on the shuttle.

A month later the shuttle Endeavour took up the Canadarm2 robot arm and Raffaello, another Italian-built logistics module. Addition of the arm (derived from the earlier Canadarm carried on the shuttle since 1981) would let the ISS crew position new modules as they arrived. Because Canadarm2 could relocate itself along rails on the ISS exterior, it could reach virtually any location where work had to be done. More capability was added in July when Atlantis

took up the Joint Airlock (called Quest), which allowed the ISS crew to conduct space walks independent of the shuttle. Further outfitting was conducted in August by the crew of Discovery, which delivered Leonardo to the ISS a second time. The mission also took the Expedition Three crew to relieve the Expedition Two crew. In September, using an expendable launcher, Russia sent up a Docking Compartment; the module carried an additional docking port for Soyuz and Progress spacecraft and an airlock for space walks. Previously the ISS had only two Soyuz/Progress-style ports, which had necessitated some juggling when new craft arrived. On December 5, after a six-day delay caused by an ISS docking problem with a Progress cargo ferry, Endeavour lifted off for the space station to carry out another crew exchange and deliver cargo in Raffaello once again.

The future of the ISS became clouded with the revelation in early 2001 that budget estimates were running $4 billion over plan. In response, NASA moved to cancel the U.S. habitat module and Crew Return Vehicle, or lifeboat, that would allow the station to house a crew of seven. With the crew restricted to three, virtually no crew time would be left for research, and the station would effectively be crippled as a science tool. At year's end NASA was negotiating with its European partners to have them pick up the responsibilities for finishing the habitat and lifeboat.

Russia's aging space station, Mir, was deliberately destroyed when mission controllers remotely commanded a docked Progress tanker to fire rockets and lower the station into Earth's atmosphere, where it burned up on March 23. Mir, whose core module was launched in 1986 and served as the nucleus of an eventual six-module complex, had operated long beyond its planned five-year lifetime.

China continued development of a human spaceflight capability with the second unmanned flight test of its Shenzhou ("Divine Ship" or "Magic Vessel") spacecraft in early January. The Shenzhou design was derived from Russia's Soyuz craft. The descent module returned to Earth after a week in orbit, but the little news that was released afterward raised doubts about its success. Analysts disagreed on when China would conduct its first manned space mission but expected it to happen within a few years.

Space Probes. The high point of the year occurred on February 12 when the Near

Earth Asteroid Rendezvous spacecraft (NEAR; officially, NEAR Shoemaker) touched down on asteroid 433 Eros, becoming the first spacecraft to land on a small body. NEAR had been orbiting Eros since Feb. 14, 2000, while taking thousands of video images and laser rangefinder readings to map the asteroid in detail. As the spacecraft ran low on fuel, controllers moved it into a lower orbit that let it collide gently with the surface of the rotating rock—a "soft" hard landing, a task for which it was not designed—and gather data on the surface. (See Astronomy, above.)

NASA launched the 2001 Mars Odyssey spacecraft on April 7 on a mission to study Mars from orbit and serve as a communications relay for U.S. and international landers scheduled to arrive in 2003 and 2004. On October 23 Mars Odyssey entered into a Mars orbit, where it spent the next several weeks using the Martian atmosphere as a brake to reshape its orbit for a 917-day mapping mission. Visible-light, infrared, and other instruments would collect data on the mineral content of the surface, including possible water locations, and the radiation hazards in the orbital environment.

The Cassini mission to Saturn, which carried the European-built Huygens probe designed to explore Saturn's moon Titan, continued toward its goal following a trajectory-assist flyby of Jupiter in late 2000 and early 2001 and returned images in conjunction with the Galileo spacecraft orbiting Jupiter. Cassini was to arrive at Saturn in 2004. Although finished with its official primary and extended missions, Galileo continued to operate during the year with additional flybys of Jupiter's moons Callisto and Io.

NASA's Microwave Anisotropy Probe (MAP) was launched on June 30 into a temporary Earth orbit and later moved to its permanent station in space about 1.5 million km (930,000 mi) from Earth, where it would use a pair of thermally isolated microwave telescopes to map small variations in the background radiation of the universe. These irregularities, discovered by the Cosmic Background Explorer (launched 1989), were believed to correspond to density differences in the early universe that gave rise to today's galaxies. NASA launched the Genesis probe on August 8 to gather 10–20 micrograms of particles of the solar wind. The material would be captured on ultrapure collector arrays exposed for more than two years in space and then returned to Earth for analysis in 2004. The collected particles could

provide clues to the composition of the nebula that formed the solar system.

Unmanned Satellites. On February 20 Russia launched Sweden's Odin satellite, which carried a 1.1-m (43-in) radio telescope as its main instrument. Using two separate operating modes, the dual-mission craft was designed to observe radiation from a variety of molecular

species to elucidate ozone-depletion mechanisms in Earth's atmosphere and star-formation processes in deep space. The Ukrainian-built Coronas-F satellite, launched by Russia on July 31, carried X-ray, radio, and particle instruments to study solar activity.

Other launches included the Geosynchronous Lightweight Technology

Launches in support of human spaceflight, 2001

Country	Flight	Crew[1]	Dates	Mission/payload
China	Shenzhou 2	—	January 9	second test flight of manned spacecraft
U.S.	STS-98, Atlantis	Kenneth Cockrell Mark Polansky Robert Curbeam Thomas Jones Marsha Ivins	February 7–20	delivery of Destiny laboratory module to ISS
Russia	Progress	—	February 26	ISS supplies
U.S.	STS-102, Discovery	James Wetherbee James Kelly Andy Thomas Paul Richards Yury Usachyov (u) Susan Helms (u) James Voss (u) William Shepherd (d) Yury Gidzenko (d) Sergey Krikalyov (d)	March 8–21	delivery of Leonardo logistics module to ISS; station crew exchange
U.S.	STS-100, Endeavour	Kent Rominger Jeffrey Ashby Chris Hadfield Scott Parazynski John Phillips Umberto Guidoni Yury Lonchakov	April 19–May 1	delivery of Canadarm2 and Raffaello logistics module to ISS
Russia	Soyuz-TM 32	Talgat Musabayev Yury Baturin Dennis Tito[2]	April 28–May 6	exchange of Soyuz return craft for ISS crew (TM 31 with TM 32)
Russia	Progress	—	May 20	ISS supplies
U.S.	STS-104, Atlantis	Steven Lindsey Charles Hobaugh Michael Gernhardt James Reilly Janet Kavandi	July 12–24	delivery of Joint Airlock to ISS
U.S.	STS-105, Discovery	Scott Horowitz Rick Sturckow Daniel Barry Patrick Forrester Frank Culbertson (u) Vladimir Dezhurov (u) Mikhail Tyurin (u) Yury Usachyov (d) Susan Helms (d) James Voss (d)	August 10–22	delivery of Leonardo logistics module to ISS; station crew exchange
Russia	Progress	—	August 21	ISS supplies
Russia	Progress-type	—	September 15	delivery of Docking Compartment-1 to ISS
Russia	Soyuz-TM 33	Viktor Afanasyev Konstantin Kozeyev Claudie Haigneré	October 21–30	exchange of Soyuz return craft for ISS crew (TM 32 with TM 33)
Russia	Progress	—	November 26	ISS supplies
U.S.	STS-108, Endeavour	Dominic Gorie Mark Kelly Linda Godwin Daniel Tani Frank Culbertson (d) Vladimir Dezhurov (d) Mikhail Tyurin (d) Yury Onufriyenko (u) Daniel Bursch (u) Carl Walz (u)	December 5–17	delivery of Raffaello logistics module to ISS; station crew exchange

[1] Commander and pilot (or flight engineer for Soyuz) are listed first.
[2] Flew as paying passenger.
u = ISS crew member carried up to station (ISS commander listed first).
d = ISS crew member returned to Earth (ISS commander listed first).

Experiment (GeoLITE; May 18), an advanced technology demonstration satellite carrying experimental and operational communications equipment for the U.S. military, and a twin payload (December 7) comprising Jason-1, a French-U.S. ocean-surface topography satellite designed as a follow-on to the highly successful TOPEX/Poseidon satellite launched in 1992, and the Thermosphere-Ionosphere-Mesosphere Energetics and Dynamics (TIMED) satellite, which would study the effects of the Sun and human activity on Earth's middle and upper atmosphere.

Launch Vehicles. NASA's plans to reduce the cost of getting payloads to orbit were set back by the cancellation of two high-profile reusable launch vehicle (RLV) projects. The X-33 subscale test craft was to have been a technology demonstrator for a larger single-stage-to-orbit Venture-Star RLV. The aircraft-launched X-34 RLV test rocket would have demonstrated technologies for low-cost orbiting of smaller payloads. Both projects ran into technical problems that led NASA to decide that further investment would not save either project. In their place NASA set up the Space Launch Initiative to focus on advancing individual technologies rather than complete systems while continuing to pursue a next-generation RLV.

Boeing's new Delta IV launcher moved toward its maiden flight in 2002 with the delivery in 2001 of the first common booster core to Cape Canaveral, Florida, and successful ground tests of its new RS-68 hydrogen-oxygen liquid-fueled engine. The Delta IV family would be able to boost payloads of 8,000–23,000 kg (17,600–50,600 lb) into low Earth orbit. India successfully launched its Geosynchronous Satellite Launch Vehicle on April 18 and thereby took an important step closer to entering the commercial space market. On August 29 Japan's National Space Development Agency launched its first H-2A rocket, a revamped version of the troubled H-2 that was intended to compete with Europe's Ariane launcher and support Japan's partnership in the ISS. The H-2 family used a liquid-hydrogen–fueled first stage and twin solid rocket boosters. On September 29 NASA and the state of Alaska inaugurated a new launch complex on Kodiak Island with the launch of the Kodiak Star payload (comprising four small satellites) by an Athena I launcher. The Kodiak location, which faced south across the open Pacific Ocean, was ideal for launching satellites into a variety of polar (north-south) orbits.   (DAVE DOOLING)

Milestones in Spaceflight

April 12, 2001, marked the anniversaries of two landmark events in space travel: the 40th anniversary of the first human spaceflight—U.S.S.R. cosmonaut Yury Gagarin's single orbit of Earth in 1961—and the 20th anniversary of the U.S. launch of the first space shuttle, *Columbia*, in 1981. Gagarin's feat and the subsequent goading by Soviet leadership sparked a chain of events that started on May 25, 1961, when U.S. Pres. John F. Kennedy petitioned Congress to commit the nation to landing a man on the Moon "before this decade is out." Though that goal was achieved on July 20, 1969, when the Apollo 11 Lunar Module carried astronauts Neil Armstrong and Edwin ("Buzz") Aldrin to the surface of the Moon, aspirations for space travel continued to expand.

Ironically, the manned space race that had started between the U.S. and the U.S.S.R. 40 years earlier was replaced by a spirit of cooperation in 2001; the former competitors worked together to build the International Space Station (ISS) with other nations that became space farers in the 1960s, '70s, and '80s. On a more sombre note, the year also marked the 30th anniversary (April 19, 1971) of the first space station, the U.S.S.R.'s Salyut 1, and the death of its first three-man crew on their return to Earth (June 30, 1971); it was also the 15th anniversary (Jan. 28, 1986) of the explosion of the space shuttle *Challenger*, which killed seven astronauts.

The year 2001 also evoked the bolder vision of space activity painted by Stanley Kubrick and Arthur C. Clarke in their 1968 motion picture *2001: A Space Odyssey*. Not only was the ISS far smaller than its movie counterpart, it was likely to be even less than what had been planned; budget overruns threatened to reduce its crew size and science facilities. Exploration beyond the immediate vicinity of Earth was by automated spacecraft. No plans were in sight for large-scale lunar exploration as depicted in the film. The first government-industry venture to develop a reusable space liner, somewhat similar to its film version, faltered amid technical and financial problems.

These endeavours highlighted the technical, economic, and political challenges facing space explorers. For instance, descendants of the R-7 rocket that launched Gagarin continued to launch the three-man Soyuz and other spacecraft for Russia. The 20-year-old *Columbia* remained operational along with three other shuttles, and all four were expected to remain in service at least through 2020.

Nevertheless, humans continued to push at the frontier. American businessman Dennis Tito became the first space tourist when he rode a Russian Soyuz to the ISS in May 2001. In addition, Russia was considering more tourist flights, and several private American ventures were trying to develop affordable space tourism as a business.

(DAVE DOOLING)

Media and Publishing

Consolidation and MERGERS continued in the broadcast and publishing industries, while the TERRORIST and ANTHRAX attacks brought a new SERIOUSNESS as well as new challenges for all media content. SATELLITE and CABLE TV dominated even as INTERACTIVE TV and STREAMING media carved out niches for themselves.

TELEVISION

Organization. By 2001 the late 1990s rush to complete megamergers seemed to have ended in the United States, as each of the six leading American broadcast networks had aligned with a much larger entertainment/business company. With the smoke cleared and regulatory approval granted, ABC was part of the Disney empire, NBC was part of General Electric, CBS and UPN belonged to Viacom, WB was primarily part of AOL Time Warner, and Fox had been taken over by Rupert Murdoch's News Corp. Such alignments provided vital protection for the business model of network television, still the nation's most powerful aggregator of audiences for advertisers but increasingly seen by analysts as outdated for having only one revenue stream—advertising—which was vulnerable to economic fluctuations.

The year's major deal involving a network saw NBC in October making a nearly $2 billion acquisition of Telemundo Communications, the Spanish-language network with a 20% share of the Hispanic audience. The move was significant because of the booming U.S. Hispanic population. (*See* WORLD AFFAIRS: *United States*: Special Report.) NBC outbid Viacom for Telemundo, owned by Sony Pictures and Liberty Media Corp., and said the companies were planning to combine advertising sales efforts and offices and share some news resources. NBC's costly Olympic telecasts would have an additional outlet, and Telemundo could draw on NBC expertise to develop comedy series. Meanwhile, Univision, which reached 80% of Hispanic viewers, was moving forward with plans to launch Telefutura, a Spanish-language network targeting younger viewers, in early 2002.

News Corp. had long been considered the leading suitor of Hughes Electronics, owner of the top American satellite television service, DIRECTV. In October, however, General Motors Corp., the controlling shareholder of Hughes, accepted a surprise $25.8 billion bid by DIRECTV's major rival in consumer satellite programming, EchoStar Communications. If granted regulatory approval, the merger would make the new company the country's largest provider of television subscriptions, with 16.7 million customers totaling 17% of the pay-TV market, compared with cable operator AT&T's 14 million. Analysts and legislators expressed doubt that the merger would pass muster because it effectively killed competition in rural areas not served by cable.

In December the French company Vivendi Universal announced it was picking up USA Networks Inc's TV and film production units, including the USA and Sci-fi cable networks—as well as executive Barry Diller—for some $10.3 billion (*see* Book Publishing, *below*). Cable TV tycoon John C. Malone strengthened Liberty Media's German holdings by adding six cable systems, including those servicing Berlin, Hamburg, and Bavaria, for $5 billion. Meanwhile, AOL Time Warner became the first foreign broadcaster licensed by China. Its Hong Kong-based China Entertainment Television (CETV) broadcast a Chinese-language channel over cable systems in Guangdong. In exchange, Time Warner Cable carried China Central Television's (CCTV's) English-language channel in New York City, Los Angeles, and Houston, Texas. Having obtained 29% of China's Sun Television Cybernetworks, the Chinese-language online network SINA.com became the company's largest shareholder. Sun TV, a major satellite TV broadcaster and cable TV program syndicator, owned restricted

land rights to operate two satellite TV channels in China. Phoenix satellite TV, which broadcast from Hong Kong in Mandarin Chinese, also received rights to transmit, but only in the Pearl River Delta area of southern China, where foreign broadcasts were allowed. Phoenix was partly owned by News Corp.'s satellite TV network, STAR. Murdoch reported a 15% drop in News Corp.'s fiscal-third-quarter revenue, while losses in film, magazine, and newspaper sectors were somewhat offset by gains in cable network programming and TV businesses. Chief executive Mark Schneider of Europe's cable operator United Pan-Europe Communications NV resigned after reporting huge losses beginning the second quarter.

New York cosmetics heir and owner of Central European Media Enterprises (CME) Ronald S. Lauder won his complaint against the government of the Czech Republic, which failed to protect CME from being squeezed out of TV Nova, the Czechs' most popular TV station. An international arbitration panel in Stockholm ordered the government to pay CME some $500 million.

Germany's second-largest TV network, Zweites Deutsches Fernsehen (ZDF), signed an agreement to cooperate with T-Online International AG as a way of getting around new regulations banning advertising on the news and information Web sites of public institutions (such as ZDF) funded by TV license fees. T-Online's parent company, Deutsche Telekom, proposed to team with the Kirch Group, Europe's largest producer of entertainment, sports, and news content, to develop hardware and software platforms for TV set-top boxes, but the deal fell through. RTL New Media took over Bertelsmann AG's interactive-TV and broadband division for $12 million. Bertelsmann then started BeBroadband for its e-commerce activities with a "preferred partner" relationship with RTL.

American Programming. The September 11 terrorist attacks in the United States dramatically altered the American television ratings picture. Before that date NBC was riding high, having finished first among young adults during the 2000–01 television season completed in May. CBS was looking forward to a ratings bonanza from the third edition of the reality game show *Survivor*, scheduled for October. The annual Emmy

Reuters/TimePix

The October 3 episode of **The West Wing** *dealt with issues of the September 11 terrorist attacks.*

Awards, announced in September, would recognize top prime-time achievers and give the networks a promotional boost going into the new season. The networks and other television producers were also feeling happy to have averted potential disaster in the spring of 2001 by reaching contract agreements with actors and writers unions, which had seemed poised to go out on strike. Some networks had prepared for a walkout by stockpiling new series episodes, but most admitted that if it had occurred, they would have had to fill their most popular hours, prime time, with reruns, reality series, and newsmagazines.

The September attacks forced first one and later a second postponement of the Emmys, as well as the delay of the TV season's debut by one week. When things finally got started, it seemed that the television order had changed. Television news organizations drew plaudits for selflessness in the immediate aftermath of the terrorist attacks. In addition to agreeing to share video, they provided nonstop commercial-free coverage from the attacks on the World Trade Center and the Pentagon beginning on Tuesday morning until Saturday, September 15. In the process all three of the old-line networks—ABC, CBS, and NBC—broke their previous records for continuous coverage, established during the first Moon walk and after the assassination of Pres. John F. Kennedy. In the first three days, CBS anchor Dan Rather and ABC counterpart Peter Jennings each put in 44 on-air hours.

High ratings continued for cable news provider CNN, which earlier in the year had modernized its format and brought in new anchors in response to growing competition from the likes of Murdoch's Fox News Channel. In the first three weeks after the attacks, CNN's ratings were up 500% from what they had been during the first eight months of 2001.

The prime-time landscape was also altered by the terrorist attacks. Viewers were now drawn to established quality series, which resulted in record ratings for such shows as CBS's *Everybody Loves Raymond* and NBC's *Friends, Law & Order,* and *The West Wing.* The producers of *The West Wing,* a dramatic series about a fictional but realistic White House, even hustled to put together a special episode directly responding to the acts of terrorism; it drew the series' highest ratings ever. Meanwhile, reality series other than *Survivor* drew very few viewers. This type of programming, so popular in 2000, had succeeded in stanching the steady loss of network audience share to cable. In September and October it was flailing, however. People coping with dramatic realities in their own lives had no patience for the ersatz danger in "reality" shows, which typically staged grueling competitions amid harsh living conditions for their nonactor participants. Even *Survivor,* while still drawing top-10 ratings, saw its popularity shrink considerably from the previous winter's edition, which had led the series to first place in the 2000–01 season ratings race.

On top of all of this, the decline in the American economy hit advertising-dependent television networks particularly hard even before September 11

and the several days without advertising that ensued. Afterward, the economy reeled, ad spending dropped even further, and the networks were talking openly about the need for major changes. The top four broadcast networks—ABC, CBS, Fox, and NBC—had increased their ad revenue by an average of almost 7% a year for five years straight, building up to a total of more than $16 billion during 2000. According to the *Los Angeles Times,* however, what analysts had projected to be a 2% drop during 2001 looked after September to be more like a 6% drop, a decline the paper called "unprecedented." This blow to the networks came against a backdrop of escalating production costs and loss of market share to cable. In response the networks vowed to slash costs, develop fewer new series, and possibly even eliminate Saturday-night prime-time programming altogether—a very drastic move.

When the *Primetime Emmy Awards* ceremony finally was held in early November, the networks got another bit of bad news. For the first time, one of the coveted best series Emmys went to a show made for cable television, the HBO look at "30-something" single women in New York, *Sex and the City* (series star Sarah Jessica Parker [*see* BIOGRAPHIES] was herself an Emmy nominee). Another HBO series, the critically acclaimed *The Sopranos,* saw two of its actors take two of the other top honours, best actor in a drama (James Gandolfini) and best actress in a drama (Edie Falco). *The West Wing* otherwise held off *The Sopranos* to win the best drama Emmy for the second year in a row. Best comedy actress went to repeat winner Patricia Heaton of *Everybody Loves Raymond,* and best comedy actor went to first-timer Eric McCormack of NBC's *Will & Grace.*

International Programming. When the private Independent Television (NTV) network was taken over by Russian government-owned Gazprom in April, after a protracted struggle with its cofounder and original owner, tycoon Vladimir Gusinsky (*see* BIOGRAPHIES), a majority of the news team (including general director Yevgeny Kiselyov) transferred to TV6. That station later faced court-mandated liquidation, however, in the wake of a lawsuit by energy giant Lukoil, whose daughter company, Lukoil-Garant, was a 15% shareholder. Boris Berezovsky, another of Russia's "oligarchs," who was now living in exile and who controlled 75% of TV6, had offered to buy out Lukoil-Garant, which then countered with an offer to buy out Berezovsky.

TV—Too Big a Dose of Reality?

Strictly speaking, reality programming—unscripted and unrehearsed programs in the form of sporting events, talk shows, documentaries, *Candid Camera*, and the like—had been part of the television landscape from the earliest days of broadcasting. Later, in 1973, it became more deliberate when, on PBS's *An American Family*, the innermost secrets of the William C. Loud family unfolded before the TV audience in 12 hour-long segments culled from 300 hours of footage shot in the family's home. Then, beginning in 1992, the American cable station MTV scored a hit by having seven young people, strangers to each other, live together for several months in a house under constant camera scrutiny, with the highlights broadcast weekly. Nevertheless, it was not until the American television network CBS in 2000 peopled an island with a band of castaways and had them vote to expel one member each week until the last person claimed a million-dollar prize that the world took notice. *Survivor*, CBS's version of a Swedish TV success, set summer viewership records, and television executives everywhere rushed to launch their own offerings. CBS itself followed later in the summer by isolating 10 persons in a house and having the audience vote them out until only one was left in *Big Brother*, its version of a Dutch hit. Not only did this type of show grab audience attention, but it was relatively cheap to produce because it did not depend on professional screenwriters and actors but instead used ordinary people. A second (and later a third) version of *Survivor* and a second *Big Brother* appeared in 2001, along with such shows as ABC's *The Mole*, in which a group facing various challenges had a saboteur in its midst, and Fox's *Temptation Island*, in which unmarried couples were separated and their fidelity was tested. PBS broadcast the British *The 1900 House*, in which a family lived for three months with no modern amenities.

The concept emerged worldwide. Great Britain, which already in 2000 had presented *Castaway*, recounting the experiences of a group that created a community for a year on a Scottish island, launched *Castaway 2001*. In addition, France had *Loft Story;* Canada offered *Pioneer Quest;* at least 18 countries had a version of *Big Brother;* and more than 20 countries had shown or were considering their own *Survivor* series.

Perhaps inevitably, with all this popularity came controversy. Accusations were made that some scenes were staged, edited, shown out of sequence, or reenacted with body doubles, that voting was rigged or influenced by show officials, that copyrights were infringed, or that the backgrounds of some participants were not checked carefully enough. Even though such shows as NBC's *Fear Factor*, with contestants subjected to stunts involving whatever scared them, and *Spy TV*, where the staged situations often were designed to evoke terror, were very popular, their mean-spiritedness also drew many complaints. Nonetheless, reality shows continued to proliferate worldwide, and there was no sign that they would disappear soon.   (BARBARA WHITNEY)

Winners of the French reality-TV show Loft Story, *Christophe and Loana, leave their studio lot near Paris on July 5.*

Olivier Morin/AFP Worldwide

"Canada's Own" CBC Television, launched its new season with theme nights accompanied by on-air hosts, as well as new branding that tied together drama, comedy, news, and sports programming on both the main network and CBC Newsworld. Hockey Night in Canada provided leaguewide coverage, including highlights, features, and analysis. Australian rugby fans in 300 households participated in a four-month interactive-TV trial by Cable & Wireless Optus beginning in August. Viewers of Seven Network's Bledisloe Cup broadcast chose match data they wanted displayed and participated in live polls. Nine Network unveiled plans to elevate Friday nights in its programming with headline matches of the Australian Football League (AFL). Seven lost its 45-year association with the AFL earlier in the year.

Seven Network could expect significant cost savings once its new $40 million broadcast centre in Melbourne—the first such digital facility in the country—began operations by the end the year. The capacious centre had 100-hour video servers and on-line storage that could contain one full year's programming.

France's first reality-TV show, *Loft Story,* garnered 5.2 million viewers daily, most between 15 and 25 years old, since it aired early in the year. Its creators, Holland-based Endemol Entertainment, had been told that *telepoubelle,* or "garbage TV," would never catch on in France. Earlier, *Big Brother* had hit it big all over Europe except France. *Loft Story* was *Big Brother* with a twist; five women and six men, in their 20s, agreed to live in a loft for 10 weeks and be filmed around-the-clock. TV watchers voted by telephone each week to eliminate one of two participants. The lone woman and lone man who remained by July won a $416,000 Parisian apartment—but had to live together in it for the next six months. (*See* Sidebar.)

India's state-owned Doordarshan television network aired before a live audience the country's first matchmaking TV show, *Swayamvar* ("Own Groom"). The program, based on a common practice in northern India in which princes vie for the most beautiful princesses, gave women participants the prerogative to choose their own men. The program featured 26 women, one per episode, from cities across India. The biggest hit on Indian TV, however, was the Hindi-language version of *Who Wants to Be a Millionaire,* starring the popular film star Amitabh Bachchan. (*See* BIOGRAPHIES.)

In other media news, Fernando Dutra Pinto, wanted for the kidnapping of Patricia Abravanel, the 24-year-old daughter of Brazilian TV baron Silvio Santos, broke into the magnate's mansion and held the 70-year-old Santos hostage for

Media Voices of the Muslim World

The terrorist attacks of Sept. 11, 2001, and the military actions against Osama bin Laden, the alleged mastermind of the operation, brought increased visibility and international attention to the news media in the Middle East and Central Asia. This was especially true of the satellite television network Al-Jazeera, which was perceived as Bin Laden's media voice when it broadcast taped interviews with him and others of the al-Qaeda terrorist group. Al-Jazeera also became the major supplier to Western media of TV footage from inside Afghanistan. Questions were raised in the U.S., however, about the propriety of the media's giving terrorists a soapbox from which to argue their views, as well as about the assertions of objectivity by Al-Jazeera and others of Al-Jazeera's reporting on Middle East issues. Al-Jazeera was founded in 1996 by Sheikh Hamad ibn Khalifah ath-Thani, the emir of Qatar, and symbolized his desire to modernize the country. Based in Doha, Qatar, Al-Jazeera was by far the most international of the Arabic-language broadcasters, reaching 35 million viewers in 20 countries. Although the staff claimed adherence to the journalistic values of free speech and fair play—and indeed they were most likely among regional broadcasters to present non-Islamic points of view—there was never any question about where the network's sympathies lay. Still, the tone of Al-Jazeera's independent reporting of the Palestinian *intifadah* in 2000, for example, contrasted significantly with that of government-controlled Arab networks.

Hezbollah-owned Lebanon-based Al-Manar TV was established in 1997 to promote the Palestinian *intifadah* and highlight the plight of Palestinians. It proudly expanded its mission in 2001, denouncing what in its broadcasts it tagged "The American Aggression on Afghanistan." Program intermission snippets, which showed the U.S. A-bomb attacks in Japan and military actions in Vietnam, Iraq, and Lebanon,

were billed as "Terrorism Without Borders." In May Palestinian TV came under scrutiny when it ran commercials asking children to drop their toys, pick up rocks, and do battle with Israel. Actors re-created the well-publicized and shocking death of 12-year-old Muhammad Dura in his father's arms during crossfire between Israelis and Palestinians and showed the boy in paradise, urging other children to follow.

An Osama bin Laden videotape airs on the Al-Jazeera television network on December 26.

AP/Wide World Photos

Opposition TV channels Pars TV and National Iranian Television (NITv), beamed from Los Angeles, encouraged Iranian viewers to step up reform efforts. The Iranian government confiscated satellite dishes receiving these broadcasts and apparently jammed NITv signals in October 2000. The opposition Iraqi National Congress opened a new front with a daily hour-long broadcast via satellite of Television Hurriah (Liberty TV). Funded by the U.S. but beamed from London, Liberty TV brought news, political profiles, music videos, and even call-in shows. In early October a bill was introduced in the U.S. Congress to create a Radio Free Afghanistan to join Radio Free Europe, Radio Liberty, Radio Martí, and other "surrogate" stations. Few remembered that there once had been a Radio Free Afghanistan but that it was discontinued by the U.S. government in 1992.

(RAMONA MONETTE SARGAN FLORES)

company, five-year-old Hong Kong broadcaster Phoenix (through its parent company Fox News), was first in its live coverage and Chinese translation of September 11 in New York City, by going on air within minutes of the attack.

Technology. New television sets in the U.S. were equipped with secondary audio programming technology that, when activated by the remote control, allowed Spanish-speaking viewers to hear TV dialogue in Spanish. The system could also provide auditory assistance to the visually impaired by describing what was happening on the screen. The U.S. Federal Communications Commission required American broadcasters to provide descriptive video service (DVS) for the blind, equivalent to closed-captioning for the deaf. DVS allowed for a second audio track in which a narrator describes visual action. Pioneered by public TV station WGBH in Boston, DVS was commercially available only on the Turner Classic Movies channel on cable TV.

It was reported that V-chip technology—which allowed the blocking of program material and had been standard equipment on all television sets manufactured since January 2000—was being used by only 7% of American parents to regulate children's viewing habits.

In December flat-panel TVs from Sharp's new Aquos line in 76-cm (1 cm=0.39 in) and 56-cm liquid crystal display (LCD) panels were introduced. Sharp also unveiled its first consumer plasma display panel (PDP) TV prototypes in 109-cm and 127-cm models.

Hitachi and Sanyo had earlier exhibited high-definition 107-cm PDP TVs, while Toshiba rolled out its 107-cm and 127-cm PDP TVs in November. Sony offered rear-projection LCD "Grand Wega" TVs, including a 152-cm prototype. HDNet, the world's first high-definition national TV network, debuted with a major league baseball game. Sports and entertainment programming was seen as the key to increasing sales of digital high-definition TV.

Microsoft Corp.'s long-delayed Interactive TV software debuted in June on Portugal's TV Cabo. Interactive TV subscribers received e-mail, banked, shopped, placed bets, and played games on TV, using a set-top box. ReplayTV technology was to be integrated in Motorola set tops for its DigiCable business. ReplayTV enabled users to record 60 hours of television on a hard drive and eliminate commercials with a 30-second skip button. TiVo won patents for its digital video recording (DVR) technology, which AOL Time Warner

seven hours (telecast live) before surrendering to the police.

Kim Ahyun, who complained that she was not allowed to cover "male" subjects such as politics and business, quit her job on South Korean TV. She founded

Fasonaki, a company that shot and sold footage of international fashion shows to local TV and cable companies. Sally Wu, Phoenix news anchor in Hong Kong, was praised as a model journalist by Chinese Premier Zhu Rongji. Her planned to include in next-generation set-top boxes to be developed and marketed jointly with Samsung Electronics. Japan launched its e-platform, and a startup company to broadcast data services for it, at the CEATEC consumer show in October. Japan's ep Corp. promised the first service in the world that would seamlessly combine digital broadcasting, Internet access, and data storage in a hard-disk drive. Princeton Graphic System's high-definition TV receiver and Channel 1's companion service enabled Web surfing without a set-top box, using Internet hardware that was built into the set. The 91-cm HDTV-ready AI3.6HD display supplied connections for every TV service and device.

A report from Scarborough Research found that almost one-quarter of adult Americans were watching less TV since they started using the Internet. On the other hand, Nielsen//NetRatings found that heavy Internet users were big consumers of all media and might not necessarily have decreased time spent watching TV or reading newspapers. Scarborough's findings showed that Americans had increased radio listening since going on-line.

RADIO

The dominant news in American radio was the potentially debilitating ailments suffered by two of the medium's biggest stars. Paul Harvey (*see* BIOGRAPHIES), fresh off a 10-year contract to continue his lucrative work with ABC Radio Networks, was off the air for about four months in midyear after an apparent viral infection cost him the temporary use of his voice. Harvey's daily news reports and commentary were heard on more than 1,200 stations. More shocking, conservative talk host Rush Limbaugh revealed in October that he had gone virtually deaf because of a rare autoimmune disease that attacks the inner ear, and there was little chance of recovery. A few listeners thought they detected a change in the rhythm and timbre of Limbaugh's talk. During the summer the popular Limbaugh had signed a contract with Premiere Radio Networks reportedly paying him $250 million through 2009, and he vowed to continue with his work, using technological aids to help him hear listeners or read what they had said—or simply to stop taking calls and do his daily show as a monologue. "Nothing's stopped me from talking, and that's what I get paid to do," he told the Associated Press. "Nobody's paying me to listen."

Recent years' consolidation waves in the radio business seemed to have ebbed, perhaps because there was little left to consolidate. Like other advertiser-dependent businesses during 2001, Clear Channel Communications Inc., which had emerged as the largest American radio broadcaster, with 1,180 stations, was undergoing a rough year, posting a large third-quarter loss. Toward year's end Radio One Inc., with 65 stations the largest owner and operator of urban radio stations, and ABC Radio Networks, with 163 urban affiliates the largest urban programmer, combined forces in a partnership creating the leading African American radio service.

The most intriguing radio story of the year, however, might have been the first stirrings of Internet-based radio as a force. The technology awaited cheap and ubiquitous Internet access to really come into its own, but some experts believed there was a huge potential audience of disaffected local radio listeners, troubled by ever-narrowing formats and ever-increasing commercial time. An executive with Arbitron Webcast Services, which rated Internet radio stations' popularity, told *Time* magazine that the proportion of Americans who had listened to Web radio had grown to 20% from 6% in just two years. A competing company, MeasureCast, reported that listening to the stations whose Internet broadcasts it measured had more than tripled during 2001.

In the latest incident in press crackdowns by authoritarian African regimes, Zambia's popular private station Radio

The future of popular radio talk show host Rush Limbaugh was cast in doubt during the year after an illness left him virtually deaf.

Phoenix was shut down for having allegedly defamed Pres. Frederick Chiluba. Many silenced journalists flocked to the Internet, which was relatively safe from censorship.

Following a federal parliamentary inquiry, the Australian government was tasked with funding a "black-spots" scheme to improve radio services in certain areas. The inquiry also highlighted concerns about a lack of local content due to networked or syndicated programs.

(RAMONA MONETTE SARGAN FLORES; STEVE JOHNSON)

NEWSPAPERS

A severe advertising recession that forewarned a global economic downturn overtook newspapers in 2001, even as the September 11 attacks in the United States produced some of the most dramatic news coverage by the press in more than a half century.

Advertising sectors—notably employment advertising and so-called dot-com advertising—were exposed to economic whims after having led the newspaper-industry revenue surge in the late 1990s, and their vulnerability served as an early-warning system for the overall economy. In the first half of 2001, newspaper employment advertising in the U.S. plunged 25%. Dot-com advertising, which had begun declining after the April 2000 crash of Internet stocks, was virtually nonexistent in newspapers.

Sharp contractions in classified, retail, and national advertising began in February in the U.S. and continued to decline throughout the year—a pattern repeated in Europe and the Asia-Pacific area later in the year. In some non-U.S. regions, national advertising was the first recessed sector as media buyers in global economic capitals, already reeling from an economic contraction, began pulling back advertising plans. In Latin America the already-poor economic situation from the previous four years was made worse by sinking economies in Brazil and Argentina, and the Western downturn made matters even worse.

Meanwhile, newspapers worldwide chafed at the unpredictability of newsprint prices, which made up 20–30% of the total cost of the publishing business. After successive price hikes in 2000, newspapers entered 2001 with projections of a 10–20% rise in prices, a sharp increase coming from a paper-manufacturing industry that had rapidly consolidated during the previous four years. The price increases did not materialize, however, at least not to predicted levels; the advertising recession, combined with the threat of higher newsprint prices, forced newspapers to reduce print consumption sharply.

Overall, the combination of an advertising pullback and the unpredictability of newsprint prices produced a sharp decrease in financial performance by newspapers. In the first half of 2001, American publicly traded newspaper companies saw revenues decline 4.7%, operating profits drop 30%, and profit margins contract nearly seven percentage points to 16.6%—albeit from record highs in 2000.

Throughout the year newspapers responded to the economic distress with layoffs, employee buyouts, a cutback in the number of pages printed, and the elimination of sections no longer supported by advertising. The trend toward small physical page widths, which had begun in the late 1990s as a cost-saving measure, continued in 2001. Critics noted that while all economy-exposed media were undergoing turbulent times, the defensive nature of the newspaper response was similar to how newspapers responded to the previous economic recession in 1990–91. After that recession, newspapers lost advertising market share to targeted and measurable media such as direct mail, cable television, and local radio.

In the U.S. the immediate cutbacks by newspaper companies provoked cries of corporate greed from quarters within the journalism community, notably by the publisher of the *San Jose Mercury News;* he resigned his prominent position within the industry instead of following through on cutbacks made by corporate giant Knight Ridder.

It was against this backdrop that newspapers responded immediately to the September terrorist attacks in the U.S. Many newspapers in the Americas published extra editions in the afternoon of the attacks, some for the first time since the Japanese attack on Pearl Harbor in 1941. Newspapers worldwide published among the most memorable newspapers of all time the day after the attacks and subsequently boosted circulation. Newspapers also mobilized their large staffs in editorial, circulation, production, and marketing departments to produce unique print newspapers, Web-site updates, instant-message alerts, e-mail newsletters, and other ways to deliver the news. Newspaper Web sites, like other Internet ventures, saw record hit counts in the immediate aftermath of September 11.

With the exception of Japan, leading industrialized countries saw a 1% annual decrease in paid daily circulation during much of the past decade. Analysts suggested that this downward trend might end because young people had become intensely interested in the news events, and they drove up circulation sales.

Though newspapers reported record circulation sales in the aftermath of the terrorist attacks, the same could not be said of advertising. Historically, advertisers pulled back media commitments in such situations for fear of being associated with negative news events. The pullback after September 11, however, was more severe because the economic foundation was already in place to encourage lower marketing expenditures.

Meanwhile, traditional publishers continued to face a third consecutive year of rapid expansion from the newest publishing sector—free commuter newspapers. As Stockholm-based Modern Times Group (MTG) launched new editions of its advertiser-supported free newspapers aimed at subway and bus-system customers, traditional publishers launched competing products, with varying degrees of success. Europe remained the focal point of MTG strategy and subsequent countermeasures by traditional publishers, though expansions were also seen in Canada, the U.S., Argentina, and Singapore.

"Convergence" remained a hot topic among newspaper executives in 2001, even if definitions varied. Though American newspapers struggled to get regulatory officials to abandon local cross-media ownership rules, newspapers in countries where such rules were nonexistent or less stringent began toying seriously with notions of re-positioning themselves as "information mills" with different distribution platforms—print newspapers, Web sites, e-mail, instant messaging, and even television, radio, and other venues. Publishers eyed the possibilities of future cost savings in news gathering as well as cross-media advertising packages. The allure of such future convergence was among the driving forces behind multimedia giant Tribune Co.'s purchase of Times Mirror properties in the United States and cable operator CanWest's purchase of Hollinger properties in Canada in 2000.

Over a 20-year period, the newspaper ownership landscape in Australia, Canada, New Zealand, the United Kingdom, and the U.S. changed dramatically, with similar trends—far fewer owners and far more public ownership of a constitutionally and legally protected industry. The

daily newspaper markets for Australia and New Zealand, for example, were now dominated by two companies; those in Canada, by four companies. The U.K., with clear distinctions between regional newspapers and national newspapers, continued to see sharp contraction in ownership. In the United States 20% of the country's 1,500 newspapers, including almost all metropolitan dailies, were owned by publicly traded companies.

In a challenging economic environment, newspapers continued to seek a more immediate return on investment from the high level of Internet activities started in the late 1990s. With the sharp downturn in the advertising market not supportive of Web-site profitability, newspaper managements turned to the more difficult issue of the degree to which readers should pay subscription fees. In early 2001 anecdotal evidence was mounting that providing free content on-line while charging for the same content in print was beginning to hurt print circulation. Two alternative models emerged—one required an individual to register for continued free access to content, another allowing free access to online content only to paid subscribers of the print newspaper. Many newspapers charged for access to archived materials.

In late 2001 American newspaper offices were gripped by fear of anthrax attacks. After two *New York Post* employees tested positive for anthrax and several newspapers reported anthrax scares, many newspapers changed mail-handling procedures.

The issue of copyright in the digital age challenged newspapers during the year. In a landmark decision the United States Supreme Court ruled that newspaper and magazine publishers broke copyright law when they failed to secure freelance writers' permission to include their works in digital databases—a decision that affected hundreds of thousands of articles stored in electronic archives as well as those republished in CD-ROM and other digital formats. In response to the decision and subsequent lawsuits by freelances, newspapers such as the *New York Times* and the *San Diego Union-Tribune* removed from their archives materials subject to review in light of the court ruling. Similar copyright issues faced newspaper publishers in Europe. In Germany the Bundestag (lower house of parliament) considered a European payment standard of between 10% and 30% for electronic reusage, outraging newspaper publishers.

Though commercial concerns overwhelmed newspapers in 2001, other pub-

Outside the News Corp. building in New York City on October 20, an electronic sign announces that anthrax had been found in the offices of the **New York Post.**

lishers struggled to maintain an environment in which they could publish. In South Korea the government of Pres. Kim Dae Jung charged and jailed three opposition newspaper owners on tax-evasion and embezzlement charges, which observers charged was a heavy-handed attempt to silence government critics. New press restrictions were adopted in Chile, Sri Lanka, Venezuela, Argentina, Malaysia, Mongolia, and Vietnam. According to the Committee to Protect Journalists, Iran, Liberia, and China remained the most oppressive enemies of a free press. Meanwhile, journalists working within Russia reported that a corrupt general environment, combined with actions by the government of Pres. Vladimir Putin, had created an atmosphere of deteriorating press freedom.

Two prominent figures in the American newspaper industry died during the year, Katherine Graham, owner of the *Washington Post*, and John Bertram Oakes, an editorial-page editor for the *New York Times*. (*See* OBITUARIES.)

(EARL J. WILKINSON)

MAGAZINES

The magazine industry faced a bad year that got worse after the Sept. 11, 2001, terrorist attacks in the U.S. "The 11th" hastened the decline of an industry already suffering lowered revenues and resulted in the closure of some well-known magazines. During the first nine months of 2001, total ad pages declined about 10%, and revenue slipped slightly more than 1%.

The good news for 2001 was that 2000 was an unusually healthy year (U.S. and worldwide advertising revenue rose by 13.5% and 4%, respectively), which meant that the decline in 2001 was probably not as precipitous as it appeared.

The only winners were the newsweeklies. *Newsweek* increased its newsstand sales sixfold after the terrorist attacks, and *Time* and *U.S. News & World Report* tripled theirs. All three published special advertisement-free editions within days of the attacks. *Fire Engineering* was most directly affected by the tragedies. The 125-year-old magazine lost 10 of its contributors, nine New York City firefighters and one Port Authority officer, who had served as both writers and trainers at the magazine's fire department instruction conferences. Among the dead was Ray Downey, the battalion chief of the New York Fire Department special operations command and a key member of the magazine's advisory board.

The implications of the attacks reverberated throughout the magazine industry, and several trade magazines, including *Pit & Quarry*, *Convenience Store News*, and *Cheese Market News*, covered the events and how their industries were affected. Later in the year, magazines were also involved in the anthrax scare. In early October Iowa police called Thomas Ryder, chief executive of Reader's Digest Association, Inc., after an Iowa subscriber notified police about a white powdery substance on her magazine. The residue was cornstarch, commonly used in the printing process to help ink dry faster and reduce static cling. A series of similar false alarms elsewhere forced some magazine printers, including R.R. Donnelley & Sons, to search for a substitute to cornstarch.

The Magazine Publishers of America (MPA) and the American Society of Magazine Editors moved their annual American Magazine Conference, scheduled for late October, from Phoenix, Ariz., to New York City. MPA president Nina Link explained that "many of our member attendees as well as speakers expressed their reluctance to leave their New York-based offices during such challenging times."

The most notable closure of the year was that of 66-year-old *Mademoiselle*, which ended its run with the November 2001 issue; subscribers were sent *Glamour* in its place. Condé Nast closed the 1.1-million-circulation magazine, stating, "Current economic conditions have produced a situation where . . . the magazine is no longer viable." Other closures included *Brill's Content, George, Working Woman, Expedia Travels, Family PC, Mode, Nova, Individual Investor, Lingua Franca, Asiaweek, Golf & Travel, Maximum Golf, The Industry Standard, Silicon Alley Reporter,* and *Woman's Realm. McCall's,* a venerable title among the women's magazines, published its last issue in March, but its publisher, Gruner+ Jahr USA Publishing, successfully relaunched it a month later as *Rosie;* by the end of June, it ranked 12th in total circulation. A prominent Russian news magazine, *Itogi,* was a casualty of the struggle between the new government of Vladimir Putin and oligarch Vladimir Gusinsky. (*See* BIOGRAPHIES.) After corporate shareholders aligned with Putin fired the editor in chief, Sergey Parkhomenko, most of the staff departed and *Newsweek* severed its partnership with the magazine; its last issue was dated April 17.

O: The Oprah Magazine, launched in May 2000, became one of the most successful magazine launches in history. After two press runs the initial May–June issue sold out of 1.6 million copies on newsstands. By the end of June 2001, the average paid circulation reached 2.7 million—20th among all magazines.

Making the rounds at *The Nation,* the most venerable left-leaning political magazine in the U.S., was a joke about its increase in circulation: "What's bad for the country is good for *The Nation.*" After George W. Bush became president, the magazine's circulation rose 4%. *Mother Jones,* another liberal magazine, increased its circulation by 6%, and two smaller left-leaning magazines, *American*

Prospect and *In These Times,* also registered healthy increases. Likewise, conservative magazines had profited from the election of Bill Clinton in the 1990s. *The American Spectator* had experienced a sevenfold circulation jump and *National Review* had increased its readership by 66% during the Clinton years.

Internet publishing was another bright spot for publishers. On-line advertising grew faster than that in any other medium and continued to increase during times of recession, according to Danny Meadows-Klue, chairman of the Interactive Advertising Bureau. At an October conference in Geneva, Meadows-Klue reported that sustained growth had more than doubled each year for three years.

Hubert Burda, president of the Association of German Magazine Publishers, received the annual Freedom of Commercial Speech medal from the European Association of Communication Agencies at its October conference in Berlin. Burda had been a prominent champion of advertising and press freedom in Europe.   (DAVID E. SUMNER)

BOOK PUBLISHING

United States. The American book-publishing industry was profoundly affected by the Sept. 11, 2001, terrorist attacks in the U.S. In the immediate aftermath local bookstores reported that they had become "de facto" community centres crowded with people seeking information, connection, and whatever comfort might be found. There was a surge in sales of books about Islam, including the Qur'an, as well as such topics as religious fundamentalism, terrorism, the Taliban, the Middle East, and biological and chemical warfare. Rutgers University Press, publisher of a pictorial history of the World Trade Center, was overwhelmed with orders for the book. Plans for stepped-up media exposure for upcoming books and their authors were derailed. Some books slated for fall publication had their publication dates pushed back until 2002, and a number of publishers used their Web sites (chat rooms, audio readings, and pictures) in an attempt to compensate for the lost

Magazine covers following September 11 reflect the impact of the terrorist attacks.

AP/Wide World Photos

face-to-face contact between authors and their audience.

Even before the terrorist attacks, some publishing segments failed to live up to expectations, especially the electronic-book (e-book) market. Though a 2000 study had projected that under the right conditions the electronic publishing market for consumer books could reach $2.3 billion–$3.4 billion by 2005, accounting for 10% of all book sales, the e-book market was slowed by ongoing technical issues, including the lack of "interoperability." The Association of American Publishers took the lead to develop open standards for the e-book marketplace in an effort to provide authors, publishers, retailers, and consumers with the widest possible array of choices in developing, selling, and utilizing information in digital form. Standards were developed in the areas of metadata and numbering, along with recommendations on digital-rights management standards. In April 2001 an agency was selected (Content Directions, Inc.) to register digital object identifiers, or DOIs, a system used by book publishers to identify and exchange electronic content.

The issue of copyright protection, especially as it applied to digital information, remained paramount for publishers; two important copyright cases dealt with electronic rights. In June in *New York Times Co. v. Tasini,* the Supreme Court ruled 7–2 in favour of a group of freelance journalists who had sued news-

paper and magazine publishers for copyright infringement. The plaintiffs objected to the defendants' reproduction and distribution in a database of their previously published print articles. The court found that the articles in an electronic database "as presented to and perceptible by" a database user could not be considered a permissible part of a "revision of a collective work," as claimed by the defendants, because the articles were reproduced in the database "clear of the context" provided either by the original periodical editions or any revision of them.

In *Random House* v. *RosettaBooks,* the plaintiff publisher sought to enjoin the defendant publisher from issuing e-book versions of works previously published by the plaintiff under contracts to "print, publish, and sell the work in book form." The federal district court, however, denied the injunction request, finding that the contract language did not convey electronic rights to the plaintiff for the works at issue.

Two of the industry's highest priorities—the protection of intellectual property and the defense of intellectual freedom—met head-on in a highly publicized court case. In May the U.S. Court of Appeals for the 11th Circuit overturned a preliminary injunction that had banned the publication of *The Wind Done Gone* by Alice Randall. The case began in April when trustees of the Margaret Mitchell estate brought a copyright and trademark infringement action against the Houghton Mifflin Co. The complaint sought to enjoin publication of that book, which it claimed used elements of *Gone with the Wind* and was therefore a misappropriation of a copyrighted work. Randall and Houghton Mifflin maintained that the book, told from the point of view of a former slave, was a work of social commentary and parody protected by the First Amendment and allowable under copyright law. In the wake of the appellate court ruling, the book was published in June.   (PATRICIA S. SCHROEDER)

Fan Fiction—TV Viewers Have It Their Way

Television shows had long captivated audiences and provided a temporary escape from reality for viewers who could vicariously live another life. Some devoted viewers would often discuss their favourite dramas and begin to play out "what-if" scenarios: What if Agent Mulder never returned to *The X-Files* and Agent Scully began having an affair with Assistant Director Walter Skinner? What if Captain Kirk of *Star Trek* had never met Spock? What if the title character of *Buffy the Vampire Slayer* found true love in a demon?

When surfing on the Internet became popular in the 1990s, fans began taking their fantasies on-line and publishing "fan fiction" or "fanfic," a practice that had started with "fanzines" (magazines or books created by fans). The year 2001 saw a burgeoning of Web sites devoted to tale-tellers who spun their imaginations and transported TV characters into a different universe. The Internet had become their vanity press.

Henry Jenkins, author of *Textual Poachers: Television Fans & Participatory Culture* (1992), had kept a watchful eye on the fan community for a number of years. He found that though there was initial anxiety and resistance to digital media, "even those who were actively . . . resistant to moving on-line five years ago are now not only putting new stuff on-line, but are archiving stories going back 20 years."

The Internet was a powerful tool; a fan could instantly enter fandom with a couple of clicks. Those looking for *Star Trek* stories could surf to trekiverse.org; prose focusing on *Star Wars* could be found at FanfiX.com. The free site Fanfiction.net was a clearinghouse for all fan-based fiction, and monthly it boasted 1.2 million authors and readers, all digesting or sharing stories—both short stories and novel-length works—based on preexisting characters.

Though many purists believed that "real" fiction came completely from the imagination, Jenkins disagreed: "What would Shakespeare have done without dealing with preexisting characters? All of his stories were based on characters that already existed." Jenkins believed that fan fiction was another way of continuing the folk process that dominated the storytelling tradition long before "we began to think of stories as legal property of individuals or companies rather than the shared property of a culture."

For producers, fan fiction was viewed as a compliment, not a threat. *The X-Files* executive producer Frank Spotnitz remarked, "Somebody said to [creator Chris Carter] early on . . . when he first started to see fan fiction about Mulder and Scully on the Internet, 'You know you've got a hit because the characters have taken hold in the imagination of the audience.'"   (NANCY SCHULZ)

Europe, Asia, Australia. In the European book-publishing industry, consolidation was the byword in 2001. Bertelsmann AG, the giant German publishing company headed by Thomas Middelhoff (*see* BIOGRAPHIES), announced in May that in an effort to compete with Amazon.com, it would integrate BOL.com, its on-line bookstore in 16 European countries, into its multichannel book club division.

In August Vivendi Universal acquired Houghton Mifflin for about $2.2 billion, which included Houghton Mifflin's $500 million debt. The purchase greatly strengthened Vivendi's position in the

Alice Randall, author of **The Wind Done Gone,** *and her husband unpack copies of her novel at a bookstore in Nashville, Tenn., after an injunction that had banned the release of the* **Gone with the Wind** *parody was overturned.*

English-language markets and propelled the company to the number two position (behind Pearson PLC) in worldwide educational publishing. (See *Television*, above.) Although Macmillan Publishers Ltd. of the U.K. bought from Pearson Education the right to use the Macmillan name in the U.S., it would continue to use Palgrave as its global academic imprint.

The traditional balance of power between publishers and booksellers was threatened after a survey of 291 publishers in France revealed that although only 30% of titles originated from the top six publishers, these accounted for nearly 70% of total turnover. In response the 10-year-old Cahart agreements between French publishers and booksellers were revamped to give the latter more control over the number of books received and to include mass-market paperbacks in the formula for determining discounts.

In May public sentiment was squashed when the Swedish Riksdag (parliament) refused to cut the value-added tax (VAT) on books from 25% to 6%. Elsewhere in Europe there was concern that e-books, which were not subject to sales tax in the U.S., would be treated as services rather than goods (printed versions were treated as goods) and attract VAT.

The abolition of price-fixing on new editions and reprints began to show results in Denmark, where publishing houses Gyldendal and Cicero launched popular novels at half the customary

price and the Dansk Supermarked sold low-priced versions of remaindered books under its own label. In Switzerland the royalty payment mechanism (rpm) was verging on collapse after it had been declared illegal by the antitrust authorities. Europe, nevertheless, remained as divided as ever on the virtues of rpm; Italy reimposed it in February but permitted discounts of up to 10% for trade books, and Belgium considered whether to follow suit.

Copyright remained a vexing issue in a wide variety of contexts. In January police raids to stem rampant book piracy in India revealed the existence of modern, well-stocked bookshops in which not one single title was found to be original. In Australia the Copyright Amendment (Parallel Importation) Bill 2001 amended the 1968 law and allowed the "parallel importing of books, periodicals and sheet music in both electronic and print form." Meanwhile, agreement was reached on the wording of the European Union (EU) digital copyright directive, which sought to balance the rights of copyright owners with those of users. The directive harmonized the reproduction, distribution, and communication of digitally stored material as well as the legal protection of anticopying devices, including encryption. Copying by individuals for educational or private purposes remained legal. EU member states had only 18 months to convert the directive into national law.   (PETER CURWEN)

Military Affairs

The **ATTACKS** on Sept. 11, 2001, opened a **NEW CHAPTER** in the history of warfare. A coalition of forces toppled the regime of the **TALIBAN** in Afghanistan. New **ANTITERRORISM** legislation was passed, and countries increased their defense **BUDGETS.**

The devastating aerial attacks by terrorists in the United States on Sept. 11, 2001, caused untold chaos and horror and initiated a flood of events that affected all aspects of life in all corners of the world. The United States declared a "war on terrorism" and promptly focused on the international al-Qaeda group and its Taliban protectors in Afghanistan. The antiterrorist coalition included contributions from Germany and Japan, countries that were largely able to overcome their post-World War II angst about deploying armed forces abroad.

SEPTEMBER 11 AND AFTERWARD

Within days of the attacks on the World Trade Center and the Pentagon, NATO, for the first time in its history, invoked Article 5 of its charter, declaring that the atrocities were an attack on the alliance. As a demonstration of support, Australia invoked the ANZUS Pact, putting elements of its armed forces on a higher state of readiness in case they were called upon to assist the U.S. On September 19 the Organization of American States agreed by acclamation to invoke the Rio Treaty, also a mutual-defense pact.

The week after the attacks was a period of shock and rage for most Americans, but there was also a feeling of helplessness because of great uncertainty about who exactly had attacked, where precisely in the world they could be found, and how they could be punished. On September 19 the U.S. dispatched more than 100 combat and support aircraft to various bases in the Middle East and the Indian Ocean. A large naval task force was sent to join what was first called Operation Infinite Justice but later, after complaints were received from Muslims, was renamed Operation Enduring Freedom. Japan sent three warships to support the effort, although they were restricted to a noncombat role according to the terms of Japan's pacifist constitution.

Allied air strikes in Afghanistan began on October 7. Later U.S. special forces, including Delta Force and Rangers, launched ground raids inside the country. The U.S. enlisted as an ally the anti-Taliban Northern Alliance, the principal remaining opposition to the Taliban takeover of Afghanistan, relying on them to provide the bulk of ground troops for the campaign. The northern city of Mazar-e Sharif fell a month later, and on November 13 the Northern Alliance entered Kabul as Taliban forces fled the capital. On December 9, with the fall of the Taliban's principal city of Kandahar imminent, American B-52s began carpet bombing a network of caves in the Tora Bora mountains of eastern Afghanistan, the last stronghold of forces loyal to Osama bin Laden and the Taliban. On December 15 anti-Taliban Afghan troops, backed by British and American commandos, surrounded a cave where they thought Bin Laden and a dwindling force of al-Qaeda fighters were hiding, but he was not found. His whereabouts were still unknown at year's end.

Smoke pours from a Taliban-controlled village in Afghanistan after a bombing raid by U.S. aircraft on November 9.

OTHER CONFLICTS AND CONFRONTATIONS

The U.S. and China. A U.S. Navy surveillance aircraft made an emergency landing in China after colliding with a Chinese fighter jet on April 1 and thereby initiated a diplomatic confrontation. The aircraft and its crew of 24 were detained on Hainan Island until April 11. The aircraft was not returned until July, after the United States, in a carefully worded diplomatic note, said it was "very sorry" that the pilot of the Chinese jet had died. At the height of the dispute, U.S. Pres. George W. Bush announced that the U.S. would sell Taiwan up to eight diesel submarines, four *Kidd*-class destroyers, and 12 antisubmarine aircraft to bolster its defenses against China. The $4 billion weapons package was the most expensive sale to Taiwan since 1992.

The Balkans. In March tension increased along the border between Macedonia and the Serbian province of Kosovo following a series of armed clashes between Macedonian security forces and ethnic Albanian gunmen. The situation prompted the deployment of international peacekeeping soldiers from the NATO-led Kosovo Force (KFOR). The fighting spread round the country, however, including in and around Macedonia's capital, Skopje. After a peace agreement was brokered in August, NATO was given a one-month mandate in Macedonia to collect and destroy more than 3,000 weapons that the ethnic Albanian guerrillas of the National Liberation Army had agreed to surrender. Sporadic violence continued for the remainder of the year.

Russia. The Russian army's war against Chechen secessionists remained at a stalemate in 2001. Tens of thousands of Russian troops stationed in the mountainous republic were unable to eliminate the rebels, whose sporadic attacks against Russian forces and pro-Russian Chechens resulted in a steady flow of fatalities. Moscow claimed that the Chechen rebels had links to Afghanistan's Taliban regime and Bin Laden, which made it all the more palatable for Russian Pres. Vladimir Putin to pledge support for U.S. President Bush's call for a war on global terrorism. In December Russia stepped up military operations in response to Chechen raids on its forces.

Middle East. The situation in Israel and the Palestinian Autonomous Areas devolved into a war in all but name. Palestinian militants used small arms, mortars, and suicide bombers, mostly against civilian targets. The Israeli military used weapons ranging from F-16 fighter jets and missile-equipped attack helicopters to tank-fired flechette rounds, which contained thousands of 5-cm (2-in)-long steel darts. Also, both sides used assassination as a weapon; for example, Palestinian gunmen shot Israel's tourism minister, Rechavam Ze'evi, dead in October in retaliation for the death of Palestinian nationalist Abu Ali Mustafa (*see* OBITUARIES) in a rocket attack in August, and an Israeli helicopter gunship destroyed a car carrying Mahmoud Abu Hanoud, a Hamas leader, and two others on November 24.

During the year U.S. and British war planes attacked numerous sites in southern Iraq to prevent Iraqi Pres. Saddam Hussein from reconstituting his air defenses. According to the U.K. Royal Air Force, there were nearly 400 incidents of Iraqi surface-to-air-missile and antiaircraft fire against U.S. and British aircraft operating over the southern no-fly zone during the first eight months of 2001. German and U.S. intelligence agencies reported that since the 1990–91 Persian Gulf War, Iraq had been able to reconstruct a significant number of its production facilities for weapons of mass destruction. The U.S. also believed that Iraq was continuing work on a ballistic missile with a range of 3,000 km (1 km=about 0.62 mi) that could be operational as early as 2005.

South Asia. The long-festering dispute over Kashmir continued to poison relations between India and Pakistan, and the two nuclear-armed countries were virtually at war at the end of 2001. India blamed Kashmiri separatists for an assault on the Indian Parliament in December in which five attackers killed eight people with guns and grenades before being killed themselves. India accused Pakistan's secret service of having assisted the attackers. In retribution India considered punitive military strikes on what they said were militant training camps in Pakistan. Pakistan denounced India's test launch of an Agni-2 ballistic missile in January. The Agni-2 was capable of carrying a nuclear warhead, and its 2,000-km range meant it could reach targets anywhere in Pakistan or deep inside China.

King Gyanendra of Nepal declared a state of emergency after the worst violence in the nearly six years the Himalayan nation had been contending with a Maoist insurgency. The Maoists had stepped up their campaign in the months following the June 1 massacre of King Birendra (*see* OBITUARIES) and other members of the Nepalese royal family.

Since 1983 the Liberation Tigers of Tamil Eelam (LTTE) had fought for an independent homeland for Sri Lanka's Tamil population. In April the Sri Lankan military launched a major assault on guerrilla positions south of the Jaffna Peninsula after the collapse of a four-month-old cease-fire. More than 300 government soldiers were killed or reported missing in action, however, and the assault was terminated after only three days. In July the LTTE attacked the country's only international airport and a nearby military base, leaving at least 18 dead and destroying several aircraft. Following the election of a new prime minister in Sri Lanka on December 5, talks with the LTTE resumed, yielding a truce agreement that entered into effect on December 24.

Southeast Asia. A new military operation began in Aceh province on the Indonesian island of Sumatra and resulted in an intensification of the conflict. There were reports of many civilians' being killed by security forces and the Gerakan Aceh Merdeka. Despite a cease-fire agreement by Indonesia and the separatist organization signed on May 12, the violence by both sides continued throughout the year. (*See* WORLD AFFAIRS: *Indonesia:* Special Report.)

Philippine Pres. Gloria Macapagal Arroyo (*see* BIOGRAPHIES) declared all-out war on Muslim extremists in April. Fighting in the southern island of Jolo pitted thousands of army troops against guerrillas loyal to a rebellious Muslim governor and head of the Moro National Liberation Front, and more than 100 people were left dead.

Sub-Saharan Africa. In 2001 the government of Burundi agreed to direct cease-fire talks with the main ethnic Hutu rebel group, Forces for the Defense of Democracy, in an attempt to end seven years of civil war. The talks, brokered by South African statesman Nelson Mandela, led to the installation of a transitional power-sharing government backed by a South African peacekeeping force under a UN mandate. The Burundian army gained control of the whole of the capital, Bujumbura, after two weeks of heavy fighting in April.

In the neighbouring Democratic Republic of the Congo (DRC), a cease-fire monitored by the UN Mission in the Democratic Republic of the Congo (MONUC) largely held during the year, although there was intermittent violence. The South African National Defence Force contributed several dozen specialist support personnel to MONUC. This was the South African force's first substantial deployment in a UN operation since the Korean War. By September approximately 15,000 guerrillas had turned in their weapons as part of a cash-for-arms scheme. The conflict was called "Africa's First World War," because Zimbabwe, Angola, and Namibia had sent troops to fight on the side of the DRC government while soldiers from Rwanda and Uganda supported the rebels. In the autumn Uganda and Rwanda began pulling their troops out of the country, and troops from Zimbabwe followed suit. None of the belligerents fully respected their commitments under the 1999 Lusaka cease-fire agreement, however. By December renewed killings and the redeployment of Ugandan troops in parts of the DRC were heightening fears of escalating violence.

Underage soldiers were a growing concern in many countries of the world; the Congolese government released a first group of child soldiers into the care of the United Nations in December. The 235 youths, aged 15 to 19, had spent up to five years in the Congolese army.

The United Nations Mission in Sierra Leone peacekeeping force deployed 17,500 troops across the country. At least 26,000 insurgents were said to have given up their weapons following a peace accord signed in May between the government, the rebels, and the UN to end the civil war, which began in 1991.

Peace talks held in Nairobi, Kenya, in June failed to make any progress toward resolving the 18-year civil war in The Sudan, but a short-lived cease-fire allowed some food aid to be delivered in the country for the first time in a decade.

In order to allow for the deployment of the UN Mission to Ethiopia and Eritrea (UNMEE) peacekeeping force established in June 2000, both sides agreed to the creation of a 25-km-wide security zone in February 2001. Delays prevented this from occurring until mid-April, however. The UNMEE included the first-ever deployment of the UN's Standing High-Readiness Brigade—a multinational unit that had been under development since 1995. Despite accusations about preparations for war, both countries had respected the 2000 Algiers agreement, but tension between the two countries remained high through the end of the year.

MILITARY TECHNOLOGY

Under the most lucrative defense contract ever awarded, the Pentagon selected the Lockheed Martin Corp. to build the Joint Strike Fighter (JSF). The contract had a potential total value of over $200 billion during the life of the program. The U.S. planned to buy nearly 3,000 JSFs for its air force, navy, and Marine Corps, while the U.K. was expected to procure up to 150.

At the beginning of the new millennium, the era of ray guns was fast approaching. A laser device designed to destroy ballistic missiles as they were boosted on their flight produced its first test beam. The Airborne Laser (ABL) was designed to patrol near the borders of hostile countries. Tests of a weapon designed to heat a person's skin with a microwave beam showed that it can disperse crowds. The U.S. Air Force Research Laboratory finished testing the system on human volunteers. It wanted to use this Active Denial Technology, which was claimed to be nonlethal, for peacekeeping or riot control.

After nearly 24 hours of flight, a Global Hawk unmanned aerial vehicle (UAV) landed successfully in South Australia after having taken off from its base in California, over 13,000 km away. This was the first nonstop flight across the Pacific Ocean by a UAV. The jet-powered Global Hawk was designed for surveillance of enemy territory. Its sensor package included a synthetic aperture radar, which can provide detailed photographs even through cloud cover. Although still in development, the Global Hawk was used during operations over Afghanistan. Also reportedly used in that conflict was a prototype armed version of the U.S.'s propeller-driven RQ-1 Predator UAV. It was said to have fired Hellfire antitank missiles at enemy positions. If true, this was the first time a UAV had fired a weapon against a target in war.

The British test ship RV Triton, the world's largest powered trimaran, completed its first transatlantic crossing in September. The 90-m (295-ft)-long Triton was launched in 2000 to prove the triple-hull concept on a full-size ship. It was being evaluated by the Royal Navy and was attracting the attention of other navies. Trimarans offer greater speed and stability over conventional hull designs, especially in rough seas.

Traditional military technologies also made news in 2001. The Belgian small arms manufacturer FN Herstal launched its new 5.56-mm-calibre F2000 rifle. This modular assault rifle included a 40-mm low-velocity grenade launcher and a computerized fire-control system with a laser rangefinder.

The list of countries producing their own advanced weapons continued to grow. Iran announced that it had successfully flight-tested an indigenously produced solid-fuel short-range ballistic missile named Fateh 110. Solid propellants are harder to manufacture than liquid fuels but offer advantages in terms of superior storage, safety in handling, and faster launch times. According to Israeli and U.S. officials, Iran began serial production of its Shahab-3 liquid-fueled ballistic missile, which had a range of 1,300 km. Taiwan deployed the Tien Chi, a new ballistic missile capable of reaching China. It was believed that as many as 50 could already be in service.

The RV Triton *sails on its first transatlantic voyage, which it completed in September.*

ARMS CONTROL AND DISARMAMENT

In December 2001 President Bush announced that the United States would withdraw from the 1972 Anti-Ballistic Missile Treaty with Russia. Bush considered the treaty a roadblock to building the National Missile Defense (NMD) system and an anachronism from the Cold War that allowed so-called rogue states to develop long-range ballistic missiles. Despite months of negotiations, Russia and the U.S. failed to agree on how to amend the treaty or move beyond it. At a meeting in Texas in November, Bush and Russian President Putin agreed to reduce their nuclear arsenals by up to two-thirds over the next decade. Bush met NATO leaders in June to try to win endorsement for the NMD. Spain, Hungary, Italy, Poland, the Czech Republic, and the U.K. offered support, but France, Germany, and others were opposed, arguing that American defense needs would be better served by strengthening existing arms-control agreements.

Meeting in New York City in July, the UN Conference on the Illicit Trade in Small Arms and Light Weapons failed to agree on a treaty to curb the spread of such weapons following U.S. opposition. The U.S. argued that a distinction had to be made between firearms used for traditional and cultural reasons and those that were traded illegally and led to or fueled wars. The U.S. also dropped its support for a protocol intended to include verification powers in the 1972 Biological and Toxin Weapons Convention. The document, already accepted by more than 50 other countries, would require member states to permit international inspection of sites that could be used for the development of biological weapons.

Under a revised agreement with the U.S., South Korea was given the go-ahead to develop ballistic missiles capable of hitting targets in most of North Korea. Seoul would also be permitted to develop civilian rockets for research and commercial purposes. A 1979 agreement with the U.S. limited the range of South Korea's missiles to 180 km. Also, South Korea joined the Missile Technology Control Regime, which bars its members from providing any other country with technology to build missiles with a range over 300 km.

A gratifying example of how arms-control treaties can work occurred when Turkey agreed to join the 1997 Ottawa Convention banning antipersonnel land mines, and in response the Greek Parlia-ment dropped its opposition to ratifying the convention. Greece and Turkey also agreed to clear mines along their border. On January 29 Turkey and Georgia had agreed to remove land mines along their common border.

Although it received little attention from news media, the last inspection under the 1987 Intermediate-Range Nuclear Forces Treaty (INF) took place in Russia. Under the treaty, signed by the Soviet Union and the United States during the height of the Cold War, an entire class of nuclear missiles and related equipment was eliminated. During 13 years of inspections (540 by the United States and 311 by the Soviet Union and its successor states), the INF established a new standard for openness in arms control by including short-notice inspections and around-the-clock monitoring of missile-assembly plants.

Defense ministers from 10 of 14 Southern African Development Community countries in late July approved a draft of a mutual-defense pact that aimed to prevent conflict in the region and establish a collective approach to security.

MILITARY AND SOCIETY

A growing number of countries were looking abroad to fill in the ranks of their armed forces. The British army was recruiting foreign Commonwealth citizens in an attempt to reduce a shortage. South Africans, Australians, Canadians, and West Indians helped bring the strength of the army back up to 108,000 from 100,000. Spain actively recruited in Latin America to help make up for a shortfall in recruits resulting from the phasing out of conscription, and more than 300 Argentines and Uruguayans traveled there to enlist in the Spanish armed forces. France announced that it would end conscription in 2001, 18 months ahead of schedule.

The German government bowed to an order by the European Court of Justice and henceforth would allow women to serve in combat units of its armed forces. The court ruled on January 11 that the German ban on women in combat violated the principles enshrined in the 1976 guidelines on sexual equality adopted by the European Union (EU). The Canadian armed forces lifted restrictions barring women from serving aboard submarines. An Australian Defence Force study recommended that women be allowed to serve in ground combat units. Women already served aboard Australian warships and were allowed to pilot combat aircraft.

ARMED FORCES, POLITICS, AND THE ENVIRONMENT

The movement against live-fire military training gained momentum during the year. President Bush announced that the U.S. Navy would cease using the island of Vieques, off the coast of Puerto Rico, for bombing exercises by 2003. A group of islanders had filed a $100 million lawsuit claiming that the bombing caused significant damage to the environment and public health. The U.S. Navy maintained that it would not be able to find a suitable alternative site for amphibious warfare training. Protesters in Seoul called on the U.S. to close a bombing range it operated along the coast of South Korea. The protesters argued that the range was noisy and dangerous to local citizens. Opposition to foreign military training also surfaced in Kenya, where lawyers attempted to bring legal action against the British army over its use of two training areas. The complainants said that people had been injured and livestock killed as a result of unexploded munitions left by the British forces.

The year was also one of contrasts. While Turkey announced the establishment of a National Space Agency to help develop policy for the military and civilian uses of space, New Zealand said it would scrap its air-combat capability by retiring its aging A-4K Skyhawk fighters and give priority to the army's ability to participate in peacekeeping operations. As a sign of growing European integration and independence from NATO, the EU Military Staff, formed to provide military analysis and advice, was declared operational. Nonaligned Austria hosted armed troops from several NATO countries on its soil for the first time for a Partnership for Peace exercise.

Previous wars also continued to haunt the planet. Russian soldiers discovered several thousand German artillery shells dating from World War II buried at a military base in Kaliningrad. The stockpile was found next to chemical warfare warehouses belonging to the Russian Baltic Fleet.

After years of negotiations the U.S. and Vietnam agreed to research jointly the effects of the chemical defoliant Agent Orange. Vietnam alleged that the health of up to one million people had been severely damaged by Agent Orange, which was used by U.S. forces in Vietnam between 1962 and 1971. Some U.S. veterans groups also believed that their members suffered from exposure to dioxin, a known carcinogen found in Agent Orange.   (PETER SARACINO)

Performing Arts

CONTROVERSIES dominated the performing arts in 2001.
A WAGNER performance caused a furor in Israel. A STORM OF
CRITICISM swirled around a landmark TV documentary on
JAZZ. Violent RAP LYRICS provoked outrage. Nevertheless,
after SEPTEMBER 11, artists of all stripes demonstrated their
capacity to respond to TRAGEDY.

MUSIC

Classical Music. More than a century after his death in 1883, German composer Richard Wagner continued to generate controversy. In Bayreuth, Ger., at the opera festival Wagner established to preserve and promote his music, the composer's descendants were engaged in a bitter struggle for power. In Israel a performance of a piece by Wagner revealed deep divisions among the nation's music lovers.

Wagner was notoriously anti-Semitic, the author of a diatribe against "Jewishness" in music that was largely an attack on his operatic rival, Giacomo Meyerbeer. This attitude, as well as his German chauvinism and his ideas on "racial purity," endeared him to Adolf Hitler and the Nazi regime. In Israel, on the other hand, an unofficial ban on live performances of Wagner's music had been loosely in effect for more than half a century, though recordings were readily available. Feelings on the subject ran deep, as Zubin Mehta, conductor of the Israel Philharmonic, had been shown at a concert in 1981 when, as he was about to lead the orchestra in a Wagner selection, a concentration camp survivor rushed on stage and stopped the proceedings, displaying Nazi-inflicted wounds he had suffered. No Wagner was played on that occasion.

Israel's traditional ban on Wagner performance was shattered in July by pianist and conductor Daniel Barenboim, a citizen of Israel who led orchestras in Berlin and Chicago. During a concert given on tour in Jerusalem by the Berlin Staatskapelle (orchestra), Barenboim conducted the Prelude to Wagner's *Tristan und Isolde* as an encore, creating a furor. Barenboim, a vigorous advocate of Wagner's music,

said he was hopeful that "this opens the door a little bit." Mehta, a close friend of Barenboim, expressed "100 percent" support.

Meanwhile, the Bayreuth Festival, which had been inaugurated in 1876, observed its 125th anniversary very quietly. Wolfgang Wagner, a grandson of the composer, ran the festival for half a century, originally in partnership with his brother Wieland, who died in 1966. Though he was 81 years old and obviously near the end of his tenure, Wolfgang Wagner steadfastly refused to name any successor except for his sec-

During a concert in Jerusalem, conductor Daniel Barenboim looks on while a man in the audience tries to calm protesters who objected to Barenboim's decision to perform a work by Richard Wagner.

ond wife, Gudrun, and their daughter, Katharina. Pressure was building in the family, the German government, and the news media to open up the possibility of new leadership for the Bayreuth Festival.

A particularly vigorous campaign was launched by Nike Wagner, daughter of Wieland and author of a book that criticized many family traditions, *The Wagners: The Dramas of a Musical Dynasty.* Among the changes Nike Wagner proposed for the festival was an enlarged repertoire, which was traditionally limited to the 10 operas of Richard Wagner's maturity. Under the direction of Nike Wagner, the festival might expand to include not only such early operas as *Rienzi* but even the work of other composers, such as Meyerbeer. In any case, significant changes in the Bayreuth Festival were postponed by Wolfgang Wagner, who announced his plans for the next five years at a press conference. Those plans included contracting Danish film director Lars von Trier to direct a new production of the *Ring* cycle, to be conducted by Christian Thielemann, beginning in 2006.

Meanwhile, other major festivals were going through transitions; at Salzburg, Austria, Gerard Mortier concluded a stormy decade as festival director with a bitter prediction that after his departure the festival would revert to "Strauss waltzes and yodeling contests." In London, for the first time in history, an American—Leonard Slatkin—conducted the popular *Last Night at the Proms.* In the wake of the terrorist attacks on the World Trade Center and the Pentagon, Slatkin omitted the traditional singalong of "Land of Hope and Glory" and "Rule, Britannia" that customarily concluded *Proms* programs and substituted Samuel Barber's *Adagio for Strings* and a selection of spirituals. In Australia another American, Peter Sellars, was forced to resign as artistic director of the Adelaide Festival of the Arts. He was replaced by former Melbourne Festival director Sue Nattrass. The board had asked Sellars to broaden his program for the upcoming year, but he refused. "I have made my share of mistakes since coming to Adelaide two and a half years ago, but I deeply believe in the principles for which this festival stands," he said in a statement issued in Paris. Marin Alsop, yet another American, was the first woman to become principal conductor of a British symphony when she was named to that post at the Bournemouth Symphony Orchestra in June.

The September 11 terrorist attacks in the U.S. climaxed a series of financial crises in the performing arts. Travel plans were disrupted, concerts were canceled, ticket sales plummeted, and various bankruptcies and reorganizations were announced. The San Jose (Calif.) Symphony and the Toronto Symphony Orchestra were the latest additions to the list of financially troubled North American orchestras. In the past 20 years a dozen orchestras—including those in Denver, Colo., Birmingham, Ala., and the California cities of Oakland, Sacramento, and San Diego—had confronted serious money problems. The Toronto Symphony players, faced with the need to cut expenses, agreed to a 15% salary reduction.

Alberto Vilar, a Cuban emigré who had become enormously wealthy investing in technology stocks, gave $25 million to the Berlin Philharmonic's musician-training program. The German orchestra was only one of many musical organizations that benefited from Vilar's largesse at a rate of more than $1 million; others included the Metropolitan Opera in New York City, the Vienna State Opera, the Royal Opera House at Covent Garden in London, the Mozart Festival in Salzburg, the Kirov Opera in St. Petersburg, and the Los Angeles and Washington, D.C., opera companies. Besides the Vilar contribution, the Berlin Philharmonic was reluctantly given $11.7 million, half of its annual operating budget, by the Berlin city government. The contribution, which would help to increase the players' salaries, was demanded by Sir Simon Rattle before he signed a 10-year contract as the orchestra's music director to begin in 2002.

In New York City the Lincoln Center for the Performing Arts launched a billion-dollar renovation program that promptly disintegrated into bickering between the constituent organizations. The Metropolitan Opera, geographically but not administratively part of the complex, was conducting its own redevelopment program. James Levine, artistic administrator of the Met, planned to keep that position while he succeeded Seiji Ozawa as music director of the Boston Symphony Orchestra. Ozawa was to become director of the Vienna State Opera. Tony Hall, a BBC executive, was named to replace Michael Kaiser as director of the Royal Opera House in London; Kaiser was slated to head the John F. Kennedy Center for the Performing Arts in

Washington, D.C. Other major personnel changes included Raymond Leppard's retirement as music director of the Indianapolis (Ind.) Symphony Orchestra, Jesús López-Cobos's departure as music director of the Cincinnati (Ohio) Symphony Orchestra, Christopher Hogwood's retirement as music director of the Handel and Haydn Society of Boston, and Lotfi Mansouri's leaving the general directorship of the San Francisco Opera. In January the New York Philharmonic announced that Lorin Maazel would replace Kurt Masur (who was ill and awaiting an organ transplant at year's end) as music director beginning with the 2002–03 season, and in May the Minnesota Orchestra announced that the Finnish conductor Osmo Vanska would replace Eiji Oue as its music director in 2003. In September American conductor James Conlon announced that he would not renew his contract with the Paris Opera; the contract was to end in 2004.

Popular Korean soprano Sumi Jo (see BIOGRAPHIES) broadened her audience, singing half Broadway songs and half works for the operatic repertory in her Carnegie Hall concert in February.

World premieres included three cello concertos. Elliott Carter's second concerto (the first had been written some 30 years earlier), written for and played by Yo-Yo Ma, was premiered by Barenboim and the Chicago Symphony Orchestra in September as part of the conductor's Wagner and Modernism series. The second, Concerto for Cello and Orchestra, was written by Philip Glass for Julian Lloyd Webber and had its premiere in Beijing in October. The third was Concerto for Cello and Orchestra: In Memoriam F.D.R. by Peter Schickele, commissioned by New Heritage Music and performed in February by Paul Tobias and the Chamber Symphony of the Manhattan School of Music. Hans Werner Henze's L'Heure bleue, a serenade for 16 players, received its first performance in Frankfurt, Ger., in September. Sir Peter Maxwell Davies's Antarctic Symphony (Symphony No. 8) was premiered by the Philharmonia Orchestra at the 50th anniversary celebration of the Royal Festival Hall in London on May 6. The Philharmonia Orchestra had also commissioned and performed Ralph Vaughn Williams's Sinfonia Antarctica for the sound track to the 1948 film Scott of the Antarctic. (See WORLD AFFAIRS: Antarctica.) On a less-serious note, British comedian and composer Richard Thomas and his Kombat Opera Company altered the musical landscape with

Jerry Springer: The Opera, a musical setting of material from a popular television show often punctuated with outbreaks of violence. The most unusual musical event of the year, and perhaps of the century, however, took place in Halberstadt, Ger.—the preparations for a performance of John Cage's Organ 2/ASLSP. It was to be played, in accordance with the instruction "as slow as possible," at the ultraslow rate of two notes per year, and estimates were that the piece, which would have its first notes played in January 2003, would be finished in 639 years.

John Corigliano (see BIOGRAPHIES) was honoured with the 2001 Pulitzer Prize in Music for his Symphony No. 2 for String Orchestra; the work had first been performed by the Boston Symphony Orchestra in November 2000. The gold medalists in the 11th Van Cliburn International Piano Competition (May 25–June 10, 2001) were Stanislav Ioudenitch from Uzbekistan and Olga Kern of Russia. In New York City the Avery Fisher Career Grants were awarded in March to violinist Timothy Fain, cellists Daniel Lee and Hai-Ye Ni, and flutist Tara Helen O'Connor.

Violinist Isaac Stern, who was generally credited with saving Carnegie Hall from demolition, died in September of heart failure. Giuseppe Sinopoli died on the podium in April while conducting Aïda at the Berlin Opera House. Japanese conductor Takashi Asahina died on December 29. Among other musicians who died in 2001 were composers Iannis Xenakis and Douglas Gordon Lilburn, pianist Yaltah Menuhin, harmonica virtuoso Larry Adler, and Canadian operatic baritone Victor Braun. (See OBITUARIES.)

(JOSEPH MCLELLAN)

Jazz. The precarious condition of jazz in 2001 was best dramatized by the extended uproar surrounding Ken Burns's documentary Jazz, which aired on the PBS television network in January. Ten episodes long—each episode lasted nearly two hours—and costing a reported $13 million to produce, Jazz attempted to portray the art form's development from its beginnings early in the 20th century. Burns used a wealth of historic film clips and photos, many of them rare, and the sources of most of the series music were recordings, many of them classic. Over half of Jazz was devoted to the quarter century between World Wars I and II, when jazz was one of the U.S.'s most popular styles of music among black and white audiences. An important nonmusical theme was the changing relations between black and white Americans. The lives of Louis Armstrong and Duke Ellington, two of the greatest jazz musicians, provided recurring story lines throughout the series; commentators, especially musician Wynton Marsalis and critics Stanley Crouch and Gary Giddins, offered frequent perspectives.

Praise for Burns's *Jazz* centred on the quality of the music and illustrations, including the historic dance styles exhibited; on the fact that many singers, musicians, and bands were profiled in each episode; and especially on the very fact that the documentary was broadcast at all—jazz had all but disappeared from American television networks, apart from cable's Black Entertainment Television. As with any history of jazz, criticism centred on the important figures and events that were omitted. Many of the omissions followed a pattern; the influence of Europe and European music on jazz was downgraded, as were white performers, especially after World War II. In addition, cool and West Coast jazz played very minor roles in Burns's history. A storm of criticism swirled around the only episode devoted to jazz of the past 40 years. In that episode later idiomatic developments, including free jazz and fusion music, played only a secondary role. Instead, Burns profiled older musicians and the revival of older styles by Marsalis and other younger musicians. After viewing Burns's grand documentary, viewers were left with a sense that jazz was something historic—such as French Impressionist painting or epic poetry—an art form that at best now only lingered on long after its natural life span.

Was it true? Was jazz a vanishing art? At one point early in 2001, according to *Billboard* magazine, of the 25 best-selling jazz albums, only 7 were current releases. In the course of the year, *Down Beat*'s usually effusive reviewers awarded five stars to only two jazz albums, *Black Dahlia* by arranger Bob Belden and *Not for Nothin'* by the Dave Holland Quintet. Although jazz still accounted for only about 3% of all U.S. compact-disc (CD) sales, the flood of new recordings continued, the vast majority of them from independent labels. The public appetite for live jazz, at least, remained high. Younger generations of listeners predominated in nightclub audiences in cities with busy jazz scenes. Jazz festivals thrived in the Americas, Europe, Asia, and Australia—*JazzTimes* listed 422 festivals that featured jazz and blues in 2001.

Roger Viollet/Liaison

Louis Armstrong—one of the central figures depicted in Ken Burns's 2001 TV documentary Jazz—*is surrounded by (from left to right) Mezz Mezzrow, Claude Luter, and Duke Ellington in a 1960 photo.*

In a generally uneventful year, 23-year-old singer Jane Monheit, an Ella Fitzgerald devotee, sparked attention with her CD *Come Dream with Me*. Chicago's cult favourite Patricia Barber (*see* BIOGRAPHIES) sang standards on her hit sixth album, *Nightclub* (2000). While revivalism and eclecticism prevailed among younger musicians, urgent personal statements could be heard in albums by tenor saxophonist Mark Turner (*Dharma Days*) and trumpeter Dave Douglas, whose *Witness* was devoted to songs of freedom and nonviolent protest. Turner, torn between cool and hard bop styles, also played on veteran altoist Lee Konitz's *Parallels*. Other outstanding albums were the Italian Instabile Orchestra's *Litania Sibilante*, the freely improvising Boston trio of Maneri-Morris-Maneri in *Out Right Now*, and the *Yet Can Spring* duets by pianist-composer Myra Melford and clarinetist-saxophonist Marty Ehrlich. A growing phenomenon was the release of albums of long-ago concerts by important artists, including woodwind improviser Anthony Braxton's *Quintet (Basel) 1977*, tenorist Fred Anderson's *Dark Day: Live in Verona 1979*, and Chris McGregor's Brotherhood of Breath big band, comprising English and South African exile musicians, in *Travelling Somewhere* from

1973. Albums began appearing from Sunday jam sessions produced by the Left Bank Jazz Society (Baltimore, Md.) during 1965–80; the first four were by Stan Getz, Sonny Stitt, Cedar Walton, and Al Cohn and Zoot Sims.

While outstanding new albums were few, there were some extraordinary reissues. A singular project was the discovery of a major composer's rarest recordings, Charles ("Baron") Mingus's *West Coast 1945–49* (2000). *The Complete in a Silent Way Sessions*, from Miles Davis's first fusion music project, was the latest of Columbia's many Davis collections. From 1919 came *Lieut. Jim Europe's 369th U.S. Infantry "Hell Fighters" Band: The Complete Recordings* (1996), a historic African American big ragtime band at the very border of early jazz. Art Pepper's *The Hollywood All-Star Sessions*, released as Japanese albums in the early 1980s, at last appeared in the U.S. as a boxed set. Two of the finest swing-era singers had their finest recordings collected. *Lady Day: The Complete Billie Holiday on Columbia (1933–1944)* was a 10-CD boxed set gathering 230 of her joy-infused early recordings. *The Complete Columbia Recordings of Mildred Bailey* was offered by Mosaic, the busy mail-order outfit that also released boxed sets of 1950s Max Roach and 1960s Gerald Wilson big band in 2001.

The year's death toll included pianist-composer John Lewis, who during the year had released the concert album *Evolution II*, trombonist J.J. Johnson, swing bandleader Les Brown, pianist Tommy Flanagan, singers Al Hibbler and Susannah McCorkle, drummer Billy Higgins, saxophonists Joe Henderson and Buddy Tate and impresario Norman Granz. (*See* OBITUARIES.) Other notable deaths included those of trumpeter Conte Candoli, saxophonists Harold Land, Billy Mitchell, Ken McIntyre, and Flip Phillips, popular Canadian flutist Moe Koffman, Latin jazz arranger Chico O'Farrill, arranger Manny Albam, record producer Milt Gabler, and author Helen Oakley Dance.   (JOHN LITWEILER)

Popular. The fortunes of American popular music in 2001 were in a decline even before the terrorist attacks of September 11. In the first half of the year, overall music sales were reportedly down 5.4%, and concert ticket sales dropped 15.5%, compared with the same period in 2000.

Pop artists responded to the tragedy with performances dedicated to remembering victims and helping survivors. *America: A Tribute to Heroes* aired without commercial interruption on radio and television in more than 210 countries. The tribute was filmed on soundstages in Los Angeles, New York, and London and featured performances by Bruce Springsteen, Neil Young, Céline Dion, and Faith Hill (see BIOGRAPHIES), among others; it generated $150 million in pledges and a two-CD set. Paul McCartney helped organize the Concert for New York City at Madison Square Garden. The Who, Eric Clapton, Mick Jagger, Keith Richards, James Taylor, Macy Gray, and many other artists performed before an audience that included 5,000 rescue workers. George Strait, Hank Williams Jr., Tim McGraw, and Alan Jackson were part of the Country Freedom Concert in Nashville, Tenn.

The Grammy nomination of rapper Eminem's *The Marshall Mathers LP* for Album of the Year sparked a huge controversy owing to its violent content. Though the award went to rock veterans Steely Dan for *Two Against Nature,* Eminem performed a duet with Elton John on the awards show and won three Grammys in rap categories.

The most popular band in the U.S., *NSYNC, sold 1,880,000 copies of its fourth album, *Celebrity,* during its first week of release. Many believed that the quintet had adopted a more mature attitude with its latest release. Since the automated tracking of sales was established in 1991, only the band's previous album, *No Strings Attached,* had sold more during its first week—2.4 million copies in March 2000. The Backstreet Boys postponed a national tour when a member of the group sought help for alcohol abuse and depression. On her third album, *Britney,* 19-year-old Britney Spears sent mixed messages as she

lingered between teen innocence and womanhood.

Alicia Keys, a 20-year-old native of New York City, sold three million copies of her debut album, *Songs in A Minor,* spurred by the hit single "Fallin'." Keys's music mixed hip-hop, soul, and classical styles. The precocious singer and actress Aaliyah, 22, released her third album, *Aaliyah,* just weeks before her death in an airplane crash in The Bahamas. (*See* OBITUARIES.) Destiny's Child—Beyonce Knowles, Kelly Rowland, and Michelle Williams—cemented their status as major pop stars with *Survivor,* which sold more than three million copies by year's end. Rock band Staind connected with disaffected youth on its dark album *Break the Cycle;* System of a Down explored political stances on *Toxicity;* and Christian rap-metal band P.O.D. found an audience with *Satellite.*

Michael Jackson returned to the top of the pop-album chart with *Invincible,* his first release in six years. Though his first single, "You Rock My World," performed poorly, peaking at number 10, the album sold 366,000 copies during its first week of release. Jackson staged two New York City concerts, titled "The Thirtieth Anniversary Celebration," at Madison Square Garden and combined them in a network TV special. Pop icon Bob Dylan turned 60 and issued *Love and Theft,* his 43rd album, to critical acclaim.

A sound-track album, *O Brother, Where Art Thou?,* with a large musical cast that included Emmylou Harris, Ralph Stanley, John Hartford (*see* OBITUARIES), Gillian Welch, and Chris Thomas King, dominated the country album chart and shipped three million copies. The Country Music Association and the International Bluegrass Music

Association both named *O Brother, Where Art Thou?* Album of the Year.

After having announced his retirement at a 2000 press conference, Garth Brooks, country's biggest all-time seller, released *Scarecrow,* his first album of new material in four years. To boost sales of the new release, Brooks appeared for three consecutive weeks in hour-long network TV specials.

A new Country Music Hall of Fame and Museum opened in Nashville and inducted a large class of members, including Bill Anderson, the Delmore Brothers, the Everly Brothers, Don Gibson, Homer & Jethro, Waylon Jennings, the Jordanaires, Don Law, the Louvin Brothers, Ken Nelson, Webb Pierce, and Sam Phillips.

The Latin Grammys were moved and then postponed. The awards ceremony was moved in August from Miami, Fla., to Los Angeles when security problems arose, stemming from anti-Fidel Castro demonstrators protesting the appearance of Cuban artists, but planned to keep its scheduled date of September 11. The terrorist attacks on that day forced a postponement, however, and the awards were finally presented in late October. The big winners were Spanish pop star Alejandro Sanz, who picked up four awards, including Record of the Year and Song of the Year, and Colombian singer Juanes, a newcomer who won three awards, including best new artist. "Queen of Salsa" singer Celia Cruz captured the award for best traditional tropical album for *Siempre Viviré.*

The Rock and Roll Hall of Fame welcomed Aerosmith (*see* BIOGRAPHIES), Solomon Burke, the Flamingos, Michael Jackson, Queen, Paul Simon, Steely Dan, and Ritchie Valens.

The popular music of North Africa continued to attract a wider global audience, thanks partly to the work of the fiery and highly political Algerian exile Rachid Taha. He was influenced by British punk, French chanson, and even Jamaican reggae, and his album *Made in Medina,* which was recorded in both Paris and New Orleans, was a rousing blend of Arabic and Western styles that had much of the wild fervour of punk or early rock and roll. This sense of danger and the unexpected was repeated in Taha's exuberant live shows.

Thanks to the North African immigrant community, Paris had developed into a world music centre and home for both Taha and Khaled, who was the best-known exponent of Algerian *rai.* Another such exile, Cheb Mami (*see* BIOGRAPHIES), developed a considerable

James Taylor (second from left), Melissa Etheridge (centre), and Bon Jovi band member Richie Sambora (right) are joined by other singers for a final number during the Concert for New York City at Madison Square Garden on October 20.

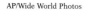
AP/Wide World Photos

audience across Europe, North Africa, and elsewhere with his more easygoing commercial blend of *rai* and Western pop. His album *Dellali* and his collaboration with British star Sting, with whom he toured and recorded "Desert Rose," increased his audience. Senegalese singer Baaba Maal released a classic new album, *Missing You* (*Mi Yeewnii*). After having mixed West African styles with experimental Western pop in his recent work, Maal returned to the acoustic music he had popularized earlier in his career with his *Djam Leelii* album, but with more subtle and sophisticated treatment. Recorded in a village in Senegal by the British producer John Leckie (best known for his work with Radiohead), the album made use of the *kora* (the West African lute) and acoustic guitar work from Maal's longtime friend and musical associate Mansour Seck, the blind griot, or hereditary singer.

The move back to delicate easygoing songs was also reflected in Senegal with the return of Orchestra Baobab, a band that had pioneered the fusion of African and Cuban styles two decades earlier and had enormous influence on the subsequent development of West African music. The group also rereleased its celebrated album *Pirate's Choice*—recorded in 1982 but not released until 1989—which still sounded as mellow and as fresh as ever. In the war-torn Democratic Republic of the Congo, there was a similar development with the emergence of Kekele, a fine semiacoustic band that included such veteran guitarists as Papa Noel and Syran Mbenza, famous for their work in the classic era of Congolese rumba back in the 1960s and '70s. Mbenza also toured with Sam Mangwana, a celebrated singer from that era. From Zimbabwe, another crisis-torn African state, there were fine performances from the soulful vocalist Oliver Mtukudzi, the star of the year's WOMAD festival in the U.K., and from the veteran guitar band the Bhundu Boys, who released *The Shed Sessions*, an anthology of early recordings.

In the Caribbean and Latin America, the fashion for Cuban music sparked by the success of the Buena Vista Social Club had eased a little, though there was one outstanding spin-off album; *Cachaito*, a solo set from the bass player Orlando ("Cachaito") López, was a brave and experimental mixture of Latin, jazz, and even Jamaican dub influences. Though Brazil—traditionally a powerhouse of Latin music—had been somewhat overshadowed by the fashion for

Cuba in recent years, it made a comeback, thanks partly to a new work from the long-established singer Gilberto Gil, who provided the sound track for the much-praised Brazilian feature film *Me, You, Them*, which featured songs of Luiz Gonzaga, his boyhood hero. The more experimental side of the new Brazilian scene was shown by Andrea Marquee, who mixed Latin and contemporary Western pop styles in her rousing, adventurous album *Zumbi*.

The Beatles' newest album, *1* (2000), a compilation of its greatest hits, broke an unofficial record when it topped the charts in 34 countries early in 2001. The death in November of George Harrison, known to many as the quiet Beatle, saddened the music world after he succumbed to a long battle with cancer. (*See* OBITUARIES.)

The Irish band U2 posted yet another classic year; the group embarked on a world tour in support of its album *All That You Can't Leave Behind*, which marked a return to the grand soulful ballads of its early years. One of the most promising newcomers in the U.K. was Susheela Raman, whose album *Salt Rain* was a cool, soulful blend of jazz and North African and Indian styles. Raman was nominated for the U.K.'s Mercury Music Prize, but the award was won by the more emotional female singer P.J. Harvey with her compelling album *Stories from the City, Stories from the Sea*.

Iranian pop diva Googoosh, banned from her homeland following the 1979 Islamic revolution, embarked in March on what she called a "homecoming tour"; she performed in March in Dubayy, U.A.E., before a crowd of some 30,000 people, most of whom flew there from Iran. In 2000, after a 20-year absence from the stage, she had performed to appreciative audiences in Canada and the U.S.

Those fleeing the war in Afghanistan reported that the Taliban government's extremist policies included a ban on the country's once-celebrated popular songs. Anyone found listening to a cassette was fined in proportion to the length of the offending tape and was forced to confess in public. In a climate such as this, it was little surprise that the country's best-known performers, Nashenas and Naghma, had fled abroad.

Among the other major music figures who died during the year were Joey Ramone, John Phillips (of the Mamas and the Papas), Chet Atkins, and John Lee Hooker. (*See* OBITUARIES.)

(ROBIN DENSELOW; JAY ORR)

DANCE

North America. In June the innocently titled *Free to Dance*—a selective, three-hour documentary chronicling African American influences in modern dance—was telecast nationally in the U.S. on the Public Broadcasting System. Once the terror events of September came and went, the chronicle's simply stated focus on freedom and dancing began to resonate throughout dance in general and suggest more complicated dimensions.

The big ballet troupes lived through both status-quo activity and stressful times. Early in 2001 New York City Ballet (NYCB) unveiled a new work by Eliot Feld. Called *Organon*, the 63-dancer work proved overly grandiose and, many thought, a large-scale waste of the company's time and personnel. Ballet master in chief Peter Martins's new ballet, *Burleske*, was as inconsequential as Feld's was awful.

Happily, Christopher Wheeldon, who recently had retired as an NYCB dancer and turned full time to choreography, gave the repertory a plummy new work called *Polyphonia*, and by the summer, shortly before the premiere of another engaging new work of his called *Variations Sérieuses*, he had been named the troupe's first-ever "resident choreographer." American Ballet Theatre (ABT) began the year by unveiling at the John F. Kennedy Center for the Performing Arts in Washington, D.C., Paul Taylor's savvy Depression-era suite, *Black Tuesday*.

In its lengthier New York City season, the company offered another modern dance-based work, the somewhat dry *Gong* by Mark Morris. (*See* BIOGRAPHIES.) Though David Parsons's *The Pied Piper* arrived with great hoopla, because of its technologically advanced digitally worked decor and modernist trappings, it turned out to be a dud. More successfully, the company also unveiled its first staging of John Cranko's *Onegin*, which showcased a good number of ABT's stellar dancers. By the summer, however, trouble was unsettling the administration, and executive director Louis Spisto resigned under pressure, partly in the wake of the *Pied Piper* fiasco. The smaller fall season featured a revival of Antony Tudor's *Dim Lustre* and the premiere of Stanton Welch's *Clear*.

Similar shifts and uncertainty befell Boston Ballet (BB) when early in the year Maina Gielgud, though due to take over from departing artistic director Anna-Marie Holmes in July, quit her post even before she started. Later,

Jeffrey Babcock left his general director's post with BB for a position at Boston University. By September Mikko Nissinen, artistic director of Canada's Alberta Ballet, had been hired as BB artistic director and was due to commence full duties in July 2002. Prior to his appointment Nissinen actively participated in a Balanchine celebration at the Banff (Alta.) Arts Festival, possibly a preview of the vision he would bring to Boston. Houston (Texas) Ballet (HB) also suffered some natural and artistic disasters.

After presenting James Kudelka's lavish *Firebird* (from the National Ballet of Canada), the HB sustained damage to a good deal of its scenery and costumes as a result of heavy flooding in Houston. In addition, long-standing director Ben Stevenson resigned but then returned to artistic direction in a more limited capacity. The company's English tour to Stevenson's homeland, however, was not much of an artistic success.

Dance Theatre of Harlem performed in June at New York City's famous Apollo Theatre and in the fall for two weeks at New York's City Center, followed by a later stint at the Kennedy Center. Miami (Fla.) City Ballet added a ballet by Sir Frederick Ashton to its repertory but had to cancel planned additions of Balanchine and Jerome Robbins ballets owing to financial cutbacks. Nonetheless, artistic director Edward Villella was able to make progress toward a full-evening creation with the first two parts of a four-act work in progress celebrating *The Neighborhood Ballroom*. Kansas City (Mo.) Ballet (KCB) held a Stravinsky Festival that showcased a reconstruction of Balanchine's *Renard*, put together by octogenarian Todd Bolender, former KCB director.

The Joffrey Ballet of Chicago led off its fall season with an all-Nijinsky ballet bill, including the American premiere of the recently reconstituted *Jeux*, which the company billed as *Games*. Carolina Ballet presented the world premiere of Lynne Taylor-Corbett's *Carmina Burana*. Pacific Northwest Ballet, which relocated to the Mercer Arts Arena during renovations at the Seattle (Wash.) Opera House, marked the 20th anniversary of favourite company ballerina Patricia Barker. San Francisco Ballet got *A Garden*, the newest freelance ballet from Morris.

Morris, who moved into a specially renovated headquarters (replete with classrooms, rehearsal studios, and other amenities) near the Brooklyn

(N.Y.) Academy of Music (BAM), celebrated his 20th anniversary at BAM with an ambitious three-week season, capped by glorious performances of his present-day classic, *L'Allegro, il penseroso, ed il moderato*. Twyla Tharp, who had previously announced that she too would relocate and set up a company and school in Brooklyn not far from Morris's building, later pulled out of the project. The Merce Cunningham Dance Company gave New York City a world premiere of the master iconoclast's *Way Station* in a run that also featured Cunningham's most recent

Carolina Ballet's Timour Bourtasenkov and Melissa Podcasy in the world premiere of Lynne Taylor-Corbett's Carmina Burana.

Nina Alovert (201) 615-1780

collaboration with Robert Rauschenberg, *Interscape*. During the year Paul Taylor presented two new works, *Dandelion Wine* and *Fiends Angelical*.

A contingent of 10 French modern dance groups presented a festival called "France Moves" throughout New York City. The American Dance Festival commissioned modern works from John Jasperse, Ronald K. Brown, Shen Wei,

Meredith Monk, and Garth Fagan, who also received the festival's Scripps Award. Brown also worked again for the Alvin Ailey American Dance Theatre; its winter season also featured a premiere by company director Judith Jamison. Mikhail Baryshnikov's White Oak Dance Project (WODP) took its *PASTForward* program of works by postmodern dance innovators from the 1960s and '70s on tour nationally and internationally. BAM's annual Next Wave Festival included a concentration of performance groups from Australia, as well as offerings that included the work of such leading lights of European dance as Anne Teresa De Keersmaeker, Pina Bausch, and William Forsythe. Though the Martha Graham Dance Company was still in "suspended operations" owing to legal battles between the Martha Graham Center for Contemporary Dance and Ron Protas, head of the trust overseeing the staging of Graham's work, the school reopened in January even as legal wrangling over the use of Graham's copyrighted name continued. In August a court ruling favoured the Graham Center and ruled against the trust's claim to exclusive rights to Graham's name.

England's Royal Ballet (RB) played both the Kennedy Center and Boston, marking the engagements as a kind of "farewell tour" for its retiring director Anthony Dowell. (ABT's gifted Ethan Stiefel performed with the RB as a guest artist.) With ambitious new ideas for the Kennedy Center, newly arrived head Michael Kaiser planned a high-profile season for his first year at the helm, notably buoyed by financial support from arts patron Alberto Vilar. In addition to presenting both the National Ballet of Cuba, which also toured elsewhere, Kaiser backed plans to expand the number of dancers and performances for the Suzanne Farrell Ballet, which began an East Coast tour with two weeks of offerings at the Kennedy Center.

In other touring ventures, the Paris Opéra Ballet played San Francisco and Orange county, Calif., and La Scala Ballet performed as part of Lincoln Center Festival 2001, with Sylvie Guillem's staging of *Giselle* proving a big draw in New York City after having gained similar attention in its Orange county season. Starting in St. Paul, Minn., Matthew Bourne's Adventures in Motion Pictures presented a run of *The Car Man*, the British choreographer's take on Georges Bizet's *Carmen*.

National Ballet of Canada launched its 50th anniversary with a repertory headed by director James Kudelka's *The Contract*, a work partly based on *The Pied Piper of Hamelin*. Les Grands Ballets Canadiens de Montréal added to its store of Balanchine works by mounting *Episodes* and reviving *Concerto Barocco*. The 10th outing of the Festival International de Nouvelle Danse offered a total of 32 productions and works by Boris Charmatz, Cunningham, Trisha Brown, and WODP. A number of events that had been scheduled for presentation in New York City during September and October had to be canceled, notably many offerings of the Québec New York 2001 festival.

Changeovers included the departure from Fort Worth (Texas) Ballet (FWB) of Benjamin Houk and the assumption by Paul Mejia, formerly with FWB, of the executive directorship of Ballet Arlington (Texas). After years of relocation in temporary quarters, the New York Public Library for the Performing Arts moved back to its fully renovated

site at Lincoln Center, with the Jerome Robbins Dance Division one of its brightest jewels, holding a king's ransom of written and visual records, including countless moving-picture items.

Deaths during the year included those of dancers Pauline Koner (*see* OBITUARIES), Willam Christensen (*see* OBITUARIES), Sonia Arova, Maria Karnilova, Mario Delamo, Jamake Highwater, Barton Mumaw, Laura Foreman, Nicholas Orloff, Robert Pagent, and Jane Dudley; choreographer and director Herbert Ross (*see* OBITUARIES); writer Robert Garis; lighting designer Nananne Porcher; and costumer Barbara Matera.

(ROBERT GRESKOVIC)

Europe. The most noticeable feature of the year 2001 in Europe was the number of directorship changes among the leading companies. Some were carefully planned, but several others resulted from artistic differences between the current director and company boards or funding bodies.

In London the Royal Ballet's final season under the direction of Sir Anthony Dowell showed many ballets closely associated with his distinguished career as a dancer. The final program had four pieces created by Sir Frederick Ashton for Dowell, including perhaps his most famous role, Oberon in *The Dream*. In the absence of Darcy Bussell and Sylvie Guillem (due to pregnancy and injury, respectively), attention focused on less-well-known dancers, one of whom, 19-year-old Romanian Alina Cojocaru, was promoted to principal dancer after her debut performances in *Giselle*. The new artistic director, Ross Stretton, made his first mark on the company by replacing the existing production of *Don Quixote*, by Mikhail Baryshnikov, with the Rudolf Nureyev version; his second innovation was the company premiere of John Cranko's *Onegin*.

The Birmingham Royal Ballet, touring more than planned while awaiting the reopening of its home theatre, presented the second part of director David Bintley's *Arthur*, which completed the story of the legendary king. English National Ballet's retiring director, Derek Deane, made a new version of *Swan Lake* for his last production; described originally as a staged adaptation of his in-the-round choreography, it was in fact largely new, closely resembling the Royal Ballet's former readings except in the last act, which was Deane's own. It was very well received. Incoming director Matz Skoog was faced with the company's ongoing financial problems.

The Rambert Dance Company, the oldest company in Great Britain, celebrated its 75th anniversary with a number of specially devised programs. Northern Ballet Theatre was another company that saw a change of director; David Nixon moved from BalletMet in Columbus, Ohio. Its first new production of the year, Massimo Moricone's *Jekyll and Hyde*, was a failure with both critics and the public, and it was withdrawn during the company's spring tour. A new company, George Piper Dances, was formed by Michael Nunn and William Trevitt—two of the dancers who had left the Royal Ballet to join Tetsuya Kumakawa's K-Ballet Company—and they made a successful debut with programs featuring contemporary ballets. Michael Clark, once the "bad boy" of British dance, reformed his company after a three-year absence and introduced a program that contrasted his older style with new work.

Scottish Ballet announced that the contract of director Robert North would not be renewed and that the company would make a major change of direction in the upcoming season, moving away from classical works toward a more contemporary style. The change would make audiences for traditional ballet dependent on visits from companies from south of the border, and there were many protests.

London had visits from both major Russian companies. The Bolshoi Ballet, represented by a group of 50 dancers, presented programs that each contained one ballet and a selection of pas de deux and solos; the performances were greeted by very sparse houses. The Mariinsky Ballet, at Covent Garden for a four-week season, also initially played to smaller audiences than expected, but enthusiasm built up during the season. The San Francisco Ballet, a London favourite, made a welcome return visit; New York City Ballet appeared at the Edinburgh International Festival, bringing three programs containing only recent works, with nothing by George Balanchine.

Elsewhere in Europe, both the Dutch National Ballet and the Stuttgart (Ger.) Ballet celebrated 40th anniversaries. The Dutch company marked the occasion with a program that included works new to the company by William Forsythe and Toer van Schayk, as well as one of the company's own signature works, Rudi van Dantzig's *Four Last Songs*. Earlier in the year the company premiered *Kurt Weill* by choreographer Krzysztof Pastor, and revivals included

The Paris Opéra Ballet dancers perform Pierre Lacotte's **Paquita.**

© Colette Masson/Agence Enguérand

Léonide Massine's 1933 masterwork *Choreartium* and Ashton's *Cinderella*. The Stuttgart company focused mainly on new work, but its season also included a fresh production of *Don Quixote* by dancer Maximiliano Guerra; it was the first new full-length ballet it had staged in five years.

In Russia the Bolshoi Ballet, rebuilding after its leadership problems in 2000, invited Roland Petit to make a new ballet based on Aleksandr Pushkin's *Queen of Spades*. Entitled *Three Cards*, it played in repertoire alongside Tchaikovsky's opera on the same subject. The Bolshoi Theatre celebrated its 225th anniversary, but there was grave concern about the physical state of the building, and much effort was concentrated on raising money for a reconstruction fund. In St. Petersburg in February, the Mariinsky Ballet hosted the first International Ballet Festival, which included a program of excerpts of ballets from the Soviet era and a controversial new version of *The Nutcracker*, with choreography by company soloist Kyrill Simonov; the work was masterminded by conductor Valery Gergiev and designer Mihail Chemyakin. Much of the year was taken up by extensive foreign tours.

Another change of management saw the Finnish National Ballet replacing di-

rector Jorma Uotinen, after 10 years, with the Dane Dinna Bjørn; the company mounted a ballet based on British novelist J.R.R. Tolkien's *The Hobbit*. In Sweden ballerina Natalia Makarova staged a new version of *Giselle* for the Royal Swedish Opera Ballet; later in the year that company also mounted *Swan Lake* in the Peter Wright–Galina Samsova production originally made for the Birmingham Royal Ballet. Aage Thordal-Christensen resigned his position as director of the Royal Danish Ballet after only two years; he was replaced by Frank Andersen, who had directed the company from 1985 to 1994. At the same time, American Lloyd Riggins, a former company dancer, was appointed first guest instructor. Thordal-Christensen mounted his own new version of *The Nutcracker* in December. The company of Peter Schaufuss devoted an entire evening to the Danish storyteller Hans Christian Andersen.

The Paris Opéra Ballet started the year with a major new production by Pierre Lacotte of the 19th-century classic *Paquita*, using the fragments that remained of Marius Petipa's original but with much additional choreography by Lacotte. The ballet provided many striking roles for the company's dancers and was greeted with much acclaim. Later in the season the company added a new work by Jiri Kylian to its repertory and

also gave the world premiere of Jean-Claude Gallotta's *Nosferatu*, a ballet inspired by Friedrich Wilhelm Murnau's classic film *Nosferatu, eine Symphonie des Gravens*. Under the Opéra's rules, a number of étoiles reached compulsory retirement at the age of 40; Isabelle Guerin, Fanny Gaida, and Carole Arbo gave their last performances. In the new season the company took part in a mixed opera and ballet bill, including Balanchine's *Prodigal Son*, paying homage to librettist Boris Kochno, and showed a program that contained both Vaslav Nijinsky's *L'Après-midi d'un faune* and Jerome Robbins's version of the same ballet, *Afternoon of a Faun*.

New technology began to play a part in the dance world; the annual competition for young dancers, the Prix de Lausanne, was transmitted live on the Internet for the first time.

British ballet mourned the death of Dame Ninette de Valois (*see* OBITUARIES), founder of the Royal Ballet. Other deaths included Kirov ballerina, teacher, and coach Inna Zubkovskaya (*see* OBITUARIES), longtime Royal Ballet dancer Leslie Edwards, dancer and choreographer Terry Gilbert, and critic and writer Richard Buckle.

(JANE SIMPSON)

World Dance. African war dances and the hoarse pleading and staccato heel rhythms of Spanish gypsies in the flamenco passion were emblematic themes of the world dance scene in 2001, primarily in New York City, Chicago, London, and Paris. There was also renewed interest in Irish dance, made popular by the *Riverdance* extravaganza, an engagement of which played in New York City in the summer.

The small Trinity Irish Dance Company (trained and directed by Mark Howard) outshone all competitors at the National Irish Dance Competition in Toronto; it won five gold, two silver, and four bronze medals. At competitions and in the traditional dances of the repertoire, the Trinity dancers performed in the classic Irish dance style—arms motionless and held straight at the sides—but in noncompetitive performances they freely used their arms. For the troupe's touring repertoire, Howard choreographed dances on modern subjects, notably the plight of Irish miners in Pennsylvania in the 19th century.

The intricate movements and flashy speed of the Argentine tango found renewed interest in the U.S., where TangoDanza drew crowds in the Midwest. The company consisted of three couples and one additional woman; the latter was needed when an additional character appeared in narrative works. The leading couple, Leandro Palou and Andrea Missé, performed double duty;

Palou was the company's choreographer, and Missé designed the many elegant costumes. In addition to the traditional tango, they introduced the playful milonga and the valsa criolla, the latter danced in the light romantic mood of the waltz.

In London, Manuel Santiago Maya, known as Manolete, directed a Spanish dance company that presented innovative Spanish dance, classical dance, and the expected flamenco. Choreographer-dancer Joaquín Cortés presented his troupe in a piece titled *Pura Pasión*, which London critics called "a cacophony of wailing." In New York, Pilar Rioja headed her flamenco group in several appearances. Spanish dance was highly visible at the Noche Flamenca at Jacob's Pillow, the annual summer dance festival in Becket, Mass., and at the New World Flamenco Festival in Irvine, Calif.

The Ballet Folklórico de México, founded and directed for many years by Amalia Hernández, was prominent on world stages throughout the season despite the death of Hernández in 2000. The Ballet Fiesta Mexicana de Yloy Ybarra was a colourful folkloric show that performed primarily in American locales populated with Mexican immigrants.

Choreographer-educator Chuck Davis, who delved into the African American

search for roots, established Dance-Africa festivals in Chicago and New York (at the Brooklyn Academy of Music [BAM]). Sabar Ak Ru Afriq ("Dream and Spirit of Africa"), a New York-based troupe directed by African American Obara Wali Rahman Ndiaye and his wife, presented Senegalese dances at BAM. Forces of Nature, another New York-based group, and Ndere Troupe, from Uganda, also performed at BAM. Lincoln Center in New York City hosted *Africa Out Loud*, which presented groups from the Democratic Republic of the Congo, Mali, Senegal, and South Africa.

The Muntu Dance Theatre of Chicago toured the U.S. and made an especially successful appearance at Lincoln Center Out of Doors. Directed by choreographer Aboulaye Camara, Muntu presented *Ancestral Memories*, dances of Mali, Guinea, and Senegal. Compagnie Käfig, a French-based hip-hop group of seven dancers of North African descent, appeared at Jacob's Pillow. Their combined break dance and poetry with scenic elements was presented to North African melodies.

Tibetan monks living in exile in Paris explained their threatened culture in sacred ritual dances that were forbidden in China. In addition to the ethnic rites and tribal folklore of its modern polyglot population, the Bayanihan Philippine National Dance Company presented the preserved Spanish-influenced dances of a past era.

The dances of India were a staple in Chicago. The Kalapriya Center for Indian Performing Arts regularly presented visiting and immigrant dancers, and the Dance Center of Columbia College presented Bharatanatyan in the Diaspora, a series of programs that illustrated several Indian dance forms.

The 10th annual Chicago Human Rhythm Project, conceived and directed by tap artist Lane Alexander, showcased leading American tap dancers, notably Broadway star Savion Glover. At that gala opening the Israeli Sheketak troupe—consisting of three highly trained dancers and two musicians—produced percussive sounds on their bodies, on the floor, and on a hanging line of pots and pans. They won standing ovations and ecstatic newspaper reviews.

In an effort to resurrect the dances of the Khmer, the New England Foundation for the Arts, in partnership with the Asia Society, sponsored a Cambodian group, which toured 12 cities.

(ANN BARZEL)

Photo © 2001 Jack Vartoogian

Amampondo, a South African-based percussion and dance ensemble, performs during the **Africa Out Loud** *series at Lincoln Center in New York City on July 13.*

THEATRE

Great Britain and Ireland. Upheaval was the byword behind the scenes at the Royal Shakespeare Company (RSC), where artistic director Adrian Noble announced far-reaching changes that affected the structure and ambitions of the company in 2001. The RSC withdrew from its residency at the Barbican Centre and initiated short seasons in other London venues. Confusion reigned among the public, which was uncertain when the Stratford-upon-Avon seasons would begin or end, and resentments grew among the company over layoffs in the technical "plant" in Stratford.

The RSC had a fine new Hamlet in Samuel West, who led a lively full-text production by Steven Pimlott. The company also debuted a remarkable new play, Martin McDonagh's *The Lieutenant of Inishmore*, in which IRA terrorist activity was the stuff of black and very bloody comedy. The RSC, however, once again played second fiddle to the Royal National Theatre (RNT).

The big RNT talking point was an impeccable revival of *My Fair Lady*, directed by Trevor Nunn, starring the pop singer Martine McCutcheon as Eliza. McCutcheon was afflicted with a severe throat infection and missed so many performances that her understudy, 18-year-old Alexandra Jay, became a new star in her own right. When Jay herself became indisposed, the show's Professor Higgins, Jonathan Pryce, while announcing another actress in the role, asked that night's audience if anyone out there fancied giving it a go. Still, the show was a resounding success and transferred to the Theatre Royal, Drury Lane, under the auspices of the producer Sir Cameron Mackintosh.

The RNT announced that Nicholas Hytner, the director of *Miss Saigon*, *Carousel*, and the award-winning movie *The Madness of King George*, would succeed Trevor Nunn in April 2003. Hytner clinched his appointment with two outstanding productions, Shakespeare's *The Winter's Tale* and Mark Ravenhill's *Mother Clap's Molly House*.

Though both plays were highly polished, there was evidence that Hytner took some risks, one of his trademarks. *The Winter's Tale* featured a modern dysfunctional royal marriage at the court of Leontes (Alex Jennings) and a sheep-shearing festival in Bohemia presented as a hippie-style rock concert. Ravenhill's play was an outrageous attempt to mix a bawdy, Restoration comedy of sexual party time in an 18th-century male

brothel with a contemporary gay scenario. Nunn himself directed Alex Jennings as Lord Foppington in a generous, colourful revival of *The Relapse* by Sir John Vanbrugh. John Caird directed one of the best plays of the year, *Humble Boy* by Charlotte Jones; it was a modern shadow play inspired by the RNT's 2000 production of *Hamlet*, with Simon Russell Beale and Cathryn Bradshaw playing contemporary equivalents of their own Hamlet and Ophelia. Russell Beale portrayed Felix Humble, a university research fellow, and Bradshaw was cast as a former girlfriend who arrives to arouse him in the long grass of a gorgeous garden deep in the English countryside. Bees and flowers figured large, as did the superstrand theory of universal matter. Dame Diana Rigg and Denis Quilley played, respectively, Felix's mother and her long-standing lover. The play had fine acting from leading players, lots of good jokes, a gloriously seductive design (by Tim Hatley), and an abundance of strong, poetic writing.

Another RNT new play, *Howard Katz*—from Patrick Marber, author of *Closer* (1999)—was a disappointing tale of a nasty show business agent's rise and fall, meticulously charted in Ron Cook's mesmerizing performance. The experience was like watching *Death of a Salesman* rewritten as *King Lear*, but the final effect was strangely unsatisfying.

The Royal Court Theatre, viewed by many as the home of new British playwriting, had another poor year. Kevin Elyot's *Mouth to Mouth* sustained an impression of poetic virtue. On transferring to the West End, however, the tragicomedy of lost love and misdirected passion—in a tangled domestic drama played backward to the point of crisis, then forward again (like a theatrical palindrome)—seemed paper thin, despite the acting talents of Lindsay Duncan and Michael Maloney.

The Royal Court presented a retrospective season of the work of Sarah Kane, who had committed suicide in 1999, but her notorious *Blasted* was drained of impact in a cool, dispassionate production. Though playwright Leo Butler premiered *Redundant*, his work about dead-end life in a northern town had none of the vitality of similar, more groundbreaking Royal Court plays of the 1960s. This was enclosed, self-indulgent drama, unexcitingly staged until, almost gratuitously, at the end the ceiling rose slowly into the flying area. Why?

No such doubts surrounded American playwright Neil LaBute's *The Shape of Things* at the Almeida Theatre, tem-

porarily rehoused in an abandoned bus depot in the King's Cross district while the home base underwent an overhaul. This world premiere was for many the play of the year, a brilliant dissection of the exploitation of trust in the cause of art and a Frankenstein morality for our media-savvy age. LaBute himself directed a quartet of hot young actors—Rachel Weisz, Gretchen Mol, Paul Rudd, and Frederick Weller—in a dozen pungent scenes punctuated by the blaring rock music of Smashing Pumpkins.

The Almeida also presented an ambitious but finally disappointing revival of Frank Wedekind's *Lulu*, with Anna Friel as a sexy but spiritually underpowered heroine, and a stunning new version by Sir David Hare of Anton Chekhov's unwieldy apprentice piece *Platonov*. Jonathan Kent's production of a play best known in recent years as *Wild Honey* in Michael Frayn's rewrite was extravagant and filmic. The vast stage area contained a revolving dacha, a forest of silver birches, another of head-high sunflowers, and a long canal that concealed the railway line. Aidan Gillen played Chekhov's feckless hero, a 27-year-old wastrel teacher who attracted women like a magnet does iron filings. It was a magnificent, panoramic evening, with superb performances from Gillen, Helen McCrory, Jhodi May, and Adrian Scarborough, among many others.

It was a mightily subdued first-night audience—the play opened on September 11, the day of the terrorist attacks in the United States. In addition, the Almeida's co-directors, Jonathan Kent and Ian McDiarmid, had previously announced that they would leave their posts in 2002, after 12 years.

The other London powerhouse, the Donmar Warehouse, had a quiet year in comparison. David Mamet's *Boston Marriage* proved a slight, though beautifully written, letdown, even if Zoë Wanamaker and Anna Chancellor acted their socks off. Sam Shepard's *A Lie of the Mind*, a demanding and convulsively depressing play, was given the works by a fine cast led by Sinéad Cusack and Catherine McCormack. It failed to attract the usual Donmar crowds. Christopher Hampton's *Tales from Hollywood* was another revival from the 1980s. The writing shimmered with sharp dialogue and wit as the European intellectual émigrés in the lotusland of Los Angeles formed a metaphor of artistic homelessness. The play seemed cramped, however, in the small theatre.

Feelgood by Alistair Beaton was a stinging satire on British Prime Minister

291

Tony Blair's government, with Henry Goodman in electrifying form as a devious spin doctor trying to keep the troops "on message" as the prime minister prepares a conference speech. His job is complicated by the revelation that one of the prime minister's inner circle, a hapless life peer—played with glorious deadpan by Nigel Planer—was responsible for the inadvertent introduction of genetically modified hops grown on his family estate that produced beer with a strange side effect on male drinkers all over Europe—they began to grow large breasts.

Feelgood originated at the Hampstead Theatre but quickly moved to the West End. Other commercial highlights were *Caught in the Net* by Ray Cooney, a hilarious, if old-fashioned, farce starring Russ Abbot and Eric Sykes; *Japes* by Simon Gray, a strong comedy of sibling rivalry across the decades, with powerful performances by Toby Stephens and Jasper Britton; and a sensationally costumed revival by Philip Prowse of Sir Noël Coward's *Semi-Monde* (1926), a forgotten play about the sexual misdemeanours and wholesale bitchiness that takes place in the foyer of a hotel; it was the second time that Prowse had rescued the play from oblivion—the first time having been 25 years earlier in Glasgow.

The classics made surprisingly big inroads on Shaftesbury Avenue. Fiona Shaw was ferocious, pitiless, and extraordinary in the title role in *Medea*, a stunning modern-dress version of the Euripides tragedy directed by Deborah Warner. Dawn French, the very large and popular television comedienne, played Bottom in a mildly daring gender-bending *A Midsummer Night's Dream*. Hollywood stars Brendan Fraser and Frances O'Connor headlined in Tennessee Williams's *Cat on a Hot Tin Roof*, with Ned Beatty as a ferocious Big Daddy. Ian Holm was an electrifying Max in Harold Pinter's *The Homecoming*. Alan Rickman and Lindsay Duncan teamed languidly in Coward's *Private Lives*.

There were no new musicals to speak of apart from *Peggy Sue Got Married*, a lively-enough stage version of the Francis Ford Coppola movie, with new music by Bob Gaudio and a vibrant Ruthie Henshall in the title role; she was sensational while traveling in time from 1980s torch songs to '50s jive and jitterbug. Playwright Jonathan Harvey's *Closer to Heaven*, at the newly refurbished Arts Theatre, was a nonevent aimed at a gay niche market, and it was inefficiently molded around a few trite numbers by the Pet Shop Boys.

Ryan Philpott and Emma Powell perform in one of the Agathie Christie plays staged at the Palace Theatre in Westcliff, Eng., during the year.

The ever-popular open-air Globe at Southwark gave a solid showing of *Macbeth* in tuxedos and *King Lear*. The Open Air Theatre in Regent's Park scored with a truly magical *Love's Labour's Lost*, directed by Rachel Kavanaugh, and an irresistible revival of *Where's Charley?*, the 1948 Broadway version of the 1892 farce *Charley's Aunt*. The other summer musical treat was *My One and Only*, with Janie Dee and Tim Flavin tapping and sloshing (there was water on the stage) their way to happiness in the 1983 romantic hybrid of Ira Gershwin songs.

Other notable productions beyond London included Christopher Marlowe's *Edward II* at the Sheffield Crucible, starring Joseph Fiennes; a long summer season of Dame Agatha Christie plays— all of them—were at the Palace Theatre, Westcliff; *King Lear*, directed by Terry Hands and featuring Nicol Williamson as an erratic but gloriously compelling Lear at the Theatre Clwyd, Mold, Flintshire, north Wales; a brilliant cut-up job of Shakespeare's *Henry VI* trilogy—set in an abattoir—directed by Edward Hall (Sir Peter's son) at the Watermill, Newbury; and *Uncle Vanya*, featuring Tom Courtenay in manic mode in the title role in the 25th-anniversary season of the Royal Exchange, Manchester.

A strong candidate for best production of the year was Aleksandr Pushkin's great epic play *Boris Godunov*, performed in Russian by an ad-hoc company of Russian actors, directed by Declan Donnellan, at the Brighton Festival and the Riverside Studios in London.

Notable new plays premiered at the Traverse Theatre during the Edinburgh International Festival included Gregory Burke's *Gagarin Way*, a tense thriller set in a factory storeroom where a kidnapping went wrong, and Iain Heggie's *Wiping My Mother's Arse*, a bright and funny comedy about the problems of old age in a nursing home, with more than a touch of Joe Orton.

The Dublin Theatre Festival also concentrated on new work, with a trilogy of short plays by Brian Friel, Conor McPherson, and filmmaker Neil Jordan and a first stage play by novelist Roddy Doyle loosely inspired by the movie *Guess Who's Coming to Dinner?* The Abbey Theatre presented a season of works by Tom Murphy ranging from his first success, *A Whistle in the Dark*, to his denser, more knotted and poetic plays *The Gigli Concert* and *The Sanctuary Lamp*. (MICHAEL COVENEY)

U.S. and Canada. The most startling and talked-about event of the American theatre year was the premiere in mid-December 2001 of Tony Kushner's new play *Homebody/Kabul*, which debuted at Off-Broadway's New York Theatre Workshop. The ballyhoo was not so much related to Kushner's return to the New York stage with a major work nearly 10 years after his Pulitzer Prize-winning *Angels in America* AIDS epic had catapulted him into the ranks of the nation's literary elite—making him as close to a household name as American dramatists ever get to be—but to the play's setting and its subject—Afghanistan.

In fact, it was more coincidence than calculation that Kushner's three-and-a-half-hour drama about the West's contemporary and historic relationship to Afghanistan arrived onstage a scant two months after the U.S. had all but declared war on that country. A writer with an ongoing interest in international affairs (wartime Germany in *A Bright Room Called Day* and corruption in the Soviet Union in *Slavs!*), Kushner had long indulged a fascination with Afghanistan and its geopolitical plight, and he had finished the initial version of *Homebody/Kabul* the previous winter. Nevertheless, the play's events—it follows the journey of a British woman who disappears into the chaos of Afghan life—seemed eerily prescient, and director Declan Donnellan's Off-Broadway production generated avid international attention.

As in other sectors of American life, the September 11 terrorist attacks reverberated throughout the nation's theatre community. Performances were postponed, canceled, modified, and reexamined as theatres in New York and Washington, D.C., struggled with logistic problems, and those in other parts of the country deferred to the mood of a shocked and mourning public. Some plays no longer seemed appropriate—a Broadway revival of Stephen Sondheim's dark musical *Assassins* was delayed, for example—and others took on surprising new resonances. In the wake of widespread uncertainty, one thing seemed certain: the economic consequences for theatre would be severe. The New York City commercial theatre, which suffered disastrously during the first weeks after the attack, continued to post below-average ticket sales through the end of the year, and the not-for-profit theatre prepared to bear the brunt of a vastly diminished pool of resources available for the arts.

In some locales existing prosperity compensated for worries about future want. California's Berkeley Repertory Theatre opened a new $20 million, 600-seat second theatre with a grand-scale two-part production of *The Oresteia*, co-directed by artistic director Tony Taccone and opera specialist Stephen Wadsworth (who said he viewed the Aeschylus tragedy as a "totemic dysfunctional family saga"). Outsized productions of the Greeks were also de rigueur in Washington, D.C., where Arena Stage artistic director Molly Smith put her lightly feminist brand on a new compilation of classic texts called *Agamemnon and His Daughters*, and Shakespeare Theatre artistic director Michael Kahn staged *The Oedipus Plays* in an African mode, with the gifted Avery Brooks in the title role.

A number of established playwrights debuted important works. Edward Albee had a success d'estime with his esoteric and literate theatrical fable *The Play About the Baby*, directed by David Esbjornson in an Off-Broadway production that made glorious use of the turn-on-a-dime talents of veteran actors Marian Seldes and Brian Murray. Suzan-Lori Parks, best known for poetic abstraction in works such as *The America Play*, favourably surprised critics with an ostensibly realistic comedy-drama *Topdog/Underdog*, in which a

Playwright Tony Kushner stands in front of the set (still under construction) of his new play, Homebody/Kabul, *at the New York Theatre Workshop in November.*

pair of down-and-out brothers fret and feud. (George C. Wolfe's taut Public Theater production was expected to return for a Broadway run during the next season.) Historian-turned-playwright Charles L. Mee made "love" the operative word in a trilogy of dissimilar plays—*Big Love, First Love,* and *True Love*—that alternately engaged and puzzled audiences across the country with their collagelike texts and juggled time frames.

Playwright Richard Nelson would mark 2001 as a prime year. He debuted a new play, *Madame Melville*, in London and New York, featuring Macaulay Culkin, the former child movie star, in the role of a 15-year-old American lad seduced by his Parisian teacher, and wooed audiences with his book and lyrics for the unusual musical play *James Joyce's The Dead*, which was widely produced across the country and on national tour.

Much attention was also paid to a national tour of *The Tragedy of Hamlet*, auteur British director Peter Brook's elegant condensation of Shakespeare's expansive tragedy, pared down to two and a half intermissionless hours and rendered with passionate restraint by a mere eight actors. Audiences in Seattle, Wash., New York City, and Chicago debated the merits of Brook's agenda, but there was general agreement that the agile black actor Adrian Lester was a thrilling prince of Denmark.

The sensation of the commercial theatre season—and the only show to take the September 11 slump in box-office stride—was comedian Mel Brooks's deliriously tasteless musicalization of his own 1967 cult film *The Producers*. The sure-fire casting of Nathan Lane (*see* BIOGRAPHIES) as the hard-luck showman Max Bialystock and Matthew Broderick as his nebbishy accountant Leo Bloom (roles played in the film by Zero Mostel and Gene Wilder), abetted by a dazzling supporting cast and Brooks's own silly-sophisticated songs and lyrics, proved irresistible to ticket buyers, who lined up around the block from the St. James Theatre and jammed Ticketmaster phone lines. Among the records broken were the biggest advance sale ever ($33 million), the most Tony nominations (15), and the most Tonys won (12). Of the 12 awards won, 2 went to Susan Stroman, its director and choreographer. (*See* BIOGRAPHIES.)

David Auburn's Pulitzer-confirmed drama *Proof*, produced by Manhattan Theatre Club, was the second most honoured Broadway show of the season, with Tonys for best play, best director (Daniel Sullivan), and best actress (Mary-Louise Parker). The actors that played the old and young British poet A.E. Housman in Tom Stoppard's *The*

Invention of Love, Richard Easton and Robert Sean Leonard, respectively, also won acting awards, as did Viola Davis of August Wilson's wordy but well-received drama *King Hedley II*.

The post-Tony arrival of an unlikely but high-spirited musical, Mark Hollmann's and Greg Kotis's savvy Bertolt Brecht–Kurt Weill parody *Urinetown*, enlivened the theatre year, as did a crowd-pleasing, all-star New York City staging in Central Park's Delacorte Theatre of Anton Chekhov's *The Seagull*, directed by Mike Nichols and reuniting long-ago stage confederates Meryl Streep and Kevin Kline. On the West Coast a revival of the tuneful 1958 Rodgers and Hammerstein musical *Flower Drum Song*, politically revamped via David Henry Hwang's rewritten book, earned high marks at the Mark Taper Forum.

In Canada, southern Ontario's Stratford Festival continued its economic and artistic upswing under the artistic direction of former actor Richard Monette. Although on the financial ropes 10 years earlier (Monette said he almost closed one of Stratford's three theatres), now—thanks in part thanks to an endowment campaign that had topped $10 million—the festival was opening a fourth theatre and planning an ambitious 50th anniversary season in 2002, with Christopher Plummer signed to star in *King Lear*. Just 90 minutes away in Toronto, the four-year-old Soulpepper Theatre Company, founded by a cluster of Canada's best-known actors, tapped ever more successfully into the depth of the city's audience for serious theatre. A September run of two Eugène Ionesco plays, *The Bald Soprano* and *The Lesson*, for example, was a sellout.

Among the losses to the theatre community in 2001 were stage and film actress Kim Stanley, famous for her roles in *Bus Stop* and *Picnic*, and rubber-faced comedienne Imogene Coca. (*See* OBITUARIES.) Other notable deaths included actress Gloria Foster, known for her expertise in classic and contemporary roles, and producer Arthur Cantor, who in the course of a long career presented more than 50 productions in New York, London, and Paris.   (JIM O'QUINN)

MOTION PICTURES

United States. It seemed the sign of troubled times that in 2001 the world film-going public seized hungrily upon two adaptations of children's books of mythical tales about the conflict of Good and Evil. *Harry Potter and the Sorcerer's Stone* ("Philosopher's Stone" in the international release), directed by Chris Columbus with an all-British cast, faithfully translated into images the story and the visions of J.K. Rowling's 1997 best-seller. The film of J.R.R. Tolkien's trilogy *The Lord of the Rings*—first published in 1954–55 and adapted in 1978 as an animated film—was directed by the once-maverick New Zealand director Peter Jackson. The first installment, *The Fellowship of the Ring*, was released in 2001; the other two parts, already filmed, were scheduled for Christmas release in 2002 and 2003. The spirit of childhood legend also imbued the future-world science fiction of Steven Spielberg's *Artificial Intelligence: AI*, a quasi-collaboration based on a long-time idea of the late filmmaker Stanley Kubrick.

Another outstanding success of mixed national progeny was *Bridget Jones's Diary*, directed by Sharon Maguire from Helen Fielding's original newspaper column. The 30ish heroine found a response on both sides of the Atlantic, and the film offered a change-of-pace role for Hugh Grant. (*See* BIOGRAPHIES.) The sequel to 1991's *The Silence of the Lambs*, *Hannibal*, directed by Ridley Scott, was a predictable box-office winner. The Australian director

A scene from the hit film Harry Potter and the Sorcerer's Stone *("Philosopher's Stone" in the international release).*

Baz Luhrmann excelled his own previous tours de force with his Parisian musical fantasy *Moulin Rouge*. Veteran Woody Allen directed a modest tribute to cinema of the 1940s, *The Curse of the Jade Scorpion*, while Robert Altman's *Gosford Park* resembled an old-style Agatha Christie whodunit, with a murder at a 1930 country house whose divided society Altman observed with pleasure but not much depth. Lasse Hallström brought E. Annie Proulx's novel *The Shipping News* to the screen.

The Coen brothers, Joel and Ethan, attempted, with only mixed success, a pastiche of 1940s film noir with *The Man Who Wasn't There*. David Lynch's *Mulholland Dr.*, developed out of a rejected TV series pilot, was a characteristic assembly of offbeat characters and enigmatic incidents, set in Los Angeles. Satire was healthily in evidence in Peter Howitt's *AntiTrust*, in which Tim Robbins patently based his performance as a computer supermogul on Bill Gates. After two Oscar-nominated dramas in 2000 (and an Oscar for one, *Traffic*), director Steven Soderbergh returned with the lively crime caper *Ocean's Eleven*. (*See* BIOGRAPHIES.)

Two sober and distinguished biopics were Michael Mann's *Ali*, with Will Smith in the role of Cassius Clay/Muhammad Ali, and Ron Howard's *A Beautiful Mind*, with Russell Crowe (*see* BIOGRAPHIES) as John Nash, the mathematical genius who conquered schizophrenia to become a Nobel Prize winner in 1994. The most spectacular critical failure of the year was the costly but banal three-hour spectacle *Pearl Harbor*.

A few interesting works appeared from the independent sector of production. Actor Todd Field made a distinguished directing debut with *In the Bedroom*, a sensitive and expansive study of the effect of a family tragedy. The off-Broadway success *Hedwig and the Angry Inch*, the musical saga of a transsexual entertainer, was brought to the screen by its writer-star creator John Cameron Mitchell.

Shrek, the outstanding animated story of a reluctantly kindly ogre directed by Andrew Adamson and Vicky Jenson, was aimed at adult as well as infant audiences and, with the year's other animated hit, *Monsters, Inc.*, confirmed the current thirst for myth and fairy tale.

In 2001 Hollywood said farewell to legendary director Stanley Kramer, as well as two double Oscar-winning actors, Jack Lemmon and Anthony Quinn, actress Dorothy McGuire, and director-choreographer Herbert Ross, among others. (*See* OBITUARIES.)

British Isles. The first apparent effect of the "New Labour" administration's initiative to centralize film activities under a Film Council was overproduction; of a total of more than 100 feature films, a substantial proportion were undeniably lamentable. British directors favoured character comedy, with Mel Smith's crime farce *High Heels and Low Lifes*, Jez Butterworth's *Birthday Girl*, about a prim bank teller who acquires a mail-order bride from Russia, and Steve Barron's *Mike Bassett: England Manager*, a self-deprecatory comedy about a disastrous English international football (soccer) team. Alan Taylor's *The Emperor's New Clothes* was a witty and likable speculation about an imagined incident in the life of Napoleon; the film offered a rewarding dual role to Ian Holm. Ken Loach made one of his most brilliant works of social criticism, *The Navigators*, describing with rich comedy the effect on the lives of a little group of workers of the disastrous degeneration of Britain's railway system after privatization.

John Boorman's *The Tailor of Panama* was a stylish adaptation of John le Carré's 1996 novel. Other successful literary adaptations were Fred Schepisi's *Last Orders*, from Brian Swift's prizewinning novel; and Michael Apted's thriller *Enigma*, adapted by the dramatist Tom Stoppard from a novel by Robert Harris, set in the wartime codebreaking headquarters at Bletchley Park. The British taste for biopics brought Richard Eyre's study of the novelist Iris Murdoch, *Iris*.

In Ireland the gifted Yugoslav director Goran Paskaljevic made *How Harry Became a Tree*, a tale of neighbour hate in 1920s Ireland that was an open metaphor for the Bosnian conflict.

Canada. One of the year's greatest surprises was *Atanarjuat, the Fast Runner*, the first film to be made in the Inuktitut language, directed by Zacharias Kunuk. Drawing upon legend and the ancient Inuit storytelling tradition, the film vividly presented an integral culture, beautifully filmed (on digital video) against the Arctic landscapes of an island in the north Baffin region.

Australia. In a lean year Ray Lawrence's *Lantana* brought to the screen Andrew Bovell's play *Speaking in Tongues*, which shrewdly probed the frustrations of 10 middle-class people. Robert Connolly's *The Bank* mined a currently popular theme—ordinary people's battle with corporate villainy. David Caesar's *Mullet* looked at a small-town community in an increasingly unfriendly world, seen through the eyes of a young man returning home after life in Sydney. Australia's hit hero of the 1980s, Crocodile Dundee, made a somewhat weary comeback in Simon Wincer's *Crocodile Dundee in Los Angeles*.

France. Among world filmmakers France remained a leader in terms of variety, invention, and craftsmanship. Jean-Pierre Jeunet's *Le Fabuleux Destin d'Amélie Poulain* (*Amélie*), an exquisitely visualized story of a young woman driven to adjust the reality of her Montmartre neighbours, enjoyed international success. One of the more controversial productions, Patrice Chéreau's English-language *Intimacy* (2000; called *Intimité* in the 2001 French release) was an uneasy combination of frank sex and overly artificial dialogue. Claude Miller triumphantly translated Ruth Rendell's 1984 novel *The Tree of Hands* to a French setting, as *Betty Fisher et autres histoires* (*Betty Fisher and Other Stories*). Another of the year's most talented films was Anne Fontaine's *Comment j'ai tué mon père*, about the disruption of a bourgeois family by the return of their prodigal paterfamilias. Of the veterans of the 1960s nouvelle vague, Jean-Luc Godard made a characteristic essay on history, politics, and, unusually, love, in *Éloge de l'amour* (*In Praise of Love*). The 81-year-old Eric Rohmer made a charming and elegant costume picture, *L'Anglaise et le duc* (*The Lady and the Duke*). The veteran Jacques Rivette returned to direction with *Va savoir* (*Go Figure*, or *Who Knows?*), an ensemble piece set in the context of a theatrical production.

Germany. Among the few outstanding films of the year was Hungarian director István Szabó's Franco-German (but English-language) production *Taking Sides*, adapting Ronald Harwood's 1995 play about the postwar investigations of conductor Wilhelm Furtwängler's relations with the Nazi elite. Roland Suso Richter's *Der Tunnel*, reconstructing one of the biggest escape attempts from East to West Berlin in Cold War days, successfully made the transition from television miniseries to theatrical release. Franziska Buch's new adaptation revealed the perennial attractions of Erich Kastner's often-filmed children's book *Emil und die Detektive*.

Italy. Nanni Moretti's *La stanza del figlio* (*The Son's Room*), a very human story about the private grief of a couple at the death of their teenage son, won

295

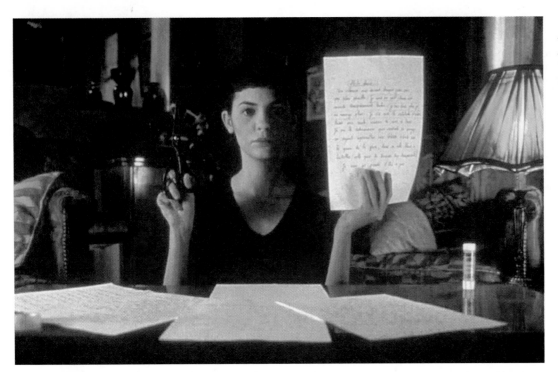

French actress Audrey Tautou plays the lead character in Jean-Pierre Jeunet's Le Fabuleux Destin d'Amélie Poulain *(*Amélie*).*

AP/Wide World Photos

for Italy the Cannes Festival Palme d'Or. Other, senior filmmakers turned to remote history. Pupi Avati's *I cavalieri che fecero l'impresa* (*The Knights of the Quest*) followed the adventures of five young 13th-century Crusaders in search of the Holy Shroud. Ermanno Olmi's *Il mestiere delle armi* (2000; *Profession of Arms*) recounted the final days and death, in 1521, of Giovanni de' Medici.

Comedy flourished. A major commercial success in the home market was *Chiedimi se sono felice* (2000; *Ask Me if I'm Happy*), directed, written, and performed by the popular comedy trio Aldo, Giovanni, and Giacomo; while the idiosyncratic Maurizio Nichetti made intelligent use of digital facilities and multilingual dialogue (with most of the comedy being visual) for his comedy about the tribulations of a Milanese office worker, *Honolulu Baby* (2000).

Iberia. Spanish films had rarely tackled contemporary social issues, so Javier Balaguer's *Sólo mía* (*Only Mine,* or *Mine Alone*), a forthright drama about domestic violence, was exceptional. The talented Joaquín Oristrell's *Sin vergüenza* (*No Shame*) explored the ambitions and relationships of an acting school.

Two Catalan directors made notable films; Ventura Pons's *Anita no perd el tren* (*Anita Takes a Chance*) related a romantic middle-aged woman's discovery of love, while Marc Recha, using a minimalist style, directed a sensitive and positive study of the effect of a death

upon a family, *Pau i el seu germà* (*Pau and His Brother*).

The nonagenarian Manoel de Oliveira produced another surprise and change of direction with a French co-production, *Je rentre à la maison,* featuring a majestic performance by Michel Piccoli as an aged actor.

Nordic Countries. A major box-office hit for Sweden was Josef Fares's *Jalla! Jalla!* (2000), relating the stories of two friends, an immigrant from Lebanon striving to evade a family-arranged marriage and his Swedish friend suffering a bad attack of impotence. The expatriate Briton Colin Nutley made an elaborate comedy about the human maneuverings in the entertainment business, *Gossip* (2000).

Denmark had an international success with Lone Scherfig's *Italiensk for begyndere* (2000; *Italian for Beginners,* 2001), showing six lonely working-class people in a Copenhagen suburb learning an emotional language along with the verbal one in their evening Italian courses.

Two notable Danish-Swedish co-productions were Bille August's delicate adaptation of Ulla Isaksson's novel *En sång för Martin* (*A Song for Martin*), about a late love affair that endures through the perils and problems of life, and Jan Troell's *Så vit som en snö* (*As White as in Snow*), which re-creates the story of Sweden's first aviatrix, Elsa Andersson.

Russia. The lawlessness of contemporary Russian urban life was featured in

Andrey Nekrasov's *Lyubov i drugiye koshmary* (2000; *Lubov and Other Nightmares*), which centred on a transvestite professional assassin, and Sergey Bodrov's effective drama *Syostry* (*Sisters*), about two women on the run from the mob enemies of their gangster father. In a lighter vein, Karen Shakhnazarov's comedy *Yady, ili vsemirnaya istoriya otravleniy* (*Poisons, or the World History of Poisoning*) described a modest would-be wife killer who seeks the aid of some of the great poisoners of history.

Eastern Europe. In a generally weak year for Hungarian production, one outstanding film was Árpád Sopsits's *Torzók* (*Abandoned*), a largely autobiographical account of a small boy's sufferings in a Cold War-era orphanage.

In the Czech production *Tmavomodrý svet* (*Dark Blue World*), the gifted Jan Sverák looked back, with a very human mixture of humour and sadness, at the experience of Czech pilots in Britain in World War II and their subsequent sufferings under communism.

The Romanian director Lucian Pintilie revisited the dark days of the Ceaușescu regime with *L'Après-midi d'un tortionnaire* (*The Afternoon of a Torturer*), based on the true confessions of a man formerly implicated in torturing political prisoners. The debutant Cristi Puiu's *Marfa și banii* (*Stuff and Dough*) provided an object lesson for filmmakers in all economically depressed national cinema industries—a film made on a minimal budget but triumphing by imagination, invention, verve, and craftsmanship. This road movie was the story of a young would-be entrepreneur undertaking a delivery to Bucharest and discovering too late that he is in thrall to petty mafiosi.

Albanian films are few in number and rarely seen abroad. Gjergj Xhuvani's *Slogans*, a tragicomedy ridiculing official postures in the late days of communist rule, and Fatmir Koçi's apocalyptic portrayal of Albanian society in the late 1990s, *Tirana, année zéro* (*Tirana Year Zero*), were welcome exceptions.

Greece. Among debutant feature writer-directors, Christos Demas's *I akrovates tou kipou* (*The Cistern*) offered an inventive rite-of-passage story of five 11-year-old boys in the fateful summer of 1974, while Christos Georgiou's *Kato apo ta asteria* (*Under the Stars*) was a road movie set in the aftermath of the division of Cyprus following the Turkish invasion of 1974. Of films by established directors, the most notable were Constantine Giannaris's *Dekapentaugoustos* (2000; *One Day in August*) and Andrea Pantzis's *To tama* (2000; *Word of Honor*). Giannaris's film was a virtuoso and occasionally visionary interweaving of the four stories of a disturbed young burglar and the absent occupants of the three apartments he devastates. Pantzis's epic was a Cypriot *Pilgrim's Progress*, set in the 1940s—the story of a devout man who encounters every kind of temptation on his journey to give thanks at the shrine of Saint Andreas for the birth of his son.

Turkey and Iran. The Turkish writer-director Kasım Öz created an epitome of the Kurdish tragedy in *Fotograf* (*The Photograph*), the story of the encounter and brief friendship on a bus journey of two young men, unaware that they will soon find themselves on opposing sides of a war. Yılmaz Erdoğan and Ömer Faruk Sorak made an auspicious debut with *Vizontele*, a comedy about the arrival of television in a back-of-beyond township.

A marked new phase in Iranian cinema was the appearance of films of open social criticism. Maziar Miri's *Qateh-ye natamam* (*The Unfinished Song*) ironically portrayed an ethnomusicologist's efforts to record the songs of peasant women when Islamic law makes it a crime for women to sing or dance in public. Rakhshan Bani-Etemad's *Zir-e poost-e shahr* (2000; *Under the Skin of the City*) was a ranging examination of social conditions in contemporary Tehran, seen through the daily problems of neighbouring families and concluding with a remarkable interrogation of the

role of cinema in Iran as the tormented woman protagonist turns on the cameraman and asks him why he is making this film. Seyyed Reza Mir-Karimi's *Zir-e noor-e maah* (*Under the Moonlight*) told the story of a young student mullah who accidentally finds himself with a group of homeless people and discovers greater fulfilment in this human contact than in the religious life. Film director and reform parliamentarian Behrooz Afkhami directed an intelligent dramatic examination of the custom of "temporary marriage" in Islamic society, *Shokaran* (*Hemlock*). Comedy is not a common commodity in Iranian cinema, but Babak Payami's *Raye makhfi* (*Void Votes*, or *Secret Ballot*) found fun in the first unaccustomed exercise of democracy. The Afghan troubles figured in several films. Mohsen Makhmalbaf's *Safar e Ghandehar* (*Kandahar*) exposed, with a remarkable poetic atmosphere, the sufferings of the Afghan people under Taliban oppression. Majid Majidi's gentle bittersweet fable *Baran* related the love story of an Iranian boy and a young Afghan girl who disguises herself as a boy to find meanly paid work on a building site. Abolfazl Jalili applied his meticulous film craft to the story of an Afghan child refugee in *Delbaran*.

Israel. An exceptionally accomplished debut film, Joseph Cedar's *Ha-Hesder* (2000; *Time of Favor*) used a personal drama about a good rabbi and his child and followers to explore troubling philosophical divisions. Dover Kosashvili's *Hatuna meuheret* (*Late Marriage*) offered a wry comedy of manners about a conventional Jewish family's desperation to marry off their 32-year-old son, who has other ideas than the "suitable" virgins they propose.

East and Southeast Asia. In Japan the major theatrical sensation of the year was 70-year-old Kinji Fukasaku's *Battle Royale* (2000), based on a best-selling novel by Koshun Takami. Its violent story of a high-school project in which pupils are compelled to kill one another led to political calls for restraints on violent films. Less controversially, another veteran, Shohei Imamura, adapted a novel by Henmi Yo, *Akai hashi no shita no nurui mizu* (*Warm Water Under a Red Bridge*), about a beautiful young woman whose body is stimulated by sex to release a magical spring gushing forth streaks of water. In a comparable vein, Gō Rijū's *Chloe* effectively and touchingly orientalized Boris Vian's novel *L'Écume des jours*, about a young women who discovers a flower bud growing in her lung.

Few films of international interest emerged from China, where the production of propaganda-loaded feature films had moved into a new and more sophisticated stage. The country's finest director, Zhang Yimou, produced an endearing character comedy, *Xingfu shiguang* (2000; *Happy Times*), which told of a dyed-in-the wool con man whose heart is moved by the young blind daughter of the woman whose hand and cash he is striving to win.

Artists in the new Hong Kong could still make films on political themes. Herman Yau's *From the Queen to the Chief Executive* (2000) argued the case of a real-life young offender who had spent 12 years detained "at Her Majesty's pleasure" and who now faced further imprisonment at the pleasure of the chief executive. Stanley Kwan's *Lan Yu* was also controversial for the new Hong Kong, depicting a homosexual love affair between the son of a communist official and a lad from the country. The biggest box-office successes of the year, however, were a Jackie Chan action thriller, *Te wu mi cheng* (*The Accidental Spy*), directed by Teddy Chan, and Johnnie To's costume comedy *Wu Yen*.

From Taiwan, Hsiao Ya-chuan's *Ming dai ahui zhu* (2000; *Mirror Image*) was essentially no more than a sketch, loosely constructed but full of wit and promise in its observation of the comings and goings of the clients of a pawnbroker's shop, left in charge of the sick proprietor's odd son.

In South Korea, Kwak Kyung-Taek drew on often painful personal memories for *Chin goo* (*Friend*), tracing the histories of four young men from boyhood in the 1970s to the present. The film proved the country's all-time box-office winner.

Thailand's runaway box-office successes were period stories dealing with Thai-Burmese conflicts of the 18th century, Thanit Jitnukul's *Bangrajan* (2000) and Chatrichalerm Yukoi's *Suriyothai*.

India. The Indian commercial cinema styled "Bollywood" broke significantly into the international market thanks to Ashutosh Gowariker's remarkable *Lagaan* (*Land Tax*). Using indigenous conventions, this skillfully related story of a group of Indian peasants challenged to compete at cricket with the arrogant British military establishment provided gripping and intelligent entertainment at any level. More limited international acceptance was earned by Santosh Sivan's Bollywood epic *Asoka* (*Ashoka*

(continued on page 299)

INTERNATIONAL FILM AWARDS 2001

Golden Globes, awarded in Beverly Hills, Calif., in January 2001

Best motion picture drama	*Gladiator* (U.K./U.S.; director, Ridley Scott)
Best musical or comedy	*Almost Famous* (U.S.; director, Cameron Crowe)
Best director	Ang Lee (*Wo hu zang lon* [*Crouching Tiger, Hidden Dragon*], China/Hong Kong/Taiwan/U.S.)
Best actress, drama	Julia Roberts (*Erin Brockovich*, U.S.)
Best actor, drama	Tom Hanks (*Cast Away*, U.S.)
Best actress, musical or comedy	Renée Zellweger (*Nurse Betty*, Germany/U.S.)
Best actor, musical or comedy	George Clooney (*O Brother, Where Art Thou?*, U.K./France/U.S.)
Best foreign-language film	*Wo hu zang lon* (*Crouching Tiger, Hidden Dragon*) (China/Hong Kong/Taiwan/U.S.; director, Ang Lee)

Sundance Film Festival, awarded in Park City, Utah, in January 2001

Grand Jury Prize, dramatic film	*The Believer* (U.S.; director, Henry Bean)
Grand Jury Prize, documentary	*Southern Comfort* (U.S.; director, Kate Davis)
Audience Award, dramatic film	*Hedwig and the Angry Inch* (U.S.; director, John Cameron Mitchell)
Audience Award, documentary	*Dogtown and Z-Boys* (U.S.; director, Stacy Peralta); *Scout's Honor* (U.S.; director, Tom Shepard)
Audience Award, world cinema	*Wode fuqin muqin* (*The Road Home*) (China; director, Zhang Yimou)
Best director, dramatic film	John Cameron Mitchell (*Hedwig and the Angry Inch*, U.S.)
Best director, documentary	Stacy Peralta (*Dogtown and Z-Boys*, U.S.)
Special Jury Prize, dramatic film	*In the Bedroom* (U.S.; director, Todd Field)
Special Jury Prize, documentary	*Children Underground* (U.S.; director, Edet Belzberg)

Berlin International Film Festival, awarded in February 2001

Golden Bear	*Intimacy* (*Intimité*) (France/U.K./Germany/Spain; director, Patrice Chéreau)
Silver Bear, Grand Jury Prize	*Shiqi sui de dan che* (*Beijing Bicycle*) (China/Taiwan/France; director, Wang Xiaoshuai)
Silver Bear, Jury Prize	*Italiensk for begyndere* (*Italian for Beginners*) (Denmark; director, Lone Scherfig)
Best director	Lin Cheng-sheng (*Ai ni ai wo* [*Betelnut Beauty*], Taiwan/France)
Best actress	Kerry Fox (*Intimacy* [*Intimité*], France/U.K./Germany/Spain)
Best actor	Benicio Del Toro (*Traffic*, Germany/U.S.)

Césars (France), awarded in February 2001

Best film	*Le Goût des autres* (France; director, Agnès Jaoui)
Best director	Dominik Moll (*Harry, un ami qui vous veut du bien* [*Harry, He's Here to Help*], France)
Best actress	Dominique Blanc (*Stand-by*, France)
Best actor	Sergi López (*Harry, un ami qui vous veut du bien* [*Harry, He's Here to Help*], France)
Best new director of a feature film	Laurent Cantet (*Ressources humaines* [*Human Resources*], France/U.K.)

British Academy of Film and Television Arts, awarded in London in February 2001

Best film	*Gladiator* (U.K./U.S.; director, Ridley Scott)
Best director	Ang Lee (*Wo hu zang lon* [*Crouching Tiger, Hidden Dragon*], China/Hong Kong/Taiwan/U.S.)
Best actress	Julia Roberts (*Erin Brockovich*, U.S.)
Best actor	Jamie Bell (*Billy Elliot*, U.K./France)
Best supporting actress	Julie Walters (*Billy Elliot*, U.K./France)
Best supporting actor	Benicio Del Toro (*Traffic*, Germany/U.S.)
Outstanding British film	*Billy Elliot* (U.K./France; director, Stephen Daldry)
Best foreign-language film	*Wo hu zang lon* (*Crouching Tiger, Hidden Dragon*) (China/Hong Kong/Taiwan/U.S.; director, Ang Lee)

Academy of Motion Picture Arts and Sciences (Oscars, U.S.), awarded in Los Angeles in March 2001

Best film	*Gladiator* (U.K./U.S.; director, Ridley Scott)
Best director	Steven Soderbergh (*Traffic*, Germany/U.S.)
Best actress	Julia Roberts (*Erin Brockovich*, U.S.)
Best actor	Russell Crowe (*Gladiator*, U.K./U.S.)
Best supporting actress	Marcia Gay Harden (*Pollock*, U.S.)
Best supporting actor	Benicio Del Toro (*Traffic*, Germany/U.S.)
Best foreign-language film	*Wo hu zang lon* (*Crouching Tiger, Hidden Dragon*) (China/Hong Kong/Taiwan/U.S.; director, Ang Lee)

Cannes International Film Festival, France, awarded in May 2001

Palme d'Or	*La stanza del figlio* (*The Son's Room*) (Italy/France; director, Nanni Moretti)
Grand Jury Prize	*La Pianiste* (*The Piano Teacher*) (Austria/France; director, Michael Haneke)
Best director	David Lynch (*Mulholland Dr.*, France/U.S.); Joel Coen (*The Man Who Wasn't There*, U.S.)
Best screenplay	Danis Tanovic (*No Man's Land*, Belgium/Bosnia and Herzegovina/France/Italy/Slovenia/U.K.)
Best actress	Isabelle Huppert (*La Pianiste* [*The Piano Teacher*], Austria/France)
Best actor	Benoît Magimel (*La Pianiste* [*The Piano Teacher*], Austria/France)
Caméra d'Or	*Atanarjuat, the Fast Runner* (Canada; director, Zacharias Kunuk)

Locarno International Film Festival, Switzerland, awarded in August 2001

Golden Leopard	*Alla rivoluzione sulla due cavalli* (Italy; director, Maurizio Sciarra)
Special Jury Prize	*Delbaran* (Iran/Japan; director, Abolfazl Jalili)
Silver Leopard	*L'Afrance* (France/Senegal; director, Alain Gomis); *Love the Hard Way* (Germany/U.S.; director, Peter Sehr)
Best actress	Kim Ho Jung (*Nabi* [*The Butterfly*], South Korea)
Best actor	Andoni Gracia (*Alla rivoluzione sulla due cavalli*, Italy)
Audience Award	*Lagaan* (*Land Tax*) (India; director, Ashutosh Gowariker)

Montreal World Film Festival, awarded in September 2001

Best film (Grand Prix of the Americas)	*Baran* (Iran; director, Majid Majidi); *Torzók* (*Abandoned*) (Hungary; director, Árpád Sopsits)
Best actress	Sandrine Kiberlain, Nicole Garcia, and Mathilde Seigner (*Betty Fisher et autres histoires* [*Betty Fisher and Other Stories*], France/Canada)
Best actor	Robert Stadlober (*Engel & Joe*, Germany)
Best director	Oliver Hirschbiegel (*Das Experiment* [*The Experiment*], Germany)
Grand Prix of the Jury	*El hijo de la novia* (*The Son of the Bride*) (Argentina; director, Juan José Campanella)
Best screenplay	*Mariage* (Canada; writer, Catherine Martin)
International Critics' Award	*Betty Fisher et autres histoires* (*Betty Fisher and Other Stories*) (France/Canada; director, Claude Miller)

Toronto International Film Festival, awarded in September 2001

Best Canadian feature film	*Atanarjuat, the Fast Runner* (director, Zacharias Kunuk)
Best Canadian first feature	*Inertia* (director, Sean Garrity)
Best Canadian short film	*Film(dzama)* (director, Deco Dawson)
Discovery award	*Chicken Rice War* (Singapore; director, Chee Kong Cheah)
International Critics' Award	*Inch'Allah dimanche* (France; director, Yamina Benguigui)
People's Choice Award	*Le Fabuleux Destin d'Amélie Poulain* (*Amélie*) (France/Germany; director, Jean-Pierre Jeunet)

Venice Film Festival, awarded in September 2001

Golden Lion	*Monsoon Wedding* (India; director, Mira Nair)
Grand Jury Prize	*Hundstage* (*Dog Days*) (Austria; director, Ulrich Seidl)
Special Jury Prize	*Raye Makhfi* (*Secret Ballot*, or *Void Votes*) (Canada/Iran/Italy/ Switzerland; director, Babak Payami)
Volpi Cup, best actress	Sandra Ceccarelli (*Luci dei miei occhi*, Italy)
Volpi Cup, best actor	Luigi Lo Cascio (*Luci dei miei occhi*, Italy)

San Sebastián International Film Festival, Spain, awarded in September 2001

Best film	*Taxi para 3* (*A Cab for Three*) (Chile; director, Orlando Lubbert)
Special Jury Prize	*En construcción* (*Work in Progress*) (Spain; director, José Luis Guerín)
Best director	Jean-Pierre Améris (*C'est la vie*, France)
Best actress	Pilar López de Ayala (*Juana la Loca*, Spain)
Best actor	Düzgün Ayhan (*Escape to Paradise*, Switzerland)
Best photography	Roman Osin (*The Warrior*, U.K.)
New Directors Prize	Gerardo Tort (*De la calle* [*Streeters*], Mexico)
International Critics' Award	*En construcción* (*Work in Progress*) (Spain; director, José Luis Guerín)

Chicago International Film Festival, awarded in October 2001

Best feature film	*À ma soeur!* (*For My Sister*, or *Fat Girl*) (France/ Italy/Spain; director, Catherine Breillat)
Grand Jury Prize	*Ni neibian jidian* (*What Time Is It There?*) (Taiwan/ France; director, Tsai Ming-Liang)
Best director	Tsai Ming-Liang (*Ni neibian jidian* [*What Time Is It There?*], Taiwan/France)
Best actress	Sandrine Kiberlain and Nicole Garcia (*Betty Fisher et autres histoires* [*Betty Fisher and Other Stories*], France/Canada)
Best actor	Koji Yakusho (*Akai hashi no shita no nurui mizu* [*Warm Water Under a Red Bridge*], Japan/France)
Silver Hugo	*Qianxi manbo* (*Millennium Mambo*) (Taiwan/France; director, Hou Hsiao-hsien)
International Critics' Award	*Anyangde guer* (*The Orphan of Anyang*) (China; director, Wang Chao)

Vancouver International Film Festival, Canada, awarded in October 2001

Federal Express Award for Most Popular Canadian Film	*Obaachan's Garden* (director, Linda Ohama)
Air Canada Award for Most Popular Film	*Promises* (U.S./Israel; directors, B.Z. Goldberg, Justine Shapiro, and Carlos Bolado)
NFB Award (documentary feature)	*Jung* (*War*): *In the Land of the Mujaheddin* (Italy/Afghanistan; directors, Alberto Vendemmiati and Fabrizio Lazzaretti)
Telefilm Canada Award for Best Western Canadian Feature	*Turning Paige* (director, Robert Cuffley)
Telefilm Canada Award for Best Western Canadian Short Film	*10-Speed* (directors, Jeff Cunningham and Adam Locke-Norton)
Dragons and Tigers Award for Young Cinema	*Ming dai ahui zhu* (*Mirror Image*) (Taiwan; director, Hsiao Ya-chuan)

Tokyo International Film Festival, awarded in November 2001

Grand Prize	*Slogans* (Albania/France; director, Gjergi Xhuvani)
Special Jury Prize	*Zir-e noor-e maah* (*Under the Moonlight*) (Iran; director, Sayed Reza Mir-Karimi)

European Film Awards, awarded in Berlin, December 2001

Best European film	*Le Fabuleux Destin d'Amélie Poulain* (*Amélie*) (France; director, Jean-Pierre Jeunet)
Best actress	Isabelle Huppert (*La Pianiste* [*The Piano Teacher*]), France/Austria)
Best actor	Ben Kingsley (*Sexy Beast*, U.K./Spain)

(continued from page 297)
the Great), the story of a historical hero of the 3rd century BC. Contemporary subjects were treated in Digvijay Singh's *Maya*, a shocking tale of child abuse sanctified as religious ceremony; in Rituparno Ghosh's *Utsab* (2000; "The Festival"), which chronicled the family crises brought to a pitch in the course of an annual festive reunion; and in the Bengali Nabyendu Chatterjee's *Mansur mian aur ghora* (*The Last Ride*), the touching story of an old man forced to give up his horse-drawn cab under pressure from his limo chauffeur son. Mira Nair's *Monsoon Wedding* was a perceptive, witty, fast-moving ensemble work about the romantic problems of a large Punjab family assembled for a wedding. Two of India's most enduring film stars died during the year: Ashok Kumar, one of Bollywood's best-loved actors for more than 60 years, and Sivaji Ganesan, a legendary star in southern India's Tamil movie industry. (*See* OBITUARIES.)

Latin America. Gerardo Tort's unsparing picture of street children in Mexico City, *De la calle* (*Streeters*), was based on a play by Jesús González Dávila. Marysa Sistach's *Perfuma de violetas, nadie te oye* (*Violet Perfume: Nobody Hears You*) dealt intelligently with rape in working-class Mexico City. Guillermo del Toro's Spanish co-production *El espinazo del diablo* (*The Devil's Backbone*) ingeniously combined a story of the perils of the Civil War and a ghost story.

Argentine cinema was seeing a marked revival with the appearance of a generation of new and distinctive filmmakers. Ana Poliak's *La fé del volcán* (*The Faith of the Volcano*) looked at the effects of the country's recent history through the friendship of two social outcasts, a 12-year-old cleaning girl and a middle-aged knife grinder. Sergio Bizzio's *Animalada* was the startling tale of a bourgeois gentleman who abandons his wife for a pretty young sheep. The biggest box-office hit in more than a decade, writer-director Fabián Bielinsky's *Nueve reinas* (*Nine Queens*), combined a brilliantly structured script and fine characterization in its depiction of small-time con men.

Brazil enjoyed its biggest-ever box-office success with Gurel Arraes's *O auto da compadecida* (2000; *A Dog's Will*), a comedy adapted from a stage success and veering between surreality and traditions of picaresque in its tale of an amiable rogue drifting through society. In *Abril despedaçado* (*Behind the Sun*), Walter Salles, director of *Central Station*, brought the weight of classical tragedy to a story of deathly feuding, based on a novel by the Albanian writer Ismail Kadare.　　　(DAVID ROBINSON)

Nontheatrical Films. *Clive Alive*, directed by Anders Envall and produced by the Swedish company Dockhouse Film & Television AB, creatively depicted the thorough safety testing of Volvo cars. The film, which starred a test dummy named Clive, beat out nine other nominees to earn the 2001 Best of Festival award at the U.S. International Film and Video Festival in Chicago. This was the third time since 1995 that Dockhouse had garnered the Best of Fest. *Clive Alive* also took the Grand Prize at three other festivals, one in Sweden and two in Germany. Swedish documentary filmmaker Arne Sucksdorff died in May at age 84. (*See* OBITUARIES.)

A young Jewish baseball player who challenged Babe Ruth's home-run record and became an American hero was chronicled in *The Life and Times of Hank Greenberg* (2000), a documentary produced by Aviva Kempner. The film was named best overall at the Columbus (Ohio) International Film & Video Festival. Film critics in Chicago, Las Vegas, Nev., New York City, and Florida voted it best documentary of the year.

Bean Cake, a 12-minute student film by David Greenspan of the University of Southern California, won high praise during the year. The film, which featured Japanese narration with English subtitles, earned the Palme d'Or for short film at the Cannes (France) International Film Festival in addition to a College Emmy and numerous other awards.

The Pigeon Murders, produced by Sean Fine for *National Geographic*, departed from the style and subject matter of traditional environmental films. The documentary depicted a detective's hunt to find out who was poisoning pigeons by the thousands in New York City. *The Pigeon Murders* won the CINE Golden Eagle, two Emmys, and numerous wildlife awards in England and the U.S.　　　(THOMAS W. HOPE)

The life of Detroit Tiger star Hank Greenberg, shown here with legendary New York Yankee Lou Gehrig, was the subject of a celebrated documentary.

Greenberg Family Collection

Religion

Relations between MUSLIMS and members of other faiths dominated the world of religion during 2001. Churches continued to tackle controversies over ORDINATION of homosexuals and sexual ABUSE by clergy, and some religious organizations found themselves examining basic beliefs on such matters as CREATION and SALVATION.

The Teachings of Islam. The September 11 terrorist attacks in the United States spurred a worldwide examination of Islamic doctrine, particularly after the FBI discovered a document left behind by a key organizer of the airplane hijackers that cited Islamic teachings in urging them to ask God for help and assuring them that by dying for the faith they would be assured entry into paradise. Muslim scholars pointed out, however, that terrorist violence is an interpretation of Islam that most adherents of the faith reject.

Attention soon focused on Afghanistan, where Osama bin Laden, the Saudi Arabian businessman and alleged mastermind of the attacks, was receiving asylum. Afghanistan's fundamentalist Islamic Taliban government had stirred controversy throughout the year because of its policies toward non-Muslims. In January Taliban leader Mullah Mohammad Omar warned that any Muslim who converted to another faith and any non-Muslim trying to win converts would face the death penalty.

In August authorities detained eight aid workers on charges of preaching Christianity and notified all Western aid organizations and the United Nations that they would be carefully watched for evidence of proselytizing. The foreign aid workers were airlifted out of the country after the Taliban fled Kabul. In March the Taliban announced that it had destroyed as idols all Buddha statues in Afghanistan, including a 53.3-m (175-ft)-high statue above the Bamian Valley that was believed to be the world's largest Buddha statue. Two months later the government said all non-Muslims had to wear distinctive marks on their clothing to set them apart from the country's Muslims, who formed an overwhelming majority. Although the ruling seemed to be especially directed against Afghanistan's largest religious minority, the tiny Hindu community, the Taliban said it was intended to protect Hindus from religious police who enforce Islamic law.

Fighting between Christians and Muslims in September in the northern Nigerian city of Jos took more than 500 lives and reportedly destroyed tens of thousands of churches, mosques, homes, and shops. Pres. Olusegun Obasanjo called out the army to restore order and declared that true believers in God must not start killing other human beings. The Catholic Bishops Conference of Nigeria said the introduction of Islamic law in some states violated the human rights of non-Muslims and was a threat to peace in the country. In June Pakistan's military ruler, Gen. Pervez Musharraf, denounced radical Islamic groups for misappropriating money collected in the name of jihad, or holy war. Addressing a gathering of Muslim leaders to mark the birthday of the Prophet Muhammad, he urged them to stop issuing "irresponsible statements" calling for holy war against the U.S. and Russia.

Interfaith Relations. Pope John Paul II became the first pope to enter a mosque when he toured a 1,300-year-old Islamic house of worship in May in Damascus, Syria. He was greeted by Mufti Ahmed Kuftaro, Syria's top Muslim cleric, and the pontiff urged joint forgiveness by Christians and Muslims for all the times they had offended one another. In September the pope arrived in Kazakhstan, a predominantly Muslim state in Central Asia, with a message of good wishes for Islamic leaders. Dato Seri Mahathir bin Mohamad, the Muslim prime minister of Malaysia, told 600 Christian leaders from 82 nations attending the 11th General Assembly of the World Evangelical Fellowship in Kuala Lumpur that "we should be careful that we don't propagate religions at the cost of conflicts and violence."

Christian-Jewish relations suffered in July when a commission of Catholic and Jewish historians suspended its study of the church's actions during the Holocaust because the Vatican had not released all of its archives from the era. The Rev. Peter Gumpel, speaking for the Vatican, subsequently said that some Jewish historians on the commission had helped mount a "slanderous campaign" against the Roman Catholic Church and that the panel's work had failed because of "irresponsible" actions by some of its members. Discussions at a meeting of Christians and Muslims in Rome organized in October by the liberal lay Catholic Community of Sant'Egidio turned raw as concord was sought over recent events in the Middle East and offended Jews (who were not represented) with talk of "arrogant Zionists."

Poland's Roman Catholic bishops apologized in May for a 1941 massacre of Jews in northeastern Poland and for wrongs committed by Polish Catholics against Jews during World War II. In *Constantine's Sword*, a book on the history of Christian anti-Semitism, however, former Catholic priest James Carroll suggested that such apologies failed to grapple with how Christian teaching created a climate that led to mob violence against Jews. The Israeli army's occupation of part of the premises of the Evangelical Lutheran Church of the Reformation in August in the West Bank town of Beit Jala was denounced by the Lutheran World Federation. The federation's general secretary, the Rev. Ishmael Noko, said the troops had invaded "one of the holy places of the Christian community."

The Israeli government came into conflict with Greek Orthodox leaders in July when Prime Minister Ariel Sharon tried to disqualify 5 of the 15 candidates vying to succeed the late Diodoros I as Greek Orthodox patriarch of Jerusalem. Although Sharon cited a centuries-old church law that allowed governmental authorities to disqualify candidates for the position, the church subsequently elected Irineos I, one of the five the Israeli leader had rejected.

Pope John Paul II (left) embraces Catholicos Karekin II, patriarch of the Armenian Apostolic Church, at the church's seat, Ejmiadzin, on September 25.

The opening of the Holy Land Experience, a Christian theme park in Orlando, Fla., stirred concern among some Jewish leaders, who saw it as an attempt to convert Jews to Christianity. The founder of the $16 million theme park, Marvin Rosenthal, was a Baptist minister who was raised Jewish and became a Christian as a teenager.

Pope John Paul II won praise from Greek Orthodox leaders when, during a visit to Athens in May, he apologized for Roman Catholic sins of "action or omission" against Orthodox Christians. He specifically offered "deep regret" for the sacking by Catholic crusaders of Constantinople, now Istanbul, in 1204. A spokesman for Greek Orthodox Archbishop Christodoulos said the pope's words would "help heal one thousand years of mistrust between the two churches and create the possibility for new dialogue."

The pope's visit to Ukraine in June, however, drew fire from Russian Orthodox Patriarch Alexey II and Metropolitan Volodymyr of the Ukrainian Orthodox Church. They warned that John Paul's embrace of Ukraine's five million members of the Greek Catholic Church would hinder ecumenical relations. In Ukraine the number of Orthodox parishes outnumbered Catholic parishes by about three to one, but the Orthodox churches were divided into three denominations, of which the largest was loyal to Moscow. Alexey also rebuked

the pope for his later visit to Kazakhstan, saying the Catholic leader should have asked his permission before making the trip.

After leaving Kazakhstan, John Paul visited Armenia and made ecumenical history by celebrating mass at the altar of an Orthodox church for the first time. The outdoor mass was held at Ejmiadzin (Echmiadzin), the seat of the Armenian Apostolic Church, an independent Oriental Orthodox church that was celebrating the 1,700th anniversary of Christianity's becoming the country's state religion.

Pope John Paul II made a number of other formal apologies during the year as well. In October he acknowledged "errors" by historical Roman Catholic missions to China (relations between China and the Holy See had been particularly tense since October 2000, when the Roman Catholic Church canonized as martyrs 120 Chinese people whom China regarded as criminals), and a month later the pontiff transmitted a document (by means of the first official papal e-mail—from a laptop computer in the pope's office in the Vatican) to dioceses around the world, which included an apology for past injustices to South Pacific islanders committed by Catholic missionaries.

Ecumenism. Representatives of Catholic, Lutheran, and Reformed churches met in Rome in February to exchange views on indulgences, the Catholic practice of

remitting punishment for sins in exchange for prayer and repentance. The Vatican said it was the first ecumenical consultation on the subject since the Protestant Reformation. In March representatives of the Presbyterian Church (U.S.A.) met with Vatican officials and issued a joint statement pledging to work toward agreement on the doctrine of justification, mutual recognition of baptisms, and the removal of mutual condemnations that went back to the Reformation. Also in March the Church of England's House of Bishops issued a statement criticizing the Catholic Church's ban on receiving communion in Anglican churches as "an ecumenical, theological and pastoral affront." A bishop of the Evangelical Lutheran Church in America (ELCA) and his Episcopal counterpart presided in June at joint ordinations of each's churches in Chicago for the first time since their two denominations joined in a full communion agreement in 2000. The Anglican Church of Canada and the Evangelical Lutheran Church in Canada approved a similar accord in July. The ELCA's national convention in August in Indianapolis, Ind., modified the agreement, however, by voting to allow clergy to be ordained by pastors rather than bishops on grounds of conscience. The Lutheran Church–Missouri Synod declared at its national convention in July in St. Louis, Mo., that it could not consider the ELCA to be "an orthodox Lutheran body" because of its full communion agreements with non-Lutheran churches. Two pastors filed charges against the president of the Missouri Synod in November for joining with ECLA clergy in worship and supporting an interfaith prayer service. Representatives of the Mennonite Church and the General Conference Mennonite Church agreed to a merger in July, forming a denomination of about 125,000 members in 1,100 congregations. The merging groups resolved differences on standards for membership by leaving such questions up to individual congregations in consultation with their local conferences.

Ministry and Membership. The General Assembly of the Presbyterian Church (U.S.A.) voted in June in Louisville, Ky., in favour of repealing a five-year-old ban on ordination of homosexuals to the ministry. The resolution was then sent to the denomination's 173 regional presbyteries for approval, in the wake of their failure to ratify a ban on same-sex unions that had been passed by the 2000 assembly. The ELCA began a four-year study of whether to ordain active homosexuals and bless same-sex unions, and an Anglican catechism commissioned by Archbishop David Hope of York said homosexuality might have "divinely ordered and positive qualities." Four bishops defied church law in the ELCA in April when they joined in the ordination of Anita C. Hill, a lesbian. One of the four, Paul W. Egertson, subsequently resigned as bishop of the Southern California (West) Synod over what he described as his "act of ecclesiastical disobedience." In June in Denver, Colo., two Anglican archbishops defied Archbishop George Carey of Canterbury in consecrating as bishops four American priests who opposed the Episcopal Church's positions on homosexuality and biblical authority. Gwynne Guibord, chief ecumenical officer of the predominantly homosexual Universal Fellowship of Metropolitan Community Churches, became the first openly gay person to head a state ecumenical council in the United States when she was appointed president of the California Council of Churches in January. The Reform Jewish movement in the United

Worldwide Adherents of All Religions by Six Continental Areas, Mid-2001

	Africa	Asia	Europe	Latin America	Northern America	Oceania	World	%	Number of Countries
Christians	368,244,000	317,759,000	559,359,000	486,591,000	261,752,000	25,343,000	2,019,052,000	32.9	238
Affiliated Christians	342,819,000	312,182,000	536,588,000	481,132,000	213,038,000	21,600,000	1,907,363,000	31.1	238
Roman Catholics	123,467,000	112,086,000	285,554,000	466,226,000	71,391,000	8,327,000	1,067,053,000	17.4	235
Protestants	90,989,000	50,718,000	77,497,000	49,008,000	70,164,000	7,478,000	345,855,000	5.6	232
Orthodox	36,038,000	14,219,000	158,375,000	564,000	6,400,000	718,000	216,314,000	3.5	134
Anglicans	43,524,000	735,000	26,628,000	1,098,000	3,231,000	5,428,000	80,644,000	1.3	163
Independents	85,476,000	157,605,000	25,850,000	40,357,000	81,032,000	1,536,000	391,856,000	6.4	221
Marginal Christians	2,502,000	2,521,000	3,606,000	6,779,000	10,747,000	468,000	26,623,000	0.4	215
Unaffiliated Christians	25,425,000	5,577,000	22,771,000	5,459,000	48,714,000	3,743,000	111,689,000	1.8	232
Baha'is	1,779,000	3,538,000	132,000	893,000	799,000	113,000	7,254,000	0.1	218
Buddhists	139,000	356,533,000	1,570,000	660,000	2,777,000	307,000	361,985,000	5.9	126
Chinese folk religionists	33,100	385,758,000	258,000	197,000	857,000	64,200	387,167,000	6.3	89
Confucianists	250	6,277,000	10,800	450	0	24,000	6,313,000	0.1	15
Ethnic religionists	97,762,000	129,005,000	1,258,000	1,288,000	446,000	267,000	230,026,000	3.8	140
Hindus	2,384,000	813,396,000	1,425,000	775,000	1,350,000	359,000	819,689,000	13.4	114
Jains	66,900	4,207,000	0	0	7,000	0	4,281,000	0.1	10
Jews	215,000	4,476,000	2,506,000	1,145,000	6,045,000	97,600	14,484,000	0.2	134
Muslims	323,556,000	845,341,000	31,724,000	1,702,000	4,518,000	307,000	1,207,148,000	19.7	204
New-Religionists	28,900	101,065,000	160,000	633,000	847,000	66,900	102,801,000	1.7	60
Shintoists	0	2,669,000	0	6,900	56,700	0	2,732,000	0.0	8
Sikhs	54,400	22,689,000	241,000	0	535,000	18,500	23,538,000	0.4	34
Spiritists	2,600	2,000	134,000	12,169,000	152,000	7,100	12,466,000	0.2	55
Taoists	0	2,658,000	0	0	11,200	0	2,670,000	0.0	5
Zoroastrians	910	2,519,000	670	0	79,100	1,400	2,601,000	0.0	22
Other religionists	67,300	63,100	238,000	99,600	605,000	9,500	1,082,000	0.0	78
Nonreligious	5,170,000	611,876,000	105,742,000	16,214,000	28,994,000	3,349,000	771,345,000	12.6	236
Atheists	432,000	122,408,000	22,555,000	2,787,000	1,700,000	369,000	150,252,000	2.5	161
Total population	**802,150,000**	**3,730,168,000**	**728,270,000**	**525,878,000**	**311,877,000**	**30,164,000**	**6,128,512,000**	**100.0**	**238**

Continents. These follow current UN demographic terminology, which now divides the world into the six major areas shown above. See United Nations, *World Population Prospects: The 1998 Revision* (New York: UN, 1999), with populations of all continents, regions, and countries covering the period 1950–2050. Note that "Asia" includes the former Soviet Central Asian states and "Europe" includes all of Russia extending eastward to Vladivostok, the Sea of Japan, and the Bering Strait.

Countries. The last column enumerates sovereign and nonsovereign countries in which each religion or religious grouping has a numerically significant and organized following.

Adherents. As defined in the 1948 Universal Declaration of Human Rights, a person's religion is what he or she says it is. Totals are enumerated for each of the world's 238 countries following the methodology of the *World Christian Encyclopedia*, 2nd ed. (2001), using recent censuses, polls, surveys, reports, Web sites, literature, and other data.

Christians. Followers of Jesus Christ affiliated with churches (church members, including children: 1,907,363,000, shown divided among the six standardized ecclesiastical megablocs), plus persons professing in censuses or polls to be Christians though not so affiliated. Figures for the subgroups of Christians do not add up to the totals in the first line because some Christians adhere to more than one denomination.

Independents. This term here denotes members of churches and networks that regard themselves as postdenominationalist and neo-apostolic and thus independent of historic, organized, institutionalized, denominationalist Christianity.

Marginal Christians. Members of denominations on the margins of organized mainstream Christianity (e.g., Church of Jesus Christ of Latter-day Saints, Jehovah's Witnesses, and Christian Science).

Buddhists. 56% Mahayana, 38% Theravada (Hinayana), 6% Tantrayana (Lamaism).

Chinese folk religionists. Followers of traditional Chinese religion (local deities, ancestor veneration, Confucian ethics, universism, divination, and some Buddhist and Taoist elements).

Confucianists. Non-Chinese followers of Confucius and Confucianism, mostly Koreans in Korea.

Ethnic religionists. Followers of local, tribal, animistic, or shamanistic religions, with members restricted to one ethnic group.

Hindus. 70% Vaishnavites, 25% Shaivites, 2% neo-Hindus and reform Hindus.

Jews. Adherents of Judaism. For detailed data on "core" Jewish population, see the annual "World Jewish Populations" article in the American Jewish Committee's *American Jewish Year Book*.

Muslims. 83% Sunnites, 16% Shi'ites, 1% other schools. Until 1990 the Muslims in the former U.S.S.R. who had embraced communism were not included as Muslims in this table. After the collapse of communism in 1990–91, these Muslims were once again enumerated as Muslims if they had returned to Islamic profession and practice.

New-Religionists. Followers of Asian 20th-century New Religions, New Religious movements, radical new crisis religions, and non-Christian syncretistic mass religions, all founded since 1800 and most since 1945.

Other religionists. Including a handful of religions, quasi-religions, pseudoreligions, parareligions, religious or mystic systems, and religious and semireligious brotherhoods of numerous varieties.

Nonreligious. Persons professing no religion, nonbelievers, agnostics, freethinkers, uninterested, or dereligionized secularists indifferent to all religion but not militantly so.

Atheists. Persons professing atheism, skepticism, disbelief, or irreligion, including the militantly antireligious (opposed to all religion).

Total population. UN medium variant figures for mid-2001, as given in *World Population Prospects: The 1998 Revision*.

States urged families and synagogues to sever ties with the Boy Scouts of America in January to protest the scouts' ban on homosexuals in leadership positions.

The General Council of the Assemblies of God voted in August in Springfield, Mo., to permit divorced people to be ordained to the ministry if they were divorced before becoming Christians.

The Rev. William Sinkford of Cambridge, Mass., became the first African American person to win the presidency of the Unitarian Universalist Association when he was elected in June at its General Assembly in Cleveland, Ohio. In November, Bishop Wilton Gregory of Belleville, Ill., became the first black elected to lead the U.S. Conference of Catholic Bishops.

A French court sentenced Catholic Bishop Pierre Pican of Bayeux-Lisieux to a three-month suspended prison term in September for having concealed information that a priest was sexually abusing children. The Vatican said in March that it was investigating allegations that some priests had regularly forced nuns to have sex with them. A report commissioned by the Catholic

Religious Adherents in the United States of America, AD 1900–2000

	Year 1900	%	mid-1970	%	mid-1990	%	Annual Change, 1990–2000 Natural	Conversion	Total	Rate (%)	mid-1995	%	mid-2000	%
Christians	73,270,000	96.4	191,182,000	91.0	217,719,000	85.7	2,081,000	−278,000	1,802,000	0.80	227,586,000	85.2	235,742,000	84.7
Affiliated Christians	54,425,000	71.6	153,299,000	73.0	175,820,000	69.2	1,680,000	−79,500	1,601,000	0.88	184,244,000	69.0	191,828,000	68.9
Protestants	35,000,000	46.1	58,568,000	27.9	60,216,000	23.7	575,000	−140,000	435,000	0.70	62,525,000	23.4	64,570,000	23.2
Roman Catholics	10,775,000	14.2	48,305,000	23.0	56,500,000	22.2	540,000	−390,000	150,000	0.26	56,715,000	21.2	58,000,000	20.8
Anglicans	1,600,000	2.1	3,196,000	1.5	2,450,000	1.0	23,400	−28,400	−5,000	−0.21	2,445,000	0.9	2,400,000	0.9
Orthodox	400,000	0.5	4,163,000	2.0	5,150,000	2.0	49,200	12,000	61,200	1.13	5,472,000	2.1	5,762,000	2.1
Multiple affiliation	0	0.0	−2,704,000	−1.3	−24,336,000	−9.6	−233,000	−87,300	−320,000	1.24	−25,360,000	−9.5	−27,534,000	−9.9
Independents	5,850,000	7.7	35,645,000	17.0	66,900,000	26.3	639,000	526,000	1,165,000	1.62	72,943,000	27.3	78,550,000	28.2
Marginal Christians	800,000	1.1	6,126,000	2.9	8,940,000	3.5	85,400	28,600	114,000	1.21	9,502,000	3.6	10,080,000	3.6
Evangelicals	*32,068,000*	*42.2*	*31,516,000*	*15.0*	*37,349,000*	*14.7*	*357,000*	*−27,800*	*329,000*	*0.85*	*39,314,000*	*14.7*	*40,640,000*	*14.6*
evangelicals	*11,000,000*	*14.5*	*45,500,000*	*21.7*	*87,656,000*	*34.5*	*838,000*	*263,000*	*1,101,000*	*1.19*	*93,457,000*	*35.0*	*98,662,000*	*35.4*
Unaffiliated Christians	18,845,000	24.8	37,883,000	18.0	41,899,000	16.5	400,000	−199,000	202,000	0.47	43,342,000	16.2	43,914,000	15.8
Baha'is	2,800	0.0	138,000	0.1	600,000	0.2	5,700	9,600	15,300	2.30	682,000	0.3	753,000	0.3
Buddhists	30,000	0.0	200,000	0.1	1,880,000	0.7	18,000	39,000	57,000	2.68	2,150,000	0.8	2,450,000	0.9
Chinese folk religionists	70,000	0.1	90,000	0.0	76,000	0.0	730	−480	250	0.32	77,000	0.0	78,500	0.0
Ethnic religionists	100,000	0.1	70,000	0.0	280,000	0.1	2,700	12,800	15,500	4.50	387,000	0.1	435,000	0.2
Hindus	1,000	0.0	100,000	0.1	750,000	0.3	7,200	21,000	28,200	3.24	930,000	0.4	1,032,000	0.4
Jains	0	0.0	0	0.0	5,000	0.0	48	150	200	3.36	6,000	0.0	7,000	0.0
Jews	1,500,000	2.0	6,700,000	3.2	5,535,000	2.2	52,900	−44,300	8,600	0.15	5,600,000	2.1	5,621,000	2.0
Muslims	10,000	0.0	800,000	0.4	3,560,000	1.4	34,000	23,200	57,200	1.50	3,825,000	1.4	4,132,000	1.5
Black Muslims	0	0.0	200,000	0.1	1,250,000	0.5	12,700	17,300	30,000	2.29	1,400,000	0.5	1,650,000	0.6
New-Religionists	0	0.0	110,000	0.1	575,000	0.2	5,500	18,100	23,600	3.50	690,000	0.3	811,000	0.3
Shintoists	0	0.0	0	0.0	50,000	0.0	480	140	620	1.18	53,900	0.0	56,200	0.0
Sikhs	0	0.0	1,000	0.0	160,000	0.1	1,500	5,900	7,400	3.87	192,000	0.1	234,000	0.1
Spiritists	0	0.0	0	0.0	120,000	0.1	1,100	690	1,800	1.44	133,000	0.1	138,000	0.1
Taoists	0	0.0	0	0.0	10,000	0.0	96	17	110	1.08	10,600	0.0	11,100	0.0
Zoroastrians	0	0.0	0	0.0	42,400	0.0	410	630	1,000	2.20	47,500	0.0	52,700	0.0
Other religionists	10,000	0.0	450,000	0.2	530,000	0.2	5,100	−390	4,700	0.85	550,000	0.2	577,000	0.2
Nonreligious	1,000,000	1.3	10,070,000	4.8	21,414,000	8.4	205,000	162,000	366,000	1.59	23,150,000	8.7	25,078,000	9.0
Atheists	1,000	0.0	200,000	0.1	770,000	0.3	7,400	30,600	37,900	4.09	950,000	0.4	1,149,000	0.4
Total population	75,995,000	100.0	210,111,000	100.0	254,076,000	100.0	2,428,000	0	2,428,000	0.92	267,020,000	100.0	278,357,000	100.0

Methodology. This table extracts and analyzes a microcosm of the world religion table. It depicts the United States, the country with the largest number of adherents to Christianity, the world's largest religion. Statistics at five points in time across the 20th century are presented. Each religion's *Annual Change* for 1990–2000 is also analyzed by *Natural* increase (births minus deaths, plus immigrants minus emigrants) per year and *Conversion* increase (new converts minus new defectors) per year, which together constitute the *Total* increase per year. *Rate* increase is then computed as percentage per year.

Structure. Vertically the table lists 30 major religious categories. The major religions (including nonreligion) in the U.S. are listed with largest (Christians) first. Indented names of groups in the "Adherents" column are subcategories of the groups above them and are also counted in these unindented totals, so they should not be added twice into the column total. Figures in italics draw adherents from all categories of Christians above and so cannot be added together with them. Figures for Christians are built upon detailed head counts by churches, often to the last digit. Totals are then rounded to the nearest 1,000. Because of rounding, the corresponding percentage figures may sometimes not total exactly 100%.

Christians. All persons who profess publicly to follow Jesus Christ as Lord and Saviour. This category is subdivided into **Affiliated Christians** (church members) and **Unaffiliated** (nominal) **Christians** (professing Christians not affiliated with any church). *See also* the note on Christians to the world religion table.

Evangelicals/evangelicals. These two designations—italicized and enumerated separately here—cut across all of the six Christian traditions or ecclesiastical megablocs listed above and should be considered separately from them. **Evangelicals** are mainly Protestant churches, agencies, and individuals that call themselves by this term (for example, members of the National Association of Evangelicals); they usually emphasize 5 or more of 7, 9, or 21 fundamental doctrines (salvation by faith, personal acceptance, verbal inspiration of Scripture, depravity of man, Virgin Birth, miracles of Christ, atonement, evangelism, Second Advent, et al). The **evangelicals** are Christians of evangelical conviction from all traditions who are committed to the evangel (gospel) and involved in personal witness and mission in the world; alternatively termed Great Commission Christians.

Jews. Core Jewish population relating to Judaism, excluding Jewish persons professing a different religion.

Other categories. Definitions are as given under the world religion table.

(DAVID B. BARRETT; TODD M. JOHNSON)

Church in England and Wales recommended that all clergy, staff, and volunteers be subject to police checks to stamp out sexual abuse of children. A consortium of eight missionary organizations reported that nearly 7% of more than 600 former missionary children said they had been sexually abused during their elementary school years.

Doctrine. Two Presbyterian denominations debated matters of biblical interpretation during 2001. The General Assembly of the 2.5-million-member Presbyterian Church (U.S.A.) adopted a statement affirming salvation through Jesus Christ but leaving unanswered the eternal destiny of non-Christians. In another resolution the PCUSA said the theology of the popular Left Behind fiction series "is not in accord with our Reformed understanding" of the biblical book of Revelation. The General Assembly of the 300,000-member Presbyterian Church in America, meeting in Dallas, Texas, in June, rejected an attempt to require members to view the six days of biblical creation as literal 24-hour days. Reflecting a growing interest in tradition, the rabbinical arm of Judaism's liberal Reform movement adopted voluntary guidelines on conversion in June in Monterey, Calif. In taking the action, the Central Conference of American Rabbis urged that converts be immersed in ritual baths and affiliated with synagogues. The Conservative movement of Judaism adopted its first official Torah commentary, a 1,560-page volume that was designed to replace a commentary written in 1937 by Rabbi J.H. Hertz.

Personalities. Zambian Catholic Archbishop Emmanuel Milingo broke his celibacy vow in May in marrying a Korean woman in a group wedding in New York City conducted by the Rev. Sun Myung Moon of the Unification Church. Threatened with excommunication, however, Milingo announced three months later that he was ending the marriage. The Rev. Paul Collins of Australia resigned from the Catholic priesthood in March after having been under investigation for three years by the Vatican's Congregation for the Doctrine of the Faith. His resignation coincided with his publication of a book titled *From Inquisition to Freedom*, a critical examination of the Vatican agency with chapters written by six other prominent Catholics who had been investigated by the congregation. The Rev. Kevin Mannoia resigned the presidency of the (U.S.) National

At the Baha'i Shrine of the Bab in Haifa, Israel, 19 terraces with gardens, waterfalls, and staircases were dedicated in May, marking the completion of a project that began in the 1930s.

Association of Evangelicals (NAE) in June over what the organization's board described as "divergent perspectives about certain operational and fiscal matters." Mannoia, a bishop emeritus in the Free Methodist Church, said a bylaw change allowing denominations affiliated with the more liberal National Council of Churches to affiliate with the NAE had stirred controversy among some of the NAE's 50 denominational and 250 ministry affiliates.

In February the board of National Religious Broadcasters voted unanimously in Dallas to end its 57-year relationship with the NAE.

The North American convention of the Antiochian Orthodox Christian Church voted in July in Los Angeles to ask its mother church in Syria for autonomy. Archbishop Philip Saliba, the church's North American primate, declared that the United States and Canada represent "the new Antioch," referring to the ancient city (located in present-day Turkey) in which followers of Christ were first called Christians.

The Rev. Arthur Peacocke, an English biochemist and Anglican priest, received the $1 million Templeton Prize for Progress in Religion for his work exploring the relationship between science and theology. (*See* BIOGRAPHIES.) In July officials in Nepal installed Preeti Shakya, a four-year-old girl from Kathmandu, as the new Kumari, a virgin goddess revered by both Hindus and Buddhists.

Preserving Religious Heritage. The UN General Assembly adopted a resolution in May calling on governments to "exert their utmost efforts to ensure that religious sites are fully respected and protected" through initiatives including national legislation. Earlier during May representatives of the Vatican and an umbrella organization of Jewish groups issued a similar appeal, in which they said, "We are all the more disturbed when members of our own religious communities have been the offenders" against religious freedom.

The dedication in May of the Baha'i faith's 19 terraced shrine gardens in Haifa, Israel, drew about 4,500 people from 200 countries. The $250 million project began in the 1930s and was designed to represent the 19th-century religious leader known as the Bab and his first 18 followers. The Jewish Museum Berlin was officially opened in September with an exhibition emphasizing Jewish contributions to German culture. In August Tibetan Buddhist monks dedicated a 33-m (108-ft)-tall stupa, a commemorative shrine, in a Rocky Mountain valley in Colorado. It contained the ashes of Chogyam Trungpa Rinpoche, a Tibetan exile who took Buddhist teachings to the West, and was the largest religious project undertaken by native-born Americans who had embraced Buddhism.

Church and State. Reports from international monitoring groups indicated that Chinese authorities had forced thousands of Tibetan Buddhist monks and nuns to leave a religious study centre in Sichuan province in June because of what an official of the Sichuan Religious Affairs Bureau called "concerns about social stability." A Belgian court sentenced two Catholic nuns in June to 12 and 15 years in prison for complicity in the genocide in Rwanda in 1994 in which 800,000 people were killed. In Guatemala in June three military officers and a priest were convicted of the 1998 murder of Catholic

Bishop Juan Gerardi, who headed the church's human rights office in that country.

Shoko Asahara, the leader of Japan's AUM Shinrikyo (Supreme Truth) sect, was ordered in July to pay $3.7 million in compensation to the families of four people killed in a 1994 nerve gas attack in the town of Matsumoto. The attack had been perpetrated by Asahara's group, which was also behind a better-known attack the following year in the Tokyo subway system in which 12 people were killed.

Catholic bishops in the Philippines issued a statement in June supporting what they called "the government's all-out war policy against lawless elements" of the Abu Sayyaf, a radical Islamic movement that attacked churches and clergy. Jagjit Singh Chauhan, a Sikh separatist, returned to India in June after 21 years of self-imposed exile in London and said he would continue to work for Khalistan, a homeland for Sikhs.

In the United States, federal officials took control of the Indianapolis Baptist Temple in February to satisfy a $6 million tax debt in what was believed to be the first time the federal government had seized a church. The independent congregation had stopped withholding federal income taxes and Social Security deductions from employee paychecks in 1984, claiming that it was not a legal entity and therefore not subject to taxation. Pres. George W. Bush proposed allowing religious organizations to receive government grants and contracts for social services. The proposal was approved by the House of Representatives in July but was stalled in the Senate. More than 250 leaders of faith-based groups organized a Progressive Religious Partnership in April in Washington, D.C., saying they wanted "to restore a progressive religious presence to its rightful place in the public square." The U.S. Supreme Court ruled 6–3 in June that public schools could not discriminate against student religious clubs on the basis of religion. In March a federal appeals court in Cincinnati ruled 9–4 that the Ohio state motto, "With God, all things are possible," was constitutionally acceptable if the state did not attribute the words to their biblical source.

(continued on page 308)

At the Rocky Mountain Shambhala Center near Red Feather Lakes, Colo., a Buddhist stupa, or commemorative shrine, was dedicated in August.

AP/Wide World Photos

Christianity's Newest Converts

by Kenneth L. Woodward

Though 2001 will undoubtedly be remembered as the year that the terrorist attacks in the U.S. were attributed to Islamic radicals, that action reminded Christians in the U.S. and other Western countries that Islam claims the allegiance of 1.2 billion people worldwide, second only to Christianity itself, which claims some 2 billion devotees. During the year there was another significant revelation—that Christianity itself is now an essentially non-Western religion. In 1900, at the dawn of what American Protestants imagined would be "the Christian century," 80% of Christians were either European or North American. In 2000 statistics showed that 60% of Christians were citizens of the "two-thirds world"— Africa, Asia, and Latin America.

Specific comparisons demonstrate some of the dimensions of this demographic shift. In Nigeria alone, for example, there are seven times as many Anglicans as there are Episcopalians in the U.S. South Korea boasts a population of Presbyterians four times that of the U.S., and as of 2001 it was the first Asian country since the Philippines to have become majority Christian. In the past 10 years, the Assemblies of God have gained 438,000 new American members, but in Africa alone this Pentecostal denomination quadrupled its size, adding nearly 7,000,000 converts. More than 90% of Seventh-day Adventists, a 150-year-old millenarian movement that began in New York, now live outside North America, most of them in Brazil and sub-Saharan Africa.

As Christianity prospers in the less-developed world, it is shrinking in the West. Northern Europe is essentially post-Christian, a society in which religious affiliation functions essentially as an identity tag, and church attendance is declining in once staunchly Catholic Spain. In Scotland fewer than 10% of Christians attend church regularly, but in the Philippines the figure is nearly 70%. Even in the U.S., still the most religious of the world's advanced industrial societies, most of the growth in Christianity is attributed to immigration from Latin America and various non-Western countries. Within the Presbyterian Church (U.S.A.), for instance, the only growth has come through immigrants from South Korea. The effects on American Catholicism are especially pronounced. One in six priests serving in U.S. Catholic parishes in 2000 was imported from abroad, and among native-born Catholic seminarians, a disproportionate number were Asian Americans. Though the U.S. was once the primary source of new recruits for the Jesuits, India now reigns as the largest supplier of Jesuit seminarians.

In short, the map of world Christianity has been redrawn. For the first time in history, the majority of Christians can be found mainly among the poor, the marginalized, the powerless, and—in parts of Asia and the Middle East—the oppressed. The face of Christianity has also changed—it is no longer the white man's religion. As a result of this massive demographic shift, areas that were once considered Christian homelands have become the mission territories of the new millennium. Evangelists from Latin America, Asia, and Africa now hold crusades in cities such as London and Berlin. Aware that the future of the church lies in part in Africa, Pope John Paul II has made 10 pastoral visits to various countries there, more than to any other continent outside Europe. On February 21 the pope expanded the Sacred College of Cardinals to a record 184 members. Of the 135 cardinals eligible to elect the next pope, 41% hail from non-Western nations.

The changing face of the church was also manifest in shifting spheres of influence within mainline American Protestant denominations. In early 2001 the presiding bishops of the worldwide Anglican Communion met in North Carolina amid a rift between the liberal Anglican churches of the West, notably the Episcopal Church, U.S.A., and the more conservative Anglican churches of Asia and Africa, over issues that included the ordination of women and homosexuals and the blessing of same-sex marriages. Unless a resolution is reached, there could be a major split within the Communion. The liberal Presbyterian Church (U.S.A.) was also feeling a rightward pull from its Korean American faithful, who also opposed the ordination of homosexuals.

The emergence of Christianity as a predominantly non-Western religion had many causes. In Latin America, Christianity arrived with the conquistadors in the 16th century and has continued to expand in part because of population explosion. Though South America is the largest Catholic continent in the world, in recent decades evangel-

Children at the Sacred Heart Roman Catholic Church in New Delhi light candles during Good Friday services on April 13.

AP/Wide World Photos

native religions the Spaniards never really extinguished. Many Christians in China include veneration of their deceased but "living" ancestors as part of the worship services at certain times of the year. In India, where sin is traditionally identified with bad karma in this and previous lives, many converts interpret the cross to mean that Jesus's self-sacrifice removes their own karmic deficiencies and thus liberates their souls from future rebirths. Millions of Christians in Africa still turn to rituals of their tribal religions in time of crisis, especially toward warding off evil spirits. There, as in many other parts of the "two-thirds world," the fastest-growing form of Christianity is Pentecostalism, which offers exorcisms and other forms of healing, though in this case they are done in the name of Jesus Christ and against the native religions themselves. Conversely, many Christians who migrate from Asian countries where they were persecuted find American Christianity too secular, individualistic, and accepting of secular mores—especially the sexual variety—for their taste. In sum, Christianity for the first time in its history is truly a global religion—but it is also becoming increasingly diverse. The problem for the pope and other church leaders in the West is how to decide which elements of Western thought and culture are essential to the faith. Put differently, the question remains how far Christianity can bend toward accepting non-Western world views without compromising its own traditional doctrines about the nature of God and the uniqueness of Jesus Christ as Savior.

Kenneth L. Woodward, the religion editor of Newsweek *magazine, is also the author of* The Book of Miracles: The Meaning of the Miracle Stories in Christianity, Judaism, Buddhism, Hinduism, and Islam *(2000). This report is adapted from his article "The Changing Face of the Church," which first appeared in* Newsweek.

ical and Pentecostal Protestantism have made impressive inroads there. In India the spread of Christianity is mainly among the outcasts, who find in Christianity hope and dignity denied them by the caste system. In China, Christianity answers problems of meaning that Marxism fails to address. In Africa, where Christianity is growing faster than at any time or place in history, the faith originally introduced by missionaries has boomed following the collapse of European colonialism. Since then, sub-Saharan Africa has seen a wild proliferation of indigenous Christian churches and cults, many of them inspired by personal visions and prophesies. According to the *World Christian Encyclopedia*, there are now 33,800 different Christian denominations, the fastest growing of which are independent churches that have no ties

to the historic Catholic and Protestant churches. Wherever it spreads, Christianity is also seen as the religion of the successful West—a spiritual way of life that is compatible with higher education, technology, and globalization.

From its very beginning, Christianity has always been a migratory religion, seeking to plant the gospel at the centre of whatever alien culture its missionaries could penetrate. In the process the gospel has been not only transplanted but also repeatedly reinterpreted according to the previously existing religious understandings. The same process exists today. In officially Roman Catholic Brazil, for instance, many church members still appease the old tribal deities brought over from Africa by slaves. In other parts of Latin America, Christians practice a hybrid form of piety that includes elements of

Religion

(continued from page 305)

Gatherings. The Maha Kumbh Mela, or "Great Pitcher Festival," drew some 110 million people to the city of Prayagraj (Allahabad), India, over 42 days in January and February. (*See* Sidebar.) The Hindu festival, held every 12 years, was also attended by the Dalai Lama, spiritual leader of Tibetan Buddhists, who joined the Shankaracharya of Kanchi, one of India's top four Hindu religious leaders, in a prayer on the banks of the Ganges River. The Dalai Lama also met with leaders of the World Hindu Council and criticized efforts to persuade adherents of one religious faith to convert to another. "I always believe it's safer and better and reasonable to keep one's

own tradition or belief," he said. More than 150 cardinals from around the world assembled at the Vatican in May in the largest such gathering in history, during which several called for more power sharing and frank debate on important issues.

Demographics. Christianity remained the world's largest religion, claiming over two billion followers—nearly 33% of the Earth's population—in mid-2001. The most dramatic growth in Christianity in recent years had been registered in Asia, Africa, and Latin America. (*See* Special Report.)

In September Cardinal Cormac Murphy-O'Connor told a gathering of priests in Leeds, Eng., that Christianity

had "almost been vanquished" as a backdrop for people's lives in Great Britain. A World Council of Churches delegation to the Middle East reported in August that violence in the region was leading Christians to emigrate, spurring fears that "the holy sites of Christianity will become museums." The American Jewish Identity Survey found that the number of American Jews who identified with another religion had more than doubled in the past decade, to 1.4 million, while an additional 1.4 million American Jews said they are secular or have no religion at all, leaving just 51% of American Jews who say they are Jewish by religion.

(DARRELL J. TURNER)

Maha Kumbh Mela

Millions of pilgrims, many of whom had traveled for days to participate in the Maha Kumbh Mela—"Great Pitcher Festival"—walked to the various camps set up on the sandy plains along the Ganges River. About 110 million people, including more than 65,000 foreigners, gathered for the Hindu festival; this was believed to be the largest-ever congregation of people on the planet for a single purpose. The pilgrims went to the city of Allahabad (newly renamed Prayagraj), where the holy rivers Ganges, Yamuna, and the invisible, mythical Saraswati converge, to wash away their sins. A dip in the river, Hindus believe, ensures *moksha*, liberation

from the cycle of life, death, and rebirth. According to Hindu mythology, gods and demons fought a battle in the sky over a pot containing the nectar of immortality. During the battle four drops of nectar fell at four different sites. Accordingly, Maha Kumbh Mela is held, on a rotation basis, every three years in one of four different cities (Nasik, Ujjain, Haridwar, and Allahabad) and thus returns to the same city every 12 years. The Allahabad festival is considered the holiest, and the 2001 event was considered especially propitious because of an unusual alignment of the Sun, Moon, and Jupiter that occurred only every 144 years. (SHANTHA UDDIN)

AP/Wide World Photos

Social Protection

The economic **SLOWDOWN** and September 11 terrorist attacks delayed anticipated **REFORMS** for welfare, Social Security, and Medicare in the U.S.; human rights **TRIBUNALS** pursued cross-nation **PROSECUTIONS**; and refugees, particularly those from **AFGHANISTAN,** strained international resources.

BENEFITS AND PROGRAMS

The financial viability of social protection programs continued to be a matter of worldwide concern. In 2001 many countries restructured their various schemes with a view to ensuring their long-term stability. In the process the pros and cons of private elements in public social protection programs were debated as well as the question of what was the "right" public-private mix for each scheme. Governments and social security administrators also strove to improve the delivery of social services and to give more people access to benefits.

North America. As with so many other areas of life, social protection was deeply affected by the terrorist attacks in the United States on September 11 and by the nation's prolonged economic downturn. High-priority legislation to provide prescription drug assistance for Medicare patients and federal support for faith-based charities was relegated, at least temporarily, to a back burner. Pledges that the Social Security Trust Fund would not be used to finance other needs were broken. Greater stress was put on the welfare system by an explosion of jobless workers. For the most part, as the federal government turned to more immediate concerns, social welfare activity was limited to debate, studies, and postponed action.

The two giant social programs for the elderly, Social Security and Medicare, had received good news early in the year when the funds' trustees reported that both would be solvent longer than previously predicted—until 2038 for Social Security, a year longer than had been forecast earlier, and 2029 for Medicare, four years longer. Nevertheless, concerns about the financial health of Social Security, which in 2001 covered some 45,526,000 retired and disabled persons, continued because of the approaching retirement of approximately 77,000,000 baby boomers and the increasing life span of beneficiaries. In 2001 three to four workers supported one retiree; that ratio was expected to be just two to one by about 2030. Past strategies for dealing with the developing demographic problems centred mainly on such "tune-ups" as reducing benefits, increasing payroll taxes, and raising the retirement age (already slated to rise gradually from 65 to 67).

U.S. Pres. George W. Bush favoured a plan for totally overhauling the system by partially privatizing it and allowing individual workers to invest a percentage of their payroll taxes in personal accounts. These, it was argued, would earn greater returns than the Trust Fund's more conservative investments. Opponents of that idea contended that it would deplete the Trust Fund more quickly and could be disastrous for individuals if stock values collapsed.

Bush appointed a 16-member bipartisan commission in May to explore the issue and recommend solutions. Although it was a bipartisan group, critics charged that it was stacked with proponents of privatization. The commission announced in December that it had agreed unanimously on three options, all of which would rely on personal retirement investment accounts, reduce traditional benefits for retirees, and require further actions for long-term sustainability.

The government announced a cost-of-living increase of 2.6% in Social Security benefits starting in January 2002. The average retiree would get $874 a month, up $22 from the $852 in 2001, and the average couple would receive $1,458 a month, an increase of $36. By law, annual increases in Social Security payments must equal increases in the consumer price index.

Disagreement also flared over a cornerstone of the president's "compassionate conservatism," his faith-based initiative for dealing with social problems. The administration wanted to extend federal financing for the charitable work of religious groups and make it easier for individuals to contribute to them. Proponents of the plan argued that religious organizations could reach some individuals with food, housing, job training, and additional assistance when many other types of social initiatives could not. Critics voiced concerns about violating First Amendment guarantees of separation of church and state. They raised the possibility that the plan would permit religious organizations to hire only members of their own faith and would exempt them from state and local laws that forbid discrimination in hiring based on sexual orientation.

In a delicate constitutional balancing act, the U.S. House of Representatives narrowly approved a watered-down version of the Bush plan. It would allow faith-based groups to use federal aid for religious activities if they received it indirectly (through vouchers, for example) and if they kept religious activities separate from social services and allowed those they helped to refrain from religious observances. The measure also allowed tax deductions for small donations for taxpayers who did not itemize their deductions. Late in 2001, faced with strong Democratic opposition in the Senate and pressures from the war on terrorism, Bush dropped the most controversial aspects of his proposal.

The upbeat report on Medicare's financial condition was tempered by studies showing that dramatic increases in the cost of prescription drugs could create serious problems. One study by a nonprofit, nonpartisan group found that spending on these drugs had risen 18.8% in 2000 to $131.9 billion. With large budget surpluses forecast early in 2001, both political parties backed legislation to add some kind of prescription drug coverage for the 40 million elderly and disabled Americans who had Medicare, but they disagreed on how to do it. Democrats generally favoured working through Medicare, while the administration looked to private insurers. By the end of the year, however, the window of opportunity that was open earlier had been closed by the recession and the costs of fighting terrorism. No action was taken, and hopes faded for any in 2002, which was a midterm election year.

In addition, the administration pushed to increase enrollment of Medicare recipients in health maintenance organizations (HMOs). In 2001 slightly more than 14% of Medicare beneficiaries were already enrolled. A potential setback to greater participation occurred when 58 HMOs serving 536,000 people announced that they would withdraw from the Medicare program in 2002.

As efforts bogged down at the federal level, states began setting up programs of their own to help low-income Medicare recipients buy prescription drugs. For example, Pennsylvania paid part of the cost of each prescription, while California and Florida put caps on how much pharmacies could charge elderly customers. By the end of the year, more than half of the states had taken steps to help with drug costs.

Welfare moved back into the spotlight in the U.S. Massive layoffs of workers following the terrorist attacks created unexpected problems for the social protection system just as Congress began to gear up for reauthorization of the 1996 welfare reform act in 2002. Pulled by the booming job market and pushed by tighter laws that limited their eligibility for welfare, nearly seven million people had left welfare rolls since 1996. Meanwhile, the U.S. Census Bureau reported that the number of people in the

nation living in poverty fell in 1999 for the fourth consecutive year—to 11.8%, compared with 13.7% in 1996.

Despite those encouraging numbers and even before the terrorist impact, critics of the new welfare system had questioned how well it could withstand a weakening of the national economy. Moreover, they argued, people still on welfare rolls were those who had the most serious problems and needed as much, or more, federal spending to help them escape. There was also concern about many of those who had left welfare. The Urban Institute in Washington, D.C., reported that one-third of former recipients had to skip meals or eat less and that 46% had not been able to pay their rent or utility bills during the previous year. Supporters of the 1996 overhaul, on the other hand, claimed that the new safety net was the strongest ever and pointed out that welfare rolls continued to decline in some states even as unemployment there rose.

In September Health and Human Services Secretary Tommy G. Thompson announced a series of national "listening and discussion" sessions to air issues and ideas about the coming welfare reauthorization. One of those issues was poverty among the young. Although conditions had improved since 1993, when child poverty reached its peak, children under 18 continued to have a higher poverty rate than any other age group. Democrats pressed for action in areas such as affordability and availability of day care, restoration of cuts in food stamps and Medicaid for immigrants, and an increase in the minimum wage, which had not been raised since 1997.

Republicans generally favoured tax credits and more money for policies that emphasized work and reductions in single-parent families.

Welfare reform also was a major issue in Canada, where Ontario, the most populous province, announced plans to impose the toughest rules ever in Canada for welfare recipients. Persons would be required to pass a literacy test before they could receive public assistance, and benefits would be cut off to those who had drug or alcohol problems and had refused treatment for them. Anyone who failed the literacy test would be required to enroll in a workfare program.

Critics labeled the measure mean-spirited and overly harsh and said it was a possible violation of Ontario's human rights code. Officials responded that those receiving assistance needed to be pushed toward independence. They said that welfare rolls in Ontario had been cut by 60% in six years, but those who remained on them were the toughest cases.

In other action the Canadian government raised the maximum pensionable earnings for 2001 under the Canada Pension Plan by Can$700 (Can$1 = about U.S. $0.63) to Can$38,300. The contribution rate was increased to 4.3% for employees and 3.9% for employers, which brought the maximum employee contribution, after a basic Can$3,500 exemption, to Can$1,496.40 per year.

Europe. Portugal endowed itself with a new framework law on social protection, which came into force in February. France modernized its social protection system by introducing new benefits, such as a "parental attendance allowance," to allow the parents of seriously ill children to take time off from work. In Romania the social protection system was adapted to new socioeconomic realities in that survivors' pensions were now also granted not only to widows but also to widowers.

In Poland a discussion was under way to reform agricultural social insurance in order to build in mechanisms for structural reform based on solutions used in the European Union. The Netherlands took another step toward integrating the special system for civil servants into the general system for employee benefits when special unemployment regulations for employees in public service were abolished. Earlier, civil servants had been covered under the general Disability Benefits Act.

Ireland took measures to reduce long-term costs related to disability benefits. The government encouraged disabled

A senior citizen purchases drugs at a pharmacy in Springfield, Ill., in May; how to add prescription drug coverage for the 40 million elderly and disabled Americans who had Medicare was the subject of debate during the year.

AP/Wide World Photos

An elderly opponent of a proposed pension-reform program in Russia attempts to tear a banner from the hands of pension-reform supporters in front of the State Duma in Moscow on July 5.

people to return to work by allowing them to retain part of their benefits during the first few years of employment after having been on government disability benefits. Beginning in April social security contributions in Italy were waived for those employees eligible for a seniority pension who postponed their retirement.

In Russia a pension-reform program that would create a three-pillar system was brought before the State Duma (parliament) in the summer and was expected to come into force in 2002. Latvia made progress in the construction of its three-pillar pension program. The law on funded state pensions went into force in July, establishing the legal basis for a capital-funded second pillar of the system that, together with the first pay-as-you-go pillar, formed the compulsory government scheme.

In the United Kingdom "stakeholder pensions" became a reality in April. The stakeholder pension was initially foreseen as a low-cost supplement to the basic government pension for people without an occupational pension or other form of privately funded pension arrangements, but its scope was broadened to allow the inclusion of people who either had personal pensions or were members of occupational programs.

In Germany pension-reform legislation was enacted in May, providing for government support for supplementary pensions in the form of cash subsidies or tax relief. At the same time, it was decided to reduce slightly and gradually the main (first) pillar of the system, essentially by introducing changes in the pension adjustment so that the replacement rate would decline from 70% to 67% of average net wages by 2030. Low-income pensioners were granted entitlement to a minimum income equal to 115% of the social assistance payment to a head of household. Workers were given the right to have a percentage of their wages paid into an occupational pension scheme. Vesting rights were modified, with employer-financed benefits becoming legally vested after five years and benefits from deferred remuneration becoming vested immediately. Earlier, one had to work for a company for 10 years to qualify for a pension.

To cut health care costs, Switzerland developed a new payment model for medicines; beginning in January advisory services provided by pharmacists and dispensing physicians were to be refunded by the social sickness insurance separately from the preparation and sales element of the costs of medicines in order to eliminate mechanisms that

made it advantageous to dispense large quantities or particularly expensive medications. Austria restricted access to illness benefits as of January. Earlier, an employee's partner who was not covered in his or her own right by social sickness insurance automatically received coverage through the working partner. This coverage was now restricted to people with children. The European Court of Justice declared during the year that medical services fell within the freedom to provide services, one of the four basic freedoms in the Maastricht Treaty.

Industrialized Asia and the Pacific. In June Australia passed legislation that provided for the split of superannuation (mandatory occupational pension) entitlements upon the breakdown of a marriage, whether by agreement or court order. Either a new account would be created in the superannuation fund for the nonmember spouse, or the nonmember's interest would be rolled over into a savings account or similar regulated product.

Thailand's Securities and Exchange Commission formally approved the framework for a new system of individual retirement mutual funds, and the Revenue Department made it known that it would grant tax deductions for personal contributions to those funds. In Singapore the health minister announced the creation of a voluntary long-term-care program based on insurance underwriting principles, which the government would subsidize.

In Japan the Ministry of Health and Welfare and the Ministry of Labour were merged in January to create a more transparent administration with more effective political leadership. Also in January the Medical Care Insurance Reform Act went into force. It was designed to cope with rising health care expenditures, essentially by revising the co-payment system. A new cost-sharing system for patients over the age of 70 was introduced, moving from flat-rate to percentage contributions; the "high-cost medical benefits scheme" was also revised, with people now having to self-finance larger shares of medical expenses before receiving a benefit.

South Korea's government proposed to introduce a system of individual medical savings accounts. It would be possible to withdraw funds from the account, up to a specified limit, to pay for medical expenses. The public health care system would cover amounts exceeding that limit. Hong Kong's Social Welfare Department made a similar proposal in relation to medical expenses after retirement.

Emerging and Less-Developed Countries. Many social protection systems in less-developed countries in Africa and Asia continued to suffer from financial imbalances stemming from unfavourable economic conditions. Nonetheless, efforts were made to extend coverage, provide better benefits and services, and proceed to structural reform.

Uganda worked on implementing legislation adopted in 2000 to transform the National Social Security Fund, established in 1967 as a provident fund, into a social insurance pension scheme. In order to be able to finance future unemployment benefits in addition to existing retirement benefits, the Board of the Nigeria Social Insurance Trust Fund approved a new broader basis for calculating members' contributions, setting higher contribution rates and a new ceiling on insurable earnings.

A health insurance program for civil servants was established in Rwanda and became operational in March. The program was designed to provide protection for the whole family; in cases where both spouses were civil servants, only one was required to contribute. In Tunisia a major reform of health insurance was under way. At the end of the process, Tunisia would possess a basic unified compulsory scheme (covering both public and private sectors) that would guarantee coverage for the most prevalent forms of sickness and an optional complementary program whose management would be open to both social security funds and private insurance companies.

The Indonesian government announced that it would abolish the rules that prevented a pension fund from investing more than 20% of its assets in securities of any single issuer, a move essentially aimed at stimulating pension fund investment in government bonds. To speed up administrative procedures and increase client satisfaction, the Social Security Organization of Iran worked on a database that would cover all of the people that it insured, an exercise concerning approximately 26 million employees.

Several Caribbean nations were able to improve their social benefits and services. In Belize a package to modernize social security was introduced. The access to a number of benefits was eased in the British Virgin Islands, and in the Netherlands Antilles the Law on Medical Insurance was amended so as to extend its coverage to retired workers and their family members aged 60 and over.

In Latin America the trend continued for countries to introduce private elements into government-operated social protection programs. In Ecuador the pros and cons of such a mixed system for retirement pensions were discussed throughout the year. In Venezuela a presidential commission tabled a proposal that provided for a substantial proportion of a person's social security contribution to go into funded personal pension accounts that would be managed by the pension fund administrator of the individual's choice.

(CHRISTIANE KUPTSCH; DAVID M. MAZIE)

HUMAN RIGHTS

Special attention was given during 2001 to racial discrimination, efforts to end the impunity of major human rights abusers, the expansion of the ethnic conflicts in southeastern Europe to Macedonia, and problems associated with the rapidly growing number of refugees in the world community. In addition, for the first time, major economic and health issues took their place as the focus of international human rights attention. Concerns about economic globalization and the HIV/AIDS pandemic and its treatment received long-overdue recognition as major human rights issues. Finally, the September 11 attacks in the United States and their aftermath raised a number of major issues of human rights concern related to terrorism and to resulting antiterrorism efforts.

Racial and Ethnic Discrimination. The United Nations targeted racial and ethnic discrimination as an issue deserving special attention through the convening of a World Conference Against Racism in Durban, S.Af., in August. A major controversy arose at the conference and in the regional preparatory meetings that preceded it over language proposed for inclusion in the conference report that sought to equate Zionism with racism and also that called for financial reparations for the practice of slavery, particularly in the context of the transatlantic slave trade in the 16th through the early 19th century. Compromise language finally was adopted that deleted mention of Zionism but did condemn the treatment of the Palestinians by Israel in the first instance and, in the second, that replaced references to monetary compensation for the practice of slavery with demands for debt forgiveness, greater access to markets, and poverty relief for countries in Africa and the less-developed world that were targets of the slave trade. That

settlement was not reached, however, until after U.S. and Israeli government representatives withdrew from the conference in protest. Many other government delegates and nongovernmental organization participants also expressed concern that the emphasis given to the Zionism and reparations issues tended to undercut efforts to give attention to a broader range of problems associated with ongoing practices of racism, including the treatment of indigenous peoples.

Human Rights Abusers. The broadening application of criminal sanctions to major human rights abuses represented an important emerging trend in the international community. In addition to indictments and trials by the tribunals for former Yugoslavia and Rwanda established by the UN Security Council, a number of individual nations, such as Belgium and Spain, instituted criminal prosecutions under legislation that provided for the exercise of universal jurisdiction over torture and other major human rights violations by every nation in the world. The principles of criminal accountability and universal jurisdiction established by the tribunals for former Yugoslavia and Rwanda and by the case in the U.K. of former Chilean dictator Augusto Pinochet Ugarte resulted in the conviction by a Belgian court of four individuals accused of participation in the 1994 genocide of the Tutsi in Rwanda, the arrest and trial of former Yugoslav president Slobodan Milosevic by the International Criminal Tribunal for the Former Yugoslavia (ICTY), and the sentencing by the ICTY of Gen. Radislav Krstic, the most senior Bosnian Serb military official prosecuted thus far, to 46 years in prison for genocide and crimes against humanity associated with mass ethnic executions at Srebrenica. The extradition of Milosevic by Yugoslavia to the ICTY in The Netherlands and the initial hearings in his case marked the first time that a former head of state had been subjected to criminal trial for violation of international human rights standards. Milosevic was charged with having authorized and supervised the massacre and forced displacement and deportation of thousands of ethnic Albanians in Kosovo by Serbian forces acting under his control and direction as part of a campaign of terror and violence that included shelling and destruction of homes and villages and mass executions of unarmed civilians. The stakes were raised even further when he was charged with genocide during the 1992–95 war in Bosnia and Herzegovina. This was the first time that a head of state had been prosecuted for genocide violations. By the end of 2001, the former Yugoslavia and Rwanda tribunals had indicted 101 and 51 individuals, respectively.

Military action erupted in Macedonia in February when the frustrations of ethnic Albanians, who constituted over 22% of the population, bubbled over and both sides resorted to military means. An agreement brokered by NATO in August called for the ethnic Albanians to surrender their arms in return for a more substantial political role and greater rights to use their own language, especially in education. The Macedonian legislature began consideration of constitutional amendments guaranteeing minority rights.

An investigation of Israeli Prime Minister Ariel Sharon for massacres at Palestinian refugee camps in Lebanon was instituted by Belgian courts under the very broad criminal prosecution statute adopted in that country. Ricardo Miguel Cavallo, a naval officer during the period of the "dirty war" in Argentina, was ordered extradited from Mexico to Spain to stand trial for kidnapping and torture violations. Mexico

was believed to be the first country in Latin America to have applied the doctrine of universal jurisdiction. (*See* LAW, CRIME, AND LAW ENFORCEMENT: *International Law.*)

Efforts were also under way to establish special courts to try individuals suspected of massive human rights crimes in Cambodia, East Timor, and Sierra Leone and to constitute a permanent international tribunal, the International Criminal Court, that would have ongoing jurisdiction to apply criminal sanctions to a wide variety of international crimes wherever they might occur. Cambodia's National Assembly, after months of negotiation, approved the creation of a special court with both international and domestic judges to prosecute top members of that country's Khmer Rouge regime who supervised the extermination of an estimated 1.7 million people in the 1970s.

Economic and Social Rights. Increased recognition of economic and social rights as part of the human rights equation was observed throughout the year. Health needs associated with HIV and AIDS received attention as a result of a

series of meetings in Africa following the XIII International AIDS Conference, held in South Africa in 2000. Several countries challenged pharmaceutical companies to make HIV medications more readily available in the less-developed world by permitting the manufacture of those medications in generic form. This would substantially reduce the cost of the treatments and make them more accessible to very-low-income populations, particularly in Africa, where the incidence of HIV/AIDS exceeded 25% of the population in many countries. Cipla Ltd., an Indian company that made generic drugs, announced just such a plan in February, and in April a lawsuit brought by 39 major pharmaceutical firms that had sought to block a law allowing South Africa to manufacture or import low-priced versions of anti-AIDS drugs was dropped.

Large-scale antiglobalization demonstrations took place in a number of cities, including Washington, D.C.; Quebec City; and Genoa, Italy, targeting major international trade and banking institutions such as the World Trade Organization (WTO), the World Bank,

The rising incidence of human trafficking in Western Europe led Britain during the year to install X-ray scanners in ports around the country that could detect passengers hidden inside trucks.

AFP Worldwide

and the International Monetary Fund. The demonstrators sought improved trade and credit policies for countries in the less-developed world and a greater voice by poor nations in determining international credit and development assistance policies. The demonstrators in Quebec City in April objected to consideration at the third Summit of the Americas of a proposed Free Trade Area of the Americas that would strengthen protections for foreign investments and patents and thereby make it more difficult for poor nations to secure loans and provide social services for their citizens. In July Italian police were accused of having used particularly brutal tactics against demonstrators at the Group of Eight economic summit meeting in Genoa. One protester was fatally shot; more than 200 were reported injured; and nearly 300 were arrested. Similar disruptions were threatened for the WTO meetings that began November 9 in Doha, Qatar, particularly in light of the terrorism concerns in that part of the world raised as a result of the international bombing campaign in Afghanistan, but massive security preparations kept protests to a minimum in Qatar.

Terrorism. The September 11 terrorist attacks in the U.S. and the American reaction to them generated a number of human rights concerns. The extensive aerial bombardment of Afghanistan raised fears about deaths and injury to civilians caused by "collateral damage," possibly in violation of the humanitarian protections of the Geneva Conventions. Within the U.S. there were a number of incidents of harassment, hate crimes, and discriminatory treatment aimed at those of Middle Eastern or South Asian appearance. The concern with increased security in airports, government offices, postal facilities, and public buildings was also accompanied by questions of freedom of access, individual rights in cases of searches of persons or property, and racial and ethnic profiling. Large-scale detention of suspected terrorists and a presidential order authorizing the use of military tribunals to prosecute aliens, including those residing in the U.S., drew wide criticism from Congress and civil liberties groups. In November a proposed UN treaty designed to combat terrorism was blocked by the demand of the 57-member Organization of the Islamic Conference that anti-Israeli militants and other national liberation groups be exempted from the pact's provisions.

(MORTON SKLAR)

REFUGEES AND INTERNATIONAL MIGRATION

At the beginning of 2001, the worldwide number of refugees and persons of concern to the Office of the United Nations High Commissioner for Refugees (UNHCR) decreased slightly, from 22,300,000 in 1999 to 21,800,000 in 2000. The latter figure included some 12,000,000 recognized refugees, 786,000 returnees, 914,000 asylum seekers, and about 8,000,000 other persons requiring protection or assistance.

During the year a process was launched to revitalize the international protection regime; Global Consultations on International Protection coincided with the 50th anniversary of the 1951 Convention Relating to the Status of Refugees. These wide-ranging consultations involved states, legal experts, nongovernmental organizations, regional bodies, and refugees themselves.

The challenges facing humanitarian responses to refugee and international migration issues continued to be spread across the globe. The main durable solutions for refugees—i.e., repatriation and local integration and resettlement—were consistently pursued. Encouragingly, there were many successful resolutions of the dilemmas facing exiled or displaced persons, such as in East Timor (a former Portuguese colony that had been invaded by Indonesia in 1975) and in the Balkans. In other instances the desire to return to the country of origin—the preferred solution for many—was dashed by persistent or new outbreaks of conflict or political and economic disruption.

In Africa the areas of particular concern remained Guinea, Sierra Leone, and Liberia, where ongoing conflict plagued the northern area, particularly in Lofa county. Violence and insecurity along Guinea's border with Sierra Leone posed considerable challenges. The issues of "safe access" to refugees for humanitarian workers and "safe passage" for the displaced were priorities for all concerned. Since early 2001 UNHCR, working together with governmental and fellow agency partners, had successfully relocated 58,000 Sierra Leonean refugees to new and more secure sites away from the border and had facilitated the repatriation of another 27,000 Sierra Leonean refugees by boat.

In the Democratic Republic of the Congo (DRC), war displaced an estimated 1,800,000 people internally and forced another 350,000 refugees to seek sanctuary in neighbouring countries.

Following Joseph Kabila's installation in January as president of the DRC (*see* BIOGRAPHIES), the international community hoped for continued progress in the implementation of the Lusaka cease-fire agreement. An accord would help pave the way for reinforced humanitarian protection and assistance to refugees from neighbouring countries who had sought safe haven within the DRC as well as for the commencement of a repatriation operation for hundreds of thousands of Congolese nationals who had fled the conflict in the DRC.

The Arusha peace process in Burundi continued to move forward, but many obstacles remained. When conditions became settled, UNHCR, with the support of the governments of Burundi and Tanzania, would work toward the voluntary repatriation of 567,000 Burundian refugees, most of whom were in Tanzania.

Other long-standing conflicts, however, showed fewer signs of progress. The civil war in The Sudan dragged on—leaving some 443,000 refugees in exile and huge numbers internally displaced. Peace initiatives showed limited progress. Angola presented one of the continent's most acute humanitarian crises, with an estimated four million displaced and war-affected people. Nearly 350,000 Angolan refugees were outside their country, mainly in the DRC and Zambia.

Afghanistan continued to be the source of one of the largest, most complex, and intractable humanitarian situations ever known. More than 20 years after the first exodus to Iran and Pakistan—and even after the repatriation of more than four million people—Afghans constituted the world's largest refugee population. By late October 2001, an estimated 1.2 million or more people were displaced within the country, and approximately 7.5 million Afghans required assistance, protection, or both. Even before the international military strikes began in Afghanistan in October, Afghans were on the move. Beginning in late August the Australian government triggered an international furor when it refused entry to boatloads of asylum seekers, mainly Afghans, who had sailed from Indonesia in an attempt to reach Australian territory, and forcibly transferred them to refugee camps in other South Pacific countries. (*See* WORLD AFFAIRS: *Australia.*) Afghan refugees were uprooted by myriad factors, including the cumulative pressures of an endless war; the lack of respect for basic human rights, particularly for women; the most severe drought in decades; and the lack of ready

Some of the more than 400 refugees who were rescued from a stranded Indonesian ferry in the Indian Ocean gather on the deck of a Norwegian cargo ship off the coast of Christmas Island on August 27.

AP/Wide World Photos

mained extremely high between ethnic Albanians and non-Albanians, particularly with the small remaining Serb community. UNHCR and its partners had to strike a balance between upholding the fundamental right of people to go home and the need to ensure their safety. A limited number of Serb returns to safe areas in Kosovo raised hopes for the reestablishment of multiethnic collaboration and reintegration.

In Western Europe an alarming growth was noted in the number of asylum seekers and the extent and nature of irregular migration issues, including human smuggling and trafficking. These trends indicated further evidence of a continuing cycle of violence, persecution, and ethnic conflict. Even stringent controls failed to dissuade desperate people from using desperate means—including employing the services of human smugglers—in an attempt to reach safety. There was a pressing need for consultation and collaboration in developing high-quality asylum systems among the European nations.

The major concern in the Americas during the first part of the year was the worsening conflict in Colombia, which resulted in escalating levels of violence and an increase in forced displacement. Struggles for territorial control in strategically important border areas intensified, which increased concerns in neighbouring countries over national security and possible mass influxes of refugees. The number of individual Colombians recognized as refugees continued to rise. From January to August, 121,115 persons left the country permanently by air, compared with approximately 125,000 during all of 2000. In addition, in Europe and North America, Colombians constituted the 12th largest group of asylum seekers, whereas in 2000 they had ranked only 21st.

Following the terrorist attacks in the United States, the U.S. government announced new rules that would allow its Immigration and Naturalization Service to detain immigrants suspected of committing crimes for 48 hours without filing charges against them and to deport terrorist suspects without submitting any evidence. Another new antiterrorist law granted the U.S. attorney general authority to certify and detain the spouses and children of asylum seekers who were found inadmissible on terrorism-related grounds. These measures were likely to have a far-reaching effect on the asylum process, both in the U.S. and elsewhere, with a risk of increased xenophobia and racist reactions.   (UNHCR)

sources of income. Prior to September acute asylum and donor fatigue had compounded the challenges facing humanitarian efforts to address these needs. The first priority was to provide immediate assistance for the coming winter months. At the same time, future needs were being assessed in the event that the conflict was resolved; a return movement would likely be large-scale and require the mobilization of huge resources to ensure sustainable return, reintegration, and stability.

In Southeast Asia UNHCR completed its shelter program in East Timor and began phasing down activities during the second half of the year. After the murder of UNHCR staff in Atambua in September 2000, West Timor remained for many months under UN security Phase V, which precluded any permanent UN presence. In mid-2001 UNHCR, working together with other concerned parties, reviewed its position in light of the changing security situation and the peaceful Timorese elections in August. Given the increased postelection interest in voluntary repatriation among the refugees in West Timor and cooperation by the Indonesian government, many believed that the remaining refugees would return home by mid-2002.

The Balkans continued to cause serious concern. By August the conflict in Macedonia between the government and ethnic Albanians had already displaced more than 140,000 people, including some 81,000 persons to neighbouring Kosovo (a province of Serbia, Yugos.), 12,000 others to the south of Serbia, and more than 50,000 who were internally displaced. The cease-fire agreement negotiated by NATO in mid-August was enforced over the next few months, and as a result, by late 2001 some 57,000 refugees had been able to return from Kosovo and southern Serbia. The processes of democratic change in Yugoslavia and Croatia raised new hopes of achieving durable solutions for the 1.2 million people still displaced from their homes in these countries and in Bosnia and Herzegovina. UNHCR anticipated that of the 700,000 refugees and displaced people in Serbia, most would not return home. National reconstruction and development programs gave priority to the integration needs of these people. Nevertheless, ongoing efforts to make return a real option were also essential in order to consolidate peace in the region.

The return of displaced persons, notably the Serb minority, to Kosovo was a more problematic issue. Tensions re-

Sports and Games

In 2001 the year in sports was **DIVIDED** into two—the events held **PRIOR** to the September 11 terrorist **ATTACKS** in the U.S. and those that occurred afterward, many of which were **POSTPONED** or went on without **AMERICAN** athletes.

In the wake of the Sept. 11, 2001, terrorist attacks in the U.S., the sporting world paused momentarily to pay its respects. Stadiums across North America stood empty and silent as professional football, ice hockey, and baseball and college games were postponed or canceled. The National Association for Stock Car Auto Racing's (NASCAR's) mighty race cars were similarly silenced, and Major League Soccer's regular season came to a premature close. The Ryder Cup in golf was postponed until 2002, and though the world archery championships took place as scheduled in Beijing, the Americans stayed home.

At the start of the year, football fans witnessed a blowout in the Super Bowl, the National Football League championship, held in Tampa Bay, Fla., on Jan. 28, 2001. Quarterback Trent Dilfer, aided by standout middle linebacker Ray Lewis (*see* BIOGRAPHIES), led the American Football Conference champion Baltimore Ravens to a 34–7 romp over the National Football Conference New York Giants.

Auto-racing fans mourned the death in February of seven-time NASCAR Winston Cup champion Dale Earnhardt, Sr., who perished in a fatal car accident in the final moments of the Daytona 500. (*See* OBITUARIES.)

American tennis player Jennifer Capriati made an impressive comeback, winning the Australian Open and the French Open, her first Grand Slam singles titles (*see* BIOGRAPHIES), and National Basketball Association superstar Michael Jordan made headlines in October when he abandoned retirement to play for the Washington Wizards.

In baseball the final game of the World Series drew the largest viewership in years as the New York Yankees faced the Arizona Diamondbacks, who won their first World Series in a thrilling seven-game finish and ended the Yankees' streak of three straight titles. San Francisco Giants slugger Barry Bonds (*see* BIOGRAPHIES) notched 73 home runs to break the record set just three seasons earlier by Mark McGwire of the St. Louis Cardinals.

An outbreak of foot-and-mouth disease in Europe led to the postponement in April of the last games of the Rugby Union Six Nations championship, which was finally won by England in October. In steeplechasing the disease forced the cancellation of numerous races in Great Britain and Ireland.

Preparations continued for the 2002 Winter Olympic Games in Salt Lake City, Utah, under new International Olympic Committee (IOC) chairman Jacques Rogge of Belgium. (*See* BIOGRAPHIES.) Meanwhile, China rejoiced when the IOC awarded Beijing the 2008 Summer Games, the country's first-ever Olympics. In association football (soccer), 32 nations qualified for the upcoming World Cup finals in 2002.

(GAVIN FORBES EHRINGER)

ARCHERY

In world archery competition, U.S. senior teams won two gold and two silver medals at the Fédération Internationale de Tir à l'Arc (FITA) world indoor target championships in Florence in March 2001. The U.S. junior teams held their own by winning two gold and one silver.

The senior men's recurve team of Richard ("Butch") Johnson, Joseph McGlyn, and Vic Wunderle defeated Russia in the gold medal round. The senior women's team took the silver medal in the recurve, behind the victorious Russians. The junior women's recurve team also earned the silver, losing to Ukraine in the final.

In the compound bow division, the senior women's team of Ashley Kamuf, Michelle Ragsdale, and Mary Zorn (who also won gold in the individual competition) edged France in the final. The Italians prevailed over the Americans to take the men's compound gold. The U.S. junior teams both won gold in the compound division.

The FITA world outdoor championships, held in Beijing, were not so kind to the U.S. team. Team members were scheduled to fly to China on the morning of September 11 but found themselves grounded after the terrorist attacks on the East Coast. The competition went on as scheduled on September 16–22, but without the Americans. Dejan Sitar of Slovenia won the men's individual compound title, and Ulrika Sjöwall of Sweden captured the women's. In the recurve championships, South Koreans showed the way, with Yeon Jung Ki and Park Sung Hyun winning the men's and women's divisions, respectively. Team gold medals went to Norway in the men's compound division and France in the women's compound. The South Korean men won the recurve gold, while in an upset the Chinese women gained the recurve team title for the host country.

At the U.S. National Field Archery Association (NFAA) indoor championships March 31–April 1, Ragsdale and George Ryals each won a shoot-off to break ties for the champions bowls in the professional freestyle competition. At the NFAA outdoor championships in July, Ragsdale made it a clean sweep, and the men's champions bowl went to Michael Anderson in a shoot-off.

(LARRY WISE)

AUTOMOBILE RACING

Grand Prix Racing. Grand Prix racing sustained its globally televised momentum throughout the 2001 season, although there was precious little evidence that this high-profile international sport could remain insulated from the turbulent events in the wider world over the next few years.

Sponsors and investors who bankrolled the high-technology sport in the belief that its global reach equated to something close to a commercial bargain in terms of TV viewership were nevertheless understandably nervous about committing sums that could approach an annual $70 million for title sponsorship of one of the top teams.

Second-guessing the future was a fruitless task, of course. As for the immediate past, in Formula One (F1) terms, 2001 was another season of decisive domination for the remarkable Michael Schumacher at the wheel of his scarlet Italian Ferrari. (*See* BIOGRAPHIES.) The 32-year-old German racked up another nine Grand Prix wins out of 17 races, memorably breaking Alain Prost's all-time career record of 51 wins.

By the end of the season, Schumacher had 53 race wins to his credit, in addition to a record number of Grand Prix Championship points scored. The only remaining barrier to be cleared was matching—and exceeding—the five world championships won by the legendary Juan Manuel Fangio of Argentina between 1951 and 1957. Few would doubt that Schumacher was on course to break that record.

Scottish driver David Coulthard drove his best season ever but was let down by uncharacteristic unreliability on the part of his machinery. His McLaren-Mercedes teammate Mika Hakkinen had a patchy year and decided to take a sabbatical in 2002. Both men won two races apiece, although it certainly should have been more.

By contrast, the Williams-BMW squad was on the rise. Ralf Schumacher won three races and his dynamic new teammate Juan Pablo Montoya just one. Montoya, nevertheless, was probably the most exciting new talent to emerge on the F1 scene since Michael Schumacher himself in 1991.

A telling index of the generally unremarkable performances delivered by most of the teams could be gauged from the fact that the Sauber-Petronas squad finished fourth in the Constructors' Championship behind Ferrari, McLaren, and Williams. Sauber, a staid and normally somewhat average team, had benefitted from a decent chassis and two motivated young drivers in Kimi Raikkonen and Nick Heidfeld.

By the end of the season, the chill winds of financial reality seemed to be blowing through the ranks of the F1 teams. Prost Grand Prix finished the season on the commercial ropes, battling for its very survival. Toyota might have been looming large on the horizon for 2002, but even the top team principals conceded there could be bumpy times ahead.

The 2001 season was also marked by the reintroduction of electronic control systems, most notably traction control. Ferrari had raised its rivals' suspicions by insisting that the reintroduction of such systems be deferred until the fifth race of the season in Spain.

When it came to it, nothing changed in terms of F1's status quo, and it was clear that Ferrari had no problems adapting to the new rules. Its rivals' hoped-for advantage under this new technical initiative simply did not materialize.

Grand Prix racing's popularity was challenged in Europe by the advent of two U.S.-style oval track races held at the Lausitzring in Germany and at Rockingham in Great Britain. Both were purpose-built brand-new facilities specifically catering to Championship Auto Racing Teams (CART) single-seaters, and both races were hugely well received. Sadly, a terrible accident in the German race ended the career of popular former Williams F1 driver Alex Zanardi, who had to have both legs amputated as a result of a high-speed collision with another competitor.

Although the standard of CART racing was of a very high quality, the American domestic series finished the year under a cloud of commercial and economic uncertainty. The economic consequences of the September 11 terrorist attacks formed only part of the downside. The split five years earlier between CART and the Indy Racing League (IRL), headed by Indianapolis (Ind.) Motor Speedway president Tony George, inevitably diluted both categories, but with Penske—American racing's blue-ribbon team and the

U.S. equivalent of Ferrari—poised to desert CART to join the IRL full-time in 2002, CART faced a bleak future.

The one man who won, of course, was George. Not only would his Indianapolis 500 continue to thrive in the future, but the track also now played host to the U.S. Grand Prix, which was held in the immediate aftermath of the terrorist attacks. The race was won superbly by Hakkinen in the McLaren-Mercedes, but not before Montoya challenged at the front of the field.

Montoya had been the winner of the 2000 Indianapolis 500, so the crowds knew him and could identify with him. That in itself gave F1 a long-overdue boost in the U.S. Signs were that the American fans had reignited their interest in F1 for the first time since the late 1980s. It certainly seemed a promising development for the sport as a whole.

(ALAN HENRY)

U.S. Auto Racing. Tragedy and off-track turmoil notwithstanding, U.S. auto racing's major organizations posted another stirring—if less profitable—season. The death of Dale Earnhardt, Sr. (*see* OBITUARIES), a quarter of a mile from the finish of the Daytona 500—which was won by Chevrolet stablemate Michael Waltrip, with Earnhardt's son, Dale, Jr., second and Ford's Rusty Wallace third—began a season that

Michael Schumacher of Germany leaves the pit after refueling during the French Formula One Grand Prix on July 1.

AP/Wide World Photos

Increasing Safety in Auto Racing: A Winning Formula?

AP/Wide World Photos

Automobile racing aficionados had never denied that part of the attraction of their favourite sport was the element of perceived danger. The skill of the drivers, the talent of the car constructors, and the rules of auto racing's sanctioning bodies were designed to balance the danger and thus maintain the element of exciting competition.

In 2000–01 that balance was sorely tested by four deaths within nine months in National Association for Stock Car Auto Racing (NASCAR) events; among those killed was Dale Earnhardt, Sr.—one of the icons of the sport—during the Daytona 500, an annual classic watched by millions via television. (*See* OBITUARIES.) Adding to the problem was the postponement at Texas Motor Speedway of an entire Championship Auto Racing Teams (CART) event because the drivers said they could not stand gravity loads at speeds in excess of 370 km/h (230 mph). The race had been scheduled despite a CART official's warning that the speedway's tight corners and high banks were unsuitable for CART vehicles.

In truth, NASCAR, CART, the Indy Racing League, and Grand Prix (Formula One) racing organizations had been keenly aware of the thin boundary between excitement and mortality for years. Money and racing's own success had altered the equation, however. Auto racing had become desirable entertainment for vast television audiences and filled racetracks accommodating crowds in excess of 100,000. The fan base reached far beyond the original cadre of enthusiasts. NASCAR, for instance, negotiated an eight-year contract for $212 million with NBC-TV and Fox TV. The races regularly won weekend ratings battles.

Drivers in the top series, who could earn more in one afternoon than the president of the U.S. did annually, remained the most frangible components of the man-machine combinations that provided the excitement and the dollars. The challenge facing auto-racing organizers was to find ways to enhance driver protection without lessening the sport's entertainment value.

To accomplish this, the sanctioning bodies continually refined rules prescribing vehicle construction, driver attire, the manner of racing, and the conditions on the track. In Earnhardt's accident, however—as well as in other crashes that had claimed the lives of

What proved to be a fatal collision occurred on the last lap of the Daytona 500: Dale Earnhardt, Sr.'s car (3) is hit by one driven by Ken Schrader.

NASCAR drivers Adam Petty and Kenny Irwin—the forces generated on the vehicle and other safety equipment upon impact were not survivable. Among the solutions floated for increasing driver safety were construction of "softer" walls at racetracks, but the idea that had attracted the most attention was the HANS (head and neck support) device. Now mandated for CART and its subsidiary series, the device was developed in the early 1980s by engineer Robert Hubbard and former sports car champion Jim Downing. The device, a collar-and-yoke system worn around the driver's neck and down the front of the shoulders, permitted normal movement of the head and neck but limited the extreme front-to-back and side-to-side movements that could make a crash fatal. Downing stated that his company equipped over 800 drivers from all series with the HANS device in the months immediately following Earnhardt's death. NASCAR made HANS-type devices voluntary, but most drivers, including Dale Earnhardt, Jr., and other stars, utilized it. NASCAR also announced the establishment of a research facility at Hickory, N.C., to develop new technology for race cars and driver equipment.

(ROBERT J. FENDELL)

changed the National Association for Stock Car Auto Racing (NASCAR) forever. It dragged the most uniquely American sanctioning body into major actions to increase driver safety. (*See* Sidebar.) Waltrip won $1,331,185 of the $9,291,741 Daytona 500 purse as 14 drivers shared 49 lead changes; the victory margin was a scant 0.124 sec.

The tragedy overshadowed the return after a 16-year absence of Dodge, which fielded three cars that finished in the Daytona top 10. Chevrolet's Jeff Gordon, the eventual Winston Cup season champion, went out 88 km (55 mi) from the finish. Gordon became a four-time season champ; he collected victories in the Brickyard 400 at the Indianapolis (Ind.) Motor Speedway, the second richest NASCAR event, and five

other races. Gordon won nearly $11 million for the season.

CART pilots again invaded the IRL's domain and won the 85th Indianapolis 500. They swept the first six places. Brazilian Helio Castroneves, driving a Marlboro Team Penske Dallara Oldsmobile, beat teammate Gil de Ferran by 1.74 sec, followed by Michael Andretti, Jimmy Vasser, Bruno Junqueira, and NASCAR regular Tony Stewart. The first IRL finisher, a lap back, was Eliseo Salazar. IRL's Greg Ray led at the halfway point but completed only 192 of the 200 laps, and pole sitter Scott Sharp spun on the first lap. Castroneves took home $1,270,475 of the $9,610,325 purse. For Penske this was the 11th Indy 500 victory in 28 attempts; to become eligible to compete, he and the other two CART car owners, Chip

Ganassi and Barry Green, had had to acquire IRL-conforming vehicles.

De Ferran in a Marlboro Team Penske Reynard Honda defended his CART season championship after a 21-event battle with ex-IRL champion Kenny Brack in a Team Rahal Lola Ford-Cosworth. Andretti, the lone American in the top 10, finished third in a Reynard Honda for Team Motorola.

Brack won four of CART's oval-track races, significant because major CART sponsor Marlboro announced that it would shift to the rival IRL, which competed only on ovals. CART was facing the ultimate loss of all three of its engine suppliers, angered over a late-season switch from a turbocharged to a normally aspirated formula for 2003. Honda and Ford said they could not produce such an engine so quickly. Toyota already had announced a shift to the IRL. During the season CART canceled two scheduled races, one in Brazil because of local politics and the other—which allegedly cost it a settlement in excess of $3.5 million—at the Texas Motor Speedway.

While the lure of the Indy 500 to sponsors and carmakers alike strengthened the IRL, the 13-race series for normally aspirated single-seaters continued to develop exciting new drivers. One of them, 22-year-old Sam Hornish, Jr., of Ohio, won the season championship for Panther Racing in a Pennzoil Dallara Oldsmobile. His closest competitor was Buddy Lazier; Sharp was third.

NASCAR's Busch Series, usually the Saturday feature at Winston Cup weekends, crowned Chevrolet's Kevin Harvick as champion. The Craftsman Truck title was won by Jack Sprague of Chevrolet over Ted Musgrave and Joe Ruttman, both in Dodges.   (ROBERT J. FENDELL)

Rallies and Other Races. In the world rally championship circuit, Finnish driver Tommi Mäkinen (Mitsubishi) won his third straight Rally of Monte Carlo in January 2001. Mäkinen became the first driver to win the rally three years in a row since German Walter Rohrl accomplished the feat in 1984.

In late November British driver Richard Burns (Subaru), winner of the Rally New Zealand earlier in the year, became World Rally champion for the season. The schism in professional road racing in the U.S. continued with two distinct series. The Rolex 24 Hours of Daytona, a Grand American Road Racing Association event, was plagued by bad weather and the inability of the allegedly fastest SportsRacing Prototypes (SRPs) to survive that length of time. Instead, the winner came from the Grand Touring Super class, a Chevrolet Corvette driven by Ron Fellows, Chris Kneifel, Franck Freon, and Johnny O'Connell. Second was a Porsche-supported GT3R. The first SRP was 11th overall.

The rival American Le Mans Series watched Audi factory R8s dominate, beginning with the 12 Hours at Sebring and ending with the 1,611-km (1,001-mi) Petit Le Mans at Road Atlanta. Audi's Emanuele Pirro won the driver crown.

(ROBERT J. FENDELL; EDITOR)

BADMINTON

In 2001, for the first time in 21 years, a badminton player from India captured the prestigious All-England Championships. Pullela Gopichand defeated world number one Peter Gade of Denmark 17–14, 17–15 in a thrilling semifinal and Chinese national champion Chen Hong 15–12, 15–6 in the final. Gong Zhichao of China easily dismissed her teammate Zhou Mi for the women's singles crown, and in an all-Indonesian men's doubles final, Halim Haryanto and Tony Gunawan topped Sigit Budiarto and Chandra Wijaya. The championships also featured Chinese winners in women's doubles and mixed doubles.

The Sudirman Cup, a best-of-five-match mixed-team competition held every other year, was contested in Seville, Spain, on May 28–June 2. In the semifinals, China edged Denmark 3–2 in a match that included Gong Zhichao's demolition of reigning world champion Camilla Martin of Denmark 11–1, 11–0. China faced Indonesia in the final and, after losing the opening men's doubles match, won three matches in a row to capture the title 3–1.

The world championships were staged in Seville immediately after the Sudirman Cup. In the men's singles semifinals, Taufik Hidayat of Indonesia was leading his teammate Hendrawan until a groin injury forced him to retire. Hendrawan then defeated Gade for his first world championship title. In the men's doubles competition, Gunawan and Haryanto conquered defending champions Kim Dong Moon and Ha Tae Kwan of South Korea. When Martin fell victim to an early-round upset, Gong Zhichao became the favourite but lost to teammate and eventual women's champion Gong Ruina in the semifinals. Chinese players accounted for the remaining two titles as Gao Ling and Huang Sui won the women's doubles and Zhang Jun and Gao Ling took the mixed doubles.

At the World Grand Prix Finals held in Brunei in August, Xia Xuaneze became the first Chinese man to win a major badminton title in 2001 with a final-round victory over Indonesia's Marleve Mainaky. Gong Zhichao lost to Zhou Mi in the women's singles final. Gunawan and Wijaya successfully defended their doubles title, and Huang Nanyan and Yang Wei of China took the women's doubles. The only European winners were the Danish mixed-doubles team of Jens Eriksen and Mette Schjoldager.

(DONN GOBBIE)

BASEBALL

The eventful 2001 major league baseball season, delayed one week by the attacks on September 11, extended into November for the first time in history and featured a new home-run record by the San Francisco Giants' Barry Bonds (see BIOGRAPHIES) and a new World Series champion—the National League (NL) Arizona Diamondbacks, who ended the three-year reign of the American League (AL) New York Yankees in a dramatic seven-game series.

Bonds hit 73 home runs to shatter the mark of the St. Louis Cardinals' Mark McGwire, who hit 70 in 1998. At the same time, however, major league offensive totals decreased. Runs per game fell from 10.28 in 2000 to 9.55 in 2001, and only 12 players hit 40 or more home runs, 4 fewer than the previous season. Despite the debut of new stadiums in Milwaukee, Wis., and Pittsburgh, Pa., overall attendance was up only slightly, to an average of just over 30,000 per game.

World Series. The Diamondbacks scored two runs in the bottom of the ninth inning of game seven at home to defeat the Yankees 3–2 and win the World Series four games to three. By doing so, the Arizona team, which debuted in 1998, staged the quickest trip to a title of any franchise in major league history. The previous mark of five years to a championship was established by the Florida Marlins in 1997.

In the Series opener in Phoenix on October 27, the Diamondbacks routed the Yankees 9–1 before a record home crowd of 49,646. Curt Schilling, the team's star right-handed pitcher, worked seven strong innings for Arizona, while the Diamondbacks collected five runs off New York starter Mike Mussina in three innings. Craig Counsell and Luis Gonzalez hit home runs for the Diamondbacks.

In game two pitcher Randy Johnson, the left-handed ace for Arizona, authored a 4–0 shutout, yielding just three hits and striking out 11 in a complete-game performance. The Diamondbacks held a slim 1–0 lead into the seventh inning when Matt Williams clubbed a three-run home run off the Yankees' starter and loser, Andy Pettitte.

On October 30 the Series moved to Yankee Stadium, where Pres. George W. Bush tossed out the first pitch before an emotional crowd of 55,820 and Mariano Rivera threw the last pitch in a 2–1 game-three victory for the Yankees. New York's Roger Clemens pitched seven innings, by which time the Yankees had broken a 1–1 tie on a single by Scott Brosius. Earlier, Jorge Posada had hit a homer for the Yankees against Arizona's Brian Anderson.

The Diamondbacks were one out away from winning game four in Yankee Stadium on October 31 when Tino Martinez clubbed a two-out, two-run home run in the bottom of the ninth inning. In the bottom of the 10th, Derek Jeter hit a home run to provide the Yankees a dramatic 4–3 triumph that tied the Series at two games each. Both home runs came against Arizona's star relief pitcher, Byung-Hyun Kim, who came on in the eighth inning trying to protect a 3–1 lead for Schilling.

The Yankees accomplished another remarkable comeback in game five at Yankee Stadium the next night, which was the first time a World Series game ever had been played in November. Home runs by Steve Finley and Rod Barajas off Mussina staked Arizona to a 2–0 lead in the fifth inning. The Yankees, for the second consecutive night, were down by two runs with two outs in the ninth inning when Brosius hit a game-tying two-run home run off Kim. By the time the defending champions achieved a 3–2 triumph in 12 innings, it was, in fact, early the next morning. Few fans had departed, however, when Alfonso Soriano slashed a single to right field to score the winning run from second base and provide the Yankees a three-games-to-two lead.

When the Diamondbacks returned home for game six before a record Bank One Ballpark crowd of 49,707, they demolished the Yankees 15–2 to square the Series at three games each. The Diamondbacks knocked out Pettitte in two-plus innings and mounted a 12–0 margin by the third for Johnson, who cruised to his second Series victory with a seven-inning stint. The Diamondbacks' 22 hits broke a single-game Series record of 20, and the 13-run margin of victory was the second largest in Series history.

To win the final game on November 4, the Diamondbacks had to mount a rally against Rivera, one of the most accomplished relief pitchers in history. Arizona had fallen behind by 2–1 on an eighth-inning home run by Soriano. Tony Womack doubled-in one run to forge a 2–2 tie, and then Gonzalez hit a bases-loaded bloop single to score the winning run for the Diamondbacks. Johnson was credited with the victory, his third of the Series, by pitching 1¹/₃ innings of relief one night after he had hurled the Diamondbacks to victory in game six. In game seven he finished for Schilling, who had made his third start of the series. Johnson and Schilling shared Most Valuable Player (MVP) honours for the Series.

Play-offs. The Diamondbacks won the NL pennant by defeating the Atlanta Braves four games to one. Arizona clinched the pennant in Atlanta's Turner Field on October 21 by winning 3–2 on a two-run pinch home run by Erubiel Durazo and strong pitching by Johnson, who worked seven innings before giving way to Kim. Counsell was voted MVP of the National League Championship Series.

The Yankees claimed their 38th pennant one night later by routing the Seattle Mariners 12–3 at home to win the American League Championship Series (ALCS) four games to one. Paul O'Neill, Bernie Williams, and Martinez hit home runs for the Yankees, and Pettitte pitched 6¹/₃ innings to register his second victory of the ALCS, for which he was named series MVP.

The Diamondbacks won the first round of the NL play-offs, defeating the Cardinals three games to two, while the Braves advanced by sweeping the Houston Astros. In the AL the Yankees defeated the Oakland Athletics (A's) three games to two, despite losing the first two games at home, the first time a team had won a best-of-five series in that fashion. After losing game three 17–2, the Mariners had to win the last two games of their series against the Cleveland Indians to prevail three games to two.

The Mariners posted a regular-season record of 116–46 to win the AL West division by 14 games over the A's, who had the second best record in the major leagues (102–60) and qualified as the AL wild-card team. The 116 victories by Seattle tied the 1906 Chicago Cubs for the most ever. The Yankees romped in

the AL East by 13¹/₂ games, and Cleveland won the AL Central by six games.

The Diamondbacks won the NL West division with a mark of 92–70, two games better than the Giants. The Braves won an unprecedented 10th consecutive division title by finishing first in the NL East. The Astros and Cardinals tied for first in the NL Central at 93–69. The Astros were crowned champions by virtue of winning the season series against the Cardinals, who earned a wild-card berth.

Individual Accomplishments. Ichiro Suzuki, a 28-year-old rookie from Japan, won the AL batting title for the Mariners by amassing 242 hits for a .350 average. Seattle's Bret Boone led the league with 141 runs batted in, and Alex Rodriguez of the Texas Rangers hit the most home runs, 52. Mark Mulder of Oakland led AL pitchers with 21 victories, though two others won 20 games, Seattle's Jamie Moyer and Clemens. Clemens won 16 straight decisions at one point, tying an AL record. Rivera of the Yankees led relief pitchers with 50 saves.

Larry Walker of the Colorado Rockies led the NL with a .350 batting average. Sammy Sosa of the Chicago Cubs batted in 160 runs and 64 home runs in his fourth straight season of 50 or more homers. Schilling and Matt Morris of the Cardinals each posted 22 victories; Johnson had 21; and Chicago's Jon Lieber had 20. Robb Nen of the Giants led NL relief pitchers with 45 saves. In an achievement that rivaled Bonds's, Rickey Henderson of San Diego broke Ty Cobb's all-time runs record by scoring his 2,246th; he finished the season with 2,248.

Pitchers Randy Johnson (left) and Curt Schilling of the Arizona Diamondbacks hold aloft the World Series Most Valuable Player trophy.

In postseason honours Suzuki was voted MVP and Rookie of the Year in the AL, a feat accomplished by only one other player—Fred Lynn of the Boston Red Sox in 1975. Albert Pujols of St. Louis was the NL Rookie of the Year. Bonds earned MVP honours in the NL for a record fourth time. Clemens won a record sixth Cy Young Award in the AL; Johnson earned his third straight NL Cy Young Award. Lou Piniella of Seattle and Larry Bowa of the Philadelphia Phillies were voted Manager of the Year in the AL and NL, respectively. Cal Ripken, Jr., of the Baltimore Orioles, Tony Gwynn of the Padres, and McGwire, each a decorated veteran, retired after the 2001 season.

Little League World Series. The Tokyo-Kitasuna team scored two runs in the sixth and final inning to beat Apopka, Fla., 2–1 on August 26 in South Williamsport, Pa., and win the Little League World Series title. Nobuhisa Baba delivered the winning hit as Japan won its fifth Little League championship. Tokyo-Kitasuna had advanced by beating Curaçao, Netherlands Antilles, 2–1; Apopka had advanced by whipping the Bronx, N.Y., team 8–2 for the U.S. championship. Earlier in the tournament, Florida had been victimized by a perfect game thrown by Danny Almonte of the Bronx, the first in the Little League World Series since 1957. After the conclusion of the tournament, it was discovered that Almonte was 14, an infraction of the Little League rules requiring players to turn 13 no earlier than August 1 in the season they are competing. Little League Baseball declared that the Bronx team had to forfeit all victories for the season as well as the team's third-place finish in the World Series. Rolando Paulino, the team's founder, and Felipe de Jesus Almonte, father of the pitcher, were banned for life from any further involvement in Little League.

(BOB VERDI)

Latin America. The 2001 Caribbean Series was held in Culiacán, Mex., on February 2–8. The Cibao Eagles (Aguilas Cibaeñas), representing the Dominican Republic, compiled a 4–2 record and won their third title. Mexico (Hermosillo Orangegrowers [Naranjeros]) and Venezuela (Lara Cardinals [Cardenales]) tied for second with 3–3 marks, while Puerto Rico (Caguas Creoles [Criollos]) was last with a 2–4 record.

Santiago de Cuba won its third consecutive Cuban championship. It defeated Granma in the quarterfinals, beat Camagüey in the semifinal round, and took four out of five games from

Atsushi Mochizuki of Tokyo delivers a pitch against the Apopka, Fla., team en route to a 2–1 victory in the Little League World Series final game on August 26.

AP/Wide World Photos

Pinar del Río in the finals to win the title. Maels Rodríguez, a pitcher from the Sancti Spiritus team, set the Cuban all-time single-season record for strikeouts with 263. In addition to leading the league in strikeouts, Rodríguez also had the best earned run average (1.77) and was tied for the most victories (15).

Nelson Barrera, player-manager with Oaxaca, broke the Mexican League all-time home-run record held by Hector Espino when he hit his 454th homer. Barrera, aged 43, had played 25 years in the league. The Mexico City Tigers defeated the Mexico City Red Devils four games to two in the league's championship series. It was the Tigers' eighth—and second consecutive—league title.

During March, Major League Baseball sponsored exhibition games between big league teams in Valencia, Venez., and three Mexican cities (Culiacán, Hermosillo, and Mexico City) as part of its "Month of the Americas." The event was capped off by a regular-season opening series featuring the Toronto Blue Jays and Texas Rangers in San Juan, P.R.

(MILTON JAMAIL)

Japan. The Yakult Swallows beat the Osaka Kintetsu Buffaloes four games to one in the 2001 Japan Series. The Swallows claimed their fifth Japan Series title and their fourth in nine years. Swallows catcher Atsuya Furuta was named series Most Valuable Player (MVP) after having hit .500 with seven hits and one home run. He also finished second in the Central League's (CL's) 140-game regular season with a batting average of .324, behind the Yomiuri Giants' Hideki Matsui, who had a .333 average. The Swallows finished the regular season with 76 wins, one more than the defending champion Giants, who came close late in the season before suffering four straight losses at the very end. The

Swallows' Roberto Petagine, leading the league with 39 home runs and 127 runs batted in, was named CL regular-season MVP. Left-handed starting pitcher Shugo Fujii and closer Shingo Takatsu led the league with 14 wins and 37 saves, respectively, for the team.

In the Pacific League (PL) the Buffaloes won their first crown since 1989 after having finished last in 1999 and 2000. The hard-hitting team ended the regular season two and a half games ahead of the Fukuoka Daiei Hawks. Buffaloes outfielder Karl ("Tuffy") Rhodes, who was named the PL's MVP, blasted 55 home runs to tie the all-time single-season Japanese record set by home-run king Sadaharu Oh in 1964. The biggest news for Japanese baseball in 2001 was Shigeo Nagashima's retirement as Giants manager. Nagashima had been extremely popular both as a player and as a manager. (HIROKI NODA)

BASKETBALL

United States. *Professional.* In 2001 the Los Angeles Lakers continued to dominate the National Basketball Association (NBA). Head coach Phil Jackson at times during the season had to serve as both mediator and conciliator while trying to defuse the animosity between his superstars, Shaquille O'Neal and Kobe Bryant. Well before the 2001 play-offs opened, however, the Lakers again were functioning like a finely tuned machine, winning their last eight regular-season games.

The Lakers breezed through the Western Conference play-offs; the team won 11 straight games to reach the NBA finals unscathed. Heavily favoured over Eastern Conference representative Philadelphia, the Lakers were expected to sweep the 76ers in the best-of-seven series and repeat as NBA champions with a 15–0 record in postseason play. That would have made Jackson's team the first in NBA history to go unbeaten in every play-off round. The grand plan got derailed, however, by a 107–101 overtime loss to the inspired 76ers in game one.

Although the 2.16-m (7-ft 1-in), 143-kg (315-lb) O'Neal towered over him, 1.8-m (6-ft), 75-kg (165-lb) 76ers point guard Allen Iverson (see BIOGRAPHIES) was virtually unstoppable in the play-offs, as he had been all season. Iverson outscored O'Neal 48–44 in the opener, but injuries and fierce Los Angeles defensive pressure prevented the superquick guard from carrying his team to another victory. The next four games went to the Lakers, who wrapped up the title with a 108–96 victory in Philadelphia on June 15.

The NBA's youth movement accelerated sharply in the 2001 draft. The search to find another Michael Jordan dipped more deeply into the high-school ranks even while Jordan, who had become president of the Washington Wizards, made his second comeback as a player at age 38, also bringing back sellout crowds to see him. Of the first eight players drafted, four were making the jump directly from high school to the pros. They included the top two picks, Kwame Brown and Tyson Chandler, along with the fourth and eighth picks, Eddy Curry and DeSagana Diop, respectively.

The NBA also brought its Developmental League (NBDL) plans to fruition. Eight teams, with players at least 20 years old, opened a 56-game inaugural season in November. The NBDL play-offs were set for March 2002.

In the Women's National Basketball Association (WNBA), the Los Angeles Sparks swept to their first championship, defeating the Charlotte (N.C.) Sting in the finals. The Sparks' victory ended the Houston (Tex.) Comets' domination in each of the WNBA's first four seasons.

College. Duke University basketball coach Mike Krzyzewski and his Blue Devils were the consensus favourites to win the 2001 National Collegiate Athletic Association (NCAA) championship, but sentimental fans and media alike were pulling for the Arizona Wildcats and their coach, Lute Olson. The death of Olson's wife, Bobbi, on January 1 had brought an outpouring of sympathy from across the country. After Bobbi's death, Olson's top assistant, Jim Rosborough, had taken over

the reins temporarily, but Olson soon discovered that returning to work was therapy for grief. When he went back to the team, the Wildcats went on an emotional winning streak that launched them into the Final Four. That gave Olson—at 66 years and six months—a chance to become the oldest coach to capture an NCAA title; legendary Kansas coach Phog Allen was two months younger when he steered the Jayhawks to the 1952 crown.

It was not to be. Olson, whose Wildcats had won the title in 1997, was denied his second national championship when Arizona and Duke met on April 2 in the Minneapolis (Minn.) Metrodome. Duke was led by swingman Mike Dunleavy, who hit three straight three-

Jed Jacobsohn/Allsport

Lisa Leslie of the Los Angeles Sparks drives past Yolanda Griffith of the Sacramento Monarchs in the first game of the WNBA Western Conference finals.

point baskets in a second-half spree. After hitting just one basket in six attempts in the opening half, Dunleavy found the mark for 18 of his 21 points after the intermission. That sort of clutch shooting made the difference in the game. Dunleavy totaled five three-pointers in the championship showdown, and Blue Devil team captain Shane Battier played a critical role at the end of the game. The senior scored the

needed baskets to help the Blue Devils survive repeated Arizona rallies and go on to clinch the final 82–72.

Battier became only the fourth player in college basketball history to compile over 1,500 career points, 500 rebounds, 200 assists, 200 steals, and 200 blocked shots. Along with the retirement of his jersey by Duke, Battier was named the outstanding player of the 2001 NCAA Final Four. The unanimous first-team All-American also swept other major honours, including the Wooden and Naismith Player of the Year awards. His accomplishments reflected the way Krzyzewski had been able to recruit athletes who excelled on the court as well as in the classroom. The 54-year-old Krzyzewski had taken the Blue Devils to the Final Four 9 times in 21 years. The victory over Arizona was the third national championship of his career.

Bobby Knight largely avoided the media in the aftermath of his controversial departure from Indiana University. He did, however, accept another coaching position, becoming the new head basketball coach at Texas Tech. Soft-spoken Mike Davis, a former assistant to Knight at Indiana, stepped successfully into the position vacated by his mentor. After leading the Hoosiers to a stunning 59–58 upset of top-ranked Michigan State on January 7 and steering the team into the NCAA tournament at the close of the season, Davis was rewarded with a four-year contract.

In the women's ranks, it was Notre Dame's year. The Fighting Irish captured their first NCAA championship by prevailing over Purdue in a 68–66 thriller in St. Louis, Mo. Fittingly, Notre Dame star senior Ruth Riley hit the decisive free throws in the final seconds of the game. Riley's 28 points and 13 rebounds fueled her team's run to the title. Perennial powerhouse Connecticut had beaten the Irish 11 straight times in previous years but lost to them twice during the 2000–01 season. A major factor in that turnabout was Riley, who also earned NCAA Player of the Year honours. (ROBERT G. LOGAN)

International. In 2001 the Fédération Internationale de Basket (FIBA) was unable to reach an agreement with the Union des Ligues Européenes de Basketball (ULEB), which had organized a European league apart from the FIBA, resulting in competition between the ULEB's Euroleague and the FIBA's SuproLeague. In November the FIBA announced its reorganization into five continental zones beneath the umbrella FIBA-World group.

The focus of international basketball in 2001 was on the continental championships, which were qualifying tournaments for the 2002 world championships in Indianapolis, Ind. The hotly contested 2001 European championship yielded five qualifiers for the world championships: Yugoslavia, Turkey, Spain, Germany, and Russia, in that order. In the African championship Angola and Algeria qualified. In the Americas competition Venezuela, Brazil, Argentina, Puerto Rico, and Canada advanced to the worlds; the U.S., as host country of the 2002 event, automatically qualified, despite placing last in the region. In the Asian championship Lebanon mounted a spectacular 75–72 semifinal upset of South Korea to advance to its first world championships, despite losing in the final game to the other Asian qualifier, China. In the Oceania region New Zealand advanced at the cost of Australia, which it defeated in the best-of-three tournament.

Automatic qualifiers for the women's 2002 world championships were the host country, China, and the 2000 Olympic champion, the U.S. The qualifiers from the European championship were France, Russia, Spain, Lithuania, and Yugoslavia, while Brazil, Cuba, and Argentina advanced from the Americas. China dominated the Asian tournament, with distant contenders Japan, South Korea, and Taiwan also qualifying for the event. Australia bested New Zealand for the qualifying spot in the Oceania championship.

In August Yugoslavia captured the gold medal in the men's World University Games, defeating China in the final game. For the bronze Germany was bested by the U.S., which had earned a medal in every biennial tournament since 1965, six years after the games were founded in 1959. On the women's side the U.S. won handily, despite an early tournament loss to Canada. China and the Czech Republic took home the silver and bronze medals, respectively.

The FIBA world championship for young men was hosted in August by Japan, where the U.S. captured the gold with a victory over Croatia. Argentina won the bronze medal game over the Dominican Republic. The world championship for junior women, held in the Czech Republic, was won by the host country in the final seconds over Russia. In the semifinals the Czech Republic had defeated the U.S., which later wrested the bronze medal from Australia. With National Basketball Association pros playing, the U.S. dominated the Goodwill Games in Australia in September, with a gold-medal win over Argentina.

In club play Maccabi Tel Aviv of Israel won its first European title in 20 years, defeating Panathinaikos BSA of Greece for the SuproLeague championship in May. The Maccabi coach was asked to step down in July after making racial slurs. In the British Basketball League (BBL), the Chester Jets claimed the 2001 trophy over the Newcastle Eagles, while in the BBL championship finals, the Leicester Riders defeated the Sheffield Sharks, who shortly afterward lost their franchise. In the ULEB's Euroleague finals Kinder Bologna of Italy defeated TAU Cerámica of Spain in the five-game series.

(TOM MICHAEL)

BILLIARD GAMES

Carom Billiards. Swedish carom billiards star Torbjörn Blomdahl defeated American Pedro Piedrabuena in the International Dutch Open, held in Barendrecht, Neth., on January 12–14, 2001. The champion compiled an average of 1.794, with a high run of 12.

On February 4 South Korean-born Sang Chun Lee of New York City captured his 12th consecutive U.S. Billiard Association three-cushion championship. Lee finished the tournament with a 9–0 record and a high run of 12 and averaged 2.667 in the final game against American runner-up Carlos Hallon.

The first event of the 2001 Carom Corner Tour was held in Peabody, Mass., in March, with Dick Jaspers of The Netherlands defeating Piedrabuena for the title. Jaspers had a high run of 15, scoring 4.286 in his best game.

Greece played host to the three-cushion stars in February. Semih Sayginer of Turkey beat a strong field for the title. At the Billiards Worldcup Association tournament in Bogotá, Colom., in May, Sayginer won for the second straight year, prevailing over Jaspers in the final.

Shane Battier of Duke University slams home two points in the NCAA championship game against Arizona on April 2.

Brian Bahr/Allsport

In June Frédéric Caudron of Belgium captured the title at the St. Willebrord (Neth.) Invitational, with Blomdahl taking second. The Monte Carlo Crystal Kelly tournament also was held in June. Jaspers avenged his earlier loss to Sayginer for the win.

In July Las Vegas, Nev., hosted the Carl Conlon Memorial Worldcup. It was the largest three-cushion event ever held in the U.S., with 152 competitors representing 21 countries. Blomdahl defeated Jaspers 3–1 for the title and posted an impressive grand average of 2.039 with a high run of 14. Legendary Belgian three-cushion star Raymond Ceulemans, who lost to Blomdahl in the second round, was inducted into the Billiard Congress of America (BCA) Hall of Fame just days earlier. Ceulemans had captured over 100 international titles in his 40-year career and was the first non-U.S. player to enter the hall since Alfredo de Oro of Spain was inducted in 1967.

Pocket Billiards. The 2001 pool season kicked off in January with Shannon Daulton defeating former U.S. Open champion Johnny Archer in the Music City Open in Nashville, Tenn. In the Derby City Classic, held in Louisville, Ky., later that month, Jose Parica took the nine-ball banks title, Buddy Hall the one-pocket crown, and Daulton both the nine-ball title and the all-around championship. At the Lexington (Ky.) All Star Championships, Jeremy Jones defeated Corey Deuel and Parica for the nine-ball crown, while John Brumback captured the nine-ball banks title.

Efren Reyes of the Philippines pocketed $20,000 for his 13–9 victory over Earl Strickland in the Masters Nine-Ball Championships in Chesapeake, Va., in April. One week later Reyes lost to fellow Filipino Francisco Bustamante in the finals of the Turning Stone Classic in Verona, N.Y. May saw the players head for the desert and the BCA nine-ball event in Las Vegas. Rising star Deuel knocked off Parica 7–5 in the final. Eight invited players descended on Uncasville, Conn., during July 11–12 for the International Challenge of Champions. Chao Fong-pang of Taiwan brushed aside Bustamante in a one-game sudden-death final.

At the World Pool–Billiard Association (WPA) men's world championships, held July 14–22 in Cardiff, Wales, Mika Immonen of Finland defeated Ralf Souquet of Germany 17–10 in the final to take home $65,000.

Back in Chesapeake in September, Deuel crushed Immonen 11–0 to cap-ture the U.S. Open nine-ball championship. At season's end Deuel was the highest-ranked man in points, but Reyes, with more than $230,000 in winnings, topped the money list.

The Women's Professional Billiard Association (WPBA) seemed like a two-woman show in 2001 as Karen Corr, originally from Northern Ireland, and England's Allison Fisher between them won nearly everything in sight. The tour kicked off in March with Corr capturing the Players Championship in Valley Forge, Pa. She followed with another title a month later in the Spring Classic in Alpine, Calif., where she defeated Taiwan's Jennifer Chen for the second consecutive event.

Taiwan hosted the Amway Cup in early April, with Fisher pocketing $20,000 and the title. At the BCA championship in Las Vegas in May, American Jeanette Lee relegated Corr to a second-place finish with a 7–5 victory in the final. It was the year's only major women's event that neither Fisher (who finished third) nor Corr won.

In a battle of former snooker professionals, Corr defeated Fisher 7–3 at the Cuetec Cues Carolina Classic in Charlotte, N.C., in June. With this victory, Corr's third of the season, she overtook Fisher atop the WPBA rankings. Fisher had held the number one spot since September 1996. By season's end Corr had swept the WPBA tour, winning all six official events. Fisher, however, captured the $25,000 prize at the International Tournament of Champions in Uncasville on November 8 and then bested Corr 11–8 in the final of the WPA world nine-ball championship in Quebec two weeks later. Though Corr held onto her number one ranking in points, Fisher outearned her on the year's money list.

Snooker. England's Ronnie O'Sullivan capped off a sensational season in May 2001 by defeating former champion John Higgins of Scotland 18–14 to capture his first world professional snooker championship. O'Sullivan's title was his fifth of the season and added £250,000 (about $350,000) to push his season earnings to nearly £700,000 (almost $1 million). O'Sullivan, described by many observers as the greatest natural talent ever to play the game, climbed to number two in the world rankings, just ahead of Higgins. Though defending champion Mark Williams of Wales had crashed out in the second round, he retained his number one ranking for the 2001–02 season. In January Higgins, with teammates Stephen Hendry and Alan McManus, defeated a team from Ireland 6–2 to win the 2001 Nations Cup for Scotland.

Canadian Cliff Thorburn, who remained the only overseas player to have won the world snooker championship (1980), celebrated his return to the amateur snooker ranks with a dramatic 4–3 last-ball victory over another former professional, Tom Finstad, to capture the Canadian amateur snooker championship. (BILL BRADLEY)

BOBSLEDDING AND LUGE

Bobsledding. The top story of the 2000–01 bobsled season was the success of Jean Racine (and her brakeman, Jennifer Davidson) of the U.S. The duo combined to win six gold medals out of seven World Cup races, and for the second year in a row, Racine won the women's World Cup season title. Sandra Prokoff of Germany was second, and American Bonny Warner finished third. At the 2001 world championships, held in Calgary, Alta., in February, Racine and Davidson were edged out, however, losing by only 0.02 sec to Switzerland's Françoise Burdet and Katharina Sutter. Susi Erdmann and Tanja Hees of Germany placed third.

In men's bobsled action, the World Cup tour had seven stops throughout Europe and the U.S. Germany's André Lange won both the four-man title and the combined season title. In four-man season standings, Sandis Prusis of Latvia took second, with Matthias Benesch of Germany finishing in third. Martin Annen of Switzerland won the two-man season title, followed by Germans René Spies and Lange. Christoph Langen of Germany dominated the men's world championship in St. Moritz, Switz., winning his fifth two-man world title (with brakeman Marco Jakobs) and the four-man gold medal.

Skeleton. American Lincoln DeWitt and Alex Coomber of Great Britain won the men's and women's skeleton World Cup season titles, respectively, after they both won the World Cup finals at Utah Olympic Park. On the men's side, Kazuhiro Koshi of Japan placed second, and American Jim Shea, Jr., won the bronze. Steffi Hanzlik of Germany finished second in the women's World Cup standings, with Switzerland's Maya Pedersen in third. At the world championships in Calgary, Austria's Martin Rettl took the crown by 0.88 sec over Jeff Pain of Canada. DeWitt finished third. Pedersen rallied to gain the women's crown, while Coomber finished second and Tricia Stumpf of the U.S. placed third.

Luge. Throughout the 2000–01 luge season, Italy's Armin Zöggeler (*see* BIOGRAPHIES) controlled the men's singles action, winning his third men's singles luge world championship title and the overall World Cup title. Georg Hackl of Germany finished second in both the world championships and the World Cup standings. Austrian Marcus Prock finished third in the World Cup.

In women's singles, Germany grabbed the top two positions in the overall World Cup standings with their duo of Silke Kraushaar and Sylke Otto. Otto also successfully defended her world championship title, while Kraushaar secured second place. Austria's Angelika Neuner finished third in the World Cup.

André Florschütz and Torsten Wustlich of Germany captured the doubles title at the 35th luge world championships. Fellow Germans Steffen Skel and Steffen Wöller raced to a silver-medal finish. Markus Schiegl and Tobias Schiegl of Austria finished in the bronze-medal position—only 0.268 sec back. In the overall World Cup standings, Germany swept the top three positions, led by Skel and Wöller. Florschütz and Wustlich took second, while Patric Leitner and Alexander Resch finished third.

In the team competition of the world championships, Germany I, comprising Hackl, Kraushaar, and the duo of Leitner and Resch, raced to the gold medal. Germany II, consisting of Karsten Albert, Otto, and the pair of Skel and Wöller, won the silver. The U.S., which came in third, captured its first non-Olympic team medal. The American team comprised Tony Benshoof, Becky Wilczak, and the duo of Mark Grimmette and Brian Martin.   (JULIE URBANSKY)

BOWLING

World Tenpins. In June 2001 the Fédération Internationale des Quilleurs (FIQ), the world governing body for the sport of tenpin bowling, reported at its biennial congress, held in Ålborg, Den., that 123 national member federations, with close to 15 million individual members, were affiliated with the FIQ. Traditionally, the FIQ was formed by three geographic zones—American, Asian, and European. The forming of a new African zone was under consideration, however, because the number of tenpin countries on that continent had reached 15.

In October 2000, at the beginning of the 2000–01 season, the 36th AMF Bowling World Cup took place in Lisbon. The field included 67 female and 88 male national qualifiers from as many countries. Mel Isaac of Wales and Tomas Leandersson of Sweden won the women's and men's titles, respectively.

The world youth championships, held in Santo Domingo, Dom.Rep., ended on Nov. 4, 2000. The American team took home 12 of the 21 medals awarded (5 gold, 5 silver, and 2 bronze). Kelly Kulick of the U.S. won the girls' singles and all-events titles, finished second to teammate Diandra Hyman in the masters, and teamed with Hyman to take silver behind England in the doubles. South Korea's Kim Jae Hoon captured gold in the boys' singles, all-events, and doubles (with partner Kong Sun Jong).

After two postponements the FIQ's 24 top-ranked men and women gathered in Abu Dhabi, U.A.E., in mid-April 2001 to determine the world's best amateur bowlers. Jesmine Ho of Singapore and Sunny Hui of Hong Kong won the women's and men's titles, respectively. At the European championships in June,

Finland captured the most medals (12), while England won the most gold (5). Top bowlers Kirsten Penny of England and Mika Luoto of Finland each won four golds and a bronze. Women competitors broke 14 tournament records, while the men broke 9.

In 2001, for the first time, the national coaches elected an International Bowler of the Year—Clara Juliana Guerrero of Colombia.   (YRJÖ SARAHETE)

U.S. Tenpins. In July 2001 the new owners of the Professional Bowlers Association (PBA) presented a 20-tournament schedule for the 2001–02 season, with all of the events to be carried on ESPN cable television as part of a three-year contract. In March 2000 the troubled PBA had been purchased by a trio of former computer software executives, Chris Peters, Mike Slade, and Rob Glaser. In the process the nonprofit PBA was converted into a for-profit corporation.

ESPN guaranteed a set time for the 10-tournament first half of the season, to be broadcast on Tuesday evenings from September to December with only a few variations. The second half of the season would be shown on Sunday afternoons, beginning on Jan. 6, 2002, and concluding with the "Battle of Little Creek" in Norfolk, Va., on March 17. The finals of the PBA world championship, with a top prize of $120,000, would be televised March 3.

To attract bowlers who had withdrawn from competition because of insufficient incentive, the PBA boosted the prize fund from $1.8 million in 2000–01 to approximately $4 million in 2001–02. Ian Hamilton, the new PBA commissioner, who previously had directed the Nike global tennis program for 14 years, said that the TV finals of the PBA tournaments would have a completely different look "without affecting the integrity of the sport." Spectators would be seated on both sides of the tournament lanes and would be encouraged to participate vocally at all times. An indefinite number of summer events would be scheduled.

During the year a joint task force began to explore the feasibility of combining five American governing bodies—the men's American Bowling Congress, the Women's International Bowling Congress, the Young American Bowling Alliance, Bowling, Inc., and USA Bowling—into one single-membership organization for amateur bowling.

In August Earl Anthony, the PBA's most prolific champion and six-time Player of the Year, died at age 63. (*See* OBITUARIES.)   (JOHN J. ARCHIBALD)

Matthew Stockman/Allsport
Jean Racine and Jennifer Davidson of the U.S. compete in the women's bobsled event at the Park City (Utah) World Cup in February.

BOXING

In 2001 Lennox Lewis (U.K.) brought a measure of continuity to a year filled with unexpected results when he regained the World Boxing Council (WBC) and International Boxing Federation (IBF) heavyweight titles by knocking out Hasim Rahman (U.S.) in the fourth round of their November 17 rematch in Las Vegas, Nev. Lewis ended the fight with a single right hand to the jaw that floored Rahman for the 10 count. The unheralded Rahman had sprung a stunning upset on April 22, knocking out Lewis in the fifth round of a bout held in Johannesburg, S.Af., to win the WBC and IBF belts.

John Ruiz (U.S.) became the first boxer of Latino heritage to win a heavyweight title when he annexed the World Boxing Association (WBA) title with a 12-round decision over Evander Holyfield (U.S.) on March 3 in Las Vegas. A rematch in Mashantucket, Conn., on December 17 ended in a draw. Former heavyweight champion Mike Tyson (U.S.) fought only once during the year, scoring a seventh-round knockout of Brian Nielsen (Den.) on October 13 in Copenhagen. The victory ensured Tyson a title bout in 2002.

In another stunning upset, Bernard Hopkins (U.S.) became the first unified middleweight champion in 14 years when he knocked out Félix Trinidad (P.R.) in the 12th round on September 29 in front of a capacity crowd of more than 19,000 fans at Madison Square Garden in New York City. The match was the final bout in a middleweight championship tournament promoted by Don King. In the first bout of the tournament, IBF middleweight champion Hopkins added the WBC title by winning a 12-round decision over Keith Holmes (U.S.) on April 14 at Madison Square Garden. In the next round of the tournament, Trinidad won the WBA middleweight title with a fifth-round knockout of William Joppy (U.S.) on May 12 at the Garden. Trinidad was heavily favoured to win the finale, but the bout was dominated by Hopkins, who gave one of the finest performances in middleweight history. Approximately 475,000 households purchased the Hopkins-Trinidad television pay-per-view, making it the largest pay-per-view sale of the year. It was Trinidad's first loss in 41 professional bouts and left Hopkins in possession of all three major middleweight titles—IBF, WBA, and WBC.

Undisputed light heavyweight champion Roy Jones, Jr. (U.S.), defended his WBA, WBC, and IBF titles twice in 2001.

Bernard Hopkins of the U.S. knocks down Félix Trinidad of Puerto Rico en route to unifying the middleweight titles on September 29.

Jones scored a 10th-round knockout of Derrick Harmon (U.S.) on February 24 in Tampa, Fla., then tallied a 12-round decision over Julio Gonzalez (U.S.) on July 28 in Los Angeles. Despite these two relatively easy victories, Jones lost prestige owing to the mediocre quality of his challengers.

Box-office attraction Oscar de la Hoya (U.S.), who had been without a world title since June 17, 2000, when he lost the WBC welterweight title to Shane Mosley (U.S.), moved up to the super welterweight (junior middleweight) class, where he won the WBC title with a 12-round decision over Francisco Castillejo (Spain) on June 23 in Las Vegas. The undefeated Mosley enhanced his standing as one of the sport's finest practitioners by making two defenses of the WBC welterweight title. Mosley scored a fifth-round knockout of Shannon Taylor (Australia) on March 10 in Las Vegas, then followed with a third-round knockout of Adrian Stone (U.K.) on July 21 in Las Vegas.

The first major upset of the year came on April 7 when featherweight Marco Antonio Barrera (Mex.) won a 12-round decision over previously undefeated Naseem Hamed (U.K.) in Las Vegas. Hamed, known for his outspoken personality and extravagant ring entrances, was exposed as a one-dimensional fighter by

Barrera's clever boxing and accurate punching. The bout drew 12,847 live spectators, and close to 250,000 homes purchased the pay-per-view program, which made it the largest-grossing featherweight bout in history. Barrera followed up with a sixth-round knockout of Enrique Sánchez (Mex.) on September 8 in Reno, Nev., to further establish his credentials as the world's foremost featherweight.

The theme of unification and upsets continued when WBA/WBC 140-lb titleholder Kostya Tszyu (Australia) became the first undisputed junior welterweight champion since Nicolino Locche, in 1968, by stopping favoured IBF champion Zab Judah (U.S.) in the second round of a bout held on November 3 in Las Vegas. After the fight was halted, an enraged Judah shoved his glove under referee Jay Nady's chin and threw a stool. In a disciplinary action, the Nevada State Athletic Commission suspended Judah's boxing license for six months and fined him $75,000.

In a bizarre match between the offspring of two famous rivals, Laila Ali (U.S.), the daughter of former heavyweight champion Muhammad Ali, won a spirited eight-round decision over Jacqui Frazier-Lyde (U.S.), the daughter of former heavyweight champion, Joe Frazier, on June 8 in Verona, N.Y. Although

Timothy A. Clary/AFP Worldwide

panned by the media beforehand, the pay-per-view event was sold to approximately 100,000 households, which made the surprisingly entertaining contest the richest women's boxing match in history.

(NIGEL COLLINS)

CHESS

The chess world settled down to a threefold division of influence in 2001—Vladimir Kramnik was considered world champion by many after his match victory over fellow Russian Garry Kasparov, while Viswanathan Anand was the official world champion, authorized by the world ruling body Fédération Internationale des Échecs after the Indian was successful in the knockout contest organized by FIDE in New Delhi and Tehran in late 2000. Meanwhile, there was Kasparov himself, still recognized by many as the strongest player in the world and certainly the undisputed leader of the international rating list.

Kasparov's aspirations for a return match against Kramnik foundered early in the year when the contractual obligations of the two players to the Brain Games Network private company came to an end. BGN planned instead an eight-game match between Kramnik and the Fritz computer program to be held in Bahrain in October. After the Sep-

Judit Polgar of Hungary contemplates a move in her match against Vladimir Kramnik of Russia during the City of Dos Hermanas (Spain) chess tournament in April.

Emilio Morenatti/AFP Worldwide

tember 11 terrorist attacks in the U.S., the match was postponed until 2002.

Tension between the players on the international circuit and FIDE intensified after the introduction of a new faster time limit for the top tournaments. "Classical chess" had traditionally been played at the rate of 40 moves in two and a half hours, a rate introduced by José Raúl Capablanca in the 1920s. This had given way in the 1990s to the slightly quicker rate of 40 moves in two hours, then 20 moves in an hour plus half an hour to finish the game. Such standard rates naturally involved playing only one game a day, so that top tournaments and matches lasted several weeks or even longer.

The initial proposal by FIDE was for the 2001 world championship cycle to be run at the rate of 40 moves in 40 minutes plus 20 minutes to finish or, with the new digital clocks, at 40/40 and a 30-second bonus for every move made. This was eased somewhat in the face of protests, but those events that had been run on this modified basis had been replete with complaints by the players that the standard of the games was very disappointing. Too many games had had farcical finishes for true lovers of chess to be satisfied with the innovation.

It was assumed that the long-term plan was to have two games a day and generally reduce the costs of contests. FIDE argued that shorter games would stand a better chance of gaining television coverage. Attempts continued to have chess admitted to the Olympic Games, with the first step being the admission of chess as an exhibition sport in the 2002 Winter Olympics.

Another bone of contention arose between FIDE and traditional organizers in Western Europe when the former tried to incorporate their events in a new World Chess Grand Prix. The "Big Three" of the tournament circuit—Wijk aan Zee, Neth.; Linares, Spain; and Dortmund, Ger.—rejected the overtures and in a joint statement indicated their intention to remain independent and preserve the character of their events. This rebuff was met by threats of FIDE's running parallel spoiler contests at the usual times in the calendar for the traditional events.

At the Wijk aan Zee event, held January 13–28, the top scores were Kasparov (9 points out of 13), Anand (8.5), Kramnik and Vasily Ivanchuk of Ukraine (both 8), and Michael Adams of England, Russian Aleksandr Morozevich, and Aleksey Shirov representing Spain (all 7.5). At the Linares tournament, which took

In a rapid-play tournament at Zürich, Switz., in late April 2001, Garry Kasparov showed up well. Here is a position in which he defeated the great veteran Viktor Korchnoi. Korchnoi, Black, appears to have won the loose knight at g6, but Kasparov continued: 1 Rf3+ Kxg6 (or 1 . . . Kg8 2 Ne7+ and 3 Nxc8) 2 Bd3+ Kh5 3 Rh3+ Kg4 4 f3+ Kf4 5 Kf2 g4 6 g3+ and Black resigned in view of 6 . . . Kg5 7 f4 mate.

place from February 23 to March 6, Kasparov (7.5 out of 10) scored an overwhelming victory in a double-round contest, followed by a unique tie for second-to-last place between Judit Polgar of Hungary, Anatoly Karpov of Russia, Shirov, Peter Leko of Hungary, and the new teenage Russian star Aleksandr Grischuk (all 4.5). The Dortmund Sparkassen Chess Meeting, on July 12–22, was also a double rounder and ended with Kramnik and Veselin Topalov of Bulgaria tied at 6.5 out of 10, followed by Leko (5.5), Morozevich (5), Adams (3.5), and Anand (3).

Anand's failure to win a single game and his lowly placing somewhat undermined the credibility of his FIDE title. The other significant result was Kasparov's first place at the six-man tournament at Astana, Kazakhstan, to celebrate the 10th anniversary of the independence of that Central Asian country. This was played as yet another double rounder and was won by Kasparov (7 points out of 10), followed by Kramnik (6.5), Boris Gelfand of Israel (5.5), Shirov and Morozevich (both 4.5), and Darmen Sadvakasov of Kazakhstan (2).

Kasparov also played a short match at odds in London, conceding two pawns to the English businessman Terry Chapman in a reversion to 19th-century practice. The Russian won 2.5–1.5. A sign of the times came in mid-March in Seattle, Wash., when China beat the U.S. 21–19 in a four-round, 10-board match, with the Chinese junior players clinching the victory.

The Najdorf Memorial was held in Buenos Aires, Arg., on September 4–13. For the first time in a top tournament, two female players were invited: the women's world champion, Xie Jun of China, and Polgar, a former child prodigy long considered the strongest woman player in the world. Both finished mid-table with 4.5 points out of 9 in the 10-player contest, which was won by Karpov (6.5). He had recently celebrated his 50th birthday, and the event marked his comeback to the world elite. Even more remarkable was the age range in the joint second-place finishers with 6 points—70-year-old Viktor Korchnoi of Switzerland and 14-year-old Teimur Radjabov of Azerbaijan, who thereby gave notice that he could be the world's best player within the next few years.

The chess world lost two significant figures late in the year. On November 12 Anthony John ("Tony") Miles died in his native Birmingham, Eng., at age 46, two years after being diagnosed with diabetes. Miles became the first English grandmaster at over the board play in 1976, after winning the junior world championship in 1974. His 10-year run of success against top players such as Karpov helped England to rise from a mediocre position in the international chess rankings to challenge the mighty Soviet Union. John W. ("Jack") Collins, a respected American chess teacher whose students had included former world champion Bobby Fischer, died on December 2 at age 89.

(BERNARD CAFFERTY)

CONTRACT BRIDGE

The two major 2001 world championships for contract bridge, the Bermuda Bowl and, for women, the Venice Cup, were originally scheduled to be played in Bali, Indonesia. Following the September 11 attacks in the United States, however, the tournaments were transferred to Paris. In the Bermuda Bowl, contested October 21 through November 3, the final was a dramatic match between Norway, which had defeated cofavourite Italy in the semifinals, and USA-2; cofavourite USA-1 had lost to Italy in the quarterfinals. With 16 deals remaining, Norway led by two points. In the final session Norway bid a small slam that went down only when both the opposing cards were distributed unfavourably and Peter Weichsel found the killing trump lead. Consequently, USA-2 won 286–265. An outstanding feature of the competition was that Rose Meltzer became the first woman to play

on a victorious Bermuda Bowl team. The USA-2 team consisted of Meltzer–Kyle Larsen, Chip Martel– Lew Stansby, and Alan Sontag–Peter Weichsel, with Jan Martel the nonplaying captain.

The final of the Venice Cup was even more closely contested than the Bermuda Bowl. After trailing by 46.5 points with 16 deals remaining, Germany defeated France 218–215.5. The winning

```
                North
                ♠ 10 9
                ♥ A 9 5 2
                ♦ K Q 9 7 2
                ♣ 9 8
West                        East
♠ K Q 2                     ♠ 7 5
♥ 7 4 3                     ♥ K Q J 10 6
♦ 8 3                       ♦ J 10 6
♣ A Q 6 5 4                 ♣ J 10 3
                South
                ♠ A J 8 6 4 3
                ♥ 8
                ♦ A 5 4
                ♣ K 7 2
```

Dealer: South
Vulnerable: North-South

South	West	North	East
Von Seida	Verhees	Eskes	Jansma
1 ♠	Pass	1NT	Pass
2 ♠	Pass	3 ♠	Pass
4 ♠	Pass	Pass	Pass

Opening lead: ♥7

West, Louk Verhees from The Netherlands, opened with a heart. South called for dummy's ace, and East signaled with the king to show his king-queen-jack sequence. South ran dummy's ♠10 to West's queen. What did Verhees lead next? (Erik Kirchhoff found the same play.)

For his raise to game, South was marked with the ♦A and ♣K. And as his two-spade rebid guaranteed at least a six-card suit, declarer was threatening to score 10 tricks via four spades, one heart, and five diamonds. It was tempting to lead another heart, expecting East to win the trick and to shift to a club through declarer's king. Verhees, however, judged that to accept his partner's game-invitational raise with a minimum point count, South was more likely to have 6=1=3=3 distribution than 6=2=3=2 or 6=2=2=3. And if that was true, there was only one hope: that his partner had the ♣J. Consequently, there was only one correct card to lead: the ♣Q.

What could South do after winning with the ♣K? If he returned a low club, East would win and push through a trump. If South cashed the ♠A and tried to get a discard on the fourth round of diamonds, West would ruff the third diamond, cash the ♣A, and lead a low club to his partner's jack. Similarly, if South played a diamond to dummy and took another spade finesse, Verhees would win, take the ♣A, and play another club. In all cases, the defense wins two spades and two clubs. Yes, a shift to a low club works here, but not if declarer has ♣K-10-x. If that is the situation, declarer wins East's ♣J with his king and continues with the ♣10, forcing West to win the trick. Then South either ruffs his last club in the dummy (and loses only two spades and one club) or holds his trump losers to one (if West returns a spade to stop that club ruff).

players were Sabine Auken–Daniela von Arnim and Pony Nehmert–Andrea Rauscheid, with Christoph Kemmer the nonplaying captain. (Katrin Farwig and Barbara Hackett were also on the team but did not play in the final round.)

From July 6 to 8 the world junior pairs tournament took place in Stargard Szczecinski, Pol. The winners were Andreas Gloyer and Martin Schifko of Austria with a score of 15,132 points. Finishing second was the Dutch pair of Sjoert Brink and Bas Drijver with a score of 14,821. Fabio Lo Presti and Francesco Mazzadi of Italy placed third with 14,266. Gloyer completed an impressive double, having won in 1999 with Bernd Saurer.

The world youth team championship was contested in Mangaratiba, Braz., August 6–15. In the final USA-1 defeated Israel 262–156. The USA-1 team consisted of Brad Campbell, Joe Grue, John Hurd, John Kranyak, Kent Mignocchi, and Joel Wooldridge, with Robert Rosen as nonplaying captain and Dennis McGarry as coach. To qualify for both of these tournaments, a player had to be born after Dec. 31, 1974. (PHILLIP ALDER)

CRICKET

On Feb. 25, 2001, cricket lost its most famous player. Sir Don Bradman, who was recognized throughout the world as the supreme batsman in the game, died at the age of 92, and Australia mourned. Had Bradman not been out for 0 in the very last of his 80 Test innings, he might have stretched his final average of 99.94 beyond 100. (See OBITUARIES.)

The morning following the news, the Australian team, led by Steve Waugh, stood to observe a minute's silence before the first Test against India in Mumbai (Bombay). The match proved to be the last in a record-breaking sequence of 16 straight Australian victories stretching back almost two years. Australia's only series defeat of the 2000–01 season came after a remarkable turnaround in the second Test in Kolkata (Calcutta), in which V.V.S. Laxman's innings of 281 allowed the home team to become only the third in Test history to win after following on its first innings. The decisive Test in Chennai (Madras) was as dramatic a game of cricket as any in the year as India scrambled home to victory by two wickets. The young Indian off spinner Harbhajan Singh took 15 wickets in the match and 32 in the series, including a hat trick.

The standard of Australia's cricket helped to divert attention away from the issue of match fixing, which continued to dog the sport. The dismissed Pakistan coach, Javed Miandad, openly hinted that his players had fixed matches during the one-day series against New Zealand, and the Pakistan Cricket Board appointed a judge to look into allegations that Pakistan fixed a defeat against Bangladesh in the 1999 World Cup. An interim report of the independent commission chaired by Sir Paul Condon, the former chief commissioner of the Metropolitan Police in London and the recently appointed head of the International Cricket Council's Anti-Corruption Unit, highlighted the difficulty in proving allegations against individuals and teams. The report suggested that the proliferation of one-day internationals, particularly in neutral venues such as Ash-Shariqah, U.A.E., had encouraged a more relaxed attitude to betting and match fixing. It also touched on possible links to organized crime and referred to a kidnapping and a murder linked to match fixing. The report was widely criticized for lacking proper jurisdiction or authority and for not being thorough enough in interviewing players accused of taking money from bookmakers. The commission's recommendations included more stringent contracts for players, better security (including fewer mobile phones in dressing rooms), and wider powers for the Anti-Corruption Unit. In October a court in South Africa upheld the lifetime ban imposed on Wessel Johannes ("Hansie") Cronje, the former South African captain, whose admission that he had taken

At the Oval in London on August 24, Steve Waugh bats for the Australian team in a Test match against England.

William West/AFP Worldwide

money from an Indian bookmaker in April 2000 initially pitched the game into crisis.

England won its Test series in both Pakistan and Sri Lanka, showing a resilience and organization under captain Nasser Hussain that augured well for the Ashes against Australia, cricket's oldest and most prestigious rivalry. Australia once again proved too strong, however, as leg spinner Shane Warne recovered his form and passed 400 career Test wickets during the five-Test series and Glenn McGrath proved to be an equally potent bowler. The pattern was set in the opening Test at Edgbaston, Birmingham, Eng., when England was bowled out twice cheaply, while Waugh, Damien Martyn, and Adam Gilchrist all made centuries for Australia. Only three times in 10 innings did England's batsmen score more than 300; four times in the first six innings they were bowled out for less than 200. England salvaged some vestige of pride in the fourth Test when, with the Ashes already lost once again, Mark Butcher scored an unbeaten 173 in the fourth innings to lead England to an unlikely target (315). Waugh, who was denied the right to take home the original 19th-century Ashes urn by the authorities at Lord's cricket ground in London, unsuccessfully tried to burn a bail so that the Australians could return home with an urn containing some ashes.

Bangladesh became the 10th Test-playing nation in November 2000, marking its debut with a defeat to India. Aminul Islam made the country's first Test century. Zimbabwe produced two record-breaking batsmen in a busy year. Just 11 days before his 18th birthday, Hamilton Masakadza became the youngest debutant to score a Test century—119 against the West Indies in Harare, Zimb. Andrew Flower totaled 1,324 runs for the year, including a double century, three centuries, and seven 50s in 15 innings. Masakadza's record was later beaten by Mohammad Ashraful of Bangladesh, who scored 114 at the age of 17 years and 63 days against Sri Lanka in Colombo.

The West Indies endured a depressing year, losing 5–0 to Australia and 2–1 to South Africa. Courtney Walsh, the great West Indian fast bowler, bowed out on his home ground in Jamaica, finishing with a record 519 Test wickets in his career. Former England captain Michael Atherton also retired from first-class cricket.

Pressure continued to grow for cricket to use more television technology to aid

in making decisions on the field. Pakistan's defeat of England at Old Trafford, Manchester, Eng., was marred by the subsequent discovery that at least three of England's wickets had fallen to no balls shown clearly by TV. Television replays were used only for run-outs, but it was argued that they could also be used by umpires to judge catches close to the wicket or even lbws.

In domestic cricket, Yorkshire won the county championship in England for the first time in 33 years, and Somerset captured the one-day C&G Cup. Other four-day champions were Western Province (South Africa), Queensland (Australia), and Wellington (New Zealand). KwaZulu/Natal in South Africa and New South Wales in Australia won one-day trophies, and the Western Warriors from Perth, Australia, won the inaugural Champions Cup for the one-day champions of the Southern Hemisphere. New Zealand triumphed in the women's World Cup, beating Australia by four runs in the final.

(ANDREW LONGMORE)

CURLING

Peter Lindholm of Sweden finally regained his international curling crown in 2001 after having made it to the men's final in four of the past five world championships. Playing in Lausanne, Switz., the 1997 world champion and 1989 world junior winner defeated Swiss skip Andreas Schwaller 6–3 in the men's final on April 8. Lindholm had finished second at the worlds in 2000 and 1998. The silver medal for Schwaller was significant in that it qualified Switzerland for the 2002 Winter Olympic Games in Salt Lake City, Utah. Norway finished third in the men's competition, pushing fourth-place Canada out of the men's medals for only the fifth time in 30 years at the worlds. Rounding out the top 10 were Finland, France, Germany, the U.S., New Zealand, and Denmark.

Colleen Jones of Halifax, N.S., earned Canada its second consecutive women's world title by defeating Anette Norberg of Sweden 5–2 in the final. Jones had first made it to the worlds in 1982 and returned in 1999, finishing fifth in both those attempts. Denmark won the bronze medal by defeating Scotland. The other women's finishers, in order, were Germany, the U.S., Japan, Norway, Russia, and Switzerland.

In June Finland announced it had pulled its women's curling entry from the 2002 Olympics because of the country's poor international results. Finnish women failed to qualify for either the 2000 or 2001 world championships but still held the 10th Olympic qualifying berth. Finland was to be replaced on the women's side in Salt Lake City by Russia, which had qualified 11th after a ninth-place finish in Lausanne—the country's first appearance at the world curling championships.

The 2001 world junior curling championships took place in March at the 2002 Olympic curling venue in Ogden, Utah. Brad Gushue of Canada defeated Casper Bossen of Denmark for the men's championship, while the U.S. defeated Scotland for the bronze. The women's junior title was won by Canada's Suzanne Gaudet, who defeated Matilda Mattsson of Sweden in the final. Switzerland won bronze, relegating Japan to fourth place.   (BRUCE CHEADLE)

CYCLING

In 2001 American rider Lance Armstrong sealed his place in cycling history when he became the fifth man to win the Tour de France, the sport's premier event, in at least three successive years, joining Louison Bobet (1953–55), Jacques Anquetil (1961–64), Eddy Merckx (1969–72), and Miguel Indurain (1991–95). The Texan finished 6 min 44 sec ahead of Germany's Jan Ullrich after 3,454 km (about 2,146 mi) of racing, establishing his superiority with a commanding display of strength on the mountain stages. Armstrong won successive road-race and time-trial legs in the Alps before taking the overall lead for the first time three days later in the Pyrenees. A fourth win followed in the last time-trial stage, two days before the event finished in Paris. Erik Zabel of Germany won the points competition, based on daily finishing positions over the 20 stages and intermediate sprints, for a record sixth time.

The sport's governing body, the Union Cycliste Internationale (UCI), in April introduced a new "health check" in the quest to eradicate the use of the human hormone erythropoietin (EPO). The UCI required any rider whose blood test showed a hematocrit level—the functional level of red blood cells as a percentage of total blood plasma—above the considered-safe level of 50% to submit to a urine test. Italy's Fabiano Fontanelli was the first rider to be excluded from a race, the Tour of Flanders on April 8, for an overly high hematocrit reading and to then take a urine test, which did not reveal any trace of EPO.

Riding in the Pyrenees, American cyclist Lance Armstrong leads the pack during the 14th stage of the Tour de France on July 22.

Pascal Rondeau/Allsport

At the Tour of Italy (Giro d'Italia), second in importance to the Tour de France, police and customs officials mounted raids on hotels where riders were staying after the June 6 stage in San Remo. The riders refused to race the following day, in protest against their treatment, which led to the cancellation of stage 18 between Imperia and San Anna di Vinadio. Italy's Dario Frigo, who was in second place overall, was dismissed by his team and left the race after doping products were found in his room. After an analysis of substances taken away in the raid, 86 people, including doctors and team managers, were later placed under investigation.

The world track championships were held at the indoor Sportpaleis velodrome in Antwerp, Belg., in September. Arnaud Tournant of France won the individual kilometre time trial for the fourth successive year and gained gold medals in the individual sprint and three-man-team Olympic sprint. Nancy Contreras Reyes won Mexico's first-ever senior world title, in the women's 500-m time trial. In October Tournant became the first rider to beat one minute for a standing-start kilometre, covering the distance in 58.875 sec with an average speed of 61.146 km/h (about 38 mph) on the La Paz, Bol., track, which had an altitude of 3,417 m (11,211 ft).   (JOHN R. WILKINSON)

EQUESTRIAN SPORTS

Thoroughbred Racing. *United States.* The thoroughbred breeding industry in the United States was dealt a severe setback in the spring of 2001 when Kentucky farms were ravaged with an outbreak of mare reproductive loss syndrome. Several thousand late-term foals and early-term fetuses, including thoroughbreds and other equine breeds, were lost. Long-term damage to the thoroughbred breeding industry was estimated at about $350 million. Speculation among veterinarians and other equine experts was that Eastern tent caterpillars had transferred cyanide from wild black cherry trees to grass, which was then ingested by the pregnant mares. Unusual spring weather conditions were thought to have caused a high production of cyanogenic material by the trees, which were common in central Kentucky.

Louisiana Downs in Bossier City, La., received permission from the state gaming board on March 19 to open an on-track casino. Another casino was planned at Delta Downs in Vinton, La. Other states that had previously legalized on-track casinos included West Virginia, Iowa, Delaware, New Mexico, and Minnesota. In October the New York legislature voted overwhelmingly to allow video lottery terminals (slot machines) at two of the state's thorough-bred tracks, Aqueduct and Finger Lakes, as well as at three of the state's harness tracks.

California became the 12th state to allow account wagering on horse racing when Gov. Gray Davis signed a bill approving it on August 13. Attached to the bill was a provision that would allow grooms, exercise riders, and hot walkers to unionize. Earlier that month, New York City Mayor Rudy Giuliani had awarded the right to buy a majority interest in the New York City Off-Track Betting Corp. to a group led by Magna Entertainment Corp. The group was selected over the New York Racing Association.

The National Thoroughbred Racing Association (NTRA) and Breeders' Cup Ltd., which had merged in 2000, announced on June 26 that the title World Thoroughbred Championships would be a permanent addition to the name of the Breeders' Cup. It was also announced that the Bessemer Trust, one of the country's leading investment banking companies, had signed on as title sponsor of the Breeders' Cup Juvenile and a new series for two-year-olds on the CNBC financial television network.

Racetracks across the country ceased operation for at least a day after the September 11 terrorist attacks, while Belmont Park in Elmont, N.Y., and the Meadowlands in East Rutherford, N.J. (the track closest to the New York City attack site), shut down for a week. The Breeders' Cup races, however, went on as planned at Belmont on October 27. Jockeys, trainers, and owners who participated in the event donated $2,760,000 of the money they earned to the New York Heroes Fund, which was established by the NTRA.

Racetrack attrition continued with the closing and planned demolition of historic Garden State Park in Cherry Hill, N.J. Opened in 1942, it was destroyed by fire in April 1977 and reopened as "the racetrack of the 21st Century" eight years later. The site was to be redeveloped into a residential and commercial complex.

The Racing Network (TRN) ceased operation abruptly on July 30, citing a lack of an adequate number of subscribers. TRN was a 24-hour multichannel satellite-based network that carried horse and dog races on a subscription basis.

Monarchos, who captured the 2001 Kentucky Derby, was sidelined in July when a hairline fracture was discovered in his right knee. He was expected to re-

sume his racing career as a four-year-old. Point Given, winner of the Preakness and Belmont stakes, was retired on August 31 with a strained tendon in his left front leg. Tiznow, the reigning Horse of the Year and three-year-old colt champion, became the first two-time Breeders' Cup Classic winner by successfully defending his title in the $4 million, 1¼-mi event. Battling between horses, he surged in the final strides to defeat Sakhee by a nose following a stretchlong battle.

Pat Day, age 47, became only the third jockey in American racing history to win 8,000 races; his landmark victory came on May 31. Only Laffit Pincay, Jr., still active with more than 9,100 career wins, and the retired Bill Shoemaker (8,833) had more victories. Russell Baze reached career win number 7,500 on September 15, and Chris McCarron captured his 7,000th victory on April 28. Jerry D. Bailey became the first jockey in history to surpass $20 million in purse earnings in a single year.

Earlie Fires, the leading apprentice jockey in the United States in 1965 and still active with more than 6,150 victories, and West Coast-based trainer Richard Mandella were inducted into the Racing Hall of Fame on August 6. Also entering the Hall was the 1994 Horse of the Year, Holy Bull.

Hall of Famer Horace Allyn ("Jimmy") Jones, trainer of 1948 Triple Crown

Point Given, ridden by Gary Stevens, crosses the finish line in first place to win the Preakness Stakes on May 19.

Matthew Stockman/Allsport

champion Citation and 53 other stakes winners and the son of the great trainer Ben Jones, died at age 94 on September 2. Affirmed, America's 11th and most recent Triple Crown champion, was euthanized at age 26 on January 12. Nureyev, one of thoroughbred racing's most successful sires, died on October 29 at age 24.   (JOHN G. BROKOPP)

Thoroughbred Racing. *International.* Two stables—the Ireland-based racing division of Coolmore Stud, the world's largest owners of stallions, and Godolphin, which deployed the pick of the horses owned by the Maktoum family—divided the European 2000–01 thoroughbred racing season between them. Godolphin, which spent the months from late October to late April in Dubayy, U.A.E., before returning to Newmarket in England, appeared to hold an advantage after a rainy winter and spring. Their luck ran out, however. Dubai Millennium, winner of the 2000 Dubayy World Cup and Godolphin's best-ever horse, died of grass sickness on April 29, halfway through his first season at stud, and their three-year-olds were disappointing. Noverre, Godolphin's only classic winner, was disqualified two months after his victory in the French Poule d'Essai des Poulains because he tested positive for methylprednisolone.

Aidan O'Brien, who trained the Coolmore horses, dominated the classics and ended the season with 23 Group 1 victories in Europe, including 7 of the 15 English, French, or Irish classics. Galileo, who easily won the Epsom and Irish Derbys, was his best horse. The three-year-old colt went on to defeat Godolphin's Fantastic Light in the King George VI and Queen Elizabeth Diamond Stakes. The Godolphin five-year-old turned the tables in the Irish Champion Stakes, however; Fantastic Light was too good for Galileo in the two-furlong-shorter race and held on by a head. Two-year-old racing also was dominated by O'Brien, whose horses won 9 of the 10 European Group 1 races open to juvenile colts. O'Brien became the first British champion trainer since 1977 to be based abroad.

Among four- and five-year-old horses, the pendulum swung to Godolphin. Sakhee had won the Juddmonte International by seven lengths 18 days before the Irish Champion Stakes, and he went on to win the Prix de l'Arc de Triomphe in Paris by six lengths. Kutub followed a hat trick of Group 1 victories in Germany and Italy by winning the Singapore Gold Cup. Slickly was a

Group 1 winner in France and Italy. Hatha Anna gave the stable its first success in Australia in the Group 2 Queen Elizabeth II Stakes, while Give the Slip led until the final 50 yards of the Melbourne Cup before losing to Ethereal by three-quarters of a length.

Irish prize money rose by 18% in 2000 and was projected to increase again in 2001 with government help. The British government attempted similar help by abolishing the off-course betting tax (on-course betting had been tax-free since 1987) and by replacing the betting levy. Negotiations on a new system to contribute extra finance proved difficult, however, and were nowhere near a solution at the end of the season.

Betting turnover increased in Great Britain, Ireland, and France, but French racing had other problems. It had allowed most Group race prizes to fall behind British ones, while a protest by pari-mutuel workers caused the postponement of the Grand Prix de Paris meeting. It was run two days later but without betting. André Fabre was the champion trainer in France for the 15th consecutive year, helped by two Group 1 disqualifications from each of which Vahorimix was the beneficiary. Italy enjoyed a better season, with prizes the highest since 1997.

German racing, which suffered from low betting turnover and static prize money, had a champion horse in Silvano, which won the Singapore Cup in March, the Queen Elizabeth II Cup in Hong Kong in April, and the Arlington Million in the U.S. in August. Silvano also was placed in other rich prizes in Dubayy, the U.S., and Australia. He was third to the Japanese-trained Stay Gold in the Dubayy Sheema Classic, on a race day that challenged the claim of the U.S.-based Breeders' Cup to be the "World Thoroughbred Championships."

Captain Steve from the U.S. beat rivals from Japan and France in the 2001 Dubayy World Cup, while Jim and Tonic, from France, bested Fairy King Prawn from Hong Kong and Sunline from New Zealand in a thrilling finish to the Dubayy Duty Free. Caller One in the Dubayy Golden Shaheen was another American winner at the most international meeting to date.

Three horses divided the 2001 Canadian Triple Crown. Dancethruthedawn, whose dam, Dance Smartly, had won the series in 1991, defeated Win City by half a length in the Queen's Plate Stakes in June, then lost to her rival by the same distance in the Prince of Wales Stakes in July. Both horses skipped the third

jewel, the Breeders' Stakes, which was won easily by Sweetest Thing.

Ethereal, who gave New Zealand-bred horses their 12th Melbourne Cup win in 20 years, earlier had triumphed in the Caulfield Cup. The four-year-old mare was the 11th horse to complete the double and the first Melbourne Cup winner to be trained by a woman, Sheila Laxon. Northerly won the Cox Plate just ahead of Sunline, with Silvano fourth.

(ROBERT W. CARTER)

Harness Racing. Two European trotters went to North America in 2001 and in just four races beat the U.S.'s best and took more than a million dollars back to the continent.

The Italian sensation Varenne won the $1 million Breeders Crown at the Meadowlands in New Jersey on July 28. Driver Giampaolo Minnucci raced his champion with the utmost confidence, reaching the wire $4^{1}/2$ lengths ahead of his closest pursuer. Verenne's time of $1:51^{1}/5$ was the fastest race-mile ever trotted. Earlier in the 2001 season the six-year-old trotter had won the Prix d'Amerique in France, the Lotteria in his native Italy, and the Elitlopp in Sweden. No horse had swept those events in a single year in many decades. Varenne returned to Europe after winning the Breeders Crown, then traveled back to North America for the Can$500,000 (about U.S. $320,000) Trot Mondial at the Hippodrome in Montreal in September. He again prevailed over North America's finest and sealed his claim as the greatest trotter in the world. In his two starts in North America, Varenne earned U.S. $750,000.

On the same day that Varenne won the Breeders Crown, a photographer-turned-horseman from Sweden named Stefan Melander started his colt Scarlet Knight in a qualifying heat for the $1 million Hambletonian. Scarlet Knight won the heat and thus earned a chance to compete for the biggest prize for three-year-old trotters. Melander had purchased Scarlet Knight in 1999 at an auction in Pennsylvania, then returned to Sweden. The colt showed remarkable ability, and Melander began to dream of winning the Hambletonian. No horse had ever come from Europe to win the Hambletonian, but Melander's dream came true on August 4. Banker Hall stole off to a huge early lead but began to tire. Melander guided Scarlet Knight to the outside and past Banker Hall in the stretch, raising his whip in jubilation as he crossed the finish line first. In his two starts at the Meadowlands, Scarlet Knight earned $535,000.

A pair of American three-year-old fillies also enjoyed impressive seasons. The trotter Syrinx Hanover cruised through the season unbeaten; her victories included the Hambletonian Oaks and the Breeders Crown. She was raced sparingly, however, as her owner wanted to conserve her for future years. The popular three-year-old pacing filly Bunny Lake used her base in New York as a springboard to success, winning major races in New Jersey, Kentucky, Ontario, and Pennsylvania.

Bettor's Delight and Real Desire gave racing fans thrills whenever they battled in the classic events for three-year-old pacers. Bettor's Delight won the North America Cup in June, but Real Desire rebounded to victory in a hard-fought stretch duel in the Meadowlands Pace in July. In September Bettor's Delight won a two-heat victory in the Little Brown Jug over Real Desire, but Real Desire got revenge when he led all the way to take the Breeders Crown in October.

Although Scarlet Knight won the Hambletonian, the king of the three-year-old trotters was a colt named SJ's Caviar. He had been so sick as a two-year-old that his owner wondered if the colt would survive an early illness, but he blossomed into the best of his class in 2001. The trotter's owners had dropped his Hambletonian eligibility when he was deemed too sick to compete, but SJ's Caviar still earned over $1.2 million in 2001.

(DEAN A. HOFFMAN)

Steeplechasing. Foot-and-mouth disease led to the cancellation of British racing for 10 days in March 2001 and the loss of many other meetings, including the Cheltenham Festival. There was no racing in Ireland between February 25 and April 16, and only three Irish horses were permitted to race in Great Britain in the Grand National, which was won by Red Marauder. Only 2 out of 40 entries completed that race without mishap, but 2 horses, Blowing Wind and 2000 National winner Papillon, were remounted and finished. Free traffic across the Irish Sea resumed in early May.

French-trained First Gold won the King George VI Chase and Martell Cup Chase but was only fifth in the Grand Steeplechase de Paris behind Kotkijet, winning his sixth consecutive race. Kotkijet was one of many champion horses owned by Daniel Wildenstein. (See OBITUARIES.) The New Zealand-trained Rand won the inaugural Pegasus Jump Stakes at Nakayama, Japan, in March but then was brought down in the Nakayama Grand Jump won by Gokai three weeks later.

(ROBERT W. CARTER)

Show Jumping and Dressage. Ludger Beerbaum of Germany rode Gladdy's S to victory in the European individual show jumping championship at Arnhem, Neth., in July 2001, and ended the season as undisputed world number one in the Fédération Equestre Internationale/Gandini world riders rankings. The pair lost, however, to Brazilian Rodrigo Pessoa on Gandini Lianos in the Nortel Networks Grand Prix, the world's richest show jumping prize, at Calgary, Alta., in September. Ireland's team of four won the Nations Cup at both Arnhem and Calgary.

The U.K. surpassed France and Italy to win the European three-day event championship at Pau, France, in October. The U.K.'s Pippa Funnell captured the individual gold medal on Supreme Rock. Riders from Germany and Spain took silver and bronze.

Ulla Salzgeber of Germany rode the Russian-bred Rusty to win both the World Cup and European championship dressage. The pair were also part of the winning German team in the Nations Cup at Aachen, Ger., in June and at Verden, Ger., in August.

(ROBERT W. CARTER)

Polo. In the 2001 U.S. high-handicap season, held in Palm Beach, Fla., from January to April, Outback, led by Argentine Adolfo Cambiaso, prevailed at the U.S. Open for the third straight year, and Boca Polo triumphed in the Gold Cup in Boca Raton, Fla. Peter Brant's White Birch, led by Mariano Aguerre and Carlos Gracida, won the Sterling Cup and the Gold Cup of the Americas. In the summer season, held in Long Island, N.Y., White Birch won the Hampton Butler Handicap Cup.

In the English high-handicap season, Cambiaso conducted Dubai to three victories in a row. With his teammates—patron Ali Abwardy of Saudi Arabia, Bartolomé ("Lolo") Castagnola, and Ryan Pemble—the polo star captured the Indian Empire Shield, the Warwickshire Cup, and the Gold Cup. The Queen's Cup was suspended as a consequence of the outbreak of foot-and-mouth disease.

In Australia, Brazil outclassed the local quartet 10–9 in the final of the low-handicap (14 goals) world championship. Château La Cardonne was the winner of the French Open, held in Chantilly, France. In Sotogrande, Spain, Talandracas, led by Milo Fernández Araujo, was the champion of the Gold Cup for the first time. Prior to this tournament, Sebastián Merlos and Santiago Chavanne, who also stood out in the U.S. season as Cambiaso's Outback teammate,

were the key for Geebung to reach victory in the Silver Cup.

In a rainy season in Argentina, La Dolfina (Cambiaso, Castagnola, and brothers Sebastián and Juan Ignacio Merlos) won the Hurlingham Open. The quartet was beaten 17–16 in the final of the Argentine Open, however, by Indios Chapaleufú I. The champions (Aguerre and brothers Bautista, Marcos, and Horacio Heguy) won the Open, the world's most important polo tournament, for the sixth time after a six-year losing streak.

(JORGE ADRIÁN ANDRADES)

FENCING

Proposed rule changes to foil were debated within the Fédération Internationale d'Escrime (FIE) during 2001. Since the foil target was restricted to the trunk, a white light traditionally had been used in the scoring apparatus to indicate an off-target nonvalid hit. As with an on-target hit, this resulted in a pause in play, leading to confusion for spectators and irritation for the media, especially television. The FIE sought to make the sport more media- and spectator-friendly, and the "white light" problem in foil had proved to be among the most difficult to resolve. Many experts believed that removing the white light and allowing play to continue after nonvalid hits would transform foil. Others thought this would destroy the essence of foil and that other measures, such as altering the blade flexibility and the pressure needed to register a hit, would

prove equally effective. In December the FIE congress decided to establish a working committee to examine the "white light" issue, with a brief report to the General Assembly due in April 2002.

The special commission formed in 2000 finally authorized transparent masks from three European manufacturers. The masks were passed as safe and technically satisfactory in all three weapons (foil, épée, and sabre) but were not made compulsory, and many fencers still would not accept them. The other continuing major concern, wireless scoring equipment, made further progress with the approval of apparatus for sabre developed by Ukrainian engineers and manufactured by the German company Allstar/Uhlmann.

While the countries traditionally strong in fencing maintained their dominant positions through the year, others, especially China, South Korea, and the U.S., continued to challenge. The U.S. particularly showed strength in women's and men's junior sabre. The 2001 senior world championships were held on October 26–November 1 in Nîmes, France, inside the covered Roman amphitheatre and amid tight security. France, Italy, Germany, and Russia took most of the glory, but encouragingly the U.S. and Sweden also won medals.

In July Gian Carlo Brusati of Italy, one of the grand old men of fencing, died at age 91. Brusati won épée team gold at the 1936 Olympic Games and was FIE president in 1981–84.

(GRAHAM MORRISON)

Paolo Milanoli of Italy (right), having scored a hit against Basil Hoffman of Switzerland, moves to evade his opponent en route to winning the mens' épée final at the world fencing championships in Nîmes, France, on October 29.

FIELD HOCKEY

On April 21, 2001, Els van Breda Vriesman of The Netherlands became the first woman president of the Fédération Internationale de Hockey (FIH). At the FIH congress in Brussels, the first round of voting, against Alain Danet of France, ended 40–40. In the second round the majority opted for van Breda Vriesman, who had been named the first woman secretary-general in 1994. Australian Peter Cohen was unanimously elected secretary-general. Van Breda Vriesman took the reins of the FIH's restructured 21-member Executive Board. She was elected to the International Olympic Committee in July.

On the field it was an eventful year, highlighted by the World Cup qualifying competitions for men and women and the World Cup finals for juniors (under 21). South Korea stunned many by winning the junior women's competition in May against host team Argentina in a tiebreaker (4–3) after being 2–2 at the end of regulation time. The 16-team, four-pool system introduced in Argentina continued for the men's junior event in Hobart, Australia, in October. India won the cup for the first time, beating Argentina 6–1. Germany defeated England 5–1 to gain the bronze.

Seven countries (Argentina, Belgium, India, Japan, New Zealand, Poland, and Spain) qualified for the 2002 World Cup from the men's championship, held in Edinburgh in July. The women's qualifier, held in Amiens and Abbeville, France, in September, concluded with England taking the top spot, followed by Russia, Ukraine, Japan, and Scotland. Ireland was declared the winner for the sixth place after Lithuania was disqualified for refusing to participate in a replayed tiebreaker. The U.S. missed the event as a result of the disrupted flight schedules after the September 11 terrorist attacks in the U.S. The FIH gave the American women a chance to fight for the seventh spot in a three-Test series against India. On an appeal from Lithuania, the disciplinary commission of the FIH recommended the four countries—Ireland, Lithuania, India, and the U.S.—play in the Challenge Cup in Randburg, S.Af., to determine the sixth and seventh qualifiers.

Argentina defeated The Netherlands 3–2 to claim the women's Champions Trophy at Amstelveen, Neth., in August. The men's competition was shifted to Rotterdam, Neth., from Lahore, Pak., in the wake of the September 11 attacks. Two goals by Florian Kunz, the top scorer with 10 goals, helped Germany regain the Champions Trophy against Australia (2–1). The Netherlands beat Pakistan 5–2 for the bronze.

Stephan Veen of The Netherlands and Alyson Annan of Australia were named the Players of the Year for the second straight year. (S. THYAGARAJAN)

FOOTBALL

Association Football (Soccer). *Europe.* In 2001 the majority of European national association football (soccer) teams concerned themselves with qualifying matches for the 2002 Fédération Internationale de Football Association (FIFA) World Cup, to be held in Japan and South Korea. Nine European nations qualified for the World Cup finals by winning their respective Union des Associations Européennes de Football (UEFA) groups: Croatia, Denmark, England, Italy, Poland, Portugal, Russia, Spain, and Sweden. By year's end five second-place teams also had qualified: Belgium, Germany, Ireland, Slovenia, and Turkey. The prospects for England, led by captain David Beckham (*see* BIOGRAPHIES), had improved with the appointment of a Swede, Sven-Goran Eriksson, as its first foreign coach.

France, the defending champion and therefore exempt from the preliminaries, was able to add another trophy to its 1998 World Cup and Euro 2000 titles by winning the FIFA 2001 Confederations Cup for area champions, which also was staged in Japan and South Korea. The triumphant French beat Japan 1–0 in the final on June 10. In September young players representing France defeated Nigeria 3–0 to capture the under-17 world championship.

At club level, despite moves toward more freedom of contract, the scramble for first-class players continued to escalate transfer fees. In July the Spanish club Real Madrid paid some $64 million to Italy's Juventus for French forward Zinedine Zidane, the reigning FIFA World Player of the Year. England, with eight current French internationals playing in its Premier League, saw champions Manchester United pay £19 million (about $28.1 million) for Dutch striker Ruud Van Nistelrooy from PSV Eindhoven and a British-record fee of £28.1 million (about $41.6 million) for Argentine midfield player Juan Sebastián Verón from Italy's Lazio, Eriksson's former club.

Manchester United's record third championship in succession—and its

David Beckham of England scores on a free kick in a World Cup qualifying match against Greece.

Gary M. Prior/Allsport

seventh in the nine years of Premier League football—produced an average crowd attendance of 67,544, the highest ever achieved in 112 years of professional football in the country.

United's league title achievement was overshadowed by the three cup victories of Liverpool, which had also managed twice to beat United in league games. Under the tutelage of French coach Gerard Houllier, Liverpool annexed the League Cup, the Football Association (FA) Cup, and the UEFA Cup for a unique treble. In August it defeated Manchester United 2–1 in the annual Charity Shield match between FA league and cup winners and then added the European Super Cup to its list of honours, beating Germany's Bayern Munich 3–2.

By the conclusion of its UEFA Cup venture, Liverpool had completed 63 competitive games during the season. The UEFA final in Dortmund, Ger., on May 16 against the Spanish finalist, Alavés, was an absorbing encounter full of goals.

For Alavés, only six years out of the third division, it was a fairy-tale scenario, but when the team found itself a goal down in three minutes to Liverpool's first serious attack, the Spanish players' prospects seemed poor. Scotsman Gary McAllister's free kick was headed in for Liverpool by Germany's Markus Babbel, and worse followed for the team from Spain's Basque region. Liverpool's other German international, Dietmar Hamann, combined with Michael Owen after 17 minutes to produce a goal for Steven Gerrard to make the score 2–0.

Rather than lapse into free fall, Alavés shrugged off these early setbacks. Coach José Manuel Esnal ("Mané") brought on striker Iván Alonso for defender Dan Eggen and switched from a 4-5-1 formation to an attacking 3-5-2 system. In the 27th minute the substitute headed in Cosmin Contra's cross to reduce the deficit to one. Alavés goalkeeper Martín Herrera then tripped Owen, and McAllister restored Liverpool's two-goal advantage at 3–1 from the resulting penalty kick in the 41st minute. Surprisingly, Herrera received only a yellow card for his indiscretion.

By the 51st minute Alavés had evened the score at 3–3 through two goals by Javi Moreno early in the second half. In the 48th minute he headed in Contra's centre and then converted a free kick for his second successful effort. Houllier then changed tactics, bringing on Vladimir Smicer in midfield for defender Stephane Henchoz, shuffling the team around, and replacing Emile Heskey

with Robbie Fowler up front. Mané's response was to withdraw Moreno, a move that arguably cost them the chance of taking the initiative. In the 73rd minute Fowler ran through to make it 4–3 for Liverpool, only to have Alavés tie the score in the dying seconds of normal time. From a corner kick from Pablo Gómez, Jordi Cruyff headed in to force the game into overtime.

Alas, the Spaniards then fell apart. Magno Mocelin of Brazil was shown the red card for a foul on Babbel in the 99th minute. Captain Antonio Karmona, already on a yellow card, was cautioned again for pulling back Smicer in the 117th minute, and Alavés was left with only nine players. From McAllister's resulting free kick, the ball clipped the head of defender Delfí Geli and found the corner of the net to give Liverpool a 5–4 sudden-death victory.

In contrast, the European Champions League final a week later between Bayern Munich and Valencia of Spain in Milan's San Siro Stadium was dominated by penalties and caution, although there was a similar 5–4 score from the final shoot-out. The Spaniards took a dramatic lead in the second minute when Swedish international defender Patrik Andersson was adjudged to have handled the ball in a scramble at the mouth of the goal. Gaizka Mendieta drove the penalty kick past goalkeeper Oliver Kahn's right hand. Four minutes later Bayern had the opportunity to level the score with a penalty of its own. Jocelyn Angloma tripped Stefan Effenberg, and although Mehmet Scholl's penalty kick was on target, the ball hit Valencia goalkeeper Santiago Cañizares's legs and rebounded over the crossbar.

Both teams made second-half changes, and Bayern equalized from the game's third penalty award in the 50th minute. Amedeo Carboni handled the ball in a panic, and Effenberg put the teams into a tie at 1–1. Neither team seemed ambitious enough to take undue risks from then on as the game drifted toward the end of 90 minutes. It was only in overtime that the Bayern players stirred themselves more than the opposition, who seemed content to await the fate of the inevitable shoot-out. Paulo Sergio missed for Bayern with the first penalty attempt, but the Germans emerged 5–4 victors after Mauricio Pellegrino's effort was saved by Kahn with what was the 17th penalty kick of the match.

In purely domestic terms Bayern had won the German Bundesliga on the last day of the season. The team needed at

least a draw at Hamburg to prevent Schalke 04 from overtaking it, and it did so 1–1. It was Bayern's 17th championship and its third in succession.

In Azerbaijan there was a closer contest, which had to be determined by a play-off in which Shamkir beat Neftchi Baku after both teams had finished level on goal difference. Boavista became only the fifth different team in 66 years to win the title in Portugal, while the French first division club Toulouse was relegated to the third division when it was unable to make adequate financial guarantees. French cup winner Strasbourg also suffered relegation to the second division. Europe's ace marksman was Swedish international striker Henrik Larsson of Scotland's Celtic. He scored 35 league goals and 52 in all competitions as the Glasgow club won all three domestic trophies. Cypriot champion Omonia Nicosia saw its German striker Rainer Raufmann head the leading scorers for the fourth season in succession.

(JACK ROLLIN)

The Americas. There were some significant changes in association football (soccer) in Latin America during 2001. While Argentina easily won the South American World Cup qualifying group, Brazil—which lost its number one spot in the FIFA ranking for the first time in years—struggled all the way and managed to make sure of a top-four automatic qualifying place only at the end. Uruguay, the other usual powerhouse, reached the finals only after a play-off against Oceania winner Australia. Ecuador made the finals for the first time ever.

The South American championship, the Copa América, held in Colombia in July, lost stature when it was canceled owing to local terrorist activity and then reinstated with six days to go (owing to pressure from television-rights holders). By that time Argentina, the favourite, had disbanded its squad and withdrawn, and guest nations and most other countries sent weak squads. Colombia took the cup for the first time, winning all six of its games with no goals against, but there were plans to revitalize the tournament, which was next scheduled for Peru in 2003.

Argentina's Boca Juniors retained the South American club championship, the Libertadores de América Cup, beating Mexico's Cruz Azul on penalties in the two-legged final, which finished with a 1–1 aggregate score. The Argentine team could not retain the Intercontinental Cup against the European champions, however, and lost 1–0 to Germany's Bayern Munich.

The made-for-TV Mercosur and Merconorte cups were played for the fourth and last time. In spite of lucrative prizes, rising from $200,000 per home match in the first round to $3 million for the final winner, many clubs fielded virtual teams, and crowds were small at most games—only six tickets were sold for one match—in spite of reduced admission prices. All four Merconorte tournaments were won by Colombian clubs, with Bogotá's Millonarios crowned in 2001. The Mercosur Cup, which had been won by Brazilian clubs on the three previous occasions, could not be completed in 2001. Flamengo (Brazil) and San Lorenzo (Argentina) drew the first leg 0–0 in Rio de Janeiro. The second leg in Buenos Aires was scheduled on the day an uprising started that brought down the Argentine government. The match was postponed until January 2002.

In domestic leagues it was the year of the small club. Atlético Paranense took the Brazilian title for the first time, beating another small club, São Caetano, in the final. In Chile the Wanderers triumphed for the first time in 33 years. While Nacional retained the Uruguayan championship, it had to face modest opening-tournament winner Danubio in the final. Alianza Lima took the Peruvian title after winning the opening tournament and then beating Cienciano of Cusco, which won the closing tournament. Both clubs were celebrating their 100th anniversary.

Though popular Racing Club was one of Argentina's big clubs, its opening-tournament title, without established stars, was its first success in 35 years. Racing Club was Argentina's only top-division club run by a company; other Argentine clubs, as well as some in Brazil and other South American countries, were close to bankruptcy through bad management, in spite of the continued sale of star players to European clubs.

In the Confederation of North, Central American and Caribbean Association Football (CONCACAF), Costa Rica, Mexico, and the U.S. qualified for the 2002 World Cup finals. On October 21 the San Jose Earthquakes won their first Major League Soccer (MLS) Cup, scoring a sudden-death overtime goal to defeat the Los Angeles Galaxy 2–1. There were reports, however, that two MLS teams—possibly the Tampa Bay Mutiny and Miami Fusion—could soon be eliminated. The eight-team professional Women's United Soccer Association finished its first year of play, with the Atlanta Beat defeating the Bay Area CyberRays on penalty kicks in the final on August 25.　　(ERIC WEIL)

U.S. Football. *College.* The University of Miami (Fla.) won its fifth national championship of college football by defeating the University of Nebraska 37–14 in the Rose Bowl at Pasadena, Calif., on Jan. 3, 2002. This was the first Rose Bowl contest since 1946 that did not match the Big Ten and Pacific conference winners. Big East champion Miami (12–0) had the only undefeated record in Division I-A of the National Collegiate Athletic Association (NCAA), which it led with 45 turnovers on defense and the lowest regular-season defensive yields: 9.4 points per game and a 75.6 passing-efficiency rating.

Although Miami was the fourth undisputed champion in four years of the Bowl Championship Series (BCS), Nebraska's inclusion in the title game generated the third controversy in identifying the two finalists. The BCS computer formula ranked Nebraska (11–2) second, but both the media reporters' and coaches' regular-season polls ranked it behind Pacific-10 champion Oregon (11–1) and Colorado (10–3), which had defeated Nebraska 62–36 during the season and won the Big 12 championship before losing to Oregon 38–16 in the Fiesta Bowl.

With Miami's victory, its third in four national championship games against Nebraska, both final polls ranked Oregon, Orange Bowl winner Florida (10–2), Tennessee (11–2), Texas (11–2), and Cotton Bowl champion Oklahoma (11–2) next in the top six. The media's Associated Press poll followed in order with Southeastern Conference champion Louisiana State (10–3), Nebraska, Colorado, Washington State (10–2), Atlantic Coast champ Maryland (10–2), and Big Ten winner Illinois (10–2), which lost to Louisiana State in the Sugar Bowl. The coaches' *USA Today*-ESPN poll flipped two pairs of those rankings with higher positions for Nebraska and Maryland; Maryland's Ralph Friedgen was the consensus Coach of the Year. Other I-A conference winners were Louisville (11–2) in Conference USA, Toledo (11–2) in the Mid-American, Brigham Young (12–2) in the Mountain West, and Louisiana Tech (7–5) in the Western Athletic, while North Texas (5–7) and Middle Tennessee State (8–3) shared the Sun Belt title.

Quarterbacks for Miami and Nebraska each won Player of the Year honours, with the Maxwell Award going to Miami's Ken Dorsey and Nebraska's Eric Crouch winning the Heisman Trophy, the Walter Camp Award, and the Davy O'Brien Award for quarterbacks. Nebraska also led Division I-A with 314.7 yd rushing per game. Oregon's 11 turnovers lost were the fewest. Miami offensive tackle Bryant McKinnie won the Outland Trophy for interior linemen.

Florida and Brigham Young were the top offensive teams. Florida passed for 405.2 yd per game behind quarterback Rex Grossman, the leader with 9.9 yd per pass attempt, 354.9 yd total offense per game, and an efficiency rating of 170.8. Brigham Young averaged 542.8 yd and 46.8 points per game, with a division-high 28 touchdowns by Luke Staley, the Doak Walker Award-winning running back.

Fresno State quarterback David Carr's 42 touchdown passes and 4,299 yd passing were best, as was Wes Counts's .726 completion percentage for Middle Tennessee State. The receiving leaders were Hawaii's Ashley Lelie with 19 touchdowns, Utah State's Kevin Curtis with 100 catches, and Fred Biletnikoff Award winner Josh Reed with 1,740 yd for Louisiana State. Nevada freshman Chance Kretschmer's 1,732 yd rushing and Levron Williams's 200.1 all-purpose yards per game for Indiana also were tops.

North Carolina defensive end Julius Peppers won the Chuck Bednarik Award for best defender and the Vince Lombardi Award for linemen. Oklahoma teammates Rocky Calmus and Roy Williams, respectively, won the Dick Butkus Award for linebackers and the Jim Thorpe Award for defensive backs. Miami's Edward Reed led with nine interceptions, and Texas allowed the fewest yards per game, 236.2.

Ray Guy Award winner Travis Dorsch of Purdue led punters with a 48.4-yd average. New Mexico's Vladimir Borombozin had the best field-goal percentage, .944 on 17-for-18, just ahead of Lou Groza Award winner Seth Marler's 15-for-16 for Tulane.

Among schools with smaller football budgets, 15–1 Montana defeated 12–3 Furman for the Division I-AA championship, 14–1 North Dakota won the Division II championship game over 12–1 Grand Valley State (Mich.), 14–0 Mount Union (Ohio) won its fifth Division III title in six years (and its 82nd game out of 83) by beating Bridgewater (Va.), and 14–0 Georgetown (Ky.) won its second straight National Association of Intercollegiate Athletics (NAIA) championship game against 12–2 Sioux Falls (S.D.). The Walter Payton and Buck Buchanan awards for Division I-AA recognized Villanova running back Brian Westbrook and James Madison linebacker Derrick Lloyd, respectively, as the top overall and

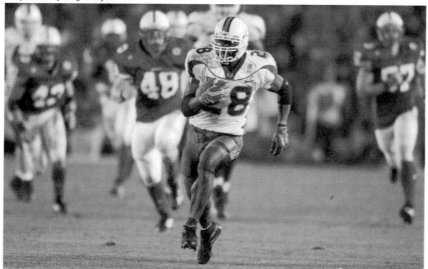

Clinton Portis of the University of Miami outsprints Nebraska defenders in the Rose Bowl on January 3.

defensive players. Valdosta State (Ga.) quarterback Dusty Bonner won his second Harlon Hill Trophy for Division II; Mount Union running back Chuck Moore received the John Gagliardi Trophy for Division III; and Georgetown quarterback Eddie Eviston won his third NAIA Player of the Year award.

Professional. On Feb. 3, 2002, in a surprisingly thrilling Super Bowl XXXVI, the American Football Conference (AFC) New England Patriots upset the heavily favoured National Football Conference (NFC) St. Louis Rams 20–17 before a crowd of 72,922 in the New Orleans Superdome. New England started with a 47-yd interception touchdown by Ty Law and unexpectedly led 14–3 at the half; St. Louis came back in the fourth quarter to tie the game at 17. Then Adam Vinatieri kicked a 48-yd field goal in the final seconds to give New England its first National Football League (NFL) championship in the franchise's 42-year history. Most Valuable Player (MVP) honours went to the Patriots' 24-year-old quarterback Tom Brady. During the play-offs, the Patriots had upset Oakland 16–13 with a game-ending 45-yd field goal and then beat Pittsburgh 24–17 with veteran Drew Bledsoe filling in for an injured Brady. St. Louis crushed Green Bay 45–17 and then defeated Philadelphia 29–24 to reach the final matchup.

In regular-season play NFC West champion St. Louis had the league's best offense with per-game averages of 31.4 points, 418.1 yd, and 306.4 yd passing. That was more than five points and 35 yd ahead of Indianapolis, the AFC leader in each category. AFC Central winner

Pittsburgh ran for the most yards on offense with 173.4 per game, allowed the fewest yards on defense with 258.6 per game total and 74.7 on the ground, ranked second to NFC Central champion Chicago's league-low yield of 12.7 points per game, and led the NFL with 55 sacks. Dallas's top-ranked pass defense allowed 188.7 yd per game. Other NFC defensive leaders were St. Louis in total yards and Chicago in rushing yards.

Other division winners were Philadelphia in the NFC East, New England in the AFC East, and Oakland in the AFC West, which repeated as division champion. Of the five other division winners in 2000, only Miami made the play-offs as a "wild-card" team, as did defending champion Baltimore and the New York Jets in the AFC, along with San Francisco, Green Bay, and Tampa Bay in the NFC. Miami's five consecutive play-off appearances led the league. Chicago won its division for the first time since 1990 with a league-best improvement of eight games, and Philadelphia won its first since 1988. Like Chicago, New England improved from last place to first, matching San Francisco's improvement of six games, and all three were among the six play-off teams that had missed the tournament in 2000–01, joining Green Bay, Pittsburgh, and the New York Jets.

New York Giants defensive end Michael Strahan set an NFL record with 22.5 sacks. Other records included Emmitt Smith's 11th season with at least 1,000 yd rushing for Dallas and Marshall Faulk's fourth with at least 2,000 yd from scrimmage. Faulk was 22 yd behind that category's leader, Kansas City's Priest Holmes,

who gained 2,169 yd from scrimmage and also led the NFL with 1,555 yd rushing. Faulk had the best average gain with 5.3 yd per rush and led the league with 21 touchdowns and 128 points, one more than teammate and top-scoring kicker Jeff Wilkins. San Francisco's Terrell Owens and Seattle's Shaun Alexander had league highs of 16 touchdowns receiving and 14 rushing, respectively.

Kurt Warner of St. Louis, the regular-season MVP, led most passing categories with a 101.4 efficiency rating, 4,830 yd, 8.85 yd per attempt, and 36 touchdowns with an .066 touchdown percentage. Oakland's Rich Gannon's nine interceptions were the fewest, as was his .016 percentage. The receiving leaders were Denver's Rod Smith with 113 catches and Arizona's David Boston with 1,598 yd. Tampa Bay's Ronde Barber and Cleveland's Anthony Henry shared the interception lead with 10 apiece.

The league's top kick returners were Ronney Jenkins of San Diego with 26.6 yd per kickoff return and Troy Brown of New England with 14.2 yd per punt return. Todd Sauerbrun of Carolina had the best punting averages, 47.5 yd gross and 38.9 yd net. Jason Elam's 31 field goals for Denver were the NFL's most, while Miami's Olindo Mare had the best percentage, .905 on 19 for 21.

In spring and summer leagues, the Grand Rapids Rampage defeated the Nashville Kats 64–42 for the 15th Arena Football League championship, and the Berlin Thunder won the NFL's developmental NFL Europe championship by beating the Barcelona Dragons 24–17. The XFL, a winter-spring league standing for extreme football, folded after its only season, which included the lowest-rated prime-time telecast in network history.   (KEVIN M. LAMB)

Canadian Football. The Calgary Stampeders won the 2001 Canadian Football League (CFL) championship by upsetting the favoured Winnipeg Blue Bombers 27–19 in the Grey Cup on November 25 at Montreal. Calgary's championship was its second in four years and the second in a row by a team with a losing regular-season record, something that never had happened in the cup's previous 87 years. Calgary, with a won-lost record of 8–10, overpowered West Division champion Edmonton (9–9) by 34–16 for the division title before beating East Division winner Winnipeg (14–4) in the cup final.

Calgary led the league with 136.9 yd rushing per game, and Grey Cup Most Outstanding Player Marcus Crandell led the quarterback field with 61.9% pass completions. Winnipeg led CFL defenses with per-game yields of 336 yd, 83.8 yd rushing, and 21.3 points. The Blue Bombers also had four top-ranked players: quarterback Khari Jones, the league's Most Outstanding Player, had CFL passing highs of 4,545 yd and 30 touchdowns, as well as an 87.8 efficiency rating; Milt Stegall led the league with 14 touchdown catches; tackle Dave Mudge was the Most Outstanding Offensive Lineman; and defensive lineman Doug Brown was Most Outstanding Canadian.

Other league award winners included Most Outstanding Defensive Player Joe Montford of Hamilton with 19 sacks and Most Outstanding Rookie Barrin Simpson of British Columbia with 115 tackles. (KEVIN M. LAMB)

Australian Football. In 2001 the Brisbane Lions ended a historic year by winning the Australian Football League (AFL) premiership for the first time. Once the Cinderella club of the AFL and the worst-performing club in a 16-team competition as late as 1998, the Lions beat 2000 titleholder Essendon 15.18 (108) to 12.10 (82) in the Grand Final at the Melbourne Cricket Ground on September 29 before a crowd of 91,482. The win also brought much joy to the former Fitzroy supporters, whose club had dropped from the competition after the 1996 season and merged with the former Brisbane Bears to form the Lions in 1997.

The Grand Final victory was the Lions' 16th successive win, easily breaking the previous club record of 10. Five days earlier Brisbane had also been on centre stage when it was announced that team member Jason Akermanis was the upset winner of the Brownlow Medal, awarded to the fairest and best player in the 22 home-and-away rounds as adjudged by the field umpires.

Essendon started the Grand Final a slight favourite, but it could not withstand the pressure. The defending champions opened up an early lead, but the Lions produced a sizzling third quarter of 6.2 to 1.2 that virtually won it the match. Shaun Hart, the Brisbane on-baller, was voted best man on the ground and won the Norm Smith Medal.

(GREG HOBBS)

Rugby Football. Australia's global domination of Rugby Union continued in 2001, as it again won the Tri-Nations Championship and gained the first series victory over the Lions (a team comprising the best players from England, Scotland, Ireland, and Wales) in its history. The Lions—in Australia with Rugby League convert Jason Robinson

Brisbane and Essendon players vie for the ball during the Australian Football League Grand Final match.

Mark Dadswell/Allsport

as one of their stars—opened the series with a stunning 29–13 win in Brisbane, only to fall to Australia in Melbourne (35–14) and Sydney (29–23) as the Wallabies took the series 2–1.

The Lions tour was unfortunately marred by a number of players' open criticism of the management—headed by Graham Henry and Donal Lenihan—and one player's launch of a tirade against the Australian side. These outbursts led to two English players, Austin Healey and Matt Dawson, being fined. Australia's victory in the Tri-Nations was confirmed with a dramatic 29–26 win over New Zealand on September 1. The triumph was sealed with a last-minute try from Toutai Kefu in a game that was legendary captain John Eales's last match. Eales ended his career as possibly the most successful Rugby Union captain of all time, with two World Cups (1991 and 1999), the Tri-Nations title, and a series victory over the Lions.

England's failure to win a Six Nations (formerly Five Nations) grand slam (a clean sweep of all five wins) continued, as it suffered its only loss on the final day of the championship for the third

successive season. In 2001 it was Ireland that exposed England's inability to win under pressure, and the Irish won a pulsating encounter 20–14. England still walked off with the Six Nations title, but it was scant reward for its efforts. The championship—usually staged between February and April—was finished in October owing to the foot-and-mouth crisis, which caused the postponement of three Ireland matches.

In domestic competition the ACT Brumbies struck a big blow for Australia in the Super 12 championship (contested by the best sides in New Zealand, Australia, and South Africa), winning the final against the South African Sharks 36–6. Most of the previous competitions had been dominated by sides from New Zealand, but this time none of the Kiwi teams made the semifinals. The Leicester Tigers won the championship in England for a third successive year and lifted the Heineken (European) Cup in an exciting 34–30 win over Stade Français in Paris, with centre Leon Lloyd scoring two tries. Newcastle took the Tetley's Bitter Cup in England, beating Harlequins 30–27. Swansea was confirmed as the Welsh champion, winning the title over Cardiff by six points, while Newport lifted the Principality Cup. In Scotland Hawick was champion, and in Ireland it was Dungannon. In France Christian Califano said goodbye to Toulouse—before he moved to Auckland—by delivering the French championship in a 34–22 final win over Montferrand in Paris.

In Rugby League's Super League, the Bradford Bulls defeated the Wigan Warriors 37–6 to be crowned English champions. In Australia the Newcastle Knights won the National Rugby League premiership in front of a sellout crowd of more than 90,000 at Stadium Australia, beating the Parramatta Eels 30–24.　　　　　(PAUL MORGAN)

GOLF

In the immediate aftermath of the Sept. 11, 2001, terrorist attacks in the U.S., at a time of national mourning, American players collectively decided not to travel to England. The Ryder Cup was postponed until September 2002.

In April Eldrick ("Tiger") Woods became the first player in the sport's history to hold all four of the modern major championships—the Masters, the U.S. Open, the British Open, and the Professional Golfers' Association of America (PGA) Championship—at the same time. The Masters, always held at the Augusta (Ga.) National Golf Club, was the only one of the four that Woods did not have in his possession at the start of the year.

Woods set the stage perfectly by winning his two preceding events. In Augusta his opening round of 70, two under par, left him five strokes behind fellow American Chris DiMarco. A second-round 66 heightened the excitement going into the weekend and brought the 25-year-old Woods into a share of second place, only two behind DiMarco. When he added a 68 on the third day, Woods moved into a one-stroke lead. Four years earlier the first major title of his career had come by a record 12-shot margin and with a record 18-under-par aggregate of 270, but completing his "Tiger Slam" was to prove much more difficult. A bogey on the first hole of the final round dropped Woods level with American Phil Mickelson, and David Duval, also of the U.S., made four successive birdies from the fifth hole and another birdie at the 10th to tie for the lead.

With three holes to play, Woods and Duval were 15 under par and Mickelson

14 under. Both Duval and Mickelson bogeyed the short 16th, and Duval missed a 1.5-m (5-ft) birdie chance on the final green. A drive and pitch to within 5.6 m (18 ft) of the final hole left Woods with two putts needed for victory. He holed for a birdie and finished at 16 under par for a two-stroke win over Duval.

The next opportunity came with the U.S. Open, at Southern Hills Country Club in Tulsa, Okla., in June. Woods had won the event in 2000 by a major championship record margin of 15 strokes, but his title defense was to be the start of a disappointing summer. An opening round of 74, four over par, left him eight behind the surprise leader, Retief Goosen. The 32-year-old South African, a member of the European circuit, had missed the halfway cut in seven of his previous nine majors in the U.S., but although he was caught on the second day by Americans Mark Brooks and J.L. Lewis, he dug his heels in.

With a round to go, Goosen shared the lead with American Stewart Cink, and with one hole to play, the two were locked together with Brooks, who had not won a tournament since he captured the PGA championship in 1996. What followed ensured that the event would be remembered for more than the simple fact that Woods did not win (he was joint 12th). Brooks three-putted for a bogey five, and Cink then took a double-bogey six. Goosen had hit his second shot to within 3.7 m (12 ft) and had two putts with which to become champion. His first went past the hole, and to the astonishment of the millions watching on television, he missed the next putt as well. This left Goosen and Brooks tied on the four-under-par total of 276 and meant that the pair faced an 18-hole play-off the next day. Not having to go into sudden death gave Goosen the opportunity to regroup, and he did so superbly, winning by two strokes with a par 70 to become only the sixth overseas player to take the title since 1927.

Much less of a surprise was Duval's victory in the British Open, held at Royal Lytham and St. Annes in Lancashire, Eng., in July. Coming into the event he had had eight top-10 finishes in the space of 13 majors. Scotland's Colin Montgomerie led for the first two days, and at the halfway point Duval was seven shots behind. On the third day the American shot a 65, good enough to bring him into a four-way tie as Montgomerie and others fell back, and with a final-round 67 the 29-year-old Duval triumphed by three with a 10-under-par total of 274.

The final day of the British Open, however, had another extraordinary story. On the second tee Wales's Ian Woosnam, joint leader after a birdie at the first hole, was told by his caddie that he had 15 clubs in his bag, one more than the rules permitted. A driver with which Woosnam had been practicing, but which he had decided not to use, was still in the bag. A two-stroke penalty was imposed, and the former world number one player, mortified and furious, finished joint third. The blunder was calculated to have cost him more than $312,000—and a place on Europe's Ryder Cup team. Two weeks later the same caddie was late in arriving for a round at the Scandinavian Masters in Malmö, Swed.—forcing Woosnam to find a last-minute replacement—and was fired.

The final major of the year, the PGA championship, held at the Atlanta Athletic Club in Duluth, Ga., in August, had no such incident, but it did include a record-breaking performance. Mickelson shot one stroke under the previous lowest aggregate in major history with a 14-under-par 266, but fellow American David Toms's closing pitch and 3-m (10-ft) putt for par, after a calculated decision not to go for the green in two at the par four, lowered that one more to a 15-under-par 265 and gave Toms, like Goosen and Duval, his first major title.

The win also qualified Toms for a Ryder Cup debut, but that had to be put on hold after September 11. Discussions

Annika Sörenstam chips onto the green on her way to shooting a record 59 (13-under-par) in March.

Scott Halleran/Allsport

eventually led to the decision that the match between the U.S. and Europe would be put back 12 months. Subsequent matches were changed to even-numbered years to restore the two-year cycle, with the Presidents Cup matches (the U.S. versus an international side comprising all countries outside Europe) switching to odd-numbered years starting in 2003.

The loss of three of his major titles did not stop Woods from maintaining a commanding lead in the world rankings to the end of the year or from topping the PGA Tour money list for the third successive season and the fourth time in five years, with a final total of $5,687,777. Goosen was the leading money winner on the European tour at £1,779,975 (about $2,537,000).

If Woods's victory in the Masters was the performance of the year, the round of the year was surely that by Sweden's Annika Sörenstam (*see* BIOGRAPHIES) during the Standard Register Ping tournament at the Moon Valley Country Club in Phoenix, Ariz, in March. Sörenstam became the first woman to break 60 in an official event. Not surprisingly, she went on to win the tournament and did so with a Ladies Professional Golf Association (LPGA) record total of 261, 27 under par.

The Swedish player won the Nabisco Championship, the first women's major of the season, by three shots the following week at Missions Hills Country Club in Rancho Mirage, Calif., and regained the world's number one position from Australian Karrie Webb before Webb hit back with an eight-stroke win in the U.S. Women's Open, held in June at the Pine Needles Lodge and Golf Club in Southern Pines, N.C. Three weeks later Webb gained a two-stroke victory at the McDonald's LPGA championship at the DuPont Country Club in Wilmington, Del.

That gave Webb her fifth victory in eight majors and made her at 26 the youngest woman golfer to record a career Grand Slam. The fourth and final major, the Weetabix Women's British Open held at Sunningdale, Eng., in August, resulted in a South Korean one-two finish. Pak Se Ri, who won both the U.S. Women's Open and the LPGA championship in 1998, beat Kim Mi Hyun by two strokes. Despite the tough competition, Sörenstam finished the season as the LPGA's top money winner with a record $2,105,868.

The high spot of the amateur season was the Walker Cup, which matched the U.S. against Great Britain and Ireland at the Ocean Forest course in Sea Island,

Ga. The home side led by a point after the first day, but just as they had been at Nairn, Scot., in 1999, the Americans were totally outplayed on the second day and again lost 15–9. It was Britain and Ireland's first-ever successful defense of the trophy and only their second away win. (MARK GARROD)

GYMNASTICS

The 2001 artistic gymnastics world championships were held in Ghent, Belg., on October 27–November 4. The Belarus men's team won its first world championship title with a score of 169.622, rounding out its collection of medals, which included a team silver medal in 1997 and a team bronze in 1999. The U.S. earned its first men's team medal since 1979, winning the silver; Ukraine took the bronze. China's 16-year-old Feng Jing, competing in his first world championship event, won the all-around title with a score of 56.211. Belarusian Ivan Ivankov, a two-time world and European all-around champion, had to settle for the silver, followed by Bulgaria's Jordan Jovtchev with the bronze.

Jovtchev and Romania's Marian Dragulescu tied for the gold medal on the floor exercise with a pair of 9.550 scores. Dragulescu also won gold on the vault (9.668), and Jovtchev secured the title on the still rings (9.775). Marius Urzica, the 2000 Olympic gold medalist, repeated his success on the pommel horse (9.800). U.S. national champion Sean Townsend claimed top honours on the parallel bars (9.70). Vlasios Maras of Greece won gold on the horizontal bar (9.737) in his first world championship.

On the women's side, Romania, with a score of 110.209, won its sixth team title, followed by Russia and the U.S. Russia's Svetlana Khorkina, the 1997 world champion and two-time Olympic gold medalist, won yet another all-around title at the 2001 worlds, scoring 37.617. Her teammate Nataliya Ziganshina took second. Romania's Andreea Raducan—who was initially declared the all-around gold medalist at the 2000 Olympic Games but then was disqualified for having a positive drug test—finished third in Ghent.

Khorkina went on to win two individual events in addition to the all-around title, scoring a 9.412 on the vault and a

Chinese phenomenon Feng Jing competes at the artistic gymnastics world championships.

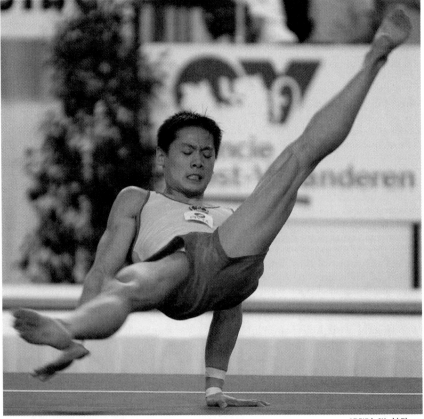

9.437 on the uneven bars. Raducan grabbed the gold medals on the balance beam and the floor exercise, with scores of 9.662 and 9.550, respectively.

The rhythmic world championships took place on October 18–21 in Madrid. Former Soviet countries earned all three team medals. Russia dominated the team competition, scoring 275.900, more than 16 points over its nearest competitor, Ukraine, which claimed the silver. Belarus captured the bronze. Russia's Alina Kabayeva won her second world all-around title, with a score of 113.025, followed by her teammate Irina Chashina and Ukraine's Tamara Yerofeyeva.   (LUAN PESZEK)

ICE HOCKEY

North America. The National Hockey League (NHL) delivered one of the most heartwarming human interest stories of the 2000–01 season when the Colorado Avalanche dethroned the New Jersey Devils on June 9, 2001, at Denver, Colo., in a historic showdown for the Stanley Cup. The championship series went to a seventh game for only the third time in 30 seasons as Colorado clinched the Stanley Cup for the second time since 1996 with a 3–1 victory. The Avalanche thus became the first NHL team since the 1971 Montreal Canadiens to overcome a three-games-to-two deficit in the final series.

The biggest story of the play-offs was 40-year-old Colorado defenseman Ray Bourque. The captain of the winning team usually skates around the rink with the Cup in his grasp, but Colorado's Joe Sakic ignored tradition and immediately handed it to Bourque as the sellout crowd of 18,007 cheered ecstatically. This marked the first time in a career that spanned a record 1,826 games that Bourque, who spent almost 21 seasons with Boston before he went to Colorado in a trade in March 2000, had celebrated victory in the final game of the season. It was also the last game of Bourque's career, as he announced his retirement 17 days later.

Of the 30 teams that contested the 82-game regular season prior to the play-offs, Colorado led the NHL in victories (52) and points (118) to capture its division by a huge 25-point margin over Edmonton. Detroit and New Jersey (111 points each), Ottawa (109), Dallas (106), and Washington (96) were the other division champions that advanced to the 16-team play-offs. Colorado advanced to the Stanley Cup finals by routing Vancouver in four straight games and

beating Los Angeles four games to three before taking the Western Conference title over St. Louis four games to one. New Jersey reached the Stanley Cup finals for the second straight season by beating Carolina four games to two, Toronto four games to three, and Pittsburgh four games to one for the Eastern Conference title.

In addition to the motivation the Avalanche players had in trying to bring Bourque his first Stanley Cup, their title quest was greatly energized by Sakic, the high-scoring centre, and Patrick Roy, their accomplished goaltender. Sakic won both the Hart Trophy as the league's Most Valuable Player (MVP) and the Lady Byng Trophy for good sportsmanship, having been penalized only 30 minutes during the regular season. Roy finished the season as the first three-time winner of the Conn Smythe Trophy awarded to the MVP of the play-offs. Roy also reached an enviable milestone on Oct. 17, 2000, when he led Colorado to a 4–3 overtime win at Washington to become the NHL all-time leader in regular-season victories. It was Roy's 448th victory in his 847th game. Terry Sawchuck of Detroit had set the former record in 1970, achieving his 447th victory in his 968th game.

The 51st NHL All-Star game, played in Denver on February 4, produced more goals than any previous All-Star match when the North Americans defeated the World team 14–12. The American trio of Bill Guerin, Tony Amonte, and Doug Weight combined for six goals and seven assists to raise North America's record to three games to one under the game format adopted in 1998. In his first All-Star game appearance, Guerin scored three goals and had two assists to win MVP honours.

Mario Lemieux of Pittsburgh ran Bourque a close second on the human-interest front during the season, reentering the NHL on Dec. 27, 2000, after a 3¹⁄₂-year retirement dictated by a long recovery from serious back injuries and Hodgkin disease. Lemieux proved that the layoff hardly had diminished his skills by scoring 35 goals and posting 41 assists in only 43 games.

Off the ice, controlling interest in the storied Montreal Canadiens was sold to George Gillett, Jr., an American businessman and ski-resort developer, for Can$275 million ($183 million). The franchise had received no offers from any Canadian buyer.

International. Taking another step toward dynasty status, the men's team from the Czech Republic and the Cana-

dian women's team dominated their respective international ice hockey rivals once again in 2001. Each team graced its season by winning a world championship in what was a familiar achievement for both organizations.

The Czech men captured their third straight world ice hockey championship at Hannover, Ger., with a 3–2 overtime victory against Finland on May 13. David Moravec scored the game-winning goal on a backhand shot that flew past Pasi Nurminen, the Finland goalie, after 10 minutes 38 seconds of overtime. Finland goals by Juha Lind and Juha Ylonen left the Czechs trailing 2–0 after the first two periods, but Martin Prochazka and Jiri Dopita beat Nurminen to square the score in the third period and send the game into overtime. That set the stage for Moravec, a Czech League journeyman whose NHL career consisted of one game with the Buffalo Sabres.

He scored off a pass from Pavel Patera. Moments later the crowd of 10,513 at Hannover's Preussag Arena roared its approval while Moravec and Czech goalie Milan Hnilicka were joyously mobbed by their teammates. It marked the sixth time in nine world tournament games that the resilient Czechs had overcome a deficit score to win. With the victory the Czech Republic became the first team to win three world titles in succession since the Soviet Union dominated from 1981 through 1983. Moravec was named MVP of the 2001 world championships.

The Finns, who similarly suffered an overtime loss to the Czechs in 1999, went home with their third silver medal in four years. Sweden took the bronze medal with a 3–2 victory over the United States.

Team Canada showed even greater domination in capturing the women's world championship for the seventh time in a row at Minneapolis, Minn., on April 8. The Canadian women claimed the world title with a 3–2 victory over the U.S. at the University of Minnesota's Marriucci Arena. In their fifth meeting of the season, the U.S. women outshot their rivals 35–18, but that barrage was not enough to beat Kim St. Pierre, the Canadian goalkeeper. She stopped 33 shots and stymied a U.S. power play in the second period when she blocked three shots and saw two others bounce off the pipes of her goalie cage.

The Canadian offense was led by Tammy Shewchuck and Jennifer Botterill, a pair of Harvard University teammates. Shewchuck scored the go-ahead goal with 9 minutes 45 seconds left in the second period after Canada's Dana Antal and Carisa Zaban of the U.S. matched goals in the first. Botterill, the world tournament MVP, gave Canada a two-goal lead when she tipped in a shot by Theresa Brisson with 3 minutes 45 seconds to go. The U.S. got its second goal from A.J. Mleczko with 79 seconds remaining after pulling its goalie, but the Americans failed to score again.

The victory was Canada's 100th in international play, raising the team's record to 35–0 in world championship games, and it demonstrated Canada's superior depth in women's ice hockey. The U.S. team had lived and trained together at Lake Placid, N.Y., for seven months preceding the world championships; the Canadian team was assembled only a week before the tournament began. The North American rivals had met 14 times since the U.S. beat Canada for the women's hockey gold medal at the 1998 Winter Olympic Games in Nagano, Japan. Including the 2001 world championship, the Canadians raised their record in the rivalry to 10–4.

(RON REID)

ICE SKATING

Figure Skating. Michelle Kwan of the U.S. and Yevgeny Plushchenko of Russia celebrated an extraordinary figure-skating season during 2001, a year in which each once again captured a world championship.

Kwan, aged 21, gave an indication of what she would achieve on January 20 in Boston, where she won her fourth straight U.S. women's championship and the fifth of her career. Kwan's remarkable free-skating performance earned a total of nine perfect 6.0 marks from the judges. She tied her record of seven 6.0s for her short program and added two more in the longer free skate to become the first woman to win four consecutive U.S. titles since Linda Fratianne (1977–80).

Plushchenko, aged 18, also got off to a superb start by winning the men's title for the second straight year at the European championships in Bratislava, Slovakia, on January 25. Plushchenko skated a bold program that included an extremely difficult quadruple toe loop and seven superbly executed triple jumps to win an emotional rivalry with fellow Russian Aleksey Yagudin, who also landed two quads and seven triple jumps. The intensity of the Russians' competition was so close that two judges gave first place to Yagudin. The European women's title went to Irina Slutskaya for the fourth time, even

Doug Pensinger/Allsport

Yevgeny Plushchenko skates his way to a world title in March.

though the Russian champion, who had beaten Kwan twice earlier in the year, hardly looked in top form as she struggled with the flu. Russia made it a clean sweep in the women's competition for the third consecutive year when Mariya Butyrskaya won the silver medal, despite two falls, and Viktoriya Volchkova took the bronze.

With her victory in the world championships at Vancouver, B.C., on March 24, Kwan was hailed as the dominant skater in her sport. She started the final night in second place, trailing Slutskaya, and responded with one of the greatest performances of her career. It brought Kwan her fourth world title (her second in a row). While Slutskaya managed the first triple Salchow/triple loop/double toe combination ever witnessed in a ladies' world championship, she finished as the silver medalist for the second straight year. Sarah Hughes, the runner-up to Kwan at the U.S. championships, rallied from fourth place after her short program to capture the bronze medal; Angela Nikodinov took fifth.

Plushchenko picked off the men's title that had eluded him the previous two seasons. He landed a quadruple jump during a strong free-skating program that included eight triple and two double jumps to leave Yagudin, a three-time world champion, as a runner-up once again. Todd Eldredge, the 1996 world champion and five-time U.S. champion,

captured the bronze medal. At 29 he became the oldest man to medal since Roger Turner took the silver in 1931 three days short of his 30th birthday.

The pairs title went to hometown favorites Jamie Salé and David Pelletier, the first Canadian duo to win the gold since 1993. Barbara Fusar Poli and Maurizio Margaglio of Italy, the ice-dancing gold medalists of the European championships, took their first world title in what was the first-ever world figure-skating medal for their nation.

Speed Skating. Rintje Ritsma of The Netherlands captured the men's all-around title at the 2001 world speed-skating championships contested February 9–11 in Budapest. A second-place finish in the 10,000-m race on the final day of competition enabled Ritsma to move past his countryman Ids Postma to secure the fourth world title of his career. Anni Friesinger of Germany took the women's all-around championship, holding off teammate Claudia Pechstein. Friesinger increased her first-day point total by winning the woman's 1,500-m final in 2 min 3.38 sec as a prelude to a sixth-place finish in the 5,000 m for a final total of 169.690 points. Pechstein finished second for the fifth time in her career by a centimetre or so, with 169.791 points. The women's competition might have evolved more predictably had Gunda Niemann-Stirnemann, the European all-around champion and eight-time world champion from Germany, not been disqualified in the 3,000 m for an inexplicable lane-change mistake.

Pechstein rebounded in a big way on March 2 in Calgary, Alta., where she won a World Cup 3,000-m race in 3 min 59.27 sec—a world record. Canada's Michael Ireland set another world record on the same track one day later when he covered 1,000 m in 1 min 8.34 sec. Ireland's Canadian teammate Jeremy Wotherspoon finished second by one one-hundredth of a second in what may have been the most exciting race of the year. Chris Witty of the U.S. lowered the women's world record for 1,000 m to 1 min 14.58 sec later that day.

Chinese athletes dominated the world short-track speed-skating championships at Chonju, S.Kor., during the final week of March. Yang Yang (A) topped the women's final standing for the fifth straight year, winning the 1,500-, 1,000-, and 3,000-m finals, in that order. (*See* BIOGRAPHIES.) Li Jiajun took the men's overall title for the second time since 1999, winning the 500-m and 1,000-m finals.

(RON REID)

JUDO

The world judo championships, held July 26–29 in Munich, Ger., was the standout judo event of 2001. Shinichi Shinohara of Japan emerged as the heavy favourite in the men's over-100-kg competition when David Douillet of France—who had faced Shinohara in the finals at the 2000 Olympic Games in Sydney, Australia—retired after winning gold in that event. In a stunning upset in the quarterfinals, however, Aleksandr Mikhaylin of Russia took only 12 seconds to score an *ippon* (full-point) victory over Shinohara, the defending world champion. Mikhaylin proceeded to beat Fashandi Miran of Iran and Selim Tataroglu of Turkey to claim the world title and then went on to victory in the open-weights event. Kosei Inoue of Japan became the only man to win gold at both the Sydney Olympics and the 2001 world championships when he successfully defended his under-100-kg world title at Munich. Olympic champion Ryoko Tamura of Japan continued her dominance in women's judo, winning her fifth straight world title in the under-48-kg event. In the overall medal count, the Japanese team placed first with 10 medals, including 4 golds, followed by Cuba (8 medals) and South Korea (5).

The 2001 Individual Grand Prix was held on October 13 in Moscow for men and on November 24 in Seville, Spain, for women. Mikhaylin placed second behind fellow Russian Tameryan Tmenov in the over-100-kg competition, and Nicolas Gill of Canada claimed the under-100-kg title. Tamura sat out the tournament, but another Japanese woman, Kayo Kitada, took the under-48-kg title.

(EDITOR)

RODEO

In 2001 the Professional Rodeo Cowboys Association's Wrangler Pro Rodeo Tour wrapped up its second year with a sold-out concert-rodeo at the new American Airlines Center in Dallas, Texas. Billed as the Texas Stampede, the finale to the pro tour season featured $700,000 in prize money, second only to the world-championship-deciding Wrangler National Finals Rodeo (NFR), which was held December 7–16 in Las Vegas, Nev.

The NFR featured a $4.6 million purse, the largest in the event's 42-year history. Topping the list of competitors was Cody Ohl of Stephenville, Texas, who earned $296,419 in three events to claim the all-around world title. In addition, Ohl

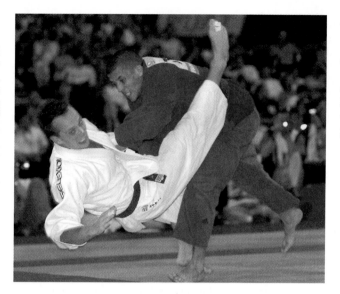

Anis Lounifi of Tunisia throws Cedric Taymans of Belgium in their world judo championships final match on July 29.

Peter Kneffel/AFP Worldwide

claimed the third calf-roping world title of his career with $222,026 in earnings. In the ninth round of the NFR, however, the cowboy tore ligaments in his right knee, an injury that was expected to keep him out of competition for at least six months. Ohl did not anticipate a title defense in 2002; world championships in professional rodeo were based on prize money won over the yearlong rodeo season as well as the money made at the season-ending NFR. In addition to the all-around—awarded to the cowboy who won the most money in a combination of events—individual event world championships were bestowed in bareback riding, steer wrestling, team roping (heading and heeling), saddle-bronc riding, calf roping, bull riding, and women's barrel racing.

In the steer-wrestling world title race, Rope Myers of Van, Texas, rose from 14th place to first after racking up $117,774 at the 10-round NFR, bringing his total season earnings to $176,584. Bareback rider Lan LaJeunesse of Morgan, Utah, earned his second world championship (his first was in 1999), defeating newcomer Bobby Mote in the final round. His earnings for the year totaled $185,556. Saddle-bronc rider Tom Reeves of Stephenville, Texas, collected his first world championship while competing at his 17th straight NFR; he topped the field with $204,008.

Janet Stover of Rusk, Texas, rode a horse owned by former NFR competitor Peyton Rainey to the barrel racing title after her own horse, Gotowin Bo, was sidelined with a leg injury. Stover won $126,934 at the finals, the most in a single event, to finish the year with $186,812.   (GAVIN FORBES EHRINGER)

ROWING

The preparation cycle for the 2004 Olympic Games in Athens began by extending the World Cup series in 2001, with a new opening round in the U.S. in April. The Fédération Internationale des Sociétés d'Aviron (FISA) international rowing congress also took a step along the road to championship status for student rowing by renaming the Nations Cup the "World Under 23 Regatta." A new regulation was introduced for the automatic removal of a boat class from the world championship program if there were fewer than seven starters for three consecutive years. A Cuban proposal to give the FISA executive discretion in sentencing first-time doping offenders was overwhelmingly rejected. FISA, almost alone among international sports federations, imposed an automatic life ban for serious doping offenses.

Germany, winner of the team title, and Great Britain were the most successful of the 10 nations that won gold medals at the FISA world championships in Lucerne, Switz., in August. In men's events Romania captured the eights by 0.99 sec over Croatia, while France and Great Britain won the coxed and coxless fours, respectively. The German men's sole victory was in quadruple sculls. Hungary finished just 0.13 sec ahead of France in double sculls, and Olaf Tufte became Norway's first world single sculls champion by only 0.32 sec. Germany won the three sculling titles in the women's events, while Australia triumphed in eights and coxless fours, with Romania taking the coxless pairs. Ireland had triple winners in the lightweight events, with Italy claiming two titles. The remainder of the 24 gold medals at stake were won by Australia, Austria, France, Germany, and Great Britain.

The biggest drama of the championships was provided by Great Britain's second bid for a golden double in men's coxed and coxless pairs. This had never been achieved, and Britain's previous attempt with Steven (later Sir Steven) Redgrave in the 1988 Olympic Games had only narrowly failed. James Cracknell and Matthew Pinsent—two members of Redgrave's 2000 Olympic gold medal coxless fours—had already won coxless pairs in the 2001 World Cup convincingly enough to be persuaded to go for the elusive double at the world championships. With an interval of only two hours for physical recovery between finals, it was a risky challenge. The British pair led all the way to win the coxed event by 0.42 sec, but in the coxless final they were never ahead until the last stroke, where a photo finish gave them the verdict and a unique world record by 0.02 sec.

At the 152nd Henley Royal Regatta in England, Redgrave won the Queen Mother Challenge Cup (quadruple sculls) for his 20th Henley medal. Overseas entries from seven countries, led by Australia, harvested 11 trophies. Duncan Free of Australia took the Diamond Challenge Sculls; Australia also captured the Princess Elizabeth Challenge Cup (eights), Henley Prize (eights), and Fawley Cup (quaduple sculls). The U.S. won twice in eights in the Ladies' Challenge Plate and the Temple Challenge Cup. The Grand Challenge Cup (eights) went to H.A.V.K. Miladost and V.K. Croatia of Croatia, while Belgium won the Thames Cup (eights). Two-time world champions Tomasz Kucharski and Robert Scez of Poland won the Double Sculls Cup. Champion women scullers included Germany in Quadruple Sculls and Yekaterina Karsten of Belarus in the Princess Royal Cup (single sculls).

In the 147th University Boat Race, Cambridge avenged Oxford's interruption in 2000 of Cambridge's seven straight wins. After 20 strokes the race was stopped for the first time since 1829 before Cambridge won by 2½ lengths to bring its overall lead in the series to 77–69.   (KEITH L. OSBORNE)

SAILING (YACHTING)

Technology was central to sailing in 2001, with dramatic effect on the sport. At the upper end a relative handful of professionals sailed boats built to aircraft specifications and using space-age materials, most of them financed by commercial sponsors that gained display platforms for their logos. In September the 2001–02 Volvo Ocean Race (formerly the Whitbread Round-the-World Race) started eight entries, all 18.3-m (60-ft) water-ballasted boats built for the event and financed by sponsorship. The Vendee Globe Race, for 18.3-m (60-ft) boats built to a different but similar rule, fielded 24 starters for a nonstop circumnavigation. Fifteen of the boats finished, and Michel Desjoyeaux established a new record, completing the voyage in 93 days 3 hr 57 min. An even faster time occurred in a new event, titled simply "the Race." Six giant catamarans, limited in size only by the availability of sponsorship funds, started this nonstop "Around" race; five entries finished. The winning *Club Med* required only 62 days 6 hr 56 min for the circumnavigation. By year's end 10 challengers had registered to contest New Zealand's hold on the America's Cup in late 2002. The America's Cup had always been a technological contest, and teams were already on New Zealand's Hauraki Gulf testing boats and sails. A successful challenge was expected to cost at least $80 million.

The official report on the storm-ravaged 1998 Australian Sydney–Hobart

In 2001 World Sailor of the Year Ellen MacArthur became the fastest—and youngest—woman to sail around the world.

Gerry Penny/AFP Worldwide

race was issued in the spring and suggested that the race management team had "abdicated its responsibility at the time of crisis." A long series of recommendations was included in the report, which was being studied worldwide for its legal implications. In the Sydney–Hobart race that ended at the beginning of January 2001, the racing fleet again met challenging conditions, and 24 of the 82 starters were forced to retire. Four crew were swept overboard in the race, but they were recovered successfully. *Nicorette* and *SAP Ausmaid* (both sponsored boats) won the line honours and the overall race, respectively.

On the administrative front the International Sailing Federation (ISAF) took the Offshore Racing Council under its wing and began providing oversight for all sail racing in the world. A controversial decision dropped the men's three-man (spinnaker) keelboat from the Olympic program and added a women's keelboat fleet racing event. This left the men without a spinnaker keelboat—when even the Olympic catamaran employed these colorful and powerful sails—and denied women the match-racing venue many of them had sought. The French youth team won the ISAF world championship for the fourth consecutive year. The ISAF's World Sailors of the Year were Ellen MacArthur of Great Britain and Robert Scheidt of Brazil.

Two notable speed records were established by Steve Fossett's giant catamaran, *Playstation*. Sailing ahead of a strong weather front, the boat logged 687 nautical miles in 24 hours and completed a transatlantic crossing in 4 days 17 hr 28 min at an average speed of 25.86 knots.   (JOHN B. BONDS)

SKIING

Alpine Skiing. In 2000–01, for the second straight season, Austrian icon Hermann ("the Herminator") Maier won four World Cup titles—overall, downhill, supergiant slalom (super G), and giant slalom (GS). Although he did not win any gold medals at the 2001 Alpine world championships in St. Anton, Austria, the Herminator did not miss much else. He finished more than 740 points ahead of teammate Stephan Eberharter for the overall title, collecting a record-tying 13 World Cup victories. In August Maier broke his leg seriously in a motorcycle accident, and it was uncertain if he would compete in the 2002 Winter Olympics in Salt Lake City, Utah.

On the women's side, Croatian teenager Janica Kostelic earned her first two

World Cup titles, despite having injured ligaments in her left knee in the final month of the season. Austrian Renate Götschl fell in several races and failed to defend her overall crown. Kostelic, who later underwent three knee surgeries, had won the first eight World Cup slaloms and cruised to the slalom title before edging Götschl in overall points. Isolde Kostner of Italy won the women's downhill title; France's Régine Cavagnoud was the super G champion; and Sonja Nef of Switzerland captured the GS title.

The world championships started with heavy snowstorms and a surprise gold medal in the men's super G for American Daron Rahlves. Austria dominated, collecting 14 medals though only 3 golds. Michaela Dorfmeister led an Austrian medals sweep in the women's downhill; "local boy" Mario Matt took the men's slalom championship on the final day; and Hannes Trinkl won the men's downhill title. Swiss great Michael von Grünigen won the GS. Martina Ertl of Germany sparkled in the combined, despite having injured her right knee a month earlier. Cavagnoud won the super G gold medal, and Nef claimed the GS title. The world champion in slalom was Sweden's Anja Paerson. In October the outlook for the 2002 Olympics changed again when Cavagnoud was killed. (See OBITUARIES.)

Nordic Skiing. The overriding story for the 2000–01 Nordic season was the doping scandal at the world championships in Lahti, Fin. Six Finns—including national icons Mika Myllylä and Harri Kirvesniemi—were caught using a banned drug, hydroxyethyl starch, a blood thinner that could boost endurance and could mask other illegal drugs. Myllylä and Kirvesniemi retired; Jari Isometsä and Janne Immonen received two-year suspensions. Virpi Kuitunen, who had won the "pursuit" gold medal at the championships, and Milla Jauho received three-month suspensions when an arbitrator ruled that they may have been innocent victims of coaches and doctors. The Fédération Internationale de Ski (FIS) had caught Isometsä and Immonen in routine postrace drug tests. The World Anti-Doping Agency (WADA) had uncovered the other four in a surprise test after the relays.

In the last two weeks of the season, Russian Yuliya Chepalova overtook two-time champion Bente Skari (formerly Martinsen) of Norway for the women's World Cup cross-country title. Per Elofsson, despite a month off to prepare for the world championships, gave Sweden its first men's crown since the great Gunde Svan's win in 1989.

Freestyle Skiing. American aerialist Eric Bergoust, who already had won everything else in his sport, won the first two World Cup events and edged teammate Joe Pack by four points for his first World Cup title. Jacqui Cooper of Australia breezed to her third straight women's aerials crown. At the world championships at Blackcomb, B.C., Canadian Veronika Bauer won the women's aerials championship; Belarusian Aleksey Grishin collected the men's title.

Norwegian Kari Traa secured a unique trifecta: the World Cup moguls title plus world championship gold in moguls and dual moguls. Mikko

Karine Ruby speeds to victory in the women's parallel slalom during the World Cup snowboarding finals on January 11.

Laurent Gillieron/AFP Worldwide

Ronkainen made it three straight World Cup titles for Finnish men, winning both the World Cup and the world championship title.

Snowboarding. The many-prismed world of snowboarding featured World Cup tours run by the FIS and the International Snowboard Federation (ISF) plus the U.S. Open and a variety of non-Cup contests. As a result, some athletes rode both World Cup circuits, some rode just one, and others stayed in the U.S. and competed in non-World Cup events.

On the FIS tour Karine Ruby of France, the most dominant woman rider for years, won two gold medals at the world championships plus the World Cup overall, GS, and snowboardcross titles; Canadian Jasey Jay Anderson was the World Cup overall champion and gold medalist in the GS at the worlds. On the ISF tour Olympic champion Gian Simmen of Switzerland was the men's halfpipe titleholder. Norway's Stine Brun Kjeldaas won the first three FIS women's halfpipes (en route to finishing second for the season), then switched to the ISF tour and easily won that halfpipe title.

(PAUL ROBBINS)

SQUASH

Australian David Palmer started 2001 ranked eighth in the world and ended it as number one. Another Australian, Sarah Fitz-Gerald, returned to the top 10 and finished at number one.

The British Open in June was indicative of how the year would go for the erstwhile top two men, Peter Nicol of Scotland and Canadian Jonathon Power. Both disappeared early in the tournament, and it was left to English veteran Chris Walker to celebrate reaching 34 years of age and reaching the final. There—tired after having played in the qualification rounds—he succumbed to the 24-year-old Palmer.

Power struggled as ever with a series of leg and back injuries in 2001, but Nicol's loss of edge emanated from a different quarter. The defending world champion surprised the squash world in February by announcing a change of allegiance from Scotland to England (based on residential qualification) in a bid to benefit from more favourable National Lottery funding. The furor seemed to affect his form, but as the year closed, wins in Cairo and Qatar took Nicol to the brink of regaining the number one spot.

After losing in the semifinals of the women's World Open in November 2000, Fitz-Gerald was beaten only once in the next 14 months—by New Zealander Leilani Joyce in the semifinals of the Hong Kong Open in August. In June Fitz-Gerald won the British Open, the only title that had threatened to elude her, and by early October she was back at number one. Later that month she traveled home to Melbourne, where she cruised to victory over Joyce in the final to win her fourth World Open title.

Australia beat defending champion Egypt 3–0 in the final of the men's team World Open after the young Egyptian side had swept past Scotland and Canada in earlier rounds. The men's World Open, due to be staged in Mumbai (Bombay), India, in December, was postponed owing to economic difficulties.

(ANDREW SHELLEY)

SWIMMING

As 2001 dawned—three months after the Sydney, Australia, Olympic Games, with 14 world records and historic performances by Inge de Bruijn and Pieter van den Hoogenband of The Netherlands and Australian phenomenon Ian Thorpe—many assumed that the new year would be anticlimactic. "The Thorpedo," however, repeatedly obliterated his already mind-boggling world records. (See BIOGRAPHIES.)

At the Australian national championships in Hobart, Tas., in March, Thorpe and Grant Hackett engaged in a stroke-for-stroke duel for the first 700 m of the 800-m freestyle. Then Thorpe left Hackett in his wake. When he touched the wall, Thorpe had clocked 7 min 41.59 sec, almost four and a half seconds under Kieren Perkins's seven-year-old mark. Hackett also finished well under the old standard. The next night Thorpe regained the 200-m world mark he had lost to van den Hoogenband in Sydney, lopping an extraordinary 0.66 sec off "Hoogie's" world record.

Meanwhile, at the U.S. national championships, 15-year-old Michael Phelps became the youngest man ever to set a world swimming record when he clocked 1 min 54.92 sec in the 200-m butterfly. Ed Moses took the 100-m breaststroke standard away from Russia's Roman Sludnov, touching in 1 min 00.29 sec. Anthony Robinson lowered the 50-m breaststroke record to 27.49 sec, but it lasted only two days until Moses reduced it again to 27.39 sec.

At the Russian national championships in June, Sludnov responded to Moses's challenge, first reducing the American's record in the 100-m breaststroke by three-hundredths of a second and then breaking the one-minute barrier with a historic 59.97-sec performance. On April 13 China's Qi Hui took the global mark in the women's 200-m breaststroke to 2 min 22.99 sec; it was the year's only women's record set in a 50-m pool.

The Fédération Internationale de Natation Amateur (FINA) world cham-

Michael Klim competes in a 50-m butterfly heat at the world swimming championships in Fukuoka, Japan.

AP/Wide World Photos

pionships, held on July 16–29 in Fukuoka, Japan, saw eight men's world records broken, four by Thorpe. He lowered his own world record in the 400-m freestyle to 3 min 40.17 sec, beating Hackett, whose 3-min 42.51-sec finish made him the second fastest man in history. In the 800-m freestyle the result was the same, with both men again under the old record. In the 200-m freestyle Thorpe exacted his revenge for his Olympic upset loss to van den Hoogenband, thrashing his Dutch rival and taking the world mark down to 1 min 44.06 sec.

The next day Thorpe, Hackett, Michael Klim, and William Kirby cut two seconds off Australia's 4 × 200-m freestyle relay record set in Sydney. Thorpe also swam legs on Australia's gold-medal-winning 4 × 100-m freestyle and medley relay teams. Not surprisingly, at year's end *Swimming World* magazine named him World Swimmer of the Year.

There were three other world-record swims in Fukuoka. Hackett took a phenomenal seven seconds off Perkins's 1994 global standard in the 1,500-m freestyle. Phelps destroyed the strongest 200-m butterfly field in history, taking his own mark down to 1 min 54.58 sec. Sludnov easily defeated Moses, as well as Olympic champion Domenico Fioravanti of Italy, in the 100-m breaststroke. American Anthony Ervin was the only man besides Thorpe to win more than one individual event, sweeping the 50-m and 100-m freestyle sprints.

In women's events de Bruijn won the 50-m and 100-m freestyle and the 50-m butterfly. Ukraine's Yana Klochkova, Germany's Hannah Stockbauer, China's Luo Xuejuan, and Australia's Petria Thomas were double winners in individual events, with Thomas adding a

third gold medal in the medley relay. In the women's 4 × 200-m freestyle, both the Australians and the Americans were disqualified, leaving the third-place British quartet as the gold medalists.

An amazing 16 new world records were set in short-course (25-m pool) competition during 2001, with five falling during the FINA World Cup series early in the year. Although she set no new records, Slovakia's Martina Moravcova was easily the most dominant swimmer on the World Cup circuit, winning 29 of 34 races and taking second in the other five.

Five world records were erased at the Australian short-course championships in Perth, only a week after the world championships. Hackett took nine seconds off Perkins's 800-m freestyle mark and lowered his own 1,500-m freestyle standard with astonishing times of 7 min 25.28 sec and 14 min 10.10 sec, respectively. An hour after setting the 1,500-m record, Hackett teamed with Thorpe, Klim, and Kirby to clock 6 min 56.41 sec in the 4 × 200-m freestyle relay, almost five full seconds under the old mark held by the U.S. Three more global standards fell at the European Short Course Championships in December, while Natalie Coughlin (U.S.) lowered the 100- and 200-m backstroke marks in the FINA World Cup series in November.

Diving. China extended its decade-long dominance in diving in 2001 and won 8 of the 10 events contested at the world swimming championships in Fukuoka. Only Russian Olympic champion Dmitry Sautin and Canadian Blythe Hartley could dent the Chinese machine. The Russian won his specialty, the men's 3-m springboard, narrowly defeating China's Wang Tianling and Japan's Ken Terauchi. A "shocked" Hartley eked out a three-point win on the women's 1-m springboard over China's Wu Minxia.

China's Wang Feng took the men's 1-m title, with teammate Wang Tianling 11 points behind. Tian Liang was an 18-point victor in the 10-m platform. The men's 3-m synchronized diving title fell to Bo Peng and Wang Kenan. The 10-m synchro crown went to China's Tian and Hu Jia.

Guo Jingjing and Wu Minxia of China teamed up to take the women's 3-m synchro crown, and Guo followed up by breezing to a 44-point victory in the women's 3-m springboard, with Olympian Irina Lashko, a Russian-turned-Australian, second. Fourteen-year-old Xu Mian of China won the 10-m platform over her fellow 14-year-old teammate Duan Qing, and Duan and Sang Xue, age 17, added the 10-m synchro title with little difficulty.

Synchronized Swimming. The year's focus for synchronized swimming was also in Fukuoka. Olga Brusnikina breezed to the solo gold medal to go with her 2000 Olympic duet title. The 22-year-old Russian scored 99.434 points, well ahead of France's Virginie Dedieu (98.287), who also had finished second, to Olga Sedakova of Russia, at the 1998 world championships. Japan's Miya Tachibana was third (97.870).

Tachibana and Miho Takeda combined to win the duet title. The victory marked the first time Japan had ever won gold at a world championship level in any aquatic discipline.

In 2000 Russia had won the Olympic gold in the team competition using an experienced team. In 2001, in a daring move, the Russians fielded a team of juniors who performed to the same music. The result, however, was the same; Russia won with 98.917 points. Japan was second, and Canada finished third.

(PHILLIP WHITTEN)

TABLE TENNIS

At the 2001 table tennis world championships held April 23–May 6 in Osaka, Japan, the Chinese were totally dominant. They scored easy victories in the team events—the men defeated Belgium (which had upset defending champion Sweden in the semifinals), and the women topped North Korea. Pro Tour grand final winner Wang Liqin won the men's singles and, with his partner from the 2000 Olympic Games, Yan Sen, captured the men's doubles. Olympic gold medalist Wang Nan won the women's singles and, with her Olympic partner, Li Ju, secured the women's doubles. Qin

Zhijian and Yang Ying took the mixed title. World Cup winners were Belarus's Vladimir Samsonov and China's Pro Tour grand final women's champion Zhang Yining. The Europe Top 12 men's and women's champions were Samsonov and Hungary's Csilla Batorfi, respectively.

On September 1 the International Table Tennis Federation (ITTF) changed the scoring in its tournaments from the traditional 21-point game to an 11-point game and increased match play to best three-out-of-five or four-out-of-seven games. As of Sept. 1, 2002, a new service rule would ensure that the receiver sees the server make contact with the ball—that is, the server would not be permitted to interpose part of his or her body to hide, and so delay the receiver from seeing, the spin applied to the ball. It was likely that the ITTF's 186 member countries would observe these new rules in their domestic competitions.

(TIM BOGGAN)

TENNIS

Although the men produced four different champions at the illustrious Grand Slam events in 2001, the "man of the year" label was worn deservedly by a pugnacious 20-year-old from Australia named Lleyton Hewitt. He captured the first major title of his career at the U.S. Open; recorded an impressive six tournament triumphs, including the season-ending Tennis Masters Cup at Sydney, Australia, in November; and became the youngest man ever to conclude a year as the number one ranked player in the world. American Andre Agassi continued his late-career exploits by claiming the Australian Open crown for the second year in a row. Brazil's Gustavo Kuerten came through at the French Open for the third time. The enigmatic Croatian Goran Ivanisevic ruled at Wimbledon.

The women, meanwhile, garnered more than their share of the public's imagination, particularly a trio of prominent Americans. Venus Williams replicated her immense feat of 2000, sweeping to triumphs at both Wimbledon and the U.S. Open. Lindsay Davenport collected seven tournament titles and finished a year ranked number one for the second time. Arguably the year's most inspiring player in the game—man or woman—was Jennifer Capriati, who completed an astounding career comeback at 25 and surged to Australian Open and French Open triumphs in a sterling 2001 campaign. (See BIOGRAPHIES.) Capriati earned a number two status on the official

Women's Tennis Association computer, but she was rewarded by an International Tennis Federation panel as "world champion" because no one else could match her consistency in the major championships. Kuerten was the men's leader in prize money for the second straight year with $4,091,004, while Williams earned top prize money for the women at $2,662,610.

Australian Open. In an unprecedented personal feat, Switzerland's wily Martina Hingis toppled both Venus and Serena Williams in the same tournament. She upended Serena in a spirited quarterfinal clash 6–2, 3–6, 8–6 after Williams built a 4–1, two service-break lead in the final set. Then Hingis crushed Venus Williams 6–1, 6–1 to set up a final-round appointment with the number 12 seed, Capriati. Capriati had ousted four-time former champion Monica Seles of the U.S. and defending champion Davenport to reach the title match. Capriati's weight of shot was too much for Hingis as the American overcame her Swiss adversary for the first time, majestically casting aside the favourite 6–4, 6–3.

Agassi was seeded sixth in his bid to rule "Down Under" for the third time, but three months before he turned 31 the American performed with the panache of a man much younger. In the semifinals he prevailed in a magnificent five-set collision with Australia's Patrick Rafter. Agassi obliterated Frenchman Arnaud Clement 6–4, 6–2, 6–2 with meticulous ground-stroke execution to win the seventh Grand Slam tournament title of his uneven yet estimable career.

French Open. In the middle of his bid for a second consecutive crown on the slow red-clay courts of Roland Garros, Kuerten found himself on the edge of elimination. Facing American qualifier Michael Russell, the 24-year-old Brazilian was match point down before recouping to win 3–6, 4–6, 7–6 (7–5), 6–3, 6–1 in a pivotal fourth-round showdown. Revitalized, Kuerten soared to the title, cutting down Russian Yevgeny Kafelnikov and two Spaniards, Juan Carlos Ferrero and Alex Corretja. The resourceful Corretja picked an uneasy Kuerten apart in the first set with a brisk wind blowing. As the weather conditions became calmer, however, Kuerten's slow court artistry took over and carried him to a 6–7 (3–7), 7–5, 6–2, 6–0 victory.

Capriati was pushed to her physical and emotional limits in a spectacular final against Belgium's rapidly improving Kim Clijsters. After holding back Serena Williams in a three-set quarterfinal and Hingis in a straight-set semifinal, Capriati came into the title-round confrontation with immense confidence. The number four seed from the U.S. was the heavy favourite, but Clijsters, who turned 18 the day before the match, was undaunted in her first major final. Her big-hitting, free-wheeling style of play unsettled the American. In the final set of an uncommonly suspenseful struggle, Capriati was two points away from defeat four times before she prevailed 1–6, 6–4, 12–10.

Wimbledon. At the All-England Club, all eyes were focused on Capriati. In the semifinals she took on number eight seed Justine Henin of Belgium. The American was blazing off both sides at the beginning but in the end Henin's exquisite one-handed backhand enabled the 19-year-old to move past Capriati 2–6, 6–4, 6–2 and into the final. Henin gave Venus Williams sporadic problems during the final, but the number two seed retained her title with a convincing 6–1, 3–6, 6–0 victory.

Ivanisevic was greatly relieved when he was given a wildcard into the main draw. The three-time former finalist had suffered from severe shoulder problems the previous year and had fallen in the qualifying rounds at the Australian Open in January. The towering left-hander had one of the biggest serves ever, however, and over the Wimbledon fortnight his shoulder pain was minimal. Breaking a record he had set in 1992, Ivanisevic released an amazing 212 aces in his seven-match run past (among others) defending U.S. Open champion Marat Safin of Russia, Briton Tim Henman, and Rafter. American Pete Sampras, the victor for seven of the previous eight years, was beaten in five sets by the gifted Roger Federer of Switzerland in the fourth round. Rafter and Ivanisevic confronted each other in a rare Monday final after rain disrupted the schedule. Two points

from defeat at 6–7 in the fifth set, Ivanisevic emerged with a 6–3, 3–6, 6–3, 2–6, 9–7 win.

U.S. Open. Sampras had struggled all year long to find his customary drive and inspiration, but with the American crowds boosting him vociferously, the 30-year-old put on some dazzling displays in New York City. Sampras knocked out three former champions in a row to reach the final—Rafter, Agassi in a classic 6–7 (7–9), 7–6 (7–2), 7–6 (7–2), 7–6 (7–5) quarterfinal, and Safin in a straight-set semifinal. Sampras lost his chance to become the first man to win at least one major title for nine consecutive years when he fell 7–6 (7–4), 6–1, 6–1 to Hewitt in a disappointing final.

The women's event did not sparkle as promised. Venus Williams overpowered her younger sister, Serena, 6–2, 6–4 in a battle between the 2000 and 1999 champions, respectively. It was the first time since 1884 that two sisters had clashed in the final of a major championship. In one-sided semifinals Venus had defeated Capriati 6–4, 6–2, and Serena had routed Hingis 6–3, 6–2.

Other Events. Hewitt took the Tennis Masters Cup. In this eight-player round-robin tournament, Hewitt did not lose a match, defeating Sebastien Grosjean of France in straight sets in the final. Serena Williams was victorious at the women's season-ending Sanex Championships, which was moved from New York City to Munich, Ger. Davenport suffered a knee injury during her semifinal win over Clijsters and was forced to default the title match to Williams.

France upset Australia in Melbourne 3–2 to take the Davis Cup for the ninth time. Belgium defeated Russia 2–1 to capture the Fed Cup.

Off the court the story of the year was that of Agassi and Germany's Steffi Graf, who were married in Las Vegas, Nev., on

October 22, four days before the birth of their son. Between them, Agassi and Graf had secured 29 major singles titles.

(STEVE FLINK)

TRACK AND FIELD SPORTS (ATHLETICS)

The year 2001 was highlighted by both indoor and outdoor world championships, as well as high-profile world records. A Czech decathlete, Roman Sebrle, took the global standard in track and field's "jack-of-all-trades" event from his countryman Tomas Dvorak; American Stacy Dragila, the reigning queen of the women's pole vault, rewrote the record books eight times; and a single autumn week saw the first two women's marathon clockings under 2 hours 20 minutes. The year also saw the farewell tour of Michael Johnson, the American world-record holder at 200 m and 400 m and history's most successful championship long sprinter.

World Indoor Championships. At the International Association of Athletics Federation (IAAF) world indoor championships, held in Lisbon on March 9–11, Cuban long jumper Iván Pedroso jumped 8.43 m (27 ft 8 in) to become the first athlete to win five world indoor golds in a career. Only two other champions from the 2000 Olympic Games in Sydney, Australia—Mozambican Maria Mutola in the women's 800 m and Tereza Marinova of Bulgaria in the women's triple jump—won titles in Lisbon.

Hicham El Guerrouj of Morocco, dominant in the 1,500-m and mile runs since 1997 (with the exception of his loss at the Sydney Olympics), set his eye on the 3,000 m. He had run the second fastest indoor two-mile in history, 8 min 9.89 sec, just two weeks before. In Lisbon he made winning look easy again with a time of 7 min 37.74 sec. Hoping to defend her 3,000-m title on the heels of a women's world record 8 min 32.88 sec three weeks earlier, Romania's Gabriela Szabo wound up more than two seconds behind Russian Olga Yegorova's final-lap burst of speed.

World Outdoor Championships. On August 3–12 Edmonton, Alta., hosted the first world outdoor championships held in North America. In the men's and women's 100-m sprints, two Americans sought to extend their winning streaks in world and Olympic dashes. Maurice Greene succeeded, hobbling the last 15 m as his left thigh muscles cramped painfully. His 9.82-sec clocking into a minor headwind (–0.2 m/sec) was the

Viva Guga! Gustavo Kuerten triumphs in the French Open.

third fastest in history, inferior only to two of his own times, and it led a U.S. medal sweep in the men's event.

Marion Jones had won 42 consecutive 100-m finals dating back to a loss in September 1997. In Edmonton, however, Zhanna Pintusevich-Block, a Ukrainian whose training was guided by her American husband in Johnson City, Tenn., bested Jones by 0.03 second, at 10.82 sec. Pintusevich-Block had celebrated what she at first thought was a victory over Jones before, at the 1997 world championships in Athens, only to learn when official times were posted that the American had edged her by 0.02 second. After that disappointment, Pintusevich-Block had gone on to win the world 200-m title in Athens. This time, as Pintusevich-Block limited herself to the 100 m, Jones won the 200-m gold in 22.39 sec and ran the anchor leg on the victorious U.S. 4 × 100-m relay.

American John Godina, the outdoor world shot-put champion in 1995 and 1997, scored a third gold, throwing 21.87 m (71 ft 9 in). German discus thrower Lars Riedel picked up his fifth world title. The 34-year-old Riedel stood fourth after the third round, in which 2000 Olympic champion Virgilijus Alekna of Lithuania had thrown a meet record 69.40 m (227 ft 8 in). In rounds four and five, though, Riedel whirled off throws of 69.50 m (228 ft) and 69.72 m (228 ft 9 in), the longest marks ever in world championships or Olympic competition. Javelin world-record holder Jan Zelezny of the Czech Republic showed the form that had won him two previous world titles and three Olympic golds since 1992. Finnish rival Aki Parviainen opened with a meet record, 91.31 m (299 ft 7 in), but Zelezny answered with an arching throw of 92.80 m (304 ft 6 in) to win his third world gold at age 35.

In a tense women's pole vault, Dragila cleared 4.75 m (15 ft 7 in), higher than any woman other than herself had ever gone, and then watched as Russian Svetlana Feofanova matched her. Dragila won the gold on the basis of fewer misses.

Men's 10,000-m world-record holder Haile Gebrselassie of Ethiopia had not raced in more than 10 months since Sydney, and 23-year-old Kenyan policeman Charles Kamathi outsprinted him to gold in 27 min 53.25 sec. Gebrselassie took bronze for his first 10,000-m loss in eight seasons and his first defeat at any distance above 1,500 m since 1996. Pedroso, on the other hand, kept his streak going and won the long jump for his fourth outdoor world title.

Drug-testing controversies enveloped the men's and women's 5,000-m races but not men's winner Richard Limo. Limo and his Kenyan teammates used team tactics to blunt the finishing speed of opponents, and Limo took gold in 13 min 0.77 sec. Ali Saïdi Sief, the 2000 Olympic silver medalist, finished second, but later came word that the Algerian had tested positive for the banned steroid nandrolone. Pending an appeals process likely to take months, Saïdi Sief faced disqualification.

Yegorova arrived for the women's 5,000 m under the cloud of a positive test for banned synthetic erythropoietin (EPO) following a win at the Paris Golden League meet. French drug testers, however, had failed to administer a required blood test along with the urinalysis, and the IAAF exonerated her on that basis. Among others in the final, Yegorova met 1,500-m winner and defending 5,000-m champion Szabo, who at one point threatened to withdraw if the Russian competed. Szabo, looking fatigued, faded to eighth place. Yegorova sprinted to victory in 15 min 3.39 sec as jeers rained down from the stands. Regarding the question of EPO use, she maintained her innocence in a postrace press conference.

Men's International Competition. The decathlon world record had belonged to a Czech since Dvorak scored 8,994 points in 1999. At Götzis, Austria, in May, Sebrle outdid Dvorak, scoring 9,026 as the first decathlete in history to surpass 9,000 points. The new champion produced personal bests in the long jump, discus, and javelin and equaled his fastest-ever 100-m time; no decathlete had ever matched his 8.11 m (26 ft 7¼-in) with legal wind. A groin injury hampered Sebrle at the world championships, however, and he placed 10th as Dvorak defended his world title and Olympic gold medalist Erki Nool of Estonia finished second.

Moroccan Brahim Boulami finished 10th in the steeplechase at the world championships, but he followed up at Grand Prix events in Zürich, Switz., and Brussels with wins in 7 min 58.50 sec and a world-record 7 min 55.28 sec, respectively. El Guerrouj assuaged in part his Olympic disappointment with an undefeated year. Briton Jonathan Edwards, the triple-jump world-record holder, won 13 straight meets between June 17 and September 9, including European Cup and world championships victories.

Swiss runner André Bucher, victor in the overall men's IAAF Grand Prix worth $150,000, won 11 of 12 outdoor meets at 800 m and 1,000 m, including the 800-m world title. Russian Yury Borzakovsky had to run the fifth fastest 800 m in history (1 min 42.47 sec) to hand Bucher his only defeat in Brussels. Bucher and El Guerrouj, along with American hurdler Allen Johnson, each garnered one-fifth shares in the Golden League series jackpot of 50 kg (110 lb) of gold.

Women's International Competition. For consistent excellence Dragila, with 25 meets and just three losses, stood out. She matched four indoor world records with four outdoors, topped by a 4.81-m (15-ft 9¼-in) vault in Palo Alto, Calif., in June. From May through the season-ending Grand Prix final in Melbourne, Australia, she never lost.

Yegorova went undefeated at 5,000 m, with just one 3,000-m loss. Her one championship failing was to lose the European Cup 1,500-m final to Romanian Violeta Szekely, herself the past recipient of a drug ban. Szekely won 11 of 12 outdoor 1,500-m races and the women's overall Grand Prix title. She and Yegorova each earned a one-fifth share of the Golden League gold. Jones, supreme star of the three preceding seasons, went undefeated except for her world championships loss, compiling 14 wins in 15 finals at 100 m and 200 m.

Cross Country and Marathon Running. In Berlin on September 30, Olympic champion Naoko Takahashi of Japan became the first woman to break 2 hr 20 min in the women's marathon, knocking 57 seconds from the previous world record. The 2-hour 20-minute barrier had loomed ever since Norwegian Grete Waitz broke 2 hours 30 minutes in 1979, but Takahashi held the record for just a week before Catherine Ndereba of Kenya ran 2 hr 18 min 47 sec at the Chicago Marathon. So strong was Ndereba's finish that she ran from 40 km (24.9 mi) to the finish faster than the top male finishers, Kenyans Benedict Kimondiu and Paul Tergat.

Tergat drew attention with his marathon debut in April, when he ran 2 hr 8 min 15 sec to place second in London. In Chicago Kimondiu, in the race as a pacemaker, elected to finish and defeated Tergat by 4 seconds in 2 hr 8 min 52 sec.

At the world cross country championships in Ostend, Belg., Kenya won four of six team titles, and Ethiopia captured the other two. Belgian Mohamed Mourhit repeated as men's long-course champion. Radcliffe won the women's long-course race over Ethiopian Gete Wami, with positions reversed and Wami defeating Radcliffe in the short-course race. (SIEG LINDSTROM)

VOLLEYBALL

The U.S. women's volleyball team made a large step toward reestablishing itself as a world power with a victory in the ninth World Grand Prix, held in Macau, China, in August 2001. It defeated the host country 3–1 in the final. The U.S. had won the team title in 1995 and had not returned to the final since. Russia, which swept Cuba to capture the bronze medal, finished among the top three for the sixth consecutive World Grand Prix season. In the semifinals the Americans had upset Russia, and China beat defending champion Cuba. Danielle Scott of the U.S. was named the best scorer and blocker; teammates Stacy Sykora and Robyn Ah Mow were tabbed the best digger and best setter, respectively.

In the men's $15 million World League finals, held in Katowice, Pol., in June, Brazil captured its first team title since 1993 as it dethroned Italy 3–0. Italy had won the previous two titles and 8 of the 11 championships. Russia downed Yugoslavia to garner the bronze medal, its fifth World League medal in six campaigns. The 2001 campaign also marked the largest field of nations (16) competing in the World League since its inception in 1990. Yugoslavia's Ivan Milijkovic was named the best scorer, and Mauricio Lima of Brazil was tabbed the best setter.

In beach volleyball the Brazilian duo of Adriana Behar and Shelda won their second straight world title. Mariano Baracetti and Martin Conde of Argentina defeated Brazilians Ricardo and Loiola to win the men's world championship.

(RICHARD S. WANNINGER)

WEIGHT LIFTING

The 2001 International Weightlifting Federation world championships were held in Antalya, Turkey, on November 3–11. A total of 265 athletes entered the competition: 151 men representing 47 countries in eight body-weight classes and 114 women representing 34 countries in seven body-weight classes.

In the men's division Turkey topped the medal rankings with 8 (5 gold, 2 silver, and 1 bronze), followed by Qatar (6 medals, 5 of them gold), Bulgaria (5), Russia (10), and Georgia (3). Superheavyweight Saeed Salem Jaber of Qatar won the overall world champion title with a 460-kg (1,012-lb) overall total. Two-time Olympic superheavyweight champion Andrey Chemerkin of Russia

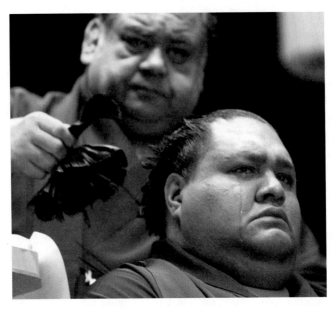

Akebono sheds a tear as his stable master chops off his topknot on September 29.

AP/Wide World Photos

finished third. Henadzy Aliyashchuk of Belarus, Vladimir Smorchkov of Russia, and Halil Mutlu of Turkey each broke one world record.

Russia topped the women's rankings with 9 medals (6 gold, 2 silver, and 1 bronze), followed by China (14, including 5 gold), Poland (8), Hungary (7), and Taiwan (10). Albina Khomitch of Russia won the superheavyweight class with a 282.5-kg (622.8-lb) overall total. Agatha Wrobel of Poland was second.

(DRAGOMIR CIOROSLAN)

WRESTLING

Freestyle and Greco-Roman. In 2001 the world wrestling championships attracted most of the attention in freestyle and Greco-Roman wrestling. The joint event was originally scheduled for New York City's Madison Square Garden on September 26–29, but it was canceled after the terrorist attacks on September 11. The freestyle championships for men and women were later held simultaneously in Sofia, Bulg., on November 22–25. In the men's division Russia won the team race with 51 points. Second place went to host country Bulgaria (46 points); Iran came in third (37 points). In the women's division China won the team title with 36 points. Close behind for second and third places were Japan and Ukraine, both with 33 points. Japan broke the tie and took second place by having more gold medals than Ukraine.

The Greco-Roman championships were held in Patras, Greece, on December 6–9. Cuba pulled a big upset by ousting Russia for the team title with 54 points to Russia's 38. Third place went

to the United States, the first time in history the U.S. had won a team medal. This bronze-medal performance was made possible by the efforts of reigning Olympic superheavyweight (130-kg [286-lb]) champion Rulon Gardner, 1996 Olympic 54-kg (119-lb) silver medalist Brandon Paulson, and 2000 Olympic 85-kg (187-lb) silver medalist Matt Lindland, who won gold, silver, and silver, respectively, in Patras. (JOHN HOKE)

Sumo. Professional sumo's popularity in Japan continued to slip in 2001. The slump was partially attributed to the country's faltering economy and the resultant decline in domestic consumption. The aging of the popular top *rikishi* of the 1990s, however, and the inability of a new generation of *rikishi* to advance to the higher ranks also contributed to reduced popularity.

The most dramatic event in sumo in 2001 was the abrupt retirement of American-born *yokozuna* (grand champion) Akebono after missing the New Year's tournament (Hatsu Basho) in January. Akebono retired at a topknot-cutting ceremony in September with an impressive career record of 566 wins, 198 losses, and 181 days absent in the *makuuchi* division.

Takanohana, the strongest *yokozuna* of the 1990s, won the Hatsu and Natsu (summer) bashos, but he suffered a severe kneecap injury on the next-to-last day of the May tournament and was unable to compete for the rest of the year. *Ozeki* (champion) Kaio won the Haru Basho in March and the Nagoya Basho in July, but he was unable to move up to *yokozuna* because of back trouble.

(CLYDE NEWTON)

Sporting Record

ARCHERY

FITA Outdoor World Target Archery Championships*

Year	Men's individual		Men's team	
	Winner	**Points**	**Winner**	**Points**
1997	Kim Kyung Ho (S.Kor.)	108	South Korea	254
1999	Hong Sung Chil (S.Kor.)	115	Italy	252
2001	**Yeon Jung Ki (S.Kor.)**	**115**	**South Korea**	**247**

Year	Women's individual		Women's team	
	Winner	**Points**	**Winner**	**Points**
1997	Kim Du Ri (S.Kor.)	105	South Korea	242
1999	Lee Eun Kyung (S.Kor.)	115	Italy	240
2001	**Park Sung Hyun (S.Kor.)**	**111**	**China**	**232**

*Olympic (recurve) division.

AUTOMOBILE RACING

Tommi Mäkinen after winning the Monte-Carlo Rally on January 21.

AP/Wide World Photos

Formula One Grand Prix Race Results, 2001

Race	Driver	Winner's time (hr:min:sec)
Australian GP	M. Schumacher	1:38:26.533
Malaysian GP	M. Schumacher	1:47:34.801
Brazilian GP	D. Coulthard	1:39:00.384
San Marino GP	R. Schumacher	1:30:44.817
Spanish GP	M. Schumacher	1:31:03.305
Austrian GP	D. Coulthard	1:27:45.927
Monaco GP	M. Schumacher	1:47:22.561
Canadian GP	R. Schumacher	1:34:31.522
European GP	M. Schumacher	1:29:42.724
French GP	M. Schumacher	1:33:35.636
British GP	M. Hakkinen	1:25:33.770
German GP	R. Schumacher	1:18:17.873
Hungarian GP	M. Schumacher	1:41:49.675
Belgian GP	M. Schumacher	1:08:05.002
Italian GP	J. Montoya	1:16:58.493
United States GP	M. Hakkinen	1:32:42.840
Japanese GP	M. Schumacher	1:27:33.298

WORLD DRIVERS' CHAMPIONSHIP: M. Schumacher 123 points, Coulthard 65 points, Barrichello 56 points.
CONSTRUCTORS' CHAMPIONSHIP: Ferrari 179 points, McLaren/Mercedes 102 points, Williams/BMW 80 points.

Le Mans 24-Hour Grand Prix d'Endurance

Year	Car	Drivers
1999	BMW V12 LMR	Y. Dalmas, P. Martini, J. Winkelhock
2000	Audi R8	F. Biela, T. Kristensen, E. Pirro
2001	**Audi R8**	**F. Biela, T. Kristensen, E. Pirro**

International Cup for Formula One Manufacturers

Year	Car	Year	Car
1996	Williams/Renault	1999	Ferrari
1997	Williams/Renault	2000	Ferrari
1998	McLaren/Mercedes	**2001**	**Ferrari**

World Championship of Drivers

Year	Winner	Car
1999	M. Hakkinen (Fin.)	McLaren/Mercedes
2000	M. Schumacher (Ger.)	Ferrari
2001	**M. Schumacher (Ger.)**	**Ferrari**

National Association for Stock Car Auto Racing (NASCAR) Winston Cup Champions

Year	Winner
1999	D. Jarrett
2000	B. Labonte
2001	**J. Gordon**

Indy Car Champions*

Year	Driver
1999	J. Montoya
2000	G. de Ferran
2001	**G. de Ferran**

*CART champion.

Indianapolis 500

Year	Winner	Avg. speed in mph
1999	K. Brack	153.176
2000	J. Montoya	167.607
2001	**H. Castroneves**	**153.601**

Monte-Carlo Rally

Year	Car	Driver
1999	Mitsubishi Lancer	T. Mäkinen (Fin.)
2000	Mitsubishi Lancer	T. Mäkinen (Fin.)
2001	**Mitsubishi Lancer**	**T. Mäkinen (Fin.)**

BADMINTON

All-England Championships—Singles

Year	Men	Women
1999	P. Gade Christensen (Den.)	Ye Zhaoying (China)
2000	Xia Xuanze (China)	Gong Zhichao (China)
2001	**P. Gopichand (India)**	**Gong Zhichao (China)**

Uber Cup (women)

Year	Winner	Runner-up
1995–96	Indonesia	China
1997–98	China	Indonesia
1999–2000	China	Denmark

Thomas Cup (men)

Year	Winner	Runner-up
1995–96	Indonesia	Denmark
1997–98	Indonesia	Malaysia
1999–2000	Indonesia	China

World Badminton Championships

Year	Men's singles	Women's singles	Men's doubles	Women's doubles
1997	P. Rasmussen (Den.)	Ye Zhaoying (China)	B. Sigit, C. Wijaya (Indon.)	Ge Fei, Gu Jun (China)
1999	Sun Jun (China)	C. Martin (Den.)	Kim Dong Moon, Ha Tae Kwon (S.Kor.)	Ge Fei, Gu Jun (China)
2001	**Hendrawan (Indon.)**	**Gong Ruina (China)**	**T. Gunawan, H. Haryanto (Indon.)**	**Gao Ling, Huang Sui (China)**

BASEBALL

Final Major League Standings, 2001

AMERICAN LEAGUE

East Division

Club	W.	L.	G.B.
*New York	95	65	—
Boston	82	79	13½
Toronto	80	82	16
Baltimore	63	98	32½
Tampa Bay	62	100	34

Central Division

Club	W.	L.	G.B.
*Cleveland	91	71	—
Minnesota	85	77	6
Chicago	83	79	8
Detroit	66	96	25
Kansas City	65	97	26

West Division

Club	W.	L.	G.B.
*Seattle	116	46	—
*Oakland	102	60	14
Anaheim	75	87	41
Texas	73	89	43

NATIONAL LEAGUE

East Division

Club	W.	L.	G.B.
*Atlanta	88	74	—
Philadelphia	86	76	2
New York	82	80	6
Florida	76	86	12
Montreal	68	94	20

Central Division

Club	W.	L.	G.B.
*Houston	93	69	—
*St. Louis	93	69	—
Chicago	88	74	5
Milwaukee	68	94	25
Cincinnati	66	96	27
Pittsburgh	62	100	31

West Division

Club	W.	L.	G.B.
*Arizona	92	70	—
San Francisco	90	72	2
Los Angeles	86	76	6
San Diego	79	83	13
Colorado	73	89	19

*Gained play-off berth.

Caribbean Series

Year	Winning team	Country
1999	Licey Tigers	Dominican Republic
2000	Santurce Crabbers	Puerto Rico
2001	**Cibao Eagles**	**Dominican Republic**

World Series*

Year	Winning team	Losing team	Results
1999	New York Yankees (AL)	Atlanta Braves (NL)	4–0
2000	New York Yankees (AL)	New York Mets (NL)	4–1
2001	**Arizona Diamondbacks (NL)**	**New York Yankees (AL)**	**4–3**

*AL—American League; NL—National League.

Japan Series*

Year	Winning team	Losing team	Results
1999	Fukuoka Daiei Hawks (PL)	Chunichi Dragons (CL)	4–1
2000	Yomiuri Giants (CL)	Fukuoka Daiei Hawks (PL)	4–2
2001	**Yakult Swallows (CL)**	**Osaka Kintetsu Buffaloes**	**4–1**

*CL—Central League; PL—Pacific League.

BASKETBALL

NBA Final Standings, 2000–01

EASTERN CONFERENCE

Atlantic Division

Team	Won	Lost
*Philadelphia	56	26
*Miami	50	32
*New York	48	34
*Orlando	43	39
Boston	36	46
New Jersey	26	56
Washington	19	63

Central Division

Team	Won	Lost
*Milwaukee	52	30
*Toronto	47	35
*Charlotte	46	36
*Indiana	41	41
Detroit	32	50
Cleveland	30	52
Atlanta	25	57
Chicago	15	67

WESTERN CONFERENCE

Midwest Division

Team	Won	Lost
*San Antonio	58	24
*Utah	53	29
*Dallas	53	29
*Minnesota	47	35
Houston	45	37
Denver	40	42
Vancouver	23	59

Pacific Division

Team	Won	Lost
*L.A. Lakers	56	26
*Sacramento	55	27
*Phoenix	51	31
*Portland	50	32
Seattle	44	38
L.A. Clippers	31	51
Golden State	17	65

*Gained play-off berth.

National Basketball Association (NBA) Championship

Season	Winner	Runner-up	Results
1998–99	San Antonio Spurs	New York Knicks	4–1
1999–2000	Los Angeles Lakers	Indiana Pacers	4–2
2000–01	**Los Angeles Lakers**	**Philadelphia 76ers**	**4–1**

Women's National Basketball Association (WNBA) Championship

Season	Winner	Runner-up	Results
1999	Houston Comets	New York Liberty	2–1
2000	Houston Comets	New York Liberty	2–0
2001	**Los Angeles Sparks**	**Charlotte Sting**	**2–0**

Division I National Collegiate Athletic Association (NCAA) Championship—Men

Year	Winner	Runner-up	Score
1999	Connecticut	Duke	77–74
2000	Michigan State	Florida	89–76
2001	**Duke**	**Arizona**	**82–72**

Division I National Collegiate Athletic Association (NCAA) Championship—Women

Year	Winner	Runner-up	Score
1999	Purdue	Duke	62–45
2000	Connecticut	Tennessee	71–52
2001	**Notre Dame**	**Purdue**	**68–66**

National Invitation Tournament (NIT) Championship

Year	Winner	Runner-up	Score
1999	California	Clemson	61–60
2000	Wake Forest	Notre Dame	71–61
2001	**Tulsa**	**Alabama**	**79–60**

World Basketball Championship—Men

Year	Winner	Runner-up
1996	United States	Yugoslavia
1998	Yugoslavia	Russia
2000	United States	France

World Basketball Championship—Women

Year	Winner	Runner-up
1996	United States	Brazil
1998	United States	Russia
2000	United States	Australia

BILLIARD GAMES

WPA World Nine-Ball Championships

Year	Men's champion	Year	Women's champion
1999*	N. Varner (U.S.) E. Reyes (Phil.)	1999	Lu Shin-Mei (Taiwan)
2000	Fong Pang Chao (Taiwan)	2000	J. Kelly (Ire.)
2001	**M. Immonen (Fin.)**	**2001**	**A. Fisher (U.K.)**

*1999 men's tournament played twice.

World Professional Snooker Championship

Year	Winner	Year	Winner
1996	S. Hendry	1999	S. Hendry
1997	K. Doherty	2000	M. Williams
1998	J. Higgins	**2001**	**R. O'Sullivan**

BOWLING

ABC Bowling Championships—Regular Divisions

Year	Singles	Score	All-events	Score
1999	D. Winter	825	T. Jones	2,158
2000	G. Hein	811	R. Daniels	2,181
2001	**N. Hoagland**	**798**	**D.J. Archer**	**2,219**

WIBC Bowling Championships—Classic Division

Year	Singles	Score	All-events	Score
1999	N. Gianulias	746	H. Mizobuchi	2,065
2000	C. Krasner	729	C. Dorin-Ballard	2,147
2001	**L. Wagner**	**756**	**J. Armon**	**2,044**

Professional Bowlers Association (PBA) Tournament of Champions

Year	Champion	Year	Champion
1996	D. D'Entremont	1999	J. Couch
1997	J. Gant	2000	J. Couch
1998	B. Goebel	**2001**	**not held**

FIQ World Bowling Championships—Men

Year	Singles	Pairs	Triples	Team (fives)
1991	Ying Chieh Ma (Taiwan)	United States	United States	Taiwan
1995	M. Doi (Can.)	Sweden	Netherlands	Netherlands
1999	G. Verbruggen (Belg.)	Sweden	Finland	Sweden

FIQ World Bowling Championships—Women

Year	Singles	Pairs	Triples	Team (fives)
1991	M. Beckel (Ger.)	Japan	Canada	South Korea
1995	D. Ship (Can.)	Thailand	Australia	Finland
1999	K. Kulick (U.S.)	Australia	South Korea	South Korea

BOXING

World Heavyweight Champions
No Weight Limit

WBA

Lennox Lewis (U.K.; 11/13/99)
  stripped of title in 2000
Evander Holyfield (U.S.; 8/12/00)
John Ruiz (U.S.; 3/3/01)

WBC

Lennox Lewis (U.K.; 2/7/97)
Hasim Rahman (U.S.; 4/22/01)
Lennox Lewis (U.K.; 11/17/01)

IBF

Lennox Lewis (U.K.; 11/13/99)
Hasim Rahman (U.S.; 4/22/01)
Lennox Lewis (U.K.; 11/17/01)

World Cruiserweight Champions
Top Weight 195 Pounds

WBA

Virgil Hill (U.S.; 12/9/00)

WBC

Juan Carlos Gómez (Ger.; 2/21/98)

IBF

Vassily Jirov (Kazakh.; 6/5/99)

World Light Heavyweight Champions
Top Weight 175 Pounds

WBA

Roy Jones, Jr. (U.S.; 7/18/98)
  declared super champion in 2001
Bruno Girard (Fr.; 12/22/01)

WBC

Roy Jones, Jr. (U.S.; 8/7/97)

IBF

Roy Jones, Jr. (U.S.; 6/5/99)

World Super Middleweight Champions
Top Weight 168 Pounds

WBA

Bruno Girard (Fr.; 4/8/00)
  stripped of title in 2001
Byron Mitchell (U.S.; 3/3/01)

WBC

Davey Hilton (Can.; 12/15/00)
  stripped of title in 2001
Eric Lucas (Can.; 7/10/01)

IBF

Sven Ottke (Ger.; 10/24/98)

World Middleweight Champions
Top Weight 160 Pounds

WBA

William Joppy (U.S.; 1/31/98)
Félix Trinidad (P.R.; 5/12/01)
Bernard Hopkins (U.S.; 9/29/01)
  declared super champion in 2001
William Joppy (U.S.; 11/17/01)

WBC

Keith Holmes (U.S.; 4/24/99)
Bernard Hopkins (U.S.; 4/14/01)

IBF

Bernard Hopkins (U.S.; 4/29/95)

World Junior Middleweight Champions
Top Weight 154 Pounds
(also called super welterweight)

WBA

Félix Trinidad (P.R.; 3/3/00)
  gave up title in 2001
Fernando Vargas (U.S.; 9/22/01)

WBC

Javier Castillejo (Spain; 1/29/99)
Oscar de la Hoya (U.S.; 6/23/01)

IBF

Félix Trinidad (P.R.; 12/2/00)
  gave up title in 2001
Ronald Wright (U.S.; 10/12/01)

BOXING (continued)

World Welterweight Champions
Top Weight 147 Pounds

WBA

James Page (U.S.; 10/10/98)
  stripped of title in 2000
Andrew Lewis (Guyana; 2/17/01)

WBC

Shane Mosley (U.S.; 6/17/00)

IBF

Félix Trinidad (P.R.; 6/19/93)
  gave up title in 2000
Vernon Forrest (U.S.; 5/12/01)
  stripped of title in 2001

World Junior Welterweight Champions
Top Weight 140 Pounds
(also called super lightweight)

WBA

Sharmba Mitchell (U.S.; 10/10/98)
Kostya Tszyu (Austl.; 2/3/01)
  declared super champion in 2001

WBC

Kostya Tszyu (Austl.; 8/21/99)

IBF

Zab Judah (U.S.; 2/12/00)
Kostya Tszyu (Austl.; 11/3/01)

World Lightweight Champions
Top Weight 135 Pounds

WBA

Takanori Hatakeyama (Japan; 6/11/00)
Julien Lorcy (Fr.; 7/1/01)
Raul Balbi (Arg.; 10/8/01)

WBC

José Luis Castillo (Mex.; 6/17/00)

IBF

Paul Spadafora (U.S.; 8/20/99)

World Junior Lightweight Champions
Top Weight 130 Pounds
(also called super featherweight)

WBA

Joel Casamayor (Cuba; 5/21/00)

WBC

Floyd Mayweather, Jr. (U.S.; 10/3/98)

IBF

Steve Forbes (U.S.; 12/3/00)

World Featherweight Champions
Top Weight 126 Pounds

WBA

Derrick Gainer (U.S.; 9/9/00)

WBC

Gustavo Espadas (Mex.; 4/14/00)
Erik Morales (Mex.; 2/17/01)

IBF

Mbulelo Botile (S.Af.; 12/16/00)
Frankie Toledo (U.S.; 4/6/01)
Manuel Medina (Mex.; 11/16/01)

Lennox Lewis jabs at Hasim Rahman en route to regaining the WBC and IBF heavyweight championship belts on November 17 in Las Vegas, Nev.

Matthew Stockman/Allsport

World Junior Featherweight Champions
Top Weight 122 Pounds
(also called super bantamweight)

WBA

Clarence Adams (U.S.; 3/4/00)
  stripped of title in 2001
Yober Ortega (Venez.; 11/17/01)

WBC

Willie Jorrin (U.S.; 9/9/00)

IBF

Lehlohonolo Ledwaba (S.Af.; 5/29/99)
Manny Pacquiao (Phil.; 6/23/01)

World Bantamweight Champions
Top Weight 118 Pounds

WBA

Paulie Ayala (U.S.; 6/26/99)
  stripped of title in 2001
Eidy Moya (Venez.; 10/14/01)

WBC

Veeraphol Sahaprom (Thai.; 12/29/98)

IBF

Tim Austin (U.S.; 7/19/97)

World Junior Bantamweight Champions
Top Weight 115 Pounds
(also called super flyweight)

WBA

Leo Gámez (Venez.; 10/9/00)
Shoji Kobayashi (Japan; 3/11/01)

WBC

Masanori Tokuyama (Japan; 8/27/00)

IBF

Félix Machado (Venez.; 7/22/00)

World Flyweight Champions
Top Weight 112 Pounds

WBA

Eric Morel (U.S.; 8/5/00)

WBC

Malcolm Tunacao (Phil.; 5/19/00)
Pongsaklek Wongjongkam (Thai.; 3/2/01)

IBF

Irene Pacheco (Colom.; 4/10/99)

World Junior Flyweight Champions
Top Weight 108 Pounds

WBA

Bebis Mendoza (Colom.; 8/12/00)
Rosendo Alvarez (Nic.; 3/3/01)

WBC

Choi Yo Sam (S.Kor.; 10/17/99)

IBF

Ricardo López (Mex.; 10/2/99)

World Mini-flyweight Champions
Top Weight 105 Pounds
(also called strawweight)

WBA

Keitaro Hoshino (Japan; 12/6/00)
Chana Porpaoin (Thai.; 4/16/01)
Yutaka Niida (Japan; 8/25/01)
  gave up title in 2001

WBC

José Antonio Aguirre (Mex.; 2/11/00)

IBF

Zolani Petelo (S.Af.; 12/27/97)
  gave up title in 2000
Roberto Leyva (Mex.; 4/29/01)

CHESS

FIDE Chess Championship—Men

Year	Winner	Runner-up
1998	A. Karpov (Russia)	V. Anand (India)
1999	A. Khalifman (Russia)	V. Akopyan (Arm.)
2000	V. Anand (India)	A. Shirov (Spain)

FIDE Chess Championship—Women

Year	Winner	Runner-up
1996	Z. Polgar (Hung.)*	Xie Jun (China)
1999	Xie Jun (China)	A. Galyamova (Russia)
2000	Xie Jun (China)	Qin Karying (China)

*Stripped of title in 1999.

FIDE Olympiad—Men

Year	Winner	Runner-up
1996	Russia	Ukraine
1998	Russia	United States
2000	Russia	Germany

FIDE Olympiad—Women

Year	Winner	Runner-up
1996	Georgia	China
1998	China	Russia
2000	China	Georgia

CONTRACT BRIDGE

World Team Olympiad

Year	Open winner	Open runner-up	Women's winner	Women's runner-up
1992	France	United States	Austria	United Kingdom
1996	France	Indonesia	United States	China
2000	Italy	Poland	United States	Canada

World Contract Bridge Pair Championship

Year	Open winners	Women's winners	Mixed winners
1994	Marcin Lesniewski, Marek Szymanowski (Pol.)	Carla Arnolds, Bep Vriend (Neth.)	Danuta Hocheker, Apolinare Kowalski (Pol.)
1998	Michal Kwiecien, Jacek Pszczola (Pol.)	Jill Meyers, Shawn Quinn (U.S.)	Enza Rossano, Antonio Vivaldi (Italy)

Bermuda Bowl

Year	Winner	Runner-up
1997	France	United States
2000	United States	Brazil
2001	**United States**	**Norway**

CRICKET

Cricket World Cup

Year	Result			
1992	Pakistan	249–6	England	227
1996	Sri Lanka	245–3	Australia	241
1999	Australia	133–2	Pakistan	132

Mufty Munir/AFP Worldwide

Bangladeshi wicket keeper Khaled Masood (right) during a match against Pakistan. Bangladesh became a Test nation in 2001.

All-Time First-Class Test Cricket Standings (as of Sept. 30, 2001)

	England			Australia			South Africa			West Indies			New Zealand		
	Wins	Draws	Losses	W	D	L	W	D	L	W	D	L	W	D	L
England v.	—	—	—	94	86	121	50	47	23	31	43*	52	37	39	6
Australia v.	121	86	94	—	—	—	34	17	14	42	22†	31	18	12	7
South Africa v.	23	47	50	14	17	34	—	—	—	7	2	2	15	9	3
West Indies v.	52	43*	31	31	22†	42	2	2	7	—	—	—	10	14	6
New Zealand v.	6	39	37	7	12	18	3	9	15	6	14	10	—	—	—
India v.	14	38	32	13	18†	29	2	4	6	7	35	28	14	20*	7
Pakistan v.	10	34	16	11	17	18	1	1	2	10	14	13	19	17	6
Sri Lanka v.	3	1	5	1	5	7	1	4	6	0	2	1	4	7	7
Zimbabwe v.	0	3	1	0	0	1	0	1	4	0	1	3	0	6	5
Bangladesh v.	‡	‡	‡	‡	‡	‡	‡	‡	‡	‡	‡	‡	‡	‡	‡

	India			Pakistan			Sri Lanka			Zimbabwe			Bangladesh		
	W	D	L	W	D	L	W	D	L	W	D	L	W	D	L
England v.	32	38	14	16	34	10	5	1	3	1	3	0	‡	‡	‡
Australia v.	29	18†	13	18	17	11	7	5	1	1	0	0	‡	‡	‡
South Africa v.	6	4	2	2	1	1	6	4	1	4	1	0	‡	‡	‡
West Indies v.	28	35	7	13	14	10	1	2	0	3	1	0	‡	‡	‡
New Zealand v.	7	20*	14	6	17	19	7	7	4	5	6	0	‡	‡	‡
India v.	—	—	—	5	33	9	8	12	3	3	2	2	1	0	0
Pakistan v.	9	33	5	—	—	—	13	9*	5	6	5*	2	1	0	0
Sri Lanka v.	3	12	8	5	9*	13	—	—	—	5	5	0	1	0	0
Zimbabwe v.	2	2	3	2	5*	6	0	5	5	—	—	—	2	0	0
Bangladesh v.	0	0	1	0	0	1	0	0	1	0	0	2	—	—	—

*Including one match abandoned. †Including one tie. ‡No matches.

CRICKET (continued)

Test Match Results, October 2000–September 2001

Host/Ground	Date	Scores	Result
Bangladesh/Dhaka	Nov. 10–13	Bangl. 400 and 91; India 429 and 64 for 1	India won by 9 wickets
Pakistan/Lahore	Nov. 15–19	Eng. 480 for 8 dec and 77 for 4 dec; Pak. 401	Match drawn
Pakistan/Faisalabad	Nov. 29–Dec. 3	Pak. 316 and 269 for 3 dec; Eng. 342 and 125 for 5	Match drawn
Pakistan/Karachi	Dec. 7–11	Pak. 405 and 158; Eng. 388 and 176 for 4	Eng. won by 6 wickets; Eng. won series 1–0
South Africa/Bloemfontein	Nov. 17–21	S.Af. 471 for 9 dec and 103 for 5; N.Z. 229 and 342	S.Af. won by 5 wickets
South Africa/Port Elizabeth	Nov. 30–Dec. 4	N.Z. 298 and 148; S.Af. 361 and 89 for 3	S.Af. won by 7 wickets
South Africa/Johannesburg	Dec. 8–12	N.Z. 200; S.Af. 261 for 3 dec	Match drawn; S.Af. won series 2–0
India/Delhi	Nov. 18–22	Zimb. 422 for 9 dec and 225; India 458 for 4 dec and 190 for 3	India won by 7 wickets
India/Nagpur	Nov. 25–29	India 609 for 6 dec; Zimb. 382 and 503 for 6	Match drawn; India won series 1–0
Australia/Brisbane	Nov. 23–25	W.Ind. 82 and 124; Austl. 332	Austl. won by an innings and 126 runs
Australia/Perth	Dec. 1–3	W.Ind. 196 and 173; Austl. 396 for 8 dec	Austl. won by an innings and 27 runs
Australia/Adelaide	Dec. 15–19	W.Ind. 391 and 141; Austl. 403 and 130 for 5	Austl. won by 5 wickets
Australia/Melbourne	Dec. 26–29	Austl. 364 and 262 for 5 dec; W.Ind. 165 and 109	Austl. won by 352 runs
Australia/Sydney	Jan. 2–6	W.Ind. 272 and 352; Austl. 452 and 174 for 4	Austl. won by 6 wickets; Austl. won series 5–0
New Zealand/Wellington	Dec. 26–30	N.Z. 487 for 7 dec and 153 for 4 dec; Zimb. 340 for 6 dec and 60 for 2	Match drawn
South Africa/Durban	Dec. 26–30	S.Af. 420 and 140 for 7 dec; SriL. 216 and 149 for 6	Match drawn
South Africa/Cape Town	Jan. 2–4	SriL. 95 and 180; S.Af. 504 for 7 dec	S.Af. won by an innings and 229 runs
South Africa/Centurion	Jan. 20–22	S.Af. 378; SriL. 119 and 252	S.Af. won by an innings and 7 runs; S.Af. won series 2–0
Sri Lanka/Galle	Feb. 22–26	SriL. 470 for 5 dec; Eng. 253 and 189	SriL. won by an innings and 28 runs
Sri Lanka/Kandy	March 7–11	SriL. 297 and 250; Eng. 387 and 161 for 7	Eng. won by 3 wickets
Sri Lanka/Colombo	March 15–17	SriL. 241 and 81; Eng. 249 and 74 for 6	Eng. won by 4 wickets; Eng. won series 2–1
India/Mumbai	Feb. 27–March 1	India 176 and 219; Austl. 349 and 47 for 0	Austl. won by 10 wickets
India/Kolkata	March 11–15	Austl. 445 and 212; India 171 and 657 for 7 dec	India won by 171 runs
India/Chennai	March 18–22	Austl. 391 and 264; India 501 and 155 for 8	India won by 2 wickets; India won series 2–1
New Zealand/Auckland	March 8–12	Pak. 346 and 336 for 5 dec; N.Z. 252 and 131	Pak. won by 299 runs
New Zealand/Christchurch	March 15–19	N.Z. 476 and 196 for 1 dec; Pak. 571 for 8 dec	Match drawn
New Zealand/Hamilton	March 27–30	Pak. 104 and 118; N.Z. 407 for 4 dec	N.Z. won by an innings and 185 runs; Series drawn 1–1
West Indies/Guyana	March 9–13	W.Ind. 304 and 333 for 7 dec; S.Af. 332 and 142 for 2	Match drawn
West Indies/Trinidad	March 17–21	S.Af. 286 and 287; W.Ind. 342 and 162	S.Af. won by 69 runs
West Indies/Barbados	March 29–April 2	S.Af. 454 and 197 for 9 dec; W.Ind. 387 and 88 for 7	Match drawn
West Indies/Antigua	April 6–10	S.Af. 247 and 215 for 7 dec; W.Ind. 140 and 240	S.Af. won by 82 runs
West Indies/Jamaica	April 19–23	W.Ind. 225 and 301; S.Af. 141 and 255	W.Ind. won by 130 runs; S.Af. won series 2–1
Zimbabwe/Bulawayo	April 19–22	Bangl. 257 and 168; Zimb. 457	Zimb. won by an innings and 32 runs
Zimbabwe/Harare	April 26–30	Bangl. 254 and 266; Zimb. 421 for 9 dec and 100 for 2	Zimb. won by 8 wickets; Zimb. won series 2–0
England/London (Lord's)	May 17–20	Eng. 391; Pak. 203 and 179	Eng. won by an innings and 9 runs
England/Manchester	May 31–June 4	Pak. 403 and 323; Eng. 357 and 261	Pak. won by 108 runs; Series drawn 1–1
Zimbabwe/Bulawayo	June 7–10	Zimb. 173 and 328; India 318 and 184 for 2	India won by 8 wickets
Zimbabwe/Harare	June 15–18	India 237 and 234; Zimb. 315 and 157 for 6	Zimb. won by 4 wickets; Series drawn 1–1
England/Birmingham	July 5–8	Eng. 294 and 164; Austl. 576	Austl. won by an innings and 118 runs
England/London (Lord's)	July 19–22	Eng. 187 and 227; Austl. 401 and 14 for 2	Austl. won by 8 wickets
England/Nottingham	Aug. 2–4	Eng. 185 and 162; Austl. 190 and 158 for 3	Austl. won by 7 wickets
England/Leeds	Aug. 16–20	Austl. 447 and 176 for 4 dec; Eng. 309 and 315 for 4	Eng. won by 6 wickets
England/London (The Oval)	Aug. 23–27	Austl. 641 for 4 dec; Eng. 432 and 184	Austl. won by an innings and 25 runs; Austl. won series 4–1
Zimbabwe/Bulawayo	July 19–22	Zimb. 155 and 228; W.Ind. 559 for 6 dec	W.Ind. won by an innings and 176 runs
Zimbabwe/Harare	July 27–31	Zimb. 131 and 563 for 9 dec; W.Ind. 347 and 98 for 1	Match drawn; W.Ind. won series 1–0
Sri Lanka/Galle	Aug. 14–17	India 187 and 180; SriL. 362 and 6 for 0	SriL. won by 10 wickets
Sri Lanka/Kandy	Aug. 22–25	SriL. 274 and 221; India 232 and 264 for 3	India won by 7 wickets
Sri Lanka/Colombo	Aug. 29–Sept. 2	India 234 and 299; SriL. 610 for 6 dec	SriL. won by an innings and 77 runs; SriL. won series 2–1
Pakistan/Multan	Aug. 29–31	Bangl. 134 and 148; Pak. 546 for 3 dec	Pak. won by an innings and 264 runs
Sri Lanka/Colombo	Sept. 6–8	Bangl. 90 and 328; SriL. 555 for 5 dec	SriL. won by an innings and 137 runs
Zimbabwe/Harare	Sept. 7–11	S.Af. 600 for 3 dec and 79 for 1; Zimb. 286 and 391	S.Af. won by 9 wickets
Zimbabwe/Bulawayo	Sept. 14–18	Zimb. 419 for 9 dec and 96 for 3; S.Af. 519 for 8 dec	Match drawn; S.Af. won series 1–0

CURLING

World Curling Championship—Men

Year	Winner	Runner-up
1999	Scotland	Canada
2000	Canada	Sweden
2001	**Sweden**	**Switzerland**

World Curling Championship—Women

Year	Winner	Runner-up
1999	Sweden	United States
2000	Canada	Switzerland
2001	**Canada**	**Sweden**

CYCLING

Cycling Champions, 2001

Event	Winner	Country
WORLD CHAMPIONS—TRACK		
Men		
Sprint	A. Tournant	France
Individual pursuit	A. Symonenko	Ukraine
Kilometre time trial	A. Tournant	France
40-km points	B. Risi	Switzerland
Team pursuit	S. Chernyavsky, O. Fedenko, A. Symonenko, L. Polotayko	Ukraine
Keirin	R. Bayley	Australia
Olympic sprint	L. Gane, F. Rousseau, A. Tournant	France
60-km Madison	J. Neuville, R. Sassone	France
Women		
Sprint	S. Grankovskaya	Russia
Individual pursuit	L. Zijlaard-Van Moorsel	Netherlands
500-m time trial	N. Contreras Reyes	Mexico
25-km points	O. Slyusareva	Russia
WORLD CHAMPIONS—ROAD		
Men		
Individual road race	O. Freire Gomez	Spain
Individual time trial	J. Ullrich	Germany
Women		
Individual road race	R. Polikeviciute	Lithuania
Individual time trial	J. Longo-Ciprelli	France
WORLD CHAMPION—CYCLO-CROSS		
Men	E. Vervecken	Belgium
Women	H. Kupfernagel	Germany

Event	Winner	Country
WORLD CHAMPIONS—MOUNTAIN BIKES		
Men		
Cross-country	R. Green	Canada
Downhill	N. Vouilloz	France
Women		
Cross-country	A. Dunlap	United States
Downhill	A.-C. Chausson	France
MAJOR ELITE ROAD-RACE WINNERS		
Tour de France	L. Armstrong	United States
Tour of Italy	G. Simoni	Italy
Tour of Spain	A. Casero Moreno	Spain
Tour of Switzerland	L. Armstrong	United States
Milan–San Remo	E. Zabel	Germany
Tour of Flanders	G. Bortolami	Italy
Paris–Roubaix	S. Knaven	Netherlands
Liège–Bastogne–Liège	O. Camenzind	Switzerland
Amstel Gold	E. Dekker	Netherlands
San Sebastian Classic	L. Jalabert	France
HEW–Cyclassics Cup	E. Zabel	Germany
Zurich Championship	P. Bettini	Italy
Paris–Tours	R. Virenque	France
Tour of Lombardy	D. Di Luca	Italy
Paris–Nice	D. Frigo	Italy
Ghent–Wevelgem	G. Hincapie	United States
Flèche Wallonne	R. Verbrugghe	Belgium
Tour of Romandie	D. Frigo	Italy
Dauphiné Libéré	C. Moreau	France
Tirreno–Adriatico	D. Rebellin	Italy

Tour de France

Year	Winner	Kilometres
1999	L. Armstrong (U.S.)	3,687
2000	L. Armstrong (U.S.)	3,663
2001	**L. Armstrong (U.S.)**	**3,454**

EQUESTRIAN SPORTS

The Kentucky Derby

Year	Horse	Jockey
1999	Charismatic	C. Antley
2000	Fusaichi Pegasus	K. Desormeaux
2001	**Monarchos**	**J. Chavez**

The Preakness Stakes

Year	Horse	Jockey
1999	Charismatic	C. Antley
2000	Red Bullet	J. Bailey
2001	**Point Given**	**G. Stevens**

The Belmont Stakes

Year	Horse	Jockey
1999	Lemon Drop Kid	J. Santos
2000	Commendable	P. Day
2001	**Point Given**	**G. Stevens**

2,000 Guineas

Year	Horse	Jockey
1999	Island Sands	L. Dettori
2000	King's Best	K. Fallon
2001	**Golan**	**K. Fallon**

The Derby

Year	Horse	Jockey
1999	Oath	K. Fallon
2000	Sinndar	J. Murtagh
2001	**Galileo**	**M. Kinane**

The St. Leger

Year	Horse	Jockey
1999	Mutafaweq	R. Hills
2000	Millenary	R. Quinn
2001	**Milan**	**M. Kinane**

EQUESTRIAN SPORTS (continued)

Triple Crown Champions—U.S.

Year	Horse
1973	Secretariat
1977	Seattle Slew
1978	Affirmed

Triple Crown Champions—British

Year	Winner
1918	Gainsborough
1935	Bahram
1970	Nijinsky

Melbourne Cup

Year	Horse	Jockey
1999	Rogan Josh	J. Marshall
2000	Brew	K. McEvoy
2001	**Ethereal**	**S. Seamer**

The Hambletonian Trot

Year	Horse	Driver
1999	Self Possessed	M. Lachance
2000	Yankee Paco	T. Ritchie
2001	**Scarlet Knight**	**S. Melander**

Major Thoroughbred Race Winners, 2001

Race	Won by	Jockey
United States		
Acorn	Forest Secrets	C. McCarron
Alabama Stakes	Flute	E. Prado
Apple Blossom	Gourmet Girl	C. Borel
Arlington Million	Silvano	A. Suborics
Ashland Stakes	Fleet Renee	J. Velazquez
Beldame	Exogenous	J. Castellano
Belmont	Point Given	G. Stevens
Beverly D.	England's Legend	C. Nakatani
Blue Grass Stakes	Millennium Wind	L. Pincay, Jr.
Breeders' Cup Juvenile	Johannesburg	M. Kinane
Breeders' Cup Juvenile Fillies	Tempera	D. Romero Flores
Breeders' Cup Sprint	Squirtle Squirt	J. Bailey
Breeders' Cup Mile	Val Royal	J. Valdivia, Jr.
Breeders' Cup Distaff	Unbridled Elaine	P. Day
Breeders' Cup Turf	Fantastic Light	L. Dettori
Breeders' Cup Filly and Mare Turf	Banks Hill	O. Peslier
Breeders' Cup Classic	Tiznow	C. McCarron
Champagne	Officer	V. Espinosa
Charles Whittingham Handicap	Bienamado	C. McCarron
Cigar Mile Handicap	Left Bank	J. Velazquez
Coaching Club American Oaks	Tweedside	J. Velazquez
Donn Handicap	Captain Steve	J. Bailey
Eddie Read	Redattore	A. Solis
Florida Derby	Monarchos	J. Chavez
Flower Bowl Invitational	Lailani	J. Bailey
Fountain of Youth	Songandaprayer	E. Prado
Gulfstream Park Handicap	Sir Bear	E. Coa
Haskell Invitational	Point Given	G. Stevens
Hollywood Derby	Denon	C. McCarron
Hollywood Futurity	Siphonic	J. Bailey
Hollywood Gold Cup	Aptitude	L. Pincay, Jr.
Hollywood Starlet	Habibti	V. Espinoza
Hollywood Turf Cup	Super Quercus	A. Solis
Hopeful Stakes	Came Home	C. McCarron
Jim Dandy Stakes	Scorpion	J. Bailey
Jockey Club Gold Cup	Aptitude	J. Bailey
Kentucky Derby	Monarchos	J. Chavez
Kentucky Oaks	Flute	J. Bailey
Man o' War	With Anticipation	P. Day
Matriarch Stakes	Starine	J. Velazquez
Metropolitan	Exciting Story	P. Husbands
Mother Goose	Fleet Renee	J. Velazquez
Oaklawn Handicap	Traditionally	P. Day
Pacific Classic	Skimming	G. Gomez
Pimlico Special	Include	J. Bailey
Preakness	Point Given	G. Stevens
Queen Elizabeth II Challenge Cup	Affluent	E. Delahoussaye
Santa Anita Derby	Point Given	G. Stevens
Santa Anita Handicap	Tiznow	C. McCarron
Secretariat Stakes	Startac	A. Solis
Spinaway Stakes	Cashier's Dream	D. Meche
Spinster	Miss Linda	R. Migliore
Super Derby	Outofthebox	L. Meche
Swaps Stakes	Congaree	G. Stevens
Travers	Point Given	G. Stevens
Turf Classic Invitational	Timboroa	E. Prado
United Nations Handicap	Senure	R. Davis
Whitney	Lido Palace	J. Bailey
Woodward	Lido Palace	J. Bailey
Yellow Ribbon Stakes	Janet	D. Romero Flores
England		
One Thousand Guineas	Ameerat	P. Robinson
Two Thousand Guineas	Golan	K. Fallon
Derby	Galileo	M. Kinane
Oaks	Imagine	M. Kinane
St. Leger	Milan	M. Kinane
Coronation Cup	Mutafaweq	L. Dettori
Ascot Gold Cup	Royal Rebel	J. Murtagh
Coral-Eclipse Stakes	Medicean	K. Fallon
King George VI and Queen Elizabeth Diamond Stakes	Galileo	M. Kinane
Sussex Stakes	Noverre	L. Dettori
Juddmonte International Stakes	Sakhee	L. Dettori
Dubayy Champion Stakes	Nayef	R. Hills
France		
Poule d'Essai des Poulains	Vahorimix	C. Soumillon
Poule d'Essai des Pouliches	Rose Gypsy	M. Kinane
Prix du Jockey-Club	Anabaa Blue	C. Soumillon
Prix de Diane	Aquarelliste	D. Boeuf
Prix Royal-Oak	Vinnie Roe	P. Smullen
Prix Ganay	Golden Snake	P. Eddery
Prix Jacques Le Marois	Vahorimix	O. Peslier
Grand Prix de Paris	Chichicastenango	A. Junk
Grand Prix de Saint-Cloud	Mirio	C. Soumillon
Prix Vermeille	Aquarelliste	D. Boeuf
Prix de l'Arc de Triomphe	Sakhee	L. Dettori
Grand Criterium	Rock of Gibraltar	M. Kinane
Ireland		
Irish Two Thousand Guineas	Black Minnaloushe	J. Murtagh
Irish One Thousand Guineas	Imagine	S. Heffernan
Irish Derby	Galileo	M. Kinane
Irish Oaks	Lailani	L. Dettori
Irish St. Leger	Vinnie Roe	P. Smullen
Irish Champion Stakes	Fantastic Light	L. Dettori
Italy		
Derby Italiano	Morshdi	P. Robinson
Gran Premio del Jockey Club	Kutub	L. Dettori
Germany		
Deutsches Derby	Boreal	J. Reid
Grosser Preis von Baden	Morshdi	P. Robinson
Europa Preis	Kutub	L. Dettori
Australia		
Melbourne Cup	Ethereal	S. Seamer
Cox Plate	Northerly	D. Oliver
Caulfield Cup	Ethereal	S. Seamer
United Arab Emirates		
Dubayy World Cup	Captain Steve	J. Bailey
Japan		
Japan Cup	Jungle Pocket	O. Peslier
Canada		
Queen's Plate Stakes	Dancethruthedawn	G. Boulanger
Prince of Wales Stakes	Win City	C. Montpellier
Breeders Stakes	Sweetest Thing	J. McAleney

FENCING

World Fencing Championships—Men

Year	Individual			Team		
	Foil	Épée	Sabre	Foil	Épée	Sabre
1999	S. Golubitsky (Ukr.)	A. Schmitt (Ger.)	D. Touya (Fr.)	France	France	France
2000	Kim Young Ho (S.Kor.)	P. Kolobkov (Russia)	M.C. Covaliu (Rom.)	France	Italy	Russia
2001	**S. Sanzo (Italy)**	**P. Milanoli (Italy)**	**S. Pozdnyakov (Russia)**	**France**	**Hungary**	**Russia**

World Fencing Championships—Women

Year	Individual			Team		
	Foil	Épée	Sabre	Foil	Épée	Sabre
1999	V. Vezzali (Italy)	L. Flessel-Colovic (Fr.)	E. Jemaeva (Azer.)	Germany	Hungary	Italy
2000	V. Vezzali (Italy)	T. Nagy (Hung.)	E. Jemaeva (Azer.)	Italy	Russia	United States
2001	**V. Vezzali (Italy)**	**C. Bokel (Ger.)**	**A.-L. Touya (Fr.)**	**Italy**	**Russia**	**Russia**

FIELD HOCKEY

World Cup Field Hockey Championship—Men

Year	Winner	Runner-up
1990	Netherlands	Pakistan
1994	Pakistan	Netherlands
1998	Netherlands	Spain

World Cup Field Hockey Championship—Women

Year	Winner	Runner-up
1990	Netherlands	Australia
1994	Australia	Argentina
1998	Australia	Netherlands

FOOTBALL

FIFA World Cup—Men

Year	Result			
1990	West Germany	1	Argentina	0
1994	Brazil*	0	Italy	0
1998	France	3	Brazil	0

*Won on penalty kicks.

FIFA World Cup—Women

Year	Result			
1991	United States	2	Norway	1
1995	Norway	2	Germany	0
1999	United States*	0	China	0

*Won on penalty kicks.

Association Football National Champions, 2001

Nation	League Champions	Cup Winners	Nation	League Champions	Cup Winners
Albania	Vllaznia	SK Tirana	Italy	Roma	Fiorentina
Andorra	Santa Coloma	Santa Coloma	Latvia	Skonto Riga	Skonto Riga
Argentina	San Lorenzo		Liechtenstein	(no league)	Vaduz
Armenia	Araks	Mika	Lithuania	Kaunas	Atlantas
Austria	Tirol Innsbruck	Kärnten	Luxembourg	Dudelange	Etzella
Azerbaijan	Shamkir	Shafa	Macedonia	Sloga	Pelister
Belarus	Slavia	Belshina	Malta	Valletta	Valletta
Belgium	Anderlecht	Westerlo	Moldova	Serif Tiraspol	Serif Tiraspol
Bolivia	Oriente Petrolero		Netherlands	PSV Eindhoven	Twente
Bosnia	Zeljeznicar	Zeljeznicar	Northern Ireland	Linfield	Glentoran
Brazil	Atlético Paranaense	Gremio	Norway	Rosenborg	Odd Grenland
Bulgaria	Levski	Liteks	Paraguay	Cerro Porteño	
Chile	Santiago Wanderers		Peru	Alianza Lima	
Colombia	América Cali		Poland	Wisla	Polonia
Croatia	Hajduk Split	Dynamo Zagreb	Portugal	Boavista	Porto
Cyprus	Omonia	Apollon	Romania	Steaua	Dinamo Bucharest
Czech Republic	Sparta Prague	Viktoria Zizkov	Russia	Spartak Moscow	Lokomotiv Moscow
Denmark	FC Copenhagen	Silkeborg	San Marino	Cosmos	Domagnano
Ecuador	Emelec		Scotland	Celtic	Celtic
England	Manchester United	Liverpool	Slovakia	Inter	Inter
Estonia	Levadia	Trans Narva	Slovenia	Maribor	Gorica
Faroe Islands	VB Vagur	GI Gøtu	Spain	Real Madrid	Zaragoza
Finland	Haka	HJK Helsinki	Sweden	Halmstads	Elfsborg
France	Nantes	Strasbourg	Switzerland	Grasshoppers	Servette
Georgia	Torpedo Kutaisi	Torpedo Kutaisi	Turkey	Fenerbahce	Genclerbirligi
Germany	Bayern Munich	Schalke	Ukraine	Dynamo Kiev	Shakhtar Donetsk
Greece	Olympiakos	PAOK Salonika	Uruguay	Nacional	
Hungary	Ferencvaros	Debrecen	Venezuela	Estudiantes	
Iceland	KR Reykjavik	IA Akranes	Wales	Barry Town	Caersws
Ireland	Bohemians	Bohemians	Yugoslavia	Red Star Belgrade	Partizan Belgrade
Israel	Maccabi Haifa	Maccabi Tel Aviv			

FOOTBALL (continued)

Libertadores de América Cup

Year	Winner (country)	Runner-up (country)	Scores
1999	Palmeiras (Braz.)	Deportiva Cali (Colom.)	0–1, 2–1, 4–3*
2000	Boca Juniors (Arg.)	Palmeiras (Braz.)	2–2, 0–0, 4–2*
2001	**Boca Juniors (Arg.)**	**Cruz Azul (Mex.)**	**1–0, 0–1, 3–1***

*Winner determined in penalty shootout.

U.S. College Football National Champions

Season	Champion
1999–2000	Florida State
2000–01	Oklahoma
2001–02	**Miami**

Rose Bowl

Season	Result			
1999–2000	Wisconsin	17	Stanford	9
2000–01	Washington	34	Purdue	24
2001–02	**Miami**	**37**	**Nebraska**	**14**

Cotton Bowl

Season	Result			
1999–2000	Arkansas	27	Texas	6
2000–01	Kansas State	35	Tennessee	21
2001–02	**Oklahoma**	**10**	**Arkansas**	**3**

European Cup of Champion Clubs

Season	Result			
1998–99	Manchester United (Eng.)	2	Bayern Munich (Ger.)	1
1999–2000	Real Madrid (Spain)	3	Valencia (Spain)	0
2000–01	**Bayern Munich (Ger.)***	**1**	**Valencia (Spain)**	**1**

*Won on penalty kicks.

Fiesta Bowl

Season	Result			
1999–2000	Nebraska	31	Tennessee	21
2000–01	Oregon State	41	Notre Dame	9
2001–02	**Oregon**	**38**	**Colorado**	**16**

Orange Bowl

Season	Result			
1999–2000	Michigan	35	Alabama	34
2000–01	Oklahoma	13	Florida State	2
2001–02	**Florida**	**56**	**Maryland**	**23**

Sugar Bowl

Season	Result			
1999–2000	Florida State	46	Virginia Tech	29
2000–01	Miami	37	Florida	20
2001–02	**Louisiana State**	**47**	**Illinois**	**34**

NFL Final Standings, 2001–02

AMERICAN CONFERENCE

Eastern Division	W	L	T
*New England	11	5	0
*Miami	11	5	0
*New York Jets	10	6	0
Indianapolis	6	10	0
Buffalo	3	13	0

Central Division	W	L	T
*Pittsburgh	13	3	0
*Baltimore	10	6	0
Cleveland	7	9	0
Tennessee	7	9	0
Jacksonville	6	10	0
Cincinnati	6	10	0

Western Division	W	L	T
*Oakland	10	6	0
Seattle	9	7	0
Denver	8	8	0
Kansas City	6	10	0
San Diego	5	11	0

NATIONAL CONFERENCE

Eastern Division	W	L	T
*Philadelphia	11	5	0
Washington	8	8	0
New York Giants	7	9	0
Arizona	7	9	0
Dallas	5	11	0

Central Division	W	L	T
*Chicago	13	3	0
*Green Bay	12	4	0
*Tampa Bay	9	7	0
Minnesota	5	11	0
Detroit	2	14	0

Western Division	W	L	T
*St. Louis	14	2	0
*San Francisco	12	4	0
New Orleans	7	9	0
Atlanta	7	9	0
Carolina	1	15	0

*Qualified for play-offs.

Super Bowl

	Season	Result			
XXXIV	1999–2000	St. Louis Rams (NFC)	23	Tennessee Titans (AFC)	16
XXXV	2000–01	Baltimore Ravens (AFC)	34	New York Giants (NFC)	7
XXXVI	**2001–02**	**New England Patriots (AFC)**	**20**	**St. Louis Rams (NFC)**	**17**

Grey Cup*

Year	Result			
1999	Hamilton Tiger-Cats (ED)	32	Calgary Stampeders (WD)	21
2000	British Columbia Lions (WD)	28	Montreal Alouettes (ED)	26
2001	**Calgary Stampeders (WD)**	**27**	**Winnipeg Blue Bombers (ED)**	**19**

*ED—Eastern Division; WD—Western Division.

AFL Final Standings, 2001 (League ladder after round 22)

Team*	W	L	D	Points
Essendon	17	5	0	68
Brisbane	17	5	0	68
Port Adelaide	16	6	0	64
Richmond	15	7	0	60
Carlton	14	8	0	56
Hawthorn	13	9	0	52
Sydney	12	10	0	48
Adelaide	12	10	0	48

*Teams that qualified for play-offs.

FOOTBALL (continued)

Record of International Rugby Union Test Matches 1871 to Oct. 31, 2001

	England			Scotland			Ireland			Wales			British Isles*		
	Wins	Draws	Losses	Wins	Draws	Losses	Wins	Draws	Losses	Wins	Draws	Losses	Wins	Draws	Losses
England v.	—	—	—	61	17	40	67	8	39	46	12	49	—	—	—
Scotland v.	40	17	61	—	—	—	61	5	46	45	3	57	—	—	—
Ireland v.	39	8	67	46	5	61	—	—	—	39	6	60	—	—	—
Wales v.	49	12	46	57	3	45	60	6	39	—	—	—	—	—	—
British Isles* v.															
South Africa v.	12	1	7	9	0	3	12	1	1	12	1	1	19	4	10
New Zealand v.	18	1	4	21	2	0	13	1	0	14	0	3	23	2	6
Australia v.	16	1	8	12	0	7	14	0	6	12	0	8	4	0	9
France v.	28	7	43	37	3	33	43	5	27	33	3	41	†	†	†

	South Africa			New Zealand			Australia			France		
	Wins	Draws	Losses	Wins	Draws	Losses	Wins	Draws	Losses	Wins	Draws	Losses
England v.	7	1	12	4	1	18	8	1	16	43	7	28
Scotland v.	3	0	9	0	2	21	7	0	12	33	3	37
Ireland v.	1	1	12	0	1	13	6	0	14	27	5	43
Wales v.	1	1	12	3	0	14	8	0	12	41	3	33
British Isles* v.	10	4	19	6	2	23	9	0	4	†	†	†
South Africa v.	—	—	—	25	3	25	27	1	14	19	5	6
New Zealand v.	25	3	25	—	—	—	71	5	33	26	0	9
Australia v.	14	1	27	33	5	71	—	—	—	11	2	13
France v.	6	5	19	9	0	26	13	2	11	—	—	—

*The British Isles ("British Lions") is a combined team from the four "Home Unions" (England, Ireland, Scotland, and Wales).   †No matches.

Rugby League World Cup

Year	Result			
1992	Australia	10	Great Britain	6
1995	Australia	16	England	8
2000	Australia	40	New Zealand	12

Rugby Union World Cup

Year	Result			
1991	Australia	12	England	6
1995	South Africa	15	New Zealand	12
1999	Australia	35	France	12

Six Nations Championship*

Year	Result
1999	Scotland
2000	England
2001	**England**

*Five Nations until 2000.

GOLF

Masters Tournament

Year	Winner
1999	J.-M. Olazábal (Spain)
2000	V. Singh (Fiji)
2001	**T. Woods (U.S.)**

United States Open Championship (men)

Year	Winner
1999	P. Stewart (U.S.)
2000	T. Woods (U.S.)
2001	**R. Goosen (S.Af.)**

British Open Tournament (men)

Year	Winner
1999	P. Lawrie (Scot.)
2000	T. Woods (U.S.)
2001	**D. Duval (U.S.)**

U.S. Professional Golfers' Association (PGA) Championship

Year	Winner
1999	T. Woods (U.S.)
2000	T. Woods (U.S.)
2001	**D. Toms (U.S.)**

United States Amateur Championship (men)

Year	Winner
1999	D. Gossett (U.S.)
2000	J. Quinney (U.S.)
2001	**B. Dickerson (U.S.)**

British Amateur Championship (men)

Year	Winner
1999	G. Storm (U.K.)
2000	M. Ilonen (Fin.)
2001	**M. Hoey (Ire.)**

United States Women's Open Championship

Year	Winner
1999	J. Inkster (U.S.)
2000	K. Webb (Austl.)
2001	**K. Webb (Austl.)**

Women's British Open Championship

Year	Winner
1999	S. Steinhauer (U.S.)
2000	S. Gustafson (Swed.)
2001	**Pak Se Ri (S.Kor.)**

Ladies Professional Golf Association (LPGA) Championship

Year	Winner
1999	J. Inkster (U.S.)
2000	J. Inkster (U.S.)
2001	**K. Webb (Austl.)**

United States Women's Amateur Championship

Year	Winner
1999	D. Delasin (U.S.)
2000	M. Newton (U.S.)
2001	**M. Duncan (U.S.)**

Ladies' British Amateur Championship

Year	Winner
1999	M. Monnet (Fr.)
2000	R. Hudson (U.K.)
2001	**M. Prieto (Spain)**

Walker Cup (men; amateur)

Year	Result
1997	United States 18, Britain and Ireland 6
1999	Britain and Ireland 15, United States 9
2001	**Britain and Ireland 15, United States 9**

David Duval shows off his winning form in the British Open.

Harry How/Allsport

GOLF (continued)

World Cup (men; professional)

Year	Winner
1999	United States (T. Woods and M. O'Meara)
2000	United States (T. Woods and D. Duval)
2001	**South Africa (E. Els and R. Goosen)**

Ryder Cup (men; professional)

Year	Result
1997	Europe 14½, United States 13½
1999	United States 14½, Europe 13½
2001	**postponed until 2002**

Curtis Cup (women; amateur)

Year	Result
1996	Britain and Ireland 11½, United States 6½
1998	United States 10, Britain and Ireland 8
2000	United States 10, Britain and Ireland 8

GYMNASTICS

World Gymnastics Championships—Men

Year	All-around team	All-around individual	Horizontal bar	Parallel bars
1999	China	N. Krukov (Russia)	J. Carballo (Spain)	Lee Joo Hyung (S.Kor.)
2000	China	A. Nemov (Russia)	A. Nemov (Russia)	Li Xiaopeng (China)
2001	**Belarus**	**Feng Jing (China)**	**V. Maras (Greece)**	**S. Townsend (U.S.)**

Year	Pommel horse	Rings	Vault	Floor exercise
1999	A. Nemov (Russia)	Dong Zhen (China)	Li Xiaopeng (China)	A. Nemov (Russia)
2000	M. Urzica (Rom.)	S. Csollany (Hung.)	G. Deferr (Spain)	I. Vihrons (Latvia)
2001	**M. Urzica (Rom.)**	**J. Jovtchev (Bulg.)**	**M. Dragulescu (Rom.)**	**J. Jovtchev (Bulg.)***
				M. Dragulescu (Rom.)*

* Tied.

World Gymnastics Championships—Women

Year	All-around team	All-around individual	Balance beam
1999	Romania	M. Olaru (Rom.)	Ling Jie (China)
2000	Romania	S. Amanar (Rom.)	Liu Xuan (China)
2001	**Romania**	**S. Khorkina (Russia)**	**A. Raducan (Rom.)**

Year	Uneven parallel bars	Vault	Floor exercise
1999	S. Khorkina (Russia)	Ye. Zamolodchikova (Russia)	A. Raducan (Rom.)
2000	S. Khorkina (Russia)	Ye. Zamolodchikova (Russia)	Ye. Zamolodchikova (Russia)
2001	**S. Khorkina (Russia)**	**S. Khorkina (Russia)**	**A. Raducan (Rom.)**

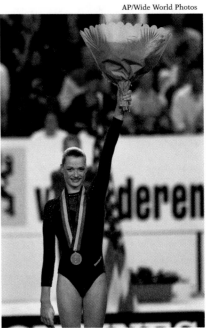

AP/Wide World Photos

Svetlana Khorkina acknowledges the crowd after winning the all-around individual gold medal at the world gymnastics championships in Brussels on November 2.

ICE HOCKEY

NHL Final Standings, 2001

EASTERN CONFERENCE

Northeast Division	W	L	T	OTL*
†Ottawa	48	21	9	4
†Buffalo	46	30	5	1
†Toronto	37	29	11	5
Boston	36	30	8	8
Montreal	28	40	8	6

Atlantic Division	W	L	T	OTL*
†New Jersey	48	19	12	3
†Philadelphia	43	25	11	3
†Pittsburgh	42	28	9	3
New York Rangers	33	43	5	1
New York Islanders	21	51	7	3

Southeast Division	W	L	T	OTL*
†Washington	41	27	10	4
†Carolina	38	32	9	3
Florida	22	38	13	9
Atlanta	23	45	12	2
Tampa Bay	24	47	6	5

WESTERN CONFERENCE

Central Division	W	L	T	OTL*
†Detroit	49	20	9	4
†St. Louis	43	22	12	5
Nashville	34	36	9	3
Chicago	29	40	8	5
Columbus	28	39	9	6

Northwest Division	W	L	T	OTL*
†Colorado	52	16	10	4
†Edmonton	39	28	12	3
†Vancouver	36	28	11	7
Calgary	27	36	15	4
Minnesota	25	39	13	5

Pacific Division	W	L	T	OTL*
†Dallas	48	24	8	2
†San Jose	40	27	12	3
†Los Angeles	38	28	13	3
Phoenix	35	27	17	3
Anaheim	25	41	11	5

*Overtime losses, worth one point. †Qualified for play-offs.

The Stanley Cup

Season	Winner	Runner-up	Games
1998–99	Dallas Stars	Buffalo Sabres	4–2
1999–2000	New Jersey Devils	Dallas Stars	4–2
2000–01	**Colorado Avalanche**	**New Jersey Devils**	**4–3**

World Ice Hockey Championship—Men

Year	Winner
1999	Czech Republic
2000	Czech Republic
2001	**Czech Republic**

World Ice Hockey Championship—Women

Year	Winner
1999	Canada
2000	Canada
2001	**Canada**

ICE SKATING

World Figure Skating Champions—Men

Year	Winner
1999	A. Yagudin (Russia)
2000	A. Yagudin (Russia)
2001	**Ye. Plushchenko (Russia)**

World Figure Skating Champions—Women

Year	Winner
1999	M. Butyrskaya (Russia)
2000	M. Kwan (U.S.)
2001	**M. Kwan (U.S.)**

World Figure Skating Champions—Pairs

Year	Winners
1999	Ye. Berezhnaya, A. Sikharulidze (Russia)
2000	M. Petrova, A. Tikhonov (Russia)
2001	**J. Salé, D. Pelletier (Can.)**

World Ice Dancing Champions

Year	Winners
1999	A. Krylova, O. Ovsyannikov (Russia)
2000	M. Anissina, G. Peizarat (Fr.)
2001	**B. Fusar Poli, M. Margaglio (Italy)**

World Ice Speed-Skating Records Set in 2001 on Major Tracks*

Event	Name	Country	Time
MEN			
500 m	Hiroyasu Shimizu	Japan	34.32 sec
1,000 m	Michael Ireland	Canada	1 min 8.34 sec
	Jeremy Wotherspoon	Canada	1 min 8.28 sec
	Jeremy Wotherspoon	Canada	1 min 7.72 sec
1,500 m	Lee Kyu Hyuk	South Korea	1 min 45.20 sec
WOMEN			
500 m	Catriona LeMay-Doan	Canada	37.40 sec
	Catriona LeMay-Doan	Canada	37.29 sec
	Catriona LeMay-Doan	Canada	37.22 sec
1,000 m	Christine Witty	United States	1 min 14.58 sec
	Monique Garbrecht-Enfeldt	Germany	1 min 14.13 sec
	Sabine Völker	Germany	1 min 14.06 sec
1,500 m	Anna Friesinger	Germany	1 min 54.38 sec
3,000 m	Gunda Niemann-Stirnemann	Germany	4 min 0.26 sec
	Claudia Pechstein	Germany	3 min 59.26 sec
5,000 m	Gunda Niemann-Stirnemann	Germany	6 min 52.44 sec

*Subject to ISU ratification.

World Ice Speed-Skating Records Set in 2001 on Short Tracks*

Event	Name	Country	Time
MEN			
500 m	Jeffrey Scholten	Canada	41.514 sec
1,000 m	Steve Robillard	Canada	1 min 25.985 sec
1,500 m	Eric Bédard	Canada	2 min 15.393 sec
	Steve Robillard	Canada	2 min 15.383 sec
	Fabio Carta	Italy	2 min 13.533 sec
5,000-m relay	Canada National Team	Canada	6 min 43.730 sec
WOMEN			
500 m	Evgenia Radanova	Bulgaria	43.671 sec
1,000 m	Yang Yang (A)	China	1 min 31.871 sec
3,000-m relay	China National Team	China	4 min 13.541 sec

*Subject to ISU ratification.

World Speed-Skating Sprint Championships

Year	Men	Women
1999	J. Wotherspoon (Can.)	M. Garbrecht (Ger.)
2000	J. Wotherspoon (Can.)	M. Garbrecht (Ger.)
2001	**M. Ireland (Can.)**	**M. Garbrecht-Enfeldt (Ger.)**

World All-Around Speed-Skating Champions—Men

Year	Winner
1999	R. Ritsma (Neth.)
2000	G. Romme (Neth.)
2001	**R. Ritsma (Neth.)**

World All-Around Speed-Skating Champions—Women

Year	Winner
1999	G. Niemann-Stirnemann (Ger.)
2000	C. Pechstein (Ger.)
2001	**A. Friesinger (Ger.)**

World Short-Track Speed-Skating Championships—Overall Winners

Year	Men	Women
1999	Li Jianjun (China)	Yang Yang (A) (China)
2000	Ryoung Min (S.Kor.)	Yang Yang (A) (China)
2001	**Li Jianjun (China)**	**Yang Yang (A) (China)**

JUDO

World Judo Championships—Men*

Year	Open weights	60 kg	65 kg (66 kg)	71 kg (73 kg)
1997	R. Kubacki (Pol.)	T. Nomura (Japan)	Kim Hyuk (S.Kor.)	K. Nakamura (Japan)
1999	S. Shinohara (Japan)	M. Poulot (Cuba)	L. Benboudaoud (Fr.)	J. Pedro (U.S.)
2001	**A. Mikhaylin (Russia)**	**A. Lounifi (Tun.)**	**A. Miresmaeili (Iran)**	**V. Makarov (Russia)**

Year	78 kg (81 kg)	86 kg (90 kg)	95 kg (100 kg)	+95 kg (+100 kg)
1997	Cho In Chul (S.Kor.)	Jeon Ki Young (S.Kor.)	P. Nastula (Pol.)	D. Douillet (Fr.)
1999	G. Randall (U.K.)	H. Yoshida (Japan)	K. Inoue (Japan)	S. Shinohara (Japan)
2001	**Cho In Chul (S.Kor.)**	**F. Demontfaucon (Fr.)**	**K. Inoue (Japan)**	**A. Mikhaylin (Russia)**

*Figures in parentheses represent new weight classes established in 1999.

World Judo Championships—Women*

Year	Open weights	48 kg	52 kg	56 kg (57 kg)
1997	D. Beltran (Cuba)	R. Tamura (Japan)	M.-C. Restoux (Fr.)	I. Fernández (Spain)
1999	D. Beltran (Cuba)	R. Tamura (Japan)	N. Narasaki (Japan)	D. González (Cuba)
2001	**C. Lebrun (Fr.)**	**R. Tamura (Japan)**	**Kye Sun Hui (N.Kor.)**	**Y. Lupetry (Cuba)**

Year	61 kg (63 kg)	66 kg (70 kg)	72 kg (78 kg)	+72 kg (+78 kg)
1997	S. Vandenhende (Fr.)	K. Howey (U.K.)	N. Anno (Japan)	C. Cicot (Fr.)
1999	K. Maeda (Japan)	S. Veranes (Cuba)	N. Anno (Japan)	B. Maksymow (Pol.)
2001	**G. Vandecaveye (Belg.)**	**M. Ueno (Japan)**	**N. Anno (Japan)**	**Yuan Hua (China)**

*Figures in parentheses represent new weight classes established in 1999.

RODEO

Men's World All-Around Rodeo Championship

Year	Winner	Year	Winner
1996	J. Beaver	1999	F. Whitfield
1997	D. Mortensen	2000	J. Beaver
1998	T. Murray	**2001**	**C. Ohl**

ROWING

World Rowing Championships—Men

Year	Single sculls	Min:sec	Double sculls	Min:sec	Quadruple sculls	Min:sec	Coxed pairs	Min:sec
1999	R. Waddell (N.Z.)	6:36.68	L. Spik, I. Cop (Slvn.)	6:04.37	Germany	6:24.37	J. Neil, P. Henry (U.S.)	6:48.56
2000	R. Waddell (N.Z.)	6:48.90	L. Spik, I. Cop (Slvn.)	6:16.63	Italy	5:45.56	K. Borcherding, M. Guerrieri (U.S.)	7:07.15
2001	**O. Tufte (Nor.)**	**6:43.04**	**A. Haller, T. Peto (Hung.)**	**6:14.16**	**Germany**	**5:40.89**	**J. Cracknell, M. Pinsent (Gr.Brit.)**	**6:49.33**

Year	Coxless pairs	Min:sec	Coxed fours	Min:sec	Coxless fours	Min:sec	Eights	Min:sec
1999	D. Ginn, J. Tomkins (Austl.)	6:19.00	United States	6:38.31	Great Britain	5:48.57	United States	6:01.58
2000	M. Andrieux, J.-C. Rolland (Fr.)	6:32.97	Great Britain	6:16.82	Great Britain	5:56.24	Great Britain	5:33.08
2001	**J. Cracknell, M. Pinsent (Gr.Brit.)**	**6:27.57**	**France**	**6:08.25**	**Great Britain**	**5:48.98**	**Romania**	**5:27.48**

World Rowing Championships—Women

Year	Single sculls	Min:sec	Double sculls	Min:sec	Quadruple sculls	Min:sec
1999	Ye. Karsten (Bela.)	7:11.68	J. Thieme, K. Boron (Ger.)	6:41.98	Germany	7:06.53
2000	Ye. Karsten (Bela.)	7:28.14	J. Thieme, K. Boron (Ger.)	6:55.44	Germany	6:19.58
2001	**K. Rutschow-Stomporowski (Ger.)**	**7:19.25**	**K. Boron, K. Kowalski (Ger.)**	**6:50.20**	**Germany**	**6:12.95**

Year	Coxless pairs	Min:sec	Coxless fours	Min:sec	Eights	Min:sec
1999	E. Robinson, T. Luke (Can.)	7:00.85	Belarus	6:26.25	Romania	6:47.66
2000	G. Damian, D. Ignat (Rom.)	7:11.00	Belarus	6:44.90	Romania	6:06.44
2001	**G. Damian, V. Susanu (Rom.)**	**7:01.27**	**Australia**	**6:27.23**	**Australia**	**6:03.66**

James Cracknell and Matthew Pinsent compete in the world rowing championships in Lucerne, Switz., on August 19.

Jamie McDonald/Allsport

The Diamond Challenge Sculls

Year	Winner	Min:sec
1999	M. Hacker (Ger.)	7:59
2000	A.H. Abdullah (U.S.)	8:12
2001	**D.S. Free (Austl.)**	**8:18**

Grand Challenge Cup

Year	Winner	Min:sec
1999	Hansa Dortmund and Berlin, Ger.	6:15
2000	Institute of Sport, Australia	6:19
2001	**H.A.V.K. Mladost and V.K. Croatia, Croatia**	**6:29**

SAILING (YACHTING)

America's Cup

Year	Winning yacht	Owner	Skipper	Losing yacht	Owner
1992	*America³* (U.S.)	America³ Foundation	B. Koch	*Il Moro di Venezia* (Italy)	Compagnia della Vela di Venezia
1995	*Black Magic* (N.Z.)	P. Blake and Team New Zealand	R. Coutts	*Young America*	Pact 95 syndicate
2000	*Black Magic* (N.Z.)	Team New Zealand	R. Coutts	*Luna Rossa* (Italy)	Prada Challenge

World Class Boat Champions, 2001

Class	Winner	Country
Etchells 22	S. Childerley	Great Britain
Europe	S. Multala	Finland
Finn	S. Godefroid	Belgium
2.4 Metre	H. Kroger	Germany
470 (men)	Y. Braslavets/I. Matviyenko	Ukraine
470 (women)	S. Bekatorou/E. Tsoulfa	Greece
49er	J. McKee/C. McKee	United States
Laser	R. Scheidt	Brazil
Mistral (men)	N. Kaklamanakis	Greece
Mistral (women)	Lee Lai Shan	Hong Kong
J/24	K. Hyodo	Japan
Optimist	L. Calabrese	Argentina
Star	F. Lööf/C. Finnsgård	Sweden
Tornado	D. Bundock/J. Forbes	Australia
Yngling	C. Skolaut	Austria

Admiral's Cup

Year	Winning team
1997	United States
1999	Netherlands
2001	**canceled**

Bermuda Race

Year	Winning yacht	Owner
1996	*Boomerang*	G. Coumantaros
1998	*Kodiak*	L. Ecclestone
2000	*Restless*	E. Crawford

Transpacific Race

Year	Winning yacht	Owner
1997	*Ralphie*	J. Montgomery
1999	*Grand Illusion*	J. McDowell
2001	***Bull***	**S. Radow**

SKIING

World Alpine Skiing Championships—Slalom

Year	Men's slalom	Men's giant slalom	Men's supergiant	Women's slalom	Women's giant slalom	Women's supergiant
1998	H.-P. Buraas (Nor.)	H. Maier (Austria)	H. Maier (Austria)	H. Gerg (Ger.)	D. Compagnoni (Italy)	P. Street (U.S.)
1999	K. Palander (Fin.)	L. Kjus (Nor.)	L. Kjus (Nor.)* H. Maier (Austria)*	Z. Steggall (Austl.)	A. Meissnitzer (Austria)	A. Meissnitzer (Austria)
2001	**M. Matt (Austria)**	**M. von Grünigen (Switz.)**	**D. Rahlves (U.S.)**	**A. Paerson (Swed.)**	**S. Nef (Switz.)**	**R. Cavagnoud (Fr.)**

*Tie.

World Alpine Skiing Championships—Downhill

Year	Men	Women
1998	J.-L. Cretier (Fr.)	K. Seizinger (Ger.)
1999	H. Maier (Austria)	R. Götschl (Austria)
2001	**H. Trinkl (Austria)**	**M. Dorfmeister (Austria)**

World Alpine Skiing Championships—Combined

Year	Men	Women
1998	M. Reiter (Austria)	K. Seizinger (Ger.)
1999	K.A. Aamodt (Nor.)	P. Wiberg (Swed.)
2001	**K.A. Aamodt (Nor.)**	**M. Ertl (Ger.)**

Alpine World Cup

Year	Men	Women
1999	L. Kjus (Nor.)	A. Meissnitzer (Austria)
2000	H. Maier (Austria)	R. Götschl (Austria)
2001	**H. Maier (Austria)**	**J. Kostelic (Cro.)**

World Nordic Skiing Championships—Men

Year	Sprint	10-km	15-km	30-km	50-km	Relay
1998		B. Dæhlie (Nor.)	T. Alsgaard (Nor.)	M. Myllylä (Fin.)	B. Dæhlie (Nor.)	Norway
1999		M. Myllylä (Fin.)	T. Alsgaard (Nor.)	M. Myllylä (Fin.)	M. Myllylä (Fin.)	Austria
2001	**T.A. Hetland (Nor.)**	**P. Elofsson (Swed.)**	**P. Elofsson (Swed.)**	**A. Veerpalu (Est.)**	**J. Mühlegg (Spain)**	**Norway**

World Nordic Skiing Championships—Women

Year	Sprint	5-km	10-km	15-km	30-km	Relay
1998		L. Lazutina (Russia)	L. Lazutina (Russia)	O. Danilova (Russia)	Yu. Chepalova (Russia)	Russia
1999		B. Martinsen (Nor.)	S. Belmondo (Italy)	S. Belmondo (Italy)	L. Lazutina (Russia)	Russia
2001	**P. Manninen (Fin.)**	**V. Kuitunen (Fin.)**	**B. Skari Martinsen (Nor.)**	**B. Skari Martinsen (Nor.)**	**canceled**	**Russia**

World Nordic Skiing Championships—Ski Jump

Year	Normal hill*	Large hill†	Team jump (normal hill)	Team jump (large hill)	Combined (7.5-km)	Combined (15-km)	Team combined
1998	J. Soininen (Fin.)	K. Funaki (Japan)		Japan		B.E. Vik (Nor.)	Norway
1999	K. Funaki (Japan)	M. Schmitt (Ger.)		Germany	B.E. Vik (Nor.)	B.E. Vik (Nor.)	Finland
2001	**A. Malysz (Pol.)**	**M. Schmitt (Ger.)**	**Austria**	**Germany**	**M. Baacke (Ger.)**	**B.E. Vik (Nor.)**	**Norway**

*90-m. †120-m through 1999, 116-m in 2001.

Nordic World Cup

Year	Men	Women
1999	B. Dæhlie (Nor.)	B. Martinsen (Nor.)
2000	J. Mühlegg (Spain)	B. Martinsen (Nor.)
2001	**P. Elofsson (Swed.)**	**Yu. Chepalova (Russia)**

Zoom Sports/Allsport

Sonja Nef races to a first-place finish in the women's giant slalom event at the world alpine skiing championships in February.

SQUASH

British Open Championship—Men

Year	Winner
1998–99	J. Power (Can.)
1999–2000	D. Evans (Wales)
2000–01	**D. Palmer (Austl.)**

British Open Championship—Women

Year	Winner
1998–99	L. Joyce (N.Z.)
1999–2000	L. Joyce (N.Z.)
2000–01	**S. Fitz-Gerald (Austl.)**

World Open Championship—Men

Year	Winner
1999	P. Nicol (Scot.)
2000	not held
2001	**canceled**

World Open Championship—Women

Year	Winner
1999	C. Campion (Eng.)
2000	C. Owens (Austl.)
2001	**S. Fitz-Gerald (Austl.)**

SWIMMING

World Swimming Records Set in 2001 in 25-m Pools

Event	Name	Country	Time
MEN			
50-m freestyle	Mark Foster	United Kingdom	21.13 sec
800-m freestyle	Grant Hackett	Australia	7 min 25.28 sec
1,500-m freestyle	Grant Hackett	Australia	14 min 10.10 sec
50-m breaststroke	Roman Sludnov	Russia	29.90 sec
50-m butterfly	Mark Foster	United Kingdom	22.87 sec
	Geoff Huegill	Australia	22.84 sec
100-m butterfly	Thomas Rupprath	Germany	50.26 sec
200-m butterfly	Franck Esposito	France	1 min 51.58 sec
	Thomas Rupprath	Germany	1 min 51.21 sec
4 × 50-m medley relay	German National Team	Germany	1 min 35.14 sec
	German National Team	Germany	1 min 34.78 sec
4 × 200-m freestyle relay	Australia National Team	Australia	6 min 56.41 sec
WOMEN			
800-m freestyle	Chen Hua	China	8 min 15.15 sec
1,500-m freestyle	Rebecca Cooke	United Kingdom	15 min 52.97 sec
50-m backstroke	Li Hui	China	26.83 sec
100-m backstroke	Mai Nakamura	Japan	58.45 sec
	Natalie Coughlin	United States	57.08 sec
200-m backstroke	Sarah Price	United Kingdom	2 min 4.44 sec
	Natalie Coughlin	United States	2 min 3.62 sec
50-m breaststroke	Li Wei*	China	30.56 sec
	Luo Xuejuan*	China	30.56 sec
200-m breaststroke	Qi Hui	China	2 min 19.25 sec
50-m butterfly	Anna-Karin Kammerling	Sweden	25.36 sec
4 × 200-m freestyle relay	British National Team	United Kingdom	7 min 58.69 sec

*Tied.

World Swimming Records Set in 2001 in 50-m Pools

Event	Name	Country	Time
MEN			
200-m freestyle	Ian Thorpe	Australia	1 min 44.69 sec
	Ian Thorpe	Australia	1 min 44.06 sec
400-m freestyle	Ian Thorpe	Australia	3 min 40.17 sec
800-m freestyle	Ian Thorpe	Australia	7 min 41.59 sec
	Ian Thorpe	Australia	7 min 39.16 sec
1,500-m freestyle	Grant Hackett	Australia	14 min 34.56 sec
50-m breaststroke	Anthony Robinson	United States	27.49 sec
	Ed Moses	United States	27.39 sec
100-m breaststroke	Ed Moses	United States	1 min 0.29 sec
	Roman Sludnov	Russia	1 min 0.26 sec
	Roman Sludnov	Russia	59.97 sec
	Roman Sludnov	Russia	59.94 sec
50-m butterfly	Geoff Huegill	Australia	23.44 sec
200-m butterfly	Michael Phelps	United States	1 min 54.92 sec
	Michael Phelps	United States	1 min 54.58 sec
4 × 200-m freestyle relay	Australia Olympic Team	Australia	7 min 4.66 sec
WOMEN			
200-m breaststroke	Qi Hui	China	2 min 22.99 sec

World Swimming and Diving Championships—Men

	Freestyle					
Year	50 m	100 m	200 m	400 m	800 m	1,500 m
1994	A. Popov (Russia)	A. Popov (Russia)	A. Kasvio (Fin.)	K. Perkins (Austl.)		K. Perkins (Austl.)
1998	B. Pilczuk (U.S.)	A. Popov (Russia)	M. Klim (Austl.)	I. Thorpe (Austl.)		G. Hackett (Austl.)
2001	**A. Ervin (U.S.)**	**A. Ervin (U.S.)**	**I. Thorpe (Austl.)**	**I. Thorpe (Austl.)**	**I. Thorpe (Austl.)**	**G. Hackett (Austl.)**

	Backstroke			Breaststroke		
	50 m	100 m	200 m	50 m	100 m	200 m
1994		M. López Zubero (Spain)	V. Selkov (Russia)		N. Rozsa (Hung.)	N. Rozsa (Hung.)
1998		L. Krayzelburg (U.S.)	L. Krayzelburg (U.S.)		F. De Burghgraeve (Belg.)	K. Grote (U.S.)
2001	**R. Bal (U.S.)**	**M. Welsh (Austl.)**	**A. Piersol (U.S.)**	**O. Lisogor (Ukr.)**	**R. Sludnov (Russia)**	**B. Hansen (U.S.)**

	Butterfly			Individual medley		Team relays
	50 m	100 m	200 m	200 m	400 m	4 × 100-m freestyle
1994		R. Szukala (Pol.)	D. Pankratov (Russia)	J. Sievinen (Fin.)	T. Dolan (U.S.)	United States
1998		M. Klim (Austl.)	D. Silantyev (Ukr.)	M. Wouda (Neth.)	T. Dolan (U.S.)	United States
2001	**G. Huegill (Austl.)**	**L. Frölander (Swed.)**	**M. Phelps (U.S.)**	**M. Rosolino (Italy)**	**A. Boggiatto (Italy)**	**Australia**

	4 × 200-m freestyle	4 × 100-m medley	Diving				
			1-m springboard	3-m springboard	Platform	3-m synchronized	10-m synchronized
1994	Sweden	United States	E. Stewart (Zimb.)	Yu Zhuocheng (China)	D. Sautin (Russia)		
1998	Australia	Australia	Yu Zhuocheng (China)	D. Sautin (Russia)	D. Sautin (Russia)	China	China
2001	**Australia**	**Australia**	**Wang Feng (China)**	**D. Sautin (Russia)**	**Tian Liang (China)**	**China**	**China**

SWIMMING (continued)

World Swimming and Diving Championships—Women

Year	Freestyle 50 m	100 m	200 m	400 m	800 m	1,500 m
1994	Le Jingyi (China)	Le Jingyi (China)	F. van Almsick (Ger.)	Yang Aihua (China)	J. Evans (U.S.)	
1998	A. Van Dyken (U.S.)	J. Thompson (U.S.)	C. Poll (C.Rica)	Chen Yan (China)	B. Bennett (U.S.)	
2001	**I. de Bruijn (Neth.)**	**I. de Bruijn (Neth.)**	**G. Rooney (Austl.)**	**Ya. Klochkova (Ukr.)**	**H. Stockbauer (Ger.)**	**H. Stockbauer (Ger.)**

Year	Backstroke 50 m	100 m	200 m	Breaststroke 50 m	100 m	200 m
1994		He Cihong (China)	He Cihong (China)		S. Riley (Austl.)	S. Riley (Austl.)
1998		L. Maurer (U.S.)	R. Maracineanu (Fr.)		K. Kowal (U.S.)	A. Kovacs (Hung.)
2001	**H. Cope (U.S.)**	**N. Coughlin (U.S.)**	**D. Mocanu (Rom.)**	**Luo Xuejuan (China)**	**Luo Xuejuan (China)**	**A. Kovacs (Hung.)**

Year	Butterfly 50 m	100 m	200 m	Individual medley 200 m	400 m	Team relays 4 × 100-m freestyle
1994		Liu Limin (China)	Liu Limin (China)	Lu Bin (China)	Dai Guohong (China)	China
1998		J. Thompson (U.S.)	S. O'Neill (Austl.)	Wu Yanyan (China)	Chen Yan (China)	United States
2001	**I. de Bruijn (Neth.)**	**P. Thomas (Austl.)**	**P. Thomas (Austl.)**	**M. Bowen (U.S.)**	**Ya. Klochkova (Ukr.)**	**Germany**

Year	4 × 200-m freestyle	4 × 100-m medley	Diving 1-m springboard	3-m springboard	Platform	3-m synchronized	10-m synchronized
1994	China	China	Chen Lixia (China)	Tan Shuping (China)	Fu Mingxia (China)		
1998	Germany	United States	I. Lashko (Russia)	Y. Pakhalina (Russia)	O. Zhupina (Ukr.)	Russia	Ukraine
2001	**United Kingdom**	**Australia**	**B. Hartley (Can.)**	**Guo Jingjing (China)**	**Xu Mian (China)**	**China**	**China**

TABLE TENNIS

World Table Tennis Championships—Men

Year	St. Bride's Vase (singles)	Iran Cup (doubles)	Swaythling Cup (team)
1999	Liu Guoliang (China)	Kong Linghui, Liu Guoliang (China)	not held
2000	not held	not held	Sweden
2001	**Wang Liqin (China)**	**Wang Liqin, Yan Sen (China)**	**China**

World Table Tennis Championships—Women

Year	G. Geist Prize (singles)	W.J. Pope Trophy (doubles)	Corbillon Cup (team)
1999	Wang Nan (China)	Wang Nan, Li Ju (China)	not held
2000	not held	not held	China
2001	**Wang Nan (China)**	**Wang Nan, Li Ju (China)**	**China**

World Table Tennis Championships—Mixed

Year	Heydusek Prize
1997	Liu Guoliang, Wu Na (China)
1999	Ma Lin, Zhang Yingying (China)
2001	**Qin Zhijian, Yang Ying (China)**

2001 Table Tennis World Rankings*

Men	Women
1. Wang Liqin (China)	1. Wang Nan (China)
2. Liu Guozheng (China)	2. Zhang Yining (China)
3. Kong Linghui (China)	3. Li Ju (China)
4. Ma Lin (China)	4. Mihaela Steff (Rom.)
5. Chiang Peng-Lung (Taiwan)	5. Tamara Boros (Cro.)

*ITTF ranking as of September 2001.

Table Tennis World Cup

Year	Men
1999	V. Samsonov (Bela.)
2000	Ma Lin (China)
2001	**V. Samsonov (Bela.)**

Year	Women
1999	Wang Nan (China)
2000	Li Ju (China)
2001	**Zhang Yining (China)**

TENNIS

Australian Open Tennis Championships—Singles

Year	Men	Women
1999	Ye. Kafelnikov (Russia)	M. Hingis (Switz.)
2000	A. Agassi (U.S.)	L. Davenport (U.S.)
2001	**A. Agassi (U.S.)**	**J. Capriati (U.S.)**

Australian Open Tennis Championships—Doubles

Year	Men	Women
1999	J. Bjorkman, P. Rafter	M. Hingis, A. Kournikova
2000	E. Ferreira, R. Leach	L. Raymond, R. Stubbs
2001	**J. Bjorkman, T. Woodbridge**	**S. Williams, V. Williams**

TENNIS (continued)

French Open Tennis Championships—Singles

Year	Men	Women
1999	A. Agassi (U.S.)	S. Graf (Ger.)
2000	G. Kuerten (Braz.)	M. Pierce (Fr.)
2001	**G. Kuerten (Braz.)**	**J. Capriati (U.S.)**

All-England (Wimbledon) Tennis Championships—Singles

Year	Men	Women
1999	P. Sampras (U.S.)	L. Davenport (U.S.)
2000	P. Sampras (U.S.)	V. Williams (U.S.)
2001	**G. Ivanisevic (Cro.)**	**V. Williams (U.S.)**

United States Open Tennis Championships—Singles

Year	Men	Women
1999	A. Agassi (U.S.)	S. Williams (U.S.)
2000	M. Safin (Russia)	V. Williams (U.S.)
2001	**L. Hewitt (Austl.)**	**V. Williams (U.S.)**

Davis Cup (men)

Year	Winner	Runner-up	Results
1999	Australia	France	3–2
2000	Spain	Australia	3–1
2001	**France**	**Australia**	**3–2**

Fed Cup (women)

Year	Winner	Runner-up	Results
1999	United States	Russia	4–1
2000	United States	Spain	5–0
2001	**Belgium**	**Russia**	**2–1**

French Open Tennis Championships—Doubles

Year	Men	Women
1999	M. Bhupathi, L. Paes	S. Williams, V. Williams
2000	T. Woodbridge, M. Woodforde	M. Hingis, M. Pierce
2001	**M. Bhupathi, L. Paes**	**V. Ruano Pascual, P. Suarez**

All-England (Wimbledon) Tennis Championships—Doubles

Year	Men	Women
1999	M. Bhupathi, L. Paes	L. Davenport, C. Morariu
2000	T. Woodbridge, M. Woodforde	S. Williams, V. Williams
2001	**D. Johnson, J. Palmer**	**L. Raymond, R. Stubbs**

United States Open Tennis Championships—Doubles

Year	Men	Women
1999	S. Lareau, A. O'Brien	S. Williams, V. Williams
2000	L. Hewitt, M. Mirnyi	J. Halard Decugis, A. Sugiyama
2001	**W. Black, K. Ullyet**	**L. Raymond, R. Stubbs**

TRACK AND FIELD SPORTS (ATHLETICS)

World Track and Field Championships—Men

Event	1999	2001
100 m	M. Greene (U.S.)	M. Greene (U.S.)
200 m	M. Greene (U.S.)	K. Kederis (Greece)
400 m	M. Johnson (U.S.)	A. Moncur (Bahamas)
800 m	W. Kipketer (Den.)	A. Bucher (Switz.)
1,500 m	H. El Guerrouj (Mor.)	H. El Guerrouj (Mor.)
5,000 m	S. Hissou (Mor.)	R. Limo (Kenya)
10,000 m	H. Gebrselassie (Eth.)	C. Kamathi (Kenya)
steeplechase	C. Koskei (Kenya)	R. Kosgei (Kenya)
110-m hurdles	C. Jackson (U.K.)	A. Johnson (U.S.)
400-m hurdles	F. Mori (Italy)	F. Sánchez (Dom.Rep.)
marathon	A. Antón (Spain)	G. Abera (Eth.)
20-km walk	I. Markov (Russia)	R. Rasskazov (Russia)
50-km walk	G. Skurygin (Russia)	R. Korzeniowski (Pol.)
4 × 100-m relay	United States (J. Drummond, T. Montgomery, B. Lewis, M. Greene)	United States (M. Grimes, B. Williams, D. Mitchell, T. Montgomery)
4 × 400-m relay	United States (J. Davis, A. Pettigrew, A. Taylor, M. Johnson)	United States (L. Byrd, A. Pettigrew, D. Brew, A. Taylor)
high jump	V. Voronin (Russia)	M. Buss (Ger.)
pole vault	M. Tarasov (Russia)	D. Markov (Austl.)
long jump	I. Pedroso (Cuba)	I. Pedroso (Cuba)
triple jump	C.M. Friedek (Ger.)	J. Edwards (U.K.)
shot put	C.J. Hunter (U.S.)	J. Godina (U.S.)
discus throw	A. Washington (U.S.)	L. Riedel (Ger.)
hammer throw	K. Kobs (Ger.)	S. Ziolkowski (Pol.)
javelin throw	A. Parviainen (Fin.)	J. Zelezny (Cz.Rep.)
decathlon	T. Dvorak (Cz.Rep.)	T. Dvorak (Cz.Rep.)

World Track and Field Championships—Women

Event	1999	2001
100 m	M. Jones (U.S.)	Z. Pintusevich-Block (Ukr.)
200 m	I. Miller (U.S.)	M. Jones (U.S.)
400 m	C. Freeman (Austl.)	A. Mbacke Thiam (Senegal)
800 m	L. Formanova (Cz.Rep.)	M. Mutola (Mozam.)
1,500 m	S. Masterkova (Russia)	G. Szabo (Rom.)
5,000 m	G. Szabo (Rom.)	O. Yegorova (Russia)
10,000 m	G. Wami (Eth.)	D. Tulu (Eth.)
100-m hurdles	G. Devers (U.S.)	A. Kirkland (U.S.)
400-m hurdles	D. Pernía (Cuba)	N. Bidouane (Mor.)
marathon	Jong Song Ok (N.Kor.)	L. Simon (Rom.)
20-km walk	Liu Hongyu (China)	O. Ivanova (Russia)
4 × 100-m relay	Bahamas (S. Fynes, C. Sturrup, P. Davis, D. Ferguson)	United States (K. White, C. Gaines, I. Miller, M. Jones)
4 × 400-m relay	Russia (T. Chebykina, S. Goncharenko, O. Kotlyarova, N. Nazarova)	Jamaica (S. Richards, C. Scott, D.-A. Parris, L. Fenton)
high jump	I. Babakova (Ukr.)	H. Cloete (S.Afr.)
pole vault	S. Dragila (U.S.)	S. Dragila (U.S.)
long jump	N. Montalvo (Spain)	F. May (Italy)
triple jump	P. Tsiamita (Greece)	T. Lebedeva (Russia)
shot put	A. Kumbernuss (Ger.)	Y. Korolchik (Bela.)
discus throw	F. Dietzsch (Ger.)	N. Sadova (Russia)
hammer throw	M. Melinte (Rom.)	Y. Moreno (Cuba)
javelin throw	M. Tzelili (Greece)	O. Menéndez (Cuba)
heptathlon	E. Barber (Fr.)	Ye. Prokhorova (Russia)

TRACK AND FIELD SPORTS (ATHLETICS)
(continued)

2001 World Indoor Records—Men

Event	Competitor and country	Performance
60 m	Maurice Greene (U.S.)	6.39 sec*
3,000-m walk†	Andreas Erm (Ger.)	10 min 31.42 sec

*Equaled existing world record. †Not an officially ratified event; best performance on record.

2001 World Indoor Records—Women

Event	Competitor and country	Performance
3,000 m	Gabriella Szabo (Rom.)	8 min 32.88 sec
Pole vault	Stacy Dragila (U.S.)	4.63 m (15 ft 2¼ in)
	Stacy Dragila (U.S.)	4.65 m (15 ft 3 in)
	Stacy Dragila (U.S.)	4.66 m (15 ft 3½ in)
	Stacy Dragila (U.S.)	4.70 m (15 ft 5 in)

2001 World Outdoor Records—Men

Event	Competitor and country	Performance
Steeplechase	Brahim Boulami (Mor.)	7 min 55.28 sec
Decathlon	Roman Sebrle (Cz.Rep.)	9,026 pts

2001 World Outdoor Records—Women

Event	Competitor and country	Performance
Steeplechase	Justyna Bak (Pol.)	9 min 25.31 sec
20-km walk	Susana Feitor (Port.)	1 hr 29 min 36.4 sec
	Olimpiada Ivanova (Russia)	1 hr 26 min 52.3 sec
Half-marathon*	Susan Chepkemei (Kenya)	1 hr 5 min 44 sec
Marathon*	Naoko Takashi (Japan)	2 hr 19 min 46 sec
	Catherine Ndereba (Kenya)	2 hr 18 min 47 sec
Pole vault	Stacy Dragila (U.S.)	4.65 m (15 ft 3 in)
	Stacy Dragila (U.S.)	4.70 m (15 ft 5 in)
	Stacy Dragila (U.S.)	4.71 m (15 ft 5½ in)
	Stacy Dragila (U.S.)	4.81 m (15 ft 9¼ in)
Javelin throw	Osleidys Menéndez (Cuba)	71.54 m (234 ft 8 in)

*Not an officially ratified event; best performance on record.

Maurice Greene celebrates his victory in the 100-m event at the world track and field championships on August 5.

Don Emmert/AFP Worldwide

IAAF World Cup—Men

	100 metre	200 metre	400 metre	800 metre	1,500 metre
1992	L. Christie (Gr.Brit.)	R. Caetano da Silva (Amer.)	S. Bada (Africa)	D. Sharpe (U.K.)	M. Suleiman (Asia)
1994	L. Christie (Gr.Brit.)	J. Regis (Gr.Brit.)	A. Pettigrew (U.S.)	M. Everett (U.S.)	N. Morceli (Africa)
1998	O. Thompson (Amer.)	F. Fredericks (Africa)	I. Thomas (Gr.Brit.)	N. Schumann (Ger.)	L. Rotich (Africa)
	3,000 metre	**5,000 metre**	**10,000 metre**	**Steeplechase**	**110-m hurdles**
1992	—	F. Bayesa (Africa)	A. Abebe (Africa)	P. Barkutwo (Africa)	C. Jackson (U.K.)
1994	—	B. Lahlafi (Africa)	K. Skah (Africa)	M. Kiptanui (Africa)	T. Jarrett (Gr.Brit.)
1998	D. Baumann (Ger.)	D. Komen (Africa)	—	D. Kallabis (Ger.)	F. Balzer (Ger.)
	400-m hurdles	**4 × 100-m relays**	**4 × 400-m relays**	**Triple jump**	**High jump**
1992	S. Matete (Africa)	United States	Africa	J. Edwards (U.K.)	Y. Sergeyenko (UT)
1994	S. Matete (Africa)	Great Britain	Great Britain	Y. Quesada (Amer.)	J. Sotomayor (Amer.)
1998	S. Matete (Africa)	Great Britain	United States	C. Friedek (Ger.)	C. Austin (U.S.)
	Pole vault	**Long jump**	**Shot put**	**Discus throw**	**Hammer throw**
1992	I. Potapovich (UT)	I. Pedroso (Amer.)	M. Stulce (U.S.)	T. Washington (U.S.)	T. Gecsek (Europe)
1994	O. Brits (Africa)	F. Salle (Gr.Brit.)	C.J. Hunter (U.S.)	V. Dubrovshchik (Europe)	A. Abduvaliyev (Asia)
1998	M. Tarasov (Europe)	I. Pedroso (Amer.)	J. Godina (U.S.)	V. Alekna (Europe)	T. Gecsek (Europe)
	Javelin throw	**Team**			
1992	J. Zelezny (Europe)	Africa			
1994	S. Backley (Gr.Brit.)	Africa			
1998	S. Backley (Gr.Brit.)	—			

TRACK AND FIELD SPORTS (ATHLETICS)
(continued)

IAAF World Cup—Women

	100 metre	200 metre	400 metre	800 metre	1,500 metre
1992	N. Voronova (UT)	M.-J. Pérec (Europe)	J. Miles (U.S.)	M. Mutola (Africa)	Y. Podkopayeva (UT)
1994	I. Privalova (Europe)	M. Ottey (Amer.)	I. Privalova (Europe)	M. Mutola (Africa)	H. Boulmerka (Africa)
1998	M. Jones (U.S.)	M. Jones (U.S.)	F. Ogunkoya (Africa)	M. Mutola (Africa)	S. Masterkova (Russia)

	3,000 metre	5,000 metre	10,000 metre	100-m hurdles	400-m hurdles
1992	D. Tulu (Africa)	—	D. Tulu (Africa)	A. López (Amer.)	S. Farmer-Patrick (U.S.)
1994	Y. Murray (Gr.Brit.)	—	E. Meyer (Africa)	A. López (Amer.)	S. Gunnell (Gr.Brit.)
1998	G. Szabo (Europe)	S. O'Sullivan (Europe)	—	G. Alozie (Africa)	N. Bidouane (Africa)

	4 × 100-m relays	4 × 400-m relays	Triple jump	High jump	Long jump
1992	Asia	Americas	—	I. Quintero (Amer.)	H. Drechsler (Ger.)
1994	Africa	Great Britain	A. Biryukova (Europe)	B. Bilac (Europe)	I. Kravets (Europe)
1998	United States	Germany	O. Vasdeki (Europe)	M. Iagar-Dinescu (Europe)	H. Drechsler (Ger.)

	Shot put	Discus throw	Javelin throw	Team	
1992	B. Laza (Amer.)	M. Marten (Amer.)	T. Sanderson (U.K.)	Unified Team	
1994	Zhihong Huang (Asia)	I. Wyludda (Europe)	T. Hattestad (Europe)	Europe	
1998	V. Pavlysh (Europe)	F. Dietzsch (Ger.)	J. Stone (Oceania)	—	

World Cross Country Championships—Men

Year	Individual	Team
1999	P. Tergat (Kenya)	Kenya
2000	M. Mourhit (Belg.)	Kenya
2001	**M. Mourhit (Belg.)**	**Kenya**

World Cross Country Championships—Women

Year	Individual	Team
1999	G. Wami (Eth.)	Ethiopia
2000	D. Tulu (Eth.)	Ethiopia
2001	**P. Radcliffe (U.K.)**	**Kenya**

Boston Marathon

Year	Men	h:min:s
1999	J. Chebet (Kenya)	2:09:52
2000	E. Lagat (Kenya)	2:09:47
2001	**Lee Bong Ju (S.Kor.)**	**2:09:43**

Year	Women	h:min:s
1999	F. Roba (Eth.)	2:23:25
2000	C. Ndereba (Kenya)	2:26:11
2001	**C. Ndereba (Kenya)**	**2:23:53**

New York City Marathon

Year	Men	h:min:s
1999	J. Chebet (Kenya)	2:09:14
2000	A. El Mouaziz (Mor.)	2:10:09
2001	**T. Jifar (Eth.)**	**2:07:43**

Year	Women	h:min:s
1999	A. Fernández (Mex.)	2:25:06
2000	L. Petrova (Russia)	2:25:45
2001	**M. Okayo (Kenya)**	**2:24:21**

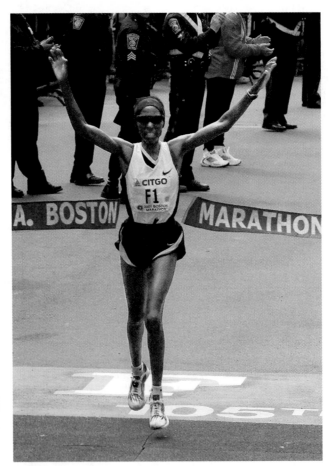

Catherine Ndereba wins the Boston Marathon on April 16.

© Mike Segar/Reuters 2001

VOLLEYBALL

World Volleyball Championships

Year	Men	Women
1996	Netherlands	Cuba
1998	Italy	Cuba
2000	Yugoslavia	Cuba

WEIGHT LIFTING

World Weight Lifting Champions, 2001

MEN

Weight class	Winner and country	Performance
56 kg (123 lb)	Halil Mutlu (Turkey)	300 kg (660 lb)
62 kg (136.5 lb)	Henadzy Aliyashchuk (Bela.)	317.5 kg (698.5 lb)
69 kg (152 lb)	Galabin Boevski (Bulg.)	340 kg (748 lb)
77 kg (169.5 lb)	Abbas Nader (Qatar)	365 kg (803 lb)
85 kg (187 lb)	George Asanidze (Georgia)	390 kg (861.9 lb)
94 kg (207 lb)	Kouroush Bagheri (Iran)	407.5 kg (896.5 lb)
105 kg (231 lb)	Vladimir Smorchkov (Russia)	422.5 kg (929.5 lb)
+105 kg (+231 lb)	Saeed Salem Jaber (Qatar)	460 kg (1,012 lb)

WOMEN

Weight class	Winner and country	Performance
48 kg (105.5 lb)	Wei Gao (China)	190 kg (418 lb)
53 kg (116.5 lb)	Li Feng-ying (Taiwan)	210 kg (462 lb)
58 kg (127.5 lb)	Aleksandra Klejnowska (Pol.)	215 kg (473 lb)
63 kg (138.5 lb)	Xiao Ying (China)	230 kg (506 lb)
69 kg (152 lb)	Valentina Popova (Russia)	257.5 kg (566.5 lb)
75 kg (165 lb)	Gyorgy Likerecz (Hung.)	255 kg (561 lb)
+75 kg (+165 lb)	Albina Khomitch (Russia)	282.5 kg (621.5 lb)

Valentina Popova hoists 142 kg (314 lb) in the clean-and-jerk en route to a first-place finish in her weight class at the world weight lifting championships in November.

AP/Wide World Photos

WRESTLING

World Wrestling Championships—Freestyle

Year	54 kg	58 kg	63 kg	69 kg
1999	Kim Woo Yong (S.Kor.)	H. Dogan (Tur.)	E. Tedeyev (Ukr.)	D. Igali (Can.)
2000	N. Abdullayev (Azer.)	A.R. Dabier (Iran)	M. Umakhanov (Russia)	D. Igali (Can.)
2001	**H. Kantoyeu (Bela.)**	**G. Sissaouri (Can.)**	**S. Barzakov (Bulg.)**	**N. Paslar (Bulg.)**

Year	76 kg	85 kg	97 kg	130 kg
1999	A. Saytyev (Russia)	Y. Romero (Cuba)	S. Murtasaliyev (Russia)	S. Neal (U.S.)
2000	B. Slay (U.S.)	A. Saytyev (Russia)	S. Murtasaliyev (Russia)	D. Musulbes (Russia)
2001	**B. Saytyev (Russia)**	**K. Magomedov (Russia)**	**G. Gogchelidze (Russia)**	**D. Musulbes (Russia)**

World Wrestling Championships—Greco-Roman Style

Year	54 kg	58 kg	63 kg	69 kg
1999	L. Rivas (Cuba)	Kim In Sub (S.Kor.)	M. Manukyan (Kazakh.)	Son Sang Pil (S.Kor.)
2000	Sim Kwon Ho (S.Kor.)	A. Nazaryan (Bulg.)	V. Samurgashev (Russia)	F. Azcuy (Cuba)
2001	**H. Rangraz (Iran)**	**D. Aripov (Uzbek.)**	**V. Galustyan (Arm.)**	**F. Azcuy (Cuba)**

Year	76 kg	85 kg	97 kg	130 kg
1999	N. Avluca (Tur.)	L. Méndez (Cuba)	G. Koguashvili (Russia)	A. Karelin (Russia)
2000	M. Kardanov (Russia)	H. Yerlikaya (Tur.)	M. Ljungberg (Swed.)	R. Gardner (U.S.)
2001	**A. Abrahamian (Swed.)**	**M. Vakhrangadze (Georgia)**	**A. Bezruchkin (Russia)**	**R. Gardner (U.S.)**

2001 Sumo Tournament Champions

Tournament	Location	Winner	Winner's record
Hatsu Basho (New Year's tournament)	Tokyo	Takanohana	14–1
Haru Basho (spring tournament)	Osaka	Kaio	13–2
Natsu Basho (summer tournament)	Tokyo	Takanohana	13–2
Nagoya Basho (Nagoya tournament)	Nagoya	Kaio	13–2
Aki Basho (autumn tournament)	Tokyo	Kotomitsuki	13–2
Kyushu Basho (Kyushu tournament)	Fukuoka	Musashimaru	13–2

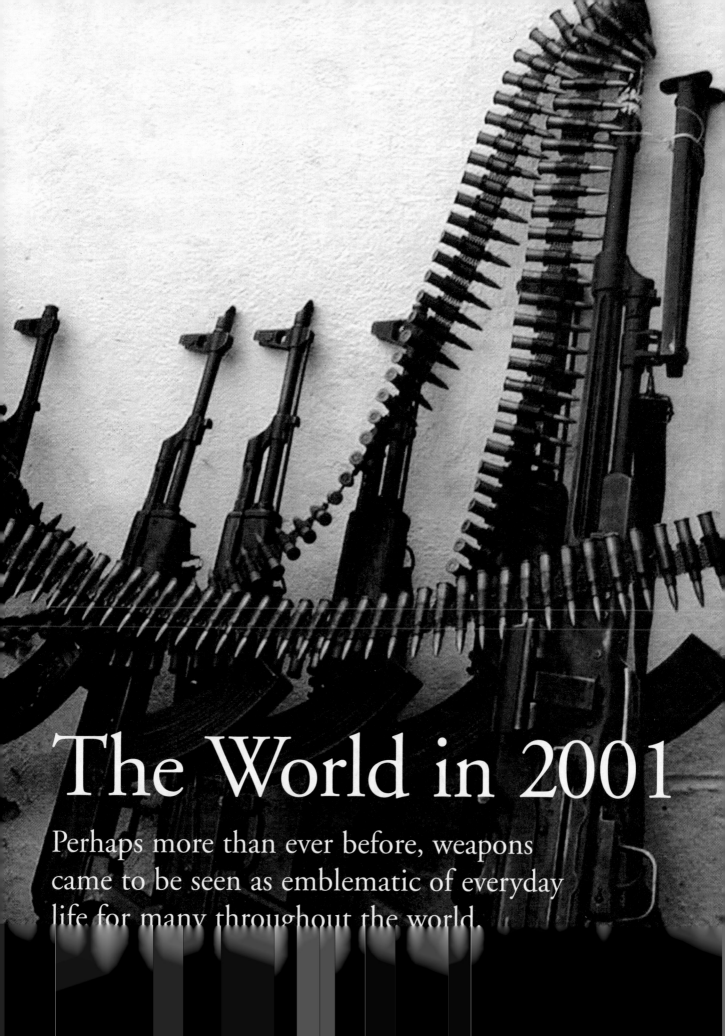

The World in 2001

Perhaps more than ever before, weapons
came to be seen as emblematic of everyday
life for many throughout the world.

World Affairs

WAR in Afghanistan; possible PEACE in Northern Ireland and Sri Lanka; CRISIS in Argentina, Israel/Palestine, and India/Pakistan; NEW LEADERS in Japan, Peru, Italy, Bulgaria, and the U.S.—these were a few of the highlights of 2001.

UNITED NATIONS

Though UN Secretary-General Kofi Annan's term was scheduled to end on Dec. 31, 2001, he announced on March 22 his availability for five more years. UN delegates credited him with having strengthened internal management, gained control over the organization's budget, and improved ties with the U.S., and they reelected him by acclamation on June 29. He was praised for his levelheadedness, clarity of vision, modesty, talent for listening, and negotiating ability.

At 5 AM on October 12, Annan received a telephone call, and he knew from experience that such an early-morning summons usually meant "something disastrous." This time, however, he learned that he and the UN had been awarded the Nobel Prize for Peace. The citation lauded Annan for "bringing new life to the organization," for moving beyond the UN's traditional responsibility for peace and security to emphasize its obligations to promote human rights, for assuming new challenges such as fighting HIV/AIDS and international terrorism, and for using the UN's "modest resources" more efficiently. The prize committee observed that the end of the Cold War "has at last made it possible for the United Nations to perform more fully the part it was originally intended to play." (*See* NOBEL PRIZES.)

War Crimes. For the first time, the UN War Crimes Tribunal in The Hague defined rape as a war crime. On June 28 former Yugoslav head of state Slobodan Milosevic was brought to trial on charges of genocide and crimes against humanity in Bosnia and Herzegovina, Croatia, and Kosovo. In September the UN Security Council ended the three-year-old arms embargo against Yugoslavia because it had satisfied the conditions for terminating the ban.

Refugees. Ruud Lubbers, former prime minister of The Netherlands, succeeded Sadako Ogata of Japan as UN High Commissioner for Refugees on January 3. He immediately tried to provide a "safe corridor" for tens of thousands of refugees from border fighting between Sierra Leone and Liberia who had sought shelter in dense rain forests and were trapped there. At year's end he faced a growing crisis in Afghanistan, where refugees, fleeing the effects of U.S. bombing, massed on the Pakistani border, joining thousands who had previously attempted to escape the country's drought. In December the World Food Programme delivered an unprecedented 114,000 metric tons of food to Afghanistan, enough to feed six million displaced persons for two months. The UN Children's Fund was also providing food

and water to help an estimated 1.5 million children survive the effects of conflict, drought, disease, and displacement.

Lubbers reduced his staff by 800, following a more than $100 million budget cut, and he chided Europeans for reducing their contributions to refugees. A pledging conference in Geneva on December 3 left a shortfall of $100 million for the next fiscal year. (*See* SOCIAL PROTECTION: *Refugees and International Migration.*)

Afghanistan. On several occasions during the year, the UN rebuked Afghanistan's ruling Taliban. Annan and Koichiro Matsuura, director general of UNESCO, pointed out that the Taliban interpreted Islam in a way that no one else recognized. When the government proposed to require non-Muslims to wear yellow badges in an effort to "protect" Sikhs and Hindus from being subject to strict Islamic rules enforced by "religious police," Annan called the measure reminiscent of "some of the most deplorable acts of discrimination in history." In August, when the Taliban detained eight foreign aid workers for the capital offense of propagating Christianity, Annan deplored the authorities' failure to allow the detainees consular access and legal representation and warned them that their act could have "severe consequences on critical human-

Shortly after learning that he and the UN had been awarded the Nobel Prize for Peace, UN Secretary-General Kofi Annan appears at a news conference.

itarian assistance." The Taliban said that they intended to try the detainees, but in November, as they retreated before attacks by the Northern Alliance, U.S. helicopters rescued the detainees and ferried them to Pakistan. On September 18 the Security Council president called on the Taliban to surrender Osama bin Laden for his alleged connections to the August 1998 bombings of U.S. embassies in Africa and to the attacks in the U.S. on September 11.

When the Taliban fled Kabul after ground attacks by the Northern Alliance and air attacks by the U.S., Lakhdar Brahimi, UN special representative for Afghanistan, proposed that the Security Council convene a meeting of Afghan representatives to devise a provisional administration and to deploy an international security presence in the capital. That meeting opened on November 27 in Bonn, Ger., and on December 5 the delegates agreed to create a broad-based Governing Council that they hoped would end more than 20 years of internal warfare. The Security Council endorsed the agreement on December 6, and the Governing Council, led by Hamid Karzai, a Pashtun tribal leader who previously fought the Taliban in southern Afghanistan, took power on December 22. Britain offered on December 19 to take the lead in organizing and commanding an International Security Assistance Force for six months, and the Security Council accepted the offer on December 20, the same day the first British Marines arrived in Kabul to maintain it as a neutral zone.

Health. On June 25 the General Assembly opened a special three-day session on HIV/AIDS and invited pledges to a "global superfund" of $7 billion–$10 billion that Annan proposed to fight the disease. By year's end the pledges amounted to $1.6 billion. UN estimates indicated that 25 million people were infected with HIV in sub-Saharan Africa, 4.8 million needed treatment, and all but 30,000 of them could expect to die without drugs commonly prescribed in the West. (*See* HEALTH AND DISEASE.)

Human Rights. China on February 28 ratified the International Convention on Economic, Social and Cultural Rights one day after UN High Commissioner for Human Rights Mary Robinson visited the country. In ratifying the measure the government seemed to hedge its support of workers rights to form and join free labour unions. China recognized just one union; the state-sanctioned All China Federation of Trade Unions forbade the formation of inde-

pendent groups and did not recognize the right to strike. Nevertheless, on May 17 China agreed to work with the International Labour Organization to promote workers' rights and well-being.

In elections on May 3 for the UN Commission on Human Rights, the U.S. lost a seat it had held since the UN was founded in 1945. The defeat was attributed to the growing strength of less-developed states opposed to U.S. policies, the U.S. failure to lobby for the seat, widespread dismay at U.S. failure to support important international treaties, and U.S. resistance to plans to allow poor countries to make generic versions of anti-AIDS drugs. Members were also upset by a perceived U.S. inattention to the UN after Pres. George W. Bush (*see* BIOGRAPHIES) took office in January and did not at once appoint an ambassador to the UN. Not until September 13, when the Senate approved the nomination of John D. Negroponte, was the U.S. represented by an ambassador at the UN.

The UN World Conference Against Racism, held in Durban, S.Af., from August 31 to September 7, declared that slavery and the slave trade were "a crime against humanity and should always have been so" and called on states to reverse the lasting consequences of slavery, apartheid, and genocide. It expressed concern "about the plight of the Palestinian people under foreign occupation" and recognized their right to self-determination and to establishment of an independent state; the conference also called for governments to ensure that Roma (Gypsies) received equal access to education, to guarantee religious freedom to minorities, to ensure access to services for people with AIDS, and to see that police did not engage in racial or ethnic profiling. The conferees asked the UN to appoint a panel of five experts to help countries carry out these objectives and to review progress.

Budget. On December 24 the General Assembly approved an increase of nearly 4% in the UN budget for the next two years to finance a modest increase in peacekeepers. It was the first increase in eight years apart from inflation adjustments. The budget authorized spending $2,625,000,000 for regular operations through 2003, an increase of $92 million over the current two-year budget of $2,533,000,000. The UN collected $4.2 billion in current and overdue payments by December 31.

Climate. On December 18 the World Meteorological Organization confirmed that Earth's temperature in 2001 was the second highest in the 140 years of

record-keeping. Temperatures were getting hotter faster than ever before and causing more storms, droughts, and other weather extremes.

East Timor. On September 10 the UN certified the results of East Timor's first democratic election, and a newly chosen constituent assembly started drafting a constitution as a step toward full independence. (See *Dependent States:* Indian Ocean and Southern Asia, below.)

Iraq. On November 29 the Security Council unanimously extended the "oil for food" program in Iraq for six months on the understanding that Russia would agree before May 30, 2002, to a new list of goods requiring UN review before being shipped to Iraq and that the U.S. would comply with Russia's demand to specify steps leading to the lifting of the embargo on the condition that Iraq allowed UN weapons inspectors to resume their work. Earlier in the year the Council had failed to devise a "smart sanctions plan" for Iraq that might do more to help civilians and restrict the military, and the proposals were dropped on July 2.

UN officials revealed on March 6 that some Iraqi officials were demanding kickbacks on contracts for food, medicine, and other essential civilian goods bought from foreign companies under the UN oil for food program and that Saddam Hussein was diverting money intended to help the civilian population into a slush fund for himself and his associates and possibly for his weapons program. Profiting from a UN-supervised program was illegal, and Annan warned Iraq and buyers of crude oil that surcharges were not permitted and that they should pay nothing to non-UN accounts.

Palestine/Israel. During a visit to the UN on March 21, Israeli Prime Minister Ariel Sharon (*see* BIOGRAPHIES) warned the Security Council against sending an observer force to the Middle East lest its presence increase violence in the West Bank and Gaza. Annan urged Sharon to reduce restrictions on Palestinians working in Israel, and Sharon replied that he was prepared to do so. On March 27 the U.S. vetoed a Security Council resolution requested by the Palestinians, calling for a UN observer force in Israeli-occupied territories. In a speech to the General Assembly in November, Israeli Foreign Minister Shimon Peres called creating an independent Palestinian state "the best bet" for settling the problems of the Middle East. On December 15 the U.S. vetoed a draft resolution in the Security Council that would have demanded an immediate end to all acts of violence, provocation, and destruction in the area and would have required the parties to return to the positions existing before September 2000. The draft asked the two sides to implement the recommendations in the Mitchell report for building confidence measures and to establish a monitoring mechanism to help the parties implement the recommendations. The U.S. objected to the resolution's not condemning recent acts of terrorism against Israel. On December 20 the General Assembly adopted the text of the rejected resolution by a vote of 124–6 with 25 abstentions.

Biological Weapons. Negotiations in Geneva in May aimed at establishing a verification scheme for the 1972 Biological Weapons Convention were jarred by U.S. statements that the treaty's verification measures could not detect cheating and might allow foreign governments to try to steal U.S. secrets. On July 25 the U.S. confirmed that it would not sign the draft protocol. The proposals, 10 years in the making and already signed by 140 countries, were designed to strengthen the convention outlawing germ warfare. They would oblige signatories to allow inspectors into sites that could be used to manufacture biological weapons. On November 18 the U.S. stated that Iran, Iraq, Libya, North Korea, and Syria were all developing germ weapons and violating the 1972 treaty. On the last day of a three-week review of the treaty in Geneva that opened on November 19, the U.S. proposed ending negotiations. The delegates then chose to adjourn until Nov. 11, 2002, rather than admit failure.

International Law. A two-week conference in New York City opened on July 9 to consider drafting a pact curtailing the international flow of illegal small arms. At the opening session the U.S. backed away from the conference objective, saying that "the responsible use of firearms is a legitimate aspect of national life" and that it intended to retain its "cultural tradition of hunting and sport shooting." China, India, and Russia, all of which had large arms industries, supported the U.S. UN officials insisted that the conference would in no way contradict the Second Amendment to the U.S. Constitution and that it was not about taking guns away from Americans but about keeping an estimated 500 million weapons, 40–60% of which had been acquired illegally, out of the hands of child soldiers and pickup armies, often in the poorest countries.

Terrorism. Annan said on September 11 that there was no doubt that the attacks in the U.S. that day were "deliberate acts of terrorism, carefully planned and co-ordinated," and he condemned them "utterly." The next day both the Security Council and the General Assembly condemned the terrorist acts, and the Assembly expressed its "condolences and solidarity with the people and government of the U.S." The Security Council called on "all states to work together," stressed that "those responsible for aiding, supporting, or harbouring the perpetrators, organizers and sponsors of these acts will be held accountable," and expressed its readiness to take all necessary steps to respond to the terrorist attacks. On September 21 Annan offered the UN as a forum for building a universal coalition against terrorism and for ensuring global legitimacy for the long-term response to terrorism. A week later the Security Council unanimously adopted a U.S.-sponsored resolution obliging all UN members to freeze bank accounts of suspected terrorists, to provide them with no training, to monitor their movements, and to cooperate in any campaign against them, including one involving the use of force. The resolution marked an enhanced U.S. appreciation of the importance of the UN. On November 30 the Security Council Counter-Terrorism Committee began receiving reports from member states on their antiterrorism measures. On December 19 the secretary-general cautioned against expanding the war against terrorism into Iraq lest it lead to a major escalation in the region.

Armaments. On December 13 President Bush served notice that in six months the U.S. would withdraw from the Anti-Ballistic Missile Treaty, generally regarded as a cornerstone of global arms control since 1972. He had concluded that the treaty hindered his government's ability to protect the U.S. from "future terrorist or rogue-state missile attacks." The announcement met with scarcely concealed dismay around the world.

On December 21 arms control experts from nearly 90 countries met in Geneva and agreed to take the first steps to reduce civilian casualties caused by explosives long after conflicts end. They established an expert group to report back in 2002 on whether to open negotiations on the subject.   (RICHARD N. SWIFT)

COMMONWEALTH OF NATIONS

The Sept. 11, 2001, terrorist attacks in the U.S. profoundly disrupted the Commonwealth. An immediate consequence was the cancellation of its finance ministers' meeting, which had been about to convene in St. Lucia. Much more serious was the postponement, for the first time in its long history, of the Commonwealth Heads of Government Meeting (CHOGM). These meetings, the longest running of all international summits and rooted in the late 19th-century imperial conferences, had been held biennially since 1969. The 2001 CHOGM had been planned for October 6–9 in Brisbane, Australia. When it became evident that many heads could not attend because of the world crisis, the gathering of an expected 52 leaders was rescheduled for 2002.

Tens of millions of Muslims lived in Commonwealth countries, most notably in India, Pakistan, and Bangladesh. Other members, such as Nigeria, Malaysia, and Brunei, contained large Muslim communities. Politically embarrassing circumstances for the Commonwealth developed when Pakistan emerged as a critical player in the war against terrorism. In its drive to secure democracy in all member countries, the Commonwealth had succeeded over the years in eliminating military rule. A setback had come in 1999 when Gen. Pervez Musharraf seized power in Pakistan. The Commonwealth had suspended Pakistan from its councils, barring its attendance at official meetings until democracy was restored. After two years it faced expulsion.

Musharraf vowed to end army rule by 2002 and held local elections during 2001. This looked set to secure agreement at the Brisbane summit to give Pakistan a year's grace. As a vital member of the alliance against terrorism, however, Musharraf came centre stage globally, with British Prime Minister Tony Blair and others needing to buttress him in power rather than persuade him to restore civilian rule.

Another consequence of the global concentration on Afghanistan was to distract international attention from the deteriorating situation in Zimbabwe. Farm seizures and a breakdown in law and order there violated Commonwealth principles, but when the eight-member Commonwealth Ministerial Action Group tried to send three ministers to Zimbabwe, Pres. Robert Mugabe refused to let them in.

Threatened stability of the southern African region increasingly worried Commonwealth African governments. After months of diplomacy Pres. Olusegun Obasanjo of Nigeria convened a meeting in Abuja of nine Commonwealth ministers, including the foreign minister of Zimbabwe, on September 6. Zimbabwe agreed to restore order and to implement a sustainable, transparent, and just program of land reform, in return for British and UN funding.

Nevertheless, the Abuja meeting changed nothing. Farm takeovers and violence continued. The Brisbane postponement meant the leaders lost the opportunity to confront Mugabe personally. Part of the Abuja deal had been the dispatch of seven Commonwealth ministers to Zimbabwe. This happened on October 25–27. The result was disappointing. Mugabe berated the ministers, and they left fearing little would change. It did not.

Despite the leaders' absence, the rest of Brisbane's Commonwealth program went ahead. An elaborate People's Festival, intended to take place alongside the summit, showcased the huge range of work of the nongovernmental organizations and the arts. A meeting of 250 business leaders in Melbourne had to be canceled.

Continuing disputes between Commonwealth countries and the Organisation for Economic Co-operation and Development (OECD) over tax havens led to a stormy conference in Barbados chaired by Prime Minister Owen Arthur, at which the OECD backed down on a Memorandum of Understanding imposing new tax procedures on small states.

(DEREK INGRAM)

EUROPEAN UNION

As 2001 began, the European Union (EU) looked forward to a solid 12 months of steady progress on the road toward a united continent. Europe's leaders had much to do as they prepared to expand membership into Eastern Europe and introduce euro notes and coins in 12 member states in 2002. Preparations for these historic developments, however, were eclipsed by unexpected events. Unforeseen tensions, pressures, and disasters on a global scale stole the headlines and overshadowed the EU's internal work. Alarmingly for the pro-EU lobby, antiglobalization protests that caused havoc at summits exposed how much the EU still had to do to win broad-based public support. In addition, the diplomatic fallout from the September 11 terrorist attacks in the U.S. exposed how far the EU was from being taken seriously as a key player in foreign policy and global diplomacy.

In January the focus was on how to restructure the EU's institutions if new member states were admitted from former communist Eastern Europe, as well as Cyprus, Malta, and Turkey. The worry was that an overly large EU would slow

The graphic symbol for the euro was inspired by the Greek letter epsilon and refers to the cradle of European civilization and to the first letter of the word Europe.

European Central Bank

down decision making even more and take government too far from the citizen. How could Europe expand, how could the goal of creating a wider market and area of peace be achieved while making its ever-expanding institutions more democratic at the same time?

Early in the year there was also an undercurrent of concern about the euro's sickly performance. Its price against the dollar did not bode well. Would the public refuse to accept a weak new currency in exchange for strong ones, such as the Deutsche Mark, that had served them so well? During its first two years as a noncash currency, the euro had lost over 30% of its value against the dollar. The hope was that the launch of notes and coins on Jan. 1, 2002—the thrill of handling the new money and the realization of the convenience it would bring—would lift confidence in the euro on the markets and among a skeptical public.

German Chancellor Gerhard Schröder was the first to offer his vision for a new Europe. In a speech made in the spring, he called for the creation of a European government that would involve the transformation of the European Commission (EC) into a strong executive, a reform of the Council of Ministers to make it a chamber of European states, and the drafting of an EU constitution. Germany, which had been a strong proponent of greater political integration, had already sunk the rock-steady Deutsche Mark into the euro and was looking to its partners—primarily France—to deliver their side of the bargain—political union. Schröder's "federal" vision for the EU won swift support from the leaders of Belgium, Finland, and Luxembourg, and it was in keeping with the ideas of EC

Pres. Romano Prodi of Italy. Schröder's recommendations, however, did not chime with the messages coming from London and Paris, where the British and French prime ministers, Tony Blair and Lionel Jospin, respectively, were quick to reject the German vision. Presenting his own ideas for a revitalized Europe, Jospin put the emphasis on strong ties between the national governments under which power remained firmly vested with the member states.

While European leaders were busy pondering the future architecture of Europe, the message dominating headlines was that the EU was losing touch with its 376 million citizens. The first wake-up call came when on June 8 Ireland voted in a referendum to reject (by 54%) the Treaty of Nice, an agreement that had been made in 2000 by the 15 heads of state to begin a reform of the EU's decision-making procedures to allow it to enlarge. Voters, fearing that enlargement would weaken Ireland's influence in the EU and that participation in peacekeeping forces could threaten the country's military neutrality, rejected the treaty. The shock was all the more stark coming from Ireland, traditionally one of the EU's most loyal and pro-European members.

A few days later the EU was shaken once again, this time by riots at its summit in Göteborg, Swed., during which one antiglobalization protester was seriously injured by police. Important agreements concerning enlargement and the environment were utterly overshadowed by the violent protests that cast strong doubts over the viability of holding such summits in the future. Ironically, the outcome of the summit was in tune with what many of the peaceful demonstrators there were demanding—a commitment to sustainable development, including measures on climate change and energy conservation. Together with the Irish "no" vote, the episode graphically underscored the growing sense of disconnection between the EU's institutions and its citizens and the need for its leaders to explain their objectives better.

As a result, EU leaders and the Brussels commission initiated a debate on the need to make the EU more relevant to its people. In early September foreign ministers agreed that in 2002 a convention should start preparing a large-scale reform of the EU's responsibilities and institutions to allow it to connect better with its citizens and cope with enlargement.

Such issues, however, were totally eclipsed by the September terrorist attacks in the U.S. As the horror of the events sank in, EU leaders took the opportunity to emphasize that such global crises demanded a global response. The need for EU member nations to work together on cross-border crime, intelligence sharing, and immigration was given a new urgency. In the 10 days that followed, the outraged member states broke new ground in foreign policy and dropped long-held taboos in the areas of justice and home affairs. Agreements that would normally have taken months, even years, to conclude were swiftly adopted. Though the political will to work together was strong, the EU's clumsy instruments for making policy, particularly on foreign and defense issues, were quickly exposed as inadequate. It soon became clear that in the short term the EU would be unable to make an effective collective contribution to the war against terrorism.

This fact was underscored by the flow of EU leaders to Washington, D.C. Though Javier Solana had been an energetic "high representative" of the EU's common foreign and security policy, it was Blair, Schröder, and French Pres. Jacques Chirac who set the pace in bilateral discussions with U.S. Pres. George W. Bush.

In addition, leaders of the 15 member states circumvented the EU institutions in their dealings with one other. Amid the frantic diplomacy, new tensions between the large and small member states arose. Many of the smaller countries felt sidelined by the efforts of the more powerful member states that were committed to making military contributions to the war against terrorism. They were particularly incensed by Blair's de-

cision, four weeks into the war, to abandon the usual EU summit formula in favour of a meeting in London to which only certain member states were invited.

Among those most angered by developments was Prodi, who was furious at the way Brussels was being ignored. A series of gaffes earlier in the year, however, had put Prodi on weak ground, and many were losing faith in his effectiveness as a leader. He barely figured in the headline-grabbing initiatives that followed September 11. Earlier, following the Irish "no" vote on the Treaty of Nice, Prodi had infuriated the Irish government and forced the EC into a damage-control mode when he stated that EU enlargement could continue in spite of the Irish vote—a remark that left EU leaders even more open to charges of being detached from the electorate. More questions about his political judgment were raised when he refused to appear at a press conference in October with Belgian Prime Minister Guy Verhofstadt, one of the few EU leaders who could still be considered his supporter. Prodi's office issued a statement saying he had stayed away because he could not compete with Verhofstadt's verbose accounts of events in Dutch and French.

Amid the uncertainty created by the war against terrorism, preparations for the introduction of euro notes and coins continued on schedule. While plans for deploying troops to help distribute the new currency were finalized, retailers protested that the first few days would be chaotic because of the European Central Bank's refusal to authorize the distribution of notes, as well as coins, ahead of January 1. A sense of unease about the impending switchover (and a fear that people were not focusing on the task at hand) was exacerbated by the euro's persistent failure to strengthen against the dollar even after the terrorist attacks and as the U.S. economy slipped into recession.

Optimistic talk earlier in the year that Europe would somehow be able to insulate itself from an economic downturn in the U.S. was also proving to be unfounded. Throughout the year Germany revised growth forecasts downward to the point where, by the autumn, there were fears that the country was entering a recession.

By year's end the expected publicity campaign about the introduction of the euro and the excitement generated by its imminent arrival unexpectedly failed to dominate the news. Even though this was to be the biggest peacetime operation of any kind in Europe since

1945, like everyone else the EU was thinking more about its role in the post-September 11 world.   (EMMA TUCKER)

MULTINATIONAL AND REGIONAL ORGANIZATIONS

March 26, 2001, marked the 10th anniversary of Mercosur, the Southern Cone Common Market (Argentina, Brazil, Paraguay, and Uruguay). The group was the world's third largest market, with production reaching more than $1 trillion annually.

From April 20 to 22, the third Summit of the Americas met in Quebec City to discuss a Free Trade Area of the Americas that would reduce or eliminate tariffs and encourage trade from the Canadian Arctic to southern Argentina. Hemispheric leaders adopted an "action plan" to strengthen democratic foundations in the Americas and to prepare for free trade. An Organization of American States fact-finding mission arrived in Haiti on May 10 to meet with Pres. Jean-Bertrand Aristide and other local leaders and to investigate the state of democracy there.

Another organization that marked its 10th anniversary during the year was the Commonwealth of Independent States (CIS). At its November 30 summit meeting, the organization, which comprised 12 of the 15 republics of the former U.S.S.R., reiterated "the common quest of its member states for stable socioeconomic development and dignified integration into the world community." The CIS also urged improved cooperation between the members' security agencies in an effort to provide unified support for the CIS antiterror centre.

China, Russia, Kazakhstan, Kyrgyzstan, Tajikistan, and Uzbekistan formed the Shanghai Cooperation Organization on June 15. Formerly called the Shanghai Five, the group changed its name to accommodate the inclusion of Uzbekistan into the organization. Its general aim was to safeguard regional security and to fight Islamic terrorism. On December 25 China called for the foreign ministers of Russia and Central Asian countries to meet with the organization on Jan. 7, 2002, to discuss Afghanistan's future, the struggle against religious extremism, and separatism and terrorism in each country.

After 38 years the Organization of African Unity (OAU) met on July 9 in Lusaka, Zambia, for its last session before starting a one-year transition period into the African Union. The AU would be modeled on the EU, with its own parliament, executive committee, court, currency, and laws. Former Côte d'Ivoire foreign minister Amara Essy was elected secretary-general on July 10 to take responsibility for steering the OAU during its critical transition period. In late November Kenya, Tanzania, and Uganda reestablished the East African Community, a group that was founded in 1967 but dismantled in 1977 owing to regional strife. The main goal of the revived group was to reduce trade barriers and stimulate economic growth in the region.

The 10 countries along the Nile River that formed the Nile Basin Initiative (Burundi, the Democratic Republic of the Congo, Egypt, Eritrea, Ethiopia, Kenya, Rwanda, The Sudan, Tanzania, and Uganda) continued to promote the sustainable development of the river and safeguard its future. The two-year-old program was aimed at bolstering hydropower and food production; improving transportation, industry, and trade; and conserving Lake Victoria and the vast wetlands of the Sudd. In June the members called a meeting of donors and development agencies in Geneva to launch an international consortium to raise funds for the initiative.

At a July 23–27 meeting in Hanoi, the Association of Southeast Asian Nations (ASEAN) faced problems arising out of a sense that the region's security and political arrangements were in flux owing to political feuding in Indonesia, its largest member; the members feared that the fighting there might lead to a breakup of the country and cause instability elsewhere. (See *Indonesia:* Special Report, below.) The members were also concerned over tensions between the U.S. and China, U.S. plans to build missile defenses, and the growing ties between the U.S. and Japan. The ASEAN Regional Forum held its annual meeting at the ministerial level on July 25. The group still hoped to launch a Southeast Asian free-trade zone by 2003 in an effort to make its countries more attractive to investors. At ASEAN's November meeting held in Brunei, talks between Chinese Prime Minister Zhu Rongji and the 10 leaders of ASEAN ended in approval for the establishment of the world's largest free-trade area within 10 years; the area would encompass about two billion people.

In March at the Arab League's summit in Amman, Jordan, the 22-member group appointed former Egyptian foreign minister Amr Moussa as its new secretary-general and agreed to support the Palestinian uprising against Israel but failed to issue a statement on the

decade-long estrangement between Kuwait and Iraq. In November Moussa renounced Osama bin Laden's latest call for a holy war but urged that a Palestinian state be established.

The Organization of the Islamic Conference met on August 27–28 in Tehran, and delegates from 22 Muslim nations agreed to encourage tourism among member countries and to facilitate residents' travel to other member countries. They met again in an emergency meeting in Doha, Qatar, on October 10 to reject "the targeting of any Islamic or Arab state under the pretext of fighting terrorism." They also stated that the terrorist attacks in the U.S. on September 11 contradicted "the teaching of all religions and human and moral values." Some delegates called for an internationally led campaign against terrorism in preference to the one led by the U.S.

The six-nation Gulf Cooperation Council (Bahrain, Kuwait, Oman, Qatar, Saudi Arabia, and the United Arab Emirates) signed an agreement on December 31 paving the way to establish joint customs tariffs in 2003 and a single market and currency by 2010. The European Union pressed for the decision as a precondition of a free trade agreement that the two organizations have discussed for 13 years.   (RICHARD N. SWIFT)

DEPENDENT STATES

Europe and the Atlantic. On May 7, 2001, the British nuclear submarine HMS *Tireless,* which had been stranded in Gibraltar for repairs for nearly a year, finally set sail. The crippled *Tireless* had limped into Gibraltar, the nearest port, on May 19, 2000, with a leak in the nuclear reactor's coolant system; repairs took far longer than anticipated. Concern over possible radiation leaks had triggered months of demonstrations by environmental activists in Gibraltar and in nearby Spain, as well as formal protests from Madrid. In November, Gibraltar Chief Minister Peter Caruana boycotted new talks between the U.K. and Spain on the territory's future status. London and Madrid declared that an agreement on Gibraltar would be reached by mid-2002, but Caruana reiterated that no settlement could be valid unless it was approved by Gibraltarians, who would never accept Spanish sovereignty.

In the South Atlantic a fire inadvertently started by British troops on tiny South Jason Island seriously damaged a major seabird nesting site in January; it was feared that hundreds of black-browed albatross and rockhopper pen-

guin chicks might have perished. In March the last British troops were withdrawn from the island of South Georgia to make way for the new British Antarctic Survey base. Future security for the island would be provided by troops based in the Falkland Islands/Islas Malvinas. A month earlier 59 young reindeer, part of a herd introduced in the early 19th century, had been transferred to the Falklands from South Georgia. After the remote island of Tristan da Cunha sustained severe hurricane damage in May, Falkland Islanders sent more than £9,000 (about $13,000) in disaster aid.

Faroe Islands Prime Minister Anfinn Kallsberg in March announced that the semiautonomous territory's referendum on independence from Denmark, scheduled for May, would be postponed indefinitely.

Caribbean and Bermuda. Sila María Calderón of the Popular Democratic Party was sworn in as governor of Puerto Rico on January 2. (*See* BIOGRAPHIES.) Although Calderón supported Puerto Rico's status as a commonwealth with the U.S., she pledged in July to hold another referendum in 2002 on whether the territory's 3.8 million people wished to retain their present status, become a full-fledged state of the U.S., or opt for independence. In the last such vote, in 1998,

Dependent States[1]

Australia	United Kingdom
Christmas Island	Anguilla
Cocos (Keeling) Islands	Bermuda
Norfolk Island	British Virgin Islands
Denmark	Cayman Islands
Faroe Islands	Falkland Islands
Greenland	Gibraltar
	Guernsey
France	Isle of Man
French Guiana	Jersey
French Polynesia	Montserrat
Guadeloupe	Pitcairn Island
Martinique	Saint Helena
Mayotte	Tristan da Cunha
New Caledonia	Turks and Caicos
Réunion	Islands
Saint Pierre and	**United Nations**
Miquelon	East Timor
Wallis and Futuna	
Netherlands, The	**United States**
Aruba	American Samoa
Netherlands Antilles	Guam
New Zealand	Northern Mariana Islands
Cook Islands	Puerto Rico
Niue	Virgin Islands
Tokelau	(of the U.S.)

[1]Excludes territories (1) to which Antarctic Treaty is applicable in whole or in part, (2) without permanent civilian population, (3) without internationally recognized civilian government (Western Sahara), or (4) representing unadjudicated unilateral or multilateral territorial claims.

the majority came out strongly for maintaining the commonwealth relationship.

The antibombing lobby in Puerto Rico prevailed against the U.S. government in June when Washington announced it would cease using Vieques Island for target practice by navy pilots from May 2003. Opposition to the bombing policy had been increasing since 1999, when one civilian was killed and four persons were injured. The White House had previously insisted that Vieques was critical to maintaining U.S. military readiness. This position might still cause the deadline to be pushed back, however, especially in light of the war against terrorism following the September 11 terrorist attacks in the U.S.

Seven policemen were injured during violent protests in Pointe-à-Pitre, Guadeloupe, in June. The situation was triggered by the refusal of shop owners to observe May 27 as the anniversary of the abolition of slavery on the island. The union had urged businessmen to shut up shop on that day and reacted strongly against those who did not. The arrest of a union leader sparked the demonstrations.

As a sign of the gradual disappearance of the artificial barriers that had long existed between Caribbean territories with different colonial histories, Saba, a Dutch Antillean territory with a population of only 2,000, indicated in August its keen interest in joining the English-speaking Organization of Eastern Caribbean States.

The self-governing Dutch territory of Aruba was commended by the International Monetary Fund in September for having improved surveillance and detection procedures relating to its growing offshore-banking sector. The opposition People's Electoral Movement (MEP) emerged victorious in the September election, taking 12 of the 21 seats in the Aruba legislature. MEP leader Nelson Oduber became prime minister.

The New People's Liberation Movement, led by former chief minister John Osborne, won the April general election in the volcano-ravaged island of Montserrat, taking seven seats in the nine-seat legislature. The National Progressive Party obtained the other two. The new government said it would concentrate on restoring jobs lost as a result of the still-active Soufrière Hills volcano, which erupted again in July following a partial collapse of the lava dome.

In June the Cayman Islands was removed by the Paris-based Financial Action Task Force (FATF) from the "blacklist" of states said to be lax in tackling money laundering in the Caribbean region. Inclusion on the list had affected the Caymans' reputation as a respectable offshore tax haven. The FATF commended the Caymanian authorities for having made "significant improvements" to anti-money-laundering systems. In Bermuda former prime minister Pamela Gordon resigned as leader of the opposition in October.

Pacific. In May elections in French Polynesia, the pro-autonomy Tahoeraa Huiaatira (TH) party was again successful, winning 28 of 49 seats; the leading pro-independence party secured 13 seats. Gaston Flosse of the TH was returned as territorial president by the assembly, which for the first time was chaired by a woman, Lucette Taero, a former minister of employment with responsibility for women's affairs. The new government placed a high priority on economic development, with special emphasis on tourism, pearl farming, fisheries, and agriculture. Earlier in the year the government had introduced financial incentives for tourism investment, but in the wake of the terrorist attacks in the U.S. on September 11, tourist numbers fell by nearly one-quarter. Flosse advocated an expansion of local responsibilities under the constitutional arrangements with France, as well as increased formal representation in the French government through the Senate.

In New Caledonia rivalries within the pro-independence movement created a degree of political uncertainty. In April Pierre Frogier was elected president of the territory's government. Tourism development struggled, with a continuing decline in air services from France and, as a consequence, fewer tourists from Europe. There were further difficulties in the latter part of the year arising from the impact of international terrorism on major airlines and related tourism activity. Potential for growth in the nickel industry was confirmed with major new investments proposed for nickel and cobalt deposits in both the northern and the southern regions.

Both the Cook Islands and Niue were warned by the Organisation for Economic Co-operation and Development that continuing failure to ensure tighter controls on money laundering would give rise to sanctions. Niue's prime minister, Sani Lakatani, called for small Pacific nations to stand together against bullying from large and powerful countries. Tourism in Niue had been affected in March, and some resorts closed when the airline responsible for most international links was grounded for safety reasons. Subsequent negotiations with other airlines were affected by the events of September 11, which added to—but did not originally cause—difficulties faced by other regional carriers. In the Cook Islands, where tourism accounted for half of gross domestic product, the economy also suffered a serious downturn resulting from the fall in tourist travel and other airline difficulties after September 11. In an attempt to stimulate economic growth and address rising inflation, the government had earlier approved the introduction of a consumption tax.

The terrorist attacks on September 11 had a major impact on U.S. dependencies in the Pacific. Andersen Air Force Base in Guam assumed greater importance for both staging and training, while the bombing range on the uninhabited Farallon de Mendinilla in the Northern Mariana Islands was put to greater use. Tourism was seriously affected in all dependencies but particularly in Micronesia, which depended on tourists from Japan, South Korea, and Taiwan. The U.S. Office of the Inspector General criticized the Guam Economic Development Authority for unauthorized tax rebates and abatements that affected tax revenues for the territory. In October Guam experienced a magnitude-7 earthquake, which caused only minor damage to buildings but disrupted power and water supplies.

In American Samoa, Gov. Tauese Sunia expressed concern over the possible implications for the territory of tax cuts proposed by U.S. Pres. George W. Bush, and legislation to prevent flow-on of any such measures was introduced. The government also attempted to tighten immigration controls by deporting those who were discovered after a brief amnesty to have overstayed their visas and proposing to hold the passports of visitors. It also adjusted employment laws to facilitate employment in the fish-canning and garment-manufacturing industries.

Indian Ocean and Southern Asia. In July 2001 Mayotte officially became a French dependent collectivity. The change to a full French departmental collectivity would take place over 10 years, with the administrative and political systems adapting to a basically Muslim society. Although French since 1841, the island had historic links to the Comoros. Illegal immigration to Mayotte (about 2,000 people annually) persisted in 2001, especially from the island of Anjouan, where a secessionist movement continued to disrupt life. (See Comoros, below.)

In Réunion local elections in March gave a large victory to the right, which

AP/Wide World Photos

East Timorese residents, with their identity cards in hand, crowd a polling station in Dili on August 30 to vote for a Constituent Assembly.

was generally hostile to the island's being divided into two separate departments. The government withdrew the bill proposed in 2000. Administrative reforms were not the population's first concern, however; high unemployment and the rapidly expanding population were the root causes of the island's social problems.

In October Diego Garcia, the largest atoll in the Chagos Archipelago, or British Indian Ocean Territory (BIOT), once again became a strategically important military base, as it had been in 1991 during the Gulf War. Diego Garcia was the main American naval and air backup base in the war in Afghanistan. In November, exactly a year after a U.K. High Court ruling in their favour, the Ilois, the BIOT's former population, continued to demand the right to return to the 65-island group.

Christmas Island was in the news several times during the year. Australia in June announced plans to build a space launch centre on the island. In August the Norwegian cargo ship *Tampa*, having picked up a boatload of illegal immigrants in distress, was refused permission by Australia to disembark them on Christmas Island. (See *Australia*, below.) An Australian military ship eventually transported the immigrants to Nauru and New Zealand, which had accepted them temporarily. By mid-November, however, several hundred

other asylum seekers had been placed in a detention centre on Christmas Island.

In East Timor the UN mandate ended in 2001 and prepared the way for independence. Indonesian Pres. Megawati Sukarnoputri recognized the island's sovereignty by making the first official visit to the capital, Dili, in September. The Timorese voted in August by universal suffrage for a Constituent Assembly of 88 members, who within three months were to prepare the first constitution of the new state. Of the 16 rival parties, the Revolutionary Front of an Independent East Timor (Fretilin), the former movement for national independence, won a comfortable majority. Fretilin's charismatic leader, Xanana Gusmão, was expected to win the presidential elections in April 2002, and East Timor was scheduled to gain independence a month later.
(CHARLES CADOUX; BARRIE MACDONALD; DAVID RENWICK; MELINDA C. SHEPHERD)

ANTARCTICA

Ice averaging 2,160 m (7,085 ft) in thickness covers more than about 98% of the continent of Antarctica, which has an area of 14 million sq km (5.4 million sq mi). There is no indigenous human population, and there is no land-based industry. Human activity consists mainly of scientific research. The 45-nation Antarctic Treaty is the managerial mechanism for the region south of latitude 60° S, which includes all of Antarctica. The treaty reserves the area for peaceful

purposes, encourages cooperation in science, prescribes environmental protection, allows inspections to verify adherence, and defers the issue of territorial sovereignty.

Conferences in Australia and the U.K. in 2001 commemorated the 40th anniversary of the Antarctic Treaty. The treaty, which entered into force on June 23, 1961, with 12 member nations, in late 2001 had 45 signatories, including Estonia, which joined in 2001. Of the 45 nations, 27 pursued programs of Antarctic scientific research. Some 8,000 scientists and supporting personnel in these national programs were in Antarctica and aboard ship in the adjacent Southern Ocean. They operated 38 year-round stations and additional temporary research camps. The austral summer continental population peaked at around 4,000; the isolated wintering crews in 2001 numbered about 1,000. In an unprecedented winter rescue mission, a Canadian aircraft landed at the U.S. Amundsen-Scott research station in April to evacuate Ronald Shemenski, who was seriously ill, and to deliver a replacement physician.

In September, Russian Prime Minister Mikhail Kasyanov called for an assessment of the country's polar research— apparently shelving a decision whether to invest more in the program or shut it down. The Soviet Union was one of the original 12 members of the Antarctic Treaty, and Western observers doubted a shutdown. The Czech Republic announced that it would establish its first science program in Antarctica, relying on Poland for help in building a station. Chile said that by 2003–04 it would scale up Antarctic tourism by expanding its landing strip on King George Island and would expand research, transferring the Chilean polar institute from Santiago to the University of Magallanes in the country's far south.

France and Italy continued to build a new research station, Concordia, on Dome C, far inland on the continental ice sheet at an altitude of 3,200 m (1 m=3.28 ft). The site was regarded as exceptionally clear for astronomy because of its high altitude, absence of humidity, and mild winds. The station was to be ready in 2003. Science already under way included ice-core drilling to 1,458 m by an international team funded by the European Union; the goal of 3,250 m in two more drilling seasons would enable study of the evolution of climate back to 500,000 BP. At the British Antarctic Survey station Rothera, fire destroyed the biology laboratory in September; a replacement was planned.

Tourism decreased from the 1999–2000 season, which had had 14,762 tourists, of whom 14,402 were shipborne. For the period November 2000 to March 2001, 12,248 persons traveled to the Antarctic on privately organized expeditions, comprising 11,997 passengers aboard 21 commercial vessels, 112 persons on chartered yachts, and 139 land-based visitors. American, German, and British visitors accounted for over two-thirds of the tourists.

The krill catch in the Southern Ocean around Antarctica in the 2000–01 season was 98,209 metric tons, down slightly from the previous season's 101,286 metric tons. Catches of other species (finfish, sharks and rays, crustaceans, and squid) totaled 14,725 metric tons. Of this, the Patagonian toothfish and the Antarctic toothfish totaled 12,733 and 626 metric tons, respectively. Illegal, unreported, and unregulated fishing took, by one estimate, 8,376 metric tons of the two toothfish species—nearing the amount of the legal take and up a thousand metric tons from the previous year.

Scientists found that the eastern Pacific Ocean warming known as El Niño and its counterpart, La Niña, appeared to be behind the periodic advance and retreat of Antarctic sea ice. The finding had implications for global climate because sea ice reflects solar energy; when there is less sea ice, the ocean absorbs the sun's heat and warming is amplified. French researchers linked a 50% reduction in some emperor penguin numbers to reduced sea ice in the 1970s, calling their find the first identification of consequences of major oceanic changes in an Antarctic large predator.

American cosmologists released new findings based on data collected from a ground-based instrument operating at the South Pole and a high-altitude balloon. The data provided the strongest evidence to date for the theory of inflation, the leading model for the formation of the universe, and supported the model that the universe experienced a tremendous spurt of growth shortly after the big bang. Another U.S. observatory, with 677 photodetectors buried deep in ice beneath the South Pole to create one of the world's largest particle detectors, became the first in the world to detect high-energy neutrinos, subatomic particles created by cataclysmic collisions.

An iceberg designated B-15A, which had calved from the Ross Ice Shelf in early 2000, drifted to the western Ross Sea, where it went aground, enabling a buildup of sea ice between it and Victoria Land that could jeopardize ship access to the U.S.'s McMurdo station, Antarctica's largest settlement, and threatened penguin populations that depend on open water for food. The Russian icebreaker *Kapitan Khlebnikov* entered the Bay of Whales, where the berg had calved, establishing a record southern latitude for a surface ship of 78° 37′ S. Satellite data showed that 31 cu km (7.4 cu mi) of ice was lost from the fast-flowing Pine Island Glacier, which demonstrated that this part of the Antarctic ice sheet was thinning and suggesting that Pine Island Glacier would be lost to the ocean within a few hundred years. Another satellite image revealed a crack 25 km (15.5 mi) long, which stretched more than two-thirds across the glacier. The crack had formed in less than five weeks, which led to the prediction that an iceberg might calve within 18 months.

An ice core from Siple Dome revealed the largest and most abrupt warming spike yet found in the Southern Hemisphere and provided evidence that climate change can be dramatically fast. The 4.5 °C (18 °F) hike over a few decades had come as the last ice age began to wane 19,000 years ago. The timing of the warming correlated with an abrupt sea-level rise and belied previous evidence that Antarctic warming events were much more gradual than Northern Hemisphere events.

Sir Peter Maxwell Davies's *Antarctic Symphony*, composed on a commission by the British Antarctic Survey after the British composer's visit south in 1997, was played for the first time by the Philharmonia Orchestra at the Royal Festival Hall in London on May 6. In addition to classical instruments, the score required pebbles, tuned brandy glasses (with water), a biscuit tin (filled with broken glass), and a plastic soap dish scraped across a tam tam. Inspiration for the work included sounds of ice breaking, the silence of the continent, and the lament of the wind. (GUY G. GUTHRIDGE)

ARCTIC REGIONS

The Arctic regions may be defined in physical terms (astronomical [north of the Arctic Circle, latitude 66° 30′ N], climatic [above the 10 °C (50 °F) July isotherm], or vegetational [above the northern limit of the tree line]) or in human terms (the territory inhabited by the circumpolar cultures—Inuit [Eskimo] and Aleut in North America and Russia, Sami [Lapp] in northern Scandinavia

NSF/U.S. Antarctic Program photo by Kristan Hutchison

An aerial photograph shows a section of the U.S.'s new elevated station in Antarctica (right); the finished arches for a garage, shop, cargo warehouse, and power plant (centre); and the silver dome of the old station (left).

and Russia, and 29 other peoples of the Russian North, Siberia, East Asia). No single national sovereignty or treaty regime governs the region, which includes portions of eight countries: Canada, the United States, Russia, Finland, Sweden, Norway, Iceland, and Greenland (part of Denmark). The Arctic Ocean, 14,090,000 sq km (5,440,000 sq mi) in area, constitutes about two-thirds of the region. The land area consists of permanent ice cap, tundra, or taiga. The population (2001 est.) of peoples belonging to the circumpolar cultures is about 375,000. International organizations concerned with the Arctic include the Arctic Council, institutions of the Barents Region, and the Indigenous Peoples' Secretariat. International scientific cooperation of the Arctic is the focus of the International Arctic Research Center of the University of Alaska at Fairbanks.

Although the Arctic was one of the most complicated and expensive areas in the world in which to operate, petroleum, mining, and transportation companies were aggressively exploring North America's last great frontier in 2001. From BP Exploration (Alaska) Inc.'s Northstar project in the Beaufort Sea to three large oil and gas fields discovered inside the 9.3-million-ha (23-million-ac) National Petroleum Reserve–Alaska, oil and gas exploration and development were surging. Throughout 2001 Alaskan and western Canadian Arctic natural gas producers went forward with government lobbying and with plans to build huge new pipeline projects to move northern natural gas reserves to U.S. markets. In a related development, U.S. Pres. George W. Bush proposed opening Alaska's Arctic National Wildlife Refuge to oil and gas exploration. There was also renewed interest in building a Canada-Alaska railway that would run parallel to one of the pipeline proposals and that could eventually be linked to Russia via a tunnel across the Bering Strait.

Early in the year a draft agreement was reached between the Canadian government, the Northwest Territories, and aboriginal groups to establish a one-stop regulatory process and streamline a review of two potential natural gas pipelines. One proposal was for a stand-alone pipeline that would only carry the estimated reserves of 254.8 billion cu m (1 cu m=about 35.3 cu ft) of Mackenzie (River) Delta Canadian natural gas. The other was for the so-called over-the-top Beaufort Sea route, in which gas from the much larger Prudhoe Bay gas fields in northern Alaska would be piped offshore along the northern coast of the Yukon Territory to the Mackenzie Delta

in the Northwest Territories; from there it would be sent to southern markets with the Canadian gas.

During the summer doubt was cast on the Canadian pipeline because of the withdrawal of support by key native groups unless developers agreed to certain conditions, including resource revenue agreements and an equal role for native groups in monitoring the environmental impacts of the project. In June a proposal was endorsed by which native groups would own the pipeline while one of the competing pipeline companies, Arctic Resources Co., would manage it under a long-term contract. The native groups also considered a proposal from an ExxonMobil group that would have given them a one-third stake in a proposed $3 billion pipeline. It was possible that the massive project to take Alaska natural gas reserves—estimated to hold about 991 billion cu m of gas—to markets in the U.S. would hinge on a Canada-U.S. treaty signed in 1977. Foothills Pipe Lines Ltd. claimed that, on the basis of the treaty, they had sole authority to transport Alaska natural gas to market, using the land-based Alaska Highway pipeline route. A consortium of Alaska gas producers—a partnership of ExxonMobil, BP (formerly British Petroleum), and Phillips—initiated a $100 million study of all the alternative pipeline routes that they initially estimated would cost $15 billion–$20 billion.

In August the Alaska Gas Producers announced that their early analysis showed that none of the pipeline options was economically feasible. Their early conclusions were that costs would be too high—$15 billion if the pipeline ran through the Beaufort Sea to the Mackenzie Delta or $17.2 billion if the pipeline was routed along the Alaska Highway through the Yukon to the continental U.S. A separate feasibility study, begun in early 2000, on how to exploit natural gas reserves in the Mackenzie Delta was also expected by the end of the year.

In September the World Wildlife Fund called for the eight countries sharing the Arctic to set aside at least 20% of the region as nature preserves and protected areas by 2010. The conservation call came as pressure for industrial development in the North intensified. Canadian government analysts announced in January that they believed that the eastern Arctic territory of Nunavut had huge reserves of precious metals, including scarce platinum and palladium and diamonds. In Iceland there were proposals to develop major new hydroelectric fa-

cilities. Norilsk, Russia, had emerged as one of the most prosperous cities in the former Soviet Union, while achieving a reputation as the world's most polluted Arctic metropolis. Studies showed that traces of heavy metal from Norilsk's vast nickel, copper, and palladium smelters were among the leading sources of toxic pollutants in the Canadian North.

According to a two-decade study based on NASA satellite images, the northern part of the world—from Alaska to Canada and Russia—was becoming warmer and greener and the growing season was longer as global temperatures rose. The increased vegetation growth was especially pronounced in woodlands and forests, ranging from Central Europe to Siberia and the eastern edge of Russia. Average temperatures could increase about 2–6 °C (3.6–10.8 °F) over the next century, however, and plant life might not be able to adjust to such dramatic changes. *The Wall Street Journal* reported that the thawing of polar ice and the opening of the once unnavigable Northwest Passage in the Canadian Arctic was creating a potential boon for shipping and other commerce, but it also presented an increased security problem. Canadian defense facilities had detected undeclared foreign submarine activity in the Far North. According to a June report from the University of Alaska at Fairbanks, the warming trend had melted about 2,490,000 sq km (960,000 sq mi), or roughly 10% of the Arctic's sea ice. The resulting rise in sea level had forced some Alaskan communities to make plans to move their coastal villages inland to higher ground.

In September the journal *Nature* reported that stone tools, animal bones, and an incised mammoth tusk found at a site on the Usa River at the Arctic Circle in Russia had provided what a team of Russian and Norwegian researchers said was the first evidence that modern humans or Neanderthals lived in the Arctic more than 30,000 years ago. This was at least 15,000 years earlier than previously reported.

The Nunavik Commission, created in November 1999, presented its recommendations for a new form of government for the Arctic region of Quebec, which was largely populated by Inuit. Among the important recommendations was the creation of nonethnic public institutions for the region, such as a Nunavik Assembly, a Council of Elders, and a Court of Justice, as well as the recognition of English, French, and Inuktitut (Inuit) as Nunavik's official languages.

(KENNETH DE LA BARRE)

AFGHANISTAN

Area: 652,225 sq km (251,825 sq mi)
Population (2001 est.): 26,813,000 (including Afghan refugees estimated to number about 2,000,000 in Pakistan and about 2,000,000 in Iran)
Capital: Kabul
Chief of state: de facto Taliban Supreme Leader (Amir-ul-Momenin), Mullah Mohammad Omar; President Burhanuddin Rabbani from November 13 to December 22, and, from December 22, Chairman of the Interim Administration Hamid Karzai
Head of government: heads of the Supreme Council Mullah Mohammad Rabbani, and, acting from April 16 to November 13, Mawlawi Abdul Kabir

Northern Alliance soldiers advance toward Kunduz, Afg., on November 13.

Sion Touhig/Getty Images

Crippling drought and unending internal fighting characterized the first half of 2001 in Afghanistan, but the terrorist attacks of September 11 in the U.S. set off a chain reaction that reversed fortunes and produced Afghanistan's first peaceful change of government in decades. A year that saw the rigid control of the Taliban on the verge of total victory also witnessed its military defeat and political marginalization.

Though humanitarian aid continued to reach Afghanistan, Taliban attitudes toward the public role of women and sensitivity to foreign influences frustrated the work of aid agencies. Its unyielding policies also provoked international condemnation and economic sanctions. In May the U.S. announced increased assistance for Afghanistan, but in that same month the Taliban closed several UN political offices in the country. UN efforts to distribute food in Kabul were threatened in a dispute over the use of Afghan women in this work. In August eight foreign relief workers were detained on charges of promoting Christianity and threatened with the death penalty; after three months in custody, however, they were rescued by U.S. forces in November.

Farmers across Afghanistan were severely affected when the winter rains failed for the third consecutive year. It was estimated that half of Afghanistan's irrigated land was out of use and that livestock herds had been reduced by as much as 70%. Unable to sustain themselves on the land, large numbers of the rural population became refugees in Afghanistan's cities or fled to neighbouring countries.

UN Secretary-General Kofi Annan reported in August that the opium poppy had almost completely disappeared from Taliban-controlled areas. Though the international community welcomed the news, the hardship it brought to local farmers contributed to the flow of refugees, both internal and international.

After overcoming bitter resistance, the Taliban retook Bamiyan in central Afghanistan in February. In March Mullah Mohammad Omar ordered that two large statues of Buddha hewn from a cliff at Bamiyan be destroyed because they were offensive to Islam. Although there were almost no Buddhists in Afghanistan, the statues, dating from the 4th and 5th centuries, were esteemed throughout the world as cultural treasures. The colossal figures were destroyed with explosives, and Taliban officials expressed dismay that so much concern was given statues when Afghans themselves were in such want. Taliban second-in-command Mullah Mohammad Rabbani died of cancer in April. (*See* OBITUARIES.)

On September 9 Ahmad Shah Masoud (*see* OBITUARIES), military leader of the Northern Alliance and the most respected hero of Afghan resistance to Soviet invasion and Taliban advances, was killed by suicide bombers thought to have been sent by Osama bin Laden. (*See* BIOGRAPHIES.) This major setback to anti-Taliban resistance appeared to leave the Northern Alliance more vulnerable than ever.

Blaming Bin Laden for the September 11 attacks on New York City and Washington, D.C., the U.S. turned its military wrath against the Taliban for continuing to protect him. A bombing campaign begun by U.S. and British forces on October 7 was aimed at Taliban military targets and coordinated to support a Northern Alliance offensive. Later that month the Taliban executed Abdul Haq, a military commander and potential threat. (*See* OBITUARIES.)

Taliban fighters were pushed out of Mazar-e Sharif and Kunduz in the north with significant losses, and on November 12 they abandoned Kabul. Soon the Taliban seat of power in Kandahar had been surrendered, and many Taliban had disappeared into the countryside, fled to Pakistan, or shifted their allegiance. U.S. bombing continued in the mountainous Tora Bora area near the border with Pakistan, where Bin Laden and many of his al-Qaeda fighters were thought to have fled. At year's end neither Bin Laden nor Taliban leader Mohammad Omar had been located.

International moves to solve the resulting political crisis focused on avoiding the chaos and destruction that had followed the mujahideen takeover from the Communist government of Mohammad Najibullah in 1992. On November 27 a UN-sponsored conference in Bonn, Ger., convened to settle on an interim government to replace the Taliban. The largest share of delegates represented the Northern Alliance,

whose political leader, Burhanuddin Rabbani, had retained international recognition even after being driven from Kabul in 1996. Supporters of former king Zahir Shah also participated. The result was an agreement that Hamid Karzai (*see* BIOGRAPHIES), a Pashtun tribal leader and supporter of the former king, would lead an interim administration for six months, when a Loya Jirga, a traditional Afghan assembly of notables, would choose a new government. On December 22 Karzai and a cabinet that included two women were installed in a peaceful ceremony joined by outgoing President Rabbani and most of the country's ethnic and political factions.

(STEPHEN SEGO)

ALBANIA

Area: 28,703 sq km (11,082 sq mi)
Population (2001 est.): 3,091,000 (not including Albanians living abroad)
Capital: Tirana
Chief of state: President Rexhep Meidani
Head of government: Prime Minister Ilir Meta

Relations with neighbouring Macedonia, where members of the large ethnic Albanian minority staged an armed rebellion in March, were of prime concern in Albania in 2001. Although Prime Minister Ilir Meta supported international peace negotiations, which led to a truce and a peace settlement in late August, there was evidence to suggest that Albanian border guards had at first failed to seal the border completely to arms smugglers supplying the rebels in Macedonia.

The focus of domestic politics was on the country's fourth democratic general elections, held June 24 and July 8. The Socialist Party (PS—the former Communists), with a reform-oriented program, gained an absolute majority in the parliament with 73 of the 140 seats. The opposition coalition Union for Victory (BpF), dominated by the Democratic Party (PD) of former president Sali Berisha, received only 46 seats. The opposition had been split since 2000, when the New Democrat Party split off from the PD. Its leader, Genc Pollo, charged Berisha with failing to offer convincing answers to the country's essential problems. His leadership

appealed to many PD voters who were looking for a group among the opposition that could demonstrate some political competence. The new party won six seats in the new parliament. Berisha and PD legislators continued to boycott the parliament and called for early elections. In September the BpF itself launched a new boycott of the parliament, charging the government with having manipulated the elections. Observers from the Organization for Security and Cooperation in Europe dismissed suggestions, however, that irregularities during the voting had affected the overall outcome. It took the parliament nearly three months—until September 12—to give Prime Minister Meta's new coalition government a vote of confidence. The delays were due to vote recounts in some districts.

Within the governing coalition the PS controlled all key ministries. Arta Dade became the first woman in Albanian history to serve as foreign minister. Former prime minister Pandeli Majko became defense minister. The interior, justice, public economy, and finance portfolios all went to Socialists as well. The chairman of the Social Democratic Party, Skender Gjinushi, took charge of labour and social affairs, while another Social Democrat, former foreign minister Paskal Milo, became minister of Euro-Atlantic integration. Former justice minister Arben Imami became minister of local government and decentralization, pledging to focus on strengthening the role of cities and towns; Niko Kacalidha (of the Union Party, which represents many ethnic Greeks) was appointed to the new post of state minister for minorities and the diaspora. For his part, Prime Minister Meta pledged to upgrade power supplies, proceed with privatization, fight corruption and organized crime, improve ties with Western Europe and neighbours in the Balkan region, and promote free trade.

Albania's economy suffered a slight recession in 2001. The national statistical institute expected an inflation rate of 2–4% at the end of the year and 7.3% growth in gross domestic product, just slightly less than the 7.8% registered in 2000. Nonetheless, unemployment dropped from 17.1% in 1999 to 13.3% in 2001, thanks to a government-supported job-creation program that included infrastructure-development projects within the framework of the Stability Pact for South Eastern Europe.

(FABIAN SCHMIDT)

ALGERIA

Area: 2,381,741 sq km (919,595 sq mi)
Population (2001 est.): 30,821,000
Capital: Algiers
Chief of state: President Abdelaziz Bouteflika
Head of government: Prime Minister Ali Benflis

Wearing black tape over their mouths to protest government restrictions on freedom of the press and to express support for those killed in earlier riots, Algerian journalists march in the streets of Tizi Ouzou on May 23.

AP/Wide World Photos

In 2001 Algeria continued to suffer from the chronic and endemic violence of the past decade. Though the levels of violence had diminished from the peaks of 1998, the Armed Islamic Group and the Salafist Group for Preaching and Combat continued to attack civilians and military targets. Violence even returned to the hearts of the cities, including the capital, Algiers. In July car bombs exploded and an assassination was carried out in Zeralda, and a spate of attacks on civilians took place in Annaba.

More worrying for Pres. Abedelaziz Bouteflika was a protest in Kabylia in April on the 21st anniversary of the "Berber Spring" riots. This time the violence was triggered by the killing of a teenager in gendarmerie custody; the government claimed the death was accidental. In the aftermath in May and June, some 80 persons were killed and hundreds were injured. Massive demonstrations—more than 100,000 people protested in the provincial capital, Tizi Ouzou, in late May—spilled over into the capital. At the end of May, 300,000 Socialist Forces Front supporters demonstrated in Algiers, and more than one million people clogged the streets in mid-June. In the ensuing violence 4 persons died and 1,000 were injured. An independent commission established by the government reported in August that the gendarmerie was to blame for the teenager's death. In October the government reluctantly conceded that Berber languages should be given the status of "national languages," but all political demands were refused. By September Berber demonstrators had been cleared from the capital, but the government was then faced with continuing confrontations in Kabylia and a widening circle of mass protest. Algerians elsewhere in the country, particularly in the east, protested worsening economic and social conditions.

There was also growing discontent in the Council of the Nation, Algeria's up-per house of the parliament, where one-third of the members were appointed by the president. The presidential choice for speaker was approved unanimously in April, but two members resigned in July, complaining of governmental indifference to the role of the parliament. In May the government lost one of its coalition partners; the Rally for Culture and Democracy, a Berber party, left over the conduct of the government during the riots in Kabylia. The army command—considered the country's power base—was faced with another problem when Gen. Khalid Nezzar was threatened with arrest for human rights abuses in France. The beleaguered president, at odds with the army command, visited the U.S. in July. Following the September terrorist attacks in the U.S., Algiers offered to hand over details of the Algerian nationals involved in the al-Qaeda movement. Though the economy benefited from high oil prices—foreign reserves rose to $15.4 billion in midyear—economic restructuring ensured that unemployment remained disturbingly high. In November massive flooding led to the deaths of some 700 persons.   (GEORGE JOFFÉ)

ANDORRA

Area: 468 sq km (181 sq mi)
Population (2001 est.): 66,900
Capital: Andorra la Vella
Chiefs of state: Co-princes of Andorra, the president of France and the bishop of Urgell, Spain
Head of government: Chief Executive Marc Forné Molné

Led by Chief Executive Marc Forné Molné, the ruling Liberal Party of Andorra (PLA) swept to victory in parliamentary elections held on March 4, 2001. With a turnout of 81.6% of the electorate, the PLA won an absolute majority—15 of the 28 seats; the Social Democratic Party garnered 6 seats, the Democratic Party 5, and the Lauredian Union 2 seats. Forné had led Andorra since December 1994.

Smuggling in Andorra continued with a new wrinkle in 2001. Older, retired people who had stashed their money under the mattress to avoid paying tax on it were flocking to Andorra with their carefully hoarded stashes of pesetas, francs, marks, and lire. There they hoped to exchange their banknotes on the black market for goods before July 2002, when the introduction of the euro would make them for the most part valueless.

Andorra also began exploring the construction of a subway system to alleviate traffic congestion.   (ANNE ROBY)

ANGOLA

Area: 1,246,700 sq km (481,354 sq mi)
Population (2001 est.): 10,366,000 (excluding about 300,000 refugees in the Democratic Republic of the Congo and Zambia)
Capital: Luanda
Chief of state and head of government: President José Eduardo dos Santos

With inflation for the 12-month period to Jan. 1, 2001, having reached 241% and with the currency showing every sign of continuing to depreciate rapidly,

Angola's annual budget, published on February 20, made depressing reading for a country with such ample resources of oil and minerals. Despite pledges given in the previous April to promote measures to alleviate poverty, the government felt it necessary to warn that there might have to be cuts in spending on health and education. Meanwhile, donors and aid agencies complained of corruption in government circles and of the diversion of money to military activities in the Democratic Republic of the Congo (DRC), as well as to the continuing struggle against the National Union for the Total Independence of Angola (UNITA) rebels at home.

The two military operations were, in fact, closely linked. Unlike most of the other countries involved in the Congo war, Angola did not aim to exploit the situation for its own financial gain but was trying to ensure that the UNITA rebels, who had devastated so much of their homeland, did not use the DRC as a secure base for their operations.

Accusations of official corruption were not so easily justified. In March ongoing investigations in France into corruption and illegal arms deals with Angola that had taken place in 1993–94 were reported to have uncovered documents demonstrating the existence of personal contacts between Angolan Pres. José Eduardo dos Santos and Charles Pasqua, one of those alleged to have been involved in illegal arms trafficking.

In April serious flooding in Benguela province rendered 13,000 families homeless, and in May the economy suffered a further unwelcome setback when De Beers Consolidated Mines, Ltd., suspended its investment and prospecting operations after having failed to agree to the revival of contracts with the Angolan government.

Nevertheless, it was the long-running war against UNITA rebels that mainly hampered the country's development. In January the president replaced his military chief of staff. Then early in June, in spite of a marked escalation of rebel activity in Uíge and Bengo provinces during the previous month, the government claimed that the civil war had virtually ended.

UNITA quickly challenged that assertion by shooting down a United Nations World Food Programme cargo plane. On August 10 UNITA forces attacked a railway train near Luanda, killing more than 250 people, and 14 days later 50 passengers in a bus were massacred in a rebel ambush. In the face of such evidence of the government's inability to contain the threat from UNITA, and with acute economic mismanagement causing tensions even among ruling-party loyalists, the president's announcement on the same day as the ambush that he would not stand in any future presidential elections gave rise to considerable speculation about his motives for making the statement. Opposition commentators suggested that, there being no obvious successor, it was a deliberate gamble aimed at reawakening support for himself and uniting the ruling party behind him, an opinion with which even some government loyalists were inclined to concur.

(KENNETH INGHAM)

ANTIGUA AND BARBUDA

Area: 442 sq km (171 sq mi)
Population (2001 est.): 71,500 (including evacuees from Montserrat)
Capital: Saint John's
Chief of state: Queen Elizabeth II, represented by Governor-General James Carlisle
Head of government: Prime Minister Lester Bird

Following a sharp rebuke by the International Monetary Fund (IMF) over what it said was a deficit of 12% of gross domestic product in public-sector finances during 2000, Prime Minister Lester Bird in March 2001 suspended ministerial traveling allowances and announced a variable cut in public servants' salaries. In April an IMF team visited the country to discuss aspects of "tax reform" designed to help the government bring its finances back into balance.

In May Bird fired both Attorney General Errol Cort and Minister of Health Bernard Percival for "a lapse of

Demonstrators in Luanda, Angola, stage a protest on August 18 against UNITA rebels, who one week earlier had attacked a train near the city and massacred more than 250 people.

Afonso Francisco/AFP Worldwide

good judgement" regarding the government's Medical Benefits Scheme. Though Bird initially had resisted a call for a commission of inquiry into the matter, he announced in June that one would occur "to maintain public confidence in the working of the scheme."

In July the U.K. government lifted its two-year-old financial advisory against Antigua and Barbuda, which had been under scrutiny by British financial institutions paying "special attention" to its transactions amid allegations of money laundering. The U.S. followed suit in August.   (DAVID RENWICK)

ARGENTINA

Area: 2,780,092 sq km (1,073,400 sq mi)
Population (2001 est.): 37,487,000
Capital: Buenos Aires
Head of state: Presidents Fernando de la Rúa (assisted by Ministerial Coordinator Chrystian Colombo), Ramón Puerta (acting) from December 21, Adolfo Rodríguez Saá (interim) from December 23 until December 30, and, acting from December 31, Eduardo Camaño

In 2001 the Argentine recession entered its fourth year, with the embattled government of Pres. Fernando de la Rúa under mounting political and social pressure. The country's gross domestic product shrank by 3%; consumer prices dropped 1%; and the unemployment rate increased from an already high 15% to 17%.

Owing to his inability to reverse the country's continued economic decline, Minister of Economy José Luis Machinea resigned in March. He was replaced by Ricardo López Murphy. López Murphy's economic reform plan, designed to reduce the fiscal deficit and restore economic growth, was, however, deemed too extreme (especially the spending cuts it entailed) by the moderate and progressive wings of the governing Alliance. López Murphy resigned after only two weeks in office.

De la Rúa replaced López Murphy with Domingo Cavallo. (See BIOGRA-PHIES.) Cavallo was former president Carlos Saúl Menem's minister of economy between 1991 and 1996 and was, along with Menem (who in June was placed under house arrest owing to corruption charges but was freed in

November), the co-architect of the country's impressive economic turnaround in the early 1990s. As a member of Menem's cabinet, Cavallo had been widely criticized, if not demonized, by a large majority of the members of the Alliance (then in opposition). His reappointment by de la Rúa provoked considerable discontent among virtually all of the members of the Alliance's junior partner, the Front for a Country in Solidarity (Frepaso), as well as among a substantial portion of the Alliance's senior partner, the Radical Civic Union (UCR), the party of de la Rúa.

Once in office, Cavallo immediately launched a series of important, albeit piecemeal, economic reforms. These included implementing a tax on bank transactions, extending the value-added tax to previously exempt activities, and modifying the country's 1991 Convertibility Law. By July it was clear that Cavallo's reforms had been ineffective, with a lack of investor confidence pushing interest rates to such a level that the external credit market was, for all intents and purposes, closed to Argentina. In a move designed to restore investor confidence and obtain additional external financial support, principally from the International Monetary Fund, Cavallo introduced a "zero deficit law," which was approved by Congress in late July. The law stipulated that Argentine government expenditures equal government revenues, with deficit spending prohibited. As a result, the government had to reduce its expenditures to keep them in line with revenues. During the third quarter this adherence resulted in a 13% reduction in government employee salaries and pensions and a considerable cutback in government purchases of goods and services.

The combination of 39 months of recession and the fallout from the implementation of the zero deficit law did not augur well for de la Rúa and the Alliance in the October 14 midterm elections. In these elections the entire 72-member Senate (the first direct Senate election since 1973) was renewed along with one-half of the Chamber of Deputies. De la Rúa's UCR, the remnants of Frepaso, and a few minor parties presented a joint Alliance list of candidates in 16 provinces, while in the remaining 8 provinces the UCR and Frepaso ran separately. The Alliance-UCR and Frepaso received a strong rebuke at the polls, garnering a meager 23% of the popular vote in the Chamber election (down from 44% in

1999) and an equally scant 24% in the Senate election. The principal opposition Justicialist Party (PJ) won 37% (up from 32%) and 40% of the Chamber and Senate vote, respectively.

In spite of the Alliance's dismal showing in the popular vote, owing to a combination of the rules governing the direct election of senators (two for the plurality winner and one for the first runner-up in each province) and the previous mode of Senate election (by provincial legislatures), the Alliance increased its Senate representation from 23 to 26. Likewise, while its number of Chamber seats won (35) represented a considerable drop from 1999 (63), the Alliance still remained a substantial force in the Chamber with 88 seats total. The PJ retained its majority in the Senate, winning 40 seats, while improving its presence in the Chamber by winning 65 seats (up from 50 in 1999) for a total of 116.

In the fourth quarter the continuing economic decline sparked a political crisis. Antigovernment protesters rioted in the capital in late December, and Cavallo resigned on December 20. After President de la Rúa unsuccessfully attempted to patch up his shaky coalition by appealing to the opposition Peronist Party to join a government of national unity, he too resigned on the 20th. On December 23 Adolfo Rodríguez Saá was installed as interim president, and that same day he suspended payment on the country's $132 billion debt. The rioting continued, however, and Saá was forced to step down on December 30 after he was unable to secure political support from his party.

(MARK P. JONES)

ARMENIA

Area: 29,743 sq km (11,484 sq mi). Some 12–15% of neighbouring Azerbaijan (including the 4,400-sq-km [1,700-sq-mi] disputed region of Nagorno-Karabakh [Armenian: Artsakh]) has been under Armenian control since 1993.
Population (2001 est.): officially 3,807,000; actually about 3,000,000 (plus 100,000 in Nagorno-Karabakh)
Capital: Yerevan
Chief of state: President Robert Kocharyan
Head of government: Prime Minister Andranik Markaryan

The configuration of forces within the Armenian parliament underwent sweeping changes during 2001. In February former prime minister Aram Sarkisyan and several supporters quit the Republican Party of Armenia to form a new opposition party named Hayastan ("Armenia"). During the summer several deputies, including parliament speaker Armen Khachatryan and one of his deputies, Gagik Aslanyan, quit the People's Party of Armenia, the Republican Party's partner in the majority Unity bloc. Aslanyan founded the new People's Democratic Party. The Communist Party of Armenia expelled two of its senior leaders. Two leading members left Vazgen Manukyan's National Democratic Union and established rival parties.

On September 5 People's Party chairman Stepan Demirchyan officially declared the Unity bloc defunct, and two days later he, together with Sarkisyan and National Unity Party chairman Artashes Geghamyan, announced their shared intention to impeach Pres. Robert Kocharyan for violating the Armenian constitution, condoning terrorism, precipitating a crisis in the country, and thwarting the investigation into the October 1999 parliament shootings. (The trial of the five perpetrators of those murders began in February.) President Kocharyan announced on September 8 that he would seek a second presidential term in 2003. Members of his bodyguard were implicated in the death in a Yerevan cafe on September 25 of an ethnic Armenian from Georgia.

Armenia's economy performed quite well, with 9.1% gross domestic product growth during the first 11 months and an 11.5% increase in agricultural output. The World Bank warned in July, however, that economic growth had still not translated into an improvement in living and social conditions for the majority of the population. Visiting Yerevan in September, Russian Defense Minister Sergey Ivanov and Pres. Vladimir Putin both stressed the strategic significance of military cooperation with Armenia. The Russian government nonetheless insisted on Armenia's prompt repayment of debts for supplies of gas and nuclear fuel.

In January Armenia was accepted into full membership of the Council of Europe. President Kocharyan's visit to Iran in November reaffirmed the importance both countries attached to economic cooperation.

In late September Pope John Paul II traveled to Armenia to participate in celebrations to mark the 1,700th anniversary of the country's adoption of Christianity as the state religion.

(ELIZABETH FULLER)

AUSTRALIA

Area: 7,692,030 sq km (2,969,910 sq mi)
Population (2001 est.): 19,358,000
Capital: Canberra
Chief of state: Queen Elizabeth II, represented by Governors-General Sir William Deane and, from June 29, the Right Rev. Peter Hollingworth
Head of government: Prime Minister John Howard

Domestic Affairs. Australia celebrated the Centenary of Federation in 2001. Amid a year of festivities, a grand meeting of all the elected members of the state and commonwealth parliaments took place on May 9. The gala event was held in the Royal Exhibition Building in Melbourne, where 100 years earlier the Australian states had formally convened the first federal Parliament. On June 29 the Right Rev. Peter Hollingworth, the Anglican archbishop of Brisbane, replaced Sir William Deane as governor-general.

Prime Minister John Howard's government faced its biggest crisis in office when the Norwegian freighter *Tampa* picked up a boatload of more than 430 refugees on August 26 and sailed with them to Christmas Island, an Australian dependency. The mainly Afghan asylum seekers had sailed from Indonesia on August 24 in a decrepit Indonesian fishing boat, which was sinking. Howard took a hard line and declared that none of the refugees would be allowed to set foot on Australian soil. Despite international protests, Australian Special Air Service troops boarded the *Tampa* on September 3 and forcibly transferred its passengers to the troopship HMAS *Manoora* for transport to Nauru and New Zealand, which had agreed to hold these and other asylum seekers temporarily while their claims were being processed. On September 12 an Australian federal court ruled that the refugees were being illegally detained, but the government remained adamant and pushed through legislation that would tighten Australia's laws on refugees. The HMAS *Tobruk* later picked up and transported 260 additional "boat people" to Nauru, and more than 200 others were taken to Papua New Guinea for processing. A large number of Australian voters—around 75%—supported the prime minister's decision, which was perhaps the most popular act his government had ever made.

The dramatic turnaround in public opinion gave Howard the opportunity to buck the trend of normal politics and win an historic third term in office. With the strong assistance of Immigration Minister Philip Ruddock, Howard stood against world opinion, and his strong line on Australian sovereignty was endorsed by the electorate on November 10. The prime minister's decisive support of U.S. Pres. George W. Bush's administration, and his decision to commit Australian armed forces to the war against terrorism, also gained popular approval. Howard's coalition enjoyed a strong working majority after the election, which saw high-profile Australian Labor Party (ALP) frontbencher Cheryl Kernot lose her seat and led the ALP's Kim Beazley to resign as the leader of the opposition. The Greens' national vote was a record, and party leader Bob Brown was returned as a senator from Tasmania, while Pauline Hanson's One Nation party lost support.

Howard went into the federal election leading a divided and demoralized Liberal Party of Australia (LPA). Successive election losses in the states had left Australia with only one LPA premier, John Olsen of South Australia. Even in the Northern Territory, where the Country Liberal Party had governed for 26 years, Clare Martin defeated Denis Burke and formed the territory's first ALP government. To make matters worse, the LPA president, Shane Stone, in a leaked memorandum, described Howard's coalition government as mean, tricky, and out of touch.

The government faced continued problems with riots in its three refugee detention centres at Port Hedland, Curtin, and Woomera. In June, exactly a year after a mass breakout from the Woomera camp, asylum seekers who had been unsuccessful in their attempts to remain in Australia smashed windows and broke furniture; shortly afterward, seven Iranian refugees burrowed under perimeter fencing and escaped. In response to the criticism of the centres—which suffered from riots, allegations of child abuse, and remote desert locations—Ruddock proposed a Swedish-style improvement under which the women and children among the refugees could be released from detention and allowed to live in the wider community in Woomera. In December, in the worst violence in 18 months, asylum seekers shouting "visa, visa, visa" set fire to 15 buildings (5 were incinerated) at the Woomera facility. At year's end more than 100 bush fires, about half of which had been set deliberately by arsonists, threatened the largest city, Sydney, and destroyed about 150 homes.

Before the federal elections Australia's major political parties had faced a resurgence of the One Nation movement in 2001. The ALP in Western Australia swept to power on the back of One Nation. Senior Minister Bob Katter resigned from the National Party to stand as an independent, declaring it was time to stand up for the bush. In a major change in national politics, Sen. Natasha Stott Despoja was elected to lead Australia's third political force, the Australian Democrats. Sen. Aden Ridgeway became deputy leader; he was the first Aboriginal politician elected to a party leadership position in what the press described as the "Dream Team."

The Economy. In 2001 Treasurer Peter Costello produced a budget with increased spending on welfare, older Australians, and health care. To make it clear to the electorate that they should take the budget concessions into account when voting, the government launched a saturation television campaign to emphasize the budget's positive features, which were largely aimed at winning back voters unhappy with the goods and services tax introduced in 2000.

The Civil Aviation Safety Authority grounded Ansett Australia's fleet of Boeing 767 aircraft in April, saying that service documents for the aircraft had to be inspected. Once this was completed, Ansett resumed normal services, but it remained under a cloud caused by negotiations between Air New Zealand, Singapore Airlines, and Qantas Airways over how best to structure future international, Australian, and regional airline ownership. The managing director of Singapore Airlines revealed that Singapore Airlines had invested in Air New Zealand Ansett for the long term. Impulse Airlines, Flightwest Airlines, and Air Pacific, which operated under a franchise as Qantas New Zealand, all ceased to be viable and ended operations. Matters were further complicated by the successful entry of Richard Branson's Virgin Blue Airlines into Australian aviation.

Serious corporate collapses marred the overall improved Australian economic performance. The government was forced to rescue policy holders when the HIH Casualty and General Insurance company went bankrupt with debts of $A 4 billion ($A 1 = about U.S. $0.51). HIH underwrote compulsory third-party indemnity insurance in the building industry, and the government accordingly provided a $A 500 million bailout package to protect consumers who were in the process of building homes. Equally important was the liquidation of One.Tel, one of Australia's biggest telephone service providers. One.Tel went into voluntary liquidation in June with debts of more than $A 600 million.

Foreign Affairs. Australia tried to improve relations with Indonesia in 2001. As part of the process, Indonesian Pres. Abdurrahman Wahid arrived in Australia on June 25. It was the first visit by an Indonesian leader to Australia in more than a quarter of a century. Howard hoped that the two countries could overcome Indonesian resentment of Australia's leadership role in peacekeeping during the East Timor crisis in 1999, and Wahid reassured Australia that Indonesia would find political stability in a short time. When Wahid was replaced by Megawati Sukarnoputri, however, relations took a step backward. The newly installed Indonesian president refused to negotiate over the refugee crisis or to accept any responsibility for the Afghan asylum seekers who had set sail from Indonesia.

Australia and Thailand began a new era in their relationship by exploring a free-trade deal in return for help from Thailand in overcoming Australia's exclusion from such key regional bodies as the Association of Southeast Asian Nations. Singapore and Australia improved economic cooperation when Canberra gave Singapore's government-controlled company SingTel permission to buy Australia's second largest telecommunications carrier, Cable & Wireless Optus.

Australia reinforced good relations with the U.S. during the year. U.S. Defense Secretary Donald Rumsfeld and Secretary of State Colin Powell were leaders of a distinguished team sent to Australia in August to thank the Howard government for its support of U.S. policy on missile defense and the Kyoto Protocol on global warming. After the September 11 terrorist attacks in the U.S., both Howard and Beazley affirmed their support for the U.S. and sought to reassure Indonesia, a predominantly Muslim country, that the U.S. and its allies were waging a fight against terrorism and not against Islam.

(A.R.G. GRIFFITHS)

Asylum seekers who had unsuccessfully attempted to enter Australia prepare for the day at a refugee camp on the island of Nauru in September.

AP/Wide World Photos

AUSTRIA

Area: 83,858 sq km (32,378 sq mi)
Population: (2001 est.): 8,069,000
Capital: Vienna
Chief of state: President Thomas Klestil
Head of government: Chancellor Wolfgang Schüssel

Austria's right-of-centre coalition government, comprising the moderate People's Party (ÖVP) and the populist—and occasionally xenophobic—Freedom Party (FPÖ), completed its first full year in office in 2001. Allaying early fears that the inclusion of the FPÖ in government heralded a lurch to the reactionary right in Austria, the coalition's policies and actions remained on a moderate and largely uncontroversial course throughout the year. This was largely because the ÖVP continued to dominate the arrangement, remaining in almost complete control of the political and policy agenda, while the inexperienced FPÖ made an impact only occasionally.

This inability to make its mark contributed to a significant loss of support for the FPÖ and led to calls from within the party for a return to opposition. More moderate elements successfully resisted this, helped by an understanding among members and supporters that withdrawal from the government would likely precipitate an election in which the party would lose considerable ground. To add to its woes during 2001, the FPÖ was bedeviled by unsightly public squabbles, often over trivial personal rivalries.

Vienna was the only one of the nine federal provinces to go to the polls in 2001. As expected, the opposition Social Democrats (SPÖ) and the Green Party made gains at the expense of the FPÖ, while ÖVP support remained static. The result allowed the centre-left SPÖ to win outright control of the city's legislature and end its former coalition arrangement with the ÖVP.

The most fundamental change undertaken by the federal government was its continued efforts to limit the role of Austria's powerful social partnership, which had traditionally given trade unions, employers, and other interest groups an important role in the formulation of economic and social policies. Since coming to power in 2000, the government had sought to wrest from the

SPÖ the leverage it had on policy (even while in opposition) via its close links with the trade union movement and to remove those individuals not affiliated with either the ÖVP or the FPÖ from positions of power in public institutions. The trade unions fought a rearguard action, however, and this resulted in the souring of the industrial relations climate and in occasional street demonstrations—unusual occurrences in socially stable Austria.

A government attempt to forge closer links with former communist countries attempting to join the European Union had little success, probably because those countries were sensitive to any appearance that Austria would take a leading role in the region. Meanwhile, the government moved closer to NATO. Although the country had been militarily neutral since 1955, both government parties had supported Austrian membership in NATO since the end of the Cold War in the early 1990s, arguing that neutrality no longer served Austria's security interests. Given public opposition, however, the government conceded that NATO membership would not be contemplated in the foreseeable future.

The rate of economic growth slowed throughout 2001. Despite this, unemployment remained below 5%—one of the lowest rates in the industrialized world. Inflation, though higher than in 2000, remained low and stable, easing back during the course of the year. Although some progress was made in reducing the deficit level in 2001, the slowdown in the economy depressed tax revenues and pushed expenditure above expected levels.   (DAN O'BRIEN)

AZERBAIJAN

Area: 86,600 sq km (33,400 sq mi), including the 5,500-sq-km (2,100-sq-mi) exclave of Nakhichevan and the 4,400-sq-km (1,700-sq-mi) disputed region (with Armenia) of Nagorno-Karabakh
Population (2001 est.): 8,105,000
Capital: Baku
Head of state and government: President Heydar Aliyev, assisted by Prime Minister Artur Rasizade

Speculation over who would succeed 78-year-old Pres. Heydar Aliyev intensified

in 2001. Media reports identified presidential administration chief Ramiz Mekhtiyev as a potential rival to Ilham Aliyev, the president's son and preferred successor. The authorities continued to suppress opposition activity, evicting the Azerbaijan National Independence Party from its headquarters and either closing or bringing libel proceedings against independent and opposition media outlets. Nine participants of a hunger strike in February by war invalids demanding an increase in their pensions that degenerated into fighting with police were tried and sentenced to up to six years' imprisonment. New restrictions were imposed on all religious organizations and communities. In late December President Aliyev proposed measures to loosen constraints on the media.

Four international consortia engaged in oil extraction in Azerbaijan's sector of the Caspian Sea reported that trial wells failed to yield hydrocarbons. Disagreements over transit tariffs delayed the planned signing of an agreement with Georgia on the export of natural gas to Turkey from late July to late September. Cooperation in the Caspian with international oil companies was called into question in July after Iranian military aircraft and gunboats threatened a prospecting vessel leased to British Petroleum, which promptly suspended operations. A long-proposed visit by President Aliyev to Iran was postponed yet again. Also postponed until early in 2002 was a visit by Aliyev to Moscow during which an agreement allowing Russia to continue using the Gabala radar facility was expected to be signed.

The unauthorized publication in February of confidential Organization for Security and Cooperation in Europe proposals for resolving the conflict over Azerbaijan's Armenian-populated breakaway Nagorno-Karabakh region triggered widespread demands for a military campaign to reconquer the region. Talks between Pres. Aliyev and his Armenian counterpart, Robert Kocharyan, in Paris in March and in Florida in early April were billed as heralding a formal agreement ending the conflict, but Aliyev subsequently denied that any agreement in principle had been reached. In January Azerbaijan was admitted to full membership of the Council of Europe.

As of August 1, Azerbaijan gave up the Cyrillic alphabet and adopted Latin letters (in a variant similar to Turkish) for the national language, Azeri. The changeover caused substantial confusion, especially because of a lack of computer fonts and keyboards.   (ELIZABETH FULLER)

BAHAMAS, THE

Area: 13,939 sq km (5,382 sq mi)
Population (2001 est.): 298,000
Capital: Nassau
Chief of state: Queen Elizabeth II, represented by Governors-General Orville Turnquest and, from November 13, Ivy Dumont (acting)
Head of government: Prime Minister Hubert Ingraham

The Bahamian government moved smartly against dubious offshore banks in February 2001; it closed down two operations and revoked the licenses of five others following the publication of a U.S. Senate report that described them as conduits for money laundering. In June The Bahamas was removed from the Paris-based Financial Action Task Force list of countries with inadequate laws to fight money laundering. The government had launched several initiatives, including the banning of anonymous ownership of the more than 100,000 international business companies registered in the country.

In May the government announced budget spending of $1,035,000,000 designed to stimulate economic growth. The International Monetary Fund (IMF) had forecast growth of 3.5%, down from about 5% in 2000. The reduction was partly based on the sluggish U.S. economy. The Bahamas was dependent on the U.S. for tourists and property investors.

Tommy Turnquest, leader of the governing Free National Movement, was designated at an internal party poll in August to succeed Prime Minister Hubert Ingraham upon his forthcoming retirement. (DAVID RENWICK)

BAHRAIN

Area: 694 sq km (268 sq mi)
Population (2001 est.): 701,000
Capital: Manama
Chief of state: Emir Hamad ibn Isa al-Khalifah
Head of government: Prime Minister Khalifah ibn Sulman al-Khalifah

In 2001 Emir Hamad ibn Isa al-Khalifah accelerated the constitutional and political reforms that he had begun the previous year. On February 14–15 Bahrainis approved by referendum the National Action Charter by an overwhelming majority—98.4%. The charter, proposed by the government, promised democratic reforms, including parliamentary elections and a separation of powers. Subsequently, the emir released 900 political prisoners and allowed hundreds of exiled Bahrainis and their families to return from abroad. The emir also abolished the unpopular state security law and the state security court, both of which had given "exceptional powers" to the government. The government further promised a law to allow the establishment of professionals' and workers' unions.

Despite reforms, however, unemployment remained high—10% among men and much higher among women. It still constituted the main source of social tension in Bahrain. Political stability was essential, since Bahrain aimed to become a centre of trade and finance in the Persian Gulf.

On March 16 the International Court of Justice in The Hague reached its verdict on the Bahrain-Qatar border dispute. Since the 1930s the two countries had disputed ownership of several territories, chief among them the Hawar Islands, which were reputed to be a rich source of natural gas. The court ruled in favour of Bahrain on the Hawar Islands but awarded Qatar some smaller islands. Both Bahrain and Qatar welcomed the decision, and relations between the two countries improved to the point where they agreed to link their countries with a 45-km (28-mi) bridge. (LOUAY BAHRY)

BANGLADESH

Area: 147,570 sq km (56,977 sq mi)
Population (2001 est.): 131,270,000
Capital: Dhaka
Chief of state: Presidents Shahabuddin Ahmed and, from November 14, A.Q.M. Badruddoza Chowdhury
Head of government: Prime Ministers Sheikh Hasina Wajed, Latifur Rahman from July 15, and, from October 10, Khaleda Zia

In a stunning upset in the parliamentary elections held on Oct. 1, 2001, the

Khaleda Zia of the Bangladesh Nationalist Party casts her vote—with help from her granddaughter—in Bangladesh's parliamentary elections on October 1.

four-party opposition alliance headed by the Bangladesh Nationalist Party (BNP) won a two-thirds majority, taking 214 of the 300 seats. The Awami League (AL), which had run the country since 1996, suffered its worst-ever defeat, securing only 62 seats. The BNP itself claimed 191 seats. In order to isolate the AL and capture the bloc votes of the religious parties, the BNP had allied with the Jamaat-e-Islami Party, which took 17 seats, the Jatiya Party (4 seats), and Islami Okiya Jote (2 seats). The election saw a massive voter turnout that was estimated at nearly 75%. Women turned out in heavy numbers and were thought to have had a decisive impact on the outcome. The AL rejected the election results, however, and declared that it would boycott Parliament and not cooperate with the future government.

During much of the rest of the year, violence dominated the news. The trouble began on January 20 when 4 people died and 50 were injured in a bomb blast in the capital, Dhaka, during a rally of the Communist Party of Bangladesh. Then on April 14 in Dhaka, a bomb killed at least 9 people and injured some 50. On June 16 an explosion in the AL party office in Narayanganj (on the outskirts of the capital) killed 22 people.

Just two days before presidential elections were to be held on November 14, independent candidate Mohammad

Raushan Ali withdrew from the race; running unopposed, Foreign Minister A.Q.M. Badruddoza Chowdhury was named president by the Election Commission.

Relations between Bangladesh and India took a totally unexpected turn on April 17 when Bangladesh's border security force suddenly took control of an outpost at Padua, which had been under Indian occupation for 30 years. In retaliation, Indian troops crossed into the Bangladesh territory on April 19 and tried to capture Boroibari, another border post. The clash resulted in the death of 16 Indian soldiers. A serious strain on relations with India followed, and Bangladesh returned Padua to Indian control. Signs of tension remained, however, with intermittent border incidents continuing throughout the year.

The news from the economic front was mixed. Bangladesh achieved a gross domestic product growth rate of 6.04%—its highest ever—while the inflation rate remained at an impressive low of 1.59%. Industry also grew at 9.1%. As in 2000, agriculture performed exceptionally well, and with another bumper crop, Bangladesh turned its food deficit into a food surplus. This was a significant change, with both economic and psychological implications. For the first half of the year, exports grew at an impressive 14% following a yearlong lean period, but they slowed down after July, triggering fears of recession. Throughout the year government borrowing remained at a high level, and the foreign-exchange reserve hit its lowest point ever at $1,050,000,000 in July.

(MAHFUZ ANAM)

BARBADOS

Area: 430 sq km (166 sq mi)
Population (2001 est.): 269,000
Capital: Bridgetown
Chief of state: Queen Elizabeth II, represented by Governor-General Sir Clifford Husbands
Head of government: Prime Minister Owen Arthur

The dangers posed to Caribbean exporters by drug traffickers were illustrated in April 2001 when Canadian garment manufacturer Gildan Activewear Inc. shut down its newly opened Barbados operation after marijuana was found in one of its export containers.

The 2001 sugar crop, the country's main export, was again a disappointment; only 49,796 metric tons were produced, well down from the 2000 level of 58,373 metric tons. Excessive dry weather was blamed for the poor showing. The diminished sugar crop and sluggish output in manufacturing had an impact on economic growth, which was expected to shrink to 1–1.5% from an average of 3% in the previous three years.

Prime Minister and Minister of Finance Owen Arthur, faced with increased unemployment of 10%, in August outlined measures to improve growth, including an "employment fund" to strengthen manufacturing, $10 million to promote the country's tourist attractions, and a 2.5% corporate tax cut for 2002. On September 28 government and public-sector officials met to discuss emergency measures to minimize fallout from the terrorist attacks in the U.S.

In August the Inter-American Development Bank moved to help Barbados modernize and reform its justice system by approving a $8,750,000 loan for that purpose.

(DAVID RENWICK)

BELARUS

Area: 207,595 sq km (80,153 sq mi)
Population (2001 est.): 9,986,000
Capital: Minsk
Head of state and government: President Alyaksandr G. Lukashenka, assisted by Prime Ministers Uladzimir Yarmoshyn and, from March 14 (acting until October 10), Henadz Navitski

The year in Belarus was dominated by a controversial presidential election campaign and the vote on Sept. 9, 2001, which resulted in a victory for incumbent Pres. Alyaksandr Lukashenka. Initially 22 candidates filed applications, including prominent opposition leaders Zyanon Paznyak, exiled leader of the Conservative Christian Party of the Belarusian Popular Front; Mikhail Marinich, the Belarusian ambassador to Latvia, Estonia, and Finland; and Natalya Masherova, daughter of a former Communist Party leader. The Central Election Commission accepted

A Belarusian election official collects ballots in a farm field near the village of Osovo on September 9.

AP/Wide World Photos

only four candidates, but several political parties banded together to nominate a single opposition candidate, trade unionist Uladzimir Hancharyk.

Despite promises made to the Organization for Security and Cooperation in Europe (OSCE), the government did not allow a democratic election process. Opposition candidates were permitted two prerecorded 30-minute broadcasts on television but were otherwise deprived of a voice in the media. During the campaign Lukashenka threatened to expel the OSCE's chief observer and place restrictions on opposition rallies. About 15% of the electorate voted early, and government workers were threatened with dismissal unless they voted for the president. The results were predictable. With a reported turnout of 83.9%, 75.6% voted for Lukashenka, while Hancharyk was second with 15.6%. The OSCE refused to recognize the election as democratic, and the United States described it as "meaningless," although Russia accepted the results.

Russia continued to spend about $1 billion annually to support the Belarusian economy through debt relief, cheap supplies of oil and gas, and purchases of Belarusian goods that would be unlikely to find a market elsewhere. In the first half of 2001 Belarus reported a rise of 3% in gross domestic product and of 4.1% in industrial production. At the same time, although exports rose by 3.9% between January and July, imports decreased by 11.4%. In June the World Bank approved a loan of $22.6 million for Belarus to improve heating, lighting, and insulation in schools, hospitals, and orphanages, the first such loan in seven years.

Human and political rights continued to be a major concern in Belarus. The opposition Magic printing press was closed down on January 9. Notable incarcerations included that of 60-year-old parliamentary deputy and journalist Valery Shchukin, who was beaten by the police and imprisoned for three months for having attempted to attend a press conference. Two foreigners were accused, Cold War style, of espionage: German citizen Christopher Letz, who was sentenced to seven years in prison in July but was subsequently pardoned, and Angelo Antonio Piu, an Italian businessman, who was sentenced to four and a half years in a high-security prison in September along with a Belarusian "accomplice." Lukashenka's continuing dependence on the secret service was illustrated by the promotion of Ural Latypau,

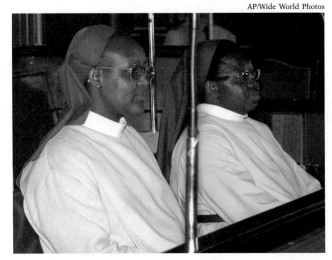

Two nuns, Sister Gertrude and Sister Maria Kisito, appear in a court in Brussels on April 17 to face charges of complicity in genocide in Rwanda.

who had served as secretary of the State Security Council since November 2000, to the position of chief of staff in September.   (DAVID R. MARPLES)

BELGIUM

Area: 30,528 sq km (11,787 sq mi)
Population (2001 est.): 10,268,000
Capital: Brussels
Chief of state: King Albert II
Head of government: Prime Minister Guy Verhofstadt

The Belgian Parliament approved a further decentralization of power to the country's three regions during 2001. After six months of intense negotiations between the major political parties, it was agreed in July that responsibility for agricultural policy, foreign trade, development cooperation, and control over communal and provincial councils would pass from the national to the regional level at the beginning of 2002. Regional governments in Flanders, Wallonia, and Brussels were also being given increased fiscal autonomy with the power to raise or lower tax rates by 6.7%—considerably more than the 3.25% leeway they previously enjoyed. Under the four-part agreement, the federal government would also increase funding to the Dutch- and French-speaking language communities, which were responsible for running the country's education system. Some estimates suggested that by 2020 this would mean the transfer of an extra BF 250 billion

(about $5.7 billion). The final element of the package provided for increased representation for Dutch speakers in the Brussels region.

Belgium's Liberal-led coalition continued to implement its social agenda. It legalized the use of cannabis for those over 18 years old; passed legislation to allow gay and lesbian partners to marry, which made Belgium the second country, after The Netherlands, to do so; and was preparing to decriminalize euthanasia. The government also took the first step toward reducing the country's tax burden over the next five years. From 2003 the top two rates of 52.5% and 55% would be reduced to a maximum rate of 50%, and existing thresholds would also be raised. Despite these changes and the introduction of more generous tax allowances, Belgium would remain one of the most heavily taxed European countries.

Belgium's legal system broke new ground during 2001 with the trial of four Rwandans—two nuns, a factory manager, and a university professor. They were accused and found guilty of complicity in the genocide of 800,000 members of Rwanda's Tutsi minority in 1994. The judgment was the first time that powers granted by a 1993 act allowing Belgian courts to prosecute serious crimes against humanity had been used.

On the business front, it proved to be a good year for Belgian brewing giant Interbrew. The Leuven-based company, the world's second largest brewer, bought Germany's fourth largest brewer, Beck's, and thereby strengthened its position in the U.S. After months of negotiations Interbrew overcame the British government's concerns regarding the company's acquisition of Bass Brewers by preparing to sell off the latter's top brand, Carling. During the first six months of 2001,

Interbrew posted its best half-yearly results in 10 years. It was turbulent times, however, for another of Belgium's corporate flagships, Sabena. The airline, jointly owned by the Belgian state and Swissair, announced drastic plans in August to shed staff, dispose of larger planes and certain assets, and cut back on long-haul operations. On October 2 Swissair, faced with financial collapse, grounded all of its flights indefinitely. The next day Sabena filed for bankruptcy protection, which sent Swissair stock plummeting. Though the Belgian government vowed to work to save the national airline, in November the struggle became too great, and Sabena became the first European carrier to be declared bankrupt. The government and financial community moved quickly to support as its successor DAT (Delta Air Transport), formerly Sabena's regional subsidiary. By year's end, however, DAT itself was facing a battle for survival as it struggled to raise the finances necessary to guarantee its survival.

Belgium's presidency of the European Union in the second half of the year ensured the country and its leading politicians a place in the international limelight.

The country's premier sporting achiever was probably Jacques Rogge, who in July was elected the eighth president of the International Olympic Committee. (*See* BIOGRAPHIES.) Former prime minister Paul Vanden Boeynants died at age 81 in January. (*See* OBITUARIES.) At the end of October Princess Mathilde gave birth to a daughter, Elisabeth Thérèse Marie Hélène, who would be second in line to the throne after her father, Prince Philippe. (RORY WATSON)

BELIZE

Area: 22,965 sq km (8,867 sq mi)
Population (2001 est.): 247,000
Capital: Belmopan
Chief of state: Queen Elizabeth II, represented by Governor-General Colville Young
Head of government: Prime Minister Said Musa

In September 2001 Belize celebrated its 20th anniversary of independence in a relatively low-key fashion in the wake of the terrorist attacks in the U.S. In his state of the nation address, Prime Minister Said Musa highlighted the accomplishments of the People's United Party government during its three years of rule. These included a booming tourist industry, which had been a central force behind Belize's rapidly growing economy, and increased cocoa production, which showed promise of one day rivaling the citrus, banana, and sugar industries in terms of foreign-exchange earnings for Belize. Cocoa growers requested additional land in order to meet the European market requests for more cocoa. For the first time, a new public-private-sector model of patient-centred health care delivery got under way during the year. The emphasis was on preventive medicine. A pilot project was scheduled for a three-year period.

On October 8 Hurricane Iris struck southern Belize with winds as strong as 225 km/h (140 mph). The storm, which forced the evacuation of Belize City, pummeled coastal towns and left some 13,000 persons homeless. (*See* DISASTERS.) (INES PARKER)

BENIN

Area: 114,760 sq km (44,300 sq mi)
Population (2001 est.): 6,591,000
Capital: Porto-Novo (executive and ministerial offices remain in Cotonou)
Head of state and government: President Mathieu Kérékou

Incumbent Pres. Mathieu Kérékou won a plurality in the first round of the presidential elections that were held in Benin on March 4, 2001. His triumph in the second round was virtually ensured when two of the four candidates withdrew after citing the large number of votes that seemed to have disappeared. Kérékou took 84% of the vote in the second round of balloting on March 24, defeating the sole remaining candidate, cabinet minister Bruno Amoussou. There was, however, widespread criticism of the handling of the poll, and nine members of the national electoral commission resigned. Nonetheless, Kérékou was expected to maintain his grip upon a nation that he had ruled for all but five years since 1972. The National Assembly granted an amnesty on June 25 to all those arrested for allegedly having caused trouble during the election campaign.

Two separate reports of child trafficking from Benin into Gabon and Côte d'Ivoire were investigated by government authorities. On April 17 a number of children believed to have been destined for slavery were said to have been removed from a Nigerian ship then docked in Cotonou. On May 9, 10 adults were arrested and charged with having attempted to smuggle another 23 children by bus across the Benin frontier. On June 26 Japan donated nearly $1 million to Benin to combat poverty and child trafficking.

With at least one-third of the population living below the poverty line, much attention was focused in 2001 on boosting economic growth. Sixty experts from West African institutions met in Cotonou on May 15 to propose new development strategies. (NANCY ELLEN LAWLER)

BHUTAN

Area: 47,000 sq km (18,150 sq mi)
Population (2001 est.): 692,000 (excluding more than 100,000 refugees in Nepal)
Capital: Thimphu
Head of state: Druk Gyalpo (King) Jigme Singye Wangchuk
Head of government: Chairmen of Council of Ministers Lyonpo Yeshey Zimba and, from August 8, Lyonpo Khandu Wangchuk

The close working relationship between the king of Bhutan, the Council of Ministers (Lhengye Zhungtshog), and the National Assembly continued throughout 2001. On August 8 Lyonpo Khandu Wangchuk took over as chairman of the council from Lyonpo Yeshey Zimba, but most council ministers retained their posts. A Civil and Criminal Procedure Code, under which the powers of the judiciary were expanded and the judicial process defined, was passed on July 23 by the National Assembly.

Discussions with Nepal continued on the status of refugees from Bhutan in seven refugee camps in southeastern Nepal. Some headway was made with a verification process, but it was evident by midyear that it would take at least another year to complete the work. Little progress was made in persuading the Assamese militants in southeastern Bhutan to withdraw their forces back into India.

The economy continued to flourish in 2001, owing primarily to the expansion of hydropower resources. Much of the power generated was sold to India, and enough currency was earned to make Bhutan's economy self-supporting. Some economic problems emerged as the number of foreign tourists declined substantially after the September 11 terrorist attacks in the United States.

(LEO E. ROSE)

BOLIVIA

Area: 1,098,581 sq km (424,164 sq mi)
Population (2001 est.): 8,516,000
Capitals: La Paz (administrative) and Sucre (judicial)
Head of state and government: Presidents Hugo Bánzer Suárez and, from August 7, Jorge Quiroga Ramírez

In Bolivia the year 2001 was marked by renewed protests over economic and social grievances and by the illness and subsequent resignation of unpopular Pres. Hugo Bánzer Suárez. The 75-year-old Bánzer, a major figure in Bolivian public life for 30 years, was treated in the U.S. for lung and liver cancer and resigned for health reasons on August 6. Vice Pres. Jorge Quiroga Ramírez, a Texas-educated industrial engineer and former IBM executive, was sworn in as president the next day. Quiroga, aged 41 and considered a moderate in Bánzer's conservative National Democratic Action party, said he represented a new generation in Bolivian politics. He named 12 new cabinet ministers and kept only 4 from Bánzer's team.

Opposition leader Felipe Quispe Huanca organized protests against Bánzer's market-oriented economic policies. Quispe's supporters included street vendors in La Paz as well as trade unionists, teachers, health workers, and growers of coca, the raw material for cocaine. Most of the illegal coca crop had been forcibly eradicated in a U.S.-supported

campaign, and farmers said they feared starvation as a result. The protests, which also included road blockades, were hampered by conflicts among the organizers. A truce was reached in August, and the government agreed to talks on land reform and other social issues. The protests indicated deep discontent with policies that attracted foreign investment but provided few jobs and little relief from economic hardship. The International Monetary Fund acknowledged that despite 15 years of adjustment programs under its supervision, nearly two-thirds of Bolivians lived in poverty.

Bánzer's political troubles continued after he stepped down. His former defense minister accused him of corruption, charging that Bánzer had inflated the amount paid for a government aircraft, and human rights campaigners threatened to prosecute him for abuses committed during his military dictatorship in the 1970s. Meanwhile, Bolivia pushed ahead with judicial reform, and the first "citizen judges" appointed under a new criminal procedure code began hearing cases in September.

Bolivian coca farmers stage a protest against the government on February 22 by scattering thousands of coca leaves along the main street of the city of Chimore.

Quiroga hoped revenues from natural gas exports would replace economic losses from coca eradication and a crackdown on smuggling. Gas exports in the first six months of the year rose by 151% over 2000, but demand in Brazil, Bolivia's major customer, was lower than expected because of economic and regulatory difficulties there. Finance Minister Jacques Trigo Loubiere said in September that the economy would register no growth during 2001. Quiroga and gas producers promoted a scheme in which liquefied Bolivian gas would be exported to Mexico, converted back to gas, and piped to the energy-hungry United States. Quiroga also hoped to further capitalize on Bolivia's vast gas fields by producing petrochemicals and issuing bonds backed by future exports.

(PAUL KNOX)

BOSNIA AND HERZEGOVINA

Area: 51,129 sq km (19,741 sq mi)
Population (2001 est.): 3,922,000
Capital: Sarajevo
Heads of state: Tripartite presidency headed by Zivko Radisic and, from June 14, Jozo Krizanovic
Head of government: Prime Ministers Martin Raguz, Bozidar Matic from February 22, and, from July 18, Zlatko Lagumdzija

In 2001 Bosnia and Herzegovina began to stand on its own administratively without extensive international supervision. Moderate parties took over the leadership of the Bosniak (Muslim)-Croat Federation and won considerable influence in Republika Srpska (Serb Republic). Prime Minister Zlatko Lagumdzija advised the world that "the role of the international community is to help us, but not to work, think, and decide for us."

In January the reform-oriented 10-party Alliance for Change succeeded in getting its members appointed speaker, deputy speaker, and parliamentary secretary of the legislative assembly by narrowly outvoting the two dominant Croat and Muslim nationalist parties, the Croatian Democratic Union (HDZ) and the Party of Democratic Action (SDA). The House of Representatives also passed a bill that standardized procedures for all elected offices—though

the nationalist Serb Democratic Party (SDS) and the HDZ boycotted the vote. Local organizations were beginning to take over from international organizations in monitoring voter education and human rights, but the nongovernment sector remained too weak to monitor elections and develop a civic society. Meanwhile, the three nationalist parties were cooperating closely in order to maintain their grip on power. In March Wolfgang Petritsch, head of the Office of the High Representative (OHR), sacked HDZ leader Ante Jelavic from the Bosnian tripartite presidency after Jelavic called for the formation of two predominantly Croat cantons; in October Jelavic was reelected HDZ president despite repeated warnings from the OHR. The OHR advised the federation government that more progress would be required in electoral laws before Bosnia and Herzegovina could be admitted to the Council of Europe.

The spurt of growth that came with postwar reconstruction faltered in 2001. Dissatisfied workers staged daily work stoppages, and much of the country's economic activity was forced underground owing to irrational tax codes and business regulations. Almost 50% of the active labour force was unemployed, in large part because of cutbacks in international aid and the lack of foreign capital investment.

In August the United Nations International Criminal Tribunal for the Former Yugoslavia (ICTY) released former Bosnian Serb president Biljana Plavsic from detention until the start of her trial. The same month, Gen. Radislav Krstic received a 46-year prison sentence for having planned, prepared, and carried out the killings of thousands of Muslim men at Srebrenica. In September Sefer Halilovic, the highest-ranking Bosnian Muslim to appear before the war crimes court, pleaded not guilty to charges of having failed to prevent the 1993 killings of Bosnian Croat civilians by his troops.

In the wake of the September 11 attacks in the U.S., Bosnia and Herzegovina found itself on a list of favourite destinations for terrorists. Interior Minister Muhamed Besic admitted that his country attracted terrorists—some with ties to Osama bin Laden—and that some had been granted Bosnian passports by militant elements of the former Sarajevo government. He denied the existence of terrorist training camps in the country, however.

(MILAN ANDREJEVICH)

BOTSWANA

Area: 581,730 sq km (224,607 sq mi)
Population (2001 est.): 1,586,000
Capital: Gaborone
Head of state and government: President Festus Mogae

Economic growth continued unabated in Botswana in 2001, with employment still expanding ahead of population growth. Government revenue from diamonds continued to rise, and new highways, administrative buildings, and large shopping malls were constructed. A challenge to the style of governmental paternalism established in the late colonial period was becoming evident, however.

In the annual Transparency International survey, Botswana was ranked the least-corrupt state in Africa (and 26th in the world), but there was increasing evidence of management laxity. An extensive north-south scheme of water articulation could not be commissioned because of defective piping. As many as 10,000 university students had to be sent to South Africa, Australia, Great Britain, and North America because the capacity of local universities had been overestimated. A complete census of households was held in August.

The death penalty made news in March when a white South African woman was hanged for having murdered her lover's wife. The most controversial issue, however, was that of ethnic minorities, whose representation in the upper house of Parliament was recommended by a report in March from the commission headed by Patrick Balopi, a former cabinet minister. Subsequent debate challenged established policies of national integration. In August Survival International, an organization devoted to the rights of tribal peoples, picketed the Botswana embassy in London over the San (Bushman) minority in the Kalahari. For 15 years the Botswana government had been inducing residents to leave the Central Kalahari Game Reserve, and wildlife officials harassed people who stayed.

In August former president Ketumile Masire started peace negotiations for the Democratic Republic of the Congo by bringing warring factions together in Gaborone, Botswana's capital.

(NEIL PARSONS)

BRAZIL

Area: 8,547,404 sq km (3,300,171 sq mi)
Population (2001 est.): 172,118,000
Capital: Brasília
Head of state and government: President Fernando Henrique Cardoso

Leadership elections in the Senate and the Chamber of Deputies in 2001 strained Brazilian Pres. Fernando Henrique Cardoso's fragile governing coalition, which included the Brazilian Social Democratic Party (PSDB), the Liberal Front Party (PFL), the Brazilian Democratic Movement Party (PMDB), and the Brazilian Progressive Party. The PMDB candidate for Senate president, Jader Barbalho of Pará state, won the election by a narrow majority (receiving 41 of 81 votes) on February 14 after having traded charges of corruption with his rival, the incumbent Senate president, Antônio Carlos Magalhães (PFL). Though the victory earned Barbalho the title of president of Congress, it exacerbated his feud with Magalhães, which carried on throughout the year and impeded progress relating to Cardoso's agenda. The Chamber of Deputies elected Aécio Neves (PSDB) of Minas Gerais state to head the lower house.

On January 25–30 Pôrto Alegre, the capital of Brazil's Rio Grande do Sul state, hosted the World Social Forum, an event that shadowed the annual World Economic Forum in Davos, Switz. The Pôrto Alegre conference attracted more than 10,000 people, including representatives of approximately 900 nongovernmental organizations from Europe, Africa, and Latin America. The forum criticized the policies of international multilateral financial institutions and called for international debt amnesty and a financial transactions tax levied on behalf of citizens.

On February 18 riots broke out in 29 state penitentiaries involving around 28,000 inmates and more than 5,000 visitors. Angered by the transfer of its leaders from São Paulo's Carandiru prison, a gang of convicts used mobile phones to order simultaneous riots during weekend visiting hours. By the time order was restored on February 19, at least 15 persons had been killed and 8 injured.

The federal government then sought to avoid a parliamentary commission of in-

quiry (CPI) into government corruption that would occupy Congress and the executive branch. Adding fuel to the opposition's call for a CPI, on February 22 Magalhães gave an interview to state prosecutors in which he hinted at corruption involving Cardoso, Barbalho, the PMDB, the PFL, and the Supreme Court. The interview, which was leaked to the press, prompted Cardoso to begin sacking government appointments linked to Magalhães.

With public opinion favouring investigation into allegations of government corruption, the opposition sought the votes of 27 senators and 171 federal deputies necessary to constitute a CPI. On May 8, after the opposition had apparently secured these votes, Barbalho canceled a joint session of Congress and thereby prevented the opposition from bringing the issue to the floor. Afterward, political maneuverings persuaded enough legislators to change their

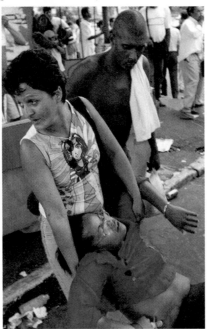

An injured female prison guard is dragged away from the scene of rioting at São Paulo's Carandiru prison on February 19.

Mauricio Lima/AFP Worldwide

minds, and the CPI threat was ended. On May 16 Saturnino Braga, the rapporteur of the Senate Ethics Committee, concluded that Magalhães and the government leader in the Senate, José Roberto Arruda of the Federal District, were guilty of having violated secrecy rules in the June 2000 vote that expelled Federal

District Sen. Luis Estevão from Congress. After damaging testimony from the director of the Senate data-processing system, who stated that she broke into the voting system under orders from Magalhães and Arruda, the Senate Ethics Committee recommended the impeachment of Magalhães and Arruda for having broken Senate decorum. Rather than risk impeachment and a loss of political rights for eight years, Arruda resigned on May 24; Magalhães followed suit on May 30.

With Arruda and Magalhães out of office, Congress, at risk of becoming ineffectual, continued to be mired in scandal as more allegations of past corruption involving Barbalho surfaced. A growing number of investigations into fraud in the state Bank of Pará, the Superintendency for Development of the Amazon, and the National Land Reform Institute revealed the involvement of Barbalho when he was governor of Pará and minister of land reform. Barbalho took a leave of absence from his post as senate president on July 20. In the face of mounting evidence and the likelihood of impeachment, he resigned from the Senate on October 4, following the same path of Magalhães and Arruda. For Barbalho the loss of immunity opened up the possibility of indictment by federal police.

In late April and May, Brazil faced a looming energy crisis, which threatened to cause blackouts. The federal government formed an energy crisis task force chaired by the presidential chief of staff, Pedro Parente. On May 18 the energy crisis team introduced a rationing plan, which included incentives, surcharges, rate hikes, and the threat of disconnection to persuade households and businesses to curb power usage by approximately 20%. Among the factors contributing to the energy crisis were insufficient rainfall to sustain hydroelectric power generation, rising demand for energy, and weak transmission infrastructure. Plans to privatize the energy sector were temporarily halted as the government announced its short-term rationing plan with medium-term plans to increase capacity by auctioning hydroelectric-power-generation and gas-turbine units.

A breakdown of law and order ensued in June and July when armed police officers protesting low wages went on strike in the states of Tocantins, Alagoas, Pernambuco, and Bahia. On August 10 Cardoso issued temporary measures to tighten public security, permitting state governors to borrow police from neighbouring states during strikes and authorizing federal intervention of the armed forces.

On September 14 the International Monetary Fund approved a new agreement with Brazil, making more than $15 billion available through December 2002. The agreement was conditioned on the federal government's reaching primary budget surpluses of 3.35% of gross domestic product (GDP) in 2001 and 3.5% in 2002. By October the Brazilian census bureau was estimating that inflation for 2001 would reach 5.8% (±2%). Over the course of the year, the central bank raised the benchmark interest rate from 15.25% in January to 19% in October. By midyear Brazil's GDP had increased an estimated 3.12% from a year earlier.   (JOHN CHARLES CUTTINO)

BRUNEI

Area: 5,765 sq km (2,226 sq mi)
Population (2001 est.): 344,000
Capital: Bandar Seri Begawan
Head of state and government: Sultan and Prime Minister Haji Hassanal Bolkiah Mu!izzaddin Waddaulah

The fallout from the scandal involving former finance minister Prince Jefri Bolkiah, the youngest brother of Hassanal Bolkiah, the sultan of Brunei Darussalam, continued in 2001. As finance minister the prince had been in charge of the Brunei Investment Agency (BIA), which was responsible for investing the nation's oil wealth, and of the Amedeo Development Corp., Brunei's largest private company. By 1998 Amedeo had collapsed under heavy debts, and reports surfaced that $15 billion in BIA funds had disappeared. The prince was sued by the state for having squandered the funds on Amedeo projects, including palaces and luxury hotels. Though an out-of-court settlement was reached in 2000, with the prince agreeing to hand over his remaining assets in exchange for a $300,000 monthly allowance, the royal family endured further embarrassment in August 2001 as 10,000 items once owned by Jefri Bolkiah were sold at a debtor's auction in Bandar Seri Begawan. Meanwhile, the prince faced a multimillion-dollar civil court action by his creditors.

New press laws went into effect on October 1 requiring newspapers in Brunei to obtain a publishing license each year from the government; under the new legislation, editors and journalists also faced jail terms if they were found guilty of publishing "false news."   (EDITOR)

BULGARIA

Area: 110,971 sq km (42,846 sq mi)
Population (2001 est.): 7,953,000
Capital: Sofia
Chief of state: President Petar Stoyanov
Head of government: Prime Ministers Ivan Kostov and, from July 24, Simeon Saxecoburggotski

In the spring of 2001, the government of Ivan Kostov became the first postcommunist administration in Bulgaria to run its full four-year course. It was not returned to power. Early in the year rumours had circulated that the former king, Simeon II, would return to Bulgaria and contest the presidential elections to be held in the fall. The constitution forbade this, however, and he decided to compete in the parliamentary campaign instead. In the elections of June 17, his National Movement for Simeon II, formed in April, secured 120 of the 240 seats. In July Simeon agreed to take the post of prime minister; Bulgaria thereby became the first country ever to elect its exiled king as head of government. Simeon henceforth officially used the surname Saxecoburggotski from his lineage in the royal house of Saxe-Coburg-Gotha, but he was universally known as "the King." (See BIOGRAPHIES.) His government's parliamentary majority was to be guaranteed by support from the Movement for Rights and Freedoms (MRF), a party representing primarily Bulgaria's ethnic Turkish minority.

The victory of the movement was based on Simeon's dramatic promise that his movement would restore the country to economic and political health within 800 days of taking office. This goal was to be accomplished by easing tax burdens on business, promoting enterprise, widening privatization, and reducing state involvement in the economy. Both economic and political health were to be gained by eliminating corruption. A re-

On a campaign swing through the town of Blagoevgrad on June 13, Simeon II, Bulgaria's former king, accepts a gift of flowers from a child.

form program to promote these objectives was announced in August.

To spearhead the economic campaign, the prime minister appointed to key economic ministries young men who had spent time working in Western financial institutions. The foreign minister was from the small Jewish minority, and two ministers were ethnic Turks from the MRF. Surprisingly, Saxecoburggotski gave ministerial posts to two members of the Bulgarian Socialist Party, which did not support his government in the parliament.

In the second round of presidential elections held on November 18, Socialist Party leader Georgi Parvanov defeated centre-right Pres. Petar Stoyanov by capturing more than 50% of the vote. Parvanov would take office after Stoyanov's term expired on Jan. 22, 2002.

In foreign policy the new administration differed little from its predecessor in making admittance to NATO and the European Union its prime objectives. With its long historic association with Macedonia, Bulgaria could not be indifferent to the growing crisis in that country, but the Sofia government insisted that solutions had to be found by peaceful means. Unilateral action by Bulgaria was ruled out. The fate of six Bulgarian medics charged in Libya with having deliberately infected 393 children with HIV became a matter of great concern when the trial began on June 2. Though a decision was expected in late December, the hearing was postponed until Feb. 17, 2002.   (RICHARD J. CRAMPTON)

BURKINA FASO

Area: 274,400 sq km (105,946 sq mi)
Population (2001 est.): 12,272,000
Capital: Ouagadougou
Chief of state: President Blaise Compaoré
Head of government: Prime Minister Ernest
Paramanga Yonli

Tensions between Burkina Faso and Côte d'Ivoire continued throughout 2001 as thousands of Burkinabe citizens returned home, complaining of persistent harassment at the hands of Ivorian officials. On July 4, at a meeting brokered by Libyan leader Muammar al-Qaddafi, Pres. Blaise Compaoré and his Ivorian counterpart, Laurent Gbagbo, agreed to take steps to restore good relations between the two nations. Nonetheless, in August Côte d'Ivoire decided to send three extra battalions to safeguard its frontiers, and on September 6 Compaoré responded by deploying additional troops along Burkina's southern border.

On February 5 the government finally acted to resolve the uncertainty surrounding the death in 1998 of journalist Norbert Zongo when the former chief of the Presidential Guard was charged with the murder.

A severe meningitis epidemic struck the country, with over 7,000 cases reported by the beginning of April. There remained a crippling shortage of vaccine. In June international donors pledged $85 million for a five-year campaign against the spread of AIDS; more than 7% of Burkinabe adults were considered HIV-positive. In August grants for poverty alleviation totaling $45 million were approved by the World Bank and the International Monetary Fund. A $70 million water project for Ouagadougou was to be undertaken with further World Bank funding.   (NANCY ELLEN LAWLER)

BURUNDI

Area: 27,816 sq km (10,740 sq mi)
Population (2001 est.): 6,224,000 (including 400,000 refugees in Tanzania)
Capital: Bujumbura
Head of state and government: President Pierre Buyoya

Widespread fighting between the government and rebel groups continued throughout 2001 amid efforts to implement the Arusha, Tanz., peace plan brokered in 2000 by former South African president Nelson Mandela. The peace process foundered, however, when the parties failed to agree on the composition of a transitional government.

On April 18 a group of junior army officers calling themselves the Patriotic Youth Front attempted to seize power in Bujumbura, but soldiers loyal to the government quickly suppressed the mutiny. Opposition leaders charged that Pres. Pierre Buyoya staged the uprising as a pretext for strengthening internal security measures.

A breakthrough came in July when Mandela announced a transition plan. Under the arrangement, Buyoya (a Tutsi) would continue as president for the first 18 months of a three-year transition period. Domitien Ndayizeye (a Hutu) would serve alongside him as vice president. During the second half of the transition, a Hutu would occupy the presidency, and a Tutsi would serve as vice president. The plan also called for the transitional government to include all 19 parties that signed the Arusha accord. It also required that the transitional government accept international peacekeeping forces and lift restrictions on political activity. The transition plan was endorsed by regional leaders and Burundian parties at a July 23 meeting in Arusha.

While Pres. Buyoya was attending a regional summit to endorse the transition, soldiers opposed to the Arusha process attempted a coup in Bujumbura. Though the uprising was quickly put down, many Burundians feared for the stability of the government. Armed rebel groups not party to the Arusha agreement vowed to continue fighting. Throughout the year government troops clashed with rebels of the National Forces of Liberation and the Forces for the Defense of the Democracy.

As a result of attacks on aid workers, humanitarian agencies frequently suspended their operations in parts of the country. An estimated 400,000 Burundian refugees were in Tanzania, and approximately 800,000 persons were displaced internally. Though Burundi and Tanzania agreed to a plan for the return of refugees, few were repatriated.

The transitional government was sworn in on November 1 amid continued fighting by Hutu rebels. The UN Security Council approved a 700-man international peacekeeping force to help protect the new government. The first contingent, 230 South African troops, was deployed just before the new government's inauguration.
          (MATTHEW A. CENZER)

AP/Wide World Photos

A Burundian woman walks past a house in Bujumbura destroyed in fighting between government troops and armed rebel forces in April.

CAMBODIA

Area: 181,035 sq km (69,898 sq mi)
Population (2001 est.): 12,720,000
Capital: Phnom Penh
Chief of state: King Norodom Sihanouk
Head of government: Prime Minister Hun Sen

In 2001, with the problems of insurgency and political quarrels within the government under control, the administration of Cambodian Prime Minister Hun Sen was able to focus on helping the economy grow. At last the country seemed to be in a place where it could move beyond its turbulent and often bloody past and build a viable environment for business. Since 1999 gross domestic product growth had been healthy; in 2001 the GDP growth rate clocked in above 5%, with expectations of more than 6% for 2002. Although analysts still described Cambodia as a "predeveloped" country, at least certain industries were flourishing.

Some 80% of the population still worked in agriculture, a sector where inefficient farming methods and problematic distribution held back its growth and shrank its importance to the national coffers. Garment manufacturing became a star industry, growing by around 50% annually since 1998. In 2001 the kingdom exported $1 billion in clothes to the U.S. and Europe; the amount represented some 70% of Cambodia's exports. Factories were located mostly near the capital, Phnom Penh. The garment business boomed as Asian companies set up shop to subcontract for Western labels. With factory workers earning $45 a month, Cambodia owned a niche as a cheap-labour destination. Revelations of sweatshoplike conditions and certain instances of the use of child labour, however, prompted several international companies to withdraw from the market.

The other sector that enjoyed vigorous growth was tourism. Nearly 500,000 travelers visited Cambodia in 2001. The government hoped for one million arrivals by 2003. The travel and hospitality industry posted a record $200 million in annual earnings, half the government budget. The primary draw for travelers was Siem Reap province and its temples. To lure even more visitors, the government made it a new policy to welcome high-profile Hollywood film productions to Angkor Wat—the 1,000-year-old World Heritage monument Cambodians considered to be sacred ground—and other sites.

On the political front, after four years of wrangling and numerous postponements, King Norodom Sihanouk in August finally signed a law providing for some surviving Khmer Rouge leaders to be tried in court before foreign and local judges. When the likes of Nuon Chea, Pol Pot's second-in-command, and former Khmer Rouge head of state Khieu Samphan might actually face the justice process was uncertain. Both men made fresh public denials of responsibility for the deaths and suffering of millions during their rule in the 1970s, placing all the blame on Pol Pot. The international community, which funneled $500 million in aid annually into Cambodia, demanded that the trial—expected to cost upwards of $50 million—take place so that a dark chapter in history could be closed and the struggling nation could face its future in a new light.

(ALEXANDRIA A. SENO)

CAMEROON

Area: 475,442 sq km (183,569 sq mi)
Population (2001 est.): 15,803,000
Capital: Yaoundé
Chief of state: President Paul Biya
Head of government: Prime Minister Peter Mafany Musonge

Following an inquiry into a February 18 explosion and fire at Yaoundé's armory, Col. Jean-Paul Mengot, chief of the Presidential Guard, was dismissed on Feb. 23, 2001, and an unspecified number of soldiers were arrested. Fears that a military coup might be under way had created near panic in the city. On July 26, in an effort to defuse reports of growing discontent within the military, Pres. Paul Biya ordered a total reorganization of the nation's armed forces.

The disappearance of nine men arrested in Douala in January for theft caused widespread anger against the Operational Command (OC), a special paramilitary crime-fighting unit that had been created by presidential decree in February 2000. On April 7 President Biya fired the OC commander, Brig.-Gen. Philippe Mpay. Several other officers of the unit, which was suspected of having carried out hundreds of summary executions, were arrested on April 7–8. On June 15 the OC was disbanded.

Six men charged with high treason for membership in the Anglophone secessionist Southern Cameroon National Council were freed on March 20 after 14 months in prison, but authorities termed the releases temporary while investigations continued. Relations between the main opposition party, Ndi's Social Democratic Front (SDF), and the government deteriorated further when the SDF accused the state-controlled media of exercising partisan censorship over its broadcasts.

In February scientists from around the world began removing poisonous gases from Lake Nyos; emissions from the volcanic crater had killed several thousand people over the past 15 years.

The government took vigorous action to reduce its internal debt, and full payment of all outstanding salary arrears was made to civil servants.

(NANCY ELLEN LAWLER)

CANADA

Area: 9,970,610 sq km (3,849,674 sq mi)
Population (2001 est.): 31,002,000
Capital: Ottawa
Chief of state: Queen Elizabeth II, represented by Governor-General Adrienne Clarkson
Head of government: Prime Minister Jean Chrétien

Domestic Affairs. After having won three elections in eight years, the Liberal Party government under Prime Minister Jean Chrétien dominated Canadian politics in 2001. Chrétien's grasp on power came from his long experience and unrivaled political skills. It was also helped by the fragmented nature of his opposition in Parliament.

In 2001, with the Liberals holding 172 of 301 seats in the House of Commons, this opposition seemed the weakest ever. During the previous year a determined effort had been made to unite the right around a Western protest movement, the Reform Party. The new grouping, the Canadian Alliance, had turned away from Reform's founder, Preston Manning, and chosen Stockwell Day as its leader. Day had served successfully as provincial treasurer of Alberta, but he was inexperienced in national politics. He led the Alliance to 66 seats in the November 2000 election and became official leader of the opposition.

Criticism of Day came forward soon after Parliament resumed sitting in the new year. Statements and actions by the Alliance leader raised questions about his political judgment. He was accused of disregarding the views of his caucus and being out of touch with the party membership. On April 24 Deborah Grey, deputy leader of the Alliance and its longest-serving member of Parliament, stated she no longer had confidence in Day. By July, amid rancorous quarreling, 11 other Alliance MPs had left the caucus, threatening to set up a new party. Some had been supporters of Manning.

The divisions within the Alliance damaged it seriously in the eyes of the public. Support dropped everywhere in Canada to a 6% approval rating in late June. By contrast, Liberal support rose to 60%. Some Alliance members talked of cooperating electorally with the rival Progressive Conservative Party (PCP), which had formed the government before Chrétien came to power in 1993.

By the end of the summer, Day had had enough. He delivered an ultimatum to the dissident Alliance members: return to the party caucus and accept his leadership by September 10, or be expelled. Four of the dissidents returned, while the other eight entered into a working coalition with the PCP, acknowledging PCP leader Joe Clark as head of the new grouping. It was the first opposition coalition in Canadian history.

If the Alliance was in disarray, the other opposition parties were also enfeebled. The separatist Bloc Québécois (BQ) held 38 seats but faced declining sentiment at home for Quebec's independence. The PCP was engaged in rebuilding itself as a national party but had still only 12 seats in the Commons. The socialist New Democratic Party (NDP), with 13 seats, appeared to be a victim of Canada's prosperity.

The BQ faced additional stress when Lucien Bouchard, the outspoken leader of the Parti Québécois and provincial premier in Quebec, abruptly announced his resignation on January 11. His successor, Bernard Landry, was sworn in on March 8 and promised to continue the fight for sovereignty. (*See* BIOGRAPHIES.)

The steadily rising costs of public health care brought about labour un-

rest in several provinces during the year. Nurses and health care providers engaged in noisy job action in Nova Scotia and British Columbia, while in New Brunswick physicians and nursing-home staffs went on strike to press demands for higher salaries. The federal government, eager to investigate possible changes to the system that would bring about greater efficiency, appointed Roy Romanow, the recently retired premier of Saskatchewan, to conduct a thorough probe.

In the meantime, other provinces, including Ontario, which spent 45% of its revenues on medical costs, argued that the federal government's share of health care funding was declining. Ottawa responded that in the previous year it had offered a Can$23.4 billion (Can$1=about U.S. $0.65) increase over five years in health and social transfers. Ontario pressed ahead with a demand for an immediate additional grant of Can$7 bil-

Lucien Bouchard, provincial premier of Quebec, wipes his eyes before announcing his resignation on the floor of the Canadian province's National Assembly on January 11.

Marcos Townsend/AFP Worldwide

lion. This demand was endorsed by the other nine provinces in a meeting in Victoria, B.C., on August 2–3. Ottawa rejected the demand as "unrealistic."

In December the federal government passed a constitutional amendment that officially changed the name of the province of Newfoundland to Newfoundland and Labrador.

The Economy. A strong Canadian economy faltered by midyear. Exports to the United States, Canada's principal market, were hurt by the downturn in the American economy. During the first quarter the Canadian gross domestic product, the total value of all goods and services produced in the country, expanded by 2%. Economic growth in the second quarter came virtually to a standstill at only 0.4%. The unemployment rate remained steady at 7% for the first half of the year but rose slightly in August.

A drought, perhaps the worst in Canadian history, gripped the country from coast to coast during the summer months. All sectors of agriculture were affected, with prairie wheat production expected to be cut by 20%.

The struggle against international terrorism led to a federal budget on December 10. Earlier, Finance Minister Paul Martin had seen no need for a 2001 budget, owing to the strong economic performance during the first half of the year, but September 11 dramatically changed the course of events both politically and economically.

The budget provided for new spending of more than $12 billion over the next five years, of which $7.7 billion would be devoted to strengthening Canada's security. Funds would be spent for tighter screening of passengers and baggage at Canada's airports, for armed undercover air marshals to man selected domestic and international flights, and for improved counterterrorism operations by the Royal Canadian Mounted Police and the military. Although there was no evidence that the terrorists who carried out the September hijackings had entered the U.S. through Canada, closer attention would be paid to immigrant and refugee screening. Procedures would be adopted for easing the massive flow of goods across the Canada-U.S. border, estimated to be worth $1.3 billion a day.

The 9.4% increase in government expenditures for the current year would eliminate the surplus that Martin had predicted earlier, but he insisted that the budget would be kept in balance over the next three years. Although the economy had languished in recession since midyear, Martin estimated a growth of 1.3% in gross domestic product during 2001.

Foreign Affairs. The historic old city of Quebec played host to the third Summit of the Americas, held April 20–22, with 34 countries taking part. Emphasizing the need for democratic government as the basis for hemispheric cooperation, the summit did not extend an invitation

Anticapitalist demonstrators face police during the Summit of the Americas in Quebec on April 22.

to Cuba. In a "democratic clause" issued at the end of the meeting, the summit made it plain that only states with democratic institutions would be permitted to take part in the hemispheric movement for economic integration. Although elaborate precautions were taken to maintain order in Quebec, including the construction of a perimeter fence around the site of the meeting, more than 25,000 demonstrators converged on the city. Linking the expansion of free trade with the growth of capitalism, the protestors held parallel seminars and study sessions as well as marches and demonstrations.

The more serious protests that marred the Group of 8 (G-8) summit of industrialized nations at Genoa, Italy, in July influenced Chrétien's choice of a meeting place for the G-8 summit to be held in Canada in 2002. He chose the Rocky Mountain resort of Kananaskis, 100 km (62 mi) west of Calgary, Alta. The resort had been the site of the 1998 Winter Olympic Games. Isolated in the mountains and with limited hotel facilities, Kananaskis was expected to provide a more intimate atmosphere for the next meeting of the world's leaders. Its location would also discourage the gathering of protesters.

Canada did not follow the example of the U.S. in withdrawing from the Kyoto Protocol of 1997 for the reduction of carbon emissions. Instead, it worked with a group of like-minded states, including Scandinavian nations, Australia, and Japan, in urging that states find their own ways of achieving lower emission standards. In a conference in Bonn, Ger., in mid-July, Canada pressed for the freedom to carry out emission reductions in its own way. Its large forests constituted "sinks" that soaked up carbon gasses. Domestic reductions would also represent a large part of the Canadian program. Collectively, the states meeting in Bonn agreed to work toward a 5.2% cut in 1990 emission levels by 2010. Canada, which promised to achieve a 6% reduction over the same period, hoped to ratify the Kyoto agreement in 2002.

Canada sent a junior minister responsible for multiculturalism to the UN World Conference Against Racism held in Durban, S.Af., for nine days in early September. Although it assisted nongovernmental organizations (NGOs) in attending the meeting, Ottawa disassociated itself sharply from views expressed by some of the NGOs. In commenting on the final declaration approved by the conference, Canada took the "strongest objections" to mention of the Israeli-Arab conflict in the Middle East. Ottawa also had serious reservations regarding the assertion that 19th-century slavery constituted a crime against humanity. It did not approve of the proposal that compensation be paid for the wrongs of slavery. Behind the scenes the Canadian delegation at Durban worked to moderate the language of the conference's final text.

During 2001 Canada cautiously considered new directions in U.S. foreign policy. The new administration of U.S. Pres. George W. Bush immediately made it clear that it considered relations with Mexico a top priority. Within a decade, it was surmised, Mexico might become the U.S.'s largest trading partner. To Canada, which had occupied this position for many years, this was a sobering reassessment. Chrétien wasted no time in traveling to Washington, D.C., to meet with Bush on February 5, only 11 days before Bush visited his Mexican counterpart. Canadian spokesmen pointed out that Canada possessed a more substantial bilateral relationship with the U.S. than did Mexico. It was also a longstanding partner with the U.S. in important international organizations, including NATO.

Canada, as the junior partner in its links with the U.S., had always preferred to work with other countries in dealing with its giant neighbour. Canada was frustrated, therefore, when the Bush administration prepared to abandon international agreements, notably the 1972 Anti-Ballistic Missile Treaty, and pressed ahead with a missile defense system unpopular with America's allies. U.S. action or lack of action on multilateral agreements to discourage trafficking in small arms and on the creation of an international criminal court also worried Canada. It was apparent, therefore, that the Bush administration's preference for unilateral action in the international sphere would be a cause of concern in Canada in the immediate future.

An old trade dispute reemerged to trouble Canada-U.S. relations in 2001. Softwood lumber—pine, cedar, spruce—had long been a principal export, valued at $10 billion a year, of Canada to the U.S. This trade was not conducted under the North American Free Trade Agreement but was governed by a 1996 bilateral arrangement under which the U.S. applied a quota on Canadian lumber imports. This agreement expired on March 31, and on August 10 the U.S. Department of Commerce imposed a preliminary 19.3% duty on Canadian lumber imports from all but the four Atlantic provinces. The nub of the dispute was the price Canadian provinces charged for the right to cut timber on Crown (public) lands. The U.S. charged that this fee, called stumpage, was set below world market levels and thus constituted a subsidy to Canadian lumber exporters, allowing them to undercut American lumber producers. Canada vigorously rejected this claim, stating that there was no basis for it in fact or in law. The economic consequences were serious to both parties. Forestry was still the largest industry in Canada, with over 380,000 employees and 337 communities dependent on the sale of lumber. For the U.S., dependent on Canada for one-third of its lumber needs, the imposition of a duty, even though the proceeds were to be paid to American lumber producers, would result in higher costs to U.S. homebuilders.

(DAVID M.L. FARR)

CAPE VERDE

Area: 4,033 sq km (1,557 sq mi)
Population (2001 est.): 446,000
Capital: Praia
Chief of state: Presidents Antonio Mascarenhas Monteiro and, from March 22, Pedro Pires
Head of government: Prime Ministers António Gualberto do Rosário and, from February 1, José Maria Neves

The year 2001 marked the end of 10 years of rule by the Movement for Democracy and the return to power of the African Party for the Independence of Cape Verde (PAIVC). In legislative elections held in January, the PAIVC won the majority of seats, and its leader, José Maria Neves, became the new prime minister. In the second round of the presidential election, held in February, Pedro Pires, the PAIVC candidate and a former prime minister, emerged as the winner by a very narrow margin of votes.

For both major parties the chief issue was the archipelago's troubled economy. Though Neves underscored the need to reduce unemployment and tackle poverty, the means by which he intended to accomplish this remained far from clear. The economy, hard hit by drought, remained heavily reliant on agriculture and fishing. Cape Verde continued to depend on international aid, most notably from the European Union and Portugal. In July Cape Verde signed two financial agreements with Portugal aimed at strengthening the convertibility of the currency and promoting the restructuring of the economy and of the country's debt.

(CHRISTOPHER SAUNDERS)

CENTRAL AFRICAN REPUBLIC

Area: 622,436 sq km (240,324 sq mi)
Population (2001 est.): 3,577,000
Capital: Bangui
Chief of state: President Ange-Félix Patassé
Head of government: Prime Ministers Anicet Georges Dologuélé and, from April 1, Martin Ziguélé

Army rebels loyal to former president André Kolingba attempted to overthrow the government on May 28, 2001. The mutineers, reportedly aided by several hundred Rwandan and Angolan mercenaries, attacked the Bangui palace of Pres. Ange-Félix Patassé; the assault resulted in at least 20 deaths. The government received swift military assistance from Libya, and reinforcements also arrived from Chad and the neighbouring Democratic Republic of the Congo (DRC); those from the latter were a group seeking to overthrow the DRC government. Fighting continued in the capital for more than a week, and unofficial estimates put the number of persons killed at between 250 and 300. Many rebel soldiers caught by government forces were thought to have been summarily executed. On June 7 the government claimed complete success at suppressing the coup, although sporadic outbreaks of violence continued. Kolingba and other suspected coup leaders re-

mained at large. The government appealed for relief supplies to aid the nearly 80,000 people who had fled the fighting.

Kolingba's Central African Democratic Rally, once the sole legal political party, was ordered dissolved on June 22. Accused of implication in the coup attempt, Defense Minister Jean-Jacques Demafouth was dismissed on August 25. Two days later Kolingba's wife and children were abducted from the French embassy in Bangui, where they, along with an estimated 300 others, had taken refuge after the coup. Their fate was unknown. (NANCY ELLEN LAWLER)

CHAD

Area: 1,284,000 sq km (495,755 sq mi)
Population (2001 est.): 8,707,000
Capital: N'Djamena
Chief of state: President Lieut. Gen. Idriss Déby
Head of government: Prime Minister Nagoum Yamassoum

Chadian Pres. Idriss Déby won 63% of the vote in the May 2001 presidential election, securing for himself another five-year term, but this was only after many irregular electoral practices. Opposition members of the electoral commission resigned before the results

Cesaria Evora, whose sad, lilting mornas *have put Cape Verde on the world music map, performs at the Palace of Culture in Warsaw on May 26.*

were announced, maintaining that the election had been rigged. The opposition parties continued to refuse to accept the results, but their appeal to the constitutional court failed, protest meetings were banned, and demonstrations were broken up. Such actions cost Déby support, both within the country and in the international community. He postponed the legislative elections until 2002, and the opposition feared that in the interval he would use his patronage to strengthen his party, the Patriotic Salvation Movement.

By mid-2001 the Office of the UN High Commissioner for Refugees was approaching the end of the voluntary repatriation of thousands of people who had fled Chad for Cameroon in the 1980s. More than 40,000 Chadian refugees in Cameroon did not return to their homeland, however, in part because of the deteriorating political situation in northern Chad. The Movement for Democracy and Justice in Chad (MDJT) continued fighting in the Tibesti region in the northwest, close to the Libyan border, under Youssouf Togoimi, a former defense minister. In July the MDJT claimed to have captured the strategic town of Fada and opened a new front 900 km (560 mi) northeast of the capital, N'Djamena. President Déby suspected that Libyan leader Muammar al-Qaddafi was helping the rebels.

(CHRISTOPHER SAUNDERS)

CHILE

Area: 756,626 sq km (292,135 sq mi)
Population (2001 est.): 15,402,000
Capitals: Santiago (national) and Valparaíso (legislative)
Head of state and government: President Ricardo Lagos Escobar

The year 2001 posed both economic and political challenges for Chile and for the government of Ricardo Lagos Escobar. The case of former Chilean president Gen. Augusto Pinochet Ugarte remained in the spotlight. Pinochet, who had been charged with human rights abuses, underwent a series of medical exams after his lawyers allowed them to go forward. Although the Chilean appeals courts decided that Pinochet was not fit to stand trial, the general was not out of the le-

Police in Santiago, Chile, apprehend student demonstrators during a protest against a delay in the reduction of public transportation fares for students on April 20.

gal morass. Other actions continued against him in Chile and elsewhere. Judicial proceedings in France led to his indictment, along with six other senior Chilean military officers, including former intelligence chief Gen. Manuel Contreras, who had spent seven years incarcerated in Chile for the 1976 murder of Chilean diplomat Orlando Letelier in Washington, D.C.

On the political front, the Lagos government had to face a stronger political opposition—the activist mayor in Santiago, Joaquín Lavín Infante. Lavín, who narrowly lost to Lagos in 2000, continued to position himself to run again for the presidency. Much to the dismay of the Lagos government, Lavín had increased his popularity by focusing on issues such as public safety. Lavín's activities bore fruit in the December parliamentary elections when his right-wing Independent Democratic Union (UDI) party overtook the Christian Democratic Party (PDC) by winning more than 25% of the vote. The right-wing Alliance for Chile coalition, which included the UDI, won 44.3% of the vote, compared to the ruling Concertación coalition's 47.9%. As a result, the two political forces were tied in the Senate (24–24), and the Concertación's majority in the lower house was reduced to 63–57 from 70–50.

The PDC suffered an earlier embarrassment when it somehow missed the deadline for registering its candidates for the congressional elections. Although the situation was rectified via congressional action and PDC candidates were included

in the Concertación electoral slate, the event demonstrated a shocking lack of internal organization and led to a shakeup within the party. There were also growing intracoalition conflicts between the PDC and its coalition ally, the Socialist Party (PS). These came to light when the PS announced that it had reached an agreement to share some of its electoral seats with the Communist Party, which was not a member of the coalition. The strongly anticommunist PDC was outraged by the agreement, which had been negotiated without the prior consent of coalition members.

In addition, the Lagos government faced difficulties on the economic front. Although Chile's economy continued to grow, the rate of growth was lower than had been originally predicted—3.5% instead of the 5% estimate. That was a much lower number than the vigorous 7% growth rates Chile had experienced prior to the 1997 Asian financial crisis, which negatively affected Chile's export-dependent economy. Unemployment remained stubbornly high, reaching 9.7% in Santiago by October. Prices for two major exports, copper and wood pulp, also sank to record lows. Although Chile tried to insulate itself from the severe economic problems across the Andes in Argentina, its peso was affected, dropping in value to an exchange rate of about 670 pesos to the dollar by December. On the plus side, Chile had virtually no foreign debt, which allowed it to offer for sale $650 million in government bonds.

(LOIS HECHT OPPENHEIM)

CHINA

Area: 9,572,900 sq km (3,696,100 sq mi), including Tibet and excluding Taiwan and the special autonomous regions of Hong Kong and Macau
Population (2001 est., excluding Taiwan, Hong Kong, and Macau): 1,274,915,000
Capital: Beijing
Chief of state: President Jiang Zemin
Head of government: Premier Zhu Rongji

Three external events diverted the attention of the Chinese government and people from their primary focus on domestic affairs in 2001. The first was a contretemps with the U.S. in April over the crash of a Chinese military jet after a midair collision with an American surveillance plane over the South China Sea. The second was the International Olympic Committee's decision in July to award the 2008 Summer Olympics to Beijing. The third was the cataclysmic September 11 terrorist attacks in the U.S. that presented China with an opportunity to get in step with the global campaign to combat terrorism. For the most part, however, China focused inward on the formidable task of maintaining domestic prosperity, the indispensable precondition for stability in a system perennially threatened by social divisions, ethnic fragmentation, endemic corruption, and political fatigue. As the global economy slowed even before September 11, China managed to sustain a still-impressive rate of economic growth, though it was lower than in previous years.

Politics and the Economy. The ruling Communist Party of China (CPC) continued to prepare for its 16th Congress in 2002, at which time Pres. Jiang Zemin, National People's Congress head Li Peng, and Premier Zhu Rongji were slated to retire from their party posts. The 75-year-old Jiang was almost certain to retain his chairmanship of the vital Central Military Commission, however, and to wield considerable behind-the-scenes influence over his designated successor, Hu Jintao, as long as he remained in good health. Meanwhile, Political Bureau member Li Ruihuan, a relative moderate who was several years younger than the members of the ruling troika, successfully resisted pressure from party conservatives to join Jiang, Li, and Zhu in retirement.

For 20 years, while brooking no organized political opposition, the CPC had struggled to regain the authority and prestige it once enjoyed. The party's internal corruption and the effects of rapid social and economic change in Chinese society had called into question the CPC's leading role and eroded its legitimacy. In order to bring in new blood, on July 1, the CPC's 80th anniversary, Jiang called on the party to open its ranks to the once-reviled capitalists, who had been responsible for most of China's economic growth since the mid-1980s. Old-guard party members, faithful to Karl Marx's dictum that communist parties were the political instrument of the proletariat (working class), gagged at this bold initiative to recruit members of the "class enemy," but Jiang brushed aside all objections and shut down an orthodox party theoretical journal that dared to question his decision. In September the Central Committee dutifully en-

On March 28, during a rally in support of China's bid to host the 2008 Summer Olympics, dragon dancers perform at the Great Wall of China near Beijing.

AP/Wide World Photos

dorsed Jiang's proposal to revise the party constitution and thereby opened the door for capitalists to enter the CPC.

Earlier in the year the first CPC Work Conference since 1988—attended by 2,000 top officials—endorsed the leadership's campaign to suppress the Falun Gong and reaffirmed once again the leadership's decision 12 years earlier to crush the spring 1989 student-led democracy movement. This may have been in response to the publication, first in English in the U.S. and later in Chinese in Hong Kong, of *The Tiananmen Papers.* Edited by American scholars Andrew J. Nathan and Perry Link, this documentary collection was the authenticated secret record of high-level CPC discussions that culminated in the decision to use lethal force against unarmed demonstrators on June 3–4, 1989 (the Tiananmen Square massacre). The book cast many of the party's old guard, including then premier Li Peng and paramount leader Deng Xiaoping, in a particularly unflattering light. Additional secret evidence concerning this still-controversial decision leaked out in the course of the year and fed Beijing's paranoia that Washington was trying to split the CPC and overturn communism in China.

After four years as a special administrative region of China, Hong Kong felt the collar of Chinese control tighten ever so slowly around its neck. Such at least was the perception among that section of Hong Kong public opinion concerned with defending the autonomy promised at the time of the handover in 1997. In July Hong Kong's Legislative Council, chosen in elections that favoured elite occupational groups over direct popular representation, voted by a 2–1 margin to give Beijing the right to fire the chief executive. This seemingly small action enhanced the power of Chinese central authorities responsible for selecting Chief Executive Tung Chee-hwa, who had proved to be a faithful, if locally unpopular, executor of Beijing's wishes.

Like an indelible stain on the fabric of Chinese society, the reality of Chinese human rights abuses continued to resist Beijing's detergent action. In late November 2000, during a visit by Mary Robinson, the UN High Commissioner for Human Rights, who was openly critical of China's human rights record, China signed an agreement providing for UN advice and assistance to upgrade its criminal justice system, including the police, legal procedures, courts, and prisons. The effects, if any, of this and similar prior expressions of China's intention to bring its human rights practices into

© John Hillery/Reuters 2001

Sociologist Gao Zhan, accompanied by her husband, speaks to reporters in Detroit on July 26 after being expelled from China following her arrest and detention on charges of revealing state secrets to Taiwan.

conformity with international norms and practices were not evident during 2001. In February Amnesty International, the bellwether international human rights organization, issued a report alleging that China was stepping up its use of torture in police interrogations of dissidents, Tibetan nationalists, migrants, and other criminal defendants. As always, Chinese authorities rejected this report, as they did the U.S. State Department's annual review of human rights that said the human rights situation in China was getting worse. To deal with rising social discontent, Beijing instructed Chinese municipal authorities to beef up their antiriot police units, which, along with the million-strong People's Armed Police, were the instruments of first choice to deal with the contingency of urban riots, worker and student strikes, and other threats to public order. The police and paramilitary assault on the village of Yuntang in Jiangxi province demonstrated that such preparations were more than contingency planning. Villagers in Yuntang, unable to get relief from exorbitant taxes levied by local officials, seized and held control of their village until overwhelmed by lethal force from outside. Such popular indignation was widespread, and the default response of authorities was more likely to be the application of force than the satisfaction of grassroots demands for equity and social justice.

For several years Beijing had targeted pervasive networks of corruption that linked venal local officials with unscrupulous entrepreneurs. Despite massive arrests and numerous well-publicized public executions, corruption persisted and exacted not only an economic cost but also a heavy toll on ordinary workers. For example, when safety inspectors ignored hazardous working conditions and failed to enforce safety standards in

unsafe local mines, thousands of miners paid with their lives, as happened again in 2001. Children were also victimized. In a case that drew international attention and provoked some soul-searching on the part of Premier Zhu Rongji, 42 people, including 38 schoolchildren, were killed in an explosion in a Fanglin township (Jiangxi province) primary school whose pupils were forced to make fireworks as part of their regular activities. (*See* DISASTERS.)

In their ongoing campaign against Falun Gong, the eclectic Buddhist-influenced meditation and exercise association that was outlawed in 1999 as a supposed threat to public order, Chinese authorities added psychiatric internment to their familiar repertoire of arrests, beatings, incarceration, torture, and coercive reeducation. On June 20 at least 14 Falun Gong prisoners either hanged themselves or were tortured to death in a prison camp in northern Heilongjiang province. The apparent effect of President Jiang's quixotic but brutal campaign to destroy the Falun Gong had been to weaken the organization considerably and drive it underground.

The arrest and detention of American permanent resident Gao Zhan, a sociologist, and Li Shaomin, a naturalized American citizen teaching in Hong Kong, on charges of revealing state secrets indicated the bureaucratic power of China's Ministry of State Security. Their detention sent a chill through the large community of overseas Chinese students and scholars. Under pressure from the U.S. government and Western scholars, Gao and Li were expelled from China after being convicted in dubious trials. Less fortunate was Stanford research scholar Hua Di, who—though his 15-year prison sentence on similar charges was overturned—was retried and received a 10-year sentence.

Environmental concerns commanded the attention of policy makers and the public in a country whose huge population and rapid industrialization had pressed against the limits of natural resources, particularly water, wood, and air. China made some progress in curbing emissions of carbon dioxide, carbon monoxide, and nitrous oxide. The switchover from coal to natural gas and the ongoing conversion of Beijing's bus and taxi fleet from diesel fuel and gasoline to liquefied petroleum gas contributed to the amelioration of the air in the capital city. Beijing announced plans to address the severe water shortage affecting all of northern China by encouraging less-water-intensive agricultural practices, shutting factories that polluted groundwater and surface water, and constructing new sewage-treatment plants.

The determination of national and municipal officials to improve Beijing's environment was motivated in part by the desire to show the city's best face to the world. In July the International Olympic Committee announced that it was awarding the 2008 Summer Olympics to Beijing. Upon receiving the news, jubilant Communist Party and government leaders as well as ordinary citizens joined in a rare spontaneous mass celebration in Tiananmen Square. In this connection Beijing unveiled plans to invest $34 billion in new stadiums, parks, transportation systems, housing, and pollution-abatement measures.

According to official statistics, China's gross domestic product grew by 7.9% in the first half of the year, with domestic demand, accounting for fully 93% of growth, the primary engine of expansion. At the end of the third quarter, consumer prices had risen a modest 1%, and foreign exchange reserves stood at $195.8 billion. China's currency was stable, but its trade balance, while still positive, declined by $5.6 billion compared to the previous year at that point. Longstanding problems of liquidity and bad loans in the banking system and the mammoth task of converting state-owned enterprises into profitable firms remained mostly unresolved. However, these problems loomed ever larger as the World Trade Organization finally certified China for membership following 15 years of difficult multilateral negotiations that culminated in agreement in mid-September.

Foreign Relations. A decade earlier Chinese leaders had greatly valued the pragmatism of then U.S. president George H.W. Bush, who cooperated with them to stabilize Sino-American rela-

tions after the shock of Tiananmen. They were understandably leery, however, of the new U.S. president, George W. Bush. The younger Bush not only lacked foreign policy experience but also had surrounded himself with advisers who for the most part viewed China as a strategic adversary that threatened American interests and the U.S.'s friends in Asia, including Taiwan. An unfortunate aerial confrontation over the South China Sea on April 1 near China's southernmost province of Hainan sorely tested Sino-American relations just three months into the new Bush administration. While on a routine patrol over international waters off the South China coast, a lumbering, propeller-driven American EP-3 surveillance plane, crammed with sophisticated electronic eavesdropping equipment, collided with one of two Chinese jet fighters that were shadowing its flight. Washington claimed that the daredevil Chinese pilot had approached too closely and struck the American craft; Beijing countered that the U.S. plane had deliberately veered into the path of the Chinese fighter. Badly damaged, the EP-3 made an arguably unauthorized emergency landing at a Chinese military airfield on Hainan Island, where the 24-person crew was taken into custody by Chinese authorities. The Chinese F-8 jet involved in the collision crashed into the sea. The Chinese government and media immediately transformed the missing pilot, Wang Wei, into a national hero who had sacrificed his life for the motherland. As Chinese anti-American sentiment reached fever pitch, expressed, among other ways, in vituperative postings on Chinese Internet chat rooms, Beijing demanded that Washington admit responsibility for the incident and offer a public apology before it would release the sequestered crew members. American public opinion was equally incensed. After a shaky start, Chinese and American officials eventually agreed on a carefully worded official U.S. statement whose linguistic legerdemain enabled Beijing to claim it was an American apology and Washington to deny that it was anything of the sort. After 11 days of detention, the crew was released in good condition, and the disassembled U.S. plane, which Chinese intelligence officers had carefully examined, was eventually returned to its home base. Tempers abated, but many Chinese criticized their government for caving in to the Americans.

Later in April Beijing again had occasion to censure Washington for President Bush's decision to supply Taiwan

with many, though not all, of the items on its high-tech military shopping list deemed necessary to preserve a rough military balance of power across the Taiwan Strait in the face of Beijing's military modernization and offensive ballistic-missile buildup. Speaking extemporaneously, President Bush said the U.S. "would do whatever it took" to defend Taiwan, although his advisers quickly asserted that there had been no change in the U.S. policy of strategic ambiguity regarding what Washington would do in the event of a Chinese attack on the island, which Beijing claimed as its inalienable territory. In an August interview with executives of the *New York Times*, President Jiang tried to defuse tension by speaking soothingly of the bright prospects for good relations with the U.S. Following the September 11 terrorist attacks, China expressed condolences and offered verbal support to the U.S.-led antiterrorist coalition. The reduction or elimination of Islamic fundamentalist terror networks in Central Asia would help ease Beijing's worries regarding the vast northwestern province of Xinjiang, where small groups of Uighur militants, supported from across the border, had challenged Chinese power.

These ups and downs in Sino-American relations bracketed a major Chinese effort to consolidate its relations with Russia. Beijing and Moscow shared a common strategic interest in containing the further extension of American power, and China was Russia's largest customer for high-performance Russian military aircraft and other equipment. At a summit meeting in Moscow in July, Jiang and Russian Pres. Vladimir Putin signed a new "strategic partnership" that fell well short of a military alliance but nevertheless enhanced cooperation between the two countries. Among other things, Russia agreed to sell China 38 SU-30 ground attack fighters worth $2 billion. (STEVEN I. LEVINE)

COLOMBIA

Area: 1,141,568 sq km (440,762 sq mi)
Population (2001 est.): 43,071,000
Capital: Santafé de Bogotá, D.C.
Head of state and government: President Andrés Pastrana Arango

During 2001 real change in Colombia appeared tantalizingly close on a variety of fronts, but in every instance only incremental gains were made or the prospects for progress vanished altogether. Observers gave the government of Pres. Andrés Pastrana Arango high marks on international relations, foreign commerce, and modernization of the armed forces. On the other hand, there were plenty of disappointments in the form of unproductive negotiations with guerrillas, government corruption, and weak economic performance. Political reform was dashed in Congress. The administration had pushed several ideas, including campaign finance reform, the use of roll-call votes in Congress (to increase transparency), the end to intraparty competition in general elections (to make party labels more meaningful), and tougher punishments for corruption. Opponents of reform watered down proposals until they were considered a waste of time.

The government continued to negotiate with the two major guerrilla groups, the Revolutionary Armed Forces of Colombia (FARC) and the National Liberation Army (ELN). One positive note was a prisoner exchange in June between the government and the FARC in which the guerrillas released a far larger number of police and soldiers than had been expected—363 in exchange for 15 guerrillas. The FARC, however, pointed out that the estimated 1,000–1,500 guerrillas who had been guarding these prisoners were now free to return to fighting. A disturbing development in the conflict was the increased use of urban bombings. Despite the prisoner release, talks between the government and the FARC moved very slowly. In addition, the likelihood for success of a proposed six-month ceasefire (part of a plan developed by a "commission of notables") seemed dim.

In August talks with the ELN broke down completely after the government refused to grant the group a demilitarized safe haven in the department of Bolívar (the FARC already had a far larger zone in the southeastern part of the country). The ELN's demand had been opposed vociferously by local residents who received prompting from right-wing paramilitary units, the United Self-Defense Forces of Colombia. The government's resolve was also bolstered by the belief in some circles of the military that the group could be defeated militarily. There was some speculation that shunning of the ELN's demand and the breakdown of talks would lead the group to step up its violent activities to reinforce the sense that it was a force with which to be reckoned.

Fits and starts on negotiations coincided with a series of indications that an escalation of combat was likely. The guerrillas showed no sign of getting out of the kidnapping business, and they displayed their resolve to use bombings to open up the urban front of their conflict. For its part, despite concerns that the way was being cleared for human rights abuses, the government adopted a Law of National Security and Defense that increased the military's power to adjudicate in issues surrounding the conflict and gave the president power to expedite an antiterrorism statute and regulation of the "theatres of operations." Implementation of Plan Colombia, a U.S.-supported effort to counteract the drug trade (and the guerrillas), got under way in earnest. Dusting of drug crops with weed killer was temporarily suspended, however, owing to legal challenges based on a lack of study regarding its unintended effects on humans, livestock, nondrug crops, and the environment generally.

After a recession in 1999, the modest growth achieved in 2000 was expected to continue in 2001 at a rate of 3% or less. Private investment was slow to recover after the recession, and the banking industry remained particularly weak. Oil and coal sectors looked strong, but they

A Colombian special forces policeman takes aim during a raid against guerrilla forces in the city of Barrancabermeja on March 3.

© Jose Miguel Gomez/Reuters 2001

were dominated by foreign investors. Coffee, on the other hand, continued to struggle.   (BRIAN F. CRISP)

COMOROS

Area: 1,862 sq km (719 sq mi), excluding the 375-sq-km (145-sq-mi) island of Mayotte, a de facto dependency of France since 1976
Population (2001 est.): 566,000 (excluding 159,000 on Mayotte)
Capital: Moroni
Chief of state and head of government: Col. Azali Assoumani

The crisis brought about by the island of Anjouan's secession from the Comoros federation continued throughout 2001. Organization of African Unity (OAU) envoy José Francisco Madeira Caetano led intensive talks that produced a reconciliation agreement. Federal and Anjouan government officials, as well as opposition parties, signed the agreement on February 17. It provided greater autonomy for individual island governments but reserved defense and foreign policy for the national government. In March the reconciliation process stalled amid disputes over the composition of a committee to implement the agreement provisions. The OAU reaffirmed its commitment to ending the secession and vowed to maintain economic sanctions to this end.

On August 9 soldiers on Anjouan deposed the island's ruler, Lieut. Col. Said Abeid Abdermane. The three-member military committee that took power cited Abdermane's alleged corruption and the government's failure to pay soldiers and civil servants. By August 28 the coup leaders had nominated chief of the gendarmerie Cmdr. Mohamed Bacar as head of state. In early November Abdermane attempted to retake power but was defeated by forces loyal to Bacar. In a referendum on December 23, 77% of voters backed a new constitution that would grant increased autonomy to the three Indian Ocean states that made up the country but keep them part of the federation.

The economy continued to struggle despite the World Bank's approval of an $11.4 million credit in March for improving basic infrastructure.

(MATTHEW A. CENZER)

CONGO, DEMOCRATIC REPUBLIC OF THE

Area: 2,344,858 sq km (905,354 sq mi)
Population (2001 est.): 53,625,000 (including 1998–2001 war deaths approaching 3 million in eastern DRC [mostly from starvation, disease, and deprivation] and an unknown figure in the western DRC)
Capital: Kinshasa (executive and ministerial); Lubumbashi (legislative from August 2000)
Head of state and government: Presidents Laurent-Désiré Kabila and, from January 17 (acting until January 26), Joseph Kabila

On Jan. 16, 2001, Pres. Laurent-Désiré Kabila was shot and killed, reportedly by a bodyguard. (*See* OBITUARIES.) The circumstances of his death were unclear, but there were few signs of regret even among his political allies. A report released on May 23 by the chief state prosecutor concluded that the assassination was part of an attempted coup involving Uganda, Rwanda, and rebel Congolese—a claim immediately denied by all parties.

Officials quickly announced that Kabila's son, Joseph, would succeed his father. Joseph Kabila, who had been born and brought up in Tanzania, proved a successful guerrilla commander in the campaign that had brought his father to power, but he spoke neither French nor Lingala, the language of the inhabitants of Kinshasa and the surrounding region. (*See* BIOGRAPHIES.)

His first actions impressed Western observers. He had a cordial meeting with Pres. Paul Kagame of Rwanda and between January and March undertook a round of visits to Brussels, Paris, Berlin, London, and Washington, D.C. At a meeting of the signatories of the Lusaka Accord in the Zambian capital on February 15, he also expressed his willingness to negotiate directly with the rebels.

At home one of his first significant decisions was to pay the salary arrears of his army. On April 4 Kabila dismissed the corrupt cabinet members appointed by his father, replacing them 10 days later with men who appeared better qualified to direct the country's affairs. With inflation running at 500%, he also set about reorganizing the economy. He revoked a much-criticized monopoly awarded by his father to Israel's International Diamond Industries and renegotiated concessions to work some of the country's copper and cobalt resources. On May 27 Jean-Claude Masangu, governor of the central bank, announced that the currency would be allowed to float with an opening rate of 315 Congolese francs (FC) to the U.S. dollar instead of the hitherto official rate of FC 50. Masangu also removed price controls on fuel, allowing the cost to rise from the unrealistic FC 70 to FC 280 per litre.

Kabila had made an early promise of free elections, and on May 4 government representatives met with leaders of three main rebel groups in Lusaka and signed a declaration containing 14 principles that would form the basis for an Inter-Congolese National Dialogue. The opening phase of the dialogue took place in Botswana in August, and a full meeting was convened in the Ethiopian capital, Addis Ababa, on October 15. The meeting broke up after a week without any progress being made, but it was proposed that it should reassemble, probably in South Africa, on Jan. 28, 2002.

On the eastern front there were signs that Uganda and Rwanda were beginning to withdraw their troops. A UN Security Council resolution of June 15, while welcoming the apparent ceasefire in the region, called upon all foreign governments to accelerate the total withdrawal of their forces.

(KENNETH INGHAM)

CONGO, REPUBLIC OF THE

Area: 342,000 sq km (132,047 sq mi)
Population (2001 est.): 2,894,000
Capital: Brazzaville
Head of state and government: President Denis Sassou-Nguesso

The search for national reconciliation continued during 2001 following the ravages of the 1997 civil war, in which an estimated 20,000 people perished. Nevertheless, opposition parties boycotted the first phase of inter-Congolese talks launched on March 22 by Pres. Denis Sassou-Nguesso and mediated by Gabonese Pres. Omar Bongo. The government announced four days later that regional assemblies had approved a draft constitution as a first step in the restoration of the democratic process. Representatives of political parties, including some opposition groups, community leaders, and members of the government, attended the second round of the peace conference, which opened on April 10. Although the conference ended with a symbolic burning of 800 rifles, its success was marred by the ab-

Military officials escort the coffin of slain DRC president Laurent-Désiré Kabila from the People's Palace in Kinshasa on January 23.

AP/Wide World Photos

sence of deposed former president Pascal Lissouba and former prime minister Bernard Kolelas. The latter, sentenced to death in absentia in April 2000, was threatened with arrest if he returned to participate. Constitutional Minister Martin Mberi, in the cabinet since 1977 and a close associate of Lissouba, resigned on May 8; he criticized the draft constitution for placing too much personal power in the hands of the president. The parliament adopted the draft constitution on September 2, and the nation was expected to vote on it in January 2002. If the referendum was approved, presidential and legislative elections would follow. Sixty-four refugees from the civil war returned from Gabon to Brazzaville on August 7, but an estimated 14,000 people still remained in self-imposed exile there.

Despite an increase in public debt, fueled by loss of revenues through evasion of customs duties and poor management of oil revenues, the government achieved a level of economic growth. On May 18 the European Union (EU), citing its support for Congo's efforts to restore civil stability and democracy, resumed economic aid to the country. The EU granted Congo €41.3 million (about $37.1 million) for humanitarian and development projects. The World Bank announced on May 10 that Congo, having repaid all outstanding service charges on loans, would once again be eligible for development credits.

(NANCY ELLEN LAWLER)

COSTA RICA

Area: 51,100 sq km (19,730 sq mi)
Population (2001 est.): 3,936,000
Capital: San José
Head of state and government: President Miguel Ángel Rodríguez Echeverría

Because national elections were set to take place in early February 2002, both of the two main political parties in Costa Rica spent much of the first half of 2001 gearing up for what proved to be hotly contested primary elections. The National Liberation Party (PLN) held its primary on June 3, with some 250,000 party members casting their ballots. Rolando Araya Monge won

handily over his opponents José Miguel Corrales Bolaños and Antonio Álvarez Desanti. Corrales, who was making his third run for the presidency and who had been the party's losing candidate in the 1998 presidential election, declared that this was his last attempt. Araya, a nephew of Luis Alberto Monge Álvarez, who had served as president of Costa Rica from 1982 to 1986, emerged from the core of the traditional PLN leadership and had the support of the party standard-bearer, former president and Nobel laureate Oscar Arias Sánchez.

On June 10 the Social Christian Unity Party nominated Abel Pacheco de la Espriella by an overwhelming margin. Pacheco hoped to continue his party's grip on the presidency, but he was well aware that there was a long tradition of alternation in power between the two leading parties. Thus, he would have to work very hard to prevail against Araya.

Of major concern to voters was the sharp decline in the growth rate, which was estimated to end in 2001 at about 3%. A growth spurt created by the opening of a large Intel computer-chip production plant in the late 1990s had increased exports but had not had the spillover into the larger economy that had been anticipated. One major drag on the economy was the decline in world coffee prices to their lowest level in seven years. Inflation had been running at 10% annually, among the highest in Latin America, but there was some good economic news as Costa Rica signed a trade pact with Canada in April. (MITCHELL A. SELIGSON)

CÔTE D'IVOIRE

Area: 322,463 sq km (124,504 sq mi)
Population (2001 est.): 16,393,000
Seats of government: predominantly Abidjan; some ministries have relocated to Yamoussoukro
Chief of state: President Laurent Gbagbo
Head of government: Prime Minister Affi N'Guessan

Political turmoil continued throughout 2001 in a nation that had once been hailed as a model of stability and tolerance. On January 7 disaffected soldiers occupied radio and television stations in the capital as part of an

apparent military coup. Troops loyal to the government, however, regained control of the city after a night of heavy fighting, in which an unknown number of people were killed. Migrant traders were attacked on January 10 following accusations by the government that unnamed bordering countries had backed the coup. Thousands of foreigners, who make up an estimated 40% of the Ivorian population, fled the city. Opposition leader Alassane Ouattara's Rally of Republicans (RDR) denied any part in the coup. The government's refusal, however, to allow the northern politician to run in the October 2000 presidential election or the January 2001 parliamentary elections (presumably over doubts about his Ivorian nationality) led to a series of protests in which more than 200 people lost their lives. In the parliamentary elections the ruling Ivorian Popular Front (FPI), aided by the electoral boycott by the RDR, won a majority of seats. On January 22, in what was seen as a gesture of reconciliation, the parliament elected former finance minister Mamadou Koulibaly, also a northerner, as its speaker. In regional elections held on March 24–25, Ouattara's RDR won control of 64 local councils, the former ruling Democratic Party (PDCI-RDA) another 60, and the FPI 34.

On August 3 eight policemen were acquitted of the massacre of 57 civilians in the aftermath of the 2000 presidential elections. President Gbagbo proposed broad-based reconciliation talks between Ivorian political leaders past and present but they were postponed from September. In November Quattara returned from a year in self-imposed exile to take part in the rescheduled forum.

On April 5 secondary-school teachers ended a three-day strike over pay and working conditions. The following day police closed all campuses of the University of Abidjan after battles between two rival student unions, one backing the RDR and the other the FPI, resulted in one death and many injuries. The prospect of yet another voided year for higher education impelled the two factions to sign an agreement on May 14; they pledged to discontinue all demonstrations on university grounds.

Abuses of migrant child labourers who were sold into virtual slavery to cocoa farmers in Côte d'Ivoire captured headlines around the world. Traffickers in children were arrested in Benin, Burkina Faso, and Gabon. It was estimated that more than 15,000 children from Mali alone were working on

Child labour was an important issue throughout West Africa in 2001; here, a youngster works on a cocoa farm in Côte d'Ivoire on June 12.

Ivorian cocoa farms. On May 4 the government accused multinational chocolate companies of keeping cocoa prices low, a factor that would lead impoverished farmers to use slave labour.

(NANCY ELLEN LAWLER)

CROATIA

Area: 56,542 sq km (21,831 sq mi)
Population (2001 est.): 4,393,000
Capital: Zagreb
Chief of state: President Stipe Mesic
Head of government: Prime Minister Ivica Racan

Croatia's six-party governing coalition frayed in 2001, revealing deep division over both the country's role during the violent breakup of former Yugoslavia and the government's inability to invigorate a moribund economy.

On December 5 Parliament approved the Stabilization and Association Agreement, putting the country on track to possible future membership in the European Union. Croatia's relationship with the United Nations International Criminal Tribunal for the Former Yugoslavia dominated foreign policy, however. Two senior military officers, Gen. Ante Gotovina and Gen. Rahim Ademi, were indicted by the tribunal on June 8 for alleged crimes against ethnic Serbs committed during military campaigns in the mid-1990s to recover seized territories. The indictments sparked outrage among Croatian veteran groups, opposition parties, coalition members, and others who considered the officers war heroes. Prime Minister Ivica Racan, an advocate of cooperation with the court, criticized the indictment for its factual errors and reliance on indirect responsibility. In May Croatia had been the first Eastern European country to ratify the International Criminal Court Treaty.

The ensuing political fracas forced Racan to call an emergency session of the parliament. The government decision to deliver both generals to The Hague prompted Drazen Budisa, leader of the centre-right Croatian Social-Liberal Party (HSLS)—the Social Democratic Party of Croatia's junior ruling partner—to resign his post as party head. Though the coalition survived a no-confidence vote on July 15, Budisa's resignation emboldened local HSLS leaders to seek coalitions with the opposition Croatian Democratic Union (HDZ), the party displaced by the coalition two years earlier. Many considered this a prelude to a possible HSLS-HDZ-led centre-right bloc. The indictment in September of Serbian strongman Slobodan Milosevic for war crimes in Croatia and another against four Serbian senior military officers in October for the shelling of Dubrovnik did little to allay public distrust of the tribunal.

Nationwide local elections on May 20 revealed growing public dissatisfaction with government underperformance;

the country had an unemployment rate of 22% and an economy that was growing at a rate of only about 3%. Voter turnout was low, but the coalition won 15 of 20 county governments as well as the capital city, Zagreb. Voters gave more than a quarter of their votes to the nationalist HDZ, confirming it as still the country's largest party. On June 4 the regional Istrian Democratic Party left the coalition after it failed to gain coalition support for a controversial law that would make Italian the second official language in the province. On March 28 Parliament's lower house abolished the upper House of Counties.

Tourism revenues were one of the few economic bright spots, approaching prebreakup levels with $4 billion in revenues, a 14% increase. Deutsche Telekom purchased 16% of Croatian Telecom, giving it a 51% majority stake and bringing the Croatian government €500 million (about $425 million) in revenues. This deal was an exception to the general reluctance to sell even uneconomical parastatals to foreigners. With limited revenues from privatization and taxes, the government faced chronic budget deficits and was forced to make unpopular cuts in social spending and public-sector salaries and dismiss state employees. Reform of the bankrupt pension system stayed on track, however, as preparations went forward for the introduction of mandatory private pension funds.

Croatian sports figures helped counter the widespread national malaise. On March 11 Janica Kostelic took the World Cup in women's skiing. Tennis star Goran Ivanisevic received a hero's welcome from 100,000 fans in his hometown of Split after winning at Wimbledon. (MAX PRIMORAC)

CUBA

Area: 110,861 sq km (42,804 sq mi)
Population (2001 est.): 11,190,000
Capital: Havana
Head of state and government: President of the Council of State and President of the Council of Ministers Fidel Castro Ruz

In 2001 intense speculation about who would become Cuba's next head of state dominated both the domestic and international fronts after 74-year-old Pres. Fidel Castro Ruz suffered a fainting spell in late June. Though Cuban authorities claimed the aging ruler was in good health, there were some signs of planning for a post-Castro transition. Among the candidates who could take major roles in a new government were First Vice Pres. Gen. Raúl Castro Ruz, who was also Fidel's brother and his most likely successor; the Council of State vice president, Carlos Lage Dávila; and the president of the National Assembly, Ricardo Alarcón de Quesada.

Owing to its internal politics, Cuba remained isolated from important international events in 2001. It was the only country in the Americas not invited to the third Summit of the Americas in Quebec City. President Castro claimed the U.S. would use the Summit to co-opt its neighbours into signing a trade deal at unfavourable terms. He used his time at home for high-profile celebrations marking the 40th anniversary of the defeat of the Bay of Pigs invasion. Despite tense relations with most of Latin America, Cuba consolidated its friendship with Venezuelan Pres. Hugo Chávez Frías. After signing an oil accord at favourable terms for Cuba in October 2000, the two countries participated in a series of cultural, scientific, and academic exchanges.

The George W. Bush administration's nominations of anti-Castro exiles to high-level government posts led to increased friction between the two countries, despite the fact that Bush continued former president Bill Clinton's practice of waiving the controversial Title III of the 1996 Helms-Burton Act. The act would have allowed Americans to seek damages against foreign companies that benefited from confiscated property in Cuba. In July the Bush administration also oversaw new regulations that would allow limited agricultural sales to Cuba for the first time in the nearly 40-year embargo. In November four American companies signed deals to supply food to replenish Cuba's food stocks in the wake of Hurricane Michelle, which had killed five people earlier that month. The deals were made on a one-time basis only.

The Cuban economy grew for the seventh consecutive year despite high oil-import prices and a low sugar output. Real gross domestic product (GDP) growth for 2000 was 5.6%. Early estimates for GDP growth in 2001 varied from 3.5% to 5% for the year. A 13% decline in the 2000–01 sugar harvest due to economic inefficiencies as well as a severe drought, coupled with an increasing foreign-trade deficit, made it unlikely that the year's GDP would come close to the government's target of 5%. The government was also disappointed by the decision of Brazilian state oil company Petrobrás to pull out of oil exploration in Cuba after it discovered an offshore well that came up dry. Producing domestic oil was a major goal of the Cuban government, which now imported two-thirds of the island's energy needs.

Tourism, the main engine of the economy for the past five years and one of the biggest earners of hard currency (along with remittances), had trouble

A new hotel in Havana nears completion on January 5.

earning double-digit growth in 2001. Though authorities expected a total of two million tourists, a strong dollar in the middle of the year made travel for Europeans more expensive. Finally, though the full effect had yet to be determined, the September 11 terrorist attacks in the U.S. were expected to affect tourism negatively in general, as people were more wary of airplane travel. Cuban authorities, recognizing that government regulation of the tourism industry had been inefficient, announced in 2001 that all new high-end hotels would be managed in partnership with foreign companies.

International human rights organizations as well as press-freedom organizations continued to condemn Cuba's record on free speech and harassment of dissidents. In its report for 2000, Amnesty International noted that hundreds of people remained imprisoned for political offenses and that critics of the government were subject to "short term detention, house arrest, threats and harassment." The government claimed that limited repression was justified to maintain national unity against the U.S. embargo. (SANDRA A. GROSSMAN)

Louisa Gouliamaki/AFP Worldwide

Escorted by Greek Pres. Konstantinos Stephanopoulos (far left), Cypriot Pres. Glafcos Clerides (centre, forefront) reviews an honour guard in Athens on May 2.

CYPRUS

Area: 9,251 sq km (3,572 sq mi) for the entire island; the area of the Turkish Republic of Northern Cyprus (TRNC), proclaimed unilaterally (1983) in the occupied northern third of the island, 3,355 sq km (1,295 sq mi)

Population (2001 est.): island 873,000; TRNC only, 198,000 (including recent Turkish settlers and Turkish military)

Capital: Lefkosia/Lefkosa (also known as Nicosia)

Head(s) of state and government: President Glafcos Clerides; of the TRNC, President Rauf Denktash

Greek Cyprus reported in 2001 that it had provisionally completed two-thirds of the accession requirements for European Union (EU) membership. Completion of the requirements was expected in 2002, with full membership in 2004. The EU planned to provide significant economic support for the transition. While the EU was prepared to accept Greek Cyprus despite partition, the is-

sue added complication to the island's already-complex situation. In May parliamentary elections in the Greek sector, the socialist Progressive Party of the Working People (AKEL) secured the largest number of seats—20 of the 56 seats, up from 19. Pres. Glafcos Clerides's Democratic Rally dropped from 20 seats to 19.

While the island saw little violence in 2001, tension continued. In May the European Court of Human Rights found Turkey guilty of human rights violations when it invaded northern Cyprus in 1974, a finding rejected by both Turkey and Turkish Cyprus. After a pause lasting more than a year, Clerides and Turkish-Cypriot Pres. Rauf Denktash met on December 4 under UN auspices and agreed to resume negotiations in early 2002.

Moved by environmental and health concerns, about 1,000 Greek Cypriots protested construction of a 190-m (about 620-ft) radio antenna on the British Sovereign Base at Akrotiri. The incident left some 40 people injured and caused more than £300,000 (about $430,000) in damage. A later survey found that the antenna met EU standards, and the issue was somewhat defused.

Turkish Cypriot bank failures in 2000 were joined by a 2001 economic crisis

in Turkey, resulting in serious inflation and currency devaluation. The per capita gross national product (GNP) of Turkish Cyprus was less than a third of that of the Greek sector. By contrast, the Greek Cypriot economy was solid, with 4.5% GNP growth and unemployment of approximately 3.3% expected in 2001. Tourist arrivals increased more than 5%. Perhaps more important, a second desalination plant opened, with removal of all restrictions on the water supply. (GEORGE H. KELLING)

CZECH REPUBLIC

Area: 78,866 sq km (30,450 sq mi)
Population (2001 est.): 10,269,000
Capital: Prague
Chief of state: President Vaclav Havel
Head of government: Prime Minister Milos Zeman

Czech political life was not without conflict but was relatively stable in 2001, while the economy improved considerably. The country continued to be ruled by a minority Czech Social Democratic Party (CSSD) government, which had been in power since the June 1998 elections, thanks to that party's power-sharing "opposition agreement" with its rival, the Civic Democratic Party (ODS). The CSSD and ODS frequently bickered in public, but they often managed to agree in private.

Two government ministers left office in 2001; Finance Minister Pavel Mertlik was replaced by Jiri Rusnok in April, while Jaroslav Tvrdik took over from Vladimir Vetchy as defense minister in May. Mertlik resigned over his frustration at having failed to persuade the government to carry out his privatization and fiscal-reform plans. Vetchy was replaced because of alleged financial mismanagement, and Tvrdik set out to professionalize the army and abolish compulsory military service. Leadership changes also took place within several key parties. As expected, Vladimir Spidla was chosen CSSD chairman at the party's congress in early April, taking over from Prime Minister Milos Zeman. Changes also took place in the leadership of the opposition Quad Coalition (4K) as well as of the two major parties within that group, the Christian Democrat Union–Czech People's Party (KDU-CSL) and the Freedom Union (US). Cyril Svoboda was elected KDU-CSL chairman in May, while Hana Marvanova was chosen US leader in June, becoming the first woman to head a Czech parliamentary party.

In late January the Constitutional Court struck down elements of a controversial electoral reform bill that the CSSD and ODS had hoped would push small parties out of the parliament by raising the threshold. The court upheld a provision obliging coalitions to obtain at least 5% of the vote for each of its member parties, a requirement apparently aimed at the 4K. As a result, the extraparliamentary Democratic Union decided in early December to merge with the US as of January 1, 2002, thereby reducing the coalition's required vote from 20% to 15%.

The ruling parties started the year in a poor position as a wave of public protests continued over the appointment of Jiri Hodac as head of the state-owned Czech Television in December 2000. The resulting drop in support was especially apparent in the case of the ODS, the party with which Hodac was associated. Although the 4K topped popularity polls in the first months of 2001, internal squabbling over personnel and the coalition's future direction sent its public support down. Many polls later in the year put the 4K, CSSD, and ODS at approximately equal levels, with the Communists farther behind.

An issue that drew considerable attention in 2001 was the decision of British immigration officials in July to check passengers at Prague's Ruzyne airport before they boarded flights to London. That step was taken because Great Britain had faced an increasing inflow of Czech Roma (Gypsies) seeking asylum, and the CSSD viewed the immigration checks as preferable to the imposition of visas for Czech citizens. Critics argued that the Czech government was caving in to British demands and failing to defend the right of Czech citizens to travel abroad.

The biggest economic problem faced by the Czech Republic in 2001 related to fiscal reform, and the CSSD appeared unconcerned about the rising budget deficit and soaring public debt. Following Mertlik's departure, economic policy took a more leftist direction, led by Rusnok and Industry and Trade Minister Miroslav Gregr, who replaced Mertlik as deputy prime minister for economy. In July the cabinet approved a scaled-down version of Gregr's "big bang" plan; the new plan would devote more than $4 billion over two years to bail out of struggling industries and support transport and housing construction.

By early December the Czech Republic had closed 22 of 31 chapters of the *acquis communautaire*, the body of legislation needed for membership in the European Union. The country hoped to become a full EU member by early 2004. The Czechs were forced to compromise on the free movement of people chapter after Germany and Austria proposed a seven-year moratorium for new EU members, a move that was perceived by Czechs as an attempt to make their country a second-class member of the European Union. Tensions also mounted between the Czech Republic and Austria over the Temelin nuclear power plant near Ceske Budejovice. The two countries reached a historic agreement on November 29, however. While Prague vowed to introduce stricter safety measures, Vienna promised not to block Czech negotiations with the EU on the energy chapter of the *acquis communautaire*.

(SHARON FISHER)

DENMARK

Area: 43,096 sq km (16,639 sq mi)
Population (2001 est.): 5,358,000
Capital: Copenhagen
Chief of state: Queen Margrethe II
Head of government: Prime Ministers Poul Nyrup Rasmussen and, from November 27, Anders Fogh Rasmussen

The issue of immigration topped the agenda in Denmark in 2001. The country's impeccable record as a bastion of democracy, human rights, and egalitarianism was tarnished by a barrage of international criticism that cited racial intolerance and maltreatment of asylum seekers amid an atmosphere of growing xenophobia at home. Government plans, though later scrapped after much furor, to confine asylum seekers on remote islands while their applications were being processed, coupled with the revelation that many would-be immigrants were being housed in container homes (albeit well-appointed), further dented Denmark's reputation abroad. In addition, fewer than 5% of Denmark's population were foreigners, and most of that figure represented citizens from European Union (EU) states or the U.S.; there were only about 165,000 Muslims in the country.

The prevailing trepidation among many Danes about their country's becoming a multiethnic society and fears that their culture or "Danishness" were threatened helped anti-immigration groups gain a foothold, notably the xenophobic Danish People's Party (DF) led by Pia Kjaersgaard. The DF—campaigning on a direct anti-Muslim, anti-foreigner platform—made solid progress in opinion polls and forced other parties, including the ruling Social Democrats and the main opposition Liberals, to adopt tougher stances on immigration. Taxes and dwindling welfare services were the other main themes of a short and bitter campaign, which ended as predicted with a landslide victory for the Liberal Party of Anders Fogh Rasmussen. The Liberals, with the support of the Conservatives and centrist and rightist groups, won 98 seats in Folketing (parliament); the Social Democrats and the centre-left bloc garnered 77 seats, down from the 89 held in the previous parliament. On

Anders Fogh Rasmussen and his wife, Anne-Mette, celebrate the victory of Rasmussen's Liberal Party in Denmark's national elections on November 20.

November 27 Anders Fogh Rasmussen announced that he would head a Liberal-Conservative minority-rightist coalition government, which called for a major tightening of immigration laws, cuts in overseas development aid, an income-tax freeze, improvements in hospital services and social welfare, tougher law-and-order provisions, and a reduction by half of Denmark's $70 billion gross public debt by 2002.

On the economic front, Denmark's historic "no" vote in 2000 to participation in the European Economic and Monetary Union did not have the predicted damaging effect—unemployment hit its lowest level in 25 years; inflation was moderate; the krone currency remained firm; and foreign trade and current account surpluses stayed buoyant. A draft budget for 2002 showed a surplus in state finances for the sixth consecutive year amid forecasts that Denmark would not be as hard hit by the world economic downturn as some of its neighbours.

Following the September terrorist attacks in the U.S., the Danish government pledged to take action to abolish Denmark's exemptions from joint defense and legal cooperation within the EU, citing the need for closer international efforts to fight terrorism.

Relations between Denmark and the Faroe Islands remained strained following the postponement in the spring of a planned local referendum on the issue of independence. Prime Minister Poul Nyrup Rasmussen had threatened to cut off Copenhagen's annual $120 million grant to the islands, about one-third of Faroese public expenditure. Undeterred by this development and the inconclusive results from the first test drillings for oil off the islands, the Faroese home-rule government announced plans to phase out Danish aid and influence gradually, starting in 2002. (CHRISTOPHER FOLLETT)

DJIBOUTI

Area: 23,200 sq km (8,950 sq mi)
Population (2001 est.): 461,000 (excluding an unknown number of refugees)
Capital: Djibouti
Chief of state and head of government: President Ismail Omar Guelleh, assisted by Prime Ministers Barkat Gourad Hamadou and, from March 4, Dileita Muhammad Dileita

In February 2001 Prime Minister Barkat Gourad Hamadou, who had served in the post since 1978, resigned for health reasons. On March 4 Pres. Ismael Omar Guelleh named Dileita Muhammad Dileita, a senior civil servant and Djibouti's ambassador to Ethiopia, as the new prime minister.

In May the government concluded a peace agreement with the radical wing of the Front for the Restoration of Unity and Democracy (FRUD). This group had battled on behalf of the Afar ethnic group after FRUD moderates had reached an accord with the government. Although details of the agreement were not announced, FRUD leader Ahmad Dini Ahmad talked about decentralization, the establishment of local governance councils, and recognition of more political parties. The disarmament of FRUD fighters and a ceremonial destruction of weapons followed in June. In July President Guelleh formed the second government of his six-year term. To the surprise of many observers, the 20-member cabinet omitted representatives from FRUD's radical wing.

Throughout the year Djibouti suffered from drought. In addition, by September Djibouti's towns had absorbed nearly 100,000 refugees, including migrants from neighbouring countries. The influx strained Djibouti's urban infrastructure. The UN World Food Programme announced a relief package, including 11,000 tons of supplies. To add to the country's woes, various missions from the International Monetary Fund and the European Union criticized the government for its growing debt.

In December the country hosted a high-level German delegation to discuss stationing German troops in Djibouti. These forces would support the U.S.-led campaign against terrorism.

(MATTHEW A. CENZER)

DOMINICA

Area: 750 sq km (290 sq mi)
Population (2001 est.): 71,700
Capital: Roseau
Chief of state: President Vernon Shaw
Head of government: Prime Minister Pierre Charles

Dominica Prime Minister Pierre Charles told the parliament in April 2001 that the preliminary findings of an inquiry into allegations of corruption against the former United Workers Party (UWP) government had shown "clear prima facie evidence" that the UWP had engaged in "illegal and unethical conduct" while in office. Opposition leader Edison James made no immediate response to the statement.

Acknowledging the uncertain long-term future of the country's main export crop, bananas, the government in May agreed to provide EC$4 million (about U.S. $1.4 million) in soft loans to help local farmers rehabilitate or replant their banana holdings. Banana production had fallen by 23.5% in 2000.

Dominica fell in line with the rest of the Caribbean in June when it stiffened its money-laundering legislation to permit more wide-ranging inspection by the supervisory authority. Despite these efforts, Dominica remained on the Paris-based Financial Action Task Force's list of "uncooperative" countries.

Dominica came under pressure in July from the International Monetary Fund to tighten government expenditure and find ways to boost revenues. The IMF proposed the introduction of a value-added tax, restraint in wage increases, and a hike in fuel prices; the government categorically rejected the latter measure.   (DAVID RENWICK)

DOMINICAN REPUBLIC

Area: 48,671 sq km (18,792 sq mi)
Population (2001 est.): 8,693,000
Capital: Santo Domingo
Head of state and government: President Hipólito Mejía Dominguez

Within a few months of the inauguration of Pres. Hipólito Mejía Dominguez in August 2000, the relatively smooth waters upon which the Dominican Repub-

lic had been sailing turned choppy. After the start of 2001, gross domestic product growth projections dropped close to zero, reflecting the downturn in the U.S. economy, the temporary shutdown of the Falconbridge nickel plant, and softening tourism figures. The September 11 terrorist attacks in the U.S. inflicted further damage on the tourism industry, a principal source of foreign exchange and employment growth in the Dominican Republic. Partial recovery from the impact of the attacks suffered a setback with the November 12 crash in New York City of a Santo Domingo-bound passenger aircraft. (*See* DISASTERS.)

Disillusionment with Mejía's administration set in. His extravagant campaign promises looked hollow. No structured program for poverty reduction appeared, nor for problems of infant mortality and low literacy. The misery quotient in the traditional sugar-producing areas and the regions bordering Haiti remained acutely high. Mejía promised transparency in public administration but was unable to reconcile his commitment with the pent-up appetite for patronage by his Dominican Revolutionary Party supporters after 16 years out of power. The leading opposition contender, the Dominican Liberation Party, defeated by Mejía in 2000, positioned itself strongly for municipal and congressional elections scheduled for May 2002. Although good news for the government was sparse, patchwork progress was made toward solving the country's chronic power outages, a few holes in the porous income tax regime were filled, and falling oil prices provided some solace.

Recognizing that poverty and environmental degradation required Hispaniola-

wide solutions, Mejía gave priority to improving relations with Haiti and asked international donors to examine the challenge through this lens. In November Juan Bosch died; he was the country's first democratically elected president. (*See* OBITUARIES.)

(JOHN W. GRAHAM)

ECUADOR

Area: 272,045 sq km (105,037 sq mi), including the 8,010-sq-km (3,093-sq-mi) Galápagos Islands
Population (2001 est.): 12,879,000 (Galápagos Islands, about 17,000)
Capital: Quito
Chief of state and head of government: President Gustavo Noboa Bejarano

Armed conflict in Colombia, Ecuador's northern neighbour, spilled across the border in 2001. The Ecuadoran army discovered several abandoned training camps set up by leftist Colombian guerrillas, as well as jungle laboratories for producing cocaine. In January right-wing Colombian paramilitary units forced hundreds of Indians in Sucumbios province to leave their homes. In June the army clashed in Carchi province with suspected members of the Colombian National Liberation Army. Thousands of Colombians fled to Ecuador to escape fighting and the U.S.-supported aerial spraying of illegal coca plantations. The government said the spraying had afected food crops in Ecuador and appealed to Colombia to stop fumigating areas close to the frontier.

There was speculation that former guerrillas had been responsible for kidnapping 10 foreign oil workers in Ecuador late in 2000. In February, after more than four months in captivity, seven of the hostages were released in exchange for a $13 million ransom. Two

On July 4 Hipólito Mejía (second from left), president of the Dominican Republic, talks with a group of tourists in The Bahamas, where he later gave a speech on environmental degradation at the 22nd Conference of the Caribbean Heads of Government.

others had escaped earlier. One was shot dead in January to underscore the ransom demand. Fifty-two people, five of whom the U.S. sought to extradite, were later arrested in connection with the case.

U.S. military aircraft began flying anti-drug-trafficking surveillance missions from the air force base at Manta under a 10-year agreement. U.S. authorities said the base would not be used for operations against the Colombian guerrillas, but some Ecuadorans feared the agreement would draw them further into Colombia's conflicts.

The Colombia-related troubles overshadowed political and economic developments. The adoption of the U.S. dollar as Ecuador's currency in 2000 (see *El Salvador:* Special Report, below) and high oil prices helped stabilize the economy. Construction began on a second oil pipeline. The government made progress on fiscal reform but met heavy opposition from Congress and the Supreme Court. Pres. Gustavo Noboa responded by proposing political reforms, including a new electoral system and a second legislative chamber. Early in the year Indian protests forced the government to stabilize fuel prices and sign an agreement on indigenous rights. Hundreds of thousands of Ecuadorans continued to live outside the country, and the press devoted considerable attention to their difficulties.

Fears for the rare fauna of the Galápagos Islands were raised in January when a tanker ran aground and spilled 655,000 litres (173,000 gal) of fuel, but winds blew much of the slick out to sea.

(PAUL KNOX)

EGYPT

Area: 997,690 sq km (385,210 sq mi)
Population (2001 est.): 65,239,000
Capital: Cairo
Chief of state: President Hosni Mubarak
Head of government: Prime Minister Atef Ebeid

During 2001 Pres. Hosni Mubarak sought to play a mediatory role in the Middle East peace process. Palestinian leader Yasir Arafat made numerous visits to Egypt, but the violence that had begun when the Palestinian *intifadah*

Peter Endig/AFP Worldwide

Egyptian Pres. Hosni Mubarak (left) is received in Berlin by German Pres. Johannes Rau on September 25 for discussions on world terrorism.

erupted and the subsequent election of Ariel Sharon (*see* BIOGRAPHIES) as prime minister of Israel rendered all Egyptian mediatory efforts futile.

Mubarak made his annual visit to the United States in early April. The deadlocked peace process and economic relations were uppermost on his agenda. Egypt's ties with the U.S. were vital if only for the continued $2 billion in military and economic aid Egypt received.

In late February Egypt hosted a summit of the Developing Eight Group, or D-8, which included Egypt, Nigeria, and six non-Arab Muslim Asian countries. The leaders called for greater cooperation in international communication and set guidelines for a doubling of trade between the member states. On June 25 Egypt and the European Union signed an association agreement to establish a free-trade area for manufactured goods, with trade barriers to be phased out over 12 years.

On February 5 a court in the town of Sawhaj in Upper Egypt convicted four Muslims and sentenced them to prison terms varying from one to 10 years for the execution-style killings in January 2000 of 21 Christian Copts. The lightness of the sentences was held up by many as an illustration of official discrimination against Christians—in this instance, by the Egyptian judiciary. In May Sa'd ad-Din Ibrahim, a professor at the American University in Cairo who had been arrested by the government in June 2000 for speaking out in seminars about this particular incident, was sentenced to seven years' hard labour by the Egyptian State Security Court. (*See* BIOGRAPHIES.)

The September 11 terrorist attacks in the United States led to a flurry of visits by Arab leaders to Egypt. These included Arafat, King Abdullah II of Jordan, and Syrian Pres. Bashar al-Assad. Mubarak's reaction to the acts of terrorism was to support the U.S.—but with reservations. He advised the U.S. to restrict its military actions against those accused of terrorism and not to extend terrorism to others. Egypt sought to shield its close allies, such as Libya and Syria, which had been known to sponsor terrorism in the past. Many Egyptians expressed their disbelief that Saudi Arabian-born businessman Osama bin Laden was behind the September 11 atrocities. (*See* BIOGRAPHIES.) The general lack of freedom of communication in Egypt and the anti-Western tirades that had been the hallmark of the Egyptian media, including the government-owned press, contributed during the year to the spread of anti-Jewish conspiracy theories in which Israel loomed large.

Following the September tragedy, President Mubarak embarked on a European tour, which included stops in France, Italy, and Germany. He spoke of Egypt's need to coordinate actions with Western countries to combat terrorism. The intelligence information provided by the Egyptian authorities might be very valuable indeed; many leading members of Bin Laden's al-Qaeda organization, including Ayman az-Zawahiri and Muhammad Atef (*see* OBITUARIES), were Egyptian. (MARIUS K. DEEB)

EL SALVADOR

Area: 21,041 sq km (8,124 sq mi)
Population (2001 est.): 6,238,000
Capital: San Salvador
Head of state and government: President Francisco Flores Pérez

On Jan. 13, 2001, a major earthquake rocked much of El Salvador. (*See* DISASTERS.) Thousands of aftershocks and another major quake in February added to the destruction, which was especially heavy in the populous region around the capital, San Salvador. In addition to direct damage from the earthquakes, massive mud slides left hundreds of thousands homeless and disrupted communications, transportation, and public services. The quakes claimed the lives of 1,259 persons and caused an estimated $1.6 billion in damage. A massive international relief effort followed, but charges of corruption and misappropriation of funds clouded the relief effort.

The earthquake imperiled El Salvador's economy and added to the confusion that had begun on January 1 when the country adopted the U.S. dollar as its official currency. (*See* Special Report, below.) Confusion and difficulty in converting the Salvadoran colón accompanied dollarization, as many Salvadorans resisted the change. Polls reflected that up to 80% of the population expressed preference for the colón. By the middle of the year, only a third of the currency had been converted to dollars, and at least two lawsuits challenged the constitutionality of the new system in the courts. The government insisted that the new system was working and contributing to economic growth by lowering interest rates, checking inflation, expanding credit, increasing dollar remittances from the U.S.—which rose 13.3% during the first five months of dollarization—and increasing foreign investment. Labour and leftist groups especially opposed dollarization. High oil prices, low coffee prices, and a serious drought slowed economic progress. Agricultural interests complained that the government's emphasis on expanding manufacturing and foreign trade was responsible for a serious decline in agricultural production, with rising rural poverty and hunger the result.

Beginning on March 15, El Salvador joined with Guatemala and Honduras in a new free-trade agreement with Mexico, which promised new jobs and Mexican investment, but since it excluded the export to Mexico of coffee, sugar, or bananas, there was fear that the treaty benefitted Mexico much more than El Salvador. In April Pres. Francisco Flores Pérez argued that economic liberty was the key to saving democratic development in the region. While El Salvador made progress in improving its bleak human rights record during 2001, extrajudicial killings, kidnappings, and allegations of police abuse continued. A United Nations Development Programme report for 2001 ranked El Salvador 95th among 162 countries for human development on the basis of its poverty, low rate of tax collection, and meagre spending on social programs.

(RALPH LEE WOODWARD, JR.)

EQUATORIAL GUINEA

Area: 28,051 sq km (10,831 sq mi)
Population (2001 est.): 486,000
Capital: Malabo
Chief of state: President Brig. Gen. Teodoro Obiang Nguema Mbasogo
Head of government: Prime Ministers Ángel Serafín Seriche Dougan and, from March 4, Cándido Muatetema Rivas

At the end of February 2001, the government of Prime Minister Ángel Serafín Seriche Dougan, which had been accused by the ruling Democratic Party of Equatorial Guinea of corruption and mismanagement, resigned. Pres. Teodoro Obiang Nguema Mbasogo then appointed a new prime minister, Cándido Muatetema Rivas, and cabinet.

As President Nguema's health deteriorated in 2001, there was speculation about a contest for power between his two eldest sons. Teodorín Nguema Obiang Mangué spent much of his time abroad and was rarely seen in Malabo; his half brother, Gabriel Nguema Lima, had been an effective minister of mines and energy but lacked charisma. By mid-year the Nguema family, head of the dominant Mongomo clan, seemed to be looking to Gen. Agustín Ndong Ona, a conservative with close links to the president, as a possible successor.

Oil production increased to almost 200,000 bbl a day, with Exxon Mobil the main producer. Other companies invested millions of dollars in oil exploration offshore. Although Equatorial Guinea had the world's fastest-growing economy in 2001, few had reaped any benefits from the oil bonanza.

(CHRISTOPHER SAUNDERS)

Triggered by a major earthquake in El Salvador on January 13, a mud slide rips through the town of Santa Tecla, near the country's capital, San Salvador.

AP/Wide World Photos

Dollarization

Is it worth it?

by Guillermo A. Calvo

By mid-2001 a number of Latin American countries had officially adopted the U.S. dollar as their currency. Ecuador replaced its sucre with the dollar in September 2000. On Jan. 1, 2001, El Salvador followed suit, and Guatemala elevated the dollar to equal status with its quetzal on May 1. Panama had been officially dollarized since the beginning of the 20th century. In 1999 Argentina had seriously considered adopting the dollar, but after much heated debate the proposal was dropped. Argentina had, however, already pegged its peso one-to-one with the U.S. dollar back in 1991. As Latin American countries continued to negotiate with the U.S. for a hemispheric trade agreement, the move to the dollar was expected only to accelerate.

Dollarization Costs. To many analysts the trend toward dollarization was unexpected, since adopting a new currency can be quite costly. One major expense is the loss of seigniorage, the profit that a country earns when it issues a currency. For example, the cost to the U.S. of printing its currency is estimated at less than 0.1% of the currency's face value, yet the notes are sold at face value to banks. If a foreign country dollarizes, it will no longer earn seigniorage and will have to buy the dollars—not an insubstantial budgetary consideration. In addition, a dollarized country will lack an independent monetary policy and, in particular, will not be capable of printing money to rescue banks in case of a liquidity crisis. Given these negatives, why would a country consider dollarization?

The Benefits. It is important to note that many countries in Latin America and elsewhere are already unofficially dollarized. In particular, countries that have experienced high and erratic inflation for long periods of time have tended to set prices in dollars (especially on big-ticket items like cars and real estate). Some governments have imposed controls on the use of the dollar, but they have proved to be very difficult to enforce. This phenomenon, where a local currency and the dollar circulate side by side, is called currency substitution. In places where currency substitution exists and the dollar is already legally recognized, conversion to a completely dollarized system will be relatively simple. Dollarized countries, in effect, import the monetary policy of the U.S. This usually results in the dropping of inflation rates toward U.S. levels. Already in Ecuador, for example, inflation has plummeted from more than 90% in 2000 to a projected rate of 30% in 2001. The drop in inflation rates and the elimination of the risk of devaluation, in turn, help boost domestic savings and attract foreign investment. Dollarization reduces interest-rate volatility as well. The monetary system stabilizes, and with less skittishness over possible devaluations, the risk of bank runs lessens—a situation common in economies that have exhibited poor monetary discipline.

Considerations for the U.S. Thus far the U.S. government has neither encouraged nor discouraged dollarization. The Federal Reserve has simply requested that it be notified in advance when a country plans such a move. Clearly, however, the more countries that use the U.S. dollar, the more the U.S. government stands to earn by gaining additional seigniorage revenue. Many experts have suggested that, in order to encourage dollarization, the U.S. could repay some of the seigniorage to countries that are officially dollarizing. This has the potential to create a "win-win" situation, with the U.S. benefiting from the expansion of the use of its currency and dollarized countries minimizing one of the biggest costs of replacing their currency. In 1999, in fact, U.S. Sen. Connie Mack put forward a proposal to share seigniorage with countries that adopt the dollar, but the bill did not pass out of committee.

To Dollarize or Not to Dollarize? The countries best suited for successful dollarization are those in which currency substitution already exists and that have ample international reserves. In many cases the reserves are so great that they would be sufficient to buy up the entire supply of domestic currency and thus dollarize.

Dollarization costs will vary from country to country and from period to period, depending in part on the interest rates prevailing in the U.S. Estimates show that in most cases the seigniorage cost is less than 1% of a country's gross domestic product. Another possible drawback, however, is that once dollarization has been adopted, it may be hard to undo—i.e., to "de-dollarize". In contrast, fixed exchange rates such as Argentina's can be modified at the stroke of a pen. There a r e circum-stances in which a deval-uation could help restore international competitiveness, as when an economy is faced with a sharp deterioration in its trade terms. This relative advantage of fixed exchange rates is lost, however, in periods in which devaluation does not take place. This is so because the knowledge that a devaluation could happen at any time leads to what has been called the "peso problem"—that is, domestic-currency interest rates substantially higher than dollar interest rates. For example, in Argentina interest rates for the peso have exceeded dollar domestic interest rates by about 3% during tranquil periods (and reached astronomical numbers during periods of turmoil). Two other issues that countries must consider before dollarizing are, first, the likelihood that larger amounts of counterfeit currency will surface and, second, that time and effort will be required for overcoming the resistance of a population to the conversion. Therefore, the decision to dollarize is not trivial or even straightforward, and each country's currency structure needs to be assessed on its own terms.

The main experiment in currency replacement of modern times is the adoption of the euro simultaneously by several countries in the European Union (EU), a process that started in 1999 and will come to fruition in 2002 as euro bills and coins begin to circulate. The EU machinery provides for member countries to share seigniorage, and access to credit lines is available if a member state finds itself in a liquidity crunch. The several countries involved have agreed to coordinate banking regulations. It is too early to tell how the system will operate, but sharply lower interest rates have already been registered in Italy and Spain, countries that prior to the adoption of the euro suffered from the peso problem. Actually, lower interest rates account for much of the fiscal adjustment that Italy had to implement to comply with the Maastricht Treaty, which outlined the EU's economic unification. In contrast to the situation in the EU, dollarization is being considered in the less-developed world mostly by individual countries and is therefore more costly. The issue of dollarization is certain to resurface in connection with the negotiations for the Free Trade Area of the Americas, a scheme that will extend the North American Free Trade Agreement to the entire hemisphere. Countries that belong to a large free-trade area and share the same currency can be less concerned about the vagaries of the exchange rate. For them, dollarization will be attractive.

Guillermo A. Calvo is chief economist at the Inter-American Development Bank in Washington, D.C., and director of the Center for International Economics at the University of Maryland. Opinions are those of the author and do not necessarily represent those of the institutions with which he is affiliated.

ERITREA

Area: 121,144 sq km (46,774 sq mi)
Population (2001 est.): 4,298,000
Capital: Asmara
Head of state and government: President Isaias Afwerki

On May 24, 2001, Eritrea celebrated the 10th anniversary of its effective independence from Ethiopia. Nevertheless, Eritrea's triumphal claims to exceptionalism from the African continent's postcolonial malaise of dictatorship were exposed to scrutiny during the year. In 2000 a group of reformists had emerged from within the ranks of the ruling People's Front for Democracy and Justice (PFDJ) and had demanded that the constitution (ratified in 1997) be implemented and that national elections be held in December 2001. In May 2001 the group published an *Open Letter to the PFDJ,* which exposed the absence of accountability and transparency in the regime led by Pres. Isaias Afwerki. The group, which was made up of 14 men and one woman and included several high-profile government officials, came to be known as the G-15. Among other demands, the G-15 called for establishing a pluralist system of government, amending laws governing the national economy, instituting a merit-based civil service system in lieu of existing patronage systems and tokenism, and preventing further degradation of women and ethnic and religious minorities.

Stung by the criticism, the ruling regime moved to crack down on the G-15. On September 18–19, 11 of the 15 were jailed without being charged. At the same time, the government announced that it was shutting down privately run newspapers in the country. In October international outcries against the crackdown irked the regime such that it expelled the European Union representative in Asmara and incarcerated local personnel at the U.S. embassy. Average Eritreans, who were unaccustomed to witnessing the airing of differences between their leaders, began to voice their concerns, which further threatened the hegemony of the PFDJ loyalists.

One member of the G-15, Mesfin Hagos, a former defense minister and a cofounder of the Eritrean People's

AP/Wide World Photos

Former Estonian president Lennart Meri (left) hangs the presidential regalia on his successor, Arnold Rüütel, during inaugural ceremonies in Tallinn on October 8.

Liberation Front, had been in the U.S. at the time his 11 fellow dissidents were jailed. Although his diplomatic passport was subsequently revoked by the regime, Hagos announced his intention to return to Eritrea—regardless of the threat of arrest—and publicly urged the Eritrean people to rise up against tyranny. In an interview on the Internet Hagos called Afwerki "an old-fashioned dictator, who reacts to any form of criticism with arbitrary, cruel and excessive measures." After 10 years of sovereignty Eritreans, too, joined postcolonial Africa's battle against home-grown dictatorship. (RUTH IYOB)

ESTONIA

Area: 45,227 sq km (17,462 sq mi)
Population (2001 est.): 1,363,000
Capital: Tallinn
Chief of state: Presidents Lennart Meri and, from October 8, Arnold Rüütel
Head of government: Prime Minister Mart Laar

On Sept. 21, 2001, Arnold Rüütel, a leading former communist and candidate of the rural-oriented People's Union, was elected Estonia's second postcommunist president for a five-year term by gaining a bare majority (186 votes) in the 367-member electoral college, composed of the 101 members of the Riigikogu (parliament) and 266 representatives of local government assemblies. As in 1996, the initial attempt to elect a president in the parliament failed because no candidate achieved the required two-thirds majority. At age 73 the oldest candidate in the field, Rüütel had been presidential runner-up twice in the 1990s, but his election this time was a surprise, since he had trailed in nearly all opinion polls. He won because of the failure of the ruling national coalition to agree on a single candidate, the strong rural representation in the electoral college, and a protest vote against the policies of the current national government. On December 27 Rüütel began negotiations with chairmen of the Coalition Reform and Center Party Siim Kallas and Edgar Savisaar to form a new government.

Estonia's overall economic performance, as suggested by various macroeconomic indicators, remained strong during 2001, but growing unemployment and the highest rate of inflation in the Baltic States were cause for concern. Privatization of various branches of the economy had proceeded quite smoothly in previous years, but Prime Minister Mart Laar's centre-right coalition faced strong criticism for its handling of the privatization of a major railroad and the electrical energy industry, especially the lack of transparency in the latter case.

Rüütel's election did not signify any change in Estonia's strongly Western-oriented foreign policy. Although NATO's next summit meeting on expansion was not scheduled until November 2002, the three Baltic States moved closer to membership as various Western leaders, notably U.S. Pres. George W. Bush and French Pres. Jacques Chirac, offered the most explicit statements to date on Baltic inclusion. In the aftermath of the events of September 11, Russia also softened its opposition to NATO membership for the Baltic States.   (TOIVO U. RAUN)

ETHIOPIA

Area: 1,133,882 sq km (437,794 sq mi)
Population (2001 est.): 65,892,000
Capital: Addis Ababa
Chief of state: Presidents Negasso Gidada and, from October 8, Girma Wolde-Giyorgis
Head of government: Prime Minister Meles Zenawi

Local elections were held across Ethiopia in February and March 2001. *Woreda* (county) elections in February resulted in the overwhelming victory of the ruling Ethiopian People's Revolutionary Democratic Front (EPRDF) coalition. Criticisms that the elections were not free and fair led to an opposition boycott of the March *kebele* (township) elections, which the EPRDF also won handily.

Beginning on April 18, student protests over the right to form a union and opposition to police presence on the Addis Ababa University campus led to one of the worst incidents of civil disturbance in Ethiopian history. In an effort to dispel the protesters, police stormed the university dormitories, killing between 30 and 41 students. There were hundreds of additional casualties, and 3,000 more students were detained in army camps for several weeks. The university was closed for several weeks and many students chose not to return when it reopened. Additionally, some university students sought refuge in Djibouti and Kenya.

Almost immediately following the riots, there was a critical split in the ruling Tigrayan People's Liberation Front (TPLF) faction within the EPRDF coalition. The split emerged over the government's anticorruption agenda as well as the capitalist path being taken by the government of Meles Zenawi—a sharp break from the previous Marxist-Leninist

Students at Addis Ababa University listen as one of their colleagues reads a list of demands during student protests in April.

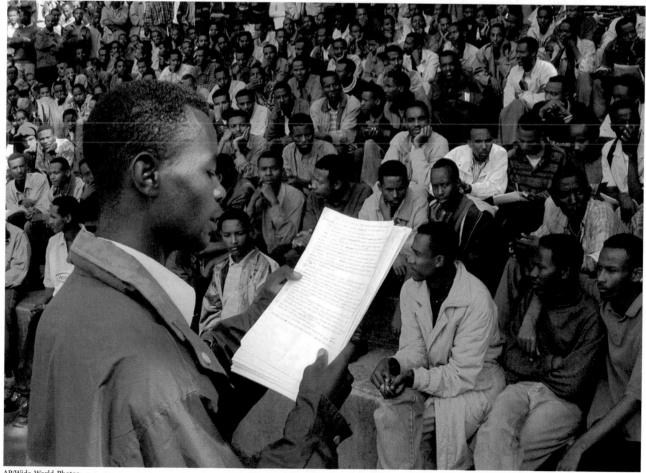

AP/Wide World Photos

ideology of the party. The 12 TPLF members who opposed the Meles regime were purged from the party and held under house arrest. Shortly thereafter, Kinfe Gebremedhin, the head of the Ethiopian Federal Security and Immigration Authority, was shot dead by a military officer as he walked out of an officers club in Addis Ababa. Kinfe had been a strong supporter of the Meles government.

In further fallout from the party split, Pres. Negasso Gidada aligned himself with the splinter group of the TPLF and was ousted from the leadership of his party, the Oromo People's Democratic Organization, though he maintained his position as federal president until his term was up in September. In October Girma Wolde-Giorgis was elected by the parliament as the second president. The year ended with a much-weakened EPRDF regime.

The economy grew at a brisk 6.5% in 2001, favoured by a good harvest and the end of the violent conflict with Eritrea, which was estimated to have cost the Ethiopian state $2.9 billion. International coffee prices remained low, however, and farmers in the south of the country were affected. Ethiopia benefited from a canceling of 67% of its $430 million debt to Paris Club countries under the World Bank's HIPC (Heavily Indebted Poor Countries) program.

Despite the end of active fighting, tensions with Eritrea remained high as both countries rejected the temporary security zone (TSZ) proposed by the United Nations in an attempt to demarcate the border between the two states. UN troops remained fully deployed in the TSZ, and the UN chose not to renew its arms embargo against Ethiopia. Ethiopian troops were involved in border skirmishes with both Kenya and Somalia. Relations with Djibouti remained good in spite of a significant increase in port fees for Ethiopian exports.

(SANDRA F. JOIREMAN)

FIJI

Area: 18,272 sq km (7,055 sq mi)
Population (2001 est.): 827,000
Capital: Suva
Chief of state: President (interim until March 15) Ratu Josefa Iloilo
Head of government: Prime Minister (interim until March 15) Laisenia Qarase

On Oct. 1, 2001—after more than a year of political instability stemming from a coup in May 2000, when Fiji's Parliament was stormed by ethnic-Fijian armed nationalists—newly elected lawmakers were sworn in amid tight security. Coup leader George Speight remained in prison on treason and firearms charges, but he was nonetheless elected to Parliament. His absence from proceedings, however, prompted the speaker of the house to vacate his seat.

Following general elections in August and September, in which Prime Minister Laisenia Qarase's nationalist United Fiji Party won 32 seats and 26% of the vote and the Indian-dominated Fiji Labour Party (FLP) of former prime minister Mahendra Chaudhry won 27 seats and 34.8% of the vote, Qarase refused to follow a constitutional provision requiring representation in the cabinet for all parties securing 10% of the vote. Chaudhry challenged the Qarase government in court and awaited a decision. In recognition of Fiji's return to democracy, the country was readmitted as a full member of the Commonwealth in December.

Fiji declined a request by Australia to establish a refugee-processing centre, owing to strong public sentiment against it. The gradual recovery of the economy, especially tourism, was challenged following the September terrorist attacks in the U.S.   (BARRIE MACDONALD)

FINLAND

Area: 338,145 sq km (130,559 sq mi)
Population (2001 est.): 5,185,000
Capital: Helsinki
Chief of state: President Tarja Halonen
Head of government: Prime Minister Paavo Lipponen

Though other countries in the region made plans in 2001 to join NATO, Finland maintained its nonalliance stance but welcomed NATO's open-door policy and pledged to cooperate closely within NATO's Partnership for Peace.

During his visit in September, Russian Pres. Vladimir Putin remarked in Helsinki that he understood the feelings of Finns who demanded the restoration of Karelia, which was ceded to the Soviet Union after World War II, but he maintained that closer cross-border contacts would be a better way to address the issue. Though he saw no need for NATO enlargement, he understood that Estonia, Latvia, and Lithuania wished to join the organization; he pledged not to launch a hysterical campaign against their efforts.

Finnish Pres. Tarja Halonen became involved in a tiff with the Baltic States following her interview in the German

Finnish Pres. Tarja Halonen (right) shares a toast with Russian Pres. Vladimir Putin during his visit to Helsinki in September.

Martti Kainulainen/AFP Worldwide

press. Critics maintained that she had indicated that she was opposed to the Baltics' joining NATO. She denied taking that position, and her later talks with Baltic leaders evidently smoothed over the matter. Accession of Estonia, Latvia, and Lithuania would leave Finland as the sole nonallied country along the immediate sea approaches to St. Petersburg.

While visiting Finland, Putin laid a wreath at the tomb of Marshal of Finland C.G.E. Mannerheim, a courtesy that had not been observed by previous visiting leaders from the former Soviet Union. In a speech made while visiting St. Petersburg, Finnish Prime Minister Paavo Lipponen remarked that Putin's gesture could exemplify a new dimension in bilateral relations. Lipponen was also hoping to secure funds from the European Union to make railroad-track improvements, which could reduce to three hours the train journey between St. Petersburg and Helsinki.

Finnish Foreign Minister Erkki Tuomioja came under criticism after an interview in which he asserted that Israel's policy was to suppress, humiliate, and impoverish the Palestinians with the kind of treatment that the Nazis had meted out to Jews in the 1930s. He later denied any intention to compare Israelis to Nazis.

The Finnish economy surged early in 2001 before sliding toward zero growth. The governor of the central bank, Matti Vanhala, warned that a higher employment rate would be necessary if the welfare state was to be maintained. By year's end the threat of a prolonged recession made it likely that Finnish industry would remain weak.

(EDWARD SUMMERHILL)

FRANCE

Area: 543,965 sq km (210,026 sq mi)
Population (2001 est.): 59,090,000
Capital: Paris
Chief of state: President Jacques Chirac
Head of government: Prime Minister Lionel Jospin

The year 2001 was one of transition and transformation for France. Tensions arose inside the coalition government of Socialist Prime Minister Lionel Jospin as economic growth dipped below 3% for the first time in four years and as the 2002 presidential and parliamentary elections approached. Tension also naturally increased between the expected two main rivals for the presidency—Jospin and Gaullist Pres. Jacques Chirac. The 2001 municipal elections showed left and right evenly matched, and at the personal level the electoral impact of allegations of past corruption surrounding the president appeared to be offset by the downturn in the prime minister's popularity that accompanied a downturn in the economy.

The year marked the passing of two elements of French statehood—the franc, which was scheduled to give way to the euro in January 2002, and military conscription, which was finally phased out in December in favour of a smaller volunteer army. Both changes could be seen in the context of a France far more willing to cooperate—at least with its European neighbours—than it had been under Charles de Gaulle. The integration was obvious in the case of the euro, to be shared with 11 other countries in the European Union (EU), but it was also an element in France's acceptance that defense of its territory was better ensured by a smaller professional army working in close cooperation with allies than by a mass army maintained on its own.

Domestic Affairs. The only formal political contest of the year was in March for control of the country's 36,000 communes. It was essentially a draw. The first round of voting (which historically was the fullest measure of political parties' standing) gave the opposition Rally for the Republic (RPR) Gaullists and their centre-right Union for French Democracy allies 46.9% of the vote and the governing left-wing coalition of the Socialist, Green, and Communist parties 44.9%. The right won control of a majority of big towns but lost two of their historic strongholds, Lyon and Paris, where Bertrand Delanoë (see BIOGRAPHIES) became the first Socialist mayor since 1871. Several government ministers lost their mayoral seats.

Of all the parties, the Communists fared the worst. To compensate and to show their supporters that they could make a difference in the government coalition, Communist leaders subsequently pushed Jospin into toughening the law on layoffs. Laurent Fabius, the powerful finance minister and former prime minister who was in the right wing of the Socialist party, made little secret of his view that if the government raised the cost to companies of dismissing workers, then the companies would think twice about hiring.

Scandal, as usual in France, provided much of the year's political theatre. In March Chirac rejected a summons from a magistrate investigating allegations that contractors for the city of Paris had "kicked back" a portion of their proceeds into the coffers of the governing RPR party. The magistrate, Eric Halphen, said he had plausible evidence that Chirac had been involved with the kickbacks while he was mayor of Paris from 1977 to 1995. In rejecting the summons, Chirac relied on a recent Constitutional Court ruling that sitting presidents were immune from "ordinary" judicial action. The president gained further time when on September 4 senior judges took Halphen off the kickbacks case, which he had been investigating for seven years. The dossier was passed to a magistrate who earlier in the year had been given the job of investigating the origin of F 2.4 million (F 1 = about $0.14) that Chirac had spent on holiday travel for himself, his family, and his entourage in 1992–95. The president said the money came not from any kickbacks but rather from secret legal funds that as prime minister in 1986–88 he had controlled.

The left suffered its own public embarrassment, one that stemmed from the trial of Roland Dumas, the Socialist former foreign minister and president of

Roland Dumas, a former French foreign minister, arrives for his trial on corruption charges at a court in Paris on February 5.

the Constitutional Court. Dumas, his mistress, Christine Deviers-Joncour, and five others were charged with having misused the funds of Elf Aquitaine in 1989–93. The trial started on January 22 but was adjourned on the dramatic news that Alfred Sirven, one of those who had been charged in absentia, had been arrested in the Philippines. When the trial resumed, Sirven, once a senior Elf employee, proved a disappointment to the press by refusing to testify; he claimed the whole process should have been restarted for him. For his silence Sirven was given the heaviest sentence—four years' imprisonment and a fine of F 2 million. Dumas received a 30-month jail term, of which 24 months was suspended, and a fine of F 1 million.

Of concern to all sides in French politics was the unsettled situation of Corsica, despite Jospin's moves to neutralize nationalist sentiment on the island by giving it more autonomy. The National Assembly in Paris voted to give Corsicans the right to amend tax, budget, environment, and tourist laws on an experimental basis. This amending right would be enshrined in the French constitution after the 2002 elections and would enter into force in 2004 if there was also an end to violence. The difficulty of meeting this precondition was brutally underlined, however, by continuing acts of violence, notably the assassination on August 17 of François Santoni, a Corsican nationalist leader. The suspects were other nationalists whom Santoni had accused of having Mafia connections. As a result, Jospin faced further criticism that he was playing into the hands of those who would never give up violence.

The Economy. After a buoyant start to the year, the government found itself steadily scaling back its growth estimates for 2001, from 3.3% to 2.3%. This still left France one of the fastest-growing European countries but meant that the government found itself with a rising budget deficit for the first time since 1993. Unemployment also was rising again as more companies, including Danone, Marks and Spencer, Moulinex, Alcatel, and Philips, announced layoffs.

The government moved not only to make layoffs more difficult but also to extend youth-employment programs, made all the more necessary by the ending of military conscription. The funding of these programs, as well as of the incentives accompanying the lowering of the standard workweek in France to 35 hours, became more difficult within the budgetary constraints of Euro-

pean monetary union. The government dragged its feet on structural economic reform of the pension system and energy markets. At the EU summit in Stockholm in March, Jospin led the successful opposition to the European Commission's plan to accelerate liberalization of the gas and electricity sectors.

Antinuclear militants march toward the railway station of Mezidon-Canon in northeastern France on October 21 to protest the resumption of the transport of nuclear waste by rail from Germany.

Foreign Policy. In common with most EU states, France complained about the "unilateral" approach to foreign policy of U.S. Pres. George W. Bush's administration and its rejection of international arms and pollution-control treaties. Indeed, France was probably the most outspoken EU critic of Bush's rejection of the Kyoto climate-change protocol and of his plan to develop a "national missile defense" (NMD). As the U.S. made clear that whatever the objections of others, it would press ahead to build NMD, designed to protect the U.S. against missile threats from so-called rogue states, Paris moderated its criticism somewhat. In September Chirac was the first foreign head of state to meet with Bush after the terrorist attacks in the U.S. and the first to survey the devastation in New York City. Chirac pledged French solidarity with the U.S. in support of an international coalition against terrorism.

Within the EU, France made no progress toward restoring its former

close relationship with Germany, despite a special meeting in January between Chirac and German Chancellor Gerhard Schröder. The meeting was designed to patch up their rift over EU reform at the December 2000 summit in Nice, France. Jospin subsequently came up with his vision of EU reform, which, in common

with Chirac, favoured a strengthening of the intergovernmental Council of Ministers as distinct from supranational institutions such as the European Parliament preferred by Germany.

The year showed that some French were as resistant as ever to various aspects of economic globalization, despite—or perhaps because of—the fact that the country was one of the most successful in exporting its goods, services, and style around the world. In January Yahoo! said it would obey a landmark ruling by a French court on Internet access and would block French users' access to Web sites selling Nazi memorabilia banned by French law. In mid-March the first case of foot-and-mouth disease in continental Europe was recorded near Paris. An EU ban on French exports was immediately imposed, but it was lifted in April. The cause of the outbreak was almost certainly imports from the U.K., where the disease raged all year. (*See* AGRICULTURE: *Special Report.*) Nonetheless, radical farm groups were more excited by genetically modified organisms developed by multinational food companies, many of them American. The protesters ripped up plants in experimental plots.

The antiglobalization movement got some backing from the prime minister. Having had the luxury of not attending the riot-torn G-8 summit in Genoa, Italy, in July, Jospin surprised many by expressing sympathy for the antiglobalization protesters there. He recalled that France had always sought to instill order into trade and monetary policy, rather than leaving everything to the free market. Earlier in the year, Jospin admitted that he had retained far-left Trotskyist connections into the 1970s, but his support for taxing international capital flows seemed more a political ploy designed to rally the left for the 2002 elections.　　(DAVID BUCHAN)

GABON

Area: 267,667 sq km (103,347 sq mi)
Population (2001 est.): 1,221,000
Capital: Libreville
Chief of state: President Omar Bongo
Head of government: Prime Minister Jean-François Ntoutoume-Emane

Amid a rising wave of urban crime, on March 1, 2001, Gabon's minister of the interior suspended the import and sale of firearms. Prime Minister Jean-François Ntoutoume-Emane addressed the National Assembly on May 16 to answer deputies' concerns about public safety. Despite the creation during the year of a special crime squad, the incidents of armed robbery and other violent crimes continued to escalate.

On May 8 unemployed workers staged a peaceful demonstration in the nation's commercial capital, Port-Gentil. Although a special commission was established to hear their grievances, it apparently made little impact, because on June 20 police had to use tear gas to disperse youths who rioted. The authorities regained control on the next day, and it was announced that meetings between the unemployed and a government official would soon take place. In legislative elections held on December 9 and 23, the ruling Gabonese Democratic Party won 84 of the 120

seats in the legislature. In December there was also an outbreak of Ebola fever, which killed at least 11 persons.

Relations between Benin and Gabon cooled when the former accused Gabonese farmers of using thousands of underage Benin nationals in conditions of virtual slavery. Despite Gabon's adoption on June 16 of a new law imposing severe penalties on those exploiting children under age 16 as forced labour, the smuggling of children into the country appeared to continue unabated.　　(NANCY ELLEN LAWLER)

GAMBIA, THE

Area: 10,689 sq km (4,127 sq mi)
Population (2001 est.): 1,411,000
Capital: Banjul
Head of state and government: President Col. Yahya Jammeh

The Gambian government spent much of the first half of 2001 dealing with calls for the scrapping of Decree 89, which banned the former main parties—including Sir Dawda Jawara's People's Progressive Party, which Pres. Col. Yahya Jammeh had ousted from power in 1994—from participating in elections. Opposition parties also called for the repeal of the decrees muzzling the press and civil society. On July 22 President Jammeh finally lifted the restrictive Decree 89.

Former president Jawara, who was living in exile in London, was ineligible to stand for election because he was older than 65. Some of the opposition parties formed a coalition in August and chose a popular lawyer, Ousainou Darboe of the United Democratic Party, as their presidential candidate. Earlier in the year Darboe had been charged with murder in an attempt to disqualify him from running. In the election held on October 18, Jammeh captured 53% of the vote, compared with Darboe's 32%. Though the opposition claimed that a number of irregularities had occurred, including the registration of foreign nationals from Casamance, it accepted the election results, which was a significant victory for Jammeh, whose win in the 1996 election had been tainted by allegations of fraud. Legislative elections were planned for January 2002.

Jammeh had earlier rejected the findings of a commission of inquiry, led by a senior judge, into the fatal shooting in April 2000 of 14 demonstrators. Brushing aside the commission's criticisms of the interior minister and the police intelligence unit, the government pushed legislation through the National Assembly to indemnify those involved in the shooting.　　(CHRISTOPHER SAUNDERS)

GEORGIA

Area: 69,700 sq km (26,911 sq mi)
Population (2001 est.): 4,989,000
Capital: T'bilisi
Head of state and government: President Eduard Shevardnadze, assisted by Secretary of State Giorgi Arsenishvili

Reformist members of the majority Citizens' Union of Georgia (SMK) criticized Pres. Eduard Shevardnadze repeatedly during the first half of the year for failing to crack down on corruption within the government. In late August, after Shevardnadze rejected a bill drafted by Justice Minister Mikhail Saakashvili that would have required ministers to prove that their wealth was acquired legally, Parliament Chairman Zurab Zhvania warned Shevardnadze that the country was on the verge of a major crisis and demanded the dismissal of allegedly corrupt police and security officials. The SMK Parliament faction failed to support Zhvania's demand, however, and the faction collapsed, leaving Parliament without a majority.

On October 30 thousands of T'bilisi residents took to the streets to protest a raid by security officials on the TV station Rustavi-2. At an emergency Parliament session on November 1, Shevardnadze offered to step down if deputies demanded the resignation of Interior Minister Kakha Targamadze and Prosecutor General Gia Meparishvili, but after both they and Zhvania quit, Shevardnadze announced that he would not resign. Shevardnadze then fired the entire government, but he included most outgoing ministers in the new government. On November 10 Parliament elected as its new speaker the Foreign Relations Committee chair, Nino Burdzhanadze, and on December 21 it finally approved Avtandil Djorbenadze as minister of state.

Gross domestic product growth during the first half of the year amounted to 5.2%, but during the first seven months industrial production fell by 2.6% compared with 2000. In late October a large tax-revenue shortfall necessitated slashing projected budget spending by 15%.

In early October several hundred armed men advanced into the Kodori gorge on the territory of the unrecognized Republic of Abkhazia, but they retreated after two weeks of sporadic fighting with Abkhaz forces. During the incident more than 100 of the interlopers were killed, a helicopter belonging to the UN Observer Mission was shot down with the loss of nine lives, and unidentified aircraft bombed remote Georgian villages but inflicted no injuries. The alleged participation of Chechen fighters in that raid further soured the strained relations between Russia and Georgia, as did Moscow's failure to comply with its commitment to withdraw all personnel from its military base in Gudauta, Abkhazia, by July 1 and Russian air raids in October and November on uninhabited border areas.

On November 18 Lyudvig Chibirov failed to win reelection as president of the unrecognized Republic of South Ossetia. Moscow-based businessman Eduard Kokoyev was elected in a runoff ballot on December 6.

(ELIZABETH FULLER)

GERMANY

Area: 357,021 sq km (137,847 sq mi)
Population (2001 est.): 82,386,000
Capital: Berlin; some ministries remain in Bonn
Chief of state: President Johannes Rau
Head of government: Chancellor Gerhard Schröder

For Germany, 2001 was marked by increased involvement in world affairs but a slowdown in the pace of economic growth and reform. As the country's Social Democratic government entered the second half of its four-year term, Chancellor Gerhard Schröder lost the lustre that he had acquired as a market reformer. In some respects the year was more remarkable for what did not hap-

pen than for what Germany accomplished in its economic-reform process. The government passed an overhaul of the pension system but shied away from further reforms in an apparent effort to preserve the support of Germany's powerful trade unions for the 2002 election. Partly as a result, Germany's became the slowest-growing economy in Europe and job creation diminished, taking Schröder's personal approval ratings down with it. At the same time, the chancellor gained in stature as a statesman as Germany embarked on a more active and assertive foreign policy course after more than half a century of restraint. Throughout the year Europe's most populous nation assumed a greater leadership role in European affairs and grew more active in other international trouble spots such as Macedonia and the Middle East. In the wake of the terrorist attacks in the United States in September, Germany said it would support the American response with both diplomatic and military means if necessary. In the past the country had shirked military intervention, especially outside Europe.

Domestic Politics. An issue inherited from the previous year dominated the early days of 2001; bovine spongiform encephalopathy (BSE, or "mad cow" disease), an animal infection that could kill humans, occupied public and political attention. Millions of Germans stopped eating beef, which helped bring Europe's beef market to the brink of collapse. Mad cow disease also claimed political victims in Germany when in January the country's health and agriculture ministers stepped down amid accusations of having mishandled the crisis. BSE faded from the public limelight when another

animal illness, foot-and-mouth disease, spread across Europe. The disease did not appear in Germany, but the meat crisis created an adverse political atmosphere as Chancellor Schröder's government, just past its midterm mark, acquired an aura of instability. (*See* AGRICULTURE AND FISHERIES: *Special Report.*)

Only a day before the cabinet resignations over mad cow disease, Schröder had been obliged to make a public statement in support of Foreign Minister Joschka Fischer, a member of the Green Party who was under fire for his militant past. A series of photographs published in the newsmagazine *Stern* in January showed Fischer using violence against a police officer during a political protest in the early 1970s. Fischer appeared before a special question period in the parliament and apologized for his actions. The affair lingered for weeks, even though Fischer was one of Germany's most popular politicians. Fischer was subsequently forced to testify in the terrorist trial of a former friend, and his court appearance then prompted a perjury probe to investigate whether he had given false testimony in the trial. The inquiry was eventually dropped, and the revelations about Fischer's past did not cloud his first meetings in Washington, D.C., in February with the new U.S. administration.

The government's midterm wobbles did not affect two key regional elections in Baden-Württemberg and Rhineland-Palatinate in March. Both of these prosperous regions in the western part of the country reelected their incumbent governments, run respectively by the conservative Christian Democratic Union

German Foreign Minister Joschka Fischer (left) and Chancellor Gerhard Schröder in the Bundestag in August. Earlier in the year the chancellor had defended Fischer when his colourful past came under intense public scrutiny.

AP/Wide World Photos

German army troops guard a convoy on August 28 in Baumholder, Ger., as part of their training for the NATO mission in Macedonia known as Operation Essential Harvest.

(CDU) and Chancellor Schröder's centre-left Social Democratic Party (SPD).

A principal reason for the government's strength despite political mismanagement, scandals, and a worsening economic outlook was the persistent weakness of the Christian Democratic Union–Christian Social Union (CSU) opposition. Throughout 2001, as for most of the year before, the CDU-CSU was haunted by the fallout of a major financing scandal that broke in late 1999 and led to the fall from grace of former chancellor Helmut Kohl, once one of Europe's most respected elder statesmen. In the spring Kohl agreed to pay a fine that closed the criminal case against him. It ended an important chapter in the affair, but the former leader's reputation and the party's fortunes did not fully recover.

The new postscandal party leadership spent much of 2001 involved in political infighting, which was dominated by the question of who would be the candidate to challenge Schröder in the 2002 election. The most prominent combatants were CDU chair Angela Merkel, a Protestant, childless, once-divorced woman from the former East Germany, and Edmund Stoiber, the Catholic, ultraconservative CSU chief and prime minister of Bavaria. Another competitor was Friedrich Merz, the CDU-CSU floor leader in the Bundestag (lower house of parliament) who clashed with Merkel over political strategy and claimed his own right to run for chancellor.

The Christian Democrats scored only one political victory, when they ousted the long-standing SPD government in the city-state of Hamburg in a September election. The real winner, however, was Ronald Schill, a former judge who campaigned on a law-and-order platform and won almost 20% of the vote for his own—newly founded—party. Otherwise, the strife within the opposition yielded Schröder several political victories, including the passage of his pension package and parliamentary approval for military participation in the autumn mission of NATO in Macedonia.

The federal government enacted several minor reforms in 2001. They included a new recycling law and a measure that improved the legal standing for same-sex couples, which resulted in a series of so-called gay marriages. Berlin also moved to attract talented foreign workers, proposing legislation that would allow it for the first time to compete with the U.S., Canada, and other industrialized nations for highly skilled professionals, scientists, and technicians from the less-developed world. Faced with a growing shortage of skilled labour and an aging workforce, Germany decided to move toward a radical break with past immigration policies. The new measures included the creation of the country's first-ever immigration law and the granting of permanent immigration status for qualified foreigners. Passage of the law was delayed past year's end, however, by a debate about a stricter security regime, notably for foreigners in Germany, after the terrorist attacks in the U.S.

Germany closed a chapter in the unending struggle with its own history. In May a fund created by several thousand large and small German companies said it would begin making payments to compensate slave labourers who worked in German factories under the Nazi regime. The announcement came after the companies felt they had sufficient protection against future lawsuits, especially from the U.S. Two years of haggling, much of it about legal details, had left many of the hopeful beneficiaries bitter and dissatisfied with what was originally intended to be a gesture of German goodwill and generosity.

The Economy. One of Germany's most pressing economic problems, a makeover of its overburdened 120-year-old pension system, was finally addressed in 2001. In May the parliament reformed the retirement law in an effort to deflect the demographic time bomb ticking in the country's pay-as-you-go pension scheme, where ever-fewer workers supported a rapidly rising number of pensioners. After years of bipartisan bickering and a last-minute protest by the trade unions, Germany introduced a dramatic change in its retirement regime. Under the new law the government would for the first time support private provisions while at the same time cutting state pension benefits. Economists and the business community welcomed the reform as an important step toward addressing the problems of Germany's graying population, stretched public finances, and high labour costs, but they warned that the reform had been so diluted by political compromise that it would not provide lasting relief for the state system. The Schröder government also abolished a restriction, dating from the time of Adolf Hitler, on retail store discounts and, under pressure from the conservative opposition, provided tax relief for small and medium-sized enterprises that tax reforms in 2000 had neglected.

Another item on Schröder's reform agenda gained prominence because it did not materialize—a renovation of the labour market. Burdened with rigid regulations and high labour costs, German companies were reluctant to hire new workers. As a result, few new jobs were being created, and Germany's unemployment rate was among the highest in Europe. The stubbornly high number of jobless presented a growing political problem for Schröder because he had explicitly tied his political future to job creation. Yet the government did little to make hiring easier or cheaper for businesses; in several respects it made it harder. Soon after entering office Schröder undid the reform efforts of the previous government by boosting sick pay and worker protection against layoffs. Later he imposed restrictions on employers trying to hire workers on fixed-term contracts. In 2001 he expanded labour's role in management and instituted a right to part-time work.

The new regulations were an apparent effort by Schröder to reconcile labour unions with pension reform and to court the traditionalist left wing of his SPD. His jockeying alienated German industry, however—especially small companies, which complained that the new labour laws added red tape and cost. The move dealt a major blow to Schröder's image as a market reformer and threatened one of his biggest political assets—the hard-won support of Germany's business community, which traditionally sided with the Christian Democrats or the small, pro-market Free Democrats. Another blow to Schröder's reform credentials came from his reluctance to reform Germany's expensive and inefficient health care system despite continually rising contributions to public health insurance.

The unsolved structural problems in the German economy became more visible with the economic slump that ended nearly a decade of unprecedented growth and productivity gains across the industrialized world. Heavily dependent on exports, Germany was hit hard by the slowdown, especially that in the U.S., one of its most important markets. The September terrorist attacks in the U.S. put additional strain on the world's third largest economy.

The outlook steadily worsened throughout 2001. The government and economists were forced into several downward adjustments of their growth forecasts for the year. By the fall Germany—already the slowest-growing economy in Europe—began to fear a recession. At the same time, inflation hit an eight-year high and unemployment continued to rise. In March Schröder promised to push the number of jobless to under three million Germans. One month later he adjusted that pledge to under 3.5 million. By the autumn that goal also appeared impossible to reach, and the chancellor merely said there would be

fewer unemployed Germans than when he took office in 1998.

Schröder's perceived inaction yielded him lower approval ratings and negative newspaper headlines. "Do something, Chancellor," said *Bild*, Germany's leading tabloid, in a large summer headline. "For the first time in Schröder's term, voters feel like they're back in the paralyzing stagnation of the Kohl era," echoed the news magazine *Der Spiegel* in September. Schröder responded to the growing pressure by announcing a "calm hand" policy, free of short-term activism, fresh debt, and costly economic stimuli.

With his image as a reformer stained, Schröder was certain to face a tougher-than-hoped-for leap into the election year of 2002. Throughout 2001 he repeated well-worn and ambiguous campaign slogans, such as "Innovation and justice" and "Security in change." It was uncertain whether he could continue to walk a tightrope between needed reforms and reassurance of his left-leaning core clientele. The months to come also held another challenge for which Germany meticulously planned throughout 2001—the introduction of the euro, Europe's common currency, as legal tender in January 2002.

Foreign Relations. The government's weakening domestic performance was offset by Schröder's growing standing as a statesman in a newly self-confident Germany that took greater responsibility in world affairs than it had in decades past. Following the terrorist attacks in the United States in September, Schröder jumped ahead even of the U.S. in defining what had happened as a "conflict of cultures" and a "declaration of war on the free world." He announced an international coalition against terror and promised "the unlimited, I stress, the unlimited solidarity of Germany." That promise put a strain on the pacifist Greens, the junior member of Schröder's governing coalition, which had long opposed the use of military force. Leading Greens said they supported the military strikes against Afghanistan that began in October, but many more warned against military "adventures" and restrictions on civil liberties once domestic security was tightened to prevent terrorist activity on German soil. Germany had served as an operational base for several of the suspects in the raids on the U.S.

Tensions within the government grew so strong that in November, Schröder called a confidence vote in the parliament. He won the vote along with the

freedom to assist as he saw fit the international coalition against terror. The terrorist attacks effectively ended the transatlantic tensions that had been simmering for months and came to the fore in the early months of the administration of George W. Bush. Like other Europeans, Germans were dismayed by the Americans' insistence on building a missile defense shield, the U.S. rejection of an international treaty against global warming, and other policies perceived as selfish and unilateralist. Even before the terrorist strikes, the German government had grown more active in international affairs. A long list of foreign visitors went to Berlin, and unlike in previous years, they went not only for money but also for German mediation, support, and political intervention. Schröder nurtured his close relations with Russian Pres.Vladimir Putin. Early in the year he celebrated Orthodox Christmas with the Russian leader, and he was the first to lobby him face-to-face for support in the battle against international terrorism.

Meanwhile, Foreign Minister Fischer became an active interlocutor in the struggling Middle East peace process. The government also scored a success when in August the parliament approved the participation of German troops in NATO's Macedonia mission. An hour after the vote, the first soldiers left their air base in Bavaria for Macedonia, and a few weeks later Germany took command of the NATO mission. The country's readiness to assume leadership in the Balkan conflict was another sign of its effort to expand its international responsibilities, both military and diplomatic.

Schröder also stepped up his involvement in the process of European integration. In April he presented a blueprint for the future of Europe that sketched out a restructuring of the European Union's (EU) governing institutions to advance political unity. He proposed to widen the executive role of the European Commission, strengthen the European Parliament by giving it full control over the EU finances—including the large agriculture budget—and make the secretive Council of Ministers more transparent. The ideas also served Germany's self-interest because they preserved the powers of its federal states and duplicated the structure of Germany's two-house parliament on a European level. Partly as a result, the German proposals met with a cool response from France and the U.K.

(CECILIE ROHWEDDER)

Relatives of victims killed in a stampede at a soccer match on May 9 in Accra, Ghana, observe a moment of silence at a memorial service four days after the incident.

AP/Wide World Photos

GHANA

Area: 238,533 sq km (92,098 sq mi)
Population (2001 est.): 19,894,000
Capital: Accra
Head of state and government: Presidents Jerry John Rawlings and, from January 7, John Kofi Agyekum Kufuor

For Ghana 2001 began with the first peaceful transfer of power between democratically elected governments in the country's 44-year history. On January 7 John Kofi Agyekum Kufuor (*see* BIOGRAPHIES) commenced his first term as president. His New Patriotic Party also gained a majority in Parliament.

Kufuor's government immediately turned its attention to Ghana's economy, which in 2000 had struggled with high unemployment, inflation, and a major devaluation of the cedi, the national currency. Soon after his installation, Kufuor declared that the state of the economy was worse than expected. In spite of criticism from many Ghanaians, he announced that Ghana would join the Heavily Indebted Poor Countries program for debt relief, and he increased prices of petroleum and utilities. Kufuor's reforms had some success. The cedi stabilized, and investment in the country increased. Kufuor also instituted political reforms, setting up a National Reconciliation Committee to look into past corruption and abuses of power.

Tragedy struck during a May 9 soccer match in Accra. Accra's Hearts of Oak was beating its longtime rival, Kumasi's Asante Kotoko, 2–1 when Kotoko fans began throwing bottles and chairs onto the field. Police fired tear gas into the crowd, and a rush to the stadium's locked gates resulted. In the ensuing confusion and stampede, around 130 people died and dozens more were injured. It was the worst sporting disaster in Africa's history. President Kufuor canceled his engagements, declared a three-day period of national mourning, and announced a government investigation into the incident.

(AMY SETTERGREN)

GREECE

Area: 131,957 sq km (50,949 sq mi)
Population (2001 est.): 10,975,000
Capital: Athens
Chief of state: President Konstantinos Stephanopoulos
Head of government: Prime Minister Konstantinos Simitis

On April 6, 2001, the Greek Parliament adopted a thorough constitutional revision, which changed 78 articles of the country's basic law. Many amendments were passed jointly by the two biggest political parties, the ruling Panhellenic Socialist Movement (Pasok) and the centre-right New Democracy (ND). Changes to the constitution included better protection of citizens' private data, the constitutional guarantee of alternative service for conscientious objectors, and the abolition of the death penalty in times of peace. Another key amendment stipulated that changes to the electoral legislation would affect the next elections only if passed by a two-thirds majority. Previously, the ruling party had often changed the election law in order to bolster its majority or limit its defeat in upcoming elections. Parliament, however, failed to separate state and church completely and to change the provision that automatically triggered early parliamentary elections in the event that Parliament failed to elect a new head of state in three rounds of voting.

Another of the government's key projects, a reform of the pension system, triggered the strongest antigovernment protests in years. In particular, plans to raise the retirement age and reduce pensions were rejected by trade unions, opposition parties, and leading Pasok members. In the midst of a general strike on April 26 and massive antigovernment demonstrations on May 1, Prime Minister Konstantinos ("Kostas") Simitis announced that a dialogue "on everything and without preconditions" with relevant social groups would be initiated, but the reform was put on hold.

On October 13–15 Pasok held its sixth congress. Simitis was reelected Pasok president, and Environment and Public Works Minister Konstantinos Laliotis was named party secretary.

Simitis reshuffled his government extensively on October 23; he promoted so-called reformers at the expense of "traditionalists." Apostolos Tsochatzopoulos was moved from the Defense Ministry to the Development Ministry. He was succeeded by Yiannos Papantoniou, who was replaced as finance and economy minister by Nikolaos Christodoulakis, previously the development minister. Vasso Papandreou was moved from the Interior Ministry to the Environment and Public Works Ministry; Konstantinos Skandalidis, Pasok secretary until the congress, became interior minister. Foreign Minister Georgios Papandreou and Public

Order Minister Michalis Chrysochoidis retained their portfolios.

The main opposition ND held its regular congress on March 30–April 1. The congress strengthened the position of party leader Konstantinos ("Kostas") Karamanlis and welcomed the return of senior politicians who had left the party following disagreement with Karamanlis.

On March 6 Athens Mayor Dimitris Avramopoulos, who had left the ND the previous year, announced the establishment of a new political party, the Movement of Free Citizens (KEP). Although he maintained that the KEP was open for cooperation with other political forces, Avramopoulos ruled out any alliance with other parties in the next parliamentary elections, due by 2004.

The government's decision to remove any reference to religious affiliation from personal identity documents continued to strain relations between the government and the Greek Orthodox Church. The church collected more than three million signatures, which Archbishop of Athens and All Greece Christodoulos submitted to Pres. Konstantinos ("Kostis") Stephanopoulos on August 29. The president, however, rejected for constitutional reasons the church leader's request for a referendum on the issue.

On May 4–5 Pope John Paul II visited Greece. Despite protests by some Orthodox clerics and believers, the first visit by a pontiff since the Schism of 1054 was widely considered a success.

As the crisis in Macedonia unfolded, Greece made clear its support of the country's integrity, calling for a political settlement. Greece also contributed some 400 troops to the "Operation Essential Harvest." Though the dispute over Macedonia's name remained unsettled, UN-mediated talks continued in 2001. Relations with other neighbours remained largely unchanged, although there was further atmospheric improvement in relations with Turkey, witnessed by the signing of the first Greek-Turkish city partnership, by the government's support for plans to jointly host Euro 2008, the European association football (soccer) championships, and by the signing of a landmark treaty allowing Greece to return illegal immigrants to Turkey.

Preparations for the 2004 Olympic Games in Athens continued at a slow pace. International Olympic Committee representatives visited Greece repeatedly and urged Greek officials to speed up preparations. On March 27 the new Athens International Airport, one of the largest infrastructure projects in Greece in recent years, started operations. No solution was found for Olympic Airways, Greece's ailing national carrier. Deadlines for a privatization tender were extended repeatedly, but no buyer was identified. Meanwhile, Olympic Airways staff staged several strikes against the airline's privatization and inherent restructuring. Two private Greek airlines, Cronus Airlines and Aegean Airlines, announced their merger in March.

The Greek economy continued to grow. In the first half of 2001, gross domestic product grew by 4.9% over the same period in 2000; investments and exports also increased. Year-on-year inflation stood at 3.8% in August. The Athens Stock Exchange continued its downward slide, however; by the end of September, the index had lost two-thirds of its value compared with its all-time high in 1999.

On February 4 composer Iannis Xenakis died in Paris. (*See* OBITUARIES.)

(STEFAN KRAUSE)

GRENADA

Area: 344 sq km (133 sq mi)
Population (2001 est.): 102,000
Capital: Saint George's
Chief of state: Queen Elizabeth II, represented by Governor-General Daniel Williams
Head of government: Prime Minister Keith Mitchell

Grenada was as active as any other Caribbean state against undesirable offshore banks in 2001, closing down 17 in one day in March. They were all linked to the First International Bank of Grenada, which collapsed in October 2000, taking $150 million worth of mainly American depositors' money along with it. A U.S. Senate committee had described First International as "one of the most notorious rogue banks" in the Caribbean offshore industry. In June another six banks had their licenses to operate canceled.

Despite its actions against offshore banks, Grenada was added in September to the list of countries deemed by the Paris-based Financial Action Task Force (FATF) to have failed in cooperating with international efforts to stop money laundering. The FATF described Grenada's system for dealing with money laundering as having "serious deficiencies." The task force pointed out that regulators in Grenada did not have adequate access to customer account information and lacked the authority to cooperate with overseas counterparts. The government reacted angrily, calling the FATF decision "shocking."

Also in September Grenada's UN ambassador, Lamuel Stanislaus, urged the UN to restore Taiwan's membership in the world body, which had been revoked in 1971. In common with other small Caribbean countries, Grenada was a recipient of generous Taiwanese aid.

(DAVID RENWICK)

GUATEMALA

Area: 108,889 sq km (42,042 sq mi)
Population (2001 est.): 11,687,000
Capital: Guatemala City
Head of state and government: President Alfonso Portillo Cabrera

Scandals eroded support for the government of Alfonso Portillo Cabrera during 2001, beginning with the continuing legislative investigation known as "Guategate." The governing Guatemalan Republican Front sought to prevent the trial of 24 indicted members of its congressional delegation, including President of the Congress Efraín Rios Montt. In April a court exonerated Rios Montt, but controversy continued along with other charges of government corruption, financial mismanagement, and conflict of interest. Portillo's frequent foreign journeys and the high crime rate were further sources of criticism, and rumours spread of an impending coup d'état.

On the positive side, despite repeated death threats to judges and witnesses, a Guatemalan court on June 8 convicted and sentenced three military officers to 30 years in prison for the 1998 murder of human rights advocate Bishop Juan Gerardi Conedera. The murder on May 5, 2001, of a former investigator for Gerardi, Barbara Ann Ford, an American nun who had worked in Guatemala for two decades to promote social justice, prompted new outcries against human rights violations.

Declining coffee prices and high oil prices hurt the Guatemalan economy during the year, although increased banana exports helped offset lower banana prices. On March 15 Guatemala began a limited free-trade agreement with Mexico and other Central American states, but it excluded Guatemalan coffee and sugar. Free circulation of the dollar and other hard currencies began on May 1 in a measure designed to improve Guatemala's trading position. On August 1 the sales tax rose from 10% to 12%, accompanied by social improvements mandated by the 1996 peace accord, including a higher minimum wage and regulations to bring Guatemala into compliance with international labour standards. Mass protests resulted as opponents charged that these measures increased inflation and discouraged investment. Most employers ignored the minimum-wage increase. Many measures agreed to in the peace accord had yet to be implemented. The UN's 2001 Human Development Index, based on life expectancy, educational attainment, and per capita GDP, ranked Guatemala lower than any other country in the Americas except Haiti. (RALPH LEE WOODWARD, JR.)

GUINEA

Area: 245,857 sq km (94,926 sq mi)
Population (2001 est.): 7,614,000
Capital: Conakry
Head of state and government: President Gen. Lansana Conté, assisted by Prime Minister Lamine Sidimé

The conflicts in neighbouring Liberia and Sierra Leone, which had spilled over into Guinea at the end of 2000, led to a refugee problem in Guinea in 2001. In February the governments of Liberia and Sierra Leone agreed to cooperate with the UN in establishing safe corridors for any refugees who wished to return home. The various upheavals also led to the displacement of about 70,000 Guineans. Pres. Gen. Lansana Conté appealed for increased international aid to all the victims of the conflicts. The UN High Commissioner for Refugees twice suspended all deliveries of food as a result of the fighting. By May 27 the UN had nevertheless managed to complete

the evacuation of 57,000 refugees from the Guinean border villages around an area in the southeast known as Parrot's Beak before closing down its operations there. Under pressure from other West African countries, defense and security ministers from Guinea, Liberia, and Sierra Leone met on September 26–28 in Monrovia, Liberia, to attempt to resolve the problems.

Political tensions mounted as President Conté's ruling party launched efforts to alter the constitution to enable a president to serve more than two terms. In late July members of three opposition parties flew to Paris in search of French support to discourage Conté's bid for a third term. Longtime opposition leader Alpha Conde, who had been arrested in December 1998 and found guilty of capital crimes at his trial in September 2000, was released from prison on May 18. He took up his seat in the parliament on September 25.

The economy experienced little growth during the year, largely because of the border conflicts. On May 7 the International Monetary Fund under-

wrote a three-year, $82 million aid package designed to finance antipoverty measures and accelerate economic development; on July 24 and 26 the World Bank approved $120 million in credits for education reforms and the alleviation of poverty; and on September 27 the African Development Fund announced that it would loan Guinea nearly $16 million for a new structural-adjustment program.

(NANCY ELLEN LAWLER)

GUINEA-BISSAU

Area: 36,125 sq km (13,948 sq mi)
Population (2001 est.): 1,316,000
Capital: Bissau
Chief of state: President Kumba Ialá (Yalla)
Head of government: Prime Ministers Caetano N'Tchama, Faustino Imbali from March 21, and, from December 8, Alamara Nhassé

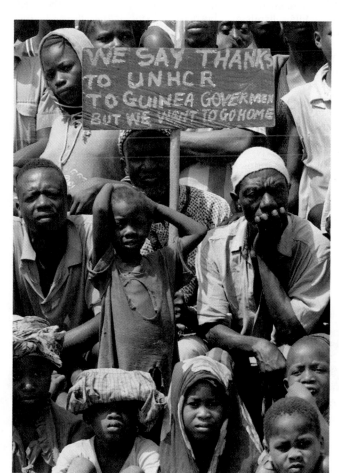

At a camp in southwestern Guinea on February 11, refugees from Sierra Leone and Liberia wait to return home.

AP/Wide World Photos

In January 2001 the coalition between the Guinea-Bissau Resistance–Bah Fatah Movement and the Party for Social Renewal collapsed. A period of uncertainty followed until Pres. Kumba Ialá appointed Faustino Imbali the new prime minister. The new government soon ran into trouble, however, when $15 million disappeared from the treasury, and the opposition called for its resignation.

After inquiries into the matter by Imbali and the National People's Assembly proved fruitless and the arrest of two Ministry of Finance employees by the attorney general's office outraged a parliamentary commission, calls for the government's resignation mounted. On December 8 Interior Minister Alamara Nhassé was appointed the new prime minister.

President Ialá was roundly criticized for suspending the activities of the Ahmadiyya Islamic group and deporting its leaders. He claimed that the Ahmadiyya was destabilizing the country's Muslim community, almost half the population. A Bissau court declared his decision unconstitutional, and both the judiciary and the parliament declared unconstitutional Ialá's dismissal of four Supreme Court judges and its president and the appointment of new ones. In August President Ialá dismissed Attorney General Rui Sanha and replaced him with former prime minister Caetano N'Tchama, who began threatening journalists from a private radio station. Meanwhile, public servants' salaries were not paid. An opposition forum warned that stability was threatened and demanded that municipal elections be held by March 2002. A rumour that Ialá wanted to replace Armed Forces Chief of Staff Verissimo Correia Seabra with Umberto Gomis led some officers to threaten war if Ialá carried out this plan.

(CHRISTOPHER SAUNDERS)

GUYANA

Area: 215,083 sq km (83,044 sq mi)
Population (2001 est.): 776,000
Capital: Georgetown
Chief of state: President Bharrat Jagdeo
Head of government: Prime Minister Sam Hinds

Guyana's ruling People's Progressive Party (PPP)/Civic alliance was returned to office in the general election held on March 19, 2001. The victory gave the alliance's leader, Bharrat Jagdeo, another five-year term as president and head of state. PPP/Civic, which took 209,031 of the 393,709 votes cast, secured 34 of the nation's 65 parliamentary seats. The opposition People's National Congress (PNC)/Reform Party won 164,074 votes and claimed 27 seats.

Sporadic violence and looting followed the announcement of the election results, and a 43-year-old woman lost her life after being shot by an unknown gunman. PNC/Reform filed a motion to prevent Jagdeo from taking office, but this was dismissed by the High Court. In an effort to prevent further violence, Jagdeo and PNC/Reform leader Desmond Hoyte met in April and several times thereafter. They agreed to the formation of six joint committees to deal with contentious issues, including local government reform and the distribution of public land and housing.

Guyana's long-standing border row with Venezuela—an issue both sides had previously relegated to the back burner—suddenly came alive in July when Venezuela's foreign minister visited the disputed Essequibo region and denounced the 1899 treaty that ceded it to Guyana, then a British colony. It was the first visit by a Venezuelan government minister to the border area in almost 20 years. That same month heads of government from Caribbean Community and Common Market countries had reiterated support for Guyana's "sovereignty" and "territorial integrity."

(DAVID RENWICK)

HAITI

Area: 27,700 sq km (10,695 sq mi)
Population (2001 est.): 6,965,000
Capital: Port-au-Prince
Chief of state and government: Presidents René Préval and, from February 7, Jean-Bertrand Aristide, assisted by Prime Ministers Jacques-Édouard Alexis and, from March 2, Jean-Marie Chérestal

The new government of Haitian Pres. Jean-Bertrand Aristide faced several political challenges in 2001. Leaders of 15 political organizations that had boy-

On March 22 police officers stand guard along a street in Buxton Village, near Georgetown, after riots erupted following the announcement of election results in Guyana.

AP/World Wide Photos

A Haitian man stands in an alley between tin shacks in Port-au-Prince. Haiti, with a gross national income per capita of $480, remained one of the world's poorest countries in 2001.

cotted the November 2000 presidential election formed an alliance known as Convergence Démocratique and challenged his legitimacy by establishing an alternative national unity government headed by educator Gérard Gourgue as provisional president. Most of these organizations were quite small and had a very limited constituency within the country. Nevertheless, their leaders were articulate enough to gather broad international backing. The roots of the confrontation ran to the May 2000 legislative elections, when Aristide's Lavalas Family party swept more than 80% of about 7,000 elected posts but failed to hold a runoff for 10 disputed Senate seats. The U.S. and international financial organizations withheld more than $500 million in scheduled foreign aid and pressured Aristide and his prime minister, Jean-Marie Chérestal, to negotiate with the opposition. In July both sides agreed to hold new elections, but they had not set a date for them by year's end.

Meanwhile, on December 17, Haitian commandos stormed the presidential palace in an attempted coup, but they were subdued after battling the police for several hours.

The economy continued to decline in 2001. The World Bank listed Haiti's gross national income per capita as $480. About 80% of the rural Haitian population lived below the poverty line. The cost of living rose sharply with the price of gasoline, going up by 40%. The gourde, the local currency, barely recovered after losing half of its value,

which made staples such as rice and beans much more expensive to the average Haitian. Macroeconomic and structural reforms successfully initiated since 1994 stagnated in 2001. Poor state management of Haiti's ports and road network and public utilities such as electricity, water, and telephones continued to discourage new private investment and limit employment opportunities. Earlier privatization efforts did not succeed because of a lack of political will to carry them out.

(JEAN-CLAUDE GARCIA-ZAMOR)

HONDURAS

Area: 112,492 sq km (43,433 sq mi)
Population (2000 est.): 6,490,000
Capital: Tegucigalpa
Head of state and government: President Carlos Roberto Flores Facussé

The national elections held on Nov. 25, 2001, were the sixth since 1981, marking an unprecedented two decades of democracy in Honduras. The presidential election was won by Ricardo Maduro of the National Party. The new government was scheduled to take office in January 2002. The campaign was marred by mutual accusations by the Liberal and National parties re-

garding the eligibility of front-running presidential aspirants. Conflict began in October 2000 when the National Elections Tribunal, dominated by the incumbent Liberals, claimed that Maduro was not a native Honduran and thus was ineligible to run for president. The dispute was finally resolved on Feb. 23, 2001, when the Congress reinterpreted the constitutional requirements for citizenship and allowed Maduro to run.

With reconstruction from the massive damage caused in October 1998 by Hurricane Mitch still ongoing in 2001, Honduras suffered an extensive drought that the UN World Food Programme called the worst natural disaster to hit Central America since Mitch. More than 316,000 people were severely affected, and some 128,000 were to receive food aid. The drought also caused severe water shortages in the capital.

Internationally several events were important. On February 21 the archbishop of Tegucigalpa, Oscar Rodríguez Maradiaga, became a cardinal. Rodríguez was the first Honduran, and only the third Central American, appointed to the Sacred College of Cardinals. On March 15 the free-trade agreement signed with Mexico, Guatemala, and El Salvador in 2000 took effect. In May the U.S. government renewed the Temporary Protected Status of 105,000 Hondurans living in the U.S. for an additional year (until July 2002) as part of continued U.S. efforts to help Honduras recover from the economic effects of Hurricane Mitch. Finally, the border disputes and economic sanctions that arose between Honduras and Nicaragua in 2000 continued during 2001.

(MICHELLE M. TAYLOR-ROBINSON)

HUNGARY

Area: 93,030 sq km (35,919 sq mi)
Population (2001 est.): 10,190,000
Capital: Budapest
Chief of state: President Ferenc Madl
Head of government: Prime Minister Viktor Orban

The Sept. 11, 2001, terrorist attacks in the U.S. did not have a major impact on Hungary's political or economic life. On the other hand, the numerous po-

435

litical scandals during the year led to a de facto, if not actual, breakup of the coalition that held power in Budapest. A bribery scandal in February triggered a wave of allegations against the Independent Smallholders' Party (FKGP), the junior coalition partner, although it did not affect the Federation of Young Democrats (Fidesz)–Hungarian Civic Party, the senior governing party. The affair resulted in the ousting of Jozsef Torgyan from both the FKGP presidency and the top position in the Ministry of Agriculture.

The level of public support for political parties generally stagnated, even with general elections anticipated in 2002. Fidesz and the former governing Hungarian Socialist Party ran neck and neck in opinion polls for most of the year, both attracting about 26% of the electorate. According to a September poll by the Gallup organization, however, support for a joint Fidesz–Hungarian Democratic Forum party list would enjoy the approval of 33% of the voters, with the Socialists drawing 28% and other opposition parties 3%. Meanwhile, public support for the FKGP plunged from 14% in 1998 to 1% in 2001. As many as 40% of the voters remained undecided, however. Although the Socialists had picked their candidate for prime minister—former finance minister Peter Medgyessy—the opposition largely remained at sixes and sevens, unable to attract political support in light of Fidesz's overwhelmingly professional political communication campaign. The Socialist Medgyessy

seemed most likely to stand alone against Prime Minister Viktor Orban in the May 2002 elections.

Still, much could depend on the radical nationalist Hungarian Justice and Life Party (MIEP), whose parliamentary support for the government Orban had accepted, notwithstanding MIEP leader Istvan Csurka's fiercely anti-Semitic rhetoric. MIEP was in opposition, but it could not be ruled out that it could be kingmaker in 2002.

Hungary attracted international media attention during the year for its passage of a law that extended education and health benefits as well as employment rights to the estimated three-million-strong Magyar (ethnic Hungarian) minority in neighbouring countries. Governments in adjacent states, particularly Romania, were insulted by the so-called status law, which they saw as a direct interference in their domestic affairs. A report in March by the Brussels-based International Federation of Journalists criticized the Hungarian government for improper political influence in the media as the country's public service broadcaster teetered close to bankruptcy.

The year 2001 was one of economic downturn. The government continued to weather criticism for being nontransparent and for operating on an unprecedented two-year budget. Despite troubling macroeconomic indicators, the long budgetary term promoted excessive social spending, including augmented state pensions and higher minimum wages. Largely owing to the

government's reversal of Hungary's traditionally liberal financial policy, trading on the Budapest stock exchange was weaker compared with 2000—so much so that in the autumn the government suggested merging the Central European stock exchanges in order to create a better environment for foreign, and particularly American, investors. The idea was turned down by exchange officials in other countries, however.

(ZSOFIA SZILAGYI)

ICELAND

Area: 102,819 sq km (39,699 sq mi)
Population (2001 est.): 284,000
Capital: Reykjavík
Chief of state: President Ólafur Ragnar Grímsson
Head of government: Prime Minister Davíd Oddsson

Iceland's economic growth slowed to 2% in 2001 after five years of more than 4.5% growth. The economy began overheating in 2000; inflation increased and a current account deficit widened. Economic activity, which had peaked late in 2000, began shrinking during 2001. Signs of recession emerged late in the year, though employment continued to be virtually full.

In December 2000 the Supreme Court ruled that the government had unconstitutionally reduced the disability benefits of individuals who were part of a married couple. In response, legislation was passed that increased disability benefits from $170 a month to $402, retroactive for four years.

The policy of managing fish stocks through fishing quotas came under increased scrutiny. Despite many years of quota management, the stocks of important fish species, such as cod and haddock, were shrinking, a factor that called into question this management method and initiated a debate about whether illegal fishing was at fault for the decline. On the other hand, the system of allocating fishing quotas for free, which in turn could be sold in the open market for a windfall profit, came under increased criticism. A government-appointed commission reported that fishing quotas should be subject to a modest charge, and the government

A news broadcast airs on Hungarian television; the state media suffered from stiff financial and political pressures during the year.

Photo by MTI Katalin Sándor

promised to introduce legislation to that effect.

The plan to build a hydroelectric dam at Kárahnjúkar, in the northeast of the country, received a setback when it failed to pass environmental scrutiny. The power company appealed the verdict. As a result, the decision to build the dam and an aluminum plant at Reydarfjördur was postponed. Construction could not begin until 2003 at the earliest.   (BJÖRN MATTHÍASSON)

INDIA

Area: 3,166,414 sq km (1,222,559 sq mi)
Population (2001 est.): 1,029,991,000
Capital: New Delhi
Chief of state: President Kocheril Raman Narayanan
Head of government: Prime Minister Atal Bihari Vajpayee

In 2001 it was the year of the terrorist in India; secessionists and raiders from across the borders stepped up their activities in Jammu and Kashmir state, India's northeastern region, and the capital itself. On December 13 five terrorists, armed with automatic weapons and explosives, made a daring bid to enter Parliament House in New Delhi. Security guards prevented their entrance, and in the exchange of fire all five raiders and nine others were killed. India held two Pakistan-based organizations, Jaish-e-Mohammad and Lashkar-e-Taiba, responsible. Earlier, on October 1, a car-bomb attack on the Jammu and Kashmir Assembly killed 38 persons. Jaish-e-Mohammad claimed responsibility.

Early in the year the government made a serious attempt at peace by halting its antiterrorist drive and holding talks with militant organizations, especially those that it suspected were encouraged by Pakistan. The talks yielding no results, Prime Minister Atal Bihari Vajpayee made the bold decision to negotiate directly with the chief executive of Pakistan, Gen. Pervez Musharraf, and invited him to New Delhi. The general arrived on July 14. His discussions with Vajpayee, which were held in Agra over the next two days, remained deadlocked, with Pakistan maintaining that a political solution to the Kashmir issue should be found first and India insist-

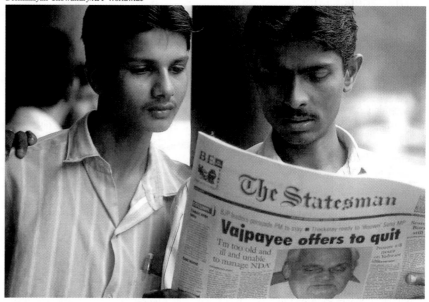
Deshakalyan Chowdhury/AFP Worldwide

Young men in Kolkata (Calcutta) on August 1 read about Indian Prime Minister Atal Bihari Vajpayee's offer to step down, which was rejected by the ruling National Democratic Alliance.

ing that cross-border terrorism should be first stopped.

India was deeply shaken by the events of September 11 and hastened to assure the U.S. of its full cooperation, as did Pakistan. Although Pakistan and India found themselves on the same side, there was no abatement in mutual rancour. One benefit that both derived by responding to the call to fight terrorism was that the U.S. ended the economic embargoes it had imposed after both countries carried out nuclear tests in 1998. India emphasized that it had long been pointing out the need for international action against cross-border terrorism. It handed over to the U.S. information about the Taliban's training camps in Afghanistan and Pakistan. Vajpayee went to Washington in November on invitation from Pres. George W. Bush for talks on the campaign against terrorism. Vajpayee also met Pres. Vladimir Putin in Russia on his way to the U.S. On his way back he had talks with Prime Minister Tony Blair in Britain. Blair had earlier paid a short visit to India. In December Vajpayee also visited Japan.

In the last week of September, India banned the Students Islamic Movement of India on the grounds that it had close links with the Taliban and arrested more than 200 of its leaders. In October a Prevention of Terrorism Ordinance was promulgated with one of its provisions enabling detention without trial for a period of six months,

but the government was unable to secure parliamentary endorsement for it.

Domestic Affairs. On January 26, the western state of Gujarat suffered an earthquake of magnitude 7.9. (*See* DISASTERS.) Over 14,000 people died, and more than 166,000 were injured. Some 370,000 houses were totally destroyed. The coalition government set aside 2% of the nation's income tax revenue to meet the expenditures for relief.

A political earthquake was soon to hit the government itself. In March a Web site, Tehelka.com, issued an extensively documented report that included videotapes of senior officials and prominent members of the ruling National Democratic Alliance (NDA) accepting money in exchange for defense contracts. (*See* Sidebar.) Tehelka.com revealed later that its reporters had posed as representatives of nonexistent foreign arms dealers. Bangaru Laxman, president of the Bharatiya Janata Party (BJP), resigned from his post on March 13; Jaya Jaitly, president of the Samata Party, and George Fernandes, India's defense minister, followed suit two days later. The defense portfolio was assigned to Foreign Minister Jaswant Singh as an additional responsibility. Several other NDA officials were suspended. Fernandes was reappointed as minister of defense in October.

More discomfiture was in store for the ruling coalition. In elections for four state legislative assemblies and a union territory in May, the NDA could not win

The Tehelka Tapes

In 2001 a stunning exposé by a New Delhi news portal claimed the jobs of India's defense minister, senior party functionaries of the ruling coalition, and at least five high-ranking members of the armed forces. The exposé, which appeared on Tehelka.com in March, included videotapes showing senior government officials accepting money in exchange for defense contracts.

In Tehelka.com's sting operation, reporters posed as representatives of nonexistent foreign arms dealers. The reporters' modus operandi involved offering to sell thermal cameras and other equipment to the Indian army. The ensuing encounters—including kickbacks accepted by politicians and army officials—were filmed by hidden cameras. The investigation, which lasted more than six months, culminated in a press conference by Tehelka.com on March 13, during which the editor in chief, Tarun Tejpal, showed the footage assembled by his team.

The exposé came during a crucial budget session of Parliament and paralyzed the proceedings. Bangaru Laxman, president of the Bharatiya Janata Party, had to resign after being caught on camera accepting money. Defense Minister George Fernandes had to resign after his Samata Party colleague Jaya Jaitly was shown meeting arms brokers at his official residence. Three of the five implicated army officers faced a court martial, while another's services were terminated.

The government-appointed commission of inquiry probing the scandal consisted of a single member, Justice K. Venkataswami, a retired Supreme Court judge. Tehelka.com submitted all of its videotapes and transcripts to Venkataswami, who on October 12 ruled that the tapes were genuine and that they had not been doctored. The commission probe was still underway at year's end.

On August 22 the *Indian Express* reported that Tehelka.com had employed prostitutes as a "honey trap" to cement the arms deals, a fact not disclosed earlier by the portal. The encounters between defense personnel, middlemen, Tehelka reporters posing as arms dealers, and the women were also captured on camera. Subsequent reports revealed that Tehelka had filmed sexual encounters, allegedly without the consent of the prostitutes, a fact admitted by the portal. This revelation put Tehelka's credibility in question—the portal was accused of violating individuals' rights to privacy, selectively editing, and erroneously transcribing the tapes to suit the story. The government was quick to denounce Tehelka's investigative methods. Tejpal's defense was that his reporters, to maintain their cover, had to accede to demands for paid sex made by the army officers.

Tejpal's "end-justifies-the-means" argument found as many supporters as critics. For the latter, Tehelka's nondisclosure of having used prostitutes and then filming the sex was proof of mala fide intent. To Tehelka supporters the tactics that were employed represented a genuine effort not to let sleaze sidetrack the main issue of corruption and to protect the women on the tapes.

(SHALAKA PARADKAR)

even one. Three of the five new chief ministers belonged to the Congress (I) party—A.K. Anthony in Kerala, Tarun Gogoi in Assam, and P. Shanmugam in the union territory of Pondicherry. Shanmugam later made way for N. Rangaswamy. In West Bengal the Communist Party of India (Marxist) won for the sixth time. In Tamil Nadu the All-India Anna Dravida Munnetra Kazhakam swept the polls and its leader, J. Jayalalitha, was sworn in as chief minister. The Supreme Court, however, removed her from the post on the grounds that as a convicted person she should not have been allowed to contest the election in the first place. O. Panneerselvam took over as chief minister. Soon thereafter, Jayalalitha's appeal against her original conviction was upheld in the Madras High Court, clearing the way for her return.

Gujarat also had a new chief minister. Poor showings in by-elections forced the ruling BJP to replace Keshubhai Patel with Narendra Modi in October. In Manipur frequent party hopping on the part of legislators prompted the coalition government to place the state under president's rule. In September the Supreme Court ruled that Sonia Gandhi, opposition leader and president of Congress (I), was an Indian citizen and upheld her election to Parliament.

The Economy. A fall in exports slowed both agricultural and industrial production during the year. The International Monetary Fund in September placed India's growth rate in 2001 at 4.5%, compared with 6% the previous year. Owing to numerous instances of irregularities, all stock markets languished throughout the year in spite of several attempts to prop them up.

In February the finance minister presented the central budget, which provided several incentives for industries, including a 15-year tax holiday for software firms. The revenue receipts of the central government in 2001–02 were placed at about Rs 2.3 trillion (1 Rs = about $0.02) and revenue expenditure at some Rs 3.1 trillion, which left a revenue deficit of Rs 788.2 billion, or 3.2% of India's gross domestic product.

Disinvestment plans made slow progress. In the first nine months of 2001, only one public-sector company, the Bharat Aluminium Co., was privatized. The terms of sale gave rise to accusations of underevaluation and corruption, but Parliament approved the deal. In September the government declared its determination to go ahead with plans to allow private participation, wholly or partially, in 13 more companies, including the State Trading Corp., Videsh Sanchar Nigam (international telecommunications), and Maruti (automobile manufacturing). It reiterated its resolve to sell Air India and Indian Airlines. The government also decided to appoint a single regulatory authority to cover information technology, telecommunications, and broadcasting, merging the ministries.

(H.Y. SHARADA PRASAD)

INDONESIA

Area: 1,922,570 sq km (742,308 sq mi)
Population (2001 est.): 212,195,000
Capital: Jakarta
Head of state and government: Presidents Abdurrahman Wahid and, from July 23, Megawati Sukarnoputri

In Indonesia the year 2001 was dominated by politics. Abdurrahman Wahid was removed as president by Indonesia's supreme decision-making body, the People's Consultative Assembly (MPR), on July 23, which thereby ended months of political crisis over his tenure.

The drawn-out dismissal process was initiated early in the year when a parliamentary inquiry found circumstantial evidence that Wahid had been complicit in the misuse of some $4 million from the state logistics agency. The findings led to a constitutional showdown. Wahid denied the charges and disputed the authority of the parliament to sit in judgment of him. The parliament asserted its right to monitor the executive and triggered the dismissal proceedings in the MPR (the MPR comprised the 500 members of the parliament plus 195 regional and community group representatives). Facing certain defeat, and against the advice of most of his cabinet, Wahid declared a state of emergency in the early hours of July 23 and tried to suspend the MPR. Political leaders and the security services ignored his declaration, and the MPR met in emergency session and removed him later that day. Wahid claimed he had acted to defend the constitution, but most legal experts believed that he had acted unconstitutionally, a view supported by the Supreme Court.

Wahid's downfall was due more to disillusionment with his leadership style than to any alleged corruption. Upon his election in October 1999, he had attracted a diverse coalition of parties into his government, but he proved unable to maintain its unity. His idiosyncratic and often gratuitously provocative remarks and his removal of several powerful ministers undermined cabinet solidarity and alienated many of the parties that had supported his presidential bid. He also showed himself to be an inept manager of government business. His grasp of key policy areas such as economics, justice, and defense was weak, and his approach to policy making tended to be ad hoc and inconstant.

His replacement, Vice Pres. Megawati Sukarnoputri, came to the presidency with a strong popular mandate and a public expectation that she would restore a measure of stability after the turmoil of Wahid's term. Her party, the Indonesian Democratic Party of Struggle (PDI-P), had won 34% of the national vote at the 1999 general election, by far the largest of any party. Much of PDI-P's success was due to Megawati's own personal following. Her popularity derived not only from her status as the eldest daughter of Indo-

On September 8 Indonesian Pres. Megawati Sukarnoputri, wearing traditional Acehnese attire, arrives at the house of the governor of Aceh on her first official visit to the troubled province.

nesia's founding president, Sukarno, but also from her image as a person of quiet integrity who had stoically resisted the manipulations of the Suharto regime in the mid-1990s. Her personality traits were atypical of a leading politician; she was reserved, cautious, and averse to confrontation and political deal making—characteristics that critics said were hindrances to successful leadership. Megawati's government comprised representatives from secular nationalist and Islamic parties as well as military officers and technocrats. Though ideologically nationalist, she pursued pragmatic policies during her first months in office.

The political tumult surrounding the presidency had drawn attention away from more fundamental issues related to political, economic, and legal re-

form. This reform process, which had begun after the fall of Suharto's New Order in May 1998, had been fitful and uneven. The transition to democracy continued, though elements of the political culture had changed little from the Suharto era. Parties remained elite-dominated and driven by personalities and patronage rather than ideology or grassroots participation. The parliament provided close scrutiny of government activities, but it remained tardy in passing legislation and prone to graft. Constitutional reform was badly needed, particularly in defining the relationship between the legislature and the executive, but appeared in danger of stalling. Confidence in the judiciary and police was low, and this contributed to rising vigilantism by local communities against suspected wrongdoers. Civilian control over the military improved, but the armed forces continued to be an important, but not dominant, element in Indonesian politics. Corruption still permeated Indonesian life but was no longer as blatant or extreme as during the Suharto era. A range of government anticorruption measures helped to ensure greater transparency, and regular press exposure of improper practices raised the risks of engaging in corruption. On November 28 Tommy Suharto, the fugitive son of Suharto, was arrested after more than a year on the lam. He was facing an 18-month prison term for corruption when he fled.

One of the most radical reforms was that of decentralization. Under this program, which began in January 2001, extensive political and economic powers were being devolved to the second tier of regional government (i.e., regency or municipality). Within two years the central government was supposed to cede to the regions authority in all administrative areas except defense, justice, fiscal controls, religion, and matters relating to technical standards. So far, the devolution process had been surrounded by controversy and confusion. Poorly drafted legislation and complex, often contradictory enabling regulations had been core problems and had been compounded by a lack of central government supervision and local government disregard for existing national laws and administrative protocols. The Megawati government announced that it would revise the legislation in early 2002. The decentralization process was likely to strengthen democracy in the regions and ease re-

(continued on page 442)

Resisting Disintegration in
Post-Suharto Indonesia

by Greg Fealy

Since the fall of Suharto's authoritarian New Order regime in May 1998, Indonesia has undergone a number of dramatic changes. At the political level, there has been a rapid and rather chaotic transition to democracy, including a significant dismantling of state controls over social and political expression. At the same time, the level of communal violence and secessionist demands has risen sharply. Many observers have seen a link between the two processes and questioned whether a society as heterogeneous as Indonesia's can survive these fissiparous tendencies intact without a strong, even repressive, central government.

For much of its independent history, Indonesia has been seen as a nation at high risk of disintegration. It has one of the world's most ethnically, culturally, and religiously diverse populations. Among the groups dispersed across a sprawling archipelago of some 13,000 islands are the staunchly Muslim Acehnese in far-north Sumatra, Catholics of Flores and Timor in the east, the Hindu Balinese, and animists in Irian Jaya and Kalimantan. In the late 1940s and 1950s, regional rebellions broke out on Java, Sumatra, Sulawesi, and Ambon, most of which were put down militarily. Under Sukarno's Guided Democracy regime (1959–66) and Suharto's New Order (1967–98), tight central control was imposed over the regions and separatist tendencies were suppressed, often harshly.

The rise in communal conflict and secessionist pressures since Suharto's downfall has led to renewed speculation about Indonesia's possible breakup. The former Portuguese colony of East Timor, effectively annexed by Indonesia in 1975, seceded in 1999. Separatist activity in Aceh and Irian Jaya—both of which have had long-standing independence movements—has grown rapidly in scope and popular support, prompting a forceful response from Indonesian security services. Aceh has experienced by far the worst violence. Separatist rebels there have been conducting a bloody guerrilla war against Indonesian forces and by 2001 controlled large areas of the rural hinterland. It is estimated that since 1999 more than 2,000 people have died, victims not only of the fighting but also of brutality by the Indonesian police and army as well as by the rebels. Armed conflict in Irian Jaya is far more sporadic, but military intervention and intimidation of pro-independence groups are common. Secessionist calls have also emerged from several other provinces, including Riau, South Sulawesi, and Bali, but these are aimed at pressuring the central government and do not have serious separatist intent. Even so, the use of such appeals shows that the earlier taboo on separatist rhetoric no longer applies.

The most severe nonseparatist violence has taken place in the Maluku archipelago, where a virtual civil war has been waged between Christian and Muslim communities since early 1999. More than 5,000 people have lost their lives in this bitter conflict, and over 500,000 have been displaced. In Kalimantan, tensions between indigenous Dayaks and Madurese internal migrants have led to a series of massacres of Madurese since 1997. In a violent outbreak in February 2001, some 500 Madurese were killed and roughly 100,000 fled to other regions. In addition to this, there has been an upsurge in attacks on places of worship across the nation. During the New Order, an average of 14 churches were attacked each year; the figure since 1998 has been about 140 per annum, in addition to the damage inflicted on scores of mosques.

While these events represent a serious challenge to Indonesia's cohesion, there are strong grounds for arguing that the nation is not in imminent danger of breakup. Despite Indonesia's diverse population, commitment to national unity is strong across most regions and

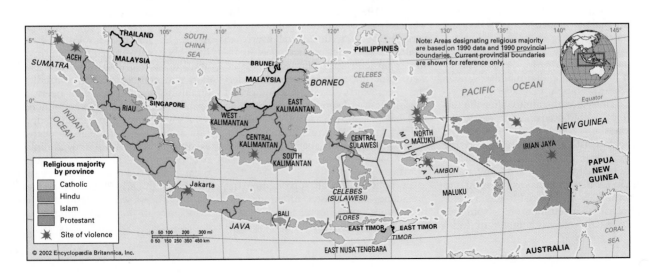

Note: Areas designating religious majority are based on 1990 data and 1990 provincial boundaries. Current provincial boundaries are shown for reference only.

Religious majority by province
Catholic
Hindu
Islam
Protestant
Site of violence

0 50 100   200   300 mi
0 50 150 250 350 450 km

© 2002 Encyclopædia Britannica, Inc.

Rioters overturn a van during a massive labour demonstration outside the State Palace in Bandung, Indon., on June 13.

AP/Wide World Photos

sections of society, judging by responses to the loss of East Timor and separatist calls in Aceh and Irian Jaya.

Ethnic and religious animosities are clearly important factors in communal and separatist unrest, though closer examination of Indonesia's social composition and dynamics suggests that most Indonesians accept diversity as an essential element of their national character. Ethnographers disagree on exactly how many ethnic groups exist in Indonesia, but most estimates put the number at about 200. There are no accurate figures on the size of each ethnic group, though some indication of ethnicity can be gained from census statistics on the "mother tongue" of citizens. The most recent available census data (1995) suggest that the main ethnic groupings are Javanese (about 40% of the population), Sundanese (14%), Madurese (4%), and Batak, Bugis, Banjarese, and Balinese (each less than 2%). There are also diasporas of Chinese (3%) and Arabs, South Asians, and Europeans (each less than 1%). Javanese are the most widely dispersed and politically dominant group, with four of Indonesia's five presidents having been Javanese. The Chinese, though a small minority, are economically dominant and constitute the wealthiest ethnic group.

Indonesia has five "officially recognized" religions. Islam is by far the largest; according to the 1990 census, it was the faith of 87% of Indonesians. This makes Indonesia the world's largest Muslim nation. The minority religions are Catholicism (6%), Protestantism (3%), and Hinduism and Buddhism (each less than 1%). In addition, animism is widely practiced among more traditional communities.

Indonesia's dispersion of ethnic and religious groups is highly complex. There are few restrictions on internal migration, and Indonesians have proved highly mobile in pursuing career or commercial opportunities outside their home provinces. The large cities are especially heterogeneous. This has led to extensive intermarriage between ethnic groups and, to a much lesser extent, religious groups (strict rules apply to marriage between Muslims and non-Muslims). Most urban Indonesians live or work in environments that are ethnically and religiously mixed. Before the upsurge in communal violence, Indonesia enjoyed a reputation for tolerance and pluralism, and the great majority of the population still coexists in relative harmony.

Ethnic and religious tensions, although important elements in social conflict and separatism, are seldom the only factors. Often there are deepseated social, economic, or political issues that take on an ethnic or religious expression. A key driver of divisive tendencies has been that of socioeconomic grievance. This has been most evident in Aceh and Irian Jaya, both of which are rich in natural resources but receive from the central government only a small percentage of the wealth extracted from their provinces. Infrastructure and government services and facilities are poor in both regions, and employment opportunities in local oil and mineral developments have been limited. New regional autonomy laws should result in a significant rise in the share of revenue going to these and other resource-rich provinces. The greater political autonomy flowing from these laws should also ease resentment toward Jakarta.

The violence in Maluku and Kalimantan also has an economic dimension. Malukan Christians have been angered by what they see as Muslim encroachment into traditionally Christian-dominated sectors of the economy and also by a perceived Islamization of local government. The Dayaks in Kalimantan have felt marginalized by Madurese settlers taking over their traditional lands and depriving them of positions in the local economy and bureaucracy.

Another important factor in provoking unrest and separatist demands has been large-scale human rights abuses by the security services. In both Aceh and Irian Jaya, police and military brutality has alienated large sections of the community against Jakarta's rule and played a major role in galvanizing support for the independence cause.

Indonesia's ethnic and religious complexities are not, in themselves, inherently destabilizing elements. They can, however, in combination with other grievances, add to the country's volatility. Appropriate government responses in addressing economic disparities, political disenfranchisement, and human rights abuses by military and police could do much to reduce regional and intracommunal tensions. Furthermore, there is no a priori reason why a democratizing and decentralizing Indonesia should be less stable than an authoritarian and centralizing one. In fact, many of Indonesia's current problems derive from the excesses of the Suharto regime.

Greg Fealy is a research fellow in Indonesian history at the Research School of Pacific and Asian Studies, Australian National University, Canberra.

(continued from page 439)
sentiment toward Jakarta, but it would also increase the disparities of wealth between resource-rich, industrially developed regions and the poorer, less-developed areas.

Indonesia's economy continued its weak recovery from the 1997 Asian financial crisis, though it remained vulnerable to an international downturn. Although growth in 2000–01 was 3.5%, better than most of its Southeast Asian neighbours, this was due largely to increased output from small and medium-sized businesses. Many of Indonesia's corporations remained heavily indebted, and much of the financial sector was in need of restructuring. The budget deficit remained large at $4.2 billion, or 2.5% of the nation's gross domestic product, and the slow pace of privatizing state enterprises and selling assets of bankrupt banks was expected to put pressure on the government to take unpopular measures such as cutting fuel and transport subsidies. A return to the robust growth rates of the Suharto era was impossible without large-scale foreign investment, and this was unlikely to occur in the short term.

The Megawati government faced daunting challenges in restoring Indonesia's economic health and political stability as well as in improving internal security. It would be undertaking these tasks in an increasingly uncertain international environment. The world economy was facing a slowdown, and the U.S.-led war against terrorism had already aroused strong protests within Indonesia's majority Islamic community. If Megawati did not provide stable and effective government, public confidence in her leadership and in democratic government could be seriously undermined.　　　　(GREG FEALY)

IRAN

Area: 1,629,918 sq km (629,315 sq mi)
Population (2001 est.): 63,442,000 (excluding roughly 2,000,000 Afghan refugees and fewer than 400,000 Iraqi refugees)
Capital: Tehran
Supreme political and religious authority: *Rahbar* (Spiritual Leader) Ayatollah Sayyed Ali Khamenei
Head of state and government: President Mohammad Khatami

The two wings of the Iranian political establishment remained firmly at loggerheads in 2001. Liberals and reformists were inhibited in their programs of economic privatization and development of a more open social regime by hard-line Islamic conservatives' opposition to change. The judiciary in particular rigorously repressed free speech. On January 13 a Revolutionary Court gave prolonged jail terms or heavy fines to 10 Iranian reformists who had participated in a proscribed conference in Berlin. The aggressive crackdown on reform-oriented Islamic factions and student groups culminated in March and April in the arrest of more than 60 eminent political figures associated with the banned Iran Freedom Movement. In addition, many reformist journals were closed down and reporters silenced by judicial organs controlled by the right wing. During the year 60 reformers in the parliament had been called before the courts on a variety of charges. In December a pro-reform member of the parliament was sentenced to 13 months in jail for insulting the courts.

The hard-line offensive against the press and the reformists was part of a sustained campaign to frustrate Pres. Mohammad Khatami and his cabinet but was also a tactic used to weaken the pro-Khatami wing of the regime in advance of the presidential election that took place on June 8. The election, however, proved a major success for the Khatami camp. The president was returned to power with an overwhelming 77% of the votes—an outcome that rebutted the hard-line contention that Khatami and his followers had lost the support of the nation. Khatami's political platform was extremely modest, promising only that he would continue within a formula of extreme moderation to pursue reform and move Iran toward an Islamic democracy.

The new presidential term was expected to bring about significant strengthening of the reformist component within the Majlis (parliament). Khatami declined as a matter of policy to confront the hard-liners, and his postelection cabinet was little changed from his original group of ministers. Indeed, the entire tone of policy in the wake of the June election was one of continuity of deference to conservative clerics, even on issues such as the hard-liners' introduction of regulations in midyear for the public flogging of persons found guilty of social/religious offenses.

Opposition to and alienation from the Islamic government was apparent during the presidential election when almost a third of the electorate opted not to vote. Active dissent was manifest in sporadic urban unrest. Officially reported cases included demonstrations in north Tehran against press controls, student protests in Tehran against the hardliners in January, and a major confrontation against the use of foreign labour at the Assaluyeh refinery in September. In April there was an intensive Iranian missile attack on Mujahedin-e Khalq Organization camps in Iraq, which indicated a continuing apprehension of MKO influence by the Iranian authorities.

Iran struggled to make headway in its key foreign policy aims, impeded by the domestic stalemate between the president and the conservatives. The U.S. renewed its Iran-Libyan Sanctions Act in mid-2001 for a period of five years. In June allegations were made in Washington that Iran had been involved in the 1996 bombing of the al-Khobar Towers in Saudi Arabia, which claimed the lives of 19 U.S. personnel. Although the Iranian leadership, notably President Khatami, was quick to condemn the September 11 terrorist attacks in the United States, hopes that the campaign against terrorism would offer some degree of rapprochement with the U.S. were dimmed in late September when the Iranian spiritual leader, Ali Khamenei, made a hard-line anti-American speech. In the speech Khamenei explicitly rejected, except under a UN banner, Iranian participation in any actions against the Taliban government in Afghanistan or in a global antiterrorist movement. Meanwhile, Iranian diplomatic relations with Central Asia, the Arabian peninsula, China, and the European Union were generally lukewarm. Arms purchases were negotiated with Russia in early October.

The economy enjoyed mixed fortunes. Oil revenues remained high at approximately $24 billion for the year ended March 2001, and foreign borrowing was estimated at a modest $12.8 billion. There were continuing difficulties, however, with real growth in the economy, which was estimated at 5.6%. Moreover, structural reform through privatization almost totally stalled, and price inflation was still running at 12.6%. Iran suffered its third straight year of severe drought in 2001; losses in agriculture were put at $2.6 billion.
　　　　(KEITH S. MCLACHLAN)

IRAQ

Area: 435,052 sq km (167,975 sq mi)
Population (2001 est.): 23,332,000
Capital: Baghdad
Head of state and government: President and Prime Minister Saddam Hussein

In the wake of the terrorist attacks in the U.S. on Sept. 11, 2001, Iraq was virtually alone among countries in failing to offer official condolences to the U.S. In line with his adversarial relationship with the U.S., Pres. Saddam Hussein publicly opposed the U.S.-led war on terrorism and called on other Islamic countries to help defeat it. He also decried the military action in Afghanistan, calling it a spark that could set "the world on fire." In response, U.S. Secretary of State Colin Powell suggested that once the U.S. had concluded its campaign in Afghanistan, it would deal with Iraq's weapons program as part of its effort against terrorism. Meanwhile, the U.S. focused on persuading Russia to sign off on a "smart sanctions" package that would ease the restrictions on civilian goods imported into Iraq but tighten restrictions on military supplies. The package also included measures to prevent Iraq from smuggling oil to the outside world, as it continued to do. Pending action on new UN measures, in November the existing "oil for food" program was renewed, while the U.S. and its allies dealt with Afghanistan. Hussein reiterated that UN arms inspectors would not be allowed to return to Iraq unless international sanctions against the country were lifted.

U.S. and British airplanes continued to attack Iraqi radar installations and other military targets throughout the year. The Iraqis strengthened their military capacity and announced that they had downed three unmanned U.S. surveillance planes patrolling the no-fly zone in southern Iraq. The Pentagon confirmed in September that it had lost contact with the planes.

Iraq put major efforts into improving relations with its neighbours, with considerable success. Relations between Iraq and Syria warmed considerably during the year. Railroad links between the two countries were reestablished in May. In June Syria abolished visa requirements for Iraqis visiting Syria, and in August, accompanied by a huge del-

egation, Syrian Prime Minister Mustafa Mero made a three-day visit to Iraq. The two countries signed several trade agreements. Regular commercial air travel resumed between Damascus (Syria) and Baghdad and between Amman (Jordan) and Baghdad.

Relations between Turkey and Iraq also improved during the year despite continued Turkish military incursions into northern Iraq in pursuit of Turkey's Kurdish rebels. The two countries resumed railway links, and the first train to go from Turkey to Iraq in more than 20 years arrived in Baghdad in early May. In July the two countries agreed to open a second border crossing in northern Iraq, at a point yet to be determined. A new Turkish ambassador presented his credentials to Baghdad on January 19 and thereby upgraded diplomatic relations between the two countries.

Relations between Iraq and Iran remained strained, however. Each country accused the other of continuing to hold

food items and most consumer goods remained beyond the reach of the general public because of high prices. Iraqis were paid very low salaries, and inflation remained high. The government made efforts to stimulate the economy. It announced loan programs for Iraqi businessmen to establish local industries and created free-trade zones with Syria and Egypt, which were designed to increase the flow of Egyptian and Syrian goods to Iraq. Smuggling operations of various kinds remained strong, providing Iraqi local markets with goods that were not allowed under the sanctions, such as electronics and computers. Smuggling of Iraqi archaeological treasures out of the country continued. The Iraqi government admitted the existence of such operations and announced severe measures to curb them.

Politically, the year saw the consolidation of power in the hands of Hussein's youngest son, Qusay. The 34-year-old

A mosaic in central Baghdad depicts Iraqi leader Saddam Hussein on horseback (centre), flanked by his sons Uday (left) and Qusay.

AP/Wide World Photos

prisoners of war from the 1980–90 Iran-Iraq War, and each country harboured organized groups opposed to the other's regime.

The economic situation inside Iraq did not improve substantially during the year. There were increases in the basic monthly food rations, sold to the population at nominal prices, but other

Qusay headed elite units of army and security forces. On May 17 he was elected to membership of the Regional Command of the ruling Arab Socialist Ba'th Party, and on May 19 Hussein named him one of the two deputy commanders of the influential military branch of the Ba'th Party. The rise of Qusay's star strengthened the prospect that he would succeed his father. Previously, Hussein's eldest son, Uday, had been thought to be next in line, but his prospects dimmed after he was badly wounded in an assassination attempt in 1996.

(LOUAY BAHRY)

IRELAND

Area: 70,273 sq km (27,133 sq mi)
Population (2001 est.): 3,823,000
Capital: Dublin
Chief of state: President Mary McAleese
Head of government: Prime Minister Bertie Ahern

Voters in Dublin celebrate the rejection of a referendum to endorse the Treaty of Nice on June 8.

AP/Wide World Photos

The year 2001 saw expectations in Ireland adjusting sharply downward after five years of rapid growth. With the slide in the U.S. economy and in the aftermath of the September 11 terrorist attacks, leading analysts in Ireland estimated the country's economic growth for the year at about 6%.

Even before September the slowdown in the U.S. had begun to have an impact on Ireland. As Silicon Valley companies shrank operations, up to 10,000 job losses were predicted for Ireland's information-technology sector. Big-name closures such as Gateway sent a shock through the community and unsettled government planners.

The effects of September 11 were immediate. The state airline, Aer Lingus, announced a 25% cut in services and said it would drop 2,500 employees. The wider implications were signaled later when Waterford Crystal—one of the jewels of Irish industry—put its operation on a three-day workweek.

The factors that had facilitated Ireland's progress suddenly made it vulnerable. Ireland had had the best of both worlds—European Union (EU) support and American investment. By year's end, however, European transfers had all but ended. With no clarity as to when the U.S. economy might start to turn around, Ireland wondered whether it had yet to feel the full brunt of the downturn.

Domestic factors added to the Irish economic worries. Inflation ran ahead of EU averages at 5%. A series of strikes disrupted schools and rail and air services. On the positive side, unemployment remained below 4%.

The spread of bovine spongiform encephalopathy (BSE), or "mad cow" disease, in Great Britain was held at bay in Ireland but at the cost of closing the countryside. Tourism revenues and farm exports fell. Meanwhile, although cases of BSE had been few, exporters struggled to hold international markets. Some optimism emerged late in the year when the Egyptian beef market partially reopened. (*See* AGRICULTURE AND FISHERIES: *Special Report.*)

Public finances suffered. In September, for the third quarter in succession, the Department of Finance reduced its forecast for taxation revenues. At that point the government still hoped for a budget surplus of perhaps £Ir 1 billion (about $1.1 billion).

A general election was due by May 2002. The centre-right government was led by Prime Minister Bertie Ahern. His Fianna Fail party and its partners, the Progressive Democrats, were determined to complete their five-year term and to seek reelection after having jump-started the slowing economy. Even if they were successful on the economic front, other problems loomed. In particular, social services and infrastructure had not kept pace with the economic growth of the past few years. There was widespread concern over the health services, while problems of transport, housing, and the environment continued. The government planned a network of new motorways, an underground and light-rail system for Dublin, an overhaul of the health system, and a special pension fund for Ireland's future elderly.

Not all of these objectives could be met. The budget presented to the Dail

(parliament) in December masterfully balanced spending against revenues without borrowing, but it seemed clear that future spending would involve some deficit budgeting. For Ireland, this prompted fearful recollections of the 1980s, when the national debt reached crisis proportions.

The economy was not the only disappointment. In June voters rejected a referendum to endorse the Treaty of Nice, which provided for EU expansion. The rejection signaled the end of Ireland's love affair with the EU. Paradoxically, the Economic and Monetary Union had given stability to the Irish economy, and the business community eagerly welcomed the advent of the euro in 2002.

Meanwhile, the future of the Belfast Agreement, which envisaged a lasting peace in Northern Ireland, appeared more secure after the illegal Irish Republican Army destroyed or "put beyond use" at least part of its armoury. Northern Ireland's elected assembly and administration was thus enabled to get down to the routine business of government.

Throughout 2001 a series of judicial tribunals continued to investigate allegations of corruption involving politicians and business figures. Central to these was the investigation of former prime minister Charles Haughey, who allegedly had received substantial sums of money from prominent businesspeople while he was in office.

In October the government announced plans for a referendum on the country's abortion laws. Abortions were illegal in Ireland unless giving birth threatened the life of the mother. Debate on this deeply divisive issue was gathering momentum as the year drew to a close. Simultaneously, the government sought a way forward after the electorate's rejection of the Treaty of Nice. Ahern established a forum in October to redefine policy on Europe. Notwithstanding encouraging sentiments from the government, Ireland found itself cast in the unwelcome role of obstructing EU expansion. (CONOR BRADY)

ISRAEL

Area: 21,671 sq km (8,367 sq mi), including the Golan Heights and disputed East Jerusalem, excluding the Emerging Palestinian Autonomous Areas
Population (2001 est.): 6,258,000
Capital: Jerusalem is the proclaimed capital of Israel (since Jan. 23, 1950) and the actual seat of government, but recognition has generally been withheld by the international community
Chief of state: President Moshe Katzav
Head of government: Prime Ministers Ehud Barak and, from March 7, Ariel Sharon

---

The Emerging Palestinian Autonomous Areas (the West Bank and the Gaza Strip)
Total area: West Bank 5,900 sq km (2,270 sq mi), of which (prior to September 2000) 342 sq km is under Palestinian administration, 3,369 sq km under Israeli administration, and 2,189 sq km under joint administration; Gaza Strip 363 sq km (140 sq mi), of which about 236 sq km is under Palestinian administration and about 127 sq km under Israeli administration
Population (2001 est.): West Bank 2,268,000, including 2,069,000 Arabs and 199,000 Jews; Gaza Strip 1,203,000, including 1,196,000 Arabs and 7,000 Jews
Principal administrative centres: Ram Allah and Gaza
Head of government: President Yasir Arafat

Following the Sept. 11, 2001, terrorist attacks in the U.S., Palestinian Authority leader Yasir Arafat declared a cease-fire in the yearlong Palestinian confrontation with Israel—known as the second *intifadah*—but the violence soon resumed, and it reached a crescendo in December.

On February 6 the hawkish Ariel Sharon (*see* BIOGRAPHIES), leader of the right-wing Likud, was elected prime minister, defeating Ehud Barak by 62.4% to 37.6%. The Israeli electorate swung dramatically to the right in the wake of the eruption of the September 2000 *in-tifadah*. Despite his sweeping victory, Sharon had only 19 Likud members in the 120-member Knesset (parliament), but he formed a broad-based coalition government supported by 77 Knesset members from seven political parties, including Labor.

The power-sharing arrangement with Labor in the "government of national unity" was reflected in the distribution of cabinet posts; Labor's Shimon Peres and Benjamin Ben-Eliezer secured the key foreign and defense portfolios, respectively. Another Labor Knesset member, Salah Tarif, of the minority Druze sect, became the first non-Jewish cabinet minister.

One of the new coalition's first acts was to amend the electoral law. The two-ballot system, in which Israelis cast one vote for prime minister and another for a party, was abolished. The system had been designed to create a more stable government, but it had strengthened small one-issue groupings at the expense of the two major national parties, Labor and Likud. It was replaced by a return to one-vote proportional representation, with the key addition of a constructive no-confidence mechanism, by which the opposition would have to muster 61 of the 120 Knesset votes and present an alternative candidate in order to oust a sitting prime minister.

Three days before Sharon took office on March 7, a Palestinian suicide bomber blew himself up in the seaside town of Netanya. The fundamentalist Hamas organization announced that the bomber was the first of 10 "martyrs" waiting to greet Sharon's new government. Other bombings followed in Hadera, Binyamina, Tel Aviv, Haifa, and Jerusalem. Israel responded with a policy of "targeted killings," arguing that the only way to preempt the bombers was to assassinate the men planning to send them. Palestinian ambushes and drive-by shootings, which took a heavy toll in Jewish settler lives in the occupied West Bank, prompted Israeli troops to seal off Palestinian towns and villages to restrict Palestinian movement, but the measures failed to curb the violence.

According to the Israeli army, there were about 8,000 "serious" Palestinian attacks during the first year of the *intifadah*, 84 of them inside Israel proper. A total of 176 Israelis lost their lives, and 1,742 were injured; the number of Palestinians killed was 604, and between 8,500 and 10,000 were injured.

After taking office, Sharon announced two major policy changes: no negotiations with the Palestinians as long as violence continued and interim rather than final arrangements when the shooting stopped. Two weeks later he visited the U.S. and persuaded the administration of Pres. George W. Bush to back his demand for a cease-fire as a precondition for talks with the Palestinians. Sharon's aim was to contain the *intifadah* through a combination of military action and international pressure on Arafat. The policy suffered from an inherent contradiction, however; the tougher the measures that Israel took, the less international support it got. In addition, the Israelis demanded an end to violence before new peace proposals would be put on the table, and the Palestinians insisted on some idea of the direction that a new peace process might lead before calling an end to the *intifadah;* as a result, the fighting continued.

On May 21 a fact-finding committee led by former U.S. senator George Mitchell presented its report on the causes of the violence, and both the Israelis and the Palestinians expressed readiness to accept Mitchell's call for a four-phase process leading to political reengagement: a cease-fire, a cooling-off period, confidence-building measures, and resumption of negotiations.

On June 1 a suicide bomber blew himself up outside a Tel Aviv discotheque, killing 20 Israeli teenagers. The outrage drew widespread international condemnation, and German Foreign Minister Joschka Fischer, who was in Tel Aviv near the scene of the carnage, pressured Arafat into calling a cease-fire. U.S. CIA Director George Tenet flew in to negotiate the terms, and on June 13 both sides announced a cease-fire designed to jump-start the Mitchell process; it failed to hold, however.

Achieving a durable cease-fire proved elusive. The Palestinians demanded international observers to oversee any truce, but Israel refused, agreeing only to reactivate the existing Supreme Security Coordination Committee, consisting of Israeli, Palestinian, and CIA officials. More important, the Palestinians sought reassurance that negotiation with the Sharon government would lead to a final settlement, at the very least along the lines of the understandings reached with the government of Ehud Barak in Taba, Egypt, in late January. Those discussions were based on the so-called "Clinton parameters," the bridging proposals announced by then U.S. president Bill Clinton in December 2000. The parameters allocated 94–96% of the West Bank to the Palestinians with an exchange of land in Israel proper to compensate for the remaining 4–6% and made equally far-reaching proposals on the core issues of Jerusalem and refugees. Sharon declared that he would be ready to discuss only a string of less-ambitious interim agreements, but he also said he would be ready to accept the establishment of a Palestinian state.

The ongoing *intifadah* led to an erosion of Israel's position in the Arab world and to widespread criticism of Israeli countermeasures by the international community. A wave of anti-Israel sentiment came to a head at the UN-sponsored World Conference Against Racism in Durban, S.Af., in early September. Arab and Muslim countries pressed for strong anti-Israel language in the final communiqué, including a statement equating Zionism with racism. The United States and Israel walked out.

On October 17 Tourism Minister Rehavam Ze'evi was assassinated in retaliation for the killing in August of Palestinian Popular Front leader Abu Ali Mustafa. (*See* OBITUARIES.) The action led Israeli forces to invade Bethlehem and five other West Bank cities. The violence escalated, and Sharon cut short a visit to the U.S. when 26 Israelis were killed and more than 270 injured in a string of suicide and car bombings in a crowded Jerusalem shopping mall late on the night of December 1 and on a bus in Haifa the following morning. By mid-December, under pressure from the United States and other countries, Arafat called for a halt to "terrorist activities," and he ordered the closure of about a dozen Hamas and Islamic Jihad offices.

The *intifadah* brought great hardship on the Palestinians, but it also hurt Israel's economy. In the third quarter of 2000, before the fighting erupted, there had been an economic upsurge, with a staggering 9.1% increase in gross domestic product; but in the fourth quarter GDP was down by 8%, and it continued to slide by a further 0.6% in the first half of 2001. Tourism slumped to unprecedented lows, and foreign investment fell by about 70%. As the economic slowdown deepened, unemployment topped the 9% mark.

The global downturn in high-tech activity also had a devastating economic effect. Exports were down by 26.5% in the first half of the year, owing mainly to the fall in high tech and in the diamond trade. In September, partly as a result of the slump in world money markets in the wake of the terrorist attacks in the U.S., the shekel lost about 6% of its value against the dollar. Inflation, however, remained under control, at an annual rate of about 1.5–2%.

(LESLIE D. SUSSER)

Israeli policemen search the scene outside a discotheque in Tel Aviv where a Palestinian suicide bomber blew himself up and killed 20 Israeli teenagers on June 1.

© Reinhard Krause/ Reuters 2001

ITALY

Area: 301,337 sq km (116,347 sq mi)
Population (2001 est.): 57,892,000
Capital: Rome
Chief of state: President Carlo Azeglio Ciampi
Head of government: Prime Ministers Giuliano Amato and, from June 11, Silvio Berlusconi

In Italy six and a half years of rule by centre-left governments came to an end in 2001 when elections swept into power a centre-right coalition led by media magnate Silvio Berlusconi, the richest man in the country. (*See* BIOGRAPHIES.) Shortly afterward, violence broke out in the northern port city of Genoa during antiglobalization protests staged while a Group of Eight (G-8) summit was being held in the city. What ultimately overshadowed these events, however, was a deep anxiety in Italy over possible repercussions from the U.S.-led war on terrorism.

The elections in May, with 630 seats at stake in the Chamber of Deputies and 315 in the Senate, were essentially a fight between two alliances—Berlusconi's House of Freedoms and the centre-left Olive Tree partnership led by Francesco Rutelli, a former mayor of Rome. The campaign centred on a highly personalized duel between the leaders of the two alliances, with Berlusconi branding his opponents "communists" and Rutelli applauding the British magazine *The Economist* for describing Berlusconi as "unfit to rule" in part because he had recently come under investigation for money laundering, tax evasion, and bribery, among other charges. Whereas Rutelli struggled to pull together partners split by chronic bickering, however, Berlusconi's alliance, led by his own Forza Italia party—the country's biggest—maintained unity. Commentators noted that superior financial resources also greatly helped Berlusconi's cause; for instance, he was able to send a biographical photo album of himself to every household in the country. In a television spot aired shortly before the elections, Berlusconi brandished a huge parchmentlike scroll bearing pledges that bound him—over five years—to lower taxes, create more than a million new jobs, embark on a major public-works program, and increase the minimum monthly pension to 1 million lire (about $465). He called this his "con-tract" with Italians.

The outcome was a triumph for Berlus-coni, who had already enjoyed seven months of premiership in 1994. The House of Freedoms scooped up 368 seats in the Chamber against the Olive Tree's 242, while in the smaller Senate the fig-ures were 177 to 125, respectively. Forza Italia increased its share of the House's cake by 9%, while another alliance mem-ber, Umberto Bossi's Northern League—which championed more autonomy for the north of Italy—fared worse than pre-dicted. It took Berlusconi a month to put together a 23-member cabinet, in which Bossi, after much haggling, became min-ister for devolution, while the foreign minister's post went to a nonpolitician, Renato Ruggiero. The new prime minis-ter's team won a vote of confidence in June by 351–261. Before the vote Berlus-coni had promised an unspecified solu-tion to a much-aired issue, that of the "conflict of interest" he faced as a polit-ical leader involved in big business.

Trouble came in July when Genoa was for three days ravaged and turned into a virtual theatre of war during pitched battles between 19,000 police and tens of thousands of antiglobal-ization demonstrators besieging a summit of the G-8. One protester was killed when a police officer whom he had threatened with a fire extinguisher shot him. The reported number of per-sons injured in the mayhem amounted to more than 200, and about 280 ar-rests were made. Police met assaults, stone throwing, and molotov cocktails with baton charges and tear gas, but both protest organizers and the gov-ernment ascribed most of the violence to black-clad intruders, including many non-Italians, who belonged to a group known as the Black Bloc; this was the same group that had first attracted headlines by rioting at a World Trade Organization summit in Seattle, Wash., in 1999. Accused of muscling in on a protest meant to be peaceful, the Black Bloc members were generally identified as the ones who set cars and rubbish bins ablaze in Genoa, vandalized banks, shops, and supermarkets, and attacked the local jail. Another incident during the Genoa protests contributed to na-tionwide dismay. Police conducted a midnight raid on a school housing scores of protesters, after which the Ital-ian media showed pools and splashes of blood on the floors and walls of the school. Later the opposition noisily ac-cused police of "brutal violence," but Interior Minister Claudio Scajola ig-nored cries for his resignation, claim-ing that the raid was justified because the school had harboured troublemak-ers. A parliamentary commission, un-der a Forza Italia chairman, eventually declared the summit "a success," as-cribed police "excesses" to individuals, and charged that "peaceful protesters" were guilty of tolerating violent ele-ments in their midst.

Fearing a repetition of violence at other planned international meetings in Italy, the government proposed chang-ing the locations of a September NATO conference in Naples—which, as a re-sult, was held in Brussels instead—and a November UN Food and Agricul-ture Organization (FAO) conference in Rome. After contemplating a switch to the Adriatic resort of Rimini, the FAO opted not to relocate its conference from Rome after all.

Uproar then broke out in Parliament when, in August and October, it passed legislation explained by the government as a step toward sweeping away obso-lescence and helping business but de-nounced by an angry opposition as meant to serve the interests of the prime minister or his friends. One new law replaced a prison term for render-ing false tax returns with a pecuniary penalty. A left-wing leader, Pierluigi Castagnetti, told Parliament that no country in the world would "pass a measure to solve its leader's problems with the law." At the time he spoke, Berlusconi faced penal proceedings for alleged financial misdeeds. Another new law, which dealt with rules of evi-dence, decreed as inadmissible docu-mentation acquired from abroad if the procedure followed to obtain it differed from Italy's. The government refuted the charges against it, terming its opponents "guardians of lies."

The prime minister stuck to his pledge on pensions but urged followers to vote "no" in an October referendum on devolution called by the previous government. Nevertheless, Italians, by a margin of 64%–34%, voted "yes" to the referendum and thus approved proposed changes in the working of the Italian state. The central government would relinquish powers to the country's regions in, for example, the spheres of education and the environment. City councils would also be able to raise certain taxes.

Following the September 11 terrorist attacks in the U.S., Berlusconi was among the European leaders who lined up to pledge support for the U.S.-led war on terrorism. The prime minister put the country on heightened alert and promised that Italy was "by the side of the United States and all who are committed to the battle against terrorism." Italy offered troops as well as the use of its ports and airports, but many in the country were anxious over possible repercussions from the conflict. Berlusconi hardly helped allay these anxieties with his statement to reporters in late September that the West was "superior" to Islamic civilization because it provided wealth and guaranteed respect for human rights. While the prime minister maintained that his comments had been taken out of context, European Union leaders took pains to distance themselves from his remarks.

Disaster struck Italy in October at Milan's Linate airport when, in heavy fog, a Scandinavian airliner collided during takeoff with a small jet taxiing across its path, killing a total of 118 people. (See DISASTERS.) Terrorism was initially suspected, but aviation experts later ruled it out, putting part of the blame instead on the absence of a working ground-level radar at the airport.   (DEREK WILSON)

JAMAICA

Area: 10,991 sq km (4,244 sq mi)
Population (2001 est.): 2,624,000
Capital: Kingston
Chief of state: Queen Elizabeth II, represented by Governor-General Sir Howard Cooke
Head of government: Prime Minister Percival J. Patterson

Tourism was dealt a severe blow when in March and April 2001 four cruise lines dropped Jamaica from their itineraries following complaints about visitor harassment. The reduction in tourist revenue was expected to amount to as much as $22 million. In May the government unveiled a $2 billion "master plan" for development of the tourist industry.

The electricity problems plaguing Jamaica and hampering development seemed on their way to being rectified in March when the government sold 80% of the Jamaica Public Service Co., the country's power generator and transmitter, to the American company Mirant, which promised to add another 385 MW of power to the existing 660 MW.

In a report issued in April by London-based Amnesty International, Jamaica's police service was sharply criticized for its violations of human rights. The report said that the police had unlawfully killed 140 people in 2000—a rate of about 5.4 per 100,000 persons, which, Amnesty said, was one of the highest in the world. The government described the report as "one-sided, false, and misleading."

Jamaica was bedeviled by spasmodic gang violence during much of the year, particularly in the West Kingston area, where in July at least 25 persons were killed in street violence. The government set up a commission of inquiry in September to look into gangs and links with the drug trade and organized crime.

(DAVID RENWICK)

JAPAN

Area: 377,837 sq km (145,884 sq mi)
Population (2001 est.): 127,100,000
Capital: Tokyo
Symbol of state: Emperor Akihito
Head of government: Prime Ministers Yoshiro Mori and, from April 26, Junichiro Koizumi

Domestic Affairs. For nearly five decades the Liberal-Democratic Party (LDP)—either alone or in coalition—had formed the government in Tokyo. Early in 2001, however, the party looked forward to the next national poll with unease. An election for 121 contested seats in the 247-seat (upper) House of Councillors was scheduled for the end of July. LDP leaders considered the real possibility of a loss in the vote.

In April 2000 Prime Minister Yoshiro Mori had been, as usual, selected in secret by LDP faction bosses. In 10 months of service, he had averaged one major blunder per month. On one occasion he referred to Japan as a "divine country," a phrase that called up memories of militarist rhetoric during the Pacific wars. In February 2001, after an American submarine collided with a Japanese trawler off the coast of Hawaii, with nine persons aboard the trawler missing, Mori continued to play golf for two hours after hearing about the accident.

A month later Mori bore a public approval rating of 6.5%, the lowest ever for a Japanese prime minister. On March 5 he survived a no-confidence vote in the (lower) House of Representatives, but rumours spread that he would soon step down. On April 6 Mori notified his cabinet that he would resign. In four days no fewer than five LDP leaders announced their candidacies for party president. At the head of popularity polls was Makiko Tanaka (see BIOGRAPHIES), the daughter of former prime minister Kakuei Tanaka. Her outspoken, often acerbic, comments on politics and politicians struck a responsive chord with the Japanese public. Tanaka once referred to her closest rival, Junichiro Koizumi, as a "crank." She eventually withdrew her candidacy and supported Koizumi, however.

A two-hour television debate on April 18 featured the four remaining candidates. Three veteran politicians faced off with Koizumi, the rising star. He seized the opportunity to air his platform. Instead of fiscal expenditures, which would result in additions to Japan's towering deficits, he urged economic reform and restraint. Koizumi was especially critical of Japan's debt-laden banking community; he also proposed privatization of the sacrosanct postal savings system.

In the LDP primaries, held on April 22–23, Koizumi took the first step toward power. He won a majority of votes (298 of 487) representing the 2.3 million party members and 346 LDP legislators. On April 24 he was elected president of the LDP. Two days later the Diet (parliament) confirmed him as prime minister. (See BIOGRAPHIES.)

Koizumi's victory, which was remarkable, considering he had denounced party factions, put him on a collision course with vested interests within the LDP itself. Faction bosses represented branches of the postal service, local construction firms, small retailers, and rice farmers all over Japan. In forming his administration, the new leader kept in mind the nature of his support. He led a three-party coalition that included the New Komeito (backed by the nation's largest Buddhist group) and the New Conservative Party. Only 6 of the 17 members of his cabinet came from the LDP's three main factions. An unprecedented number of women—five, including Tanaka, Japan's first female foreign minister—were given portfolios. For his minister of economic policy, Koizumi chose Heizo Takenaka, an economist from Keio University, Tokyo. In a surprise he named Masajuro Shiokawa finance minister. The 79-year-old Shiokawa had served in several governments but never as an adviser on finance matters.

The new regime enjoyed popular support, with surveys showing approval over the 80% level. At first Koizumi avoided controversial economic issues, concentrating instead on proposals attractive to the centre and the right. He called for a review of the so-called MacArthur constitution, imposed on Japan by the Allied powers in 1946. He advocated a more democratic system, including the direct election of the prime minister. Most important, Koizumi joined nationalists in urging that Japan allow its military forces to exercise a full-fledged (rather than only defensive) security policy. This last goal guaranteed opposition from a coalition ally, the pacifist New Komeito. Moreover, many Japanese, especially elders with grim wartime memories, were uneasy with the idea of increased military forces.

A preliminary but important endorsement of the new regime was received on June 24 in the Tokyo municipal poll. The coalition won a majority in an urban area where the LDP had always been weak. The next challenge was the scheduled upper house election set for July 29. Normally, Japanese political campaigns were mercifully short and discreet. In this case, however, there was an explosion of posters heralding Koizumi, as well as vigorous debates between local candidates. The LDP enjoyed its best victory since 1992; its coalition won 78 of the 121 contested seats.

On December 1 the royal family celebrated the birth of the first child—a daughter—to Crown Princess Masako and Crown Prince Naruhito; although the emperor traditionally would have decided the name, the couple themselves chose it—Princess Aiko.

The Economy. Japan's recession lingered during the year, with few signs that the country would emerge from it soon. The Finance Ministry announced that in December 2000 Japan's trade surplus had shrunk to $7 billion, the lowest monthly level since March 1997. Officials later identified the first two quarters of 2001 as marking the sharpest trade decline on record, with the surplus down 44% from the same two quarters of the previous year.

In similar fashion the current account surplus (the difference between income from foreign sources and payments on foreign obligations) for fiscal year 2000 fell 4.5%, the second consecutive annual decline. The month of July 2001

was the eighth straight in which this surplus fell, down 28% from a year earlier. Slowing global growth had reduced demand for Japan's exports.

Trade was by no means the only problem. On September 3 Tokyo stocks dove to a 17-year low, with the benchmark 225-issue Nikkei index down to 10,409.68—its worst showing since August 1984. On September 17, in the wake of the terrorist attacks in the U.S., the index sank to an 18-year low of 9,504.41. By October year-on-year industrial output had fallen by 11.9% to a 13-year low. Consumer spending, usually an engine of Japanese growth, was sluggish despite a deflation in retail prices.

Among the world's industrial powers, Japan traditionally expected low levels of unemployment. Corporations often provided lifetime employment to their workers. Therefore, one of the biggest shocks in the country's economic downturn had been the spread of unemployment. In October the unemployment rate reached 5.4%, a postwar high. Japan's demography, marked by an aging population and a sharply declining birthrate, exacerbated the problem.

The national census, released in October 2000, set Japan's population at 126,920,000 and cited only a 0.2% per annum rise in population from the prior count (1995). This was the smallest increase since World War II. Just as significant, the proportion of elderly Japanese (17.5% at age 65 and older) surpassed youngsters (14.5% at 15 or younger). The dilemma was that a shrinking number of working-age Japanese would be expected to support an exploding number of people at retirement age. Indeed, Japan had become the fastest-aging society among advanced industrial powers.

Foreign Affairs. With new executive leaders, Japan and the U.S. continued their discussions of familiar issues. U.S. Pres. George W. Bush (see BIOGRAPHIES), during his election campaign of 2000, had urged reinforcement of security ties with Japan. He recognized the problems generated by the presence of some 47,000 American troops based in Okinawa and promised adjustments. Before his election Bush had referred only indirectly to the economic downturns in both countries.

In fact, shortly after his inauguration Bush met with Koizumi's predecessor, Yoshiro Mori, already a lame duck. On March 18 the embattled Mori arrived in Washington, D.C., carrying a portfolio of problems. In January an American

On April 26, the day of his inauguration, Japanese Prime Minister Junichiro Koizumi (front row, centre) appears with his newly appointed cabinet.

AP/Wide World Photos

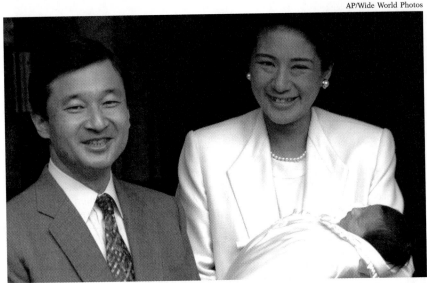

On December 8 Crown Prince Naruhito and Crown Princess Masako leave the palace hospital in Tokyo with their infant daughter, Princess Aiko.

marine corporal stationed in Okinawa had harassed a local girl. The local assembly immediately issued a resolution calling for a reduction of American forces in the area. On January 23 the senior U.S. commander there, Lieut. Gen. Earl Hailston, fired off an e-mail to fellow officers, referring to the local officials as "nuts" and "wimps." When this was leaked to the press, Hailston apologized. The assembly nevertheless issued a demand for his dismissal on February 7. Local leaders insisted on a revised U.S.-Japan Status of Forces Agreement, and on February 22—for the first time—Okinawa Gov. Keiichi Inamine, who had hitherto supported the American military, joined the requests for an adjustment to the agreement.

Meanwhile, Washington and Tokyo faced another, more bizarre challenge. On February 9 the USS *Greeneville*, an American submarine, collided with the *Ehime-maru*, a Japanese fishing trawler, near Hawaii. The submarine, which had been executing a quick surface drill, sliced the Japanese vessel in half and helplessly watched as it sank. Teachers and students from a fisheries-vocation school in Japan were aboard the ship, and after the accident nine persons remained missing.

The next day the commander in chief of the U.S. Pacific fleet, Adm. Thomas Fargo, apologized to Tokyo, as did Secretary of State Colin Powell (*see* BIOGRAPHIES), who passed along President Bush's condolences. In presenting his formal farewell to Emperor Akihito, retiring Ambassador Thomas Foley also expressed regret. On February 28 the captain of the submarine, Comdr. Scott D. Waddle, sent a letter of regret to the victims' families through Japan's consulate in Hawaii.

On March 26 Bush named a former senator, Howard H. Baker, Jr., to be ambassador to Japan. Before Baker arrived, however, a range of new issues arose.

The April 1 incident involving a collision between an American reconnaissance plane and a Chinese fighter jet over the South China Sea seemed to some observers to have only marginal interest to the Japanese. The American plane had, however, taken off from the U.S. Air Force base at Kadena, Okinawa. After the collision—which caused the crash of the Chinese jet and the death of its pilot—the American plane made an emergency landing on Hainan Island. The plane's crew members, detained for a time by Chinese authorities, were eventually released. Japanese opinion was divided over the incident. For some it represented a warning about growing threats—posed not only by China but also by North Korea, which supported Beijing.

On May 8 U.S. Deputy Secretary of State Richard Armitage publicly urged Japan to form a strategic partnership like that between the U.S. and Great Britain. Some Japanese worried about the "overwhelming presence" of U.S. military forces already on Okinawa, and many were concerned about Tokyo's tacit support of a deliberately vague Washington policy toward Taiwan.

On June 30 Koizumi made his first visit as prime minister to the U.S., meeting President Bush at Camp David, Mary-

land. On the very eve of Koizumi's arrival, yet another incident involving U.S. military personnel based on Okinawa emerged to overshadow the summit. Japanese police picked up an American air force sergeant in a small village near Kadena. He was questioned about an encounter with a local woman but was released. After she claimed she was raped, local officials demanded that the man be returned to them. For only the second time, the U.S. released a serviceman on active duty for trial in a local court. The sergeant pleaded not guilty, and the trial dragged on.

Meanwhile, the Koizumi-Bush summit turned out to be somewhat of an anticlimax. A communiqué listed the topics informally discussed by the two leaders. These included continued security cooperation, economic partnership for growth, and cooperation on global change. The prime minister visited Washington again on September 25, when he promised the president help in logistics and intelligence in the U.S. campaign against terrorism.

The subject of textbooks came to dominate diplomatic relations between Japan, South Korea, Taiwan, and China. In Seoul on February 28—the day before the 82nd anniversary of a Korean uprising against Japanese rule—South Korean Foreign Minister Lee Joung Binn gave a warning to Ambassador Terusuke Terada of Japan, stating that Tokyo's approval of a textbook praising Imperial Japan's record as a colonial ruler of Korea and much of China would undermine relations. Some 19 groups demonstrated in front of the Japanese embassy in Seoul, and demonstrators in Pusan burned a Japanese flag and destroyed an effigy of a right-wing Japanese politician.

In Japan Foreign Minister Tanaka admitted that the textbook controversy was having a negative impact. Indeed, on May 8 Seoul canceled a scheduled joint military exercise with Japan. Koreans were particularly upset over the fact that Japan had never confessed to the mobilization of thousands of Koreans to be "comfort women" for Japanese troops. Koizumi nevertheless replied that Tokyo could not "revise again" textbooks approved by the Education Ministry. On June 11 hundreds of protesters—including Japanese, Chinese, Koreans, and Filipinos—surrounded the ministry and sang "We Shall Overcome."

To make matters worse, Koizumi remarked that he was considering a visit, as prime minister, to the Yasukuni Shrine in Tokyo on August 15, the anniversary of Japan's surrender at the end of World War II. The shrine memorialized the sacrifices of Japan's dead veterans, including several well-known convicted war criminals. This plan met the opposition of Tanaka, who had received warnings from Taiwan, China, and the Philippines. As it turned out, Koizumi retreated a bit but on August 13 did officially, though briefly, pay homage at the shrine. China and South Korea filed protests. On December 22 Japanese Coast Guard ships exchanged fire with and sank a vessel suspected of being a North Korean spy boat. Tokyo later announced that it planned to seek Beijing's permission to salvage the boat from waters claimed to be in China's economic zone.

In a telephone conversation on June 6, Tanaka and her Russian counterpart, Foreign Minister Igor S. Ivanov, agreed to resume talks toward signing a formal peace treaty. No such accord had been reached since 1945, when Russian forces occupied small islands—long claimed by Japan—between Hokkaido and the Russian-held Kuril Islands. Japan referred to these islets as the Northern Territories. In June, Voice of Russia radio announced that South Korean fishing vessels would be welcome to work in the area. Japan's Fisheries Ministry had threatened to bar Korean fishing in Japanese waters if the Korean vessels did fish there. By September tempers had cooled, and senior officials in Tokyo and Moscow predicted that they could settle the dispute.   (ARDATH W. BURKS)

JORDAN

Area: 89,342 sq km (34,495 sq mi)
Population (2001 est.): 5,133,000 (including more than 1,500,000 Palestinian refugees, most of whom hold Jordanian citizenship)
Capital: Amman
Head of state and government: King Abdullah II, assisted by Prime Minister 'Ali Abu ar-Raghib

Jordan hosted the 13th ordinary session of the Arab League summit on March 27–28, 2001. The Arab leaders, who decided to meet annually, regarded this conference as a milestone to safeguarding "the vital interests of Arab countries within the context of achieving Arab accord and pan-Arab security."

On June 16 the Jordanian cabinet, headed by Prime Minister 'Ali Abu ar-Raghib, was reshuffled. Eleven cabinet ministers were replaced, but the total membership remained at 29. Among the newcomers were two independent Islamists.

On July 22 the State Security Court, in a retrial ordered in April, passed life sentences against nine defendants, all members of the radical Islamic Reform and Challenge organization, who had been accused of a series of car-park bombings in Amman in 1998. Amnesty International denounced the proceedings and called for a retrial by a criminal court.

King Abdullah II was the first Arab leader to visit the U.S. following the terroist attacks of September 11. In talks with Pres. George W. Bush, Abdullah fully supported the war against terrorism and pointed to Jordan's successful foiling of Osama bin Laden's terrorist operations in Jordan in 1999.

Although Palestinian leader Yasir Arafat, who made numerous visits to Amman, sought Abdullah's help to revive the Middle East peace process, Jordanian opposition parties headed by the Islamic Action Front had a different agenda. On September 28 these parties marked the first anniversary of the Palestinian *intifadah* by declaring "that the strategic option of peace with Israel is no longer valid." The Islamic Action Front, the political arm of the Muslim Brotherhood Movement, was the largest and most influential political group among Jordan's 25 registered parties.

On October 8, one day after U.S. air strikes began against Afghanistan, the Jordanian government adopted amendments to the penal code with restrictive measures against the press, including fines and prison sentences up to three years. The new law stipulated the permanent or temporary closure of publications that carried "false or libelous information that can undermine national unity or the country's reputation."

During the year Jordan further improved its excellent relations with Egypt, Syria, and Iraq. On March 14 King Abdullah, Egyptian Pres. Hosni Mubarak, and Syrian Pres. Bashar al-Assad inaugurated the Dair Ali power station, located at the Jordanian-Syrian border. The joint power grid linked the three countries. On June 5 Royal Jordanian Airlines resumed regular flights to Baghdad, Iraq, and in August a delegation headed by the Jordanian minister of industry and trade and four other members of the cabinet made an official visit to Iraq.   (MARIUS K. DEEB)

KAZAKHSTAN

Area: 2,724,900 sq km (1,052,090 sq mi)
Population (2001 est.): 14,868,000
Capital: Astana
Head of state and government: President Nursultan Nazarbayev, assisted by Prime Minister Kasymzhomart Tokayev

In 2001 Kazakhstan's efforts to integrate into the international community beyond the Commonwealth of Independent States (CIS) were stymied by the country's worsening human rights record. In early March a delegation from the Parliamentary Assembly of the Council of Europe arrived in Almaty to examine the human rights and social situation in connection with Kazakhstan's application for observer status in the Council. Opposition activists publicly criticized the government for allowing only meetings with pro-government groups, which portrayed the progress of democratization in the country as far rosier than warranted by reality. Kazakhstan's application was subsequently denied by the Council.

The opposition and international observers were also critical of draft amendments to laws on the media and on religion. The latter included a provision for banning extremist sects and unauthorized missionary activity. In March the National Security Committee complained of an increase in Islamic religious and extremist activities in southern Kazakhstan. Shortly thereafter a group of adherents of the banned Muslim sect Hizb ut-Tahrir were put on trial for terrorism.

Leaders of the opposition Republican People's Party and members of seven other opposition groups told foreign contacts that they had been harassed by the authorities because of their objections to the revised media law. Kazakhstan's international reputation was further damaged when security officials prevented two opposition politicians from taking part in a congressional hearing in the United States in July, though the country's image received a boost at the end of that month when the abolition of exit visas for Kazakhstani citizens was announced.

Kazakhstan's economic outlook improved with the commissioning in March of the pipeline linking the Tengiz oil field in western Kazakhstan to the Russian Black Sea oil port of Novorossiysk. The pipeline, fully operational by December, significantly increased the amount of Kazakhstani oil that could be exported. An official proposal to raise money by accepting nuclear waste from abroad for burial in Kazakhstan set off protests by the country's influential environmental lobby.

In May Kazakhstan agreed with Russia, Kyrgyzstan, and Tajikistan to set up a rapid reaction force under the CIS Collective Security Treaty. In the wake of the September 11 attacks in the U.S., Kazakhstani Pres. Nursultan Nazarbayev ordered intensified security on Kazakhstan's borders and offered use of the country's airspace and ground facilities to the U.S.-led antiterrorism coalition. In a step that caused considerable friction within the region, Kazakhstan's borders were closed to citizens of Tajikistan.   (BESS BROWN)

KENYA

Area: 582,646 sq km (224,961 sq mi)
Population (2001 est.): 30,766,000
Capital: Nairobi
Head of state and government: President Daniel arap Moi

In January 2001 Kenyan Pres. Daniel arap Moi joined with the presidents of Tanzania and Uganda to launch a new East African Economic Community. Conditions at home were far from propitious for such a venture, however. The economy was shrinking; the value of the Kenyan shilling (K Sh) had declined and now stood at about 79 to the U.S. dollar; and the price of petroleum had risen to K Sh 56 per litre (about $2.68 per gallon). Meanwhile, the International Monetary Fund (IMF) and the World Bank continued to withhold aid because of the government's failure to control corruption.

Early in February hopes were raised when the government selected a consortium led by South Africa-based Econet Wireless to buy 49% of the state-owned telecommunications company, Telkom, which the IMF had insisted should be privatized. To the disgust of the World Bank, which blamed the Kenyan government, the deal fell through, but other

donors had already warned that, even if the plan had materialized, aid would not be forthcoming until an effective anti-corruption policy was in place.

The resignation as head of the Kenyan Civil Service on March 26 of Richard Leakey, who had been appointed to lead the campaign against corruption, was seen at first to have been another serious setback to the reform program. Leakey's campaign, however, had been faltering for some months because of the opposition of senior officials and other members of the government who feared for their own reputations. Leakey's own reputation was threatened when it became known that his resignation followed upon allegations by a British-born businessman that Leakey had written a letter to the attorney general of Kenya urging him to halt proceedings on a charge of fraud that the businessman had brought against a Dutch bank. Leakey, who was known to have close links with the Dutch royal family, had argued that the case would put a strain on Kenya's relations with The Netherlands. He was replaced as head of the civil service by Sally Kosgei, a highly respected civil servant and former high commissioner in London.

On June 17 President Moi began engineering a merger between the ruling Kenya African National Union and the National Development Party (NDP), Kenya's second largest opposition party. He then appointed Raila Odinga, the leader of the NDP, together with Adhu Owiti, another prominent figure in the party, to a reshuffled cabinet.

Opponents of the government were not slow to respond. On June 24 Charity Kaluki Ngilu, the Social Democratic Party's candidate in the 1997 presidential election, launched a new party, the National Party of Kenya, claiming that gender equality would feature prominently in the party's manifesto. More significantly, on August 14 opposition members in the National Assembly prevented the government from achieving the two-thirds majority needed to enact a bill ostensibly aimed at combating corruption. The opposition claimed that the bill was a sham, intended to deceive the IMF into renewing aid. The following day the IMF announced that it would remain in dialogue with the government but would be unable to resume aid payments. This meant that help from other sources would not be forthcoming. A few days later the government joined with six other eastern African countries to launch an African Trade Insurance Agency, to be based in Nairobi and intended to undercut the high premiums demanded from African companies by foreign insurance agencies, which regarded Africa as a high-risk area.

Early in December disturbances broke out in the most deprived locality in Nairobi, ostensibly in support of a demand for reduced rents, though there were suggestions that the violence had political undertones. Later that month the government agreed that U.S. and U.K. troops might use Kenya as a base for operations against alleged terrorist cells in Somalia.

(KENNETH INGHAM)

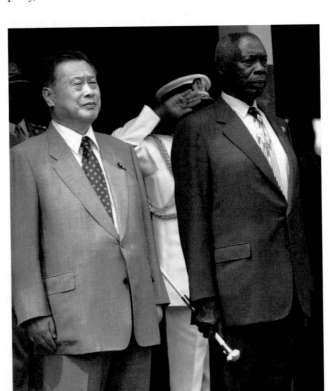

Japanese Prime Minister Yoshiro Mori and Kenyan Pres. Daniel arap Moi listen to the Japanese national anthem upon Mori's arrival in Nairobi on January 10.

AP/Wide World Photos

KIRIBATI

Area: 811 sq km (313 sq mi)
Population (2001 est.): 94,100
Capital: Bairiki, on Tarawa
Head of state and government: President Teburoro Tito

In Kiribati, with stability in domestic politics and the economy remaining largely dependent on foreign aid and trust investments derived from previous phosphate mining, the high points of 2001 had an international dimension. In October the government joined Australia in investigating the establishment of a processing centre for asylum-seeking refugees on Kanton (Canton), an island 1,900 km (about 1,200 mi) southeast of Tarawa. Kanton, a part of Kiribati formerly governed under a British-U.S. condominium, had been used for transpacific civil aviation from the 1930s and as a U.S. military base.

During the year Kiribati opened its first overseas diplomatic mission (in Fiji), while the U.K. reopened its mission in Kiribati. Early in the year Kiribati hosted a meeting on the implications of global warming for itself and other low-lying atoll nations facing the possibility of land loss and an increased frequency of cyclonic storms. The country was also one of the signatories to the Waigani Convention—a 1995 Pacific Islands initiative banning the importation of radioactive waste and placing controls on the shipment of hazardous materials; it finally went into effect in late 2001. Pres. Teburoro Tito announced plans for an airline with service links to neighbouring countries.   (BARRIE MACDONALD)

KOREA, DEMOCRATIC PEOPLE'S REPUBLIC OF

Area: 122,762 sq km (47,399 sq mi)
Population (2001 est.): 21,968,000
Capital: Pyongyang
Chief of state: Chairman of the National Defense Commission Kim Jong Il
Head of government: Chairman of the Council of Ministers (Premier) Hong Sang Nam

Work progresses toward reconnecting a railway across the border between North and South Korea on June 15.

Reclusive North Korean chief of state Kim Jong Il made several state visits to other countries in the year 2001. In January Kim visited Shanghai, China's financial capital, touring several companies and holding economic discussions. In late July–early August he made a 10-day trip to Russia, meeting with Russian Pres. Vladimir Putin. North Korea had been dismayed at the growing economic cooperation between Russia and South Korea; on the military front the two leaders spoke of limitations on North Korean missile testing. Kim pledged to continue a moratorium on missile testing until at least the year 2003. Western nations hoped that Putin would be able to persuade North Korea to become more open and more willing to contact Western countries directly.

Relations between North Korea and the U.S. had been developing through negotiations during the final years of Bill Clinton's administration, but all negotiations were put on hold after George W. Bush took office. The new Bush administration initially announced that it was going to review the relationship before proceeding. Secretary of State Colin Powell later called for resumed talks, but North Korea demanded to set the agenda before any meetings took place.

North Korea continued to struggle with a failing economy and agriculture shortfalls domestically. In mid-May at a UNICEF conference in Beijing, remarkable statistics revealing conditions inside North Korea were reported by Deputy Foreign Minister Choe Su Hon. The report indicated that life expectancy had fallen from 73.2 years in 1993 to 66.8 by 1999. Mortality rates for children under five rose during those years from 27 to 48 per 1,000. Infant mortality rose from 14 to 22.5 per 1,000 births. Per capita gross national product dropped from $991 per year to $457. The percentage of children getting vaccinations for diseases such as polio and measles fell from 90% to 50% between 1990 and 1997. The percentage of the population with access to safe water fell from 86% to just 53% between 1994 and 1996. The report at the UNICEF conference confirmed some of the worst fears the outside world had had of the situation inside the closed and secretive country.

(MARK PETERSON)

KOREA, REPUBLIC OF

Area: 99,461 sq km (38,402 sq mi)
Population (2001 est.): 47,676,000
Capital: Seoul
Head of state and government: President Kim Dae Jung

In late 2000 South Korean Pres. Kim Dae Jung was awarded the Nobel Peace Prize for his efforts to bring peace to the peninsula by way of negotiations with North Korea. In early 2001, however, cold water was thrown on these efforts by none other than Korea's closest ally—the United States. Soon after his inauguration in January, U.S. Pres. George W. Bush announced that the U.S. wanted to review its policy toward North Korea. In March President Kim visited the Bush White House but was unable to persuade the Americans to again get on board his program for negotiations. The situation eventually improved, and Secretary of State Colin Powell announced at midyear that the U.S. would be interested in reopening discussions with North Korea.

South Korean–Russian relations took a step forward in February when Russian Pres. Vladimir Putin visited Seoul. The two countries agreed to increase economic cooperation, and South Korea joined Russia in expressions of opposition to American development of a missile-defense system. Within a few weeks, however, American protests had pushed the South Korean government into rethinking its position. By late March the confusion over foreign policy had led to a shuffle of the president's cabinet; among the changes were the office of foreign minister—Lee Joung Binn was replaced by Han Seung Soo, formerly trade minister and ambassador to the U.S.

South Korea opened a new airport in late March. Incheon International Airport, located outside Seoul and built at a cost of $5.5 billion, could handle 27 million passengers per year.

Relations with Japan took a turn for the worse when the textbook controversy again flared up. As in the past, Japan's officially sanctioned textbooks played down the aggressive role of the Japanese in their invasions of Asian countries during World War II. The controversy hit the press in April and in protest South Korea canceled a planned joint military exercise in May. The National Assembly passed a resolution condemning the Japanese action. The dispute had a peaceful resolution by the end of the year, when

Japanese Prime Minister Junichiro Koizumi (*see* BIOGRAPHIES) visited Seoul and apologized for the errors.

There was both good news and bad news on the economic front. The best of the good news was that South Korea paid off the last of the loans from the International Monetary Fund (IMF) bailout. The economic disaster that hit the country in December 1997—and was thereafter referred to in South Korea as the "IMF period"—was officially over, although there were still many economic problems. In mid-August the government announced that 40 companies were going to collapse. By November the Central Bank and Finance Ministry announced that the economy would likely grow a meagre 2.5% during the year.

South Korea, though disappointed in the lack of progress in talks with North Korea and the U.S., pushed ahead with contacts with the North. Although Red Cross talks and family visits were suspended, South Korea continued its humanitarian aid to North Korea on the one hand and tourism to the special tourist zone in the Diamond Mountains on the other. Tourism was an important source of income for North Korea, and South Korean aid, together with aid from many other countries, had become essential to preventing even greater human suffering in the North.

(MARK PETERSON)

KUWAIT

Area: 17,818 sq km (6,880 sq mi)
Population (2001 est.): 2,275,000
Capital: Kuwait City
Head of state and government: Emir Sheikh Jabir al-Ahmad al-Jabir as-Sabah, assisted by Prime Minister Crown Prince Sheikh Saad al-Abdullah as-Salim as-Sabah

Prior to the terrorist attacks in New York City and Washington, D.C., on Sept. 11, 2001, strength in oil prices had led economic analysts to predict another year of prosperity for Kuwait. The strong oil market had boosted gross domestic product growth in the country for a second year in a row. Following September 11, however, slumping demand in Kuwait's principal markets, Asia and Europe, exposed the fragility of the economy. The one bright spot in

the domestic sector was a boom in house construction. Government housing programs were so far behind demand that Kuwaitis increasingly had been availing themselves of interest-free loans and building homes on their own.

The stagnant economy reflected a deeper problem: government paralysis due to the age and debility of the nation's leaders. In late September Emir Sheikh Jabir al-Ahmad al-Jabir as-Sabah suffered a brain hemorrhage and was taken to London for medical treatment. The caretaker government—constrained from taking initiatives without the emir's backing—was thus stymied with regard to continued Islamist agitation, including fallout from the revelation following the September 11 attacks that a member of the inner circle of the al-Qaeda terrorist organization was a Kuwaiti.

A January 2001 request by Uday Hussein, son of Pres. Saddam Hussein, to the Iraqi parliament to revise the country's maps to include Kuwait within Iraq's borders served as a grim reminder that, despite having signed a treaty recognizing Kuwait as an independent state, Iraq remained a threat to its continued independence. Even so, the Kuwaiti government had backed down repeatedly in confrontations with Islamists. In a startling statement about government laxity in this regard, a former oil and information minister and member of the ruling family, Sheikh Saud Nasir as-Sabah, connected the government's tepid support for U.S. antiterrorism measures following September 11 to the successful "hijacking" of the government by Islamist militants. "We should remove the veil of secrecy that protects these groups and their financial and political activities in Kuwait and abroad," the sheikh declared.

(MARY ANN TÉTREAULT)

KYRGYZSTAN

Area: 199,900 sq km (77,200 sq mi)
Population (2001 est.): 4,883,000
Capital: Bishkek
Head of state and government: President Askar Akayev, assisted by Prime Minister Kurmanbek Bakiyev

In mid-January 2001 Kyrgyzstan's Defense Council concerned itself with repelling attacks by Muslim extremists.

South Korean Pres. Kim Dae Jung (right) is greeted by Chinese Pres. Jiang Zemin at the Science and Technology Museum in Shanghai prior to an Asia-Pacific Economic Cooperation meeting on October 21.

Top priority was given to strengthening defense, and Kyrgyzstan joined the Central Asian rapid reaction force that was set up in Bishkek in August.

In July fighting was reported in the south between Kyrgyz troops and the Islamic Movement of Uzbekistan. Tajikistan, whence the militants were supposed to have come, questioned the accuracy of the reports, however, and the head of Kyrgyzstan's National Security Council asserted that the fighting had actually involved an armed gang of drug smugglers. Later reports emerged of an attempt by presumed militants to seize control of a television relay station in the mountains of Batken region.

There was also growing concern in Kyrgyzstan over the possibility that extremism would develop among the population in the southern part of the country, which had a large Uzbek component and had long felt itself neglected by the more developed north. In April Prime Minister Kurmanbek Bakiyev stated that many mosques had been built recently in the south and the government was intensifying its supervision of religion. The state commission on religious affairs was moved to Osh, the "southern capital," in an effort to counter extremist tendencies, including the growth of the banned Hizb ut-Tahrir sect. A number of persons in the south were put on trial for their membership in the sect, which was officially regarded in all Central Asian states as a terrorist organization, although its adherents insisted that they rejected violence and sought to set up an Islamic state through peaceful means.

Relations with Uzbekistan remained cool throughout the year, partly because of the Uzbek practice of shutting off the gas supply to Kyrgyzstan. A Kyrgyz proposal to exchange gas for water was rejected by Tashkent. In February the Kyrgyz government signed a secret memorandum that would give Uzbekistan easier access to an exclave in southern Kyrgyzstan, but the Kyrgyz parliament rejected the transfer of land that would be involved and sharply criticized the government for its secret dealings. Lawmakers also attacked the leadership for striking an agreement with China to settle a long-standing border dispute by handing over some mountainous territory. In September the parliament refused to ratify an agreement with Uzbekistan on fighting terrorism, demanding that the Uzbeks first remove their land mines from the common border. In December the parliament approved the use of the Manas Airport by the U.S.-led antiterrorist coalition.   (BESS BROWN)

LAOS

Area: 236,800 sq km (91,429 sq mi)
Population (2001 est.): 5,636,000
Capital: Vientiane (Viangchan)
Chief of state: President Khamtai Siphandon
Head of government: Prime Ministers Sisavath Keobounphanh and, from March 27, Boungnang Vorachith

The seventh congress of the Lao People's Revolutionary Party was opened on March 12, 2001, by Pres. Khamtai Siphandon, who, as anticipated, was unanimously reelected party chairman. Contrary to widespread predictions that Vientiane's increasingly market-oriented policies would lead to a more reform-minded leadership, most of the secretive political and military chiefs retained their positions. On March 27 the compliant National Assembly chose Finance Minister Boungnang Vorachith to replace Sisavath Keobounphanh as prime minister, but Sisavath kept his seat on the all-powerful Political Bureau. President Khamtai was uncharacteristically frank about the failure of the previous government to bring about increased prosperity and outlined an ambitious 20-year program for economic growth and better education, health, and living standards. Few impartial observers, including analysts at the international lending agencies, put

much faith in the promised outcome, however, pointing out that Laos's dependence on foreign aid had doubled over the previous 15 years to about half of the annual budget in 2001. In April the International Monetary Fund approved a $40 million loan for financial stability.

Laos and Thailand signed an agreement in March to construct a second bridge over the Mekong River at Savannakhet, about 500 km (310 mi) downstream from the existing bridge near Vientiane. New roads were envisaged to promote trade with Vietnam. In August Laos and Cambodia approached Japan for financial backing for yet another Mekong bridge. Laos's largest source of foreign exchange—the income from selling hydroelectricity to Thailand—was dealt a blow when Bangkok, blaming an economic slowdown, reduced the number of purchases it promised to make. In June the problem of refugees was addressed at a UN-sponsored conference in Louangphrabang, the old royal capital. Human rights groups in the U.S. heavily criticized the continuing forced repatriation of refugees from Thailand. A simmering row over the detention of two Australian business executives for what Vientiane claimed to be fraud in a gem-mining business threatened to damage relations with one of the country's leading aid donors. Eventually the two were released to the Australian ambassador. During the course of this controversy, Vientiane introduced new controls over both local and foreign media.

(ROBERT WOODROW)

At a press conference in Brisbane on November 9, Kerry Danes and his wife, Kay—the two Australian business executives who had been accused of fraud in Laos—describe the relief they felt at being allowed to return home.

William West/AFP Worldwide

LATVIA

Area: 64,589 sq km (24,938 sq mi)
Population (2001 est.): 2,358,000
Capital: Riga
Chief of state: President Vaira Vike-Freiberga
Head of government: Prime Minister Andris Berzins

Latvians and foreign visitors joined to celebrate Riga's 800th anniversary in 2001; commemorative cultural events took place throughout the summer. Latvians were buoyant with optimism as the country neared membership in the European Union (EU) and NATO and generally enjoyed fine foreign relations. The economy had recovered, with predictions that the 6.6% growth rate in 2000 would even be exceeded in 2001. Politics, too, seemed to have stabilized, with Prime Minister Andris Berzins's government having held office since May 2000, which set some kind of Latvian record for longevity. The most popular leaders in the country represented the centre-right, but the local elections on March 11 demonstrated the vigour of the left as well.

In acknowledgment of Latvia's adherence to the principles of human rights and integration of its noncitizens (mostly ethnic Russians), the Council of Europe Parliamentary Assembly ended its monitoring procedures in the country, and the Organization for Security and Cooperation in Europe announced in December that it would close its mission in January 2002. Nonetheless, Russia continued to accuse Latvia of violating the rights of its Russian-speaking population. Latvian diplomatic missions in Russia were targeted for vandalism on the occasions of war-crimes trials against World War II Soviet officers and when young National Bolsheviks from Russia were sentenced for having tried to blow up a church in Riga in November 2000. The Latvian and Russian presidents met in Austria on February 10, but little progress was registered overall on substantive issues such as Russia's not signing the border accords with Latvia, which had been ready since 1997. Squabbling picked up again after Latvia's supportive response to the U.S. call for a worldwide campaign against terrorism. Russia claimed that Latvia was aiding Chechen terrorists, but Latvia countered that the Russians were simply trying to impede Latvia's membership in the EU and NATO.   (DZINTRA BUNGS)

LEBANON

Area: 10,400 sq km (4,016 sq mi)
Population (2001 est.): 3,628,000 (excluding Palestinian refugees estimated to number about 330,000)
Capital: Beirut
Chief of state: President Gen. Émile Lahoud
Head of government: Prime Minister Rafiq al-Hariri

Before the events of Sept. 11, 2001, Lebanon was consumed to a large extent with its own internal affairs. In August state security forces, apparently with the approval of Pres. Émile Lahoud, conducted a wave of arrests of anti-Syrian activists, some of whom were accused of conspiring with Israel. Although most of them were released later, two journalists and a political adviser to Samir Geagea, the imprisoned leader of disbanded right-wing Lebanese forces, remained in custody because security forces said they had hard evidence linking them to Israel. The episode triggered a crisis between the Lebanese president and the prime minister, Rafiq al-Hariri, since the cabinet was not consulted and did not approve the steps taken by the security forces. Normalcy did not return to relations between Lahoud and al-Hariri until Syrian officials intervened and asked the two to put aside their differences. A year after the Israeli withdrawal from southern Lebanon, Hezbollah—Lebanon's main resistance force in the region—refused to consider that the country had regained its full sovereignty, since Israel still controlled the Sheba' farms enclave and had not released all Lebanese prisoners of war, and Israeli warplanes patrolled Lebanese skies at will. A military attack by Hezbollah in June on Israeli targets in the Sheba' farms region was countered by an Israeli attack on Syrian military targets in the Lebanese Al-Biqa' (Bekaa Valley). At the end of July, the UN Security Council voted unanimously to downgrade the UN interim force in southern Lebanon to an observer mission and cut its military personnel from 4,500 to 3,600.

In its first steps toward privatization, the government laid off all the employees of the official television network. It also laid off one-third of the employees of Middle East Airlines, the national carrier. Privatization was also being considered for other state-run utilities, such as electricity. Lebanon's mounting public debt was expected to reach 170% of the country's gross domestic product by the end of the year.

In the aftermath of the September 11 terrorist attacks in the U.S., Lebanon tried to walk a tightrope. Lebanese officials were at pains to stress their condemnation of the attacks against civilians, while at the same time, they emphasized the distinction between terrorism and the struggle for liberation. U.S. Pres. George W. Bush's statement in early October in support of establishing a Palestinian state was welcomed by Lebanese officials, who had been fearful of what they perceived as international pressure on them to naturalize about 330,000 Palestinian refugees living on Lebanese soil. The same officials were uneasy, however, about mixed signals from Washington over the possibility of targeting Hezbollah for attack as a terrorist organization. Although certain Lebanese sectors —particularly tourism—were negatively affected by the September 11 attacks and the U.S.-led retaliation on Afghanistan in October, some saw a glimmer of hope, since many Lebanese and Arabs living in the West felt unwelcome there and many were starting to transfer part of their liquid wealth to Lebanese banks, while Arab students who were targets of harassment were expected to transfer to Lebanese universities that followed Western educational systems. On a different note, and owing to the tense situation in the Middle East, the Francophone Summit that was scheduled to meet in Beirut in October 2001 was postponed to October 2002.   (MAHMOUD HADDAD)

LESOTHO

Area: 30,355 sq km (11,720 sq mi)
Population (2001 est.): 2,177,000
Capital: Maseru
Chief of state: King Letsie III
Head of government: Prime Minister Bathuel Pakalitha Mosisili

More than two years of wrangling over the way an election should be held was ended in February 2001 when the country's political parties endorsed a plan that was drawn up by the Independent Electoral Commission for the holding of elections. Preparations for voter registration were then made, and registration itself took place in August and September. An election was to be held in 2002.

A power struggle within the ruling Lesotho Congress for Democracy party, which had itself emerged as a breakaway from the Basotho Congress Party in 1997, began with the election of a new national executive committee in January. The election was disputed and referred to the Court of Appeal to settle. At the end of September, the deputy prime minister and minister of law, justice, and constitutional affairs, Kelebone Maope, resigned from the cabinet. He had long been a critic of Prime Minister Bathuel Pakalitha Mosisili, and in October he formed an opposition party, the Lesotho People's Congress.

There was much disillusion within the country about the political infighting, which distracted attention from the real issues of poverty and HIV/AIDS. One bright note was a grant of $15,240,000 by the World Bank to the governments of South Africa and Lesotho for a five-year Maloti-Drakensberg Transfrontier Conservation and Development Project. This was to protect an area on Lesotho's eastern border and develop small businesses involved with ecotourism. With further retrenchments in the South African mines causing unemployment in Lesotho to reach perhaps 50%, the government saw new foreign direct investment, especially in the textile sector, as one hope for the future.

(CHRISTOPHER SAUNDERS)

LIBERIA

Area: 97,754 sq km (37,743 sq mi)
Population (2001 est.): 3,226,000
Capital: Monrovia
Head of state and government: President Charles Taylor

In March 2001 the UN Security Council voted to impose sanctions on Liberia unless it stopped supporting

In Monrovia, Liberia, on September 10, men repair shoes beneath a billboard protesting UN-imposed sanctions against the West African country.

Sierra Leone's Revolutionary United Front rebels. The sanctions, which included a worldwide ban on Liberian diamonds and travel restrictions on senior government officials, took effect in May despite Liberian claims of compliance with UN demands. Some humanitarian groups called for sanctions against Liberian timber, alleging that Pres. Charles Taylor was diverting timber profits to military use.

Beginning in April there was an increase in fighting between the army and antigovernment rebels in Lofa county in the north of the country. President Taylor claimed that Guinea and Sierra Leone supported the rebels and expelled those countries' ambassadors, although they were later allowed to return. In September defense ministers from the three countries met in an effort to find ways to end the conflict. Though rebels captured two towns in Gbarpolu county, northwest of Monrovia, in November, the government forces later retook the towns. Fighting remained heavy at year's end, and some humanitarian organizations withdrew from the worst areas. According to humanitarian sources, more than 40,000 people had fled this latest round of fighting. The UN World Food Programme reported feeding nearly 300,000

people in Liberia, including internally displaced persons and refugees from Sierra Leone.

The government imposed numerous restrictions on the press. Several newspapers were closed, and journalists were arrested after criticizing the government. In March security forces entered the University of Liberia and arrested students who were rallying in support of detained journalists. Students and faculty members reported being beaten.

In April former deputy information minister Milton Teahjay disappeared after trying to leave the country. Teahjay, a former opposition activist, had been taken into the government by President Taylor but was later dismissed for opposing logging activities in parts of the country. Human rights organizations and opposition groups alleged a government role in Teahjay's disappearance, and they demanded a full investigation into the matter. Also in April the sports minister, François Massaquoi, who was himself a former faction leader, was killed when rebels allegedly fired on his helicopter. President Taylor appointed a commission to investigate the killing, as some opposition figures charged that the government was involved.

(MATTHEW A. CENZER)

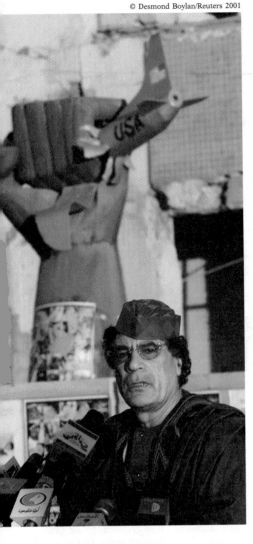

Muammar al-Qaddafi speaks to reporters in Tripoli on February 5 regarding the trial of two Libyan officials accused of the December 1988 downing of a Pan Am jetliner over Lockerbie, Scot.

LIBYA

Area: 1,757,000 sq km (678,400 sq mi)
Population (2001 est.): 5,241,000
Capital: Tripoli (policy-making body and many secretariats intermittently meet in Surt)
Chief of state: (de facto) Col. Muammar al-Qaddafi; (nominal) Secretary of the General People's Congress Zentani Muhammad az-Zentani
Head of government: Secretary of the General People's Committee (Prime Minister) Mubarak Abdallah ash-Shamikh

In Libya January 2001 was dominated by the trial in The Netherlands of two Libyan officials charged with having downed Pan Am Flight 103 over Lockerbie, Scot., on Dec. 21, 1988. The trial, conducted under Scottish law, found Lamin Khalifa Fhimah not guilty, but 'Abd al-Baset al-Megrahi was jailed for life. A preliminary administrative hearing of the appeal was held on October 15, and a full hearing was anticipated in January 2002. After 12 years of intense inquiry and an 84-day trial, the case ended abruptly when the defense failed to obtain evidence from the Syrian government. On March 14 the French high court exempted the Libyan leader, Col. Muammar al-Qaddafi, from prosecution in connection with the bombing of a French UTA DC-10 airliner that killed 170 people over Niger in 1989.

In March the U.S. and Great Britain conducted a closed-door meeting to discuss the requirements that Libya would have to meet before UN sanctions could be lifted. The U.S. refused to lift its own sanctions, although there was strong evidence that American companies were keen to gain access to the expanding Libyan market and, especially, to oil interests. On October 1 the head of Libya's national oil company met in Vienna with officials of the American oil companies Conoco, Marathon, Amerada Hess, and Occidental.

In late February Syrian Pres. Bashar al-Assad met with Qaddafi in Tripoli. Qaddafi later attended meetings in Africa, and his assistance to South Africa was rewarded by public statements of support by Nelson Mandela and Pres. Thabo Mbeki. At the Arab League summit in Amman, Jordan, in March, Qaddafi's speech shocked participants by calling on Arabs to "forget about Jerusalem and join Africa."

Libya's economy was strengthened by improved oil prices. Annual growth rates of 6.5% had fallen to about 5.5% in 2001, but it was sufficient as oil-exploration deals were struck with European and Asian interests. Commitment to the once-derided tourist sector was reinforced. Technical problems with the Great Man-Made River (GMMR) were overcome, as were the consequent embarrassing contractual relations with the project's bankrupt South Korean contractor. By 2000 desalination costs had fallen to below those of water delivered by the GMMR, however, and a fierce debate became public between the advocates of desalination and those backing the GMMR approach.

After the terrorist attacks of September 11, the U.S.-Libyan international discourse on terrorism shifted. In early October U.S. and British security officials met in London with a Libyan contingent headed by Musa Kusa, who had been implicated in the shooting of a London policewoman outside the Libyan embassy in 1984.   (J.A. ALLAN)

LIECHTENSTEIN

Area: 160 sq km (62 sq mi)
Population (2001 est.): 33,000
Capital: Vaduz
Chief of state: Prince Hans Adam II
Head of government: Mario Frick and, from April 5, Otmar Hasler

In 2001, as Prince Hans Adam II reiterated his threat to "sell up" if constitutional changes vastly increasing his powers were not accepted, a survey found that 60% of the people favoured the status quo, only 20% wanted to give the prince more power, and 20% favoured less power. In parliamentary elections on February 9–11, the Progressive Citizens' Party (FBP), which had ignored the dispute during the campaign, won 13 of the 25 seats with 49.9% of the vote. The Fatherland Union (41.1%) won 11 seats, and the Free List party took the remaining seat. Otmar Hasler of the FBP was sworn in as the new head of government on April 5.

After two years of diplomatic maneuvering, on June 1 Liechtenstein filed a complaint against Germany at the International Court of Justice in The Hague demanding reparations for alleged violation of its sovereignty and property rights of its citizens. At issue was the confiscation of land, artwork, and other property of the prince's family by Czechoslovakia at the end of World War II to pay war debts to Germany. The Czechs had refused to negotiate, while Germany, which considered the property German-owned, had used the assets to pay war reparations. (*See* LAW, CRIME, AND LAW ENFORCEMENT: *International Law.*)

Liechtenstein faced new indictments for money laundering in July. Two financial advisers were charged with conspiracy to hide millions of dollars for the drug cartel based in Cali, Colom. (ANNE ROBY)

LITHUANIA

Area: 65,300 sq km (25,212 sq mi)
Population (2001 est.): 3,691,000
Capital: Vilnius
Chief of state: President Valdas Adamkus
Head of government: Prime Ministers Rolandas Paksas, Eugenijus Gentvilas (acting) from June 20, and, from July 3, Algirdas Brazauskas

Lithuania's Prime Minister Rolandas Paksas, the leader of the Liberal Union, resigned in June 2001, principally over disagreements with his coalition partners, the populist New Union (Social Liberals), over the supply of oil to the Mazeikui Nafta oil refinery, privatization of the state-owned natural gas monopoly, and tax and pension reforms. A new coalition between the Social Liberals and the Social Democratic Party was formed, with Algirdas Brazauskas, the Social Democrat leader (and former Communist) and former president of Lithuania, as head of government.

Despite election promises, the government failed to address social prob-

Vytautas Landsbergis, head of the Homeland Union Party and former Lithuanian president, receives an award from the University of Wales, Cardiff.

Darius Furmonavičius

lems. Average annual wages remained at approximately $3,300, and the rate of unemployment topped 12%. The majority of pensioners and people in rural areas found themselves in particularly difficult straits. On the other hand, gross domestic product increased by nearly 5%. The volume of foreign trade in the first half of the year was $5.2 billion. The largest proportion of Lithuanian exports and imports was directed to and from European Union countries—49.4% and 42.5%, respectively; exports increased by 24% and imports by 15% over 2000 levels.

The NATO Parliamentary Assembly spring session, held in Vilnius on May 27–31, was the largest international event in Lithuania in a decade and the first such meeting held outside NATO territory. Some 270 parliamentarians from NATO and NATO-associated states gathered in the Lithuanian capital. The assembly approved a declaration on NATO enlargement, and Lithuania once again declared its commitment to join the organization during its 2002 summit in Prague. (DARIUS FURMONAVIČIUS)

LUXEMBOURG

Area: 2,586 sq km (999 sq mi)
Population (2001 est.): 444,000
Capital: Luxembourg
Chief of state: Grand Duke Henri
Head of government: Prime Minister Jean-Claude Juncker

In 2001, his first year as head of state, Grand Duke Henri sought to make his own mark as leader of Luxembourg. In an emotional ceremony on June 21, he presented his father, Grand Duke Jean, with the Croix de la Résistance in honour of his father's service with the British army during World War II. Then on October 10, stating that he wished to underscore the importance of its work, Grand Duke Henri broke with tradition by officially opening the parliament in person. The last time the parliament had been opened by a royal was in 1877.

The parliament voted unanimously on June 28 to extend and upgrade the European Parliament complex. It planned to expand the conference centre, build new office blocks, and add a concert hall. Also in June, the head of Luxem-

bourg's army proposed to increase its size, to purchase a military transport plane, and, with Belgium, to buy a transport ship. There were again proposals to establish a University of Luxembourg, but government officials felt a full university in the country would discourage its citizens from studying abroad and have a negative effect on their overall education.

In the wake of the September 11 terrorist attacks in the U.S., several Luxembourg banks acknowledged that some of their customers might have ties to Osama bin Laden (*see* BIOGRAPHIES), and the bank accounts of such depositers were placed under investigation. (ANNE ROBY)

MACEDONIA

Area: 25,713 sq km (9,928 sq mi)
Population (2001 est.): 2,046,000
Capital: Skopje
Chief of state: President Boris Trajkovski
Head of government: Prime Minister Ljubco Georgievski

In 2001 Macedonia's fragile interethnic balance collapsed. Fighting between government security forces and the self-styled ethnic Albanian National Liberation Army (UCK) brought the country to the verge of all-out civil war and cast doubts over its very future.

A bomb attack on a police station in the village of Tearce on January 22 was followed by armed clashes between government forces and UCK fighters near Tanusevci in February. Fighting soon erupted in and around Tetovo, the country's second largest city, with a largely ethnic Albanian population. Throughout the spring and summer, government forces and rebels were fighting around Tetovo, Skopje, and Kumanovo. More than 100 persons lost their lives, often indiscriminately, in the early months of the year, and large numbers of persons were displaced within the country as a result of the fights. Many Albanians also fled across the border to Kosovo. Anti-Albanian riots occurred in several towns.

Government threats throughout the spring to launch counteroffensives led only to short-lived cease-fires. Meanwhile, UCK demands for negotiations on

In Krivolak, Macedonia, on September 10, a metal worker cuts apart a machine gun surrendered to NATO forces by ethnic Albanian rebels.

the future status of Macedonia were rejected by the government. The international community, which initially condemned the UCK attacks, later called on the government to address the problems of Macedonia's ethnic Albanian community.

On May 13 a government of national unity was formed that included all relevant parties from both ethnic groups. Negotiations between ethnic Macedonian and ethnic Albanian parties brought little result, nor was Western shuttle diplomacy between the government and the UCK eminently successful. July and August saw renewed fighting and killings of soldiers and civilians. Ethnic Macedonians stormed the parliament building on June 25, and one month later rioters attacked Western embassies, accusing the West of pro-Albanian bias. Finally, European Union (EU) and U.S. mediators assembled the leaders of the main political parties in Ohrid for peace talks. The Ohrid Agreement, signed on August 13, provided for constitutional amendments raising the status of the ethnic Albanian community, increased local self-government, the disarmament of ethnic Albanian rebels to be followed by an amnesty, and increased participation of ethnic Albanians in state structures, including the

police. The parties also agreed on early parliamentary elections in January 2002.

In August the North Atlantic Council decided to deploy 3,500 troops to collect UCK weapons, and a month later NATO began "Amber Fox," the 1,000-troop-strong follow-up mission designed to protect Western monitors in Macedonia. While UCK weapons were being successfully collected, parliamentary debates on constitutional amendments were delayed repeatedly by legislators from both ethnic groups and were not concluded on schedule. Complaining that the Macedonian government and parliament had failed to meet their part of the peace plan, the EU twice cancelled a planned donors' conference. Finally, Parliament also decided to postpone holding early elections. On November 23, the Social Democrats and two smaller parties left the government, but Prime Minister Ljubco Georgievski managed to form a new cabinet.

The interethnic conflict severely hurt Macedonia's economy and resulted in a sharp drop of industrial output, agricultural production, and imports and exports; widening trade and budget deficits; and increasing unemployment.

(STEFAN KRAUSE)

MADAGASCAR

Area: 587,041 sq km (226,658 sq mi)
Population (2001 est.): 15,983,000
Capital: Antananarivo
Chief of state and head of government:
President Didier Ratsiraka, assisted by Prime Minister Tantely Andrianarivo

At the beginning of May 2001, Pres. Didier Ratsiraka reinstated the country's Senate, which he had suspended after he came to power in 1975. The Senate was inaugurated in new $6 million premises in Antananarivo. The 90 senators elected a former director of the civil service as Senate leader. It remained to be seen what role the new body would play in checking executive power, for the president's Association for the Rebirth of Madagascar, with its allies, retained an overwhelming majority in the parliament. Though early results from the mid-December presidential elections suggested that Antananarivo Mayor Marc Ravalomanana had a slight lead over

460

President Ratsiraka, neither had a majority of votes and a second round of elections would be needed in February 2002.

One of the president's projects aimed at providing as many as possible of the almost 16 million people of the island with glasses to protect them against the solar eclipse in June. A special budget of 23 billion Malagasy francs (about $3.6 million) was established.

Bringing Madagascar some international attention during the year was the discovery of the 70-million-year-old remains of several specimens of dinosaurs.

(CHRISTOPHER SAUNDERS)

MALAWI

Area: 118,484 sq km (45,747 sq mi)
Population (2001 est.): 10,491,000
Capital: Lilongwe (legislative, ministerial, and financial), Blantyre (executive and judicial)
Head of state and government: President Bakili Muluzi

In February 2001 Judge Edward Twea sentenced John Chikakwiya, mayor of Blantyre and a prominent member of the ruling United Democratic Front, together with three senior policemen, to two weeks in prison, suspended for 18 months. Chikakwiya had ordered the teargassing of a legal and peaceful gathering of the National Democratic Alliance, deliberately disregarding a court ruling that barred him from disrupting opposition party meetings.

On February 21 four government officials were arrested—followed by two more the following day—and charged with having embezzled funds from the Ministry of Education. Also on February 22 former cabinet member Cassim Chilumpha was arrested and charged with corrupt practices during the campaign that led up to the elections in June 1999. On March 26 six people were charged with treason as a result of their alleged involvement in a plot to overthrow the government.

After this internal cleansing the government took part in the replacement of the Organization of African Unity by a new African Union at a July meeting in Lusaka, Zambia. The following month Malawi joined with six other East African governments to create the African Trade Insurance Agency (ATI) in

an attempt to counter the high premiums demanded by foreign companies that considered Africa a high-risk area. In December the ATI signed an agreement with Gerling, the world's third largest credit insurance group, which offered protection to companies trading to and within Africa against nonpayment by buyers.

(KENNETH INGHAM)

MALAYSIA

Area: 329,845 sq km (127,354 sq mi)
Population (2001 est.): 22,602,000
Capital: Kuala Lumpur; head of government office in Putrajaya (the future planned capital) from 1999
Chief of state: *Yang di-Pertuan Agongs* (Paramount Rulers) Tuanku Salahuddin Abdul Aziz Shah ibni al-Marhum Sultan Hisamuddin Alam Shah, Tuanku Mizan Zainal Abidin ibni al-Marhum Sultan Mahmud (acting) from October 8 and (interim) from November 21, and, from December 13, Tuanku Syed Sirajuddin ibni al-Marhum Tuanku Syed Putra Jamalullail
Head of government: Prime Minister Datuk Seri Mahathir bin Mohamad

The ruling United Malays National Organization (UMNO), led by Prime Minister Datuk Seri Mahathir bin Mo-

hamad, began the year 2001 under stress. A diverse new opposition coalition had emerged called the Alternative Front, which included many younger generation Malaysians and counted among its members both Malays and non-Malays as well as Muslims and non-Muslims. The UMNO was also under unprecedented scrutiny from the newly created Human Rights Commission for its recourse to harsh measures limiting the rights of assembly and freedom of speech. Elements within the judiciary had begun to reassert their independence from the executive, and Mahathir faced mounting criticism over the government's continuing protection of UMNO-connected corporations with close ties to Finance Minister Tun Daim Zainuddin and his protégés.

Although Mahathir's legitimacy among the nation's demographically and politically dominant Malay citizens was threatened by these issues and developments, by year's end he had turned the situation around decisively. He had accepted Tun Daim's resignation as finance minister and had further allayed public disquiet by removing from the personal grasp of Tun Daim's protégés the great national and party assets they controlled.

Mahathir also turned up the pressure on the Alternative Front coalition by exploiting the deep and unresolved tensions between the coalition's two largest partners: the Islamic Party of Malaysia (PAS), which wanted Malaysia to become a Shar'iah-based Islamic state, and

Malaysian Prime Minister Mahathir bin Mohamad warns in a radio address on July 6 of a possible crackdown on student activists in the country.

AP/Wide World Photos

the stridently anticlericalist Democratic Action Party (DAP), which held explicitly non-Malay-centric views of Malaysian society and identity. By September the Alternative Front had cracked.

To the UMNO's great advantage, Malaysian voters were once again likely to be faced in 2004 with the hardly attractive choice between the UMNO's crude regimen of statist authoritarianism and the PAS's increasingly assertive neotraditionalist Islamism.

Arrests and detentions ensued of young PAS activists and other Islamic militants allegedly involved in jihad-type actions throughout Southeast Asia. Initially greeted with skepticism, this government action was placed beyond questioning by the September 11 terrorist attacks in the U.S. If the PAS/DAP entente had not already been dead, this would have killed it.

Far from boasting of any vindication, Mahathir coolly asserted that the arrests were unconnected with the search for Osama bin Laden's associates and pointedly questioned U.S. strikes against Afghanistan. Mahathir's political enemies were suddenly tainted by association with deeds far exceeding the most lurid UMNO propaganda. Domestic criticism of his strong-handed government was discredited, and, as a prominent Muslim moderate, Mahathir could be confident that international—especially U.S.—criticism of his rule as repressive would end.   (CLIVE S. KESSLER)

MALDIVES

Area: 298 sq km (115 sq mi)
Population (2001 est.): 275,000
Capital: Male
Head of state and government: President
 Maumoon Abdul Gayoom

Sustainable development remained the single most important objective of Maldives in 2001. In his address at the opening session of the Majlis (parliament) on February 22, Pres. Maumoon Abdul Gayoom listed poverty alleviation, rural development, and expansion and modernization of education as priority areas. Liberalization of the fishing industry and private-sector participation in development plans were also proposed. In August Gulf Craft Inc., a company based

Pres. Maumoon Abdul Gayoom (right) welcomes Chinese Premier Zhu Rongji to Maldives on May 16.

in the United Arab Emirates, was allowed to set up a boatbuilding and repair centre at Thilafushi in Male Atoll. Maldives decided to ratify an agreement establishing the Islamic Corporation for the Development of the Private Sector under the control of the Islamic Development Bank. Considering the importance of foreign investment in sustaining economic progress, the government promised to take steps to inspire confidence among investors.

An important diplomatic event was the visit of Chinese Premier Zhu Rongji on May 16–17. An agreement on economic and technical cooperation was signed between Maldives and China. Population growth and environmental degradation were other areas of concern. On July 11—World Population Day—President Gayoom underlined the need to control the population growth in order to reduce pressure on trees, coastlines, and reefs.   (PONMONI SAHADEVAN)

MALI

Area: 1,248,574 sq km (482,077 sq mi)
Population (2001 est.): 11,009,000
Capital: Bamako
Chief of state: President Alpha Oumar Konaré
Head of government: Prime Minister Mande
 Sidibe

Thousands of hunters from West Africa converged on Bamako on Jan. 27, 2001, carrying handmade shotguns and bows and arrows to celebrate the millennium of hunting. Their mission was to call attention to the role of hunters in the new global economy.

On May 7 Mali and Namibia became the first two member states of the Organization of African Union (OAU) to agree to join the Pan-African Parliament, which was established on May 26 and would form part of the new organization that would replace the OAU.

The annual meeting of foreign ministers from member countries of the Islamic Conference Organization opened in Bamako on June 25, and on July 11 Mali became the first country to sign a binding international agreement designed to halt the proliferation of small arms.

On August 9—pursuant to a law passed by the parliament on June 29 making those convicted of child trafficking subject to prison sentences of 5–20 years—the government enacted legislation that required all children under 18 years of age to carry travel passes. Pres. Alpha Oumar Konaré canceled a December 23 referendum that would give the president immunity from prosecution after critics decried the reform.

Ibrahim Bahanga, one of the last Tuareg rebel chiefs to defy the government after the official end of the uprising, announced on September 24 that he was laying down his arms for the good of the people of northern Mali.

(NANCY ELLEN LAWLER)

MALTA

Area: 316 sq km (122 sq mi)
Population (2001 est.): 384,000
Capital: Valletta
Chief of state: President Guido de Marco
Head of government: Prime Minister Eddie Fenech Adami

Speaking in February 2001 on Malta's application to become a member of the European Union, Günter Verheugen, the EU commissioner for enlargement, remarked that the progress Malta had made in the previous two years was surprising. Though EU accession was the top foreign-policy priority for the government, the opposition Labour Party held that it was not in Malta's interest to join the EU. Nonetheless, negotiations were expected to be concluded by the end of 2002.

In May, after having visited Greece and Syria, Pope John Paul II arrived in Malta to beatify three persons—a nun, a priest, and a layman. They were the first-ever Maltese to be so honoured. He urged the Maltese to cherish their Christian vocation.

During his July 1–8 visit to China, Pres. Guido de Marco invited Chinese Pres. Jiang Zemin to Malta. Jiang readily accepted the offer and arrived for a state visit on July 23. The two leaders agreed to establish in Malta a Chinese cultural centre for the Mediterranean region, to maintain cultural cooperation between the two countries during 2001–03, and to list Malta as a tourist destination for Chinese citizens.

In April the neolithic temple at Mnajdra, a World Heritage site, was vandalized; about 60 megaliths were dislodged. The government condemned in the strongest terms the September terrorist attacks in the United States, and it pledged to cooperate fully in the effort to eradicate international terrorism.

(ALBERT GANADO)

MARSHALL ISLANDS

Area: 181 sq km (70 sq mi)
Population (2001 est.): 52,300
Capital: Majuro
Head of state and government: President Kessai Note

Having reestablished his position in January 2001 by defeating a motion of no-confidence brought by the supporters of former president Imata Kabua, Marshall Islands Pres. Kessai Note held his majority in the Nitijela (legislative assembly) throughout the year. Financial relations with the U.S. remained a priority with the Compact of Free Association between the two countries due to expire in 2001 and negotiations over the future relationship already in train. The U.S.—through direct allocations, funding under the compact, and special federal grants—contributed more than 53% of the total Marshall Islands government expenditure of $106.6 million. The government's financial administration, though improved over recent years, remained weak. The U.S. General Accounting Office criticized the government for its lack of compliance and accountability and for the misdirection of funds. The government also had a shortfall in social security funds against anticipated future drawing rights.

In February the Marshall Islands High Court rejected 10 of 11 charges brought by the government against major American tobacco companies to seek compensation for health costs related to smoking; this decision was upheld in a further hearing in June. The judge was critical of the government's legal team for its poor presentation of its client's case. (BARRIE MACDONALD)

MAURITANIA

Area: 1,030,700 sq km (398,000 sq mi)
Population (2001 est.): 2,591,000
Capital: Nouakchott
Chief of state: President Col. Maaouya Ould Sidi Ahmad Taya
Head of government: Prime Minister Cheikh El Afia Ould Mohamed Khouna

On April 8, 2001, police arrested Mohamed Lemine Ch'Bih Ould Cheikh Melainine, leader of the Popular Front. Despite widespread criticism by opposition parties and international human rights organizations, he was brought to trial in Nouakchott on May 9 and charged with criminal conspiracy. Defense lawyers resigned in protest after the proceedings were abruptly moved to Aioun, near the Malian border, 800 km (500 mi) south of the capital. Though critics condemned the trial as nothing more than a show, Melainine was sentenced on June 14 to five years' imprisonment.

On August 4 an agreement on fishing rights was renewed between the government and the European Union. Despite the fears of environmentalists that

Spectators crowd the Floriana Granaries square in Valletta, Malta, for an open-air mass performed by Pope John Paul II on May 9.

increased fishing would further reduce the already sharply depleted stocks, the revised protocol nevertheless allowed for an increased number of European vessels to fish the area around the island of Agadir off the northern Mauritanian coast.

King Muhammad VI of Morocco began a three-day state visit to Mauritania on September 10. Ties had been strained between the two countries since 1975, when in a dispute over independence for Western Sahara, claimed by Morocco, Mauritania had actively supported the Western Saharan Polisario Front; Mauritania later shifted to neutrality, and the king's visit was seen as an indication of the importance that both countries attached to improving relations.

In the legislative and municipal elections held on October 19 and 26, the ruling Democratic and Social Republican Party garnered 51% of the vote and captured 64 of the 81 seats in the National Assembly.   (NANCY ELLEN LAWLER)

MAURITIUS

Area: 2,040 sq km (788 sq mi)
Population (2001 est.): 1,195,000
Capital: Port Louis
Chief of state: President Cassam Uteem
Head of government: Prime Minister Sir Anerood Jugnauth

Throughout 2001 there were signs of rivalry between Prime Minister Sir Anerood Jugnauth of the Mauritian Socialist Movement and Deputy Prime Minister Paul Berenger of the Mauritian Militant Movement. Despite clashes over government appointments and other matters, however, their ruling coalition remained intact.

Mauritius made a concerted effort during the year to develop a high-technology economy. In January Berenger announced the creation of the Infocom Development Authority to manage growth in the information-technology sector. India agreed to provide Mauritius with a $100 million line of credit for the development of a "cybercity" technology-development centre. A number of Indian software companies also announced that they would invest in the project.

The Mauritian government offered a variety of tax incentives for Indian businesses to establish export operations on the island. While visiting India, Prime Minister Jugnauth noted that Mauritius had preferential access to the U.S. and European Union markets under, respectively, the Africa Growth and Opportunity Act and the Cotonou Agreement. The country's export earnings remained strong, with the Export Processing Zone increasing 7% over the previous year while the Mauritius Freeport registered 43% growth over a similar period.

(MATTHEW A. CENZER)

MEXICO

Area: 1,964,375 sq km (758,449 sq mi)
Population (2001 est.): 99,969,000
Capital: Mexico City
Head of state and government: President Vicente Fox Quesada

The inauguration of Vicente Fox Quesada as president of Mexico on Dec. 1, 2000, ended 71 years of uninterrupted national rule by the Institutional Revolutionary Party and opened a new historical era. Although economic and political constraints slowed change in some areas, perhaps disappointing some domestic and foreign observers expecting a more rapid transformation, Fox's personal-approval ratings remained in the 60% range throughout 2001.

As the candidate of the opposition National Action Party (PAN), Fox had promised quick resolution of the long-simmering conflict in southern Chiapas state, and in his first months in office he devoted substantial political capital to seeking a peaceful resolution of the matter. In his inaugural address to the Mexican Congress, Fox announced his commitment to the restarting of negotiations with the rebel Zapatista National Liberation Army (EZLN), the withdrawal of army troops from several controversial postings in Chiapas, and the appointment of a cabinet-level indigenous rights coordinator. Fox also submitted to Congress a constitutional-reform initiative congruent with the terms of a peace accord that the EZLN and the federal government had reached in 1996. In July this initiative, known as the Law on Indigenous Rights and Culture, was ratified by the required number of state legislatures. The EZLN and its allies,

however, harshly denounced the measure, claiming that it broke with the earlier peace accord by not creating an autonomous territorial base for the exercise of indigenous rights. Legislatures in states with some of Mexico's largest indigenous populations rejected the constitutional reform for this same reason.

The Fox administration's other major legislative initiative concerned fiscal reform. The proposal sought to stabilize (and make more transparent) the Mexican banking system and modify the federal budgetary-approval process in order to prevent executive-legislative political deadlock from threatening continued government operations at the end of each calendar year. The measure's most controversial components concerned taxes, however. The administration touted its proposal with the phrase "Because it is just" and underscored the importance of expanding the country's tax base for future social spending, education, infrastructure development, and the national savings rate. Nevertheless, the prospect of significant tax increases generated considerable opposition, much of it focusing on the proposal to eliminate value-added-tax exemptions for food and medicines. It appeared by year's end that there would be substantial modifications to the government's reform proposal before it won final congressional approval.

As a presidential candidate, Fox had also promised significant measures to reduce poverty, but during 2001 a sharp downturn in the Mexican economy constrained a number of social-policy initiatives. The downturn followed an economic slump in the U.S.—the market for approximately 90% of Mexico's exports. Fox had promised 7% economic growth on a sustained basis and the creation of 1,350,000 new formal-sector jobs each year, yet it was projected that inflation-adjusted growth in 2001 would be close to zero, and there was a loss of more than 600,000 jobs in the first eight months of the Fox administration. Most experts anticipated continued low inflation (4–6%) and moderate interest rates in 2002, but they also predicted a real increase in gross domestic product of only about 2%.

It was in the foreign-affairs arena that the Fox administration initially made most rapid progress. In a high-profile gesture of the signal importance that both leaders attached to Mexican-U.S. relations, Fox and U.S. Pres. George W. Bush met at Fox's ranch in the state of Guanajuato on February 16. The two recently inaugurated leaders agreed to closer bilateral cooperation in a num-

AP/Wide World Photos

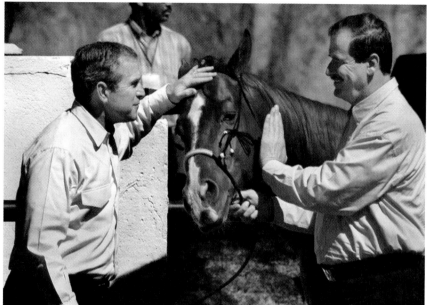

Mexican Pres. Vicente Fox and U.S. Pres. George W. Bush chat during Bush's visit to Fox's ranch in San Cristobal in February.

were realized when Mexico won a seat on the UN Security Council; it was the first time in two decades that Mexico would serve on the council. The country attracted unfavourable headlines in late November when a National Human Rights Commission released a report that held the Mexican government responsible for the detention and torture of hundreds of those who "disappeared" in the 1970s in the "dirty war" against leftist groups. Fox acknowledged the government role and appointed a special prosecutor to investigate the cases.

(KEVIN J. MIDDLEBROOK)

MICRONESIA, FEDERATED STATES OF

Area: 701 sq km (271 sq mi)
Population (2001 est.): 118,000
Capital: Palikir, on Pohnpei
Head of state and government: President Leo A. Falcam

Negotiations for the renewal of the Federated States of Micronesia's (FSM) Compact of Free Association with the U.S. continued in 2001. The governments agreed that the FSM's defense and security relationship with the U.S. should remain, private enterprise should be strengthened, and greater financial accountability should be achieved. FSM negotiators sought an annual grant and an annual payment to the FSM Trust Fund, both inflation protected; the U.S. agreed to the payments in principle, but at a lower level and without inflation adjustment. Negotiations were ongoing. A special session of Congress was called in March to consider business pending from the previous session, including the establishment of a retirement plan and housing allocations.

Voters in the district of Faichuuk overwhelmingly passed a referendum to declare the district a separate state within the FSM. A proposal envisaged a transition phase of three years, although the FSM legislature had yet to decide on the matter. In March Pres. Leo A. Falcam made a state visit to Japan. In October he offered the U.S. use of FSM facilities for staging points in the U.S.-led "war on terrorism" following the September 11 attacks.

(BARRIE MACDONALD)

---

ber of areas, and in the months following the meeting, there was indeed evidence of more effective collaboration against drug traffickers and immigrant smugglers. Responding to Bush's commitment to reviewing U.S. drug-certification policy (in which the U.S. Congress required the executive branch to certify that countries were collaborating effectively with the U.S. in the battle against drug traffickers), Mexico broke with long-established precedent by extraditing suspected drug traffickers to the U.S. for trial. The two governments also made efforts to resolve long-standing disagreements concerning the sharing of Rio Grande water.

Immigration policy was the area in which the most novel developments occurred. The U.S. had vetoed consideration of immigration issues during negotiations of the North American Free Trade Agreement in the early 1990s, and when President-elect Fox traveled to Washington, D.C., in August 2000, his call for a more open border between Mexico and the U.S. was greeted with considerable skepticism. Nevertheless, Bush and Fox established a cabinet-level working group composed of senior officials from the U.S. Department of State and Department of Justice and the Mexican Ministry of Foreign Affairs and Ministry of the Interior. In the following months, discussions focused primarily on expanded visa quotas for temporary workers (especially in agriculture but also in construction, food processing,

and the hotel and restaurant industries) and ways to normalize over time the status of the estimated 3.5 million undocumented Mexican migrants in the U.S. Bush and leading Republican strategists appeared eager both to consolidate a highly positive bilateral relationship with Mexico and the Fox administration and to win support from the increasingly influential Latino electorate while simultaneously reducing opposition from conservative forces adamantly opposed to the amnesty of illegal immigrants. When domestic political opposition in the U.S. threatened to stall negotiations, Fox used his state visit to Washington, D.C., on September 5–6 to highlight the importance of the issue.

In this area as well, unanticipated events intervened. The September 11 terrorist attacks in the U.S. immediately reordered American foreign-policy priorities, and relations with Mexico were forced onto the back burner. American attitudes toward border enforcement also shifted dramatically, accompanied by stringent new border and visa controls. Bush reassured Fox that he remained committed to changing immigration policy, and Fox attempted to regain momentum in this area by proposing a continentwide security area in which Mexico would actively combat cross-border terrorist activities. The prospects for rapid action on immigration issues dimmed considerably, however.

In October Fox's efforts to move Mexico away from an isolationist position

MOLDOVA

Area: 33,700 sq km (13,000 sq mi)
Population (2001 est.): 4,211,000 (including some 600,000 persons working abroad)
Capital: Chisinau
Chief of state: Presidents Petru Lucinschi and, from April 7, Vladimir Voronin
Head of government: Prime Ministers Dumitru Braghis and, from April 19, Vasile Tarlev

Following early general elections on Feb. 25, 2001, Moldova became the first former Soviet republic in which unreformed Communists returned to power. Playing on widespread dissatisfaction with the post-Communist transition, the Communist Party of the Republic of Moldova garnered 50.1% of the votes, taking 71 of the 101 seats in Parliament. The remaining seats were divided between the Braghis Alliance, a loose centre-left bloc led by incumbent Prime Minister Dumitru Braghis, and the right-wing Christian Democratic Popular Party. On April 4 Parliament elected Communist leader Vladimir Voronin as Moldova's president, and he set up a government of technocrats led by Vasile Tarlev, a 37-year-old manager. One main goal was to increase the role of the state in the economy. Another was the introduction of Russian as the country's second official language, but this evoked protests, especially among the intelligentsia.

As might be expected, the Communists advocated a reorientation toward Moscow and favoured joining the Russia-Belarus Union. On November 19 Voronin and Russian Pres. Vladimir Putin signed a basic bilateral treaty covering cooperation in many fields and favouring the special status of the Russian language in Moldova. The Moldova Parliament ratified the treaty on December 27. Moldova was admitted to the Stability Pact for South Eastern Europe in June, and in July it became a full member in the World Trade Organization. Neighbouring Romania introduced strict passport controls for Moldovan citizens effective July 1, and in October Romanian Prime Minister Adrian Nastase canceled an official visit to Chisinau following statements by Moldovan Justice Minister Ion Morei, who accused Romania of interference in Moldova's internal affairs and of "expansionism."

The Communists' pledge to find a firm resolution to the Transnistria conflict proved unrealistic. In September the breakaway heavily Slavic-populated region suspended negotiations with Moldovan authorities, whom it accused of imposing an economic blockade. In early October Putin disbanded the Russian State Commission for Transnistria, and in mid-November Russian officials announced that the withdrawal of heavy military equipment from the region had been completed.

(DAN IONESCU)

MONACO

Area: 1.95 sq km (0.75 sq mi)
Population (2001 est.): 31,800
Chief of state: Prince Rainier III
Head of government: Minister of State Patrick Leclercq

As health problems continued to sideline Prince Rainer III, his son, Prince Albert, took the spotlight in 2001, making a number of official trips abroad. In March Albert chaired a convention on air-pollution monitoring in Rabat, Morocco. In Cuba on a five-day visit in April, he attended a sports conference and, after meeting with Pres. Fidel Castro, opened Monaco's first consulate in Cuba. Albert also traveled to Moscow, where he met with Russian Prime Minister Mikhail Kasyanov to discuss cooperation in business, finance, culture, and sports. The July visit was the first by a prince of Monaco to Russia since 1913. In New York City in October, Albert attended a benefit in tribute to his late mother, Princess Grace, and gave Mayor Rudolph Giuliani a check for $710,000 to be contributed to the Twin Towers Fund.

An ambitious building program to attract more visitors to Monaco continued during the year. The new Grimaldi Forum provided conference facilities with space for such special events as trade fairs. Monte-Carlo announced its intention to develop more family-oriented activities, especially attractions for children. Government data showed that the number of people who spent at least one night in Monaco hit a record high of 300,185 in 2000.

(ANNE ROBY)

MONGOLIA

Area: 1,564,116 sq km (603,909 sq mi)
Population (2001 est.): 2,435,000
Capital: Ulaanbaatar
Chief of state: President Natsagiyn Bagabandi
Head of government: Prime Minister Nambaryn Enhbayar

Consolidating its victory in the July 2000 elections to the Great Hural (parliament), the reformed communist Mongolian People's Revolutionary Party (MPRP) won the May 2001 presidential elections. Standing for a second term, MPRP candidate Natsagiyn Bagabandi with 58.1% of the ballot easily beat the 36.5% gained by the Mongolian National Democratic Party's choice, Radnaasumbereliyn Gonchigdorj. After a two-year power struggle between presidency and legislature, President Bagabandi finally stamped his seal on the Great Hural's first

Newly reelected Mongolian Pres. Natsagiyn Bagabandi, standing before a portrait of Mongolian People's Revolutionary Party founder Sukhbaatar, welcomes members of the media to the Government House in Ulaanbaatar on May 22.

amendments to the constitution. Prime Minister Nambaryn Enhbayar was unanimously reelected party chairman by the MPRP's 23rd congress in March. The 626 delegates approved a new Little Hural of 244 members, who elected a new 15-member Leadership Council. Chinese Foreign Minister Tang Jiaxuan, visiting Mongolia in July, expressed support for Mongolian membership in the Shanghai Cooperation Organization—China, Russia, Kazakhstan, Kyrgyzstan, Tajikistan, and Uzbekistan. The new group had just issued a declaration in Dushanbe, Tajikistan, opposing "international terrorism, religious extremism, and national separatism." The Ulaanbaatar Declaration, signed during the visit to Mongolia of Russian Pres. Vladimir Putin in November 2000, had pledged Mongolia and Russia not to allow their territory "to be used by any third state for purposes of aggression or other acts of violence" against the other.

The September 11 terrorist attacks in the U.S. were condemned by President Bagabandi and Prime Minister Enhbayar, who visited the U.S. embassy to express Mongolia's condolences. In a broadcast to the nation, Bagabandi called the attacks a crime against democracy, freedom, and humanity. A Great Hural resolution supported the "world community's fight against terrorism."

The Paris meeting in May of the Consultative Group on aid for Mongolia agreed to a new package worth $330 million for one year. A second successive autumn drought and hard winter had killed another 3.3 million head of livestock.

Lhamsurengiyn Enebish, the Great Hural speaker and secretary-general of the MPRP, died of a stroke on September 29. (*See* OBITUARIES.)

(ALAN J.K. SANDERS)

MOROCCO

Area: 710,850 sq km (274,461 sq mi), including the 252,120-sq-km (97,344-sq-mi) area of the disputed Western Sahara annexation
Population (2001 est.): 29,237,000, of which Western Sahara 251,000
Capital: Rabat
Head of state and government: King Muhammad VI, assisted by Prime Minister 'Abd ar-Rahman Youssoufi

Moroccans became worried during 2001 over a slowdown in political liberalization after the banning of three newspapers (*Le Journal, Demain,* and *Assahifa*) in December 2000 and the arrest of three French TV journalists. The newspapers had published information about a letter from a veteran opposition leader, Muhammad Basri, admitting links between the Socialist Union of Popular Forces (USFP) and the organizer of an unsuccessful coup in 1972. Though the USFP dominated the government coalition and vehemently objected to the accusation, the newspaper ban was lifted after international protest in January.

Anxiety over basic rights mounted with the arrest of Hannouda Taibi, a journalist on the USFP newspaper *Al-Ittihad al-Ishtiraki,* and the king's decision in January to cancel a planned meeting with the directors of the International Federation for Human Rights. In May 36 human rights activists from the Association Marocaine des Droits Humains—who had been arrested during a protest the previous December—were sentenced to three months in prison. Concerns were heightened when the interior minister was replaced in September by former businessman Driss Jettou in a move to reassert royal control.

The Moroccan government welcomed the appointment of Margaret Tutwiler as U.S. ambassador to Morocco; she had been a close associate of James Baker, the U.S. secretary of state under the former George H.W. Bush administration, and her appointment was seen as an expression of American confidence in King Muhammad VI. Baker, serving as special envoy for the UN secretary-general in resolving the 25-year-long territorial dispute between Morocco and the Polisario Front over the Western Sahara, put forward a new peace plan in June, just before the UN Security Council granted a five-month extension to the peacekeeping force there.

The plan envisioned limited autonomy for the region under Moroccan sovereignty for a five-year period, after which the promised referendum for self-determination could be held. Algeria, the Polisario Front's main backer, objected to the plan, and the Polisario Front rejected it. In the first visit of his reign, King Muhammad VI traveled to the Western Sahara in November to underscore Morocco's claim to the disputed area.

(GEORGE JOFFÉ)

MOZAMBIQUE

Area: 812,379 sq km (313,661 sq mi)
Population (2001 est.): 19,371,000
Capital: Maputo
Head of state and government: President Joaquim Chissano, assisted by Prime Minister Pascoal Mocumbi

When an interview given to a Portuguese newspaper by Afonso Dhlakama, leader of the Mozambique National Resistance (Renamo) opposition movement, was published on Jan. 2, 2001, it added fuel to the dispute between his party and the Mozambique Liberation Front (Frelimo) government that had flared up in the north of the country the previous November. In the interview Dhlakama accused the ruling party of orchestrating violence against opposition supporters.

The problem was immediately overshadowed when the Zambezi River on January 3 again burst its banks after a week of heavy rains; the downpour continued through February and March. As many as 180,000 people were reported to have been displaced, and the situation was made worse when the floodgates on the Cabora Bassa Dam were partially opened to reduce pressure on the wall and thereby added to the volume of water sweeping over the Zambezi plain.

Though help was quickly forthcoming from the South African air force, many farmers were reluctant to leave their homes in spite of exhortations, and even threats of arrest, from the government. Donor agencies in Germany, The Netherlands, Portugal, Sweden, the U.K., and the U.S. were quick to respond to the government's appeal for financial assistance, but Mozambique found it difficult to recover from such an overwhelming setback. The annual growth rate of the economy had dropped from 9% in the 1990s to 1.7% in 2000, and the estimated growth rate for 2001 was not expected to exceed 3%. The country was suffering from the general decline in investment in Africa, and though it received $700 million in aid in 2001 in addition to flood-relief payments, that sum represented 90% of all foreign investment in the country and accounted for 60% of government spending, a state of dependency that discouraged enterprise.

Midyear, Pres. Joaquim Chissano announced that he would not run for re-election in 2004. Under the terms of the constitution, he was entitled to be reelected twice, and since he had been first elected in 1994 and reelected in 1999, there was no reason why he should not run again in 2004. Because, however, he had already been president for eight years before the 1994 election, he considered that to campaign again would be contrary to the spirit, if not the letter, of the law. A final decision on the issue would not be made until the eighth party congress in 2002.

Mozambique's relations with South Africa were strengthened when the two countries signed a "protocol of cooperation" on December 6.

(KENNETH INGHAM)

MYANMAR (BURMA)

Area: 676,577 sq km (261,228 sq mi)
Population (2001 est.): 41,995,000
Capital: Yangon (Rangoon)
Head of state and government: Chairman of the State Peace and Development Council Gen. Than Shwe

Along with some of his followers, 13-year-old Luther Htoo (centre)—who with his twin brother, Johnny, led the rebel group God's Army in Myanmar—is heavily guarded by police after laying down arms in Thailand.

AP/Wide World Photos

In Myanmar the year 2001 saw the continuation of the ruling military junta's talks aimed at resolving the 10-year standoff with opposition National League for Democracy (NLD) leader Daw Aung San Suu Kyi. Since talks began in October 2000, almost 200 political prisoners had been released (though about 1,500 still remained in detention), and the media's virulent attacks on the opposition had ceased. Frustrated with the slow pace of the talks, and with little hope of a breakthrough after 12 months, the NLD in September called for the immediate release of Suu Kyi from house detention and the recognition of the party's 1990 election victory.

Following a fact-finding team's visit to Myanmar in early 2001, the European Union (EU) renewed sanctions on the country for a further six months, citing human rights violations. The EU, however, increased humanitarian aid funding. Myanmar allowed access to an International Labor Organization delegation to evaluate progress on banning forced labour. Religious riots between Buddhists and Muslims claimed the lives of an unknown number of people in October.

The first half of the year saw a marked deterioration in Myanmar-Thai relations, with fierce border skirmishes taking place. After 19 years of being oriented toward Thailand's eastern border, Thai and U.S. Special Forces staged joint military exercises on Thailand's western border with Myanmar in May. Myanmar troops also exchanged fire in the west with Bangladeshi forces.

While China remained the main supplier of military hardware and economic aid to Myanmar, the junta also strengthened its ties with Russia, North Korea, Pakistan, and India. Yangon was reportedly purchasing a nuclear reactor and sophisticated MiG-29 fighters from Russia and conventional arms from North Korea. Pakistani chief executive Gen. Pervez Musharraf's visit on May 1–3 was preceded by calls by three Pakistani naval ships to Myanmar ports. India's external affairs minister visited Myanmar to strengthen economic ties and inaugurated an Indian-built highway. A joint Indo-Myanmar military offensive against rebel groups operating in India's northeast was also undertaken. On December 12–15 Chinese Pres. Jiang Zemin visited Myanmar, the first such trip by a Chinese chief of state since 1988.

Political uncertainty, high inflation, declining foreign investment, and sluggish agricultural growth worsened Myanmar's economic situation. The value of the kyat slipped more than 20% in mid-August, and tourism declined significantly. (MOHAN MALIK)

NAMIBIA

Area: 825,118 sq km (318,580 sq mi)
Population (2001 est.): 1,798,000
Capital: Windhoek
Chief of state and head of government: President Sam Nujoma, assisted by Prime Minister Hage Geingob

The security situation in northeastern Namibia remained tense in 2001 in the aftermath of Angolan attacks from Namibian soil on National Union for the Total Independence of Angola (UNITA) rebels and the failed secessionist attempt in the Caprivi Strip. Tourism, one of the country's main foreign-currency earners, was badly affected. In mid-October a dusk-to-dawn curfew was reimposed along a stretch of the border with Angola.

At the first cabinet meeting of the year, Pres. Sam Nujoma criticized unnecessary expenditure by top officials and instructed them to give up their Mercedes-Benz vehicles and limit their overseas trips. By August most of the Namibian troops in the Democratic Republic of the Congo had been withdrawn. The president and some of his ministers were criticized for using strong words against human rights organizations, foreigners, and homosexuals. In March President Nujoma announced that the police had orders to imprison and deport homosexuals. Some suggested that he was frustrated by the increase in AIDS deaths; at least one in five Namibian adults was infected with HIV.

Though legislation was introduced to establish an anticorruption commission with wide powers to investigate and uncover corruption in public and private bodies, the president was specifically excluded from its provisions. After sending out contradictory signals about his intention to stand for a fourth term in 2004, President Nujoma finally bowed to pressure and announced in late 2001 that he would not seek another term of office.   (CHRISTOPHER SAUNDERS)

NAURU

Area: 21.2 sq km (8.2 sq mi)
Population (2001 est.): 12,100
Capital: Government offices in Yaren district
Head of state and government: Presidents Bernard Dowiyogo and, from March 30, Rene Harris

Rene Harris returned as president following a vote of no-confidence against Pres. Bernard Dowiyogo in Nauru's Parliament on March 29, 2001. Dowiyogo lost his job over international criticism of Nauru's financial system and in particular over allegations of money laundering for the Russian mafia. Russia's central bank claimed that about $70 billion had been lost in transactions processed through Nauru's 400 offshore banks. In December the Financial Action Task Force on Money Laundering announced that it would take countermeasures against Nauru's failure to meet a November 30 deadline to address the shortcomings of its laws against money laundering.

Relations with the U.S. proved difficult for Nauru in 2001. Nauru's ambassador to the UN, Vinci Clodumar, led regional opposition to a proposed U.S. missile-defense system. Clodumar said that the development of the system was not in the best interest of the Pacific region, as it could lead to radioactive fallout from missile intercepts landing on Pacific islands.

In September Nauru received UN approval to process several hundred refugees denied access to Australia and temporarily settled on Nauru. Under an agreement with Australia, Nauru would receive about $10 million in financial aid in exchange for processing the asylum seekers, most of whom were from Iraq or Afghanistan. (See *Australia,* above.)   (A.R.G. GRIFFITHS)

NEPAL

Area: 147,181 sq km (56,827 sq mi)
Population (2001 est.): 25,284,000
Capital: Kathmandu
Head of state: Kings Birendra Bir Bikram Shah Dev and, from June 4, Gyanendra Bir Bikram Shah Dev
Head of government: Prime Ministers Girija Prasad Koirala and, from July 21, Sher Bahadur Deuba

Nepal seemed on the brink of political chaos and even disintegration in mid-2001. The assassination of King Birendra (see OBITUARIES) and eight other members of the royal family by Crown Prince Dipendra threatened the traditional monarchical system. Divisions within the ruling Nepali Congress Party led to changes in the prime ministership in July, and the Maoist insurgency in the western hill area posed a major challenge to the democratic parliamentary system of government. By October King Gyanendra, the late king's brother, was

The bodies of Nepalese King Birendra, Queen Aiswarya, and other relatives shot and killed by Birendra's eldest son, Crown Prince Dipendra, are cremated in Kathmandu on June 2.

AP/Wide World Photos

functioning effectively as a constitutional monarch, the Nepali Congress government was in control, and all the political parties, including the Maoists, were engaged in political dialogues. In late November, however, in the wake of renewed Maoist violence, the king and Prime Minister Sher Bahadur Deuba declared a state of emergency. The army and the Maoists were still battling at year's end.

Nepal's difficult but essential relationship with neighbouring India also caused major problems. Their vital 1996 trade treaty, due to expire in December 2001, was extended until March 2002 as negotiations continued to iron out a few basic differences between the two sides.

The economic-growth rate remained low, owing to a limited resource base, rapid population growth, environmental degradation, low levels of social development, and widespread poverty. Nepal's vast hydropower resources also were at an early stage of development—despite a variety of agreements with India and others on the subject—primarily because of political division within Nepal. In September Deuba's government announced major land-reform programs that could provide land to the large landless population.

(LEO E. ROSE)

NETHERLANDS, THE

Area: 41,526 sq km (16,033 sq mi)
Population (2001 est.): 15,968,000
Capital: Amsterdam; seat of government, The Hague
Chief of state: Queen Beatrix
Head of government: Prime Minister Wim Kok

The Dutch economy was strong in 2001—jobs were plentiful; incomes went up across the board; and the government continued to invest in public projects and in strengthening the economy. Though growth seemed to be slowing, the government planned to invest more than €3.5 billion (about $3.1 billion) in 2002 to improve health care, education, and safety. The government also planned to continue to pay down the national debt.

The year began with a catastrophic fire during New Year's celebrations in a

café in Volendam, in which more than 180 people were hurt; at least 12 people eventually died of their injuries. The number of casualties was much higher than expected because proper safety precautions had been ignored. An estimated 2,000 individuals were traumatized to such an extent that they would need ongoing psychological treatment. In the aftermath—with memories still fresh from the explosions in a fireworks factory in Enschede the previous year—renewed interest surfaced in the enforcement of safety standards.

The agricultural sector suffered from an outbreak of foot-and-mouth disease, which dampened farmers' morale and had adverse effects on their income. Beyond the sphere of agriculture, travel restrictions interfered with commerce and led to the cancellation of some celebrations of the national holiday (Koninginnedag, or Queen's Day) and some World War II memorial events. Bovine spongiform encephalopathy (also referred to as "mad cow" disease) was also detected in The Netherlands.

Though the euro was about to become the only legal tender in January 2002, The Netherlands nonetheless celebrated its tradition of creating beautifully designed currency by issuing one "last" guilder coin in mid-June. One side was drawn by a 12-year-old boy, whose design, selected from more than 50,000 submissions, sported a cartoonish flag-waving "Dutch lion." Sixteen

million copies of the popular coin were put into circulation.

The royal family turned its attention to matrimony. Prince Constantijn, the third son of Queen Beatrix, married Laurentien Brinkhorst. Crown Prince Willem-Alexander announced his engagement to Máxima Zorreguieta. The proposed marriage was approved by the States-General after skillful negotiation by Prime Minister Wim Kok. At issue was the fact that Zorreguieta's father had been the minister of agriculture in Argentina during the Jorge Rafaél Videla regime. Kok authorized an independent study to explore the extent of her father's involvement in human rights violations. Zorreguieta denied having known of any such violations by his government at the time and stated that he would not attend the nuptials, scheduled for Feb. 2, 2002. Máxima Zorreguieta publicly expressed regret that her father had "worked hard" for a regime that had engaged in unacceptable practices. The fact that she was able to make such statements in Dutch helped establish her credibility with the Dutch public.

The Netherlands made news around the world on April 1 when the first four gay and lesbian couples were legally

Gay couples celebrate at City Hall in Amsterdam on April 1 after exchanging wedding vows under a new law allowing same-sex marriages.

AP/Wide World Photos

married in Amsterdam. Almost 400 couples followed suit that month. Of those, 80% were already registered as domestic partners, an option that had been available since 1998.

(JOLANDA VANDERWAL TAYLOR)

NEW ZEALAND

Area: 270,534 sq km (104,454 sq mi)
Population (2001 est.): 3,861,000
Capital: Wellington
Chief of state: Queen Elizabeth II, represented by Governors-General Sir Michael Hardie-Boys, Dame Sian Elias (acting) from March 22, and, from April 4, Dame Silvia Cartwright
Head of government: Prime Minister Helen Clark

Pierre Vinet/New Line Cinema

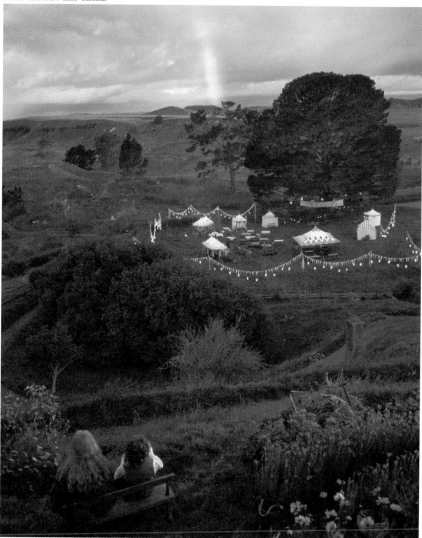

The spectacular landscape of New Zealand provided the backdrop for the popular 2001 film **The Fellowship of the Ring.**

In 2001, the Labour Party's second full year in power, Prime Minister Helen Clark continued to have the support of her coalition deputy, Jim Anderton of the liberal Alliance, and the less-reliable support of various fragmentary groupings, which came and went on different issues. Anderton's personal ambition to convert the national post office to a People's Bank came closer with his appointment of former National Party (NP) prime minister Jim Bolger as that project's leader. The mildly conservative NP provided a dull parliamentary opposition, and it was no surprise to insiders when NP leader Jenny Shipley paid the price. On October 8 her colleagues produced the numbers to persuade her it was time to step down. Deputy party leader Bill English, minister of health and then of finance in past NP governments, stepped up.

In the wake of the attacks in the United States on September 11, New Zealand offered deployment of its elite Special Air Service (SAS) to an antiterrorism operation coordinated and led by the U.S. The SAS force specialized in undercover long-range reconnaissance and counterterrorism missions, and a New Zealand government spokesman acknowledged that it might serve in Afghanistan. Anderton's support for New Zealand's involvement triggered some dissent within the Alliance. The situation also provoked some New Zealanders to recall the country's post-World War II treaty with the U.S. and Australia, the ANZUS Pact, which New Zealand had effectively jettisoned when it barred nuclear-age U.S. warships from its ports in the 1980s. In May the government had announced plans to scrap all of New Zealand's combat aircraft. A legal challenge to the decision was rejected by a High Court judge in November, and the squadrons were disbanded in December.

In the second half of the year, the government passed initiatives to help Australia place Afghan and other refugees and also to save New Zealand's international airline. Beginning in late August Afghan "boat people" bearing down on northern and western Australia were refused permission to land. New Zealand agreed to accept a quota for settlement, and in late September more than 140 refugees were flown to Auckland from a transshipment centre on Nauru. At the same time, New Zealand Muslims announced plans to combat perceived harassment and met with a government-appointed race relations conciliator. Air New Zealand's (ANZ) crisis was partly attributable to world reaction against flying, as well as to a failed attempt to digest fully the Australian airline Ansett in a many-sided takeover op-

eration. For the New Zealand government it meant returning to the business of running an airline 12 years after privatization. In early October it assumed control of ANZ, with a cost of NZ$885 million (about U.S. $366.5 million), 83% ownership, and a less-than-buoyant market. ANZ chief executive Gary Toomey immediately resigned. John Palmer replaced him in late November.

The engineering of genetically modified (GM) organisms became a tentative new issue with the release at the end of July of a Royal Commission report backing commercial use of GM products in New Zealand. One reviewer said the commission had balanced the need for progress with the need for robust safety controls. In October the government allowed a moratorium on GM research, including experimental field trials, to lapse, but it announced a new two-year moratorium on the commercial release of GM organisms under development.

In November yachtsman Sir Peter Blake was killed by bandits. (*See* OBITUARIES.)   (JOHN A. KELLEHER)

NICARAGUA

Area: 130,373 sq km (50,337 sq mi)
Population (2001 est.): 4,918,000
Capital: Managua
Head of state and government: President Arnoldo Alemán Lacayo

In Nicaragua socioeconomic conditions worsened in 2001 as the world recession, poor commodity prices, administrative malfeasance and incompetence, bank failures, and drought caused economic growth to slow to an estimated 2.1%. Unemployment, poverty, and income inequality grew. At midyear starving peasants from the north erected protest encampments along major highways and in Managua. In acknowledgment of the country's dire conditions, the international donor community had finally admitted Nicaragua to the Heavily Indebted Poor Countries Initiative in December 2000 and canceled much of its foreign debt. The government was to make fiscal reforms and combat corruption, but medications donated by the international community to the government were soon found being distributed in ruling party campaign offices. The U.S. chose to deliver its food aid through nongovernmental organizations.

It was also an election year. The 1999 "pact" between Sandinista Daniel Ortega and Constitutionalist Liberal Arnoldo Alemán Lacayo had resulted in 2000 in the packing of the Supreme Electoral Council. Controlled by partisans, the council rejected all attempts by third parties to qualify to compete in the next presidential elections except that of the Conservative Party, whose bid was apparently saved by U.S. pressure. As the unofficial campaign heated up early in 2001, however, with Ortega seven points in the lead, the U.S. successfully pressured the Conservatives to withdraw in order not to split the anti-Sandinista vote.

Though the Conservatives later named new candidates, the contest narrowed to a tight two-way race. While the Liberal candidate, 73-year-old businessman Enrique Bolaños Geyer, sought to establish his concern for Nicaragua's impoverished majority, erstwhile revolutionary Ortega presented himself as a "new man" able to coexist with practically anyone. Unmoved, the Catholic hierarchy and various American officials—including Secretary of State Colin Powell—made strong anti-Sandinista declarations. Following the September 11 attacks in the U.S., Washington even drew connections between Ortega and world "terrorism," and one American official predicted a "vicious" U.S. response should an Ortega government be found to have links to terrorism. On November 4 Bolaños trounced Ortega 56.3%–42.3%, while the Conservatives claimed 1.4% of the vote. Hours before the election, former U.S. president Jimmy Carter, heading an observer team in Nicaragua, commented: "I personally disapprove of statements or actions by any country . . . to influence the vote . . . in another sovereign nation." In December, citing that the statute of limitations had run out, a judge dismissed charges of rape brought against Ortega by his stepdaughter.

(THOMAS W. WALKER)

NIGER

Area: 1,267,000 sq km (489,000 sq mi)
Population (2001 est.): 10,355,000
Capital: Niamey
Head of state and government: President Tandja Mamadou, assisted by Prime Minister Hama Amadou

Thousands of University of Niamey students, protesting against government plans to reduce their grants, clashed with security forces on Feb. 21, 2001. One policeman later died of head wounds received during the violence, and nearly 50 persons from both sides were injured. Sixteen students were arrested after the demonstration, and the university was closed. On March 24 the government easily defeated an opposition no-confidence vote over its handling of the unrest. The Niamey students rejected an agreement signed on March 28 between the government and their parent organization, the Union of Niger Students, that would have reopened the university and restored full financial support. They demanded the release of the arrested students as a precondition for negotiations. At a court appearance on April 3, however, only four were released; the remaining 12 were charged with murder. On April 28 the imprisoned students began a hunger strike, and in May 100 other students staged a sit-down strike outside the parliament building. The action was abandoned after 11 days, and students staged a peaceful demonstration through the streets of Niamey. The prisoners' hunger strike continued for several more days.

Niger's food crisis remained at critical levels throughout the summer, though the year's increased rainfall held promise of an improved harvest. On July 25 the UN World Food Programme launched an appeal for donors to give Niger $5 million for emergency purchases of grain. The government announced on August 15 that, in order to try to halt ongoing desertification, it would more than double the number of tree seedlings to be planted during the year.   (NANCY ELLEN LAWLER)

At a special forum on child slavery held during the World Conference Against Racism in Durban, S.Af., Mariama Oumarou tearfully recounts her experiences as a child slave in Niger.

NIGERIA

Area: 923,768 sq km (356,669 sq mi)
Population (2001 est.): 126,636,000
Capital: Abuja; judiciary and some ministries remain in Lagos, the former capital
Head of state and government: President Olusegun Obasanjo

George Esiri/TimePix

A burnt-out church in Kano, Nigeria, on October 17, attests to the Muslim-Christian fighting in the area that reportedly claimed more than 100 lives.

Throughout 2001 Nigeria experienced ethnic and religious violence. In June and July battles between the Tiv minority and Hausa majority left approximately 50,000 people displaced in Nassarawa state. In August Christians and Muslims fought in Bauchi state over the state government's efforts to institute Shari'ah (Islamic law). Similar clashes in the central city of Jos claimed an estimated 1,000 lives in September. Violence flared in October between Muslims and Christians in Kano following Muslim protests against U.S.-led military action in Afghanistan. Official reports put the death toll at 18, though the unofficial tally reached more than 100.

The oil-producing Niger Delta region was again the site of environmental problems and political conflicts. A blown-out well in the Yorla oil field released crude oil for nine days before being capped. Residents fled several surrounding villages as their crops were destroyed and drinking water was poisoned by the oil. Shell Oil Co. officials charged that they were prevented from taking adequate safety precautions by the Movement for the Survival of Ogoni People (MOSOP), a group formed to protect the interests of the delta region's inhabitants. For its part MOSOP claimed that Shell failed to consult local people about the oil fields.

In January the federal government asked the Supreme Court to clarify a constitutional provision allowing state governments to keep a portion of profits from oil produced in their territory. The federal government claimed the proceeds of offshore oil production, money that oil-producing states had attempted to keep. In July the court sided with the federal government. As a result, oil-producing states received 7.8% of the national oil revenue rather than the 13% they had claimed.

In April Pres. Olusegun Obasanjo announced the simultaneous replacement of the heads of the army, navy, and air

force. The move was widely interpreted as a result of Obasanjo's desire to remove Army Chief of Staff Lieut. Gen. Victor Malu from office. Malu caused controversy when he publicly criticized military training and cooperation arrangements between Nigeria and the U.S. The new top military men were Maj. Gen. Alexander Ogomudia (army), Air Vice Marshal James Wuyep (air force), and Rear Adm. Samuel Afolayan (navy).

In March the police arrested Gilbert Okoye in connection with the murder of a politician in Anambra state. Okoye led the Anambra Vigilance Services, better known as the Bakassi Boys, a vigilante group that was revived in 2000 and supported by the Anambra government. That support ended amid criticism that the group killed suspected criminals instead of turning them over to the authorities. In April police in Lagos exchanged fire with members of the Oodua Peoples' Congress, a banned Yoruba militia.

In September serious flooding struck northern parts of the country. The Taura dam in Jigawa state overflowed following heavy rains, killing more than 100 people and leaving 40,000 homeless. Another 60 lives were lost and 10,000 people rendered homeless by floods in nearby Kano state. Late in the year a cholera outbreak claimed more than 700 lives.

The Human Rights Violation Investigation Commission (HRVIC) continued to look into alleged abuses by the country's

former military governments. In July Justice Chukwudifu Oputa, chairman of the HRVIC, called on three former military rulers to appear before the commission. The three, Generals Muhammadu Buhari, Ibrahim Babangida, and Abdulsalam Abubakar, all refused and challenged the commission summons in court. President Obasanjo appeared before the commission in September to answer charges stemming from his tenure as a military ruler in 1978. In December gunmen assassinated Attorney General and Justice Minister Bola Ige. The attack was blamed on a power struggle between political factions in Ige's home state of Osun.   (MATTHEW A. CENZER)

NORWAY

Area: 323,758 sq km (125,004 sq mi)
Population (2001 est.): 4,516,000
Capital: Oslo
Chief of state: King Harald V
Head of government: Prime Ministers Jens Stoltenberg and, from October 19, Kjell Magne Bondevik

Norway's long-dominant Labour Party lost much of its grip on power after a miserable showing in the general election held on Sept. 10, 2001. In its worst showing since 1924, the party won only 24.4% of the popular vote and managed to secure just 43 seats in the 165-member Storting (parliament), down from the 65 seats the party had won four years earlier. The big winners were the Conservatives and the Socialist Left Party. The Conservatives obtained 38 seats—a gain of 15 from 1997—while the Socialist Left Party increased its number of seats from 9 to 23. The Labour government chose to resign as a result of the elections. On October 17 a minority government was formed that included the Conservatives, the Christian People's Party (22 seats), and the Liberal Party (2 seats). Kjell Magne Bondevik of the Christian People's Party became prime minister for the second time in his career, and Conservative leader Jan Petersen was named foreign minister. The populist right-wing Progress Party (26 seats) pledged its support for the new government.

The marriage of Crown Prince Haakon to the beautiful, courageous, but controversial Mette-Marit Tjessem Høiby on August 25 in Oslo captured the nation's attention. (*See* BIOGRAPHIES.) The prince's choice of bride had raised eyebrows not only because she was a commoner but because she had a four-year-old son by a convicted drug dealer. Public opinion, however, began to swing in her favour after Mette-Marit held a news conference only days before the wedding to publicly apologize for aspects of her past and to condemn drug use. The hour-long wedding in Oslo Cathedral was relayed via a giant screen to thousands of people who had gathered outside the building. On December 13 the second heiress to the throne, Princess Märtha Louise, and author Ari Behn declared their engagement. At the end of the year support for the monarchy was strongly expressed in most of the press.

Prices in the global oil market continued to influence the Norwegian economy. Average daily oil production was an estimated three million barrels. Until October the average oil spot price per barrel of Brent Blend was $26. It then dropped to around $20. The negative effect from the oil price reductions that followed was counterbalanced by Norway's long-term contracts of gas deliveries by pipelines to the European market.

Surplus state income from the oil industry went into a Petroleum Fund that was set up in part to ensure pensions for the elderly. In March the government declared that future interest income from the fund should be used to cover state budget deficits.

Unemployment remained relatively low at about 3.6% during the year. The consumer price index rose by 4.3% in May but declined to 2.5% in July owing to tax cuts. In June the Bank of Norway decided to maintain the interest rate at 7% (the highest level in Western Europe) and even declared that it would raise the rate should inflation once more approach 4%. By the end of November the bank had reduced the rate by 0.25%.

(GUDMUND SANDVIK)

OMAN

Area: 309,500 sq km (119,500 sq mi)
Population (2001 est.): 2,497,000
Capital: Muscat
Head of state and government: Sultan and Prime Minister Qabus ibn Sa'id

In the immediate aftermath of the terrorist attacks in the U.S. on Sept. 11, 2001, Oman, in fulfillment of preparations launched two and a half years earlier, hosted a joint military exercise with Great Britain. The presence of some 30,000 British troops in the sultanate facilitated the U.S.-led coalition's military campaign against the Taliban regime and al-Qaeda terrorist network in Afghanistan. Throughout the campaign Oman remained supportive of the coalition, allowing the deployment of American B-1 bombers to bases in the sultanate and agreeing to serve as a staging area for British and American special forces.

Sultan Qabus ibn Sa'id was more visible in 2001 than in previous years. He was among the regional leaders who met personally with U.S. Secretary of Defense Donald Rumsfeld during Rumsfeld's three-day swing through the Middle East in early October to garner international support for the war on terrorism. At the end of the year, the sultan was elected chairman of the Gulf Cooperation Council's (GCC's) Supreme Council for 2002. The GCC, established in 1981 and committed to enhancing economic, defense, and political cooperation between its six member states, had become one of the world's most prominent subregional organizations. The members—Bahrain, Kuwait, Oman, Qatar, Saudi Arabia, and the United Arab Emirates—possessed nearly half the planet's proven petroleum reserves.

Domestically, Oman continued along the path of its previous political reforms. In addition to the cabinet and government headed by the sultan, a 52-member State Council helped determine national development strategies. As part of a larger Oman Council, the State Council also rendered advice regarding the sultanate's economic and financial policies. The uncertain future of oil revenues continued to underpin the government's resolve to diversify the economy. This entailed further development of the country's liquefied natural gas industry, tourism, and the southernmost port of Salalah, one of the world's largest container terminals.

(JOHN DUKE ANTHONY)

PAKISTAN

Area: 796,095 sq km (307,374 sq mi), excluding the 84,159-sq-km Pakistani-administered portion of Jammu and Kashmir
Population (2001 est.): 144.6 million (excluding 4 million residents of Pakistani-administered Jammu and Kashmir as well as 2 million Afghan refugees)
Capital: Islamabad
Head of state and government: President and Chief Executive Gen. Pervez Musharraf

The leader of Pakistan's military regime, Gen. Pervez Musharraf, found himself walking a political tightrope in 2001. After having consolidated his grip on power by declaring himself president in June, Musharraf risked a highly unpopular move with his decision—in the wake of the terrorist attacks in the United States on September 11—to side with the U.S. in its war against the Taliban government in Afghanistan and the al-Qaeda terrorist network led by Saudi-born Osama bin Laden. (*See* BIOGRAPHIES.) Pakistan had been one of only three countries ever officially to recognize the Afghan Islamists, and the Taliban enjoyed the sympathies and support of many of Pakistan's 140 million Muslims. In the aftermath of September 11, Islamic militants staged protests in dozens of cities throughout

Pakistan, burning U.S. Pres. George W. Bush in effigy and promising a "holy war" against any American troops that set foot in the country. Some 10,000 Pakistanis were thought to have crossed the Suleman Mountains into Afghanistan to fight alongside the Taliban against the U.S.-led forces.

Musharraf appeared on nationwide television on September 19 to defend his decision to side with the U.S., and as time went on, he appeared more confident in his ability to restrain the vocal Muslim clerics and militant groups responsible for the rash of angry protests. In fact, Musharraf all but abandoned his initial calls for a political settlement to the conflict that had included uniting so-called moderate Taliban members with rival Afghan groups in a new government. Instead, he expressed support for removing the Taliban outright and, at home, went about purging Taliban-friendly officers in the Pakistani military. Moreover, he ordered a complete ban on any public gathering that included what he described as seditious conduct or language. By December these measures appeared to have had an impact. The militants had failed to ignite anything close to a real threat to Musharraf. As the military rout of the Taliban progressed, the Pakistani government began to devote considerable attention to the role it might play in the establishment of a post-Taliban government in Afghanistan. Islamabad clearly wanted to ensure that Pashtuns—who made up the largest ethnic group in Afghanistan and dominated Pakistani regions on the Afghan border—had a major voice in any future Kabul government.

Pakistan's dispute with India over Jammu and Kashmir state remained essentially unsettled despite several attempts at negotiation. Alarmed by an increase in secessionist violence in the region, Indian Prime Minister Atal Bihari Vajpayee invited Musharraf to India for talks on the matter. Musharraf accepted the invitation and arrived in New Delhi on July 14. Discussions were held in Agra over the following two days. India pushed for help in ending cross-border terrorism, but Pakistan continued to insist that a political solution to the Jammu and Kashmir issue needed to be reached before effective change could be brought about. While no final agreement was reached, Vajpayee accepted an invitation to visit Pakistan later in the year. A meeting scheduled for September in New York City was canceled owing to the terrorist attacks. After both countries had pledged their support for the U.S.-led war on terrorism following the events of September 11, the U.S. decided to end the economic embargoes it had imposed on Pakistan and India for carrying out nuclear tests in 1998. Pakistani and Indian relations deteriorated severely after India blamed two Pakistan-based organizations for the terrorist attack on Parliament House in New Delhi on December 13.

On the economic front, Pakistan's attempt to follow an International Monetary Fund reform program met with mixed results. Although recession continued and unemployment steadily climbed, Pakistan successfully secured loan guarantees from the World Bank, which promised to deliver $350 million for bank restructuring and a like amount to help reduce the country's current-account deficit. Gross domestic product growth, which had been targeted at 4.5% for 2001, was revised down to 3.8%. The government plans to privatize some 50 companies over the next two years were still intact, despite the fact that few investors had expressed interest in the state-owned banks and corporations slated for sale.   (EDITOR)

PALAU

Area: 488 sq km (188 sq mi)
Population (2001 est.): 19,700
Provisional capital: Koror; a site on Babelthuap was designated to be the permanent capital
Head of state and government: Presidents Kuniwo Nakamura and, from January 19, Tommy Remengesau

Pakistani paramilitary troops check their ammunition while patrolling the Indian border near Wagah on December 28.

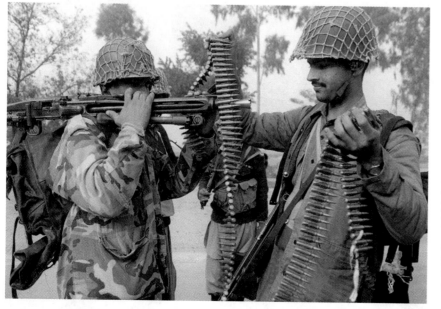

Voters in Palau elected a new president. Tommy Remengesau began his four-year term on Jan. 19, 2001, and replaced Kuniwo Nakamura, who enthusiastically endorsed his successor. Remengesau moved quickly to strengthen economic relations with Taiwan, especially in the tourism industry, and Taiwan sent a delegation to attend his inauguration.

In April Palau and Saga University, Saga City, Japan, signed an agreement for technical cooperation in the implementation of a power-generation method developed by the university. Under the agreement, Palau would generate its electric power through ocean thermal energy conversion (OTEC). In the South Pacific region, water temperatures can differ by as much as 11 °C (20 °F) between the surface and depths of several hundred metres, a factor that was ideally suited to the environmentally friendly OTEC method using ocean temperature differentials.
                              (A.R.G. GRIFFITHS)

PANAMA

Area: 74,979 sq km (28,950 sq mi)
Population (2001 est.): 2,903,000
Capital: Panama City
Head of state and government: President
Mireya Moscoso

The year 2001 marked the second anniversary of Panamanian Pres. Mireya
Moscoso's administration. Four issues
dominated the domestic agenda: the
slowing economy, the reorganization of
the state-owned water company, growing charges of corruption, and problems stemming from an effort to modernize public transportation.

Panama's economy continued a downward trend during the year. The finance
minister was forced to admit that economic growth would not exceed 2%.
Economists attributed the downturn in
the economy to a slowdown in activity
in the Colón Free Trade Zone and reduced foreign investment. In addition,
the government announced that the September 11 terrorist attacks in the U.S.
would depress Panama's tourism sector.

Throughout the year a battle ensued
between the president and the Legislative Assembly over the reorganization
of the state-owned water and sewer
company IDAAN. During the presidential campaign, Moscoso had promised
that she would never privatize IDAAN.
Once in office, however, she was faced
with the company's massive operating
deficit. Initially, she sought to pump
$150 million from the Fiduciary Fund
into IDAAN. The opposition-controlled
Congress refused to support the idea
without a major overhaul of the way
the company was run. Efforts to reach
a compromise were under way.

The media and opposition party leaders highlighted charges of nepotism
and misuse of public funds. A leading
adviser to Moscoso quit the administration, alleging that "crooks disguised
as businessmen" surrounded the president. Additional problems surfaced
when Moscoso commuted the sentence
of a known drug trafficker whose
brother worked at the Ministry of the
Presidency. Moscoso later rescinded the
commutation.

Mass protests were sparked by a 67%
transit hike that had been part of a government effort to modernize public

transportation. The demonstrations,
which blocked many key streets in
Panama City, led the education minister
to temporarily close down all public
schools in the city and the adjoining district of San Miguelito. Under pressure,
the government formed a negotiating
commission and in the end backed away
from the hike.   (ORLANDO J. PÉREZ)

PAPUA NEW GUINEA

Area: 462,840 sq km (178,704 sq mi)
Population (2001 est.): 5,287,000
Capital: Port Moresby
Chief of state: Queen Elizabeth II, repre-
sented by Governor-General Silas Atopare
Head of government: Prime Minister Sir
Mekere Morauta

Papua New Guinea's secessionist province of Bougainville ended a decade-
long war when final terms for peace

were negotiated on June 1, 2001. Under
an agreement signed by the minister for
Bougainville affairs, Moi Avei, on behalf
of the national government, the island
was to have statelike autonomy and the
option of total independence by 2011–16.

Widespread breakdowns in law and
order caused by difficult economic conditions and popular hostility to the
Papua New Guinea Privatization Commission, the World Bank, and the International Monetary Fund posed serious
problems in 2001. In the most serious
incident, rebellious soldiers stole weapons from armouries in Port Morseby.
The soldiers were angered by a Commonwealth Eminent Persons Group
recommendation that the size of the
army be halved and that the army headquarters be sold off as commercial real
estate. To defuse the situation, Prime
Minister Sir Mekere Morauta gave an
unconditional amnesty to all those who
took part in the uprising.

In Port Moresby four students died
during protests against privatization.
The government promised a commission of inquiry into the killings.
Violent squabbling between rival tribes
over potential royalties from an

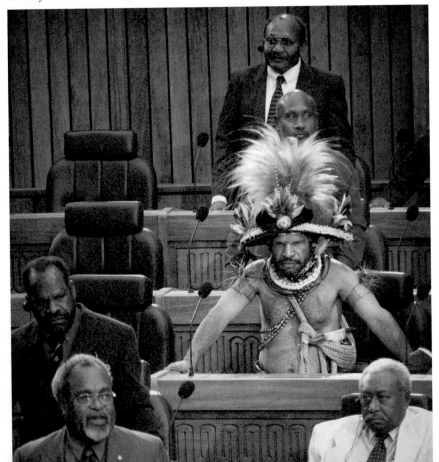

*Alfred Kaibe, a member of Parliament in Papua New Guinea, wears
traditional clothing from the Southern Highlands during a legislative session
on July 25.*

A\$8,590,000,000 (U.S. \$4,278,000,000) project worried possible investors in a gas consortium. At least 25 people died during tribal fighting sparked by land ownership claims along the projected route of the PNG-Queensland (Australia) gas pipeline. In December clashes near Mendi between the Ujimap and Tugumap tribesmen killed at least 36 persons. (A.R.G. GRIFFITHS)

PARAGUAY

Area: 406,752 sq km (157,048 sq mi)
Population (2001 est.): 5,636,000
Capital: Asunción
Head of state and government: President Luis Ángel González Macchi

During 2001 Paraguay faced a series of political and socioeconomic challenges—largely dealing with corruption scandals and ineffective economic policies—that threatened to overwhelm the country's weak democracy and fragile economic system. A general feeling of uncertainty and despair contributed to rumours of presidential resignation, coups, and social violence. In March, after the collapse of the National Unity government, unconfirmed rumours spread that Pres. Luis Ángel González Macchi had resigned in the face of demands from several labour groups and opposition parties that he "step down because of incompetence." Vice Pres. Julio César Franco and Miguel Abdon Saguier of the opposition Authentic Radical Liberal Party organized several protests and lobbied the legislature to have the president impeached and removed from office.

González was further weakened by a series of corruption scandals involving his family, including an allegation that the president's siblings were involved in the illegal diversion of offshore accounts of nearly \$16 million in assets from two failed banks. Also, it was disclosed in March that the president's official car had been illegally imported after apparently having been stolen in Brazil.

The political crisis was exacerbated by a continued decline in economic and social conditions. Approximately a dozen strikes and roadblocks were staged during the year, most of them by landless peasants, teachers, labour unions, bus drivers, and owners of small businesses. The one thing that all of them had in common was a demand for a coherent and just economic policy and the resignation of González. Paraguay's economy grew by less than 1% during the year, while unemployment was expected to increase from 18% in 2000 to about 25% in 2001.

The domestic, political, and economic crisis overwhelmed the attention of the government and did not allow for many foreign-policy initiatives. Paraguay hosted the summit of the Southern Cone Common Market (Mercosur) members in Asunción June 21–22. During the summit Paraguay expressed concern about the consequences of exchange-rate adjustments in Argentina, demanding that a compensation mechanism be created to alleviate the negative effects on Paraguayan exports. After the September attacks in the U.S., Paraguay was one of only two countries in Latin America to consider offering troops in the U.S.-led effort to stamp out international terrorism. (FRANK O. MORA)

PERU

Area: 1,285,216 sq km (496,225 sq mi)
Population (2001 est.): 26,090,000
Capital: Lima
Head of state and government: Presidents Valentín Paniagua (interim) and, from July 28, Alejandro Toledo

The year 2001 finally brought some stability and order to Peru after a tumultuous period of political upheaval. In 2000 Pres. Alberto Fujimori had stood for a third election, in which he claimed victory despite universal outcries of fraud and ballot manipulation. Shortly after his apparent victory, however, a series of scandals involving him and Vladimiro Montesinos, his chief intelligence officer, brought about his downfall, which ended with Fujimori's faxing in his resignation as president from Japan, where he sought and received asylum.

Following Fujimori's fall from power, the Peruvian Congress had named Valentín Paniagua as interim president. He was able to bring a certain calm to Peru, stabilize a chaotic political situation, and shepherd elections through a

Vladimiro Montesinos (in handcuffs), former Peruvian president Alberto Fujimori's chief intelligence officer, arrives for a criminal hearing at a naval base in Callao on September 7.
AFP Worldwide

first round in May 2001 and then a second round some weeks later. The first round saw Alejandro Toledo, an independent candidate from Peru's highlands, and former president Alan García Pérez finish first and second, respectively, but neither won the required simple majority. In the second round Toledo won a close (52–48%) race and was inaugurated on July 28. (*See* BIOGRAPHIES.)

In the meantime, Montesinos was finally captured after having fled Peru to Venezuela. He was returned to Lima, where he faced dozens of charges ranging from money laundering and drug smuggling to human rights abuses and murder. Several congressional committees as well as an independent investigator were overseeing the investigation, which was expected to take some years. Montesinos had made numerous videotapes that incriminated perhaps hundreds of high-ranking military officers, politicians, judges, businessmen, and others. At the same time, Peru was attempting to persuade Japan to extradite Fujimori, a first-generation Peruvian of Japanese descent, so that he could also face numerous charges, including murder and embezzlement. Whether Japan would accede to such requests was open to question.

As president, Toledo inherited a difficult political and economic situation. He did not have a majority in Congress, and since Peru's political party system was highly fluid, politics was largely a game of personalities—inherently unstable and dependent on shifting and uncertain coalitions. The centre-left American Popular Revolutionary Alliance (APRA) was probably the best organized party in the country, although nowhere near as strong as it had been in its past. APRA showed restraint as the major opposition early in Toledo's term, but how long such a truce could last was anyone's guess. In addition, the presidency was Toledo's first elected position; he had to learn a great deal quickly in order to be able to govern successfully. Following his first 100 days in office, critics began to scrutinize his work habits and private life unfavourably; as a result, Toledo slashed his pay by one-third—from $18,000 to $12,000 a month.

In any case, Toledo's presidency promised to be a departure from his predecessors; his ethnic background as an indigenous non-European made him distinctive and gave him a certain popularity among Peru's poor. His cabinet was nevertheless composed of well-known individuals, for the most part from Peru's economic, financial, and political establishment.

Economically, Peru was in the midst of a significant recession; new investment was low, meaning that job creation was scarce and unemployment and poverty levels were high. To add to the misery, a severe earthquake struck southern Peru on June 23 in and around the city of Arequipa, causing widespread damage to houses, highways, and other infrastructure. On December 29 a demonstration that went awry at a Lima fireworks shop caused an explosion that killed at least 290 persons. (*See* DISASTERS.)

(HENRY A. DIETZ)

PHILIPPINES

Area: 300,076 sq km (115,860 sq mi)
Population (2001 est.): 78,609,000
Capital: Quezon City (designated national government centre and the location of the lower house of the legislature and some ministries); many government offices are in Manila or other suburbs
Head of state and government: Presidents Joseph Estrada and, from January 20, Gloria Macapagal Arroyo

Angered by corruption charges against Philippines Pres. Joseph Estrada, demonstrators drove him from office on Jan. 20, 2001. That same day Vice Pres. Gloria Macapagal Arroyo was installed as president. (*See* BIOGRAPHIES.)

The Philippines Senate had begun trying Estrada on impeachment charges in late 2000. When the trial was abandoned because some senators blocked the admission of evidence, protesters poured into the streets of Manila. After four increasingly tense days, the army chief of staff, Gen. Angelo Reyes, informed Estrada on Jan. 19, 2001, that the military was "withdrawing its support" from him. Without troops to protect the presidential palace, Estrada fled that night. The Supreme Court declared the presidency to be vacant and swore Arroyo in as his successor.

Estrada later claimed that he had only temporarily vacated the presidency, not resigned, but the Supreme Court unanimously upheld Arroyo's succession. As accusations against Estrada piled up, Arroyo, vice president since 1998, distanced herself from him and became an opposition leader.

Using evidence from the impeachment proceedings, authorities arrested Estrada on April 25. In protest some 20,000 of his supporters marched on the presidential palace on May 1. Four people were

Life goes on for residents of a house in Jolo, Phil., damaged in an attack by Moro National Liberation Front rebels on November 21.

killed as riot police stopped them. Arroyo declared a "state of rebellion" that lasted five days.

More than 100 people were killed in the bloodiest congressional and local elections in more than a decade. In voting on May 14, Arroyo's supporters won 8 of the 13 open Senate seats, and the new president was given a Senate majority.

Estrada's trial on charges of plundering the country began in October. It could take years, during which he was to remain behind bars. The charges carried a possible death penalty, but few observers expected that sentence if he was convicted. Estrada's wife and son also faced charges.

Rumours of corruption involving Arroyo's husband, a wealthy businessman and lawyer, were denied by the president. She asked for official investigations to clear their names.

In her first state of the nation address, given on July 22, Arroyo tackled the issue of poverty. She announced plans to create at least one million jobs as part of agricultural modernization and to distribute 200,000 ha (494,000 ac) of land annually to landless farmers. Just 5% of Filipinos owned nearly 90% of all the land in the country.

On Basilan Island in the southern Philippines, 7,000 army troops fought a long jungle campaign against a bandit group known as Abu Sayyaf, which the U.S. government said had links to terrorist Osama bin Laden. The group, estimated at 1,000 strong, comprised former guerrillas who had fought for a separate Muslim state in the south and had turned to kidnapping. The troops stormed an Abu Sayyaf camp on nearby Jolo Island on April 12 and freed a kidnapped American, Jeffrey Schilling. On May 27 the bandits raided a resort off Palawan Island and abducted 20 people to Basilan, including three Americans. They later beheaded one of the Americans and raided villages, beheading 10 Filipino Christians.

On August 7 the government signed a cease-fire agreement with the main Muslim group still seeking independence in the south, the Moro Islamic Liberation Front. After at least 12 cease-fire violations, another agreement was signed on October 18. In November a rebel faction of the Moro National Liberation Front that was loyal to Nur Misuari—governor of the Autonomous Region of Muslim Mindanao—broke a five-year peace agreement and launched an attack on Jolo Island to prevent elections for Misuari's successor. (HENRY S. BRADSHER)

POLAND

Area: 312,685 sq km (120,728 sq mi)
Population (2001 est.): 38,647,000
Capital: Warsaw
Chief of state: President Aleksander Kwasniewski
Head of government: Prime Ministers Jerzy Buzek and, from October 19, Leszek Miller

The focal point in Poland during 2001 was the September 23 parliamentary election. In the spring and summer, a number of new right-wing parties began to coalesce, including the new Right-Wing Alliance in March and the centre-right pro-business party Civic Forum–Christian Democracy in July. A new election bill with a provision that would admit to the Sejm (lower house of the legislature) only parties that won at least 5% of the vote was adopted in April.

The elections attracted a low voter turnout (46%), but the left won a decisive victory. The big winner was the Democratic Left Alliance (SLD), led by former communist Leszek Miller, which took 216 of 460 seats. Second was the Civic Platform (65 seats), followed by Self Defense, a radical farmers group that opposed Poland's joining the European Union (EU), with 53, and the right-wing Law and Justice party (44). The incumbent Solidarity Electoral Action of the Right (AWSP) was routed, failing to meet the required threshold and therefore not able to claim a single Sejm seat. Despite its big win, the SLD found itself 15 seats short of a majority, and a coalition agreement was struck with the Polish Peasant Party (PSL), which had taken 8.9% of the vote. The same two parties had shared power uneasily from 1993 to 1997. Miller named his cabinet on October 10. SLD members took the key portfolios of finance (Marek Belka) and the economy (Jacek Piechota); PSL leader Jaroslaw Kalinowski was deputy prime minister and minister of agriculture. A new Infrastructure Ministry, embracing transportation, communications, and regional policy, was also created. At his inauguration Prime Minister Miller pledged continuity, "not to start or pursue any revolutions." An amendment to the civil service regulations passed by the Sejm in December raised eyebrows, as it seemed to open the way for more

political appointments to administrative positions.

AWSP's big losses were principally chalked up to Poland's sinking economy. Prime Minister Jerzy Buzek was under severe pressure to trim the $20 billion budget deficit, and the government floundered throughout the spring and summer trying to do so. Shares in the state telecom company Telekomunikacja Polska had to be sold to raise cash in March. The government tried to raise the budget deficit by $2 billion in July. Finance Minister Jaroslaw Bauc was fired in late August, ostensibly for not having warned of the magnitude of the problem. In September the Sejm rejected Buzek's report on the budget. Picking up the struggle to balance the budget, the new government adopted a 20% tax on interest from savings and investments and froze income tax thresholds in order to postpone an expected loss of revenue from that quarter. On October 20 state expenditures were ordered cut by about $2 billion, and salaries of central administration employees were frozen. In the austerity draft budget for 2002, adopted on November 20, the deficit was limited to 5% of gross domestic product. Projected 2001 GDP growth figures of 2.3% were reduced to 1%; inflation figures were estimated at 4.5%, down from the 4.7–4.8% forecast earlier. By December unemployment had soared to 16.8%, a record for the postcommunist period.

Poland's foreign policy focused on trying to accelerate the process of joining the European Union. The new foreign minister, Wlodzimierz Cimoszewicz, ran into trouble with the Sejm in late November because of concessions he had made in EU negotiations earlier that month. Poland signed a gas deal with Denmark in July, trying to reduce the country's dependence on Russian energy supplies. Miller visited Russia on December 20 to discuss the imbalance of trade and a planned new oil pipeline from Russia through Poland to Western Europe.

The return of a leftist government was not the only reminder of Poland's past during the year. Former leader Gen. Wojciech Jaruzelski was placed on trial in May for having given orders, when he was defense minister in 1970, to shoot striking workers. In June the first checks from a German fund set up to reimburse workers from Nazi-occupied countries who had been impressed into slave labour were distributed in Poland. Meanwhile, public debate continued over the question of the proper apportionment—between the Nazi occupiers, the Polish Roman Catholic Church, and the local populations—of responsibility for a number of massacres of Polish Jews during World War II. On July 10 Pres. Aleksander Kwasniewski voiced a formal apology on behalf of the Polish people for one such massacre, in the village of Jedwabne, in 1941.

(EDITOR)

PORTUGAL

Area: 92,365 sq km (35,662 sq mi)
Population (2001 est.): 10,328,000
Capital: Lisbon
Chief of state: President Jorge Sampaio
Head of government: Prime Minister António Guterres

Against a backdrop of slowing growth, rising inflation, and growing public deficits, Portugal's government lost its popular appeal in 2001; opposition parties remained fragmented, however, and were unable to capitalize on the Socialist government's woes. Though the government won reelection in January, it looked particularly shaky in the first half of the year. Finance Minister Joaquim Pina Moura was forced to resign at the end of June after issuing a "corrective" supplementary budget to get the economy back on track. The reshuffle also brought changes at the Health, Economy, Defense, Education, and Culture ministries but did not—as some observers expected—spark snap elections.

The economic problems continued in the fall, exacerbated by global fallout from the September 11 terrorist attacks in the U.S. Drafts for the 2002 budget indicated that the government deficit would rise to 1.7% of gross domestic product by year's end. Along with other European Union (EU) partners, Portugal blamed the deficit slippage on the global economic troubles. The new finance minister, Guilherme de Oliveira Martins, stressed that the 2002 budget would cut back sharply on ministerial spending but would boost state investment in an attempt to make the economy grow. In addition, efforts to fight tax fraud and tax evasion would be stepped up. The Socialist government—which held 115 seats in the 230-seat

Assembly of the Republic (parliament)—would once again be forced to forge a deal with at least one of the opposition parties in order to pass the 2002 budget.

In the December local and municipal elections, the main interest was the Lisbon mayoral race between Portuguese Socialist Party (PSP) incumbent João Soares—son of former president Mário Soares—and centre-right Social Democratic Party (PSD) candidate Pedro Santana Lopes. Though Lisbon had long been a Socialist stronghold, Santana Lopes had found support there for his urban-renewal platform, and he emerged victorious. The PSD also won elections in Porto and the Lisbon suburb of Sintra. After the PSD won control of 144 councils, compared to the 98

In northern Portugal a bridge collapsed and four vehicles plunged into the Douro River.

captured by the PSP, Prime Minister António Guterres took responsibility for the poor PSP showing and resigned. Pres. Jorge Sampaio dissolved the parliament and called a general election for March 17, 2002.

One of the country's deadliest accidents claimed the lives of 59 persons in March when a bridge spanning the northern Douro River collapsed while a bus and three cars were passing over it. The collapse was blamed on erosion and extensive sand dredging in the area, as well as on a stronger river current due to the unusually rainy winter. The incident spurred inspection of all the country's bridges, and, as a result, a handful of spans were either closed or reinforced.

Late in the year the government moved to tighten drunk-driving and speeding laws in hopes of reducing the country's troubling rate of road deaths, one of the highest in the EU. Vehicular accidents in Portugal annually killed about 240 of every million persons, compared with an EU average of about 110 per million population. Wine producers protested the new blood-alcohol limit of 0.2 g per litre from the previous 0.5 g per litre limit, complaining that it would severely cut consumption. In addition, professional truck drivers staged a one-day strike, saying that they had been unfairly targeted by the new laws.

Another legal change that drew criticism from a number of quarters was a decision to treat drug use as an ill-

ness rather than a crime. In July the parliament voted that drug users would not face jail sentences, a law that effectively decriminalized drugs and replaced prison time with counseling and monitoring of addicts. Though the changes focused mainly on heroin and Portugal's growing population of heroin users, other drugs such as cannabis and ecstasy were also covered. Trafficking and drug dealing remained a criminal offense punishable with jail time, but the changes brought a rash of foreign media coverage touting Portugal as a "paradise" for "drug tourism," an accusation swiftly and forcefully challenged by the government.

(ERIK T. BURNS)

QATAR

Area: 11,427 sq km (4,412 sq mi)
Population (2001 est.): 596,000
Capital: Doha
Head of state and government: Emir Sheikh Hamad ibn Khalifah ath-Thani, assisted by Prime Minister Sheikh Abdullah ibn Khalifah ath-Thani

In 2001 Qatar continued its increasingly prominent role in regional, interregional, and global affairs. In November 2000 Qatar had succeeded Iran as head of the 57-member-state Organization of the Islamic Conference. During its three-year term, Qatar would enjoy unprecedented standing among the world's 1.2 billion Muslims.

In addition, Qatar's Al-Jazeera television station remained the Arab world's most prominent media force in publicizing the al-Aqsa *intifadah* (Palestinian uprising). In the aftermath of the September 11 terrorist attacks in the U.S., Al-Jazeera became the leading source for news and analysis, with reports about Osama bin Laden and his al-Qaeda network. (*See* MEDIA AND PUBLISHING: *Television:* Sidebar.)

In November Qatar hosted the meeting of the World Trade Organization, the WTO's first summit since 1999 in Seattle, Wash. In December, at the annual heads of state summit in Muscat, Oman, Qatar was elected to head the Gulf Cooperation Council's Secretariat-General in Riyadh, Saudi Arabia. As a result, a Qatari would be the senior-most official responsible for the day-to-day administration of the six member-states' (Bahrain, Kuwait, Oman, Qatar, Saudi Arabia, and the United Arab Emirates) efforts to establish a common market and customs union by 2003.

In March the International Court of Justice resolved a long-standing territorial dispute between Qatar and Bahrain; Bahrain was awarded the Hawar Islands, and Qatar retained sovereignty over the Zubarah town and land strip in the northern part of the country. Qatar also continued to make progress in widening the base of its elected representatives and in developing its niche as the Gulf region's leading exporter of natural gas.

(JOHN DUKE ANTHONY)

ROMANIA

Area: 237,500 sq km (91,699 sq mi)
Population (2001 est.): 22,413,000
Capital: Bucharest
Chief of state: President Ion Iliescu
Head of government: Prime Minister Adrian Nastase

Stability returned to Romania in 2001 after a shock in the November 2000 presidential elections in which Corneliu Vadim Tudor, a populist demagogue with close links to a number of Middle Eastern radical regimes, won almost one-third of the vote. In October 2001 the ruling Social Democratic Party of Romania (PDSR) took steps to lift Vadim's parliamentary immunity after he made unsubstantiated claims that in 1995 members of the Palestinian extremist group Hamas had been given training in Romania by the security forces.

The Romanian economy grew by nearly 5%, and the privatization of Sidex, the country's largest steelmaker and biggest loss-making plant, was announced in July. Two-thirds of the economy was still state-owned, however, and overall production was still only 75% of its level in 1989. Foreign investors remained wary of Romania, but there was an increasing willingness by the government to reduce the multiple layers of bureaucracy that were discouraging investment. Membership in the European Union (EU) remained a key goal, which meant that the left-wing PDSR was prepared to accept many EU recommendations for moving away from a state-led economy.

Romania was also keen to join NATO. In 2001 spending on defense was boosted to 4% of gross domestic product in anticipation of the next phase of NATO expansion in 2002. Romania's NATO hopes may have been dented, however, by revelations about the continuing influence of the feared communist-era secret police, the Securitate, in business, politics, and no fewer than nine different intelligence services in the state structure.

The PDSR strengthened its credentials as moderate by being more receptive to the demands of the 1.6-million-strong ethnic Magyar (Hungarian) minority, whose parliamentarians helped sustain Adrian Nastase's minority government,

In 2001 former Romanian king Michael demanded the return of royal family property, including Peles Castle (above) in the mountain resort of Sinaia.

AP/Wide World Photos

and showing a new disinclination to flirt with extremist figures like Vadim, which it did for much of the 1990s. Nonetheless, relations with the Hungarian government were strained following the passage in the Hungarian parliament on June 19 of the Status Law. This law extended to Magyar minorities in neighbouring countries education, health, and employment rights that may not be available to other ethnic groups in these countries. On July 2 Pres. Ion Iliescu branded the Status Law "a diversionary, provocative, antidemocratic and discriminatory document."

Relations with Moldova (part of Romania from 1918 to 1940) were strained after the return to power there in February of the communists. Moldova resented the view, long held in Romania, that the majority of its population was ethnically Romanian. On October 3 Nastase canceled a visit to Chisinau following charges by the Moldovan minister of the interior of unwarranted interference by Romania in the affairs of his country.

One unexpected reconciliation occurred in the spring, however, between President Iliescu and former king Michael, whom the communists forced to abdicate in 1947. The 80-year-old former monarch was given back part of the royal family's property, and he decided to return to Romania to live.

(TOM GALLAGHER)

481

RUSSIA

Area: 17,075,400 sq km (6,592,800 sq mi)
Population (2001 est.): 144,417,000
Capital: Moscow
Chief of state: President Vladimir Putin
Head of government: Prime Minister Mikhail Kasyanov

Domestic Affairs. Russian Pres. Vladimir Putin's popularity remained consistently high in 2001, and Russians drew renewed confidence from the fact that their country was headed by a young and vigorous leader. Putin's efforts to bring Russia's rebellious regions to heel were particularly successful. Central control was tightened over tax collection, the police, and the law courts. Regional governors were compensated for the loss of their seats in the Federation Council (upper house of the parliament) by the adoption in January of a law allowing the leaders of 69 of the country's 89 regions to stand for a third or even fourth term in office. In February Putin used his new power to remove regional governors to secure the resignation of the controversial governor of Primorsky *kray* in Russia's Far East. Regional legislatures gradually brought local laws into accord with federal legislation, though some of the larger republics, notably Tatarstan and Bashkortostan, continued to drag their feet in this respect.

Putin's strong support in the parliament enabled him to promote potentially far-reaching reforms. Promising to make the law apply equally to everyone, Putin in May announced a reform of the judicial system. Bills submitted to the State Duma (lower house of the parliament) sought to raise the status and powers of judges and defense lawyers and to enhance the rights of defendants. A revised Code of Criminal Procedure promised to transfer the right to issue arrest and search warrants from prosecutors to judges and to institute trial by jury nationwide. Educational reform was also promised.

Putin continued his campaign to wrest the mass media from the control of the "oligarchs." Tycoons Vladimir Gusinsky (*see* BIOGRAPHIES) and Boris Berezovsky were stripped of their electronic media holdings. Gusinsky lost control of the independent television network, NTV, the only major national electronic media outlet not controlled by the state, while Berezovsky was removed from his position of influence at Russian Public Television, Russia's most widely watched TV channel. Threatened with arrest on corruption charges, both men went into self-imposed exile. Legislation was passed to restrict foreign ownership of the Russian media.

In July a Kremlin-inspired law on political parties was adopted. Parties would be officially registered and permitted to compete in national elections only if they had a minimum of 10,000 members and registered offices in at least half of Russia's regions. Those that met the criteria would receive federal funding after the 2003 legislative elections. As many as 60% of Russia's existing 180 parties were not expected to meet the criteria and would therefore be forced to disband. The Kremlin argued that the law would prevent corrupt businessmen from fund-

Russian media tycoon Vladimir Gusinsky leaves the Valdemoro prison near Madrid on March 26.

AP/Wide World Photos

ing pocket parties, but regional political movements were also expected to be hard hit. In October the pro-Kremlin Unity party merged with its erstwhile archrival, the Fatherland movement led by Moscow Mayor Yury Luzhkov. The merger was expected to produce Russia's dominant political organization.

Economy. Economic growth continued in 2001, though at a reduced rate from that of 2000. Revised official data put gross domestic product (GDP) growth in 2000 at 8.3% above 1999. In the first half of 2001, the increase in output was about 5% up from the level of first-half

2000. The government revised its medium-term forecasts (through 2004) down to around 3.5–4% a year.

Growth revived somewhat in mid-2001, and the government remained bullish, maintaining that in the longer term (through 2010) output could be expected to grow at an average annual rate of 5%. Independent economists in Moscow were more skeptical, and there were good reasons to question the sustainability of rapid growth. The output recovery that followed the August 1998 financial crisis had been jump-started by the massive devaluation from 6 rubles to the dollar before the crisis to an average of 25 in 1999 and 28 in 2000. By the end of 2001 the rate was 30.5. With inflation still quite high (heading for a rise in consumer prices of some 18.6% in 2001), the leveling off of the exchange rate meant that Russian producers were gradually losing the competitive advantage they had gained from devaluation. Similarly, Russian external finances, company profits, and tax revenues had all benefited from the steep rise in international oil prices in 1999. A downturn in oil prices in late 2001 reduced those gains.

The state both of Russia's balance of payments and of public finances in 2000–01 reflected the combination of a devalued currency and a high oil price. Imports fell dramatically as their ruble prices inside Russia soared. Producers in the hitherto severely depressed manufacturing sector—especially in textiles, clothing, food processing, and engineering—suddenly found life much easier as competition from imports dried up. That, plus the higher oil and gas prices on world markets, had given Russia a current-account balance of payments surplus of over $46 billion in 2000—an extraordinary 17% of GDP. Gold and foreign exchange reserves grew to $35 billion by July 2001. That level, enough to finance almost nine months' imports, was far above what was needed on grounds of prudence.

The federal budget moved into surplus in 2000 and (with some fluctuations) in 2001. This enabled Moscow to service its external debt without significant new borrowing. Having paid off some of its external sovereign debt in 2000, Russia went on in 2001 to make debt-service payments (repayment of principal plus payment of interest) equivalent to 5% of GDP. Western governments and international financial institutions, faced with this revival in Russian fortunes, were less disposed than before to charitable giving. Until spring 2001 the Russian government had been counting on rolling over its inherited Soviet-era debt to Western governments while keeping current with its servicing of post-Soviet debt. Western governments, negotiating with Moscow in the framework of the Paris Club, began instead to insist on payment in full, and they got their way. The International Monetary Fund (IMF), negotiating with the Russian government over IMF approval (and associated loan facilities) for Russian economic policies, held out for a reform agenda that was quite demanding. Eventually, a compromise was reached: Russian reforms would be monitored by the Fund, without formal approval of them; Moscow would forgo new IMF loans.

The government and the central bank were pushed to pursue more liberal policies than they had perhaps wished at the beginning of 2001. Domestic critics (notably Putin's economic adviser Andrey Illarionov) and foreign governments wanted external-debt service in full and got it. They also wanted to see the implementation of structural reforms: tax reform, including a lowering of profits tax; land reform to allow a free market in all land; measures to strengthen corporate governance; the introduction of competition into the gas, electricity, and rail industries; banking reform; an easing of foreign exchange controls; and a general reduction in the bureaucratic (read "bribery") burden on producers.

Putin, most notably in a state of the nation address to the Russian parliament in April, espoused the cause of radical economic reform. Strikingly, he spoke of the precarious nature of Russia's economic recovery and the urgent need to improve the business environment. It appeared that, in his concern to see Russia strong again, he had become convinced that free-market reforms were needed to provide the economic sinew that a revived Russia would require—hence his resolve to back economic liberalization. Legislative progress was achieved in all the measures mentioned, though with concessions over land reform and banking reform.

In September the Duma gave its approval to a land code that would pave the way for the creation of a property market in Russia for the first time since the establishment of Soviet power. Communist and nationalist parliamentarians vehemently opposed the bill, warning that it would lead to the country's being bought up by foreigners and wealthy Russians, and the bill's first reading saw a punch-up among parliamentarians. The final version of the code was a compromise, setting rules for the sale only of commercial land in towns and cities (about 2% of the total) and leaving the vexing issue of farmland to the discretion of regional authorities.

Promising to introduce a wide-ranging restructuring of the natural gas industry, the Kremlin in May asserted control over Russia's state-controlled natural gas monopoly, Gazprom, by replacing veteran Rem Vyakhirev as chief executive with its own appointee, 39-year-old Aleksey Miller. Anatoly Chubais—chief executive of the state-controlled United Energy Systems (UES), which controlled Russia's electricity grid—launched a series of reforms aimed at separating the distribution of electricity from its generation and gradually privatizing the latter. Minority investors expressed concern over some of Chubais's proposals to break up UES. Regional governors were also wary of the reforms, which would reduce the power hitherto enjoyed by local politicians to manipulate electricity prices.

Plans were accelerated to raise charges for the maintenance of urban housing and for the provision of electricity, gas, water, and sewerage to cost-recovery (that is, unsubsidized) levels by 2003. Low-income families would continue to receive housing subsidies, but others would be required to pay their own way.

Defense and Foreign Policy. In March a cabinet reshuffle saw Putin's close associate Sergey Ivanov shifted laterally from the post of Security Council secretary to head the Defense Ministry as its first civilian minister. Ivanov was expected to spearhead a long-awaited reform of the armed forces. In October Putin met with top military leaders and told them bluntly to speed up reform. He promised to increase defense spending in response to the terrorist attacks in the U.S. He also announced that Russia would close two relics of the Cold War—its electronic reconnaissance centre in Cuba and its last big overseas naval base at Cam Ranh Bay in Vietnam.

Russia's military campaign in the breakaway Chechen Republic dragged on. The rebels showed no sign of giving up the fight. Polling data suggested that the Russian population was growing unhappy with the failure to bring the conflict to a close. Optimists spied light at the end of the tunnel when, in June, Putin told a press conference that Chechnya's independence was not the issue; what was vital, he said, was to ensure that Chechen territory would never again be used as a bridgehead for an attack on Russia. In September Putin issued an "ultimatum" that was essentially a proposal to begin talks with those rebels prepared to lay down their arms. Although the offer expired without visible effect and the fighting continued, the two sides did begin to negotiate about negotiating. It seemed unlikely, however, that Chechnya's relatively moderate [res-ident, Aslan Maskhadov, would be able to negotiate on behalf of uncompromising rebel leaders who controlled their own armies and territory.

In October after a difficult three-month operation, the remains of the nuclear submarine *Kursk* were salvaged from the Barents Sea, where it had sunk after an explosion in August 2000.

During the year Putin maintained a busy program of foreign meetings and visits. In a speech in January, he defined Russia's major foreign policy objective as creating stable and secure conditions on Russia's borders to allow the government to concentrate on solving the country's social and economic problems. He identified Europe as an important partner for Russia.

Putin shifted Russia's relations with its closest allies, the Commonwealth of Independent States, from the multilateral focus that had characterized the years of Boris Yeltsin's presidency to highlight bilateral relations. Russian analysts interpreted this as a sign that Putin recognized that the close ties that had existed during the Soviet period could not be reestablished. Meanwhile, Russia maintained and in some cases strengthened ties with former allies and markets for Soviet and Russian arms—India, Iraq, Cuba, Libya, Vietnam, and North Korea. In July a 20-year friendship treaty was signed with China.

Relations with the new U.S. administration were initially strained. Missile defense (NMD), U.S. plans to abandon the 1972 Anti-Ballistic Missile (ABM) Treaty, and NATO's possible enlargement to include Estonia, Latvia, and Lithuania were the main bones of contention. Russia opposed U.S.-British plans for revised sanctions against Iraq. Russia planned too to continue arms sales to Iran and to finish construction work on the controversial Iranian nuclear power reactor at Bushehr in the Persian Gulf, identifying Iran as a key ally in the struggle against fundamentalist Islamic movements on Russia's southern borders.

Relations with the U.S. improved in May when Moscow responded positively to a call by U.S. Pres. George W. Bush for new nuclear arms reductions and for improved relations. A breakthrough occurred in June when the two presidents met in Slovenia for direct talks and established an immediate rapport.

The remains of the Russian nuclear submarine Kursk, *which sank after an explosion in 2000, are raised for examination in a dock at the port of Roslyakovo, near Murmansk.*

AP/Wide World Photos

The terrorist attacks of September 11 brought a further improvement in U.S.-Russian relations. Putin was the first world leader to call Bush after the attacks, pledging Russia's support and cooperation in the U.S.-led campaign against terrorism, and offering use of Russia's airspace for humanitarian deliveries and help in search and rescue operations. Overruling his defense minister, Putin said Russia would not object if the former Soviet republics of Central Asia made their airspace and military facilities available to the U.S. In October Putin became the first Russian leader to visit NATO headquarters in Brussels, where he spoke of "qualitatively new" relations between Russia and the alliance. Also in October Putin attended a Russia–European Union (EU) summit at which it was decided to hold monthly consultations on security issues. The European Commission said afterward that it and the U.S. would work to give fresh impetus to Russia's eight-year-old bid to join the World Trade Organization.

(ELIZABETH TEAGUE)

RWANDA

Area: 26,338 sq km (10,169 sq mi)
Population (2001 est.): 7,313,000
Capital: Kigali
Head of state and government: President Maj. Gen. Paul Kagame, assisted by Prime Minister Bernard Makuza

On March 6, 2001, Rwandans participated in the country's first-ever local elections. Voters chose 2,765 district representatives, and an electoral college selected 106 mayors and 424 district executives. The vote was a step toward political decentralization and part of the country's postgenocide reconstruction plan. Observers reported that the voting was generally free from irregularities, and nearly 90% of those eligible voted. Opposition groups charged that the National Electoral Commission unfairly favoured candidates from the ruling Rwandan Patriotic Front. During the year the government introduced a new flag and a new anthem that emphasized national unity.

After a two-year peaceful interval, elements of the extremist Hutu Interahamwe militia launched attacks in May near Ruhengeri in the northwest of the country. The clashes continued, and the army reported 150 rebels killed in a June battle. Security forces scored a major victory in July when they captured Pierre Habimana, the Interahamwe's chief of staff. The Rwandan government charged that the rebels were operating from bases in the Democratic Republic of the Congo (DRC). Though Rwanda had begun to withdraw its troops from the DRC in late February, it halted the withdrawal in June and demanded that the DRC stop aiding Rwandan rebels. Some progress was made toward easing tensions in September when the DRC announced that it would hand over 3,000 Rwandan rebels to UN observers.

Relations between Rwanda and Uganda soured in March when the Ugandan government listed its southern neighbour as a "hostile nation." In July Pres. Maj. Gen. Paul Kagame met his Ugandan counterpart in an effort to mend relations. Though their meeting was described as cordial, tensions persisted over both countries' military involvement in the DRC.

In May former president Pasteur Bizimungu planned the creation of a new political party, the Democratic Party for Renewal. Security forces interrupted the party's launch and placed Bizimungu under house arrest. Though he was quickly released, the new party remained outlawed.

In June the UN-sponsored International Criminal Tribunal for Rwanda issued its first acquittal, finding Ignace Bagilishema, the former mayor of Mabanza, innocent of genocide and crimes against humanity. In an attempt to clear the backlog of 115,000 genocide suspects awaiting trial, the government announced plans to establish courts according to the traditional justice system. The move would create 11,000 courts that could handle some genocide suspects, though the most serious offenders would continue to be tried in higher courts. In June a Belgian court found four Rwandans, including two Roman Catholic nuns, guilty of having committed war crimes during the 1994 genocide. In December the government reported that over one million people had died during the genocide and other violence between 1991 and 1994.

(MATTHEW A. CENZER)

SAINT KITTS AND NEVIS

Area: 269 sq km (104 sq mi)
Population (2001 est.): 38,800
Capital: Basseterre
Chief of state: Queen Elizabeth II, represented by Governor-General Cuthbert Sebastian
Head of government: Prime Minister Denzil Douglas

Prime Minister Denzil Douglas reshuffled his cabinet in August 2001 in an effort to instill new dynamism into government programs. He kept the key portfolios of finance and national security for himself.

St. Kitts and Nevis saw its hope of being removed from the Paris-based Fi-

Villagers in Ryinyo, Rwanda, sit in front of some of the arms and ammunition captured by government troops in a clash with Hutu rebels in May.
AP/Wide World Photos

nancial Action Task Force's (FATF's) list of states not doing enough to combat money laundering dashed when the task force met in September. St. Kitts and Nevis expected to be given a clean bill of health, but despite the country's establishment of a Financial Services Commission to oversee the offshore banking industry, the FATF was unsatisfied with the overall effort to identify tainted funds.

The Concerned Citizens Movement, led by Vance Amory, was returned to office in the September local elections in Nevis. The party had consistently been elected to run local affairs in Nevis since 1992. It won four of the five seats in the Island Assembly, with the Nevis Reformation Party retaining one.

Following the September 11 terrorist attacks in the U.S., Douglas extended to all New York City and Washington, D.C., firefighters, police officers, and emergency medical service workers the offer of a free one-week vacation in St. Kitts. More than 170,000 tourists had visited the islands in the first six months of 2001.　　(DAVID RENWICK)

SAINT LUCIA

Area: 617 sq km (238 sq mi)
Population (2001 est.): 158,000
Capital: Castries
Chief of state: Queen Elizabeth II, represented by Governor-General Pearlette Louisy
Head of government: Prime Minister Kenny Anthony

485

The opposition moved to shore up its forces in May when controversial left-winger George Odlum, who had been fired by Prime Minister Kenny Anthony from his St. Lucia Labour Party government, joined forces with former prime minister Sir John Compton and the United Workers' Party (UWP) to form the National Alliance. The partnership proved to be short-lived, however. In December elections to the House of Assembly, the Labour Party won 14 of the 17 seats. Morella Joseph resigned as UWP leader and was replaced by Marius Wilson.

Even before the events of September 11, tourism in St. Lucia was experiencing a downturn, mainly brought on by the weakening U.S. economy. August was described by the St. Lucia Hotel and Tourism Association as "extremely bad." Three hotels actually closed for the summer. The decrease in tourist revenue was predicted to be as much as 18% for the year, representing a loss of $35.5 million in national income.

In October Prime Minister Anthony came down firmly against any sale of St. Lucia bananas to Libya, as had been touted during a visit to the North African state by three Caribbean leaders in September. He insisted that St. Lucia could not "compromise" its long-standing trading relationships with other countries, particularly the U.K.

(DAVID RENWICK)

SAINT VINCENT AND THE GRENADINES

Area: 389 sq km (150 sq mi)
Population (2001 est.): 113,000
Capital: Kingstown
Chief of state: Queen Elizabeth II, represented by Governor-General Sir David Jack
Head of government: Prime Ministers Arnhim Eustace and, from March 29, Ralph Gonsalves

The Unity Labour Party, led by left-wing firebrand Ralph Gonsalves, won the general election in St. Vincent and the Grenadines in March 2001, grabbing 12 of the 15 seats in the parliament and decisively ousting the New Democratic Party (NDP) of Prime Minister Arnhim Eustace, who only narrowly held on to his own seat.

The election had not been constitutionally due until 2003, but Eustace agreed to move it up following antigovernment protests. The NDP had been in office since 1984. Gonsalves assumed several portfolios, including finance, economic development, labour, and Grenadines Affairs, as well as the prime ministership.

The country's lack of strong legislative and supervisory systems for offshore financial institutions kept it on the Paris-based Financial Action Task Force's list of uncooperative states, even though the government promised to "rewrite" the entire package of laws governing offshore operations. The licenses of two offshore banks were revoked in June.

St. Vincent and the Grenadines signed a "comprehensive cooperation accord" with Cuba in September, covering matters such as health, tourism, trade, and language training, following an official visit to Havana by Gonsalves. The prime minister had earlier raised eyebrows by going to Libya on a controversial trip from which other Caribbean leaders had withdrawn.

(DAVID RENWICK)

SAMOA

Area: 2,831 sq km (1,093 sq mi)
Population (2001 est.): 179,000
Capital: Apia
Chief of state: *O le Ao o le Malo* (Head of State) Malietoa Tanumafili II
Head of government: Prime Minister Tuila'epa Sa'ilele Malielegaoi

Samoa's general election in March 2001 saw the return of the governing Human Rights Protection Party led by Prime Minister Tuila'epa Sa'ilele Malielegaoi, although the new government relied on the support of independent members for its majority. There was a strong emphasis on local issues and the record of the government in an election cam-

paign that saw a number of members elected unopposed and, at the same time, petitions alleging election fraud in 10 of the 49 seats. Three women were elected to the new parliament. Longtime opposition leader Tuiatua Tupua Tamasese Efi gave way to Le Mamea Ropati.

In international affairs, Samoa was one of two South Pacific nations that did not support the establishment of a whale sanctuary. It denied allegations from Australia and New Zealand as well as environmental groups that this stance was related to the fact that Japan, Samoa's largest aid donor, sought to expand its whaling activity in South Pacific and Antarctic waters.

The economy remained heavily dependent on remittances from Samoans living overseas, tourism revenue, and agricultural production (which acounted for some 16% of the country's gross domestic product).

(BARRIE MACDONALD)

SAN MARINO

Area: 61.2 sq km (23.6 sq mi)
Population (2001 est.): 27,200
Capital: San Marino
Heads of state and government: The republic is governed by two *capitani reggenti*, or coregents, appointed every six months by a popularly elected Great and General Council.

The major focus in San Marino in 2001 was debate by opposition parties over the government's proposal to privatize the country's public utilities company, which was founded in 1981 to furnish electricity, gas, and drinking water. The opposition was concerned about the impact the action might have on San Marino's poorer population.

In the June 10 parliamentary elections the ruling Christian Democratic-Socialist coalition stayed in power, winning 40 of the 60 seats in the Great General Council.

Another area of sensitivity involved European Union plans to close up loopholes in European tax law to make it impossible for EU citizens to utilize San Marino as a tax haven for investments. San Marino believed that the new tax laws would unfairly penalize the 5,000 Italians who worked there. San Marino and Italy were both preparing to adopt the new euro, which would replace the Italian lira as the domestic currency in 2002.

On another front San Marino took measures to thwart a possible terrorist attack and created a special team to safeguard its mail system.

(GREGORY O. SMITH)

SÃO TOMÉ AND PRÍNCIPE

Area: 1,001 sq km (386 sq mi)
Population (2001 est.): 147,000
Capital: São Tomé
Chief of state: Presidents Miguel Trovoada and, from September 3, Fradique de Menezes
Head of government: Prime Ministers Guilherme Posser da Costa and, from September 26, Evaristo de Carvalho

Until September 2001 the country's two main parties, the Independent Democratic Action (ADI) and the Movement for the Liberation of São Tomé and Príncipe (MLSTP), had enjoyed seven years of cooperation. The ADI held the presidency, and the MLSTP, which had won the parliamentary elections of 1994 and 1999, claimed the prime ministership. Though Pres. Miguel Trovoada was barred from running for a third term in the July 2001 presidential election, the ADI's new candidate, businessman Fradique de Menezes, won with a considerable majority (56% to 39%) over former president Manuel Pinto da Costa in an election that was generally regarded as free and fair. After being sworn in as Trovoada's successor on September 3, de Menezes demanded a cabinet reshuffle. When Prime Minister Guilherme Posser da Costa refused to sack certain MLSTP ministers, he was himself dismissed and the cabinet dissolved.

A new government was then formed under Evaristo de Carvalho, whose 10-member cabinet was drawn exclusively from the two parties that had supported de Menezes in the presidential election. In December de Menezes dissolved parliament and announced that legislative elections would take place on March 3, 2002.

(CHRISTOPHER SAUNDERS)

SAUDI ARABIA

Area: 2,248,000 sq km (868,000 sq mi)
Population (2001 est.): 22,757,000
Capital: Riyadh
Head of state and government: King Fahd

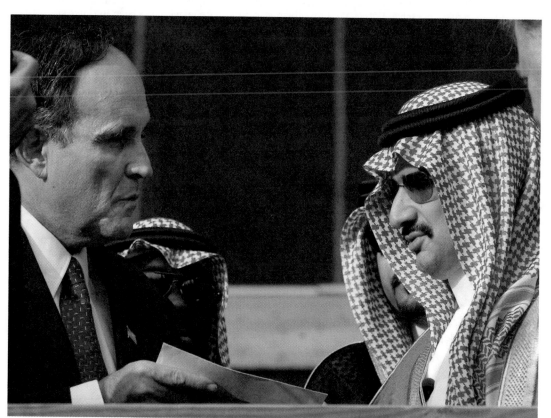

Saudi Prince Alwaleed bin Talal presents New York City Mayor Rudolph Giuliani with a $10 million check for relief efforts following September 11; Giuliani later returned the check after the prince said America's relationship with Israel was partly to blame for the attacks.
AP/Wide World Photos

In Saudi Arabia the year 2001 was dominated by security and regional political issues. During the year four British nationals, as well as a Canadian and a Belgian, confessed to involvement in a series of car bombings in what authorities described as a "Mafia war" between resident aliens who were illegally trafficking in alcohol. In late August Prince Turki al-Faisal, who headed the kingdom's General Intelligence Directorate, was replaced by Prince Nayif ibn 'Abd al-'Aziz. Relations with Washington were not at their best. On September 5, less than a week before the attacks by militant Islamists in the U.S., Prince Saud al-Faisal, Saudi Arabia's minister of foreign affairs, said that the peace process between the Palestinians and the Israelis had failed because of "the policies of Israel" and declared that it was "time especially for the U.S. to assume its own responsibility and prevent Israeli aggression against the Arab world."

The September 11 attacks had a profound impact on Saudi Arabia, since the primary suspect was Osama bin Laden, a wealthy Saudi national who had been stripped of his citizenship some years before. Saudi authorities were quick to condemn the attacks. The government was reluctant to permit U.S. warplanes to use Prince Sultan Airbase, the most sophisticated such installation south of Riyadh, to launch attacks on Afghanistan, but it played the role of "silent partner" in the American-led coalition against Afghanistan's Taliban government. At a summit meeting of foreign ministers of the countries attending the Organization of the Islamic Conference in Qatar on October 10, Saudi Arabia was instrumental in passing a resolution that condemned terrorism and the September 11 attacks but—in reference to the situation of the Palestinians in the West Bank and Gaza—drew a distinction between terrorism and what were labeled acts of self-defense. The organization warned against targeting any other Muslim or Arab country by the Western coalition under the pretext of fighting terrorism.

On the economic front, Saudi Arabia was still far from gaining admittance to the World Trade Organization, because the country had not fully liberalized its economy. Saudi reforms introduced in May 2000 that permitted total outside ownership in some sectors were, however, able to attract pledges of about $10 billion in foreign investment in 2001. There was every reason to believe that the country's gross domestic investment was keeping pace with the 21.3% of gross domestic product in nominal terms realized in 2000 before the fourth quarter, which witnessed a slowdown due to the fallout from the war in Afghanistan and the decrease in crude oil prices. Real GDP growth for 2001 was projected to be 1%. This figure was expected to rise to 2.5% in 2002 and 4.5% in 2005 on account of the returns from the $25 billion in investments made in gas projects. (MAHMOUD HADDAD)

SENEGAL

Area: 196,712 sq km (75,951 sq mi)
Population (2001 est.): 10,285,000
Capital: Dakar
Chief of state: President Abdoulaye Wade, assisted by Prime Ministers Moustapha Niasse and, from March 3, Mame Madior Boye

On April 29, 2001, Sopi ("Change")—a coalition of 40 parties, led by Pres. Abdoulaye Wade, won an overwhelming victory in the country's parliamentary elections, taking 89 of the National Assembly's 120 seats. The Alliance of Progressive Forces, led by former prime minister Moustapha Niasse, won 11 seats, while the former ruling Socialist Party managed to hold only 10. On May 12 the new prime minister, Mame Madior Boye, announced her 24-member cabinet, which was dominated by ministers from Wade's own Democratic Party. In January Wade also won a referendum on constitutional reforms.

Efforts to end 19 years of unrest in the Casamance region once again encountered setbacks. On February 16, rebels attacked a convoy of trucks north of Ziguinchor, killing at least 13 civilians. The Movement of Democratic Forces of Casamance (MFDC), the main separatist group, signed two peace agreements with the government on March 16 and 23, but several other rebel factions announced that they would continue the armed conflict. Despite this pact, the army renewed its efforts to crush the MFDC after April 6, when a second rebel attack on a convoy of cars near Ziguinchor took place. The government's offensive was suspended on May 25 in order to provide a more secure atmosphere for peace talks between the MFDC and hard-line rebel groups. After several postponements the three-day forum of the separatist groups was held in Banjul, Gambia, on August 7–9, but apparently no consensus was reached, and the scheduled closing ceremony was canceled. On August 10 Augustia Diamacoune, the MFDC's longtime leader, was replaced by Jean-Marie François Biagui.

Léopold Sédar Senghor—the first president of Senegal, the first African to be elected to the French Academy, and the first head of state in post-colonial Africa to relinquish power voluntarily—died on December 20 in his retirement home in Normandy, France. (See OBITUARIES.)

(NANCY ELLEN LAWLER)

SEYCHELLES

Area: 455 sq km (176 sq mi)
Population (2001 est.): 80,600
Capital: Victoria
Head of state and government: President France-Albert René

In September 2001, the Seychelles held its closest-fought presidential election since independence. Pres. France-Albert René, who had been in office since 1977, took 54% of the vote to win another five-year term. His opponent, Wavel Ramkalawan of the Seychelles National Party, took 45% of the vote. Approximately 50,000 of the islands' 60,000 registered voters decided a contest that had been dominated by economic issues.

An International Monetary Fund report published at the end of 2000 pointed to slow economic growth and falling foreign exchange reserves. The report also called on the government to remove exchange rate controls on the Seychelles rupee. Unofficial markets were trading foreign currencies with a 100% premium over the official rate.

In February the Seychelles reached an agreement with the Organisation for Economic Co-operation and Development (OECD) to reform its banking sector. The agreement provided greater regulation of accounts held by offshore companies. The Seychelles also agreed to cooperate with criminal and tax investigators from OECD member states.

Also in February the government announced it was considering membership in the Common Market for Eastern and Southern Africa, a free-trade zone. (MATTHEW A. CENZER)

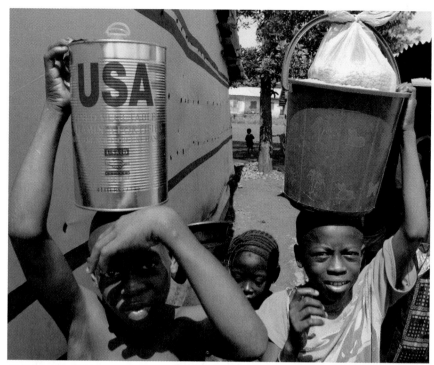

Children in Sierra Leone carry a can of oil and bucket of corn distributed by the World Food Programme in November.

Issouf Sanogo/AFP Worldwide

ures to help rebuild the country. In March the European Union pledged €11 million (about $10 million) in humanitarian aid, and the African Development Fund provided $13 million for economic recovery. The U.S. government pledged $14.5 million to support the reintegration of society.

In March, Pres. Ahmad Tejan Kabbah replaced five cabinet members, including the foreign and finance ministers. Citing the ongoing disarmament process, the National Electoral Commission announced that presidential voting slated for December would be postponed until May 2002. Despite a shortfall in funds, the UN proceeded with plans for the establishment of a tribunal for those accused of war crimes in Sierra Leone's civil war.

(MATTHEW A. CENZER)

SINGAPORE

Area: 683 sq km (264 sq mi)
Population (2001 est.): 3,322,000 (excluding 808,000 newly arrived nonresidents)
Chief of state: President S.R. Nathan
Head of government: Prime Minister Goh Chok Tong

SIERRA LEONE

Area: 71,740 sq km (27,699 sq mi)
Population (2001 est.): 5,427,000 (including about 185,000 Sierra Leonean refugees temporarily residing in Guinea and other West African countries)
Capital: Freetown
Head of state and government: President Ahmad Tejan Kabbah

Throughout 2001 the United Nations Mission in Sierra Leone (UNAMSIL) attempted to implement a compromise peace based on the Lomé agreement. UNAMSIL had occasional success disarming Revolutionary United Front (RUF) rebels and the Civil Defense Force (CDF), a pro-government militia. During May some RUF and CDF fighters surrendered their weapons to the UN in Kambia and Port Loko, and other RUF forces disarmed in October. In March UNAMSIL forces occupied Lunsar, their first deployment into an area where the RUF had taken 500 UN troops hostage in 2000. In August

UNAMSIL began deployment in the diamond-rich Kono district, an RUF stronghold. By year's end over 45,000 fighters had been disarmed.

The U.K. government ended its training program for Sierra Leone's army in September but pledged to continue assisting with the reintegration of former rebels into the army. In May the army had occupied formerly RUF-held areas around Kambia, north of Freetown.

Despite ongoing efforts, violence continued in parts of the country. In April RUF and CDF forces clashed near Tonga, a diamond-producing area in the east. In May the two groups agreed to a cease-fire, but this was broken within a week by fighting in the eastern town of Jagbwema. During July serious violence flared between the RUF and the CDF in the northern and eastern parts of the country. In one incident 22 civilians were reported killed when the RUF attacked the town of Henekuma.

Aid organizations continued efforts to remedy the damage caused by years of war. Humanitarian groups, including the Save the Children Fund, helped to secure the release of child soldiers and aid their reintegration into society. Donors announced a number of meas-

Pres. S.R. Nathan formally dissolved the Singaporean Parliament on Oct. 18, 2001, and called for new general elections to be held on November 3, well in advance of an August 2002 deadline. Most observers believed the elections were called early in anticipation of an economic downturn that was sure to reflect badly on the ruling People's Action Party (PAP). A new opposition coalition, made up of four previously unallied parties, emerged to challenge the PAP; among other measures, the Singapore Democratic Alliance (SDA) called for the establishment of a welfare system for the unemployed and a demonstration by the government of greater fiscal responsibility. The SDA proved unable to take advantage of public discontent over the deteriorating economy, however. On election night the PAP won a landslide victory, taking 82 of the 84 parliamentary seats. The opposition complained that tight government control of the media made it difficult, if not impossible, to make serious headway against the PAP. Nonetheless, despite the country's economic woes, Singapore still ranked as one of the wealthiest states in Southeast Asia, and few Singaporeans were willing to risk a change in leadership.

The country was hit hard by slumping worldwide demand for electronic products, which made up some 60% of Singapore's manufacturing output, and by a downturn in the economies of key trading partners such as the U.S. and Japan. Singapore officially entered a recession in the second quarter, which saw a steep 10% drop in growth figures. Before the election the government unveiled a $6.2 billion stimulus package intended to reactivate the flagging economy. The package allowed for an array of tax cuts and an increase in government spending; at year's end it was still too early to tell whether the measures had begun to have their intended effect.

Aside from the economy, government officials were alarmed at the country's rapidly declining birthrate, which had fallen to 1.5 children per woman. An estimated 2.5 children per woman were needed to maintain Singapore's current population level. (EDITOR)

SLOVAKIA

Area: 49,035 sq km (18,933 sq mi)
Population (2001 est.): 5,410,000
Capital: Bratislava
Chief of state: President Rudolf Schuster
Head of government: Prime Minister Mikulas Dzurinda

Although Slovakia continued to struggle with political uncertainty and economic difficulties in 2001, the country also made considerable progress in reforms. The ruling parties showed remarkable unity when necessary, which was demonstrated by the adoption in February of 85 constitutional amendments, the most important of which allowed for public administration reforms and the introduction of an ombudsman.

The parliament approved territorial and public administration reforms in July aimed at granting more power to municipalities. Slovakia's first regional elections were held on December 1 and 5. The centre-right ruling coalition parties won a clear majority in just three of the eight regions and obtained the post of regional leader in only two. The other regions went to former prime minister Vladimir Meciar's Movement for a Democratic Slovakia, sometimes in coalition with the left-wing ruling parties and the extra-parliamentary Smer ("Direction"). The turnout was disappointingly low, at just 26% in the first round and 23% in the second.

The government experienced two major upheavals in 2001. The first was a squabble on the centre-right in May over who would appoint a replacement for Interior Minister Ladislav Pittner. Prime Minister Mikulas Dzurinda eventually prevailed, putting forward his close ally Ivan Simko. In the summer the five-party ruling coalition faced collapse when the Party of the Hungarian Coalition (SMK) threatened to leave the government because of its disagreement over the territorial reforms. The parliament had voted to retain the 8 regions established by the previous government rather than switch to the 12-region model preferred by the SMK. However, the SMK finally decided to stay in the government after the parliament approved all the relevant laws on administrative reforms by early October, transferring approximately 300 powers from the central government to regions and municipalities.

On the economic front the government pushed forward quickly with privatization, completing the sales of the country's major banks and making significant headway into privatizing the energy sector. Nonetheless, economic growth continued to be slowed by weak household consumption, a sign that ordinary Slovaks had yet to benefit from the government's reforms.

Slovakia remained on the fast track for membership in NATO and the European Union (EU). Defense Minister Jozef Stank worked hard to push forward military reforms, and Slovakia was seen as one of the two favourites to receive an invitation to NATO in 2002. Slovakia caught up with the first-round countries in preparations for EU membership, closing 22 of 31 chapters of the *acquis communautaire*, the body of legislation that regulates the activities of EU member states. The one major setback was related to a scandal in May over the alleged misuse of EU PHARE funds, which led to the resignation of the deputy prime minister for European integration, Pavol Hamzik; he was replaced by Maria Kadlecikova.

(SHARON FISHER)

SLOVENIA

Area: 20,273 sq km (7,827 sq mi)
Population (2001 est.): 1,991,000
Capital: Ljubljana
Chief of state: President Milan Kucan
Head of government: Prime Minister Janez Drnovsek

On June 16, 2001, Slovenia played host to the first meeting between U.S. Pres. George W. Bush and his Russian counterpart, Vladimir Putin. The two met at Brdo, a government-owned guest house northwest of Ljubljana.

The left-centre coalition government formed by Prime Minister Janez Drnovsek of the Liberal Democracy of Slovenia—by far the largest party in the parliament following the Oct. 15, 2000, election—was stable during 2001. In October Drnovsek confirmed the possible return of the cancer for which he had undergone successful surgery in 1999 but said he planned to run for president in late 2002.

Slovenia devoted much attention to improving relations with its immediate neighbours. On February 14 Italy's Parliament approved a law protecting its Slovene minority, alleviating a decades-long source of tension. On July 23 Drnovsek and Croatian Prime Minister Ivica Racan signed an agreement defining the sea and land border between the two countries, but opposition arose in Croatia, and by year's end it was clear that Croatia would not ratify the agreement. The impasse was likely to require international arbitration, which Slovenia opposed. On September 17 Slovenia opened an embassy in Belgrade and thus normalized relations with Yugoslavia; the latter reciprocated on November 2. Relations with Austria remained touchy, however, in large part because of Slovenia's concerns about treatment of the Slovene minority in the Austrian province of Kärnten.

Slow implementation of the nearly 10-year-old law on denationalization caused problems for Slovenia in its relations with the European Union (EU) and the United States. Government-approved decisions to return large tracts of land and major properties to the Catholic Church led to court appeals delaying the transfers, while Archbishop Franc Rode, head of the Slovene Church, spoke out against

AP/Wide World Photos

On June 16 in Ljubljana, Slovenia, U.S. Pres. George W. Bush and Russian Pres. Vladimir Putin share a laugh during the first meeting between the two heads of state.

SOMALIA

Area: 637,000 sq km (246,000 sq mi, including the 176,000-sq-km [68,000-sq-mi] area of the unilaterally declared [in 1991] and unrecognized Republic of Somaliland)
Population (2001 est.): 7,489,000 (including Somaliland); about 300,000 refugees are registered in neighbouring countries
Capital: Mogadishu; Hargeysa is the capital of Somaliland
Head of state and government: Somalia's government under President Abdiqassim Salad Hassan was barely functioning in 2001, with opposition forces controlling parts of the country.

what he viewed as the antireligious attitude of the predominantly leftist political establishment and mass media. Slovenia seemed to make progress in its effort to meet the conditions for membership in the EU. A similar effort continued with respect to gaining an invitation to join NATO in 2002, with less-obvious results.　　(RUDOLF M. SUSEL)

SOLOMON ISLANDS

Area: 28,370 sq km (10,954 sq mi)
Population (2001 est.): 480,000
Capital: Honiara
Chief of state: Queen Elizabeth II, represented by Governor-General John Lapli
Head of government: Prime Ministers Manasseh Sogavare and, from December 17, Sir Allan Kemakeza

Despite the peace agreement reached in 2000 that ended two years of ethnic conflict in the Solomon Islands, the government led by Prime Minister Manasseh Sogavare struggled to function in 2001. The economy remained in a state of near collapse, and the government was unable to meet its financial obligations or provide basic services. The power supply was irregular, civil servants went unpaid, businesses closed, and there were few exports in an economy where consumption was already heavily dependent on imports. The situation was exacerbated by the murder of a former commander of the Isatambu Freedom Movement and by violent attacks on politicians and government officials. In July the first $8 million tranche of a soft loan from Taiwan to compensate victims of ethnic violence led to disputes concerning distribution.

The government passed legislation granting amnesty to those who had taken part in ethnic violence since October 1998. A possible move from a provincial and national system of government to a federation of states remained under consideration. Despite concern over a lack of funds and administrative capacity, elections for the new 50-seat parliament took place on December 5. Former minister of foreign affairs Sir Allan Kemakeza was sworn in as prime minister.　　(BARRIE MACDONALD)

By the end of 2001 the economic situation of Somalia was critical. The failure of the main seasonal rains led to crop failure, and in December the UN Food and Agriculture Organization estimated that some 800,000 people were experiencing food difficulties, while 300,000, mainly in the southern regions, were threatened by starvation. The Gulf states still banned livestock from the region on health grounds, thus killing the country's main export. In February and April continued deliveries of unauthorized Somali shilling banknotes led to hyperinflation. Nevertheless, at the beginning of the year business thrived, supported largely by remittances from abroad. Financial and telephone services functioned well, and in April Mogadishu's first Internet cafe opened. A crippling blow was dealt in November when the U.S. authorities closed down Al Barakat, the company that handled most of the money-transfer and overseas telecommunications services, on the grounds that it supported terrorism.

The new Transitional National Government (TNG) under Pres. Abdiqassim Salad Hassan appeared from the outside to be working; it occupied Somalia's seat in the UN and was backed by the Organization of African Unity, the Arab League, and the European Union, which pledged aid. At home, however, it failed to control even the capital, Mogadishu, let alone the rest of the country.

In an effort to establish law and order in Mogadishu, the TNG began enrolling former gunmen into a new army and recalled former police officers, but most of the city remained in the hands of faction leaders; two deputies of the Transitional

National Assembly were assassinated, and spasmodic clan and faction fighting continued. In November the prime minister, Ali Khalif Ghalayr, was voted out of office by the Transitional National Assembly in a vote of no confidence; he was replaced by Hasan Abshir Farah.

Outside Mogadishu, clans divided into factions; some supported the TNG, but others opposed it. The breakaway regions of Somaliland in the northwest and Puntland in the northeast totally rejected the TNG, though it contained members from those regions and claimed to represent the whole country. (*See* Sidebar.) The result was the formation of a new alliance in opposition to the TNG, the Somalia Reconciliation and Restoration Council (SRRC), which was inaugurated in April at a meeting in Ethiopia and with the backing of the Ethiopian government. The TNG, backed by Egypt and Saudi Arabia, accused Ethiopia of sending troops to support the SRRC, though Ethiopia denied the charge. At the end of the year, reconciliation talks between the TNG and various factions opposed to it were held in Kenya, where a peace deal was signed on December 24. However, this was followed by fighting in Mogadishu between supporters and opponents of the deal.

In the southern port of Kismaayo, a new administration was organized by the pro-TNG Juba Valley Alliance. The area around Luuk and Bardera in the Gedo region remained under the control of al-Ittihad al-Islami, a hard-line Islamic group.   (VIRGINIA LULING)

How Many Somali States?

For the past decade there has been one island of relative stability in the sea of clan warfare and political uncertainty that is the Horn of Africa. On May 18, 2001, the "Republic of Somaliland" celebrated its 10th anniversary. This territory in the northwest of Somalia comprises the former British Somaliland protectorate (which was independent for six days in 1960 before it amalgamated with the former Italian Somalia to form the Somali Republic). So far, however, it has failed to win international recognition.

In 1991, after the fall of Somalia's military dictator Muhammad Siad Barre, the victorious Somali National Movement unilaterally reasserted the independent status of the northwest area and claimed the old protectorate frontiers. The bustling capital, Hargeysa, was rebuilt after its destruction by Siad Barre's forces. Muhammad Ibrahim Egal (who had been Somalia's prime minister at the time of independence in 1960) was elected president in 1993 at a conference of traditional elders. In 2001 he was seeking a third term but faced strong opposition. In a referendum held on June 1, 97% of the eligible voters supported the new constitution, which affirmed the region's independence from the rest of Somalia.

In 1998 the northeastern area of Somalia also proclaimed itself the "autonomous region" of Puntland, but, unlike Somaliland, its stated goal was eventual incorporation into a federal Somali state. Puntland is governed by a house of representatives and a traditional elders' council. The inland town of Garoowe is the official capital, while the thriving port of Boosaaso is the commercial centre. Col. Abdullahi Yusuf was elected president by the elders' council. Yusuf's mandate was to have expired on June 30, 2001, but was extended for another three years by the elders' council and the house of representatives. Opposition leaders claimed, however, that the vote was manipulated. In July Chief Justice Yusuf Haji Nur issued a decree deposing him. A general conference called in November elected Col. Jama Ali Jama president; Yusuf and his supporters responded by attacking Garoowe, and a standoff ensued.

Women in Somaliland sing as they wait to cast their ballots in the constitutional referendum held on June 1.

Pedro Ugarte/AFP Widewide

So far, beyond the creation of Eritrea from Ethiopia in 1993, the international community has not been willing to sanction the political fragmentation of the Horn by recognizing these secessionist states. As long as the jockeying and fighting between clan groups continues to paralyze government in Somalia, however, the delicate balance between multiple Somali states is likely to continue.

(VIRGINIA LULING)

SOUTH AFRICA

Area: 1,219,090 sq km (470,693 sq mi)
Population (2001 est.): 43,586,000
Capitals (de facto): Pretoria/Tshwane (executive); Bloemfontein/Mangaung (judicial); Cape Town (legislative)
Head of state and government: President Thabo Mbeki

Domestic Affairs. The key words in South Africa in 2001 were *privatization* and *corruption*. In his annual address to Parliament, Pres. Thabo Mbeki enumerated the improvements made in South Africa since the inception of democratic government in 1994: 1,129,612 houses had been or were being built, and nearly 7 million people had been furnished with clean water. During 2000 some 397,019 homes were connected to the electricity grid, 412,000 new telephones were installed, and 127 clinics were built. Mbeki planned to speed up delivery of services and to accelerate economic growth by lowering costs through a continued policy of privatization. He also stressed that he would combat corruption in the ruling African National Congress (ANC) government. For most of the year the main opposition party, the Democratic Alliance (DA), was making strides in becoming an important alternative to the ANC and hoped to win 30% of the vote by 2004, particularly by gaining support from blacks. DA leader Tony Leon stressed the country's need for strong leadership in the fight against crime and poverty and in the creation of jobs, and he demanded faster privatization. In October, however, a split occurred between the two components which had formed the DA, the New National Party (NNP) and the Democratic Party (DP). The catalyst for this was the expulsion from the DA of Cape Town Mayor Peter Marais. In April Marais had proposed that two principal streets in the city be renamed after former president Nelson Mandela and former president F.W. de Klerk. The proposal proved controversial, and fraud was detected in the final vote. Following the expulsion of Marais, Marthinus van Schalkwyk led much of the NNP out of the DA and into an alliance with the ANC.

Privatization threatened the alliance between the ANC, the Congress of South African Trade Unions (COSATU), and the South African Communist Party (SACP). In August COSATU and other trade unions, supported by ANC-aligned civic and student organizations, launched a two-day general strike against privatization. Nonetheless, the government severely criticized the strike and vowed that it would not change its policy. The COSATU president, Willie Madisha, cited a class struggle inside the alliance. In October the government narrowly averted a strike by public-sector workers over wages and retrenchment procedures.

The arms deal concluded in 1999, whose cost had escalated from R 30 billion (R 1=about $0.12) to more than R 60 billion due to the decline in value of the rand, continued to provoke controversy. After allegations of corruption, the government set up a joint investigating team into the deal which cleared government ministers of any wrongdoing. Opposition parties, however, believed that the investigation was compromised, and its mode of establishment had undermined the independence of parliament. Several people, including the ANC chief whip, Tony Yengeni, were charged with offenses related to the arms deal, such as corruption or fraud, perjury, and forgery. All of the major parties encountered severe internal tensions.

In April the ANC minister of safety and security provoked considerable incredulity when he claimed that three businessmen, ANC supporters, were involved in a plot to oust President Mbeki and that they were being investigated by police and national intelligence. COSATU called the statement "highly irresponsible." The government was accused of using state resources to thwart a possible political challenge to Mbeki. Though President Mbeki regretted that the businessmen had been named, he justified a police investigation on the grounds that there were also rumours circulating that he had been involved in the 1993 assassination of SACP leader Chris Hani.

In July thousands of people who had occupied land illegally in Gauteng—they had bought plots costing R 25 each from the Pan-Africanist Congress (PAC)—were forcibly evicted by the government. This led to tensions and disagreements within the PAC.

Controversy over HIV/AIDS continued. In March the DA and COSATU wanted the government to declare the AIDS epidemic a state of emergency. Such an action would permit the acquisition of less-costly medicines, but the government refused. In April the Pharmaceutical Manufacturers' Association, representing 39 manufacturers, withdrew its 1998 court case against the government, which had empowered itself to import generic drugs, including less-expensive anti-AIDS drugs, without the permission of the patent holder. The dropping of the suit was regarded as a victory for the government and the AIDS-activist organization, the Treatment Action Campaign. The health minister, however, said that the decision did not mean that the government would purchase large quantities of the drugs. In October a Medical Research Council report—which was leaked to the *Johannesburg Sunday Times* after the government had suppressed its contents—concluded that AIDS was the chief cause of death in the country and that unless measures were taken to curb the disease, it would claim the lives of between five million and seven million South Africans by 2010.

In a stampede for seats at a soccer match on April 11 at Ellis Park stadium in Johannesburg, 43 fans died and hundreds were injured. The stadium held 62,000 persons, but thousands more went to the contest. ANC stalwart and former Robben Island prisoner Govan Mbeki, father of President Mbeki, died in early August at the age of 91. Christiaan Barnard, the first surgeon to perform a successful heart transplant, succumbed in September. (*See* OBITUARIES.) On December 4 Marike de Klerk, F.W. de Klerk's ex-wife, was found murdered in her home near Cape Town. A 21-year-old security guard in her housing complex was arrested days later, though the motive for the crime was unclear.

The Economy. From a 3.1% growth rate in 2000, the economy slowed to an increase of 1.5% in the first quarter, 1.8% in the second quarter, and 1.2% in the third quarter of 2001. The slowdown was attributed to a decline in the growth of export volume. Gross domestic fixed investment, which increased by 1.5% in 2000, grew by 5.5% in the first half of 2001. The job sector remained problematic, however. Though employment estimates rose from 9.2 million in 1996 to 10.4 million in 1999, mainly in the informal sector, unemployment as of February 2000 was 26.7% on a narrow definition, which excluded people who had not actively sought work in the previous week, and 37.3% on a broader definition.

The budget for 2001–02 provided a tax-relief package of R 8.3 billion, and it also included an economic-stimulus package of R 7.8 billion, which would be spent on infrastructure; the R 600 million allocated as tax incentives for job creation was criticized as too little by COSATU. The increases in pensions and child-

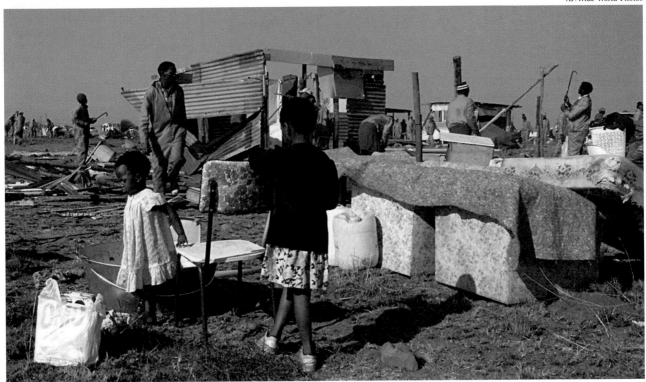

Outside Johannesburg, S.Afr., workers dismantle the shacks of squatter families on July 13.

support grants were criticized as insufficient. During the year the rand slumped by near 40% against the dollar.

Foreign Affairs. President Mbeki's Millennium Africa Recovery Program, which aimed to combat poverty through investment and trade, received a warm response from developed countries during the year. Mbeki and other African leaders first presented the plan in January at the World Economic Forum summit in Davos, Switz. He then emerged from the Organization of African Unity conference in July with Senegal's proposals for a New African Initiative. Mbeki went on to present the proposal to the Group of Eight industrialized nations in July, and the measure was expected to be finalized for the group in 2002. In August–September, South Africa hosted the UN's World Conference Against Racism, which provoked controversy when the U.S. withdrew in protest against attempts to equate Zionism with racism and demands for reparations for slavery and colonialism.

Mbeki's unilateral "quiet diplomacy" to deal with the land and law-and-order crisis in Zimbabwe was supplemented by multilateral pressure from the Commonwealth of Nations and the Southern African Development Community. In February Mbeki's international investment council expressed concern that the

violence in the Zimbabwe land crisis would spill over into South Africa. South Africa's defense force assisted refugees from Mozambican floods in February, and a limited number of South African troops were deployed to the UN peacekeeping force in the Democratic Republic of the Congo. In October South Africa and Burundi signed an agreement that would deploy as many as 700 South African peacekeeping troops to monitor the installation in November of Burundi's transitional government. The first visit by a sitting Japanese prime minister to South Africa took place in January. President Mbeki visited Cuba in March; the U.K., the U.S., and Germany in June; and Japan in October.

(MARTIN LEGASSICK)

SPAIN

Area: 505,990 sq km (195,364 sq mi)
Population (2001 est.): 40,144,000
Capital: Madrid
Chief of state: King Juan Carlos I
Head of government: Prime Minister José María Aznar López

Spain was one of the fastest-growing economies in the European Union (EU) in 2001. Despite inflation nearing 4% and the clear signs of slowdown, the strong economy helped Prime Minister José María Aznar López through a rather troubled year for his centre-right Popular Party (PP) government.

The government's problems involved politics as much as policies. A number of issues were handled clumsily, including implementation of immigration legislation passed in January and a health scare over low-quality olive oil in July. Complaints that the government was steamrolling controversial university reforms through the parliament inflamed the opposition, and students all over the country joined in strikes, demonstrations, and sit-ins.

A number of senior officials were implicated in financial scandals during the year. In July Foreign Minister Joseph Piqué only narrowly escaped prosecution for his role in alleged irregularities committed in 1991 by the chemicals group Ercros, of which he was then a director. Just days later the collapse of the stockbroking house Gescartera with debts amounting to over $82 million spelled more trouble for the government. The junior finance minister, Enrique Giménez-Reyna, whose sister was managing director of Gescartera, and

Pilar Valiente, president of the stock market regulator, resigned amid accusations of official incompetence and favouritism. The PP's parliamentary majority ensured that the congressional inquiry exonerated the government from all responsibility in the case, but opposition parties called for the dismissal of the ministers of the economy and finance. These scandals also conjured up the spectre of corruption that had cost the previous government under the Spanish Socialist Workers' Party (PSOE) so dearly in the 1996 elections.

The PP's disappointing performance in the Basque regional elections on May 13 was another setback. Following the signing of an antiterrorist pact with the PSOE in December 2000, the two "constitutional" parties had fought the campaign hand-in-hand. Preelectoral polls suggested they might be able to oust the moderate Basque Nationalist Party (PNV) after 21 years in power, but the PNV won a resounding victory, taking 33 seats in the 75-seat parliament (up from 27). The main loser was Euskal Herritarrok (EH), the political wing of the Basque separatist organization Euskadi Ta Askatasuna (ETA), which apparently was punished by voters for having ended its unilateral cease-fire six months earlier.

These elections were widely seen as a personal triumph for Basque regional president Juan José Ibarretxe, as well as an endorsement for his demands for both greater regional autonomy and self-determination. The latter was rejected out of hand by the PP government, which accused the nationalist regional government—which the Basque federation of the left-wing United Left (IU) coalition joined in September—of being soft on terrorism.

ETA continued its campaign of street violence, arson, and assassination, unde-

terred by the evident electoral costs and successful police antiterrorist operations. The organization claimed 13 mortal victims in 2001, taking its death toll to well over 800 in just over three decades. Victims included bystanders as well as local politicians and members of the police, press, military, and judiciary. Late in the year José Javier Arizkurn Ruíz, who was believed to be the former military leader of the ETA, was extradited from France to face charges of plotting to kill King Juan Carlos I in 1995; Arizkurn also faced 12 murder charges.

Spain's domestic terrorist problem framed its response to the September 11 attacks in the U.S. Seeing an opportunity to consolidate ties with U.S. Pres. George W. Bush's administration as well as to secure closer international cooperation against ETA, Aznar immediately offered sympathy and full support to the U.S. Spanish bases and troops were put at the disposition of Washington, and on November 13 the Spanish police arrested 11 suspected members of the terrorist organization al-Qaeda. Spain also strongly supported initiatives to tighten the EU's antiterrorist legislation. With the exception of the IU, there was a broad consensus behind the government's response to the international crisis.

A number of long-running tensions between Spain and Morocco surfaced in 2001. Madrid's response to the events of September 11 included tightening entry controls in the North African enclaves of Ceuta and Melilla, which helped trigger a diplomatic crisis with Morocco in November. Moroccan resentment of Spanish occupation of these "colonies" was inflamed by signs of progress on Spain's claims to the British colony of Gibraltar. The collapse of talks between the EU and Morocco over European fishing rights in Moroccan waters in April was followed in September by suggestions from Ma-

drid that Rabat could do more to stem the flow of illegal immigration into Spain across the Strait of Gibraltar. Press criticism of the pace of political reform in Morocco also irritated that country, as did Spain's perceived opposition to Rabat's plans for Western Sahara, the former Spanish colony occupied by Morocco in 1975. The tension came to a head on October 27, days before Moroccan King Muhammad VI began his first official visit to Western Sahara, when Rabat unexpectedly recalled its ambassador to Madrid and canceled a bilateral summit.

(JUSTIN BYRNE)

SRI LANKA

Area: 65,610 sq km (25,332 sq mi)
Population (2001 est.): 19,399,000
Capitals: Sri Jayawardenepura Kotte (legislative and judicial); Colombo (executive)
Head of state and government: President Chandrika Kumaratunga, assisted by Prime Ministers Ratnasiri Wickramanayake and, from December 9, Ranil Wickremesinghe

Although in 2001 the Sri Lankan civil war entered its 19th year, and there was no end in view by year's end, there was new hope that a negotiated settlement might finally be attainable. In April the Liberation Tigers of Tamil Eelam (LTTE), who had long fought to establish an independent nation in the north and east of the nation, canceled the cease-fire they had unilaterally declared the previous December, blaming the government for not reciprocating. Norwegian-brokered efforts to initiate peace talks had foundered because the LTTE demanded that the political ban on its organization and economic embargo against it be lifted and a cease-fire declared by the government, which in turn insisted that peace talks proceed without preconditions.

Soon after the LTTE's cease-fire was canceled, the government launched an offensive in the area of Elephant Pass, which had been lost to rebel forces a year earlier. The offensive was repelled with heavy losses, and government troops retreated to their original lines. Sporadic fighting continued throughout the year, despite renewed efforts to start negotiations. The rebels scored a spectacular coup in July when they briefly

On May 14, a day after Juan José Ibarretxe's Basque Nationalist Party triumphed in the Basque regional elections, workers cover an election poster of one of his rivals, Jaime Mayor Oreja of the Popular Party.

Rafa Rivas/AFP Worldwide

seized Bandaranaike International Airport and its nearby air base, terrifying passengers and staff and destroying half of Air Lanka's Airbus fleet as well as military planes and an oil depot.

Meanwhile, a prolonged political crisis began in June with the withdrawal of the Sri Lanka Muslim Congress from Pres. Chandrika Kumaratunga's People's Alliance coalition. In an effort to survive, the president suspended Parliament and called for a national referendum, provoking further controversy. In August the crisis was temporarily relieved when the Marxist People's Liberation Front (JVP) agreed to support the government for one year in exchange for several concessions. In December, however, a general election returned control of Parliament to the opposition United National Party. The new government quickly declared a cease-fire, eased restrictions on internal movement, and took initial steps toward negotiations with the rebels.

Economic growth declined sharply from the 6.9% real gross domestic product growth achieved in 2000. Dampening factors included a severe drought, which caused electricity shortages, and the need to pay war-risk insurance premiums on imports and exports. Hope for economic recovery rose at the year's end, but that remained dependent on the success of the peace effort and faced severe resource depletion in any case.

(DONALD R. SNODGRASS)

SUDAN, THE

Area: 2,503,890 sq km (966,757 sq mi)
Population (2001 est.): 36,080,000
Capitals: Khartoum (executive and ministerial) and Omdurman (legislative)
Head of state and government: President and Prime Minister Lieut. Gen. Omar Hassan Ahmad al-Bashir

On Jan. 3, 2001, Pres. Omar Hassan Ahmad al-Bashir extended the existing state of emergency in The Sudan for an additional 12 months. He stressed, however, that this extension would not restrict religious freedom or freedom of speech among opposition parties. Late in February a former supporter of the president, Hassan al-Turabi, eager to reassert his authority, was arrested after signing a memorandum of under-

standing with the rebel Sudanese People's Liberation Army (SPLA). At about the same time, President Bashir began discussions with Sadiq al-Mahdi, leader of the opposition Ummah Party, who had returned to The Sudan from self-imposed exile the previous November.

During the year a number of disturbing contrasts emerged. The 25-year-old Kenana Sugar Co.—which employed some 16,000 people and provided education and health care for 100,000 others—announced record production in 2000–01. The harvest produced a large surplus that fully supplied the needs of the domestic and export markets. Meanwhile, the UN World Food Programme warned that three million people were threatened by hunger resulting from drought and civil war. Though the oil industry was earning approximately $1 million per day for the government, a report by the charity organization Christian Aid accused the government of driving hundreds of thousands of people from the land where the oil companies were operating and killing them and burning their villages if they resisted. The oil industry also funded the civil war, which continued unabated in spite of recurring disputes between the leaders of the SPLA. On the other hand, the government's military expenditures, which since 1998 had doubled, by 2001 equaled exactly its income from oil.

Nevertheless, the Sudanese government, which had been accused by the U.S. of sponsoring terrorists and which U.S. Pres. George W. Bush had described on May 3 as presiding over a country that was "a disaster area for all human rights," gave its immediate support to the antiterrorist campaign launched by the U.S. following the September terrorist attacks. In August diplomatic relations with Uganda were reestablished. In September the UN Security Council lifted sanctions imposed on The Sudan in 1996, and in November the U.S. sent an envoy with proposals to end the civil war in the country. (KENNETH INGHAM)

SURINAME

Area: 163,820 sq km (63,251 sq mi)
Population (2001 est.): 434,000
Capital: Paramaribo
Head of state and government: President Ronald Venetiaan

Into his second year of government in 2001, Pres. Ronald Venetiaan brought some improved fiscal and economic stability to Suriname, which was still recovering from the 1986–92 civil conflict that destructively polarized the coastal and interior cultures. He wrestled too with the chaotic economic legacy of his predecessor, Jules Wijdenbosch. Under Venetiaan's guidance, the currency had responded to corrective measures, inflation had been reduced, the armed forces had been largely depoliticized, and loans to underpin health, education, and social programs had been negotiated with The Netherlands and the Inter-American Development Bank. Disruptive frontier disputes with neighbouring Guyana had been positively addressed, while an expansion of oil production was anticipated.

Key to Venetiaan's modest success was his ability to keep his fragile New Front coalition of four political parties intact in the face of major challenges, notably a towering fiscal deficit, a robust informal economy of illegal mining and narcotics smuggling, a swollen and diet-resistant public service, and the accelerating global downturn on traditional export earnings, including bauxite and rice.

Although issues such as land rights and natural resources in the interior remained unresolved, in July in Paramaribo the country formally commemorated the successful eight-year Organization of American States mission to assist Suriname in finding "durable peace" and strengthening "institutions and democratic order." (JOHN W. GRAHAM)

Pres. Ronald Venetiaan of Suriname speaks at a press conference in Paramaribo on August 9.

SWAZILAND

Area: 17,364 sq km (6,704 sq mi)
Population (2001 est.): 1,104,000
Capitals: Mbabane (administrative and judicial); Lozitha and Ludzidzini (royal); Lobamba (legislative)
Chief of state: King Mswati III, with much power shared by his mother, Queen Mother Ntombi Latfwala
Head of government: Prime Minister Barnabas Sibusiso Dlamini

The high point in Swazi politics during 2001 was reached when on August 10 the Constitutional Review Commission (CRC) submitted its report to King Mswati III. The entire nation was called to Ludzidzini to witness the king's receipt of the commission's report, which provided a constitutional framework for the legal experts who would write the country's constitution.

In April 1973 Sobhuza II, King Mswati III's father, had abolished the constitution that Great Britain bequeathed when colonial rule ended on Sept. 6, 1968. Although most parts of that constitution were restored in Swaziland after independence, the sections providing a bill of rights and allowing political parties to be formed were removed. The CRC reported that the majority of the Swazi population did not favour the formation of political parties.

Pro-democracy groups, however, continued to call for the establishment of such parties and for greater open participation in governance. The Swaziland government appeared to allow open political activities in October; for the first time, campaigns in the local government elections were promoted publicly.
(ACKSON M. KANDUZA)

SWEDEN

Area: 449,964 sq km (173,732 sq mi)
Population (2001 est.): 8,888,000
Capital: Stockholm
Chief of state: King Carl XVI Gustaf
Head of government: Prime Minister Göran Persson

The first six months of 2001 were dominated by Sweden's role as president of the European Union (EU), and while the country was criticized for lacking a grand vision for its time in charge, it was praised for the efficiency with which it ran the presidency.

For the Swedes the most obvious achievement was the injection of fresh impetus to the process of EU enlargement. At the end of the Göteborg summit in June, Prime Minister Göran Persson said he hoped the most advanced candidates would complete entry negotiations by the end of 2002 with the objective of participating in the 2004 European Parliamentary elections.

Sweden's term as president also marked some bold foreign initiatives for the EU. With the U.S. under Pres. George W. Bush appearing to disengage from some of the world's most intractable political disputes, it was left to Persson to visit the Middle East and North Korea. The EU also took the lead in attempting to prevent an all-out war in Macedonia.

For all the successes, most Swedes would remember the presidency not for the long line of foreign dignitaries who visited the country but for the bloody riots that marred the Göteborg summit as groups of antiglobalization protesters and police battled in the streets of the city.

Domestic politics got under way in the second half of the year but were overshadowed by the September 11 terrorist attacks in the U.S. Persson wholeheartedly supported the U.S.-led campaign against terrorism and the bombing in Afghanistan, a position that prompted sharp criticism from some members of his Social Democratic Labour Party (SAP).

Despite the dispute, Persson remained unchallenged as party leader and was set to take the SAP into the September 2002 general election. In opinion polls the SAP claimed about 35% of the support, with its ally the Left Party at around 12–13%. The environmental Green Party, which the SAP also relied upon for its legislative majority, might struggle to return to the Riksdag (parliament) after the election. If this happened, or if support for the Left and the SAP slipped further, then the way would be open for a nonsocialist four-party coalition to take power, headed by the conservative Moderate Party leader Bo Lundgren.

Economically, the bursting of the information technology bubble had as marked implications for Sweden as for other countries. Ericsson, the world's largest producer of mobile telecommunications equipment, shed thousands of jobs, as did the country's once fast-expanding Internet consulting firms and dot-com start-ups.

Gross domestic product growth of 3.6% in 2000 was expected to have fallen to around 1.5% in 2001, and only a minor recovery was forecast for 2002. The government was hoping that measures such as tax cuts, subsidies on child-care expenses, and wage increases would boost consumer confidence with real disposable income to increase by 5.4%. Exports were also expected to pick up in 2002, helped by the weakness of the Swedish krona, which hit record lows against both the dollar and the euro in 2001.

For the time being, Sweden had decided to remain outside the European single currency, and Persson was eager to ensure that membership did not become an issue in the general election. At the earliest a referendum on the matter could be held after the election, but there was little obvious enthusiasm for the monetary project among the general public.
(NICHOLAS GEORGE)

SWITZERLAND

Area: 41,284 sq km (15,940 sq mi)
Population (2001 est.): 7,222,000
Capitals: Bern (administrative) and Lausanne (judicial)
Head of state and government: President Moritz Leuenberger

In the worst accident of its kind that Switzerland had ever experienced, 11 people lost their lives on Oct. 24, 2001, in a head-on collision between two heavy trucks and the consequent fire in the 17-km (10.5-mi) St. Gotthard tunnel, hitherto considered as having "above-average security." Traffic in the tunnel, a main route through the Swiss Alps between Göschenen and Airolo on the way to Italy, had increased significantly since a fire that resulted in 39 deaths closed the Mont Blanc tunnel—the principal Alpine link between France and Italy—in 1999. By the end of 2001, the Mont Blanc tunnel had reopened initially for light traffic. The Gotthard tunnel reopened on December 21. In a further accident on November 24, a Crossair plane crashed as it was on the point of landing at Zürich airport; 24 people died. (*See* DISASTERS.)

The Swiss public was likewise traumatized by the mass killing on September 27 in the cantonal parliament of Zug. A man wearing what looked like a police uniform and armed with a grenade and an assault rifle burst into a joint session and opened fire, killing 14 people and wounding many more, before shooting himself.

After a fairly promising start to the year, the Swiss economy was shaken by successive restructuring, entailing thousands of layoffs and bringing unemployment up to almost 2%, though inflation was at its lowest since February 1999. This culminated in the downfall of the national airline, Swissair, which since its founding in 1931 had established itself as the hallmark of Swiss efficiency. Swissair had experienced serious financial difficulties in preceding years (at a stormy shareholders meeting in April, the management was severely criticized), which were compounded by repercussions from the September 11 terrorist attacks in the U.S. Swissair grounded its fleet of 73 planes for two days in early October when two of its jets were denied fuel replenishment at London's Heathrow Airport and the company was refused further credit. Thousands of passengers were stranded.

Difficult weeks followed, leading to the collapse of the SAirGroup. Its subsidiary, Crossair, emerged as the national airline, taking over 52 flights from Swissair, which was granted a six-month protection against bankruptcy proceedings. Financial support was pledged by government, banks, and the private sector, with UBS and Credit Suisse holding 70.5% of the share capital of Crossair.

In a March referendum voters followed the government's advice to postpone a decision on joining the European Union to allow more time for reflection. In June voters approved by a narrow majority government proposals that Swiss soldiers serving abroad be armed. The electorate also narrowly voted to permit military training in NATO countries or common exercises with NATO troops on Swiss soil. Action for an Independent and Neutral Switzerland and other opponents expressed fears that the country might otherwise lose its neutrality and be drawn into a military entanglement. At the same time, voters accepted the repeal of an article in the constitution by which the creation of new bishoprics needed the blessing of

A plane of the financially troubled Swissair—part of the SAirGroup—takes off in Zürich on November 18.

the political authorities. In December limitations on budgetary indebtedness were accepted, while abolishing the army was once more rejected, as were replacing the army by a peace service, imposing a tax on energy, and another tax on capital gains.

Continuing its reform "Army XXI," the Swiss cabinet decided that new military recruits would serve for 21 weeks, up from 15. Parliamentary approval of this change was taken for granted. It would apply from 2004, by which time the strength of the army would be reduced from 350,000 to 200,000, while the annual budget would remain at Sw F 4.3 billion (about $2.6 billion).

Although a massive majority in the National Council was in favour of joining the United Nations, the final decision still depended on a referendum to be held in March 2002. By the end of 2001, the Swiss political scene had moved slightly to the right, as the Swiss People's Party had gained representation in all cantonal parliaments.

The Federal Council opened the way to simplify the procedure for foreigners of the second and third generation to acquire Swiss nationality (subject to parliamentary approval and acceptance in a future referendum). Belgium was by the end of the year the last EU country to have ratified the bilateral agreements with Switzerland. After adjustments, due largely to some donators being unable to meet their pledges, the Swiss na-

tional exhibition, Expo02, was expected to open as scheduled. It was already a year late.   (ALAN MCGREGOR)

SYRIA

Area: 185,180 sq km (71,498 sq mi)
Population (2001 est.): 16,729,000
Capital: Damascus
Head of state and government: President Bashar al-Assad, assisted by Prime Minister Muhammad Mustafa Mero

Political discussion groups blossomed throughout Syria as 2001 opened. In mid-January the reform movement published a Basic Document that called for a return to "constitutional legitimacy" and the rule of law. Immediately after this manifesto appeared, leftist reformers organized a Gathering for Democracy and Unity to encourage public debate and promote competitive parties. Influential liberals responded by forming the Social Peace Movement, committed to orderly dialogue between the regime and its critics and to opening the political arena to previously excluded viewpoints, especially those of the younger generation. At the end of

January, however, the minister of information warned that "any talk that undermines the unity of society is a threat to society as a whole" and equated the spread of Western conceptions of civil society with "neocolonialism."

Attacks on the reform movement by senior government officials and the state-run media escalated in February, and discussion forums were ordered to clear their agendas, speaker lists, and participants with the authorities in advance. By late summer outspoken dissidents were being accused of insulting the honour of the nation. The historic leader of the Syrian Communist Party, Riyad at-Turk, was arrested after he publicly criticized the Ba'th Party's economic policies and Syria's involvement in Lebanon. Prominent liberal activists were rounded up by the security services during September.

Economic and diplomatic relations with Iraq steadily improved during the year. An agreement to phase out tariffs on trade between the two countries was signed in January, and some 150,000 bbl of oil per day flowed through the long-abandoned pipeline linking northern Iraq to the docks at Baniyas. Rapprochement with Iraq accompanied heightened tensions with Israel. On April 16 and July 1, following Hezbollah operations against Israeli forces on the Golan Heights front, Israeli warplanes bombed Syrian military positions in eastern Lebanon.

Prime Minister Muhammad Mustafa Mero led a delegation of state officials and businesspeople to Baghdad, Iraq, in mid-August. The trip resulted in a mutual defense pact, along with treaties to expand bilateral commercial and technical exchanges. On September 10 the interior ministers of Syria and Turkey pledged to coordinate efforts to combat organized crime and terrorism. Foreign Minister Farouk ash-Shara' expressed regret over the attacks in the U.S. the next day, but he urged those set on eliminating international terrorism to focus their attention on Israeli policy toward the Palestinians and neighbouring states. In December the cabinet resigned, and Pres. Bashar al-Assad asked the prime minister to form a new government that could handle economic reform.

Pres. Bashar al-Assad announced on January 2 that the previous day he had married Asma Akhras, who was born in Syria and educated in the U.K. In May the couple traveled to Spain in Assad's first trip to Europe since being named president in July 2000.

(FRED H. LAWSON)

TAIWAN

Area: 36,188 sq km (13,972 sq mi)
Population (2001 est.): 22,340,000
Capital: Taipei
Chief of state: President Chen Shui-bian
Head of government: President of the Executive Yuan (Premier) Chang Chun-hsiung

Ripples from the global economic slowdown in 2001 produced a severe negative impact on Taiwan's economy and overshadowed the ongoing political turmoil that resulted from a divided government. The perennial threat from China evoked a variety of responses from within Taiwan, while the new U.S. administration of Pres. George W. Bush proved more sympathetic to Taiwan's security needs than the Bill Clinton administration had been in the preceding eight years.

Shrinking demand in the U.S. and Japan for Taiwan's high-tech exports, particularly computer chips, and the exodus of thousands of manufacturing plants to China, where labour costs were significantly lower, crippled the economy. Growth slowed from a robust 6.3% in 2000 to just over 1% in the first quarter of 2001, and the economy actually contracted by 2.35% in the second quarter compared with the previous year as the island entered recession for the first time since 1975. At midyear the unemployment rate, which had hovered around 2% for many years, shot up to 4.22%, the highest figure on record. Diminished bank credit added to the economic gloom. One of the few bright spots was that Taiwan's long-standing application to join the World Trade Organization was finally approved in mid-September, the day after China's bid to join the WTO was sealed.

The election in March 2000 of Democratic Progressive Party (DPP) presidential candidate Chen Shui-bian ended the Kuomintang's (KMT) half-century monopoly of that office, but the KMT

Taiwanese Pres. Chen Shui-bian speaks at the conclusion of economic meetings held in Taipei in late August.

Sam Yeh/AFP Worldwide

retained its majority in the Legislative Yuan pending the outcome of parliamentary elections scheduled for December 1. The inexperience of the new DPP administration combined with the determination of the KMT to make things difficult for its political nemesis made this unprecedented experiment in divided government a series of partisan political skirmishes. Former president Lee Teng-hui, who had resigned as head of the KMT after his handpicked candidate, Lien Chan, was crushed in the March 2000 election, threw his support to a new political party, the Taiwan Solidarity Union (TSU), which favoured the maintenance of Taiwan's de facto independence from China.

Meanwhile, the KMT endorsed the novel concept of confederation with China as a way out of the half-century impasse between the People's Republic and the Republic of China. In September the KMT expelled elder statesman Lee from its ranks, severing its ties with the man who had been the party's most important leader for the past dozen years. In the December 1 parliamentary elections, the KMT suffered a crushing defeat, dropping from 110 to 68 seats while its share of the vote plummeted from 46% to 31%. The DPP increased its seats from 66 to 87, and its vote share from 30% to 37%, making it the largest party in the 225-seat Legislative Yuan. The fledgling People First Party led by James Soong picked up 46 seats, and the TSU 13. Overall, these results gave the DPP and President Chen an unprecedented opportunity to create a reform-minded coalition with a small but workable majority.

In January the KMT-dominated Legislative Yuan voted to override Chen's decision to halt construction of Taiwan's fourth nuclear power plant, in fulfillment of a campaign promise, and the courts ruled that Chen had acted improperly. Over the objections of his DPP and environmentalist supporters who opposed nuclear power on principle, Chen bowed to opposition pressure and authorized resumption of construction on the contested power plant.

Taiwan's sole major power patron, the U.S., showed a more sympathetic face to the island under the new Republican Bush administration. In April Bush said he would do whatever it took to defend Taiwan. That same month, in response to Taiwan's annual request for defensive weaponry, Washington announced that it would provide Taiwan with four Kidd-class destroyers, 12 P-3C Orion surveillance aircraft, eight diesel submarines,

minesweeping helicopters, surface- and submarine-launched torpedoes, and Avenger surface-to-air missiles, while it withheld approval of the advanced Aegis antimissile defense system that was Taiwan's most coveted item. The transfers were designed to bolster Taiwan's navy in the face of a steadily growing military imbalance across the Taiwan Strait. China, as usual, objected vociferously to U.S. support for Taiwan, since it hoped to intimidate the island into surrendering its de facto sovereignty. Washington also eased restrictions on Taiwan leaders visiting the U.S., another thing that China deemed objectionable. In May, en route to a tour of Latin American allies, President Chen stopped over in New York City and Houston, where he met with municipal officials and sympathetic congresspeople.   (STEVEN I. LEVINE)

TAJIKISTAN

Area: 143,100 sq km (55,300 sq mi)
Population (2001 est.): 6,252,000
Capital: Dushanbe
Chief of state: President Imomali Rakhmonov
Head of government: Prime Minister Akil Akilov

Tajikistan continued to suffer the effects of the regionwide drought, which continued for a third year. International humanitarian assistance provided some relief, but the country's vital agricultural sector had little chance to start the process of recovery.

The post-civil war peace process was endangered by outbreaks of violence that lasted from April, when the deputy minister of internal affairs was assassinated in Dushanbe, through the summer as government troops battled two armed gangs that had formerly been part of the Islamic opposition. Members of the Islamic opposition who had become government officials stated that the cleanup operation was necessary because, since the end of the civil war, the two groups had engaged in criminal activities, including hostage taking. One former opposition official reported that the killing of civilians during the operations against the gangs had undermined the implementation of the peace process. In July the adviser to Pres. Imomali Rakhmonov was shot dead in Dushanbe. Politicians

of various parties attributed the violence to unspecified forces that wanted to destabilize the country. The minister of culture was assassinated in September.

From the beginning of the year, Tajikistan was under pressure from international humanitarian-aid agencies to admit a group of several thousand Afghan refugees stranded on islands in the Amu Darya. The Tajik authorities refused to allow the refugees into Tajikistan on the grounds that there were armed men among them and in any case Tajikistan was unable to care for its own people. In April the mayor of Dushanbe ordered all Afghan refugees out of the capital.

In January the Tajik authorities began jailing adherents of the banned Islamic sect Hizb ut-Tahrir, which was particularly strong in northern Tajikistan. In early April Kyrgyz officials asserted that militants of the Islamic Movement of Uzbekistan had returned to Tajikistan, which in previous years they had used as a launching point for attacks on Kyrgyzstan. Tajik officials denied this charge and subsequent claims that leaders of the Afghanistan-based group had been sighted in Tajikistan.

Relations with neighbouring Uzbekistan remained tense; the Uzbeks had mined the border between the two countries, and numerous Tajik citizens were killed or maimed when they stepped on mines. The Tajik military spent the summer trying to remove as many mines as possible.

Tajikistan continued to depend on the Russian military presence to protect its borders with Afghanistan. In May it joined the NATO-sponsored Partnership for Peace program. After the terrorist attacks in the U.S. in September, Dushanbe was obliged to consult with Russia before agreeing to provide help to the international antiterrorist coalition.

(BESS BROWN)

TANZANIA

Area: 945,090 sq km (364,901 sq mi)
Population (2001 est.): 36,232,000 (including nearly 1,000,000 refugees, nearly all of whom are from Burundi)
De facto capital: Dar es Salaam; the legislature meets in Dodoma, the capital designate
Chief of state and head of government: President Benjamin William Mkapa, assisted by Prime Minister Frederick Tulway Sumaye

On January 26–27, 2001, police used tear gas and live ammunition to break up demonstrations called by the opposition Civic United Front (CUF) on the islands of Zanzibar and Pemba; the CUF demanded a rerun of the October 2000 parliamentary and presidential elections. Though CUF reports of the number of people killed during the demonstrations were exaggerated, the government's estimate of 20 dead was regarded by impartial observers as too low. The U.S. and several European countries condemned the killings, and Amnesty International criticized the excessive use of force by police and called on both the Tanzanian and Zanzibari governments to institute an impartial investigation. The simultaneous demonstrations that were planned on the mainland were apparently forestalled when officials and other supporters of the CUF were arrested. Foreign Minister Jakaya Kikwete visited London, Washington, Brussels, and Stockholm in a damage-control effort, even though there were no signs that donors were threatening to withhold aid.

Tanzania's continuing dependence on foreign aid was highlighted by the budget presented by Finance Minister Basil Mramba on June 14. Estimated income for the year 2001–02 amounted to markedly less than 60% of estimated expenditure, with something less than the about 40% remaining to come from external grants and loans. Nor was external aid uniformly successful in achieving its aims. Primary-school enrollment suffered a sharp decline; the Heavily Indebted Poor Countries debt-relief program, launched jointly by the World Bank and the International Monetary Fund (IMF), insisted that poor parents contribute a part of the cost of educating their children, a condition that few could meet. Moreover, in spite of the program, Tanzania was still spending 26% of its export earnings on debt servicing. After a March meeting with the members of an IMF–World Bank mission in Tanzania, leaders of southern and central African countries called for urgent steps to be taken to encourage African exports.

Against this backdrop, the news that the British government was contemplating issuing an export license that would authorize a British company to provide a sophisticated $40 million air traffic control system for Tanzania caused the World Bank and the IMF considerable consternation in August.

There were, however, some hopeful signs for the economy. Increased investor interest in gold mining raised Tanzania's hopes of becoming the third largest gold producer in the world by 2004;

some 300 of the 400 companies that had been earmarked for privatization had achieved their aim. In addition, tourism, which in 1999 had accounted for 14% of gross domestic product, continued to expand. Telecommunications lagged well behind neighbouring countries, but the rapid growth in mobile phone ownership—more than 160,000 by midyear—meant that business development was not being held back. There was further good news on November 27 when the IMF and World Bank agreed to a reduction of $77 million in Tanzania's debt repayment for the year 2002. On the political front, however, the peace accord signed between the ruling party, Chama Cha Mapinduzi (CCM), and the CUF on October 10 ran into difficulties when the leadership of the CUF accused the CCM of lacking the will to implement it.

(KENNETH INGHAM)

THAILAND

Area: 513,115 sq km (198,115 sq mi)
Population (2001 est.): 61,251,000
Capital: Bangkok
Chief of state: King Bhumibol Adulyadej
Head of government: Prime Ministers Chuan Leekpai and, from February 9, Thaksin Shinawatra

Thailand's national elections on Jan. 6, 2001—the first held under the new code of conduct mandated by the 1997 con-

stitution—delivered a resounding victory to Thaksin Shinawatra's newly formed Thai Rak Thai Party, which took 248 of the 500 parliamentary seats. This gave Thaksin an overwhelmingly powerful role under the country's coalition-dominated political traditions. The New Aspiration Party of former prime minister Chavalit Yongchaiyudh and the Chart Thai Party of former prime minister Banharn Silapa-archa joined with Thai Rak Thai, and the cabinet was sworn in by King Bhumibol Adulyadej on February 17. The delay was caused by the independent Election Commission, which disqualified 62 winners from various parties and ordered new elections for those seats on January 29. Chavalit was appointed minister of defense, but Banharn declined a portfolio. The powerful post of interior minister went to little-known Thaksin associate Purachai Piumsombun, who promptly declared his intention to curb the excesses of the kingdom's vibrant nightlife. Another close associate of Thaksin, Somkid Jatusripitak, was given the Finance Ministry.

Thaksin, a billionaire telecommunications tycoon (see BIOGRAPHIES), campaigned on a populist platform. He promised to create a development fund for each of the country's 70,000 villages. Farmers were to be given a three-year debt moratorium. Virtually free health care was to be offered at state hospitals. In addition, 1,350,000,000,000 baht ($30,000,000,000) in bad debts from state and private banks was to be bought up by a new agency. These measures were steered through the parliament but were fiercely opposed by the opposition Democrat Party amid doubts cast by economists. Minutes be-

Thai soldiers use bamboo sticks to hack opium poppies near the Myanmar border on January 24.

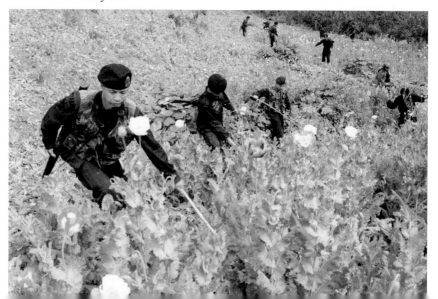

fore Thaksin was to board a domestic flight at Bangkok's airport on March 3, an explosion destroyed the aircraft. Thaksin was unharmed. Attempted assassination was at first assumed, but the U.S. National Transportation Safety Board declared the blast to have been a fuel-tank accident.

The National Countercorruption Commission on April 3 brought a charge against Thaksin before the Constitutional Court, accusing him of having understated his wealth in a mandatory assets declaration. On August 3 the court ruled 8–7 in the prime minster's favour. Meanwhile, the Election Commission completed its probe of the 2000 Senate election and ousted 10 senators, including the speaker. In new elections on April 21, only two of the senators were reelected. Addiction to methamphetamine drugs became so rampant in Thailand that death penalties were handed down to large numbers of traffickers, and tensions mounted with Myanmar (Burma), where many illicit drug factories were located. Financial and sexual scandals involving leading Buddhist clergy, including a monk revered by Thaksin, led to calls for a thorough overhaul of the tradition-bound ecclesiastic hierarchy. After the September 11 terrorist attacks in the U.S., Thailand adopted a studied neutrality, fearful of unrest among the Malay-speaking Muslims in its southern border provinces.

(ROBERT WOODROW)

TOGO

Area: 56,785 sq km (21,925 sq mi)
Population (2001 est.): 5,153,000
Capital: Lomé
Chief of state: President Gen. Gnassingbé Eyadéma
Head of government: Prime Minister Gabriel Agbéyomé Kodjo

On Jan. 30, 2001, after months of negotiations, the government announced plans to hold new parliamentary elections on October 14. In 1999 opposition parties had charged the government with fraud (following the disputed 1998 presidential election) and boycotted the parliamentary elections. On February 23 the findings of a joint Organization of African Unity–UN report on the conduct

of the 1998 presidential election revealed that the government had systematically violated human rights. Fearing that the newly announced elections would be postponed, thousands of supporters of the main opposition party, the Action Committee for Renewal (CAR), took to the streets of the capital the following day in protest. Police, using tear gas and truncheons, broke up the demonstration.

On June 5 senior journalist Lucien Messan was convicted of having published "falsehoods" about alleged killings that took place during the 1998 presidential election campaign. He was sentenced to 18 months' imprisonment.

Further controversy erupted in August when CAR leader Yawovi Agboyibo was sentenced to six months' imprisonment for having defamed Prime Minister Gabriel Abéyomé Kodjo. On August 11 riot police dispersed a large demonstration demanding Agboyibo's release. A proposed constitutional amendment that would enable President Eyadéma to stand for a third five-year term in 2003 brought new protests and threats of strong action from the opposition to prevent Africa's longest-serving leader (34 years) from extending his tenure. On August 31 Eyadéma announced that he would respect the constitution and step down at the end of his term. Nevertheless, on October 5 the electoral commission, citing insufficient time for preparation, announced that legislative elections would be postponed. The government seized issues of independent newspapers several times during the year. (NANCY ELLEN LAWLER)

TONGA

Area: 750 sq km (290 sq mi)
Population (2001 est.): 101,200
Capital: Nuku'alofa
Head of state and government: King Taufa'ahau Tupou IV, assisted by Prime Minister of Privy Council Prince 'Ulukalala Lavaka Ata

A major political and financial scandal brought Tonga to international attention in 2001. More than $20 million from Tonga's trust fund was lost following its investment in a Nevada-based "viatical" scam that involved, in effect, gambling on the death dates of 16 terminally ill patients in the U.S. The trust invested in the

scheme on the advice of American speculator Jesse Bugdonoff, who had also persuaded Tonga's king to appoint him court jester. The lost funds were part of $30.7 million raised more than a decade earlier from the sale of passports and citizenship to foreign nationals—mostly Hong Kong Chinese but also former Philippine president Ferdinand Marcos and his family. The trustees responsible for the investment included then prime minister Baron Vaea, Deputy Prime Minister Tevita Tupou, and Minister of Education Tutoatasi Fakafanua. The latter two resigned in September at the request of the regent, Princess Pilolevu, who was acting for King Taufa'ahau Tupou IV. He was in Auckland, N.Z., for medical tests; the government denied news stories that the 82-year-old king was near death. Meanwhile, investigations into the investment scheme continued.

Air transport within Tonga and to major international links in Australia, New Zealand, and Fiji was disrupted by the grounding in March for safety reasons of Royal Tongan Airlines. In July consumer protection legislation was enacted. On New Year's Eve, Tonga, and the Vava'u group expecially, were struck by Cyclone Waka. (BARRIE MACDONALD)

TRINIDAD AND TOBAGO

Area: 5,128 sq km (1,980 sq mi)
Population (2001 est.): 1,298,000
Capital: Port of Spain
Chief of state: President Arthur Napoleon Raymond Robinson
Head of government: Prime Minister Basdeo Panday

The unexpected outcome (an 18–18 parliamentary seat tie) of the general election called on Dec. 10, 2001, in Trinidad and Tobago after a United National Congress (UNC) government lost its majority in the House of Representatives created uncertainty for a period of time. The two party leaders, UNC's Basdeo Panday and the People's National Movement's (PNM's) Patrick Manning, agreed to let chief of state Pres. Arthur Robinson settle the issue. Robinson opted for Manning, a choice that did not go down well with Panday, who, at year's end, was calling loudly for a fresh election within six months.

Dhanraj Singh (centre), former minister of the local government in Trinidad and Tobago, is escorted to court in Port of Spain on February 20 to answer charges for the 1999 murder of a former local government councillor.

prove human rights observance, and a slightly more liberal press law was introduced in August. Human Rights Watch, however, continued to condemn the government for its human rights record; Tunisia had more than 1,000 political prisoners, and for the fourth year running, it was listed as one of the 10 countries most hostile to a free press.

Though the constitution limited the president to three terms in office, it seemed likely that it would be amended and that Ben Ali would run again in 2004, especially when the central committee of the governing Democratic Constitutional Rally called on him in September to run again. The cabinet was changed twice, in January and October, apparently to bring in younger talent, although veterans controlled the foreign affairs, defense, and interior portfolios. Foreign Minister Habib Ben Yahia visited London shortly after the September terrorist attacks in the U.S. to argue once again of the danger of Tunisian Islamist dissidents abroad and to call for the extradition of the an-Nahda ("Renaissance Party") leadership there.

Tunisia's economic progress continued unabated. Gross domestic product grew an estimated 6% in 2001 despite an ongoing drought. Tourism rose in 2000 by 3.5%, and direct foreign investment was up by 144% to $768 million. Unemployment, however, remained stubbornly high at 15.6%. The privatization program forged ahead; 35 of 41 firms completed privatization, with an average 5% improvement in their turnover.

(GEORGE JOFFÉ)

In January 2001, for the first time since the Tobago House of Assembly (THA) was established in 1980, the PNM had wrested control of the THA from the National Alliance for Reconstruction (NAR). In February Dhanraj Singh, the former minister of local government, was charged with the murder of a former UNC local government councillor, Hansraj Sumairsingh. At year's end his trial was still under way.

Local Muslim leader Yasin Abu Bakr, who had led a short-lived insurrection in 1990, denied in September that he had any connection with wanted terrorist Osama bin Laden. As with other areas in the Caribbean, Trinidad and Tobago had been on heightened alert since the terrorist attacks in the U.S. on September 11.   (DAVID RENWICK)

TUNISIA

Area: 164,150 sq km (63,378 sq mi)
Population (2001 est.): 9,828,000
Capital: Tunis
Chief of state: President Gen. Zine al-Abidine Ben Ali
Head of government: Prime Minister Mohamed Ghannouchi

Tunisia's human rights record was again the subject of international concern during 2001. In January veteran activist Moncef Marzouki, spokesman for the National Council for Liberties in Tunisia (CNLT), was imprisoned for one year. He had already been banned from foreign travel and had lost his professorship at the University of Sousse. His defense team walked out in protest over trial procedure—as did lawyers at proceedings in February against the Tunisian League for Human Rights after its leadership was suspended. Saida, the sister of Taoufik Ben Brik, and Sihem Ben Sédrine, CNLT spokesperson and editor of the on-line magazine *Kalima*, were arrested in June after allegedly having criticized the government during an appearance on the London-based Arab television station Al Mustaquilla; international pressure, however, ensured their speedy release.

In an open letter to Pres. Zine al-Abidine Ben Ali, Tunis judge Mokhtar Yahyaoui protested the harassment and official intimidation he had experienced. After international protest he was reinstated to the bench on August 2, but concerns over governmental judicial interference continued throughout the year. The president, in response to pressure from abroad, agreed to an early release from an eight-year sentence for veteran protester Nejib Hosni. President Ben Ali also promised to im-

TURKEY

Area: 779,452 sq km (300,948 sq mi)
Population (2001 est.): 66,229,000
Capital: Ankara
Chief of state: President Ahmet Necdet Sezer
Head of government: Prime Minister Bulent Ecevit

The financial crisis that struck Turkey in November 2000 worsened in 2001. Financial markets tumbled in February after Pres. Ahmet Necdet Sezer accused Prime Minister Bulent Ecevit of obstructing corruption inquiries involving government ministers. The Turkish lira, which had been pegged to targeted inflation under the program arranged with the International Monetary Fund (IMF) at the end of 1999, was allowed to float on February 22. By the end of the year, it had depreciated by 114% year-on-year. A number of banks failed and had to be taken over by the state. The gross national product dropped by 8% in the first nine months of the year; industrial production decreased by 14% by the end of November; imports were down by 25% (though exports rose 13%) by the end of October. Consumer prices surged 68% year-on-year by the end of December. Demonstrations by shopkeepers, tradesmen, and public employees over price rises and the sharp contraction in employment took place without incident. Calls by business associations for the government's resignation or for a change of economic policy also had little impact, and the draft budget for 2002 submitted to the parliament in October maintained a restrictionist stance by calling for a primary surplus of 6.5%.

On March 2 Kemal Dervis, vice president of the World Bank in charge of the Middle East and North Africa, was appointed minister of state in charge of the economy. He secured additional funding from the IMF for a revised program. Although some $19 billion was secured

from international financial institutions, the government's ability to service its domestic debt, swollen by bank takeovers, continued to depend on foreign help. In mid-November, however, the IMF signaled that it would approve a rescue loan to bridge a $10 billion financing gap. As a result, market confidence increased at the end of the year.

The campaign against corruption and accusations of foot-dragging in implementing the IMF program led to the resignation of several ministers. Nonetheless, the ruling coalition—made up of Ecevit's Democratic Left Party, Devlet Bahceli's Nationalist Action Party, and Mesut Yilmaz's Motherland Party—retained a solid majority of seats (338) in the 550-member single-chamber Turkish Grand National Assembly. In June the Islamist Virtue Party (FP) was banned by the constitutional court, and 2 of its 101 MPs were disqualified for engaging in activities against the secular character of the state. The remaining Islamist deputies divided between two parties: the Felicity Party, headed by former FP leader Recai Kutan, and the Justice and Development Party, established in August by former Istanbul mayor Recep Tayyip Erdogan. The courts had yet to decide whether Erdo-

gan's former conviction for antisecularist pronouncements barred him from political office, however.

Grounds for banning political parties were narrowed and wider freedoms recognized (including the freedom to use any language, and, therefore, the right to broadcast in Kurdish) under a package of constitutional amendments approved by the parliament in October. After a month of debate, the parliament ratified sweeping changes to a civil code dating to 1926. Women, who previously had not been given a voice concerning family life, including decisions about home or children, were granted equal roles in family matters. In addition, in the event of a divorce, women would be entitled under certain conditions to an equal division of marital property and assets, not just the properties that were in both names. The new code would be effective Jan. 1, 2002.

After the September 11 terrorist attacks in the U.S., Turkey—the only Muslim nation belonging to NATO—agreed immediately that Article 5 of the NATO alliance should be invoked; Turkey opened its air space to U.S. and other allied military aircraft and allowed the use of the U.S. air base at Incirlik (near Adana in southern Turkey) for antiterrorist opera-

Turkish Pres. Ahmet Nacdet Sezer reviews a Pakistani honour guard upon his arrival in Islamabad on October 25.

Saeed Khan/AFP Worldwide

tions. On October 9 the parliament authorized the dispatching of Turkish troops abroad and the stationing of foreign troops on Turkish soil at the government's discretion. Only the two Islamist parties voted against the measure. Turkish diplomacy, which had long sought to persuade Western governments to deny facilities to Kurdish, Marxist, and Islamic fundamentalist terrorists seeking to subvert the regime in Turkey, went into action in support of the coalition. President Sezer traveled to Pakistan to strengthen the hand of Pres. Pervez Musharraf, and Foreign Minister Ismail Cem sought to gain support for the initiative at the summit meeting of the Organization of the Islamic Conference in Doha, Qatar, and from the Turkic republics of the former Soviet Union, which he toured in October.

In early November Turkey and Greece signed a landmark agreement that provided for the return by Greece of illegal Turkish immigrants. The deal significantly improved relations between the two countries and lessened fears by Greece that it would face an increased influx of refugees in the wake of the U.S. bombings in Afghanistan.

Sabiha Gokcen, Turkey's first woman military pilot and the adopted daughter of the republic's founder, Mustafa Kemal Ataturk, died on March 22. A few months earlier, an airport named for her had opened on the Asian shore of Istanbul.   (ANDREW MANGO)

TURKMENISTAN

Area: 488,100 sq km (188,500 sq mi)
Population (2001 est.): 4,462,000
Capital: Ashgabat
Head of state and government: President Saparmurad Niyazov

The rapid turnover of personnel in government posts in Turkmenistan that had begun in 2000 accelerated in 2001. Ministers of both foreign affairs and defense were replaced. By the end of the year, few persons in top positions had held their jobs for more than a year. One of the most significant changes was the concentration of power in the hands of the chairman of the National Security Committee (KNB), who was appointed deputy prime minister respon-

sible for defense, law enforcement, and foreign affairs as well as the president's special adviser on legal matters. In January the KNB received a major infusion of new personnel from other law-enforcement agencies.

In February Pres. Saparmurad Niyazov presented the People's Council with a draft of the *Ruhnama*, which he intended as a sort of moral code for the Turkmen people. Its final version, with additional material on the ideal Turkmen family, was completed for the 10th anniversary of Turkmenistan's independence in October.

Official pressure continued on small unregistered religious congregations, primarily Protestant, to stop holding religious services in private homes, although such activities did not violate the law. A decree requiring that foreigners pay the state insurance company $50,000 in order to marry a citizen of Turkmenistan brought sharp international criticism. The Turkmen authorities attempted to defend the decree, saying that it was intended to prevent marriages of convenience that ended in the Turkmen partner's being abandoned without means of support.

The planned summit of heads of state of countries bordering the Caspian Sea was postponed several times in the course of the year. The summit was intended to settle the issue of the division of the Caspian seabed, which was in urgent need of resolution because the littoral states wanted to exploit the sea's natural resources, especially its oil. As discussions continued through the year, the Turkmen position shifted. A major dispute resumed with Azerbaijan in May over Azerbaijani work in oil fields claimed by Turkmenistan. Meetings of experts from the two countries were unable to resolve the dispute, and in June Turkmenistan withdrew its ambassador to Baku. Talks in Ashgabat in July ended in mutual recriminations, with each side accusing the other of unreasonableness.

The Turkmen authorities denied that the regionwide drought was having any effect on the country's agriculture, but the official claims of record wheat harvests were discounted by citizens and international observers alike.

As a neutral state, Turkmenistan refused to allow its airspace or military facilities to be used for attacks on Afghanistan, but the president's agreement to permit transit of international humanitarian aid to Afghanistan was quickly acted upon by UN and other agencies.   (BESS BROWN)

TUVALU

Area: 25.6 sq km (9.9 sq mi)
Population (2001 est.): 11,000
Capital: Government offices in Vaiaku, Fongafale islet, of Funafuti atoll
Chief of state: Queen Elizabeth II, represented by Governor-General Sir Tomasi Puapua
Head of government: Prime Ministers Lagitupu Tuilimu (acting), Faimalaga Luka from February 24, and, from December 14, Koloa Talake

Following the death of Prime Minister Ionatana Ionatana in December 2000, Lagitupu Tuilimu served as acting prime minister until Faimalaga Luka, a former civil servant, was elected in February 2001 to lead the government, but he lost office in December after a parliamentary vote of no-confidence. He was replaced by Koloa Talake, a former public servant and minister of finance. A referendum on the country's future constitutional status was scheduled to be held in early 2002.

The government's commercialization of its Internet domain—.tv—had generated revenue of some $30 million in less than two years. Some funds were invested and, with aid donors, the government embarked on major infrastructure projects, including roads, outer-island electrification, and airport development; the .tv Corp. also became a major shareholder in Air Fiji, which would have the exclusive right to provide air service to Tuvalu for five years.

Internationally, the government continued to express concern over the implications of global warming for low-lying states and criticized Australia for its unwillingness to develop a systematic relocation scheme for Tuvalu residents in the event that Tuvalu's islands became uninhabitable. Scientific evidence, however, suggested that Tuvalu had changed little in eight years.

Though Tuvalu was admitted as the 54th member of the British Commonwealth of Nations in 2000, its formal induction was deferred when the October 2001 Commonwealth Heads of Government Meeting planned for Brisbane, Australia, was canceled following the terrorist attacks in the U.S. Tuvalu established its mission at the United Nations in New York City.

(BARRIE MACDONALD)

UGANDA

Area: 241,038 sq km (93,065 sq mi)
Population (2001 est.): 23,986,000
Capital: Kampala
Head of state and government: President Yoweri Museveni, assisted by Prime Minister Apolo Nsibambi

The last victim of the Ebola virus, which had ravaged northern districts of Uganda in the previous year, recovered in January 2001. A month later the epidemic was officially declared to be at an end; of the 426 people infected, 224 of them had died.

A presidential election was held on March 12. Though there were six candidates, including Pres. Yoweri Museveni, only one, Kiiza Besigye, a founding member of Museveni's National Resistance Movement (NRM) and a former close associate of the president, appeared to offer a serious challenge. Prior to the election Besigye's supporters underwent considerable harassment, and independent observers reported numerous cases of irregularities in the conduct of the election. Nevertheless, they concluded that these instances did not have any significant impact on the election outcome. Museveni captured 69.3% of the votes to Besigye's 27.8%. Relations between Uganda and Rwanda, its former ally in the war in the Democratic Republic of the Congo (DRC), worsened after allegations were made that Besigye's campaign had been financed by Rwanda, an accusation that was vehemently denied.

On April 16 a UN panel appointed to inquire into the illegal exploitation of the DRC's natural resources called upon the UN Security Council to use "strong measures, including sanctions" against Uganda, Rwanda, and Burundi for looting the DRC's mineral reserves. These charges appeared to carry no weight with aid donors.

Approval of Uganda's campaign against HIV/AIDS was reflected in the decision to locate an international treatment and training centre in Kampala. The work there would be overseen by a coalition consisting of the Academic Alliance for AIDS Care and Prevention in Africa, Uganda's Makerere University, and the Infectious Diseases Society of America.

Minister of Finance Gerald Sendawula presented his budget on June 14. His aim was to remedy the decline in Uganda's economic growth rate, which in 2000 had fallen below the estimated 7% owing to a rise in oil prices and a fall in the price of coffee, Uganda's chief export earner. A timely boost to Uganda's economic prospects was provided by the announcement that a consortium known as Eagle Drill, led by Canada's Heritage Oil Corp., had carried out a four-year study of the Semliki River Valley on the western border and had found indications that significant reserves of oil were located there. The consortium planned to carry out tests until January 2002 and to start drilling in Lake Albert in March of that year.

On June 26 parliamentary elections were held. Once again, with all the resources of the government at its disposal and with opposition groups forbidden to operate as parties, Museveni's "no-party" NRM won an overwhelming victory, claiming 230 of the 292 seats, including those to which candidates were indirectly elected by the army, by women, and by other selected groups.

(KENNETH INGHAM)

UKRAINE

Area: 603,700 sq km (233,100 sq mi)
Population (2001 est.): 48,767,000
Capital: Kiev
Chief of state: President Leonid Kuchma
Head of government: Prime Ministers Viktor Yushchenko and, from May 29, Anatoly Kinakh

Ukraine in 2001 was marked by high-level political conflict and a notable improvement in economic performance but continuing social problems. On January 19 Pres. Leonid Kuchma dismissed Yuliya Tymoshenko, a deputy premier for the energy and fuel sector. Tymoshenko, a former colleague of disgraced former prime minister Pavlo Lazarenko, was arrested a month later and accused of having passed a bribe to Lazarenko. She was released on March 27, however, after a district court in Kiev annulled the original arrest warrant. Tymoshenko was widely regarded as a possible presidential contender when Kuchma's second term expired in 2004.

The president continued to face political fallout from the disappearance in September 2000 of dissident journalist Georgy Gongadze—who had been investigating Lazarenko—and from recordings that allegedly had captured Kuchma's voice sanctioning Gongadze's elimination. The tapes had been taken

Mikhailo Markiv/AFP Worldwide

Yuliya Tymoshenko, former deputy premier for the energy and fuel sector in Ukraine, receives flowers from well-wishers as she leaves prison in Kiev on March 27.

out of the country by a former presidential bodyguard and later made public. On January 10 officials stated that a headless corpse found outside Kiev in November 2000 was most likely that of the missing journalist. A protest movement arose, and tents pitched by activists on Kiev's main street had to be forcibly removed by the militia on March 1. The largest demonstration, on March 9—part of a new movement called Ukraine Without Kuchma—led to fierce clashes between demonstrators and the police close to the presidential administration building. By the summer the protests appeared to have died down somewhat. Several officials were dismissed in the aftermath of the Gongadze scandal, including Leonid Derkach, head of the Security Service, and Interior Minister Yury Kravchenko. In mid-April the U.S. granted political asylum to the bodyguard as well as to Gongadze's widow and two children.

The political turmoil continued when, on April 26, the parliament passed a vote of no-confidence in Prime Minister Viktor Yushchenko, probably the most pro-Western figure in Kuchma's cabinet. The parliamentary resolution, which was proposed by the Communist faction and passed 263–69, also accused the cabinet of having failed to ameliorate the economic situation. Yushchenko was replaced by Anatoly Kinakh, who subsequently formed an electoral bloc called Our Ukraine to contest the 2002 parliamentary elections. It remained unclear whether this bloc was opposed to the continuation of the Kuchma presidency.

Economic performance in Ukraine improved in the first half of 2001. Gross domestic product rose by 9% during 2001, following a growth figure of 6% for the year 2000. According to Prime Minister Kinakh, wages increased by almost 17% between January and July, and real income rose by 8.5%. Inflation remained at about 6%, and although the state debt had fallen, it continued to exceed the 50 billion hryvnia (about $9.4 billion) mark. The improved economic performance might be linked to the expansion of Russian business enterprises into Ukraine, but it had not yet offset the general decline in living standards that had characterized the independence period. By mid-August Ukraine had already surpassed its grain production target of 35 million metric tons for the 2001 harvest, which also added to the improved performance of the agricultural sector over the year 2000.

In early February Ukraine dismantled its last Tu-160 strategic bomber at a base near Kiev. The government accepted responsibility for the accidental downing of a Russian commercial airliner by a stray missile on October 4. The plane was flying from Israel to Russia but was hit while flying over the Black Sea. Defense Minister Oleksandr Kuzmuk resigned three weeks later over the incident, and he was replaced by Chief of Staff Volodymyr Shkidchenko on a temporary basis.

Pope John Paul II visited Ukraine in the summer and, in beatification ceremonies in the city of Lviv, paid tribute to some 27 Greek Catholic priests who were victims of the Soviet secret police in the early postwar years. The pontiff also tried to reconcile the Orthodox and Catholic factions in Ukraine. In the social sphere, Médicins sans Frontières (Doctors Without Borders) sponsored an AIDS-awareness campaign in March on the heels of an announcement that over 250,000 Ukrainians were HIV-positive, the highest rate per capita in the countries of the former U.S.S.R.

(DAVID R. MARPLES)

UNITED ARAB EMIRATES

Area: 83,600 sq km (32,280 sq mi)
Population (2001 est.): 3,108,000
Capital: Abu Dhabi
Chief of state: President Sheikh Zaid ibn Sultan an-Nahayan
Head of government: Prime Minister Sheikh Maktum ibn Rashid al-Maktum

On March 13, 2001, the U.A.E. Offsets Group, a government agency, signed a $3.5 billion agreement with Qatar to develop natural gas from Qatar's North Field and import it by a 350-km (217-mi) undersea pipeline to Abu Dhabi and Dubayy emirates. Though the American company Enron and the European firm TotalFinaElf were the original partners in this "Dolphin" project, Enron withdrew in May. Qatar's gas, which was expected to flow by 2004 or 2005, would meet important United Arab Emirates economic needs and help to solidify an already strong political relationship.

Meanwhile, the U.A.E. became the number-one trader among Persian Gulf states, surpassing even Saudi Arabia, due primarily to a high level of reexports, notably textiles, electronics, and gold. One-quarter of U.A.E. imports were reexported, and Iran was a major customer. Among all Arab states, the U.A.E. became the number one importer and the number two exporter. In addition, it ranked second (behind Qatar) in per capita income. The U.A.E. also led the Arab world in Internet use.

In July 2001 a high-level official U.A.E. delegation led by Minister of State for Foreign Affairs Sheikh Hamdan ibn Zayid, a son of the president, visited Tehran to congratulate Mohammad Khatami on his reelection as president of Iran. The visit was also symbolic politically—it was the first group of senior emissaries to arrive in Iran in nearly a decade. Though the U.A.E.-Iranian dispute over the islands of Abu Musa and the two Tunbs continued, the atmosphere and public rhetoric improved.

(WILLIAM A. RUGH)

UNITED KINGDOM

Area: 244,101 sq km (94,248 sq mi)
Population (2001 est.): 59,953,000
Capital: London
Chief of state: Queen Elizabeth II
Head of government: Prime Minister Tony Blair

Domestic Affairs. In 2001 Tony Blair, the United Kingdom's prime minister since 1997, confirmed his place as the towering figure in British politics both by leading the Labour Party to its second successive landslide election victory (*see* Sidebar) and by winning overwhelming political and public support for his international role in the fight against terrorism following the terrorist attacks in the United States on September 11.

Blair's year had started less auspiciously, with two major shocks. On January 24 he dismissed Peter Mandelson as Northern Ireland secretary. Mandelson had been accused of giving misleading information about his contacts with two controversial Indian businessmen, the Hinduja brothers, over their applications for British passports. For more than a decade, Mandelson had been one of Blair's closest political associates. Following Mandelson's earlier resignation in December 1998, Blair had provoked criticism by restoring his colleague to the cabinet just 10 months later. On March 9 the report of an official inquiry into the affair cleared Mandelson of any impropriety in his dealings with the Hindujas. It was too late for the former minister, however, and Mandelson acknowledged that his future lay outside the ranks of government.

By this time Blair was engulfed in a more enduring domestic crisis. On February 20 the U.K.'s first case of foot-and-mouth disease in 20 years was diagnosed among pigs at an abattoir in Essex, 64 km (40 mi) northeast of London. (*See* AGRICULTURE: *Special Report.*) It turned out that the disease had spread to many parts of the U.K. At its peak in March, over 40 new cases a day were being confirmed. For a while, town dwellers were advised to stay away from the countryside, particularly the normally popular—and heavily infected—tourist destinations of Devon, in the southwest of England, and the Lake District, in the northwest. As a result, much of rural

A pub owner in Oldham, Eng., surveys damage to her establishment that occurred during race riots in the city in late May.

Britain suffered a double loss—the destruction of millions of pigs and sheep in the infected areas and the short-term collapse of tourist income. The rest of Britain, notably London, also suffered a loss of income as overseas tourists, especially from the U.S., decided not to go to the U.K. for the time being.

So intense was the crisis that Blair took the unprecedented step (for peacetime) of obtaining parliamentary approval to postpone for five weeks local elections due to be held on May 3. This was also the widely expected date for the general election, which was postponed until June 7. By late April the number of new cases had declined to fewer than 20 a day, but the disease lingered through the summer. By September the total number of infected farms had passed 2,000, which made it the worst foot-and-mouth outbreak on record. During the last three months of the year, however, no new cases were reported, and the outbreak was officially declared to be over by year's end.

Following Labour's reelection on June 7, Blair made a number of changes to his cabinet. He promoted David Blunkett (*see* BIOGRAPHIES) from education secretary to home secretary, moved Jack Straw from home secretary to foreign secretary, and demoted Robin Cook from foreign secretary to leader of the House of Commons (a position that mainly involved managing day-to-day government business in Parliament). John Prescott and Gordon Brown retained their positions as deputy prime minister and chancellor of the Exchequer, respectively. A record 7 of the 23 members of Blair's new cabinet were women.

The front ranks of the Conservative Party took longer to sort out. At 7:30 AM on June 8, as the scale of his party's election defeat became clear, William Hague announced his intention to resign as party leader. Five candidates stood in the contest to succeed him. Following two early rounds of voting, in July three candidates remained: Kenneth Clarke, the former chancellor, who argued that the Conservatives needed to become more centrist and pro-European; Michael Portillo, the former defense secretary and onetime right-winger, who argued that the party should be less authoritarian and socially more liberal; and Iain Duncan Smith (*see* BIOGRAPHIES), who had no government experience and who retained his right-wing, anti-European Union (EU) views. On July 17, 59 Conservative MPs voted for Clarke, 54 for Duncan Smith, and 53 for Portillo.

Clarke and Duncan Smith went forward to a runoff ballot in which, for the first time, the party's 320,000 local members decided the victor. The result was announced on September 13. On a 79% turnout, Duncan Smith defeated Clarke 61–39%. Clarke and Portillo both declined to serve in Duncan Smith's shadow cabinet, as did a number of other prominent Conservative MPs, fearing that the party would be too right-wing for them. Duncan Smith's first major act was to give Blair full support in his policy toward terrorism. As a result, normal political contest was placed in abeyance, as were all attempts to make an early assessment of Duncan Smith's skills as a partisan opposition leader.

On the night of May 26, the U.K.'s generally good relations between its different racial groups were jolted by street battles between groups of whites and Asians in the northern city of Oldham. In the days that followed, riots took place in Leeds, Burnley, and Bradford. Although the riots subsequently died down, they provided a grim reminder that all was not well, especially in northern inner-city areas that contained significant amounts of poverty, bad housing, and unemployment.

On November 8 Henry McLeish resigned as Scotland's first minister following allegations that he had improperly claimed £36,000 (£1 = about $1.42) in office expenses while he was a member of Parliament at Westminster. On November 22 Jack McConnell, Scotland's education minister, became the country's new first minister, following his election as the new leader of Scotland's Labour Party.

The Economy. In common with much of the world, the British economy experienced a slowdown in 2001, starting in the summer but becoming more severe after September 11. At 2%, however, the growth recorded for the year as a whole compared well with most other industrialized countries. Before September most service sectors prospered, although the tourist-related businesses in parts of the U.K. were badly affected by the foot-and-mouth disease outbreak, which reduced access to the countryside during the spring and the early summer months. Airlines and hotels suffered in the immediate aftermath of the terrorist attacks in the U.S. in September. Many manufacturers, however, found it hard to increase sales, especially exports, at a time when the pound sterling was widely regarded as overvalued against the euro, the EU's single currency, at around £ = €1.60 throughout the year.

By midyear, unemployment had fallen below 5% (according to the definition set by the International Labour Organization), but then it started to rise gradually as the effects of the economic slowdown made themselves felt. Inflation remained steady at 2–2.5%. This allowed the Bank of England to reduce its main "repo" rate in stages from 6% in January to 5% in July. Following the events of September 11, the bank authorized two further quarter-point re-

ductions in quick succession, followed by an additional half-point reduction on November 8, to take the rate to 4%, its lowest since 1963. This helped to sustain consumer confidence as well as reduce the cost for home buyers. In addition, retail sales leading up to Christmas were well above those in 2000.

Speaking to Labour's annual conference on October 2, Blair held out the prospect of a referendum before the next election (to be held by May 2006 at the latest) on whether Great Britain should adopt the euro. He continued to say that the decision would depend on the achievement of five economic conditions, of which the most important was that there be sustained convergence between the economies of the U.K. and the 12 euro-zone countries.

In October Railtrack—a privatized company floated in 1996 to run Britain's railway tracks and stations—collapsed as the costs of improving safety in the wake of serious crashes in 1999 and 2000 spiraled beyond the company's capacity to fund improvements. This was the first failure of a major company established during the wave of privatizations in the 1980s and '90s. Stephen Byers, the transport sec-

retary, announced that a new company would be established as a nonprofit trust to run the tracks and stations.

Foreign Affairs. As soon as the terrorist attacks took place on September 11, Blair committed Great Britain to full support of the United States. The prime minister agreed to deploy British military forces, including bombers and undercover troops. Blair and Straw engaged in intense diplomatic activity, in coordination with U.S. Pres. George W. Bush's administration, in order to maximize the coalition against the al-Qaeda terrorist group in Afghanistan. Between them in the weeks following September 11, Blair and Straw visited Russia, Pakistan, India, Oman, Egypt, Iran, Syria, Saudi Arabia, and Israel. In addition, they helped to secure NATO and EU support for military action against the terrorists. Blair's visit to Damascus in October to meet Syria's president, Bashar al-Assad, was the first in modern times by a British prime minister. Despite some embarrassment at a joint press conference—when Assad and Blair made clear their different views of what constituted "terrorism," especially in the context of the dispute between Israel and the Palestinians—their private

The British Election of 2001

On June 7, 2001, the U.K.'s Labour Party won a second consecutive landslide victory over the Conservatives. Although Labour's majority in Parliament was reduced fractionally, from 179 to 167 in the 659-seat House of Commons, this was still a massive victory by historical standards. It was larger than that achieved by any party in the 60 years prior to Labour's return to power in 1997.

Labour won 413 seats (6 fewer than four years earlier), while the Conservatives claimed 166 (a net increase of just one). The Liberal Democrats took 52 seats, 6 more than in 1997. This gave the House of Commons its highest number of third-party members since 1929. Labour's victory was less emphatic in terms of votes cast. The party's share of the total vote across the U.K. was 40.7% (down 2.5% from 1997), while the Conservatives won 31.7% (up 1%) and the Liberal Democrats tallied 18.3% (up 1.5%). (Smaller parties won 9.3% of the total vote and 28 seats.) Despite its huge majority in terms of seats, Labour's share of the popular vote was lower than that achieved by any other victorious party since 1974.

Labour's main achievement during the campaign was to consolidate its support among the United Kingdom's traditionally Conservative-voting middle classes. Such voters dominate the swing seats that tend to determine the outcome of general elections. Labour's success in managing the country's economy over the previous four years—with falling unemployment, low inflation, and the lowest interest rates for home buyers in 30 years—together

with promises of significantly higher spending on health, education, and public transport in the years ahead proved decisive in retaining the support of these voters and hence almost all the seats the party had gained in 1997.

In contrast, the Conservatives were handicapped by past failings and an unpopular leader. Opinion polls found that most voters continued to blame the pre-1997 Conservative administration, rather than the post-1997 Labour government, for Britain's continuing problems, especially the inferior quality of its public services. Moreover, William Hague, who had been elected Conservative leader following the party's defeat in 1997, turned out to be a vote loser. He was a sharp, quick-witted debater in the House of Commons, but most voters watching him on television regarded him as too lightweight to become prime minister.

One feature of this election that shocked people from all parties was the sharp fall in turnout. Just 59% of registered electors cast their votes. This was 12 percentage points lower than in 1997 and by far the lowest general election turnout since the advent of universal adult suffrage in 1928. The decline of ideology and firm, class-based party loyalties, the lack of positive enthusiasm toward Labour, the continuing unpopularity of the Conservatives, and polls showing that Labour was certain to be reelected by a large majority were all cited as contributory reasons for the jump in the number of nonvoters.

(PETER KELLNER)

talks paved the way for fresh diplomatic moves, including those by the United States, to advance the peace process in the Middle East. These were subsequently disrupted, however, by continued suicide bombing raids organized by radical Palestinians and by reprisals by Israeli forces.

Blair received strong support for his antiterrorist strategy from the Conservatives and Liberal Democrats in the House of Commons, but a small minority of MPs from Blair's own Labour Party expressed opposition to military action. A substantially larger block of Labour (and also Liberal Democrat) MPs opposed Blair's willingness (announced by his media spokesman on May 2) to support the development by the U.S. of its proposed National Missile Defense system. The prime minister received widespread support, however, both within and beyond his party, for setting out an ambitious vision for global action beyond the fight against terrorism.

Northern Ireland. On October 23 the Irish Republican Army (IRA) announced that it had decommissioned a portion of its arsenal. Although no details were published, the Independent International Commission on Decommissioning (IICD) confirmed that "we have now witnessed an event—which we regard as significant—in which the IRA has put a quantity of arms completely beyond use. The material in question includes arms, ammunition, and explosives." The action was believed to have involved the injection of concrete into two IRA arms dumps in Ireland. Blair described the IRA's decision as "a very significant milestone." The following day John Reid, the Northern Ireland secretary, announced that some police and army watchtowers in Northern Ireland would be dismantled and that some terrorist escaped prisoners would be granted an amnesty. David Trimble, the leader of the Ulster Unionist Party (UUP), said his party would resume its place on the Northern Ireland Executive.

This rapid sequence of events revived the peace process at a critical time. For much of the year there had been deadlock, with the Unionists threatening to withdraw completely from the executive in protest against the IRA's refusal to start decommissioning its weapons and the IRA saying it would not be forced to act in response to Unionist ultimatums.

Trimble had to tread a narrow line between destroying the peace process and losing unionist support to the rival Democratic Unionist Party (DUP), which blamed him for conceding too much to the nationalists. The U.K. general election in June produced a shift in Northern Ireland, with its own distinct party structure, toward militancy. Among unionist parties the UUP lost 4 of its 10 seats, while the DUP gained 3 seats to end up with 5. Among nationalist parties the Social and Democratic Labour Party (SDLP) retained its three seats but, for the first time, saw its support overtaken by that of Sinn Fein, the political arm of the IRA, which doubled its representation to end up with four seats. Sinn Fein MPs, however, continued their refusal to take their seats in the House of Commons, as to do so would have required them to swear an oath of allegiance to the British crown.

On July 1 Trimble resigned as first minister in protest against the IRA's inaction; twice Reid suspended the Northern Ireland Executive for 24 hours—in August and September—in order to buy time. Under the terms of the 1998 Good Friday Agreement, such suspensions allowed a six-week breathing space without the need for more drastic action. After the September suspension, however, Reid warned that without a resumption

mounting pressure to act. Two external events helped to tilt the balance of debate inside the IRA and Sinn Fein. The first was the capture of three IRA members in Colombia, where they were accused of forging links with the Revolutionary Armed Forces of Colombia (FARC) guerrillas who financed many of their operations by dealing in drugs. This embarrassed Sinn Fein, whose tough antidrug policies in Ireland had helped them gain popular support on low-income housing estates. Second, the September 11 terrorist attacks led to increased pressure from the United States on the IRA to give up its weapons. On September 19 the IRA offered to "intensify [its] engagement" with the IICD.

One month later, and just 48 hours before the Ulster Unionist deadline, the IICD reported that decommissioning had in fact taken place. This prompted the Unionists to agree to rejoin, and therefore effectively to revive, the executive and to nominate Trimble to resume his position as first minister. A minority within his own party, together with the whole of the rival DUP, opposed him, but

A Protestant father and son stand on a railing in front of a large Loyalist mural in Belfast, N.Ire., on October 24.

AP/Wide World Photos

of cooperation between unionists and nationalists, the peace process might collapse altogether.

Trimble threatened to provoke this very outcome if decommissioning had not started by October 25. As this deadline approached, the IRA came under

he was supported by most of his party as well as the SDLP, Sinn Fein, and the small cross-community Alliance Party. On November 6 after four days of wrangling and legal maneuvers, the assembly reelected Trimble as first minister.

(PETER KELLNER)

UNITED STATES

Area: 9,363,364 sq km (3,615,215 sq mi), including 204,446 sq km of inland water but excluding the 155,534 sq km of the Great Lakes that lie within U.S. boundaries
Population (2001 est.): 286,067,000; significant revision based on the 2000 census
Capital: Washington, D.C.
Head of state and government: Presidents Bill Clinton and, from January 20, George W. Bush

Resilience had been a fundamental element of the American character from colonial times, but in 2001 the United States' ability to recover from adversity was severely tested. Its national economy, weary from years as the engine of world growth, finally slipped into recession. An energy crisis threatened further disruption, producing major bankruptcies. Terrorist attacks on September 11 coupled with a subsequent public health scare sent shock waves across the nation; the dispirited American morale slowed economic activity further, and the U.S. was soon plunged into a distant Asian war against an implacable fundamentalist regime.

Within weeks, however, the country had righted its listing self-confidence. Security measures gradually began restoring trust in public institutions. A series of government economic measures, including 11 interest-rate reductions and substantial emergency spending, established a foundation under the rocky economy. The Taliban regime in Afghanistan was rapidly uprooted and dispersed by a devastating show of American military technology. By year's end the United States was on the road to recovery, its position as the world's economic, cultural, and military leader not only restored but burnished in a year of challenges.

Security Crisis. Authorities responded immediately to the September 11 events, bolstering safety measures at public buildings, upgrading screening at airports, freezing assets of groups with suspected terrorist ties, and detaining more than 1,000 noncitizens for questioning. The measures included such extraordinary steps as the granting of authority to air force generals to shoot down hijacked civilian airliners and a provision for wartime military tribunals to try suspected alien terrorists. Some measures prompted criticism from civil liberties groups, but public opinion polls showed that the measures were widely supported.

In a September 20 address to Congress, Pres. George W. Bush announced the creation of an Office of Homeland Security under former Pennsylvania governor Tom Ridge to coordinate the antiterrorism efforts of 40 federal agencies. (*See* BIOGRAPHIES.) Within days the new agency confronted a new threat when several employees of a tabloid newspaper publisher in Florida contracted anthrax, an infectious disease ordinarily confined to farm animals, via suspicious mail. Additional anthrax spores were soon discovered in a variety of places, including the offices of Senate Majority Leader Tom Daschle (*see* BIOGRAPHIES), post offices, and various news organizations. Most of the spores were traced to mail originating near Trenton, N.J., but a connection to the September 11 terrorism was never established. By year's end two forms of anthrax had killed 5 persons and sickened 14.

Congress approved a variety of measures to counter economic and security concerns following the terrorist attacks; $15 billion was appropriated to assist U.S. airline firms, including $5 billion in grants; lawmakers appropriated an immediate $40 billion in additional spending for a variety of causes, including stepped-up military activity and assistance to affected areas, such as New York City; and President Bush received authority to expend half of the funds at his discretion. Congress also authorized the use of force to respond to the attacks, provided for federal takeover of some 28,000 airport security workers, and approved an antiterrorism law that allowed expanded law-enforcement powers over money laundering, electronic and telephone eavesdropping, and detention of suspected terrorists.

By year's end the death toll from the attacks had been revised sharply downward. At one point unofficial estimates had projected up to 10,000 deaths in New York and 500 or more at the Pentagon near Washington. Authorities in December, while cautioning that the precise number of deaths might never be known, put the toll at nearly 2,900 in New York City, with an additional 189 at the Pentagon and 44 in Pennsylvania, where another hijacked plane crashed after passengers attempted to overpower the terrorists.

Domestic Issues. The September 11 events proved to be a critical turning point for President Bush and his administration. Bush was inaugurated in January after having lost the popular vote and enjoying the weakest mandate of any recent U.S. president. (*See* Sidebar.) Congress was nominally in Republican hands but was almost evenly divided. Bush surprised many observers by pushing an aggressively conservative agenda, including a 10-year, $1.6 trillion tax cut, expanded energy exploration, a faith-based social assistance initiative, and withdrawal from several international treaties.

During a visit to an elementary school in Sarasota, Fla., on the morning of September 11, Pres. George W. Bush receives word of the terrorist attacks from his chief of staff, Andy Card.

AP/Wide World Photos

Following compromise with congressional Democrats, Bush signed an 11-year, $1,350,000,000,000 tax reduction bill on June 7 that provided instant $300–$600 rebates to most taxpayers, reduced the four major marginal rates, repealed the estate tax, increased the child-care credit, and provided relief for married couples and incentives for savings.

In late May veteran Republican lawmaker Sen. James M. Jeffords of Vermont announced that he would leave the GOP and become an Independent caucusing with Senate Democrats. That turned the Senate, previously divided 50–50 but under Republican organization, over to a 50–49–1 configuration under Democratic control. Jeffords cited disappointment with conservative GOP policies. With Congress now officially divided along partisan lines, Bush's agenda bogged down over the summer, and the president, while still enjoying general popular support, was widely viewed as tentative and ineffective in his public appearances.

Within days of September 11, however, Bush had shed that image. He delivered a thoughtful eulogy to victims at the National Cathedral service in Washington, D.C., and won praise for his presence in an early visit to the World Trade Center site. Bush's September 20 speech to a special joint session of Congress received widespread acclaim for its eloquence and delivery and helped launch Bush's personal approval ratings in public opinion polls to record levels through the remainder of the year.

During the fall, measures responding to the terrorist assault were approved by Congress with only modest opposition, particularly legislation covering military preparedness and disaster relief. In the realm of ongoing domestic policy, however, entrenched partisan arguments stopped passage of numerous bills, including several that had been debated for years. Among legislation failing to pass Congress during 2001 were the president's energy security bill (which included oil exploration in an Alaskan wilderness area), campaign finance reform, fast-track trade-negotiation authority, Bush's faith-based social initiative, an agriculture subsidy bill, a federal patients' bill of rights, and a fiscal stimulus bill that administration partisans said was vital to the national economic recovery.

At year's end Congress did approve a compromise education-reform act cosponsored by Democratic Sen. Edward Kennedy of Massachusetts. The bill required for the first time annual reading and mathematics testing for students in grades three through eight nationwide. It also required school districts to close the gap between poor and middle-class achievement and mandated that consistently underperforming schools allot part of their federal financial assistance to tutoring or providing transportation to other schools. (*See* EDUCATION: *Special Report.*)

Debate over the wisdom and ethics of advanced scientific research grew in intensity during the year. The U.S. House of Representatives approved a bill banning cloning of humans from embryos and prohibiting creation of cloned embryos for research, but the Senate delayed the measure. Under pressure to take a position, President Bush announced in August that he would allow federal funding only for research on the approximately 60 colonies of embryo cells that had been already created, saying he did not believe taxpayer dollars should support further destruction of human embryos. A National Academy of Sciences panel quickly published a report detailing problems with the Bush position, and little was settled on the subject.

Recent FBI figures revealed that the incidence of serious crime had remained virtually unchanged following eight years of significant decline. The figures showed a modest 0.3% reduction in seven index crimes during the first half of 2001. On June 11 Timothy McVeigh (*see* OBITUARIES)—the main perpetrator of the 1995 Oklahoma City, Okla., bombing of the Alfred P. Murrah Federal Building that killed 168 persons—was executed at a U.S. prison in Terre Haute, Ind. It was the first federal execution since 1963. A second federal prisoner, Juan Raul Garza, convicted of three 1993 drug-related murders, was put to death eight days later in the same prison.

Republican businessman Michael Bloomberg (*see* BIOGRAPHIES) prevailed in the highest-profile election of 2001, the race to succeed Rudolph Giuliani as mayor of New York City. Bloomberg spent a record $69 million of personal funds on the campaign. The year's most bizarre political story involved the disappearance from Washington, D.C., of a 24-year-old government intern, Chandra Levy, shortly before she was to return home to Modesto, Calif. Her parents hired lawyers and investigators and turned a glaring media spotlight on their hometown congressman, Democratic Rep. Gary Condit, who eventually admitted to a "close relationship" with the missing woman. Levy remained missing at year's end, and Condit announced that he would launch an uphill bid for reelection.

The Economy. The national economic expansion ended with a whimper during 2001. A panel of the National Bureau of Economic Research (NBER) declared in November that the nation's economic growth had ended the previous March, exactly 10 years after it had started, which made it the longest-running expansion since the organization began keeping records in 1854. Government figures showed that gross domestic product had increased by a modest 1.2% in the first quarter and an anemic 0.3% in the second, followed by a 1.3% retraction in the third quarter. Though recessions had traditionally been declared after two consecutive quarters of negative growth, NBER economists, noting continued economic deterioration, cited other factors in their assessment.

The trauma of September 11 effectively kicked the national economy while it was down. The events further shook consumer confidence, which had been declining, and markedly reduced personal and business travel, entertainment expenditures, and other economic activity. The national jobless rate, which had bottomed at 3.9% in 2000, had started to climb early in the year; it jumped from 4.9% to 5.4% in October, the biggest one-month jump in two decades. By December unemployment had soared to 5.8%, the highest level in six years. Another victim of the terrorist-exacerbated recession was the short-lived federal budget surplus: after a record $237 billion in black ink during fiscal 2000, the U.S. ended fiscal 2001 on September 30 with a fast-diminishing $127 billion surplus, with many fiscal 2002 projections anticipating a return to deficit spending.

Even so, the recession's impact was cushioned by several events. Fearing an overexuberant stock market and inflation, the nation's Federal Reserve System had nudged up interest rates six times in 1999–2000. In 2001, however, the Fed sharply reversed field and lowered its key federal funds rate on 11 occasions, from 6.5% to 1.75%, in a desperate attempt to revive the failing national economy. The actions provided a ripple effect that lowered borrowing costs across the board for credit cards, mortgages, and businesses. Additionally, as the recession reduced energy demand, oil prices began dropping worldwide, providing further relief to consumers. The nation's major automobile manufacturers began offering no-interest loans in a successful effort to maintain high demand, and new auto sales continued through the last months of 2001 at record levels. The federal government further contributed with cash tax rebates and at least $60 billion in emergency spending following the terrorist attacks.

By year's end some economists were predicting imminent resumption of national economic expansion. Two major measurements of consumer confidence were rising sharply in December. The Dow Jones Industrial Average, which had dipped as low as 8,235 in the wake of September 11, finished the year over 10,000 and rising. The national inflation rate dropped back to a modest 2.6%, and productivity gains remained strong, which led several economists to predict an end to the recession as the country put memories of the attacks behind it.

The recession helped avoid a widely predicted energy disaster in California and neighbouring states. As the year began, California was suffering under a mishandled deregulation of electricity that led to severe power shortages and the bankruptcy of a major state public utility. Rolling blackouts plagued the state during January, and many analysts predicted further outages and economic disruption during the summer, when air-conditioner use would be high. A combination of state government assistance to the utilities, a cool summer, upgrading of electrical distribution line efficiency, reduced usage due to recession and conservation, and the worldwide energy surplus largely prevented serious energy incidents.

During the height of the crisis, California Gov. Gray Davis denounced out-of-state energy companies for taking advantage of the state and its consumers, and he specifically named the Houston, Texas-based Enron Corp. Late in 2001 Enron—the seventh largest American corporation, with over $100 billion in revenue in 2000—filed for Chapter 11 bankruptcy protection. The company, listing $49.5 billion in assets, became the largest company in U.S. history to go under. The failure was only tangentially related to its long-running exploitation of deregulated markets for wholesale natural gas and electricity. Analysts discovered that key company officials, while operating largely unregulated marketplaces trading derivative energy contracts, were simultaneous running private off-book partnerships and profiting personally, even while they overstated Enron profits. The company's failure was particularly hard on employees, many of whom had retirement funds tied up in near-worthless company stock.

The world's leading software company, Microsoft Corp., avoided a court-ordered breakup by settling its antitrust case with the Bush administration Justice Department. The company had been found guilty of monopolistic practices in a case brought by the Bill Clinton administration and ordered divided into at least two parts. An appeals court panel in June confirmed that Microsoft had monopoly power but disqualified the original trial judge for injudicious comments outside the courtroom. After Microsoft allowed computer makers to disable some parts of its Windows operating system and replace them with software from other firms, the replacement

Sen. James Jeffords (centre), who in late May switched his party affiliation from Republican to Independent, shown on June 5 with Democratic senators Ted Kennedy (left), Joseph Lieberman (second from right), and Christopher Dodd (right).

AP/Wide World Photos

(continued on page 516)

The U.S. Census of 2000

by Eric Schmitt

AP/Wide World Photos

The 2000 census of the United States revealed a nation that had become ethnically and racially more diverse as cities and suburbs filled with new immigrants. It also showed that the migration from the Frost Belt to the Sun Belt was continuing. About 44% of the nation's 30.5 million foreign-born residents, or 13.3 million people, arrived in the U.S. in the 1990s. By 2000 immigrants constituted 11% of the country's population, the largest share since the 1930s, and nearly one in five Americans did not speak English at home. Overall, the nation's population grew by about 13% to 281.4 million.

The Hispanic population rose 58% in the last decade, which brought it into rough parity, or better, with African Americans as the country's largest minority. U.S. Census Bureau figures showed that the number of Hispanics, who have Spanish-speaking ancestry but may belong to any race, soared to 35.3 million from the 22.4 million in the 1990 census. By contrast, the number of African Americans increased by about 16% to 34.7 million from the 30 million counted in the 1990 census. Demographers had long anticipated that Hispanics would supplant African Americans as the nation's largest minority, but earlier census reports had forecast that this would not happen until 2005.

While Hispanics remained concentrated primarily in the Southwest, California, Florida, and New York, new immigrants from Mexico and Central America moved to states such as North Carolina, Georgia, and Iowa, where the Hispanic population was almost nonexistent a decade ago. Hispanics often became a mainstay in many low-paying, labour-intensive industries. In Atlanta, Ga., and Memphis, Tenn., for instance, they dominated the construction and landscaping trades. In eastern North Carolina they processed hogs. In Arkansas they plucked chickens.

In the 2000 census, for the first time, Americans were allowed to identify themselves as a member of more than one race, choosing from six racial categories; this option was taken by nearly seven million people, about 2% of the overall population. Demographers concluded that the growing waves of immigrants and the increasing numbers of interracial marriages accounted for this result. The new multiracial measurement was especially striking in regard to young people. For example, African Americans aged 17 and younger were nearly four times as likely as those 50 and older to identify themselves as belonging to more than one race.

By permitting people to choose an array of racial identities—white, African American, Asian, American Indian, Alaska native, Pacific islander, native Hawaiian, or "some other race"—the 2000 census presented a matrix of 63 racial categories, compared with 5 a decade ago. The American Indian category offered one of the more interesting glimpses into the census's new racial classification. The number of American Indians and Alaska natives who defined themselves by only that category grew by 26% in the past decade to 2.5 million. When, however, the number of people who said they were part Indian were added, the total ballooned to 4.1 million, a 110% increase since 1990.

The changing face of the U.S. was reflected in cities, suburbs, and rural areas. For the first time, nearly half of the nation's 100 largest cities were home to more African Americans, Hispanics, Asians, and other minorities than to non-Hispanic whites. While the population of the country's fastest-growing cities, such as Las Vegas, Nev., and Phoenix, Ariz., increased in all racial and ethnic categories, the vast majority of U.S. cities —71 of the top 100—lost non-Hispanic white residents. As whites left many urban cores in the 1990s for suburbs and beyond, the nation's largest gained 3.8 million Hispanic residents, a 43% increase from a decade ago. Many cities, including Boston, Los Angeles, and Dallas, Texas, would have lost population in the 1990s were it not for large gains in the number of Hispanics.

The mixture of white flight from urban downtowns and the influx of Hispanics, in particular, underscored the extent to which immigration and higher birthrates among the foreign-born had changed the complexion of cities, fueling a renaissance in some urban centres and forcing civic leaders to confront difficult decisions on how to cope with a new and fast-changing citizenry. Overall, the nation's largest cities grew nearly twice as fast in the 1990s as in the 1980s, with three out of every four urban centres gaining population. In the cities with more than 100,000 people, however, the growth was uneven. Reversing a 50-year

U.S. Hispanic Population

Percent increase by county

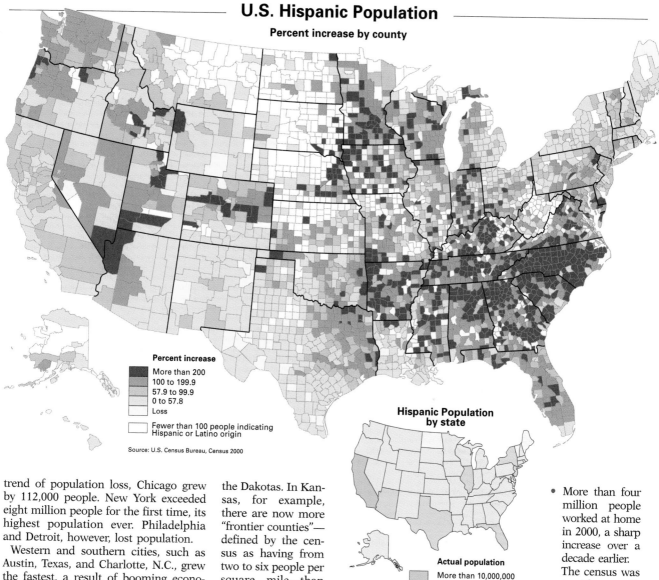

Percent increase

- More than 200
- 100 to 199.9
- 57.9 to 99.9
- 0 to 57.8
- Loss
- Fewer than 100 people indicating Hispanic or Latino origin

Source: U.S. Census Bureau, Census 2000

Hispanic Population by state

Actual population

- More than 10,000,000
- 1,000,000 to 9,999,999
- 10,000 to 999,999
- Less than 10,000

Source: U.S. Census Bureau, Census 2000

trend of population loss, Chicago grew by 112,000 people. New York exceeded eight million people for the first time, its highest population ever. Philadelphia and Detroit, however, lost population.

Western and southern cities, such as Austin, Texas, and Charlotte, N.C., grew the fastest, a result of booming economies and an influx of immigrants. Urban industrial centres in the Rust Belt, such as Cleveland, Ohio, and Pittsburgh, Pa., and such Middle Atlantic and Northeastern cities as Hartford, Conn., and Baltimore, Md., generally declined as jobs and people migrated elsewhere. A small but growing number of cities with declining populations, such as Pittsburgh and Philadelphia, began to embrace new strategies to attract immigrants to replenish shrinking neighbourhoods, fill labour shortages, and inject greater ethnic diversity into their communities.

Even as most cities were thriving in the 1990s, many rural areas, particularly in the Great Plains, continued to empty out. The Census Bureau found that 676 of the nation's 3,141 counties lost people. Most of the decline took place in wheat, ranching, and oil country in Texas, Oklahoma, Iowa, Nebraska, Kansas, Minnesota, and the Dakotas. In Kansas, for example, there are now more "frontier counties"—defined by the census as having from two to six people per square mile—than there were in 1890.

In a preview of official 2000 census data to be released in 2002 from the questionnaire known as the long form, the Census Bureau disclosed results of a test survey of 700,000 households. Highlights from that survey include the following:

- More than two million grandparents are rearing their grandchildren, the first time the Census Bureau has kept track of that statistic.
- In 2000, 82% of people aged 25 and older had graduated from high school and 25% had at least a bachelor's degree. In 1990 the figures were 75% and 20%, respectively.
- More than 90% of households owned a car, van, or truck in 2000, the highest share ever, and 18% owned three or more vehicles.

- More than four million people worked at home in 2000, a sharp increase over a decade earlier.

The census was not without political controversy. In March the Census Bureau decided against statistically adjusting the 2000 population tally. Several congressional Democrats and Democratic-leaning groups argued that adjusted figures should be used because the 2000 census, while touted as the most accurate in history, still missed millions of people, mainly racial minorities and renters, and double-counted others, mainly whites and homeowners. At stake was what population counts would be used to allocate federal aid and redraw congressional and other legislative districts. About $185 billion a year was distributed on the basis of population counts from the 1990 census.

Eric Schmitt is national immigration and census correspondent for the New York Times.

(continued from page 513)
judge approved a settlement allowing the company to stay intact.

Foreign Policy. Within hours of the September 11 attacks, the Bush administration began preparations for a military assault on the al-Qaeda network in Afghanistan and started assembling international support for the mission. The partners took pains to assure that it was international terrorists and their protectors who were targets, not Islam. In the end some 60 countries offered tangible assistance, including Muslim Pakistan as well as Russia, which provided access to military bases in nearby Tajikistan. The U.S. doubled its military presence in the region to 50,000 during the month the hostilities began.

Demands that the Afghan Taliban regime locate and turn over Osama bin Laden (*see* BIOGRAPHIES) to international forces were met by evasion, then refusal. U.S.-dominated military action started with cruise missile, bomber, and fighter jet attacks throughout Afghanistan on October 7, followed by continued military operations in support of the Northern Alliance Afghan resistance fighters. At the beginning U.S. preparations were met by a hailstorm of criticism and doubts; critics suggested that Americans would be repeating Russian mistakes in Afghanistan or would be bogged down in a Vietnam-style Asian conflict. Instead, the operation was largely completed in 11 weeks as the Taliban was driven from power, replaced by a UN-brokered coalition.

In his September 20 congressional speech, President Bush declared, "From this day forward, any nation that continues to harbor or support terrorism will be regarded by the U.S. as a hostile regime." By year's end neither Bin Laden nor Taliban leader Mullah Mohammad Omar had been located. While continuing to search for Taliban and al-Qaeda leadership in the area, the U.S. turned its attention toward other countries facilitating terrorist activity. The ongoing confrontation with rogue organizations and states, especially those believed to be developing chemical, biological, or nuclear weapons, continued to dominate world affairs.

Cooperation on Afghanistan was a highlight of improved U.S. relations with Russia. In mid-November, Russian Pres. Vladimir Putin visited Washington and Bush's ranch in Crawford, Texas. Talks appeared promising when Putin said he would consider allowing the U.S. to test a missile defense system even though the test would be an apparent violation of the 1972 Anti-Ballistic Missile (ABM) Treaty, provided the two countries could agree on nuclear weapons reductions. Bush announced that the U.S. would slash nuclear warheads from 7,000 to the 1,700–2,200 range over the next decade, and Putin hinted at similar reductions in the Russian 5,800-warhead arsenal. The two were never able to hammer out an agreement on the antimissile test, however, and in December Bush announced that the U.S. would withdraw from the treaty and thereby leave the way open for missile defense testing.

The long-running U.S. effort to broker a lasting peace in the Middle East appeared to collapse during the year. Talks between Israeli and Palestinian leaders sponsored by former president Clinton had fallen apart in late 2000, producing violence that escalated during 2001. After a period of inaction, the Bush administration attempted to revive talks but without success, and after September 11 Israeli advocates successfully likened Palestinian bombing and assaults to the terrorist attacks in the U.S. President Bush pointedly declined to condemn Israeli military responses against the Palestinian population and refused to meet with Palestinian leader Yasir Arafat.

Free-trade advocates scored a major advance at an international meeting in Doha, Qatar, when major countries agreed to begin a new three-year round of trade negotiations. The talks would be aimed at reducing agricultural trade barriers and industrial tariffs. The U.S. made concessions, putting its antidumping law under review in spite of opposition from American steel interests and agreeing that less-developed nations could override drug patents in the interests of public health. Most analysts declared that no new trade agreement could be negotiated, however, unless the U.S. Senate voted fast-track negotiating authority to President Bush. The U.S. normalized trade relations with China during the year after having cleared the way for China's membership in the World Trade Organization.

During 2001 the focus of war concerns shifted to Asia, including Afghanistan. U.S. military efforts aggravated the decades-long conflict between India and Pakistan, and the two countries, both possessing nuclear weapons, were at the brink of war at year's end. Ironically, in an effort to encourage cooperation in the Afghan operation, the U.S. had lifted sanctions imposed on both countries following their 1998 nuclear tests. Problems with North Korea, one of the world's last communist regimes, continued to fester and led to periodic threats of war against the U.S. and its allies, including Japan.

The Bush administration's efforts to build a coalition to support military measures in Afghanistan reversed what critics had labeled U.S. rejection of international solutions to world problems, including its refusal to sign the ABM Treaty and the Comprehensive Test Ban Treaty. Earlier in the year the Bush administration had officially rejected the Kyoto Protocol, suggesting that the anti-global-warming treaty would affect the global economy disproportionately. In late summer the U.S. sent a delegation to the UN World Conference Against Racism in Durban, S.Af., but walked out in protest against proposed conference resolutions calling for reparations to blacks for slavery and for condemnation of Israel for alleged racism against Palestinians.   (DAVID C. BECKWITH)

DEVELOPMENTS IN THE STATES

After close to a decade of uninterrupted sunny economic times, states were plunged into multiple new problem areas at the end of 2001. Most states started modest belt-tightening early in the year as the slackening national economy produced slow revenue growth with additional outlays remaining modest. Following the September 11 terrorist attacks, however, matters worsened dramatically, with revenues dropping as travel, commerce, incomes, and other state taxation sources were severely and adversely affected.

States also scrambled to revamp public safety and health security measures in the national emergency, beefing up security in public places and overhauling outdated emergency procedures. At year-end virtually all states were facing budget shortfalls for the year—either higher expenditures or lower revenues, or both—and many began spending cutbacks to balance their budgets. The problems complicated the always-thorny relationship between the federal government and the states over which level of government should have the authority and responsibility for handling aspects of the crisis.

All 50 states held regular legislative sessions during the year, and two dozen staged special sessions later, often to deal with budget and security problems. Democrats made gains in limited state elections, picking up governorships in New Jersey and Virginia previously held by Republicans and improving their status

Election Reform Debate in the U.S.

Amid calls for a radical overhaul of the U.S. electoral system, George W. Bush was inaugurated as president of the United States on Jan. 20, 2001. The 2000 presidential election exposed several deficiencies in the conduct of American elections: the possibility that a candidate could win more popular votes than his opponent and still lose the electoral college tally—Bush defeated Al Gore 271–266 despite winning 500,000 fewer votes nationwide; faulty and outdated election equipment—a General Accounting Office audit found that nearly three-fifths of voting sites had problems in 2000; a lack of uniform rules for election recounts; early and incorrect media projections; confusing ballot design, most notably in Florida, where possibly thousands of people were led to vote mistakenly for a candidate; and low voter turnout. As legislators throughout the U.S. debated election reform, by year's end media analyses of disputed ballots still showed the 2000 race too close to call.

Many proposed election reforms, such as the abolition of the electoral college and the creation of a national holiday for election day, were discarded quickly owing to a lack of support, though in early 2001 momentum in favour of reform suggested that major changes, such as a uniform national poll closing time, would be enacted by year's end. Of the more than 1,500 bills proposed in Congress and in all 50 states, however, few were enacted. Partisan wrangling hampered reform efforts early in the year. Receiving the most support were proposals to eliminate punch-card ballot systems, which had led to high rates of uncounted ballots and which tended to be concentrated in poorer areas, in favour of optical scanning systems. Some studies found that as many as two million votes were uncounted nationwide because of faulty election equipment. Despite the efforts of the bipartisan National Commission on Federal Election Reform, led by former presidents Gerald Ford and Jimmy Carter, by May the election reform movement had stalled in the U.S. Congress and in many states. In December, however, the House of Representatives overwhelmingly approved (362–63) a bill that provided funds to states to modernize election equipment and establish national voting standards, and at year's end many predicted that a compromise between the House and Senate would result in the enactment of election reforms in early 2002.

The most sweeping election reform package was adopted in Florida, the state that had endured a five-week standoff in the presidential election before Bush was declared the winner by a margin of only 537 votes after the Supreme Court halted a recount. On May 9 Florida Gov. Jeb Bush, the brother of the president, approved a uniform statewide ballot design and the elimination of punch cards in favour of optical scanners or other advanced technologies by 2002. The new law also established standardized procedures for the review of ballots during manual recounts—a key point of contention between the Gore and Bush camps. Nevertheless, the U.S. Commission on Civil Rights issued a report a few weeks later that criticized Florida election officials, finding them "grossly derelict" both before and during the November 2000 standoff. The commission's report, which was criticized by Republicans, also found that African Americans were 10 times more likely than white voters to have their votes uncounted and claimed that the reforms enacted in Florida would not entirely eliminate this disparity.

(MICHAEL LEVY)

Members of the Joint Selection Committee to Examine Election Issues study a sample ballot from a voting machine similar to ones used in Florida during the 2000 presidential election.

AP/Wide World Photos

in state legislatures. Entering 2002 the GOP would hold 27 governorships and the Democrats 21, with two independents. Party control of state legislatures was deadlocked, with Republicans and Democrats each controlling 17 states and 15 states under split control. (Nebraska had a nonpartisan unicameral legislature.)

Government Structures, Powers. Stung by criticism of 2000 election procedures, numerous states pursued reform measures early in 2001. (*See* Sidebar.) Florida, Georgia, and Maryland approved sweeping reforms, including complete overhauls of voting equipment statewide. Seven states, including California, either banned or phased out punch-card ballots. Ohio, Nevada, Tennessee, and Virginia clarified what counts as a vote on a punch card; Colorado, Kansas, Virginia, and Washington set up new rules for recounts; and Colorado, Florida, Indiana, Iowa, Kansas, Oregon, and South Dakota either established or upgraded statewide voter-registration databases. A consensus on proper steps was slow in arriving, however, and political considerations in Congress prevented federal assistance or leadership for state election reform. By year's end the momentum for reform had largely dissipated.

A majority of state legislatures enacted new redistricting plans for U.S. Congress and state legislative districts following tabulation of the 2000 U.S. census. (*See* Special Report.) In a key 5–4 decision, the U.S. Supreme Court ruled that states may concentrate African Americans, Hispanics, or other minorities in specific districts as long as they do so for political, not racial, reasons.

Government Relations. The U.S. Supreme Court again bolstered state powers against federal encroachment, ruling 5–4 in separate civil rights cases involving Alabama that states may not be sued for discriminating against employees with disabilities or for policies that have a "discriminatory effect" on racial minorities. In a setback for states, however, the high court ruled 5–4 in a Massachusetts case that tobacco companies have a free-speech right to advertise their products;

the federal government had preempted the issue, leaving states virtually powerless to restrict tobacco promotion, the court said.

The proper division between state and national government responsibilities was at the centre of numerous other controversies during the year. As states scrambled to fund security and health programs made necessary after September 11, they looked to the federal government for assistance, with mixed results. New York state was pledged $20 billion in U.S. aid for extraordinary expenses related to the World Trade Center disaster, but assistance to less-affected states lagged behind their expenses.

In early November, U.S. Attorney General John Ashcroft moved to invalidate Oregon's assisted-suicide law on grounds that the federal Controlled Substances Act barred doctors from prescribing lethal drugs to dying patients. Oregon voters had twice approved a Death with Dignity law, and more than 70 patients had taken advantage of it since 1997. State authorities obtained a temporary court order effectively barring federal intervention.

Security. States moved quickly to address public health and safety concerns arising from September 11 and its aftermath. Some 35 states named security directors or created task forces to help prevent and deal with terrorism, particularly biological threats. Physical security around state capitols, transportation terminals, and public buildings was stepped up.

After it was revealed that the September 11 terrorists had used driver's permits to open bank accounts and rent cars and apartments, several states immediately tightened rules for obtaining driver's licenses. A Florida executive order limited foreigners to a 30-day temporary permit while authorities investigated their identification. New Jersey stopped issuing licenses to immigrants whose visas were to expire within a year.

Finances. As the national economy slowed, legislators began modest belt-tightening measures early in the year. An unprecedented seven consecutive years of multibillion-dollar tax reductions came to an end as states enacted relatively minimal tax and spending changes during 2001 legislative sessions. The cautious outlook changed dramatically after September 11 as anticipated tax revenue plummeted, new security costs escalated, and social spending began to ascend.

Health and Welfare. Problems with managed health care continued to preoccupy state lawmakers, with a focus emerging

A San Francisco resident shops in the dark at an auto parts store during a statewide rolling blackout on March 19.

AP/Wide World Photos

on improving patient knowledge about plans and service. A majority of states set up information and complaint-resolution systems, often including publishing health maintenance organization (HMO) "report cards," provider profiles, and state-run ombudsman services. North Carolina became the 46th state to adopt a patients' bill of rights.

As states' fiscal problems mounted, additional states diverted their share of the 25-year, $207 billion tobacco settlement money away from public health and toward other needs. Maryland became the first state with a tobacco buyout, appropriating $5.9 million to wean tobacco farmers over to alternative crops such as grapes or raspberries. The 1996 federal welfare-reform act mandated a cutoff of assistance to recipients after five consecutive years, beginning in October 2001. But state welfare authorities reported that because of strong economic conditions over that period, few recipients were affected by the deadline. Massachusetts joined Maine in providing expanded services to HIV-positive patients on Medicaid, bidding to delay onset of full-blown AIDS. The Wisconsin Supreme Court upheld a novel order prohibiting a deadbeat dad from having any more children while he was on probation. The court's four male judges endorsed the court's ruling, while the three female jurists voted against it.

Law and Justice. After eight consecutive years of declining crime rates, incidence of major violent and property offenses leveled off during 2001. The number of inmates in state prisons nationwide also was flat as California inaugurated a new program to divert nonviolent drug offenders from incarceration to treatment. Nationwide, 66 convicts were executed.

By an 8–0 vote, the U.S. Supreme Court declared that federal law prohibited the use of marijuana as a medical treatment for diseases such as cancer, glaucoma, or AIDS. The ruling did not directly invalidate medical marijuana laws in nine states but allowed authorities to pursue violators even in those states on federal drug charges. Nevada became the first state to approve Internet gambling, another practice forbidden by federal law. State officials planned to overturn the federal law in court.

Energy and Environment. California's 1996 law partially deregulating the electricity industry put the state at the centre of a national crisis in early 2001. California had loosened regulation on power generators while retaining retail price caps, and that led to power shortages and financial trouble for several large utilities. In January state officials decided to buy more than $40 billion worth of electricity on behalf of Pacific Gas & Electric Co., Southern California Edison Corp., and San Diego Gas & Electric Co., all then suffering from high wholesale electricity prices. The state signed multiple-year contracts with energy producers that guaranteed delivery of electricity at set prices and thereby allowed the state to escape the spot market, where prices had soared to as high as $500 per megawatt hour. A combination of the contracts, conservation efforts, a cool summer, and declining energy prices helped the state avoid widely predicted blackouts, and by year's end the contracts were being criticized for overcommitting and overpaying for the electricity.

When California's problems spilled over into neighbouring states, Nevada repealed an electricity deregulation plan it had approved in 1999. Even so, Maryland, New York, Texas, and Virginia moved toward deregulation during the year, which brought to 24 the number of states pursuing a free market in electrical energy.   (DAVID C. BECKWITH)

URUGUAY

Area: 176,215 sq km (68,037 sq mi)
Population (2001 est.): 3,303,000
Capital: Montevideo
Head of state and government: President
Jorge Batlle Ibáñez

The year 2001 was a difficult one for Uruguay. Pres. Jorge Batlle Ibáñez's first full calendar year in office confronted him with a worsening of Uruguay's economic situation exacerbated by an outbreak of foot-and-mouth disease that seriously disrupted Uruguay's meat exports. The government had hoped that 2001 would bring modest economic growth after two years of recession. Unfortunately, the continued devaluation of the Brazilian currency—the real—and the deepening economic and political crisis in Argentina had adverse effects on both Uruguayan exports and tourism. With these internal and external conditions, unemployment skyrocketed to some 16%, and the gross domestic product rate was –1.1% for the first half of the year. The only good news on the economic front was the continued low inflation rate of 4–5%.

Batlle's approval rating remained relatively high by Uruguayan standards, owing in part to his continued support of a commission he established in 2000 to investigate the disappearance of some 180 Uruguayans during the period of military dictatorship from 1973 to 1985. The ruling Colorado Party's coalition with the Blanco Party remained intact despite strains produced by the stagnant economy. The leftist Broad Front coalition began to voice greater criticism of the administration's economic program and supported increased work stoppages by the labour unions. Nevertheless, Broad Front leader Tabaré Vázquez Rosas adopted a moderate tone on most issues in a clear effort to build on the coalition's more than 40% approval rating in the polls. He clearly had his eye on the next presidential election, which, however, would not take place until October 2004.

Uruguay qualified for the association football (soccer) World Cup finals to be held in 2002 in South Korea and Japan.

(MARTIN WEINSTEIN)

UZBEKISTAN

Area: 447,400 sq km (172,700 sq mi)
Population (2001 est.): 25,155,000
Capital: Tashkent
Chief of state and head of government:
President Islam Karimov, assisted by Prime
Minister Otkir Sultonov

Through much of 2001, Uzbekistan's position in the world community became more and more difficult. Although there was some understanding for the country's security concerns, it was criticized for its intransigence in the fields of economic reform, human rights, and restrictions on the information media and religious expression. Many international observers pointed out that the repressive policies of the Uzbek leadership were fueling the religious extremism that they feared. An international outcry occurred after the death of human rights activist Shovruk Ruzimuradov in police custody in July.

Relations with neighbouring Tajikistan and Kyrgyzstan worsened as citizens of those countries were injured or killed by Uzbek mines that were placed in border areas to hinder incursions by armed militants. Within Uzbekistan itself, arrests and trials of persons accused of religious extremism continued throughout the year. Leaflets of the banned Islamic group Hizb ut-Tahrir appeared in cities in various parts of the country, and numerous individuals were prosecuted on charges that they were members of the organization. Hizb ut-Tahrir activists insisted that they wanted to create an Islamic state in Central Asia by peaceful means, but the Uzbek authorities considered it a terrorist group.

Already in February, Uzbek officials announced that the continuing drought in the region would probably reduce the amount of cotton that would be produced in 2001, which would in turn affect Uzbekistan's foreign export earnings. In April the International Monetary Fund withdrew from Uzbekistan on the grounds that the Uzbek authorities had failed to implement genuine economic reform as prescribed by the Fund. Two months later the European Bank for Reconstruction and Development warned that it would reduce its level of invest-

ment if economic reform was not accelerated. The World Bank considered reducing its credit program for the same reason. While the international lending agencies expressed their dissatisfaction with the rate of reform, foreign investors were quietly withdrawing from Uzbekistan, and by the end of the year many international companies had either closed down or drastically reduced their activities. Many small businesses suffered when the tourism industry effectively collapsed after the beginning of the campaign against the Taliban and al-Qaeda in Afghanistan.

After the terrorist attacks in the United States, Uzbekistan quickly joined the international antiterrorist coalition, permitting U.S. forces the use of an air base near Karshi. According to official statements, the base was to be used for search and rescue operations, but by the end of October a small U.S. military presence had already been well established in Uzbekistan.

(BESS BROWN)

VANUATU

Area: 12,190 sq km (4,707 sq mi)
Population (2001 est.): 195,000
Capital: Vila
Chief of state: President John Bernard Bani
Head of government: Prime Ministers Barak
Sopé and, from April 13, Edward Natapei

Vanuatu faced a political crisis in March 2001 when Prime Minister Barak Sopé lost support in Parliament and the speaker, a Sopé supporter, refused to allow consideration of a vote of no confidence. After the acting chief justice of the Supreme Court ruled that the speaker's action was unconstitutional, Sopé's government was defeated and replaced by a coalition of the Vanua'aku Party and the Union of Moderate Parties led by Prime Minister Edward Natapei. In November police attempts to search for documents related to Sopé's controversial business dealings while in office were thwarted by armed villagers.

In late September 2001, Finance Minister Joe Carl met with representatives of the Organisation for Economic Cooperation and Development in Vila, where he expressed his concern over the pressure exerted by the OECD in demanding details of the island's international tax-haven revenue. In June 2000 the OECD had included Vanuatu on a list of nations that sheltered money-laundering activities and maintained unacceptable taxation structures and had threatened sanctions unless action was taken to address the situation. Carl complained that the OECD had not offered an alternative means whereby the country could raise revenue. In October 2001 Vanuatu was accepted for membership (effective in November) in the World Trade Organization. Vanuatu's annual exports totaled about $25 million, mostly coconut products, beef, cocoa, timber, and kava root. Tourism strengthened in the wake of violence and political instability in neighbouring Fiji and the Solomon Islands. In November Natapei rejected suggestions that Vanuatu might offer refugee-processing facilities for asylum seekers (mostly from Afghanistan and Iraq) arriving in Australian waters via Indonesia.

The release of the 1999 census report indicated that the population of Vanuatu at that time was 186,678, an increase of 31% over 1989.

(BARRIE MACDONALD)

Pope John Paul II prepares to send a message to Roman Catholics in Oceania on November 22; the message, which included a one-paragraph apology for sexual abuse by Roman Catholic clergy, was the first personally sent by a pope over the Internet.

VATICAN CITY STATE

Area: 44 ha (109 ac)
Population (2001 est.): 900
Chief of state: (sovereign pontiff) Pope John Paul II
Head of administration: Secretary of State Angelo Cardinal Sodano, who heads a pontifical commission of five cardinals

The year 2001 was important in terms of the octogenarian pontiff's desire to strengthen the Vatican's pastoral mission around the globe. Pope John Paul II visited areas of the world that had long viewed the Roman Catholic Church's activities with suspicion, if not open hostility. The pope followed in the footsteps of Saint Paul, traveling to Malta, Greece, and Damascus. He also went to Eastern Europe and Central Asia, making pastoral visits to Ukraine and Kazakhstan. The personal courage involved in undertaking the latter visit was astounding,

considering that the trip was completed only days before the U.S. began its bombing in nearby Afghanistan. As with all of his pastoral visits, the aim was to strengthen the Vatican's role as a major player in global affairs. One of the chief areas of resistance in this process was China, and it was remarkable that China manifested an open attitude during the year toward the possibility of reestablishing diplomatic relations with the Vatican after a rupture that had lasted 50 years. A low point in relations between China and the Vatican had been reached in 2000 when the pope canonized 120 Chinese martyrs to communism on the same day as China's national holiday. The pope hoped to strengthen ties with the estimated 10 million Catholics who lived in the world's most populous country. Consistent with the Vatican's mission of bringing peace to the world, the pope expressed horror at the many atrocities committed throughout the globe in 2001, and Vatican officials reiterated the urge for rich nations to devote more attention to the problem of poverty, encouraging steps such as abolishing the debt of poor countries and providing mechanisms to ensure that all nations could derive benefits from the global market. (GREGORY O. SMITH)

VENEZUELA

Area: 916,445 sq km (353,841 sq mi)
Population (2001 est.): 24,632,000
Capital: Caracas
Head of state and government: President Hugo Chávez Frías

The municipal and parish councilmen that Venezuelans elected on Dec. 3, 2000, assumed office in January 2001. This act completed Pres. Hugo Chávez Frías's demolition of the post-1958 system of the political parties that had governed Venezuela over four decades. Chávez's Fifth Republic Movement and its ally, the Movement to Socialism, as well as other political parties opposed to the previously dominant Democrat Action (AD) party and Social Christians, had captured 72% of all municipal and parish council seats. On October 25, however, the pro-Chávez parties suffered a stinging rebuke when their candidates ran for leadership positions in the Venezuelan Confederation of Workers.

The defeat was so overwhelming (unofficial tallies gave the pro-Chávez slates less than 10% of the total vote) that the National Electoral Council had not released the results as of mid-November. The victorious forces were the same groups that for more than four decades had been part of the AD and the Social Christians. Their victory did not signal the return to favour of these organizations, however. Rather, it indicated that organized labour had emerged as an autonomous political force in Venezuela, one whose support future governments could not take for granted.

Chávez saw his plans to remake Venezuela in the image of his leftist ideology derailed on several other fronts. First, in May he introduced legislation into the National Assembly that would have increased the national government's control over education, private as well as public. Proposals that required the imposition of government overseers with powers to dismiss administrators and teachers evoked intense opposition from the Roman Catholic Church and associations of middle-class parents whose children attended public schools. Chávez and the governing political party backed away from what threatened to become an ugly and possibly violent confrontation. In addition, they declined

Pres. Hugo Chávez of Venezuela hoists a youngster at the opening ceremony of a school in Caucagua on November 14.

to press the influential association of taxi drivers when the drivers resisted attempts to regulate them and to integrate them into the ruling political party. Finally, the Chávez government even had difficulty in controlling the capital city of Caracas. The 1999 constitution provided for the election of a "high mayor" to replace the appointed Federal District governor, traditionally the highest local executive authority in Caracas. The first elected high mayor of Caracas was Alfredo Peña, once Chávez's chief of staff. Peña broke with the president, successfully resisted his efforts to control the capital city police forces, and even suggested that it would be necessary to remove the president in a revocatory referendum. On December 10 the business group Fedecámaras and the one-million-strong Confederation of Venezuelan Workers staged a nationwide strike to protest new economic laws—involving the agriculture, fishing, and oil industries—that they believed would "lead the country to economic disaster."

Venezuela's central bank reported that the economic recovery that had begun in the second quarter of 2000 slowed in the third quarter of 2001. The communications sector failed to sustain earlier rates of growth, and the financial sector did not recover from the contraction that it experienced in 1999 and 2000. On November 1 the central bank reported that inflation was running at roughly 10% for the year, down slightly from 2000. Private consumption, which had fallen by 15% between May 1999 and May 2000, grew by 5% during the first half of 2001. Total public-sector debt stood at 31% of the country's gross domestic product, up from 29% for 2000.

The Chávez government's handling of foreign policy created two important problems for Venezuela. First, insurgency continued to simmer in neighbouring Colombia, and Chávez's ambiguous position toward the rebel cause raised tensions with Bogotá and Washington. The U.S. government was especially unhappy with Venezuela's unwillingness to allow overflights by military aircraft attempting to track drug-smuggling guerrillas. Second, after U.S. Pres. George W. Bush initiated the bombing of Afghanistan in October, relations between Venezuela and the U.S. deteriorated further when Chávez equated civilian casualties from the bombing with the deaths caused by terrorists on September 11. This position isolated the Chávez government within the Western Hemisphere and hardened opposition by the government's domestic critics. (DAVID J. MYERS)

VIETNAM

Area: 331,041 sq km (127,816 sq mi)
Population (2001 est.): 79,939,000
Capital: Hanoi
Chief of state: President Tran Duc Luong
Head of government: Prime Minister Phan Van Khai

In February 2001 a wave of protests among ethnic minorities swept through the central highlands of Vietnam. The demonstrators were angry over government corruption and encroachment on their ancestral lands by members of the Vietnamese majority. These developments quickly had an impact on political maneuvering prior to the ninth National Congress of the Communist Party of Vietnam. The stewardship of Secretary-General Le Kha Phieu came under challenge by senior retired leaders. Phieu also was implicated in a wiretapping scandal involving the military intelligence service.

Prior to the National Congress, party delegates decided to select Nong Duc Manh as party leader. Manh, a member of the Tay ethnic minority group, was respected for his considerable legislative experience as chairman of the National Assembly.

The National Congress was held on April 19–22. The party set a goal of doubling the country's gross domestic product by 2010 and achieving an annual growth rate of 7.5% for the first five years. Secretary-General Manh quickly stamped his authority on Vietnam's ongoing reform program. He immediately reshuffled key party and military leadership posts. He then ordered the implementation of a directive requiring all party and state officials to publicly declare their assets in an effort to curb corruption.

In June Manh obtained approval from the party's Central Committee for controversial plans to construct a costly hydroelectric scheme at Son La in the north. This project was designed to provide future energy for industry and to control flooding. It would also displace 100,000 persons who would need to be resettled. In August Manh received party endorsement to carry out a thorough reform of the state-owned enterprise sector. In September he personally addressed the problem of ethnic minority grievances by visiting the central highlands. He directed government officials to work closely with local elders, ordered a step-up in the recruitment of ethnic minorities for government service, and offered financial support for the ailing coffee-growing industry.

The National Congress reaffirmed Vietnam's commitment to a policy aimed at diversifying foreign relations. In March Vietnam hosted a visit by Russian Pres. Vladimir Putin. The two countries agreed to form a "strategic partnership" involving long-term economic cooperation and Russian arms sales. In October Russia announced that it would withdraw the last of its military forces from the Cam Ranh Bay naval station. Vietnam received visits by a number of Chinese officials, including Defense Minister Chi Haotian in February, Vice Pres. Hu Jintao in April, and National People's Congress Chairman Li Peng in September. In midyear Vietnam, as chairman of the Standing Committee of the Association of Southeast Asian Nations (ASEAN), hosted the annual meeting of ASEAN foreign ministers, a meeting of the ASEAN Regional Forum, and a meeting of the "ASEAN Plus Three" (China, Japan, and South Korea). In July Vietnam hosted a groundbreaking visit by Kim Yong Nam, president of North Korea's Supreme People's Assembly, and in October the two countries agreed to expand bilateral trade and investment. Vietnam responded to the September 11 terrorist attacks in the U.S. by offering sympathy and condemning terrorism but warned against "overreacting" to the attacks. In the final quarter of the year, Vietnam and the U.S. ratified the Bilateral Trade Agreement, which meant that Vietnamese exports would be subject to much lower tariffs. (CARLYLE A. THAYER)

YEMEN

Area: 555,000 sq km (214,300 sq mi)
Population (2001 est.): 18,078,000
Capital: San'a'
Chief of state: President Maj. Gen. 'Ali 'Abdallah Salih
Head of government: Prime Ministers 'Abd al-Karim al-Iryani and, from March 31, 'Abd al-Qadir al-Ba Jamal

In February 2001, for the first time ever, Yemen held elections for local councils; of the more than 20,000 candidates, 7,000 representatives were chosen. Voters also approved a referendum that would extend the term of the president from five to seven years, a constitutional change that could allow Pres. Maj. Gen. 'Ali 'Abdallah Salih to remain in office until 2013. On April 28 President Salih appointed 111 members to the newly created Consultative Council, which would form the upper house of the parliament.

In March 2001 President Salih reshuffled the cabinet and appointed as prime minister 'Abd al-Qadir al-Ba Jamal, a southerner from the Hadramawt; he had served as foreign minister and minister of oil when Yemen was unified in 1990. Prior to unification Ba Jamal had served in the People's Democratic Republic of Yemen's (South Yemen's) pro-Marxist government as planning and oil minister. Outgoing prime minister 'Abd al-Karim al-Iryani, a veteran politician who had served in many cabinets (before and after unity), became a senior presidential adviser. The new 35-member cabinet, all of whom belonged to the president's party, included Wahiba Fare, Yemen's first woman minister; she became minister of state for human rights.

Yemeni and U.S. authorities continued their intense investigation into the October 2000 terrorist attack on the USS *Cole;* several arrests were made. Following the September 2001 attacks in the U.S., Yemen cooperated with U.S. investigators, arrested dozens of suspects, and froze the bank accounts of two honey stores that were suspected of having links to terrorists.

(WILLIAM A. RUGH)

YUGOSLAVIA

Area: 102,173 sq km (39,449 sq mi)
Population (2001 est.): 10,677,000
Capital: Belgrade
Chief of state: President Vojislav Kostunica
Head of government: Prime Ministers Zoran Zizic and, from July 24, Dragisa Pesic

Yugoslavia made significant advances in returning to the international fold in 2001. All international sanctions were lifted; former strongman Slobodan Milosevic was extradited to the International Criminal Tribunal for the Former Yugoslavia (ICTY); the national currency was stabilized; and nearly one-fourth of the country's foreign debt was erased. Domestically, the privatization process was initiated, and an unexpectedly strong voter turnout among Serbs in Kosovo brought some measure of hope to a country ravaged by more than a decade of conflict, isolation, and economic mismanagement.

There was no progress over Yugoslavia's future status as a federation, however. The ruling coalition government was split and perpetually on the verge of collapse; the opposition was marginalized; and political parties continued to exert influence over media much as they had during the 13 years of the Milosevic regime. The government seemed far too occupied with internal rivalries to be able to push through legal, social, and economic reforms that could rid the country of the burdens of recent decades.

Milosevic's arrest on April 1 and his extradition to the ICTY on June 28 revealed the extent of government infighting. The ruling coalition, the Democratic Opposition of Serbia (DOS), led by Serbian Premier Zoran Djindjic, clashed with Yugoslav Pres. Vojislav Kostunica, whose Democratic Party of Serbia was the strongest member of the DOS, over the particulars of a draft extradition law and how Yugoslavia should cooperate with the ICTY. Kostunica demanded a thorough legal review of the draft law, while Djindjic pushed through a document on cooperation with the ICTY and authorized Milosevic's extradition.

The situation in Yugoslavia's constituent republic of Montenegro remained precarious. Pres. Milo Djukanovic's drive for Montenegro's independence from Yugoslavia was imperiled by boycotts from the opposition, pressure from the international community, the worsening economic situation, and fissures within the pro-independence bloc. In April Djukanovic's Democratic Party of Socialists of Montenegro and other parties that favoured independence for the republic barely won the parliamentary election. A broad consensus was lacking even on the rules and conditions for a proposed referendum, and there was considerable wrangling over whether a simple majority or a two-thirds majority would be needed to express the "national will." Clearly, there was no large majority that would vote in favour of Montenegrin independence; opinion surveys in November indicated 52% favoured independence, 33% opposed it, and 15% remained undecided. Observers were predicting that the economic and political situation could tilt undecided voters against independence. The referendum on the issue was tentatively scheduled to take place in April 2002.

Parliamentary elections in the Serbian province of Kosovo (under UN control) went on as planned in November without violence and with the participation of a significant number of ethnic Serbs who heeded Belgrade's call to vote and who ignored demands by their local leaders that they boycott the balloting. The Organization for Security and Cooperation in Europe conducted the elections, and international observers generally agreed that the vote was a step toward stability. Kosovar Albanians generally opted for a more moderate approach to government and independence, while the Serbs expressed hope for a negotiated future in which they might secure real power in a new provincial assembly. The international community rejected a call for independence by moderate ethnic Al-

banian leader Ibrahim Rugova, whose Democratic League of Kosovo won 47 of 120 seats in the parliament. Two other pro-independence Albanian parties headed by former guerrilla leaders won 34 seats; the only slate of Kosovo Serb candidates, called the Return coalition, took 22 seats.

The hoped-for upturn in the Yugoslav economy was not evident in 2001. According to one study, conducted by an influential nongovernmental group of economists in Serbia called G17 Plus, one out of seven citizens was worse off at the end of 2001 than the previous year. Experts suggested that Yugoslavia would require an influx of about $15 billion over the next five years to stabilize the economy. Unemployment stood at almost 30%, and officials estimated that about 40% of the population lived below the poverty line. The foreign debt rose 20% to $12 billion, and prices on basic commodities jumped 120%.

There were positive indicators, however. According to an International Monetary Fund (IMF) report in September, the Yugoslav tax system had been successfully adjusted to European standards, budgetary discipline had been restored, the central bank had taken

control over the flow of currency, and the government no longer printed money to cover the budget deficit or bail out bankrupt state companies. In addition, foreign currency exchange stabilized, foreign currency reserves continued to rise, and for the first time in nearly a decade, citizens were opening savings accounts. A key privatization law, a precondition for foreign capital investment, was also passed by the parliament. These changes led to Yugoslavia's reentry into the IMF, the World Bank, and other Western institutions. A donors' conference in June pledged $1.3 billion in developmental aid for Yugoslavia, and in November the Paris Club of creditors wrote off $3 billion of Yugoslavia's debt to that organization.

(MILAN ANDREJEVICH)

ZAMBIA

Area: 752,614 sq km (290,586 sq mi)
Population (2001 est.): 9,770,000
Capital: Lusaka
Head of state and government: President Frederick Chiluba

The companies that had taken over the Zambian government's holdings in the copper-mining industry in 2000 started 2001 in a buoyant mood, promising considerable increases in copper output. Encouraged by the apparent success of the government's privatization program, the Dutch oil company Shell resumed operations in Zambia after a 19-year interval.

Early in the year the World Bank released the first $2.5 million installment of its pledge of $30 million for major rehabilitation work on the country's railroad and freight infrastructure, and on April 17 the International Monetary Fund announced that it would make available a loan of $126 million to support Zambia's economic program. Sixteen donor groups representing various countries also made possible a government scheme to give doctors and nurses a substantial pay raise, and in June the European Union made a donation for road improvements.

There were difficulties, however. By the end of 2000, inflation had risen to 28.7%, and to counter this trend the government

Supporters of the pro-independence Liberal Alliance of Montenegro rally in Podgorica, Yugos., on April 16.

Milos Bicanski/AFP Worldwide

Zambian Pres. Frederick Chiluba (left) speaks with South African Pres. Thabo Mbeki before the opening session of the Organization of African Unity summit in Lusaka on July 9.
Alexander Joe/AFP Worldwide

began the year by ordering foreign investors to keep 75% of their earnings in Zambia. In February heavy rains caused floods at the confluence of the Zambezi and Luangwa rivers, threatening more than 30,000 people with famine. Then in October falling copper prices forced the South African Metorex Group to put its Chibuluma opencast mine on a care and maintenance basis less than a year after it had started operations.

Agitation by members of the ruling Movement for Multiparty Democracy (MMD) for a third term in office for Pres. Frederick Chiluba caused a violent reaction in many quarters and even from some members of the MMD itself. A conference of the MMD at the end of April changed the party's rules to allow the president to stand for a further term. Chiluba then dismissed a number of ministers who had opposed the change, including the vice president, Lieut. Gen. Christon Tembo, who formed his own party, the Forum for Democracy and Development. On May 4, however, Chiluba announced that he would not, after all, stand for a third term, and in August Levy Mwanawasa, a lawyer and former vice president, was adopted as the MMD's presidential candidate at the next election.

On November 22, Chiluba formally dissolved the country's National Assembly and called for presidential and general elections to be held on December 27. There were 11 presidential candidates. Even before early results suggested that both the presidential and parliamentary elections would be close, opposition parties accused the government of ballot rigging, and

clashes ensued between protesters and riot police.   (KENNETH INGHAM)

ZIMBABWE

Area: 390,757 sq km (150,872 sq mi)
Population (2001 est.): 11,365,000
Capital: Harare
Head of state and government: President Robert Mugabe

Throughout 2001 government policy in Zimbabwe was mainly focused upon victory in the elections scheduled for 2002. On January 25 a sharp fall in market interest rates was engineered in spite of urgent warnings from leading bankers. An International Monetary Fund (IMF) team that visited Zimbabwe in March—not impressed by the economic situation—refused to provide any new funds and threatened that if the government did not pay a debt of $73.6 million later in the year, it could be suspended from the IMF. Nevertheless, Finance Minister Simba Makoni, presenting his budget on November 1, said that public spending would double in the next financial year while taxation would be cut. At the same time, he admitted that gross domestic product growth would fall by 7.3% in 2001 and by a further 5.3% in 2002, largely as a result of a 12% cut in agricultural output due to the government's land-reform program.

That program, launched the previous year and involving the forcible occupation of white-owned land by men claiming to be veterans of the 1970s war of independence, was represented by the government as a fulfillment of unfinished business arising from the war. Great Britain, President Mugabe claimed, had failed to carry out the terms of the independence agreement regarding the transfer of land to black ownership and was now conducting a neocolonial campaign on behalf of white farmers. It was a point of view that won the almost unanimous sympathy of African leaders at a summit meeting held in Lusaka in July. It led, however, to clashes with the law courts. Chief Justice Anthony Gubbay was forced to resign in March after the president said that he could not offer protection against people who threatened Gubbay's life. Two other judges resigned in similar circumstances later in the year. Gubbay was replaced by Godfrey Chidyausiku, a friend of the president, and three other black judges were appointed to the bench. Late in the year the Supreme Court ruled that land reform could proceed.

Frequently, journalists of the country's only independent daily newspaper, the *Daily News*, were subjected to harassment for their criticism of government policy. In April two bills were hurried through the parliament, one strengthening the government's control over broadcasting and the other banning donations to political parties by foreign organizations. Members of opposition parties were also harassed and were sometimes subjected to violence by vigilantes. In February Morgan Tsvangirai, leader of the Movement for Democratic Change, was arrested and charged with inciting the violent overthrow of the president. Later in the year his car was attacked by a hostile crowd.

South African Pres. Thabo Mbeki consistently advocated a cooperative approach to Mugabe, and after the outbreak of further violence on white-owned farms in August, he agreed to cooperate with the president of Nigeria in organizing a meeting of Commonwealth foreign ministers aimed at effecting an accommodation between Zimbabwe and Britain over land reform. Although Mugabe accepted the meeting's recommendation that law and order should be restored in Zimbabwe, there was no letup in the activities of vigilantes, and the newly constituted Supreme Court declared the president's method of land reform legal.   (KENNETH INGHAM)

Alder, Phillip. Syndicated Bridge Columnist. Associate Editor, *The Bridge World.* Author of *Get Smarter at Bridge.* •SPORTS AND GAMES: *Contract Bridge*

Alexander, Steve. Freelance Technology Writer. •COMPUTERS AND INFORMATION SYSTEMS

Allaby, Michael. Freelance Writer. Author of *Encyclopedia of Weather and Climate* and *Basics of Environmental Science.* •THE ENVIRONMENT: *Environmental Issues; International Activities*

Allan, J.A. Professor of Geography, School of Oriental and African Studies, University of London. Author of *The Water Question in the Middle East* and *Water and Peace in the Middle East.* •WORLD AFFAIRS: *Libya*

Anam, Mahfuz. Editor, *The Daily Star,* Bangladesh. •WORLD AFFAIRS: *Bangladesh*

Andrades, Jorge Adrián. Freelance Journalist. •SPORTS AND GAMES: *Equestrian Sports:* Polo

Andrejevich, Milan. Senior Editor, *Post-Tribune* (Gary, Ind.). Adjunct Professor of Communications and History, Valparaiso University and Indiana University Northwest. Author of *The Sandžak: A Perspective of Serb-Muslim Relations.* •WORLD AFFAIRS: *Bosnia and Herzegovina; Yugoslavia*

Anthony, John Duke. President and CEO, National Council on U.S.-Arab Relations; Consultant to U.S. Departments of Defense and State. •WORLD AFFAIRS: *Oman; Qatar*

Archibald, John J. Retired Feature Writer, St. Louis (Mo.) *Post-Dispatch.* Member of the American Bowling Congress Hall of Fame. •SPORTS AND GAMES: *Bowling:* U.S. Tenpins

Aurora, Vincent. Lecturer in French and Romance Philology, Columbia University, New York City. Author of *Michel Leiris' "Failles": Immobile in mobili.* •LITERATURE: *French:* France

Bahry, Louay. Adjunct Professor of Political Science, University of Tennessee. Author of *The Baghdad Bahn.* •WORLD AFFAIRS: *Bahrain; Iraq*

Balaban, Avraham. Professor and Chairman, Department of African and Asian Languages and Literatures, University of Florida. Author of *Shiv'ah.* •LITERATURE: *Jewish:* Hebrew

Bamia, Aida A. Professor of Arabic Language and Literature, University of Florida. •LITERATURE: *Arabic*

Barrett, David B. Research Professor of Missiometrics, Regent University, Virginia Beach, Va. Author of *World Christian Encyclopedia* and *Schism and Renewal in Africa.* •RELIGION: *Tables (in part)*

Barry, John. Professor of Spanish, Roosevelt University, Chicago. Editor, *Voces en el viento: Nuevas ficciones desde Chicago.* •LITERATURE: *Spanish:* Latin America

Barzel, Ann. Senior Editor, *Dance Magazine.* •PERFORMING ARTS: *Dance:* World

Beattie, Ted A. President, American Zoo and Aquarium Association; President and CEO, John G. Shedd Aquarium, Chicago. •THE ENVIRONMENT: *Zoos*

Beckwith, David C. Vice President, National Cable Television Association. •WORLD AFFAIRS: *United States; United States:* State and Local Affairs

Benedetti, Laura. John L. Loeb Associate Professor of the Humanities, Harvard University. Author of *La sconfitta di Diana. Un percorso per la Gerusalemme liberata.* •LITERATURE: *Italian*

Bernstein, Ellen. Freelance Writer and Editor, specializing in health and medicine, Chicago. •HEALTH AND DISEASE; HEALTH AND DISEASE: Sidebar

Bird, Thomas E. The Jewish Studies Program, Queens College, City University of New York. Coeditor of *Hryhorij Savyc Skovoroda: An Anthology of Critical Articles.* •LITERATURE: *Jewish:* Yiddish

Boggan, Tim. Historian, U.S.A. Table Tennis Association (USATT). Author of *Winning Table Tennis* and *History of U.S. Table Tennis, vol. 1.* •SPORTS AND GAMES: *Table Tennis*

Bonds, John B. Adjunct Professor of History, The Citadel, Charleston, S.C. •SPORTS AND GAMES: *Sailing (Yachting)*

Bradley, Bill. Freelance Journalist; Publisher, *Billiard News.* •BIOGRAPHIES *(in part);* SPORTS AND GAMES: *Billiard Games*

Bradsher, Henry S. Foreign Affairs Analyst. Author of *Afghan Communism and Soviet Intervention.* •BIOGRAPHIES *(in part);* WORLD AFFAIRS: *Philippines*

Brady, Conor. Editor, *The Irish Times,* Dublin. •WORLD AFFAIRS: *Ireland*

Brecher, Kenneth. Professor of Astronomy and Physics; Director, Science and Mathematics Education Center, Boston University. •MATHEMATICS AND PHYSICAL SCIENCES: *Astronomy*

Brockmann, Stephen. Associate Professor of German, Carnegie Mellon University, Pittsburgh, Pa. Author of *Literature and German Reunification.* •LITERATURE: *German*

Brokopp, John G. Specialist and Writer on equestrian racing and casino gambling; Director of Public Relations, National Jockey Club. Author of *Thrifty Gambling* and *The Insider's Guide to Internet Gambling: Your Sourcebook for Safe and Profitable Gambling.* •SPORTS AND GAMES: *Equestrian Sports:* Thoroughbred Racing: *United States*

Brown, Bess. Political Officer, OSCE Centre, Ashgabat, Turkmenistan. Author of *Authoritarianism in the New States of Central Asia.* •WORLD AFFAIRS: *Kazakhstan; Kyrgyzstan; Tajikistan; Turkmenistan; Uzbekistan*

Buchan, David. International Energy Editor, *Financial Times,* London. Author of *The Single Market and Tomorrow's Europe: A Progress Report from the European Commission.* •BIOGRAPHIES *(in part);* WORLD AFFAIRS: *France*

Bungs, Dzintra. Consultant, Stiftung Wissenschaft und Politik, Berlin. Author of *The Baltic States: Problems and Prospects of Membership of the European Union.* •WORLD AFFAIRS: *Latvia*

Burks, Ardath W. Professor Emeritus of Asian Studies, Rutgers University, New Brunswick, N.J. Author of *Japan: A Postindustrial Power.* •BIOGRAPHIES *(in part);* WORLD AFFAIRS: *Japan*

Burns, Erik T. Bureau Chief, Dow Jones Newswires, Lisbon. •WORLD AFFAIRS: *Portugal*

Byrne, Justin. Researcher, Center for Advanced Study in the Social Sciences, Instituto Juan March de Estudios e Investigaciones, Madrid. •WORLD AFFAIRS: *Spain*

Cadoux, Charles. Professor of Public Law, University of Aix-Marseille III, Aix-en-Provence, Fr. •WORLD AFFAIRS: *Dependent States:* Indian Ocean and Southeast Asia

Cafferty, Bernard. Associate Editor, *British Chess Magazine.* Author of *The Soviet Championships.* •SPORTS AND GAMES: *Chess*

Calhoun, David R. Freelance Editor and Author. •BIOGRAPHIES *(in part)*

Calvo, Guillermo A. Chief Economist, Inter-American Development Bank, Washington, D.C.; Director, Center for International Economics, and Professor of Economics, University of Maryland, College Park. •WORLD AFFAIRS: *Special Report:* Dollarization: Is It Worth It?

Campbell, Paul J. Professor of Mathematics and Computer Science, Beloit College, Beloit, Wis. Author of *For All Practical Purposes.* •MATHEMATICS AND PHYSICAL SCIENCES: *Mathematics*

Campbell, Robert. Architect and Architecture Critic. Author of *Cityscapes of Boston: An American City Through Time.* •ARCHITECTURE AND CIVIL ENGINEERING: *Architecture*

Carter, Robert W. Journalist. •SPORTS AND GAMES: *Equestrian Sports:* Show Jumping and Dressage; Steeplechasing; Thoroughbred Racing: *International*

Cenzer, Matthew A. Lecturer in History, Northwestern University, Evanston, Ill. •WORLD AFFAIRS: *Burundi; Comoros; Djibouti; Liberia; Mauritius; Nigeria; Rwanda; Seychelles; Sierra Leone*

Chappell, Duncan. President, Mental Health Review Tribunal, Sydney. Author of *Violence at Work.* •LAW, CRIME, AND LAW ENFORCEMENT: *Crime*

Cheadle, Bruce. Journalist, Canadian Press news agency. •SPORTS AND GAMES: *Curling*

Cheuse, Alan. Writing Faculty, English Department, George Mason University, Fairfax, Va.; Book Commentator, National Public Radio. Author of *The Light Possessed* and *Listening to the Page: Adventures in Reading and Writing.* •LITERATURE: *English:* United States

Cioroslan, Dragomir. National Team Coach, U.S.A. Weightlifting, Inc.; Executive Board Member, International Weightlifting Federation. Author of *Banish Your Belly.* •SPORTS AND GAMES: *Weight Lifting*

Claiborn, Charles D. Professor, Division of Psychology in Education, Arizona State University. •EDUCATION: *Special Report:* Does Testing Deserve a Passing Grade?

Clark, David Draper. Managing Editor, *World Literature Today.* •LITERATURE: *English:* Other Literature in English

Clark, Janet H. Editor, Standard & Poor's, London. •NOBEL PRIZES *(in part)*

Collins, Nigel. Editor in Chief, *The Ring, KO, World Boxing,* and *Boxing 2002.* •SPORTS AND GAMES: *Boxing*

Cosgrave, Bronwyn. Associate Editor, *British Vogue.* Author of *Costume and Fashion: A Complete History.* •BIOGRAPHIES *(in part);* FASHIONS

Coveney, Michael. Theatre Critic, *The Daily Mail.* Author of *The Andrew Lloyd Webber Story* and others. •PERFORMING ARTS: *Theatre:* Great Britain and Ireland

Craine, Anthony G. Writer. •BIOGRAPHIES *(in part)*

Crampton, Richard J. Professor of East European History, University of Oxford, Oxford, Eng. Author of *A Concise History of Bulgaria* and *Eastern Europe in the Twentieth Century—and After.* •WORLD AFFAIRS: *Bulgaria*

Crisp, Brian F. Associate Professor of Political Science, University of Arizona. Author of *Democratic Institutional Design.* •WORLD AFFAIRS: *Colombia*

Curwen, Peter. Professor of Business and Management, Sheffield Hallam University, Sheffield, Eng. Author of *The U.K. Publishing Industry* and others. •MEDIA AND PUBLISHING: *Book Publishing* (international)

Cuttino, John Charles. Lyndon B. Johnson School of Public Affairs, University of Texas at Austin. •WORLD AFFAIRS: *Brazil*

Dailey, Meghan. Art Historian and Critic, New York. •ART, ANTIQUES, AND COLLECTIONS: *Art Exhibitions; Painting and Sculpture;* BIOGRAPHIES *(in part)*

Davis, Stephen P. Associate Editor, Encyclopædia Britannica. •BIOGRAPHIES *(in part)*

Deeb, Marius K. Professor of Middle East Studies, SAIS, Johns Hopkins University, Washington, D.C. Author of *Syria's War on Lebanon and the Peace Process 1974-2001* and others. •BIOGRAPHIES *(in part);* WORLD AFFAIRS: *Egypt; Jordan*

de la Barre, Kenneth. Fellow, Arctic Institute of North America; Research Associate, Yukon College, Northern Research Institute. •WORLD AFFAIRS: *Arctic Regions*

Denselow, Robin. Music Writer, *The Guardian;* Correspondent, BBC Television's *Newsnight.* Author of *When the Music's Over: The Politics of Pop.* •PERFORMING ARTS: *Music:* Popular (international)

Dietz, Henry A. Professor, Department of Government, University of Texas at Austin. Author of *Urban Poverty, Political Participation and the State: Lima 1970-1990.* •WORLD AFFAIRS: *Peru*

Dooling, Dave. Manager, NASA Microgravity Outreach, Infinity Technology, Inc. Coauthor of *Engineering Tomorrow.* •MATHEMATICS AND PHYSICAL SCIENCES: *Space Exploration; Space Exploration:* Sidebar

Dowd, Siobhan. Columnist, *Literary Review* (London); *Glimmer Train* (U.S.). Author of *This Prison Where I Live* and *Roads of the Roma*. •LITERATURE: *English:* United Kingdom

Ehringer, Gavin Forbes. Freelance Writer and Photographer; Correspondent, *People Magazine, Rocky Mountain News,* and *Western Horseman.* Coauthor of *Rodeo in America: Wranglers, Roughstock and Paydirt,* •SPORTS AND GAMES: *Introduction; Rodeo*

El Guindi, Fadwa. Adjunct Professor of Anthropology, University of Southern California. Author of *Veil: Modesty, Privacy and Resistance.* •ANTHROPOLOGY AND ARCHAEOLOGY: *Anthropology:* Cultural

Esteban, Verónica. Journalist and Judicial Interpreter. •LITERATURE: *Spanish:* Spain

Fagan, Brian. Professor of Anthropology, University of California, Santa Barbara. Author of *The Little Ice Age: How Climate Made History, 1300–1850* and *Floods, Famines, and Emperors: El Niño and the Collapse of Civilizations.* •ANTHROPOLOGY AND ARCHAEOLOGY: *Archaeology:* Western Hemisphere

Farr, David M.L. Professor Emeritus of History, Carleton University, Ottawa. •BIOGRAPHIES *(in part);* WORLD AFFAIRS: *Canada*

Fealy, Greg. Research Fellow in Indonesian History, Research School of Pacific and Asian Studies, Australian National University, Canberra. Author of *The Release of Indonesia's Political Prisoners: Domestic Versus Foreign Policy, 1975–1979.* •WORLD AFFAIRS: *Indonesia; Special Report: Resisting Disintegration in Post-Suharto Indonesia*

Fendell, Robert J. Freelance Writer on automobiles and racing. Author of *The Encyclopedia of Auto Racing Greats.* •SPORTS AND GAMES: *Automobile Racing:* Sidebar; *Automobile Racing:* U.S. Auto Racing *(in part)*

Fisher, Sharon. Central European Specialist, PlanEcon, Inc., Washington, D.C. •WORLD AFFAIRS: *Czech Republic; Slovakia*

Flink, Steve. Senior Correspondent, *Tennis Week.* Author of *The Greatest Tennis Matches of the Twentieth Century.* •SPORTS AND GAMES: *Tennis*

Flores, Ramona Monette Sargan. Professor, University of the Philippines, Quezon City. •MEDIA AND PUBLISHING: *Radio* (international); *Television* (international); *Television:* Sidebar

Follett, Christopher. Denmark Correspondent, *The Times;* Local Correspondent for Reuters News Agency, Copenhagen; Editor, *Copenhagen This Week.* Author of *Fodspor paa Cypern.* •WORLD AFFAIRS: *Denmark*

Ford, Brian J. Royal Literary Fellow, Open University, United Kingdom; Fellow, Cardiff University, Wales. Author of *BSE: The Facts.* •AGRICULTURE AND FOOD SUPPLIES: *Special Report:* Trouble on the Hoof: Disease Outbreaks in Europe

Fridovich, Irwin. James B. Duke Professor of Biochemistry, Emeritus, Duke University Medical Center, Durham, N.C. •LIFE SCIENCES: *Molecular Biology (in part)*

Fridovich-Keil, Judith L. Associate Professor, Department of Genetics, Emory University School of Medicine, Atlanta, Ga. •LIFE SCIENCES: *Molecular Biology (in part)*

Fuller, Elizabeth. Editor, *Newsline,* Radio Free Europe/Radio Liberty, Prague. •WORLD AFFAIRS: *Armenia; Azerbaijan; Georgia*

Furmonavičius, Darius. Ph.D. candidate, Department of European Studies, University of Bradford, Eng. •WORLD AFFAIRS: *Lithuania*

Gallagher, Tom. Professor of European Peace Studies, University of Bradford, Eng. Author of *Outcast Europe: The Balkans 1789–1989.* •WORLD AFFAIRS: *Romania*

Ganado, Albert. Lawyer; Chairman, Malta National Archives Advisory Committee; President, Malta Historical Society. Coauthor of *A Study in Depth of 143 Maps Representing the Great Siege of Malta of 1565* and others. •WORLD AFFAIRS: *Malta*

Garcia-Zamor, Jean-Claude. Professor of Public Administration, Florida International University. •WORLD AFFAIRS: *Haiti*

Garrod, Mark. Golf Correspondent, PA Sport, U.K. Honorary Secretary of the Association of Golf Writers. •SPORTS AND GAMES: *Golf*

Gaughan, Thomas. Library Director, Muhlenberg College, Allentown, Pa. •BIOGRAPHIES *(in part);* LIBRARIES AND MUSEUMS: *Libraries; Libraries:* Sidebar

George, Nicholas. Stockholm Correspondent, *Financial Times.* •WORLD AFFAIRS: *Sweden*

Gibbons, J. Whitfield. Professor of Ecology, Savannah River Ecology Laboratory, University of Georgia. Coauthor of *Ecoviews: Snakes, Snails and Environmental Tales.* •LIFE SCIENCES: *Zoology*

Gill, Martin J. Information and Computer Expert, F.A.O. EASTFISH; Editor, *Eurofish.* •AGRICULTURE AND FOOD SUPPLIES: *Fisheries*

Gobbie, Donn. CEO, American Badminton League. •SPORTS AND GAMES: *Badminton*

Goldsmith, Arthur. Freelance Writer. Author of *The Camera and Its Images.* •ART, ANTIQUES, AND COLLECTIONS: *Photography*

Graham, John W. Chair, Canadian Foundation for the Americas; Former Canadian Ambassador. •WORLD AFFAIRS: *Dominican Republic; Suriname*

Greskovic, Robert. Dance Critic, *The Wall Street Journal.* Author of *Ballet, 101.* •PERFORMING ARTS: *Dance:* North America

Griffiths, A.R.G. Associate Professor in History, Flinders University of South Australia. Author of *Contemporary Australia* and *Beautiful Lies.* •WORLD AFFAIRS: *Australia; Nauru; Palau; Papua New Guinea*

Grossman, Sandra A. Deputy Director, The Cuba Program, Inter-American Dialogue, Washington, D.C. •WORLD AFFAIRS: *Cuba*

Guthridge, Guy G. Manager, Antarctic Information Program, U.S. National Science Foundation. •WORLD AFFAIRS: *Antarctica*

Haddad, Mahmoud. Associate Professor of History, Balamand University, Lebanon. •WORLD AFFAIRS: *Lebanon; Saudi Arabia*

Halman, Talat S. Professor and Chairman, Department of Turkish Literature, Bilkent University, Ankara, Turkey. Author of *Doğrusu.* •LITERATURE: *Turkish*

Hammer, William R. Professor and Chair, Department of Geology, Augustana College, Rock Island, Ill. Author of *Gondwana Dinosaurs from the Jurassic of Antarctica.* •LIFE SCIENCES: *Paleontology*

Henry, Alan. Grand Prix Editor, *Autocar* (London). Motor Racing Correspondent, *The Guardian.* Author of *Mercedes in Motorsport* and *50 Years of World Championship Grand Prix Motor Racing.* •SPORTS AND GAMES: *Automobile Racing:* Grand Prix Racing

Hobbs, Greg. Chief Writer, *AFL Record.* Author of *One Hundred and Twenty-Five Years of the Melbourne Demons.* •SPORTS AND GAMES: *Football:* Australian

Hoffman, Dean A. Executive Editor, *Hoof Beats.* Author of *The Hambletonian: America's Trotting Classic.* •SPORTS AND GAMES: *Equestrian Sports:* Harness Racing

Hoke, John. Publisher, *Amateur Wrestling News.* •SPORTS AND GAMES: *Wrestling*

Hollar, Sherman. Assistant Editor, Encyclopædia Britannica. •BIOGRAPHIES *(in part);* DISASTERS; OBITUARIES *(in part)*

Homel, David. Freelance Writer; Lecturer, Concordia University, Montreal. Author of *Get on Top* and others. •LITERATURE: *French:* Canada

Hope, Thomas W. Owner, Hope Reports, Inc.; Former Film Producer. Author of *Large Screen Presentation Systems.* •PERFORMING ARTS: *Motion Pictures:* Nontheatrical Films

IEIS. International Economic Information Services. •ECONOMIC AFFAIRS: *World Economy; Stock Exchanges* (international)

Ingham, Kenneth. Emeritus Professor of History, University of Bristol, Eng. Author of *Politics in Modern Africa: The Uneven Tribal Dimension* and others. •WORLD AFFAIRS: *Angola; Congo; Democratic Republic of the; Kenya; Malawi; Mozambique; Sudan, The; Tanzania; Uganda; Zambia; Zimbabwe*

Ingram, Derek. President Emeritus, Commonwealth Journalists Association; Founding Editor, Gemini News Service. Author of *A Much-Too-Timid Commonwealth* and others. •WORLD AFFAIRS: *Commonwealth of Nations*

Ionescu, Dan. Broadcaster/Editor, Radio Free Europe/Radio Liberty. Contributor to *Transitions.* •WORLD AFFAIRS: *Moldova*

Isaacson, Lanae Hjortsvang. Editor, *Nordic Women Writers.* •LITERATURE: *Danish*

Iyob, Ruth. Associate Professor of Political Science, University of Missouri, St. Louis. •WORLD AFFAIRS: *Eritrea*

Jamail, Milton. Lecturer, Department of Government, University of Texas at Austin. Author of *Full Count: Inside Cuban Baseball.* •SPORTS AND GAMES: *Baseball:* Latin America

Joffé, George. Director, Centre of North African Studies, University of Cambridge. Editor, *Perspectives on Development: The Euro-Mediterranean Partnership.* •WORLD AFFAIRS: *Algeria; Morocco; Tunisia*

Johnson, Steve. Media Critic, *Chicago Tribune.* •MEDIA AND PUBLISHING: *Radio* (U.S.); *Television* (U.S.)

Johnson, Todd M. Director, World Evangelization Research Center. Coauthor of *World Christian Encyclopedia.* •RELIGION: *Tables (in part)*

Joireman, Sandra F. Associate Professor of Politics and International Relations, Wheaton College, Wheaton, Ill. Author of *Property Rights and Political Development in Ethiopia and Eritrea.* •WORLD AFFAIRS: *Ethiopia*

Jones, David G.C. Tutor, Department of Continuing Education, University of Aberystwyth, Aberystwyth, Wales. Author of *Atomic Physics.* •MATHEMATICS AND PHYSICAL SCIENCES: *Physics*

Jones, Mark P. Associate Professor of Political Science, Michigan State University. Author of *Electoral Laws and the Survival of Presidential Democracies.* •WORLD AFFAIRS: *Argentina*

Kaiser, Robert G. Associate Editor, *The Washington Post.* Author of *Why Gorbachev Happened: His Triumphs and His Failure* and others. •SPECIAL REPORT: *9-11*

Kanduza, Ackson M. Associate Professor and Chair, Department of History, University of Swaziland. Author of *Political Economy of Democratisation in Swaziland.* •WORLD AFFAIRS: *Swaziland*

Karimi-Hakkak, Ahmad. Professor of Persian Languages and Literature, University of Washington. Author of *Recasting Persian Poetry: Scenarios of Poetic Modernity in Iran.* •LITERATURE: *Persian*

Kazamaru, Yoshihiko. Literary Critic. •LITERATURE: *Japanese*

Kelleher, John A. Journalist and Editorial Consultant; Former Editor, *Dominion* and *Dominion Sunday Times* (Wellington). •WORLD AFFAIRS: *New Zealand*

Kelling, George H. Lieutenant Colonel, U.S. Army (ret.). Author of *Countdown to Rebellion: British Policy in Cyprus 1939–1955.* •WORLD AFFAIRS: *Cyprus*

Kellner, Peter. Journalist, *The Observer, London Evening Standard.* Author of *The New Mutualism* and others. •BIOGRAPHIES *(in part);* WORLD AFFAIRS: *United Kingdom; United Kingdom:* Sidebar

Kessler, Clive S. Professor of Sociology, University of New South Wales, Sydney. •WORLD AFFAIRS: *Malaysia*

Knox, Paul. International Affairs Reporter, *The Globe and Mail,* Toronto. •WORLD AFFAIRS: *Bolivia; Ecuador*

Kobliner, Beth. Journalist. Author of *Get a Financial Life.* •ECONOMIC AFFAIRS: *Stock Exchanges* (North America)

Kovel, Ralph and Terry. Publishers. Authors of *Kovels on Antiques and Collectibles*. •ART, ANTIQUES, AND COLLECTIONS: *Antiques and Collectibles*

Krause, Stefan. Freelance Political Analyst, Brussels. •WORLD AFFAIRS: *Greece; Macedonia*

Kruger, Linda M. Managing Editor, *Collectors News*. •ART, ANTIQUES, AND COLLECTIONS: Sidebar

Kuiper, Kathleen. Senior Editor, Encyclopædia Britannica. Editor, *Merriam-Webster's Encyclopedia of Literature*. •BIOGRAPHIES *(in part)*; LITERATURE: *Japanese*: Sidebar

Kuptsch, Christiane. Research Officer, International Institute for Labour Studies, International Labour Office. Coeditor of *Social Security at the Dawn of the 21st Century*. •SOCIAL PROTECTION (international)

Lamb, Kevin M. Special Projects Writer, *Dayton (Ohio) Daily News*. Author of *Quarterbacks, Nickelbacks & Other Loose Change*. •SPORTS AND GAMES: *Football*: Canadian, U.S.

Langeneckert, Sandra. Senior Copy Editor, Encyclopædia Britannica. •BIOGRAPHIES *(in part)*

Lawler, Nancy Ellen. Professor Emeritus, Oakton Community College, Des Plaines, Ill. Author of *Soldiers of Misfortune* and others. •BIOGRAPHIES *(in part)*; WORLD AFFAIRS: *Benin; Burkina Faso; Cameroon; Central African Republic; Congo, Republic of the; Côte d'Ivoire; Gabon; Guinea; Mali; Mauritania; Niger; Senegal; Togo*

Lawson, Fred H. James Irvine Professor of Government, Mills College, Oakland, Calif. Author of *Why Syria Goes to War*. •WORLD AFFAIRS: *Syria*

Le Comte, Douglas. Meteorologist, Climate Prediction Center, National Oceanic and Atmospheric Administration. •EARTH SCIENCES: *Meteorology and Climate*

Legassick, Martin. Professor of History, University of the Western Cape, Bellville, S.Af. Author of *Skeletons in the Cupboard: South African Museums and the Trade in Human Remains 1907–1917*. •WORLD AFFAIRS: *South Africa*

Levine, Steven I. Mansfield Professor of Asia Pacific Studies, The Mansfield Center, University of Montana, Missoula. •WORLD AFFAIRS: *China; Taiwan*

Levy, Michael I. Editor, Encyclopædia Britannica. •BIOGRAPHIES *(in part)*; WORLD AFFAIRS: *United States*: Sidebar

Lindstrom, Sieg. Managing Editor, *Track & Field News*. •SPORTS AND GAMES: *Track and Field Sports (Athletics)*

Litweiler, John. Jazz Critic. Author of *The Freedom Principle: Jazz After 1958* and *Ornette Coleman: A Harmolodic Life*. •BIOGRAPHIES *(in part)*; OBITUARIES *(in part)*; PERFORMING ARTS: *Music: Jazz*

Logan, Robert G. Sportswriter, *Daily Herald* (Arlington Heights, Ill.). Author of *The Bulls and Chicago: A Stormy Affair* and others. •SPORTS AND GAMES: *Basketball*: United States

Longmore, Andrew. Chief Sports Feature Writer, *The Independent*; Former Assistant Editor, *The Cricketer*. Author of *The Complete Guide to Cycling*. •SPORTS AND GAMES: *Cricket*

Luling, Virginia. Independent Researcher, Survival International. Author of *Somali Sultanate: The Geledi City-State over 150 Years*. •WORLD AFFAIRS: *Somalia; Somalia*: Sidebar

Lundin, Immi. Freelance Journalist and Literary Critic. •LITERATURE: *Swedish*

Macdonald, Barrie. Professor of History, Massey University, Palmerston, N.Z. •WORLD AFFAIRS: *Dependent States*: Pacific; *Fiji; Kiribati; Marshall Islands; Micronesia, Federated States of; Samoa; Solomon Islands; Tonga; Tuvalu; Vanuatu*

McGregor, Alan. Freelance Journalist. •WORLD AFFAIRS: *Switzerland*

McLachlan, Keith S. Professor Emeritus, School of Oriental and African Studies, University of London. Coeditor of *Landlocked States of Africa and Asia*. Author of *Boundaries of Modern Iran*. •WORLD AFFAIRS: *Iran*

McLellan, Joseph. Music Critic Emeritus, *The Washington Post*. •PERFORMING ARTS: *Music: Classical*

Malik, Mohan. Associate Professor, Asia-Pacific Center for Security Studies, Honolulu. •WORLD AFFAIRS: *Myanmar (Burma)*

Manghnani, Murli H. Professor of Geophysics, University of Hawaii at Manoa, Honolulu. •EARTH SCIENCES: *Geophysics*

Mango, Andrew. Foreign Affairs Analyst. Author of *Atatürk: The Biography of the Founder of Modern Turkey* and *Turkey: The Challenge of a New Role*. •WORLD AFFAIRS: *Turkey*

Marples, David R. Professor of History, University of Alberta. Author of *Belarus: A Denationalized Nation* and *Lenin's Revolution: Russia, 1917–1921*. •WORLD AFFAIRS: *Belarus; Ukraine*

Matthíasson, Björn. Economist, Ministry of Finance, Iceland. •WORLD AFFAIRS: *Iceland*

Mazie, David M. Freelance Journalist. •SOCIAL PROTECTION (U.S.)

Michael, Tom. Editor, Encyclopædia Britannica. •BIOGRAPHIES *(in part)*; OBITUARIES *(in part)*; SPORTS AND GAMES: *Basketball*: International

Middlebrook, Kevin J. Director, Center for U.S.-Mexican Studies, University of California, San Diego. Editor of *Conservative Parties, the Right, and Democracy in Latin America*. •WORLD AFFAIRS: *Mexico*

Mora, Frank O. Associate Professor and Chair of International Studies, Rhodes College, Memphis, Tenn. •WORLD AFFAIRS: *Paraguay*

Morgan, Paul. Editor, *Rugby World*. •SPORTS AND GAMES: *Football*: Rugby Football

Morris, Jacqui M. Freelance Editor; Lecturer, University of Sussex, Brighton, Eng.; Former Editor, *Oryx, The International Journal of Conservation*. •THE ENVIRONMENT: *Wildlife Conservation*

Morrison, Graham. Press Officer, British Fencing Association; Correspondent, *Daily Telegraph*; *Country Life*. •SPORTS AND GAMES: *Fencing*

Murphy, Colin J. Freelance Writer and Editor. •BIOGRAPHIES *(in part)*

Myers, David J. Professor of Political Science, Pennsylvania State University. •WORLD AFFAIRS: *Venezuela*

Newton, Clyde. Editor and Publisher, *Sumo World*. Author of *Dynamic Sumo*. •SPORTS AND GAMES: *Wrestling*: Sumo

Noda, Hiroki. Staff Reporter, *Jiji Press Ltd.*, Japan. •SPORTS AND GAMES: *Baseball*: Japan

O'Brien, Dan. Senior Editor/Economist (Europe), Economist Intelligence Unit. •WORLD AFFAIRS: *Austria*

Ogden, Shepherd. Founder and President, The Cook's Garden. Author of *Straight Ahead Organic* and others. •THE ENVIRONMENT: *Gardening*

O'Leary, Christopher. Senior Editor, *Investment Dealers Digest*. •ECONOMIC AFFAIRS: *Business Overview*

Oppenheim, Lois Hecht. Professor of Political Science and Vice President for Academic Affairs, University of Judaism, Los Angeles. Author of *Politics in Chile: Democracy, Authoritarianism and the Search for Development*. •WORLD AFFAIRS: *Chile*

O'Quinn, Jim. Editor in Chief, *American Theatre*. •PERFORMING ARTS: *Theatre*: U.S. and Canada

Orr, Jay. Editor and Senior Music Writer, Country.com. •BIOGRAPHIES *(in part)*; PERFORMING ARTS: *Music*: Popular (U.S.)

Orwig, Sarah Forbes. Associate Editor, Encyclopædia Britannica. •BIOGRAPHIES *(in part)*

Osborne, Keith L. Editor, *British Rowing Almanack*. Author of *Boat Racing in Britain, 1715–1975* and *One Man Went to Row*. •SPORTS AND GAMES: *Rowing*

Paarlberg, Philip L. Professor of Agricultural Economics, Purdue University, West Lafayette, Ind. •AGRICULTURE AND FOOD SUPPLIES: *Agriculture*

Paradkar, Shalaka. Content Manager, Industrial Credit and Investment Corporation of India. •BIOGRAPHIES *(in part)*; OBITUARIES *(in part)*; WORLD AFFAIRS: *India*: Sidebar

Parker, Ines. Freelance Writer. •WORLD AFFAIRS: *Belize*

Parsons, Neil. Professor of History, University of Botswana. Author of *King Khama, Emperor Joe, and the Great White Queen*. •WORLD AFFAIRS: *Botswana*

Pérez, Orlando J. Associate Professor of Political Science, Central Michigan University. Editor of *Post-Invasion Panama: The Challenges of Democratization in the New World Order*. •WORLD AFFAIRS: *Panama*

Peszek, Luan. Publications Director and Editor, *U.S.A. Gymnastics*. Author of *Gymnastics Almanac*. •SPORTS AND GAMES: *Gymnastics*

Peterson, Mark. Associate Professor of Korean Studies, Brigham Young University. Author of *Korean Adoption and Inheritance* and others. •WORLD AFFAIRS: *Korea, Dem. People's Republic of; Korea, Republic of*

Prasad, H.Y. Sharada. Vice President, Indian Council for Cultural Relations; Former Information Adviser to the Prime Minister of India. •WORLD AFFAIRS: *India*

Primorac, Max. Executive Director, Institute of World Affairs, Zagreb, Croatia. •WORLD AFFAIRS: *Croatia*

Rauch, Robert. Freelance Editor and Writer. •BIOGRAPHIES *(in part)*; NOBEL PRIZES *(in part)*; OBITUARIES *(in part)*

Raun, Toivo U. Professor of Central Eurasian Studies, Indiana University. Author of *Estonia and the Estonians*. •WORLD AFFAIRS: *Estonia*

Rebelo, L.S. Professor Emeritus, Department of Portuguese Studies, King's College, University of London. •LITERATURE: *Portuguese*: Portugal

Reid, Ron. Staff Writer, *Philadelphia Inquirer*. •SPORTS AND GAMES: *Ice Hockey; Ice Skating*

Renwick, David. Freelance Journalist. •WORLD AFFAIRS: *Antigua and Barbuda; Bahamas, The; Barbados; Dependent States: Caribbean and Bermuda; Dominica; Grenada; Guyana; Jamaica; Saint Kitts and Nevis; Saint Lucia; Saint Vincent and the Grenadines; Trinidad and Tobago*

Robbins, Paul. International Correspondent, *Ski Trax*; Nordic Correspondent, *Ski Racing*. •SPORTS AND GAMES: *Skiing*

Robinson, David. Film Critic and Historian. Author of *A History of World Cinema* and *Chaplin: His Life and Art*. •PERFORMING ARTS: *Motion Pictures*

Roby, Anne. Freelance Journalist. •WORLD AFFAIRS: *Andorra; Liechtenstein; Luxembourg; Monaco*

Rohwedder, Cecilie. Staff Reporter, *The Wall Street Journal Europe*. •WORLD AFFAIRS: *Germany*

Rollin, Jack. Editor, *Rothmans Football Yearbook*. Author of *World Cup 1930–1990* and others. •SPORTS AND GAMES: *Football*: Association Football (Soccer)

Rose, Leo E. Professor Emeritus of Political Science, University of California, Berkeley. •WORLD AFFAIRS: *Bhutan; Nepal*

Rugh, William A. President and CEO, AMIDEAST; Former U.S. Ambassador to Yemen and the United Arab Emirates. Author of *The Arab Press*. •WORLD AFFAIRS: *United Arab Emirates; Yemen*

Rutherford, Andrew. Professor of Law and Criminal Policy, University of Southampton, Eng. Author of *Transforming Criminal Policy* and others. •LAW, CRIME, AND LAW ENFORCEMENT: *Prisons and Penology*

Sabo, Anne G. Assistant Professor of Norwegian, St. Olaf College, Northfield, Minn. •LITERATURE: *Norwegian*

Sahadevan, Ponmoni. Associate Professor, Jawaharlal Nehru University, New Delhi. Author of *Conflict and Peacemaking in South Asia*. •WORLD AFFAIRS: *Maldives*

Sanders, Alan J.K. Former Lecturer in Mongolian Studies, School of Oriental and African Studies, University of London. Author of *Historical Dictionary of Mongolia*; Coauthor of *Colloquial Mongolian*. •WORLD AFFAIRS: *Mongolia*

Sandvik, Gudmund. Professor Emeritus of Legal History, Faculty of Law, University of Oslo. •WORLD AFFAIRS: *Norway*

Saracino, Peter. Freelance Defense Journalist. •MILITARY AFFAIRS

Contributors

Sarahete, Yrjö. Secretary Emeritus, Fédération Internationale des Quilleurs. •SPORTS AND GAMES: *Bowling:* World Tenpins

Saunders, Christopher. Professor of Historical Studies, University of Cape Town, S.Af. Coauthor of *Historical Dictionary of South Africa* and *South Africa: A Modern History.* •WORLD AFFAIRS: *Cape Verde; Chad; Equatorial Guinea; Gambia, The; Guinea-Bissau; Lesotho; Madagascar; Namibia; São Tomé and Príncipe*

Schmidt, Fabian. Head of the Bosnian Program, Deutsche Welle. •WORLD AFFAIRS: *Albania*

Schmitt, Eric. National Immigration and Census Correspondent, *The New York Times.* •WORLD AFFAIRS: *United States:* Special Report: The U.S. Census of 2000

Schroeder, Patricia S. President and CEO, Association of American Publishers. Author of *24 Years of House Work...and the Place Is Still a Mess.* •MEDIA AND PUBLISHING: *Book Publishing* (U.S.)

Schulz, Nancy. Freelance Journalist. •MEDIA AND PUBLISHING: *Book Publishing:* Sidebar

Schuster, Angela M.H. Director of Publications, World Monuments Fund; Contributing Editor, *Archaeology;* Editor, *The Explorers Journal.* •ANTHROPOLOGY AND ARCHAEOLOGY: *Archaeology:* Eastern Hemisphere

Sego, Stephen. Freelance Journalist; Former Director, Radio Free Afghanistan. •BIOGRAPHIES *(in part);* WORLD AFFAIRS: *Afghanistan*

Seligson, Mitchell A. Daniel H. Wallace Professor of Political Science, University of Pittsburgh. Editor of *Elections and Democracy in Central America, Revisited.* •WORLD AFFAIRS: *Costa Rica*

Seno, Alexandra A. Correspondent, *Asiaweek.* •WORLD AFFAIRS: *Cambodia*

Serafin, Steven R. Director, Writing Center, Hunter College, City University of New York. Editor of *The Continuum Encyclopedia of American Literature.* •NOBEL PRIZES *(in part)*

Settergren, Amy. Department of History, Northwestern University, Evanston, Ill. •BIOGRAPHIES *(in part);* WORLD AFFAIRS: *Ghana*

Shelley, Andrew. Director, Women's International Squash Players Association; Technical Director, World Squash Federation. Author of *Squash Rules: A Players Guide.* •SPORTS AND GAMES: *Squash*

Shepherd, Melinda C. Associate Editor, Encyclopædia Britannica. •OBITUARIES *(in part);* WORLD AFFAIRS: *Dependent States:* Europe and the Atlantic

Shubinsky, Valery. Correspondent, *Vecherny Peterburg.* •LITERATURE: *Russian*

Siler, Shanda. Editorial Assistant, Encyclopædia Britannica. •BIOGRAPHIES *(in part);* OBITUARIES *(in part)*

Simons, Paul. Freelance Journalist. Author of *The Action Plant.* •LIFE SCIENCES: *Botany*

Simpson, Jane. Freelance Writer. •PERFORMING ARTS: *Dance:* European

Sklar, Morton. Executive Director, World Organization Against Torture USA; Judge, Administrative Tribunal for OAS. Editor, *The Status of Human Rights in the United States* and *Torture in the U.S.* Author of *The Right to Travel* and others. •SOCIAL PROTECTION: *Human Rights*

Smentkowski, Brian. Associate Professor of Political Science, Southeast Missouri State University, Cape Girardeau, Mo. *(The author acknowledges research assistance of Benjamin Lowrance)* •LAW, CRIME, AND LAW ENFORCEMENT: *Court Decisions*

Smith, Gregory O. Academic Development Officer, European School of Economics. •WORLD AFFAIRS: *San Marino; Vatican City State*

Snodgrass, Donald R. Institute Fellow Emeritus, Harvard University. Coauthor of *Economics of Development,* 5th ed. •WORLD AFFAIRS: *Sri Lanka*

Sparks, Karen J. Managing Editor, Encyclopædia Britannica. •BIOGRAPHIES *(in part);* OBITUARIES *(in part);* LIBRARIES AND MUSEUMS: *Museums*

Stern, Irwin. Lecturer in Foreign Languages, North Carolina State University. Editor of *Dictionary of Brazilian Literature.* •LITERATURE: *Portuguese:* Brazil

Stewart, Alan. Freelance Journalist. Author of *How to Make It in IT.* •COMPUTERS AND INFORMATION SYSTEMS: *Microelectronics; Telecommunications*

Summerhill, Edward. Editor, Finnish News Agency; Former Part-Time Staff Member, Reuters. •WORLD AFFAIRS: *Finland*

Sumner, David E. Professor of Journalism and Head of the Magazine Program, Ball State University, Muncie, Ind. •MEDIA AND PUBLISHING: *Magazines*

Susel, Rudolph M. Editor, *American Home.* •WORLD AFFAIRS: *Slovenia*

Susser, Leslie D. Diplomatic Correspondent, *The Jerusalem Report.* Coauthor of *Shalom Friend: The Life and Legacy of Yitzhak Rabin.* •BIOGRAPHIES *(in part);* WORLD AFFAIRS: *Israel*

Swift, Richard N. Professor Emeritus of Politics, New York University. •WORLD AFFAIRS: *Multinational and Regional Organizations; United Nations*

Szilagyi, Zsofia. Freelance Writer. •WORLD AFFAIRS: *Hungary*

Tao, Amy R. Freelance Writer and Editor. •BIOGRAPHIES *(in part)*

Taylor, Jolanda Vanderwal. Associate Professor of Dutch and German, University of Wisconsin, Madison. Author of *A Family Occupation: Children of the War and the Memory of World War II in Dutch Literature of the 1980s.* •LITERATURE: *Netherlandic;* WORLD AFFAIRS: *The Netherlands*

Taylor-Robinson, Michelle M. Associate Professor of Political Science, Texas A&M University. Coauthor of *Negotiating Democracy: Transitions from Authoritarian Rule.* •WORLD AFFAIRS: *Honduras*

Teague, Elizabeth. Research Analyst, Foreign and Commonwealth Office, London. *(The opinions expressed are personal and do not necessarily represent those of the British government.)* •WORLD AFFAIRS: *Russia*

Tétreault, Mary Ann. Una Chapman Cox Distinguished Professor of International Affairs, Trinity University, San Antonio, Texas. Author of *Stories of Democracy: Politics and Society in Contemporary Kuwait* and others. •WORLD AFFAIRS: *Kuwait*

Thayer, Carlyle A. Professor of Politics, Australian Defence Force Academy, Canberra. Author of *The Vietnam People's Army Under Doi Moi.* •WORLD AFFAIRS: *Vietnam*

Thomas, R. Murray. Professor Emeritus of Education, University of California, Santa Barbara. Author of *Recent Theories of Human Development.* •EDUCATION

Thyagarajan, S. Deputy Editor and Hockey Correspondent, *The Hindu.* •SPORTS AND GAMES: *Field Hockey*

Tikkanen, Amy. Freelance Writer and Editor. •BIOGRAPHIES *(in part)*

Todd Middleton, Amy. Assistant Vice President, Sotheby's. •ART, ANTIQUES, AND COLLECTIONS: *Art Auctions and Sales*

Tucker, Emma. Correspondent, *Financial Times.* •WORLD AFFAIRS: *European Union*

Turner, Darrell J. Freelance Writer; Former Religion Writer, *The Journal Gazette* (Fort Wayne, Ind.). •RELIGION

Uddin, Shantha. Director, Research and Reference Center/Permissions, Encyclopædia Britannica. •RELIGION: Sidebar

Uhlick, Lawrence R. Executive Director and General Counsel, Institute of International Bankers. •ECONOMIC AFFAIRS: *Banking*

UNHCR. The Office of the United Nations High Commissioner for Refugees. •SOCIAL PROTECTION: *Refugees and International Migration*

Urbansky, Julie. Media and Public Relations Director, U.S. Bobsled and Skeleton Federation. •SPORTS AND GAMES: *Bobsledding and Luge*

Verdi, Robert. Senior Writer, *New York Times Magazine* group; Contributing Columnist, *Chicago Tribune.* •SPORTS AND GAMES: *Baseball* (U.S. and Canada)

Walker, Thomas W. Professor of Political Science and Director, Latin American Studies Program, Ohio University. Coauthor of *Repression, Resistance, and Democratic Transition in Central America.* •WORLD AFFAIRS: *Nicaragua*

Wallenfeldt, Jeff. Senior Editor, Encyclopædia Britannica. •BIOGRAPHIES *(in part)*

Wang Xiaoming. Professor of Chinese Literature, East China Normal University, Shanghai. Author of *The Cold Face of Reality: A Biography of Lu Xun.* •LITERATURE: *Chinese*

Wanninger, Richard S. Freelance Journalist. •SPORTS AND GAMES: *Volleyball*

Watson, Rory. Freelance Journalist specializing in European Union affairs. Coauthor of *The American Express Guide to Brussels.* •WORLD AFFAIRS: *Belgium*

Weil, Eric. Sports Editor, *Buenos Aires Herald.* •SPORTS AND GAMES: *Football:* Association Football (Soccer): Latin America

Weinstein, Martin. Professor of Political Science, William Paterson University of New Jersey, Wayne, N.J. Author of *Uruguay: Democracy at the Crossroads.* •WORLD AFFAIRS: *Uruguay*

White, Martin L. Freelance Writer, Chicago. •OBITUARIES *(in part)*

Whitney, Barbara. Copy Supervisor, Encyclopædia Britannica. •BIOGRAPHIES *(in part);* MEDIA AND PUBLISHING: *Television:* Sidebar; OBITUARIES *(in part)*

Whitten, Phillip. Editor in Chief, *Swimming World.* Author of *The Complete Book of Swimming* and others. •SPORTS AND GAMES: *Swimming*

Wilkinson, Earl J. Executive Director, International Newspaper Marketing Association. Author of *Branding and the Newspaper Consumer.* •MEDIA AND PUBLISHING: *Newspapers*

Wilkinson, John R. Sportswriter, Coventry Newspapers. •SPORTS AND GAMES: *Cycling*

Williams, Victoria C. Assistant Professor of the Humanities, Alvernia College, Reading, Pa.; Independent Consultant on International Affairs. •LAW, CRIME, AND LAW ENFORCEMENT: *International Law*

Wilson, Derek. Correspondent, BBC, Rome. Author of *Rome, Umbria and Tuscany.* •BIOGRAPHIES *(in part);* WORLD AFFAIRS: *Italy*

Wise, Larry. Freelance Writer; Former World Champion Archer and Professional Coach. Author of *Tuning Your Compound Bow* and others. •SPORTS AND GAMES: *Archery*

Woodrow, Robert. Former Assistant Managing Editor, *Asiaweek.* •BIOGRAPHIES *(in part);* WORLD AFFAIRS: *Laos; Thailand*

Woods, Elizabeth. Writer. Author of *If Only Things Were Different (I): A Model for a Sustainable Society, Bird Salad,* and others. •LITERATURE: *English:* Canada

Woods, Michael. Science Editor, *The Toledo Blade.* Author of *Ancient Technology.* •MATHEMATICS AND PHYSICAL SCIENCES: *Chemistry;* NOBEL PRIZES *(in part)*

Woodward, Kenneth L. Religion Editor, *Newsweek.* Author of *The Book of Miracles: The Meaning of the Miracle Stories in Christianity, Judaism, Buddhism, Hinduism, and Islam.* •RELIGION: *Special Report:* Christianity's Newest Converts

Woodward, Ralph Lee, Jr. Neville G. Penrose Professor of Latin American Studies, Texas Christian University. Author of *Central America, a Nation Divided.* •WORLD AFFAIRS: *El Salvador; Guatemala*

Wyllie, Peter J. Emeritus Professor of Geology, California Institute of Technology, Pasadena. Author of *The Dynamic Earth* and *The Way the Earth Works.* •EARTH SCIENCES: *Geology and Geochemistry*

Zegura, Stephen L. Professor of Anthropology, University of Arizona. •ANTHROPOLOGY AND ARCHAEOLOGY: *Anthropology:* Physical

Index

The index uses word-by-word alphabetization (treating a word as one or more characters separated by a space from the next word). Names beginning with "Mc" and "Mac" are alphabetized as "Mac"; "St." is treated as "Saint."

Entries in **boldface** are major title headings.
References to illustrations are indicated by the abbreviation *il.*

G

Jordan 451
traffic disaster 65
Jordan, Michael 49, 316, 322
José Donoso Prize (Sp. lit.) 253
José Martí Iberoamerican Prize (lit.) 254
Jospin, Lionel 425, 427
journalism: *see* Magazines; Newspapers
Jovanovich, William, *or* Vladimir Jovanovich (obit.) 126
Juan Carlos I, king of Spain 494
Juan de Fuca Ridge (geol.) 183, 185
Juan Rulfo Prize (Sp. lit.) 253
Juanes (Col. mus.) 285
Juba Valley Alliance (govt., Som.) 492
Judah, Zab 326
Judaism
Poland 480
religion 300, 301, 302, 304, 305
Russia 32
September 11 terrorist attacks 10
Temple Mount 15
Juddmonte International (horse race) 331
Judo 343
Sporting Record *tables* 363
Jugnauth, Sir Anerood 464
Juncker, Jean-Claude 459
Jung, Andrea (biog.) 86
Jun'ichirō Tanizaki Prize (lit.) *table* 243
Jupiter (planet) 267
Jupiter Media Metrix, Inc. (Am. co.) 177
Justice, U.S. Department of
Microsoft case 51, 54, 175
music industry 178
Oregon Death With Dignity Act 55
Justicialist Party (pol. party, Arg.) 388
JVA (govt., Som.): *see* Juba Valley Alliance
JVP (pol. party, Sri Lanka): *see* Marxist People's Liberation Front

K

Kabbah, Ahmad Tejan 489
Kabila, Joseph 410
biography 86
inauguration 17
Kabila, Laurent-Désiré 16, 410, *il.* obituary 126
Kabir, Mawlawi Abdul 384
Kacalidha, Niko 385
Kael, Pauline (obit.) 126
Kagame, Paul 484
Kaibe, Alfred *il.* 476
Kaiser, Robert G.
"9-11" (special report) 8
Kalapriya Center for Indian Performing Arts (Chicago, Ill.) 290
Kalymnos (is., Gr.) 24
Kananaskis (resort, Can.) 403
Kane, Sarah 291
Kansas City Ballet 287
Kanton (is., Kiri.) 453
Karadzic, Radovan 227
Karamanlis, Konstantinos ("Kostas") 432
Karan (fashion co.) 220
Karelia (reg., Russ.)
Finland 424
Karimov, Islam 519
Karmapa Lama 18
Karpov, Anatoly 327
Karsten, Yekaterina 344
Karzai, Hamid 61, 384
biography 86
Kashmir (state, India): *see* Jammu and Kashmir
Kasparov, Garry 327
Kasyanov, Mikhail 482
Kato, Shizue Hirota (obit.) 126
"Kato apo ta asteria" (motion picture) 297
Katter, Bob 390
Katzav, Moshe 445
Kaufmann Conference Center (N.Y., N.Y.) 165

Kawamura, Fujio: *see* Utaemon VI, Nakamura
Kazakhstan 451
prisons and penology 231
religion 300, 301
Shanghai Cooperation Organization 378
wildlife conservation 215
Kazanjian, Arlene Frances: *see* Francis, Arlene
Kazantzidis, Stelios (obit.) 126
"Kazus Kukotskogo" (Ulitskaya) 256
KCB (Am. ballet co.): *see* Kansas City Ballet
KDU-CSL (pol. party, Cz. Rep.): *see* Christian Democrat Union–Czech People's Party
"kedi, bir adam, bir ölüm, Bir" (Livaneli) 257
Keïta, Seydou (obit.) 126
Kekele (Af. mus. group) 286
Kemakeza, Sir Allan 60, 491
Kenana Sugar Co. (Sud. co.) 496
Kennedy Center (Wash., D.C.): *see* John F. Kennedy Center for the Performing Arts
Kentucky (state, U.S.)
equine disaster 33, 330
Kentucky Derby (horse race) 30
Sporting Record *tables* 357
Kenya 452
anthropology 158
Ethiopia 424
international law 227
military affairs 281
Kenyanthropus platyops (hominid) 25, 159
KEP (pol. party, Gr.): *see* Movement of Free Citizens
Kepes, Gyorgy (obit.) 127
Kepesh, David (fictional character) 244
keratin (paleon.) 241
Kérékou, Mathieu 25, 395
Kernot, Cheryl 389
Kerouac, Jack 172
Kerrey, Bob 26, 28
Kesey, Ken Elton (obit.) 127
Ketcham, Henry King ("Hank") (obit.) 127
Ketterle, Wolfgang 51
biography 71
KFOR (internat. armed force): *see* Kosovo Force
Khachatryan, Armen 389
Khai, Phan Van 521
Khalifah, Hamad ibn Isa al- 392
Khalifah, Khalifah ibn Sulman al- 392
Khamenei, Ayatollah Sayyed Ali 442
Khamtai Siphandon 455
Kharibian, Leo (obit.) 127
Khatami, Hojatoleslam Mohammad 35, 442
Khmer Rouge (pol. org., Camb.) 14
court cases 401
human rights abuses 313
Khorkina, Svetlana 340, 362, *il.*
Khouna, Cheikh El Afia Ould Mohamed 463
Kiam, Victor Kermit, II (obit.) 127
Kiarostami, Abbas 257
kidnapping
cricket (sport) 329
Ecuador 22, 417
Philippines 479
Kilauea volcano (Haw.) 185
Kilburn, Tom (obit.) 127
Kim Dae Jung 25, 453, *il.*
Kim Jong Il 453
China 16
terrorism 42
Kimondiu, Benedict 51, 349
Kinakh, Anatoly 33, 506, 507
"Kind of Fiction, A" (Page) 247
Kinfe Gebremedhin 31, 424
King George VI Chase (horse race) 332
King George VI Diamond Stakes (horse race) 331
"King Lear" (play) 292
king snake (zool.) 235, *il.*
"Kingdom of Monkeys" (Schroeder) 247
Kirch Group (Eur. co.) 269
Kirchhoff, Bodo 248, *il.*
Kirghizia: *see* Kyrgyzstan

Kiribati 453
"Kızlarıma mektuplar" (Kongar) 257
Klaus, Josef (obit.) 128
Klestil, Thomas 391
Klim, Michael 346, *il.*
Klimt, Gustav 169
Klossowski, Balthazar: *see* Balthus
KMT (pol. party, Tai.): *see* Kuomintang
Knapp, (Geoffrey Goodman) James ("Jimmy") (obit.) 128
KNB (Turkmenistan): *see* National Security Committee
Kneale, Matthew 17, 242
Knesset (Isr.) 445
Knight, Bobby 322
Knowles, John (obit.) 128
Knowles, William S. 51
biography 70
"Knyza' vetr" (Yuzefovich) 255
Kocharyan, Robert 388, 391
Kodiak Island (is., U.S.) 268
Kodjo, Agbéyomé 502
Kohl, Hannelore Renner 38
obituary 128
Kohl, Helmut Michael 19, 429
Koirala, Girija Prasad 40, 469
Koizumi, Junichiro 29, 34, 44, 449, *il.*
biography 87
Japan 448, 450
South Korea 454
Kok, Wim 470
Kolelas, Bernard 411
Kolingba, André 404
Komyo-ji (Japanese temple) 164
Konaré, Alpha Oumar 33, 462
Koner, Pauline (obit.) 128
"Königsmacher, Der" (Delius) 248
Koolhaas, Rem 165
Koons, Jeff 168, 172
biography 87
Korda, Alberto, *or* Alberto Díaz Gutiérrez (obit.) 128
Korea, Democratic People's Republic of 453
agriculture and food supplies 153
international relations
Japan 451
Myanmar 468
Vietnam 522
meteorology and climate 187
South Korea 453, 454
United States 516
Korea, Republic of 453
banking 203
disasters 64, 65
education 206
Japan 450, 451
meteorology and climate 187
military affairs 281
motion pictures 297
newspapers 275
social protection 311
television 272
Korean Council for University Education 211
Kosovo (aut. area, Yugos.)
border conflict 21
election 56
human rights abuses 312
military affairs 279
refugees 315
Yugoslavia 523
Kosovo Force (internat. armed force) 279
Kostelic, Janica 344, 413
Kostner, Isolde 345
Kostov, Ivan 399
"Kotkijet" (horse) 332
Kow Swamp human remains (Austl.) 158, *il.*
Kramer, Stanley Earl (obit.) 128
Kramnik, Vladimir 327
Krizanovic, Jozo 397
"Kro ukhtov" (Matalon) 256
Krstic, Radislav 42, 397
human rights 312
international law 227
Kruger National Park (S.Af.) 62, 216
"Kryp" (Nestor) 250
Krzyzewski, Mike 322
Kucan, Milan 490
Kuchma, Leonid 18, 19, 33, 506
Chernobyl memorial 212

Kuerten, Gustavo 35, 347, *il.* 348
Kufuor, John Kofi Agyekum 15, 431
biography 88
Kuitunen, Virpi 345
"Kule, En" (Kristensen) 250
"Kuma no shikiishi" (Horie) 259
Kumar, Ashok 299
obituary 129
Kumaratunga, Chandrika 39, 51, 495
Kumbh Mela (festival, India) 17, 308
Kuomintang (pol. party, Tai.) 499
Kurds (people)
marine disaster 20
"Kuroi ame" (Ibuse) 260
"Kursk" (submarine) 20, 483, *il.* 484
Kushida, Fuki (obit.) 129
Kushner, Tony 292, 293, *il.*
"Kutub" (horse) 331
Kuwa Mekki, Yousif (obit.) 129
Kuwait 454
museum 234
"Kvinden fra Sáez" (Roulund) 249
Kwan, Michelle 342
Kwasniewski, Aleksander 479
Kyllo *v.* United States (U.S. law case) 228, 229
Kyoto Protocol 25, 40
Canada 403
environment 213
France 426
United States 516
Kyrgyzstan 454
prisons and penology 231
Shanghai Cooperation Organization 378
Uzbekistan 519

L

La Niña (weather pattern) 186
La Scala (It. opera house) 61
La Scala Ballet (It. ballet co.) 288
Laar, Mart 422, 423
Labor Party (Isr.) 445
labour-management relations
Austria 391
see also employment
Labour Party (pol. party, Nor.) 473
Labour Party (pol. party, U.K.) 34, 509, 510
labour union: *see* trade union
Labrador (prov., Can.): *see* Newfoundland and Labrador
Lachmon, Jaggernath (obit.) 129
Laden, Osama bin: *see* Bin Laden, Osama
Ladies Professional Golf Association 37, 340
Lady Byng Trophy (ice hockey) 341
"Lady Day: The Complete Billie Holiday on Columbia (1933–1944)" (album) 284
"Lagaan" (motion picture) 297
Lagos Escobar, Ricardo 405
Lagumdzija, Zlatko 39, 397
Lahoud, Émile 456
Lake, Harriette: *see* Sothern, Ann
Lake Mungo human remains (Austl.) 158, *il.*
Lal, (Chaudhuri) Devi (obit.) 129
"Lan Yu" (motion picture) 297
land reform
Zimbabwe 524
land use: *see* individual countries by name
landmine
military affairs 281
Tajikistan 500
Uzbekistan 519
Landry, Bernard 22, 402
biography 88
Landsat (satellite) 236
Landsbergis, Vytautas *il.* 459
landslide
El Salvador 419, *il.*
Iran 43
natural disasters 63
Landslide Productions, Inc. (Am. co.) 180
Lane, Nathan (biog.) 88
Langen, Christoph 324

X

Y

Z